CRIMINAL PROCEDURE: INVESTIGATING CRIME

[from CRIMINAL PROCEDURE: PRINCIPLES, POLICIES AND PERSPECTIVES, FOURTH EDITION]

■ ■ ■

By

Joshua Dressler

Frank R. Strong Chair in Law
Michael E. Moritz College of Law
The Ohio State University

George C. Thomas III

Rutgers University Board of Governors Professor of Law
Judge Alexander P. Waugh, Sr. Distinguished Scholar
School of Law, Newark

AMERICAN CASEBOOK SERIES®

WEST®

A Thomson Reuters business

Mat #40793737

© West, a Thomson business, 2003, 2006
© 2010 Thomson Reuters
    610 Opperman Drive
    St. Paul, MN 55123
    1–800–313–9378
Printed in the United States of America

ISBN: 978–0–314–20277–2

To Dottie, my life's partner, for everything
To Sandy Koufax for one thing in particular:
not pitching on Yom Kippur

—J.D.

To Gretchen, for our love and friendship,
and for traveling along with me.

—G.T.

PREFACE

___

Criminal Procedure: Investigating Crime

This book is a complete, unchanged reprint of Chapters 1–10 and 14 of Dressler & Thomas, *Criminal Procedure: Principles, Policies and Perspectives* (4th ed. 2010). The pagination is the same in this softcover book as in the hardcover version.

It is a pleasure to teach Criminal Procedure. Much of the course features constitutional law, with its fascinating questions about theories of interpretation and about fidelity to text and history. Criminal procedure also brings students face to face with fundamental policy questions about the appropriate balance between protecting us *from criminals* and protecting us *from the government*. We want the criminal process to solve and prosecute crime but we also want controls that protect our privacy and autonomy. (The aftermath of the September 11 attacks, and recent disclosures about telephone surveillance by the government, make this point all too well.) Most students have had contact with the police, if only to receive a traffic ticket. Even minor events like traffic stops can lead to a search of the car and can manifest racial profiling or other abuses of police authority. Students also "know" about policing from television shows like the late *NYPD Blue* and the endless variations of *Law and Order*.

Television shows over the years have also featured the criminal trial process and the role of lawyers in it. Think of *Perry Mason* in black and white, *Perry Mason* in color, *Law and Order*, and the real-life drama of O.J. Simpson and countless other actual trials. From these shows, and news accounts, the country has acquired a set of beliefs and attitudes about the prosecution, defense, and adjudication of criminal defendants. The focus at this stage of the process shifts to finding the right balance between convicting the guilty in an efficient manner while freeing the innocent and providing fairness to all. Fundamental policy issues underlie much of the doctrine here as well. Does due process permit non-unanimous verdicts or exclusion of jurors on the basis of race? Does due process require prosecutors to turn over all favorable evidence to the defense or only that evidence likely to produce an acquittal?

If criminal procedure is as topical as today's newspaper, it is also deeply steeped in history. Criminal trials appear in Roman law and Hebrew law. The right to counsel surfaces in Roman law and reappears in the twelfth century laws of Henry I. English history is filled with criminal procedure controversies, from the dispute between Henry II and Thomas Becket in 1168 over the authority of church courts, to the Magna Carta, the reign of Henry VIII, and the Reformation. A study of criminal procedure is not just a search of now but also of our past. In our past, we find the enduring values that shape court decisions today.

A casebook cannot be all things to all people, but it should offer sufficient flexibility to accommodate diverse teaching goals and pedagogical methods. We include materials that encourage students to think about constitutional theory and judicial craftsmanship as they read cases and learn doctrine. In the selection of cases, less can be more. We have chosen not to edit cases down to their bones in order to include more cases. We offer broad coverage but also give students and professors the chance to dig deep into the important constitutional cases.

Professor Anthony Amsterdam famously observed about Supreme Court jurisprudence, that "once uttered, these pronouncements will be interpreted by arrays of lower appellate courts, trial judges, magistrates, commissioners and police officials. *Their* interpretation * * * for all practical purposes, will become the word of god." Anthony G. Amsterdam, *The Supreme Court and the Rights of Suspects in Criminal Cases*, 45 N.Y.U. L. Rev. 785, 786 (1979). We seek the "word of god" by including empirical research data where it exists, political science analyses, and news accounts that illuminate how law works "in the trenches."

We believe that students should learn early, and think often, about the overarching principles of the subject matter they are learning. In Chapter 1 we display failures of the criminal process as a way to get students to identify appropriate goals for a criminal process. Then we invite them to return again and again to those goals to understand, and sometimes to critique, Supreme Court doctrine. Why does the Sixth Amendment require appointed counsel in almost every case while the Fourth Amendment receives a grudging interpretation? We believe this, and many other, interpretational issues are illuminated by considering the importance that a criminal process places on accurate outcomes, a goal that is inevitably hindered when limitations are placed on the power of government to seek evidence.

As much as we would like the law to be neutral, we are realistic enough to know that it does not always achieve that goal. And we think it important for students to realize the ways in which law fails to achieve neutrality. Thus, we do not skirt—in fact, we confront—the effects of racism and other malignant-isms in the criminal process.

A casebook need not be forbidding to inspire students to display high standards of thought, analysis, and criticism. Users of our book will discover some informality, even humor (heresy!), in places. For us, this style has worked well. We seek balance between principal cases and the Notes and Questions that illuminate or expand on the principal cases. Thus, professors who want to teach the cases can rely on the Notes and Questions to facilitate a more traditional classroom discussion. Those who like the problem method will find enough Problems in conjunction with the Notes and Questions to keep a lively class discussion going. And those, like Dressler and Thomas, who blend the traditional case analysis with the problem method, will find the book especially well suited to that approach.

Outside reading materials. There are many useful sources for additional reading. Among the excellent general resources are Joshua Dressler & Alan C. Michaels, Understanding Criminal Procedure (5th ed. 2010); Wayne R. La-Fave, Jerold H. Israel, Nancy J. King & Orin S. Kerr, Criminal Procedure (5th ed. 2009); and Charles Whitebread & Christopher Slobogin, Criminal Procedure (5th ed. 2008). For those who want even more coverage of the Fourth Amendment, nothing can compare to Wayne R. LaFave, Search and Seizure (4th ed. 2004), an incredible six-volume treatise. For those who want a greater dose of history with their Fourth Amendment, we recommend Thomas K. Clancy, The Fourth Amendment, Its History and Interpretation (2008). We have also cited and quoted from other excellent books and articles throughout the casebook.

Editing policies. We prefer students to read judicial opinions in largely intact form. Nonetheless, deletions are necessary. Because the goal of this book is pedagogy, we have not followed all scholarly conventions in identifying omissions from the extracted materials. We have applied the following rules of thumb to extracted materials.

1. Most footnotes and citations have been omitted, always without use of ellipses to indicate their omission. Asterisks have been used, however, to indicate deletions of other textual materials.

2. Numbered footnotes are from the original materials and retain their original numbering. Our "editors' footnotes" are designated by letter.

Personal acknowledgments. Many people assisted us in producing this edition or its predecessors, or all four, including many colleagues on our respective faculties and throughout the United States and United Kingdom as well as members of the Bar and judiciary. We name a few people here: Phil Bates, Robert Batey, Doug Berman, Susan Brenner, Neil Cohen, Stan Cox, Thomas Davies, Michiael Dimino, John G. Douglass, Jim Ellis, Arnold Enker, Barry Feinstein, Stanley Z. Fisher, Clifford Fishman, Gary Francione, Jeffrey Froelich, Adam Gershowitz, Mark Godsey, Stuart Green, Kenneth Graham, David Harris, Stephen Henderson, Peter J. Henning, Charles Jones, Andy Leipold, Rory Little, Gerard Lynch, Michael Mannheimer, Bernie McShane, Alan Michaels, Sam Pillsbury, and Michael Vitiello.

We also want to credit our student research assistants who assisted us in one or more of the editions of this casebook. At McGeorge, appreciation goes to Kristine Byron, Michael Kuzmich, and most especially, Allison Martin. At Ohio State, we thank Nathan DeDino, Jennifer Dutcher, and Leigh Anne Williams. At Rutgers, we thank Jennifer Alonso, Peter Berger, Art Nalbandian, Barbara Schweiger, Gail Spence, Rebekah Wanger and, especially, Chris Alliegro, Kegan Brown, and Michael Mulligan.

Author Thomas thanks co-author Dressler for his unflagging attempts to force discipline on the project, some of which succeeded. For heroic assistance on the Fourth Edition, thanks to Henry Snee.

Author Dressler offers heartfelt thanks to co-author George for his seemingly unlimited good humor, which was put to the ultimate test by Dressler's compulsive need to send thousands of e-mail messages raising endless manuscript issues.

JOSHUA DRESSLER
Michael E. Moritz College of Law
The Ohio State University
Columbus, Ohio

GEORGE C. THOMAS III
Rutgers University School of Law
Newark, New Jersey

February 2010

ACKNOWLEDGMENTS

Janet E. Ainsworth, *The Pragmatics of Powerlessness in Police Interrogation*, 103 Yale Law Journal 259 (1993). Copyright © 1993, The Yale Law Journal Company, Inc. Reprinted by permission of the Yale Law Journal Company and Fred B. Rothman & Company from *The Yale Law Journal*, Vol. 103, pages 259–322.

Albert W. Alschuler, *Preventive Pretrial Detention and the Failure of Interest–Balancing Approaches to Due Process*, 85 Michigan Law Review 510 (1986). Copyright © 1986, Michigan Law Review Association. Reprinted by permission.

Albert W. Alschuler, *The Changing Plea Bargaining Debate*, 69 California Law Review 652 (1981). Copyright © 1981 by California Law Review, Inc. Reprinted from California Law Review, Vol. 69, No. 3, pp. 652–723.

Akhil Reed Amar, *Terry and Fourth Amendment First Principles*, 72 St. John's L. Rev. 1097 (1998). Copyright © 1998, St. John's Law Review. Reprinted by permission.

Akhil Reed Amar, *Fourth Amendment First Principles*, 107 Harvard Law Review 757 (1994). Copyright © 1994 by the Harvard Law Review Association. Reprinted by permission.

Akhil Reed Amar, *The Bill of Rights and the Fourteenth Amendment*, 101 Yale Law Journal 1193 (1992). Copyright © 1992, Yale Law Journal Company, Inc. Reprinted by permission of The Yale Law Journal Company and Fred B. Rothman & Company from The Yale Law Journal, Vol. 101, pages 1193–1284.

Vivian O. Berger, *The Supreme Court and Defense Counsel: Old Roads, New Paths—A Dead End?*, 86 Columbia Law Review 9 (1986). Copyright © 1986 by the Directors of the Columbia Law Review Association. This article originally appeared at 86 Colum. L. Rev. 9 (1986). Reprinted by permission.

Craig M. Bradley, *Murray v. United States: The Bell Tolls for the Search Warrant Requirement*, 64 Indiana Law Journal 907 (1989). Copyright © 1989, by the Trustees of Indiana University. Reprinted by permission.

Craig M. Bradley, *Two Models of the Fourth Amendment*, 83 Michigan Law Review 1468 (1985). Copyright © 1985, Michigan Law Review Association. Reprinted by permission.

Susan W. Brenner, *The Voice of the Community: A Case for Grand Jury Independence*, 3 Virginia Journal of Social Policy & Law 67 (1995). Copyright © 1995, Virginia Journal of Social Policy & Law. Reprinted by permission.

Stephen Breyer, *The Federal Sentencing Guidelines and the Key Compromises Upon Which They Rest*, 17 Hofstra Law Review 1 (1988). Copyright © 1988, by the *Hofstra Law Review Association*. Reprinted with the permission of *Hofstra Law Review*.

Alvin J. Bronstein, *Representing the Powerless: Lawyers Can Make a Difference*, originally published in the Maine Law Review, 49 Maine Law Review 1, 5–7, 12–13 (1997). Copyright © 1997, University of Maine School of Law. Reprinted by permission.

Paul D. Butler, *Race–Based Jury Nullification: Case-in-Chief*, 30 John Marshall Law Review 911 (1997). Copyright © 1997, The John Marshall Law School. Reprinted with permission from The John Marshall Law Review, Volume XXX, Issue 4 (Summer 1997).

Gerald M. Caplan, *Questioning Miranda*, 38 Vanderbilt Law Review 1417 (1985). Copyright © 1985, Vanderbilt Law Review. Reprinted by permission.

Morgan Cloud, *The Dirty Little Secret*, 43 Emory Law Journal 1311 (1994). Copyright © 1994, Emory Law Journal. Reprinted by permission.

Sherry F. Colb, *What Is a Search? Two Conceptual Flaws in Fourth Amendment Doctrine and Some Hints of a Remedy*, 55 Stan. L. Rev. 119 (2002). Copyright © 2002 by the Board of Trustees of the Leland Stanford Junior University. Reprinted by permission.

David Cole, No Equal Justice (1999). Copyright © 1999, by David Cole. Reprinted by permission of the author.

Thomas Y. Davies, *Recovering the Original Fourth Amendment*, 98 Michigan Law Review 547 (1999). Copyright © 1999, Michigan Law Review Association. Reprinted by permission of the author.

John G. Douglass, *Confronting the Reluctant Accomplice*, 101 Columbia Law Review 1797 (2001). Copyright © 2001 by the Directors of the Columbia Law Review Association. This article originally appeared at 101 Colum. L. Rev. 1797 (2001). Reprinted by permission.

Joshua Dressler, Understanding Criminal Law (Fourth edition 2006). Reprinted with permission. Copyright © 2006 Matthew Bender & Company, Inc., a member of the LexisNexis Group. All rights reserved.

Joshua Dressler & Alan C. Michaels, Understanding Criminal Procedure (Fourth Edition 2006) (Vols. 1–2). Reprinted from Understanding Criminal Procedure Vols. 1–2, 4th Ed. with permission. Copyright © 2006 Matthew Bender & Company, Inc., a member of the LexisNexis Group. All rights reserved.

Sam J. Ervin, Jr., *Foreword: Preventive Detention—A Step Backward for Criminal Justice*, 6 Harvard Civil Rights–Civil Liberties Law Review 291 (1971). Copyright © 1971 by the President and Fellows of Harvard College. Reprinted by permission.

Martha A. Field, *Assessing the Harmlessness of Federal Constitutional Error—A Process in Need of a Rationale*, 125 University of Pennsylvania

Law Review 15 (1976). Copyright © 1976 by the University of Pennsylvania. Reprinted by permission.

Barry Friedman, *A Tale of Two Habeas*, 73 Minnesota Law Review 248 (1988). Copyright © 1988, Minnesota Law Review Foundation. Reprinted by permission.

Ann Fagan Ginger, editor, Minimizing Racism in Jury Trials (1969). Copyright © 1969, Ann Fagan Ginger. Reprinted by permission of the editor.

Abe Fortas Papers, Manuscripts and Archives, Yale University Press. Used with permission.

Steven H. Goldberg, *Harmless Error: Constitutional Sneak Thief*, 71 Journal of Criminal Law & Criminology 421 (1980). Copyright © 1980, Northwestern University School of Law. Reprinted by special permission of Northwestern University School of Law, Journal of Criminal Law and Criminology, volume 71, pp. 421, 429–30 (1980).

James Goodman, Stories of Scottsboro, Random House Times Book (1994). From Stories of Scottsboro by James Goodman. Copyright © 1994 by James E. Goodman. Reprinted by permission of Pantheon Books, a division of Random House, Inc.

Joseph D. Grano, *Probable Cause and Common Sense: A Reply to the Critics of Illinois v. Gates*, 17 University of Michigan Journal of Legal Reform 465 (1984). Copyright © 1984, by the University of Michigan Journal of Law Reform. Reprinted by permission.

Bruce A. Green, *Lethal Fiction: The Meaning of "Counsel" in the Sixth Amendment*, 78 Iowa Law Review 433 (1993). Copyright © 1993, by the University of Iowa (Iowa Law Review) (reprinted with permission).

Sandra Guerra, *The Myth of Dual Sovereignty: Multijurisdictional Drug Law Enforcement and Double Jeopardy*, 73 North Carolina Law Review 1159 (1995). Copyright © 1995, North Carolina Law Review. Reprinted by permission.

Peter J. Henning, *Prosecutorial Misconduct in Grand Jury Investigations*, 51 South Carolina Law Review 1 (1999). Copyright © 1999, South Carolina Law Review. Reprinted by permission.

Lenese C. Herbert, *Can't You See What I'm Saying? Making Expressive Conduct a Crime in High–Crimes Areas*, 9 Georgetown.Journal on Poverty Law & Policy 135 (2002). Reprinted with permission of the publisher, Georgetown Journal on Poverty Law & Policy © 2002.

Lawrence Herman, *The Supreme Court, the Attorney General, and the Good Old Days of Police Interrogation*, 48 Ohio State Law Journal 733 (1987). Copyright © 1987, Ohio State Law Journal

Graham Hughes, *The Decline of Habeas Corpus*, (NYU Center for Research in Crime and Justice, 1990). Copyright © 1990, NYU Center for Research in Crime and Justice. Reprinted by permission.

Randolph N. Jonakait, *Restoring the Confrontation Clause to the Sixth Amendment*, 38 UCLA Law Review 557 (1988). Originally published in 35

UCLA L. Rev. 557. Copyright © 1988, The Regents of the University of California. All rights reserved. Reprinted by permission.

Sanford H. Kadish, *Fifty Years of Criminal Law: An Opinionated Review*, 87 Calif. L. Rev. 943 (1999). Copyright © 1999 by Sanford H. Kadish. Reprinted by permission of the author.

Michael J. Klarman, *The Racial Origins of Modern Criminal Procedure*, 99 Michigan Law Review 48 (2000). Copyright © 2000, Michigan Law Review Association. Reprinted by permission.

Charles Krauthammer—The Truth about Torture: It's Time To Be Honest About Doing Terrible Things, The Weekly Standard, 12/05/2005, Volume 011, Issue 12. Copyright © 2005, by Charles Krauthammer. Reprinted with permission.

Richard B. Kuhns, *The Concept of Personal Aggrievement in Fourth Amendment Standing Cases*, 65 Iowa Law Review 493 (1980). Copyright © 1980, by the University of Iowa (Iowa Law Review). Reprinted with permission.

Gerald B. Lefcourt, *Responsibilities of a Criminal Defense Attorney*, 30 Loyola of Los Angeles Law Review (1996). Copyright © 1996, Loyola of Los Angeles Law Review. Reprinted by permission.

Andrew D. Leipold, *Race–Based Jury Nullification: Rebuttal (Part A)*, 30 John Marshall Law Review 923 (1997). Copyright © 1997, The John Marshall Law School. Reprinted with permission from The John Marshall Law Review, Volume XXX, Issue 4 (Summer 1997).

Andrew D. Leipold, *Why Grand Juries Do Not (and Cannot) Protect the Accused*, 80 Cornell Law Review 260 (1995). Copyright © 1995, Cornell Law Review. Reprinted by permission.

Erik Luna, *Gridland: An Allegorical Critique of Federal Sentencing*, 96 Journal of Criminal Law & Criminology 25 (2005). Copyright © 2005, Northwestern University School of Law. Reprinted by special permission of Northwestern University School of Law, The Journal of Criminal Law and Criminology.

Tracey Maclin, *Terry v. Ohio's Fourth Amendment Legacy: Black Men and Police Discretion*, 72 St. John's Law Review 1271 (1998). Copyright © 1998, St. John's Law Review. Reprinted by permission.

Tracey Maclin, *When the Cure for the Fourth Amendment Is Worse Than the Disease*, 68 Southern California Law Review 1 (1994). Copyright © 1994, University of Southern California. Reprinted with the permission of the Southern California Law Review.

Tracey Maclin, *"Black and Blue Encounters"—Some Preliminary Thoughts About Fourth Amendment Seizures: Should Race Matter?*, 26 Valparaiso University Law Review 243 (1991). Copyright © 1991, by Valparaiso University Law Review. Reprinted with the permission of the publisher and author.

Michael S. Moore, Act and Crime, Oxford University Press (1993). Copyright © 1993, Oxford University Press. Reprinted by permission of Oxford University Press.

Robert B. Mosteller, *Remaking Confrontation Clause and Hearsay Doctrine Under the Challenge of Child Sexual Abuse Prosecutions*, University of Illinois Law Review 691 (1993). Copyright © 1993. The copyright to the University of Illinois Law Review is held by The Board of Trustees of the University of Illinois.

Charles E. Moylan, Jr., *Hearsay and Probable Cause: An Aguilar and Spinelli Primer*, 25 Mercer Law Review 741 (1974). Copyright © 1974, Walter F. George School of Law, Mercer University. Reprinted by permission.

Eric L. Muller, *Solving the Batson Paradox: Harmless Error, Jury Representation, and the Sixth Amendment*, 106 Yale Law Journal 93 (1996). Copyright © 1996, The Yale Law Journal Company. Reprinted by permission of The Yale Law Journal Company and Fred B. Rothman & Company from The Yale Law Journal, Volume 106, pages 93–150.

William J. Powell & Michael T. Cimino, *Prosecutorial Discretion Under the Federal Sentencing Guidelines: Is the Fox Guarding the Hen House?*, 97 West Virginia Law Review 373 (1995). Copyright © 1995, West Virginia Law Review. Reprinted by permission.

Ric Simmons, *Re-examining the Grand Jury: Is There Room for Democracy in the Criminal Justice System?*, 82 Boston University Law Review 1 (2002). Copyright © 2002, Boston University Law Review. Reprinted by permission.

David Simon, Homicide, A Year on the Killing Streets (1991). Abridged from Homicide: A Year on the Killing Streets. Copyright © 1991 by David Simon. Reprinted by permission of Houghton Mifflin Co. All rights reserved.

Abbe Smith, *Defending Defending: The Case for Unmitigated Zeal on Behalf of People Who Do Terrible Things*, 28 Hofstra L. Rev. 925 (2000). Copyright © 2000 by the *Hofstra Law Review Association*. Reprinted with the permission of the *Hofstra Law Review Association*.

Potter Stewart, *The Road to Mapp v. Ohio and Beyond: The Origins, Development and Future of the Exclusionary Rule in Search-and-Seizure Cases*, 83 Columbia Law Review 1365 (1983). Copyright © 1983 by the Directors of the Columbia Law Review Association, Inc. This article originally appeared at 83 Colum. L. Rev. 1365 (1983). Reprinted by permission.

Kate Stith and José A. Cabranes, Fear of Judging: Sentencing Guidelines in the Federal Courts (1998). Copyright © 1998, University of Chicago Press. Reprinted by permission.

Louis Stokes, *Representing John W. Terry*, 72 St. John's L. Rev. 727 (1998). Copyright © 1998, St. John's Law Review. Reprinted by permission.

William J. Stuntz, *Miranda's Mistake*, 99 Michigan Law Review. 975 (2001). Copyright © 1999, Michigan Law Review Association. Reprinted by permission.

Scott E. Sundby, *Fallen Superheroes and the Brady Mirage*, 33 McGeorge Law Review 643 (2002). Copyright © 2002, McGeorge Law Review. Reprinted by permission of the author and journal.

Scott E. Sundby, *An Ode to Probable Cause: A Brief Response to Professors Amar and Slobogin*, 72 St. John's Law Review 1133 (1998). Copyright © 1998, St. John's Law Review. Reprinted by permission.

Scott E. Sundby, A Return to Fourth Amendment Basics: Undoing the Mischief of Camara and Terry, 72 Minnesota Law Review 383 (1988). Copyright © 1988, Minnesota Law Review Foundation. Reprinted by permission.

George C. Thomas III, The Supreme Court on Trial: How the Supreme Court Sacrifices Innocent Defendants (Ann Arbor: The University of Michigan Press). Copyright © 2008, The University of Michigan Press. Reprinted by permission.

Sandra Guerra Thompson, *The Non–Discrimination Ideal of Hernandez v. Texas Confronts a "Culture" of Discrimination: The Amazing Story of Miller–El v. Texas,* 25 Chicano–Latino L. Rev. 97 (2005). Copyright © 2005, Chicano–Latino Law Review. Reprinted by permission.

H. Richard Uviller, *Evidence from the Mind of the Criminal Suspect: A Reconsideration of the Current Rules of Access and Restraint*, 87 Columbia Law Review 1137 (1987). Copyright © 1987 by the Directors of the Columbia Law Review Association, Inc. This article originally appeared at 87 Colum. L. Rev. 1137 (1987). Reprinted by permission.

Thomas Weigend, *Germany*. From Criminal Procedure: A Worldwide View, edited by Craig M. Bradley (1998). Copyright © 1998, Carolina Academic Press. Reprinted by permission of Carolina Academic Press, telephone (919) 489–7486, website www.cap-press.com.

Summary of Contents

TABLE OF CONTENTS

———————

TABLE OF CASES

The principal cases are in bold type. Cases cited or discussed in the text
are in roman type. References are to pages. Cases cited in principal
cases and within other quoted materials are not included.

TABLE OF AUTHORITIES

This table lists books, articles and other secondary authorities quoted or cited by the casebook authors. (Newspaper articles and government sources are not included.) Anonymous student notes and comments follow the alphabetical listings of the authors.

Chapter 1
The Criminal Process: Failure and Legitimacy

Akhil Reed Amar, The Bill of Rights (1998).

Akhil Reed Amar, *The Bill of Rights and the Fourteenth Amendment*, 101 Yale L.J. 1193 (1992).

Mary Sue Backus & Paul Marcus, *The Right to Counsel in Criminal Cases, A National Crisis*, 57 Hastings L. J. 1031 (2006).

Tim Bakken, *Truth and Innocence Procedures to Free Innocent Persons: Beyond the Adversarial System*, 41 U. Mich. L. Reform 547 (2008).

4 W. Blackstone's Commenatries *358 (1769).

James E. Bond, No Easy Walk to Freedom (1997).

Dan T. Carter, The Politics of Rage: George Wallace, the Origins of the New Conservatism and the Transformation of American Politics (1995).

Morgan Cloud, *A Liberal House Divided: How the Warren Court Dismantled the Fourth Amendment*, 3 Ohio State J. Crim. L. 33 (2005).

Felix Cohen, *Transcendental Nonsense and the Functional Approach*, 35 Colum. L. Rev. 809 (1935).

Michael Kent Curtis, No State Shall Abridge (1986).

Leonard Dinnerstein, The Leo Frank Case (1968).

1 Joshua Dressler & Alan C. Michaels, Understanding Criminal Procedure (4th ed. 2006).

Donald A. Dripps, *Justice Harlan on Criminal Procedure: Two Cheers for the Legal Process School*, 3 Ohio State J. Crim. L. 125 (2005).

Donald Dripps, *Akhil Amar on Criminal Procedure and Constitutional Law: Here I Go Down That Wrong Road Again*, 74 N.C. L. Rev. 1559 (1996).

Henry J. Friendly, *The Fifth Amendment Tomorrow: The Case for Constitutional Change*, 37 U. Cinn. L. Rev. 617 (1968).

Brandon L. Garrett & Peter J. Neufeld, *Invalid Forensic Science Testimony and Wrongful Convictions*, 95 Va. L. Rev. 1 (2009).

Daniel Givelber, *Meaningless Acquittals, Meaningful Convictions: Do We Reliably Acquit the Innocent?*, 49 Rutgers L. Rev. 1317 (1997).

James Goodman, Stories of Scottsboro (1995).

Fred C. Zacharias & Bruce A. Green, *The Duty to Avoid Wrongful Convictions: A Thought Experiment in the Regulation of Prosecutors*, 89 B. U. L. Rev. 1 (2009).

Chapter 2
Fourth Amendment: An Overview

Akhil Reed Amar, *Fourth Amendment First Principles*, 107 Harv. L. Rev. 757 (1994).

Anthony G. Amsterdam, *Perspectives On the Fourth Amendment*, 58 Minn. L. Rev. 349 (1974).

Dennis D. Dorin, *Justice Tom Clark's Rule in* Mapp v. Ohio*'s Extension of the Exclusionary Rule to State Searches and Seizures*, 52 Case W. Res. L. Rev. 401 (2001).

Wayne R. LaFave, Search and Seizure (4th ed. 2004).

Carolyn N. Long, Mapp v. Ohio: Guarding Against Unreasonable Searches and Seizures (2006).

Bernard Schwartz, Super Chief: Earl Warren and His Supreme Court—A Judicial Biography (1983).

Potter Stewart, *The Road to Mapp v. Ohio and Beyond: The Origins, Development and Future of the Exclusionary Rule in Search-and-Seizure Cases*, 83 Colum. L. Rev. 1365 (1983).

Chapter 3
Passing the Threshold of the Fourth Amendment

Anthony G. Amsterdam, *Perspectives on the Fourth Amendment*, 58 Minn. L. Rev. 349 (1974).

Sherry F. Colb, *What Is a Search? Two Conceptual Flaws in Fourth Amendment Doctrine and Some Hints of a Remedy*, 55 Stan. L. Rev. 119 (2002).

Eva Marie Dowdell, *You Are Here!—Mapping the Boundaries of the Fourth Amendment with GPS Technology*, 32 Rutgers Computer & Tech. L.J. 109 (2005).

Editors, *Here's Looking at You*, Scientific American, Dec. 2001, at 8.

John P. Elwood, *What Were They Thinking: The Supreme Court in Revue, October Term 2000*, 4 Green Bag 2d 365 (2001).

Edmund W. Kitch, *Katz v. United States: The Limits of the Fourth Amendment*, 1968 Sup. Ct. Rev. 133.

Yale Kamisar, *How Earl Warren's Twenty–Two Years in Law Enforcement Affected His Work as Chief Justice*, 3 Ohio St. J. Crim. L. 11 (2005).

Wayne R. LaFave, *The Fourth Amendment as a "Big Time" TV Fad*, 53 Hastings L.J. 265, 277 (2001).

Bernard Schwartz, Super Chief: Earl Warren and His Supreme Court—A Judicial Biography (1983).

David Alan Sklansky, *"One Train May Hide Another": Katz, Stonewall, and the Secret Subtext of Criminal Procedure*, 41 U.C. Davis L. Rev. 875 (2008).

Chapter 4
The Substance of the Fourth Amendment

Janice Nadler, *No Need to Shout: Bus Sweeps and the Psychology of Coercion*, 2002 Sup. Ct. Rev. 153.

Reuben M. Payne, *The Prosecutor's Perspective on Terry: Detective McFadden Had a Right to Protect Himself*, 72 St. John's L. Rev. 733 (1998).

Hope Viner Samborn, *Profiled and Pulled Over*, American Bar Association Journal, October, 1999.

Stephen J. Schulhofer, *On the Fourth Amendment Rights of the Law–Abiding Public*, 1989 Sup. Ct. Rev. 87.

Louis Stokes, *Representing John W. Terry*, 72 St. John's L. Rev. 727 (1998).

Marcy Strauss, *Reconstructing Consent*, 92 J. Crim. L. & Criminology 211 (2001).

William J. Stuntz, *Implicit Bargains, Government Power, and the Fourth Amendment*, 44 Stan. L. Rev. 553 (1992).

Scott E. Sundby, *An Ode to Probable Cause: A Brief Response to Professors Amar and Slobogin*, 72 St. John's L. Rev. 1133 (1998).

Scott E. Sundby, *A Return to Fourth Amendment Basics: Undoing the Mischief of Camara and Terry*, 72 Minn. L. Rev. 383 (1988).

James J. Tomkovicz, *California v. Acevedo: The Walls Close In On the Warrant Requirement*, 29 Am. Crim. L. Rev. 1003 (1992).

James B. White, *The Fourth Amendment as a Way of Talking About People: A Study of Robinson and Matlock*, 1974 Sup. Ct. Rev. 165.

Note, *Warrantless Searches and Seizures of Automobiles*, 87 Harv. L. Rev. 835 (1974).

Chapter 5
Remedies for Fourth Amendment Violations

Albert W. Alschuler, *The Exclusionary Rule and Causation: Hudson v. Michigan and Its Ancestors*, 93 Iowa L. Rev. 1741 (2008).

Craig M. Bradley, *Murray v. United States: The Bell Tolls for the Search Warrant Requirement*, 64 Ind. L.J. 907 (1989).

Joshua Dressler & Alan C. Michaels, Understanding Criminal Procedure (Vol. 1) (4th ed. 2006).

Eric A. Johnson, *Causal Relevance in the Law of Search and Seizure*, 88 B.U. L. Rev. 113 (2008).

Richard B. Kuhns, *The Concept of Personal Aggrievement in Fourth Amendment Standing Cases*, 65 Iowa L. Rev. 493 (1980).

Wayne R. LaFave, Search and Seizure (4th ed. 2004).

Wayne R. LaFave, *Fourth Amendment Vagaries (Of Improbable Cause, Imperceptible Plain View, Notorious Privacy, and Balancing Askew)*, 74 J. Crim. L. & Criminology 1171 (1983).

Scott Optican, *Lessons From Down Under: A Dialogue on Police Search and Seizure in New Zealand and the United States*, 3 Ohio St. J. Crim. L. 257 (2005).

Thomas Y. Davies, *Farther and Farther from the Original Fifth Amendment: The Recharacterization of the Right Against Self–Incrimination as a "Trial Right" in Chavez v. Martinez*, 70 Tenn. L. Rev. 987 (2003).

1 Joshua Dressler & Alan C. Michaels, Understanding Criminal Procedure (5th ed. 2010).

Donald Dripps, *Akhil Amar On Criminal Procedure and Constitutional Law "Here I Go Down That Wrong Road Again"*, 74 N.C. L. Rev. 1559 (1996).

Abe Fortas, *The Fifth Amendment: Nemo Tenetur Prodere Seipsum,*25 Clev. B. Ass'n J. 91 (1954).

Henry J. Friendly, *The Fifth Amendment Tomorrow: The Case for Constitutional Change*, 37 U. Cin. L. Rev. 671 (1968).

William A. Geller, *Videotaping Interrogations and Confessions*, in Miranda: Law, Justice, and Policing (Richard A. Leo & George C. Thomas III eds., 1998).

Fred P. Graham, The Self–Inflicted Wound (1970).

Joseph D. Grano, Confessions, Truth, and the Law (1993).

Kent Greenawalt, *Silence as a Moral and Constitutional Right*, 23 Wm. & Mary L. Rev. 15 (1981).

Lawrence Herman, *The Supreme Court, the Attorney General, and the Good Old Days of Police Interrogation*, 48 Ohio St. L.J. 733 (1987).

Yale Kamisar, *Can (Did) Congress "Overrule" Miranda?*, 85 Cornell L. Rev. 883 (2000).

Yale Kamisar, *The Edwards and Bradshaw Cases: The Court Giveth and the Court Taketh Away*, in 5 The Supreme Court: Trends and Developments 153 (J. Choper, Y. Kamisar, & L. Tribe, eds. 1984).

Yale Kamisar, *Equal Justice in the Gatehouses and Mansions of American Criminal Procedure: From Powell to Gideon, from Escobedo to * * **, in Criminal Justice in Our Time (A.E. Dick Howard, ed. 1965).

John H. Langbein, The Origins of Adversary Criminal Trial (2003).

Richard A. Leo, *Questioning the Relevance of Miranda in the Twenty–First Century*, 99 Mich. L. Rev. 1000 (2001).

Richard A. Leo, *Inside the Interrogation Room*, 86 J. Crim. L. & Criminology 266 (1996).

Michael J. Zydney Mannheimer, *Toward a Unified Theory of Testimonial Evidence under the Fifth and Sixth Amendments*, 80 Temple L. Rev. 1135 (2007).

Michael J. Zydney Mannheimer, *Ripeness of Self–Incrimination Clause Disputes*, 95 J. Crim. L. & Criminology 1261 (2005).

William T. Pizzi & Morris B. Hoffman, *Taking Miranda's Pulse*, 58 Vand. L. Rev. 813 (2005).

Lawrence Rosenthal, *Against Orthodoxy: Miranda Is Not Prophylactic and the Constitution Is Not Perfect*, 10 Chap. L. Rev. 579 (2007).

Stephen J. Schulhofer, *Some Kind Words for the Privilege Against Self-Incrimination*, 26 Val. U.L. Rev. 311 (1991).

Stephen J. Schulhofer, *Reconsidering Miranda*, 54 U. Chi. L. Rev. 435 (1986).

Louis Michael Seidman, *Rubashov's Question: Self–Incrimination and the Problem of Coerced Preferences*, 2 Yale J. L. & Human. 149 (1990).

David Simon, Homicide, A Year on the Killing Streets (1991).

Christopher Slobogin, *Towards Taping*, 1 Ohio St. J. Crim. L. 309 (2003).

William J. Stuntz, *Miranda's Mistake*, 99 Mich. L. Rev. 975 (2001).

William J. Stuntz, *The Substantive Origins of Criminal Procedure*, 105

Yale L.J. 393 (1995).

George C. Thomas III, *Stories About Miranda*, 102 Mich. L. Rev. 1959 (2004).

George C. Thomas III, *Miranda's Illusion: Telling Stories in the Police Interrogation Room*, 81 Texas L. Rev. 1091 (2003) (essay on Welsh S. White, *Miranda*'s Waning Protections (2001)).

Charles D. Weisselberg, *Mourning Miranda*, 96 Cal. L. Rev. 1519 (2008).

Charles D. Weisselberg, *In the Stationhouse After Dickerson*, 99 Mich. L. Rev. 1121 (2001).

Charles D. Weisselberg, *Saving Miranda*, 84 Cornell L. Rev. 1 (1998).

2 John Henry Wigmore, A Treatise on Evidence (2d ed. 1923).

Daniel Yeager, *Rethinking Custodial Interrogation*, 28 Am. Crim. L. Rev. 1 (1990).

Chapter 8
Police Interrogation: The Sixth Amendment Right to Counsel

1 Joshua Dressler & Alan C. Michaels, Understanding Criminal Procedure (5th ed. 2010).

Joseph D. Grano, *Rhode Island v. Innis: A Need to Reconsider the Constitutional Premises Underlying the Law of Confessions*, 17 Am. Crim. L. Rev. 1 (1979).

Phillip E. Johnson, *The Return of the "Christian Burial Speech" Case*, 32 Emory L.J. 349 (1983).

Yale Kamisar, *Brewer v. Williams, Massiah and Miranda: What is "Interrogation"? When Does it Matter?*, 67 Geo L.J. 1 (1978).

Michael J. Zydney Mannheimer, *Toward a Unified Theory of Testimonial Evidence under the Fifth and Sixth Amendments*, 80 Temple L. Rev. 1135 (2007).

Stephen J. Schulhofer, *Confessions and the Court*, 79 Mich. L. Rev. 865 (1980).

George C. Thomas III, *Colonial Criminal Law and Procedure: The Royal Colony of New Jersey 1749–57*, 1 N.Y.U. J. L. & Liberty 671 (2005).

Gerald B. Lefcourt, *Responsibilities of a Criminal Defense Attorney*, 30 Loyola L.A. L. Rev. 59 (1996).

Michael McConville & Chester L. Mirsky, *Understanding Defense of the Poor in State Courts*, 10 Studies in Law, Politics, and Society 217 (1990).

Michael McConville & Chester Mirsky, *Criminal Defense of the Poor in New York City*, 15 N.Y.U. L. & Social Change 581 (1986–87).

Anne Bowen Poulin, *The Role of Standby Counsel in Criminal Cases: In the Twilight Zone of the Criminal Justice System*, 75 N.Y.U. L. Rev. 676 (2000).

Martin Sabelli & Stacey Leyton, *Train Wrecks and Freeway Crashes: An Argument For Fairness and Against Self–Representation in the Criminal Justice System*, 91 J. Crim. L. & Criminology 161 (2000).

Abbe Smith, *Defending Defending: The Case for Unmitigated Zeal on Behalf of People Who Do Terrible Things*, 28 Hofstra L. Rev. 925 (2000).

George C. Thomas III, *Colonial Criminal Law and Procedure: The Royal Colony of New Jersey, 1749–57*, 1 N.Y.U. J. L. & Liberty 671 (2005).

David von Drehle, Among the Lowest of the Dead (1995).

CRIMINAL PROCEDURE: INVESTIGATING CRIME

[from CRIMINAL PROCEDURE: PRINCIPLES, POLICIES AND PERSPECTIVES, FOURTH EDITION]

UNITED STATES CONSTITUTION (SELECTED PROVISIONS)

ARTICLE I

Section 9. * * *

[2] The privilege of the Writ of Habeas Corpus shall not be suspended, unless when in Cases of Rebellion or Invasion the public Safety may require it.

[3] No Bill of Attainder or ex post facto Law shall be passed.

ARTICLE III

Section 1. The judicial Power of the United States, shall be vested in one supreme Court, and in such inferior Courts as the Congress may from time to time ordain and establish. The Judges, both of the supreme and inferior Courts, shall hold their Offices during good Behaviour, and shall, at stated Times, receive for their Services a Compensation, which shall not be diminished during their Continuance in Office.

Section 2. [1] The judicial Power shall extend to all Cases, in Law and Equity, arising under this Constitution, the Laws of the United States, and Treaties made, or which shall be made, under their Authority;—to all Cases affecting Ambassadors, other public Ministers and Consuls;—to all Cases of admiralty and maritime Jurisdiction;—to Controversies to which the United States shall be a Party;—to Controversies between two or more States;—between a State and Citizens of another State;—between Citizens of different States;—between Citizens of the same State claiming Lands under Grants of different States, and between a State, or the Citizens thereof, and foreign States, Citizens or Subjects. * * *

[3] The trial of all Crimes, except in Cases of Impeachment, shall be by Jury; and such Trial shall be held in the State where the said Crimes shall have been committed; but when not committed within any State, the Trial shall be at such Place or Places as the Congress may by Law have directed.

Section 3. [1] Treason against the United States, shall consist only in levying War against them, or, in adhering to their Enemies, giving them Aid and Comfort. No Person shall be convicted of Treason unless on the Testimony of two Witnesses to the same overt Act, or on Confession in open Court.

[2] The Congress shall have Power to declare the Punishment of Treason, but no Attainder of Treason shall work Corruption of Blood, or Forfeiture except during the Life of the Person attainted.

ARTICLE IV

Section 2. [1] The Citizens of each State shall be entitled to all Privileges and Immunities of Citizens in the several States.

[2] A person charged in any State with Treason, Felony, or other Crime, who shall flee from Justice, and be found in another State, shall on demand of the executive Authority of the State from which he fled, be delivered up, to be removed to the State having Jurisdiction of the Crime.

ARTICLE VI

[2] This Constitution, and the Laws of the United States which shall be made in Pursuance thereof; and all Treaties made, or which shall be made, under the Authority of the United States, shall be the supreme Law of the Land; and the Judges in every State shall be bound thereby, any Thing in the Constitution or Laws of any State to the Contrary notwithstanding.

* * *

AMENDMENT I [1791]

Congress shall make no law respecting an establishment of religion, or prohibiting the free exercise thereof; or abridging the freedom of speech, or of the press; or the right of the people peaceably to assemble, and to petition the Government for a redress of grievances.

AMENDMENT II [1791]

A well regulated Militia, being necessary to the security of a free State, the right of the people to keep and bear Arms, shall not be infringed.

AMENDMENT III [1791]

No Soldier shall, in times of peace be quartered in any house, without the consent of the Owner, nor in time of war, but in a manner to be prescribed by law.

AMENDMENT IV [1791]

The right of the people to be secure in their persons, houses, papers, and effects, against unreasonable searches and seizures, shall not be violated, and no Warrants shall issue, but upon probable cause, supported by Oath or affirmation, and particularly describing the place to be searched, and the persons or things to be seized.

AMENDMENT V [1791]

No person shall be held to answer for a capital, or otherwise infamous crime, unless on a presentment or indictment of a Grand Jury, except in cases arising in the land or naval forces, or in the Militia, when in actual service in time of War or public danger; nor shall any person be subject for the same offence to be twice put in jeopardy of life or limb; nor shall be compelled in any criminal case to be a witness against himself, nor be deprived of life, liberty, or property, without due process of law; nor shall private property be taken for public use, without just compensation.

AMENDMENT VI [1791]

In all criminal prosecutions, the accused shall enjoy the right to a speedy and public trial, by an impartial jury of the State and district wherein the crime shall have been committed, which district shall have been previously ascertained by law, and to be informed of the nature and cause of the accusation; to be confronted with the witnesses against him; to have compulsory process for obtaining witnesses in his favor, and to have the Assistance of Counsel for his defence.

AMENDMENT VII [1791]

In Suits at common law, where the value in controversy shall exceed twenty dollars, the right of trial by jury shall be preserved, and no fact tried by jury, shall be otherwise re-examined in any Court of the United States, than according to the rules of the common law.

AMENDMENT VIII [1791]

Excessive bail shall not be required, nor excessive fines imposed, nor cruel and unusual punishment inflicted.

AMENDMENT IX [1791]

The enumeration in the Constitution, of certain rights, shall not be construed to deny or disparage others retained by the people.

AMENDMENT X [1791]

The powers not delegated to the United States by the Constitution, nor prohibited by it to the States, are reserved to the States respectively, or to the people.

AMENDMENT XIII [1865]

Section 1. Neither slavery nor involuntary servitude, except as a punishment for crime whereof the party shall have been duly convicted, shall exist within the United States, or any place subject to their jurisdiction.

Section 2. Congress shall have power to enforce this article by appropriate legislation.

AMENDMENT XIV [1868]

Section 1. All persons born or naturalized in the United States, and subject to the jurisdiction thereof, are citizens of the United States and of the State wherein they reside. No State shall make or enforce any law which shall abridge the privileges or immunities of citizens of the United States; nor shall any State deprive any person of life, liberty, or property, without due process of law; nor deny to any person within its jurisdiction the equal protection of the laws. * * *

Section 5. The Congress shall have power to enforce, by appropriate legislation, the provisions of this article.

AMENDMENT XV [1870]

Section 1.   The right of citizens of the United States to vote shall not be denied or abridged by the United States or by any State on account of race, color, or previous condition of servitude.

Section 2.   The Congress shall have the power to enforce this article by appropriate legislation.

MEMBERS OF THE SUPREME COURT

Justice	Appointed By	State	To Replace	Judicial Oath Taken	Date Service Terminated
Jay Chief Justice	Washington	NY	New Seat	10/19/1789	6/29/1795
Cushing	Washington	MA	New Seat	2/2/1790	9/13/1810
Rutledge J.[1] Rutledge, Chief Justice	Washington	SC	New Seat Jay	2/15/1790 8/12/1795	3/5/1791 12/15/1795
Wilson	Washington	PA	New Seat	10/5/1789	8/21/1798
Blair	Washington	VA	New Seat	2/2/1790	10/25/1795
Iredell	Washington	NC	New Seat	5/12/1790	10/20/1799
Johnson, T.	Washington	MD	Rutledge, J./Jay	8/6/1792	1/16/1793
Paterson	Washington	NJ	Johnson, T.	3/11/1793	9/9/1806
Chase, S.	Washington	MD	Blair	2/4/1796	6/19/1811
Ellsworth, Chief Justice	Washington	CT	Rutledge, J	3/8/1796	12/15/1800
Washington	Adams, J.	VA	Wilson	2/4/1799	11/26/1829
Moore	Adams. J	NC	Iredell	4/21/1800	1/26/1804
Marshall, J., Chief Justice	Adams, J.	VA	Ellsworth	2/4/1801	7/6/1835
Johnson, W.	Jefferson	SC	Moore	5/7/1804	8/4/1834
Livingston	Jefferson	NY	Paterson	1/20/1807	3/18/1823
Todd	Jefferson	KY	New Seat	5/4/1807	2/7/1826
Duvall	Madison	MD	Chase, S.	11/23/1811	1/14/1835
Story	Madison	MA	Cushing	2/3/1812	9/10/1845
Thompson	Monroe	NY	Livingston	9/1/1823	12/18/1843
Trimble	Adams. J.Q.	KY	Todd	6/16/1826	8/25/1828
McLean	Jackson	OH	Trimble	1/11/1830	4/4/1861
Baldwin	Jackson	PA	Washington	1/18/1830	4/21/1844
Wayne	Jackson	GA	Johnson, W.	1/14/1835	7/5/1867
Taney, Chief Justice	Jackson	MD	Marshall, J.	3/28/1836	10/12/1864
Barbour	Jackson	VA	Duvall	5/12/1836	2/25/1841
Catron	Van Buren	TN	New Seat	5/1/1837	5/30/1865
McKinley	Van Buren	AL	New Seat	1/9/1838	7/19/1852

[1] Recess appointment; nominated 7/1/1795; rejected by Senate 12/15/1795.

Justice	Appointed By	State	To Replace	Judicial Oath Taken	Date Service Terminated
Daniel	Van Buren	VA	Barbour	1/10/1842	5/31/1860
Nelson	Tyler	NY	Thompson	2/27/1845	11/28/1872
Woodbury	Polk	NH	Story	9/23/1845	9/4/1851
Grier	Polk	PA	Baldwin	8/10/1846	1/31/1870
Curtis	Fillmore	MA	Woodbury	10/10/1851	9/30/1857
Campbell	Pierce	AL	McKinley	4/11/1853	4/30/1861
Clifford	Buchanan	ME	Curtis	1/21/1858	7/25/1881
Swayne	Lincoln	OH	McLean	1/27/1862	1/24/1881
Miller	Lincoln	IA	Daniel	7/21/1862	10/13/1890
Davis	Lincoln	IL	Campbell	12/10/1862	3/4/1877
Field[2]	Lincoln	CA	New Seat	5/20/1863	12/1/1897
Chase, S.P., Chief Justice	Lincoln	OH	Taney	12/15/1864	5/7/1873
Strong	Grant	PA	Grier	3/14/1870	12/14/1880
Bradley	Grant	NJ	New Seat	3/23/1870	1/22/1892
Hunt	Grant	NY	Nelson	1/9/1873	1/27/1882
Waite, Chief Justice	Grant	OH	Chase, S.P.	3/4/1874	3/23/1888
Harlan I	Hayes	KY	Davis	12/10/1877	10/14/1911
Woods	Hayes	GA	Strong	1/5/1881	5/14/1887
Matthews	Garfield	OH	Swayne	5/17/1881	3/22/1889
Gray	Arthur	MA	Clifford	1/9/1882	9/15/1902
Blatchford	Arthur	NY	Hunt	4/3/1882	7/7/1893
Lamar. L.	Cleveland	MS	Woods	1/18/1888	1/23/1893
Fuller, Chief Justice	Cleveland	IL	Waite	10/8/1888	7/4/1910
Brewer	Harrison. B.	KS	Matthews	1/6/1890	3/28/1910
Brown	Harrison. B.	MI	Miller	1/5/1891	5/28/1906
Shiras	Harrison. B.	PA	Bradley	10/10/1892	2/23/1903
Jackson. H.	Harrison. B.	TN	Lamar. L.	3/4/1893	8/8/1895
White E.	Cleveland	LA	Blatchford	3/12/1894	12/18/1910

[2] Longest-serving member until Douglas; apparently he was intent on remaining on the Court longer than the record held by John Marshall and he refused to step down even when asked to do so by the other Justices; he did increasingly less Court work through the 1890s, and by the time of his retirement he was practically useless to his colleagues. *See, e.g.,* CARL BRENT SWISHES, STEPHEN J. FIELD, CRAFTSMAN OF THE LAW (1930); G. EDWARD WHITE, THE AMERICAN JUDICIAL TRADITION (1976).

Justice	Appointed By	State	To Replace	Judicial Oath Taken	Date Service Terminated
White, E., Chief Justice	Taft	LA	Fuller	12/19/1910	5/19/1921
Peckham	Cleveland	NY	Jackson. H	1/6/1896	10/24/1909
McKenna	McKinley	CA	Filed	1/26/1898	1/5/1925
Holmes	Roosevelt. T.	MA	Gray	12/8/1902	1/12/1932
Day	Roosevelt, T.	OH	Shiras	3/2/1903	11/13/1922
Moody	Roosevelt. T.	MA	Brown	12/17/1906	11/20/1910
Lurton	Taft	TN	Peckham	1/3/1910	7/12/1914
Hughes	Taft	NY	Brewer	10/10/1910	6/10/1916
Hughes, Chief Justice	Hoover		Taft	2/24/1930	6/30/1941
Van Devanter	Taft	WY	White. E.	1/3/1911	6/2/1937
Lamar, J	Taft	GA	Moody	1/3/1911	1/2/1916
Pitney	Taft	NJ	Harlan I	3/18/1912	12/31/1922
McReynolds	Wilson	TN	Lurton	10/12/1914	1/31/1941
Brandeis	Wilson	MA	Lamar. J.	6/5/1916	2/13/1939
Clarke	Wilson	OH	Hughes	10/9/1916	9/18/1922
Taft, Chief Justice	Harding	CT	White, E	7/11/1921	2/3/1930
Sutherland	Harding	UT	Clarke	10/2/1922	1/17/1938
Butler	Harding	MN	Day	1/2/1923	11/16/1939
Sanford	Harding	TN	Pitney	2/19/1923	3/8/1930
Stone	Coolidge	NY	McKenna	3/2/1925	7/2/1941
Stone, Chief Justice	Roosevelt. F.		Hughes	7/3/1941	4/22/1946
Roberts	Hoover	PA	Sanford	6/2/1930	7/31/1945
Cardozo	Hoover	NY	Holmes	3/14/1932	7/9/1938
Black	Roosevelt. F.	AL	Van Devanter	8/19/1937	9/17/1971
Reed	Roosevelt. F.	KY	Sutherland	1/31/1938	2/25/1957
Frankfurter	Roosevelt. F.	MA	Cardozo	1/30/1939	8/28/1962
Douglas[3]	Roosevelt. F.	CT	Brandeis	4/17/1939	11/12/1975
Murphy	Roosevelt. F.	MI	Butler	2/5/1940	7/19/1949
Byrnes	Roosevelt. F.	SC	McReynolds	7/8/1941	10/3/1942
Jackson. R.	Roosevelt. F.	NY	Stone/Hughes	7/11/1941	10/9/1954
Rutledge, W.	Roosevelt. F.	IA	Byrnes	2/15/1943	9/10/1949
Burton	Truman	OH	Roberts	10/1/1945	10/13/1958

[3] Longest serving member to date.

Justice	Appointed By	State	To Replace	Judicial Oath Taken	Date Service Terminated
Vinson, Chief Justice	Truman	KY	Stone	6/24/1946	9/8/1953
Clark	Truman	TX	Murphy	8/24/1949	6/12/1967
Minton	Truman	IN	Rutledge. W.	10/12/1949	10/15/1956
Warren,[4] Chief Justice	Eisenhower	CA	Vinson	10/5/1953	6/23/1969
Harlan II	Eisenhower	NY	Jackson, R	3/28/1955	9/23/1971
Brennan	Eisenhower	NJ	Minton	10/16/1956	7/20/1990
Whittaker	Eisenhower	MO	Reed	3/25/1957	3/31/1962
Stewart	Eisenhower	OH	Burton	10/14/1958	7/3/198
White. B.	Kennedy	CO	Whittaker	4/16/1962	6/28/1993
Goldberg	Kennedy	IL	Frankfurter	10/1/1962	7/25/1965
Fortas	Johnson, L.	TN	Goldberg	10/4/1965	5/14/1969
Marshall, T.	Johnson, L.	NY	Clark	10/2/1967	10/1/1991
Burger, Chief Justice	Nixon	VA	Warren	6/23/1969	9/26/1986
Blackmun	Nixon	MN	Fortas	6/9/1970	8/3/1994
Powell	Nixon	VA	Black	1/7/1972	6/26/1987
Rehnquist Rehnquist, Chief Justice	Nixon Reagan	AZ	Harlan II Burger	1/7/1972 9/26/1986	9/26/1986 9/3/2005
Stevens	Ford	IL	Douglas	12/19/1975	
O'Connor	Reagan	AZ	Stewart	9/25/1981	1/31/2006
Scalia	Reagan	VA	Rehnquist /Burger	9/26/1986	
Kennedy	Reagan	CA	Powell	2/18/1988	
Souter	Bush	NH	Brennan	10/9/1990	6/29/2009
Thomas	Bush	GA	Marshall, T	10/23/1991	
Ginsburg	Clinton	NY	White, B.	8/10/1993	
Breyer	Clinton	MA	Blackmun	8/3/1994	
Roberts, Chief Justice	Bush	MD	Rehnquist	9/29/2005	
Alito	Bush	NJ	O'Connor	1/31/2006	
Sotomayor	Obama	NY	Souter	8/8/2009	

[4] Joined the Court as a recess appointment on opening day of the 1953 term, shortly after Chief Justice Fred Vinson died unexpectedly; appointment was not confirmed by the Senate until March 1, 1954.

CHAPTER 1

THE CRIMINAL PROCESS: FAILURES, CHOICES, AND LEGITIMACY

■ ■ ■

A. FAILURES

The train from Chattanooga to Memphis passed through northern Alabama on the night of March 25, 1931. Nine black youths and several white youths were riding the freight train illegally. James Goodman, Stories of Scottsboro 3–4 (1995). Four of the blacks were friends who had gotten on the train in Chattanooga. The black and white youths got into a fight, and the black youths "chased or threw" all but one of the whites from the train shortly after it pulled away from a station. *Id.* at 4. At the next stop, Paint Rock, dozens of white men armed with pistols, rifles, and shotguns grabbed the blacks, "tied them to one another with a plow line," put them on a flatbed truck, and drove them to the jail in Scottsboro. *Id.*

The charge, said a deputy, was assault and attempted murder.

JAMES GOODMAN—STORIES OF SCOTTSBORO
(1995), 5–6, 13–16, 19, 21–23.

They were in jail for hours before they found out that there would be another charge. Not until the guards took them out of their cell and lined them up against a wall and the sheriff brought two white women by and asked them to point to the boys who had "had them" did they realize that they had been accused of rape. One of the women, Victoria Price, pointed to six of them. When the other didn't say a word, a guard said that "If those six had Miss Price, it stands to reason that the others had Miss Bates." The boys protested, insisting they hadn't touched the women, hadn't even seen them before Paint Rock, when they saw them being led away from the train. Clarence Norris called the women liars. One of the guards struck him with his bayonet, cutting to the bone the hand that Norris put up to shield his face. "Nigger," the guard hollered, "you know damn well how to talk about white women."

"I was scared before," Norris recalled years later, "but it wasn't nothing to how I felt now. I knew if a white woman accused a black man of rape, he was as good as dead. My hand was bleeding like I don't know

9

what * * * but I didn't even think about it. All I could think was that I was going to die for something that I had not done." * * *

Without some luck they would have been dead already. The night they were arrested they were nearly lynched by several hundred "crackers" who had gathered around the old, dilapidated two-story jail as the news of the arrest spread through the hills of Scottsboro and the neighboring towns. The men leading the mob threatened to break down the doors if the sheriff wouldn't let them in or let the "niggers" out. The boys could hear their voices through the window of their cell. * * *

They were saved by the Jackson County sheriff, M. L. Wann, who, unable to disperse the crowd, called the governor of Alabama, Benjamin Meeks Miller, who, in turn, called the National Guard. But the boys had no way of knowing that the National Guardsmen, white men with guns, distinguishable only by their uniforms from the men threatening to hang them, were not part of the lynching bee. Nor in the weeks that followed that sleepless night could they ever be certain that the guardsmen would protect them from the crowds that gathered every time they were moved from one prison to another or back and forth between prison and court. Men with uniforms had beaten or threatened them in every jail they had been in. * * *

Everything white Alabamans heard or read in the next few days confirmed the story that spread from Paint Rock and Scottsboro the day the posse stopped the train. The day after the arrest, newspapers reported that Price and Bates had identified the Negroes who had attacked them and that all of the Negroes had either confessed or been implicated by the others. Editors repeated these stories in every piece they ran about the case for a week; local reporters and editors, who lived in Scottsboro, Paint Rock, Huntsville, and Decatur and worked as stringers for the Associated Press, wrote the dispatches that the wire service carried all over the South, the first drafts of the newspaper articles most people read.

On April 6, twelve days after the crime, Judge A. E. Hawkins called the Jackson County Court to order. Three days in a row Price and Bates told their story to four different juries, and to a standing-room-only audience, from which women of all ages and men under twenty-one were excluded. At recess and adjournments the audience passed the story on to the crowd outside; reporters rushed to the nearest phone or telegraph office, ensuring that highlights of the testimony made the front pages of papers published later the same day. The white audience listened to Price and Bates tell the white jurors how all nine of the defendants held knives at their throats, pinned down their legs, tore off their clothes, and raped them.

"There were six to me," Price told the jury in the first trial, "and three to her, and three of hers got away. It took three of them to hold me. One was holding my legs and the other had a knife to my throat while the other one ravished me. It took three of those negroes to hold me. It took two to hold me while one had intercourse. The one sitting behind [the]

defendants' counsel took my overalls off. My step-ins were torn off. * * *
This negro boy tore them off. He held me while he took them off. Six of
them had intercourse with me. The one sitting there was the first one. I
don't know the name of the next one. * * * I know them when I see them.
I can surely point out the next one. Yonder he sits, yonder. That boy had
intercourse with me. The third one was the little bit of one; yonder he is.
He held my legs while this one and that one ravished me and then he took
my legs again." In what seemed like two or three hours, each of them was
raped six times. They begged the Negroes to quit but the men ignored
them, and even after they finished they stayed in the car with them,
"telling us they were going to take us north and make us their women or
kill us." * * *

Writers and editors all over the region agreed that it was the most
atrocious crime ever recorded in that part of the country, perhaps in the
whole United States, "a wholesale debauching of society * * * so horrible
in its details that all the facts could never be printed," a "heinous and
unspeakable crime" that "savored of the jungle, the way back dark ages of
meanest African corruption." They were revolted by the story, but not
surprised. Or if surprised, surprised only by the magnitude of the crime.
They expected black men to rape white women. Blacks were savages, more
savage, many argued (with scientific theories to support them), than they
had been as slaves. Savages with an irrepressible sex drive and an appetite
for white women. They were born rapists, rapists by instinct; given the
chance, they struck. Two white women swore that they had been raped.
Even if all nine of the boys had denied it and told the same story it is
likely they would have been convicted; accusations much less serious and
less substantiated had condemned black men. Bates and Price charged
rape. Most of the boys denied it.[a] There was no question in anyone's mind
about whom to believe. * * *

Victoria Price and Ruby Bates knew two versions of the events on
that freight train, and they told one of them to the sheriff's deputies, local
reporters, solicitor, judge, and jurors. In search of work, they had traveled
to Chattanooga the only way they could afford. They had no luck in
Chattanooga, and much worse luck on their way home, when they were
brutally assaulted and repeatedly raped by nine black men. Had the posse
not stopped the train in Paint Rock, the Negroes would have raped them
again, or killed them, or taken them up north. "When I saw them nab
those Negroes," Price told reporters, "I sure was happy. Mister, I never
had a break in my life. Those Negroes have ruined me and Ruby forever.
The only thing I ask is that they give them all the law allows." * * *

Price and Bates worked in the worst mills. They came from families
that had been battered by underemployment and poverty in the best of
times. They had meager schooling if any at all. They lived with their
mothers in unpainted wooden shacks in the worst sections of town.

---

a. Two of the defendants, Wright and Patterson, testified on at least one occasion that some
of the defendants (not they or their Chattanooga friends) had had intercourse with the women.
Goodman, at 14–15.

Bates's family was the only white family on their block, and their block was in the Negro section of town.

Their lives mocked the white South's most sacred ideal. More prosperous southerners liked to boast that the color line extended from the top to the bottom of southern society, and often it did. Yet no one who looked carefully could fail to notice that by the time it reached cities like Huntsville it was frayed beyond repair. Price and Bates lived among black people, played with them as children, roamed the streets with them as teenagers, bootlegged liquor and got drunk with them as young adults. They also went out with them, slept with them, fell in and out of love with them, apparently unaware of the widespread wishful thinking that made it possible for many white southerners to call all sex between white women and black men rape. No white woman, one Mississippi editor put it, no matter how degraded or depraved, would ever willingly "bestow her favors on a black man." Price and Bates had heard the words *white supremacy*, *segregation*, and *white womanhood*, but they did not live by them. In the eyes of "respectable" southern whites, Price and Bates had sunk as low as two women with white skin could sink. Perhaps lower. One frustrated Huntsville social worker complained that the whites in the mill villages were "as bad as the niggers."

Until they were thought to have been raped. When sheriff's deputies found Price and Bates alongside the train at Paint Rock and realized they had been on it alone with the Negroes who had thrown the white boys off, their first thought was of rape. Later, no one could say for sure what came first, Price and Bates's accusation or the sheriff's interrogation. Some said that the girls had offered the charge without encouragement; others said that they had said nothing about an assault until a deputy asked if the Negroes had bothered them. Either way, Price and Bates were not deluded. They knew that the black youths had not raped them or bothered them in any way.[b] But they also knew that if they had said nothing or no—"No, those Negroes didn't even speak to us"—the people who asked would have thought of them the way respectable white men and women had always thought of them: as the lowest of the low, vagabonds, adulterers, bootleggers, tramps. If, on the other hand, they complained or said yes, the same people would suddenly have thought of them as rape victims and treated them as white southern women, poor but virtuous, for the first time in their lives. It was a rare opportunity, and the choice was not a hard one for them to make. * * *

On the witness stand there were all sorts of things about the trip to Chattanooga and the rape that Bates could not remember. She contradicted herself when asked whether she and Price had known the white boys

---

b. That Ruby Bates was lying when she testified that the defendants raped her is not open to serious doubt. She admitted in a letter dated January 5, 1932 that "those Negroes did not touch me or those white boys." Goodman, 195. Though she later recanted the letter, under police threat of one hundred days on the chain gang, *id*. at 195, she testified in a subsequent trial that "the defendants did not rape, touch, or even speak to her and Victoria." *Id*. at 132. Despite this testimony, it took the jury only moments to vote unanimously to convict (it took eleven hours to persuade one juror to vote for the death penalty). *Id*. at 145.

on the train or traveled with them the day before. And unlike Price, she couldn't say positively which of the defendants had raped her, which ones had raped Price, or in what order. But considering what she had gone through, neither juries nor spectators held her bad memory against her; she got the most important part of the story right. She remembered clearly that two of the Negroes had guns and the rest had knives and that after chasing the white boys off the train they had thrown them down in the gondola, held knives at their throats, and raped each of them six times. * * *

POWELL v. ALABAMA

Supreme Court of the United States, 1932.
287 U.S. 45, 53 S.Ct. 55, 77 L.Ed. 158.

MR. JUSTICE SUTHERLAND delivered the opinion of the Court.

These cases were argued together and submitted for decision as one case.

The petitioners, hereinafter referred to as defendants, are negroes charged with the crime of rape, committed upon the persons of two white girls. The crime is said to have been committed on March 25, 1931. The indictment was returned in a state court of first instance on March 31, and the record recites that on the same day the defendants were arraigned and entered pleas of not guilty. There is a further recital to the effect that upon the arraignment they were represented by counsel. But no counsel had been employed, and aside from a statement made by the trial judge several days later during a colloquy immediately preceding the trial, the record does not disclose when, or under what circumstances, an appointment of counsel was made, or who was appointed. During the colloquy referred to, the trial judge, in response to a question, said that he had appointed all the members of the bar for the purpose of arraigning the defendants and then of course anticipated that the members of the bar would continue to help the defendants if no counsel appeared. Upon the argument here both sides accepted that as a correct statement of the facts concerning the matter.

There was a severance upon the request of the state, and the defendants were tried in three several groups, as indicated above. As each of the three cases was called for trial, each defendant was arraigned, and, having the indictment read to him, entered a plea of not guilty. Whether the original arraignment and pleas were regarded as ineffective is not shown. Each of the three trials was completed within a single day. Under the Alabama statute the punishment for rape is to be fixed by the jury, and in its discretion may be from ten years imprisonment to death. The juries found defendants guilty and imposed the death penalty upon all. The trial court overruled motions for new trials and sentenced the defendants in accordance with the verdicts. The judgments were affirmed by the state supreme court. Chief Justice Anderson thought the defendants had not been accorded a fair trial and strongly dissented.

In this court the judgments are assailed upon the grounds that the defendants, and each of them, were denied due process of law and the equal protection of the laws, in contravention of the Fourteenth Amendment, specifically as follows: (1) they were not given a fair, impartial and deliberate trial; (2) they were denied the right of counsel, with the accustomed incidents of consultation and opportunity of preparation for trial; and (3) they were tried before juries from which qualified members of their own race were systematically excluded. These questions were properly raised and saved in the courts below.

The only one of the assignments which we shall consider is the second, in respect of the denial of counsel; and it becomes unnecessary to discuss the facts of the case or the circumstances surrounding the prosecution except in so far as they reflect light upon that question. * * *

* * * The record does not disclose [defendants'] ages, except that one of them was nineteen; but the record clearly indicates that most, if not all, of them were youthful, and they are constantly referred to as "the boys." They were ignorant and illiterate. All of them were residents of other states, where alone members of their families or friends resided.

However guilty defendants, upon due inquiry, might prove to have been, they were, until convicted, presumed to be innocent. It was the duty of the court having their cases in charge to see that they were denied no necessary incident of a fair trial. With any error of the state court involving alleged contravention of the state statutes or constitution we, of course, have nothing to do. The sole inquiry which we are permitted to make is whether the federal Constitution was contravened; and as to that, we confine ourselves, as already suggested, to the inquiry whether the defendants were in substance denied the right of counsel, and if so, whether such denial infringes the due process clause of the Fourteenth Amendment.

First. The record shows that immediately upon the return of the indictment defendants were arraigned and pleaded not guilty. Apparently they were not asked whether they had, or were able to employ, counsel, or wished to have counsel appointed; or whether they had friends or relatives who might assist in that regard if communicated with. That it would not have been an idle ceremony to have given the defendants reasonable opportunity to communicate with their families and endeavor to obtain counsel is demonstrated by the fact that, very soon after conviction, able counsel appeared in their behalf. This was pointed out by Chief Justice Anderson in the course of his dissenting opinion. "They were nonresidents," he said, "and had little time or opportunity to get in touch with their families and friends who were scattered throughout two other states, and time has demonstrated that they could or would have been represented by able counsel had a better opportunity been given by a reasonable delay in the trial of the cases, judging from the number and activity of counsel that appeared immediately or shortly after their conviction."

It is hardly necessary to say that, the right to counsel being conceded, a defendant should be afforded a fair opportunity to secure counsel of his own choice. Not only was that not done here, but such designation of counsel as was attempted was either so indefinite or so close upon the trial as to amount to a denial of effective and substantial aid in that regard. This will be amply demonstrated by a brief review of the record.

April 6, six days after indictment, the trials began. When the first case was called, the court inquired whether the parties were ready for trial. The state's attorney replied that he was ready to proceed. No one answered for the defendants or appeared to represent or defend them. Mr. Roddy, a Tennessee lawyer not a member of the local bar, addressed the court, saying that he had not been employed, but that people who were interested had spoken to him about the case. He was asked by the court whether he intended to appear for the defendants, and answered that he would like to appear along with counsel that the court might appoint. * * *

It thus will be seen that until the very morning of the trial no lawyer had been named or definitely designated to represent the defendants. Prior to that time, the trial judge had "appointed all the members of the bar" for the limited "purpose of arraigning the defendants." Whether they would represent the defendants thereafter if no counsel appeared in their behalf, was a matter of speculation only, or, as the judge indicated, of mere anticipation on the part of the court. Such a designation, even if made for all purposes, would, in our opinion, have fallen far short of meeting, in any proper sense, a requirement for the appointment of counsel. How many lawyers were members of the bar does not appear; but, in the very nature of things, whether many or few, they would not, thus collectively named, have been given that clear appreciation of responsibility or impressed with that individual sense of duty which should and naturally would accompany the appointment of a selected member of the bar, specifically named and assigned.

That this action of the trial judge in respect of appointment of counsel was little more than an expansive gesture, imposing no substantial or definite obligation upon any one, is borne out by the fact that prior to the calling of the case for trial on April 6, a leading member of the local bar accepted employment on the side of the prosecution and actively participated in the trial. It is true that he said that before doing so he had understood Mr. Roddy would be employed as counsel for the defendants. This the lawyer in question, of his own accord, frankly stated to the court; and no doubt he acted with the utmost good faith. Probably other members of the bar had a like understanding. In any event, the circumstance lends emphasis to the conclusion that during perhaps the most critical period of the proceedings against these defendants, that is to say, from the time of their arraignment until the beginning of their trial, when consultation, thoroughgoing investigation and preparation were vitally important, the defendants did not have the aid of counsel in any real sense, although they were as much entitled to such aid during that period as at the trial itself.

Nor do we think the situation was helped by what occurred on the morning of the trial. At that time, as appears from the [record], Mr. Roddy stated to the court that he did not appear as counsel, but that he would like to appear along with counsel that the court might appoint; that he had not been given an opportunity to prepare the case; that he was not familiar with the procedure in Alabama, but merely came down as a friend of the people who were interested; that he thought the boys would be better off if he should step entirely out of the case. Mr. Moody, a member of the local bar, expressed a willingness to help Mr. Roddy in anything he could do under the circumstances. To this the court responded, "All right, all the lawyers that will; of course I would not require a lawyer to appear if—." And Mr. Moody continued, "I am willing to do that for him as a member of the bar; I will go ahead and help do any thing I can do." With this dubious understanding, the trials immediately proceeded. The defendants, young, ignorant, illiterate, surrounded by hostile sentiment, haled back and forth under guard of soldiers, charged with an atrocious crime regarded with especial horror in the community where they were to be tried, were thus put in peril of their lives within a few moments after counsel for the first time charged with any degree of responsibility began to represent them.

It is not enough to assume that counsel thus precipitated into the case thought there was no defense, and exercised their best judgment in proceeding to trial without preparation. Neither they nor the court could say what a prompt and thoroughgoing investigation might disclose as to the facts. No attempt was made to investigate. No opportunity to do so was given. Defendants were immediately hurried to trial. Chief Justice Anderson, after disclaiming any intention to criticize harshly counsel who attempted to represent defendants at the trials, said: " * * * the record indicates that the appearance was rather *pro forma* than zealous and active * * *." Under the circumstances disclosed, we hold that defendants were not accorded the right of counsel in any substantial sense. To decide otherwise, would simply be to ignore actualities. * * *

It is true that great and inexcusable delay in the enforcement of our criminal law is one of the grave evils of our time. Continuances are frequently granted for unnecessarily long periods of time, and delays incident to the disposition of motions for new trial and hearings upon appeal have come in many cases to be a distinct reproach to the administration of justice. The prompt disposition of criminal cases is to be commended and encouraged. But in reaching that result a defendant, charged with a serious crime, must not be stripped of his right to have sufficient time to advise with counsel and prepare his defense. To do that is not to proceed promptly in the calm spirit of regulated justice but to go forward with the haste of the mob. * * *

Second. The Constitution of Alabama provides that in all criminal prosecutions the accused shall enjoy the right to have the assistance of counsel; and a state statute requires the court in a capital case, where the defendant is unable to employ counsel, to appoint counsel for him. The state supreme court held that these provisions had not been infringed, and with that holding we are powerless to interfere. The question, however, which it is our duty, and within our power, to decide, is whether the denial of the assistance of counsel contravenes the due process clause of the Fourteenth Amendment to the federal Constitution. * * *

It never has been doubted by this court, or any other so far as we know, that notice and hearing are preliminary steps essential to the passing of an enforceable judgment, and that they, together with a legally competent tribunal having jurisdiction of the case, constitute basic elements of the constitutional requirement of due process of law. The words of Webster, so often quoted, that by "the law of the land" is intended "a law which hears before it condemns," have been repeated in varying forms of expression in a multitude of decisions. * * *

What, then, does a hearing include? Historically and in practice, in our own country at least, it has always included the right to the aid of counsel when desired and provided by the party asserting the right. The right to be heard would be, in many cases, of little avail if it did not comprehend the right to be heard by counsel. Even the intelligent and educated layman has small and sometimes no skill in the science of law. If charged with crime, he is incapable, generally, of determining for himself whether the indictment is good or bad. He is unfamiliar with the rules of evidence. Left without the aid of counsel he may be put on trial without a proper charge, and convicted upon incompetent evidence, or evidence irrelevant to the issue or otherwise inadmissible. He lacks both the skill and knowledge adequately to prepare his defense, even though he have a perfect one. He requires the guiding hand of counsel at every step in the proceedings against him. Without it, though he be not guilty, he faces the danger of conviction because he does not know how to establish his innocence. If that be true of men of intelligence, how much more true is it of the ignorant and illiterate, or those of feeble intellect. If in any case, civil or criminal, a state or federal court were arbitrarily to refuse to hear a party by counsel, employed by and appearing for him, it reasonably may not be doubted that such a refusal would be a denial of a hearing, and, therefore, of due process in the constitutional sense. * * *

In the light of the facts outlined in the forepart of this opinion—the ignorance and illiteracy of the defendants, their youth, the circumstances of public hostility, the imprisonment and the close surveillance of the defendants by the military forces, the fact that their friends and families were all in other states and communication with them necessarily difficult, and above all that they stood in deadly peril of their lives—we think the failure of the trial court to give them reasonable time and opportunity to secure counsel was a clear denial of due process.

But passing that, and assuming their inability, even if opportunity had been given, to employ counsel, as the trial court evidently did assume, we are of opinion that, under the circumstances just stated, the necessity of counsel was so vital and imperative that the failure of the trial court to make an effective appointment of counsel was likewise a denial of due process within the meaning of the Fourteenth Amendment. Whether this would be so in other criminal prosecutions, or under other circumstances, we need not determine. All that it is necessary now to decide, as we do decide, is that in a capital case, where the defendant is unable to employ counsel, and is incapable adequately of making his own defense because of ignorance, feeble mindedness, illiteracy, or the like, it is the duty of the court, whether requested or not, to assign counsel for him as a necessary requisite of due process of law; and that duty is not discharged by an assignment at such a time or under such circumstances as to preclude the giving of effective aid in the preparation and trial of the case. To hold otherwise would be to ignore the fundamental postulate * * * "that there are certain immutable principles of justice which inhere in the very idea of free government which no member of the Union may disregard." * * *

The judgments must be reversed and the causes remanded for further proceedings not inconsistent with this opinion.

Judgments reversed.

Mr. Justice BUTLER, dissenting. * * *

If there had been any lack of opportunity for preparation, trial counsel would have applied to the court for postponement. No such application was made. There was no suggestion, at the trial or in the motion for a new trial which they made, that Mr. Roddy or Mr. Moody was denied such opportunity or that they were not in fact fully prepared. The amended motion for new trial, by counsel who succeeded them, contains the first suggestion that defendants were denied counsel or opportunity to prepare for trial. But neither Mr. Roddy nor Mr. Moody has given any support to that claim. Their silence requires a finding that the claim is groundless, for if it had any merit they would be bound to support it. And no one has come to suggest any lack of zeal or good faith on their part.

If correct, the ruling that the failure of the trial court to give petitioners time and opportunity to secure counsel was denied of due process is enough, and with this the opinion should end. But the Court goes on to declare that 'the failure of the trial court to make an effective appointment of counsel was likewise a denial of due process within the meaning of the Fourteenth Amendment.' This is an extension of federal authority into a field hitherto occupied exclusively by the several States. Nothing before the Court calls for a consideration of the point. It was not suggested below and petitioners do not ask for its decision here. The Court, without being called upon to consider it, adjudges without a hearing an important constitutional question concerning criminal procedure in state courts. * * *

Mr. Justice McREYNOLDS concurs in this opinion.

NOTES AND QUESTIONS

1.   In what sense did the defendants here lack a lawyer? The judge, after all, appointed all the members of the local bar.

2.   *Doubts about guilt.* The excerpt about the Scottsboro defendants cannot begin to capture the richness of the account in James Goodman, Stories of Scottsboro (1995), which we highly recommend. The *Powell* Court was without Goodman's historical account strongly suggesting that no rapes took place. Even without an independent historical account, the Court could easily have been skeptical of the story told by the State, given the locale and racial dimension. If you had been on the *Powell* Court, would doubt about guilt have made you more likely to find a violation of the right to counsel? Turning the question around, would you *still* have found a violation of the right to counsel on these facts, even if the evidence of guilt had been overwhelming? If not, why not?

3.   *Further proceedings not inconsistent with this opinion.* Look again at the order at the end of the majority opinion. It is a standard order when a court reverses a lower court. Alabama could then choose to dismiss the indictments or retry the defendants with effective counsel at their side. In this case, though, the order represented a test of federal power. Given the white-hot rage that the rapes and the trials provoked, would Alabama find some way to defy the federal court? (You will see state defiance of the Supreme Court in Note 5.) According to *The New York Times* correspondent in Birmingham, however, there was "little public tendency" in Alabama "to protest the new trial ordered by the Supreme Court." Indeed, "a great many Alabamians * * * suspect[ed] that the trial itself was not fair to the spirit even if it was faithful to the letter of the law." John Temple Graves 2d, *Alabama Approves Scottsboro Ruling*, The New York Times, November 13, 1932.

And there would be many retrials. A total of eleven trials involved the nine defendants during the 1930s. Alabama dropped charges against four of the defendants in 1937. The other five eventually received convictions that withstood appellate review; the sentences were twenty years, seventy-five years (two defendants), ninety-nine years, and death. The death sentence was commuted to life by Alabama Governor Bibb Graves. The Scottsboro defendants were paroled in 1943, 1946, and 1950. One escaped from prison in 1948 and was arrested in Detroit in 1950. Michigan governor G. Mennen Williams refused Alabama's request for extradition, and Alabama abandoned extradition proceedings. In 1976, Governor George Wallace pardoned the last surviving Scottsboro defendant (the one who had been sentenced to death).

4.   The irony of Wallace pardoning one of the Scottsboro defendants may be lost on many readers. Wallace was best known for his staunch pro-segregation views when he was governor of Alabama in the 1950s and 1960s. Oddly enough, in his first race for governor, he was a racial moderate but lost to a candidate endorsed by the Ku Klux Klan. After that defeat, according to at least two sources but denied by Wallace, he vowed never to be "outniggered again." Dan T. Carter, The Politics of Rage: George Wallace, the Origins of the New Conservatism and the Transformation of American Politics 96

(1995). In 1963, he sought to block "the school house door" and prevent two black students from enrolling at the University of Alabama. He moved out of the way when confronted by the Deputy Attorney General of the United States, federal marshals, and units of the Alabama National Guard that had been nationalized by President Kennedy. *Id.* at 150.

Wallace ran for president in 1968 as an independent candidate, collecting 13.5% of the popular vote and 45 electoral votes, all in the Deep South. In 1972, he campaigned for the Democratic nomination and transformed himself into a national candidate. He won primaries in Maryland and Michigan, and he finished a close second in Indiana and Wisconsin. Indeed, he finished a close third in total primary votes with 23%, trailing only Hubert Humphrey, 26%, and George McGovern, 25%.

But his chance to win the Democratic nomination effectively ended when Arthur Bremer, a young loner intent on killing either Nixon or Wallace, shot Wallace five times at a campaign rally in Wisconsin. *Id.* at 419, 437. Grievously wounded, and confined to a wheelchair, he was a spent force at the convention. Bremer was sentenced to sixty-three years in prison for the shooting. *Id.* at 444. In 2007, he was released from prison, a man who according to a Maryland corrections official "is alone. He has no one." Catharine Skipp & Arian Campo–Flores, *Arthur Bremer Is Alone*, Newsweek, November 19, 2007.

Late in his life, Wallace sought reconciliation with black politicians and African–Americans in general (primarily conducted through predominantly black churches) in Alabama. As historian Dan Carter comments, "[b]lack Alabamians wanted Wallace to be forgiven." Carter, at 463. His pardon of one of the Scottsboro defendants might have been part of this effort at reconciliation.

5. *Predecessor I to Powell.* More than a quarter century prior to *Powell*, the Court sought to intervene in a racially-flawed Southern death penalty case. The rape of a young white woman by a black man in 1906 in Chattanooga, Tennessee unleashed a storm of fury and racism. The sheriff arrested two black men and the prosecutor chose Ed Johnson, the one the victim came closer to identifying. But at the trial, the rape victim refused to say for certain that Johnson was her attacker. She would only testify, "To the best of my knowledge and belief, he is the same man." The defense team, three white lawyers, mounted an aggressive alibi defense that put the State's case in doubt.

At one point, a member of the jury rose to his feet, "tears streaming down his face * * * and in a voice trembling with emotion, he cried: 'In God's name, Miss Taylor, tell us positively—is that the guilty negro? Can you say it—can you swear it?' "

She responded: "Listen to me. I would not take the life of an innocent man. But before God, I believe this is the guilty negro."

The jury initially voted 8–4 for conviction and the judge sent them home for the evening. When the jury returned the next day, the doubts of the four dissenting jurors had somehow been laid to rest. Ed Johnson was found guilty and sentenced to hang. The Supreme Court granted a hearing on a writ of habeas corpus to examine whether the trial met due process fairness standards. To permit the hearing to proceed, the Court granted a stay of execution and issued an order that the prisoner be kept safe. The intervention by the federal court proved too much for some in the community.

The headlines in the Chattanooga News the next day, March 20, 1906, told the whole story: " 'God Bless You All—I Am Innocent,' Ed Johnson's Last Words Before Being Shot to Death By a Mob Like a Dog, Majesty of the Law Outraged by Lynchers, Mandate of the Supreme Court of the United States Disregarded and Red Riot Rampant, Terrible and Tragic Vengeance Bows City's Head in Shame."

President Theodore Roosevelt condemned the lynching as "contemptuous of the Court." Using the bloodless language of formal judicial opinions, the Court dismissed Johnson's appeal on the ground that it was "abated by the death of the appellant." Johnson v. Tennessee, 214 U.S. 485, 29 S.Ct. 651, 53 L.Ed. 1056 (1909). But prior to dismissing the appeal, the Court did something extraordinary. It ordered a federal criminal trial that resulted in contempt convictions for the Chattanooga sheriff and several other law enforcement officers.

In 2000, a Chattanooga court granted a petition to clear Mr. Johnson of the rape. Leroy Phillips, a local lawyer, noted during the proceeding that 4,708 lynchings took place in the United States from 1882 to 1944, according to an archive at Tuskegee University in Alabama. For a fuller description of the Johnson case, the heroes and villains, and its aftermath, see Mark Curriden & Leroy Phillips, Jr., Contempt of Court (1999); George C. Thomas III, The Supreme Court on Trial: How the American Justice System Sacrifices Innocent Defendants (2008).

6. *Predecessor II to Powell.* A similar story of lawlessness played itself out in Georgia in 1915. The vicious murder of a young woman in Atlanta led to sensational newspaper coverage and to the arrest of Leo Frank, her employer. From the beginning, the case attracted nationwide attention, in part because Frank was Jewish and anti-Semitism was on the rise in the United States. Frank was convicted and sentenced to death based wholly on circumstantial evidence offered in a trial that took place, according to Justice Oliver Wendell Holmes, "in the presence of a hostile demonstration and seemingly dangerous crowd, thought by the presiding judge to be ready for violence unless a verdict of guilty was rendered." Leonard Dinnerstein, The Leo Frank Case 109 (1968). Despite Holmes's due process concern, the Court, 7–2, denied Frank's habeas corpus petition. Frank v. Mangum, 237 U.S. 309, 35 S.Ct. 582, 59 L.Ed. 969 (1915). Such was the reluctance of the Supreme Court in the early twentieth century to reverse the fact finding of state courts.

A petition seeking executive clemency was filed with Georgia governor John M. Slaton. Over 100,000 letters asking for commutation arrived in the offices of the governor and the Prison Commission. *Id.* at 122. The Prison Commission voted two-to-one not to recommend clemency. After holding his own hearings into the facts of the murder, Slaton commuted Frank's death sentence to life in prison. "Privately, Slaton confided to friends that he believed Frank innocent and would have granted a full pardon if he were not convinced that in a short while the truth would come out * * *." *Id.* at 129.

Many Georgians were furious at the commutation. His political career ruined, Slaton had to call out an entire battalion of state militia to keep from being lynched. *Id.* at 132. The commutation failed to save Frank. Two months later, a mob of twenty-five men stormed the prison farm, abducted Frank, and hung him. "Hordes of people made their way to the oak tree" to view Frank's body and take pictures. *Id.* at 143. Those who planned and participated in this lawless act included a "clergyman, two former Superior Court judges, and an ex-sheriff." *Id.* at 139. The *Marietta Journal and Courier* wrote: "We regard the hanging of Leo M. Frank in Cobb County as an act of law abiding citizens." *Id.* at 145.

7. *Trying to make sense of it all.* How could clergymen, judges, and law officers have participated in the conduct described in Note 6? Consider Michael Klarman's observations about the Scottsboro case:

> If all of this seems extraordinary to modern eyes, one must remember that for white southerners defending mob-dominated trials, the relevant comparison was to lynchings rather than to elaborate court proceedings accompanied by all the trappings of due process. Thus, a local newspaper warned in connection with a mob-dominated trial conducted contemporaneously with Scottsboro that challenging the conviction was "playing with fire," since a hasty trial was preferable to a lynching and indeed was "a first step, and a very important one." Local newspapers frequently crowed with pride after a lynching was averted and congratulated local citizens on the admirable self-restraint they had demonstrated. White Alabamians seemed genuinely puzzled at outside criticism of their handling of the Scottsboro cases. Avoiding a lynching was "a genuine step forward," and thus was deserving of commendation, not condemnation. The state supreme court lauded the speed of the Scottsboro Boys' trials as likely to instill greater respect for the law. A state member of the Commission on Interracial Cooperation thought it odd that Alabama should be criticized for delivering exactly what the [Commission] had been fighting so hard to accomplish—replacement of lynchings with trials. Several southern newspapers warned in connection with Scottsboro that if outsiders continued to assail Alabama after juries had returned guilty verdicts, then there would be little incentive to resist a lynching on future occasions.

Michael J. Klarman, *The Racial Origins of Modern Criminal Procedure*, 99 Mich. L. Rev. 48, 56–57 (2000).

8. *The broader effect of Powell.* Look again at Justice Butler's dissent in *Powell*. Butler is correct that federal courts, particularly in the nineteenth and early twentieth centuries, were loathe to impose federal supervision over state criminal justice systems. And, as Justice Butler points out, the Court could have decided the case in favor of the defendants by finding insufficient time to prepare. Yet the Court also held that the failure to appoint counsel violated due process. Why do you think the Court went this additional step?

If the Court hoped that requiring counsel in cases like *Powell* would lead to better representation of blacks in southern states, and that better representation would lead to a different set of outcomes, its hopes were probably not realized. Professor Michael Klarman writes:

Even if *Powell* did ensure better legal representation for southern black defendants, how much this affected actual case outcomes is uncertain. The [Communist International Labor Defense] criticized *Powell* because the Justices apparently had selected the least significant ground for reversing the Scottsboro Boys' convictions. Indeed, the Communists accused the Court of simply providing Alabama with instructions on how properly to lynch the defendants. Even if appointed days before trial and afforded adequate opportunity to prepare a defense, counsel generally could do little to assist clients like the Scottsboro Boys. Black lawyers, who might have been willing aggressively to pursue their clients' defense, were few and far between in the South, and in any event were distinct liabilities owing to the prejudice they aroused among white judges and juries. White lawyers, on the other hand, generally refrained from pressing defenses that raised broader challenges to the Jim Crow system, such as race-based exclusion from juries. In any event, even the most earnest advocacy rarely could influence case outcomes when the system was so pervasively stacked against fair adjudication of the legal claims of black defendants. The Scottsboro Boys did enjoy outstanding legal representation in their retrials, yet it made absolutely no difference to the outcomes.

Michael J. Klarman, *The Racial Origins of Modern Criminal Procedure*, 99 Mich. L. Rev. 48, 78 (2000).

Indeed, it is not clear that the promise of *Powell* has been realized even today. Consider the following description of what the criminal process looked and felt like to one public defender.

GERALD B. LEFCOURT—RESPONSIBILITIES OF A CRIMINAL DEFENSE ATTORNEY

30 Loyola of Los Angeles Law Review 59 (1996), 59–63.

Our perspective as criminal defense lawyers is often based on a pivotal experience. Mine was as a law school honors program participant, sent to work with Legal Aid Society lawyers—New York City's public defenders. I was assigned to help a young lawyer handling arraignments. In New York City that meant a daily crush of cases. His job was to seek bail as each defendant entered the system. In disgusting pens holding as many as forty prisoners, I would interview clients. I was the first person many prisoners saw after they had spent up to four days waiting to appear before the court.

The holding pens were filled with huddling defendants, most of whom were standing because there was only one bench. Virtually the entire population of the pens was nonwhite and poor, without the resources or stable families to allow them bail. Most were in shock or panic, yelling questions and begging for help. "What am I charged with?" "When will I ever get out?" "Can you call my mother?" "What if I didn't do it; will they still keep me?" "Will you call my boss because if I don't show up I'll lose my job?"

I came to see that most of them were not really represented at all. Not only would they not make bail, but most would ultimately plead guilty to something, anything, just to move out of the system. I realized that with a lawyer who had a few days to spend with the client instead of a few minutes, a proper fight could be waged, both to get the defendant out on bail and ultimately, to get a favorable disposition. In many cases defendants would not have ended up with criminal records, a millstone that serves to keep the underclasses as underclasses.

I realized that the Legal Aid attorneys, like their counterparts across the country, were not properly trained, had no resources, and were, frankly, overwhelmed. The number of defendants was so great that there was no time for the niceties of an interview long enough to establish any relationship, much less one of trust.

So, there were two systems operating, one for the wealthy who had the resources to seek vindication of their rights and one for the rest of society, left haphazardly to lawyers who could ensure entirely less predictable results.

It was obvious that a system promising the right to counsel was a farce.

NOTES AND QUESTIONS

1. Lefcourt's anecdotal experience is borne out by the data. Researchers McConville and Mirsky concluded in 1990 that in large cities "criminal courts are places of *mass* processing," which "arraign defendants twenty-four hours a day, seven days a week." On days set for docketing cases, "lower courts commonly docket 100 or more cases a day, while superior courts often docket 60 felony indictments a day. Court business is conducted in a swirl of activity as judges seek to 'move' crowded calendars." Michael McConville & Chester L. Mirsky, *Understanding Defense of the Poor in State Courts*, 10 Studies in Law, Politics, and Society 217, 217 (1990).

Any thoughts about why public defense in large cities has become mass processing?

2. Do you think Justice Sutherland, the author of the majority opinion in *Powell*, would consider the system described by Lefcourt and in Note 1 to constitute the "Assistance of Counsel"? Does this description portend "the guiding hand of counsel at every step in the proceedings"? How is the representation described here better or worse than the representation provided by Mr. Roddy and the local bar in *Powell*?

3. *Is indigent defense really that bad?* In 2009, the National Right to Counsel Committee issued a report entitled *Justice Denied: America's Continuing Neglect of our Constitutional Right to Counsel*. The report details systemic and endemic failures of indigent defense in this country. It found "overwhelming" evidence that, in most of the country, "quality defense work is simply impossible because of inadequate funding, excessive caseloads, a lack of genuine independence, and insufficient availability of other essential resources."

The report provides twenty-two recommendations for improvement and can be found at http://tcpjusticedenied.org/. See also Mary Sue Backus & Paul Marcus, *The Right to Counsel in Criminal Cases, A National Crisis*, 57 Hastings L. J. 1031 (2006).

The committee included prosecutors, judges, defense lawyers, and academics. The honorary co-chairs were Walter Mondale, former Democratic candidate for president, and William Sessions, former director of the FBI.

The right to counsel is considered in depth in Chapter 14.

4. *After Powell came Brown v. Mississippi.* If you were surprised by the treatment of the suspects in *Powell* by officers sworn to uphold the law, prepare for an even more brutal case.

BROWN v. MISSISSIPPI

Supreme Court of the United States, 1936.
297 U.S. 278, 56 S.Ct. 461, 80 L.Ed. 682.

MR. CHIEF JUSTICE HUGHES delivered the opinion of the Court.

The question in this case is whether convictions, which rest solely upon confessions shown to have been extorted by officers of the State by brutality and violence, are consistent with the due process of law required by the Fourteenth Amendment of the Constitution of the United States.

Petitioners were indicted for the murder of one Raymond Stewart, whose death occurred on March 30, 1934. They were indicted on April 4, 1934, and were then arraigned and pleaded not guilty. Counsel were appointed by the court to defend them. Trial was begun the next morning and was concluded on the following day, when they were found guilty and sentenced to death.

Aside from the confessions, there was no evidence sufficient to warrant the submission of the case to the jury. After a preliminary inquiry, testimony as to the confessions was received over the objection of defendants' counsel. Defendants then testified that the confessions were false and had been procured by physical torture. The case went to the jury with instructions, upon the request of defendants' counsel, that if the jury had reasonable doubt as to the confessions having resulted from coercion, and that they were not true, they were not to be considered as evidence. On their appeal to the Supreme Court of the State, defendants assigned as error the inadmissibility of the confessions. The judgment was affirmed.

Defendants then moved in the Supreme Court of the State to arrest the judgment and for a new trial on the ground that all the evidence against them was obtained by coercion and brutality known to the court and to the district attorney, and that defendants had been denied the benefit of counsel or opportunity to confer with counsel in a reasonable manner. The motion was supported by affidavits. At about the same time, defendants filed in the Supreme Court a "suggestion of error" explicitly challenging the proceedings of the trial, in the use of the confessions and with respect to the alleged denial of representation by counsel, as violating the due process clause of the Fourteenth Amendment of the Constitution of the United States. The state court entertained the suggestion of error, considered the federal question, and decided it against defendants' contentions. Two judges dissented. * * *

The grounds of the decision were (1) that immunity from self-incrimination is not essential to due process of law, and (2) that the failure of the trial court to exclude the confessions after the introduction of evidence showing their incompetency, in the absence of a request for such exclusion, did not deprive the defendants of life or liberty without due process of law; and that even if the trial court had erroneously overruled a motion to exclude the confessions, the ruling would have been mere error reversible on appeal, but not a violation of constitutional right.

The opinion of the state court did not set forth the evidence as to the circumstances in which the confessions were procured. That the evidence established that they were procured by coercion was not questioned. The state court said: "After the state closed its case on the merits, the appellants, for the first time, introduced evidence from which it appears that the confessions were not made voluntarily but were coerced." There is no dispute as to the facts upon this point, and as they are clearly and adequately stated in the dissenting opinion of Judge Griffith (with whom Judge Anderson concurred)—showing both the extreme brutality of the measures to extort the confessions and the participation of the state authorities—we quote this part of his opinion in full, as follows:

"The crime with which these defendants, all ignorant negroes, are charged, was discovered about one o'clock p.m. on Friday, March 30, 1934. On that night one Dial, a deputy sheriff, accompanied by others, came to the home of Ellington, one of the defendants, and requested him to accompany them to the house of the deceased, and there a number of white men were gathered, who began to accuse the defendant of the crime. Upon his denial they seized him, and with the participation of the deputy they hanged him by a rope to the limb of a tree, and having let him down, they hung him again, and when he was let down the second time, and he still protested his innocence, he was tied to a tree and whipped, and still declining to accede to the demands that he confess, he was finally released and he returned with some difficulty to his home, suffering intense pain and agony. The record of the testimony shows that the signs of the rope on his neck were plainly visible during the so-called trial. A day or two thereafter the said deputy, accompanied by another, returned to the home of the said defendant and arrested him, and departed with the prisoner towards the jail in an adjoining county, but went by a route which led into the State of Alabama; and while on the way, in that State, the deputy stopped and again severely whipped the defendant, declaring that he would continue the whipping until he confessed, and the defendant then agreed to confess to such a statement as the deputy would dictate, and he did so, after which he was delivered to jail.

"The other two defendants, Ed Brown and Henry Shields, were also arrested and taken to the same jail. On Sunday night, April 1, 1934, the same deputy, accompanied by a number of white men, one of whom was also an officer, and by the jailer, came to the jail, and the two last named defendants were made to strip and they were laid over chairs and their backs were cut to pieces with a leather strap with buckles on it, and they were likewise made by the said deputy definitely to understand that the whipping would be continued unless and until they confessed, and not only confessed, but confessed in every matter of detail as demanded by those present; and in this manner the defendants confessed the crime, and as the whippings progressed and were repeated, they changed or adjusted their confession in all particulars of detail so as to conform to the demands of their torturers. When the confessions had been obtained in the exact form and contents as desired by the mob, they left with the parting admonition and warning that, if the defendants changed their story at any time in any respect from that last stated, the perpetrators of the outrage would administer the same or equally effective treatment.

"Further details of the brutal treatment to which these helpless prisoners were subjected need not be pursued. It is sufficient to say that in pertinent respects the transcript reads more like pages torn from some medieval account, than a record made within the confines of a modern civilization which aspires to an enlightened constitutional government.

"All this having been accomplished, on the next day, that is, on Monday, April 2, when the defendants had been given time to recuperate somewhat from the tortures to which they had been subjected, the two sheriffs, one of the county where the crime was committed, and the other of the county of the jail in which the prisoners were confined, came to the jail, accompanied by eight other persons, some of them deputies, there to hear the free and voluntary confession of these miserable and abject defendants. The sheriff of the county of the crime admitted that he had heard of the whipping, but averred that he had no personal knowledge of it. He admitted that one of the defendants, when brought before him to confess, was limping and did not sit down, and that this particular defendant then and there stated that he had been strapped so severely that he could not sit down, and as already stated, the signs of the rope on the neck of another of the defendants were plainly visible to all. Nevertheless the solemn farce of hearing the free and voluntary confessions was gone through with, and these two sheriffs and one other person then present were the three witnesses used in court to establish the so-called confessions, which were received by the court and admitted in evidence over the objections of the defendants duly entered of record as each of the said three witnesses delivered their alleged testimony. There was thus enough before the court when these confessions were first offered to make known to the court that they were not, beyond all reasonable doubt, free and voluntary; and the failure of the court then to exclude the confessions is sufficient to reverse the judgment, under every rule of procedure that has heretofore been prescribed, and hence it was not necessary subsequently to renew the objections by motion or otherwise.

"The spurious confessions having been obtained—and the farce last mentioned having been gone through with on Monday, April 2d—the court, then in session, on the following day, Tuesday, April 3, 1934, ordered the grand jury to reassemble on the succeeding day, April 4, 1934, at nine o'clock, and on the morning of the day last mentioned the grand jury returned an indictment against the defendants for murder. Late that afternoon the defendants were brought from the jail in the adjoining county and arraigned, when one or more of them offered to plead guilty, which the court declined to accept, and, upon inquiry whether they had or desired counsel, they stated that they had none, and did not suppose that counsel could be of any assistance to them. The court thereupon appointed counsel, and set the case for trial for the following morning at nine o'clock, and the defendants were returned to the jail in the adjoining county about thirty miles away.

"The defendants were brought to the courthouse of the county on the following morning, April 5th, and the so-called trial was opened, and was concluded on the next day, April 6, 1934, and resulted in a pretended conviction with death sentences. The evidence upon which the conviction was obtained was the so-called confessions. Without this evidence a peremptory instruction to find for the defendants would have been inescapable. The defendants were put on the stand, and by their testimony the facts and the details thereof as to the manner by which the confessions were extorted from them were fully developed, and it is further disclosed by the record that the same deputy, Dial, under whose guiding hand and active participation the tortures to coerce the confessions were administered, was actively in the performance of the supposed duties of a court deputy in the courthouse and in the presence of the prisoners during what is denominated, in complimentary terms, the trial of these defendants. This deputy was put on the stand by the state in rebuttal, and admitted the whippings. It is interesting to note that in his testimony with reference to the whipping of the defendant Ellington, and in response to the inquiry as to how severely he was whipped, the deputy stated, 'Not too much for a negro; not as much as I would have done if it were left to me.' Two others who had participated in these whippings were introduced and admitted it—not a single witness was introduced who denied it. The facts are not only undisputed, they are admitted, and admitted to have been done by officers of the state, in conjunction with other participants, and all this was definitely well known to everybody connected with the trial, and during the trial, including the state's prosecuting attorney and the trial judge presiding."

1.   The State stresses the statement in *Twining v. New Jersey*, 211 U.S. 78, 114, 29 S.Ct. 14, 26, 53 L.Ed. 97, that "exemption from compulsory self-incrimination in the courts of the States is not secured by any part of the Federal Constitution," and the statement in *Snyder v. Massachusetts*, 291 U.S. 97, 105, 54 S.Ct. 330, 332, 78 L.Ed. 674, 90 A.L.R. 575, that "the privilege against self-incrimination may be withdrawn and the accused put upon the stand as a witness for the State." But the question of the right of the State to withdraw the privilege against self-incrimination is not here involved. The compulsion to which the quoted statements refer is that of the processes of justice by which the accused may be called as a witness and required to testify. Compulsion by torture to extort a confession is a different matter.

The State is free to regulate the procedure of its courts in accordance with its own conceptions of policy, unless in so doing it "offends some principle of justice so rooted in the traditions and conscience of our people as to be ranked as fundamental." The State may abolish trial by jury. It may dispense with indictment by a grand jury and substitute complaint or information. But the freedom of the State in establishing its policy is the freedom of constitutional government and is limited by the requirement of due process of law. Because a State may dispense with a jury trial, it does not follow that it may substitute trial by ordeal. The rack and torture chamber may not be substituted for the witness stand. The State may not permit an accused to be hurried to conviction under mob domination— where the whole proceeding is but a mask—without supplying corrective process. The State may not deny to the accused the aid of counsel. *Powell v. Alabama*, [p. 13]. Nor may a State, through the action of its officers, contrive a conviction through the pretense of a trial which in truth is "but used as a means of depriving a defendant of liberty through a deliberate deception of court and jury by the presentation of testimony known to be perjured." And the trial equally is a mere pretense where the state authorities have contrived a conviction resting solely upon confessions obtained by violence. The due process clause requires "that state action, whether through one agency or another, shall be consistent with the fundamental principles of liberty and justice which lie at the base of all our civil and political institutions." It would be difficult to conceive of methods more revolting to the sense of justice than those taken to procure the confessions of these petitioners, and the use of the confessions thus obtained as the basis for conviction and sentence was a clear denial of due process.

2. It is in this view that the further contention of the State must be considered. That contention rests upon the failure of counsel for the accused, who had objected to the admissibility of the confessions, to move for their exclusion after they had been introduced and the fact of coercion had been proved. It is a contention which proceeds upon a misconception of the nature of petitioners' complaint. That complaint is not of the commission of mere error, but of a wrong so fundamental that it made the whole proceeding a mere pretense of a trial and rendered the conviction and sentence wholly void. We are not concerned with a mere question of state practice, or whether counsel assigned to petitioners were competent or mistakenly assumed that their first objections were sufficient. In an earlier case the Supreme Court of the State had recognized the duty of the court to supply corrective process where due process of law had been denied. * * * [T]he court said: "Coercing the supposed state's criminals into confessions and using such confessions so coerced from them against them in trials has been the curse of all countries. It was the chief iniquity, the crowning infamy of the Star Chamber, and the Inquisition, and other similar institutions. The constitution recognized the evils that lay behind these practices and prohibited them in this country. * * * The duty of maintaining constitutional rights of a person on trial for his life rises above mere rules of procedure and wherever the court is clearly satisfied that such violations exist, it will refuse to sanction such violations and will apply the corrective."

In the instant case, the trial court was fully advised by the undisputed evidence of the way in which the confessions had been procured. The trial court knew that there was no other evidence upon which conviction and sentence could be based. Yet it proceeded to permit conviction and to pronounce sentence. The conviction and sentence were void for want of the essential elements of due process, and the proceeding thus vitiated could be challenged in any appropriate manner. It was challenged before the Supreme Court of the State by the express invocation of the Fourteenth Amendment. That court entertained the challenge, considered the federal question thus presented, but declined to enforce petitioners' constitutional right. The court thus denied a federal right fully established and specially set up and claimed and the judgment must be

Reversed.

NOTES AND QUESTIONS

1. The Court in 1936 was loathe to meddle in state criminal procedure. But how could the Court have done anything other than reverse the Mississippi courts on the outrageous facts of Brown? A more difficult question is how could the state supreme court have affirmed the convictions. How did the state court justify that conclusion? Does the argument seem plausible?

In Brown, unlike *Powell*, we have no independent evidence of the innocence of the defendants. Should this matter when a court is trying to determine if a confession is coerced?

2. Notice that the Court drew the facts of the coercion/torture exclusively from the dissent in the Mississippi Supreme Court. Why do you think the Court did this?

3. Whenever some historical fact seems unbelievable—the deputies' conduct and the state court's opinion in Brown, for example—we should seek to recover what might have been different about that historic period. Re-read Professor Klarman's observations about *Powell*, p. 13, Note 7, and apply that mind set to Brown.

4. *Brown: the rest of the story.* Are you surprised to learn that, upon remand from the United States Supreme Court, the three defendants in *Brown* accepted plea bargains rather than risk a retrial? They served from three to seven years in prison. Klarman, *supra*, at 82.

Are you surprised to learn that the prosecutor in *Brown* later served forty-two years as a United States senator? He was John Stennis, who ran for office in Mississippi thirteen times and never lost. See http://www.stennis.gov/senatorpage.htm.

5. Racism, of course, is not limited to the South. Consider the New York City Draft Riots, which raged for five days in July of 1863. The riots were touched off by working-class hostility to the military draft, from which the affluent could purchase an exemption for a $300 fee. While rioters initially concentrated on institutions associated with the draft (the government, the elite, capitalism and the Republican Party), the mob's rage soon expanded to New York's African–American population, which it saw as competition for

scarce employment. The Colored Orphan Asylum, located at Fifth Avenue and Forty-third Street, was burned and looted, although most of the children were safely evacuated. One little girl was found by the mob hiding under a bed, and killed.

One city paper reported, "A perfect reign of terror exists in the quarters of this helpless people, and if the troubles which now agitate our city continue during the week it is believed that not a single negro will remain within the metropolitan limits." Peter Houston, a Mohawk Indian, was mistaken for an African–American and beaten to death. Just off the Bowery, one crowd set a building ablaze where African–Americans lived, waited for their victims to fall from the eaves of the rooftop, and beat them to death. Ann Derrickson, a white woman married to an African–American, was beaten by the mob as she saved her son's life. She died of her wounds. On Eighth Avenue, the mob re-strung the bodies of its African–American victims from lampposts after the authorities had come by and cut them down. Mobs also looted and burned the homes of whites who offered African–Americans safe-harbor, as well as businesses that catered to a racially mixed clientele.

The Union Army arrived from Gettysburg, where ten days earlier it had defeated Lee's Army of Northern Virginia, and put down the uprising. In the aftermath, New York's African–American population shrank by as much as a quarter. Many left for Hoboken, the outer boroughs, and the suburbs. See James McCague, *The Second Rebellion: The Story of the New York City Draft Riots of 1863*, The Dial Press, Inc., New York (1968); see also *Racial Violence in the United States*, Allen D, Grimshaw, ed., Aldine Publishing Company, Chicago (1968) at 37–42.

6. Nor is torture merely an unpleasant historical fact. We address contemporary uses in Chapter 6.

THE RANGE OF CHOICES FACING JUDGES

By the time a case gets into court, and certainly by the time a case makes it all the way to the United States Supreme Court, it is unlikely to be solved by an easy application of a clear legal rule. There is a clear legal rule about many things—for example, the speed limit on a particular stretch of road—but disputes about clear rules rarely make it into the courts. Instead, most cases present the judge with a range of outcomes that are plausible because they fit within the precedents that she has before her. Some judges will resist this truth, at least publicly, because they want to be seen as merely applying "the law" rather than making a quasi-legislative choice, but any realistic examination of case law will make clear that judges have choices. Otherwise, how can we explain dissents?

Once we accept that most cases present judges with a range of outcomes, we must then consider what factors move judges to choose among the possible outcomes. Many factors undoubtedly are at play here, some legitimate and some illegitimate. A prior generation of legal scholars sought to unmask the power that lies in judicial choices as well as the factors that influence how this power is wielded. See, e.g., Felix Cohen,

Transcendental Nonsense and the Functional Approach, 35 Colum. L. Rev. 809 (1935); Karl Llewellyn, *A Realistic Jurisprudence—The Next Step*, 30 Colum. L. Rev. 431 (1930). Today's scholarship about judicial choices has at least two different camps. One camp seeks to understand choices by drawing on other disciplines of knowledge—for example, law and economics, law and literature, and law and philosophy. A second camp focuses mostly on what it considers illegitimate factors and can be loosely referred to as "critical" scholarship. It seeks to show how race, sex, gender, class, and hegemony lead judges to shut the door on those who are not of the dominant political majority.

Identifying the full range of factors that move judges to make choices, and how those factors interact, is probably impossible and certainly beyond the scope of this comment. But the study of criminal procedure brings to the forefront three factors that move judges to choose one permissible outcome over another. First, American judges are citizens in a free democracy. Like every other citizen in the United States, judges bring to the task at hand a view about the importance of security and individual rights. Governments exist, in large part, to provide security from those who might harm us, but the very power of government also leads us to be fearful about how its power will be exercised when our individual rights and freedom are at stake. John Adams signed into law the Sedition Act that made it a crime to criticize the government. Richard Nixon used the Internal Revenue Service to attack his enemies. In the wake of 9/11, George W. Bush authorized wiretaps without court order. There are many possible ways to balance security and individual rights, and judges who decide criminal procedure cases will strike the balance at different points. Obviously, judges who put the balance nearer the security end of the scale will be more likely to vest discretion in police and prosecutors while judges whose tipping point is nearer the individual rights end will require more judicial supervision of those who enforce the law.

A second factor that affects criminal procedure cases is federalism. The United States has a federal government, in which states and the federal government share power in an uneasy, shifting balance. The battle over ratification of the Constitution between the Federalists and the Anti-federalists has played out in every generation since and continues to this day—think "red" states and "blue" states. The long-festering controversy over how much federal power should exist led federal judges for most of our history to be reluctant to interpose the federal Constitution in matters that might plausibly be considered "local." But where to locate the balance between too much federal supervision and not enough is also a contestable issue, one about which judges disagree.

Notice, in this regard, Justice Butler's dissent in *Powell*. He argued that the Court did not need to reach the issue of the denial of counsel, that it was enough to find a violation of due process in the failure to provide sufficient time to prepare the case. To fasten on the states some undefined obligation to provide counsel to ignorant defendants was, for Justice Butler and Justice McReynolds, "an extension of federal authority into a field hitherto occupied exclusively by the several States" that should not be done unless necessary to decide the case before the Court. This argument has, at its core, a respect for, and deference to, state actors.

Racism is a third factor that helps explain the Alabama and Mississippi decisions in *Powell* and *Brown*. The range of choices that are available to judges in one state or region may be different from the acceptable range in other parts of the country. In the Mississippi Supreme Court in 1935, only two of the five judges found the convictions flawed by the torture used to obtain "confessions." All nine members of the United States Supreme Court found the state court's decision to affirm the convictions to be an unacceptable choice. Outside the Deep South, the range of available choices was different in cases where race was a central factor.

As you read the cases in this book, you should ask yourself what range of acceptable choices the judges thought they had, how the judges came up with that range of choices, and why the judges chose one outcome over the others. You will often find the various choices best explained by the balance between security and liberty and the balance between robust and minimal federal intervention in state criminal justice. Racism is not easily seen today, unlike in Alabama's treatment of the Scottsboro defendants, but it is a powerful force nonetheless. See Sheri Lynn Johnson, *Unconscious Racism and the Criminal Law*, 73 Cornell L. Rev. 1016 (1988).

NOTES AND QUESTIONS

1. *Narrow holdings and the range of permissible choices.* It is useful to distinguish the narrow holding of a case from the rationale that informs it. What is the narrow holding in *Powell*? The Court stressed the role of the defense lawyer in helping achieve a more reliable outcome, but is that part of the narrow holding or the rationale? One way to ask this question is to ask whether the *holding* of *Powell* extends to a defendant who was not so young or uneducated and who was charged with a non-capital crime in a situation that did not involve racial hysteria. Another way to ask the question is to ask whether ruling against this new defendant is within the range of acceptable choices. Consider the following case.

> [T]here was no question of the commission of a robbery. The State's case consisted of evidence identifying the petitioner as the perpetrator. The defense was an alibi. Petitioner called and examined witnesses to prove that he was at another place at the time of the commission of the offense. The simple issue was the veracity of the testimony for the State and that for the defendant. * * * [T]he accused was not helpless, but was a man forty-three years old, of ordinary intelligence, and ability to take care of his own interests on the trial of that narrow issue. He had once before been in a criminal court, pleaded guilty to larceny and served a sentence and was not wholly unfamiliar with criminal procedure.

Does the narrow holding of *Powell* apply to this case? If not, should *Powell* be extended to cover these facts? Is this an acceptable outcome, given

Powell? What if the defendant were described as "a farm hand, out of a job and on relief," "too poor to hire a lawyer," and "a man of little education"? If you were the judge, would this description make you *more* likely to provide him a lawyer? If so, you might be interested to learn that the "ordinary intelligence" description appears in a majority opinion refusing to extend *Powell* and the "little education" description is found in Justice Black's dissent, joined by Justices Douglas and Murphy. See Betts v. Brady, 316 U.S. 455, 62 S.Ct. 1252, 86 L.Ed. 1595 (1942). This tells us, of course, that both choices were permissible ways to read *Powell* and that the Court was not (yet) willing to make the choice that Black, Douglas, and Murphy supported. Black would have the final word on this issue some twenty-one years later. See Gideon v. Wainwright, p. 950.

2. *Norms versus rules.* Another way to approach the precedential effect of *Powell* is to understand the distinction between rules and norms. Though the distinction between a norm and a rule is not always clear, it can be a useful way to classify legal argument and doctrine. Roughly, a rule requires a particular result and a norm is a way of organizing one's thinking to produce the best result in a particular case. A rule can be expressed "if X, then Y," but a norm implies a softer relationship between X and Y, sort of "if X, then we should carefully consider whether Y." It is wrong to tell a lie—a norm—suggesting that one should tell the truth. But does that mean we should tell our best friend that his wife is having an affair? Perhaps not. On the other hand if it is perjury to tell a lie under oath—a rule—then a question about the affair requires a truthful answer.

Using this admittedly oversimplified description, look again at the language from *Betts* quoted in the last Note. Can you phrase both a rule and a norm that would have governed the case?

3. The United States Supreme Court could not have been happy with the range of choices that some state courts seemed to find legitimate early in the twentieth century. *Johnson, Frank, Powell*, and *Brown* paint a frightening picture of justice in the hands of men too biased to see innocence in those perceived to be different, perceived as threatening. Even so, the power of federalism in criminal justice matters made the Court's interventions sporadic and weak for many years. The next section discusses the origin of this strong version of criminal justice federalism and its gradual decline.

B. SEEKING LEGITIMACY IN THE FOURTEENTH AMENDMENT

To understand the importance of the Fourteenth Amendment, you must return to 1790. The new central government, hotly debated and barely ratified in the key states of Virginia and New York, was but three years old. "The States eye the central government, to which they have just ceded much of their sovereignty, as a potential bully or, worse, as a tyrant." George C. Thomas III, *When Constitutional Worlds Collide: Resurrecting the Framers' Bill of Rights and Criminal Procedure*, 100 Mich. L. Rev. 149 (2001). The only central government that most colonists knew was that of King George III and the British Parliament, with whom the colonies had just fought a long, costly war. "Because of this fear of the distant, unknown government, the Bill of Rights is added in 1791, and the States grow more comfortable. They view the Bill of Rights as a wall between themselves and the central government. * * * The potential tyrant has been hobbled." *Id.*

But the potential tyrant hobbled by the Bill of Rights was not the state governments, with which the colonists had a long experience. This is made clear in 1833 in Barron v. Baltimore, 32 U.S. (7 Pet.) 243, 8 L.Ed. 672 (1833). Chief Justice John Marshall stated in *Barron* for a unanimous Court that none of the Bill of Rights guarantees binds the states.

AKHIL REED AMAR—THE BILL OF RIGHTS AND THE FOURTEENTH AMENDMENT

101 Yale Law Journal 1193 (1992), 1198–1203.

* * * Though he did not cite it by name, Marshall seems to have had in mind [in *Barron*] * * * the sweeping dictum of Hamilton's *Federalist* No. 83: "The United States, in their united or collective capacity, are the OBJECT to which all general provisions in the Constitution must necessarily be construed to refer." * * *

The legislative history of the Bill of Rights confirms that its framers and ratifiers [relied on a rule of construction like Hamilton's]. Various state conventions endorsed amendments limiting the new central government, some phrased in general language, others using words explicitly targeted at the central government * * *. * * *

Unlike state ratifying conventions, Madison believed that additional restrictions in favor of liberty should also be placed on state governments and said so on the floor of the House; but even more important for our purposes, he proposed a constitutional amendment that used explicit language to communicate this idea—the very same explicit language that John Marshall seemed to be asking for in *Barron*: "*No State shall* violate the equal rights of conscience, or the freedom of the press, or the trial by jury in criminal cases." [This amendment failed.]

So far, so good for Marshall's opinion. But what makes *Barron*'s holding compelling is * * * what Marshall near the end of his opinion called the "universally understood" historical background of the Bill of Rights. In state convention after state convention in 1787–88, Anti–Federalists voiced loud concerns about a new, distant, aristocratic, central government that was being called into existence. Many ultimately voted for the Constitution only because Federalists like Madison promised to consider a Bill of Rights soon after ratification. Madison of course kept his word, and knew that if he had not, states' rightists might have called a second constitutional convention to repudiate the basic structure of the Constitution he had labored so hard to build. In short, without the good will of many moderate Anti–Federalists, prospects for the new Constitution looked bleak in 1787–88; and a Bill of Rights was the explicit price of that good will. But the Bill of Rights that Anti–Federalists sought was a Bill to limit the *federal* government—not just for the sake of individual liberty, but also to serve the cause of states' rights. Madison and his fellow Federalists could hardly have placated their critics, or won over their skeptics, by sneaking massive new restrictions on states into apparently innocuous general language. Nor would Anti–Federalists in Congress or in states have knowingly allowed such a trojan horse through the gates. * * *

Barron's holding thus kept faith with both the letter and the spirit of the original Bill of Rights. We should not be surprised, then, that the decision in *Barron* was unanimous, or that the Court repeatedly and unanimously reaffirmed *Barron*'s rule over the next thirty-three years in cases involving the First, Fourth, Fifth, Seventh, and Eighth Amendments.

1 JOSHUA DRESSLER & ALAN MICHAELS— UNDERSTANDING CRIMINAL PROCEDURE

(5th ed. 2010), § 3.01.

The Fourteenth Amendment, adopted in 1868, imposes limits on state action. Section 1 of that amendment limits the state in three ways:

> No State shall [1] make or enforce any law which shall abridge the privileges or immunities of citizens of the United States; [2] nor shall any State deprive any person of life, liberty, or property, without due process of law; [3] nor deny to any person within its jurisdiction the equal protection of the laws.

A matter of considerable dispute is what the relationship is between the Fourteenth Amendment and the Bill of Rights. At the center of the debate, commonly called the "incorporation" debate, is the second clause of section 1, namely, the due process clause. The essential question is this: To what extent, if at all, does the Fourteenth Amendment due process clause "incorporate" (or "absorb") the Bill of Rights, so as to make the Bill's restrictions on *federal* power applicable to the *states*? A related question is whether the due process clause guarantees any rights not expressed in the Constitution. According to one scholar, "despite the importance of the topic and all the attention devoted to it, we still lack a fully satisfying account of the relationship between the first ten amendments and the Fourteenth."[c]

The incorporation debate is important for various reasons. First, the extent to which people are protected from overreaching by agents of the state depends in large measure on the extent to which the Fourteenth Amendment incorporates the Bill of Rights. At one extreme, if none of the provisions of the Bill of Rights apply to the states, a citizen may be

---

c. Akhil Reed Amar, *The Bill of Rights and the Fourteenth Amendment*, 101 Yale L.J. 1193, 1196 (1992).

subjected to (just to note a few examples) warrantless entries of the home by local police, coercive interrogation techniques, and felony trials without the assistance of counsel. On the other hand, if the due process clause incorporates the Bill of Rights in its entirety, the latter clause becomes a national code of criminal procedure; federal and state action would be restricted in identical manner.

Second, as the latter observation suggests, the values of federalism are at stake in the incorporation debate. The broader the scope of the Fourteenth Amendment due process clause, the less free are the states to develop their own rules of criminal procedure. Yet, uniformity among the states is said to be "inimical to traditional notions of federalism."

Third, incorporation raises questions regarding the proper role of the judiciary in the enforcement of constitutional rights. * * * [S]ome critics claim that certain incorporation theories exacerbate the danger that judges will apply their personal views of proper governmental action, rather than enforce the terms of the Constitution.

NOTES AND QUESTIONS

1. *Privileges or immunities.* The first clause of the Fourteenth Amendment forbids states from denying its citizens "the privileges or immunities of citizens of the United States." Would this not guarantee at least some of the rights granted in the first ten amendments? In 1873, the Court rejected this argument in dicta by a 5–4 vote. Slaughter–House Cases, 83 U.S. (16 Wall.) 36, 21 L.Ed. 394 (1873). The Court stated that this clause protected only those privileges and immunities that exist *by virtue of national citizenship*, which did not include the rights guaranteed in the Bill of Rights. A recent historical account of the *Slaughter-House Cases* describes in detail the purpose of the legislation that the Court upheld—to prevent the vast butchering operations from disposing of waste into the streets of New Orleans. At times, the streets of New Orleans were rivers of offal. Unsurprisingly, the city had cholera outbreaks every year. See Ronald M. Labbe & Jonathan Lurie, The Slaughterhouse Cases: Regulation, Reconstruction, and the Fourteenth Amendment (2003).

2. *Due process.* In 1884, the Court acknowledged that the Fourteenth Amendment due process clause applied to state criminal processes, though the Court held that the right to a grand jury indictment is not part of due process. Hurtado v. California, 110 U.S. 516, 4 S.Ct. 111, 28 L.Ed. 232 (1884). In 1900, the Court held that the right to a jury of twelve in a criminal case is not part of due process (the state constitution required a jury of eight). Maxwell v. Dow, 176 U.S. 581, 20 S.Ct. 448, 44 L.Ed. 597 (1900). Eight years later, the Court held that due process did not prohibit an instruction to the jury that it could draw a negative inference from the defendant's failure to testify. Twining v. New Jersey, 211 U.S. 78, 29 S.Ct. 14, 53 L.Ed. 97 (1908).

3. We have seen that the defendants won their due process claim in *Powell* p. 13, and *Brown*, p. 25, and that the defendants in *Hurtado* and *Twining* (Note 2) lost. Can you develop an account of due process that would explain why the *Powell* and *Brown* defendants prevailed while Hurtado and

Twining lost? How would you apply your account to the following motions by defendants: (a) to suppress an eyewitness identification as unreliable; (b) for money to pay a forensic expert to testify on behalf of an indigent defendant; and (c) to require that a jury verdict be unanimous?

4. *Developing standards of due process.* What test should the Supreme Court use to decide when a state trial or investigation has violated the Fourteenth Amendment due process clause? In Palko v. Connecticut, 302 U.S. 319, 58 S.Ct. 149, 82 L.Ed. 288 (1937), Justice Cardozo sought to articulate a test for what due process requires of a state criminal process.

> Our survey of the cases serves, we think, to justify the statement that the dividing line between them, if not unfaltering throughout its course, has been true for the most part to a unifying principle. On which side of the line the case made out by the appellant has appropriate location must be the next inquiry and the final one. Is that kind of double jeopardy to which the statute has subjected him a hardship so acute and shocking that our polity will not endure it? Does it violate those "fundamental principles of liberty and justice which lie at the base of all our civil and political institutions"?

The test announced by Cardozo was a restrictive one. Not many rights would qualify if the test were whether the lack of the right "subjected" the defendant to "a hardship so acute and shocking that our polity will not endure it." Nor would many rights qualify as "fundamental principles of liberty and justice which lie at the base of all our civil and political institutions." Which rights in the Bill of Rights do you think would qualify for inclusion under Cardozo's test?

5. *The inexorable march of incorporation.* One way to read the Fourteenth Amendment, which avoids having to develop an account of due process, is Justice Hugo Black's "total" incorporation approach. In Black's view, "one of the chief objects" of the Fourteenth Amendment "was to make the Bill of Rights applicable to the states." Adamson v. California, 332 U.S. 46, 67 S.Ct. 1672, 91 L.Ed. 1903 (1947) (Black, J., dissenting). On this view, the Fourteenth Amendment simply absorbs the entire Bill of Rights, and makes each right applicable to the states, but creates no rights other than those found in the Bill of Rights.

Justice Black never persuaded a majority to accept total incorporation, but he stayed on the Court long enough (thirty-six years) to see a step-by-step "selective" incorporation that, by Black's death in 1971, was almost complete. Here is the way the Court described the status of incorporation in 1968.

> The Fourteenth Amendment denies the States the power to "deprive any person of life, liberty, or property, without due process of law." In resolving conflicting claims concerning the meaning of this spacious language, the Court has looked increasingly to the Bill of Rights for guidance; many of the rights guaranteed by the first eight Amendments to the Constitution have been held to be protected against state action by the Due Process Clause of the Fourteenth Amendment. That clause now protects the right to compensation for property taken by the State; the rights of speech, press, and religion covered by the First Amendment; the Fourth Amendment rights to be free from unreasonable searches and

seizures and to have excluded from criminal trials any evidence illegally seized; the right guaranteed by the Fifth Amendment to be free of compelled self-incrimination; and the Sixth Amendment rights to counsel, to a speedy and public trial, to confrontation of opposing witnesses, and to compulsory process for obtaining witnesses.

Duncan v. Louisiana, 391 U.S. 145, 88 S.Ct. 1444, 20 L.Ed.2d 491 (1968).

6.   The Court has overruled *Twining v. New Jersey*, Note 2. See Malloy v. Hogan, 378 U.S. 1, 84 S.Ct. 1489, 12 L.Ed.2d 653 (1964). The Court has not, however, overruled *Hurtado v. California*, Note 2, and states are thus *not* required to provide grand juries. But what about trial juries? How would that right fit into the list in Note 5? Consider the next case.

DUNCAN v. LOUISIANA

Supreme Court of the United States, 1968.
391 U.S. 145, 88 S.Ct. 1444, 20 L.Ed.2d 491.

MR. JUSTICE WHITE delivered the opinion of the Court. * * *

* * * Appellant sought trial by jury [on the charge of simple assault], but because the Louisiana Constitution grants jury trials only in cases in which capital punishment or imprisonment at hard labor may be imposed, the trial judge denied the request. Appellant was convicted and sentenced to serve 60 days in the parish prison and pay a fine of $150. * * *

I   * * *

The test for determining whether a right extended by the Fifth and Sixth Amendments with respect to federal criminal proceedings is also protected against state action by the Fourteenth Amendment has been phrased in a variety of ways in the opinions of this Court. The question has been asked whether a right is among those "fundamental principles of liberty and justice which lie at the base of all our civil and political institutions," whether it is "basic in our system of jurisprudence," and whether it is "a fundamental right, essential to a fair trial." The claim before us is that the right to trial by jury guaranteed by the Sixth Amendment meets these tests. The position of Louisiana, on the other hand, is that the Constitution imposes upon the States no duty to give a jury trial in any criminal case, regardless of the seriousness of the crime or the size of the punishment which may be imposed. Because we believe that trial by jury in criminal cases is fundamental to the American scheme of justice, we hold that the Fourteenth Amendment guarantees a right of jury trial in all criminal cases which—were they to be tried in a federal court—would come within the Sixth Amendment's guarantee. * * *

The history of trial by jury in criminal cases has been frequently told. It is sufficient for present purposes to say that by the time our Constitution was written, jury trial in criminal cases had been in existence in England for several centuries and carried impressive credentials traced by many to Magna Carta. * * *

Jury trial came to America with English colonists, and received strong support from them. Royal interference with the jury trial was deeply resented. Among the resolutions adopted by the First Congress of the American Colonies (the Stamp Act Congress) on October 19, 1765—resolutions deemed by their authors to state "the most essential rights and liberties of the colonists"—was the declaration:

> "That trial by jury is the inherent and invaluable right of every British subject in these colonies."

The First Continental Congress, in the resolve of October 14, 1774, objected to trials before judges dependent upon the Crown alone for their salaries and to trials in England for alleged crimes committed in the colonies; the Congress therefore declared:

> "That the respective colonies are entitled to the common law of England, and more especially to the great and inestimable privilege of being tried by their peers of the vicinage, according to the course of that law."

* * * The Constitution itself, in Art. III, § 2, commanded:

> "The Trial of all Crimes, except in Cases of Impeachment, shall be by Jury; and such Trial shall be held in the State where the said Crimes shall have been committed."

Objections to the Constitution because of the absence of a bill of rights were met by the immediate submission and adoption of the Bill of Rights. Included was the Sixth Amendment which, among other things, provided:

> "In all criminal prosecutions, the accused shall enjoy the right to a speedy and public trial, by an impartial jury of the State and district wherein the crime shall have been committed."

The constitutions adopted by the original States guaranteed jury trial. Also, the constitution of every State entering the Union thereafter in one form or another protected the right to jury trial in criminal cases.

Even such skeletal history is impressive support for considering the right to jury trial in criminal cases to be fundamental to our system of justice, an importance frequently recognized in the opinions of this Court. * * *

The guarantees of jury trial in the Federal and State Constitutions reflect a profound judgment about the way in which law should be enforced and justice administered. A right to jury trial is granted to criminal defendants in order to prevent oppression by the Government. Those who wrote our constitutions knew from history and experience that it was necessary to protect against unfounded criminal charges brought to eliminate enemies and against judges too responsive to the voice of higher authority. The framers of the constitutions strove to create an independent judiciary but insisted upon further protection against arbitrary action. Providing an accused with the right to be tried by a jury of his peers gave him an inestimable safeguard against the corrupt or overzealous prosecutor and against the compliant, biased, or eccentric judge. If the defendant preferred the common-sense judgment of a jury to the more tutored but perhaps less sympathetic reaction of the single judge, he was to have it. Beyond this, the jury trial provisions in the Federal and State Constitutions reflect a fundamental decision about the exercise of official power—a reluctance to entrust plenary powers over the life and liberty of the citizen to one judge or to a group of judges. Fear of unchecked power, so typical of our State and Federal Governments in other respects, found expression in the criminal law in this insistence upon community participation in the determination of guilt or innocence. The deep commitment of the Nation to the right of jury trial in serious criminal cases as a defense against arbitrary law enforcement qualifies for protection under the Due Process Clause of the Fourteenth Amendment, and must therefore be respected by the States. * * *

Mr. Justice BLACK, with whom Mr. Justice DOUGLAS joins, concurring. * * *

* * * With [the Court's] holding I agree for reasons given by the Court. I also agree because of reasons given in my dissent in *Adamson v. California*, 332 U.S. 46, 68, 67 S.Ct. 1672, 1683, 91 L.Ed. 1903. In that dissent, I took the position, contrary to the holding in *Twining v. New Jersey* [p. 37, Note 2], that the Fourteenth Amendment made all of the provisions of the Bill of Rights applicable to the States. * * *

* * * The dissent in this case, however, makes a spirited and forceful defense of that now discredited [*Twining*] doctrine. I do not believe that it is necessary for me to repeat the historical and logical reasons for my challenge to the *Twining* holding contained in my *Adamson* dissent and Appendix to it. What I wrote there in 1947 was the product of years of study and research. My appraisal of the legislative history followed 10 years of legislative experience as a Senator of the United States, not a bad way, I suspect, to learn the value of what is said in legislative debates, committee discussions, committee reports, and various other steps taken in the course of passage of bills, resolutions, and proposed constitutional amendments. My Brother Harlan's objections to my *Adamson* dissent history, like that of most of the objectors, relies most heavily on a criticism written by Professor Charles Fairman and published in the Stanford Law Review. 2 Stan. L. Rev. 5 (1949). I have read and studied this article extensively, including the historical references, but am compelled to add that in my view it has completely failed to refute the inferences and arguments that I suggested in my *Adamson* dissent. * * *

In addition to the adoption of Professor Fairman's "history," the dissent states that "the great words of the four clauses of the first section of the Fourteenth Amendment would have been an exceedingly peculiar way to say that 'The rights heretofore guaranteed against federal intrusion by the first eight Amendments are henceforth guaranteed against state intrusion as well.'" In response to this I can say only that the words "No State shall make or enforce any law which shall abridge the privileges or immunities of citizens of the United States" seem to me an eminently reasonable way of expressing the idea that henceforth the Bill of Rights shall apply to the States. What more precious "privilege" of American citizenship could there be than that privilege to claim the protections of our great Bill of Rights? I suggest that any reading of "privileges or immunities of citizens of the United States" which excludes the Bill of Rights' safeguards renders the words of this section of the Fourteenth Amendment meaningless. * * *

* * * [In Justice Harlan's view,] the Due Process Clause is treated as prescribing no specific and clearly ascertainable constitutional command that judges must obey in interpreting the Constitution, but rather as leaving judges free to decide at any particular time whether a particular rule or judicial formulation embodies an "immutable principl[e] of free government" or is "implicit in the concept of ordered liberty," or whether certain conduct "shocks the judge's conscience" or runs counter to some other similar, undefined and undefinable standard. Thus due process, according to my Brother Harlan, is to be a phrase with no permanent meaning, but one which is found to shift from time to time in accordance with judges' predilections and understandings of what is best for the country. If due process means this, the Fourteenth Amendment, in my opinion, might as well have been written that "no person shall be deprived of life, liberty or property except by laws that the judges of the United States Supreme Court shall find to be consistent with the immutable principles of free government." It is impossible for me to believe that such unconfined power is given to judges in our Constitution that is a written one in order to limit governmental power. * * *

Mr. Justice FORTAS, concurring.

* * * I agree that the Due Process Clause of the Fourteenth Amendment requires that the States accord the right to jury trial in prosecutions for offenses that are not petty. * * *

But although I agree with the decision of the Court, I cannot agree with the implication, that the tail must go with the hide: that when we hold, influenced by the Sixth Amendment, that "due process" requires that the States accord the right of jury trial for all but petty offenses, we automatically import all of the ancillary rules which have been or may hereafter be developed incidental to the right to jury trial in the federal courts. I see no reason whatever, for example, to assume that our decision today should require us to impose federal requirements such as unanimous verdicts or a jury of 12 upon the States. We may well conclude that these and other features of federal jury practice are by no means fundamental—that they are not essential to due process of law—and that they are not obligatory on the States.

I would make these points clear today. Neither logic nor history nor the intent of the draftsmen of the Fourteenth Amendment can possibly be said to require that the Sixth Amendment or its jury trial provision be applied to the States together with the total gloss that this Court's decisions have supplied. The draftsmen of the Fourteenth Amendment intended what they said, not more or less: that no State shall deprive any person of life, liberty, or property without due process of law. It is ultimately the duty of this Court to interpret, to ascribe specific meaning to this phrase. There is no reason whatever for us to conclude that, in so doing, we are bound slavishly to follow not only the Sixth Amendment but all of its bag and baggage, however securely or insecurely affixed they may be by law and precedent to federal proceedings. To take this course, in my judgment, would be not only unnecessary but mischievous because it would inflict a serious blow upon the principle of federalism. The Due Process Clause commands us to apply its great standard to state court proceedings to assure basic fairness. It does not command us rigidly and arbitrarily to impose the exact pattern of federal proceedings upon the 50 States. On the contrary, the Constitution's command, in my view, is that in our insistence upon state observance of due process, we should, so far as possible, allow the greatest latitude for state differences. It requires, within the limits of the lofty basic standards that it prescribes for the States as well as the Federal Government, maximum opportunity for diversity and minimal imposition of uniformity of method and detail upon the States. Our Constitution sets up a federal union, not a monolith. * * *

Mr. Justice HARLAN, whom Mr. Justice STEWART joins, dissenting.

Every American jurisdiction provides for trial by jury in criminal cases. The question before us is not whether jury trial is an ancient institution, which it is; nor whether it plays a significant role in the administration of criminal justice, which it does; nor whether it will endure, which it shall. The question in this case is whether the State of Louisiana, which provides trial by jury for all felonies, is prohibited by the Constitution from trying charges of simple battery to the court alone. In my view, the answer to that question, mandated alike by our constitutional history and by the longer history of trial by jury, is clearly "no."

The States have always borne primary responsibility for operating the machinery of criminal justice within their borders, and adapting it to their particular circumstances. In exercising this responsibility, each State is compelled to conform its procedures to the requirements of the Federal Constitution. The Due Process Clause of the Fourteenth Amendment requires that those procedures be fundamentally fair in all respects. It does not, in my view, impose or encourage nationwide uniformity for its own sake; it does not command adherence to forms that happen to be old; and it does not impose on the States the rules that may be in force in the federal courts except where such rules are also found to be essential to basic fairness.

The Court's approach to this case is an uneasy and illogical compromise among the views of various Justices on how the Due Process Clause should be interpreted. The Court does not say that those who framed the Fourteenth Amendment intended to make the Sixth Amendment applicable to the States. And the Court concedes [in an omitted part of the majority opinion] that it finds nothing unfair about the procedure by which the present appellant was tried. Nevertheless, the Court reverses his conviction: it holds, for some reason not apparent to me, that the Due Process Clause incorporates the particular clause of the Sixth Amendment that requires trial by jury in federal criminal cases—including, as I read its opinion, the sometimes trivial accompanying baggage of judicial interpretation in federal contexts. I have raised my voice many times before against the Court's continuing undiscriminating insistence upon fastening on the States federal notions of criminal justice, and I must do so again in this instance. With all respect, the Court's approach and its reading of history are altogether topsy-turvy.

I * * *

A few members of the Court have taken the position that the intention of those who drafted the first section of the Fourteenth Amendment was simply, and exclusively, to make the provisions of the first eight Amendments applicable to state action. This view has never been accepted by this Court. In my view, often expressed elsewhere, the first section of the Fourteenth Amendment was meant neither to incorporate, nor to be limited to, the specific guarantees of the first eight Amendments. * * * In short, neither history, nor sense, supports using the Fourteenth Amendment to put the States in a constitutional straitjacket with respect to their own development in the administration of criminal or civil law.

Although I therefore fundamentally disagree with the total incorporation view of the Fourteenth Amendment, it seems to me that such a position does at least have the virtue, lacking in the Court's selective incorporation approach, of internal consistency: we look to the Bill of Rights, word for word, clause for clause, precedent for precedent because, it is said, the men who wrote the Amendment wanted it that way. For those who do not accept this "history," a different source of "intermediate premises" must be found. The Bill of Rights is not necessarily irrelevant to the search for guidance in interpreting the Fourteenth Amendment, but the reason for and the nature of its relevance must be articulated. * * *

Today's Court still remains unwilling to accept the total incorporationists' view of the history of the Fourteenth Amendment. This, if accepted, would afford a cogent reason for applying the Sixth Amendment to the States. The Court is also, apparently, unwilling to face the task of determining whether denial of trial by jury in the situation before us, or in other situations, is fundamentally unfair. Consequently, the Court has compromised on the ease of the incorporationist position, without its internal logic. It has simply assumed that the question before us is whether the Jury Trial Clause of the Sixth Amendment should be incorporated into the Fourteenth, jot-for-jot and case-for-case, or ignored. Then the Court merely declares that the clause in question is "in" rather than "out."

The Court has justified neither its starting place nor its conclusion. If the problem is to discover and articulate the rules of fundamental fairness in criminal proceedings, there is no reason to assume that the whole body of rules developed in this Court constituting Sixth Amendment jury trial must be regarded as a unit. The requirement of trial by jury in federal criminal cases has given rise to numerous subsidiary questions respecting the exact scope and content of the right. It surely cannot be that every answer the Court has given, or will give, to such a question is attributable to the Founders; or even that every rule announced carries equal conviction of this Court; still less can it be that every such subprinciple is equally fundamental to ordered liberty.

Examples abound. I should suppose it obviously fundamental to fairness that a "jury" means an "impartial jury." I should think it equally obvious that the rule, imposed long ago in the federal courts, that "jury" means "jury of exactly twelve," is not fundamental to anything: there is no significance except to mystics in the number 12. Again, trial by jury has been held to require a unanimous verdict of jurors in the federal courts, although unanimity has not been found essential to liberty in Britain, where the requirement has been abandoned. * * *

Even if I could agree that the question before us is whether Sixth Amendment jury trial is totally "in" or totally "out," I can find in the Court's opinion no real reasons for concluding that it should be "in." The basis for differentiating among clauses in the Bill of Rights cannot be that only some clauses are in the Bill of Rights, or that only some are old and much praised, or that only some have played an important role in the development of federal law. These things are true of all. The Court says that some clauses are more "fundamental" than others, but it turns out to be using this word in a sense that would have astonished Mr. Justice Cardozo and which, in addition, is of no help. The word does not mean "analytically critical to procedural fairness" for no real analysis of the role of the jury in making procedures fair is even attempted. Instead, the word turns out to mean "old," "much praised," and "found in the Bill of Rights." The definition of "fundamental" thus turns out to be circular.

II

Since, as I see it, the Court has not even come to grips with the issues in this case, it is necessary to start from the beginning. When a criminal defendant contends that his state conviction lacked "due process of law," the question before this Court, in my view, is whether he was denied any element of fundamental procedural fairness. * * *

The argument that jury trial is not a requisite of due process is quite simple. The central proposition of *Palko* [p. 38, Note 4], a proposition to which I would adhere, is that "due process of law" requires only that criminal trials be fundamentally fair. * * * But it simply has not been demonstrated, nor, I think, can it be demonstrated, that trial by jury is the only fair means of resolving issues of fact. * * *

It can hardly be gainsaid * * * that the principal original virtue of the jury trial—the limitations a jury imposes on a tyrannous judiciary—has largely disappeared. We no longer live in a medieval or colonial society. Judges enforce laws enacted by democratic decision, not by regal fiat. They are elected by the people or appointed by the people's elected officials, and are responsible not to a distant monarch alone but to reviewing courts, including this one. * * *

* * * Two experts have estimated that, of all prosecutions for crimes triable to a jury, 75% are settled by guilty plea and 40% of the remainder are tried to the court. * * * The Court recognizes the force of these statistics in stating,

> "We would not assert, however, that every criminal trial—or any particular trial—held before a judge alone is unfair or that a defendant may never be as fairly treated by a judge as he would be by a jury."

I agree. I therefore see no reason why this Court should reverse the conviction of appellant, absent any suggestion that his particular trial was in fact unfair, or compel the State of Louisiana to afford jury trial in an as yet unbounded category of cases that can, without unfairness, be tried to a court. * * *

In sum, there is a wide range of views on the desirability of trial by jury, and on the ways to make it most effective when it is used; there is also considerable variation from State to State in local conditions such as the size of the criminal caseload, the ease or difficulty of summoning jurors, and other trial conditions bearing on fairness. We have before us, therefore, an almost perfect example of a situation in which the celebrated dictum of Mr. Justice Brandeis should be invoked. It is, he said,

> "one of the happy incidents of the federal system that a single courageous state may, if its citizens choose, serve as a laboratory * * *."

This Court, other courts, and the political process are available to correct any experiments in criminal procedure that prove fundamentally unfair to defendants. That is not what is being done today: instead, and quite without reason, the Court has chosen to impose upon every state one means of trying criminal cases; it is a good means, but it is not the only fair means, and it is not demonstrably better than the alternatives States might devise. * * *

NOTES AND QUESTIONS

1. Justices Hugo Black and John Harlan were on the Supreme Court together for sixteen years (1955–1971). As you can see from the exchange in *Duncan*, they disagreed fundamentally over how to interpret the Fourteenth Amendment. Can you articulate Justice Harlan's view of due process? What do you think Harlan means when he charges that the "Court has compromised on the ease of the incorporationist position, without its internal logic"?

2. Part of Black's argument in favor of total incorporation is that, otherwise, judges would be tempted "to roam at large in the broad expanses

of policy and morals and to trespass, all too freely, on the legislative domain of the States as well as the Federal government." Adamson v. California, 332 U.S. 46, 67 S.Ct. 1672, 91 L.Ed. 1903 (1947) (Black, J., dissenting). Remember, Black's view of total incorporation was that the Fourteenth Amendment incorporated *all* of the Bill of Rights guarantees but otherwise created no rights against state authority. For example, he dissented in Griswold v. Connecticut, 381 U.S. 479, 85 S.Ct. 1678, 14 L.Ed.2d 510 (1965), which held that the due process clause prohibited Connecticut from enforcing its criminal law against the use of birth control. A fundamental-rights theorist could find, as the Court did, a right to privacy in the due process clause, but not an incorporationist who looked only at the relatively specific guarantees of the Bill of Rights. Can you see why?

3. Between the Harlan and Black positions in *Duncan*, which argument do you prefer? Does it matter on this issue that the Framers of the Bill of Rights considered, and rejected, an amendment that would have required states to provide jury trials?

4. One issue in the incorporation debate is what the Framers of the Fourteenth Amendment intended. For an argument that the Framers intended some form of incorporation, see Michael Kent Curtis, No State Shall Abridge (1986); Earl M. Maltz, Civil Rights, the Constitution, and Congress, 1863–1869 (1990). The contrary argument is forcefully made in Donald Dripps, *Akhil Amar on Criminal Procedure and Constitutional Law: "Here I Go Down That Wrong Road Again,"* 74 N.C. L. Rev. 1559 (1996). The congressional debate on the Fourteenth Amendment is set out thoroughly, and in chronological format in Joseph T. Sneed III, Footprints on the Rocks of the Mountains (1997).

A less frequently asked question is what the ratifying state legislatures thought. More fundamentally, does it make a difference if the states did not intend to ratify a Fourteenth Amendment that incorporated the Bill of Rights. Whose intent controls? For a provocative argument, based on an examination of all surviving original documents in the Southern states, that none of these ratifying state legislatures intended to fix the Bill of Rights on themselves, see James E. Bond, No Easy Walk to Freedom (1997). See also Bryan H. Wildenthal, Nationalizing the Bill of Rights: Revisiting the Original Understanding of the Fourteenth Amendment in 1866–67, 68 Ohio St. L.J. 1509 (2007) (proposing, as a metric for measuring state legislative intent, whether Congress "clearly, publicly, and candidly conveyed" to the country its intent to impose the first eight amendments on the states); George C. Thomas III, The Riddle of the Fourteenth Amendment: A Response to Professor Wildenthal, 68 Ohio St. L.J. 1627 (2007) (accepting Wildenthal's metric but concluding that the available evidence does not satisfy it).

5. *The role of precedent.* Justice Fortas concurred in the majority opinion in *Duncan*, yet his view seems closer to Harlan's. Suppose you joined the Court a few years after *Duncan*, and one of the first cases is a challenge to a state statute permitting verdicts by a 9–3 vote. Now assume you agree with Harlan and Stewart, who are still on the Court, that *Duncan* was wrongly decided. Fortas and another member of the original *Duncan* majority are willing to reverse *Duncan*. Alternatively, you can distinguish *Duncan* on the

theory that a 9–3 jury is at least a jury, while Duncan had no jury at all. Would you press to overrule *Duncan*, since you have five votes, or would you decide the new case by distinguishing *Duncan*? Do you think precedent ought to stand until it is necessary to overrule it, or should the Court take the first opportunity to correct doctrine when it decides a mistake has been made?

6. *What goes around, comes around.* The case described in Note 5 came to the Court, after Fortas resigned, and the Court split 4–4 on whether the Sixth Amendment required a unanimous verdict. Apodaca v. Oregon, 406 U.S. 404, 92 S.Ct. 1628, 32 L.Ed.2d 184 (1972). Justice Powell's crucial fifth vote was based on the Fortas view that unanimous jury verdicts are required by the *Sixth Amendment* but not by the *Fourteenth*. The Court, in effect, gave greater leeway to the states in interpreting the Fourteenth Amendment than it was willing to give to Congress under the Sixth Amendment.

7. Scholars have begun to question the Warren Court's decision to incorporate the Bill of Rights criminal procedure guarantees. Incorporation, Tracey Meares argued, has caused the Court to de-emphasize the "public-regarding" vision of fairness that once highlighted racial injustice in the application of criminal laws. When the Court asked itself whether convictions resulted from fundamentally fair processes, it often considered, explicitly or implicitly, the racial context of the case. Incorporation, however, led the Court to ask merely whether the defendant received the proper procedure, a focus that invited courts to ignore the racial context. Choosing incorporation "as the mechanism for criminal justice system reform" has ironically limited "prospects for addressing race-related perceptions of criminal justice system unfairness." Tracey L. Meares, *Everything Old is New Again: Fundamental Fairness and the Legitimacy of Criminal Justice*, 3 Ohio State J. Crim. Law 105, 106 (2005).

Morgan Cloud concluded that incorporation in effect replaced traditional theories of the Fourth Amendment with new doctrines that weakened protections of privacy, property, and liberty. See Morgan Cloud, *A Liberal House Divided: How the Warren Court Dismantled the Fourth Amendment*, 3 Ohio State J. Crim. L. 33 (2005). George Thomas argued that one effect of incorporation was to distract the Court from what should be its prime directive in criminal procedure—designing doctrines to protect innocent suspects and defendants. See George C. Thomas III, *The Criminal Procedure Road Not Take: Due Process and the Protection of Innocence*, 3 Ohio State J. Crim. L. 169 (2005).

In Donald Dripps's view, incorporation prevailed because there was not a strong advocate for the due process alternative. Donald A. Dripps, *Justice Harlan on Criminal Procedure: Two Cheers for the Legal Process School*, 3 Ohio State J. Crim. L. 125 (2005). While Justice Harlan was a brilliant justice and gifted writer, his stubborn view that criminal process questions could be left largely to the state legislatures doomed any chance that a majority of the Court would embrace his due process theory. Dripps argued that the due process clause could be read as requiring "proportionate police practices and reliable trial procedures" and that this would be a better criminal procedure world than incorporation has given us. *Id.* at 168.

8. *Don't forget state law.* The focus in criminal procedure books tends to be on the Bill of Rights provisions that now, mostly, apply to state suspects and defendants just as they do in federal cases. But don't make the mistake one of the casebook authors made. Fresh out of law school, the author was appointed to represent a defendant charged with second-degree murder based on a drunk driving accident. The police obtained a highly incriminating blood sample from the driver while he was unconscious in the hospital. When time came to file a motion to suppress, the young lawyer decided not to bother since the Supreme Court had decided this precise issue against the defendant in Breithaupt v. Abram, 352 U.S. 432, 77 S.Ct. 408, 1 L.Ed.2d 448 (1957). An older and wiser member of the local defense bar asked why no motion to suppress was being filed. The young lawyer said, with a touch of arrogance, "The Supreme Court has already decided this issue in *Breithaupt*."

"I don't know *Breithaupt*," sputtered the wise lawyer. "But I do know the Tennessee Code Annotated."

Yes, indeed, a Tennessee statute provided that a blood sample could not be used for any purpose if taken without consent. The motion was filed and argued on state law grounds. The judge suppressed the blood sample, and a very favorable plea offer followed. (Tennessee later amended the statute so that it did not apply in homicide cases.)

C.   THE NORMS OF THE CRIMINAL PROCESS

We spoke earlier of three factors that move judges to choose outcomes from the range of outcomes permitted by the relevant precedent. The illegitimate factor is racism. The legitimate factors are (1) how the judge balances security and individual rights, and (2) how the judge balances the need for federal supervision and the value of state autonomy in fashioning state and local criminal justice processes. These foundational factors, we believe, are the most important in explaining why a judge picks one outcome over the others. But modern judges rarely speak directly of even the legitimate factors. Instead, judges tend to cloak the foundational views in other language—the language of (1) the accuracy of verdicts; (2) the fairness of the procedure; (3) honoring the presence of certain limitations on the power of government to find or use evidence; and (4) efficiency.

Accuracy

All systems that process and evaluate information will make errors in evaluation. If the system is indifferent to the "direction" of the error (indifferent to which party is harmed by the error), it would permit a verdict based on the slightest difference in the weight of the evidence presented by the two parties. This standard of proof, called "preponderance of the evidence," is the standard used in civil court. As a consequence, the plaintiff wins if she can show the slightest additional weight of evidence on her side of the balance; the defendant wins if the evidence is in equipoise or tilted ever so slightly in the defendant's direction.

Criminal law has adopted an "innocence-weighted" procedural approach that, in theory, protects innocent defendants. See Tom Stacy, *The*

Search for Truth in Constitutional Criminal Procedure, 91 Colum. L. Rev. 1369. Blackstone put the rationale colorfully: "[T]he law holds that it is better that ten guilty persons escape than that one innocent suffer." 4 W. Blackstone's Commentaries *352 (1769). To create an "innocence-weighted" procedure, criminal law requires proof beyond a reasonable doubt.

As Professor Daniel Givelber notes, however, no one knows for certain that the reasonable-doubt standard operates to acquit a greater percentage of *innocent* defendants. It might just produce more acquittals randomly distributed among defendants generally. Daniel Givelber, *Meaningless Acquittals, Meaningful Convictions: Do We Reliably Acquit the Innocent?*, 49 Rutgers L. Rev. 1317 (1997). There are two ways in which a high standard of proof should differentially benefit innocent defendants—by encouraging more innocent defendants to stand trial rather than plea bargain, and by influencing juries to vote not guilty in cases involving innocent defendants. If more innocent defendants choose to stand trial because they have faith in the reasonable doubt standard, then even random acquittals will differentially benefit innocent defendants. But the most direct differential effect—and the one Blackstone likely meant—is that it should be more difficult to convict innocent defendants than guilty ones. This effect, however, depends crucially on whether the prosecution will have a weaker case against innocent defendants. If innocent and guilty defendants present cases of equal "strength," then the reasonable-doubt standard does not help innocent defendants any more than guilty ones. Many scholars and judges assume that our rules of procedure will permit innocent defendants to demonstrate the weakness of the prosecution case, but is it so clear?

It is not evident to Professor Givelber, who argues that our rules of adjudication "assume a guilty defendant, and focus on the task of creating a fair fight between the prosecution and the guilty defendant." For example, no current doctrine insists on "the availability of the most accurate information concerning the crime and its investigation"—such as guaranteed defense access to DNA testing. Instead, the system has "provided the defendant with a series of tactical opportunities to derail the prosecution's case." *Id.* at 1378.

Some of these opportunities to derail the State's case should, in theory, advance accurate outcomes. As we saw in Part A., providing indigent defendants with a lawyer should help avoid wrongful convictions. Other trial rights provide the lawyer with tools to test the State's case— the right to confront the prosecution witnesses, to call defense witnesses, and to have the case heard in a public trial before an impartial jury fairly soon after the events in question.

The right to confront and to call witnesses bears an obvious relationship to accuracy. The right to a speedy and public trial enhances accuracy in two ways. The sooner the trial occurs after the crime, the more accurate should be the memories of witnesses. Less obviously, the public nature of a trial should serve as a deterrent to judges who might be inclined to favor one party over another.

All of these trial rights are specifically guaranteed by the Sixth Amendment. Partly because they bear an obvious relationship to accuracy, they are much less controversial than some of the rights that are grounded more in fairness or in limited-government sentiment.

Fairness

No one denies that suspects and defendants should be treated fairly. Much debate centers, naturally, on what constitutes "fair" treatment. One famous example is Yale Kamisar's 1965 article that pre-dated the famous *Miranda* warnings requirement. Yale Kamisar, *Equal Justice in the Gatehouses and Mansions of American Criminal Procedure*, reprinted in Yale Kamisar, Police Interrogation (1980). According to Professor Kamisar, the Fifth Amendment gives everyone the right to refuse to answer police questions, but most criminal suspects do not know they have that right. Affluent suspects are able to retain counsel to advise them during interrogation. Fairness, in this context, thus meant for Kamisar that suspects should be told of their right to refuse to answer and should be provided the right to counsel during interrogation, an analysis the *Miranda* Court adopted. Fairness here implicates equality; the rich and the poor, the knowledgeable as well as the ignorant, should be able to deal with police interrogators on more or less equal terms.

Others take a different view of fairness in the interrogation room. As long as the police do not coerce a confession, one could argue that it is fair to question suspects who are under arrest, and even to take advantage of suspects who do not know of the privilege against self-incrimination. Assuming that an inconsequential number of innocent people confess when faced with non-coercive interrogation—of late, a questionable assumption—these commentators wonder why anyone cares that the police trick or encourage guilty people to confess their crimes. Moreover, to make lawyers available to all suspects, just because a very few suspects have a lawyer during interrogation, might be the wrong way to solve the inequality problem; why not ban lawyers from police interrogation, thus reaching the "equality" of zero lawyers?

To the extent equality means making all suspects as resistant to police investigation as the savvy affluent suspects, these commentators deride equality as a "sporting theory of justice"—turning the police investigation into a fox hunt where the fox must be given a fair chance. Perhaps law-abiding persons should rejoice when non-coercive police questioning causes a guilty defendant to confess.

These questions tend to divide courts and commentators because of the inherent difficulty in deciding what is fair. Of course, a procedure is not fair if it produces too many inaccurate verdicts (though defining "too many" may be difficult), but once we have identified accuracy as an independent requirement, it is much more difficult to give content to a fairness requirement. Fairness, then, is a controversial legitimacy factor precisely because fairness invites those with different views to ascribe what they please to the concept of "fairness."

Limited-Government Provisions

One could have an accurate criminal process that included the power to question defendants in court, whether or not they wished to testify, and the power to introduce evidence seized in a search later found to be too broad or too intrusive. The continental European systems typically permit the presiding judge to question the defendant at trial in front of the jury. The Canadian, European, and English systems permit evidence to be introduced even if it is seized in an unfair manner. While we may prefer our system, no one suggests that these other systems produce inaccurate verdicts.

The reason is simple enough. Physical evidence does not need to have its accuracy tested by the adversarial process; visual examination or lab tests can disclose its true meaning. And, there is no reason to believe that a system that permits defendants to be questioned in court will be less accurate than a system that permits defendants to avoid testifying. Indeed, limitations on questioning defendants and using physical evidence found in searches make the overall set of outcomes *less* accurate. So, on balance, the Fourth Amendment and the privilege against self-incrimination are accuracy-impeding provisions.

It is more controversial to assert that a process can be *fair* when it requires defendants to submit to questioning, or uses reliable evidence that was seized wrongfully. But one could plausibly argue, as Justice Cardozo did, that the question of how police obtain physical evidence is separate from the question of whether the defendant is guilty; otherwise, "[t]he criminal is to go free because the constable has blundered." People v. Defore, 242 N.Y. 13, 150 N.E. 585 (N.Y. 1926). As to questioning defendants in court, one might ask why it is unfair to expect other witnesses to testify at trial but not the one witness who probably knows more about the facts of the case than anyone else—the defendant. Judge Henry Friendly even called for the Fifth Amendment privilege against self-incrimination to be repealed by constitutional amendment. Henry J. Friendly, *The Fifth Amendment Tomorrow: The Case for Constitutional Change*, 37 U. Cinn. L. Rev. 617 (1968).

However one decides the fairness question, something more than accuracy and fairness explains why the Bill of Rights includes the Fourth Amendment. Examination of the constitutional language helps here. (The full text of the Bill of Rights can be found on pages 2–3.) The Fourth Amendment begins by recognizing the "right of the people to be secure in their persons, houses, papers and effects against unreasonable searches and seizures." It then establishes strict standards for issuing warrants, standards that include probable cause and a "particular[]" description of "the place to be searched, and the persons or things to be seized."

The Fourth Amendment is part of an overall theme in the Bill of Rights that establishes "the people" as a separate entity from the government. The First Amendment forbids a state religion and creates the right to worship freely, to speak freely, and to assemble and to petition the government. The Second Amendment provides for a militia to exist separately from the government. The Ninth and Tenth Amendments retain power in the people and the states. Viewed as part of this broad canvas, the Fourth Amendment is a statement that the government must not interfere with our daily lives (our persons, houses, papers, and effects) absent good cause. The specific requirements for warrants will keep judges from taking lightly the command that the people be "secure." The Fourth Amendment's purpose thus seems to be to limit the power of government to intrude on "the people" in this particular way.

Most of the Fifth Amendment also consists of general rights against government: it forbids re-litigating the outcome of the first trial (by forbidding double jeopardy); it forbids governmental compulsion of defendants to testify against themselves; it requires the government to obtain assent of the community through a grand jury indictment before bringing a defendant to trial; it forbids government from denying "life, liberty, or property" without due process of law, or taking private property without "just compensation." Viewed in this context, the Fifth Amendment prohibition of compelling defendants to be witnesses against themselves seems like a restriction on the power of government to invade our autonomy.

If the Fourth and Fifth Amendment rights are fundamentally to control government, rather than to enhance accuracy or fairness, it would explain why the suppression of evidence under these two provisions is more controversial than the implementation of the Sixth Amendment trial rights. Society today likely does not feel as hostile toward government as the Framers felt anti-British in 1791.

Indeed, Professor Daniel Givelber argues that these provisions actually lessen the chance that an innocent defendant can prove her innocence. "Advantages which may enhance the case of the guilty defendant such as the right to silence and to exclude relevant inculpatory evidence, work no benefit for the innocent. Instead, those advantages justify the prosecution's withholding from the accused and the factfinder evidence which might undermine the prosecution's case." Daniel Givelber, *Meaningless Acquittals, Meaningful Convictions: Do We Reliably Acquit the Innocent?*, 49 Rutgers L. Rev. 1317, 1394 (1997).

Efficiency

The political and pragmatic legitimacy of the criminal process requires a threshold level of efficiency in solving and prosecuting crime. Unfortunately police do not solve, or clear, as many crimes as society would like. Because limited-government norms are necessarily inconsistent to some degree with police efficiency, the low clearance rate has led crime control adherents to urge abolition or restriction of the limited-government provisions in the Bill of Rights. Specifically, many have urged a rethinking of the principle requiring suppression of evidence seized in violation of the Fourth Amendment, and a few scholars have suggested rethinking the *Miranda* principle requiring that suspects must be warned prior to custodial interrogation.

The criminal process following police investigation is also currently dominated by the efficiency norm. Plea bargains are much more efficient than trials, and over 90% of felony charges are bargained to guilty pleas. Most lawyers and academics contend that the system could not survive without plea bargaining. If a mere 20% of felony defendants demanded a jury trial, that would more than double the present number of trials, with the complications of choosing a jury and all the rights that attend presenting a defense. Plea bargaining, in short, is the grease that permits the wheels of justice to turn smoothly.

The Supreme Court explicitly approves of plea bargaining, and has held that prosecutors are bound by plea bargains once the defendant pleads guilty. *Santobello v. New York*, Chapter 15. These rulings have a double effect in encouraging more pleas: Judges know they can accept guilty pleas induced by plea bargains, and defendants can seek these pleas knowing that the prosecutor cannot withdraw from the bargain once the guilty plea is entered.

Efficiency is an important overlay on the legitimating norms of the American criminal process. But it must be tempered by the fairness norm and by the limited-government provisions of the Bill of Rights. How to balance these norms is always controversial. And the balance is subject to outside influences, as we witnessed in the aftermath of September 11, 2001.

The Norms Post–September 11

Larry Ellison, chief executive of Oracle Corporation, on the question of whether we should have National ID cards: "Those are political decisions that need to be made. I just think people need to ask themselves who they trust more, terrorists or the government." Robert O'Harrow Jr. & Jonathan Krim, *Is Big Brother Watching?*, The Washington Post National Weekly Edition, Dec. 24, 2001—Jan. 6, 2002, at 6, 7.

We tend to forget, when times are good, that the ultimate role of government is to protect its citizens—from crime, from anarchy, from attacks by enemies. It is particularly easy for this country to forget. From the very beginning of the Republic, we have tended to view ourselves as isolated from the political machinations in Europe and Asia. And, until Pearl Harbor, the great oceans protected us from surprise attack. But in the wake of September 11, we now know all too well that we are vulnerable. One question is how much liberty we are willing to surrender, as a society, in exchange for the hope or expectation of being made more secure.

Of course, if the relevant question when deciding how much civil liberty we should surrender is whether we trust government more than terrorists, we are likely to surrender just about all of our civil liberties. Perhaps a better way to phrase the question is how much of an intrusion is the proposed government action and how much safety will it buy, and are there any liberties or values so valuable—even sacred—that they are not susceptible to cost-benefit analysis?

A few hours after the hijacked commercial airliners struck the two World Trade Center towers and the Pentagon, the FBI was in federal court getting court orders to wiretap the phones of hundreds of persons suspected of having links with terrorist groups. Some of these phone taps produced evidence of support for the hijackers—some gave thanks to Allah for the great success of the hijackers and others gloated at the death and destruction. Did this indicate widespread conspiratorial involvement or only defiant, but lawful, speech? And we may assume that many of the phone taps produced nothing even slightly incriminating because the persons under surveillance were innocent.

Moreover, we now know that the National Security Agency soon began a two-pronged monitoring of telephone calls and e-mails, in many cases without warrants. One part included monitoring the phone calls and e-mails of people with known ties to Al Qaeda. The other aspect was described by the New York Times as mining a "vast data trove," consisting of volume and pattern phone data. Eric Lichtblau & James Risen, *Spy Agency Mined Vast Data Trove, Officials Report*, N.Y. Times, December 24, 2005, A1. These data included who called whom, how often, and how long the calls lasted. *Id*. at A12.

In the hours and days following September 11, we did not know whether additional attacks would occur, and whether those attacks might be nuclear, chemical, or biological. Did that risk justify the government's actions? Does it still justify mining "vast data troves"? And what about coercive interrogation methods used at our military base at Guantanamo Bay and other, secret locations overseas? The horrors of September 11, and the Government's response to it, bring into stark clarity the questions that must be asked and answered in *every* criminal investigation and prosecution. What is the optimal trade-off between liberty and privacy, on the one hand, and security against those who would destroy us, on the other hand? In the final analysis, what is the meaning of the middle word in "criminal justice system"?

NOTES AND QUESTIONS

1. *Police investigation problems*. In "solving" the following problems, do not use any constitutional doctrine that you might have learned in other courses (or think you have learned from television). Attempt to use only the norms and values we have identified in this section.

A. *Radar searches*. Suppose scientists develop a type of "radar" gun that can identify with 100% accuracy the existence of chemical compounds. This radar can be tuned so that it will *only* signal the existence of substances that cannot be legally possessed under federal law. If the police aim this machine at residences while driving up and down the streets, to provide the basis for search warrants, does this raise a fairness concern? Any other concern?

B. *The morality of torture.* Police arrested a kidnaping suspect and tried to persuade him to provide information about where the victim was located. He requested counsel, and police permitted him to call counsel. When counsel arrived, he refused to represent the kidnapper (who said the lawyer would only be paid from the ransom money). The kidnapper then insisted on meeting with the victim's father and arranging some kind of cash settlement for lawyer's fees, bail, and expenses. By the time the kidnapper led the police to where he had buried the victim in a coffin-like box in a shallow grave, she had suffocated. Should the police have acted more decisively? Should they have attempted to coerce from the suspect the victim's location? Should they have used physical coercion? Torture? What if police knew of the victim's fate and had every reason to believe she was clinging to life? See William J. Pizzi, *The Privilege Against Self–Incrimination in a Rescue Situation*, 76 J. Crim. L. & Criminology 567 (discussing People v. Krom, 61 N.Y.2d 187, 473 N.Y.S.2d 139, 461 N.E.2d 276 (1984)).

2. *Criminal process problems.* If you were a state legislator, would you support the following bills? Again, use the norms and values identified in the reading above, rather than anything you might know about existing constitutional or statutory provisions that are relevant to each problem.

A. *Speedy trial.* A proposed bill would require trials within 180 days after formal charges are filed. The sanction for failing to meet the deadline is dismissal of charges, which can be without prejudice to bring the same charges again if required in the interests of justice.

B. *Pretrial depositions.* A bill is proposed to require depositions of criminal defendants, on the model of civil depositions, with two differences: (1) a judge will oversee the process; (2) the defendant may refuse to answer questions. If the defendant refuses, however, the refusal is admissible in evidence at trial.

The bill also requires the State to make its witnesses available for the defense to depose, except when the prosecutor can show the potential for witness intimidation or reprisal. State funds will pay defense counsel's fee when the defendant is indigent.

C. *Pretrial detention.* A bill requires pretrial detention of all defendants charged with the most serious felonies if the hearing magistrate finds by clear and convincing evidence that no lesser restraint will reasonably assure the appearance of the defendant at trial and the safety of the community.

D. *Jury service.* A proposed bill would automatically exempt from jury service the following groups: (1) surgeons; (2) lawyers; (3) mothers with children younger than six; (4) college students. Any exempted individual can request to be included in the pool by filing a form with the court clerk.

E. *Jury composition.* The legislature is considering a bill to reduce the jury size to six, requiring unanimity, or, alternatively, to keep the number at twelve and permit verdicts by a vote of 9–3.

F. *Jury challenges.* The bill described in E. abolishes all peremptory challenges (those granted without the necessity of showing cause for dismissal).

3. *Protecting innocence.* Professor Givelber has concluded that rules of adjudication "assume a guilty defendant, and focus on the task of creating a fair fight between the prosecution and the guilty defendant." Daniel Givelber, *Meaningless Acquittals, Meaningful Convictions: Do We Reliably Acquit the Innocent?*, 49 Rutgers L. Rev. 1317 (1997). The next section suggests how true, and scary, that might be.

D. DOES THE PROCESS PROTECT THE INNOCENT?

GEORGE C. THOMAS III—THE SUPREME COURT ON TRIAL—HOW THE AMERICAN SYSTEM OF JUSTICE SACRIFICES INNOCENT DEFENDANTS

(2008) 6–8.

At 8:10 in the morning on December 29, 1991, a female bartender was found, dead, in the men's room of the C.B.S. Lounge in Phoenix. She was nude. The killer left behind no physical evidence save bite marks on her breast and neck. The victim had told a friend that Ray Krone was going to help close the bar that night. Police asked Krone to make a bite impression, and an expert witness prepared a videotape that purported to show a match by moving Krone's bite impression onto the marks on the victim. According to the Arizona Supreme Court, the videotape "presented evidence in ways that would have been impossible using static exhibits." State v. Krone, 897 P.2d 621, 622 (Ariz. 1995). Although defense counsel had been given the opportunity to examine the dental expert, counsel was not informed of the existence of the videotape until the eve of trial.

The only other evidence against Krone was that he was "evasive with the police about his relationship" with the victim. *Id.* Of course, without the bite mark identification, being "evasive" about a relationship is practically worthless as evidence. The case turned on the bite mark evidence, and the court-appointed defense expert had no experience in video production. Accordingly, counsel moved for a continuance to obtain an expert who could evaluate the videotape. Alternatively, counsel moved to suppress the videotape or to allow testimony about an earlier case in which the same expert's testimony was successfully challenged as not sufficiently scientific. The trial court overruled all the defense motions. The prosecution expert used the videotape in his testimony, and no defense expert challenged his presentation. The jury convicted Krone of murder and kidnaping. The trial judge sentenced Krone to death.

On appeal, the Arizona Supreme Court held that the trial judge had acted improperly in refusing to allow a continuance. The jury had not yet been selected when the motion was made, the court noted, and the State would have suffered little prejudice. If substantial prejudice would have been caused, the right course of action, according to the state supreme court, was to preclude use of the videotape. What the trial judge could not do was what he did—allow use of the tape without giving defense counsel ample opportunity to prepare a defense.

So far, so good. The case was remanded for a new trial, the defense secured an expert, and the jury convicted again. This time, though, the judge sentenced Krone to life in prison, "citing doubts about whether or not Krone was the true killer." See Innocence Project web site (case of Ray Krone). This borders on the unbelievable. A trial judge who had "doubts about whether or not Krone was the true killer" *sentenced him to life in prison*. Krone served over ten years in prison before DNA testing conducted on the saliva and blood found on the victim excluded him as the killer. The DNA matched a man who lived close to the bar but who had never been considered a suspect in the killing.

Ray Krone's case is an example of how the current system fails innocent defendants. Police seized on the first plausible suspect and looked no further. The prosecution built a case on a Styrofoam bite impression and mumbo-jumbo scientific evidence. That the case was so weak perhaps explains why the prosecutor did not want the defense to be able to challenge the videotaped "expert" testimony. If true, that violates the first rule of prosecution—to do justice rather than try to win all cases. "Doing justice" in Ray Krone's case meant allowing the defense to challenge the prosecution's expert testimony.

The first trial judge failed to give Krone a chance to demonstrate his innocence, and the second one sentenced him to life in prison even though he had doubts about his guilt. These are fundamental failures. To be sure, some parts of the system worked. Krone received what appears to have been effective representation by his counsel, and the Arizona Supreme Court recognized the errors of the first trial judge. Nonetheless, despite these successes, Ray Krone would have spent the rest of his life in prison for a crime he did not commit were it not for DNA testing and the Innocence Project at Cardozo Law School, founded by Barry Scheck and Peter Neufeld.

What has gone wrong? In a work published in 1713, Matthew Hale acclaimed the English common law jury trial as the "best Trial in the World." Matthew Hale, The History and Analysis of the Common Law 252 (1713). Several commendable qualities that Hale noted have truth as the goal, and three mention truth specifically. Hale said that having witnesses testify in person—subject to being questioned by the parties, the judge, and the jury—was the "best Method of searching and sifting out the Truth." Today * * * any rational system of justice should care more about protecting innocent defendants than any other value. But DNA testing has made plain that our modern adversary system just isn't very good at protecting innocent defendants.

NOTES AND QUESTIONS

1. *Is Krone a rare case?* In a study of over 10,000 cases in which the FBI compared DNA of the suspect with DNA from the crime scene, the DNA tests exonerated the prime suspect in 20% of the cases. In another 20%, the results were inconclusive. Because the inconclusive results must be removed from the sample, the police were wrong in one case in four. The lab records do not indicate whether the 20% of excluded suspects were tried using other evidence. Edward Conners, et al., Convicted by Juries, Exonerated by Science: Case Studies in the Use of DNA Evidence to Establish Innocence After Trial, in National Institute of Justice Report (1996). We don't know from these data how many innocent suspects are arrested for crimes that cannot be cleared through DNA testing.

The DNA evidence is bound to overstate the error rate in arrests overall. When the identity of the actor is known, and the argument is over whether what he did is a crime, there is no risk of convicting the wrong person and thus no reason to conduct a DNA test. These cases will not, of course, appear in the DNA database, making the error rate in all cases lower than that found in the Justice study. But even if the error rate is only 3%, that means almost half a million innocent defendants are arrested each year. See U.S. Department of Justice, Federal Bureau of Investigation, Crime in the United States, 2004, tbl. 4.1, p. 280 (showing fourteen million non-traffic arrests in 2004).

2. *Is there a reliable estimate of system-wide wrongful convictions?* The short answer is no. By "wrongful convictions," we mean convictions of factually innocent defendants. In his book, excerpted above, Thomas drew on a statistical model and a study of English convictions to produce a rough overall estimate that two percent of convictions are of innocent defendants. Thomas, at 39–40.

Michael Risinger has made a compelling argument that it is a fool's errand to attempt an estimate of a general error rate, both because we lack a methodology and because the error rate will almost certainly vary dramatically by category. See D. Michael Risinger, *Innocents Convicted: An Empirically Justified Factual Wrongful Conviction Rate*, 97 J. Crim. L. & Criminology 761 (2007). So, for example, the error rate in armed robbery cases, where identification is a critical issue, will be much higher than in cases of failing to file income tax returns, where it should be almost zero.

But Risinger has developed a methodology for estimating the error rate in rape-murder capital cases. His rigorous methodology produced a minimum error rate of 3.3%. What is your reaction to being told that of 319 capital rape-murder convictions Risinger studied, at least 10 of the men sentenced to die were factually innocent?

3. "There is no worse error in American criminal justice than the wrongful prosecution, conviction, and incarceration of an innocent person, especially in capital cases...." Richard A. Leo, False Confessions: Causes, Consequences, and Solutions, in Wrongly Convicted: Perspectives on Failed Justice (Saundra D. Westervelt & John A. Humphrey, eds. 2001). Do you have any thoughts about how to avoid these miscarriages of justice?

4. *Is there a due process right to test DNA?* The answer is "it depends." Prior to trial, the due process clause requires the State to turn over exculpatory evidence to the defendant—see Chapter 13 C. 2.—and, in most if not all cases, a DNA sample from the crime scene would be potentially exculpatory. As the Court said in District Attorney's Office for the Third Judicial District v. Osborne, 557 U.S. ___, 129 S.Ct. 2308, 174 L.Ed.2d 38 (2009): "DNA testing has an unparalleled ability both to exonerate the wrongly convicted and to identify the guilty."

But Osborne, who was convicted of kidnaping, sexual assault, and assault, did not make a request for DNA testing prior to trial. Here's what happened. The State of Alaska tested a condom found near the scene of the crime using a basic DNA test that generally cannot narrow the field of possible matches to fewer than 5% of the population. Because Osborne's lawyer believed him guilty, she did not request a more discriminating form of DNA testing. Years after Osborne's convictions were affirmed on appeal, he sought to force the State to turn over the condom so that he could, at his own expense, have it subjected to more advanced testing. Oddly, he did not utilize the Alaska procedure for post-conviction discovery of evidence, instead filing a 42 U.S.C. § 1983 suit in federal court that alleged a violation of the due process clause.

The Supreme Court held that Osbourne did *not* have the same due process right to discover exculpatory evidence that he would have had if his lawyer had sought the evidence prior to trial. The trial and conviction partially extinguished his liberty interest and thus permitted the State "more flexibility in deciding what procedures are needed in the context of postconviction relief." The Court held that the Alaska "procedures are adequate on their face, and without trying them, Osborne can hardly complain that they do not work in practice." The Court also rejected Osborne's substantive due process argument for "a freestanding right to DNA evidence untethered from the liberty interests he hopes to vindicate with it." The Court was "reluctant to expand the concept of substantive due process because guideposts for responsible decisionmaking in this uncharted area are scarce and open-ended."

Justices Stevens, Ginsburg, and Breyer dissented, arguing that Osborne had both a procedural and substantive due process right to force the State to turn over the evidence. Justice Stevens wrote:

> Although a valid criminal conviction justifies punitive detention, it does not entirely eliminate the liberty interests of convicted persons. For while a prisoners rights may be diminished by the needs and exigencies of the institutional environment[,] * * * [t]here is no iron curtain drawn between the Constitution and the prisons of this country. * * * It is therefore far too late in the day to question the basic proposition that convicted persons such as Osborne retain a constitutionally protected measure of interest in liberty, including the fundamental liberty of freedom from physical restraint.

Justice Souter also dissented.

5. *Who could be against innocent defendants?* While trying to help innocent defendants is surely uncontroversial, the innocence *movement* has generated criticism. Margaret Raymond, for example, criticizes the wrongful

conviction movement for "elevating factual innocence" over other defenses. This could lead jurors to think "that anything short of factual innocence is simply not good enough to justify an acquittal." Margaret Raymond, *The Problem with Innocence*, 49 Clev. St. L. Rev. 449, 457 (2001). Another criticism is that a focus on innocence is a distraction that "may obscure more pervasive flaws in the criminal justice system and have a series of untoward effects on (1) the trial process, (2) legislative reform, and (3) other systemic critiques." Daniel S. Medwed, *Innocentrism*, 2008 U. Ill. L. Rev. 1549, 1555. To Medwed, innocence arguments do not displace other critiques of criminal justice but, rather, reinforce many of the values that underlie procedural rights—e.g., maximizing individual dignity and minimizing the power of the State. *Id.* at 1570.

Several scholars have embraced changes in the procedures of criminal procedure that move beyond adversarial cliches like presumption of innocence and proof beyond a reasonable doubt. See Tim Bakken, *Truth and Innocence Procedures to Free Innocent Persons: Beyond the Adversarial System*, 41 U. Mich. L. Reform 547 (2008); Andrew M. Siegel, *Moving Down the Wedge of Injustice: A Proposal for a Third Generation of Wrongful Convictions Scholarship and Advocacy*, 42 Am. Crim. L. Rev. 1219 (2005); Sandra Guerra Thompson, *Beyond a Reasonable Doubt? Reconsidering Uncorroborated Eyewitness Identification Testimony*, 41 U.C. Davis L. Rev. 1487 (2008).

A particularly intriguing idea is that prosecutors may have (or at least should have) a duty to avoid wrongful convictions. Professors Fred Zacharias and Bruce Green tentatively conclude that current disciplinary procedures, if not the ethical rules they seek to enforce, are inadequate to enforce that duty. They recommend "renewed attention to alternative regulatory processes." See Fred C. Zacharias & Bruce A. Green, *The Duty to Avoid Wrongful Convictions: A Thought Experiment in the Regulation of Prosectors*, 89 B. U. L. Rev. 1 (2009). The article was motivated by Van de Kamp v. Goldstein, 555 U.S. ___, 129 S.Ct. 855, 172 L.Ed.2d 706 (2009), holding that an innocent man who served 24 years in prison could not sue prosecutors for failure to provide training that might have avoided the wrongful conviction.

6. For other thoughts on the problem of wrongful convictions, see Brandon L. Garrett & Peter J. Neufeld, *Invalid Forensic Science Testimony and Wrongful Convictions*, 95 Va. L. Rev. 1 (2009); Richard A. Leo, Steven Drizin, Peter Neufeld, Brad Hall, and Amy Vatner (2006), *Bringing Reliability Back In: False Confessions and Legal Safeguards in the Twenty–First Century*, 2006 Wis. L. Rev. 479.

CHAPTER 2

FOURTH AMENDMENT: AN OVERVIEW

■ ■ ■

A. THE TEXT AND ITS MYSTERIES

The Fourth Amendment journey begins here. The first step in that journey, as is the case in evaluating *any* provision of a constitution, is to read the text being interpreted. The Fourth Amendment is just 54 words long:

> The right of the people to be secure in their persons, houses, papers, and effects, against unreasonable searches and seizures, shall not be violated, and no Warrants shall issue, but upon probable cause, supported by Oath or affirmation, and particularly describing the place to be searched, and the persons or things to be seized.

These 54 words appear to tell us a great deal, but do they? They tell us *who* is protected by the provisions of the Amendment, *i.e.*, "the people." But, who are "the people"? Only citizens of the United States? Anyone legally present in the United States? Anyone in the country, legally or not? And, are citizens protected when they are outside the country? These questions, always important, have grown in significance in the aftermath of the September 11, 2001 terrorist attacks on the United States, the investigation of which primarily focused on persons of foreign ancestry located in and outside the United States, including some United States citizens.

What does the Fourth Amendment guarantee "the people"? The text tell us that the people are entitled "to be secure in their persons, houses, papers, and effects" (we will see that this phrase is not all-encompassing) "against unreasonable searches and seizures." But, what is an "unreasonable" search or seizure? For that matter, what are "searches" and "seizures"? These are matters of considerable complexity.

Perhaps the most controversial feature of Fourth Amendment jurisprudence relates to the relationship between the preceding language (often called the "reasonableness clause") and the remaining language of the text ("no Warrants shall issue, but upon probable cause * * *"), which constitutes the "warrant clause." Does the warrant clause mean that searches conducted without warrants are (at least, presumptively) unreasonable and, consequently, in violation of the reasonableness requirement? Or did the drafters of the Fourth Amendment mean only that *when* a warrant is issued it must meet the requirements of probable cause, oath or affirmation, and particularity, but that there is no warrant requirement, as such? And, however this question is answered, what does the text mean by "probable cause," and how particular must the warrant describe "the place to be searched, and the persons or things to be seized"?

Finally, notice what the text does *not* say. Yes, the people have a right (in their persons, houses, papers, and effects) to be free from unreasonable searches and seizures, but what is the *remedy* for violation of this right? Did the Amendment's Framers have a particular remedy in mind? Or, did they expect the judiciary or the legislature to formulate one?

All of these questions (and others that could be posed) suggest the aptness of Professor Anthony Amsterdam's characterization of the Fourth Amendment text as "brief, vague, general, [and] unilluminating." Anthony G. Amsterdam, *Perspectives on the Fourth Amendment*, 58 Minn. L. Rev. 349, 353–54 (1974). The judiciary, in particular the United States Supreme Court, has endeavored to illuminate the text. Justice Felix Frankfurter observed in 1961, however, that "[t]he course of true law pertaining to [the Fourth Amendment] * * * has not * * * run smooth." Chapman v. United States, 365 U.S. 610, 81 S.Ct. 776, 5 L.Ed.2d 828 (1961) (concurring opinion). Indeed, although the text of the Amendment has not changed over the years, the personnel of the Supreme Court and, therefore, its interpretation of the Constitution, *has* changed. As a consequence, the path you will be following in your Fourth Amendment journey includes many significant turns, including some U-turns, as well as zigs and zags. At the conclusion of your voyage, you will have a basis for determining whether Professor Akhil Amar overstated the situation when he equated Fourth Amendment case law to "a sinking ocean liner— rudderless and badly off course." Akhil Reed Amar, *Fourth Amendment First Principles*, 107 Harv. L. Rev. 757, 759 (1994).

B. THE REACH OF THE FOURTH AMENDMENT

How far does the Fourth Amendment reach? Two issues relating to the Amendment's scope—one relating to the category of persons who are searched and the other regarding the nature of persons who do the searching and seizing—deserve attention.

Consider, first, the criminal investigations that occurred in the aftermath of the September 11 attacks on the United States. Apparently all nineteen hijackers of the four airplanes were of Middle Eastern descent. After the events, the federal government investigated hundreds of persons in order to try to identify possible co-conspirators in the crimes and to identify persons who might be planning future attacks. Initial reports suggested that these investigations primarily focused on four categories of individuals: (a) American citizens of Middle Eastern descent living in the United States; (b) citizens of other countries *lawfully* in the United States on student (or other) visas; (c) citizens of other countries *unlawfully* in this country (persons who came lawfully but whose visas had expired, as well as those who illegally entered the country); and (d) non-U.S. citizens residing in other countries suspected of planning criminal activities in the United States or against U.S. interests on foreign land. Obviously, category (a) individuals are covered by the Fourth Amendment, but what rights do the other classes of suspects possess? May federal law enforcement agents conduct unlimited surveillance of such persons? May their homes be searched and their property seized with impunity? Remarkably, the Supreme Court has rarely spoken on the subject.

The Fourth Amendment provides that "the people" should "be secure in their persons, houses, papers, and effects, against unreasonable searches and seizures." It turns out, however, that the term "people" is not all-inclusive. In United States v. Verdugo–Urquidez, 494 U.S. 259, 110 S.Ct. 1056, 108 L.Ed.2d 222 (1990), Verdugo–Urquidez, a Mexican resident, was arrested on drug charges and brought to the United States for trial. While he was in a San Diego federal correctional facility, United States Drug Enforcement Agency (DEA) agents entered and seized property from defendant's Mexican residences without a search warrant. The issue presented to the Supreme Court was "whether the Fourth Amendment applies to the search and seizure by United States agents of property that is owned by a non-resident alien and located in a foreign country."

A seriously splintered Court held that Verdugo–Urquidez could not object to the DEA action on Fourth Amendment grounds, because he was not among "the people" the Framers intended to protect from unreasonable searches and seizures. Specifically, a search or seizure of property located in a foreign country, which is owned by a nonresident alien who is only briefly on U.S. soil, is not covered by the Amendment, even if the search is conducted by U.S. law enforcement agents. According to then-Chief Justice Rehnquist writing for the majority, the words "the people" found in the Fourth Amendment (and elsewhere in the Constitution) "refer[] to a class of persons who are part of a national community or who have otherwise developed sufficient connection with this country to be considered part of that community." The defendant's connection to the United States—"lawful but involuntary [presence]—is not of the sort to indicate any substantial connection with our country."

The justices left a great deal open for future resolution in category (b) and (c) cases, including whether the Fourth Amendment applies if a noncitizen's involuntary "stay in the United States were to be prolonged—by a prison sentence, for example." Also undecided—and certainly of greater significance—is whether, and to what extent, the Fourth Amendment protects a person *voluntarily* but *unlawfully living* in this country, *i.e.*, one who has "presumably * * * accepted some societal obligations," who is subjected to a search or seizure on U.S. land. Indeed, *Verdugo-Urquidez* even leaves open the issue of the scope of rights of non-U.S. citizens *lawfully* in this country temporarily or with the intention of becoming citizens. (Obviously, category (d) individuals are not protected by the Fourth Amendment.)

The second coverage issue relates to the *searching*, not searched, party. In *Verdugo-Urquidez*, the contested searches were conducted by federal law enforcement agents. But, what if a search or seizure occurs in the United States, of a United States citizen, by a *private* party? Suppose that Burglar John breaks into Jane's home while she is at work, and is arrested while fleeing the crime scene. In an effort to avoid prosecution, John hands over to the police a large quantity of illegal drugs he discovered in Jane's home. May Jane object to the Government's use of these drugs against her in a drug prosecution? Or suppose that a private detective, hired by Jack to discover evidence of wife Jill's adulterous behavior, searches through Jill's belongings and, to his surprise, discovers evidence linking Jill to a murder. If the private detective furnishes the evidence to the police, may Jill object on Fourth Amendment grounds?

The answer in both cases is "no." The Supreme Court ruled in Burdeau v. McDowell, 256 U.S. 465, 41 S.Ct. 574, 65 L.Ed. 1048 (1921), that the Fourth Amendment only limits governmental action. It does not reach private searches or seizures. Consequently, the Fourth Amendment is not violated if a landlord searches her tenant's possessions, or an airline employee searches luggage, or a private company monitors telephone calls of its employees without their knowledge. 1 Wayne R. LaFave, Search and Seizure § 1.8(a) (4th ed. 2004). On the other hand, the Amendment *is* implicated if there is police instigation or participation, such as when an officer requests a landlord to search through her tenant's belongings or assists in the process.

C. THE BIRTH OF THE EXCLUSIONARY RULE

INTRODUCTORY COMMENT

Suppose that federal law enforcement officers, without good cause and without a search warrant, enter your home without your permission, and search it for evidence of a crime. The search is thorough: They go through every room in your house, including your bedroom, opening desk and dresser drawers, reading your personal diary, rifling through private files, searching through closets, and opening containers. They find nothing and leave. We may assume for current purposes (with good reason) that this conduct constitutes an unreasonable search in violation of your Fourth Amendment rights.

What is your remedy for violation of your rights? The text of the Fourth Amendment provides no answer. Perhaps you can bring a civil suit against the police. Or, you might file a formal complaint with police authorities or seek a criminal prosecution of the officers for trespass.

Now, suppose that the same events occur, but the federal agents *do* find evidence of a crime in your home, which they seize and seek to use against you in a criminal prosecution. The Fourth Amendment guarantees "the people"—not just those innocent of criminal activity—the right to be free from unreasonable searches and seizures. Therefore, in *this* case, what should your remedy be? The same as before? Or, should you have a right to have your property—unconstitutionally taken from your home— returned to you and, therefore, the Government denied the right to introduce it into evidence in your prosecution?

At common law, and for decades after the Fourth Amendment was ratified, your only remedy was a tort suit against the agents for trespass. If the agents had no valid warrant, and entered and searched without your permission, they were automatically deemed trespassers and could offer no defense. As the North Carolina Supreme Court put the rule: "Every entry by one, into the dwelling-house of another, against the will of the occupant, is a trespass, unless warranted by such authority in law as will justify the entry." Gardner v. Neil, 4 N.C. 104 (1814). The most famous English search case from the colonial era was, after all, a tort case. See Entick v. Carrington, 19 How. State Trials 1029 (1765) (holding the king's messengers liable in tort to the victim of the search because they had an invalid, general warrant).

In Adams v. New York, 192 U.S. 585, 24 S.Ct. 372, 48 L.Ed. 575 (1904), the Supreme Court provided its initial answers to these questions under the Fourth Amendment. It stated that "the weight of authority" was that "testimony clearly competent as tending to establish the guilt of the accused of the offense charged" may be retained by the Government and used at a defendant's trial. According to *Adams*, "the courts do not stop to inquire as to the means by which the evidence was obtained."

Governmental misconduct, it may forcefully be argued, is a collateral matter in a criminal prosecution of one whom they have arrested. If the purpose of a trial is to determine the innocence or guilt of the accused, shouldn't the trial focus *exclusively* on *that* matter? If the evidence seized by the police serves to prove the defendant's guilt, why should a court exclude this probative evidence? Yet, as the following cases demonstrate, the Supreme Court has turned away from the *Adams* approach and formulated a so-called "exclusionary rule."

Note: As explained in Chapter 1, the provisions of the Bill of Rights, including the Fourth Amendment, only limit the conduct of agents of the federal, as distinguished from state and local, government. State and local police are limited, *if at all*, by the Fourteenth Amendment due process clause. Therefore, in considering the materials that follow, pay attention to the federal/state distinction.

WEEKS v. UNITED STATES

Supreme Court of the United States, 1914.
232 U.S. 383, 34 S.Ct. 341, 58 L.Ed. 652.

MR. JUSTICE DAY delivered the opinion of the court.

An indictment was returned against the * * * defendant * * *. The seventh count, upon which a conviction was had, charged the use of the mails for the purpose of transporting certain coupons or tickets representing chances or shares in a lottery or gift enterprise, in violation of [federal law]. * * *

The defendant was arrested by a police officer, so far as the record shows, without warrant, at the Union Station in Kansas City, Missouri, where he was employed by an express company. Other police officers had gone to the house of the defendant and being told by a neighbor where the key was kept, found it and entered the house. They searched the defendant's room and took possession of various papers and articles found there, which were afterwards turned over to the United States Marshal. Later in the same day police officers returned with the Marshal, who thought he might find additional evidence, and, being admitted by someone in the house, probably a boarder, * * * the Marshal searched the defendant's room and carried away certain letters and envelopes found in the drawer of a chiffonier. Neither the marshal nor the police officers had a search warrant. * * *

[The defendant unsuccessfully petitioned the district court for return of the items that were seized by the local police and United States Marshal on the ground that the property was obtained in violation of the Fourth Amendment.] Among the papers retained and put in evidence were a number of lottery tickets and statements with reference to the lottery, taken at the first visit of the police to the defendant's room, and a number of letters written to the defendant in respect to the lottery, taken by the Marshal upon his search of defendant's room. * * *

The history of this Amendment is given with particularity in the opinion of Mr. Justice Bradley, speaking for the court in *Boyd v. United States*, 116 U.S. 616, 6 S.Ct. 524, 29 L.Ed. 746 (1886). As was there shown, it took its origin in the determination of the framers of the Amendments to the Federal Constitution to provide for that instrument a Bill of Rights, securing to the American people, among other things, those safeguards which had grown up in England to protect the people from unreasonable searches and seizures, such as were permitted under the general warrants issued under authority of the Government by which there had been invasions of the home and privacy of the citizens and the seizure of their private papers in support of charges, real or imaginary, made against them. Such practices had also received sanction under warrants and seizures under the so-called writs of assistance, issued in the American colonies. Resistance to these practices had established the principle which was enacted into the fundamental law in the Fourth Amendment, that a man's house was his castle and not to be invaded by any general authority to search and seize his goods and papers. * * *

In the *Boyd Case*, after citing Lord Camden's judgment in *Entick v. Carrington*, 19 Howell's State Trials, 1029, Mr. Justice Bradley said:

> "The principles laid down in this opinion affect the very essence of constitutional liberty and security. They reach farther than the concrete form of the case then before the court, with its adventitious circumstances; they apply to all invasions on the part of the government and its employés of the sanctity of a man's home and the privacies of life. It is not the breaking of his doors, and the rummaging of his drawers, that constitutes the essence of the offence; but it is the invasion of his indefeasible right of personal security, personal liberty and private property, where that right has never been forfeited by his conviction of some public offence,—it is the invasion of this sacred right which underlies and constitutes the essence of Lord Camden's judgment." * * *

The effect of the Fourth Amendment is to put the courts of the United States and Federal officials, in the exercise of their power and authority, under limitations and restraints as to the exercise of such power and authority, and to forever secure the people, their persons, houses, papers and effects against all unreasonable searches and seizures under the guise of law. This protection reaches all alike, whether accused of crime or not, and the duty of giving to it force and effect is obligatory upon all entrusted under our Federal system with the enforcement of the laws. The tendency of those who execute the criminal laws of the country to obtain conviction by means of unlawful seizures and enforced confessions, the latter often obtained after subjecting accused persons to unwarranted practices destructive of rights secured by the Federal Constitution, should find no sanction in the judgments of the courts which are charged at all times with the support of the Constitution and to which people of all conditions have a right to appeal for the maintenance of such fundamental rights. * * *

* * * If letters and private documents can * * * be seized and held and used in evidence against a citizen accused of an offense, the protection of the Fourth Amendment * * * is of no value, and, so far as those thus placed are concerned, might as well be stricken from the Constitution. The efforts of the courts and their officials to bring the guilty to punishment, praiseworthy as they are, are not to be aided by the sacrifice of those great principles established by years of endeavor and suffering which have resulted in their embodiment in the fundamental law of the land. The United States Marshal * * * acted without sanction of law, * * * and under color of his office undertook to make a seizure of private papers in direct violation of the constitutional prohibition against such action. * * * To sanction such proceedings would be to affirm by judicial decision a manifest neglect if not an open defiance of the prohibitions of the

Constitution, intended for the protection of the people against such unauthorized action. * * *

We therefore reach the conclusion that the letters in question were taken from the house of the accused by an official of the United States * * * in direct violation of the constitutional rights of the defendant; that having made a seasonable application for their return, * * * the court should have restored these letters to the accused. In holding them and permitting their use upon the trial, we think prejudicial error was committed. As to the papers and property seized by the policemen, it does not appear that they acted under any claim of Federal authority such as would make the Amendment applicable to such unauthorized seizures. * * * What remedies the defendant may have against them we need not inquire, as the Fourth Amendment is not directed to individual misconduct of such officials. Its limitations reach the Federal Government and its agencies.

It results that the judgment of the court below must be reversed * * *.

NOTES AND QUESTIONS

1. Why does the Court conclude that the letters seized by the United States Marshal should be excluded from the defendant's trial? Why did the Court not treat the papers and property seized by the local police in the same manner?

2. Federal Rule of Criminal Procedure 41(g) provides that a "person aggrieved by an unlawful search and seizure of property or by the deprivation of property may move for the property's return." And, under Rule 41(h), "[a] defendant may move to suppress evidence in the court where the trial will occur * * *."

Suppose the police unlawfully search Jane's home and seize contraband, such as illegal narcotics. Should Jane be able to seek its return under the federal rule quoted above? If not, is the contraband admissible at her trial?

3. *"Silver platter" doctrine.* Because the Court in *Weeks* only applied the exclusionary rule to evidence seized under "federal authority," this seemingly left local police free to conduct unreasonable searches and seizures and then deliver the evidence to federal prosecutors "on a silver platter," to be used in federal prosecutions. In Byars v. United States, 273 U.S. 28, 47 S.Ct. 248, 71 L.Ed. 520 (1927), however, the Court ruled that this "silver platter" doctrine did not apply to evidence obtained unlawfully during a search that "in substance and effect" was a joint state-federal venture. In *Byars*, state police conducted their search accompanied by a federal agent. And, in Gambino v. United States, 275 U.S. 310, 48 S.Ct. 137, 72 L.Ed. 293 (1927), state officers, acting alone, conducted a search solely on behalf of the federal government. In both cases, the Court applied the *Weeks* exclusionary rule to the state officers' actions.

4. *The exclusionary rule in the states.* What if state or local police officers want to use evidence in a *state* prosecution they obtained as a result of an unreasonable search or seizure? *Weeks* recognized an exclusionary rule in

federal cases. Is there an equivalent exclusionary rule that applies in state courts through the Fourteenth Amendment due process clause? Consider the next case in this regard.

WOLF v. COLORADO

Supreme Court of the United States, 1949.
338 U.S. 25, 69 S.Ct. 1359, 93 L.Ed. 1782.

MR. JUSTICE FRANKFURTER delivered the opinion of the Court.

The precise question for consideration is this: Does a conviction by a State court for a State offense deny the "due process of law" required by the Fourteenth Amendment, solely because evidence that was admitted at the trial was obtained under circumstances which would have rendered it inadmissible in a prosecution for violation of a federal law in a court of the United States because there deemed to be an infraction of the Fourth Amendment as applied in *Weeks v. United States*, [p. 67 supra]? The Supreme Court of Colorado has sustained convictions in which such evidence was admitted, and we brought the cases here.

Unlike the specific requirements and restrictions placed by the Bill of Rights (Amendments I to VIII) upon the administration of criminal justice by federal authority, the Fourteenth Amendment did not subject criminal justice in the States to specific limitations. The notion that the "due process of law" guaranteed by the Fourteenth Amendment is shorthand for the first eight amendments of the Constitution and thereby incorporates them has been rejected by this Court again and again, after impressive consideration. * * * The issue is closed.

For purposes of ascertaining the restrictions which the Due Process Clause imposed upon the States in the enforcement of their criminal law, we adhere to the views expressed in *Palko v. Connecticut*, 302 U.S. 319, 58 S.Ct. 149, 82 L.Ed. 288. * * * In rejecting the suggestion that the Due Process Clause incorporated the original Bill of Rights, Mr. Justice Cardozo reaffirmed on behalf of that Court a different but deeper and more pervasive conception of the Due Process Clause. This Clause exacts from the States for the lowliest and the most outcast all that is "implicit in the concept of ordered liberty."

Due process of law thus conveys neither formal nor fixed nor narrow requirements. It is the compendious expression for all those rights which the courts must enforce because they are basic to our free society. But basic rights do not become petrified as of any one time, even though, as a matter of human experience, some may not too rhetorically be called eternal verities. It is of the very nature of a free society to advance in its standards of what is deemed reasonable and right. Representing as it does a living principle, due process is not confined within a permanent catalogue of what may at a given time be deemed the limits or the essentials of fundamental rights.

To rely on a tidy formula for the easy determination of what is a fundamental right for purposes of legal enforcement may satisfy a longing for certainty but ignores the movements of a free society. It belittles the scale of the conception of due process. The real clue to the problem confronting the judiciary in the application of the Due Process Clause is not to ask where the line is once and for all to be drawn but to recognize that it is for the Court to draw it by the gradual and empiric process of "inclusion and exclusion." * * *

The security of one's privacy against arbitrary intrusion by the police—which is at the core of the Fourth Amendment—is basic to a free society. It is therefore implicit in "the concept of ordered liberty" and as such enforceable against the States through the Due Process Clause. The knock at the door, whether by day or by night, as a prelude to a search, without authority of law but solely on the authority of the police, did not need the commentary of recent history to be condemned as inconsistent with the conception of human rights enshrined in the history and the basic constitutional documents of English-speaking peoples.

Accordingly, we have no hesitation in saying that were a State affirmatively to sanction such police incursion into privacy it would run counter to the guaranty of the Fourteenth Amendment. But the ways of enforcing such a rule raise questions of a different order. How such arbitrary conduct should be checked, what remedies against it should be afforded, the means by which the right should be made effective, are all questions not to be so dogmatically answered as to preclude the varying solutions which spring from an allowable range of judgment on issues not susceptible to quantitative solution.

In *Weeks v. United States, supra*, this Court held that in a federal prosecution the Fourth Amendment barred the use of evidence secured through an illegal search and seizure. * * * It was not derived from the explicit requirements of the Fourth Amendment; it was not based on legislation expressing Congressional policy in the enforcement of the Constitution. The decision was a matter of judicial implication. Since then it has been frequently applied and we stoutly adhere to it. But the immediate question is whether the basic right to protection against arbitrary intrusion by the police demands the exclusion of logically relevant evidence obtained by an unreasonable search and seizure because, in a federal prosecution for a federal crime, it would be excluded. As a matter of inherent reason, one would suppose this to be an issue as to which men with complete devotion to the protection of the right of privacy might give different answers. When we find that in fact most of the English-speaking world does not regard as vital to such protection the exclusion of evidence thus obtained, we must hesitate to treat this remedy as an essential ingredient of the right. The contrariety of views of the States is particularly impressive in view of the careful reconsideration which they have given the problem in the light of the *Weeks* decision.

[According to the Court's survey of the law, twenty-seven states prior to *Weeks* had passed on the admissibility of evidence obtained by unlawful search or seizure. Of these, all but one state rejected an exclusionary rule. After *Weeks*, forty-seven states passed on the *Weeks* doctrine. Of this number, only sixteen adopted the *Weeks* exclusionary rule. The Court also reported that of ten jurisdictions within the United Kingdom and the British Commonwealth, none had adopted a similar doctrine. The Court concluded that, although the exclusionary rule might "be an effective way of deterring unreasonable searches, it is not for this Court to condemn as falling below the minimal standards assured by the Due Process Clause a State's reliance upon other methods which, if consistently enforced, would be equally effective."] * * *

We hold, therefore, that in a prosecution in a State court for a State crime the Fourteenth Amendment does not forbid the admission of evidence obtained by an unreasonable search and seizure. * * *

Affirmed.

[Justice Black's concurring opinion is omitted. Also omitted are the dissenting opinions of Justices Douglas, Murphy, and Rutledge.]

NOTES AND QUESTIONS

1. *Wolf* represented a classic "I have good news and I have bad news" story for the defendant: "Arbitrary searches and seizures by state and local police violate the concept of ordered liberty and, therefore, violate the Fourteenth Amendment due process clause, but—sorry!—the government can still use the fruits of its agents' unconstitutional conduct in your criminal prosecution." Is there any practical value in possessing the right to be free from arbitrary or unreasonable searches and seizures if a state may use the evidence unlawfully secured in a criminal prosecution?

2. *The "Rochin" principle: the exclusionary rule in different clothing.* In Rochin v. California, 342 U.S. 165, 72 S.Ct. 205, 96 L.Ed. 183 (1952), Justice Frankfurter, author of *Wolf*, described the relevant facts in the case:

> Having "some information that [the petitioner here] was selling narcotics," three deputy sheriffs * * * made for the two-story dwelling house in which Rochin lived with his mother, common-law wife, brothers and sisters. Finding the outside door open, they entered and then forced open the door to Rochin's room on the second floor. Inside they found petitioner sitting partly dressed on the side of the bed, upon which his wife was lying. On a "night stand" beside the bed the deputies spied two capsules. When asked, "Whose stuff is this?" Rochin seized the capsules and put them in his mouth. A struggle ensued, in the course of which the three officers "jumped upon him" and attempted to extract the capsules. The force they applied proved unavailing against Rochin's resistance. He was handcuffed and taken to a hospital. At the direction of one of the officers a doctor forced an emetic solution through a tube into Rochin's stomach against his will. This "stomach pumping" produced vomiting. In

the vomited matter were found two capsules which proved to contain morphine.

Rochin was prosecuted for possession of morphine. The chief evidence against him, admitted over defense objection, were the two capsules extracted from his stomach.

Although local police conducted the search and seizure, the Supreme Court ruled that the Fourteenth Amendment due process clause prohibited admission of the capsules. Justice Frankfurter explained:

> [W]e are compelled to conclude that the proceedings by which this conviction was obtained do more than offend some fastidious squeamishness or private sentimentalism about combatting crime too energetically. This is conduct that shocks the conscience. Illegally breaking into the privacy of the petitioner, the struggle to open his mouth and remove what was there, the forcible extraction of his stomach's contents—this course of proceeding by agents of government to obtain evidence is bound to offend even hardened sensibilities. They are methods too close to the rack and the screw to permit of constitutional differentiation.

Is *Rochin* consistent with *Wolf*? If this had been a pre-*Weeks* federal prosecution, how would the case have been resolved?

3. *Wolf* was not the end of the story. . . .

MAPP v. OHIO

Supreme Court of the United States, 1961.
367 U.S. 643, 81 S.Ct. 1684, 6 L.Ed.2d 1081.

MR. JUSTICE CLARK delivered the opinion of the Court.

Appellant stands convicted of knowingly having had in her possession and under her control certain lewd and lascivious books, pictures, and photographs in violation of [state law].[a] * * *

On May 23, 1957, three Cleveland police officers arrived at appellant's residence in that city pursuant to information that "a person [was] hiding out in the home, who was wanted for questioning in connection with a recent bombing, and that there was a large amount of policy [gambling] paraphernalia being hidden in the home." Miss Mapp and her daughter by a former marriage lived on the top floor of the two-family dwelling. Upon their arrival at that house, the officers knocked on the door and demanded entrance but appellant, after telephoning her attorney, refused to admit them without a search warrant. They advised their headquarters of the situation and undertook a surveillance of the house.

The officers again sought entrance some three hours later when four or more additional officers arrived on the scene. When Miss Mapp did not come to the door immediately, at least one of the several doors to the

---

a. The materials consisted of four books (*Affairs of a Troubadour, Little Darlings, London Stage Affairs, Memories of a Hotel Man*) and "a hand-drawn picture described in the state's brief as being 'of a very obscene nature.' " Potter Stewart, *The Road to* Mapp v. Ohio *and Beyond: The Origins, Development and Future of the Exclusionary Rule in Search-and-Seizure Cases*, 83 Colum. L. Rev. 1365, 1367 (1983).

house was forcibly opened[2] and the policemen gained admittance. Meanwhile Miss Mapp's attorney arrived, but the officers, having secured their own entry, and continuing in their defiance of the law, would permit him neither to see Miss Mapp nor to enter the house. It appears that Miss Mapp was halfway down the stairs from the upper floor to the front door when the officers, in this highhanded manner, broke into the hall. She demanded to see the search warrant. A paper, claimed to be a warrant, was held up by one of the officers. She grabbed the "warrant" and placed it in her bosom. A struggle ensued in which the officers recovered the piece of paper and as a result of which they handcuffed appellant because she had been "belligerent" in resisting their official rescue of the "warrant" from her person. Running roughshod over appellant, a policeman "grabbed" her, "twisted [her] hand," and she "yelled [and] pleaded with him" because "it was hurting." Appellant, in handcuffs, was then forcibly taken upstairs to her bedroom where the officers searched a dresser, a chest of drawers, a closet and some suitcases. They also looked into a photo album and through personal papers belonging to the appellant. The search spread to the rest of the second floor including the child's bedroom, the living room, the kitchen and a dinette. The basement of the building and a trunk found therein were also searched. The obscene materials for possession of which she was ultimately convicted were discovered in the course of that widespread search.

At the trial no search warrant was produced by the prosecution, nor was the failure to produce one explained or accounted for. At best, "There is, in the record, considerable doubt as to whether there ever was any warrant for the search of defendant's home." The Ohio Supreme Court believed a "reasonable argument" could be made that the conviction should be reversed "because the 'methods' employed to obtain the [evidence] * * * were such as to 'offend "a sense of justice," ' '" but the court found determinative the fact that the evidence had not been taken "from defendant's person by the use of brutal or offensive physical force against defendant."

The State says that even if the search were made without authority, or otherwise unreasonably, it is not prevented from using the unconstitutionally seized evidence at trial, citing *Wolf v. Colorado* [p. 70], in which this Court did indeed hold "that in a prosecution in a State court for a State crime the Fourteenth Amendment does not forbid the admission of evidence obtained by an unreasonable search and seizure." On this appeal, * * * it is urged once again that we review that holding.

I.   * * *

* * * [I]n the year 1914, in the *Weeks* [*v. United States*] case, this Court "for the first time" held that "in a federal prosecution the Fourth

---

2. A police officer testified that "we did pry the screen door to gain entrance"; the attorney on the scene testified that a policeman "tried * * * to kick in the door" and then "broke the glass in the door and somebody reached in and opened the door and let them in"; the appellant testified that "The back door was broken."

Amendment barred the use of evidence secured through an illegal search and seizure." This Court has ever since required of federal law officers a strict adherence to that command which this Court has held to be a clear, specific, and constitutionally required—even if judicially implied—deterrent safeguard without insistence upon which the Fourth Amendment would have been reduced to "a form of words." Holmes, J., *Silverthorne Lumber Co. v. United States*, 251 U.S. 385, 392, 40 S.Ct. 182, 183, 64 L.Ed. 319 (1920). It meant, quite simply, that "conviction by means of unlawful seizures and enforced confessions * * * should find no sanction in the judgments of the courts * * *," and that such evidence "shall not be used at all."

There are in the cases of this Court some passing references to the *Weeks* rule as being one of evidence. But the plain and unequivocal language of *Weeks*—and its later paraphrase in *Wolf*—to the effect that the *Weeks* rule is of constitutional origin, remains entirely undisturbed. * * *

II.

In 1949, 35 years after *Weeks* was announced, this Court, in *Wolf v. Colorado*, again for the first time, * * * decided that the *Weeks* exclusionary rule would not then be imposed upon the States as "an essential ingredient of the right." The Court's reasons for not considering essential to the right to privacy, as a curb imposed upon the States by the Due Process Clause, that which decades before had been posited as part and parcel of the Fourth Amendment's limitation upon federal encroachment of individual privacy, were bottomed on factual considerations.

While they are not basically relevant to a decision that the exclusionary rule is an essential ingredient of the Fourth Amendment as the right it embodies is vouchsafed against the States by the Due Process Clause, we will consider the current validity of the factual grounds upon which *Wolf* was based.

The Court in *Wolf* first stated that "[t]he contrariety of views of the States" on the adoption of the exclusionary rule of *Weeks* was "particularly impressive" * * *. While in 1949, prior to the *Wolf* case, almost two-thirds of the States were opposed to the use of the exclusionary rule, now, despite the *Wolf* case, more than half of those since passing upon it, by their own legislative or judicial decision, have wholly or partly adopted or adhered to the *Weeks* rule. Significantly, among those now following the rule is California, which, according to its highest court, was "compelled to reach that conclusion because other remedies have completely failed to secure compliance with the constitutional provisions * * * ." *People v. Cahan*, 44 Cal.2d 434, 445, 282 P.2d 905 [1955]. In connection with this California case, we note that the second basis elaborated in *Wolf* in support of its failure to enforce the exclusionary doctrine against the States was that "other means of protection" have been afforded "the right to privacy." The experience of California that such other remedies have

been worthless and futile is buttressed by the experience of other States.
* * *

It, therefore, plainly appears that the factual considerations supporting the failure of the *Wolf* Court to include the *Weeks* exclusionary rule
when it recognized the enforceability of the right to privacy against the
States in 1949, while not basically relevant to the constitutional consideration, could not, in any analysis, now be deemed controlling.

III.

* * * Today we once again examine *Wolf*'s constitutional documenta-
tion of the right to privacy free from unreasonable state intrusion, and,
after its dozen years on our books, are led by it to close the only
courtroom door remaining open to evidence secured by official lawlessness
in flagrant abuse of that basic right, reserved to all persons as a specific
guarantee against that very same unlawful conduct. We hold that all
evidence obtained by searches and seizures in violation of the Constitution
is, by that same authority, inadmissible in a state court.

IV.

Since the Fourth Amendment's right of privacy has been declared
enforceable against the States through the Due Process Clause of the
Fourteenth, it is enforceable against them by the same sanction of
exclusion as is used against the Federal Government. Were it otherwise,
then just as without the *Weeks* rule the assurance against unreasonable
federal searches and seizures would be "a form of words," valueless and
undeserving of mention in a perpetual charter of inestimable human
liberties, so too, without that rule the freedom from state invasions of
privacy would be so ephemeral and so neatly severed from its conceptual
nexus with the freedom from all brutish means of coercing evidence as not
to merit this Court's high regard as a freedom "implicit in the concept of
ordered liberty." * * * Therefore, in extending the substantive protections
of due process to all constitutionally unreasonable searches—state or
federal—it was logically and constitutionally necessary that the exclusion
doctrine—an essential part of the right to privacy—be also insisted upon
as an essential ingredient of the right newly recognized by the *Wolf* case.
In short, the admission of the new constitutional right by *Wolf* could not
consistently tolerate denial of its most important constitutional privilege,
namely, the exclusion of the evidence which an accused had been forced to
give by reason of the unlawful seizure. To hold otherwise is to grant the
right but in reality to withhold its privilege and enjoyment. Only last year
the Court itself recognized that the purpose of the exclusionary rule "is to
deter—to compel respect for the constitutional guaranty in the only
effectively available way—by removing the incentive to disregard it."

* * * This Court has not hesitated to enforce as strictly against the
States as it does against the Federal Government the rights of free speech
and of a free press, the right to notice and to a fair, public trial, including,
as it does, the right not to be convicted by use of a coerced confession,

however logically relevant it be, and without regard to its reliability. * * * The philosophy of each Amendment and of each freedom is complementary to, although not dependent upon, that of the other in its sphere of influence—the very least that together they assure in either sphere is that no man is to be convicted on unconstitutional evidence.

V.

Moreover, our holding that the exclusionary rule is an essential part of both the Fourth and Fourteenth Amendments is not only the logical dictate of prior cases, but it also makes very good sense. There is no war between the Constitution and common sense. Presently, a federal prosecutor may make no use of evidence illegally seized, but a State's attorney across the street may, although he supposedly is operating under the enforceable prohibitions of the same Amendment. Thus the State, by admitting evidence unlawfully seized, serves to encourage disobedience to the Federal Constitution which it is bound to uphold. * * *

There are those who say, as did Justice (then Judge) Cardozo, that under our constitutional exclusionary doctrine "[t]he criminal is to go free because the constable has blundered." In some cases this will undoubtedly be the result. But, * * * "there is another consideration—the imperative of judicial integrity." The criminal goes free, if he must, but it is the law that sets him free. Nothing can destroy a government more quickly than its failure to observe its own laws, or worse, its disregard of the charter of its own existence. As Mr. Justice Brandeis, dissenting, said in *Olmstead v. United States*, 277 U.S. 438, 485, 48 S.Ct. 564, 575, 72 L.Ed. 944 (1928): "Our Government is the potent, the omnipresent teacher. For good or for ill, it teaches the whole people by its example. * * * If the Government becomes a lawbreaker, it breeds contempt for law; it invites every man to become a law unto himself; it invites anarchy." Nor can it lightly be assumed that, as a practical matter, adoption of the exclusionary rule fetters law enforcement. Only last year this Court expressly considered that contention and found that "pragmatic evidence of a sort" to the contrary was not wanting. * * *

* * * Our decision, founded on reason and truth, gives to the individual no more than that which the Constitution guarantees him, to the police officer no less than that to which honest law enforcement is entitled, and, to the courts, that judicial integrity so necessary in the true administration of justice. * * *

Reversed and remanded.

Mr. Justice BLACK, concurring. * * *

I am still not persuaded that the Fourth Amendment, standing alone, would be enough to bar the introduction into evidence against an accused of papers and effects seized from him in violation of its commands. For the Fourth Amendment does not itself contain any provision expressly precluding the use of such evidence, and I am extremely doubtful that such a provision could properly be inferred from nothing more than the basic command against unreasonable searches and seizures. Reflection on the problem, however, in the light of cases coming before the Court since *Wolf*, has led me to conclude that when the Fourth Amendment's ban against unreasonable searches and seizures is considered together with the Fifth Amendment's ban against compelled self-incrimination, a constitutional basis emerges which not only justifies but actually requires the exclusionary rule.

The close interrelationship between the Fourth and Fifth Amendments, as they apply to this problem, has long been recognized and, indeed, was expressly made the ground for this Court's holding in *Boyd v. United States*[, 116 U.S. 616, 6 S.Ct. 524, 29 L.Ed. 746 (1886)]. There the Court fully discussed this relationship and declared itself "unable to perceive that the seizure of a man's private books and papers to be used in evidence against him is substantially different from compelling him to be a witness against himself." * * * [A]lthough I rejected the argument [in *Wolf*], its force has, for me at least, become compelling with the more thorough understanding of the problem brought on by recent cases. In the final analysis, it seems to me that the *Boyd* doctrine, though perhaps not required by the express language of the Constitution strictly construed, is amply justified from an historical standpoint, soundly based in reason, and entirely consistent with what I regard to be the proper approach to interpretation of our Bill of Rights * * *.

[Justice Douglas also concurred in the majority opinion. Justice Stewart concurred in the result. He expressed "no view as to the merits of the constitutional issue which the Court today decides." Instead, he would have reversed the conviction on the ground that it violated rights of "free thought and expression assured against state action by the Fourteenth Amendment."]

Mr. Justice HARLAN, whom Mr. Justice FRANKFURTER and Mr. Justice WHITTAKER join, dissenting.

In overruling the *Wolf* case the Court, in my opinion, has forgotten the sense of judicial restraint which, with due regard for *stare decisis*, is one element that should enter into deciding whether a past decision of this Court should be overruled. Apart from that I also believe that the *Wolf* rule represents sounder Constitutional doctrine than the new rule which now replaces it.

I.

From the Court's statement of the case one would gather that the central, if not controlling, issue on this appeal is whether illegally state-seized evidence is Constitutionally admissible in a state prosecution, an issue which would of course face us with the need for re-examining *Wolf*. However, such is not the situation. For, although that question was indeed raised here and below among appellant's subordinate points, the new and pivotal issue brought to the Court by this appeal is whether * * * the Ohio Revised Code making criminal the *mere* knowing possession or control of obscene material, and under which appellant has been convicted, is consistent with the rights of free thought and expression assured against state action by the Fourteenth Amendment. That was the principal issue which was decided by the Ohio Supreme Court, * * * and which was briefed[5] and argued[6] in this Court.

In this posture of things, I think it fair to say that five members of this Court have simply "reached out" to overrule *Wolf*. * * * I can perceive no justification for regarding this case as an appropriate occasion for re-examining *Wolf*. * * *

II.

Essential to the majority's argument against *Wolf* is the proposition that the rule of *Weeks v. United States*, excluding in federal criminal trials the use of evidence obtained in violation of the Fourth Amendment, derives not from the "supervisory power" of this Court over the federal judicial system, but from Constitutional requirement. This is so because no one, I suppose, would suggest that this Court possesses any general supervisory power over the state courts. Although I entertain considerable doubt as to the soundness of this foundational proposition of the majority, I shall assume, for present purposes, that the *Weeks* rule "is of constitutional origin."

At the heart of the majority's opinion in this case is the following syllogism: (1) the rule excluding in federal criminal trials evidence which is the product of an illegal search and seizure is "part and parcel" of the Fourth Amendment; (2) *Wolf* held that the "privacy" assured against federal action by the Fourth Amendment is also protected against state action by the Fourteenth Amendment; and (3) it is therefore "logically and constitutionally necessary" that the *Weeks* exclusionary rule should also be enforced against the States.

This reasoning ultimately rests on the unsound premise that because *Wolf* carried into the States, as part of "the concept of ordered liberty" embodied in the Fourteenth Amendment, the principle of "privacy" underlying the Fourth Amendment, it must follow that whatever configurations of the Fourth Amendment have been developed in the particularizing federal precedents are likewise to be deemed a part of "ordered liberty," and as such are enforceable against the States. For me, this does not follow at all.

It cannot be too much emphasized that what was recognized in *Wolf* was not that the Fourth Amendment *as such* is enforceable against the States as a facet of due process, a view of the Fourteenth Amendment

---

5. The appellant's brief did not urge the overruling of *Wolf*. Indeed it did not even cite the case. * * * The brief of the American and Ohio Civil Liberties Unions, as *amici*, did in one short concluding paragraph of its argument "request" the Court to re-examine and overrule *Wolf*, but without argumentation. * * *

6. Counsel for appellant on oral argument, as in his brief, did not urge that *Wolf* be overruled. Indeed, when pressed by questioning from the bench whether he was not in fact urging us to overrule *Wolf*, counsel expressly disavowed any such purpose.

which, as *Wolf* itself pointed out, has long since been discredited, but the principle of privacy "which is at the core of the Fourth Amendment." It would not be proper to expect or impose any precise equivalence, either as regards the scope of the right or the means of its implementation, between the requirements of the Fourth and Fourteenth Amendments. For the Fourth, unlike what was said in *Wolf* of the Fourteenth, does not state a general principle only; it is a particular command, having its setting in a pre-existing legal context on which both interpreting decisions and enabling statutes must at least build. * * *

I would not impose upon the States this federal exclusionary remedy. The reasons given by the majority for now suddenly turning its back on *Wolf* seem to me notably unconvincing.

First, it is said that "the factual grounds upon which *Wolf* was based" have since changed, in that more States now follow the *Weeks* exclusionary rule than was so at the time *Wolf* was decided. While that is true, * * * surely all this is beside the point, as the majority itself indeed seems to recognize. Our concern here, as it was in *Wolf*, is not with the desirability of that rule but only with the question whether the States are Constitutionally free to follow it or not as they may themselves determine, and the relevance of the disparity of views among the States on this point lies simply in the fact that the judgment involved is a debatable one. * * *

The preservation of a proper balance between state and federal responsibility in the administration of criminal justice demands patience on the part of those who might like to see things move faster among the States in this respect. Problems of criminal law enforcement vary widely from State to State. One State, in considering the totality of its legal picture, may conclude that the need for embracing the *Weeks* rule is pressing because other remedies are unavailable or inadequate to secure compliance with the substantive Constitutional principle involved. Another, though equally solicitous of Constitutional rights, may choose to pursue one purpose at a time, allowing all evidence relevant to guilt to be brought into a criminal trial, and dealing with Constitutional infractions by other means. Still another may consider the exclusionary rule too rough-and-ready a remedy, in that it reaches only unconstitutional intrusions which eventuate in criminal prosecution of the victims. Further, a State after experimenting with the *Weeks* rule for a time may, because of unsatisfactory experience with it, decide to revert to a non-exclusionary rule. And so on. * * * For us the question remains, as it has always been, one of state power, not one of passing judgment on the wisdom of one state course or another. In my view this Court should continue to forbear from fettering the States with an adamant rule which may embarrass them in coping with their own peculiar problems in criminal law enforcement. * * *

A state conviction comes to us as the complete product of a sovereign judicial system. Typically a case will have been tried in a trial court, tested in some final appellate court, and will go no further. In the comparatively rare instance when a conviction is reviewed by us on due process grounds we deal then with a finished product in the creation of which we are allowed no hand, and our task, far from being one of over-all supervision, is, speaking generally, restricted to a determination of whether the prosecution was Constitutionally fair. The specifics of trial procedure, which in every mature legal system will vary greatly in detail, are within the sole competence of the States. I do not see how it can be said that a trial becomes unfair simply because a State determines that evidence may be considered by the trier of fact, regardless of how it was obtained, if it is relevant to the one issue with which the trial is concerned, the guilt or innocence of the accused. Of course, a court may use its procedures as an incidental means of pursuing other ends than the correct resolution of the controversies before it. Such indeed is the *Weeks* rule, but if a State does not choose to use its courts in this way, I do not believe that this Court is empowered to impose this much-debated procedure on local courts, however efficacious we may consider the *Weeks* rule to be as a means of securing Constitutional rights.

Finally, it is said that the overruling of *Wolf* is supported by the established doctrine that the admission of evidence of an involuntary confession renders a state conviction Constitutionally invalid. Since such a confession may often be entirely reliable, and therefore of the greatest relevance to the issue of the trial, the argument continues, this doctrine is ample warrant in precedent that the way evidence was obtained, and not just its relevance, is Constitutionally significant to the fairness of a trial. I believe this analogy is not a true one. * * *

The point * * * must be that in requiring exclusion of an involuntary statement of an accused, we are concerned not with an appropriate remedy for what the police have done, but with something which is regarded as going to the heart of our concepts of fairness in judicial procedure. * * * What is crucial is that the trial defense to which an accused is entitled should not be rendered an empty formality by reason of statements wrung from him, for then "a prisoner * * * [has been] made the deluded instrument of his own conviction." That this is a *procedural right*, and that its violation occurs at the time his improperly obtained statement is admitted at trial, is manifest. For without this right all the careful safeguards erected around the giving of testimony * * * would become empty formalities in a procedure where the most compelling possible evidence of guilt, a confession, would have already been obtained at the unsupervised pleasure of the police.

This, and not the disciplining of the police, as with illegally seized evidence, is surely the true basis for excluding a statement of the accused which was unconstitutionally obtained. In sum, I think the coerced confession analogy works strongly *against* what the Court does today. * * *

I regret that I find so unwise in principle and so inexpedient in policy a decision motivated by the high purpose of increasing respect for Constitutional rights. But in the last analysis I think this Court can increase respect for the Constitution only if it rigidly respects the limitations which the Constitution places upon it, and respects as well the principles inherent in its own processes. In the present case I think we exceed both, and that our voice becomes only a voice of power, not of reason.

NOTES AND QUESTIONS

1. *Counting votes.* You should grow accustomed to counting the votes in Supreme Court opinions. That is, you should determine how many justices signed an opinion of the Court. An opinion of five justices does not carry the same symbolic weight as a unanimous opinion and, of course, is more susceptible to erosion or outright overruling, especially as new justices join the Court.

When counting votes, it is important to distinguish between two types of concurring opinions. Sometimes, a justice will "concur in the judgment" or "concur in the result," as Justice Stewart did in this case. In such circumstances, the concurring justice has reached the same outcome as the majority (*e.g.*, reversal or affirmance of a lower court judgment), but does not want to attach his or her name to the main opinion, usually because the concurring justice reaches the result on different grounds.

Alternatively, concurring justices (here, Black and Douglas) may sign the Court's opinion, but still write separately. This is called a concurrence "in the opinion" of the Court. Typically, justices will write such a concurrence in order to clarify aspects of the main opinion that they believe need elucidation, or because they are unhappy with certain language in the principal opinion.

In view of this explanation, how many justices signed on to Justice Clark's opinion in *Mapp*?

2. Do you consider Mapp an "innocent" or "guilty" person, who was subjected to police misconduct? In regard to the admissibility of the seized evidence, should such characterization matter? For more details of the case, including a recent interview with "Miss Mapp" (Dollree Mapp), see Carolyn N. Long, Mapp v. Ohio: Guarding Against Unreasonable Searches and Seizures (2006).

3. What was the Ohio Supreme Court getting at when it stated that a "reasonable argument" could be made that the conviction should be overturned because police methods "offended a sense of justice." Why do you think it rejected that "reasonable argument"?

4. Why did Justice Harlan believe that this case was an inappropriate vehicle for overruling *Wolf*? Was he right? What should a justice who believed that *Wolf* was wrongly decided have done?

After his retirement, Justice Potter Stewart described the behind-the-scene events this way:

> At the conference following the argument, a majority of the Justices agreed that the Ohio statute violated the *first* and fourteenth amendments. Justice Tom Clark was assigned the job of writing the opinion of the Court.

What transpired in the month following our conference * * * is really a matter of speculation on my part, but I have always suspected that the members of the soon-to-be *Mapp* majority had met in what I affectionately call a "rump caucus" to discuss a different basis for their decision.[12] But regardless of how they reached their decision, five Justices * * * concluded that * * * *Wolf* was to be overruled.

I was shocked when Justice Clark's proposed Court opinion reached my desk. I immediately wrote him a note expressing my surprise and questioning the wisdom of overruling an important doctrine in a case in which the issue was not briefed, argued, or discussed by the state courts, by the parties' counsel, or at our conference following the oral argument.

Potter Stewart, *The Road to* Mapp v. Ohio *and Beyond: The Origins, Development and Future of the Exclusionary Rule in Search-and-Seizure Cases*, 83 Colum. L. Rev. 1365, 1368 (1983). For more on Justice Clark's behind-the-scenes role in *Mapp*, see Dennis D. Dorin, *Justice Tom Clark's Rule in* Mapp v. Ohio*'s Extension of the Exclusionary Rule to State Searches and Seizures*, 52 Case W. Res. L. Rev. 401 (2001).

5.   Why did Justice Clark say that the "factual grounds upon which *Wolf* was based" were "basically [ir]relevant"? If so, why did he survey post-*Wolf* state law? Can it plausibly be claimed that the results of his survey actually supported the dissent?

6.   What is the purpose of an exclusionary rule? According to the majority, why is it required in state prosecutions? How did Justice Harlan answer the majority?

7.   The majority supported its position by pointing out that coerced confessions are inadmissible at trial. What was Justice Clark's point in this regard? Why did Justice Harlan believe that this argument worked *against* the majority's position?

8.   The exclusionary rule has evoked considerable controversy, virtually from the start. Moreover, in large part because of post-*Mapp* Supreme Court misgivings, the scope of the Fourth Amendment exclusionary rule has been seriously limited. The debate regarding *Mapp* and the changes to the rule that the Court has wrought are considered in Chapter 5.

---

12.   Professor Schwartz reports that an impromptu caucus of the *Mapp* majority took place in an elevator at the Court immediately after the conference at which the case was discussed. [Bernard Schwartz, Super Chief: Earl Warren and His Supreme Court—A Judicial Biography 393 (1983).]

CHAPTER 3

PASSING THE THRESHOLD OF THE FOURTH AMENDMENT

■ ■ ■

The Fourth Amendment states that "[t]he right of the people to be secure in their persons, houses, papers, and effects, against unreasonable searches and seizures, shall not be violated * * *." In these few words we are told what interests are protected (persons, houses, papers, and effects) and what the Government must do in regard to these protected interests (conduct only reasonable searches and seizures).

But notice: The Constitution does not prohibit *all* unreasonable law enforcement practices. As far the Fourth Amendment is concerned, a police officer may act as arbitrarily or unreasonably as she wants, as long as she does not "search" or "seize"; and, even searches and seizures are unregulated by the Fourth Amendment unless "they bear the requisite relationship to 'persons, houses, papers, and effects.'" Anthony G. Amsterdam, *Perspectives on the Fourth Amendment*, 58 Minn. L. Rev. 349, 356 (1974).

This chapter considers the threshold of the Fourth Amendment. It focuses on the question: What governmental conduct constitutes a *search* or *seizure* of a *person*, *house*, *paper*, or *effect* and, therefore, triggers Fourth Amendment protection?

A. WHAT IS A "SEARCH"?

1. GENERAL PRINCIPLES

KATZ v. UNITED STATES

Supreme Court of the United States, 1967.
389 U.S. 347, 88 S.Ct. 507, 19 L.Ed.2d 576.

MR. JUSTICE STEWART delivered the opinion of the Court.

The petitioner was convicted * * * under an eight-count indictment charging him with transmitting wagering information by telephone from Los Angeles to Miami and Boston, in violation of a federal statute. At trial the Government was permitted, over the petitioner's objection, to introduce evidence of the petitioner's end of telephone conversations, overheard by FBI agents who had attached an electronic listening and recording device to the outside of the public telephone booth from which he had placed his calls. In affirming his conviction, the Court of Appeals rejected the contention that the recordings had been obtained in violation of the Fourth Amendment, because "[t]here was no physical entrance into the area occupied by [the petitioner]." We granted certiorari in order to consider the constitutional questions thus presented.

The petitioner has phrased those questions as follows:

"A. Whether a public telephone booth is a constitutionally protected area so that evidence obtained by attaching an electronic listening recording device to the top of such a booth is obtained in violation of the right to privacy of the user of the booth.

"B. Whether physical penetration of a constitutionally protected area is necessary before a search and seizure can be said to be violative of the Fourth Amendment to the United States Constitution."

We decline to adopt this formulation of the issues. In the first place, the correct solution of Fourth Amendment problems is not necessarily promoted by incantation of the phrase "constitutionally protected area." Secondly, the Fourth Amendment cannot be translated into a general constitutional "right to privacy." That Amendment protects individual privacy against certain kinds of governmental intrusion, but its protections go further, and often have nothing to do with privacy at all.[1] Other provisions of the Constitution protect personal privacy from other forms of governmental invasion.[2] But the protection of a person's *general* right to privacy—his right to be let alone by other people—is, like the protection of his property and of his very life, left largely to the law of the individual States.

Because of the misleading way the issues have been formulated, the parties have attached great significance to the characterization of the telephone booth from which the petitioner placed his calls. The petitioner has strenuously argued that the booth was a "constitutionally protected area." The Government has maintained with equal vigor that it was not. But this effort to decide whether or not a given "area," viewed in the abstract, is "constitutionally protected" deflects attention from the prob-

---

1. "The average man would very likely not have his feelings soothed any more by having his property seized openly than by having it seized privately and by stealth. * * * And a person can be just as much, if not more, irritated, annoyed and injured by an unceremonious public arrest by a policeman as he is by a seizure in the privacy of his office or home." *Griswold v. Connecticut,* 381 U.S. 479, 509, 85 S.Ct. 1678, 1695, 14 L.Ed.2d 510 [(1965)] (dissenting opinion of Mr. Justice Black).

2. The First Amendment, for example, imposes limitations upon governmental abridgement of "freedom to associate and privacy in one's associations." The Third Amendment's prohibition against the unconsented peacetime quartering of soldiers protects another aspect of privacy from governmental intrusion. To some extent, the Fifth Amendment too "reflects the Constitution's concern for * * * ' * * * the right of each individual "to a private enclave where he may lead a private life." ' " Virtually every governmental action interferes with personal privacy to some degree. The question in each case is whether that interference violates a command of the United States Constitution.

lem presented by this case. For the Fourth Amendment protects people, not places. What a person knowingly exposes to the public, even in his own home or office, is not a subject of Fourth Amendment protection. But what he seeks to preserve as private, even in an area accessible to the public, may be constitutionally protected.

The Government stresses the fact that the telephone booth from which the petitioner made his calls was constructed partly of glass, so that he was as visible after he entered it as he would have been if he had remained outside. But what he sought to exclude when he entered the booth was not the intruding eye—it was the uninvited ear. He did not shed his right to do so simply because he made his calls from a place where he might be seen. No less than an individual in a business office, in a friend's apartment, or in a taxicab, a person in a telephone booth may rely upon the protection of the Fourth Amendment. One who occupies it, shuts the door behind him, and pays the toll that permits him to place a call is surely entitled to assume that the words he utters into the mouthpiece will not be broadcast to the world. To read the Constitution more narrowly is to ignore the vital role that the public telephone has come to play in private communication.

The Government contends, however, that the activities of its agents in this case should not be tested by Fourth Amendment requirements, for the surveillance technique they employed involved no physical penetration of the telephone booth from which the petitioner placed his calls. It is true that the absence of such penetration was at one time thought to foreclose further Fourth Amendment inquiry, *Olmstead v. United States*, 277 U.S. 438, 457, 464, 466, 48 S.Ct. 564, 565, 567, 568, 72 L.Ed. 944 [(1928)]; *Goldman v. United States*, 316 U.S. 129, 134–136, 62 S.Ct. 993, 995–97, 86 L.Ed. 1322 [(1942)], for that Amendment was thought to limit only searches and seizures of tangible property. But "[t]he premise that property interests control the right of the Government to search and seize has been discredited." Thus, although a closely divided Court supposed in *Olmstead* that surveillance without any trespass and without the seizure of any material object fell outside the ambit of the Constitution, we have since departed from the narrow view on which that decision rested. Indeed, we have expressly held that the Fourth Amendment governs not only the seizure of tangible items, but extends as well to the recording of oral statements, overheard without any "technical trespass under * * * local property law." *Silverman v. United States*, 365 U.S. 505, 511, 81 S.Ct. 679, 682, 5 L.Ed.2d 734 [(1961)]. Once this much is acknowledged, and once it is recognized that the Fourth Amendment protects people—and not simply "areas"—against unreasonable searches and seizures, it becomes clear that the reach of that Amendment cannot turn upon the presence or absence of a physical intrusion into any given enclosure.

We conclude that the underpinnings of *Olmstead* and *Goldman* have been so eroded by our subsequent decisions that the "trespass" doctrine there enunciated can no longer be regarded as controlling. The Government's activities in electronically listening to and recording the petitioner's words violated the privacy upon which he justifiably relied while using the telephone booth and thus constituted a "search and seizure" within the meaning of the Fourth Amendment. The fact that the electronic device employed to achieve that end did not happen to penetrate the wall of the booth can have no constitutional significance.

The question remaining for decision, then, is whether the search and seizure conducted in this case complied with constitutional standards. [The Court went on to hold that they did not, as explained more fully in Note 6, *infra*.]

[Justice Douglas's concurring opinion, with whom Justice Brennan joined, is omitted.]

Mr. Justice HARLAN, concurring.

I join the opinion of the Court, which I read to hold only (a) that an enclosed telephone booth is an area where, like a home, and unlike a field, a person has a constitutionally protected reasonable expectation of privacy; (b) that electronic as well as physical intrusion into a place that is in this sense private may constitute a violation of the Fourth Amendment; and (c) that the invasion of a constitutionally protected area by federal authorities is, as the Court has long held, presumptively unreasonable in the absence of a search warrant.

As the Court's opinion states, "the Fourth Amendment protects people, not places." The question, however, is what protection it affords to those people. Generally, as here, the answer to that question requires reference to a "place." My understanding of the rule that has emerged from prior decisions is that there is a twofold requirement, first that a person have exhibited an actual (subjective) expectation of privacy and, second, that the expectation be one that society is prepared to recognize as "reasonable." Thus a man's home is, for most purposes, a place where he expects privacy, but objects, activities, or statements that he exposes to the "plain view" of outsiders are not "protected" because no intention to keep them to himself has been exhibited. On the other hand, conversations in the open would not be protected against being overheard, for the expectation of privacy under the circumstances would be unreasonable.

The critical fact in this case is that "[o]ne who occupies it [a telephone booth], shuts the door behind him, and pays the toll that permits him to place a call is surely entitled to assume" that his conversation is not being intercepted. The point is not that the booth is "accessible to the public" at other times, but that it is a temporarily private place whose momentary occupants' expectations of freedom from intrusion are recognized as reasonable.

In *Silverman v. United States*, we held that eavesdropping accomplished by means of an electronic device that penetrated the premises occupied by petitioner was a violation of the Fourth Amendment. That case established that interception of conversations reasonably intended to be private could constitute a "search and seizure," and that the examination or taking of physical property was not required. * * * In *Silverman* we found it unnecessary to re-examine *Goldman v. United States*, which had held that electronic surveillance accomplished without the physical penetration of petitioner's premises by a tangible object did not violate the Fourth Amendment. This case requires us to reconsider *Goldman*, and I agree that it should now be overruled. Its limitation on Fourth Amendment protection is, in the present day, bad physics as well as bad law, for reasonable expectations of privacy may be defeated by electronic as well as physical invasion. * * *

[Justice White's concurring opinion is omitted.]

Mr. Justice BLACK, dissenting.

If I could agree with the Court that eavesdropping carried on by electronic means (equivalent to wiretapping) constitutes a "search" or "seizure," I would be happy to join the Court's opinion. * * *

My basic objection is twofold: (1) I do not believe that the words of the Amendment will bear the meaning given them by today's decision, and (2) I do not believe that it is the proper role of this Court to rewrite the Amendment in order "to bring it into harmony with the times" and thus reach a result that many people believe to be desirable.

While I realize that an argument based on the meaning of words lacks the scope, and no doubt the appeal, of broad policy discussions and philosophical discourses on such nebulous subjects as privacy, for me the language of the Amendment is the crucial place to look in construing a written document such as our Constitution. * * * The first clause protects "persons, houses, papers, and effects, against unreasonable searches and seizures * * *." These words connote the idea of tangible things with size, form, and weight, things capable of being searched, seized, or both. The second clause of the Amendment still further establishes its Framers' purpose to limit its protection to tangible things by providing that no warrants shall issue but those "particularly describing the place to be searched, and the persons or things to be seized." A conversation overheard by eavesdropping, whether by plain snooping or wiretapping, is not tangible and, under the normally accepted meanings of the words, can neither be searched nor seized. In addition the language of the second clause indicates that the Amendment refers not only to something tangible so it can be seized but to something already in existence so it can be described. Yet the Court's interpretation would have the Amendment apply to overhearing future conversations which by their very nature are nonexistent until they take place. How can one "describe" a future conversation, and, if one cannot, how can a magistrate issue a warrant to eavesdrop one in the future? * * * Rather than using language in a completely artificial way, I must conclude that the Fourth Amendment simply does not apply to eavesdropping.

Tapping telephone wires, of course, was an unknown possibility at the time the Fourth Amendment was adopted. But eavesdropping (and wiretapping is nothing more than eavesdropping by telephone) was * * * "an ancient practice which at common law was condemned as a nuisance. 4 Blackstone, Commentaries 168. In those days the eavesdropper listened by naked ear under the eaves of houses or their windows, or beyond their walls seeking out private discourse." There can be no doubt that the Framers were aware of this practice, and if they had desired to outlaw or restrict the use of evidence obtained by eavesdropping, I believe that they would have used the appropriate language to do so in the Fourth Amendment. They certainly would not have left such a task to the ingenuity of language-stretching judges. * * *

Since I see no way in which the words of the Fourth Amendment can be construed to apply to eavesdropping, that closes the matter for me. In interpreting the Bill of Rights, I willingly go as far as a liberal construction of the language takes me, but I simply cannot in good conscience give a meaning to words which they have never before been thought to have and which they certainly do not have in common ordinary usage. I will not distort the words of the Amendment in order to "keep the Constitution up to date" or "to bring it into harmony with the times." It was never meant that this Court have such power, which in effect would make us a continuously functioning constitutional convention.

With this decision the Court has completed, I hope, its rewriting of the Fourth Amendment, which started only recently when the Court began referring incessantly to the Fourth Amendment not so much as a law against *unreasonable* searches and seizures as one to protect an individual's privacy. * * *

The Fourth Amendment protects privacy only to the extent that it prohibits unreasonable searches and seizures of "persons, houses, papers, and effects." No general right is created by the Amendment so as to give this Court the unlimited power to hold unconstitutional everything which affects privacy. Certainly the Framers, well acquainted as they were with the excesses of governmental power, did not intend to grant this Court such omnipotent lawmaking authority as that. The history of governments proves that it is dangerous to freedom to repose such powers in courts.

For these reasons I respectfully dissent.

NOTES AND QUESTIONS

1. Justice Stewart states that what "a person *knowingly* exposes to the public" is not protected by the Fourth Amendment. Why? Should this be the rule? Would the scope of Fourth Amendment coverage have been enlarged if the Court had used the word "purposely," rather than "knowingly"? Also, what is meant by the word "public"? If you knowingly expose your conversation to just one person, have you exposed it "to the public"? Keep these questions in mind as you proceed through this chapter.

2. *Variations on the theme.* Telephone booths are an endangered species (when did you last see one?) in the era of cell phones and other new methods of technological communication. One observer at the time of *Katz*, perhaps

thinking the question was merely rhetorical, asked, "Would the case have been different if the pay phone has not been surrounded by a booth?" Edmund W. Kitch, Katz v. United States: *The Limits of the Fourth Amendment*, 1968 Sup. Ct. Rev. 133, 140. How would Justice Stewart have answered his question?

Or, suppose that the FBI, rather than conducting electronic surveillance, had positioned a lip reader immediately outside the telephone booth, who observed Katz's lips and recorded his words on paper? Would Justice Stewart consider *this* conduct a "search"?

What if police officers, in an effort to catch men in homosexual activity, install a peephole in the ceiling so they can secretly observe activities in a public toilet stall. Is this a "search" under *Katz*? Does it matter whether the stall has doors on it? See People v. Triggs, 8 Cal.3d 884, 106 Cal.Rptr. 408, 506 P.2d 232 (1973). For a provocative analysis of the subject, see David Alan Sklansky, *"One Train May Hide Another":* Katz, Stonewall, and the Secret Subtext of Criminal Procedure, 41 U.C. Davis L. Rev. 875, 877 (2008) (contending that "homosexuality is a suppressed theme not just of the *Katz* decision but of criminal procedure law as a whole").

3. Is a telephone booth a "person, house, paper, or effect"? If not, why does the Fourth Amendment apply to Katz's conversations there? Does the majority provide a suitable answer to Justice Black's textual argument that electronic surveillance falls outside the coverage of the Fourth Amendment?

4. *The subjective prong in Justice Harlan's test: things to think about.* As the cases that follow will show, the two-prong formula set out in Justice Harlan's concurring opinion has become the primary standard for determining whether police conduct constitutes a search.

Do you see any problems with Harlan's subjective prong? Do *you* have an expectation of privacy in your home? Do you think that a person living in a high-crime area has such an expectation? Do you have an expectation of privacy in your belongings at the airport? Does a child who goes to a public school where metal detectors are used to check for hidden weapons have an expectation of privacy? Why might the answers to these questions have motivated one scholar to write that "[a]n actual, subjective expectation of privacy obviously has no place * * * in a theory of what the fourth amendment protects." Anthony G. Amsterdam, *Perspectives on the Fourth Amendment*, 58 Minn. L. Rev. 349, 384 (1974).

5. *The objective prong in Justice Harlan's test: things to think about.* How should a court apply the second prong of Justice Harlan's test? Should it consider whether the American people, in general, expect privacy in certain circumstances? If so, should a court consider public opinion polls and other reliable evidence of public attitudes in this regard? *E.g.*, Christopher Slobogin & Joseph E. Schumacher, *Reasonable Expectations of Privacy and Autonomy in Fourth Amendment Cases: An Empirical Look at "Understandings Recognized and Permitted by Society,"* 42 Duke L.J. 727 (1993) (surveying public attitudes regarding privacy, and concluding that "the Supreme Court's conclusions about the scope of the Fourth Amendment are often not in tune with commonly held attitudes about police investigative techniques"). Or, is Justice Harlan suggesting that courts should conduct a normative inquiry to deter-

mine what privacy rights people living in a democracy ought to be entitled to possess? Is it desirable to permit unelected federal judges to answer this question?

6. *If electronic surveillance is a search, what then?* Please keep in mind that in the excerpt of the *Katz* opinion set out above, the issue considered was whether the wiretapping constituted a Fourth Amendment "search," *i.e.*, whether the restrictions of the Fourth Amendment applied to the electronic surveillance. Having answered this question affirmatively, the Court next had to consider whether the FBI agents' actions complied with the Fourth Amendment.

The *Katz* Court, quoting prior case law, observed that the Fourth Amendment generally "requires adherence to judicial processes." Justice Stewart, using oft-quoted language, stated the rule that "searches conducted outside the judicial process, without prior approval by judge or magistrate [*i.e.*, in the form of a search warrant] are *per se* unreasonable under the Fourth Amendment—subject only to a few specifically established well-delineated exceptions." The Court proceeded:

> Accepting * * * the Government's [account of its] actions as accurate, it is clear that this surveillance was so narrowly circumscribed that a duly authorized magistrate, properly notified of the need for such investigation, specifically informed of the basis on which it was to proceed, and clearly apprised of the precise intrusion it would entail, could constitutionally have authorized, with appropriate safeguards, the very limited search and seizure that the Government asserts in fact took place.

All would have been well, in other words, had the FBI obtained a judicially authorized warrant to conduct the surveillance. Because no warrant was secured, however, the Court ruled that the Fourth Amendment was violated.

7. *Obtaining a search warrant to conduct electronic surveillance: special problems.* Search warrants are considered in detail in the next chapter, but it is worth noting here that the search warrant process in electronic surveillance cases creates special constitutional issues. Notice that if the police want to search a suspect's home for a tangible object, let's say a stolen painting, they can tell the magistrate, with particularity, what it is they are looking for (the painting) and where they expect to find it. Once they seize the object, the search ends. But, in an electronic surveillance case, the police must request permission to "search" and "seize" something that is not only intangible but does not even exist at the time of the warrant request, namely, a future conversation.

In Berger v. New York, 388 U.S. 41, 87 S.Ct. 1873, 18 L.Ed.2d 1040 (1967), the Supreme Court declared a New York wiretapping statute unconstitutional because it permitted law enforcement officers to obtain a judicial order to conduct electronic surveillance without particularizing the crime being investigated and the conversations they expected to hear; the statute also improperly permitted surveillance of *all* of the suspect's conversations for sixty days on the basis of a single showing of probable cause, and allowed renewal of the order without a further finding of probable cause; and the court order did not require the police to stop surveillance once the conversations they sought were "seized."

Many observers read *Berger* to signal that a warrant to seize and search a future conversation could never satisfy the Fourth Amendment requirement that warrants "particularly describ[e] the place to be searched and the persons or things to be seized." *Katz* was set for argument just days into the Court's 1967 Term and only five months after *Berger* was decided. Though *Katz* arguably expanded the scope of the protection offered by the Fourth Amendment, it also answered the critical question of whether a warrant could permit the government to intercept an electronic communication. The answer was "yes."

One year after *Berger* and *Katz*, Congress enacted legislation, the 1968 Omnibus Crime Control and Safe Streets Act, which includes warrant procedures for electronic surveillance, intended to avoid the weaknesses in the invalidated New York statute. The complicated law is set out in Appendix A. of the Supplement.

8. *Problem.* C lives in a house with a screen door and a solid wood interior front door. A police officer opens the unlocked screen door and observes an object—let's assume it is marijuana—lying between the two doors. Is this observation a search? Does it matter why the officer opened the screen door? Does it matter whether the interior front door was open or shut? Christian v. State, 172 Md.App. 212, 914 A.2d 151 (2007).

9. *"So, do I really want to be a police officer?"* The police suspect a person of rape. The suspect denies his guilt but refuses to provide a DNA sample to the police. Later, an officer observes the suspect spit on a public sidewalk. The officer retrieves the saliva for DNA testing. Search? See Commonwealth v. Cabral, 69 Mass.App.Ct. 68, 866 N.E.2d 429 (2007).

2. THE *KATZ* DOCTRINE IN APPLICATION

UNITED STATES v. WHITE

Supreme Court of the United States, 1971.
401 U.S. 745, 91 S.Ct. 1122, 28 L.Ed.2d 453.

MR. JUSTICE WHITE announced the judgment of the Court and an opinion in which THE CHIEF JUSTICE, MR. JUSTICE STEWART, and MR. JUSTICE BLACKMUN join.

In 1966, respondent James A. White was tried and convicted under two consolidated indictments charging various illegal transactions in narcotics * * *. * * * The issue before us is whether the Fourth Amendment bars from evidence the testimony of governmental agents who related certain conversations which had occurred between defendant White and a government informant, Harvey Jackson, and which the agents overheard by monitoring the frequency of a radio transmitter carried by Jackson and concealed on his person. On four occasions the conversations took place in Jackson's home; each of these conversations was overheard by an agent concealed in a kitchen closet with Jackson's consent and by a second agent

outside the house using a radio receiver. Four other conversations—one in respondent's home, one in a restaurant, and two in Jackson's car—were overheard by the use of radio equipment. The prosecution was unable to locate and produce Jackson at the trial and the trial court overruled objections to the testimony of the agents who conducted the electronic surveillance. The jury returned a guilty verdict and defendant appealed.
* * *

I * * *

Katz v. United States * * * finally swept away doctrines that electronic eavesdropping is permissible under the Fourth Amendment unless physical invasion of a constitutionally protected area produced the challenged evidence. In that case government agents, without petitioner's consent or knowledge, attached a listening device to the outside of a public telephone booth and recorded the defendant's end of his telephone conversations. In declaring the recordings inadmissible in evidence in the absence of a warrant authorizing the surveillance, the Court overruled *Olmstead* [*v. United States*, 277 U.S. 438, 48 S.Ct. 564, 72 L.Ed. 944 (1928)] and Goldman [*v. United States*, 316 U.S. 129, 62 S.Ct. 993, 86 L.Ed. 1322 (1942)] and held that the absence of physical intrusion into the telephone booth did not justify using electronic devices in listening to and recording Katz' words, thereby violating the privacy on which he justifiably relied while using the telephone in those circumstances.

The Court of Appeals understood *Katz* to render inadmissible against White the agents' testimony concerning conversations that Jackson broadcast to them. We cannot agree. *Katz* involved no revelation to the Government by a party to conversations with the defendant nor did the Court indicate in any way that a defendant has a justifiable and constitutionally protected expectation that a person with whom he is conversing will not then or later reveal the conversation to the police.

Hoffa v. United States, 385 U.S. 293, 87 S.Ct. 408, 17 L.Ed.2d 374 (1966), which was left undisturbed by *Katz*, held that however strongly a defendant may trust an apparent colleague, his expectations in this respect are not protected by the Fourth Amendment when it turns out that the colleague is a government agent regularly communicating with the authorities.[a] In these circumstances, "no interest legitimately protected by the Fourth Amendment is involved," for that Amendment affords no protection to "a wrongdoer's misplaced belief that a person to whom he voluntarily confides his wrongdoing will not reveal it." No warrant to "search and seize" is required in such circumstances, nor is it when the Government sends to defendant's home a secret agent who conceals his identity and makes a purchase of narcotics from the accused, *Lewis v. United States*, 385 U.S. 206, 87 S.Ct. 424, 17 L.Ed.2d 312 (1966), or when the same agent, unbeknown to the defendant, carries electronic equipment to record the defendant's words and the evidence so gathered is later

---

a. In *Hoffa*, the defendant talked in his hotel suite to a long-time labor associate, unaware that his colleague had become a government informant.

offered in evidence. *Lopez v. United States*, 373 U.S. 427, 83 S.Ct. 1381, 10 L.Ed.2d 462 (1963).

Conceding that *Hoffa*, *Lewis*, and *Lopez* remained unaffected by *Katz*, the Court of Appeals nevertheless read both *Katz* and the Fourth Amendment to require a different result if the agent not only records his conversations with the defendant but instantaneously transmits them electronically to other agents equipped with radio receivers. Where this occurs, the Court of Appeals held, the Fourth Amendment is violated and the testimony of the listening agents must be excluded from evidence.

To reach this result it was necessary for the Court of Appeals to hold that *On Lee v. United States* [343 U.S. 747, 72 S.Ct. 967, 96 L.Ed. 1270 (1952),] was no longer good law. In that case, which involved facts very similar to the case before us, the Court first rejected claims of a Fourth Amendment violation because the informer had not trespassed when he entered the defendant's premises and conversed with him. To this extent the Court's rationale cannot survive *Katz*. But the Court announced a second and independent ground for its decision; for it went on to say that overruling *Olmstead* and *Goldman* would be of no aid to On Lee since he "was talking confidentially and indiscreetly with one he trusted, and he was overheard. * * * It would be a dubious service to the genuine liberties protected by the Fourth Amendment to make them bedfellows with spurious liberties improvised by farfetched analogies which would liken eavesdropping on a conversation, with the connivance of one of the parties, to an unreasonable search or seizure. We find no violation of the Fourth Amendment here." We see no indication in *Katz* that the Court meant to disturb that understanding of the Fourth Amendment or to disturb the result reached in the *On Lee* case, nor are we now inclined to overturn this view of the Fourth Amendment.

Concededly a police agent who conceals his police connections may write down for official use his conversations with a defendant and testify concerning them, without a warrant authorizing his encounters with the defendant and without otherwise violating the latter's Fourth Amendment rights. *Hoffa v. United States*. For constitutional purposes, no different result is required if the agent instead of immediately reporting and transcribing his conversations with defendant, either (1) simultaneously records them with electronic equipment which he is carrying on his person, *Lopez v. United States*; (2) or carries radio equipment which simultaneously transmits the conversations either to recording equipment located elsewhere or to other agents monitoring the transmitting frequency. *On Lee v. United States*. If the conduct and revelations of an agent operating without electronic equipment do not invade the defendant's constitutionally justifiable expectations of privacy, neither does a simultaneous recording of the same conversations made by the agent or by others from transmissions received from the agent to whom the defendant is talking and whose trustworthiness the defendant necessarily risks.

Our problem is not what the privacy expectations of particular defendants in particular situations may be or the extent to which they may in fact have relied on the discretion of their companions. Very probably, individual defendants neither know nor suspect that their colleagues have gone or will go to the police or are carrying recorders or transmitters. Otherwise, conversation would cease and our problem with these encounters would be nonexistent or far different from those now before us. Our problem, in terms of the principles announced in *Katz*, is what expectations of privacy are constitutionally "justifiable"—what expectations the Fourth Amendment will protect in the absence of a warrant. So far, the law permits the frustration of actual expectations of privacy by permitting authorities to use the testimony of those associates who for one reason or another have determined to turn to the police, as well as by authorizing the use of informants in the manner exemplified by *Hoffa* and *Lewis*. If the law gives no protection to the wrongdoer whose trusted accomplice is or becomes a police agent, neither should it protect him when that same agent has recorded or transmitted the conversations which are later offered in evidence to prove the State's case.

Inescapably, one contemplating illegal activities must realize and risk that his companions may be reporting to the police. If he sufficiently doubts their trustworthiness, the association will very probably end or never materialize. But if he has no doubts, or allays them, or risks what doubt he has, the risk is his. In terms of what his course will be, what he will or will not do or say, we are unpersuaded that he would distinguish between probable informers on the one hand and probable informers with transmitters on the other. Given the possibility or probability that one of his colleagues is cooperating with the police, it is only speculation to assert that the defendant's utterances would be substantially different or his sense of security any less if he also thought it possible that the suspected colleague is wired for sound. At least there is no persuasive evidence that the difference in this respect between the electronically equipped and the unequipped agent is substantial enough to require discrete constitutional recognition, particularly under the Fourth Amendment which is ruled by fluid concepts of "reasonableness."

Nor should we be too ready to erect constitutional barriers to relevant and probative evidence which is also accurate and reliable. An electronic recording will many times produce a more reliable rendition of what a defendant has said than will the unaided memory of a police agent. It may also be that with the recording in existence it is less likely that the informant will change his mind, less chance that threat or injury will suppress unfavorable evidence and less chance that cross-examination will confound the testimony. Considerations like these obviously do not favor the defendant, but we are not prepared to hold that a defendant who has no constitutional right to exclude the informer's unaided testimony nevertheless has a Fourth Amendment privilege against a more accurate version of the events in question. * * *

The judgment of the Court of Appeals is * * * reversed.

[Justice Black concurred in the Court's judgment for the reasons set forth in his dissent in *Katz*. Justice Brennan's concurrence in the result is omitted.]

Mr. Justice DOUGLAS, dissenting. * * *

The issue in this case is clouded and concealed by the very discussion of it in legalistic terms. What the ancients knew as "eavesdropping," we now call "electronic surveillance"; but to equate the two is to treat man's first gunpowder on the same level as the nuclear bomb. Electronic surveillance is the greatest leveler of human privacy ever known. * * * [T]he concepts of privacy which the Founders enshrined in the Fourth Amendment vanish completely when we slavishly allow an all-powerful government, proclaiming law and order, efficiency, and other benign purposes, to penetrate all the walls and doors which men need to shield them from the pressures of a turbulent life around them and give them the health and strength to carry on. * * *

Today no one perhaps notices because only a small, obscure criminal is the victim. But every person is the victim, for the technology we exalt today is everyman's master. * * *

It is urged by the Department of Justice that *On Lee* be established as the controlling decision in this field. I would stand by * * * *Katz* and reaffirm the need for judicial supervision under the Fourth Amendment of the use of electronic surveillance which, uncontrolled, promises to lead us into a police state. * * *

Mr. Justice HARLAN, dissenting. * * *

I

Before turning to matters of precedent and policy, several preliminary observations should be made. We deal here with the constitutional validity of instantaneous third-party electronic eavesdropping, conducted by federal law enforcement officers, without any prior judicial approval of the technique utilized, but with the consent and cooperation of a participant in the conversation * * *. The magnitude of the issue at hand is evidenced not simply by the obvious doctrinal difficulty of weighing such activity in the Fourth Amendment balance, but also, and more importantly, by the prevalence of police utilization of this technique. Professor Westin has documented in careful detail the numerous devices that make technologically feasible the Orwellian Big Brother. Of immediate relevance is his observation that " 'participant recording,' in which one participant in a conversation or meeting, either a police officer or a cooperating party, wears a concealed device that records the conversation or broadcasts it to others nearby * * * is used tens of thousands of times each year throughout the country, particularly in cases involving extortion, conspiracy, narcotics, gambling, prostitution, corruption by police officials * * * and similar crimes."[3] * * *

---

3. A. Westin, Privacy and Freedom 131 (1967). This investigative technique is also used to unearth "political" crimes. "Recordings of the private and public meetings of suspect groups

II * * *

A

On Lee involved circumstances virtually identical to those now before us. There, Government agents enlisted the services of Chin Poy, a former friend of Lee, who was suspected of engaging in illegal narcotics traffic. Poy was equipped with a "minifon" transmitting device which enabled outside Government agents to monitor Poy's conversations with Lee. In the privacy of his laundry, Lee made damaging admissions to Poy which were overheard by the agents and later related at trial. Poy did not testify. Mr. Justice Jackson, writing for five Justices, held the testimony admissible. Without reaching the question of whether a conversation could be the subject of a "seizure" for Fourth Amendment purposes, as yet an unanswered if not completely open question, the Court concluded that in the absence of a trespass, no constitutional violation had occurred.

The validity of the trespass rationale was questionable even at the time the decision was rendered. In this respect *On Lee* rested on common-law notions and looked to a waning era of Fourth Amendment jurisprudence. * * *

III

A

That the foundations of *On Lee* have been destroyed does not, of course, mean that its result can no longer stand. Indeed, the plurality opinion today fastens upon our decisions in *Lopez*, *Lewis v. United States*, and *Hoffa v. United States*, to resist the undercurrents of more recent cases emphasizing the warrant procedure as a safeguard to privacy. But this category provides insufficient support. In each of these cases the risk the general populace faced was different from that surfaced by the instant case. No surreptitious third ear was present, and in each opinion that fact was carefully noted. * * *

The plurality opinion seeks to erase the crucial distinction between the facts before us and these holdings by the following reasoning: if A can relay verbally what is revealed to him by B (as in *Lewis* and *Hoffa*), or record and later divulge it (as in *Lopez*), what difference does it make if A conspires with another to betray B by contemporaneously transmitting to the other all that is said? The contention is, in essence, an argument that the distinction between third-party monitoring and other undercover techniques is one of form and not substance. The force of the contention depends on the evaluation of two separable but intertwined assumptions: first, that there is no greater invasion of privacy in the third-party situation, and, second, that uncontrolled consensual surveillance in an

---

[have] been growing. Police in Miami, Florida, used a hidden transmitter on a police agent to record statements made at meetings of a right-wing extremist group suspected of planning acts of terrorism. In 1964 a police undercover agent obtained recordings of incendiary statements by the leader of a Communist splinter movement in Harlem, at private meetings and at a public rally, which served as the basis for his conviction for attempting to overthrow the state government." *Ibid.*

electronic age is a tolerable technique of law enforcement, given the values and goals of our political system.

The first of these assumptions takes as a point of departure the so-called "risk analysis" approach of *Lewis*, and *Lopez*, and to a lesser extent *On Lee*, or the expectations approach of *Katz*. While these formulations represent an advance over the unsophisticated trespass analysis of the common law, they too have their limitations and can, ultimately, lead to the substitution of words for analysis. The analysis must, in my view, transcend the search for subjective expectations or legal attribution of assumptions of risk. Our expectations, and the risks we assume, are in large part reflections of laws that translate into rules the customs and values of the past and present.

Since it is the task of the law to form and project, as well as mirror and reflect, we should not, as judges, merely recite the expectations and risks without examining the desirability of saddling them upon society. The critical question, therefore, is whether under our system of government, as reflected in the Constitution, we should impose on our citizens the risks of the electronic listener or observer without at least the protection of a warrant requirement.

This question must, in my view, be answered by assessing the nature of a particular practice and the likely extent of its impact on the individual's sense of security balanced against the utility of the conduct as a technique of law enforcement. For those more extensive intrusions that significantly jeopardize the sense of security which is the paramount concern of Fourth Amendment liberties, I am of the view that more than self-restraint by law enforcement officials is required and at the least warrants should be necessary.

B

The impact of the practice of third-party bugging, must, I think, be considered such as to undermine that confidence and sense of security in dealing with one another that is characteristic of individual relationships between citizens in a free society. It goes beyond the impact on privacy occasioned by the ordinary type of "informer" investigation upheld in *Lewis* and *Hoffa*. The argument of the plurality opinion, to the effect that it is irrelevant whether secrets are revealed by the mere tattletale or the transistor, ignores the differences occasioned by third-party monitoring and recording which insures full and accurate disclosure of all that is said, free of the possibility of error and oversight that inheres in human reporting.

Authority is hardly required to support the proposition that words would be measured a good deal more carefully and communication inhibited if one suspected his conversations were being transmitted and transcribed. Were third-party bugging a prevalent practice, it might well smother that spontaneity—reflected in frivolous, impetuous, sacrilegious, and defiant discourse—that liberates daily life. Much off-hand exchange is easily forgotten and one may count on the obscurity of his remarks, protected by the very fact of a limited audience, and the likelihood that the listener will either overlook or forget what is said, as well as the listener's inability to reformulate a conversation without having to contend with a documented record. All these values are sacrificed by a rule of law that permits official monitoring of private discourse limited only by the need to locate a willing assistant. * * *

Finally, it is too easy to forget—and, hence, too often forgotten—that the issue here is whether to interpose a search warrant procedure between law enforcement agencies engaging in electronic eavesdropping and the public generally. By casting its "risk analysis" solely in terms of the expectations and risks that "wrongdoers" or "one contemplating illegal activities" ought to bear, the plurality opinion, I think, misses the mark entirely. *On Lee* does not simply mandate that criminals must daily run the risk of unknown eavesdroppers prying into their private affairs; it subjects each and every law-abiding member of society to that risk. The very purpose of interposing the Fourth Amendment warrant requirement is to redistribute the privacy risks throughout society in a way that produces the results the plurality opinion ascribes to the *On Lee* rule. Abolition of *On Lee* would not end electronic eavesdropping. It would prevent public officials from engaging in that practice unless they first had probable cause to suspect an individual of involvement in illegal activities and had tested their version of the facts before a detached judicial officer. * * *

The Fourth Amendment does, of course, leave room for the employment of modern technology in criminal law enforcement, but in the stream of current developments in Fourth Amendment law I think it must be held that third-party electronic monitoring, subject only to the self-restraint of law enforcement officials, has no place in our society.

IV * * *

What this means is that the burden of guarding privacy in a free society should not be on its citizens; it is the Government that must justify its need to electronically eavesdrop. * * *

I would hold that *On Lee* is no longer good law and affirm the judgment below.

[Justice Marshall's dissent is omitted.]

NOTES AND QUESTIONS

1. In *Katz*, the Supreme Court held that the electronic surveillance of Katz's conversations with others constituted a "search" and, therefore, was regulated by the Fourth Amendment. In *White*, however, the Court held that the Government's use of an informant "wired" with a transmitter fell outside the scope of the Fourth Amendment. As one scholar has observed:

The law treats secret surveillance of speech or other behavior largely according to whether the surveilling agent is visible or invisible to the subject. An agent, visibly present though masquerading [as a confidant], is thought to gather evidence in a fundamentally different manner than a concealed agent or a hidden electronic device. The theory is that the contents of the mind, deliberately revealed to another person, are willingly shared, while the secret eye or ear, possibly electronically enhanced, bypasses constitutional concern to spirit the evidence away.

H. Richard Uviller, *Evidence from the Mind of the Criminal Suspect: A Reconsideration of the Current Rules of Access and Restraint*, 87 Colum. L. Rev. 1137, 1151 (1987).

2. *False friends, false friends with tape recorders, and "wired" false friends*. Notice that there are various ways the Government listens to conversations of persons suspected of crime. First, it may surreptitiously eavesdrop on a conversation between *A* and *B*, as in *Katz*. Second, the Government may participate in the conversation itself, as when *A* talks to *B*, who turns out to be an undercover police officer or friend-turned-government-agent, as in *Hoffa*. In this latter case we may characterize *B* as a "false friend." Third, it is possible that false friend *B* will tape record the conversation (*Lopez*) or be "wired" with a transmitter (*On Lee, White*).

Consider first the pure false friend, *Hoffa*, situation. Should such a case fall outside the scope of the Fourth Amendment? Even dissenting Justice Harlan accepts this proposition, but should he? Consider:

> [T]he Court [has] viewed betrayal as an expected (if reprehensible) behavior among human beings * * *. Nosy neighbors and pretend friends are not unheard-of phenomena. We trust such people at our own risk. * * *
>
> By allowing the police to send out pretend friends, however, the Court does more than simply mimic the sorts of betrayals that would inevitably occur from time to time in the real world of friendship. By planting moles in our midst, the government deliberately manipulates reality to create relationships for the sole purpose of betrayal. * * * By utilizing such spies, the government therefore adds a level of unusual risk to our private lives. Even for those of us who trust our own judgment in detecting pretend friends, the government-issue friend is peculiar enough to be more like the recording device on Katz's telephone booth than like a friend in the real world who fails to keep a secret. Such creatures are more difficult to discover (since they are not naturally occurring) and could therefore chill even the savvy individual, otherwise insulated by a sixth sense, from trusting other people.

Sherry F. Colb, *What Is a Search? Two Conceptual Flaws in Fourth Amendment Doctrine and Some Hints of a Remedy*, 55 Stan. L. Rev. 119, 141–43 (2002).

Do you agree with Professor Colb's observations? If so, are you prepared to set up constitutional obstacles to the use of undercover police agents in criminal investigations?

However you feel about *Hoffa* and false friends, is there something worse about false friend *B* tape recording his conversations with *A*, or transmitting the conversations live to agents away from the scene, as in *White*? Do you think, for example, that if persons in the Nixon White House had known that their Watergate conversations were being taped by the President, that they would have been more careful with their words? If so, is this a valid reason to provide Fourth Amendment protection to such speakers?

3. Assume the Court in *Katz* had accepted petitioner's conception of the case, and had held (1) a telephone booth is a constitutionally protected area; and (2) placing a bug on a telephone booth is a trespass of that area. With this newly-formulated *Katz* doctrine, how would *White* be decided? Would it be an easier or harder case to decide under the "new *Katz*"?

4. *The objective prong of Harlan's "search" test.* Reconsider p. 90, Note 5. Based on his dissent here, how would Justice Harlan answer the questions raised in that Note?

In relation to the objective prong of the Harlan "search" test, Professor Anthony Amsterdam would phrase the issue this way:

> The ultimate question, plainly, is a value judgment. It is whether, if the particular form of surveillance practiced by the police is permitted to go unregulated by constitutional restraints, the amount of privacy and freedom remaining to citizens would be diminished to a compass inconsistent with the aims of a free and open society.

Anthony G. Amsterdam, *Perspectives on the Fourth Amendment*, 58 Minn. L. Rev. 349, 403 (1974). How would *you* decide *White* according to this standard?

5. *Historical tidbit.* In 1938, Earl Warren's father was murdered in Bakersfield, California. The police had no leads until a San Quentin prisoner came under suspicion. The Bakersfield Chief of Police wanted to put a "stool pigeon" in the cell with the suspect and wire the cell for sound with a Dictaphone. However, Warren, then District Attorney in Alameda County, flatly rejected the use of the recorder, on the ground that he considered eavesdropping an inappropriate law enforcement technique. Therefore, no taping occurred, and the murder was never solved. Bernard Schwartz, Super Chief: Earl Warren and His Supreme Court—A Judicial Biography 11–12 (1983).

Warren joined the Supreme Court in 1953 upon the death of Chief Justice Fred Vinson, one year after the Court ruled, 5–4 (with Vinson joining the majority), in *On Lee v. United States, supra,* that use of a secret microphone by an undercover agent to transmit conversations to a third party did not implicate Fourth Amendment interests. Had the case come to the Court *after* Warren had joined the Court, the outcome might have been different. Had *On Lee* been decided differently, it is intriguing to consider how the law, culminating in *White,* might have evolved.

Warren, it may also be noted, was the only dissenter in the *Hoffa* "false friend" case. Noting that the false friend in *Hoffa* had a strong incentive to distort the truth, the Chief Justice noted the "serious potential for undermining the integrity of the truth-finding process in the federal courts." He concluded that "for the dubious evidence thus obtained, the Government paid an enormous price. Certainly if a criminal defendant insinuated his informer into the prosecution's camp in this manner he would be guilty of obstructing justice."

For a fuller examination of Chief Justice Warren's law enforcement background and its likely influence on his criminal justice opinions, see Yale Kamisar, *How Earl Warren's Twenty–Two Years in Law Enforcement Affected His Work as Chief Justice*, 3 Ohio St. J. Crim. L. 11 (2005).

6. *Justice Harlan and Big Brother*. Justice Harlan expressed his concern that the plurality's approach to the Fourth Amendment "might well smother that spontaneity—reflected in frivolous, impetuous, sacrilegious, and defiant discourse—that liberates daily life." He also pointed to the risks of "Orwellian Big Brother" technology that can be "used to unearth 'political' crimes."

One person's "political" crimes and free speech is another person's incipient terrorism. One post-September 11 commentator has observed: "How the times have changed. Today the talk is of more, rather than less, surveillance. Instead of 'Big Brother is watching you,' we hear 'Big Brother is watching out for you.'" Editors, *Here's Looking at You*, Scientific American, Dec. 2001, at 8. Do you believe that the Supreme Court in *White* set the proper balance between security from crime and individual liberty?

7. The *White* plurality cited *Lewis v. United States*, a 1966 "consent" case, in which a federal agent, "misrepresenting his identity and stating his willingness to purchase narcotics, was invited into petitioner's home where an unlawful narcotics transaction was consummated." The Court found no violation in this conduct, observing that the agent did not "see, hear, or take anything that was not contemplated, and in fact intended, by [Lewis] as a necessary part of his illegal business." The Court went on to make the following observation about the use of undercover agents:

> Were we to hold the deceptions of the agent in this case constitutionally prohibited, we would come near to a rule that the use of undercover agents in any manner is virtually unconstitutional per se. Such a rule would * * * severely hamper the Government in ferreting out those organized criminal activities that are characterized by covert dealings with victims who either cannot or do not protest.

Does this represent a valid reason to uphold the *Hoffa-White* approach to false friends?

8. *Problem*. Undercover police officer Alice seeks to negotiate a drug sale with Barbara. Barbara informs Alice that she will only discuss the matter in a specified spot in a public park at 2:00 a.m., because "nobody is ever there at that hour." Alice agrees to meet her there. In the meantime, with Alice's knowledge, the police install a hidden transmitter in a tree near the meeting place, so that another officer can listen to the conversation. Is it a "search" when the officer listens to Alice's and Barbara's conversations via the transmitter? Put another way, is this *Katz* or *White*? What if agent Alice is herself unaware of the transmitter?

Suppose that the police leave the device in the tree and listen to other conversations in the park by passersby. Is the Fourth Amendment implicated by *this* surveillance?

SMITH v. MARYLAND

Supreme Court of the United States, 1979.
442 U.S. 735, 99 S.Ct. 2577, 61 L.Ed.2d 220.

MR. JUSTICE BLACKMUN delivered the opinion of the Court.

This case presents the question whether the installation and use of a pen register[1] constitutes a "search" within the meaning of the Fourth Amendment, made applicable to the States through the Fourteenth Amendment.

I

On March 5, 1976, in Baltimore, Md., Patricia McDonough was robbed. She gave the police a description of the robber and of a 1975 Monte Carlo automobile she had observed near the scene of the crime. After the robbery, McDonough began receiving threatening and obscene phone calls from a man identifying himself as the robber. On one occasion, the caller asked that she step out on her front porch; she did so, and saw the 1975 Monte Carlo she had earlier described to police moving slowly past her home. On March 16, police spotted a man who met McDonough's description driving a 1975 Monte Carlo in her neighborhood. By tracing the license plate number, police learned that the car was registered in the name of petitioner, Michael Lee Smith.

The next day, the telephone company, at police request, installed a pen register at its central offices to record the numbers dialed from the telephone at petitioner's home. The police did not get a warrant or court order before having the pen register installed. The register revealed that on March 17 a call was placed from petitioner's home to McDonough's phone. On the basis of this and other evidence, the police obtained a warrant to search petitioner's residence. The search revealed that a page in petitioner's phone book was turned down to the name and number of Patricia McDonough; the phone book was seized. * * *

Petitioner was indicted in the Criminal Court of Baltimore for robbery. By pretrial motion, he sought to suppress "all fruits derived from the pen register" on the ground that the police had failed to secure a warrant prior to its installation. The trial court denied the suppression motion, holding that the warrantless installation of the pen register did not violate the Fourth Amendment. * * * The pen register tape (evidencing the fact that a phone call had been made from petitioner's phone to McDonough's phone) and the phone book seized in the search of petitioner's residence were admitted into evidence against him. Petitioner was convicted, and was sentenced to six years. * * *

---

1. "A pen register is a mechanical device that records the numbers dialed on a telephone by monitoring the electrical impulses caused when the dial on the telephone is released. It does not overhear oral communications and does not indicate whether calls are actually completed." A pen register is "usually installed at a central telephone facility [and] records on a paper tape all numbers dialed from [the] line" to which it is attached.

II

A

* * * In determining whether a particular form of government-initiated electronic surveillance is a "search" within the meaning of the Fourth Amendment, our lodestar is *Katz v. United States*. In *Katz*, Government agents had intercepted the contents of a telephone conversation by attaching an electronic listening device to the outside of a public phone booth. The Court rejected the argument that a "search" can occur only when there has been a "physical intrusion" into a "constitutionally protected area," noting that the Fourth Amendment "protects people, not places." Because the Government's monitoring of Katz' conversation "violated the privacy upon which he justifiably relied while using the telephone booth," the Court held that it "constituted a 'search and seizure' within the meaning of the Fourth Amendment."

Consistently with *Katz*, this Court uniformly has held that the application of the Fourth Amendment depends on whether the person invoking its protection can claim a "justifiable," a "reasonable," or a "legitimate expectation of privacy" that has been invaded by government action. This inquiry, as Mr. Justice Harlan aptly noted in his *Katz* concurrence, normally embraces two discrete questions. The first is whether the individual, by his conduct, has "exhibited an actual (subjective) expectation of privacy"—whether, in the words of the *Katz* majority, the individual has shown that "he seeks to preserve [something] as private." The second question is whether the individual's subjective expectation of privacy is "one that society is prepared to recognize as 'reasonable' "—whether, in the words of the *Katz* majority, the individual's expectation, viewed objectively, is "justifiable" under the circumstances.[5]

B

In applying the *Katz* analysis to this case, it is important to begin by specifying precisely the nature of the state activity that is challenged. The activity here took the form of installing and using a pen register. Since the pen register was installed on telephone company property at the telephone company's central offices, petitioner obviously cannot claim that his "property" was invaded or that police intruded into a "constitutionally protected area." Petitioner's claim, rather, is that, notwithstanding the absence of a trespass, the State, as did the Government in *Katz*, infringed

---

5. Situations can be imagined, of course, in which *Katz'* two-pronged inquiry would provide an inadequate index of Fourth Amendment protection. For example, if the Government were suddenly to announce on nationwide television that all homes henceforth would be subject to warrantless entry, individuals thereafter might not in fact entertain any actual expectation of privacy regarding their homes, papers, and effects. Similarly, if a refugee from a totalitarian country, unaware of this Nation's traditions, erroneously assumed that police were continuously monitoring his telephone conversations, a subjective expectation of privacy regarding the contents of his calls might be lacking as well. In such circumstances, where an individual's subjective expectations had been "conditioned" by influences alien to well-recognized Fourth Amendment freedoms, those subjective expectations obviously could play no meaningful role in ascertaining what the scope of Fourth Amendment protection was. In determining whether a "legitimate expectation of privacy" existed in such cases, a normative inquiry would be proper.

a "legitimate expectation of privacy" that petitioner held. Yet a pen register differs significantly from the listening device employed in *Katz*, for pen registers do not acquire the *contents* of communications. This Court recently noted:

> "Indeed, a law enforcement official could not even determine from the use of a pen register whether a communication existed. These devices do not hear sound. They disclose only the telephone numbers that have been dialed—a means of establishing communication. Neither the purport of any communication between the caller and the recipient of the call, their identities, nor whether the call was even completed is disclosed by pen registers."

Given a pen register's limited capabilities, therefore, petitioner's argument that its installation and use constituted a "search" necessarily rests upon a claim that he had a "legitimate expectation of privacy" regarding the numbers he dialed on his phone.

This claim must be rejected. First, we doubt that people in general entertain any actual expectation of privacy in the numbers they dial. All telephone users realize that they must "convey" phone numbers to the telephone company, since it is through telephone company switching equipment that their calls are completed. All subscribers realize, moreover, that the phone company has facilities for making permanent records of the numbers they dial, for they see a list of their long-distance (toll) calls on their monthly bills. In fact, pen registers and similar devices are routinely used by telephone companies "for the purposes of checking billing operations, detecting fraud, and preventing violations of law." * * * Although most people may be oblivious to a pen register's esoteric functions, they presumably have some awareness of one common use: to aid in the identification of persons making annoying or obscene calls. Most phone books tell subscribers, on a page entitled "Consumer Information," that the company "can frequently help in identifying to the authorities the origin of unwelcome and troublesome calls." *E.g.*, Baltimore Telephone Directory 21 (1978); District of Columbia Telephone Directory 13 (1978). Telephone users, in sum, typically know that they must convey numerical information to the phone company; that the phone company has facilities for recording this information; and that the phone company does in fact record this information for a variety of legitimate business purposes. Although subjective expectations cannot be scientifically gauged, it is too much to believe that telephone subscribers, under these circumstances, harbor any general expectation that the numbers they dial will remain secret.

Petitioner argues, however, that, whatever the expectations of telephone users in general, he demonstrated an expectation of privacy by his own conduct here, since he "us[ed] the telephone *in his house* to the exclusion of all others." But the site of the call is immaterial for purposes of analysis in this case. Although petitioner's conduct may have been calculated to keep the *contents* of his conversation private, his conduct was not and could not have been calculated to preserve the privacy of the number he dialed. Regardless of his location, petitioner had to convey that number to the telephone company in precisely the same way if he wished to complete his call. The fact that he dialed the number on his home phone rather than on some other phone could make no conceivable difference, nor could any subscriber rationally think that it would.

Second, even if petitioner did harbor some subjective expectation that the phone numbers he dialed would remain private, this expectation is not "one that society is prepared to recognize as 'reasonable.'" This Court consistently has held that a person has no legitimate expectation of privacy in information he voluntarily turns over to third parties. *E.g.*, *United States v. Miller*, 425 U.S. [435, 442–444, 96 S.Ct. 1619, 1623–24, 48 L.Ed.2d 71 (1976)]; [*United States v. White, Hoffa v. United States*, and *Lopez v. United States, supra*]. In *Miller*, for example, the Court held that a bank depositor has no "legitimate 'expectation of privacy'" in financial information "voluntarily conveyed to * * * banks and exposed to their employees in the ordinary course of business." The Court explained:

> "The depositor takes the risk, in revealing his affairs to another, that the information will be conveyed by that person to the Government. * * * This Court has held repeatedly that the Fourth Amendment does not prohibit the obtaining of information revealed to a third party and conveyed by him to Government authorities, even if the information is revealed on the assumption that it will be used only for a limited purpose and the confidence placed in the third party will not be betrayed."

Because the depositor "assumed the risk" of disclosure, the Court held that it would be unreasonable for him to expect his financial records to remain private.

This analysis dictates that petitioner can claim no legitimate expectation of privacy here. When he used his phone, petitioner voluntarily conveyed numerical information to the telephone company and "exposed" that information to its equipment in the ordinary course of business. In so doing, petitioner assumed the risk that the company would reveal to police the numbers he dialed. The switching equipment that processed those numbers is merely the modern counterpart of the operator who, in an earlier day, personally completed calls for the subscriber. * * * We are not inclined to hold that a different constitutional result is required because the telephone company has decided to automate. * * *

We therefore conclude that petitioner in all probability entertained no actual expectation of privacy in the phone numbers he dialed, and that, even if he did, his expectation was not "legitimate." The installation and use of a pen register, consequently, was not a "search," and no warrant was required. * * *

Mr. Justice POWELL took no part in the consideration or decision of this case.

Mr. Justice STEWART, with whom Mr. Justice BRENNAN joins, dissenting. * * *

I think that the numbers dialed from a private telephone—like the conversations that occur during a call—are within the constitutional protection recognized in *Katz*. * * * The information captured by such surveillance emanates from private conduct within a person's home or office—locations that without question are entitled to Fourth and Fourteenth Amendment protection. * * *

The numbers dialed from a private telephone—although certainly more prosaic than the conversation itself—are not without "content." Most private telephone subscribers may have their own numbers listed in a publicly distributed directory, but I doubt there are any who would be happy to have broadcast to the world a list of the local or long distance numbers they have called. This is not because such a list might in some sense be incriminating, but because it easily could reveal the identities of the persons and the places called, and thus reveal the most intimate details of a person's life. * * *

Mr. Justice MARSHALL, with whom Mr. Justice BRENNAN joins, dissenting. * * *

Applying the standards set forth in *Katz v. United States*, the Court first determines that telephone subscribers have no subjective expectations of privacy concerning the numbers they dial. To reach this conclusion, the Court posits that individuals somehow infer from the long-distance listings on their phone bills, and from the cryptic assurances of "help" in tracing obscene calls included in "most" phone books, that pen registers are regularly used for recording local calls. But even assuming, as I do not, that individuals "typically know" that a phone company monitors calls for internal reasons,[1] it does not follow that they expect this information to be made available to the public in general or the government in particular. Privacy is not a discrete commodity, possessed absolutely or not at all. Those who disclose certain facts to a bank or phone company for a limited business purpose need not assume that this information will be released to other persons for other purposes.

The crux of the Court's holding, however, is that whatever expectation of privacy petitioner may in fact have entertained regarding his calls, it is not one "society is prepared to recognize as 'reasonable.'" In so ruling, the Court determines that individuals who convey information to third parties have "assumed the risk" of disclosure to the government. This analysis is misconceived in two critical respects.

Implicit in the concept of assumption of risk is some notion of choice. At least in the third-party consensual surveillance cases, which first

---

1. Lacking the Court's apparently exhaustive knowledge of this Nation's telephone books and the reading habits of telephone subscribers, I decline to assume general public awareness of how obscene phone calls are traced. Nor am I persuaded that the scope of Fourth Amendment protection should turn on the concededly "esoteric functions" of pen registers in corporate billing, functions with which subscribers are unlikely to have intimate familiarity.

incorporated risk analysis into Fourth Amendment doctrine, the defendant presumably had exercised some discretion in deciding who should enjoy his confidential communications. See, *e.g.*, [*Lopez, Hoffa,* and *White, supra*]. By contrast here, unless a person is prepared to forgo use of what for many has become a personal or professional necessity, he cannot help but accept the risk of surveillance. It is idle to speak of "assuming" risks in contexts where, as a practical matter, individuals have no realistic alternative.

More fundamentally, to make risk analysis dispositive in assessing the reasonableness of privacy expectations would allow the government to define the scope of Fourth Amendment protections. For example, law enforcement officials, simply by announcing their intent to monitor the content of random samples of first-class mail or private phone conversations, could put the public on notice of the risks they would thereafter assume in such communications. Yet, although acknowledging this implication of its analysis, the Court is willing to concede only that, in some circumstances, a further "normative inquiry would be proper." No meaningful effort is made to explain what those circumstances might be, or why this case is not among them.

In my view, whether privacy expectations are legitimate within the meaning of *Katz* depends not on the risks an individual can be presumed to accept when imparting information to third parties, but on the risks he should be forced to assume in a free and open society. By its terms, the constitutional prohibition of unreasonable searches and seizures assigns to the judiciary some prescriptive responsibility. As Mr. Justice Harlan, who formulated the standard the Court applies today, himself recognized: "[s]ince it is the task of the law to form and project, as well as mirror and reflect, we should not * * * merely recite * * * risks without examining the desirability of saddling them upon society." *United States v. White, supra* (dissenting opinion). In making this assessment, courts must evaluate the "intrinsic character" of investigative practices with reference to the basic values underlying the Fourth Amendment. And for those "extensive intrusions that significantly jeopardize [individuals'] sense of security * * *, more than self-restraint by law enforcement officials is required."

The use of pen registers, I believe, constitutes such an extensive intrusion. To hold otherwise ignores the vital role telephonic communication plays in our personal and professional relationships, as well as the First and Fourth Amendment interests implicated by unfettered official surveillance. Privacy in placing calls is of value not only to those engaged in criminal activity. The prospect of unregulated governmental monitoring will undoubtedly prove disturbing even to those with nothing illicit to hide. Many individuals, including members of unpopular political organizations or journalists with confidential sources, may legitimately wish to avoid disclosure of their personal contacts. Permitting governmental access to telephone records on less than probable cause may thus impede certain forms of political affiliation and journalistic endeavor that are the hallmark of a truly free society. * * * I am unwilling to insulate use of pen registers from independent judicial review.

Just as one who enters a public telephone booth is "entitled to assume that the words he utters into the mouthpiece will not be broadcast to the world," *Katz v. United States, supra,* so too, he should be entitled to assume that the numbers he dials in the privacy of his home will be recorded, if at all, solely for the phone company's business purposes. Accordingly, I would require law enforcement officials to obtain a warrant before they enlist telephone companies to secure information otherwise beyond the government's reach.

NOTES AND QUESTIONS

1. Is *Smith* consistent with *Katz*? Justice Stewart, author of *Katz*, dissented. Do his distinctions persuade you? In view of Justice Harlan's remarks in *White, supra,* regarding the two-pronged standard he developed in *Katz,* do you think he would have voted with the majority or dissent had he still been on the Court?

Justice Stewart announced in *Katz* that what a "person knowingly exposes to the public" is unprotected by the Fourth Amendment. Is the implication of *Smith* that when a person exposes private information to one person she thereby altogether loses Fourth Amendment protection in that information? In this regard, consider:

> A person going on vacation * * * might give a neighbor the key to her house and ask him to water her plants while she is gone. The neighbor now has explicit permission to observe what would otherwise be hidden from view * * *. By granting this permission that vacationer has forfeited a measure of privacy and has thus knowingly exposed part of her home to her neighbor. Still, if the neighbor were to invite his friends * * * into the apartment to see the vacationer's personal items, even just those things visible from where the plants are located, that act would go beyond the scope of the vacationer's permission and therefore represent an invasion of her privacy. There are degrees of privacy and, accordingly, degrees of exposure, and one might choose to forfeit some of her freedom of exposure without thereby forfeiting all of it.

Sherry F. Colb, *What Is a Search? Two Conceptual Flaws in Fourth Amendment Doctrine and Some Hints of a Remedy,* 55 Stan. L. Rev. 119, 122–23 (2002).

Do you agree? If so, how would *you* have the Court define "the public" in Justice Stewart's rule, or would you devise a different standard?

2. Justice Marshall noted the possibility that, in the absence of Fourth Amendment regulation, journalists, political dissenters, and others not suspected of any criminal offense might become victims of pen register surveillance. One possible example of this arose in 1991, when the *Wall Street Journal* quoted "current and former Proctor & Gamble managers" as stating that the company might sell parts of a troubled division of the corporation. Outraged by the disclosures, the Chairman of the Board of the Cincinnati-

based company enlisted the services of the local prosecutor to investigate the corporate leak.

Ultimately, pen register records were obtained by law enforcement authorities of all telephone calls made from the 513 area code (Cincinnati) to the newspaper's Pittsburgh bureau or to the home of the *Wall Street Journal's* reporter. Police interrogated those whose phone numbers were found on the list. See *A Subpoena to Punish News Leaks*, The Washington Post, Aug. 18, 1991, at C6; *The Pampers Police*, St. Petersburg Times, Sept. 9, 1991, at 10A. The sources for the story apparently were never discovered. The prosecutor stated that the investigation was appropriate because state law prohibited disclosure of trade secrets to outsiders.

3. *What the Court taketh away, Congress can giveth back.* *Smith* placed the installation and use of pen registers outside the scope of the Fourth Amendment. In 1986, however, Congress placed statutory limits on use of pen registers in law enforcement. See 18 U.S.C. §§ 3121–3126 (2008). Of course, what Congress giveth, it can also taketh back again. As a result of the September 11 terrorism attacks, Congress granted special powers to the Attorney General to authorize use of pen registers without prior court approval in emergency circumstances relating to international terrorism and foreign intelligence. 50 U.S.C. §§ 1842–1843 (2008).

4. *Beyond pen registers: other forms of technology in evidence-gathering.* *Smith* involved the use of a technological device, the pen register, installed *outside* the defendant's home, in order to obtain information regarding an activity (telephone calling) occurring *inside* his residence. Consider in this context a pair of Supreme Court cases in which the police again used modern technology—this time, a "beeper"—to gather evidence.

In United States v. Knotts, 460 U.S. 276, 103 S.Ct. 1081, 75 L.Ed.2d 55 (1983), as part of an investigation of the manufacture of illicit drugs, federal agents installed a radio transmitter (a "beeper"), which emitted periodic signals, in a five-gallon drum containing chloroform purchased by defendant Petschen (presumably for use in the production of illicit drugs). By use of the beeper, the police monitored the suspect's movements from the point of purchase in Minneapolis, Minnesota along public roads to a secluded cabin in Wisconsin belonging to co-defendant Knotts. As is turned out, the police ended visual surveillance of the Petschen car when he made evasive maneuvers, but they picked up the signals from the beeper by helicopter, where the drum had been left outside the Knotts cabin. Based on this information, the police secured a warrant to search the cabin.

Defendants Petschen and Knotts sought to suppress evidence found in the cabin, on the ground that the surveillance, conducted without a warrant, was unconstitutional. The Court concluded that the surveillance did not constitute a Fourth Amendment search:

> A person traveling in an automobile on public thoroughfares has no reasonable expectation of privacy in his movements from one place to another. When Petschen traveled over the public streets he voluntarily conveyed to anyone who wanted to look the fact that he was traveling over particular roads in a particular direction, the fact of whatever stops

he made, and the fact of his final destination when he exited from public roads onto private property. * * *

Visual surveillance from public places along Petschen's route or adjoining Knotts' premises would have sufficed to reveal all of these facts to the police. The fact that the officers in this case relied not only on visual surveillance, but also on the use of the beeper to signal the presence of Petschen's automobile to the police receiver, does not alter the situation. Nothing in the Fourth Amendment prohibited the police from augmenting the sensory faculties bestowed upon them at birth with such enhancement as science and technology afforded them in this case. * * *

We have recently had occasion to deal with another claim which was to some extent a factual counterpart of respondent's assertions here. [The Court quoted from *Smith v. Maryland, supra,* including the language from that opinion that Smith, by using his telephone, "assumed the risk that the company would reveal to police the numbers he dialed."]

Respondent does not actually quarrel with this analysis, though he expresses the generalized view that the result of the holding sought by the Government would be that "twenty-four hour surveillance of any citizen of this country will be possible, without judicial knowledge or supervision." * * * [I]f such dragnet-type law enforcement practices as respondent envisions should eventually occur, there will be time enough then to determine whether different constitutional principles may be applicable. Insofar as respondent's complaint appears to be simply that scientific devices such as the beeper enabled the police to be more effective in detecting crime, it simply has no constitutional foundation. We have never equated police efficiency with unconstitutionality, and we decline to do so now.

Respondent specifically attacks the use of the beeper insofar as it was used to determine that the can of chloroform had come to rest on his property at Shell Lake, Wis. He repeatedly challenges the "use of the beeper to determine the location of the chemical drum at Respondent's premises" * * *. * * *

We think that respondent's contentions * * * to some extent lose sight of the limited use which the government made of the signals from this particular beeper. As we have noted, nothing in this record indicates that the beeper signal was received or relied upon after it had indicated that the drum containing the chloroform had ended its automotive journey at rest on respondent's premises in rural Wisconsin. * * * [T]here is no indication that the beeper was used in any way to reveal information as to the movement of the drum within the cabin, or in any way that would not have been visible to the naked eye from outside the cabin.

Notice the Court's observation in the last sentence. Didn't the pen register in *Smith* reveal information regarding activities *inside* a residence that was otherwise "hidden"? In any case, the *Knotts* Court's observation proved critical in a second "beeper" case, United States v. Karo, 468 U.S. 705, 104 S.Ct. 3296, 82 L.Ed.2d 530 (1984). In *Karo,* federal agents installed a tracking device in a can of ether and monitored suspect Karo's movement of the beeper over public roads, as in *Knotts*, but also monitored the tracking device in Karo's home, as well as in two other houses. The Court held that the warrantless "monitoring of a beeper in a private residence, a location not open to visual surveillance, violates the Fourth Amendment rights of those who have a justifiable interest in the privacy of the residence." More specifically:

> At the risk of belaboring the obvious, private residences are places in which the individual normally expects privacy free of governmental intrusion not authorized by a warrant, and that expectation is plainly one that society is prepared to recognize as justifiable. Our cases have not deviated from this basic Fourth Amendment principle. * * * In this case, had a DEA agent thought it useful to enter the * * * residence to verify that the ether was actually in the house and had he done so surreptitiously and without a warrant, there is little doubt that he would have engaged in an unreasonable search within the meaning of the Fourth Amendment. For purposes of the Amendment, the result is the same where * * * the Government surreptitiously employs an electronic device to obtain information that it could not have obtained by observation from outside the curtilage of the house. The beeper tells the agent that a particular article is actually located at a particular time in the private residence and is in the possession of the person or persons whose residence is being watched. Even if visual surveillance has revealed that the article to which the beeper is attached has entered the house, the later monitoring not only verifies the officers' observations but also establishes that the article remains on the premises. * * *

> The monitoring of an electronic device such as a beeper is, of course, less intrusive than a full-scale search, but it does reveal a critical fact about the interior of the premises that the Government is extremely interested in knowing and that it could not have otherwise obtained without a warrant. The case is thus not like *Knotts*, for there the beeper told the authorities nothing about the interior of Knotts' cabin. The information obtained in *Knotts* was "voluntarily conveyed to anyone who wanted to look * * * "; here, as we have said, the monitoring indicated that the beeper was inside the house, a fact that could not have been visually verified.[b]

Is *Karo* consistent with *Smith v. Maryland*? You will want to reconsider the beeper cases, and *Smith*, when you read the high court's recent venture

---

b. Consider:

[T]he Court's analysis here is counterintuitive. Imagine that police officers presented you with the option of having them follow you everywhere you travel, keeping track of when you leave your house each day, where you go for recreation and how often you visit various people and places. Now imagine that as an alternative, the police propose tracking exactly where inside your garage your car is parked at any given time. Which of the two would you choose? Which of the two represents the greater invasion of privacy?

Only the most formalistic analysis would consider the threshold of the home the place where privacy begins and ends, regardless of how trivial the "hidden" data and how absolute the "public" surveillance.

Sherry F. Colb, *What Is a Search? Two Conceptual Flaws in Fourth Amendment Doctrine and Some Hints of a Remedy*, 55 Stan. L. Rev. 119, 134 (2002).

into the Fourth Amendment implications of even more modern technology, in *Kyllo v. United States*, p. 126.

5. *"Dog sniffs."* You will remember that the *Smith* Court's analysis of pen registers relied in part on the "limited capabilities" of the device (it does not acquire the contents of communications). Likewise, in the beeper cases (Note 4, *supra*), the Court observed that the beepers had a "limited use" (*Knotts*) and are "less intrusive than a full-scale search" (*Karo*). The Court has repeated this theme elsewhere. In United States v. Place, 462 U.S. 696, 103 S.Ct. 2637, 77 L.Ed.2d 110 (1983), federal drug authorities at LaGuardia Airport in New York subjected a passenger's luggage to a "sniff test" by a dog trained to identify narcotics by smell. One issue in the case was whether the dog sniff constituted a Fourth Amendment search:

> A "canine sniff" by a well-trained narcotics detection dog * * * does not require opening the luggage. It does not expose noncontraband items that otherwise would remain hidden from public view, as does, for example, an officer's rummaging through the contents of the luggage. Thus, the manner in which information is obtained through this investigative technique is much less intrusive than a typical search. Moreover, the sniff discloses only the presence or absence of narcotics, a contraband item. Thus, despite the fact that the sniff tells the authorities something about the contents of the luggage, the information obtained is limited. This limited disclosure also ensures that the owner of the property is not subjected to the embarrassment and inconvenience entailed in less discriminate and more intrusive investigative methods.

> In these respects, the canine sniff is *sui generis*. We are aware of no other investigative procedure that is so limited both in the manner in which the information is obtained and in the content of the information revealed by the procedure. Therefore, we conclude that the particular course of investigation that the agents intended to pursue here—exposure of respondent's luggage, which was located in a public place, to a trained canine—did not constitute a "search" within the meaning of the Fourth Amendment.

The Supreme Court reaffirmed *Place* and explained it further in Illinois v. Caballes, 543 U.S. 405, 125 S.Ct. 834, 160 L.Ed.2d 842 (2005). In *Caballes*, police officers used a "well-trained narcotics-detection dog" to sniff the exterior of the trunk of an automobile, which was lawfully stopped on the highway for a traffic ticket. The Court, 6–2, per Justice John Stevens, wrote:

> Official conduct that does not "compromise any legitimate interest in privacy" is not a search subject to the Fourth Amendment. [*United States v.*] *Jacobsen,* 466 U.S.[109,] at 123, 104 S.Ct. 1652, 80 L.Ed.2d 85 [(1984)]. We have held [in *Jacobsen*] that any interest in possessing contraband cannot be deemed "legitimate," and thus, governmental conduct that *only* reveals the possession of contraband "compromises no legitimate privacy interest." This is because the expectation "that certain facts will not come to the attention of the authorities" is not the same as an interest in "privacy that society is prepared to consider reasonable." * * *

Accordingly, the use of a well-trained narcotics-detection dog—one that "does not expose noncontraband items that otherwise would remain hidden from public view"—during a lawful traffic stop, generally does not implicate legitimate privacy interests. In this case, * * * [a]ny intrusion on respondent's privacy expectations does not rise to the level of a constitutionally cognizable infringement.

Justice Souter dissented:

I would hold that using the dog for the purposes of determining the presence of marijuana in the car's trunk was a search * * *. * * *

In *United States* v. *Place,* we categorized the sniff of the narcotics-seeking dog as *"sui generis"* under the Fourth Amendment and held it was not a search. The classification rests not only upon the limited nature of the intrusion, but on a further premise that experience has shown to be untenable, the assumption that trained sniffing dogs do not err. What we have learned about the fallibility of dogs in the years since *Place* was decided [is] * * * reason to call for reconsidering *Place*'s decision against treating the intentional use of a trained dog as a search. * * * [A]n uncritical adherence to *Place* would render the Fourth Amendment indifferent to suspicionless and indiscriminate sweeps of cars in parking garages and pedestrians on sidewalks * * *. We should not wait for these developments to occur before rethinking *Place*'s analysis, which invites such untoward consequences.

At the heart both of *Place* and the Court's opinion today is the proposition that sniffs by a trained dog are *sui generis* because a reaction by the dog in going alert is a response to nothing but the presence of contraband. Hence, the argument goes, because the sniff can only reveal the presence of items devoid of any legal use, the sniff "does not implicate legitimate privacy interests" and is not to be treated as a search.

The infallible dog, however, is a creature of legal fiction. * * * [T]heir supposed infallibility is belied by judicial opinions describing well-trained animals sniffing and alerting with less than perfect accuracy, whether owing to errors by their handlers, the limitations of the dogs themselves, or even the pervasive contamination of currency by cocaine. Indeed, a study cited by Illinois in this case for the proposition that dog sniffs are "generally reliable" shows that dogs in artificial testing situations return false positives anywhere from 12.5 to 60% of the time, depending on the length of the search. In practical terms, the evidence is clear that the dog that alerts hundreds of times will be wrong dozens of times.

Once the dog's fallibility is recognized, * * * that ends the justification claimed in *Place* for treating the sniff as *sui generis* under the Fourth Amendment: the sniff alert does not necessarily signal hidden contraband * * *. * * *

It makes sense, then, to treat a sniff as the search that it amounts to in practice, and to rely on the body of our Fourth Amendment cases * * * in determining whether such a search is reasonable.

6. *You and your friendly Internet Service Provider (ISP).* In light of *Smith v. Maryland*, do you have a reasonable expectation of privacy in your Internet address (which your ISP can capture and provide to the Government) when you use your home computer to access an Internet website? See State v. Reid, 194 N.J. 386, 945 A.2d 26 (2007).

"OPEN FIELDS," "CURTILAGES," AND BEYOND: WHEN IS THE FOURTH AMENDMENT IMPLICATED?

As the Supreme Court's treatment of the electronic beeper in *United States v. Karo* (p. 111, in Note 4) demonstrates, and as will become increasingly evident as you proceed on your Fourth Amendment journey, the high court treats a person's home more protectively than other sites, even including land near the residence.

Open fields. In *Hester v. United States*, 265 U.S. 57, 44 S.Ct. 445, 68 L.Ed. 898 (1924), the Supreme Court first enunciated the so-called "open fields" doctrine, which provides that entry of an open field does not implicate the Fourth Amendment. In Oliver v. United States, 466 U.S. 170, 104 S.Ct. 1735, 80 L.Ed.2d 214 (1984), the Court held that this doctrine remains good law after *Katz*. According to *Oliver*, an "open field" "may include any unoccupied or undeveloped area outside of the curtilage [of a home]. An open field need be neither 'open' nor a 'field' as those terms are used in common speech. For example, * * * a thickly wooded area nonetheless may be an open field as that term is used in construing the Fourth Amendment."

In *Oliver* and a companion case, law enforcement officers, without a warrant or probable cause, trespassed on defendants' property, as follows:

> Acting on reports that marihuana was being raised on the farm of petitioner Oliver, two narcotics agents of the Kentucky State Police went to the farm to investigate. Arriving at the farm, they drove past petitioner's house to a locked gate with a "No Trespassing" sign. A footpath led around one side of the gate. The agents walked around the gate and along the road for several hundred yards, passing a barn and a parked camper. At that point, someone standing in front of the camper shouted: "No hunting is allowed, come back up here." The officers shouted back that they were Kentucky State Police officers, but found no one when they returned to the camper. The officers resumed their investigation of the farm and found a field of marihuana over a mile from petitioner's home.* * *

> [In the second case, a]fter receiving an anonymous tip that marihuana was being grown in the woods behind respondent Thornton's residence, two police officers entered the woods by a path between this residence and a neighboring house. They followed a footpath through the woods until they reached two marihuana patches fenced with chicken wire.

In an opinion written by Justice Lewis Powell, the Court ruled, 6–3, that open fields fall outside the scope of the Fourth Amendment text, which only prohibits unreasonable searches of "persons, houses, papers, [or] effects":

> The rule announced in *Hester v. United States* was founded upon the explicit language of the Fourth Amendment. That Amendment indicates with some precision the places and things encompassed by its protections. As Justice Holmes explained for the Court in his characteristically laconic style: "[T]he special protection accorded by the Fourth Amendment to the people in their 'persons, houses, papers, and effects,' is not extended to the open fields. The distinction between the latter and the house is as old as the common law."[6]
>
> Nor are the open fields "effects" within the meaning of the Fourth Amendment. In this respect, it is suggestive that James Madison's proposed draft of what became the Fourth Amendment preserves "[t]he rights of the people to be secured in their persons, their houses, their papers, and their other property, from all unreasonable searches and seizures * * *." Although Congress' revisions of Madison's proposal broadened the scope of the Amendment in some respects, the term "effects" is less inclusive than "property" and cannot be said to encompass open fields. We conclude, as did the Court in deciding *Hester v. United States*, that the government's intrusion upon the open fields is not one of those "unreasonable searches" proscribed by the text of the Fourth Amendment.

The Court could have stopped at this point, but it did not. Five justices also concluded that entry of open fields does not constitute a "search" within the post-*Katz* meaning of that concept:

> [T]he rule of *Hester v. United States* that we reaffirm today, may be understood as providing that an individual may not legitimately demand privacy for activities conducted out of doors in fields, except in the area immediately surrounding the home. This rule is true to the conception of the right to privacy embodied in the Fourth Amendment. The Amendment reflects the recognition of the Framers that certain enclaves should be free from arbitrary government interference. For example, the Court since the enactment of the Fourth Amendment has stressed "the overriding respect for the sanctity of the home that has been embedded in our traditions since the origins

---

6. * * * Nor have subsequent cases discredited *Hester*'s reasoning. This Court frequently has relied on the explicit language of the Fourth Amendment as delineating the scope of its affirmative protections. * * * *Katz*' "reasonable expectation of privacy" standard did not sever Fourth Amendment doctrine from the Amendment's language. *Katz* itself construed the Amendment's protection of the person against unreasonable searches to encompass electronic eavesdropping of telephone conversations sought to be kept private; and *Katz*' fundamental recognition that "the Fourth Amendment protects people—and not simply 'areas'—against unreasonable searches and seizures" is faithful to the Amendment's language. As *Katz* demonstrates, the Court fairly may respect the constraints of the Constitution's language without wedding itself to an unreasoning literalism. * * *

of the Republic." *Payton v. New York*, [445 U.S. 573, 601, 100 S.Ct. 1371, 1387, 63 L.Ed.2d 639 (1980).]

In contrast, open fields do not provide the setting for those intimate activities that the Amendment is intended to shelter from government interference or surveillance. There is no societal interest in protecting the privacy of those activities, such as the cultivation of crops, that occur in open fields. Moreover, as a practical matter these lands usually are accessible to the public and the police in ways that a home, an office, or commercial structure would not be. It is not generally true that fences or "No Trespassing" signs effectively bar the public from viewing open fields in rural areas. And both petitioner Oliver and respondent Thornton concede that the public and police lawfully may survey lands from the air. For these reasons, the asserted expectation of privacy in open fields is not an expectation that "society recognizes as reasonable."[c]

The historical underpinnings of the open fields doctrine also demonstrate that the doctrine is consistent with respect for "reasonable expectations of privacy." As Justice Holmes, writing for the Court, observed in *Hester*, the common law distinguished "open fields" from the "curtilage," the land immediately surrounding and associated with the home. The distinction implies that only the curtilage, not the neighboring open fields, warrants the Fourth Amendment protections that attach to the home. At common law, the curtilage is the area to which extends the intimate activity associated with the "sanctity of a man's home and the privacies of life," *Boyd v. United States*, 116 U.S. 616, 630, 6 S.Ct. 524, 532, 29 L.Ed. 746 (1886), and therefore has been considered part of the home itself for Fourth Amendment purposes. Thus, courts have extended Fourth Amendment protection to the curtilage; and they have defined the curtilage, as did the common law, by reference to the factors that determine whether an individual reasonably may expect that an area immediately adjacent to the home will remain private. Conversely, the common law implies, as we reaffirm today, that no expectation of privacy legitimately attaches to open fields.

Justice Marshall, writing also for Justices Brennan and Stevens, rejected the majority's "search" analysis.

We have frequently acknowledged that privacy interests are not coterminous with property rights. However, because "property rights reflect society's explicit recognition of a person's authority to act as he wishes in certain areas, [they] should be considered in determining whether an individual's expectations of privacy are reasonable." * * *

---

c. Do you agree with a rule that "permits police to engage in what is criminal misconduct on the theory that they could have made the same observation by a legal, alternative means," such as viewing land from the air? Sherry F. Colb, *What Is a Search? Two Conceptual Flaws in Fourth Amendment Doctrine and Some Hints of a Remedy*, 55 Stan. L. Rev. 119, 131 (2002). Is the Court's analysis here consistent with *Katz*? Reconsider the lip-reader hypothetical raised on p. 89, Note 2.

It is undisputed that Oliver and Thornton each owned the land into which the police intruded. That fact alone provides considerable support for their assertion of legitimate privacy interests in their woods and fields. But even more telling is the nature of the sanctions that Oliver and Thornton could invoke, under local law, for violation of their property rights. In Kentucky, a knowing entry upon fenced or otherwise enclosed land, or upon unenclosed land conspicuously posted with signs excluding the public, constitutes criminal trespass. The law in Maine is similar. * * * Thus, positive law not only recognizes the legitimacy of Oliver's and Thornton's insistence that strangers keep off their land, but subjects those who refuse to respect their wishes to the most severe of penalties—criminal liability. Under these circumstances, it is hard to credit the Court's assertion that Oliver's and Thornton's expectations of privacy were not of a sort that society is prepared to recognize as reasonable. * * *

Privately owned woods and fields that are not exposed to public view regularly are employed in a variety of ways that society acknowledges deserve privacy. Many landowners like to take solitary walks on their property, confident that they will not be confronted in their rambles by strangers or policemen. Others conduct agricultural businesses on their property.[14] Some landowners use their secluded spaces to meet lovers, others to gather together with fellow worshippers, still others to engage in sustained creative endeavor. Private land is sometimes used as a refuge for wildlife, where flora and fauna are protected from human intervention of any kind. Our respect for the freedom of landowners to use their posted "open fields" in ways such as these partially explains the seriousness with which the positive law regards deliberate invasions of such spaces, and substantially reinforces the landowners' contention that their expectations of privacy are "reasonable." * * *

* * * A claim of privacy is * * * strengthened by the fact that the claimant somehow manifested to other people his desire that they keep their distance.

Certain spaces are so presumptively private that signals of this sort are unnecessary; a homeowner need not post a "Do Not Enter" sign on his door in order to deny entrance to uninvited guests. * * * Still other spaces are, by positive law and social convention, presumed accessible to members of the public *unless* the owner manifests his intention to exclude them.

Undeveloped land falls into the last-mentioned category. If a person has not marked the boundaries of his fields or woods in a way that informs passersby that they are not welcome, he cannot object if members of the public enter onto the property. There is no reason

---

14. We accord constitutional protection to businesses conducted in office buildings; it is not apparent why businesses conducted in fields that are not open to the public are less deserving of the benefit of the Fourth Amendment.

why he should have any greater rights as against government officials. * * *

A very different case is presented when the owner of undeveloped land has taken precautions to exclude the public. As indicated above, a deliberate entry by a private citizen onto private property marked with "No Trespassing" signs will expose him to criminal liability. I see no reason why a government official should not be obliged to respect such unequivocal and universally understood manifestations of a landowner's desire for privacy. * * *

A clear, easily administrable rule emerges from the analysis set forth above: Private land marked in a fashion sufficient to render entry thereon a criminal trespass under the law of the State in which the land lies is protected by the Fourth Amendment's proscription of unreasonable searches and seizures.

With which opinion—Justice Powell's or Justice Marshall's—do you agree more?

Curtilage: what is it? In *Oliver*, Justice Powell defined and distinguished the curtilage of a house from an open field. In United States v. Dunn, 480 U.S. 294, 107 S.Ct. 1134, 94 L.Ed.2d 326 (1987), the Court explained the curtilage concept further. It stated that "questions should be resolved with reference to four factors: the proximity of the area claimed to be curtilage to the home, whether the area is included within an enclosure surrounding the home, the nature of the uses to which the area is put, and the steps taken by the resident to protect the area from observation by people passing by."

Dunn warned that the four factors do not produce a "fine tuned formula that, when mechanically applied, yields a 'correct' answer to all extent-of-curtilage questions. Rather, these factors are useful analytical tools only to the degree that, in any given case, they bear upon the centrally relevant consideration—whether the area in question is so intimately tied to the home itself that it should be placed under the home's 'umbrella' of Fourth Amendment protection." Thus, even as the *Oliver* Court favored the ease of a bright-line rule that excludes all fields from the protections of the Fourth Amendment, *Dunn* requires courts to conduct case-by-case determination of whether the police have entered a "curtilage" or merely an "open field."

* * *

PROBLEM: OPEN FIELD OR CURTILAGE?

Consider the facts in *Dunn*:

Respondent's ranch comprised approximately 198 acres and was completely encircled by a perimeter fence. The property also contained several interior fences, constructed mainly of posts and multiple strands of barbed wire. The ranch residence was situated ½ miles from a public road. A fence encircled the residence and a nearby small greenhouse. Two barns were located approximately 50 yards from this fence. The front of the larger of the two barns was enclosed by a wooden fence and had an open overhang. Locked, waist-high gates barred entry into the barn proper, and netting material stretched from the ceiling to the top of the wooden gates.

* * * [L]aw enforcement officials made a warrantless entry onto respondent's ranch property. A DEA agent accompanied by an officer from the Houston Police Department crossed over the perimeter fence and one interior fence. Standing approximately midway between the residence and the barns, the DEA agent smelled what he believed to be phenylacetic acid, the odor coming from the direction of the barns. The officers approached the smaller of the barns—crossing over a barbed wire fence—and, looking into the barn, observed only empty boxes. The officers then proceeded to the larger barn, crossing another barbed wire fence as well as a wooden fence that enclosed the front portion of the barn. The officers walked under the barn's overhang to the locked wooden gates and, shining a flashlight through the netting on top of the gates, peered into the barn.

In your view, were the officers in an open field or curtilage? Should the Fourth Amendment analysis change if they had actually entered the larger barn?

* * *

Surveillance of a curtilage. It does not follow from the fact that an area is identified as a curtilage that police surveillance of it inevitably constitutes a "search." That lesson is learned from two cases of aerial surveillance of curtilages. Consider first the facts in California v. Ciraolo, 476 U.S. 207, 106 S.Ct. 1809, 90 L.Ed.2d 210 (1986):

On September 2, 1982, Santa Clara Police received an anonymous telephone tip that marijuana was growing in respondent's backyard. Police were unable to observe the contents of respondent's yard from ground level because of a 6–foot outer fence and a 10–foot inner fence completely enclosing the yard. Later that day, Officer Shutz, who was assigned to investigate, secured a private plane and flew over respondent's house at an altitude of 1,000 feet, within navigable airspace; he was accompanied by Officer Rodriguez. Both officers were trained in marijuana identification. From the overflight, the officers readily identified marijuana plants 8 feet to 10 feet in height growing in a 15– by 25–foot plot in respondent's yard; they photographed the area with a standard 35mm camera.

Based on this surveillance, the police obtained a warrant to search the premises. The issue was whether the information secured from the aerial surveillance properly was used to secure the warrant. That, in turn, raised the question of whether the surveillance was, itself, a search that may have required a warrant. Chief Justice Burger declared that the surveillance of the curtilage of Ciraolo's home was *not* a search and, therefore, fell outside the protections of the Fourth Amendment. The Court dealt briefly with the subjective prong of Harlan's "search" test before turning to the critical objective prong:

Clearly—and understandably—respondent has met the test of manifesting his own subjective intent and desire to maintain privacy as to his unlawful agricultural pursuits. However, we need not address that issue, for the State has not challenged the finding of the California Court of Appeal that respondent had such an expectation. It can reasonably be assumed that the 10–foot fence was placed to conceal the marijuana crop from at least street-level views. * * *

Yet a 10–foot fence might not shield these plants from the eyes of a citizen or a policeman perched on the top of a truck or a two-level bus. Whether respondent therefore manifested a subjective expectation of privacy from *all* observations of his backyard, or whether instead he manifested merely a hope that no one would observe his unlawful gardening pursuits, is not entirely clear in these circumstances. * * *

We turn * * * to the second inquiry under *Katz*, *i.e.*, whether that expectation is reasonable. * * *

That the area is within the curtilage does not itself bar all police observation. The Fourth Amendment protection of the home has never been extended to require law enforcement officers to shield their eyes when passing by a home on public thoroughfares. Nor does the mere fact that an individual has taken measures to restrict some views of his activities preclude an officer's observations from a public vantage point where he has a right to be and which renders the activities clearly visible. *E.g.*, *United States v. Knotts*, [p. 110, Note 4]. "What a person knowingly exposes to the public, even in his own home or office, is not a subject of Fourth Amendment protection." *Katz, supra.*

The observations by Officers Shutz and Rodriguez in this case took place within public navigable airspace, in a physically nonintrusive manner; from this point they were able to observe plants readily discernible to the naked eye as marijuana. That the observation from aircraft was directed at identifying the plants and the officers were trained to recognize marijuana is irrelevant. * * * Any member of the public flying in this airspace who glanced down could have seen everything that these officers observed. On this record, we readily conclude that respondent's expectation that his garden was protected from such observation is unreasonable and is not an expectation that society is prepared to honor. * * *

* * * In an age where private and commercial flight in the public airways is routine, it is unreasonable for respondent to expect that his marijuana plants were constitutionally protected from being observed with the naked eye from an altitude of 1,000 feet. The Fourth Amendment simply does not require the police traveling in the public airways at this altitude to obtain a warrant in order to observe what is visible to the naked eye.

Are you persuaded? Four justices were not. Justice Powell, who wrote the open-fields *Oliver* decision, explained their disagreement:

In my view, the Court's holding rests on only one obvious fact, namely, that the airspace generally is open to all persons for travel in airplanes. The Court does not explain why this single fact deprives citizens of their privacy interest in outdoor activities in an enclosed curtilage. * * *

As the decision in *Katz* held, and dissenting opinions written by Justices of this Court prior to *Katz* recognized, a standard that defines a Fourth Amendment "search" by reference to whether police have physically invaded a "constitutionally protected area" provides no real protection against surveillance techniques made possible through technology. Technological advances have enabled police to see people's activities and associations, and to hear their conversations, without being in physical proximity. Moreover, the capability now exists for police to conduct intrusive surveillance without any physical penetration of the walls of homes or other structures that citizens may believe shelters their privacy. Looking to the Fourth Amendment for protection against such "broad and unsuspected governmental incursions" into the "cherished privacy of law-abiding citizens," the Court in *Katz* abandoned its inquiry into whether police had committed a physical trespass. * * *

This case involves surveillance of a home, for as we stated in *Oliver v. United States*, the curtilage "has been considered part of the home itself for Fourth Amendment purposes." * * *

* * * [R]espondent's yard unquestionably was within the curtilage. Since Officer Shutz could not see into this private family area from the street, the Court certainly would agree that he would have conducted an unreasonable search had he climbed over the fence, or used a ladder to peer into the yard without first securing a warrant.

The Court concludes, nevertheless, that Shutz could use an airplane—a product of modern technology—to intrude visually into respondent's yard. The Court argues that respondent had no reasonable expectation of privacy from aerial observation. It notes that Shutz was "within public navigable airspace," when he looked into and photographed respondent's yard. It then relies on the fact that the surveillance was not accompanied by a physical invasion of the curtilage. Reliance on the *manner* of surveillance is directly contrary to the standard of *Katz*, which identifies a constitutionally protected privacy right by focusing on the interests of the individual and of a free society. Since *Katz*, we have consistently held that the presence or absence of physical trespass by police is constitutionally irrelevant to the question whether society is prepared to recognize an asserted privacy interest as reasonable.

The Court's holding, therefore, must rest solely on the fact that members of the public fly in planes and may look down at homes as they fly over them. The Court does not explain why it finds this fact to be significant. One may assume that the Court believes that citizens bear the risk that air travelers will observe activities occurring within backyards that are open to the sun and air. This risk, the Court appears to hold, nullifies expectations of privacy in those yards even as to purposeful police surveillance from the air.

This line of reasoning is flawed. First, the actual risk to privacy from commercial or pleasure aircraft is virtually nonexistent. Travelers on commercial flights, as well as private planes used for business or personal reasons, normally obtain at most a fleeting, anonymous, and nondiscriminating glimpse of the landscape and buildings over which they pass. The risk that a passenger on such a plane might observe private activities, and might connect those activities with particular people, is simply too trivial to protect against. It is no accident that, as a matter of common experience, many people build fences around their residential areas, but few build roofs over their backyards. Therefore, contrary to the Court's suggestion, people do not " 'knowingly expos[e]' " their residential yards " 'to the public' " merely by failing to build barriers that prevent aerial surveillance. * * * [T]he Court fails to acknowledge the qualitative difference between police surveillance and other uses made of the airspace. Members of the public use the airspace for travel, business, or pleasure, not for the purpose of observing activities taking place within residential yards. Here, police conducted an overflight at low altitude solely for the purpose of discovering evidence of crime within a private enclave into which they were constitutionally forbidden to intrude at ground level without a warrant. It is not easy to believe that our society is prepared to force individuals to bear the risk of this type of warrantless police intrusion into their residential areas.[10]

One feature of Powell's dissent focuses on the manner of surveillance. He states that "[r]eliance on the *manner* of surveillance is directly contrary to the standard of *Katz*." Is it? He also suggests that if Officer Shutz had used a ladder to peer into the yard, this uncontroversially would have constituted a Fourth Amendment search. Is he correct? Suppose Officer Shutz had received permission from Ciraolo's neighbor to peer into the backyard from the neighbor's second-floor window overlooking the curtilage. Is *that* a search? Or, suppose there was a public park across the street and Shutz climbed into a tree and looked into the backyard. Search?

Justice Powell is critical of the majority for failing "to acknowledge the qualitative difference between police surveillance and other uses made of the airspace." *Should* courts draw such a distinction? That is, even if persons do not expect freedom from private intrusions, should the issue in Fourth Amendment cases be whether a person has a reasonable expectation of privacy from purposeful *governmental* surveillance?

Ciraolo is not the Supreme Court's only effort to wrestle with the problems of aerial surveillance. In Florida v. Riley, 488 U.S. 445, 109 S.Ct. 693, 102 L.Ed.2d 835 (1989), a police officer observed the interior of a partially covered greenhouse in Riley's backyard, while circling 400 feet above the greenhouse in a police helicopter. Justice White, in an opinion joined only

---

10. The Court's decision has serious implications for outdoor family activities conducted in the curtilage of a home. The feature of such activities that makes them desirable to citizens living in a free society, namely, the fact that they occur in the open air and sunlight, is relied on by the Court as a justification for permitting police to conduct warrantless surveillance at will. Aerial surveillance is nearly as intrusive on family privacy as physical trespass into the curtilage. It would appear that, after today, families can expect to be free of official surveillance only when they retreat behind the walls of their homes.

by Chief Justice Rehnquist and Justices Scalia and Kennedy, concluded that *Ciraolo* controlled the case:

> In this case, as in *Ciraolo*, the property surveyed was within the curtilage of respondent's home. Riley no doubt intended and expected that his greenhouse would not be open to public inspection, and the precautions he took protected against ground-level observation. Because the sides and roof of his greenhouse were left partially open, however, what was growing in the greenhouse was subject to viewing from the air. Under the holding in *Ciraolo*, Riley could not reasonably have expected the contents of his greenhouse to be immune from examination by an officer seated in a fixed-wing aircraft flying in navigable airspace at an altitude of 1,000 feet or, as the Florida Supreme Court seemed to recognize, at an altitude of 500 feet, the lower limit of the navigable airspace for such an aircraft. * * *
>
>   Nor on the facts before us, does it make a difference for Fourth Amendment purposes that the helicopter was flying at 400 feet when the officer saw what was growing in the greenhouse through the partially open roof and sides of the structure. We would have a different case if flying at that altitude had been contrary to law or regulation. But helicopters are not bound by the lower limits of the navigable airspace allowed to other aircraft. Any member of the public could legally have been flying over Riley's property in a helicopter at the altitude of 400 feet and could have observed Riley's greenhouse. The police officer did no more.

In dictum, the plurality suggested some additional limitations on aerial surveillance:

> This is not to say that an inspection of the curtilage of a house from an aircraft will always pass muster under the Fourth Amendment simply because the plane is within the navigable airspace specified by law. But it is of obvious importance that the helicopter in this case was *not* violating the law * * *. Neither is there any intimation here that the helicopter interfered with respondent's normal use of the greenhouse or of other parts of the curtilage. As far as this record reveals, no intimate details connected with the use of the home or curtilage were observed, and there was no undue noise, and no wind, dust, or threat of injury. In these circumstances, there was no violation of the Fourth Amendment.

What does Justice White mean by these limitations? For example, suppose that the surveillance of Riley's greenhouse had been conducted by *airplane* at 400 feet. Because an airplane should not be at such a low altitude, has a search occurred, although the same surveillance by helicopter is permissible? Does such a distinction make sense?

Does Justice White also mean that if an officer in a helicopter simultaneously observes marijuana in a greenhouse and sexually intimate acts occurring in the same curtilage, the surveillance constitutes a search as to the latter, but not as to the former, sighting? Does such a distinction make sense? And, why is it a Fourth Amendment concern whether a helicopter is noisy or blows dust in a person's backyard?

Justice O'Connor, concurring in the judgment, and the four dissenters minimized the significance of the fact that the helicopter was in lawful navigable airspace, or even that *police* use of helicopters at that altitude may have been common. As Justice O'Connor, the fifth vote to affirm the conviction, put it:

> [T]he relevant inquiry * * * is not whether the helicopter was where it had a right to be under FAA regulations. Rather, consistent with *Katz*, we must ask whether the helicopter was in the public airways at an altitude at which members of the public travel with sufficient regularity that Riley's expectation of privacy was not "one that society is prepared to recognized as 'reasonable.' "

O'Connor stated that there was "reason to believe that there is considerable public use of airspace at altitudes of 400 feet and above, and because Riley introduced no evidence to the contrary," his subjective expectation of privacy was unreasonable.

Surveillance outside the curtilage, near a house, but not in an open field. In California v. Greenwood, 486 U.S. 35, 108 S.Ct. 1625, 100 L.Ed.2d 30 (1988), officers searched through plastic garbage bags left on the curb in front of a house for trash pickup. The Court ruled that a person does not have a reasonable expectation of privacy in garbage left outside the curtilage of a home for trash removal. Justice White explained that the objective prong of *Katz* is not satisfied in such circumstances:

> It is common knowledge that plastic garbage bags left on or at the side of a public street are readily accessible to animals, children, scavengers, snoops, and other members of the public. Moreover, respondents placed their refuse at the curb for the express purpose of conveying it to a third party, the trash collector, who might himself have sorted through respondents' trash or permitted others, such as the police, to do so. * * *
>
> Furthermore, as we have held, the police cannot reasonably be expected to avert their eyes from evidence of criminal activity that could have been observed by any member of the public. Hence, "[w]hat a person knowingly exposes to the public, even in his own home or office, is not a subject of Fourth Amendment protection." *Katz v. United States.* We held in *Smith v. Maryland* [p. 103], for example, that * * * [a]n individual has no legitimate expectation of privacy in the numbers dialed on his telephone * * * because he voluntarily conveys those numbers to the telephone company when he uses the telephone.

If you represented Greenwood, how would you try to distinguish *Katz* and *Smith* from the circumstances here?

Another look at technology in Fourth Amendment jurisprudence. As noted above, in *Ciraolo*, Officers Shutz and Rodriguez photographed the marijuana with a 35mm camera. In a companion case, Dow Chemical Co. v. United States, 476 U.S. 227, 106 S.Ct. 1819, 90 L.Ed.2d 226 (1986), agents of the Environmental Protection Agency (EPA) photographed Dow's 2000–acre outdoor industrial complex (an area the justices described as "more comparable to an open field" than to an "industrial curtilage") from altitudes of 12,000, 3,000, and 1,200 feet with a "standard, floor-mounted, precision aerial mapping camera." The Court, observing that it was important that the area photographed was "*not* an area immediately adjacent to a private home, where privacy expectations are most heightened," upheld the use of the camera to take pictures:

> Here, EPA was not employing some unique sensory device that, for example, could penetrate the walls of buildings and record conversations in Dow's plants, offices, or laboratories, but rather a conventional, albeit precise, commercial camera commonly used in mapmaking. * * *

> It may well be, as the Government concedes, that surveillance of private property by using highly sophisticated surveillance equipment not generally available to the public, such as satellite technology, might be constitutionally proscribed absent a warrant. But the photographs here are not so revealing of intimate details as to raise constitutional concerns. Although they undoubtedly give EPA more detailed information than naked-eye views, they remain limited to an outline of the facility's buildings and equipment. The mere fact that human vision is enhanced somewhat, at least to the degree here, does not give rise to constitutional problems. An electronic device to penetrate walls or windows so as to hear and record confidential discussions of chemical formulae or other trade secrets would raise very different and far more serious questions * * *.

The Court's latter observations are worth remembering as we turn to the next case.

KYLLO v. UNITED STATES

Supreme Court of the United States, 2001.
533 U.S. 27, 121 S.Ct. 2038, 150 L.Ed.2d 94.

JUSTICE SCALIA delivered the opinion of the Court.

This case presents the question whether the use of a thermal-imaging device aimed at a private home from a public street to detect relative amounts of heat within the home constitutes a "search" within the meaning of the Fourth Amendment.

I

In 1991 Agent William Elliott of the United States Department of the Interior came to suspect that marijuana was being grown in the home belonging to petitioner Danny Kyllo, part of a triplex on Rhododendron Drive in Florence, Oregon. Indoor marijuana growth typically requires high-intensity lamps. In order to determine whether an amount of heat was emanating from petitioner's home consistent with the use of such lamps, at 3:20 a.m. on January 16, 1992, Agent Elliott and Dan Haas used an Agema Thermovision 210 thermal imager to scan the triplex. Thermal imagers detect infrared radiation, which virtually all objects emit but which is not visible to the naked eye. The imager converts radiation into images based on relative warmth—black is cool, white is hot, shades of gray connote relative differences; in that respect, it operates somewhat like a video camera showing heat images. The scan of Kyllo's home took only a few minutes and was performed from the passenger seat of Agent Elliott's vehicle across the street from the front of the house and also from the street in back of the house. The scan showed that the roof over the garage and a side wall of petitioner's home were relatively hot compared to the rest of the home and substantially warmer than neighboring homes in the triplex. Agent Elliott concluded that petitioner was using halide lights to grow marijuana in his house, which indeed he was. Based on tips from informants, utility bills, and the thermal imaging, a Federal Magistrate Judge issued a warrant authorizing a search of petitioner's home, and the agents found an indoor growing operation involving more than 100 plants. Petitioner * * * unsuccessfully moved to suppress the evidence seized from his home * * *. * * *

II

* * * "At the very core" of the Fourth Amendment "stands the right of a man to retreat into his own home and there be free from unreasonable governmental intrusion." *Silverman v. United States*, 365 U.S. 505, 511 (1961). With few exceptions, the question whether a warrantless search of a home is reasonable and hence constitutional must be answered no.

On the other hand, the antecedent question of whether or not a Fourth Amendment "search" has occurred is not so simple under our precedent. The permissibility of ordinary visual surveillance of a home used to be clear because, well into the 20th century, our Fourth Amendment jurisprudence was tied to common-law trespass. Visual surveillance was unquestionably lawful because " 'the eye cannot by the laws of England be guilty of a trespass.' " *Boyd v. United States*, 116 U.S. 616, 628 (1886) (quoting *Entick v. Carrington*, 19 How. St. Tr. 1029, 95 Eng. Rep. 807 (K. B. 1765)). We have since decoupled violation of a person's Fourth Amendment rights from trespassory violation of his property, but the lawfulness of warrantless visual surveillance of a home has still been preserved. As we observed in *California v. Ciraolo*, [p. 120], "[t]he Fourth Amendment protection of the home has never been extended to require law enforcement officers to shield their eyes when passing by a home on public thoroughfares."

One might think that the new validating rationale would be that examining the portion of a house that is in plain public view, while it is a "search"[1] despite the absence of trespass, is not an "unreasonable" one under the Fourth Amendment. But in fact we have held that visual observation is no "search" at all * * *. In assessing when a search is not a search, we have applied somewhat in reverse the principle first enunciated in *Katz v. United States*. *Katz* involved eavesdropping by means of an

---

1. When the Fourth Amendment was adopted, as now, to "search" meant "[t]o look over or through for the purpose of finding something; to explore; to examine by inspection; as, to search the house for a book; to search the wood for a thief." N. Webster, An American Dictionary of the English Language 66 (1828) (reprint 6th ed. 1989).

electronic listening device placed on the outside of a telephone booth—a location not within the catalog ("persons, houses, papers, and effects") that the Fourth Amendment protects against unreasonable searches. We held that the Fourth Amendment nonetheless protected Katz from the warrantless eavesdropping because he "justifiably relied" upon the privacy of the telephone booth. As Justice Harlan's oft-quoted concurrence described it, a Fourth Amendment search occurs when the government violates a subjective expectation of privacy that society recognizes as reasonable. We have subsequently applied this principle to hold that a Fourth Amendment search does *not* occur—even when the explicitly protected location of a *house* is concerned—unless "the individual manifested a subjective expectation of privacy in the object of the challenged search," and "society [is] willing to recognize that expectation as reasonable." We have applied this test in holding that it is not a search for the police to use a pen register at the phone company to determine what numbers were dialed in a private home, *Smith v. Maryland*, [p. 103], and we have applied the test on two different occasions in holding that aerial surveillance of private homes and surrounding areas does not constitute a search, *Ciraolo, supra*; *Florida v. Riley*, [p. 123].

The present case involves officers on a public street engaged in more than naked-eye surveillance of a home. We have previously reserved judgment as to how much technological enhancement of ordinary perception from such a vantage point, if any, is too much. While we upheld enhanced aerial photography of an industrial complex in *Dow Chemical*, [p. __] we noted that we found "it important that this is *not* an area immediately adjacent to a private home, where privacy expectations are most heightened."

III

It would be foolish to contend that the degree of privacy secured to citizens by the Fourth Amendment has been entirely unaffected by the advance of technology. For example, as the cases discussed above make clear, the technology enabling human flight has exposed to public view (and hence, we have said, to official observation) uncovered portions of the house and its curtilage that once were private. The question we confront today is what limits there are upon this power of technology to shrink the realm of guaranteed privacy.

The *Katz* test—whether the individual has an expectation of privacy that society is prepared to recognize as reasonable—has often been criticized as circular, and hence subjective and unpredictable. While it may be difficult to refine *Katz* when the search of areas such as telephone booths, automobiles, or even the curtilage and uncovered portions of residences are at issue, in the case of the search of the interior of homes—the prototypical and hence most commonly litigated area of protected privacy—there is a ready criterion, with roots deep in the common law, of the minimal expectation of privacy that *exists*, and that is acknowledged to be *reasonable*. To withdraw protection of this minimum expectation would be to permit police technology to erode the privacy guaranteed by the Fourth Amendment. We think that obtaining by sense-enhancing technology any information regarding the interior of the home that could not otherwise have been obtained without physical "intrusion into a constitutionally protected area" constitutes a search—at least where (as here) the technology in question is not in general public use. This assures preservation of that degree of privacy against government that existed when the Fourth Amendment was adopted. On the basis of this criterion, the information obtained by the thermal imager in this case was the product of a search.[2]

The Government maintains, however, that the thermal imaging must be upheld because it detected "only heat radiating from the external surface of the house." The dissent makes this its leading point, contending that there is a fundamental difference between what it calls "off-the-wall" observations and "through-the-wall surveillance." But just as a thermal imager captures only heat emanating from a house, so also a powerful directional microphone picks up only sound emanating from a house—and a satellite capable of scanning from many miles away would pick up only visible light emanating from a house. We rejected such a mechanical interpretation of the Fourth Amendment in *Katz*, where the eavesdropping device picked up only sound waves that reached the exterior of the phone booth. Reversing that approach would leave the homeowner at the mercy of advancing technology—including imaging technology that could discern all human activity in the home. While the technology used in the present case was relatively crude, the rule we adopt must take account of more sophisticated systems that are already in use or in development.[3]

* * *

The Government also contends that the thermal imaging was constitutional because it did not "detect private activities occurring in private areas." It points out that in *Dow Chemical* we observed that the enhanced aerial photography did not reveal any "intimate details." *Dow Chemical*, however, involved enhanced aerial photography of an industrial complex,

---

2. The dissent's repeated assertion that the thermal imaging did not obtain information regarding the interior of the home is simply inaccurate. A thermal imager reveals the relative heat of various rooms in the home. The dissent may not find that information particularly private or important, but there is no basis for saying it is not information regarding the interior of the home. The dissent's comparison of the thermal imaging to various circumstances in which outside observers might be able to perceive, without technology, the heat of the home—for example, by observing snowmelt on the roof—is quite irrelevant. The fact that equivalent information could sometimes be obtained by other means does not make lawful the use of means that violate the Fourth Amendment. The police might, for example, learn how many people are in a particular house by setting up year-round surveillance; but that does not make breaking and entering to find out the same information lawful. In any event, on the night of January 16, 1992, no outside observer could have discerned the relative heat of Kyllo's home without thermal imaging.

3. The ability to "see" through walls and other opaque barriers is a clear, and scientifically feasible, goal of law enforcement research and development. The National Law Enforcement and Corrections Technology Center, a program within the United States Department of Justice, features on its Internet Website projects that include a "Radar–Based Through-the-Wall Surveillance System," "Handheld Ultrasound Through the Wall Surveillance," and a "Radar Flashlight" that "will enable law officers to detect individuals through interior building walls." Some devices may emit low levels of radiation that travel "through-the-wall," but others, such as more sophisticated thermal imaging devices, are entirely passive, or "off-the-wall" as the dissent puts it.

which does not share the Fourth Amendment sanctity of the home. The Fourth Amendment's protection of the home has never been tied to measurement of the quality or quantity of information obtained. In *Silverman*, for example, we made clear that any physical invasion of the structure of the home, "by even a fraction of an inch," was too much, and there is certainly no exception to the warrant requirement for the officer who barely cracks open the front door and sees nothing but the nonintimate rug on the vestibule floor. In the home, our cases show, *all* details are intimate details, because the entire area is held safe from prying government eyes. Thus, in *Karo*, the only thing detected was a can of ether in the home; and in *Arizona v. Hicks*, [p. 304], the only thing detected by a physical search that went beyond what officers lawfully present could observe in "plain view" was the registration number of a phonograph turntable. These were intimate details because they were details of the home, just as was the detail of how warm—or even how relatively warm—Kyllo was heating his residence.

Limiting the prohibition of thermal imaging to "intimate details" would not only be wrong in principle; it would be impractical in application, failing to provide "a workable accommodation between the needs of law enforcement and the interests protected by the Fourth Amendment." To begin with, there is no necessary connection between the sophistication of the surveillance equipment and the "intimacy" of the details that it observes—which means that one cannot say (and the police cannot be assured) that use of the relatively crude equipment at issue here will always be lawful. The Agema Thermovision 210 might disclose, for example, at what hour each night the lady of the house takes her daily sauna and bath—a detail that many would consider "intimate"; and a much more sophisticated system might detect nothing more intimate than the fact that someone left a closet light on. We * * * would have to develop a jurisprudence specifying which home activities are "intimate" and which are not. And even when (if ever) that jurisprudence were fully developed, no police officer would be able to know *in advance* whether his through-the-wall surveillance picks up "intimate" details—and thus would be unable to know in advance whether it is constitutional.

The dissent's proposed standard—whether the technology offers the "functional equivalent of actual presence in the area being searched"—would seem quite similar to our own at first blush. The dissent concludes that *Katz* was such a case, but then inexplicably asserts that if the same listening device only revealed the volume of the conversation, the surveillance would be permissible. Yet, if without technology, the police could not discern volume without being actually present in the phone booth, Justice Stevens should conclude a search has occurred. * * * Thus the driving force of the dissent, despite its recitation of the above standard, appears to be a distinction among different types of information—whether the "homeowner would even care if anybody noticed." The dissent offers no practical guidance for the application of this standard, and for reasons already discussed, we believe there can be none. The people in their houses, as well as the police, deserve more precision.[6]

We have said that the Fourth Amendment draws "a firm line at the entrance to the house." That line, we think, must be not only firm but also bright—which requires clear specification of those methods of surveillance that require a warrant. While it is certainly possible to conclude from the videotape of the thermal imaging that occurred in this case that no "significant" compromise of the homeowner's privacy has occurred, we must take the long view, from the original meaning of the Fourth Amendment forward. * * * Where, as here, the Government uses a device that is not in general public use, to explore details of the home that would previously have been unknowable without physical intrusion, the surveillance is a "search" and is presumptively unreasonable without a warrant. * * *

Justice STEVENS, with whom THE CHIEF JUSTICE, Justice O'CONNOR, and Justice KENNEDY join, dissenting. * * *

While the Court "take[s] the long view" and decides this case based largely on the potential of yet-to-be-developed technology that might allow "through-the-wall surveillance," this case involves nothing more than off-the-wall surveillance by law enforcement officers to gather information exposed to the general public from the outside of petitioner's home. All that the infrared camera did in this case was passively measure heat emitted from the exterior surfaces of petitioner's home; all that those measurements showed were relative differences in emission levels, vaguely indicating that some areas of the roof and outside walls were warmer than others. * * * [N]o details regarding the interior of petitioner's home were revealed. Unlike an x-ray scan, or other possible "through-the-wall" techniques, the detection of infrared radiation emanating from the home did not accomplish "an unauthorized physical penetration into the premises," *Silverman v. United States*, nor did it "obtain information that it could not have obtained by observation from outside the curtilage of the house." *United States v. Karo*.

Indeed, the ordinary use of the senses might enable a neighbor or passerby to notice the heat emanating from a building, particularly if it is vented, as was the case here. Additionally, any member of the public might notice that one part of a house is warmer than another part or a nearby building if, for example, rainwater evaporates or snow melts at different rates across its surfaces. Such use of the senses would not convert into an unreasonable search if, instead, an adjoining neighbor allowed an officer onto her property to verify her perceptions with a sensitive thermometer. Nor, in my view, does such observation become an

---

6. The dissent argues that we have injected potential uncertainty into the constitutional analysis by noting that whether or not the technology is in general public use may be a factor. That quarrel, however, is not with us but with this Court's precedent. See *Ciraolo* ("In an age where private and commercial flight in the public airways is routine, it is unreasonable for respondent to expect that his marijuana plants were constitutionally protected from being observed with the naked eye from an altitude of 1,000 feet"). Given that we can quite confidently say that thermal imaging is not "routine," we decline in this case to reexamine that factor.

unreasonable search if made from a distance with the aid of a device that merely discloses that the exterior of one house, or one area of the house, is much warmer than another. Nothing more occurred in this case.

Thus, the notion that heat emissions from the outside of a dwelling is a private matter implicating the protections of the Fourth Amendment (the text of which guarantees the right of people "to be secure *in* their * * * houses" against unreasonable searches and seizures) is not only unprecedented but also quite difficult to take seriously. Heat waves, like aromas that are generated in a kitchen, or in a laboratory or opium den, enter the public domain if and when they leave a building. A subjective expectation that they would remain private is not only implausible but also surely not "one that society is prepared to recognize as 'reasonable.'"

* * * [T]he equipment in this case did not penetrate the walls of petitioner's home, and while it did pick up "details of the home" that were exposed to the public, it did not obtain "any information regarding the *interior* of the home." In the Court's own words, based on what the thermal imager "showed" regarding the outside of petitioner's home, the officers "concluded" that petitioner was engaging in illegal activity inside the home. It would be quite absurd to characterize their thought processes as "searches," regardless of whether they inferred (rightly) that petitioner was growing marijuana in his house, or (wrongly) that "the lady of the house [was taking] her daily sauna and bath." * * *

* * * Just as "the police cannot reasonably be expected to avert their eyes from evidence of criminal activity that could have been observed by any member of the public," so too public officials should not have to avert their senses or their equipment from detecting emissions in the public domain such as excessive heat, traces of smoke, suspicious odors, odorless gases, airborne particulates, or radioactive emissions, any of which could identify hazards to the community. In my judgment, monitoring such emissions with "sense-enhancing technology," and drawing useful conclusions from such monitoring, is an entirely reasonable public service.

On the other hand, the countervailing privacy interest is at best trivial. After all, homes generally are insulated to keep heat in, rather than to prevent the detection of heat going out, and it does not seem to me that society will suffer from a rule requiring the rare homeowner who both intends to engage in uncommon activities that produce extraordinary amounts of heat, and wishes to conceal that production from outsiders, to make sure that the surrounding area is well insulated. * * *

Since what was involved in this case was nothing more than drawing inferences from off-the-wall surveillance, rather than any "through-the-wall" surveillance, the officers' conduct did not amount to a search and was perfectly reasonable.

II

* * * [T]he Court has fashioned a rule that is intended to provide essential guidance for the day when "more sophisticated systems" gain

the "ability to 'see' through walls and other opaque barriers." The newly minted rule encompasses "obtaining [1] by sense-enhancing technology [2] any information regarding the interior of the home [3] that could not otherwise have been obtained without physical intrusion into a constitutionally protected area * * * [4] at least where (as here) the technology in question is not in general public use." In my judgment, the Court's new rule is at once too broad and too narrow, and is not justified by the Court's explanation for its adoption. * * *

Despite the Court's attempt to draw a line that is "not only firm but also bright," the contours of its new rule are uncertain because its protection apparently dissipates as soon as the relevant technology is "in general public use." Yet how much use is general public use is not even hinted at by the Court's opinion, which makes the somewhat doubtful assumption that the thermal imager used in this case does not satisfy that criterion.[5] In any event, putting aside its lack of clarity, this criterion is somewhat perverse because it seems likely that the threat to privacy will grow, rather than recede, as the use of intrusive equipment becomes more readily available.

It is clear, however, that the category of "sense-enhancing technology" covered by the new rule is far too broad. It would, for example, embrace potential mechanical substitutes for dogs trained to react when they sniff narcotics. But in *United States v. Place*, [p. 113, Note 5], we held that a dog sniff that "discloses only the presence or absence of narcotics" does "not constitute a 'search' within the meaning of the Fourth Amendment," and it must follow that sense-enhancing equipment that identifies nothing but illegal activity is not a search either. Nevertheless, the use of such a device would be unconstitutional under the Court's rule, as would the use of other new devices that might detect the odor of deadly bacteria or chemicals for making a new type of high explosive, even if the devices (like the dog sniffs) are "so limited in both the manner in which" they obtain information and "in the content of the information" they reveal. * * *

Because the new rule applies to information regarding the "interior" of the home, it is too narrow as well as too broad. Clearly, a rule that is designed to protect individuals from the overly intrusive use of sense-enhancing equipment should not be limited to a home. If such equipment did provide its user with the functional equivalent of access to a private place—such as, for example, the telephone booth involved in *Katz*, or an office building—then the rule should apply to such an area as well as to a home. See *Katz* ("[T]he Fourth Amendment protects people, not places").* * *

---

5. The record describes a device that numbers close to a thousand manufactured units; that has a predecessor numbering in the neighborhood of 4,000 to 5,000 units; that competes with a similar product numbering from 5,000 to 6,000 units; and that is "readily available to the public" for commercial, personal, or law enforcement purposes, and is just an 800–number away from being rented from "half a dozen national companies" by anyone who wants one. * * *

The two reasons advanced by the Court as justifications for the adoption of its new rule are both unpersuasive. First, the Court suggests that its rule is compelled by our holding in *Katz*, because in that case, as in this, the surveillance consisted of nothing more than the monitoring of waves emanating from a private area into the public domain. Yet there are critical differences between the cases. In *Katz*, the electronic listening device attached to the outside of the phone booth allowed the officers to pick up the content of the conversation inside the booth, making them the functional equivalent of intruders because they gathered information that was otherwise available only to someone inside the private area; it would be as if, in this case, the thermal imager presented a view of the heat-generating activity inside petitioner's home. By contrast, the thermal imager here disclosed only the relative amounts of heat radiating from the house; it would be as if, in *Katz*, the listening device disclosed only the relative volume of sound leaving the booth, which presumably was discernible in the public domain.[6] * * * It is pure hyperbole for the Court to suggest that refusing to extend the holding of *Katz* to this case would leave the homeowner at the mercy of "technology that could discern all human activity in the home."

Second, the Court argues that the permissibility of "through-the-wall surveillance" cannot depend on a distinction between observing "intimate details" such as "the lady of the house [taking] her daily sauna and bath," and noticing only "the nonintimate rug on the vestibule floor" * * *. This entire argument assumes, of course, that the thermal imager in this case could or did perform "through-the-wall surveillance" that could identify any detail "that would previously have been unknowable without physical intrusion." In fact, the device could not and did not enable its user to identify either the lady of the house, the rug on the vestibule floor, or anything else inside the house * * *. * * *

III

* * * Instead of concentrating on the rather mundane issue that is actually presented by the case before it, the Court has endeavored to craft an all-encompassing rule for the future. It would be far wiser to give legislators an unimpeded opportunity to grapple with these emerging issues rather than to shackle them with prematurely devised constitutional constraints. * * *

NOTES AND QUESTIONS

1. As a matter of public policy, whom do you believe has the better side of the argument, Scalia or Stevens? Or, do you agree with Professor Wayne LaFave, who suggested that "after reading both opinions * * * I feel as if I have witnessed a sword fight in which both sides drew blood"? Wayne R.

---

6. The use of the latter device would be constitutional given *Smith v. Maryland*, which upheld the use of pen registers to record numbers dialed on a phone because, unlike "the listening device employed in *Katz* * * * pen registers do not acquire the contents of communications."

LaFave, *The Fourth Amendment as a "Big Time" TV Fad*, 53 Hastings L.J. 265, 277 (2001).

In terms of privacy from governmental intrusion, what should matter more in Fourth Amendment analysis: (1) where the government surveilling agent is physically located; or (2) where the private information is physically situated? Do you agree with Justice Scalia that in regard to the home "*all* details are intimate details," that should be "held safe from prying government eyes"?

Do you agree with one commentator who predicted that the rule announced by Justice Scalia, "despite its apparent strengthening of privacy protections, is likely to result in diluted Fourth Amendment protections in the long run"? Leading Cases, *Fourth Amendment—Warrantless Searches—Surveillance Technology,* 115 Harv. L. Rev. 346, 351 (2001). You will notice that the thermal imaging in *Kyllo* took place in 1991, a full decade before this case reached the high court. Why might that fact have caused the same commentator to observe that "the Court's rule quite possibly would not even protect Kyllo today"? *Id.* at 355.

2. Which opinion—the majority or the dissent—seems more faithful to the principles of *Katz*?

3. Beyond *Katz*, thinking back through the cases previously considered in this chapter—for example, the open-field doctrine (*Oliver*, p. 115), the aerial surveillance cases (p. 120), the beeper cases (p. 110), the garbage bag case (*Greenwood*, p. 125)—whom do you think has the better side of the argument in terms of precedent?

4. According to *Kyllo*, is it a "search" for the police to use a Geiger counter on public streets to locate plutonium (used in nuclear bomb-making) cached in someone's home?

What if some enterprising business tomorrow begins selling "pocket-thermal-imagers-'n'toenail-clippers" on cable television for $10.99 (but you get a second one free if you call within twenty minutes)? Would police use of a thermal imager *now* constitute a Fourth Amendment search? *See* John P. Elwood, *What Were They Thinking: The Supreme Court in Revue, October Term 2000*, 4 Green Bag 2d 365, 371 (2001).

5. Do you sense that if he had the votes, Justice Scalia would seek to overrule some of the pre-*Kyllo* "search" cases? If so, which ones would seem to be on his potential "hit list"?

In regard to *Katz* itself, Justice Scalia previously observed in Minnesota v. Carter, 525 U.S. 83, 119 S.Ct. 469, 142 L.Ed.2d 373 (1998) (concurring opinion):

> In my view, the only thing the past three decades have established about the *Katz* test (which has come to mean the test enunciated by Justice Harlan's separate concurrence in *Katz*) is that, unsurprisingly, those "actual (subjective) expectation[s] of privacy" "that society is prepared to recognize as 'reasonable,'" bear an uncanny resemblance to those expectations of privacy that this Court considers reasonable. When that self-indulgent test is employed * * * to determine whether a "search or seizure" within the meaning of the Constitution has *occurred* (as opposed

to whether that "search or seizure" is an "unreasonable" one), it has no plausible foundation in the text of the Fourth Amendment.

What does Scalia say about *Katz* in *Kyllo*?

6. *Kyllo* is not the only recent Supreme Court case to reverse the post-*Katz* trend of pro-law enforcement rulings. Consider Bond v. United States, 529 U.S. 334, 120 S.Ct. 1462, 146 L.Ed.2d 365 (2000), in which Border Patrol agents walked through a Greyhound bus stopped at a checkpoint and routinely squeezed the soft luggage that passengers had placed in the overhead storage bins. In Bond's case, an agent felt a brick-like object. Bond allowed the agents to open his luggage, at which point illegal drugs were discovered. At issue was the pre-consent squeezing of the luggage. Chief Justice Rehnquist, writing for seven members of the Court, held that this constituted a "search":

> [T]he Government asserts that by exposing his bag to the public, petitioner lost a reasonable expectation that his bag would not be physically manipulated. The Government relies on our [aerial surveillance] decisions in *California v. Ciraolo* and *Florida v. Riley* for the proposition that matters open to public observation are not protected by the Fourth Amendment. * * *

> But *Ciraolo* and *Riley* are different from this case because they involved only visual, as opposed to tactile, observation. Physically invasive inspection is simply more intrusive than purely visual inspection. * * *

> Our Fourth Amendment analysis embraces two questions. First, we ask whether the individual, by his conduct, has exhibited an actual expectation of privacy; that is, whether he has shown that "he [sought] to preserve [something] as private." Here, petitioner sought to preserve privacy by using an opaque bag and placing that bag directly above his seat. Second, we inquire whether the individual's expectation of privacy is "one that society is prepared to recognize as reasonable." When a bus passenger places a bag in an overhead bin, he expects that other passengers or bus employees may move it for one reason or another. Thus, a bus passenger clearly expects that his bag may be handled. He does not expect that other passengers or bus employees will, as a matter of course, feel the bag in an exploratory manner. But this is exactly what the agent did here. We therefore hold that the agent's physical manipulation of petitioner's bag violated the Fourth Amendment.

Do you agree? Justice Breyer, along with Justice Scalia, dissented:

> How does the "squeezing" just described differ from the treatment that overhead luggage is likely to receive from strangers in a world of travel that is somewhat less gentle than it used to be? I think not at all. * * *

> * * * Privacy itself implies the exclusion of uninvited strangers, not just strangers who work for the Government. Hence, an individual cannot reasonably expect privacy in respect to objects or activities that he "knowingly exposes to the public."

> Indeed, the Court has said that it is not objectively reasonable to expect privacy if "[a]ny member of the public * * * could have" used his

senses to detect "everything that th[e] officers observed." *California v. Ciraolo*. Thus, it has held that the fact that strangers may look down at fenced-in property from an aircraft or sift through garbage bags on a public street can justify a similar police intrusion. The comparative likelihood that strangers will give bags in an overhead compartment a hard squeeze would seem far greater. * * *

Nor can I accept the majority's effort to distinguish "tactile" from "visual" interventions, even assuming that distinction matters here. Whether tactile manipulation (say, of the exterior of luggage) is more intrusive or less intrusive than visual observation (say, through a lighted window) necessarily depends on the particular circumstances.

7. *A look at where we are in "search" law.* In view of post-*Katz* case law, does it seem to you that "search" law is where the *Katz* Court would have expected it to be? Consider Professor Scott Sundby's only somewhat-tongue-in-cheek observations:

To see just how far afield the Court has strayed, it is instructive to imagine compiling the Court's holdings concerning when the Fourth Amendment applies or, more accurately, does not apply into an *"Accidental Tourist's Guide to Maintaining Privacy Against Government Surveillance."* The advice would be rather astonishing:

To maintain privacy, one must not write any checks nor make any phone calls. It would be unwise to engage in conversation with any other person, or to walk, even on private property, outside one's house. If one is to barbecue or read in the backyard, do so only if surrounded by a fence higher than a double-decker bus and while sitting beneath an opaque awning. The wise individual might also consider purchasing anti-aerial spying devices if available (be sure to check the latest Sharper Image catalogue). Upon retiring inside, be sure to pull the shades together tightly so that no crack exists and to converse only in quiet tones. When discarding letters or other delicate materials, do so only after a thorough shredding of the documents (again see your Sharper Image catalogue); ideally, one would take the trash personally to the disposal site and bury it deep within. Finally, when buying items, carefully inspect them for any electronic tracking devices that may be attached.

Scott E. Sundby, *"Everyman' "s Fourth Amendment: Privacy or Mutual Trust Between Government and Citizen?*, 94 Colum. L. Rev. 1751, 1789–90 (1994).

Can you identify the cases Professor Sundby has in mind for each of the rules announced in his *Accidental Tourist* guide?

8. *Cell phones.* In light of everything you have read so far, culminating in *Kyllo*, as a matter of Fourth Amendment law is it a search if the police learn the location of a suspect based on the individual's use of her cell phone, which is equipped with GPS (Global Positioning System) technology? Is it a search if the police are able to listen to a cell phone conversation by intercepting the signals using widely available radio scanners? Regarding GPS technology generally, see Eva Marie Dowdell, *You Are Here!—Mapping the*

Boundaries of the Fourth Amendment with GPS Technology, 32 Rutgers Computer & Tech. L.J. 109 (2005).

9. Now, in light of everything you have read, do you believe that Justice Harlan's two-pronged "reasonable expectation of privacy" test is satisfactory? Is it a better test that the prior trespass doctrine? Can you come up with a better solution?

B. WHAT IS A "SEIZURE"?

UNITED STATES v. KARO

Supreme Court of the United States, 1984.
468 U.S. 705, 104 S.Ct. 3296, 82 L.Ed.2d 530.

JUSTICE WHITE delivered the opinion of the Court.

In *United States v. Knotts*, 460 U.S. 276, 103 S.Ct. 1081, 75 L.Ed.2d 55 (1983), we held that the warrantless monitoring of an electronic tracking device ("beeper") inside a container of chemicals did not violate the Fourth Amendment when it revealed no information that could not have been obtained through visual surveillance. In this case, we are called upon to address [a question] * * * left unresolved in *Knotts*: * * * whether installation of a beeper in a container of chemicals with the consent of the original owner constitutes a * * * seizure within the meaning of the Fourth Amendment when the container is delivered to a buyer having no knowledge of the presence of the beeper * * *.

I

In August 1980 Agent Rottinger of the Drug Enforcement Administration (DEA) learned that respondents James Karo, Richard Horton, and William Harley had ordered 50 gallons of ether from Government informant Carl Muehlenweg of Graphic Photo Design in Albuquerque, N. M. Muehlenweg told Rottinger that the ether was to be used to extract cocaine from clothing that had been imported into the United States. * * * With Muehlenweg's consent, agents substituted their own can containing a beeper for one of the cans in the shipment and then had all 10 cans painted to give them a uniform appearance. * * *

II

* * * It is clear that the actual placement of the beeper into the can violated no one's Fourth Amendment rights. The can into which the beeper was placed belonged at the time to the DEA * * *. The ether and the original 10 cans, on the other hand, belonged to, and were in the possession of, Muehlenweg, who had given his consent to any invasion of those items that occurred. Thus, even if there had been no substitution of cans and the agents had placed the beeper into one of the original 10 cans, Muehlenweg's consent was sufficient to validate the placement of the beeper in the can.

The Court of Appeals acknowledged that before Karo took control of the ether "the DEA and Muehlenweg presumably could do with the can and ether whatever they liked without violating Karo's rights." It did not hold that the actual placement of the beeper into the ether can violated the Fourth Amendment. Instead, it held that the violation occurred at the time the beeper-laden can was transferred to Karo. * * *

We * * * do not believe that the transfer of the container constituted a seizure. A "seizure" of property occurs when "there is some meaningful interference with an individual's possessory interests in that property." [*United States v. Jacobsen*, 466 U.S. 109, 104 S.Ct. 1652, 80 L.Ed.2d 85 (1984).] Although the can may have contained an unknown and unwanted foreign object, it cannot be said that anyone's possessory interest was interfered with in a meaningful way. At most, there was a technical trespass on the space occupied by the beeper. * * * Of course, if the presence of a beeper in the can constituted a seizure merely because of its occupation of space, it would follow that the presence of any object, regardless of its nature, would violate the Fourth Amendment. * * * .

[The concurring opinion of Justice O'Connor, with whom Justice Rehnquist joined, is omitted.]

Justice STEVENS, with whom Justice BRENNAN and Justice MARSHALL join, concurring in part and dissenting in part. * * *

I

The attachment of the beeper, in my judgment, constituted a "seizure." The owner of property, of course, has a right to exclude from it all the world, including the Government, and a concomitant right to use it exclusively for his own purposes. When the Government attaches an electronic monitoring device to that property, it infringes that exclusionary right; in a fundamental sense it has converted the property to its own use. Surely such an invasion is an "interference" with possessory rights; the right to exclude, which attached as soon as the can respondents purchased was delivered, had been infringed. That interference is also "meaningful"; the character of the property is profoundly different when infected with an electronic bug than when it is entirely germ free. * * *

* * * By attaching the beeper and using the container to conceal it, the Government in the most fundamental sense was asserting "dominion and control" over the property—the power to use the property for its own purposes. And "assert[ing] dominion and control" is a "seizure" in the most basic sense of that term. * * *

NOTES AND QUESTIONS

1. Suppose that a police officer installs a beeper inside the trunk of a suspect's automobile, parked on a public road? Does this constitute either a search or seizure? If it is a search, would it permissible for a blindfolded officer to install it in the trunk? If it is a seizure, how would you distinguish it from *Karo*?

2. Suppose that a police officer, properly inside a suspect's home, picks up a stereo turntable in order to record the serial number printed on the bottom. Is this a seizure of the turntable? See *Arizona v. Hicks*, Chapter 4.

3. *Problem*. A package is shipped from outside the country to the United States containing a photo album and cocaine. Aware of this, the government takes custody of the package when it arrives in the country. It holds it for ten days until an electronic beeper can be hidden in the cover of the photo album, after which the package is delivered to the intended recipient. Seizure? See State v. Kelly, 68 Haw. 213, 708 P.2d 820 (1985).

4. *Objects subject to seizure*. Law enforcement officers may seize what they have probable cause to believe is criminal evidence. Three categories of seizable items are: (1) contraband (evidence that may not lawfully be possessed by a private party); (2) fruits of a crime; and (3) instrumentalities used in the commission of an offense (*e.g.*, a weapon, an automobile for the getaway, etc.).

A fourth category of property is so-called "mere evidence," *i.e.*, an item of value to the police solely because it will help in the apprehension or conviction of a person for an offense. An example is a blood stained shirt in a homicide investigation. The item is not contraband, a fruit of the murder, or a criminal instrumentality. Its usefulness to law enforcement officers is limited to what it may provide in the way of evidence—such as the blood type of the killer—connecting a suspect to the crime.

Until 1967, "mere evidence" could not be seized by the police. Gouled v. United States, 255 U.S. 298, 41 S.Ct. 261, 65 L.Ed. 647 (1921). The Court's reasoning was that the Government could only seize property if it asserted a property interest superior to that of the possessor of the property. For reasons that need not detain us now, the Government was said to have a superior property interest in contraband and fruits and instrumentalities of criminal activity, but not as to "mere evidence."

The Supreme Court abandoned the "mere evidence" rule in 1967. It concluded that the doctrine was indefensible in light of the then-developing privacy principles of the Fourth Amendment. Warden v. Hayden, 387 U.S. 294, 87 S.Ct. 1642, 18 L.Ed.2d 782 (1967). Therefore, today (assuming probable cause) the police may seize contraband, fruits of a crime, criminal instrumentalities, as well as "mere evidence."

5. *Seizure of persons*. *Karo* involved seizure of property, but what constitutes a seizure of a person? According to the Supreme Court, "the quintessential 'seizure of the person' under our Fourth Amendment jurisprudence" is an arrest. California v. Hodari D., 499 U.S. 621, 111 S.Ct. 1547, 113 L.Ed.2d 690 (1991).

Although an arrest is the "quintessential" seizure of a person, a person can be "seized" for Fourth Amendment purposes short of an arrest. In Terry v. Ohio, 392 U.S. 1, 88 S.Ct. 1868, 20 L.Ed.2d 889 (1968), the Court stated that a seizure occurs "when the officer, by means of physical force or show of authority has *in some way* restrained the liberty of a citizen" (emphasis added). Even a temporary detention of a person by an officer constitutes a Fourth Amendment seizure. The law regarding seizures of persons is better understood in the context of other Fourth Amendment doctrines considered in the next chapter.

CHAPTER 4

THE SUBSTANCE OF THE FOURTH AMENDMENT

■ ■ ■

A. PROBABLE CAUSE

INTRODUCTORY COMMENT

The Fourth Amendment prohibits *unreasonable* searches and seizures. Very generally speaking, this means that searches and seizures must be supported by probable cause. Put differently, a search or seizure conducted *in the absence* of probable cause ordinarily is considered an *unreasonable one*. As the Court has put it, "probable cause" is the "traditional standard" of the Fourth Amendment. Arizona v. Hicks, 480 U.S. 321, 107 S.Ct. 1149, 94 L.Ed.2d 347 (1987).

It is easier to state the definition of "probable cause" than it is to determine whether it exists in a particular case. Probable cause to arrest "exists where 'the facts and circumstances within [the officers'] knowledge and of which they [have] reasonably trustworthy information [are] sufficient in themselves to warrant a man of reasonable caution in the belief that' *an offense has been or is being committed*" by the person to be arrested. Brinegar v. United States, 338 U.S. 160, 69 S.Ct. 1302, 93 L.Ed. 1879 (1949) (quoting Carroll v. United States, 267 U.S. 132, 45 S.Ct. 280, 69 L.Ed. 543 (1925)) (emphasis added). The same definition applies to "probable cause to search," except that the italicized language is replaced with "evidence subject to seizure will be found in the place to be searched."

Procedurally, the issue of probable cause typically arises in one of two circumstances. First, the police may apply to a magistrate for an arrest or search warrant. Warrants constitutionally may only be issued if there is probable cause to make the arrest or conduct the search. Therefore, the police must set out for the magistrate, under oath, the information in their possession that they believe justifies issuance of the warrant, *i.e.*, the facts that constitute probable cause for the arrest or search.

Alternatively, the police may conduct an arrest or search without a warrant. Assuming that it results in seizure of criminal evidence, the defendant may seek to have this evidence excluded from the trial at a suppression hearing. The defendant may argue that the police acted in violation of the Fourth Amendment because they did not obtain a warrant (an issue to which we will turn shortly), or she may argue that, warrant issues aside, the police lacked probable cause. In the latter case, the judge must decide whether the police had adequate evidence—probable cause— *before* they conducted the warrantless search or arrest. She must ask herself, in essence, "If the police *had* sought a warrant, would it have been granted?," although, as we will see, the judge should place a somewhat higher burden on the government to prove "probable cause" in such warrantless circumstances than if the police had originally sought a warrant.

SPINELLI v. UNITED STATES

Supreme Court of the United States, 1969.
393 U.S. 410, 89 S.Ct. 584, 21 L.Ed.2d 637.

MR. JUSTICE HARLAN delivered the opinion of the Court.

William Spinelli was convicted under 18 U. S. C. § 1952 of traveling to St. Louis, Missouri, from a nearby Illinois suburb with the intention of conducting gambling activities proscribed by Missouri law. At every appropriate stage in the proceedings in the lower courts, the petitioner challenged the constitutionality of the warrant which authorized the FBI search that uncovered the evidence necessary for his conviction. * * * Believing it desirable that the principles of *Aguilar* [*v. Texas*, 378 U.S. 108, 84 S.Ct. 1509, 12 L.Ed.2d 723 (1964)] should be further explicated, we granted certiorari * * *. For reasons that follow we reverse.

In *Aguilar*, a search warrant had issued upon an affidavit of police officers who swore only that they had "received reliable information from a credible person and do believe" that narcotics were being illegally stored on the described premises. While recognizing that the constitutional requirement of probable cause can be satisfied by hearsay information, this Court held the affidavit inadequate for two reasons. First, the application failed to set forth any of the "underlying circumstances" necessary to enable the magistrate independently to judge of the validity of the informant's conclusion that the narcotics were where he said they were. Second, the affiant-officers did not attempt to support their claim that their informant was " 'credible' or his information 'reliable.' " The Government is, however, quite right in saying that the FBI affidavit in the present case is more ample than that in *Aguilar*. Not only does it contain a report from an anonymous informant, but it also contains a report of an independent FBI investigation which is said to corroborate the informant's tip. We are, then, required to delineate the manner in which *Aguilar*'s two-pronged test should be applied in these circumstances.

In essence, the affidavit * * * contained the following allegations:

1. The FBI had kept track of Spinelli's movements on five days during the month of August 1965. On four of these occasions, Spinelli was seen crossing one of two bridges leading from Illinois into St.

Louis, Missouri, between 11 a.m. and 12:15 p.m. On four of the five days, Spinelli was also seen parking his car in a lot used by residents of an apartment house at 1108 Indian Circle Drive in St. Louis, between 3:30 p.m. and 4:45 p.m. On one day, Spinelli was followed further and seen to enter a particular apartment in the building.

2. An FBI check with the telephone company revealed that this apartment contained two telephones listed under the name of Grace P. Hagen, and carrying the numbers WYdown 4–0029 and WYdown 4–0136.

3. The application stated that "William Spinelli is known to this affiant and to federal law enforcement agents and local law enforcement agents as a bookmaker, an associate of bookmakers, a gambler, and an associate of gamblers."

4. Finally, it was stated that the FBI "has been informed by a confidential reliable informant that William Spinelli is operating a handbook and accepting wagers and disseminating wagering information by means of the telephones which have been assigned the numbers WYdown 4–0029 and WYdown 4–0136."

There can be no question that the last item mentioned, detailing the informant's tip, has a fundamental place in this warrant application. Without it, probable cause could not be established. The first two items reflect only innocent-seeming activity and data. Spinelli's travels to and from the apartment building and his entry into a particular apartment on one occasion could hardly be taken as bespeaking gambling activity; and there is surely nothing unusual about an apartment containing two separate telephones. Many a householder indulges himself in this petty luxury. Finally, the allegation that Spinelli was "known" to the affiant and to other federal and local law enforcement officers as a gambler and an associate of gamblers is but a bald and unilluminating assertion of suspicion that is entitled to no weight in appraising the magistrate's decision. *Nathanson v. United States*, 290 U.S. 41, 46, 54 S.Ct. 11, 12, 78 L.Ed. 159 (1933).

So much indeed the Government does not deny. Rather, * * * the Government claims that the informant's tip gives a suspicious color to the FBI's reports detailing Spinelli's innocent-seeming conduct and that, conversely, the FBI's surveillance corroborates the informant's tip, thereby entitling it to more weight. It is true, of course, that the magistrate is obligated to render a judgment based upon a common-sense reading of the entire affidavit. We believe, however, that the "totality of circumstances" approach taken by the Court of Appeals paints with too broad a brush. Where, as here, the informer's tip is a necessary element in a finding of probable cause, its proper weight must be determined by a more precise analysis.

The informer's report must first be measured against *Aguilar*'s standards so that its probative value can be assessed. If the tip is found inadequate under *Aguilar*, the other allegations which corroborate the information contained in the hearsay report should then be considered. At this stage as well, however, the standards enunciated in *Aguilar* must inform the magistrate's decision. He must ask: Can it fairly be said that the tip, even when certain parts of it have been corroborated by independent sources, is as trustworthy as a tip which would pass *Aguilar*'s tests without independent corroboration? *Aguilar* is relevant at this stage of the inquiry as well because the tests it establishes were designed to implement the long-standing principle that probable cause must be determined by a "neutral and detached magistrate," and not by "the officer engaged in the often competitive enterprise of ferreting out crime." A magistrate cannot be said to have properly discharged his constitutional duty if he relies on an informer's tip which—even when partially corroborated—is not as reliable as one which passes *Aguilar*'s requirements when standing alone.

Applying these principles to the present case, we first consider the weight to be given the informer's tip when it is considered apart from the rest of the affidavit. It is clear that a Commissioner could not credit it without abdicating his constitutional function. Though the affiant swore that his confidant was "reliable," he offered the magistrate no reason in support of this conclusion. Perhaps even more important is the fact that *Aguilar*'s other test has not been satisfied. The tip does not contain a sufficient statement of the underlying circumstances from which the informer concluded that Spinelli was running a bookmaking operation. We are not told how the FBI's source received his information—it is not alleged that the informant personally observed Spinelli at work or that he had ever placed a bet with him. Moreover, if the informant came by the information indirectly, he did not explain why his sources were reliable. In the absence of a statement detailing the manner in which the information was gathered, it is especially important that the tip describe the accused's criminal activity in sufficient detail that the magistrate may know that he is relying on something more substantial than a casual rumor circulating in the underworld or an accusation based merely on an individual's general reputation.

The detail provided by the informant in *Draper v. United States*, 358 U.S. 307, 79 S.Ct. 329, 3 L.Ed.2d 327 (1959), provides a suitable benchmark. While Hereford, the Government's informer in that case, did not state the way in which he had obtained his information, he reported that Draper had gone to Chicago the day before by train and that he would return to Denver by train with three ounces of heroin on one of two specified mornings. Moreover, Hereford went on to describe, with minute particularity, the clothes that Draper would be wearing upon his arrival at the Denver station. A magistrate, when confronted with such detail, could reasonably infer that the informant had gained his information in a reliable way.[1] Such an inference cannot be made in the present case. Here, the only facts supplied were that Spinelli was using two specified tele-

---

1. While *Draper* involved the question whether the police had probable cause for an arrest without a warrant, the analysis required for an answer to this question is basically similar to that demanded of a magistrate when he considers whether a search warrant should issue.

phones and that these phones were being used in gambling operations. This meager report could easily have been obtained from an offhand remark heard at a neighborhood bar.

Nor do we believe that the patent doubts *Aguilar* raises as to the report's reliability are adequately resolved by a consideration of the allegations detailing the FBI's independent investigative efforts. At most, these allegations indicated that Spinelli could have used the telephones specified by the informant for some purpose. This cannot by itself be said to support both the inference that the informer was generally trustworthy and that he had made his charge against Spinelli on the basis of information obtained in a reliable way. Once again, *Draper* provides a relevant comparison. Independent police work in that case corroborated much more than one small detail that had been provided by the informant. There, the police, upon meeting the inbound Denver train on the second morning specified by informer Hereford, saw a man whose dress corresponded precisely to Hereford's detailed description. It was then apparent that the informant had not been fabricating his report out of whole cloth; since the report was of the sort which in common experience may be recognized as having been obtained in a reliable way, it was perfectly clear that probable cause had been established.

We conclude, then, that in the present case the informant's tip—even when corroborated to the extent indicated—was not sufficient to provide the basis for a finding of probable cause. This is not to say that the tip was so insubstantial that it could not properly have counted in the magistrate's determination. Rather, it needed some further support. When we look to the other parts of the application, however, we find nothing alleged which would permit the suspicions engendered by the informant's report to ripen into a judgment that a crime was probably being committed. * * * [T]he allegations detailing the FBI's surveillance of Spinelli and its investigation of the telephone company records contain no suggestion of criminal conduct when taken by themselves—and they are not endowed with an aura of suspicion by virtue of the informer's tip. Nor do we find that the FBI's reports take on a sinister color when read in light of common knowledge that bookmaking is often carried on over the telephone and from premises ostensibly used by others for perfectly normal purposes. Such an argument would carry weight in a situation in which the premises contain an unusual number of telephones or abnormal activity is observed, but it does not fit this case where neither of these factors is present. All that remains to be considered is the flat statement that Spinelli was "known" to the FBI and others as a gambler. But just as a simple assertion of police suspicion is not itself a sufficient basis for a magistrate's finding of probable cause, we do not believe it may be used to give additional weight to allegations that would otherwise be insufficient.

The affidavit, then, falls short of the standards set forth in *Aguilar*, *Draper*, and our other decisions that give content to the notion of probable cause. * * * [W]e cannot sustain this warrant without diluting important safeguards that assure that the judgment of a disinterested judicial officer will interpose itself between the police and the citizenry.

The judgment of the Court of Appeals is reversed * * *. * * *

Mr. Justice MARSHALL took no part in the consideration or decision of this case. * * *

Mr. Justice WHITE, concurring.

An investigator's affidavit that he has seen gambling equipment being moved into a house at a specified address will support the issuance of a search warrant. The oath affirms the honesty of the statement and negatives the lie or imagination. Personal observation attests to the facts asserted—that there is gambling equipment on the premises at the named address.

But if the officer simply avers, without more, that there is gambling paraphernalia on certain premises, the warrant should not issue, even though the belief of the officer is an honest one, as evidenced by his oath, and even though the magistrate knows him to be an experienced, intelligent officer who has been reliable in the past. This much was settled in *Nathanson v. United States*, [*supra*,] where the Court held insufficient an officer's affidavit swearing he had cause to believe that there was illegal liquor on the premises for which the warrant was sought. The unsupported assertion or belief of the officer does not satisfy the requirement of probable cause. What is missing in *Nathanson* and like cases is a statement of the basis for the affiant's believing the facts contained in the affidavit—the good "cause" which the officer in *Nathanson* said he had. If an officer swears that there is gambling equipment at a certain address, the possibilities are (1) that he has seen the equipment; (2) that he has observed or perceived facts from which the presence of the equipment may reasonably be inferred; and (3) that he has obtained the information from someone else. If (1) is true, the affidavit is good. But in (2), the affidavit is insufficient unless the perceived facts are given, for it is the magistrate, not the officer, who is to judge the existence of probable cause. With respect to (3), where the officer's information is hearsay, no warrant should issue absent good cause for crediting that hearsay. Because an affidavit asserting, without more, the location of gambling equipment at a particular address does not claim personal observation of any of the facts by the officer, and because of the likelihood that the information came from an unidentified third party, affidavits of this type are unacceptable.

Neither should the warrant issue if the officer states that there is gambling equipment in a particular apartment and that his information comes from an informant, named or unnamed, since the honesty of the informant and the basis for his report are unknown. Nor would the missing elements be completely supplied by the officer's oath that the informant has often furnished reliable information in the past. This attests to the honesty of the informant, but *Aguilar v. Texas*, *supra*, requires something more—did the information come from observation, or did the informant in turn receive it from another? Absent additional facts for believing the informant's report, his assertion stands no better than the oath of the officer to the same effect. Indeed, if the affidavit of an officer, known by the magistrate to be honest and experienced, stating that gambling equipment is located in a certain building is unacceptable, it would be quixotic if a similar statement from an honest informant were found to furnish probable cause. * * *

If the affidavit rests on hearsay—an informant's report—what is necessary under *Aguilar* is one of two things: the informant must declare either (1) that he has himself seen or perceived the fact or facts asserted; or (2) that his information is hearsay, but there is good reason for believing it—perhaps one of the usual grounds for crediting hearsay information. The first presents few problems: since the report, although hearsay, purports to be first-hand observation, remaining doubt centers on the honesty of the informant, and that worry is dissipated by the officer's previous experience with the informant. The other basis for accepting the informant's report is more complicated. But if, for example, the informer's hearsay comes from one of the actors in the crime in the nature of admission against interest, the affidavit giving this information should be held sufficient.

I am inclined to agree with the majority that there are limited special circumstances in which an "honest" informant's report, if sufficiently detailed, will in effect verify itself—that is, the magistrate when confronted with such detail could reasonably infer that the informant had gained his information in a reliable way. Detailed information may sometimes imply that the informant himself has observed the facts. Suppose an informant with whom an officer has had satisfactory experience states that there is gambling equipment in the living room of a specified apartment and describes in detail not only the equipment itself but also the appointments and furnishings in the apartment. Detail like this, if true at all, must rest on personal observation either of the informant or of someone else. If the latter, we know nothing of the third person's honesty or sources; he may be making a wholly false report. But it is arguable that on these facts it was the informant himself who has perceived the facts, for the information reported is not usually the subject of casual, day-to-day conversation. Because the informant is honest and it is probable that he has viewed the facts, there is probable cause for the issuance of a warrant.

So too in the special circumstances of *Draper v. United States*, the kind of information related by the informant is not generally sent ahead of a person's arrival in a city except to those who are intimately connected with making careful arrangements for meeting him. The informant, posited as honest, somehow had the reported facts, very likely from one of the actors in the plan, or as one of them himself. The majority's suggestion is that a warrant could have been obtained based only on the informer's report. I am inclined to agree, although it seems quite plain that if it may be so easily inferred from the affidavit that the informant has himself observed the facts or has them from an actor in the event, no possible harm could come from requiring a statement to that effect, thereby removing the difficult and recurring questions which arise in such situations.

Of course, *Draper* itself did not proceed on this basis. Instead, the Court pointed out that when the officer saw a person getting off the train at the specified time, dressed and conducting himself precisely as the informant had predicted, all but the critical fact with respect to possessing narcotics had then been verified and for that reason the officer had "reasonable grounds" to believe also that Draper was carrying narcotics. Unquestionably, verification of arrival time, dress, and gait reinforced the honesty of the informant—he had not reported a made-up story. But if what *Draper* stands for is that the existence of the tenth and critical fact is made sufficiently probable to justify the issuance of a warrant by verifying nine other facts coming from the same source, I have my doubts about that case.

* * * [T]he proposition is not that the tenth fact may be logically inferred from the other nine or that the tenth fact is usually found in conjunction with the other nine. No one would suggest that just anyone getting off the 10:30 train dressed as Draper was, with a brisk walk and carrying a zipper bag, should be arrested for carrying narcotics. The thrust of *Draper* is not that the verified facts have independent significance with respect to proof of the tenth. The argument instead relates to the reliability of the source: because an informant is right about some things, he is more probably right about other facts, usually the critical, unverified facts. * * *

The tension between *Draper* and the *Nathanson-Aguilar* line of cases is evident from the course followed by the majority opinion. First, it is held that the report from a reliable informant that Spinelli is using two telephones with specified numbers to conduct a gambling business plus Spinelli's reputation in police circles as a gambler does not add up to probable cause. This is wholly consistent with *Aguilar* and *Nathanson*: the informant did not reveal whether he had personally observed the facts or heard them from another and, if the latter, no basis for crediting the hearsay was presented. Nor were the facts, as Mr. Justice Harlan says, of such a nature that they normally would be obtainable only by the personal observation of the informant himself. The police, however, did not stop with the informant's report. Independently, they established the existence of two phones having the given numbers and located them in an apartment house which Spinelli was regularly frequenting away from his home. There remained little question but that Spinelli was using the phones, and it was a fair inference that the use was not for domestic but for business purposes. The informant had claimed the business involved gambling. Since his specific information about Spinelli using two phones with particular numbers had been verified, did not his allegation about gambling thereby become sufficiently more believable if the *Draper* principle is to be given any scope at all? I would think so, particularly since the information from the informant which was verified was not neutral, irrelevant information but was material to proving the gambling allegation: two phones with different numbers in an apartment used away from home indicates a business use in an operation, like bookmaking, where multiple phones are needed. The *Draper* approach would reasonably justify the issuance of a warrant in this case, particularly since the police had some awareness of Spinelli's past activities. The majority, however, while seemingly embracing *Draper*, confines that case to its own facts. Pending full-scale reconsideration of that case, on the one hand, or of the *Nathanson-Aguilar* cases on the other, I join the opinion of the Court and the judgment of reversal, especially since a vote to affirm would produce an equally divided Court.

[The dissenting opinions of Justices Black, Fortas, and Stewart are omitted.]

NOTES AND QUESTIONS

1. Suppose that your professor announced in class that the dean of your law school "has cocaine in her office, which she uses every morning." Based exclusively on this statement, would you believe your professor's claim? If you were a magistrate, and if you were told this under oath by your professor, would you issue a warrant to search the dean's office? If not, why not? What more information, if any, would you demand? Are the factors you would consider in making a judgment in your dean's case similar to those set out by the Supreme Court in *Spinelli* and *Aguilar* (discussed in *Spinelli*)?

2. One highly respected Maryland judge explains the magistrate's job, as set out in *Aguilar-Spinelli*, this way:

> The simple thrust of these decisions is that whatever rules govern the evaluation of information from the primary source—the affiant— govern also the evaluation of information from the secondary source—the non-swearing, non-appearing, off-warrant declarant, *i.e.*, the informant. Whether the magistrate is dealing with a primary, a secondary or even, theoretically, a tertiary source, he must still (1) assess the credibility of that source and (2) then weigh the information furnished if he believes it to be true.

> Whether the information being evaluated is the direct observation of the affiant or is hearsay information, the issuing magistrate is required to perform the same intellectual surgery. In determining the existence *vel non* of probable cause, the magistrate must make two distinct determinations. * * * He must:

>> (1) Evaluate the truthfulness of the source of the information; and

>> (2) Evaluate the adequacy of the factual premises furnished by that source to support the validity of the source's conclusion.

> In the first instance, he is judging the integrity of a person. In the second instance, he is judging the logic of a proposition. These functions are distinct. They are the direct analogues of those other functions performed by the ultimate finder of fact who (1) assesses the credibility of

a witness and (2) then assesses the weight to be given the testimony of that witness.

Charles E. Moylan, Jr., *Hearsay and Probable Cause: An* Aguilar *and* Spinelli *Primer*, 25 Mercer L. Rev. 741, 750–51 (1974).

3.   What does Justice Harlan mean by the "two-pronged" test of *Aguilar*? What are the prongs?

4.   What does Justice White mean when he says that an informant's highly detailed information, such as existed in *Draper v. United States* (discussed in *Spinelli*), "will in effect verify itself." Do you agree?

5.   In what way did police corroboration of some of the claims made by informant Hereford in *Draper* strengthen the probable cause claim? Why does corroboration of entirely innocent conduct—*e.g.*, that Draper got off a particular train dressed in a particular way—support the critical finding that he was carrying heroin on his person?

6.   In determining credibility, Judge Moylan has observed that "[t]estimonials from friends, neighbors, and business associates as to [an informant's] reputation for 'truth and veracity' would be highly relevant. As a practical matter, 'stool pigeons' are neither Boy Scouts, princes of the church, nor recipients of testimonials." Moylan, *supra*, at 758. How, then, does a police officer convince a judge that an informant is credible? How does the officer convince the magistrate that *she* (the officer-affiant) is credible?

7.   *Bobo, a police officer's friendly four-legged informant.* In United States v. Florez, 871 F.Supp. 1411 (D.N.M.1994), a police officer's dog, Bobo, sniffed luggage in a train station and alerted the officer to the supposed presence of a controlled substance inside certain suitcases. The police seized the luggage, opened it, and discovered large quantities of cocaine.

Bobo got it right, but dogs, like humans, are imperfect. As Justice Souter stated in his dissent in Illinois v. Caballes, 543 U.S. 405, 125 S.Ct. 834, 160 L.Ed.2d 842 (2005), "[t]he infallible dog * * * is a creature of legal fiction." As a dog trainer testified in *Florez, supra*, "dogs are not unlike humans, dogs can have good and bad days just like we can." Indeed, reconsider the data on "dog sniffing" recounted by Justice Souter in *Caballes* (p. 114). How should a court go about evaluating the reliability of the Bobos of this world?

ILLINOIS v. GATES

Supreme Court of the United States, 1983.
462 U.S. 213, 103 S.Ct. 2317, 76 L.Ed.2d 527.

JUSTICE REHNQUIST delivered the opinion of the Court. * * *

II

* * * Bloomingdale, Ill., is a suburb of Chicago located in Du Page County. On May 3, 1978, the Bloomingdale Police Department received by mail an anonymous handwritten letter which read as follows:

"This letter is to inform you that you have a couple in your town who strictly make their living on selling drugs. They are Sue and

Lance Gates, they live on Greenway, off Bloomingdale Rd. in the condominiums. Most of their buys are done in Florida. Sue his wife drives their car to Florida, where she leaves it to be loaded up with drugs, then Lance flys down and drives it back. Sue flys back after she drops the car off in Florida. May 3 she is driving down there again and Lance will be flying down in a few days to drive it back. At the time Lance drives the car back he has the trunk loaded with over $100,000.00 in drugs. Presently they have over $100,000.00 worth of drugs in their basement.

"They brag about the fact they never have to work, and make their entire living on pushers.

"I guarantee if you watch them carefully you will make a big catch. They are friends with some big drugs dealers, who visit their house often.

"Lance & Susan Gates

"Greenway

"in Condominiums"

The letter was referred by the Chief of Police of the Bloomingdale Police Department to Detective Mader, who decided to pursue the tip. Mader learned, from the office of the Illinois Secretary of State, that an Illinois driver's license had been issued to one Lance Gates, residing at a stated address in Bloomingdale. He contacted a confidential informant, whose examination of certain financial records revealed a more recent address for the Gateses, and he also learned from a police officer assigned to O'Hare Airport that "L. Gates" had made a reservation on Eastern Airlines Flight 245 to West Palm Beach, Fla., scheduled to depart from Chicago on May 5 at 4:15 p.m.

Mader then made arrangements with an agent of the Drug Enforcement Administration for surveillance of the May 5 Eastern Airlines flight. The agent later reported to Mader that Gates had boarded the flight, and that federal agents in Florida had observed him arrive in West Palm Beach and take a taxi to the nearby Holiday Inn. They also reported that Gates went to a room registered to one Susan Gates and that, at 7 o'clock the next morning, Gates and an unidentified woman left the motel in a Mercury bearing Illinois license plates and drove northbound on an interstate highway frequently used by travelers to the Chicago area. In addition, the DEA agent informed Mader that the license plate number on the Mercury was registered to a Hornet station wagon owned by Gates. The agent also advised Mader that the driving time between West Palm Beach and Bloomingdale was approximately 22 to 24 hours.

Mader signed an affidavit setting forth the foregoing facts, and submitted it to a judge of the Circuit Court of Du Page County, together with a copy of the anonymous letter. The judge of that court thereupon issued a search warrant for the Gateses' residence and for their automobile. * * *

At 5:15 a.m. on March 7, only 36 hours after he had flown out of Chicago, Lance Gates, and his wife, returned to their home in Bloomingdale, driving the car in which they had left West Palm Beach some 22 hours earlier. The Bloomingdale police were awaiting them, searched the trunk of the Mercury, and uncovered approximately 350 pounds of marihuana. A search of the Gateses' home revealed marihuana, weapons, and other contraband. * * *

The Illinois Supreme Court concluded—and we are inclined to agree—that, standing alone, the anonymous letter sent to the Bloomingdale Police Department would not provide the basis for a magistrate's determination that there was probable cause to believe contraband would be found in the Gateses' car and home. The letter provides virtually nothing from which one might conclude that its author is either honest or his information reliable; likewise, the letter gives absolutely no indication of the basis for the writer's predictions regarding the Gateses' criminal activities. Something more was required, then, before a magistrate could conclude that there was probable cause to believe that contraband would be found in the Gateses' home and car. See *Aguilar v. Texas*, 378 U.S. [108, 109 n. 1, 84 S.Ct. 1509, 1511 n. 1, 12 L.Ed.2d 723 (1964)]; *Nathanson v. United States*, 290 U.S. 41, 54 S.Ct. 11, 78 L.Ed. 159 (1933).

The Illinois Supreme Court also properly recognized that Detective Mader's affidavit might be capable of supplementing the anonymous letter with information sufficient to permit a determination of probable cause. In holding that the affidavit in fact did not contain sufficient additional information to sustain a determination of probable cause, the Illinois court applied a "two-pronged test," derived from our decision in *Spinelli v. United States*, [p. 142]. The Illinois Supreme Court, like some others, apparently understood *Spinelli* as requiring that the anonymous letter satisfy each of two independent requirements before it could be relied on. According to this view, the letter, as supplemented by Mader's affidavit, first had to adequately reveal the "basis of knowledge" of the letterwriter—the particular means by which he came by the information given in his report. Second, it had to provide facts sufficiently establishing either the "veracity" of the affiant's informant, or, alternatively, the "reliability" of the informant's report in this particular case.

The Illinois court, alluding to an elaborate set of legal rules that have developed among various lower courts to enforce the "two-pronged test,"[4] found that the test had not been satisfied. First, the "veracity" prong was not satisfied because, "[t]here was simply no basis [for] conclud[ing] that

---

4. In summary, these rules posit that the "veracity" prong of the *Spinelli* test has two "spurs"—the informant's "credibility" and the "reliability" of his information. Various interpretations are advanced for the meaning of the "reliability" spur of the "veracity" prong. Both the "basis of knowledge" prong and the "veracity" prong are treated as entirely separate requirements, which must be independently satisfied in every case in order to sustain a determination of probable cause. Some ancillary doctrines are relied on to satisfy certain of the foregoing requirements. For example, the "self-verifying detail" of a tip may satisfy the "basis of knowledge" requirement, although not the "credibility" spur of the "veracity" prong. Conversely, corroboration would seem not capable of supporting the "basis of knowledge" prong, but only the "veracity" prong.

the anonymous person [who wrote the letter to the Bloomingdale Police Department] was credible." The court indicated that corroboration by police of details contained in the letter might never satisfy the "veracity" prong, and in any event, could not do so if, as in the present case, only "innocent" details are corroborated. In addition, the letter gave no indication of the basis of its writer's knowledge of the Gateses' activities. * * *

We agree with the Illinois Supreme Court that an informant's "veracity," "reliability," and "basis of knowledge" are all highly relevant in determining the value of his report. We do not agree, however, that these elements should be understood as entirely separate and independent requirements to be rigidly exacted in every case, which the opinion of the Supreme Court of Illinois would imply. Rather, as detailed below, they should be understood simply as closely intertwined issues that may usefully illuminate the commonsense, practical question whether there is "probable cause" to believe that contraband or evidence is located in a particular place.

III

This totality-of-the-circumstances approach is far more consistent with our prior treatment of probable cause than is any rigid demand that specific "tests" be satisfied by every informant's tip. Perhaps the central teaching of our decisions bearing on the probable-cause standard is that it is a "practical, nontechnical conception." *Brinegar v. United States*, 338 U.S. 160, 176, 69 S.Ct. 1302, 1311, 93 L.Ed. 1879 (1949). "In dealing with probable cause, * * * as the very name implies, we deal with probabilities. These are not technical; they are the factual and practical considerations of everyday life on which reasonable and prudent men, not legal technicians, act." * * *

As these comments illustrate, probable cause is a fluid concept—turning on the assessment of probabilities in particular factual contexts—not readily, or even usefully, reduced to a neat set of legal rules. Informants' tips doubtless come in many shapes and sizes from many different types of persons. * * * Rigid legal rules are ill-suited to an area of such diversity. * * *

Moreover, the "two-pronged test" directs analysis into two largely independent channels—the informant's "veracity" or "reliability" and his "basis of knowledge." There are persuasive arguments against according these two elements such independent status. Instead, they are better understood as relevant considerations in the totality-of-the-circumstances analysis that traditionally has guided probable-cause determinations: a deficiency in one may be compensated for, in determining the overall reliability of a tip, by a strong showing as to the other, or by some other indicia of reliability.

If, for example, a particular informant is known for the unusual reliability of his predictions of certain types of criminal activities in a locality, his failure, in a particular case, to thoroughly set forth the basis of his knowledge surely should not serve as an absolute bar to a finding of probable cause based on his tip. Likewise, if an unquestionably honest citizen comes forward with a report of criminal activity—which if fabricated would subject him to criminal liability—we have found rigorous scrutiny of the basis of his knowledge unnecessary. Conversely, even if we entertain some doubt as to an informant's motives, his explicit and detailed description of alleged wrongdoing, along with a statement that the event was observed firsthand, entitles his tip to greater weight than might otherwise be the case. Unlike a totality-of-the-circumstances analysis, which permits a balanced assessment of the relative weights of all the various indicia of reliability (and unreliability) attending an informant's tip, the "two-pronged test" has encouraged an excessively technical dissection of informants' tips, with undue attention being focused on isolated issues that cannot sensibly be divorced from the other facts presented to the magistrate.

As early as *Locke v. United States*, 7 Cranch 339, 348, 3 L.Ed. 364 (1813), Chief Justice Marshall observed, in a closely related context: "[T]he term 'probable cause,' according to its usual acceptation, means less than evidence which would justify condemnation * * *. It imports a seizure made under circumstances which warrant suspicion." More recently, we stated that "the *quanta* * * * of proof" appropriate in ordinary judicial proceedings are inapplicable to the decision to issue a warrant. Finely tuned standards such as proof beyond a reasonable doubt or by a preponderance of the evidence, useful in formal trials, have no place in the magistrate's decision. While an effort to fix some general, numerically precise degree of certainty corresponding to "probable cause" may not be helpful, it is clear that "only the probability, and not a prima facie showing, of criminal activity is the standard of probable cause."

We also have recognized that affidavits "are normally drafted by nonlawyers in the midst and haste of a criminal investigation. Technical requirements of elaborate specificity once exacted under common law pleadings have no proper place in this area." Likewise, search and arrest warrants long have been issued by persons who are neither lawyers nor judges, and who certainly do not remain abreast of each judicial refinement of the nature of "probable cause." The rigorous inquiry into the *Spinelli* prongs and the complex superstructure of evidentiary and analytical rules that some have seen implicit in our *Spinelli* decision, cannot be reconciled with the fact that many warrants are—quite properly—issued on the basis of nontechnical, common-sense judgments of laymen applying a standard less demanding than those used in more formal legal proceedings. Likewise, given the informal, often hurried context in which it must be applied, the "built-in subtleties" of the "two-pronged test" are particularly unlikely to assist magistrates in determining probable cause.

Similarly, we have repeatedly said that after-the-fact scrutiny by courts of the sufficiency of an affidavit should not take the form of *de novo* review. A magistrate's "determination of probable cause should be paid great deference by reviewing courts." *Spinelli, supra.* "A grudging or negative attitude by reviewing courts toward warrants" is inconsistent with the Fourth Amendment's strong preference for searches conducted pursuant to a warrant; "courts should not invalidate warrant[s] by interpreting affidavit[s] in a hypertechnical, rather than a commonsense, manner."

If the affidavits submitted by police officers are subjected to the type of scrutiny some courts have deemed appropriate, police might well resort to warrantless searches, with the hope of relying on consent or some other exception to the Warrant Clause that might develop at the time of the search. In addition, the possession of a warrant by officers conducting an arrest or search greatly reduces the perception of unlawful or intrusive police conduct, by assuring "the individual whose property is searched or seized of the lawful authority of the executing officer, his need to search, and the limits of his power to search." Reflecting this preference for the warrant process, the traditional standard for review of an issuing magistrate's probable-cause determination has been that so long as the magistrate had a "substantial basis for * * * conclud[ing]" that a search would uncover evidence of wrongdoing, the Fourth Amendment requires no more. We think reaffirmation of this standard better serves the purpose of encouraging recourse to the warrant procedure and is more consistent with our traditional deference to the probable-cause determinations of magistrates than is the "two-pronged test."

Finally, the direction taken by decisions following *Spinelli* poorly serves "[t]he most basic function of any government": "to provide for the security of the individual and of his property." The strictures that inevitably accompany the "two-pronged test" cannot avoid seriously impeding the task of law enforcement. If, as the Illinois Supreme Court apparently thought, that test must be rigorously applied in every case, anonymous tips would be of greatly diminished value in police work. * * * Yet, such tips, particularly when supplemented by independent police investigation, frequently contribute to the solution of otherwise "perfect crimes." While a conscientious assessment of the basis for crediting such tips is required by the Fourth Amendment, a standard that leaves virtually no place for anonymous citizen informants is not.

For all these reasons, we conclude that it is wiser to abandon the "two-pronged test" established by our decisions in *Aguilar* and *Spinelli*. In its place we reaffirm the totality-of-the-circumstances analysis that traditionally has informed probable-cause determinations. The task of the issuing magistrate is simply to make a practical, common-sense decision whether, given all the circumstances set forth in the affidavit before him, including the "veracity" and "basis of knowledge" of persons supplying hearsay information, there is a fair probability that contraband or evidence of a crime will be found in a particular place. And the duty of a reviewing court is simply to ensure that the magistrate had a "substantial basis for * * * conclud[ing]" that probable cause existed. We are convinced that this flexible, easily applied standard will better achieve the accommodation of public and private interests that the Fourth Amendment requires than does the approach that has developed from *Aguilar* and *Spinelli*.

Our earlier cases illustrate the limits beyond which a magistrate may not venture in issuing a warrant. A sworn statement of an affiant that "he has cause to suspect and does believe" that liquor illegally brought into the United States is located on certain premises will not do. *Nathanson v. United States*. An affidavit must provide the magistrate with a substantial basis for determining the existence of probable cause, and the wholly conclusory statement at issue in *Nathanson* failed to meet this requirement. * * * Sufficient information must be presented to the magistrate to allow that official to determine probable cause; his action cannot be a mere ratification of the bare conclusions of others. In order to ensure that such an abdication of the magistrate's duty does not occur, courts must continue to conscientiously review the sufficiency of affidavits on which warrants are issued. But when we move beyond the "bare bones" affidavits present in cases such as *Nathanson* and *Aguilar*, this area simply does not lend itself to a prescribed set of rules, like that which had developed from *Spinelli*. Instead, the flexible, common-sense standard * * * better serves the purposes of the Fourth Amendment's probable-cause requirement. * * *

IV

Our decisions applying the totality-of-the-circumstances analysis outlined above have consistently recognized the value of corroboration of details of an informant's tip by independent police work. * * *

Our decision in *Draper v. United States* * * * is the classic case on the value of corroborative efforts of police officials. [See p. 140 for the facts.] * * *

The showing of probable cause in the present case was fully as compelling as that in *Draper*. Even standing alone, the facts obtained through the independent investigation of Mader and the DEA at least suggested that the Gateses were involved in drug trafficking. In addition to being a popular vacation site, Florida is well known as a source of narcotics and other illegal drugs. Lance Gates' flight to West Palm Beach, his brief, overnight stay in a motel, and apparent immediate return north to Chicago in the family car, conveniently awaiting him in West Palm Beach, is as suggestive of a prearranged drug run, as it is of an ordinary vacation trip.

In addition, the judge could rely on the anonymous letter, which had been corroborated in major part by Mader's efforts—just as had occurred in *Draper*. The Supreme Court of Illinois reasoned that *Draper* involved an informant who had given reliable information on previous occasions, while the honesty and reliability of the anonymous informant in this case were unknown to the Bloomingdale police. While this distinction might be an apt one at the time the Police Department received the anonymous letter, it became far less significant after Mader's independent investigative work occurred. The corroboration of the letter's predictions that the Gateses' car would be in Florida, that Lance Gates would fly to Florida in the next day or so, and that he would drive the car north toward Bloomingdale all indicated, albeit not with certainty, that the informant's other assertions also were true. "[B]ecause an informant is right about some things, he is more probably right about other facts," *Spinelli* (White, J., concurring)—including the claim regarding the Gateses' illegal activity. This may well not be the type of "reliability" or "veracity" necessary to satisfy some views of the "veracity prong" of *Spinelli*, but we think it suffices for the practical, common-sense judgment called for in making a probable-cause determination. It is enough, for purposes of assessing probable cause, that "[c]orroboration through other sources of information reduced the chances of a reckless or prevaricating tale," thus providing "a substantial basis for crediting the hearsay."

Finally, the anonymous letter contained a range of details relating not just to easily obtained facts and conditions existing at the time of the tip, but to future actions of third parties ordinarily not easily predicted. The letterwriter's accurate information as to the travel plans of each of the Gateses was of a character likely obtained only from the Gateses themselves, or from someone familiar with their not entirely ordinary travel plans. If the informant had access to accurate information of this type a magistrate could properly conclude that it was not unlikely that he also had access to reliable information of the Gateses' alleged illegal activities. Of course, the Gateses' travel plans might have been learned from a talkative neighbor or travel agent; under the "two-pronged test" developed from *Spinelli*, the character of the details in the anonymous letter might well not permit a sufficiently clear inference regarding the letterwriter's "basis of knowledge." But, as discussed previously, probable cause does not demand the certainty we associate with formal trials. It is enough that there was a fair probability that the writer of the anonymous letter had obtained his entire story either from the Gates or someone they trusted. And corroboration of major portions of the letter's predictions provides just this probability. * * *

Reversed.

Justice WHITE, concurring in the judgment. * * *

III

* * * Abandoning the "two-pronged test" of *Aguilar v. Texas* and *Spinelli v. United States*, the Court upholds the validity of the warrant under a new "totality of the circumstances" approach. Although I agree that the warrant should be upheld, I reach this conclusion in accordance with the *Aguilar-Spinelli* framework.

A * * *

In the present case, it is undisputed that the anonymous tip, by itself, did not furnish probable cause. The question is whether those portions of the affidavit describing the results of the police investigation of the respondents, when considered in light of the tip, "would permit the suspicions engendered by the informant's report to ripen into a judgment that a crime was probably being committed." *Spinelli, supra.* The Illinois Supreme Court concluded that the corroboration was insufficient to permit such a ripening. * * *

In my view, the lower court's characterization of the Gateses' activity here as totally "innocent" is dubious. In fact, the behavior was quite suspicious. I agree with the Court that Lance Gates' flight to West Palm Beach, an area known to be a source of narcotics, the brief overnight stay in a motel, and apparent immediate return north, suggest a pattern that trained law enforcement officers have recognized as indicative of illicit drug-dealing activity.

Even, however, had the corroboration related only to completely innocuous activities, this fact alone would not preclude the issuance of a valid warrant. The critical issue is not whether the activities observed by the police are innocent or suspicious. Instead, the proper focus should be on whether the actions of the suspects, whatever their nature, give rise to an inference that the informant is credible and that he obtained his information in a reliable manner. * * *

As in *Draper*, the police investigation in the present case satisfactorily demonstrated that the informant's tip was as trustworthy as one that would alone satisfy the *Aguilar* tests. The tip predicted that Sue Gates would drive to Florida, that Lance Gates would fly there a few days after May 3, and that Lance would then drive the car back. After the police corroborated these facts, the judge could reasonably have inferred, as he apparently did, that the informant, who had specific knowledge of these unusual travel plans, did not make up his story and that he obtained his information in a reliable way. It is theoretically possible, as respondents insist, that the tip could have been supplied by a "vindictive travel agent" and that the Gateses' activities, although unusual, might not have been unlawful. But *Aguilar* and *Spinelli*, like our other cases, do not require that certain guilt be established before a warrant may properly be issued. * * * I therefore conclude that the judgment of the Illinois Supreme Court invalidating the warrant must be reversed.

B

The Court agrees that the warrant was valid, but, in the process of reaching this conclusion, it overrules the *Aguilar-Spinelli* tests and replaces them with a "totality of the circumstances" standard. As shown above, it is not at all necessary to overrule *Aguilar-Spinelli* in order to reverse the judgment below. Therefore, because I am inclined to believe that, when applied properly, the *Aguilar-Spinelli* rules play an appropriate role in probable-cause determinations, and because the Court's holding may foretell an evisceration of the probable-cause standard, I do not join the Court's holding.

The Court reasons that the "veracity" and "basis of knowledge" tests are not independent, and that a deficiency as to one can be compensated for by a strong showing as to the other. Thus, a finding of probable cause may be based on a tip from an informant "known for the unusual reliability of his predictions" or from "an unquestionably honest citizen," even if the report fails thoroughly to set forth the basis upon which the information was obtained. If this is so, then it must follow *a fortiori* that "the affidavit of an officer, known by the magistrate to be honest and experienced, stating that [contraband] is located in a certain building" must be acceptable. It would be "quixotic" if a similar statement from an honest informant, but not one from an honest officer, could furnish probable cause. But we have repeatedly held that the unsupported assertion or belief of an officer does not satisfy the probable-cause requirement. Thus, this portion of today's holding can be read as implicitly rejecting the teachings of these prior holdings.

The Court may not intend so drastic a result. Indeed, the Court expressly reaffirms the validity of cases such as *Nathanson* that have held that, no matter how reliable the affiant-officer may be, a warrant should not be issued unless the affidavit discloses supporting facts and circumstances. The Court limits these cases to situations involving affidavits containing only "bare conclusions" and holds that, if an affidavit contains anything more, it should be left to the issuing magistrate to decide, based solely on "practical[ity]" and "common sense," whether there is a fair probability that contraband will be found in a particular place.

Thus, as I read the majority opinion, it appears that the question whether the probable-cause standard is to be diluted is left to the common-sense judgments of issuing magistrates. I am reluctant to approve any standard that does not expressly require, as a prerequisite to issuance of a warrant, some showing of facts from which an inference may be drawn that the informant is credible and that his information was obtained in a reliable way. * * * Hence, I do not join the Court's opinion rejecting the *Aguilar-Spinelli* rules.

Justice BRENNAN, with whom Justice MARSHALL joins, dissenting.
* * *

I * * *

In recognition of the judiciary's role as the only effective guardian of Fourth Amendment rights, this Court has developed over the last half century a set of coherent rules governing a magistrate's consideration of a warrant application and the showings that are necessary to support a finding of probable cause. We start with the proposition that a neutral and detached magistrate, and not the police, should determine whether there is probable cause to support the issuance of a warrant. * * *

In order to emphasize the magistrate's role as an independent arbiter of probable cause and to insure that searches or seizures are not effected on less than probable cause, the Court has insisted that police officers provide magistrates with the underlying facts and circumstances that support the officers' conclusions. * * *

Although the rules drawn from the cases * * * are cast in procedural terms, they advance an important underlying substantive value: Findings of probable cause, and attendant intrusions, should not be authorized unless there is some assurance that the information on which they are based has been obtained in a reliable way by an honest or credible person. As applied to police officers, the rules focus on the way in which the information was acquired. As applied to informants, the rules focus both on the honesty or credibility of the informant and on the reliability of the way in which the information was acquired. Insofar as it is more complicated, an evaluation of affidavits based on hearsay involves a more difficult inquiry. This suggests a need to structure the inquiry in an effort to insure greater accuracy. The standards announced in *Aguilar*, as refined by *Spinelli*, fulfill that need. The standards inform the police of what information they have to provide and magistrates of what information they should demand. The standards also inform magistrates of the subsidiary findings they must make in order to arrive at an ultimate finding of probable cause. *Spinelli*, properly understood, directs the magistrate's attention to the possibility that the presence of self-verifying detail might satisfy *Aguilar*'s basis of knowledge prong and that corroboration of the details of a tip might satisfy *Aguilar*'s veracity prong. By requiring police to provide certain crucial information to magistrates and by structuring magistrates' probable-cause inquiries, *Aguilar* and *Spinelli* assure the magistrate's role as an independent arbiter of probable cause, insure greater accuracy in probable-cause determinations, and advance the substantive value identified above.

Until today the Court has never squarely addressed the application of the *Aguilar* and *Spinelli* standards to tips from anonymous informants. Both *Aguilar* and *Spinelli* dealt with tips from informants known at least to the police. And surely there is even more reason to subject anonymous informants' tips to the tests established by *Aguilar* and *Spinelli*. By definition nothing is known about an anonymous informant's identity, honesty, or reliability. * * * [T]here certainly is no basis for treating anonymous informants as presumptively reliable. Nor is there any basis for assuming that the information provided by an anonymous informant has been obtained in a reliable way. If we are unwilling to accept conclusory allegations from the police, who are presumptively reliable, or from informants who are known, at least to the police, there cannot possibly be any rational basis for accepting conclusory allegations from anonymous informants.

To suggest that anonymous informants' tips are subject to the tests established by *Aguilar* and *Spinelli* is not to suggest that they can never provide a basis for a finding of probable cause. It is conceivable that police corroboration of the details of the tip might establish the reliability of the informant under *Aguilar*'s veracity prong, as refined in *Spinelli*, and that the details in the tip might be sufficient to qualify under the "self-verifying detail" test established by *Spinelli* as a means of satisfying *Aguilar*'s basis of knowledge prong. The *Aguilar* and *Spinelli* tests must be applied to anonymous informants' tips, however, if we are to continue to insure that findings of probable cause, and attendant intrusions, are based on information provided by an honest or credible person who has acquired the information in a reliable way.

In light of the important purposes served by *Aguilar* and *Spinelli*, I would not reject the standards they establish. * * *

II * * *

At the heart of the Court's decision to abandon *Aguilar* and *Spinelli* appears to be its belief that "the direction taken by decisions following *Spinelli* poorly serves '[t]he most basic function of any government': 'to provide for the security of the individual and of his property.' " This conclusion rests on the judgment that *Aguilar* and *Spinelli* "seriously imped[e] the task of law enforcement," and render anonymous tips valueless in police work. Surely, the Court overstates its case. But of particular concern to all Americans must be that the Court gives virtually no consideration to the value of insuring that findings of probable cause are based on information that a magistrate can reasonably say has been obtained in a reliable way by an honest or credible person. I share Justice White's fear that the Court's rejection of *Aguilar* and *Spinelli* and its adoption of a new totality-of-the-circumstances test, "may foretell an evisceration of the probable-cause standard * * *."

III

The Court's complete failure to provide any persuasive reason for rejecting *Aguilar* and *Spinelli* doubtlessly reflects impatience with what it perceives to be "overly technical" rules governing searches and seizures under the Fourth Amendment. Words such as "practical," "nontechnical," and "common sense," as used in the Court's opinion, are but code words for an overly permissive attitude towards police practices in derogation of the rights secured by the Fourth Amendment. Everyone shares the Court's concern over the horrors of drug trafficking, but under our Constitution only measures consistent with the Fourth Amendment may be employed by government to cure this evil. * * *

Rights secured by the Fourth Amendment are particularly difficult to protect because their "advocates are usually criminals." But the rules "we fashion [are] for the innocent and guilty alike." By replacing *Aguilar* and *Spinelli* with a test that provides no assurance that magistrates, rather than the police, or informants, will make determinations of probable cause; imposes no structure on magistrates' probable-cause inquiries; and invites the possibility that intrusions may be justified on less than reliable information from an honest or credible person, today's decision threatens to "obliterate one of the most fundamental distinctions between our form of government, where officers are under the law, and the police-state where they are the law."

Justice STEVENS, with whom Justice BRENNAN joins, dissenting.

The fact that Lance and Sue Gates made a 22–hour nonstop drive from West Palm Beach, Florida, to Bloomingdale, Illinois, only a few hours after Lance had flown to Florida provided persuasive evidence that they were engaged in illicit activity. That fact, however, was not known to the judge when he issued the warrant to search their home.

What the judge did know at that time was that the anonymous informant had not been completely accurate in his or her predictions. The informant had indicated that "Sue * * * drives their car to Florida *where she leaves it to be loaded up with drugs * * *. Sue fl[ies] back after she drops the car off in Florida.*" Yet Detective Mader's affidavit reported that she " 'left the West Palm Beach area driving the Mercury northbound.' "

The discrepancy between the informant's predictions and the facts known to Detective Mader is significant for three reasons. First, it cast doubt on the informant's hypothesis that the Gates already had " 'over [$100,000] worth of drugs in their basement.' " The informant had predicted an itinerary that always kept one spouse in Bloomingdale, suggesting that the Gates did not want to leave their home unguarded because something valuable was hidden within. That inference obviously could not be drawn when it was known that the pair was actually together over a thousand miles from home.

Second, the discrepancy made the Gates' conduct seem substantially less unusual than the informant had predicted it would be. It would have been odd if, as predicted, Sue had driven down to Florida on Wednesday, left the car, and flown right back to Illinois. But the mere facts that Sue was in West Palm Beach with the car, that she was joined by her husband at the Holiday Inn on Friday, and that the couple drove north together the next morning[3] are neither unusual nor probative of criminal activity.

Third, the fact that the anonymous letter contained a material mistake undermines the reasonableness of relying on it as a basis for making a forcible entry into a private home.

Of course, the activities in this case did not stop when the judge issued the warrant. The Gates drove all night to Bloomingdale, the officers searched the car and found 400 pounds of marihuana, and then they searched the house. However, none of these subsequent events may be considered in evaluating the warrant, and the search of the house was legal only if the warrant was valid. I cannot accept the Court's casual conclusion that, *before the Gates arrived in Bloomingdale,* there was probable cause to justify a valid entry and search of a private home. No one knows who the informant in this case was, or what motivated him or her to write the note. Given that the note's predictions were faulty in one

---

3. Detective Mader's affidavit hinted darkly that the couple had set out upon "that interstate highway commonly used by travelers to the Chicago area." But the same highway is also commonly used by travelers to Disney World, Sea World, and Ringling Brothers and Barnum and Bailey Circus World. It is also the road to Cocoa Beach, Cape Canaveral, and Washington, D.C. I would venture that each year dozens of perfectly innocent people fly to Florida, meet a waiting spouse, and drive off together in the family car.

significant respect, and were corroborated by nothing except ordinary innocent activity, I must surmise that the Court's evaluation of the warrant's validity has been colored by subsequent events. * * *[8]

NOTES AND QUESTIONS

1. *A bit more on Sue and Lance Gates and the anonymous informant.* According to Professor Thomas Davies, the anonymous informant was Sue Gates's beautician, who was infuriated at her client's frequent boasts about not working. Davies reports that "the hairdresser called the police after the case made the Chicago papers, and said that she would have signed the letter if she knew how much trouble she was causing!" (Electronic mail correspondence from Davies to author Dressler, January 24, 2001.)

Susan and Lance Gates pleaded guilty to the drug charges. "[N]ot exactly a Bonnie & Clyde operation," according to Professor Davies, and neither Sue nor Lance has reportedly been prosecuted in the intervening years.

2. Is the *Gates* case an example of good law enforcement? The anonymous informant stated "I guarantee *if you watch them carefully* you will make a big catch. They are friends with some big drug *dealers, who visit their house often.*" According to one scholar, "[o]ut of the mouths of babes and anonymous informants sometimes comes wisdom." Yale Kamisar, Gates, *"Probable Cause," "Good Faith," and Beyond*, 69 Iowa L. Rev. 551, 576 (1984). Professor Kamisar reasons that if the police had been more patient they would have satisfied the two-pronged standard and, perhaps more importantly, might have apprehended "big drug dealers."

3. Was the Court right to abandon the two-pronged test of *Aguilar-Spinelli*? Consider the following facts from State v. Boggess, 115 Wis.2d 443, 340 N.W.2d 516 (1983), and observations of them in light of *Gates*:

> A social worker received an anonymous phone call at suppertime reporting that two children, who lived with Calvin Boggess but had different last names, may have been battered. The caller stated that one of the children was limping, that he had seen bruises on this child, and that he believed the child might need medical attention. Moreover, the caller said that he knew the Boggesses fairly well and that Mr. Boggess had a bad temper. The social worker who received the call reported it to another social worker who, along with a policeman, went to Boggess's house. Although he was told about the call, Boggess refused to let the two into his house to observe the children.
>
> Imagine, for a moment, that you are the officer. What should or would you do when Boggess refuses to let you enter?[309] Under *Spinelli's*

---

8. The Court holds that what were heretofore considered two independent "prongs"— "veracity" and "basis of knowledge"—are now to be considered together as circumstances whose totality must be appraised. * * * "[A] deficiency in one may be compensated for, in determining the overall reliability of a tip, by a strong showing as to the other, or by some other indicia of reliability." Yet in this case, the lower courts found *neither* factor present. And the supposed "other indicia" in the affidavit take the form of activity that is not particularly remarkable. I do not understand how the Court can find that the "totality" so far exceeds the sum of its "circumstances."

309. I have deliberately refrained from indicating whether any children in fact were battered. Hindsight knowledge, either way, can too easily influence analysis. Thus, you as reader are no more enlightened than the officer at the door.

test, this case is * * * difficult * * * because here both prongs are arguably deficient. The informant claimed that he personally observed only some bruises, not any beating. Moreover, the informant did not give any basis for his suspicion that one of the children possibly needed medical attention. In any event, even if we infer personal observation, the veracity prong remains unsatisfied.

My unscientific sampling of lawyers and law professors suggests that reasonable people differ in their responses to this fact situation. Some want more corroboration before concluding that a forcible entry is proper. Others, however, want to enter immediately after Boggess's refusal to cooperate. Some, like me, vacillate back and forth. If my survey is accurate, the two prong deficiency does not prevent some reasonable people from concluding that an immediate search is reasonable. For these people, the two-pronged test itself would be unreasonable as applied to these facts. * * *

This example should illustrate that the reasonably cautious person does not always require *Spinelli*'s two prongs to be satisfied before an arrest or a search can be made. Rather, * * * the reasonable person examines the totality of circumstances and balances the competing interests.

Joseph D. Grano, *Probable Cause and Common Sense: A Reply to the Critics of Illinois v. Gates*, 17 U. Mich. J.L. Reform 465, 516–18 (1984). What do you think?

4. The police often use informants to obtain critical information in criminal investigations. In one study in the San Diego Judicial District, for example, 63.9% of search warrant affidavits contained information provided by informants. Laurence A. Benner & Charles T. Samarkos, *Searching for Narcotics in San Diego: Preliminary Findings from the San Diego Search Warrant Project*, 36 Cal. Western L. Rev. 221, 239 (2000). However, in half of the cases the affiant did not personally know the informant. That is, "the officer simply related information given him by another officer who did not join in signing the affidavit. Thus, Officer A swears under oath that Officer B told him that there was [a confidential informant] who gave him certain information." *Id.* at 241. Thus, the magistrate was receiving double hearsay. What problems do you see in this?

5. *The "confidential informant": How confidential is he?* The police rarely disclose the identity of their informants—many of whom provide information on a regular basis—to magistrates in warrant applications. In McCray v. Illinois, 386 U.S. 300, 87 S.Ct. 1056, 18 L.Ed.2d 62 (1967), the Supreme Court ruled that the due process clause does not require a judge in every probable cause or evidence-suppression hearing to compel disclosure of the informant's identity. In reaching this conclusion the Court quoted the followed reasoning of the New Jersey Supreme Court in State v. Burnett, 42 N.J. 377, 201 A.2d 39 (1964):

If a defendant may insist upon disclosure of the informant in order to test the truth of the officer's statement that there is an informant or as to what the informant related or as to the informant's reliability, we can be sure that every defendant will demand disclosure. He has nothing to lose and the prize may be the suppression of damaging evidence if the State cannot afford to reveal its source, as is so often the case. * * *

The Fourth Amendment is served if a judicial mind passes upon the existence of probable cause. Where the issue is submitted upon an application for a warrant, the magistrate is trusted to evaluate the credibility of the affiant in an *ex parte* proceeding. As we have said, the magistrate is concerned, not with whether the informant lied, but with whether the affiant is truthful in his recitation of what he was told. If the magistrate doubts the credibility of the affiant, he may require that the informant be identified or even produced. It seems to us that the same approach is equally sufficient where the search was without a warrant, that is to say, that it should rest entirely with the judge who hears the motion to suppress [evidence] to decide whether he needs such disclosure as to the informant in order to decide whether the officer is a believable witness.

6. *The "oath and affirmation" requirement of the Fourth Amendment.* A police officer-affiant is ordinarily considered reliable because she provides her information under oath. But, suppose that the defendant fears that the officer lied under oath to the judge who issued a search warrant? Perhaps the defense believes that the affiant lied to the judge as to what she personally observed, or made up the existence of an informant, or lied as to a real informant's reliability, or knew or should have known that the informant's claims were false. What may the defendant do to attack a warrant in such circumstances?

The Fourth Amendment provides that warrants, founded on probable cause, must be "supported by Oath or affirmation." The Supreme Court held in Franks v. Delaware, 438 U.S. 154, 98 S.Ct. 2674, 57 L.Ed.2d 667 (1978), that in view of this requirement, a defendant may challenge the truthfulness of statements made under oath in an affidavit supporting a warrant under limited circumstances. *Franks* explains the procedure:

> [W]here the defendant makes a substantial preliminary showing that a false statement knowing and intentionally, or with reckless disregard for the truth, was included by the affiant in the warrant affidavit, the Fourth Amendment requires that a hearing be held at the defendant's request. In the event that at that hearing the allegation of perjury or reckless disregard is established * * * by a preponderance of the evidence, and, with the affidavit's false material set to one side, the affidavit's remaining content is insufficient to establish probable cause, the search warrant must be voided and the fruits of the search excluded to the same extent as if probable cause was lacking on the face of the affidavit.

Franks does not authorize a special hearing if a defendant claims that the *informant* lied to an *innocent* affiant. Do you see why this is so?

7. *Preference for the warrant process.* As noted in *Gates*, the constitutionally preferable arbiter of probable cause is a "neutral and detached magistrate," rather than a police officer "engaged in the often competitive enterprise of ferreting out crime." Johnson v. United States, 333 U.S. 10, 68 S.Ct. 367, 92 L.Ed. 436 (1948). In order to provide the police with an incentive to seek warrants, the Supreme Court has stated that "the resolution of

doubtful or marginal cases [of probable cause] * * * should be largely determined by the preference to be accorded to warrants." United States v. Ventresca, 380 U.S. 102, 85 S.Ct. 741, 13 L.Ed.2d 684 (1965). In other words, in close cases, a search pursuant to a warrant may be upheld where, without one, it would not be.

8. *How probable is "probable cause"?* Gates eschewed the quantification of any "precise degree of certainty corresponding to 'probable cause'." The Court has stated, however, that the standard does *not* "demand any showing that such a belief be * * * more likely true than false." Texas v. Brown, 460 U.S. 730, 103 S.Ct. 1535, 75 L.Ed.2d 502 (1983).

Should this be the rule? What if the police have extremely solid evidence, amounting to near certainty, that one (but only one) of two identical twins committed a particular offense? In light of *Brown*, should the police arrest *both* of the twins, even though they know one of them is innocent? If not, should they flip a coin and arrest the unlucky one? What if we are dealing with triplets? Indeed, consider this:

> Imagine * * * that the police suspect ten persons of a crime but have no way of discriminating among them. Suppose, moreover, that the police are certain, at least as certain as humanly possible, that one of the ten committed the crime. With the available evidence pointing equally to each suspect, the mathematical probability that any one suspect committed the crime is only ten percent. Indeed, for any suspect selected at random from the group, the odds are only ten percent that he is guilty but a whopping ninety percent that he is innocent. Such a probability analysis, however, distorts our perspective. It causes us to overlook the success of the police in narrowing their investigation from the universe of all possible suspects, which may include much of the population, to ten individuals. In a modern, mobile society, this should be seen as a rather significant accomplishment.

> Assume now that arresting each suspect would permit further investigation such as interrogation, a face or voice lineup, sampling blood or hair, or taking fingerprints. Or assume that the nature of the crime suggests that searching the actual offender's house or car will yield incriminating evidence. The question is whether we may reasonably expect—indeed, require—each suspect to sacrifice some liberty or privacy in order to unmask the offender. I think we can. In constitutional language, I would say that probable cause exists to arrest or search each suspect.

Joseph D. Grano, *Probable Cause and Common Sense: A Reply to the Critics of Illinois v. Gates,* 17 U. Mich. J.L. Reform 465, 496–97 (1984).

Do you agree?

9. *The one-out-of-three issue, redux.* In the last Note you were asked whether the police have probable cause, and therefore may arrest, triplets for a murder that only one committed. In this regard consider this true case recounted to the authors of this casebook by Professor Neil Cohen:

> A few years ago I got a call from a judge who had this case. Very late at night on a rural dark road a police officer spotted a car driving erratically.

The officer * * * pulled over the car. The car stopped on the side of this dark rural road. The officer then got out of the cruiser and walked up to the parked car. When the officer shined his flashlight in the car, he found three young men "asleep" in the back seat. No one was in the front seat. He "awakened" them and all said the same thing: They had been at a party, drank too much, and fell asleep in the back seat of the car. Each denied knowing who the driver was. The officer had kept the car in eyesight the entire time and was confident that no one had gotten out of it. All three of the young men were drunk.

Was there probable cause to charge anyone with driving the vehicle under the influence of alcohol?

Now consider Maryland v. Pringle, 540 U.S. 366, 124 S.Ct. 795, 157 L.Ed.2d 769 (2003). In *Pringle*, an officer lawfully stopped a speeding vehicle occupied by three men. As a result of a lawful search, the officer discovered a large amount of rolled-up money in the glove compartment, and five baggies of cocaine hidden in the back-seat armrest and elsewhere in the back seat. The officer questioned the men about the ownership of the drugs and warned them that if they did not answer he would arrest all three of them for possession of the cocaine, which he did when nobody admitted ownership. Later, Pringle, the front seat passenger, admitted ownership, and charges were dropped against the other two men. A state court, however, reversed Pringle's conviction because the officer lacked probable cause at the time he made the arrest. The Supreme Court unanimously upheld Pringle's arrest:

We think it an entirely reasonable inference from [the] facts of the case that any or all three of the occupants had knowledge of, and exercised dominion and control over, the cocaine. [Under state law, "possession" of property exists if one or more persons has "actual or constructive dominion or control" over the property—Eds.] Thus a reasonable officer could conclude that there was probable cause to believe Pringle committed the crime of possession of cocaine, either solely or jointly. * * *

* * * [Previously,] we noted that "a car passenger * * * will often be engaged in a common enterprise with the driver, and have the same interest in concealing the fruits or the evidence of their wrongdoing." Here we think it was reasonable for the officer to infer a common enterprise among the three men. The quantity of drugs and cash in the car indicated the likelihood of drug dealing, an enterprise to which a dealer would be unlikely to admit an innocent person with the potential to furnish evidence against him.

Does this case resolve the triplet hypothetical or the three-drunks-in-the-back-seat case?

10. *A "sliding scale" of probable cause?* In Schmerber v. California, 384 U.S. 757, 86 S.Ct. 1826, 16 L.Ed.2d 908 (1966), the Supreme Court observed that the taking of a blood sample from a motorist arrested for drunk driving, because it involved an intrusion into a human body, was a more offensive type of search, which requires "a clear indication that in fact such evidence [of intoxication] will be found." One can interpret this latter language as, perhaps, requiring "probable cause plus," i.e., a heightened degree of likeli-

hood of discovering evidence when the police wish to conduct such a hyper-intrusive search. And, indeed, in Winston v. Lee, 470 U.S. 753, 105 S.Ct. 1611, 84 L.Ed.2d 662 (1985), a case in which the police sought a warrant to compel a surgical intrusion into a suspect's body in order to seize a bullet that might incriminate him, the Court stated that "when the State seeks to intrude upon an area in which our society recognizes a significantly heightened privacy interest, a more substantial justification is required" to authorize such a search.

Does this suggest, therefore, a sliding scale of "probable cause"? And, if so, one may expect that the sliding scale could work in both directions. Might there be cases in which "probable cause" requires *less* than the ordinary degree of proof?

Consider this post–9/11 scenario: The police have a credible report that an atomic bomb, smaller than a suitcase, has been smuggled into New York City. The bomb, if detonated, will kill thousands of persons and make the city uninhabitable for generations. The report is confirmed by use of radiation sensors, which determine that the bomb is hidden in one of 100 homes. Therefore, Homeland Security officials search all 100 homes simultaneously. Ronald M. Gould & Simon Stern, *Catastrophic Threats and the Fourth Amendment*, 77 S. Cal. L. Rev. 777, 779 (2004). Did the government act with probable cause? Would your answer be the same if police instead searched the same houses for a small stash of cocaine, based on the same likelihood of success?

Does your response to these hypotheticals suggest that the Court is right in suggesting that "probable cause" should be a fluid concept—that there should be a sliding scale of probable cause? Can you suggest a plausible Fourth Amendment textual argument for such a distinction?

11. *Probable cause as an objective concept.* According to the Supreme Court, "evenhanded law enforcement is best achieved by the application of objective standards of conduct, rather than standards that depend upon the subjective state of mind of the [police] officer." Horton v. California, 496 U.S. 128, 110 S.Ct. 2301, 110 L.Ed.2d 112 (1990). Therefore, as will be developed more fully later, see p. 259, the Supreme Court has stated that an officer's "state of mind (except for the facts that he knows) is irrelevant to the existence of probable cause." Devenpeck v. Alford, 543 U.S. 146, 125 S.Ct. 588, 160 L.Ed.2d 537 (2004). As the Court held in *Devenpeck,* an arrest is lawful, even if an officer incorrectly believes he has probable cause to arrest a person for Crime A (and, therefore, makes such an arrest), if based on the facts known to the arresting officer, probable cause objectively exists to arrest for Crime B.

12. *Problem.* A mother reported to the police that her three-year-old son told her that *S* had sexually touched him on his penis ("he touched my pee-pee"). Is this sufficient grounds to arrest *S* for child sexual abuse? United States v. Shaw, 464 F.3d 615 (6th Cir. 2006).

13. *Problems.* Is there probable cause in either of these circumstances?

A.   United States troops in Iraq have used hand-held devices to scan the irises of tens of thousands of Iraqi men in order to create an "insurgent database." According to one military official, if the same man is found at the scene of several bombings, "now we've got probable cause." Thomas Frank, *U.S. is Building Database on Iraqis*, USA Today, July 13, 2007, at A1.

B. According to the police, *F*, who was convicted of child sex abuse eighteen years ago, "appears" to have "gained or attempted to gain" access to a Web site that distributes child pornography. Is this allegation sufficient grounds to secure a warrant to search *F*'s home for child pornography? United States v. Falso, 544 F.3d 110 (2d Cir. 2008).

14. *Problem.* Ready for a little 1940s *film noir*? Here is how Chief Justice Roberts described the facts in Pennsylvania v. Dunlap, 555 U.S. ___, 129 S.Ct. 448, 172 L.Ed.2d 321 (2008) (dissenting from denial of certiorari):

> North Philly, May 4, 2001. Officer Sean Devlin, Narcotics Strike Force, was working the morning shift. Undercover surveillance. The neighborhood? Tough as a three-dollar steak. Devlin knew. Five years on the beat, nine months with the Strike Force. He'd made fifteen, twenty drug busts in the neighborhood. Devlin spotted him: a lone man on the corner. Another approached. Quick exchange of words. Cash handed over; small objects handed back. Each man then quickly on his own way. Devlin knew the guy wasn't buying bus tokens. He radioed a description and Officer Stein picked up the buyer. Sure enough: three bags of crack in the guy's pocket. Head downtown and book him. Just another day at the office.

Do these facts support a finding of probable cause to arrest the man (who handed over cash) for the offense of possession of illegal drugs, although Officer Devlin did not see any drugs transferred?

15. *Problem.* The police pulled over *P*, an erratic driver. When an officer approached the car he smelled marijuana and properly determined that *P* had been driving under the influence of drugs. A lawful search of the car turned up one marijuana cigarette and 1.5 grams of methamphetamine. Based on this information the officer applied for a warrant to search *P*'s home for drugs. The officer's affidavit described his background in drug enforcement and included statements that, in his experience, drug users keep additional quantities of drugs at their residence. Probable cause? See People v. Pressey, 102 Cal.App.4th 1178, 126 Cal.Rptr.2d 162 (2002).

16. *Problem.* Two adult men accused *B*, an Episcopal priest and former chaplain of a boarding school, of sexual abuse sixteen years earlier when they were teenagers. The police sought a warrant to search *B*'s home (a different home) for a footlocker that the complainants stated had, by their observation at the time of the crimes, contained pornographic material, photographs of sodomy performed on them, and sexual aids used on them in the sexual abuse. Probable cause? Behrel v. State, 151 Md.App. 64, 823 A.2d 696 (2003).

17. *The Ballad of Lance and Susie (sung to the tune of the theme song to that classic television show, "The Beverly Hillbillies").* This comes to us from University of Toledo law student songstress Kate Munger. (Of course, if you don't know the tune, then it seems you have not been watching enough cable reruns, or have a weak stomach.)

Listen to the story 'bout Lance and Sue
Windy City kids who had a secret or two.
They didn't have to work, life just couldn't be better
'Til they were ratted out by an anonymous letter
Snitch, that is
Finger-pointin', betrayed.

Well the next thing you know the detective tracked their flight
And the Sunshine State hosted our perps for the night.
Corroborated details, just like in the note
Enough to get a warrant that the magistrate wrote.
Too coincidental, that is,
Modus operandi.

Well, Lance and Susie drove on home and didn't know
That the cops would soon be searchin' their happy bungalow.
Reefer in the trunk of their shiny Mercury
Sending Sue and Lance to the penitentiary.
Jail that is,
Hard time, orange pants.

Now the small Gates gang thought they might get off scot free
'Cause the warrant was invalid to search their Mercury,
But the highest court shouted out a new decree,
The circumstances would be viewed in their totality.
Probable cause, that is
Case-by-case, big picture.

18. *Probable cause and "anticipatory warrants."* "An anticipatory warrant is 'a warrant based upon an affidavit showing probable cause that at some future time (but not presently) certain evidence of crime will be located at a specified place.'" United States v. Grubbs, 547 U.S. 90, 126 S.Ct. 1494, 164 L.Ed.2d 195 (2006). For example, in *Grubbs*, *G* purchased a videotape containing child pornography from a Web site operated by an undercover postal inspector. Law enforcement officers then arranged a delivery of the package to *G*'s residence. Before it arrived, the officers sought a warrant to search the residence for the video, stating in an affidavit that "[e]xecution of this search warrant will not occur unless and until the parcel has been received by a person(s) and has been physically taken into the residence."

As the Fourth Amendment provides that "no Warrant shall issue, but upon probable cause," is a warrant invalid if it is issued by a magistrate *before* the triggering condition—here, delivery of the videotape—has taken place? No, as a unanimous Supreme Court has explained:

Anticipatory warrants are * * * no different in principle from ordinary warrants. They require the magistrate to determine (1) that it is *now probable* that (2) contraband, evidence of a crime, or a fugitive *will be* on the described premises (3) when the warrant is executed. It should be noted, however, that where the anticipatory warrant places a condition

* * * upon its execution, the first of these determinations goes not merely to what will probably be found *if* the condition is met. * * * Rather, the probability determination for a conditioned anticipatory warrant looks also to the likelihood that the condition will occur, and thus that a proper object of seizure will be on the described premises. In other words, for a conditioned anticipatory warrant to comply with the Fourth Amendment requirement of probable cause, two prerequisites of probability must be satisfied. It must be true not only that *if* the triggering condition occurs "there is a fair probability that contraband or evidence of a crime will be found in a particular place," but also that there is probable cause to believe the triggering condition *will* occur. The supporting affidavit must provide the magistrate with sufficient information to evaluate both aspects of the probable-cause determination.

B. ARREST WARRANTS

PAYTON v. NEW YORK

Supreme Court of the United States, 1980.
445 U.S. 573, 100 S.Ct. 1371, 63 L.Ed.2d 639.

MR. JUSTICE STEVENS delivered the opinion of the Court.

These appeals challenge the constitutionality of New York statutes that authorize police officers to enter a private residence without a warrant and with force, if necessary, to make a routine felony arrest.

The important constitutional question presented by this challenge has been expressly left open in a number of our prior opinions. In *United States v. Watson*, 423 U.S. 411, 96 S.Ct. 820, 46 L.Ed.2d 598 [1976], we upheld a warrantless "midday public arrest," expressly noting that the case did not pose "the still unsettled question * * * 'whether and under what circumstances an officer may enter a suspect's home to make a warrantless arrest.' "a* * *

I

On January 14, 1970, after two days of intensive investigation, New York detectives had assembled evidence sufficient to establish probable cause to believe that Theodore Payton had murdered the manager of a gas station two days earlier. At about 7:30 a. m. on January 15, six officers went to Payton's apartment in the Bronx, intending to arrest him. They had not obtained a warrant. Although light and music emanated from the apartment, there was no response to their knock on the metal door. They summoned emergency assistance and, about 30 minutes later, used crowbars to break open the door and enter the apartment. No one was there. In plain view, however, was a .30–caliber shell casing that was seized and later admitted into evidence at Payton's murder trial.

---

a. The Supreme Court held in *Watson* that as a matter of Fourth Amendment law, an arrest warrant is not required to make a felony arrest in a public place.

In due course Payton surrendered to the police, was indicted for murder, and moved to suppress the evidence taken from his apartment. The trial judge held that the warrantless and forcible entry was authorized by the New York Code of Criminal Procedure, and that the evidence in plain view was properly seized. * * *

On March 14, 1974, Obie Riddick was arrested for the commission of two armed robberies that had occurred in 1971. He had been identified by the victims in June 1973, and in January 1974 the police had learned his address. They did not obtain a warrant for his arrest. At about noon on March 14, a detective, accompanied by three other officers, knocked on the door of the Queens house where Riddick was living. When his young son opened the door, they could see Riddick sitting in bed covered by a sheet. They entered the house and placed him under arrest. Before permitting him to dress, they opened a chest of drawers two feet from the bed in search of weapons and found narcotics and related paraphernalia. Riddick was subsequently indicted on narcotics charges. At a suppression hearing, the trial judge held that the warrantless entry into his home was authorized by the revised New York statute, and that the search of the immediate area [as an incident of the arrest] was reasonable under *Chimel v. California*, 395 U.S. 752, 89 S.Ct. 2034, 23 L.Ed.2d 685. * * *

Before addressing the narrow question presented by these appeals, we put to one side other related problems that are *not* presented today. Although it is arguable that the warrantless entry to effect Payton's arrest might have been justified by exigent circumstances, none of the New York courts relied on any such justification. * * * Accordingly, we have no occasion to consider the sort of emergency or dangerous situation, described in our cases as "exigent circumstances," that would justify a warrantless entry into a home for the purpose of either arrest or search.

Nor do these cases raise any question concerning the authority of the police, without either a search or arrest warrant, to enter a third party's home to arrest a suspect. The police broke into Payton's apartment intending to arrest Payton, and they arrested Riddick in his own dwelling. We also note that in neither case is it argued that the police lacked probable cause to believe that the suspect was at home when they entered. Finally, in both cases we are dealing with entries into homes made without the consent of any occupant. In *Payton*, the police used crowbars to break down the door and in *Riddick*, although his 3–year-old son answered the door, the police entered before Riddick had an opportunity either to object or to consent.

II

It is familiar history that indiscriminate searches and seizures conducted under the authority of "general warrants" were the immediate evils that motivated the framing and adoption of the Fourth Amendment. Indeed, as originally proposed in the House of Representatives, the draft contained only one clause, which directly imposed limitations on the issuance of warrants, but imposed no express restrictions on warrantless searches or seizures. As it was ultimately adopted, however, the Amendment contained two separate clauses, the first protecting the basic right to be free from unreasonable searches and seizures and the second requiring that warrants be particular and supported by probable cause. * * *

It is thus perfectly clear that the evil the Amendment was designed to prevent was broader than the abuse of a general warrant. Unreasonable searches or seizures conducted without any warrant at all are condemned by the plain language of the first clause of the Amendment. Almost a century ago the Court stated in resounding terms that the principles reflected in the Amendment "reached farther than the concrete form" of the specific cases that gave it birth, and "apply to all invasions on the part of the government and its employees of the sanctity of a man's home and the privacies of life." *Boyd v. United States*, 116 U.S. 616, 630, 6 S.Ct. 524, 532, 29 L.Ed. 746. * * *

The simple language of the Amendment applies equally to seizures of persons and to seizures of property. Our analysis in this case may therefore properly commence with rules that have been well established in Fourth Amendment litigation involving tangible items. As the Court reiterated just a few years ago, the "physical entry of the home is the chief evil against which the wording of the Fourth Amendment is directed." And we have long adhered to the view that the warrant procedure minimizes the danger of needless intrusions of that sort.

It is a "basic principle of Fourth Amendment law" that searches and seizures inside a home without a warrant are presumptively unreasonable. Yet it is also well settled that objects such as weapons or contraband found in a public place may be seized by the police without a warrant. The seizure of property in plain view involves no invasion of privacy and is presumptively reasonable, assuming that there is probable cause to associate the property with criminal activity. The distinction between a warrantless seizure in an open area and such a seizure on private premises was plainly stated in *G. M. Leasing Corp. v. United States*, 429 U.S. 338, 354, 97 S.Ct. 619, 629, 50 L.Ed.2d 530:

> "It is one thing to seize without a warrant property resting in an open area or seizable by levy without an intrusion into privacy, and it is quite another thing to effect a warrantless seizure of property, even that owned by a corporation, situated on private premises to which access is not otherwise available for the seizing officer."

As the late Judge Leventhal recognized, this distinction has equal force when the seizure of a person is involved. Writing on the constitutional issue now before us for the United States Court of Appeals for the District of Columbia Circuit sitting en banc, *Dorman v. United States*, 140 U.S.App.D.C. 313, 435 F.2d 385 (1970), Judge Leventhal first noted the settled rule that warrantless arrests in public places are valid. He immediately recognized, however, that

> "[a] greater burden is placed * * * on officials who enter a home or dwelling without consent. Freedom from intrusion into the home or

dwelling is the archetype of the privacy protection secured by the Fourth Amendment.''

His analysis of this question then focused on the long-settled premise that, absent exigent circumstances, a warrantless entry to search for weapons or contraband is unconstitutional even when a felony has been committed and there is probable cause to believe that incriminating evidence will be found within. He reasoned that the constitutional protection afforded to the individual's interest in the privacy of his own home is equally applicable to a warrantless entry for the purpose of arresting a resident of the house; for it is inherent in such an entry that a search for the suspect may be required before he can be apprehended. Judge Leventhal concluded that an entry to arrest and an entry to search for and to seize property implicate the same interest in preserving the privacy and the sanctity of the home, and justify the same level of constitutional protection.

* * * We find this reasoning to be persuasive and in accord with this Court's Fourth Amendment decisions.

The majority of the New York Court of Appeals, however, suggested that there is a substantial difference in the relative intrusiveness of an entry to search for property and an entry to search for a person. It is true that the area that may legally be searched is broader when executing a search warrant than when executing an arrest warrant in the home. This difference may be more theoretical than real, however, because the police may need to check the entire premises for safety reasons, and sometimes they ignore the restrictions on searches incident to arrest.

But the critical point is that any differences in the intrusiveness of entries to search and entries to arrest are merely ones of degree rather than kind. The two intrusions share this fundamental characteristic: the breach of the entrance to an individual's home. The Fourth Amendment protects the individual's privacy in a variety of settings. In none is the zone of privacy more clearly defined than when bounded by the unambiguous physical dimensions of an individual's home—a zone that finds its roots in clear and specific constitutional terms: "The right of the people to be secure in their * * * houses * * * shall not be violated." That language unequivocally establishes the proposition that "[a]t the very core [of the Fourth Amendment] stands the right of a man to retreat into his own home and there be free from unreasonable governmental intrusion." In terms that apply equally to seizures of property and to seizures of persons, the Fourth Amendment has drawn a firm line at the entrance to the house. Absent exigent circumstances, that threshold may not reasonably be crossed without a warrant.

III

* * * New York argues that the reasons that support the *Watson* holding require a similar result here. In *Watson* the Court relied on (a) the well-settled common-law rule that a warrantless arrest in a public place is

valid if the arresting officer had probable cause to believe the suspect is a felon; (b) the clear consensus among the States adhering to that well-settled common-law rule; and (c) the expression of the judgment of Congress that such an arrest is "reasonable." We consider each of these reasons as it applies to a warrantless entry into a home for the purpose of making a routine felony arrest.

A * * *

It is obvious that the common-law rule on warrantless home arrests was not as clear as the rule on arrests in public places. * * * [T]he weight of authority as it appeared to the Framers was to the effect that a warrant was required, or at the minimum that there were substantial risks in proceeding without one. The common-law sources display a sensitivity to privacy interests that could not have been lost on the Framers. The zealous and frequent repetition of the adage that a "man's house is his castle," made it abundantly clear that both in England and in the Colonies "the freedom of one's house" was one of the most vital elements of English liberty.

Thus, our study of the relevant common law does not provide the same guidance that was present in *Watson*. * * * [T]he absence of any 17th-or 18th-century English cases directly in point, together with the unequivocal endorsement of the tenet that "a man's house is his castle," strongly suggests that the prevailing practice was not to make such arrests except in hot pursuit or when authorized by a warrant. * * *

B

* * * At this time, 24 States permit * * * warrantless entries; 15 States clearly prohibit them * * *; and 11 States have apparently taken no position on the question. * * *

* * * [A]lthough the weight of state-law authority is clear, there is by no means the kind of virtual unanimity on this question that was present in *United States v. Watson*, with regard to warrantless arrests in public places. Only 24 of the 50 States currently sanction warrantless entries into the home to arrest, and there is an obvious declining trend. Further, the strength of the trend is greater than the numbers alone indicate. Seven state courts have recently held that warrantless home arrests violate their respective State Constitutions. That is significant because by invoking a state constitutional provision, a state court immunizes its decision from review by this Court. This heightened degree of immutability underscores the depth of the principle underlying the result.

C

No congressional determination that warrantless entries into the home are "reasonable" has been called to our attention. None of the federal statutes cited in the *Watson* opinion reflects any such legislative judgment. Thus, that support for the *Watson* holding finds no counterpart in this case. * * *

IV

The parties have argued at some length about the practical consequences of a warrant requirement as a precondition to a felony arrest in the home. In the absence of any evidence that effective law enforcement has suffered in those States that already have such a requirement, we are inclined to view such arguments with skepticism. More fundamentally, however, such arguments of policy must give way to a constitutional command that we consider to be unequivocal.

Finally, we note the State's suggestion that only a search warrant based on probable cause to believe the suspect is at home at a given time can adequately protect the privacy interests at stake, and since such a warrant requirement is manifestly impractical, there need be no warrant of any kind. We find this ingenious argument unpersuasive. It is true that an arrest warrant requirement may afford less protection than a search warrant requirement, but it will suffice to interpose the magistrate's determination of probable cause between the zealous officer and the citizen. If there is sufficient evidence of a citizen's participation in a felony to persuade a judicial officer that his arrest is justified, it is constitutionally reasonable to require him to open his doors to the officers of the law. Thus, for Fourth Amendment purposes, an arrest warrant founded on probable cause implicitly carries with it the limited authority to enter a dwelling in which the suspect lives when there is reason to believe the suspect is within.

Because no arrest warrant was obtained in either of these cases, the judgments must be reversed and the cases remanded to the New York Court of Appeals for further proceedings not inconsistent with this opinion. * * *

[Justice Blackmun's concurring opinion is omitted.]

Mr. Justice WHITE, with whom THE CHIEF JUSTICE and Mr. Justice REHNQUIST join, dissenting. * * *

I * * *

B

The history of the Fourth Amendment does not support the rule announced today. At the time that Amendment was adopted the constable possessed broad inherent powers to arrest. The limitations on those powers derived, not from a warrant "requirement," but from the generally ministerial nature of the constable's office at common law. Far from restricting the constable's arrest power, the institution of the warrant was used to expand that authority by giving the constable delegated powers of a superior officer such as a justice of the peace. Hence at the time of the Bill of Rights, the warrant functioned as a powerful tool of law enforcement rather than as a protection for the rights of criminal suspects.

In fact, it was the abusive use of the warrant power, rather than any excessive zeal in the discharge of peace officers' inherent authority, that precipitated the Fourth Amendment. * * *

* * * [T]he background, text, and legislative history of the Fourth Amendment demonstrate that the purpose was to restrict the abuses that had developed with respect to warrants; the Amendment preserved common-law rules of arrest. Because it was not considered generally unreasonable at common law for officers to break doors to effect a warrantless felony arrest, I do not believe that the Fourth Amendment was intended to outlaw the types of police conduct at issue in the present cases. * * *

II

A

Today's decision rests, in large measure, on the premise that warrantless arrest entries constitute a particularly severe invasion of personal privacy. I do not dispute that the home is generally a very private area or that the common law displayed a special "reverence * * * for the individual's right of privacy in his house." However, the Fourth Amendment is concerned with protecting people, not places, and no talismanic significance is given to the fact that an arrest occurs in the home rather than elsewhere. * * * The inquiry in the present case, therefore, is whether the incremental intrusiveness that results from an arrest's being made *in the dwelling* is enough to support an inflexible constitutional rule requiring warrants for such arrests whenever exigent circumstances are not present.

Today's decision ignores the carefully crafted restrictions on the common-law power of arrest entry and thereby overestimates the dangers inherent in that practice. At common law, absent exigent circumstances, entries to arrest could be made only for felony. Even in cases of felony, the officers were required to announce their presence, demand admission, and be refused entry before they were entitled to break doors. Further, it seems generally accepted that entries could be made only during daylight hours. And, in my view, the officer entering to arrest must have reasonable grounds to believe, not only that the arrestee has committed a crime, but also that the person suspected is present in the house at the time of the entry.

These four restrictions on home arrests—felony, knock and announce, daytime, and stringent probable cause—constitute powerful and complementary protections for the privacy interests associated with the home. The felony requirement guards against abusive or arbitrary enforcement and ensures that invasions of the home occur only in case of the most serious crimes. The knock-and-announce and daytime requirements protect individuals against the fear, humiliation, and embarrassment of being roused from their beds in states of partial or complete undress. And these requirements allow the arrestee to surrender at his front door, thereby maintaining his dignity and preventing the officers from entering other rooms of the dwelling. The stringent probable-cause requirement would help ensure against the possibility that the police would enter when the suspect was not home, and, in searching for him, frighten members of the family or ransack parts of the house, seizing items in plain view. In short, these requirements, taken together, permit an individual suspected of a serious crime to surrender at the front door of his dwelling and thereby avoid most of the humiliation and indignity that the Court seems to believe necessarily accompany a house arrest entry. Such a front-door arrest, in my view, is no more intrusive on personal privacy than the public warrantless arrests which we found to pass constitutional muster in *Watson*.

* * * The Court substitutes, in one sweeping decision, a rigid constitutional rule in place of the common-law approach, evolved over hundreds of years, which achieved a flexible accommodation between the demands of personal privacy and the legitimate needs of law enforcement. * * *

B

While exaggerating the invasion of personal privacy involved in home arrests, the Court fails to account for the danger that its rule will "severely hamper effective law enforcement." * * *

* * * [P]olice officers will often face the difficult task of deciding whether the circumstances are sufficiently exigent to justify their entry to arrest without a warrant. This is a decision that must be made quickly in the most trying of circumstances. If the officers mistakenly decide that the circumstances are exigent, the arrest will be invalid and any evidence seized incident to the arrest or in plain view will be excluded at trial. On the other hand, if the officers mistakenly determine that exigent circumstances are lacking, they may refrain from making the arrest, thus creating the possibility that a dangerous criminal will escape into the community. The police could reduce the likelihood of escape by staking out all possible exits until the circumstances become clearly exigent or a warrant is obtained. But the costs of such a stakeout seem excessive in an era of rising crime and scarce police resources.

The uncertainty inherent in the exigent-circumstances determination burdens the judicial system as well. * * * Under today's decision, whenever the police have made a warrantless home arrest there will be the possibility of "endless litigation with respect to the existence of exigent circumstances, whether it was practicable to get a warrant, whether the suspect was about to flee, and the like," *United States v. Watson, supra.* * * *

[Justice Rehnquist's dissenting opinion is omitted.]

NOTES AND QUESTIONS

1. Justice Stevens states that it is a "basic principle" of the Fourth Amendment "that searches and seizures inside a home without a warrant are presumptively unreasonable." Look again at the text of the Fourth Amend-

ment: *Is* there a presumptive warrant requirement? Why does the majority conclude that there is one? How does the dissent answer the majority?

2. What interest is served by the arrest warrant requirement? Does *Payton* protect the arrestee's person from unlawful seizure or, instead, the resident's interest in freedom from unlawful invasion of privacy in the dwelling?

3. Warrant issues aside, *all* arrests, whether conducted in a public place (*Watson*) or made in a private residence (*Payton*), *must* be supported by probable cause. What is the Fourth Amendment textual basis for this rule?

4. *Proceedings after a warrantless arrest: a "Gerstein hearing".* Most arrests occur outside a private residence. Therefore, in light of *United States v. Watson*, warrantless arrests are exceedingly common. This means that a police officer, and not a neutral and detached magistrate, usually makes the initial probable cause determination. Does this mean that an arrestee may be required to remain in custody pending trial without any judicial determination that the arrest was lawful? No, the Supreme Court ruled in Gerstein v. Pugh, 420 U.S. 103, 95 S.Ct. 854, 43 L.Ed.2d 54 (1975):

> [A] policeman's on-the-scene assessment of probable cause provides legal justification for arresting a person suspected of crime, and for a brief period of detention to take the administrative steps incident to arrest. Once the suspect is in custody, however, the reasons that justify dispensing with the magistrate's neutral judgment evaporate. There no longer is any danger that the suspect will escape or commit further crimes while the police submit their evidence to a magistrate. And, while the State's reasons for taking summary action subside, the suspect's need for a neutral determination of probable cause increases significantly. The consequences of prolonged detention may be more serious than the interference occasioned by arrest. Pretrial confinement may imperil the suspect's job, interrupt his source of income, and impair his family relationships. Even pretrial release may be accompanied by burdensome conditions that effect a significant restraint of liberty. When the stakes are this high, the detached judgment of a neutral magistrate is essential if the Fourth Amendment is to furnish meaningful protection from unfounded interference with liberty. Accordingly, we hold that the Fourth Amendment requires a judicial determination of probable cause as a prerequisite to extended restraint of liberty following arrest. * * *

> [The lower courts] held that the [judicial] determination of probable cause must be accompanied by the full panoply of adversary safeguards— counsel, confrontation, cross-examination, and compulsory process for witnesses. * * *

> These adversary safeguards are not essential for the probable cause determination required by the Fourth Amendment. The sole issue is whether there is probable cause for detaining the arrested person pending further proceedings. This issue can be determined reliably without an adversary hearing. The standard is the same as that for arrest. That standard—probable cause to believe the suspect has committed a crime— traditionally has been decided by a magistrate in a nonadversary proceed-

ing on hearsay and written testimony, and the Court has approved these informal modes of proof. * * *

Although we conclude that the Constitution does not require an adversary determination of probable cause, we recognize that state systems of criminal procedure vary widely. There is no single preferred pretrial procedure, and the nature of the probable cause determination usually will be shaped to accord with a State's pretrial procedure viewed as a whole. * * * Whatever procedure a State may adopt, it must provide a fair and reliable determination of probable cause as a condition for any significant pretrial restraint of liberty, and this determination must be made by a judicial officer either before or promptly after arrest.

In order to satisfy the *Gerstein* timeliness requirement, a jurisdiction must provide a probable cause determination within 48 hours after a warrantless arrest, absent a bona fide emergency or other "extraordinary circumstance." County of Riverside v. McLaughlin, 500 U.S. 44, 111 S.Ct. 1661, 114 L.Ed.2d 49 (1991).

One question left unanswered by *Gerstein* and *McLaughlin* is what remedy is available if a timely hearing is not provided. Imagine that you are a prosecutor, and a defense lawyer files a motion to free her client from jail on the ground that no *Gerstein* proceeding has been held. Given that the hearing can be *ex parte* and based on hearsay evidence, what would be your likely response to this motion?

5. *Executing an arrest: use of force.* An arrest, even one based on probable cause, constitutes an unreasonable seizure of the person if the method for making the arrest is unreasonable. In Tennessee v. Garner, 471 U.S. 1, 105 S.Ct. 1694, 85 L.Ed.2d 1 (1985), a police officer shot in the head and killed a "young, slight, and unarmed" burglary suspect while the youth was running away. The officer "could not have reasonably believed" that the youth "posed any threat." The Court held that the officer's use of deadly force constituted an unreasonable seizure of the arrestee. It stated that use of deadly force to prevent the escape of a fleeing felon is unreasonable unless the officer has "probable cause to believe that the suspect poses a threat of serious physical harm, either to the officer or to others," if the suspect is not immediately taken into custody. "Thus, if the suspect threatens the officer with a weapon or there is probable cause to believe that he has committed a crime involving the infliction or threatened infliction of serious physical harm, deadly force may be used if necessary to prevent escape, and if, where feasible, some warning has been given."

Although many observers believed that the latter quoted language in *Garner* constituted a hard-and-fast rule regarding the proper use of deadly force, the case has turned out to be nothing more than a fact-specific holding. In Scott v. Harris, 550 U.S. 372, 127 S.Ct. 1769, 167 L.Ed.2d 686 (2007), the Court stated that the issue of what constitutes excessive force and, thus, what constitutes an unreasonable seizure of a person, is not susceptible to "an easy-to-apply legal test." Instead, "in the end we must still slosh though the factbound morass of 'reasonableness.'" According to Justice Scalia, "*Garner* does not establish a magical on/off switch that triggers rigid preconditions whenever an officer's actions constitute 'deadly force.'" Thus, the *Scott* Court held that a deputy sheriff did not use unreasonable force when he rammed a motorist's car from behind to end a long "public-endangering" car chase that began when the deputy sought to pull over the motorist for driving 73 miles-per-hour in a 55–mile zone. The deputy's action caused the speeding car to leave the roadway, turn over, crash, and leave its driver a quadriplegic. The Court reasoned that the fleeing driver posed a "substantial" and "immediate" risk of serious injury to innocent persons on the road, rendering the officer's action—seizure—reasonable.

As the Court put it in Graham v. Connor, 490 U.S. 386, 109 S.Ct. 1865, 104 L.Ed.2d 443 (1989), "what was implicit in *Garner*'s analysis" is "that *all* claims that law enforcement officers have used excessive force—deadly or not—in the course of an arrest, investigatory stop, or other 'seizure' of a free citizen should be analyzed under the Fourth Amendment * * * 'reasonable-ness' standard."

6. *Exceptions to the Payton rule.* In Minnesota v. Olson, 495 U.S. 91, 110 S.Ct. 1684, 109 L.Ed.2d 85 (1990), two men robbed a gas station and killed the attendant. The gunman was quickly arrested and the murder weapon retrieved. His accomplice, however, escaped. The next day, the police learned that the second man was hiding with two women in the upper unit of a duplex. Hours later, the police surrounded the dwelling and, without permission or a warrant, entered the upper unit and arrested the suspect. The State sought to justify the warrantless entry on exigency grounds. Justice White, for seven justices, disagreed:

> In *Payton v. New York*, the Court had no occasion to "consider the sort of emergency or dangerous situation, described in our cases as 'exigent circumstances,' that would justify a warrantless entry into a home for the purpose of either arrest or search." This case requires us to determine whether the Minnesota Supreme Court was correct in holding that there were no exigent circumstances that justified the warrantless entry into the house to make the arrest.

> The Minnesota Supreme Court applied essentially the correct standard in determining whether exigent circumstances existed. The court observed that "a warrantless intrusion may be justified by hot pursuit of a fleeing felon, or imminent destruction of evidence, or the need to prevent a suspect's escape, or the risk of danger to the police or to other persons inside or outside the dwelling." The court also apparently thought that in the absence of hot pursuit there must be at least probable cause to believe that one or more of the other factors justifying the entry were present and that in assessing the risk of danger, the gravity of the crime and likelihood that the suspect is armed should be considered. Applying this standard, the state court determined that exigent circumstances did not exist.

> We are not inclined to disagree with this fact-specific application of the proper legal standard. The court pointed out that although a grave crime was involved, respondent "was known not to be the murderer but thought to be the driver of the getaway car," and that the police had already recovered the murder weapon. "The police knew that [two women] were with the suspect in the upstairs duplex with no suggestion

of danger to them. Three or four Minneapolis police squads surrounded the house. The time was 3 p.m., Sunday. * * * It was evident the suspect was going nowhere. If he came out of the house he would have been promptly apprehended." We do not disturb the state court's judgment that these facts do not add up to exigent circumstances.

7. *Getting around Payton?* In *Payton*, suppose that Riddick, rather than his 3–year-old son, had come to the door. If the officers had said, "You are under arrest," would this warrantless arrest have been valid? What if they asked him to come outside, he complied, and *then* they arrested him?

Suppose that police surround an individual's residence and, with a bullhorn, order him out of the house, at which point they arrest him (again, without a warrant). Is *Payton* violated?

8. *Arrests in a third person's residence: the Steagald principle.* In Steagald v. United States, 451 U.S. 204, 101 S.Ct. 1642, 68 L.Ed.2d 38 (1981), the police secured a valid warrant to arrest Ricky Lyons, a fugitive, on drug charges. Based on information that Lyons could be found "during the next 24 hours" at the residence of acquaintance Gary Steagald, twelve officers proceeded to the house and entered without consent. They did not find Lyons, but they did observe cocaine belonging to Steagald. Steagald was later indicted on drug charges and sought to suppress the evidence discovered in the search on the ground that the officers entered the premises without a *search* warrant. The Court, per Justice Marshall, agreed:

> The question before us is a narrow one. The search at issue here took place in the absence of consent or exigent circumstances. Except in such special situations, we have consistently held that the entry into a home to conduct a search or make an arrest is unreasonable under the Fourth Amendment unless done pursuant to a warrant. * * * Here, of course, the agents had a warrant—one authorizing the arrest of Ricky Lyons. However, the Fourth Amendment claim here is not being raised by Ricky Lyons. Instead, the challenge to the search is asserted by a person not named in the warrant who was convicted on the basis of evidence uncovered during a search of his residence for Ricky Lyons. Thus, the narrow issue before us is whether an arrest warrant—as opposed to a search warrant—is adequate to protect the Fourth Amendment interests of persons not named in the warrant, when their homes are searched without their consent and in the absence of exigent circumstances.

> * * * [W]hile an arrest warrant and a search warrant both serve to subject the probable-cause determination of the police to judicial review, the interests protected by the two warrants differ. An arrest warrant is issued by a magistrate upon a showing that probable cause exists to believe that the subject of the warrant has committed an offense and thus the warrant primarily serves to protect an individual from an unreasonable seizure. A search warrant, in contrast, is issued upon a showing of probable cause to believe that the legitimate object of a search is located in a particular place, and therefore safeguards an individual's interest in the privacy of his home and possessions against the unjustified intrusion of the police.

Thus, whether the arrest warrant issued in this case adequately safeguarded the interests protected by the Fourth Amendment depends upon what the warrant authorized the agents to do. To be sure, the warrant embodied a judicial finding that there was probable cause to believe that Ricky Lyons had committed a felony, and the warrant therefore authorized the officers to seize Lyons. However, the agents sought to do more than use the warrant to arrest Lyons in a public place or in his home; instead, they relied on the warrant as legal authority to enter the home of a third person based on their belief that Ricky Lyons might be a guest there. Regardless of how reasonable this belief might have been, it was never subjected to the detached scrutiny of a judicial officer. Thus, while the warrant in this case may have protected Lyons from an unreasonable seizure, it did absolutely nothing to protect petitioner's privacy interest in being free from an unreasonable invasion and search of his home. Instead, petitioner's only protection from an illegal entry and search was the agent's personal determination of probable cause. In the absence of exigent circumstances, we have consistently held that such judicially untested determinations are not reliable enough to justify * * * a search of a home for objects in the absence of a search warrant. We see no reason to depart from this settled course when the search of a home is for a person rather than an object.

9. *Problem: Payton versus Watson.* Police officers have probable cause to arrest Alice for a drug-related offense. The officers drive to Alice's residence without a warrant, although they had time to secure one. Upon arrival in their police van, they observe Alice standing directly in the doorway ("one step forward would have put her outside, one step backward would have put her in the vestibule of her residence"). The officers get out of the van, guns drawn, shouting "police." Alice retreats into her residence. The officers follow her inside through the open door and arrest her. Inside, the police discover drugs in plain view. Should evidence of these drugs be excluded from her trial? See United States v. Santana, 427 U.S. 38, 96 S.Ct. 2406, 49 L.Ed.2d 300 (1976).

10. *Problem: Payton versus Steagald.* Police officers, armed with a warrant to arrest *B* for a felony, receive a tip that *B* is "staying" at a specific apartment building, in apartment #118; they show *B*'s picture to the apartment manager, who states that *B* "might be staying" in apartment #118; an occupant of the building informs them that *B* had been outside the building smoking a cigarette before the police arrived; another occupant tells the police that he observed *B* enter apartment #118 just before the police arrived; the officers knock at apartment #118; a female opens the door, but refuses to allow them to enter; police enter without her consent. State v. Blanco, 237 Wis.2d 395, 614 N.W.2d 512 (Wis.App.2000). Which case applies: *Payton* or *Steagald*? Suppose that the police had *not* been informed by occupants of the apartment building that they had observed *B* smoking a cigarette and then entering apartment #118. Does this affect the constitutionality of the police entry?

C. SEARCH WARRANTS

1. THE CONSTITUTIONAL DEBATE

INTRODUCTORY OVERVIEW

The Fourth Amendment contains two clauses. The first one (the "reasonableness clause") declares a right to be free from unreasonable searches and seizures of persons, houses, papers and effects. The second clause, the "warrant clause," sets out the requirements of any valid warrant (most especially, that it be supported by probable cause, and that it particularly describe "the place to be searched, and the persons or things to be seized"). What is the relationship of these two clauses? Does the second inform the first, or are they independent? More specifically, what is the role of the search warrant in Fourth Amendment jurisprudence: If the police search and seize without a warrant, have they, at least presumptively, violated the Fourth Amendment?

Consider first Justice Jackson's observations for the Court in Johnson v. United States, 333 U.S. 10, 68 S.Ct. 367, 92 L.Ed. 436 (1948) (emphasis added):

> The point of the Fourth Amendment, which often is not grasped by zealous officers, is not that it denies law enforcement the support of the usual inferences which reasonable men draw from evidence. Its protection consists in requiring that those inferences be drawn by a neutral and detached magistrate instead of being judged by the officer engaged in the often competitive enterprise of ferreting out crime. Any assumption that evidence sufficient to support a magistrate's disinterested determination to issue a search warrant will justify the officers in making a search without a warrant would reduce the Amendment to a nullity * * *. * * * *When the right of privacy must reasonably yield to the right of search is, as a rule, to be decided by a judicial officer, not by a policeman or government enforcement agent.*

> There are exceptional circumstances in which, on balancing the need for effective law enforcement against the right of privacy, it may be contended that a magistrate's warrant for search may be dispensed with. But * * * [n]o reason is offered [in this case] for not obtaining a search warrant except the inconvenience to the officers and some slight delay necessary to prepare papers and present the evidence to a magistrate. These are never very convincing reasons and, in these circumstances, certainly are not enough to by-pass the constitutional requirement.

Johnson represents the traditional position that the Fourth Amendment is better served if police officers apply for warrants, rather than act on the basis of their own probable cause determinations. *Johnson*'s reasoning has led courts often to say that there is a "search warrant requirement" in the Fourth Amendment. Stated in its most extreme version, "[t]he command of the Fourth Amendment to the American police officer and the American Prosecutor is simple: 'You always have to get a warrant—UNLESS YOU CAN'T.' " Dyson v. State, 122 Md.App. 413, 712 A.2d 573 (1998). More traditionally, the constitutional "requirement" has been described as follows: "Searches conducted outside the judicial process, without prior approval by judge or magistrate, are *per se* unreasonable under the Fourth Amendment—subject only to a few specifically established and well-delineated exceptions." Katz v. United States, 389 U.S. 347, 88 S.Ct. 507, 19 L.Ed.2d 576 (1967).

The competing view is that the proper Fourth Amendment test "is not whether it is reasonable [or practicable] to procure a search warrant, but whether the search was reasonable." United States v. Rabinowitz, 339 U.S. 56, 70 S.Ct. 430, 94 L.Ed. 653 (1950). After all, the argument goes, the text of the Amendment bars unreasonable searches and seizures; nowhere does it state that warrants are required, only that when warrants *are* sought they must meet certain specifications.

These two alternative views of the relationship of the warrant clause to the reasonableness clause have co-existed uneasily for many years. As Justice Scalia, concurring in California v. Acevedo, 500 U.S. 565, 111 S.Ct. 1982, 114 L.Ed.2d 619 (1991), has observed:

> Although the Fourth Amendment does not explicitly impose the requirement of a warrant, it is of course textually possible to consider that implicit within the requirement of reasonableness. For some years after the (still continuing) explosion in Fourth Amendment litigation that followed our announcement of the exclusionary rule in *Weeks v. United States*, [p. 67], our jurisprudence lurched back and forth between imposing a categorical warrant requirement and looking to reasonableness alone. (The opinions preferring a warrant involved searches of structures.) By the late 1960's, the preference for a warrant had won out, at least rhetorically.

> The victory was illusory. * * * [T]he "warrant requirement" had become so riddled with exceptions that it was basically unrecognizable. In 1985, one commentator cataloged nearly 20 such exceptions * * *. Since then, we have added at least two more. * * *

> * * * There can be no clarity in this area unless we make up our minds [about whether to impose a categorical warrant requirement or look to reasonableness alone], and unless the principles we express comport with the actions we take.

Justice Scalia is among those members of the current Court, apparently now constituting a majority, who reject the "warrant requirement" rule. As you read the remaining cases in this chapter, you will see the Supreme Court moving (if not lurching, as Scalia described it) back and forth between an emphasis on the warrant clause and a more generalized reasonableness analysis.

Scholars, too, have long debated the relationship between the reasonableness and warrant clauses of the Fourth Amendment. What are the historical and policy arguments in favor of a search warrant requirement? What are the arguments for looking to "reasonableness alone"? The following materials consider these important questions.

AKHIL REED AMAR—FOURTH AMENDMENT FIRST PRINCIPLES

107 Harvard Law Review 757 (1994), 762–63, 767–71.

The modern Supreme Court has claimed on countless occasions that there is a warrant requirement in the Fourth Amendment. There are two variants of the warrant requirement argument—a strict (per se) variant that insists that searches and seizures always require warrants, and a looser (modified) variant that concedes the need to craft various common-sense exceptions to a strict warrant rule. Both variants fail.

1. The Per Se Approach.—The first (per se) variant interpolates but nevertheless purports to stay true to the text. The Amendment contains two discrete commands—first, all searches and seizures must be reasonable; second, warrants authorizing various searches and seizures must be limited (by probable cause, particular description, and so on). What is the relationship between these two commands? The per se approach reasons as follows: Obviously, the first and second commands are yoked by an implicit third that no searches and seizures may take place except pursuant to a warrant. Although not expressing the point in so many words, the Amendment plainly presumes that warrantless searches and seizures are per se unreasonable. Surely executive officials should not be allowed to intrude on citizens in a judicially unauthorized manner. And the mode of proper judicial authorization is the warrant. Why else would the Warrant Clause exist?

Standing alone, this line of argument is initially plausible. But when all the evidence is in, we shall see that it is plainly wrong. * * *

If a warrant requirement was intended but not spelled out—if it simply went without saying—we might expect to find at least some early state constitutions making clear what the federal Fourth Amendment left to inference. Yet although many states featured language akin to the Fourth Amendment, none had a textual warrant requirement. Of course, it could be argued that here, too, a warrant requirement was generally presumed—it went without saying. But in leading antebellum cases, the state supreme courts of Pennsylvania, New Hampshire, and Massachusetts briskly dismissed claims of implied warrant requirements under state constitutional provisions that were predecessors of, and textually quite similar to, the federal Fourth Amendment. * * * Supporters of the warrant requirement have yet to locate any antebellum cases contra.

Nor have proponents of a warrant requirement uncovered even a handful of clear statements of the "requirement" in common law treatises, in the debates over the Constitution from 1787 to 1789, or in the First Congress, which proposed the Fourth Amendment. * * *

Of course, this hardly ends the matter. Perhaps early judges and lawmakers simply misunderstood the true spirit of the principles the Constitution embodied. * * * Is it possible that in the Fourth Amendment * * * the early implementation betrayed the underlying principle?

No. The problem with the so-called warrant requirement is not simply that it is not in the text and that it is contradicted by history. The problem is also that, if taken seriously, a warrant requirement makes no sense. Consider just a few common-sense counterexamples to the notion that all searches and seizures must be made pursuant to warrants.

* * * *Exigent Circumstances.*—In a wide range of fast-breaking situations—hot pursuits, crimes in progress, and the like—a warrant requirement would be foolish. Recognizing this, the modern Supreme Court has carved out an "exigent circumstances exception" to its so-called warrant requirement.

* * * *Consent Searches.*—If government officials obtain the uncoerced authorization of the owner or apparent owner, surely they should be allowed to search a place, even without a warrant. And the modern Supreme Court has so held. * * * The explicit logic here has been that, even though the police had neither a true warrant nor a true waiver, they acted *reasonably*. But this is a recognition that reasonableness—not a warrant—is the ultimate touchstone for all searches and seizures.

* * * *Plain View Searches.*—When a Secret Service agent at a presidential event stands next to her boss, wearing sunglasses and scanning the crowd in search of any small signal that something might be amiss, she is searching without a warrant. Yet surely this must be constitutional, and the Supreme Court has so suggested. At times, however, the Court has played word games, insisting that sunglass or naked-eye searches are not really searches. * * *

These word games are unconvincing and unworthy. A search is a search, whether with Raybans or x-rays. The difference between these two searches is that one may be much more reasonable than another. * * *

Because it creates an unreasonable mandate for all searches, the warrant requirement leads judges to artificially constrain the scope of the Amendment itself by narrowly defining "search" and "seizure." If a "search" or a "seizure" requires only reasonableness rather than warrants, however, judges will be more likely to define these terms generously. * * *

* * * *Real Life.*—Finally, consider the vast number of real-life, unintrusive, non-discriminatory searches and seizures to which modern day Americans are routinely subjected: metal detectors at airports, annual auto emissions tests, inspections of closely regulated industries, public school regimens, border searches, and on and on. All of these occur without warrants. Are they all unconstitutional? Surely not, the Supreme

Court has told us, in a variety of cases. What the Court has not clearly explained, however, is how all these warrantless searches are consistent with its so-called warrant requirement. * * *

We have now seen * * * [various] historical and commonsensical exceptions to the so-called warrant requirement. There are many others—but I am a lover of mercy. And by now I hope the point is clear: it makes no sense to say that all warrantless searches and seizures are per se unreasonable.

2. *The Modified Per Se Approach.*—At this point, a supporter of the so-called warrant requirement is probably tempted to concede some exceptions and modify the per se claim: warrantless searches and seizures are per se unreasonable, save for a limited number of well-defined historical and commonsensical exceptions.

This modification is clever, but the concessions give up the game. The per se argument is no longer the textual argument it claimed to be; it no longer merely specifies an implicit logical relationship between the reasonableness command and the Warrant Clause. To read in a warrant requirement that is not in the text—and then to read in various non-textual exceptions to that so-called requirement—is not to read the Fourth Amendment at all. It is to rewrite it. What's more, in conceding that, above and beyond historical exceptions, common sense dictates various additional exceptions to the so-called warrant requirement, the modification seems to concede that the ultimate touchstone of the Amendment is not warrants, but reasonableness.

* * * On my reading, the Framers did say what they meant, and what they said makes eminent good sense: all searches and seizures must be reasonable. Precisely because these searches and seizures can occur in all shapes and sizes under a wide variety of circumstances, the Framers chose a suitably general command.

TRACEY MACLIN—WHEN THE CURE FOR THE FOURTH AMENDMENT IS WORSE THAN THE DISEASE

68 Southern California Law Review 1 (1994), 5–11, 13, 20–21, 24–25.

The concept of reasonableness makes eminently good sense—provided it is applied in a manner that does not undermine the values embodied in the Fourth Amendment. I am not opposed to common sense when interpreting the Fourth Amendment. Who is? But Amar's readers are ill-served if they believe that the Fourth Amendment simply calls for reasonable police behavior. Further, I do not oppose consulting history when interpreting the Fourth Amendment. But the history and development of the Fourth Amendment includes a lot more than Professor Amar is willing to concede.

The history of the Fourth Amendment is about controlling executive power. Amar's thesis that the Fourth Amendment only requires that police intrusions comport with "common sense" is simply wrong. Reasonable judgment and common sense should play a role in the ongoing formulation of search and seizure law. But "reasonableness" cannot be the end of the matter. Amar's vision of the Amendment is delusive because it does not grapple with the hard reality that "the fourth amendment is quintessentially a regulation of the police—that, in enforcing the fourth amendment, courts *must* police the police."

Amar begins his critique of current Fourth Amendment doctrine by constructing several straw men, which he attacks as inimical to the notion that reasonableness "is the ultimate touchstone for all searches and seizures." Consider, for example, Amar's criticism of the "warrant preference" rule, which holds that a judicial warrant is a necessary precondition of a reasonable search unless good reasons call for proceeding without one. He argues that the Fourth Amendment does not expressly provide for such a rule. He also writes that there is no historical support for the rule in eighteenth-or nineteenth-century thinking on the subject. * * *

Professor Amar is correct: The text of the Fourth Amendment does not expressly provide for a warrant preference rule. Amar, however, cites no one who argues that "all searches and seizures must be made pursuant to warrants." Only Amar makes this claim, and he asserts it to attack a proposition that is not at issue. Many people have advocated that the Court take the warrant preference rule seriously. Proponents of the warrant preference rule, however, have never claimed that the rule is textually based or derived from express references to eighteenth-century thinking about the meaning of the Fourth Amendment. Instead, they argue that the rule is designed to promote the central premise of the Fourth Amendment, which is to control police discretion.

But Professor Amar never discusses whether the warrant preference rule reasonably restrains police investigatory power. Many of the Justices and law professors * * * have long argued that the Fourth Amendment is a "profoundly anti-government document[]" that is designed to control the discretion and authority of law enforcement personnel. Why doesn't Amar directly confront this position? * * * [I]f judges do not restrain the police when they investigate the presumed bad guys, they will have no mechanism to control the police when they decide to investigate the rest of us.

Professor Amar also cites four categories of warrantless intrusions that were permitted around the time the Fourth Amendment was adopted. * * *

Again, Amar has resolved a nonissue. Proponents of the warrant preference rule have never claimed that eighteenth- and nineteenth-century authorities share their view about the phraseology of the Fourth Amendment. Proponents of the warrant preference rule have looked to history to discover the broad themes that compelled the Framers to establish a constitutional principle against governmental searches and seizures. Those who proposed the Fourth Amendment did so because they "opposed leaving the power to search and seize solely in executive hands." In their day, the abuse of executive search and seizure powers primarily manifested itself in the form of general warrants and writs of assistance.

Today, law enforcement officials have a greater array of weapons to invade our privacy and personal security. Certain investigatory tools obviously did not exist when the Fourth Amendment was adopted; other police practices still used today existed in 1791, but were not on the revolutionary agenda, or may have never been considered subject to regulation under the Constitution. What did the Framers think about eavesdropping? What did they think about frisking suspicious persons? Was the power of subpoena a seizure? Did it require judicial authorization? Did the Framers consider undercover spies and informants a type of search that a judge could order by warrant? How would the Framers react to having the "knock and announce" rule eliminated in cases where the police suspect that contraband is inside a private home?

Following Amar's advice, we should first examine the text of the Amendment for answers to these questions. The text, of course, provides no answers. That leaves us with the views of eighteenth- and nineteenth-century legal authorities * * * under Amar's scheme. But do we really want the existence and breadth of our interests in privacy and personal security to turn on the values and understanding of the eighteenth or nineteenth century? * * * As Professor Carol Steiker wrote, the Fourth Amendment's vague text "positively invites constructions that change with changing circumstances."[38] * * *

* * * Amar is right that the Framers did not go on record as opposing all warrantless searches. Amar is also correct that the text of the Fourth Amendment does not proscribe all warrantless searches and that eighteenth-century precedents support certain types of warrantless intrusions. General, discretionary searches by government officers were widespread in the states when the Fourth Amendment was proposed. But what does this history reveal? For starters, it reveals that early Americans did not always practice what they preached. Law enforcement practices frequently did not satisfy constitutional ideals. That discretionary searches and seizures were the norm in early America provides scant evidence that they were constitutionally correct—then or now.

The Fourth Amendment makes a pledge to the American people. It states an ideal; it is not a constitutional wrench that "locks-in" search and seizure practices of a vanished era. * * *

So Amar's history lesson is really beside the point. Rather than focus solely upon particular practices that may or may not have preoccupied the Framers, historical analysis and constitutional originalism are helpful tools when they instruct us on the broad principles that motivated the Framers. Again, the broad value that inspired the Fourth Amendment is restraint of police power and discretion. * * *

---

38. Carol Steiker, *Second Thoughts About First Principles*, 107 HARV. L. REV. 820, 824 (1994).

* * * [T]he Warrant Clause defines and interprets the Reasonableness Clause. The Warrant Clause informs the judiciary of the type of search that is reasonable and therefore presumed permitted by the Amendment—a search that is consistent with the procedural safeguards of probable cause, particularity, and judicial scrutiny. An interpretation that detaches the Reasonableness Clause from the Warrant Clause runs the risk of making the Warrant Clause "virtually useless." * * *

THOMAS Y. DAVIES—RECOVERING THE ORIGINAL FOURTH AMENDMENT

98 Michigan Law Review 547 (1999), 547–56.

If American judges, lawyers, or law teachers were asked what the Framers intended when they adopted the Fourth Amendment, they would likely answer that the Framers intended that all searches and seizures conducted by government officers must be reasonable given the circumstances. That answer may seem obvious—the Amendment begins with a clause that states that "[t]he right of the people to be secure in their persons, houses, papers, and effects, against unreasonable searches and seizures, shall not be violated * * *." Indeed, this language has been identified as a prime example of how the original understanding can be gleaned directly from constitutional text—what could "unreasonable" mean if not inappropriate in the circumstances?

Of course, the reference to "unreasonable searches and seizures" does not exhaust the intended meaning of the text—the standards for valid arrest or search warrants that are set out in the second clause also show that the Framers intended to ban the use of too-loose, or "general," warrants. Thus the Framers intended to require that all searches and seizures be reasonable and also to forbid use of general warrants.

There is a difficulty embedded in the apparently obvious meanings of the two clauses, however—the text does not indicate how they fit together. It does not say whether a valid warrant should be the usual criterion for a "reasonable" police intrusion, or whether "Fourth Amendment reasonableness" should be assessed independently of use of a warrant. Put more concretely, it does not indicate whether or in what circumstances arrests or searches must be made pursuant to a warrant. Thus, it does not say when an officer should be allowed to intrude on the basis of his own judgment, or when he should be required to obtain prior approval from a judge. Largely because of this silence in the text, the need for warrants has been the central issue in the modern debate regarding search and seizure authority.

A number of the historical commentaries on the Fourth Amendment have either favored or rejected a warrant requirement. However, none have supported their answer with persuasive historical evidence. If one turns to the historical sources themselves, the mystery initially deepens: the participants in the historical controversies that stimulated the framing of the Fourth Amendment simply did not discuss when a warrant was required. Odd as it may seem, the Framers simply were not troubled by the most salient issue in the modern debate.

However, upon closer examination, the historical sources do provide a solution to the silence. They show that the Framers did not perceive the problem of search and seizure authority in the same way we now do. In fact, they reveal that the Framers did not even use the term "unreasonable searches and seizures" the way we do.

The historical statements about search and seizure focused on condemning general warrants. In fact, the historical concerns were almost exclusively about the need to ban house searches under general warrants. Thus, the Framers clearly understood the warrant standards to be the operative content of the Fourth Amendment, as well as the earlier state search and seizure provisions. [Evidence suggests that the reference to "persons, houses, papers, and effects" in the first clause was meant to define the scope of the amendment's protection so as to exclude commercial premises, such as ships and warehouses.—Eds.] Moreover, the evidence indicates that the Framers understood "unreasonable searches and seizures" simply as a pejorative label for the inherent illegality of any searches or seizures that might be made under general warrants. In other words, the Framers did not address warrantless intrusions at all in the Fourth Amendment or in the earlier state provisions; thus, they never anticipated that "unreasonable" might be read as a standard for warrantless intrusions.

Perplexing as that omission may appear from a modern perspective, it made sense in the context of the Framers' understanding of the problem of search and seizure. They saw no need for a constitutional standard to regulate the warrantless officer because they did not perceive the warrantless officer as being capable of posing a significant threat to the security of person or house. That was so because the *ex officio* authority of the peace officer was still meager in 1789. Warrant authority was the potent source of arrest and search authority. As a result, the Framers expected that warrants would be used. Thus, they believed that the only threat to the right to be secure came from the possibility that too-loose warrants might be used.

The modern interpretation of "unreasonable searches and seizures" is the product of *post-framing* developments that the Framers did not anticipate. * * *

The post-framing transformation of the original meaning into modern search and seizure doctrine is a complex story in its own right * * *. The conferral of discretionary authority on the warrantless officer during the nineteenth century was the catalyst for the transformation. [In particular, courts set aside the framing-era standard under which arrests were lawful only if it could be proven that a crime had been committed *in fact*, and instead allowed arrests to be based on probable cause that a crime had been committed, a standard that permitted police officers to take the initiative in investigating criminal activity.—Eds.] The expansion of *ex* *officio* authority marginalized the warrant process as a means of controlling police intrusions. As a result, police began to assert broader authority to make searches "incident to arrest," including warrantless searches of houses and offices. The Supreme Court responded to that novel threat to the right to be secure by creating the basic elements of modern search and seizure doctrine. The 1914 decision *Weeks v. United States* [p. 67] extended the Fourth Amendment to a federal officer's warrantless search of a house and papers, constitutionalized the common-law warrant requirement for such searches, and adopted exclusion as the means for enforcing the right to be secure. Next, the 1925 decision in *Carroll v. United States*[, 267 U.S. 132, 45 S.Ct. 280, 69 L.Ed. 543,] assumed that the Fourth Amendment broadly protected all privately owned property but adopted a relativistic reasonableness standard to assess the constitutionality of warrantless police intrusions. Notably, Chief Justice Taft's *Carroll* opinion was grounded on a historically false description of the original meaning of "unreasonable searches and seizures." The two currently competing constructions of the Fourth Amendment have emerged from the tensions arising between the doctrinal elements announced in *Weeks* and *Carroll*.

* * * [N]either of the currently competing constructions of the Fourth Amendment adheres to the historical meaning, though the warrant-preference construction is more faithful to the Framers' concerns than the generalized-reasonableness construction. In fact, the latter is nearly the antithesis of the Framers' understanding. However, I [doubt] * * * that the original meaning can be directly applied to address modern issues. In particular, * * * any attempt to return to the literal original meaning—that is, to an understanding that the text only banned general warrants but did not address warrantless intrusions—would subvert the larger purpose for which the Framers adopted the text; namely to curb the exercise of discretionary authority by officers. [It is] * * * inappropriate to employ framing-era doctrines selectively to answer specific modern issues because historic doctrines often do not accomplish the same ends in the modern context as they did during the framing era.

NOTES AND QUESTIONS

1. If the warrant clause does *not* inform the reasonableness clause—that is, if there is no Fourth Amendment "warrant requirement"—does this mean that Congress and the various states may abolish warrants altogether and thereby render the warrant clause useless? If so, does that mean that the requirement of probable cause, which is attached to the warrant provision, may also be avoided?

2. One scholar has suggested a solution for the self-created quagmire in which the Supreme Court finds itself in the search warrant debate:

> [C]urrent fourth amendment law, complete with the constant tinkering which it necessarily entails, should be abandoned altogether. Instead, there are two, and only two, ways of looking at the fourth amendment

which will provide the police with reasonably coherent direction as to how they must proceed and the courts with a consistent basis for decision.

The two models, briefly, may be called the "no lines" and the "bright line" approaches. Model I, no lines, uses tort law as a guide in proposing that the hopeless quest of establishing detailed guidelines for police behavior in every possible situation be abandoned. It suggests that the Court adopt the following view of the fourth amendment: A search or seizure must be reasonable, considering all relevant factors on a case-by-case basis. If it is not, the evidence must be excluded. Factors to be considered include, but are not limited to, whether probable cause existed, whether a warrant was obtained, whether exigent circumstances existed, the nature of the intrusion, the quantum of evidence possessed by the police, and the seriousness of the offense under investigation. This model * * * is (roughly) the current practice in Germany and other European countries. Moreover, in most cases it reflects the result, though not the reasoning, of current Supreme Court cases.

The second model may be as shocking at first glance to "law and order" advocates as the first model is to civil libertarians. It is, basically, that the Supreme Court should actually enforce the warrant doctrine to which it has paid lip service for so many years. That is, a warrant is *always* required for *every* search and seizure when it is practicable to obtain one. However, in order that this requirement be workable and not be swallowed by its exception, the warrant need not be in writing but rather may be phoned or radioed into a magistrate (where it will be tape recorded and the recording preserved) who will authorize or forbid the search orally. By making the procedure for obtaining a warrant less difficult (while only marginally reducing the safeguards it provides), the number of cases where "emergencies" justify an exception to the warrant requirement should be very small.

* * * Model I, by presenting an unabashedly *unclear* rule that provides no guidelines, will never have to be modified to suit an unusual fact situation. While not an ideal solution, it will, it is argued, work considerably better than the present system where the Court purports to set forth clear rules but does not actually do so. Model II presents a clear rule which can be lived with. If the Court required a modified, easily obtainable warrant to be used in all but true emergencies, the police would know what is expected of them and would be able to conform their conduct to the requirement of the law, much as they have accommodated their behavior to the *Miranda* requirements.

Craig M. Bradley, *Two Models of the Fourth Amendment*, 83 Mich. L. Rev. 1468, 1471–72 (1985).

3. *A reality check. Does any of this debate really matter in day-to-day affairs: the warrant application process.* If it *is* better for magistrates, rather than "officers engaged in the often competitive enterprise of ferreting out crime," to make probable cause determinations, one is left with a nagging empirical question: *Does* the warrant application process serve its intended purpose? *Do* magistrates give warrant applications careful attention?

Perhaps not. In the most thorough national study of search warrant procedures ever conducted, the National Center for State Courts reported that in one city studied, the average length of magisterial review was a mere two minutes and forty-eight seconds; ten percent of the warrant applications were approved in less than one minute. Richard Van Duizend et al., The Search Warrant Process: Preconceptions, Perceptions, and Practices 31 (1984). In a more recent study in San Diego, only a few judges handled the great majority of warrant applications because of magistrate-shopping by the police. As a "veteran officer" candidly admitted, "some judges were known for being liberal in granting search warrants." Laurence A. Benner & Charles T. Samarkos, *Searching for Narcotics in San Diego: Preliminary Findings from the San Diego Search Warrant Project*, 36 Cal. West. L. Rev. 221, 227–228 (2000). As one scholar has put it, "warrants [are] commonly issu[ed] upon something more akin to 'possible cause' rather than 'probable cause.'" Fabio Arcila, Jr., *In the Trenches: Searches and the Misunderstood Common–Law History of Suspicion and Probable Cause*, 10 U. Pa. J. Const. L. 1, 58 (2007) (also suggesting that this approach does not appreciably differ from the Framers' era).

2. ELEMENTS OF A VALID SEARCH WARRANT

Warrants must meet constitutional specifications. They must be based on probable cause and supported by oath or affirmation, matters considered in Part A. of this chapter. Two other required features are considered here.

LO–JI SALES, INC. v. NEW YORK

Supreme Court of the United States, 1979.
442 U.S. 319, 99 S.Ct. 2319, 60 L.Ed.2d 920.

MR. CHIEF JUSTICE BURGER delivered the opinion of the Court. * * *

I

On June 20, 1976, an investigator for the New York State Police purchased two reels of film from petitioner's so-called "adult" bookstore. Upon viewing them, he concluded the films violated New York's obscenity laws. On June 25, he took them to a Town Justice for a determination whether there was reasonable cause to believe the films violated the state obscenity laws so as to justify a warrant to search the seller's store. The Town Justice viewed both films in their entirety, and he apparently concluded they were obscene. Based upon an affidavit of the investigator subscribed before the Town Justice after this viewing, a warrant issued authorizing the search of petitioner's store and the seizure of other copies of the two films exhibited to the Town Justice.

The investigator's affidavit also contained an assertion that "similar" films and printed matter portraying similar activities could be found on the premises, and a statement of the affiant's belief that the items were possessed in violation of the obscenity laws. The warrant application requested that the Town Justice accompany the investigator to petitioner's store for the execution of the search warrant. The stated purpose was to allow the Town Justice to determine independently if any other items at the store were possessed in violation of law and subject to seizure. The Town Justice agreed. Accordingly, the warrant also contained a recital that authorized the seizure of "[t]he following items that the Court independently [on examination] has determined to be possessed in violation of Article 235 of the Penal Law * * *." However, at the time the Town Justice signed the warrant there were no items listed or described following this statement. As noted earlier, the only "things to be seized" that were described in the warrant were copies of the two films the state investigator had purchased. * * *

The Town Justice and the investigator enlisted three other State Police investigators, three uniformed State Police officers, and three members of the local prosecutor's office—a total of 11—and the search party converged on the bookstore. * * *

The search began in an area of the store which contained booths in which silent films were shown by coin-operated projectors. The clerk adjusted the machines so that the films could be viewed by the Town Justice without coins; it is disputed whether he volunteered or did so under compulsion * * *. The Town Justice viewed 23 films for two to three minutes each and, satisfied there was probable cause to believe they were obscene, then ordered the films and the projectors seized.

The Town Justice next focused on another area containing four coin-operated projectors showing both soundless and sound films. After viewing each film for two to five minutes, again without paying, he ordered them seized along with their projectors.

The search party then moved to an area in which books and magazines were on display. The magazines were encased in clear plastic or cellophane wrappers which the Town Justice had two police officers remove prior to his examination of the books. Choosing only magazines that did not contain significant amounts of written material, he spent not less than 10 seconds nor more than a minute looking through each one. When he was satisfied that probable cause existed, he immediately ordered the copy which he had reviewed, along with other copies of the same or "similar" magazines, seized. An investigator wrote down the titles of the items seized. All told, 397 magazines were taken.

The final area searched was one in which petitioner displayed films and other items for sale behind a glass enclosed case. When it was announced that each box of film would be opened, the clerk advised that a picture on the outside of the box was representative of what the film showed. Therefore, if satisfied from the picture that there was probable cause to believe the film in the box was obscene, the Town Justice ordered the seizure of all copies of that film. As with the magazines, an investigator wrote down the titles of the films seized, a total of 431 reels. * * *

After the search and seizure was completed, the seized items were taken to a State Police barracks where they were inventoried. Each item was then listed on the search warrant, and late the same night the completed warrant was given to the Town Justice. The warrant, which had consisted of 2 pages when he signed it before the search, by late in the day contained 16 pages. It is clear, therefore, that the particular description of "things to be seized" was entered in the document after the seizure and impoundment of the books and other articles. * * *

II

This search warrant and what followed the entry on petitioner's premises are reminiscent of the general warrant or writ of assistance of the 18th century against which the Fourth Amendment was intended to protect. Except for the specification of copies of the two films previously purchased, the warrant did not purport to "particularly describ[e] * * * the * * * things to be seized." Based on the conclusory statement of the police investigator that other similarly obscene materials would be found at the store, the warrant left it entirely to the discretion of the officials conducting the search to decide what items were likely obscene and to accomplish their seizure. The Fourth Amendment does not permit such action. Nor does the Fourth Amendment countenance open-ended warrants, to be completed while a search is being conducted and items seized or after the seizure has been carried out.

This search began when the local justice and his party entered the premises. But at that time there was not sufficient probable cause to pursue a search beyond looking for additional copies of the two specified films, assuming the validity of searching even for those. And the record is clear that the search began and progressed pursuant to the sweeping open-ended authorization in the warrant. It was not limited at the outset as a search for other copies of the two "sample" films; it expanded into a more extensive search because other items were found that the local justice deemed illegal. * * *

III

We have repeatedly said that a warrant authorized by a neutral and detached judicial officer is "a more reliable safeguard against improper searches than the hurried judgment of a law enforcement officer 'engaged in the often competitive enterprise of ferreting out crime.' " * * *

The Town Justice did not manifest that neutrality and detachment demanded of a judicial officer when presented with a warrant application for a search and seizure. We need not question the subjective belief of the Town Justice in the propriety of his actions, but the objective facts of record manifest an erosion of whatever neutral and detached posture existed at the outset. He allowed himself to become a member, if not the leader, of the search party which was essentially a police operation. Once in the store, he conducted a generalized search under authority of an invalid warrant; he was not acting as a judicial officer but as an adjunct law enforcement officer. When he ordered an item seized because he believed it was obscene, he instructed the police officers to seize all "similar" items as well, leaving determination of what was "similar" to the officer's discretion. Indeed, he yielded to the State Police even the completion of the general provision of the warrant. * * *

IV * * *

* * * Our society is better able to tolerate the admittedly pornographic business of petitioner than a return to the general warrant era; violations of law must be dealt with within the framework of constitutional guarantees. * * *

NOTES AND QUESTIONS

1. *"Neutral and detached magistrate" requirement.* What is it, precisely, that the Town Justice did wrong in *Lo-Ji Sales*? Is it that he left his regular office to make himself available to law enforcement personnel?

Should a search warrant be invalidated (and if so, why) in the following circumstances: (a) it is issued by the State Attorney General, see Coolidge v. New Hampshire, 403 U.S. 443, 91 S.Ct. 2022, 29 L.Ed.2d 564 (1971); (b) the magistrate is paid a fee for issuing a warrant, but is not paid if she denies an application for a warrant, see Connally v. Georgia, 429 U.S. 245, 97 S.Ct. 546, 50 L.Ed.2d 444 (1977); (c) the magistrate fails to read the warrant that she signs, see United States v. Decker, 956 F.2d 773 (8th Cir.1992); or (d) she spends only 2 minutes, 48 seconds considering the warrant application (see p. 194, Note 3)?

2. *The warrant particularity requirement.* This requirement is intended to prevent general searches, the immediate evil "that motivated the framing and adoption of the Fourth Amendment," *Payton v. New York*, p. 171, and to prevent "the seizure of one thing under a warrant describing another." Andresen v. Maryland, 427 U.S. 463, 96 S.Ct. 2737, 49 L.Ed.2d 627 (1976). According to *Andresen*, "nothing [should be] left to the discretion of the officer executing the warrant."

In fact, courts do not apply such a stringent standard. "A greater degree of ambiguity will be tolerated when the police have done the best that could be expected under the circumstances * * *." 2 Wayne R. LaFave, Search and Seizure 604 (4th ed. 2004). Professor LaFave has listed nine principles (*id.* at 609–13) distilled from court opinions. Among the principles are: (1) a relatively general description will be tolerated if the nature of the object to be seized could not realistically be described more specifically (*e.g.*, "paper clips" and "string" in a search for stolen property); (2) greater generality is allowed in the case of contraband; (3) greater specificity is demanded if other objects of the same general classification are likely to be found at the search site (*e.g.*, "cartons of women's clothing" will not do if the police will be searching a warehouse containing many such cartons); and (4) "scrupulous exactitude" is demanded when the search encroaches on First Amendment concerns, such as in *Lo-Ji Sales.*

Andresen v. Maryland, supra, also teaches that a court should read a search warrant in fair context. For example, in *Andresen*, a warrant authorized the police to seize a long list of specific items relating to a specific incident of false pretenses, "together with other fruits, instrumentalities, and evidence of crime at this [time] unknown." Although Andresen argued that the latter phrase permitted the search and seizure of *any* evidence of *any* crime—clearly a violation of the particularity requirement—the Court concluded that the challenged phrase, coming as part of the same sentence that included the long list of specific items, "must be read as authorizing only the search for and seizure of evidence relating to" the particular crime under investigation.

3. *Particularity by incorporation?* Suppose a search warrant fails to properly specify the property to be seized. May this constitutional failing be cured if the *application* for the warrant particularizes the items to be seized? In Groh v. Ramirez, 540 U.S. 551, 124 S.Ct. 1284, 157 L.Ed.2d 1068 (2004), the Supreme Court answered this way:

> The fact that the *application* adequately described "the things to be seized" does not save the *warrant* from its facial invalidity. The Fourth Amendment by its terms requires particularity in the warrant, not in the supporting documents. * * * We do not say that the Fourth Amendment forbids a warrant from cross-referencing other documents. Indeed, most Courts of Appeals have held that a court may construe a warrant with reference to a supporting application or affidavit if the warrant uses appropriate words of incorporation, and if the supporting document accompanies the warrant.

3. EXECUTION OF A SEARCH WARRANT

INTRODUCTORY NOTE

Consider these facts: An informant tells Atlanta police officers that he purchased two bags of crack cocaine from a man at a house the address of which he provided to the police. Based on this information, the officers obtained a warrant to search the residence. Armed with the warrant, eight members of the Atlanta police department went to the home where, in a military-type raid, broke into the house without warning—they did not knock at the door, nor did they announce their identity and purpose before breaking in. Inside the house was one person, Kathryn Johnston, a 92-year-old woman living alone.

Assume for current purposes (there is more to the story, which will be disclosed later) that the information the police received justified the search warrant. Thus, the police had a valid search warrant. And, surely the fact that the information proved wrong—this was not a house where drugs were sold—does not render the warrant invalid. Warrants are based on probable cause, not certainty. Was the *means* of execution of the warrant, however, unconstitutional? Specifically, does it violate the Fourth Amendment for agents of the government to enter a person's home forcibly, rather than giving the occupant(s) notice of their presence and allowing the resident(s) an opportunity to comply with the officers' demand for entry?

In Wilson v. Arkansas, 514 U.S. 927, 115 S.Ct. 1914, 131 L.Ed.2d 976 (1995), the Supreme Court, per Justice Clarence Thomas, ruled unanimously that the Fourth Amendment prohibition on unreasonable searches and seizures contains an implicit knock-and-announce rule previously embedded in the common law. However, the Court warned that "[t]his is not to say, of course, that every entry must be preceded by an announcement. The Fourth Amendment's flexible requirement of reasonableness should not be read to mandate a rigid rule of announcement that ignores countervailing law enforcement interests."[b] Without "attempt[ing] a comprehensive catalog" of exceptions to the requirement, Justice Thomas suggested in dictum that the knock-and-announce principle does not apply

> under circumstances presenting a threat of physical violence. Similarly, courts [have] held that an officer may dispense with announcement in cases where a prisoner escapes from him and retreats to his dwelling. Proof of "demand and refusal" was deemed unnecessary in such cases because it would be a "senseless ceremony" to require an officer in pursuit of a recently escaped arrestee to make an announcement prior to breaking the door to retake him. Finally, courts have indicated that unannounced entry may be justified where police officers have reason to believe that evidence would likely be destroyed if advance notice were given.

Soon after *Wilson*, the Supreme Court considered the exceptions to the knock-and-announce principle more fully.

RICHARDS v. WISCONSIN

Supreme Court of the United States, 1997.
520 U.S. 385, 117 S.Ct. 1416, 137 L.Ed.2d 615.

JUSTICE STEVENS delivered the opinion of the Court.

In *Wilson v. Arkansas*, we held that the Fourth Amendment incorporates the common law requirement that police officers entering a dwelling must knock on the door and announce their identity and purpose before attempting forcible entry. At the same time, we recognized that the "flexible requirement of reasonableness should not be read to mandate a rigid rule of announcement that ignores countervailing law enforcement interests," and left "to the lower courts the task of determining the circumstances under which an unannounced entry is reasonable under the Fourth Amendment."

In this case, the Wisconsin Supreme Court concluded that police officers are *never* required to knock and announce their presence when

---

b. According to one scholar, the common law did *not* recognize a flexible reasonableness standard allowing for exceptions to the knock-and-announce rule. "The Justices' decision to relax the requirements for the execution of a search warrant was not based in history; rather it was a departure from historical doctrine." Thomas Y. Davies, *Recovering the Original Fourth Amendment*, 98 Mich. L. Rev. 547, 742 n. 561 (1999).

executing a search warrant in a felony drug investigation. In so doing, it reaffirmed a pre-*Wilson* holding and concluded that *Wilson* did not preclude this *per se* rule. We disagree with the court's conclusion that the Fourth Amendment permits a blanket exception to the knock-and-announce requirement for this entire category of criminal activity. But because the evidence presented to support the officers' actions in this case establishes that the decision not to knock and announce was a reasonable one under the circumstances, we affirm the judgment of the Wisconsin court.

I

On December 31, 1991, police officers in Madison, Wisconsin obtained a warrant to search Steiney Richards' hotel room for drugs and related paraphernalia. The search warrant was the culmination of an investigation that had uncovered substantial evidence that Richards was one of several individuals dealing drugs out of hotel rooms in Madison. The police requested a warrant that would have given advance authorization for a "no-knock" entry into the hotel room, but the magistrate explicitly deleted those portions of the warrant.

The officers arrived at the hotel room at 3:40 a.m. Officer Pharo, dressed as a maintenance man, led the team. With him were several plainclothes officers and at least one man in uniform. Officer Pharo knocked on Richards' door and, responding to the query from inside the room, stated that he was a maintenance man. With the chain still on the door, Richards cracked it open. Although there is some dispute as to what occurred next, Richards acknowledges that when he opened the door he saw the man in uniform standing behind Officer Pharo. He quickly slammed the door closed and, after waiting two or three seconds, the officers began kicking and ramming the door to gain entry to the locked room. At trial, the officers testified that they identified themselves as police while they were kicking the door in. When they finally did break into the room, the officers caught Richards trying to escape through the window. They also found cash and cocaine hidden in plastic bags above the bathroom ceiling tiles.

Richards sought to have the evidence from his hotel room suppressed on the ground that the officers had failed to knock and announce their presence prior to forcing entry into the room. The trial court denied the motion, concluding that the officers could gather from Richards' strange behavior when they first sought entry that he knew they were police officers and that he might try to destroy evidence or to escape. The judge emphasized that the easily disposable nature of the drugs the police were searching for further justified their decision to identify themselves as they crossed the threshold instead of announcing their presence before seeking entry. Richards appealed the decision to the Wisconsin Supreme Court and that court affirmed.

The Wisconsin Supreme Court did not delve into the events underlying Richards' arrest in any detail, but accepted the following facts: "[O]n

December 31, 1991, police executed a search warrant for the motel room of the defendant seeking evidence of the felonious crime of Possession with Intent to Deliver a Controlled Substance in violation of [state law]. They did not knock and announce prior to their entry. Drugs were seized."

Assuming these facts, the court proceeded to consider whether our decision in *Wilson* required the court to abandon its decision in *State v. Stevens*, 181 Wis.2d 410, 511 N.W.2d 591 (1994), which held that "when the police have a search warrant, supported by probable cause, to search a residence for evidence of delivery of drugs or evidence of possession with intent to deliver drugs, they necessarily have reasonable cause to believe exigent circumstances exist" to justify a no-knock entry. The court concluded that nothing in *Wilson*'s acknowledgment that the knock-and-announce rule was an element of the Fourth Amendment "reasonableness" requirement would prohibit application of a *per se* exception to that rule in a category of cases.

In reaching this conclusion, the Wisconsin court found it reasonable—after considering criminal conduct surveys, newspaper articles, and other judicial opinions—to assume that all felony drug crimes will involve "an extremely high risk of serious if not deadly injury to the police as well as the potential for the disposal of drugs by the occupants prior to entry by the police." Notwithstanding its acknowledgment that in "some cases, police officers will undoubtedly decide that their safety, the safety of others, and the effective execution of the warrant dictate that they knock and announce," the court concluded that exigent circumstances justifying a no-knock entry are always present in felony drug cases. Further, the court reasoned that the violation of privacy that occurs when officers who have a search warrant forcibly enter a residence without first announcing their presence is minimal, given that the residents would ultimately be without authority to refuse the police entry. The principal intrusion on individual privacy interests in such a situation, the court concluded, comes from the issuance of the search warrant, not the manner in which it is executed. Accordingly, the court determined that police in Wisconsin do not need specific information about dangerousness, or the possible destruction of drugs in a particular case, in order to dispense with the knock-and-announce requirement in felony drug cases. * * *

II

We recognized in *Wilson* that the knock-and-announce requirement could give way "under circumstances presenting a threat of physical violence," or "where police officers have reason to believe that evidence would likely be destroyed if advance notice were given." It is indisputable that felony drug investigations may frequently involve both of these circumstances. The question we must resolve is whether this fact justifies dispensing with case-by-case evaluation of the manner in which a search was executed.

The Wisconsin court explained its blanket exception as necessitated by the special circumstances of today's drug culture, and the State asserted at oral argument that the blanket exception was reasonable in "felony drug cases because of the convergence in a violent and dangerous form of commerce of weapons and the destruction of drugs." But creating exceptions to the knock-and-announce rule based on the "culture" surrounding a general category of criminal behavior presents at least two serious concerns.[4]

First, the exception contains considerable overgeneralization. For example, while drug investigation frequently does pose special risks to officer safety and the preservation of evidence, not every drug investigation will pose these risks to a substantial degree. For example, a search could be conducted at a time when the only individuals present in a residence have no connection with the drug activity and thus will be unlikely to threaten officers or destroy evidence. Or the police could know that the drugs being searched for were of a type or in a location that made them impossible to destroy quickly. In those situations, the asserted governmental interests in preserving evidence and maintaining safety may not outweigh the individual privacy interests intruded upon by a no-knock entry.[5] Wisconsin's blanket rule impermissibly insulates these cases from judicial review.

A second difficulty with permitting a criminal-category exception to the knock-and-announce requirement is that the reasons for creating an exception in one category can, relatively easily, be applied to others. Armed bank robbers, for example, are, by definition, likely to have weapons, and the fruits of their crime may be destroyed without too much difficulty. If a *per se* exception were allowed for each category of criminal investigation that included a considerable—albeit hypothetical—risk of danger to officers or destruction of evidence, the knock-and-announce element of the Fourth Amendment's reasonableness requirement would be meaningless.

---

4. It is always somewhat dangerous to ground exceptions to constitutional protections in the social norms of a given historical moment. The purpose of the Fourth Amendment's requirement of reasonableness "is to preserve that degree of respect for the privacy of persons and the inviolability of their property that existed when the provision was adopted—even if a later, less virtuous age should become accustomed to considering all sorts of intrusion 'reasonable.'" *Minnesota v. Dickerson*, 508 U.S. 366, 380, 113 S.Ct. 2130, 2139, 124 L.Ed.2d 334 (1993) (Scalia, J., concurring).

5. The State asserts that the intrusion on individual interests effectuated by a no-knock entry is minimal because the execution of the warrant itself constitutes the primary intrusion on individual privacy and that the individual privacy interest cannot outweigh the generalized governmental interest in effective and safe law enforcement. While it is true that a no-knock entry is less intrusive than, for example, a warrantless search, the individual interests implicated by an unannounced, forcible entry should not be unduly minimized. As we observed in *Wilson v. Arkansas*, the common law recognized that individuals should have an opportunity to themselves comply with the law and to avoid the destruction of property occasioned by a forcible entry. These interests are not inconsequential.

Additionally, when police enter a residence without announcing their presence, the residents are not given any opportunity to prepare themselves for such an entry. The State pointed out at oral argument that, in Wisconsin, most search warrants are executed during the late night and early morning hours. The brief interlude between announcement and entry with a warrant may be the opportunity that an individual has to pull on clothes or get out of bed.

Thus, the fact that felony drug investigations may frequently present circumstances warranting a no-knock entry cannot remove from the neutral scrutiny of a reviewing court the reasonableness of the police decision not to knock and announce in a particular case. Instead, in each case, it is the duty of a court confronted with the question to determine whether the facts and circumstances of the particular entry justified dispensing with the knock-and-announce requirement.

In order to justify a "no-knock" entry, the police must have a reasonable suspicion that knocking and announcing their presence, under the particular circumstances, would be dangerous or futile, or that it would inhibit the effective investigation of the crime by, for example, allowing the destruction of evidence. This standard—as opposed to a probable cause requirement—strikes the appropriate balance between the legitimate law enforcement concerns at issue in the execution of search warrants and the individual privacy interests affected by no-knock entries.[c] This showing is not high, but the police should be required to make it whenever the reasonableness of a no-knock entry is challenged.

III

Although we reject the Wisconsin court's blanket exception to the knock-and-announce requirement, we conclude that the officers' no-knock entry into Richards' hotel room did not violate the Fourth Amendment. We agree with the trial court, and with Justice Abrahamson, that the circumstances in this case show that the officers had a reasonable suspicion that Richards might destroy evidence if given further opportunity to do so.

The judge who heard testimony at Richards' suppression hearing concluded that it was reasonable for the officers executing the warrant to believe that Richards knew, after opening the door to his hotel room the first time, that the men seeking entry to his room were the police. Once the officers reasonably believed that Richards knew who they were, the court concluded, it was reasonable for them to force entry immediately given the disposable nature of the drugs.

In arguing that the officers' entry was unreasonable, Richards places great emphasis on the fact that the magistrate who signed the search warrant for his hotel room deleted the portions of the proposed warrant that would have given the officers permission to execute a no-knock entry. But this fact does not alter the reasonableness of the officers' decision, which must be evaluated as of the time they entered the hotel room. At the time the officers obtained the warrant, they did not have evidence sufficient, in the judgment of the magistrate, to justify a no-knock warrant. Of course, the magistrate could not have anticipated in every particular the circumstances that would confront the officers when they

---

c. To satisfy the "reasonable suspicion" standard, an officer must be able to articulate something more than an "inchoate and unparticularized suspicion or 'hunch.'" *Terry v. Ohio*, p. 349. There must exist "some minimal level of objective justification" for the police conduct. This is a less demanding standard than "probable cause." See generally, *Alabama v. White*, p. 397.

arrived at Richards' hotel room. These actual circumstances—petitioner's apparent recognition of the officers combined with the easily disposable nature of the drugs—justified the officers' ultimate decision to enter without first announcing their presence and authority.

Accordingly, although we reject the blanket exception to the knock-and-announce requirement for felony drug investigations, the judgment of the Wisconsin Supreme Court is affirmed.

NOTES AND QUESTIONS

1. As a practical matter, who are the big winners in this case, the police or home dwellers? Is it fair to assert that in virtually every drug-dealer case the police will possess reasonable suspicion that persons inside are armed or that contraband will likely be destroyed if they announce their presence and intention?

Why does the *Richards* Court permit the police to apply a less demanding standard than probable cause in determining whether an exception to the knock-and-announce requirement exists? Does Justice Stevens offer an explanation?

2. *More to come.* There is much more to the story of the knock-and-announce rule, but as to that you will need to wait until we get to the next chapter. See p. 509, *infra.*

3. What interests are served by the knock-and-announce rule? What reasons did Justice Stevens give for the rule? In Hudson v. Michigan, 547 U.S. 586, 126 S.Ct. 2159, 165 L.Ed.2d 56 (2006), Justice Scalia provided the Court's most recent explanation for the requirement:

> One of [the] interests [of the knock-and-announce requirement] is the protection of human life and limb, because an unannounced entry may provoke violence in supposed self-defense by the surprised resident. Another interest is the protection of property. Breaking a house (as the old cases typically put it) absent an announcement would penalize someone who " 'did not know of the process, of which, if he had notice, it is to be presumed that he would obey it * * * .' " The knock-and-announce rule gives individuals "the opportunity to comply with the law and to avoid the destruction of property occasioned by a forcible entry." And thirdly, the knock-and-announce rule protects those elements of privacy and dignity that can be destroyed by a sudden entrance. It gives residents the "opportunity to prepare themselves for" the entry of the police. "The brief interlude between announcement and entry with a warrant may be the opportunity that an individual has to pull on clothes or get out of bed." In other words, it assures the opportunity to collect oneself before answering the door.

4. *The rest of the Atlanta story.* We promised you more to the story of the Atlanta police officers who entered a "drug house" only to find a 92-year-old woman inside. The story is more sordid than we suggested, and tragic. As it turned out, the informant lied to the police about purchasing drugs at that home. He had never been there and, it seems, picked that address at random.

The police, in turn, lied to the magistrate when they applied for the warrant: an officer under oath falsely claimed that he had personally purchased drugs at that address in his undercover status. He further perjured himself by stating that he had seen surveillance cameras in the house. (Based on these false statements, *was* the warrant valid? What case or doctrine would come into play with this new information? Hint: see p. 165, Note 6.)

The sordid story now turns tragic. The elderly and infirm (the officers might have noticed a wheelchair ramp when they arrived at the residence) Kathryn Johnston, fearful of intruders, apparently kept a gun with her, which she fired at them when the intruders entered her small house. The outcome was inevitable: She was shot to death in the ensuing hail of police bullets. And, then to finish the ugly events, one or more of the officers planted a small quantity of drugs on the premises to try to justify their actions.

The upshot: The family of the deceased has sued the city. Two police officers were charged with murder and pleaded guilty to manslaughter and federal civil rights violations. A third officer, who had been stationed at the rear of the house, was charged with violating his oath of office (acquitted), falsely imprisoning Johnston (acquitted), and lying in an official investigation (convicted). He was sentenced to 4½ years in prison. See, e.g., Shaila Dewan & Brenda Goodman, *Atlanta Officers Suspended In Inquiry on Killing in Raid*, New York Times, Nov, 28, 2006, at A16; Steve Visser, *Officer in Fatal '06 Raid Guilty of One Charge*, The Atlanta Journal–Constitution, May 21, 2008, at 1A; *Former Atlanta Cop Gets 4½ Years*, Atlanta Journal–Constitution, May 23, 2008, at 16; and Christian Boone & Marcus K. Garner, *Family Offers to Settle in Notorious Raid*, Atlanta Journal–Constitution, July 18, 2008, at 5H.

5. After knocking and announcing their presence, how long must the police wait before they forcibly enter a residence and execute a warrant to search for cocaine? In United States v. Banks, 540 U.S. 31, 124 S.Ct. 521, 157 L.Ed.2d 343 (2003), officers armed with a warrant to search Banks's two-bedroom apartment for cocaine, knocked loudly, announced their purpose, and waited fifteen to twenty seconds for a response. When nobody came to the door, the police broke open the door with a battering ram, entered, and executed their warrant. As it turned out, Banks was in the shower and had not heard the police knock.

The Court unanimously held that although the "call is a close one, * * * we think that after 15 or 20 seconds without a response, police could fairly suspect that cocaine would be gone if they were reticent any longer." In short, an exigency justified the forcible entry. The fact that Banks was in the shower was irrelevant: "[I]t is enough to say that the facts known to the police are what count in judging reasonable waiting time."

Does it matter to the analysis that the police entry required them to damage the property? The Court explained that where, as here, an exigency justifies immediate forcible entry, the police "may damage premises so far as necessary for a no-knock entrance without demonstrating the suspected risk in any more detail than the law demands for an unannounced intrusion simply by lifting the latch." However, the Court suggested that in some circumstances damage to property *could* be relevant to the reasonableness of an entry to execute a search warrant. Specifically, when immediate entry is *not* required as a result of an exigency, "the reasonable wait time" before causing damage to enter "may well be longer" than if the door to the house is open and they can enter without damaging the residence:

> Suffice it to say that the need to damage property in the course of getting in is a good reason to require more patience than it would be reasonable to expect if the door were open. Police seeking a stolen piano may be able to spend more time to make sure they really need the battering ram.

6. *In anticipation of a warrant.* What, if anything, may the police do *before* they execute a warrant—indeed, before they even have a warrant—to ensure that criminal evidence they expect to find during the search will not be destroyed or moved while they apply for the warrant? For example, in Illinois v. McArthur, 531 U.S. 326, 121 S.Ct. 946, 148 L.Ed.2d 838 (2001), police officers who were already at McArthur's home, developed probable cause at the scene to believe that he had hidden marijuana in his trailer home. Two officers asked McArthur for permission to search the premises for marijuana, but he refused. As a consequence, one officer left to apply for a search warrant. The second officer informed McArthur, who by this time was standing on the porch, that he could not reenter his trailer unless accompanied by an officer. McArthur reentered his home two or three times, to make phone calls and get cigarettes, and each time the officer stood just inside the door to observe McArthur. The first officer returned two hours later with a search warrant, which was promptly executed.

The Supreme Court, 8–1, approved the police action, although it conceded that by preventing McArthur or others from entering the trailer home, the police had effectively seized the premises without a warrant. Justice Breyer explained:

> We conclude that the restriction at issue was reasonable, and hence lawful, in light of the following circumstances, which we consider in combination. First, the police had probable cause to believe that McArthur's trailer home contained evidence of a crime and contraband, namely, unlawful drugs. * * *

> Second, the police had good reason to fear that, unless restrained, McArthur would destroy the drugs before they could return with a warrant. * * * They reasonably could have concluded that McArthur, * * * suspecting an imminent search, would, if given the chance, get rid of the drugs fast.

> Third, the police made reasonable efforts to reconcile their law enforcement needs with the demands of personal privacy. They neither searched the trailer nor arrested McArthur before obtaining a warrant. Rather, they imposed a significantly less restrictive restraint, preventing McArthur only from entering the trailer unaccompanied. They left his home and his belongings intact—until a neutral Magistrate, finding probable cause, issued a warrant.

> Fourth, the police imposed the restraint for a limited period of time, namely, two hours. As far as the record reveals, this time period was no longer than reasonably necessary for the police, acting with diligence, to obtain the warrant. Given the nature of the intrusion and the law

enforcement interest at stake, this brief seizure of the premises was permissible.

7. *Executing a warrant after entry: The scope of the search of the premises.* Once officers are lawfully on premises to execute a warrant, various search principles apply. First, the police may search containers large enough to hold the criminal evidence for which they are searching. For example, if a warrant authorizes a search of a suspect's bedroom for a stolen ring, the officer may, pursuant to the warrant, open dresser drawers, jewelry boxes, and other containers in the bedroom that could hold the ring. In contrast, if they are searching a bedroom for a stolen 42–inch plasma television set, the police would not be authorized to open drawers or to open boxes smaller than the television.

Second, while officers execute a search warrant, they may seize an object *not* described in the warrant, if they have probable cause to believe it is a seizable item (contraband, or a fruit, instrumentality or evidence of a crime).

Third, as Maryland v. Garrison, 480 U.S. 79, 107 S.Ct. 1013, 94 L.Ed.2d 72 (1987), teaches, information that becomes available to officers immediately before or during the execution of a warrant may require them to cease or narrow their search, notwithstanding the dictates of the warrant. In *Garrison*, the officers obtained a warrant to search "the premises known as 2036 Park Avenue third floor apartment" belonging to one Lawrence McWebb. What the officers did not know when they sought the warrant, or even as they entered the third floor "apartment," was that the third floor was divided into *two* apartments, one occupied by McWebb, and a second by petitioner Garrison. The officers erroneously entered Garrison's premises; only after they discovered contraband there did they realize the mistake. They immediately ceased the search of Garrison's premises. However, they sought to prosecute him on the basis of the evidence they found before they discovered their error. The Court upheld the validity of the erroneous warrant and its execution:

> Plainly, if the officers had known, or even if they should have known, that there were two separate dwelling units on the third floor of 2036 Park Avenue, they would have been obligated to exclude respondent's apartment from the scope of the requested warrant. But we must judge the constitutionality of their conduct in light of the information available to them at the time they acted. Those items of evidence that emerge after the warrant is issued have no bearing on whether or not a warrant was validly issued. * * * The validity of the warrant must be assessed on the basis of the information that the officers disclosed, or had a duty to discover and to disclose, to the issuing Magistrate. On the basis of that information * * * the warrant * * * was valid when it issued. * * *

> The question whether the execution of the warrant violated respondent's constitutional right to be secure in his home is somewhat less clear. * * * If the officers had known, or should have known, that the third floor contained two apartments before they entered the living quarters on the third floor, and thus had been aware of the error in the warrant, they would have been obligated to limit their search to McWebb's apartment. Moreover, as the officers recognized, they were required to discontinue the search of respondent's apartment as soon as

they discovered that there were two separate units on the third floor and therefore were put on notice of the risk that they might be in a unit erroneously included within the terms of the warrant. The officers' conduct and the limits of the search were based on the information available as the search proceeded. While the purposes justifying a police search strictly limit the permissible extent of the search, the Court has also recognized the need to allow some latitude for honest mistakes that are made by officers in the dangerous and difficult process of making arrests and executing search warrants.

What is the essence of the Fourth Amendment lesson of *Garrison*?

8. *Searching persons during the execution of a warrant.* A warrant may authorize the search of a person, but it should be explicit. A warrant to search a home or other premises does not provide implicit authority to search persons found at the scene, even if the criminal evidence for which the police are looking might be on them.

For example, in Ybarra v. Illinois, 444 U.S. 85, 100 S.Ct. 338, 62 L.Ed.2d 238 (1979), the police obtained a valid warrant to search a tavern and "Greg," the bartender, for "evidence of the offense of possession of a controlled substance." Seven or eight officers proceeded to the tavern in the late afternoon. While most of the officers searched the premises and bartender Greg, one officer conducted cursory searches of a dozen or so customers present and, in the case of Ventura Ybarra, conducted a more extensive search. The latter search turned up a cigarette pack, inside which were six tinfoil packets containing a brown powdery substance that later turned out to be heroin. The Court held that the warrant did not authorize the Ybarra search.

Ybarra does *not* stand for the proposition that police officers may *never* search persons coincidentally at the scene during a warranted search. However, the police must have independent probable cause to search the person ("a person's mere propinquity to others independently suspected of criminal activity does not, without more, give rise to probable cause to search that person"), as well as some justification for conducting the search without a warrant, *i.e.*, they must be able to point to an exception to the "warrant requirement."

9. *Seizure of persons during warranted searches.* Although the police may not automatically *search* persons present at the scene during the execution of a search warrant (Note 8), the Supreme Court announced a bright-line rule in Michigan v. Summers, 452 U.S. 692, 101 S.Ct. 2587, 69 L.Ed.2d 340 (1981), regarding *seizure* of persons: "[A] warrant to search [a residence] for contraband founded on probable cause implicitly carries with it the limited authority to detain the occupants of the premises while a proper search is conducted."

Moreover, the right of the police under *Summers* to detain an occupant during a warranted search of a residence necessarily includes the right to use reasonable force to secure and maintain detention of the occupant. For example, in Muehler v. Mena, 544 U.S. 93, 125 S.Ct. 1465, 161 L.Ed.2d 299 (2005), members of a SWAT team came armed with a warrant to search a house for deadly weapons and evidence of gang membership. They discovered a female, who was not a gang member, and detained her in handcuffs for up to three hours while they executed the search warrant.

The Court stated that "[i]nherent in *Summers'* authorization to detain an occupant of the place to be searched is the authority to use reasonable force to effectuate the detention." Although the handcuffing "undoubtedly" constituted a "separate intrusion in addition to detention," Chief Justice Rehnquist ruled that "[t]he governmental interests in not only detaining, but using handcuffs, are at their maximum when, as here, a warrant authorizes a search for weapons and a wanted gang member resides on the premises. In such inherently dangerous situations, the use of handcuffs minimizes the risk of harm to both officers and occupants."

Justice Kennedy, while joining the five-justice majority opinion, wrote separately to warn that it is "a matter of first concern that excessive force is not used on persons detained, especially when those persons, though lawfully detained under *Michigan v. Summers*, are not themselves suspected of any involvement in criminal activity." He also warned that "[i]f the search extends to the point when the handcuffs can cause real pain or serious discomfort, provision must be made to alter the conditions of detention at least long enough to attend to the needs of the detainee."

Justice Stevens, writing for Justices Souter, Ginsburg, and Breyer, believed that it was "clear that the jury could properly have found [as it did] that this 5–foot–2–inch young lady posed no threat to the officers at the scene, and that [the officers] used excessive force in keeping her in handcuffs for up to three hours."

10. *Problem*. Los Angeles County, California v. Rettele, 550 U.S. 609, 127 S.Ct. 1989, 167 L.Ed.2d 974 (2007):

> From September to December 2001, Los Angeles County Sheriff's Department Deputy Dennis Watters investigated a fraud and identity-theft crime ring. There were four suspects of the investigation. One had registered a 9–millimeter Glock handgun. The four suspects were known to be African–Americans. * * *

> On December 11, Watters obtained a [valid] search warrant for two houses in Lancaster, California, where he believed he could find the suspects. * * *

> What Watters did not know was that one of the houses (the first to be searched) had been sold in September to a Max Rettele. He had purchased the home and moved into it three months earlier with his girlfriend Judy Sadler and Sadler's 17-year-old son Chase Hall. All three, respondents here, are Caucasians.

> On the morning of December 19, Watters briefed six other deputies in preparation for the search of the houses. Watters informed them they would be searching for three African–American suspects, one of whom owned a registered handgun. The possibility a suspect would be armed caused the deputies concern for their own safety. * * * Around 7:15 [a.m.] Watters and six other deputies knocked on the door and announced their presence. Chase Hall answered. The deputies entered the house after ordering Hall to lie face down on the ground.

The deputies' announcement awoke Rettele and Sadler. The deputies entered their bedroom with guns drawn and ordered them to get out of their bed and to show their hands. They protested that they were not wearing clothes. Rettele stood up and attempted to put on a pair of sweatpants, but deputies told him not to move. Sadler also stood up and attempted, without success, to cover herself with a sheet. Rettele and Sadler were held at gunpoint for one to two minutes before Rettele was allowed to retrieve a robe for Sadler. He was then permitted to dress. Rettele and Sadler left the bedroom within three to four minutes to sit on the couch in the living room.

By that time the deputies realized they had made a mistake. They apologized to Rettele and Sadler, thanked them for not becoming upset, and left within five minutes.

The residents brought a federal suit against the police for violation of their Fourth Amendment rights. Based on everything you have studied so far, should they win their claim?

D. WARRANT CLAUSE: WHEN ARE WARRANTS REQUIRED?

INTRODUCTORY COMMENT

According to Katz v. United States, 389 U.S. 347, 88 S.Ct. 507, 19 L.Ed.2d 576 (1967), "searches conducted outside the judicial process, without prior approval by judge or magistrate, are *per se* unreasonable under the Fourth Amendment—subject only to a few specifically established and well-delineated exceptions." This chapter section considers the most important "exceptions" to the search warrant "requirement."

We primarily leave to Section E. of this chapter the Court's move away from "warrant requirement" jurisprudence to an explicit, flexible "reasonableness" balancing approach. Despite this sectioning of the topics, however, there is no absolute line separating the two lines of cases. One could treat the materials in Section E. as further "warrant exceptions," albeit discussed in "reasonableness" terms; or you could say that some of the "exceptions" here are, simply, examples of reasonable (warrantless) searches, albeit discussed in "warrant exception" terms.

1. EXIGENT CIRCUMSTANCES

WARDEN v. HAYDEN

Supreme Court of the United States, 1967.
387 U.S. 294, 87 S.Ct. 1642, 18 L.Ed.2d 782.

MR. JUSTICE BRENNAN delivered the opinion of the Court. * * *

I

About 8 a.m. on March 17, 1962, an armed robber entered the business premises of the Diamond Cab Company in Baltimore, Maryland.

He took some $363 and ran. Two cab drivers in the vicinity, attracted by shouts of "Holdup," followed the man to 2111 Cocoa Lane. One driver notified the company dispatcher by radio that the man was a Negro about 5'8" tall, wearing a light cap and dark jacket, and that he had entered the house on Cocoa Lane. The dispatcher relayed the information to police who were proceeding to the scene of the robbery. Within minutes, police arrived at the house in a number of patrol cars. An officer knocked and announced their presence. Mrs. Hayden answered, and the officers told her they believed that a robber had entered the house, and asked to search the house. She offered no objection.

The officers spread out through the first and second floors and the cellar in search of the robber. Hayden was found in an upstairs bedroom feigning sleep. He was arrested when the officers on the first floor and in the cellar reported that no other man was in the house. Meanwhile an officer was attracted to an adjoining bathroom by the noise of running water, and discovered a shotgun and a pistol in a flush tank; another officer who, according to the District Court, "was searching the cellar for a man or the money" found in a washing machine a jacket and trousers of the type the fleeing man was said to have worn. A clip of ammunition for the pistol and a cap were found under the mattress of Hayden's bed, and ammunition for the shotgun was found in a bureau drawer in Hayden's room. All these items of evidence were introduced against respondent at his trial.

II

We agree with the Court of Appeals that neither the entry without warrant to search for the robber, nor the search for him without warrant was invalid. Under the circumstances of this case, "the exigencies of the situation made that course imperative." The police were informed that an armed robbery had taken place, and that the suspect had entered 2111 Cocoa Lane less than five minutes before they reached it. They acted reasonably when they entered the house and began to search for a man of the description they had been given and for weapons which he had used in the robbery or might use against them. The Fourth Amendment does not require police officers to delay in the course of an investigation if to do so would gravely endanger their lives or the lives of others. Speed here was essential, and only a thorough search of the house for persons and weapons could have insured that Hayden was the only man present and that the police had control of all weapons which could be used against them or to effect an escape. * * *

It is argued that, while the weapons, ammunition, and cap may have been seized in the course of a search for weapons, the officer who seized the clothing was searching neither for the suspect nor for weapons when he looked into the washing machine in which he found the clothing. But even if we assume, although we do not decide, that the exigent circumstances in this case made lawful a search without warrant only for the suspect or his weapons, it cannot be said on this record that the officer who found the clothes in the washing machine was not searching for weapons. He testified that he was searching for the man or the money, but his failure to state explicitly that he was searching for weapons, in the absence of a specific question to that effect, can hardly be accorded controlling weight. He knew that the robber was armed and he did not know that some weapons had been found at the time he opened the machine. In these circumstances the inference that he was in fact also looking for weapons is fully justified. * * *

[The concurring opinion of Justice Fortas, with whom Chief Justice Warren concurred, is omitted. Justice Douglas dissented on unrelated grounds.]

NOTES AND QUESTIONS

1.   The officer who looked in the washing machine testified that he was searching for the suspect or the money taken in the robbery. Yet, in upholding the search, the Court only went so far as to say that exigent circumstances justified a search for the robbery suspect *and for weapons*. Obviously, the officer was not looking in the washing machine for Hayden, so that leaves his testimony that he was searching for money (as distinguished from weapons). How did Justice Brennan get around this problem? What is arguably wrong with his solution?

2.   Suppose that Mrs. Hayden had objected to the officers' entry of her home? Would the result have been different?

3.   *Warrantless entry of a home (part 1).* Various exigencies, not just those specified in *Hayden*, may justify a warrantless entry of a home. As noted earlier (see p. 181, Note 6), in Minnesota v. Olson, 495 U.S. 91, 110 S.Ct. 1684, 109 L.Ed.2d 85 (1990), the Supreme Court considered the exigencies that might justify a warrantless entry of a home to make an arrest or conduct a search. It stated:

The Minnesota Supreme Court [in this case] applied essentially the correct standard in determining whether exigent circumstances [to enter a residence] existed. The court observed that "a warrantless intrusion may be justified by hot pursuit of a fleeing felon, or imminent destruction of evidence, or the need to prevent a suspect's escape, or the risk of danger to the police or to other persons inside or outside the dwelling." The court also apparently thought that in the absence of hot pursuit there must be at least probable cause to believe that one or more of the other factors justifying the entry were present and that in assessing the risk of danger, the gravity of the crime and likelihood that the suspect is armed should be considered.

Notwithstanding these exceptions, the Supreme Court has hesitated to give the police a free rein to enter a home without a warrant. For example, in Welsh v. Wisconsin, 466 U.S. 740, 104 S.Ct. 2091, 80 L.Ed.2d 732 (1984), the police received information that *W* had been driving his vehicle in a manner that suggested either that he was inebriated or very sick. The police immediately proceeded to *W*'s nearby home and entered without consent or—despite

Payton v. New York, p. 171—an arrest warrant. Inside they discovered *W* in bed. They placed him under arrest for operating a motor vehicle under the influence of an intoxicant, a noncriminal offense that could result in a monetary fine and subject *W* to civil forfeiture of his automobile. The Supreme Court held, however, that the warrantless entry of *W*'s house was unlawful:

> It is axiomatic that the "physical entry of the home is the chief evil against which the wording of the Fourth Amendment is directed." And a principal protection against unnecessary intrusions into private dwellings is the warrant requirement imposed by the Fourth Amendment on agents of the government who seek to enter the home for purposes of search or arrest. It is not surprising, therefore, that the Court has recognized, as "a 'basic principle of Fourth Amendment law[,]' that searches and seizures inside a home without a warrant are presumptively unreasonable." * * *

> Consistently with these long-recognized principles, the Court decided in *Payton v. New York* that warrantless felony arrests in the home are prohibited by the Fourth Amendment, absent probable cause and exigent circumstances. * * *

> Our hesitation in finding exigent circumstances, especially when warrantless arrests in the home are at issue, is particularly appropriate when the underlying offense for which there is probable cause to arrest is relatively minor. Before agents of the government may invade the sanctity of the home, the burden is on the government to demonstrate exigent circumstances that overcome the presumption of unreasonableness that attaches to all warrantless home entries. When the government's interest is only to arrest for a minor offense, that presumption of unreasonableness is difficult to rebut, and the government usually should be allowed to make such arrests only with a warrant issued upon probable cause by a neutral and detached magistrate.

> * * *[T]he only potential exigency claimed by the State was the need to ascertain the petitioner's blood-alcohol level.

> Even assuming, however, that the underlying facts would support a finding of this exigent circumstance * * *, [t]he State of Wisconsin has chosen to classify the first offense for driving while intoxicated as a noncriminal, civil forfeiture offense for which no imprisonment is possible. This is the best indication of the State's interest in precipitating the arrest * * *. Given this expression of the State's interest, a warrantless home arrest cannot be upheld simply because evidence of the petitioner's blood-alcohol level might have dissipated while the police obtained a warrant.

4. *Warrantless entry of a home (part 2): the "murder scene" non-exception.* In Mincey v. Arizona, 437 U.S. 385, 98 S.Ct. 2408, 57 L.Ed.2d 290 (1978), the Supreme Court rejected a "murder scene warrant exception" to the Fourth Amendment that the Arizona Supreme Court had recognized. However, it is essential to draw a distinction between this *non*-exception to the warrant requirement and a true emergency:

After the shooting, the narcotics agents, thinking that other persons in the apartment might have been injured, looked about quickly for other victims. They found a young woman wounded in the bedroom closet and Mincey apparently unconscious in the bedroom, as well as Mincey's three acquaintances (one of whom had been wounded in the head) in the living room. Emergency assistance was requested, and some medical aid was administered to Officer Headricks. But the agents refrained from further investigation, pursuant to a Tucson Police Department directive that police officers should not investigate incidents in which they are involved. They neither searched further nor seized any evidence; they merely guarded the suspects and the premises.

Within 10 minutes, however, homicide detectives who had heard a radio report of the shooting arrived and took charge of the investigation. They supervised the removal of Officer Headricks and the suspects, trying to make sure that the scene was disturbed as little as possible, and then proceeded to gather evidence. Their search lasted four days, during which period the entire apartment was searched, photographed, and diagrammed. The officers opened drawers, closets, and cupboards, and inspected their contents; they emptied clothing pockets; they dug bullet fragments out of the walls and floors; they pulled up sections of the carpet and removed them for examination. Every item in the apartment was closely examined and inventoried, and 200 to 300 objects were seized. In short, Mincey's apartment was subjected to an exhaustive and intrusive search. No warrant was ever obtained. * * *

The State's * * * argument in support of its categorical exception to the warrant requirement is that a possible homicide presents an emergency situation demanding immediate action. We do not question the right of the police to respond to emergency situations. Numerous state and federal cases have recognized that the Fourth Amendment does not bar police officers from making warrantless entries and searches when they reasonably believe that a person within is in need of immediate aid. Similarly, when the police come upon the scene of a homicide they may make a prompt warrantless search of the area to see if there are other victims or if a killer is still on the premises. * * * And the police may seize any evidence that is in plain view during the course of their legitimate emergency activities.

But a warrantless search must be "strictly circumscribed by the exigencies which justify its initiation," and it simply cannot be contended that this search was justified by any emergency threatening life or limb. All the persons in Mincey's apartment had been located before the investigating homicide officers arrived there and began their search. And a four-day search that included opening dresser drawers and ripping up carpets can hardly be rationalized in terms of the legitimate concerns that justify an emergency search.

Notice: The emergency in *Mincey* that justified the original warrantless entry by the police was to look for injured persons. This emergency essentially falls within a police department's "community caretaking function," as distinguished from its criminal law enforcement function (as seen in *Hayden*).

Although an exigency may justify a warrantless entry in either case, and the two functions can overlap, the strict rules relating to warrants and probable cause do not apply when the police are merely exercising their community caretaking function rather than investigating crime. Can you see why this is so? For more on this subject, see John F. Decker, *Emergency Circumstances, Police Responses, and Fourth Amendment Restrictions*, 89 J. Crim. L. & Criminology 433 (1999). The next Note looks further at this point.

5. *Warrantless entry of a home (part 3): the emergency doctrine.* The Supreme Court, per Chief Justice Roberts, reaffirmed and stated clearly (unanimously, at that) the emergency doctrine mentioned in *Mincey* (Note 4):

> At about 3 a.m., four police officers responded to a call regarding a loud party at a residence. Upon arriving at the house, * * * they observed two juveniles drinking beer in the backyard. They entered the backyard, and saw—through a screen door and windows—an altercation taking place in the kitchen of the home. * * * [F]our adults were attempting, with some difficulty, to restrain a juvenile. The juvenile eventually "broke free, swung a fist and struck one of the adults in the face." The officer testified that he observed the victim of the blow spitting blood into a nearby sink. The other adults continued to try to restrain the juvenile, pressing him up against a refrigerator with such force that the refrigerator began moving across the floor. At this point, an officer opened the screen door and announced the officers' presence. Amid the tumult, nobody noticed. The officer entered the kitchen and again cried out, and as the occupants slowly became aware that the police were on the scene, the altercation ceased.

> The officers subsequently arrested respondents and charged them with contributing to the delinquency of a minor, disorderly conduct, and intoxication. In the trial court, respondents filed a motion to suppress all evidence obtained after the officers entered the home, arguing that the warrantless entry violated the Fourth Amendment. * * *

> It is a " 'basic principle of Fourth Amendment law that searches and seizures inside a home without a warrant are presumptively unreasonable.' " Nevertheless, because the ultimate touchstone of the Fourth Amendment is "reasonableness," the warrant requirement is subject to certain exceptions. * * *

> One exigency obviating the requirement of a warrant is the need to assist persons who are seriously injured or threatened with such injury. * * * [L]aw enforcement officers may enter a home without a warrant to render emergency assistance to an injured occupant or to protect an occupant from imminent injury. * * *

> Respondents * * * contend that their conduct was not serious enough to justify the officers' intrusion into the home. They rely on *Welsh* v. *Wisconsin* [Note 3, *supra*], in which we held that "an important factor to be considered when determining whether any exigency exists is the gravity of the underlying offense for which the arrest is being made." This contention, too, is misplaced. *Welsh* involved a warrantless entry by officers to arrest a suspect for driving while intoxicated. There, the "only

potential emergency" confronting the officers was the need to preserve evidence (*i.e.*, the suspect's blood-alcohol level)—an exigency that we held insufficient under the circumstances to justify entry into the suspect's home. Here, the officers were confronted with *ongoing* violence occurring *within* the home. *Welsh* did not address such a situation.

We think the officers' entry here was plainly reasonable under the circumstances. * * * [T]hey could see that a fracas was taking place inside the kitchen. A juvenile, fists clenched, was being held back by several adults. As the officers watch, he breaks free and strikes one of the adults in the face, sending the adult to the sink spitting blood.

In these circumstances, the officers had an objectively reasonable basis for believing both that the injured adult might need help and that the violence in the kitchen was just beginning. Nothing in the Fourth Amendment required them to wait until another blow rendered someone "unconscious" or "semi-conscious" or worse before entering. The role of a peace officer includes preventing violence and restoring order, not simply rendering first aid to casualties; an officer is not like a boxing (or hockey) referee, poised to stop a bout only if it becomes too one-sided.

The manner of the officers' entry was also reasonable. After witnessing the punch, one of the officers opened the screen door and "yelled in police." When nobody heard him, he stepped into the kitchen and announced himself again. Only then did the tumult subside. The officer's announcement of his presence was at least equivalent to a knock on the screen door. Indeed, it was probably the only option that had even a chance of rising above the din. Under these circumstances, there was no violation of the Fourth Amendment's knock-and-announce rule [p. 200, supra]. Furthermore, once the announcement was made, the officers were free to enter; it would serve no purpose to require them to stand dumbly at the door awaiting a response while those within brawled on, oblivious to their presence.

Brigham City, Utah v. Stuart, 547 U.S. 398, 126 S.Ct. 1943, 164 L.Ed.2d 650 (2006).

6. *Problem.* Officers came to *W*'s home based on information that *W* was involved in manufacture of methamphetamine in his home. The officers also knew that *W* had once been arrested for menacing with a knife. The officers knocked at *W*'s residence, but received no reply. As they stood there, two other persons arrived and told them that *W* was ill and probably asleep. The visitors agreed to rouse *W*. When the visitors entered, they left the front door open, and from outside the officers could see a collection of swords mounted on a wall and smelled a strong odor of iodine, which is used in the manufacture of methamphetamine. Approximately thirty seconds after the door was left open, the officers entered without a warrant. Constitutional? People v. Winpigler, 8 P.3d 439 (Colo.1999).

2. SEARCHES INCIDENT TO AN ARREST

a. General Principles

CHIMEL v. CALIFORNIA

Supreme Court of the United States, 1969.
395 U.S. 752, 89 S.Ct. 2034, 23 L.Ed.2d 685.

MR. JUSTICE STEWART delivered the opinion of the Court. * * *

The relevant facts are essentially undisputed. Late in the afternoon of September 13, 1965, three police officers arrived at the Santa Ana, California, home of the petitioner with a warrant authorizing his arrest for the burglary of a coin shop. The officers knocked on the door, identified themselves to the petitioner's wife, and asked if they might come inside. She ushered them into the house, where they waited 10 or 15 minutes until the petitioner returned home from work. When the petitioner entered the house, one of the officers handed him the arrest warrant and asked for permission to "look around." The petitioner objected, but was advised that "on the basis of the lawful arrest," the officers would nonetheless conduct a search. No search warrant had been issued.

Accompanied by the petitioner's wife, the officers then looked through the entire three-bedroom house, including the attic, the garage, and a small workshop. In some rooms the search was relatively cursory. In the master bedroom and sewing room, however, the officers directed the petitioner's wife to open drawers and "to physically move contents of the drawers from side to side so that [they] might view any items that would have come from [the] burglary." After completing the search, they seized numerous items—primarily coins, but also several medals, tokens, and a few other objects. The entire search took between 45 minutes and an hour.

At the petitioner's subsequent state trial on two charges of burglary, the items taken from his house were admitted into evidence against him, over his objection that they had been unconstitutionally seized. * * * [T]he appellate courts went on to hold that the search of the petitioner's home had been justified, despite the absence of a search warrant, on the ground that it had been incident to a valid arrest. * * *

Without deciding the question, we proceed on the hypothesis that the California courts were correct in holding that the arrest of the petitioner was valid under the Constitution. This brings us directly to the question whether the warrantless search of the petitioner's entire house can be constitutionally justified as incident to that arrest. The decisions of this Court bearing upon that question have been far from consistent, as even the most cursory review makes evident.

Approval of a warrantless search incident to a lawful arrest seems first to have been articulated by the Court in 1914 as dictum in *Weeks v. United States*, [p. 67], in which the Court stated:

"What then is the present case? Before answering that inquiry specifically, it may be well by a process of exclusion to state what it is not. It is not an assertion of the right on the part of the Government, always recognized under English and American law, to search the person of the accused when legally arrested to discover and seize the fruits or evidences of crime."

That statement made no reference to any right to search the *place* where an arrest occurs, but was limited to a right to search the "person." Eleven years later the case of *Carroll v. United States*, 267 U.S. 132, 45 S.Ct. 280, 69 L.Ed. 543, brought the following embellishment of the *Weeks* statement:

"When a man is legally arrested for an offense, whatever is found upon his person *or in his control* which it is unlawful for him to have and which may be used to prove the offense may be seized and held as evidence in the prosecution." (Emphasis added.)

Still, that assertion too was far from a claim that the "place" where one is arrested may be searched so long as the arrest is valid. Without explanation, however, the principle emerged in expanded form a few months later in *Agnello v. United States*, 269 U.S. 20, 46 S.Ct. 4, 70 L.Ed. 145— although still by way of dictum:

"The right without a search warrant contemporaneously to search persons lawfully arrested while committing crime and to search the place where the arrest is made in order to find and seize things connected with the crime as its fruits or as the means by which it was committed, as well as weapons and other things to effect an escape from custody, is not to be doubted."

[The Court then proceeded to summarize a long line of cases, including Harris v. United States, 331 U.S. 145, 67 S.Ct. 1098, 91 L.Ed. 1399 (1947) and Trupiano v. United States, 334 U.S. 699, 68 S.Ct. 1229, 92 L.Ed. 1663 (1948), in which the justices veered back and forth between an expansive and then narrow interpretation of the *Agnello* dictum (which subsequently became a holding) that police may, incident to an arrest, conduct a warrantless search of "the place where the arrest is made."]

In 1950 * * * came *United States v. Rabinowitz*, 339 U.S. 56, 70 S.Ct. 430, 94 L.Ed. 653, the decision upon which California primarily relies in the case now before us. In *Rabinowitz*, federal authorities had been informed that the defendant was dealing in stamps bearing forged overprints. On the basis of that information they secured a warrant for his arrest, which they executed at his one-room business office. At the time of the arrest, the officers "searched the desk, safe, and file cabinets in the office for about an hour and a half," and seized 573 stamps with forged overprints. The stamps were admitted into evidence at the defendant's trial, and this Court affirmed his conviction, rejecting the contention that the warrantless search had been unlawful. The Court held that the search in its entirety fell within the principle giving law enforcement authorities "[t]he right 'to search the place where the arrest is made in order to find and seize things connected with the crime * * *.' " * * * The opinion rejected the rule of *Trupiano* that "in seizing goods and articles, law enforcement agents must secure and use search warrants wherever reasonably practicable." The test, said the Court, "is not whether it is reasonable to procure a search warrant, but whether the search was reasonable."

Rabinowitz has come to stand for the proposition, *inter alia*, that a warrantless search "incident to a lawful arrest" may generally extend to the area that is considered to be in the "possession" or under the "control" of the person arrested. And it was on the basis of that proposition that the California courts upheld the search of the petitioner's entire house in this case. That doctrine, however, at least in the broad sense in which it was applied by the California courts in this case, can withstand neither historical nor rational analysis.

Even limited to its own facts, the *Rabinowitz* decision was, as we have seen, hardly founded on an unimpeachable line of authority. * * *

Nor is the rationale by which the State seeks here to sustain the search of the petitioner's house supported by a reasoned view of the background and purpose of the Fourth Amendment. Mr. Justice Frankfurter wisely pointed out in his *Rabinowitz* dissent that the Amendment's proscription of "unreasonable searches and seizures" must be read in light of "the history that gave rise to the words"—a history of "abuses so deeply felt by the Colonies as to be one of the potent causes of the Revolution * * *." The Amendment was in large part a reaction to the general warrants and warrantless searches that had so alienated the colonists and had helped speed the movement for independence. In the scheme of the Amendment, therefore, the requirement that "no Warrants shall issue, but upon probable cause," plays a crucial part. * * *

* * * Clearly, the general requirement that a search warrant be obtained is not lightly to be dispensed with, and "the burden is on those seeking [an] exemption [from the requirement] to show the need for it * * *." * * *

* * * When an arrest is made, it is reasonable for the arresting officer to search the person arrested in order to remove any weapons that the latter might seek to use in order to resist arrest or effect his escape. Otherwise, the officer's safety might well be endangered, and the arrest itself frustrated. In addition, it is entirely reasonable for the arresting officer to search for and seize any evidence on the arrestee's person in order to prevent its concealment or destruction. And the area into which an arrestee might reach in order to grab a weapon or evidentiary items must, of course, be governed by a like rule. A gun on a table or in a drawer in front of one who is arrested can be as dangerous to the arresting officer as one concealed in the clothing of the person arrested. There is ample justification, therefore, for a search of the arrestee's person and the area "within his immediate control"—construing that phrase to mean the area

from within which he might gain possession of a weapon or destructible evidence.

There is no comparable justification, however, for routinely searching any room other than that in which an arrest occurs—or, for that matter, for searching through all the desk drawers or other closed or concealed areas in that room itself. Such searches, in the absence of well-recognized exceptions, may be made only under the authority of a search warrant. The "adherence to judicial processes" mandated by the Fourth Amendment requires no less. * * *

It is argued in the present case that it is "reasonable" to search a man's house when he is arrested in it. But that argument is founded on little more than a subjective view regarding the acceptability of certain sorts of police conduct, and not on considerations relevant to Fourth Amendment interests. Under such an unconfined analysis, Fourth Amendment protection in this area would approach the evaporation point. It is not easy to explain why, for instance, it is less subjectively "reasonable" to search a man's house when he is arrested on his front lawn—or just down the street—than it is when he happens to be in the house at the time of arrest. As Mr. Justice Frankfurter put it:

> "To say that the search must be reasonable is to require some criterion of reason. It is no guide at all either for a jury or for district judges or the police to say that an 'unreasonable search' is forbidden—that the search must be reasonable. What is the test of reason which makes a search reasonable? The test is the reason underlying and expressed by the Fourth Amendment: the history and the experience which it embodies and the safeguards afforded by it against the evils to which it was a response." * * *

It would be possible, of course, to draw a line between *Rabinowitz* and *Harris* on the one hand, and this case on the other. For *Rabinowitz* involved a single room, and *Harris* a four-room apartment, while in the case before us an entire house was searched. But such a distinction would be highly artificial. The rationale that allowed the searches and seizures in *Rabinowitz* and *Harris* would allow the searches and seizures in this case. No consideration relevant to the Fourth Amendment suggests any point of rational limitation, once the search is allowed to go beyond the area from which the person arrested might obtain weapons or evidentiary items. The only reasoned distinction is one between a search of the person arrested and the area within his reach on the one hand, and more extensive searches on the other.[12]

---

12. It is argued in dissent that so long as there is probable cause to search the place where an arrest occurs, a search of that place should be permitted even though no search warrant has been obtained. This position seems to be based principally on two premises: first, that once an arrest has been made, the additional invasion of privacy stemming from the accompanying search is "relatively minor"; and second, that the victim of the search may "shortly thereafter" obtain a judicial determination of whether the search was justified by probable cause. With respect to the second premise, one may initially question whether all of the States in fact provide the speedy suppression procedures the dissent assumes. More fundamentally, however, we cannot accept the view that Fourth Amendment interests are vindicated so long as "the rights of the criminal" are

The petitioner correctly points out that one result of decisions such as *Rabinowitz* and *Harris* is to give law enforcement officials the opportunity to engage in searches not justified by probable cause, by the simple expedient of arranging to arrest suspects at home rather than elsewhere. We do not suggest that the petitioner is necessarily correct in his assertion that such a strategy was utilized here, but the fact remains that had he been arrested earlier in the day, at his place of employment rather than at home, no search of his house could have been made without a search warrant. In any event, even apart from the possibility of such police tactics, the general point so forcefully made by Judge Learned Hand in *United States v. Kirschenblatt*, 2 Cir., 16 F.2d 202, 51 A.L.R. 416, remains:

> "After arresting a man in his house, to rummage at will among his papers in search of whatever will convict him, appears to us to be indistinguishable from what might be done under a general warrant; indeed, the warrant would give more protection, for presumably it must be issued by a magistrate. True, by hypothesis the power would not exist, if the supposed offender were not found on the premises; but it is small consolation to know that one's papers are safe only so long as one is not at home."

Rabinowitz and *Harris* * * * are no longer to be followed.

Application of sound Fourth Amendment principles to the facts of this case produces a clear result. The search here went far beyond the petitioner's person and the area from within which he might have obtained either a weapon or something that could have been used as evidence against him. There was no constitutional justification, in the absence of a search warrant, for extending the search beyond that area. The scope of the search was, therefore, "unreasonable" under the Fourth and Fourteenth Amendments, and the petitioner's conviction cannot stand.

[Justice Harlan's concurring opinion is omitted.]

Mr. Justice WHITE, with whom Mr. Justice BLACK joins, dissenting.

Few areas of the law have been as subject to shifting constitutional standards over the last 50 years as that of the search "incident to an arrest." There has been a remarkable instability in this whole area, which has seen at least four major shifts in emphasis. Today's opinion makes an untimely fifth. In my view, the Court should not now abandon the old rule. * * *

II

The rule which has prevailed, but for very brief or doubtful periods of aberration, is that a search incident to an arrest may extend to those areas

---

"protect[ed] * * * against introduction of evidence seized without probable cause." The Amendment is designed to prevent, not simply to redress, unlawful police action. In any event, we cannot join in characterizing the invasion of privacy that results from a top-to-bottom search of a man's house as "minor." And we can see no reason why, simply because some interference with an individual's privacy and freedom of movement has lawfully taken place, further intrusions should automatically be allowed despite the absence of a warrant that the Fourth Amendment would otherwise require.

under the control of the defendant and where items subject to constitutional seizure may be found. The justification for this rule must, under the language of the Fourth Amendment, lie in the reasonableness of the rule. * * * [T]he Court must decide whether a given search is reasonable. The Amendment does not proscribe "warrantless searches" but instead it proscribes "unreasonable searches" and this Court has never held nor does the majority today assert that warrantless searches are necessarily unreasonable.

Applying this reasonableness test to the area of searches incident to arrests, one thing is clear at the outset. Search of an arrested man and of the items within his immediate reach must in almost every case be reasonable. There is always a danger that the suspect will try to escape, seizing concealed weapons with which to overpower and injure the arresting officers, and there is a danger that he may destroy evidence vital to the prosecution. Circumstances in which these justifications would not apply are sufficiently rare that inquiry is not made into searches of this scope, which have been considered reasonable throughout.

The justifications which make such a search reasonable obviously do not apply to the search of areas to which the accused does not have ready physical access. This is not enough, however, to prove such searches unconstitutional. The Court has always held, and does not today deny, that when there is probable cause to search and it is "impracticable" for one reason or another to get a search warrant, then a warrantless search may be reasonable. This is the case whether an arrest was made at the time of the search or not.

This is not to say that a search can be reasonable without regard to the probable cause to believe that seizable items are on the premises. But when there are exigent circumstances, and probable cause, then the search may be made without a warrant, reasonably. An arrest itself may often create an emergency situation making it impracticable to obtain a warrant before embarking on a related search. Again assuming that there is probable cause to search premises at the spot where a suspect is arrested, it seems to me unreasonable to require the police to leave the scene in order to obtain a search warrant when they are already legally there to make a valid arrest, and when there must almost always be a strong possibility that confederates of the arrested man will in the meanwhile remove the items for which the police have probable cause to search. This must so often be the case that it seems to me as unreasonable to require a warrant for a search of the premises as to require a warrant for search of the person and his very immediate surroundings.

This case provides a good illustration of my point that it is unreasonable to require police to leave the scene of an arrest in order to obtain a search warrant when they already have probable cause to search and there is a clear danger that the items for which they may reasonably search will be removed before they return with a warrant. * * * There was doubtless probable cause not only to arrest petitioner, but also to search his house. He had obliquely admitted, both to a neighbor and to the owner of the burglarized store, that he had committed the burglary. In light of this, and the fact that the neighbor had seen other admittedly stolen property in petitioner's house, there was surely probable cause on which a warrant could have issued to search the house for the stolen coins. Moreover, had the police simply arrested petitioner, taken him off to the station house, and later returned with a warrant,[5] it seems very likely that petitioner's wife, who in view of petitioner's generally garrulous nature must have known of the robbery, would have removed the coins. For the police to search the house while the evidence they had probable cause to search out and seize was still there cannot be considered unreasonable. * * *

IV

* * * Like the majority, I would permit the police to search the person of a suspect and the area under his immediate control either to assure the safety of the officers or to prevent the destruction of evidence. And like the majority, I see nothing in the arrest alone furnishing probable cause for a search of any broader scope. However, where as here the existence of probable cause is independently established and would justify a warrant for a broader search for evidence, I would follow past cases and permit such a search to be carried out without a warrant, since the fact of arrest supplies an exigent circumstance justifying police action before the evidence can be removed, and also alerts the suspect to the fact of the search so that he can immediately seek judicial determination of probable cause in an adversary proceeding, and appropriate redress.

This view, consistent with past cases, would not authorize the general search against which the Fourth Amendment was meant to guard, nor would it broaden or render uncertain in any way whatsoever the scope of searches permitted under the Fourth Amendment. The issue in this case is not the breadth of the search, since there was clearly probable cause for the search which was carried out. No broader search than if the officers had a warrant would be permitted. The only issue is whether a search warrant was required as a precondition to that search. It is agreed that such a warrant would be required absent exigent circumstances. I would hold that the fact of arrest supplies such an exigent circumstance, since the police had lawfully gained entry to the premises to effect the arrest and since delaying the search to secure a warrant would have involved the risk of not recovering the fruits of the crime. * * *

---

5. There were three officers at the scene of the arrest, one from the city where the coin burglary had occurred, and two from the city where the arrest was made. Assuming that one policeman from each city would be needed to bring the petitioner in and obtain a search warrant, one policeman could have been left to guard the house. However, if he not only could have remained in the house against petitioner's wife's will, but followed her about to assure that no evidence was being tampered with, the invasion of her privacy would be almost as great as that accompanying an actual search. Moreover, had the wife summoned an accomplice, one officer could not have watched them both.

NOTES AND QUESTIONS

1. Who has the better side of the argument, Justice Stewart or Justice White, in regard to searches incident to lawful arrests? Applying the majority's approach, what should the police have done about Chimel's wife?

2. According to Justice Stewart, what is the scope of a proper warrantless search incident to a lawful arrest? Must the police have probable cause to search the permissible areas? Answer the same questions according to the dissent.

3. Justices Stewart and White apparently disagree with each other regarding the role of the warrant clause in Fourth Amendment analysis. What does each justice believe?

4. *"Principle of particular justification."* The majority opinion in *Chimel* applied what may be described as the "principle of particular justification" (James B. White, *The Fourth Amendment as a Way of Talking About People: A Study of Robinson and Matlock*, 1974 Sup. Ct. Rev. 165, 190). According to this principle, "the police must, whenever practicable, obtain advance judicial approval of searches and seizures through the warrant procedure," and "[t]he scope of [a] search must be 'strictly tied to and justified by' the circumstances which rendered its initiation permissible." Terry v. Ohio, 392 U.S. 1, 88 S.Ct. 1868, 20 L.Ed.2d 889 (1968).

Applying this doctrine, we start from the proposition—in computer terms, the "default" position—that warrantless searches are unreasonable and, therefore, unconstitutional. If the police seek to justify a warrantless search, the burden is on them to demonstrate the existence of a justification for dispensing with the warrant requirement. Assuming that a justification exists, the scope of the permissible warrantless search (that is, the places that may be searched, and the things or persons that may be seized, without a warrant) must be no broader than the justification for the warrantless conduct compels. Once the circumstances that justify the warrantless conduct no longer exist, or once the police go beyond the legitimate scope of the warrantless search, the original obtain-a-warrant default position returns.

Can you articulate how the principle of particular justification applies in *Chimel*?

5. *Bright versus fuzzy lines.* A recurring issue in criminal jurisprudence is whether the Supreme Court, in devising rules of criminal procedure, should announce bright-line rules or rules that are "fuzzy" in nature that require case-by-case adjudication. In *Chimel*, did the Court announce a bright-line rule? If Justice White had prevailed, would the search-incident-to-lawful-arrest rule have been brighter? (In Chapter 1, we offered a similar distinction between rules and norms. See p. 34, Note 2.)

6. *Problem.* Officers Gonzalez and Rogers have probable cause to arrest Donald for murder. They come to Donald's home to arrest him, but nobody is home. They return to their car across the street, and await Donald's arrival. Ninety minutes later, Donald arrives and enters his house. Fifteen minutes later, the officers come to the door, knock, and arrest Donald at the doorway

when he opens the door. Donald is now shoeless but otherwise fully dressed. The police handcuff Donald at the door and move him into the living room, twelve feet from an open closet. The police search Donald, but they find nothing. Officer Gonzales, hoping to find the murder weapon, goes to the closet, pats down trousers on closet hangers, and shakes pairs of shoes. In one pair, the officer discovers a gun, later determined to be the murder weapon. Prior to trial, Donald moves to suppress the gun from evidence. Should the motion be granted? (The officers had neither an arrest nor a search warrant in the foregoing facts.)

7. The Supreme Court has expanded the lawful scope of a warrantless search incident to an arrest in a home. See *Maryland v. Buie*, p. 411.

UNITED STATES v. ROBINSON

Supreme Court of the United States, 1973.
414 U.S. 218, 94 S.Ct. 467, 38 L.Ed.2d 427.

MR. JUSTICE REHNQUIST delivered the opinion of the Court. * * *

On April 23, 1968, at approximately 11 p.m., Officer Richard Jenks, a 15–year veteran of the District of Columbia Metropolitan Police Department, observed the respondent driving a 1965 Cadillac near the intersection of 8th and C Streets, N.E., in the District of Columbia. Jenks, as a result of previous investigation following a check of respondent's operator's permit four days earlier, determined there was reason to believe that respondent was operating a motor vehicle after the revocation of his operator's permit. This is an offense defined by statute in the District of Columbia which carries a mandatory minimum jail term, a mandatory minimum fine, or both.

Jenks signaled respondent to stop the automobile, which respondent did, and all three of the occupants emerged from the car. At that point Jenks informed respondent that he was under arrest for "operating after revocation and obtaining a permit by misrepresentation." It was assumed by the Court of Appeals, and is conceded by the respondent here, that Jenks had probable cause to arrest respondent, and that he effected a full-custody arrest.[1]

In accordance with procedures prescribed in police department instructions, Jenks then began to search respondent. He explained at a subsequent hearing that he was "face-to-face" with the respondent, and

---

1. * * * Counsel for respondent on appeal stressed that respondent had a record of two prior narcotics convictions, and suggested that Officer Jenks may have been aware of that record through his investigation of criminal records, while Jenks was checking out the discrepancies in the birthdates on the operator's permit and on the Selective Service card that had been given to him for examination when he had confronted respondent on the previous occasion. Respondent argued below that Jenks may have used the subsequent traffic violation arrest as a mere pretext for a narcotics search which would not have been allowed by a neutral magistrate had Jenks sought a warrant. The Court of Appeals found that Jenks had denied he had any such motive, and for the purposes of its opinion accepted the Government's version of that factual question * * *. We think it is sufficient for purposes of our decision that respondent was lawfully arrested for an offense, and that Jenks' placing him in custody following that arrest was not a departure from established police department practice. We leave for another day questions which would arise on facts different from these.

"placed [his] hands on [the respondent], my right-hand to his left breast like this (demonstrating) and proceeded to pat him down thus [with the right hand]." During this patdown, Jenks felt an object in the left breast pocket of the heavy coat respondent was wearing, but testified that he "couldn't tell what it was" and also that he "couldn't actually tell the size of it." Jenks then reached into the pocket and pulled out the object, which turned out to be a "crumpled up cigarette package." Jenks testified that at this point he still did not know what was in the package:

"As I felt the package I could feel objects in the package but I couldn't tell what they were. * * * I knew they weren't cigarettes."

The officer then opened the cigarette pack and found 14 gelatin capsules of white powder which he thought to be, and which later analysis proved to be, heroin. * * * The heroin seized from the respondent was admitted into evidence at the trial which resulted in his conviction in the District Court. * * *

I

It is well settled that a search incident to a lawful arrest is a traditional exception to the warrant requirement of the Fourth Amendment. This general exception has historically been formulated into two distinct propositions. The first is that a search may be made of the *person* of the arrestee by virtue of the lawful arrest. The second is that a search may be made of the area within the control of the arrestee.

Examination of this Court's decisions shows that these two propositions have been treated quite differently. The validity of the search of a person incident to a lawful arrest has been regarded as settled from its first enunciation, and has remained virtually unchallenged until the present case. The validity of the second proposition, while likewise conceded in principle, has been subject to differing interpretations as to the extent of the area which may be searched. * * *

Throughout the series of cases in which the Court has addressed the second proposition relating to a search incident to a lawful arrest—the permissible area beyond the person of the arrestee which such a search may cover—no doubt has been expressed as to the unqualified authority of the arresting authority to search the person of the arrestee. In *Chimel* [*v. California, supra*] * * * full recognition was again given to the authority to search the person of the arrestee * * *.

* * * Since the statements in the cases speak not simply in terms of an exception to the warrant requirement, but in terms of an affirmative authority to search [the person], they clearly imply that such searches also meet the Fourth Amendment's requirement of reasonableness.

II

In its decision of this case, the Court of Appeals decided that even after a police officer lawfully places a suspect under arrest for the purpose of taking him into custody, he may not ordinarily proceed to fully search the prisoner. He must, instead, conduct a limited frisk of the outer clothing and remove such weapons that he may, as a result of that limited frisk, reasonably believe and ascertain that the suspect has in his possession. While recognizing that *Terry v. Ohio*, [p. 349], dealt with a permissible "frisk" incident to an investigative stop based on less than probable cause to arrest, the Court of Appeals felt that the principles of that case should be carried over to this probable-cause arrest for driving while one's license is revoked. Since there would be no further evidence of such a crime to be obtained in a search of the arrestee, the court held that only a search for weapons could be justified.

Terry v. Ohio did not involve an arrest for probable cause, and it made quite clear that the "protective frisk" for weapons which it approved might be conducted without probable cause. This Court's opinion explicitly recognized that there is a "distinction in purpose, character, and extent between a search incident to an arrest and a limited search for weapons."

> "The former, although justified in part by the acknowledged necessity to protect the arresting officer from assault with a concealed weapon, is also justified on other grounds, and can therefore involve a relatively extensive exploration of the person. A search for weapons in the absence of probable cause to arrest, however, must, like any other search, be strictly circumscribed by the exigencies which justify its initiation. Thus it must be limited to that which is necessary for the discovery of weapons which might be used to harm the officer or others nearby, and may realistically be characterized as something less than a 'full' search, even though it remains a serious intrusion.

> " * * * An arrest is a wholly different kind of intrusion upon individual freedom from a limited search for weapons, and the interests each is designed to serve are likewise quite different. An arrest is the initial stage of a criminal prosecution. It is intended to vindicate society's interest in having its laws obeyed, and it is inevitably accompanied by future interference with the individual's freedom of movement, whether or not trial or conviction ultimately follows. The protective search for weapons, on the other hand, constitutes a brief, though far from inconsiderable, intrusion upon the sanctity of the person."

Terry, therefore, affords no basis to carry over to a probable-cause arrest the limitations this Court placed on a stop-and-frisk search permissible without probable cause. * * *

III * * *

The Court of Appeals in effect determined that the *only* reason supporting the authority for a *full* search incident to lawful arrest was the possibility of discovery of evidence or fruits. Concluding that there could be no evidence or fruits in the case of an offense such as that with which respondent was charged, it held that any protective search would have to be limited by the conditions laid down in *Terry* for a search upon less than probable cause to arrest. Quite apart from the fact that *Terry* clearly recognized the distinction between the two types of searches, and that a different rule governed one than governed the other, we find additional reason to disagree with the Court of Appeals.

The justification or reason for the authority to search incident to a lawful arrest rests quite as much on the need to disarm the suspect in order to take him into custody as it does on the need to preserve evidence on his person for later use at trial. The standards traditionally governing a search incident to lawful arrest are not, therefore, commuted to the stricter *Terry* standards by the absence of probable fruits or further evidence of the particular crime for which the arrest is made.

Nor are we inclined, on the basis of what seems to us to be a rather speculative judgment, to qualify the breadth of the general authority to search incident to a lawful custodial arrest on an assumption that persons arrested for the offense of driving while their licenses have been revoked are less likely to possess dangerous weapons than are those arrested for other crimes.[5] It is scarcely open to doubt that the danger to an officer is far greater in the case of the extended exposure which follows the taking of a suspect into custody and transporting him to the police station than in the case of the relatively fleeting contact resulting from the typical *Terry*-type stop. This is an adequate basis for treating all custodial arrests alike for purposes of search justification.

But quite apart from these distinctions, our more fundamental disagreement with the Court of Appeals arises from its suggestion that there must be litigated in each case the issue of whether or not there was present one of the reasons supporting the authority for a search of the person incident to a lawful arrest. We do not think the long line of authorities of this Court * * *, or what we can glean from the history of practice in this country and in England, requires such a case-by-case adjudication. A police officer's determination as to how and where to search the person of a suspect whom he has arrested is necessarily a quick *ad hoc* judgment which the Fourth Amendment does not require to be broken down in each instance into an analysis of each step in the search. The authority to search the person incident to a lawful custodial arrest, while based upon the need to disarm and to discover evidence, does not depend on what a court may later decide was the probability in a particular arrest situation that weapons or evidence would in fact be found upon the person of the suspect. A custodial arrest of a suspect based on probable cause is a reasonable intrusion under the Fourth Amendment; that intrusion being lawful, a search incident to the arrest requires no

---

5. Such an assumption appears at least questionable in light of the available statistical data concerning assaults on police officers who are in the course of making arrests. The danger to the police officer flows from the fact of the arrest, and its attendant proximity, stress, and uncertainty, and not from the grounds for arrest. One study concludes that approximately 30% of the shootings of police officers occur when an officer stops a person in an automobile. The * * * Uniform Crime Reports, prepared by the Federal Bureau of Investigation, indicate that a significant percentage of murders of police officers occurs when the officers are making traffic stops. Those reports indicate that during January–March 1973, 35 police officers were murdered; 11 of those officers were killed while engaged in making traffic stops.

additional justification. It is the fact of the lawful arrest which establishes the authority to search, and we hold that in the case of a lawful custodial arrest a full search of the person is not only an exception to the warrant requirement of the Fourth Amendment, but is also a "reasonable" search under that Amendment.

IV

The search of respondent's person conducted by Officer Jenks in this case and the seizure from him of the heroin, were permissible under established Fourth Amendment law. * * * Since it is the fact of custodial arrest which gives rise to the authority to search,[6] it is of no moment that Jenks did not indicate any subjective fear of the respondent or that he did not himself suspect that respondent was armed. Having in the course of a lawful search come upon the crumpled package of cigarettes, he was entitled to inspect it; and when his inspection revealed the heroin capsules, he was entitled to seize them as "fruits, instrumentalities, or contraband" probative of criminal conduct. The judgment of the Court of Appeals holding otherwise is

Reversed.

Mr. Justice POWELL, concurring.

Although I join the opinions of the Court, I write briefly to emphasize what seems to me to be the essential premise of our decisions.

* * * I believe that an individual lawfully subjected to a custodial arrest retains no significant Fourth Amendment interest in the privacy of his person. Under this view the custodial arrest is the significant intrusion of state power into the privacy of one's person. If the arrest is lawful, the privacy interest guarded by the Fourth Amendment is subordinated to a legitimate and overriding governmental concern. No reason then exists to frustrate law enforcement by requiring some independent justification for a search incident to a lawful custodial arrest. This seems to me the reason that a valid arrest justifies a full search of the person, even if that search is not narrowly limited by the twin rationales of seizing evidence and disarming the arrestee. The search incident to arrest is reasonable under the Fourth Amendment because the privacy interest protected by that constitutional guarantee is legitimately abated by the fact of arrest.

Mr. Justice MARSHALL, with whom Mr. Justice DOUGLAS and Mr. Justice BRENNAN join, dissenting.

Certain fundamental principles have characterized this Court's Fourth Amendment jurisprudence over the years. Perhaps the most basic of these was expressed by Mr. Justice Butler, speaking for a unanimous Court in *Go-Bart Co. v. United States*, 282 U.S. 344, 51 S.Ct. 153, 75 L.Ed.

---

6. The opinion of the Court of Appeals also discussed its understanding of the law where the police officer makes what the court characterized as "a routine traffic stop," *i.e.*, where the officer would simply issue a notice of violation and allow the offender to proceed. Since in this case the officer did make a full-custody arrest of the violator, we do not reach the question discussed by the Court of Appeals.

374 (1931): "There is no formula for the determination of reasonableness. Each case is to be decided on its own facts and circumstances." As we recently held: "The constitutional validity of a warrantless search is preeminently the sort of question which can only be decided in the concrete factual context of the individual case." And the intensive, at times painstaking, case-by-case analysis characteristic of our Fourth Amendment decisions bespeaks our "jealous regard for maintaining the integrity of individual rights."

In the present case, however, the majority turns its back on these principles * * *. The majority's approach represents a clear and marked departure from our long tradition of case-by-case adjudication of the reasonableness of searches and seizures under the Fourth Amendment. * * *

II * * *

* * * As the majority itself is well aware, the powers granted the police in this case are strong ones, subject to potential abuse. Although, in this particular case, Officer Jenks was required by police department regulations to make an in-custody arrest rather than to issue a citation, in most jurisdictions and for most traffic offenses the determination of whether to issue a citation or effect a full arrest is discretionary with the officer. There is always the possibility that a police officer, lacking probable cause to obtain a search warrant, will use a traffic arrest as a pretext to conduct a search. I suggest this possibility not to impugn the integrity of our police, but merely to point out that case-by-case adjudication will always be necessary to determine whether a full arrest was effected for purely legitimate reasons or, rather, as a pretext for searching the arrestee. * * *

III

The majority states that "[a] police officer's determination as to how and where to search the person of a suspect whom he has arrested is necessarily a quick *ad hoc* judgment which the Fourth Amendment does not require to be broken down in each instance into an analysis of each step in the search." No precedent is cited for this broad assertion—not surprisingly, since there is none. * * * ["]This Court has held in the past that a search which is reasonable at its inception may violate the Fourth Amendment by virtue of its intolerable intensity and scope." *Terry v. Ohio.* As we there concluded, "in determining whether the seizure and search were 'unreasonable' our inquiry is a dual one—whether the officer's action was justified at its inception, and whether it was reasonably related in scope to the circumstances which justified the interference in the first place."

As I view the matter, the search in this case divides into three distinct phases: the patdown of respondent's coat pocket; the removal of the unknown object from the pocket; and the opening of the crumpled-up cigarette package.

A

No question is raised here concerning the lawfulness of the patdown of respondent's coat pocket. The Court of Appeals unanimously affirmed the right of a police officer to conduct a limited frisk for weapons when making an in-custody arrest, regardless of the nature of the crime for which the arrest was made. * * *

B

With respect to the removal of the unknown object from the coat pocket, the first issue presented is whether that aspect of the search can be sustained as part of the limited frisk for weapons. The weapons search approved by the Court of Appeals was modeled upon the narrowly drawn protective search for weapons authorized in *Terry*, which consists "of a limited patting of the outer clothing of the suspect for concealed objects which might be used as instruments of assault."

It appears to have been conceded by the Government below that the removal of the object from respondent's coat pocket exceeded the scope of a *Terry* frisk for weapons, since, under *Terry*, an officer may not remove an object from the suspect's pockets unless he has reason to believe it to be a dangerous weapon.

In the present case, however, Officer Jenks had no reason to believe and did not in fact believe that the object in respondent's coat pocket was a weapon. He admitted later that the object did not feel like a gun. * * * Since the removal of the object from the pocket cannot be justified as part of a limited *Terry* weapons frisk, the question arises whether it is reasonable for a police officer, when effecting an in-custody arrest of a traffic offender, to make a fuller search of the person than is permitted pursuant to *Terry*.

* * * A search incident to arrest, as the majority indicates, has two basic functions: the removal of weapons the arrestee might use to resist arrest or effect an escape, and the seizure of evidence or fruits of the crime for which the arrest is made, so as to prevent their concealment or destruction.

The Government does not now contend that the search of respondent's pocket can be justified by any need to find and seize evidence in order to prevent its concealment or destruction, for, as the Court of Appeals found, there is no evidence or fruits of the offense with which respondent was charged. The only rationale for a search in this case, then, is the removal of weapons which the arrestee might use to harm the officer and attempt an escape. This rationale, of course, is identical to the rationale of the search permitted in *Terry*. * * * Since the underlying rationale of a *Terry* search and the search of a traffic violator are identical, the Court of Appeals held that the scope of the searches must be the same. * * *

The problem with this approach, however, is that it ignores several significant differences between the context in which a search incident to arrest for a traffic violation is made, and the situation presented in *Terry*. Some of these differences would appear to suggest permitting a more thorough search in this case than was permitted in *Terry*; other differences suggest a narrower, more limited right to search than was there recognized. [Justice Marshall set out the arguments on both sides of the balancing scale, and then stated:]

As will be explained more fully below, I do not think it necessary to solve this balancing equation in this particular case. It is important to note, however, in view of the reasoning adopted by the majority, that available empirical evidence supports the result reached by the plurality of the Court of Appeals, rather than the result reached by the Court today.

The majority relies on statistics indicating that a significant percentage of murders of police officers occurs when the officers are making traffic stops. But these statistics only confirm what we recognized in *Terry*—that "American criminals have a long tradition of armed violence, and every year in this country many law enforcement officers are killed in the line of duty, and thousands more are wounded." As the very next sentence in *Terry* recognized, however, "[v]irtually all of these deaths and a substantial portion of the injuries are inflicted with guns and knives." The statistics relied on by the Government in this case support this observation. Virtually all of the killings are caused by guns and knives, the very type of weapons which will not go undetected in a properly conducted weapons frisk. * * *

C

The majority opinion fails to recognize that the search conducted by Officer Jenks did not merely involve a search of respondent's person. It also included a separate search of effects found on his person. And even were we to assume, *arguendo*, that it was reasonable for Jenks to remove the object he felt in respondent's pocket, clearly there was no justification consistent with the Fourth Amendment which would authorize his opening the package and looking inside.

To begin with, after Jenks had the cigarette package in his hands, there is no indication that he had reason to believe or did in fact believe that the package contained a weapon. More importantly, even if the crumpled-up cigarette package had in fact contained some sort of small weapon, it would have been impossible for respondent to have used it once the package was in the officer's hands. Opening the package, therefore, did not further the protective purpose of the search. * * *

It is suggested, however, that since the custodial arrest itself represents a significant intrusion into the privacy of the person, any additional intrusion by way of opening or examining effects found on the person is not worthy of constitutional protection. But such an approach was expressly rejected by the Court in *Chimel*. There it was suggested that since the police had lawfully entered petitioner's house to effect an arrest, the additional invasion of privacy stemming from an accompanying search of the entire house was inconsequential. The Court answered: "[W]e can see no reason why, simply because some interference with an individual's privacy and freedom of movement has lawfully taken place, further intrusions should automatically be allowed despite the absence of a warrant that the Fourth Amendment would otherwise require." * * *

The Government argues that it is difficult to see what constitutionally protected "expectation of privacy" a prisoner has in the interior of a cigarette pack. One wonders if the result in this case would have been the same were respondent a businessman who was lawfully taken into custody for driving without a license and whose wallet was taken from him by the police. Would it be reasonable for the police officer, because of the possibility that a razor blade was hidden somewhere in the wallet, to open it, remove all the contents, and examine each item carefully? Or suppose a lawyer lawfully arrested for a traffic offense is found to have a sealed envelope on his person. Would it be permissible for the arresting officer to tear open the envelope in order to make sure that it did not contain a clandestine weapon—perhaps a pin or a razor blade? * * *

The search conducted by Officer Jenks in this case went far beyond what was reasonably necessary to protect him from harm or to ensure that respondent would not effect an escape from custody. In my view, it therefore fell outside the scope of a properly drawn "search incident to arrest" exception to the Fourth Amendment's warrant requirement. * * *

NOTES AND QUESTIONS

1. Is *Robinson* consistent with *Chimel*?

2. How far does *Robinson* go in regard to the opening of containers found on an arrestee? Are the police entitled to open a businessman's wallet or a lawyer's sealed envelope, as Justice Marshall muses? If not, what is the distinction? If the police *are* entitled to open such containers, what possible justification is there for such a search in a traffic case such as this?

3. *Arrest inventories: another warrant "exception."* After Robinson was taken into custody, he had to be transported to the police station for booking. Any arrestee typically undergoes a second search—an "arrest inventory"—if she will be incarcerated, even temporarily, pending an appearance before a magistrate on the charges brought against her. This inventory search, which occurs without a warrant and in the absence of probable cause, is constitutionally justified on various grounds: to protect the arrestee from theft of her valuables within the jail; to reduce the risk of false claims of theft by the arrestee; and to ensure that contraband and dangerous instrumentalities that might have been missed by the police in the initial search incident to the arrest are not smuggled into the jail. Illinois v. Lafayette, 462 U.S. 640, 103 S.Ct. 2605, 77 L.Ed.2d 65 (1983). To be valid, the inventory must follow procedures standardized in that jurisdiction.

Notice the significance of this warrant exception: Even if Officer Jenks had not searched Robinson's clothing at the scene and discovered the crumpled up cigarette package, it presumably would have been discovered in a routine inventory search, assuming that Robinson was going to be jailed, even temporarily, after booking. Although inventory operating procedures of police department's vary, the police typically open containers found on arrestees, such as wallets or, as here, cigarette packages. Therefore, as a practical matter, once Robinson's custodial arrest was made, his fate was virtually sealed: If one warrant exception didn't justify the search of his person, the other would!

b. Arrests of Automobile Occupants

NEW YORK v. BELTON

Supreme Court of the United States, 1981.
453 U.S. 454, 101 S.Ct. 2860, 69 L.Ed.2d 768.

JUSTICE STEWART delivered the opinion of the Court. * * *

I

On April 9, 1978, Trooper Douglas Nicot, a New York State policeman driving an unmarked car on the New York Thruway, was passed by another automobile traveling at an excessive rate of speed. Nicot gave chase, overtook the speeding vehicle, and ordered its driver to pull it over to the side of the road and stop. There were four men in the car, one of whom was Roger Belton, the respondent in this case. The policeman asked to see the driver's license and automobile registration, and discovered that none of the men owned the vehicle or was related to its owner. Meanwhile, the policeman had smelled burnt marihuana and had seen on the floor of the car an envelope marked "Supergold" that he associated with marihuana. He therefore directed the men to get out of the car, and placed them under arrest for the unlawful possession of marihuana. He patted down each of the men and "split them up into four separate areas of the Thruway at this time so they would not be in physical touching area of each other." He then picked up the envelope marked "Supergold" and found that it contained marihuana. After giving the arrestees the warnings required by *Miranda v. Arizona* [p. 581], the state policeman searched each one of them. He then searched the passenger compartment of the car. On the back seat he found a black leather jacket belonging to Belton. He unzipped one of the pockets of the jacket and discovered cocaine. * * *

Belton was subsequently indicted for criminal possession of a controlled substance. In the trial court he moved that the cocaine the trooper had seized from the jacket pocket be suppressed. The court denied the motion. * * *

II

It is a first principle of Fourth Amendment jurisprudence that the police may not conduct a search unless they first convince a neutral magistrate that there is probable cause to do so. This Court has recognized, however, that "the exigencies of the situation" may sometimes make exemption from the warrant requirement "imperative." Specifically, the Court held in *Chimel v. California* [p. 218] that a lawful custodial arrest creates a situation which justifies the contemporaneous search without a warrant of the person arrested and of the immediately surrounding area. Such searches have long been considered valid because of the need "to remove any weapons that [the arrestee] might seek to use in order to resist arrest or effect his escape" and the need to prevent the concealment or destruction of evidence. * * *

Although the principle that limits a search incident to a lawful custodial arrest may be stated clearly enough, courts have discovered the principle difficult to apply in specific cases. Yet, as one commentator has pointed out, the protection of the Fourth and Fourteenth Amendments "can only be realized if the police are acting under a set of rules which, in most instances, makes it possible to reach a correct determination beforehand as to whether an invasion of privacy is justified in the interest of law enforcement." LaFave, *"Case–By–Case Adjudication" versus "Standardized Procedures": The Robinson Dilemma*, 1974 S.Ct. Rev. 127, 142. This is because:

> "Fourth Amendment doctrine, given force and effect by the exclusionary rule, is primarily intended to regulate the police in their day-to-day activities and thus ought to be expressed in terms that are readily applicable by the police in the context of the law enforcement activities in which they are necessarily engaged. A highly sophisticated set of rules, qualified by all sorts of ifs, ands, and buts and requiring the drawing of subtle nuances and hairline distinctions, may be the sort of heady stuff upon which the facile minds of lawyers and judges eagerly feed, but they may be 'literally impossible of application by the officer in the field.' " *Id.*, at 141.

In short, "[a] single familiar standard is essential to guide police officers, who have only limited time and expertise to reflect on and balance the social and individual interests involved in the specific circumstances they confront." *Dunaway v. New York*, 442 U.S. 200, 213–214, 99 S.Ct. 2248, 2256–57, 60 L.Ed.2d. 824.

So it was that, in *United States v. Robinson* [p. 226], the Court hewed to a straightforward rule, easily applied, and predictably enforced: "[I]n the case of a lawful custodial arrest a full search of the person is not only an exception to the warrant requirement of the Fourth Amendment, but is also a 'reasonable' search under that Amendment." In so holding, the Court rejected the suggestion that "there must be litigated in each case the issue of whether or not there was present one of the reasons supporting the authority for a search of the person incident to a lawful arrest."

But no straightforward rule has emerged from the litigated cases respecting the question involved here—the question of the proper scope of a search of the interior of an automobile incident to a lawful custodial arrest of its occupants. * * *

When a person cannot know how a court will apply a settled principle to a recurring factual situation, that person cannot know the scope of his constitutional protection, nor can a policeman know the scope of his authority. While the *Chimel* case established that a search incident to an arrest may not stray beyond the area within the immediate control of the arrestee, courts have found no workable definition of "the area within the immediate control of the arrestee" when that area arguably includes the interior of an automobile and the arrestee is its recent occupant. Our reading of the cases suggests the generalization that articles inside the relatively narrow compass of the passenger compartment of an automobile are in fact generally, even if not inevitably, within "the area into which an arrestee might reach in order to grab a weapon or evidentiary ite[m]." In order to establish the workable rule this category of cases requires, we read *Chimel*'s definition of the limits of the area that may be searched in light of that generalization. Accordingly, we hold that when a policeman has made a lawful custodial arrest of the occupant of an automobile, he may, as a contemporaneous incident of that arrest, search the passenger compartment of that automobile.[3]

It follows from this conclusion that the police may also examine the contents of any containers found within the passenger compartment, for if the passenger compartment is within reach of the arrestee, so also will containers in it be within his reach.[4] Such a container may, of course, be searched whether it is open or closed, since the justification for the search is not that the arrestee has no privacy interest in the container, but that the lawful custodial arrest justifies the infringement of any privacy interest the arrestee may have. * * *

It is true, of course, that these containers will sometimes be such that they could hold neither a weapon nor evidence of the criminal conduct for which the suspect was arrested. However, in *United States v. Robinson*, the Court rejected the argument that such a container—there a "crumpled up cigarette package"—located during a search of Robinson incident to his arrest could not be searched:

> "The authority to search the person incident to a lawful custodial arrest, while based upon the need to disarm and to discover evidence, does not depend on what a court may later decide was the probability in a particular arrest situation that weapons or evidence would in fact be found upon the person of the suspect. A custodial arrest of a suspect based on probable cause is a reasonable intrusion under the Fourth Amendment; that intrusion being lawful, a search incident to the arrest requires no additional justification." * * *

---

3. Our holding today does no more than determine the meaning of *Chimel*'s principles in this particular and problematic context. It in no way alters the fundamental principles established in the *Chimel* case regarding the basic scope of searches incident to lawful custodial arrests.

4. "Container" here denotes any object capable of holding another object. It thus includes closed or open glove compartments, consoles, or other receptacles located anywhere within the passenger compartment, as well as luggage, boxes, bags, clothing, and the like. Our holding encompasses only the interior of the passenger compartment of an automobile and does not encompass the trunk.

III

It is not questioned that the respondent was the subject of a lawful custodial arrest on a charge of possessing marihuana. The search of the respondent's jacket followed immediately upon that arrest. The jacket was located inside the passenger compartment of the car in which the respondent had been a passenger just before he was arrested. The jacket was thus within the area which we have concluded was "within the arrestee's immediate control" within the meaning of the *Chimel* case. The search of the jacket, therefore, was a search incident to a lawful custodial arrest, and it did not violate the Fourth and Fourteenth Amendments. Accordingly, the judgment is reversed. * * *

[The concurrence of Justice Rehnquist and the concurrence in the judgment of Justice Stevens are omitted.]

Justice BRENNAN, with whom Justice MARSHALL joins, dissenting.

In *Chimel v. California*, this Court carefully analyzed more than 50 years of conflicting precedent governing the permissible scope of warrantless searches incident to custodial arrest. The Court today turns its back on the product of that analysis, formulating an arbitrary "bright-line" rule applicable to "recent" occupants of automobiles that fails to reflect *Chimel's* underlying policy justifications. While the Court claims to leave *Chimel* intact, I fear that its unwarranted abandonment of the principles underlying that decision may signal a wholesale retreat from our carefully developed search-incident-to-arrest analysis. I dissent.

I * * *

The *Chimel* exception to the warrant requirement was designed with two principal concerns in mind: the safety of the arresting officer and the preservation of easily concealed or destructible evidence. * * *

The *Chimel* standard was narrowly tailored to address these concerns * * *. It * * * places a temporal and a spatial limitation on searches incident to arrest, excusing compliance with the warrant requirement only when the search " 'is substantially contemporaneous with the arrest and is confined to the *immediate* vicinity of the arrest.' " When the arrest has been consummated and the arrestee safely taken into custody, the justifications underlying *Chimel's* limited exception to the warrant requirement cease to apply: at that point there is no possibility that the arrestee could reach weapons or contraband.

* * * [T]he Court today disregards these principles, and instead adopts a fiction—that the interior of a car is *always* within the immediate control of an arrestee who has recently been in the car. * * *

II

As the facts of this case make clear, the Court today substantially expands the permissible scope of searches incident to arrest by permitting police officers to search areas and containers the arrestee could not possibly reach at the time of arrest. These facts demonstrate that at the time Belton and his three companions were placed under custodial arrest—which was *after* they had been removed from the car, patted down, and separated—none of them could have reached the jackets that had been left on the back seat of the car. * * *

By approving the constitutionality of the warrantless search in this case, the Court carves out a dangerous precedent that is not justified by the concerns underlying *Chimel*. * * *

* * * [T]he crucial question under *Chimel* is not whether the arrestee could *ever* have reached the area that was searched, but whether he could have reached it at the time of arrest and search. If not, the officer's failure to obtain a warrant may not be excused. By disregarding this settled doctrine, the Court does a great disservice not only to *stare decisis*, but to the policies underlying the Fourth Amendment as well.

III

The Court seeks to justify its departure from the principles underlying *Chimel* by proclaiming the need for a new "bright-line" rule to guide the officer in the field. As we pointed out in *Mincey v. Arizona*, [437 U.S. 385, 98 S.Ct. 2408, 57 L.Ed.2d 290 (1978)], however, "the mere fact that law enforcement may be made more efficient can never by itself justify disregard of the Fourth Amendment." Moreover, the Court's attempt to forge a "bright-line" rule fails on its own terms. While the "interior/trunk" distinction may provide a workable guide in certain routine cases—for example, where the officer arrests the driver of a car and then immediately searches the seats and floor—in the long run, I suspect it will create far more problems than it solves. The Court's new approach leaves open too many questions and, more important, it provides the police and the courts with too few tools with which to find the answers.

Thus, although the Court concludes that a warrantless search of a car may take place even though the suspect was arrested outside the car, it does not indicate how long after the suspect's arrest that search may validly be conducted. Would a warrantless search incident to arrest be valid if conducted five minutes after the suspect left his car? Thirty minutes? Three hours? Does it matter whether the suspect is standing in close proximity to the car when the search is conducted? Does it matter whether the police formed probable cause to arrest before or after the suspect left his car? * * *

The Court does not give the police any "bright-line" answers to these questions. * * *

The standard announced in *Chimel* is not nearly as difficult to apply as the Court suggests. * * * While it may be difficult in some cases to measure the exact scope of the arrestee's immediate control, relevant factors would surely include the relative number of police officers and arrestees, the manner of restraint placed on the arrestee, and the ability of the arrestee to gain access to a particular area or container. Certainly there will be some close cases, but when in doubt the police can always turn to the rationale underlying *Chimel*—the need to prevent the arrestee from reaching weapons or contraband—before exercising their judgment. A rule based on that rationale should provide more guidance than the rule announced by the Court today. Moreover, unlike the Court's rule, it would be faithful to the Fourth Amendment.

Justice WHITE, with whom Justice MARSHALL joins, dissenting.

* * * The Court now holds that as incident to the arrest of the driver or any other person in an automobile, the interior of the car and any container found therein, whether locked or not, may be not only seized but also searched even absent probable cause to believe that contraband or evidence of crime will be found. As to luggage, briefcases, or other containers, this seems to me an extreme extension of *Chimel* and one to which I cannot subscribe. * * * Here, searches of luggage, briefcases, and other containers in the interior of an auto are authorized in the absence of any suspicion whatsoever that they contain anything in which the police have a legitimate interest. This calls for more caution than the Court today exhibits, and, with respect, I dissent.

NOTES AND QUESTIONS

1.   Is *Belton* consistent with *Chimel*?

2.   *Bright-lines (part 1).* Justice Stewart notes favorably the benefits to police of bright-line rules of criminal procedure. Are there benefits of such rules to *courts*? What are the *costs* of bright-line rules?

3.   *Bright-lines (part 2).* The *Belton* majority quotes from an article written by Professor Wayne LaFave, apparently supportive of bright-line rules. In another article, this one written after *Belton*, LaFave explained his position more fully. According to him, a court should ask itself four questions before it adopts a particular bright-line rule:

> (1) Does it [the proposed rule] have clear and certain boundaries, so that it in fact makes case-by-case evaluation and adjudication unnecessary? (2) Does it produce results approximating those which would be obtained *if* accurate case-by-case application of the underlying principle were practicable? (3) Is it responsive to a genuine need to forego case-by-case application of a principle because that approach has proved unworkable? (4) Is it not readily subject to manipulation and abuse?

Wayne R. LaFave, *The Fourth Amendment In an Imperfect World: On Drawing "Bright Lines" and "Good Faith"*, 43 U. Pitt. L. Rev. 307, 325–26 (1982).

Does the *Belton* bright-line rule pass Professor LaFave's four-pronged test? If you believe a bright-line rule *is* desirable, did the Court fashion the best rule? Can you suggest a better bright-line rule?

4.   *"Search incident to lawful citation"?* In Knowles v. Iowa, 525 U.S. 113, 119 S.Ct. 484, 142 L.Ed.2d 492 (1998), an Iowa police officer stopped Knowles for speeding. State law authorized the police to arrest traffic violators and take them immediately before a magistrate, but the officer instead merely issued Knowles a traffic citation. Although the officer had no reason to

believe he would find a weapon or criminal evidence in the car, he conducted a full search of the vehicle, as expressly permitted by state law. During the search, the officer discovered a bag of marijuana and a "pot pipe" under the driver's seat. Does *Belton* apply to the search? Should it? What about *United States v. Robinson*, p. 226?

The Supreme Court, per Chief Justice Rehnquist, unanimously held that the search of the car *violated* the Fourth Amendment:

> In *Robinson*, we noted the two historical rationales for the "search incident to arrest" exception: (1) the need to disarm the suspect in order to take him into custody, and (2) the need to preserve evidence for later use at trial. But neither of these underlying rationales for the search incident to arrest exception is sufficient to justify the search in the present case.
>
>   We have recognized that the first rationale—officer safety—is " 'both legitimate and weighty.' " The threat to officer safety from issuing a traffic citation, however, is a good deal less than in the case of a custodial arrest. In *Robinson*, we stated that a custodial arrest involves "danger to an officer" because of "the extended exposure which follows the taking of a suspect into custody and transporting him to the police station." We recognized that "[t]he danger to the police officer flows from the fact of the arrest, and its attendant proximity, stress, and uncertainty, and not from the grounds for arrest." A routine traffic stop, on the other hand, is a relatively brief encounter * * *.
>
>   This is not to say that the concern for officer safety is absent in the case of a routine traffic stop. It plainly is not. But while the concern for officer safety in this context may justify the "minimal" additional intrusion of ordering a driver * * * out of the car, it does not by itself justify the often considerably greater intrusion attending a full field-type search. * * *
>
>   Nor has Iowa shown the second justification for the authority to search incident to arrest—the need to discover and preserve evidence. Once Knowles was stopped for speeding and issued a citation, all the evidence necessary to prosecute that offense had been obtained. No further evidence of excessive speed was going to be found either on the person of the offender or in the passenger compartment of the car.

5.   In *Knowles* (Note 4), the officer chose to issue a citation to a traffic violator although he could have taken the violator into custody under Iowa law. The Court disapproved the warrantless search of the car incident to the citation. However, may an officer skirt *Knowles* by simply taking traffic violators into custody, and then seeking to justify their search of the arrestee and the car on the basis of the "search incident to a lawful custodial arrest" rule? That question—and scenario—however, raises a preliminary Fourth Amendment question not considered in *Knowles*: *May* a legislature constitutionally authorize the police to take a person into custody for a very petty offense, such as a minor traffic violation that carries only a small fine? Consider the next case.

In Atwater v. City of Lago Vista, 532 U.S. 318, 121 S.Ct. 1536, 149 L.Ed.2d 549 (2001), Atwater was driving her pickup truck with her 3–year-old son and 5–year-old daughter in the front seat. None of them was wearing a seatbelt. Officer *T*, who had on a previous occasion stopped Atwater for the same reason but had let her go with a warning, again stopped Atwater's vehicle and yelled something at her, such as, "we've met before" and "you're going to jail." Atwater pleaded to take her "frightened, upset, and crying" children to a friend's house nearby, but he told her, "you're not going anywhere." (Fortunately, Atwater's friend learned what was going on and arrived to take charge of the children.) *T* handcuffed Atwater, placed her in his squad car, and drove her to the police station where booking officers required her to remove her shoes, jewelry, and eyeglasses, and empty her pockets. Officers took Atwater's "mug shot," jailed her for an hour, after which she was taken before a magistrate and released on bond.

No criminal evidence was found on Atwater's person or in her vehicle during the warrantless searches. As a result, she pleaded no contest to the misdemeanor seatbelt offenses and paid a $50 fine. Later, she filed suit under a federal statute (42 U.S.C. § 1983) for violation of her Fourth Amendment rights. She claimed that the City lacked constitutional authority to permit custodial arrests for such a minor offense.

The Court, 5–4, per Justice Souter, rejected Atwater's argument. First, it rejected the defense's claim that at common law (and, therefore, at the time of the framing of the Fourth Amendment), peace officers were forbidden to make warrantless misdemeanor arrests except for breaches of the peace. Justice Souter surveyed pre-Constitutional English common law and found sufficient disagreement among jurists and English text writers to conclude that "we simply are not convinced that Atwater's is the correct, or even necessarily the better, reading of the common-law history." The Court went on to consider and reject Atwater's non-historical argument:

> Atwater does not wager all on history. Instead, she asks us to mint a new rule of constitutional law * * *, one not necessarily requiring violent breach of the peace, but nonetheless forbidding custodial arrest, even upon probable cause, when conviction could not ultimately carry any jail time and when the government shows no compelling need for immediate detention.
>
> If we were to derive a rule exclusively to address the uncontested facts of this case, Atwater might well prevail. She was a known and established resident of Lago Vista with no place to hide and no incentive to flee, and common sense says she would almost certainly have buckled up as a condition of driving off with a citation. In her case, the physical incidents of arrest were merely gratuitous humiliations imposed by a police officer who was (at best) exercising extremely poor judgment. Atwater's claim to live free of pointless indignity and confinement clearly outweighs anything the City can raise against it specific to her case.
>
> But we have traditionally recognized that a responsible Fourth Amendment balance is not well served by standards requiring sensitive, case-by-case determinations of government need, lest every discretionary judgment in the field be converted into an occasion for constitutional

review. See, *e.g.*, *United States v. Robinson*. Often enough, the Fourth Amendment has to be applied on the spur (and in the heat) of the moment, and the object in implementing its command of reasonableness is to draw standards sufficiently clear and simple to be applied with a fair prospect of surviving judicial second-guessing months and years after an arrest or search is made. Courts attempting to strike a reasonable Fourth Amendment balance thus credit the government's side with an essential interest in readily administrable rules. See *New York v. Belton*.

At first glance, Atwater's argument may seem to respect the values of clarity and simplicity * * *. But the claim is not ultimately so simple, nor could it be, for complications arise the moment we begin to think about the possible applications of the several criteria Atwater proposes for drawing a line between minor crimes with limited arrest authority and others not so restricted.

One line, she suggests, might be between "jailable" and "fine-only" offenses * * *. The trouble with this distinction, of course, is that an officer on the street might not be able to tell. It is not merely that we cannot expect every police officer to know the details of frequently complex penalty schemes, but that penalties for ostensibly identical conduct can vary on account of facts difficult (if not impossible) to know at the scene of an arrest. Is this the first offense or is the suspect a repeat offender? Is the weight of the marijuana a gram above or a gram below the fine-only line? Where conduct could implicate more than one criminal prohibition, which one will the district attorney ultimately decide to charge? And so on.

But Atwater's refinements would not end there. She represents that if the line were drawn at nonjailable traffic offenses, her proposed limitation should be qualified by a proviso authorizing warrantless arrests where "necessary for enforcement of the traffic laws or when [an] offense would otherwise continue and pose a danger to others on the road." * * * The proviso only compounds the difficulties. Would, for instance, either exception apply to speeding? * * *

* * * [O]ne Member of this Court * * * [asked] at oral argument, "how bad the problem is out there." The very fact that the law has never jelled the way Atwater would have it leads one to wonder whether warrantless misdemeanor arrests need constitutional attention, and there is cause to think the answer is no. * * *

* * * Indeed, when Atwater's counsel was asked at oral argument for any indications of comparably foolish, warrantless misdemeanor arrests, he could offer only one. We are sure that there are others, but just as surely the country is not confronting anything like an epidemic of unnecessary minor-offense arrests. That fact caps the reasons for rejecting Atwater's request for the development of a new and distinct body of constitutional law.

The dissenters, per Justice O'Connor, expressed concern about the long-term consequences of the Court's holding:

The *per se* rule that the Court creates has potentially serious consequences for the everyday lives of Americans. A broad range of conduct falls into the category of fine-only misdemeanors. In Texas alone, for example, disobeying any sort of traffic warning sign is a misdemeanor punishable only by fine, as is failing to pay a highway toll, and driving with expired license plates. Nor are fine-only crimes limited to the traffic context. In several States, for example, littering is a criminal offense punishable only by fine.

To be sure, such laws are valid and wise exercises of the States' power to protect the public health and welfare. My concern lies not with the decision to enact or enforce these laws, but rather with the manner in which they may be enforced. Under today's holding, when a police officer has probable cause to believe that a fine-only misdemeanor offense has occurred, that officer may stop the suspect, issue a citation, and let the person continue on her way. Or, if a traffic violation, the officer may stop the car, arrest the driver, search the driver, search the entire passenger compartment of the car including any purse or package inside, and impound the car and inventory all of its contents. Although the Fourth Amendment expressly requires that the latter course be a reasonable and proportional response to the circumstances of the offense, the majority gives officers unfettered discretion to choose that course without articulating a single reason why such action is appropriate.

Such unbounded discretion carries with it grave potential for abuse. * * * Indeed, as the recent debate over racial profiling demonstrates all too clearly, a relatively minor traffic infraction may often serve as an excuse for stopping and harassing an individual. After today, the arsenal available to any officer extends to a full arrest and the searches permissible concomitant to that arrest. * * * [W]e must vigilantly ensure that officers' poststop actions * * * comport with the Fourth Amendment's guarantee of reasonableness.

Looking only at the facts of *this* case, do you believe Atwater's custodial arrest was unreasonable? If so, "we are left with a riddle: how can a clearly unreasonable arrest and an unfettered arrest power with grave potential for abuse be considered 'reasonable' under the Fourth Amendment?" Richard S. Frase, *What Were They Thinking? Fourth Amendment Unreasonableness in Atwater v. City of Lago Vista*, 71 Fordham L. Rev. 329, 335 (2002). Can you provide a suitable answer to the riddle?

6. In *Knowles v. Iowa* (Note 4), as we saw, the officer who stopped Knowles for speeding had a choice: issue a traffic citation or take the driver into custody. Now, however, change the facts in *Knowles* as follows: Assume that the officer has only one option available to him under state law, namely, to issue a citation. However, further assume that the officer, *in violation of state law*, takes the driver into custody anyway. May the officer *now* conduct a search incident to this *custodial* arrest? No way, you might think. After all, the search warrant exception we are talking about applies to a search incident to a *lawful* custodial arrest, and the hypothetical arrest here was unlawful. Right?

Wrong. It turns out that when the Supreme Court speaks of a search incident to a "lawful" arrest, one must distinguish between an arrest that is lawful (or unlawful) under the Fourth Amendment and one that is lawful (or unlawful) under local law. According to a unanimous Court in Virginia v. Moore, 553 U.S. ___, 128 S.Ct. 1598, 170 L.Ed.2d 559 (2008), an arrest based on probable cause, although in violation of state law, is "lawful" for purposes of Fourth Amendment analysis. A search conducted as an incident of such an arrest, therefore, satisfies the Fourth Amendment rules discussed in this chapter.

7. *Belton is extended * * * and questioned.* The Supreme Court extended the *Belton* rule in Thornton v. United States, 541 U.S. 615, 124 S.Ct. 2127, 158 L.Ed.2d 905 (2004). In *Thornton*, the police lawfully arrested *T*, who had just parked and exited his vehicle, for possession of illegal drugs. The police handcuffed *T* and placed him in the back seat of a patrol car, after which they conducted a warrantless *Belton* search of the car, resulting in discovery of a handgun under the driver's seat. *T* "argued that *Belton* was limited to situations where the officer initiated contact with an arrestee while he was still an occupant of the car." The Court disagreed, and ruled that the *Belton* rule applies "[s]o long as an arrestee is the sort of 'recent occupant' of a vehicle such as [*T*] was here." (Query: Should *Belton* apply if the police arrest a person as she unlocks her car door and is about to enter it?)

Justice Scalia (joined by Justice Ginsburg), while concurring in the judgment, took the opportunity to criticize the *Belton* rule and suggest that it be recast:

> [One]   defense of the [police] search is that, even though the arrestee posed no risk here, *Belton* searches in general are reasonable, and the benefits of a bright-line rule justify upholding that small minority of searches that, on their particular facts, are not reasonable. The validity of this argument rests on the accuracy of *Belton*'s claim that the passenger compartment is "in fact generally, even if not inevitably," within the suspect's immediate control. By the United States' own admission, however, "[t]he practice of restraining an arrestee on the scene before searching a car that he just occupied is so prevalent that holding that *Belton* does not apply in that setting would * * * 'largely render *Belton* a dead letter.' " Reported cases involving this precise factual scenario—a motorist handcuffed and secured in the back of a squad car when the search takes place—are legion. * * *

> The popularity of the practice is not hard to fathom. If *Belton entitles* an officer to search a vehicle upon arresting the driver despite having taken measures that eliminate any danger, what rational officer would not take those measures? If it was ever true that the passenger compartment is "in fact generally, even if not inevitably," within the arrestee's immediate control at the time of the search, it certainly is not true today. As one judge has put it: "[I]n our search for clarity, we have now abandoned our constitutional moorings and floated to a place where the law approves of purely exploratory searches of vehicles during which officers with no definite objective or reason for the search are allowed to

rummage around in a car to see what they might find." I agree entirely with that assessment. * * *

If *Belton* searches are justifiable, it is not because the arrestee might grab a weapon or evidentiary item from his car, but simply because the car might contain evidence relevant to the crime for which he was arrested. * * *

In this case, as in *Belton*, petitioner was lawfully arrested for a drug offense. It was reasonable for Officer Nichols to believe that further contraband or similar evidence relevant to the crime for which he had been arrested might be found in the vehicle from which he had just alighted and which was still within his vicinity at the time of arrest. I would affirm the decision below on that ground.

In a separate concurrence, Justice O'Connor stated that she found Justice Scalia's proposed change in the law "on firmer ground" than "*Belton*'s shaky foundation," but she indicated her reluctance to "adopt it in the context of a case in which neither the Government nor the petitioner has had a chance to speak to its merits."

The two dissenters in *Thornton*—Justices Stevens and Souter—criticized *Belton* for allowing "the police to conduct a broader search than our decision in *Chimel v. California* would have permitted."

So, the law after *Thornton* sat in an odd position: *Belton* had been extended to recent occupants of automobiles, even as five justices expressed criticism of *Belton*. In 2005, Chief Justice Rehnquist (the author of *Thornton*) died and was replaced by John Roberts, and in 2006 Justice O'Connor retired and her seat was filled by Samuel Alito.

It was not too long thereafter that the "new" Court took the opportunity to confront the *Belton* rule again, as we see immediately below.

ARIZONA v. GANT

Supreme Court of the United States, 2009.
556 U.S. ___, 129 S.Ct. 1710, 173 L.Ed.2d 485.

JUSTICE STEVENS delivered the opinion of the Court.

After Rodney Gant was arrested for driving with a suspended license, handcuffed, and locked in the back of a patrol car, police officers searched his car and discovered cocaine in the pocket of a jacket on the backseat. Because Gant could not have accessed his car to retrieve weapons or evidence at the time of the search, the Arizona Supreme Court held that the search-incident-to-arrest exception to the Fourth Amendments warrant requirement, as defined in *Chimel* v. *California*, [p. 218] and applied to vehicle searches in *New York* v. *Belton*, [p. 235], did not justify the search in this case. We agree with that conclusion.

Under *Chimel*, police may search incident to arrest only the space within an arrestees immediate control, meaning the area from within which he might gain possession of a weapon or destructible evidence. The safety and evidentiary justifications underlying *Chimel*s reaching-distance rule determine *Belton*'s scope. Accordingly, we hold that *Belton* does not authorize a vehicle search incident to a recent occupant's arrest after the arrestee has been secured and cannot access the interior of the vehicle. Consistent with the holding in *Thornton* v. *United States*, [p. 245, Note 7], and following the suggestion in Justice Scalia's opinion concurring in the judgment in that case, we also conclude that circumstances unique to the automobile context justify a search incident to arrest when it is reasonable to believe that evidence of the offense of arrest might be found in the vehicle.

I

[The police had reliable information that there was an outstanding warrant for the arrest of Rodney Gant for driving with a suspended license. Gant was discovered and arrested after he got out of his car in a driveway where two other persons had moments earlier been arrested on drug charges. Each arrestee was handcuffed and placed in a separate locked patrol car. In Gant's case, two officers searched his car and discovered cocaine in the backseat.]

Gant was charged with two offenses—possession of a narcotic drug for sale and possession of drug paraphernalia (*i.e.*, the plastic bag in which the cocaine was found). He moved to suppress the evidence seized from his car on the ground that the warrantless search violated the Fourth Amendment. * * * Gant argued that *Belton* did not authorize the search of his vehicle because he posed no threat to the officers after he was handcuffed in the patrol car and because he was arrested for a traffic offense for which no evidence could be found in his vehicle. When asked at the suppression hearing why the search was conducted, Officer Griffith responded: "Because the law says we can do it."

The trial court * * * denied the motion to suppress. Relying on the fact that the police saw Gant commit the crime of driving without a license and apprehended him only shortly after he exited his car, the court held that the search was permissible as a search incident to arrest. * * *

After protracted state-court proceedings, the Arizona Supreme Court concluded that the search of Gant's car was unreasonable within the meaning of the Fourth Amendment. The court's opinion discussed at length our decision in *Belton* * * *. The court distinguished *Belton* as a case concerning the permissible scope of a vehicle search incident to arrest and concluded that it did not answer "the threshold question whether the police may conduct a search incident to arrest at all once the scene is secure." Relying on our earlier decision in *Chimel*, the court observed that the search-incident-to-arrest exception to the warrant requirement is justified by interests in officer safety and evidence preservation. When "the justifications underlying *Chimel* no longer exist because the scene is secure and the arrestee is handcuffed, secured in the back of a patrol car, and under the supervision of an officer," the court concluded, a "warrantless search of the arrestees car cannot be justified as necessary to protect the officers at the scene or prevent the destruction of evidence." Accordingly, the court held that the search of Gant's car was unreasonable. * * *

The chorus that has called for us to revisit *Belton* includes courts, scholars, and Members of this Court who have questioned that decision's clarity and its fidelity to Fourth Amendment principles. We therefore granted the State's petition for certiorari.

II

Consistent with our precedent, our analysis begins, as it should in every case addressing the reasonableness of a warrantless search, with the basic rule that "searches conducted outside the judicial process, without prior approval by judge or magistrate, are *per se* unreasonable under the Fourth Amendment—subject only to a few specifically established and well-delineated exceptions." Among the exceptions to the warrant requirement is a search incident to a lawful arrest. The exception derives from interests in officer safety and evidence preservation that are typically implicated in arrest situations.

In *Chimel*, we held that a search incident to arrest may only include "the arrestee's person and the area 'within his immediate control'— construing that phrase to mean the area from within which he might gain possession of a weapon or destructible evidence." That limitation, which continues to define the boundaries of the exception, ensures that the scope of a search incident to arrest is commensurate with its purposes of protecting arresting officers and safeguarding any evidence of the offense of arrest that an arrestee might conceal or destroy. If there is no possibility that an arrestee could reach into the area that law enforcement officers seek to search, both justifications for the search-incident-to-arrest exception are absent and the rule does not apply.

In *Belton*, we considered *Chimel*'s application to the automobile context. * * *

* * * [W]e held that when an officer lawfully arrests "the occupant of an automobile, he may, as a contemporaneous incident of that arrest, search the passenger compartment of the automobile" and any containers therein. That holding was based in large part on our assumption "that articles inside the relatively narrow compass of the passenger compartment of an automobile are in fact generally, even if not inevitably, within 'the area into which an arrestee might reach.' "

The Arizona Supreme Court read our decision in *Belton* as merely delineating "the proper scope of a search of the interior of an automobile" incident to an arrest. That is, *when* the passenger compartment is within an arrestee's reaching distance, *Belton* supplies the generalization that the entire compartment and any containers therein may be reached. On that view of *Belton*, the state court concluded that the search of Gant's car was unreasonable because Gant clearly could not have accessed his car at the time of the search. * * *

Gant now urges us to adopt the reading of *Belton* followed by the Arizona Supreme Court.

III

Despite the textual and evidentiary support for the Arizona Supreme Court's reading of *Belton*, our opinion has been widely understood to allow a vehicle search incident to the arrest of a recent occupant even if there is no possibility the arrestee could gain access to the vehicle at the time of the search. This reading may be attributable to Justice Brennan's dissent in *Belton*, in which he characterized the Court's holding as resting on the "fiction * * * that the interior of a car is *always* within the immediate control of an arrestee who has recently been in the car." Under the majority's approach, he argued, "the result would presumably be the same even if [the officer] had handcuffed Belton and his companions in the patrol car" before conducting the search.

* * * As Justice O'Connor observed [in *Thornton*], "lower court decisions seem now to treat the ability to search a vehicle incident to the arrest of a recent occupant as a police entitlement rather than as an exception justified by the twin rationales of *Chimel*." Justice Scalia has similarly noted that, although it is improbable that an arrestee could gain access to weapons stored in his vehicle after he has been handcuffed and secured in the backseat of a patrol car, cases allowing a search in "this precise factual scenario * * * are legion." * * *

Under this broad reading of *Belton*, a vehicle search would be authorized incident to every arrest of a recent occupant notwithstanding that in most cases the vehicle's passenger compartment will not be within the arrestee's reach at the time of the search. To read *Belton* as authorizing a vehicle search incident to every recent occupant's arrest would thus untether the rule from the justifications underlying the *Chimel* exception—a result clearly incompatible with our statement in *Belton* that it "in no way alters the fundamental principles established in the *Chimel* case regarding the basic scope of searches incident to lawful custodial arrests." Accordingly, we reject this reading of *Belton* and hold that the *Chimel* rationale authorizes police to search a vehicle incident to a recent occupant's arrest only when the arrestee is unsecured and within reaching distance of the passenger compartment at the time of the search.[4]

Although it does not follow from *Chimel*, we also conclude that circumstances unique to the vehicle context justify a search incident to a lawful arrest when it is "reasonable to believe evidence relevant to the crime of arrest might be found in the vehicle." In many cases, as when a recent occupant is arrested for a traffic violation, there will be no reasonable basis to believe the vehicle contains relevant evidence. But in others, including *Belton* and *Thornton*, the offense of arrest will supply a

---

4. Because officers have many means of ensuring the safe arrest of vehicle occupants, it will be the rare case in which an officer is unable to fully effectuate an arrest so that a real possibility of access to the arrestee's vehicle remains. But in such a case a search incident to arrest is reasonable under the Fourth Amendment.

basis for searching the passenger compartment of an arrestee's vehicle and any containers therein.

Neither the possibility of access nor the likelihood of discovering offense-related evidence authorized the search in this case. * * * Because police could not reasonably have believed either that Gant could have accessed his car at the time of the search or that evidence of the offense [of driving with a suspended license] for which he was arrested might have been found therein, the search in this case was unreasonable.

IV

The State does not seriously disagree with the Arizona Supreme Court's conclusion that Gant could not have accessed his vehicle at the time of the search, but it nevertheless asks us to uphold the search of his vehicle under the broad reading of *Belton* discussed above. The State argues that *Belton* searches are reasonable regardless of the possibility of access in a given case because that expansive rule correctly balances law enforcement interests, including the interest in a bright-line rule, with an arrestee's limited privacy interest in his vehicle.

For several reasons, we reject the States argument. First, the State seriously undervalues the privacy interests at stake. * * * It is particularly significant that *Belton* searches authorize police officers to search not just the passenger compartment but every purse, briefcase, or other container within that space. A rule that gives police the power to conduct such a search whenever an individual is caught committing a traffic offense, when there is no basis for believing evidence of the offense might be found in the vehicle, creates a serious and recurring threat to the privacy of countless individuals. Indeed, the character of that threat implicates the central concern underlying the Fourth Amendment—the concern about giving police officers unbridled discretion to rummage at will among a person's private effects.

At the same time as it undervalues these privacy concerns, the State exaggerates the clarity that its reading of *Belton* provides. Courts that have read *Belton* expansively are at odds regarding how close in time to the arrest and how proximate to the arrestee's vehicle an officer's first contact with the arrestee must be to bring the encounter within *Belton*'s purview and whether a search is reasonable when it commences or continues after the arrestee has been removed from the scene. The rule has thus generated a great deal of uncertainty, particularly for a rule touted as providing a "bright line."

Contrary to the State's suggestion, a broad reading of *Belton* is also unnecessary to protect law enforcement safety and evidentiary interests. Under our view, *Belton* and *Thornton* permit an officer to conduct a vehicle search when an arrestee is within reaching distance of the vehicle or it is reasonable to believe the vehicle contains evidence of the offense of arrest. Other established exceptions to the warrant requirement authorize a vehicle search under additional circumstances when safety or evidentiary concerns demand. * * *

* * * Construing *Belton* broadly to allow vehicle searches incident to any arrest would serve no purpose except to provide a police entitlement, and it is anathema to the Fourth Amendment to permit a warrantless search on that basis. * * *

V

Our dissenting colleagues argue that the doctrine of *stare decisis* requires adherence to a broad reading of *Belton* even though the justifications for searching a vehicle incident to arrest are in most cases absent.[9] The doctrine of *stare decisis* is of course "essential to the respect accorded to the judgments of the Court and to the stability of the law," but it does not compel us to follow a past decision when its rationale no longer withstands "careful analysis."

We have never relied on *stare decisis* to justify the continuance of an unconstitutional police practice. And we would be particularly loath to uphold an unconstitutional result in a case that is so easily distinguished from the decisions that arguably compel it. The safety and evidentiary interests that supported the search in *Belton* simply are not present in this case. Indeed, it is hard to imagine two cases that are factually more distinct, as *Belton* involved one officer confronted by four unsecured arrestees suspected of committing a drug offense and this case involves several officers confronted with a securely detained arrestee apprehended for driving with a suspended license. This case is also distinguishable from *Thornton*, in which the petitioner was arrested for a drug offense. It is thus unsurprising that Members of this Court who concurred in the judgments in *Belton* and *Thornton* also concur in the decision in this case.

We do not agree with the contention in Justice Alito's dissent * * * that consideration of police reliance interests requires a different result. Although it appears that the State's reading of *Belton* has been widely taught in police academies and that law enforcement officers have relied on the rule in conducting vehicle searches during the past 28 years, many of these searches were not justified by the reasons underlying the *Chimel* exception. Countless individuals guilty of nothing more serious than a traffic violation have had their constitutional right to the security of their private effects violated as a result. The fact that the law enforcement community may view the State's version of the *Belton* rule as an entitlement does not establish the sort of reliance interest that could outweigh the countervailing interest that all individuals share in having their constitutional rights fully protected. * * *

---

9. Justice Altio's dissenting opinion * * * accuses us of "overrul[ing]" *Belton* and *Thornton* v. *United States*, "even though respondent Gant has not asked us to do so." Contrary to that claim, the narrow reading of *Belton* we adopt today is precisely the result Gant has urged. That Justice Alito has chosen to describe this decision as overruling our earlier cases does not change the fact that the resulting rule of law is the one advocated by respondent.

The experience of the 28 years since we decided *Belton* has shown that the generalization underpinning the broad reading of that decision is unfounded. We now know that articles inside the passenger compartment are rarely "within 'the area into which an arrestee might reach,'" and blind adherence to *Belton*'s faulty assumption would authorize myriad unconstitutional searches. The doctrine of *stare decisis* does not require us to approve routine constitutional violations.

VI

Police may search a vehicle incident to a recent occupant's arrest only if the arrestee is within reaching distance of the passenger compartment at the time of the search or it is reasonable to believe the vehicle contains evidence of the offense of arrest. When these justifications are absent, a search of an arrestee's vehicle will be unreasonable unless police obtain a warrant or show that another exception to the warrant requirement applies. * * * Accordingly, the judgment of the State Supreme Court is affirmed.

Justice SCALIA, concurring.

To determine what is an "unreasonable" search within the meaning of the Fourth Amendment, we look first to the historical practices the Framers sought to preserve; if those provide inadequate guidance, we apply traditional standards of reasonableness. Since the historical scope of officers' authority to search vehicles incident to arrest is uncertain, traditional standards of reasonableness govern. It is abundantly clear that those standards do not justify what I take to be the rule set forth in *Belton* and *Thornton*: that arresting officers may always search an arrestee's vehicle in order to protect themselves from hidden weapons. When an arrest is made in connection with a roadside stop, police virtually always have a less intrusive and more effective means of ensuring their safety—and a means that is virtually always employed: ordering the arrestee away from the vehicle, patting him down in the open, handcuffing him, and placing him in the squad car. * * *

Justice Stevens acknowledges that an officer-safety rationale cannot justify all vehicle searches incident to arrest, but asserts that that is not the rule *Belton* and *Thornton* adopted. (As described above, I read those cases differently). Justice Stevens would therefore retain the application of *Chimel* v. *California* in the car-search context but would apply in the future what he believes our cases held in the past: that officers making a roadside stop may search the vehicle so long as the "arrestee is within reaching distance of the passenger compartment at the time of the search." I believe that this standard fails to provide the needed guidance to arresting officers and also leaves much room for manipulation, inviting officers to leave the scene unsecured (at least where dangerous suspects are not involved) in order to conduct a vehicle search. In my view we should simply abandon the *Belton–Thornton* charade of officer safety and overrule those cases. I would hold that a vehicle search incident to arrest is *ipso facto* "reasonable" only when the object of the search is evidence of the crime for which the arrest was made, or of another crime that the officer has probable cause to believe occurred. Because respondent was arrested for driving without a license (a crime for which no evidence could be expected to be found in the vehicle), I would hold in the present case that the search was unlawful.

Justice Alito insists that the Court must demand a good reason for abandoning prior precedent. That is true enough, but it seems to me ample reason that the precedent was badly reasoned and produces erroneous (in this case unconstitutional) results. * * *

Justice Alito argues that there is no reason to adopt a rule limiting automobile-arrest searches to those cases where the search's object is evidence of the crime of arrest. I disagree. This formulation of officers' authority both preserves the outcomes of our prior cases and tethers the scope and rationale of the doctrine to the triggering event. * * * I also disagree with Justice Alito's conclusory assertion that this standard will be difficult to administer in practice; the ease of its application in this case would suggest otherwise.

No other Justice, however, shares my view that application of *Chimel* in this context should be entirely abandoned. It seems to me unacceptable for the Court to come forth with a 4–to–1–to–4 opinion that leaves the governing rule uncertain. I am therefore confronted with the choice of either leaving the current understanding of *Belton* and *Thornton* in effect, or acceding to what seems to me the artificial narrowing of those cases adopted by Justice Stevens. The latter, as I have said, does not provide the degree of certainty I think desirable in this field; but the former opens the field to what I think are plainly unconstitutional searches—which is the greater evil. I therefore join the opinion of the Court.

Justice BREYER, dissenting.

I agree with Justice Alito that *New York* v. *Belton* is best read as setting forth a bright-line rule that permits a warrantless search of the passenger compartment of an automobile incident to the lawful arrest of an occupant—regardless of the danger the arrested individual in fact poses. I also agree with Justice Stevens, however, that the rule can produce results divorced from its underlying Fourth Amendment rationale. For that reason I would look for a better rule—were the question before us one of first impression.

The matter, however, is not one of first impression, and that fact makes a substantial difference. * * * Principles of *stare decisis* must apply, and those who wish this Court to change a well-established legal precedent—where, as here, there has been considerable reliance on the legal rule in question—bear a heavy burden. I have not found that burden met. Nor do I believe that the other considerations ordinarily relevant when determining whether to overrule a case are satisfied. I consequently join Justice Alitos dissenting opinion with the exception of Part II–E.

Justice ALITO, with whom THE CHIEF JUSTICE and Justice KEN-NEDY join, and with whom Justice BREYER joins except as to Part II–E, dissenting.

* * * Today's decision effectively overrules [*Belton* and *Thornton*], even though respondent Gant has not asked us to do so.

To take the place of the overruled precedents, the Court adopts a new two-part rule under which a police officer who arrests a vehicle occupant or recent occupant may search the passenger compartment if (1) the arrestee is within reaching distance of the vehicle at the time of the search or (2) the officer has reason to believe that the vehicle contains evidence of the offense of arrest. The first part of this new rule may endanger arresting officers and is truly endorsed by only four Justices; Justice Scalia joins solely for the purpose of avoiding a "4–to–1–to 4 opinion." The second part of the new rule is taken from Justice Scalia's separate opinion in *Thornton* without any independent explanation of its origin or justification and is virtually certain to confuse law enforcement officers and judges for some time to come. The Court's decision will cause the suppression of evidence gathered in many searches carried out in good-faith reliance on well-settled case law, and although the Court purports to base its analysis on the landmark decision in *Chimel* v. *California*, the Courts reasoning undermines *Chimel*. I would follow *Belton*, and I therefore respectfully dissent.

I

Although the Court refuses to acknowledge that it is overruling *Belton* and *Thornton*, there can be no doubt that it does so. * * *

The precise holding in *Belton* could not be clearer. The Court stated unequivocally: "'[W]e hold that when a policeman has made a lawful custodial arrest of the occupant of an automobile, he may, as a contemporaneous incident of that arrest, search the passenger compartment of that automobile."

Despite this explicit statement, the opinion of the Court in the present case curiously suggests that *Belton* may reasonably be read as adopting a holding that is narrower than the one explicitly set out in the *Belton* opinion, namely, that an officer arresting a vehicle occupant may search the passenger compartment "*when* the passenger compartment is within an arrestee's reaching distance." According to the Court, the broader reading of *Belton* that has gained wide acceptance may be attributable to Justice Brennan's dissent."

Contrary to the Court's suggestion, however, Justice Brennan's *Belton* dissent did not mischaracterize the Court's holding in that case or cause that holding to be misinterpreted. As noted, the *Belton* Court explicitly stated precisely what it held. * * * [The *Belton*] "bright-line rule" has now been interred.

II

Because the Court has substantially overruled *Belton* and *Thornton,* the Court must explain why its departure from the usual rule of *stare decisis* is justified. I recognize that stare decisis is not an "inexorable command," and applies less rigidly in constitutional cases. But the Court has said that a constitutional precedent should be followed unless there is a " 'special justification' " for its abandonment. Relevant factors identified in prior cases include whether the precedent has engendered reliance, whether there has been an important change in circumstances in the outside world, whether the precedent has proved to be unworkable, whether the precedent has been undermined by later decisions, and whether the decision was badly reasoned. These factors weigh in favor of retaining the rule established in *Belton.*

A

Reliance. * * *

* * * [T]here certainly is substantial reliance here. The *Belton* rule has been taught to police officers for more than a quarter century. Many searches—almost certainly including more than a few that figure in cases now on appeal—were conducted in scrupulous reliance on that precedent. It is likely that, on the very day when this opinion is announced, numerous vehicle searches will be conducted in good faith by police officers who were taught the *Belton* rule.

The opinion of the Court recognizes [this] * * *. But for the Court, this seemingly counts for nothing. * * * [T]he Court cites no authority for the proposition that *stare decisis* may be disregarded or provides only lesser protection when the precedent that is challenged is one that sustained the constitutionality of a law enforcement practice. * * *

B

Changed circumstances. Abandonment of the *Belton* rule cannot be justified on the ground that the dangers surrounding the arrest of a vehicle occupant are different today than they were 28 years ago. * * * [S]urely it was well known in 1981 that a person who is taken from a vehicle, handcuffed, and placed in the back of a patrol car is unlikely to make it back into his own car to retrieve a weapon or destroy evidence.

C

Workability. The *Belton* rule has not proved to be unworkable. On the contrary, the rule was adopted for the express purpose of providing a test that would be relatively easy for police officers and judges to apply. The Court correctly notes that even the *Belton* rule is not perfectly clear in all situations. Specifically, it is sometimes debatable whether a search is or is not contemporaneous with an arrest, but that problem is small in comparison with the problems that the Courts new two-part rule will produce. * * *

D

Consistency with later cases. The *Belton* bright-line rule has not been undermined by subsequent cases. On the contrary, that rule was reaffirmed and extended just five years ago in *Thornton.*

E

Bad reasoning. The Court is harshly critical of *Belton*'s reasoning, but the problem that the Court perceives cannot be remedied simply by overruling *Belton. Belton* represented only a modest—and quite defensible—extension of *Chimel*, as I understand that decision.

Prior to *Chimel*, the Court's precedents permitted an arresting officer to search the area within an arrestee's "possession" and "control" for the purpose of gathering evidence. Based on this "abstract doctrine," the Court had sustained searches that extended far beyond an arrestee's grabbing area. See *United States* v. *Rabinowitz*, 339 U. S. 56 (1950) (search of entire office); *Harris* v. *United States*, 331 U. S. 145 (1947) (search of entire apartment).

The *Chimel* Court * * * overruled these cases. Concluding that there are only two justifications for a warrantless search incident to arrest—officer safety and the preservation of evidence—the Court stated that such a search must be confined to "the arrestee's person" and "the area from within which he might gain possession of a weapon or destructible evidence."

Unfortunately, *Chimel* did not say whether "the area from within which [an arrestee] might gain possession of a weapon or destructible evidence" is to be measured at the time of the arrest or at the time of the search, but unless the *Chimel* rule was meant to be a specialty rule, applicable to only a few unusual cases, the Court must have intended for this area to be measured at the time of arrest.

This is so because the Court can hardly have failed to appreciate the following two facts. First, in the great majority of cases, an officer making an arrest is able to handcuff the arrestee and remove him to a secure place before conducting a search incident to the arrest. Second, because it is safer for an arresting officer to secure an arrestee before searching, it is likely that this is what arresting officers do in the great majority of cases. * * * Thus, if the area within an arrestee's reach were assessed, not at the time of arrest, but at the time of the search, the *Chimel* rule would rarely come into play. * * *

I do not think that this is what the *Chimel* Court intended. Handcuffs were in use in 1969. The ability of arresting officers to secure arrestees before conducting a search—and their incentive to do so—are facts that can hardly have escaped the Court's attention. I therefore believe that the *Chimel* Court intended that its new rule apply in cases in which the arrestee is handcuffed before the search is conducted.

The *Belton* Court, in my view, proceeded on the basis of this interpretation of *Chimel*. * * * Viewing *Chimel* as having focused on the time of arrest, *Belton*'s only new step was to eliminate the need to decide on a case-by-case basis whether a particular person seated in a car actually could have reached the part of the passenger compartment where a weapon or evidence was hidden. For this reason, if we are going to reexamine *Belton*, we should also reexamine the reasoning in *Chimel* on which *Belton* rests.

F

The Court, however, does not reexamine *Chimel* and thus leaves the law relating to searches incident to arrest in a confused and unstable state. The first part of the Court's new two-part rule—which permits an arresting officer to search the area within an arrestee's reach at the time of the search—applies, at least for now, only to vehicle occupants and recent occupants, but there is no logical reason why the same rule should not apply to all arrestees.

The second part of the Court's new rule, which the Court takes uncritically from Justice Scalia's separate opinion in *Thornton*, raises doctrinal and practical problems that the Court makes no effort to address. Why, for example, is the standard for this type of evidence-gathering search "reason to believe" rather than probable cause? And why is this type of search restricted to evidence of the offense of arrest? It is true that an arrestee's vehicle is probably more likely to contain evidence of the crime of arrest than of some other crime, but if reason-to-believe is the governing standard for an evidence-gathering search incident to arrest, it is not easy to see why an officer should not be able to search when the officer has reason to believe that the vehicle in question possesses evidence of a crime other than the crime of arrest.

Nor is it easy to see why an evidence-gathering search incident to arrest should be restricted to the passenger compartment. The *Belton* rule was limited in this way because the passenger compartment was considered to be the area that vehicle occupants can generally reach, but since the second part of the new rule is not based on officer safety or the preservation of evidence, the ground for this limitation is obscure.[2]

III

Respondent in this case has not asked us to overrule *Belton*, much less *Chimel*. Respondent's argument rests entirely on an interpretation of *Belton* that is plainly incorrect, an interpretation that disregards *Belton*'s

---

2. I do not understand the Court's decision to reach the following situations. First, it is not uncommon for an officer to arrest some but not all of the occupants of a vehicle. The Court's decision in this case does not address the question whether in such a situation a search of the passenger compartment may be justified on the ground that the occupants who are not arrested could gain access to the car and retrieve a weapon or destroy evidence. Second, there may be situations in which an arresting officer has cause to fear that persons who were not passengers in the car might attempt to retrieve a weapon or evidence from the car while the officer is still on the scene. The decision in this case, as I understand it, does not address that situation either.

explicit delineation of its holding. I would therefore leave any reexamination of our prior precedents for another day, if such a reexamination is to be undertaken at all. In this case, I would simply apply *Belton* and reverse the judgment below.

NOTES AND QUESTIONS

1. Is *Gant* consistent with *Chimel*? With *Robinson* (p. 226)?

2. In the second paragraph of the majority opinion, Justice Stevens states that a warrantless search incident to a lawful arrest is permissible, even if the arrestee no longer has access to the passenger compartment, "when it is reasonable to believe that evidence of the offense of arrest might be found in the vehicle." In Part VI, this portion of the *Gant* test is stated as follows: when it is "reasonable to believe the vehicle contains evidence of the offense of arrest." Are these two statements functionally the same? Furthermore, Justice Alito points out that the majority did not use the term "probable cause." In this context, is "reasonable to believe" a lesser standard than "probable cause"?

c. Pretextual Stops and Arrests (Particularly in Automobiles)

INTRODUCTORY COMMENT

Consider for a moment State v. Ladson, 138 Wash.2d 343, 979 P.2d 833 (1999):

On October 5, 1995 City of Lacey police officer Jim Mack and Thurston County sheriff's detective Cliff Ziesmer were on proactive gang patrol. The officers explained they do not make routine traffic stops while on proactive gang patrol although they use traffic infractions as a means to pull over people in order to initiate contact and questioning. * * *

On the day in question Richard Fogle attracted the attention of officers Mack and Ziesmer as he drove by. Fogle and his passenger Thomas Ladson are both African–American. Although the officers had never seen Ladson before, they recognized Fogle from an unsubstantiated street rumor that Fogle was involved with drugs. * * *

The officers tailed the Fogle vehicle looking for a legal justification to stop the car. They shadowed the vehicle while it refueled at a local filling station and then finally pulled Fogle over several blocks later on the grounds that Fogle's license plate tabs had expired five days earlier. The officers do not deny the stop was pretextual.

The police then discovered Fogle's driver's license was suspended and arrested him on the spot. After securing Fogle in handcuffs in the squad car, the police conducted a full search of the car "incident to Fogle's arrest." [The police proceeded to order passenger Ladson out of the vehicle, patted him down for weapons, and found a handgun resulting in his arrest and subsequent search. A search of his person turned up baggies of marijuana.]

Notice that this entire process began with an unsubstantiated rumor that could not justify the arrest or search of Fogle, his car, or Ladson. The police strategy, therefore, was to find lawful grounds to stop the vehicle. A traffic violation was the pretext. It gave the officers the opportunity to have forced contact with Fogle, visually peer inside the car in the hope of finding incriminating evidence of drugs, and perhaps find a way to "negotiate" consent to search the car. More conveniently in this case, the expired driver's license provided police with apparent authority to take Fogle into custody and use "search incident to lawful arrest" law to conduct a nonconsensual warrantless search of him and (in the post-*Belton*, but pre-*Gant*, era) his car, and then to turn their attention to Ladson. The police had the authority, that is, unless the pretextual aspects of the case affect the analysis.

The *Ladson* scenario is not rare. It is played out often on the sidewalks and highways of the United States. Sometimes the scenario even lacks the unsubstantiated rumor that triggered the car stop in *Ladson*. A person's race, ethnicity, or national origin may motivate the police conduct. The term "DWB"—Driving While Black—describes the phenomenon in which officers target persons based on race for traffic (or other) detentions in order to follow up on hunches of criminal behavior.

Although African–Americans have disproportionately suffered from this procedure, other groups have been—or can—be targeted. For example, suppose that a law enforcement officer, post-September 11, decides to target all persons of apparent Arab ancestry, "just in case they are terrorists." She might put such persons under surveillance and use a minor traffic violation, such as failure to use a seat belt, as a pretext for further investigation and, perhaps, even for custodial arrest, as in *Atwater*, p. 241, Note 5.

All of this is possible *if* it is constitutional, which brings us to the question: *Does* the Fourth Amendment bar pretextual police conduct? The next case considers this question.

WHREN v. UNITED STATES

Supreme Court of the United States, 1996.
517 U.S. 806, 116 S.Ct. 1769, 135 L.Ed.2d 89.

JUSTICE SCALIA delivered the opinion of the Court.

In this case we decide whether the temporary detention of a motorist who the police have probable cause to believe has committed a civil traffic violation is inconsistent with the Fourth Amendment's prohibition against unreasonable seizures unless a reasonable officer would have been motivated to stop the car by a desire to enforce the traffic laws.

I

On the evening of June 10, 1993, plainclothes vice-squad officers of the District of Columbia Metropolitan Police Department were patrolling a "high drug area" of the city in an unmarked car. Their suspicions were aroused when they passed a dark Pathfinder truck with temporary license plates and youthful occupants waiting at a stop sign, the driver looking down into the lap of the passenger at his right. The truck remained stopped at the intersection for what seemed an unusually long time—more than 20 seconds. When the police car executed a U-turn in order to head back toward the truck, the Pathfinder turned suddenly to its right, without signalling, and sped off at an "unreasonable" speed. The policemen followed, and in a short while overtook the Pathfinder when it stopped behind other traffic at a red light. They pulled up alongside, and Officer Ephraim Soto stepped out and approached the driver's door, identifying himself as a police officer and directing the driver, petitioner Brown, to put the vehicle in park. When Soto drew up to the driver's window, he immediately observed two large plastic bags of what appeared to be crack cocaine in petitioner Whren's hands. Petitioners were arrested, and quantities of several types of illegal drugs were retrieved from the vehicle.

Petitioners were charged in a four-count indictment with violating various federal drug laws * * *. At a pretrial suppression hearing, they challenged the legality of the stop and the resulting seizure of the drugs. They argued that the stop had not been justified by probable cause to believe, or even reasonable suspicion, that petitioners were engaged in illegal drug-dealing activity; and that Officer Soto's asserted ground for approaching the vehicle—to give the driver a warning concerning traffic violations—was pretextual. The District Court denied the suppression motion, concluding that "the facts of the stop were not controverted," and "[t]here was nothing to really demonstrate that the actions of the officers were contrary to a normal traffic stop."

Petitioners were convicted of the counts at issue here. The Court of Appeals affirmed the convictions, holding with respect to the suppression issue that, "regardless of whether a police officer subjectively believes that the occupants of an automobile may be engaging in some other illegal behavior, a traffic stop is permissible as long as a reasonable officer in the same circumstances *could have* stopped the car for the suspected traffic violation." * * *

II * * *

Petitioners accept that Officer Soto had probable cause to believe that various provisions of the District of Columbia traffic code had been violated. See 18 D. C. Mun. Regs. §§ 2213.4 (1995) ("An operator shall * * * give full time and attention to the operation of the vehicle"); 2204.3 ("No person shall turn any vehicle * * * without giving an appropriate signal"); 2200.3 ("No person shall drive a vehicle * * * at a speed greater than is reasonable and prudent under the conditions"). They argue, however, that "in the unique context of civil traffic regulations" probable cause is not enough. Since, they contend, the use of automobiles is so heavily and minutely regulated that total compliance with traffic and safety rules is nearly impossible, a police officer will almost invariably be able to catch any given motorist in a technical violation. This creates the temptation to use traffic stops as a means of investigating other law violations, as to which no probable cause or even articulable suspicion exists. Petitioners, who are both black, further contend that police officers might decide which motorists to stop based on decidedly impermissible factors, such as the race of the car's occupants. To avoid this danger, they say, the Fourth Amendment test for traffic stops should be, not the normal one (applied by the Court of Appeals) of whether probable cause existed to justify the stop; but rather, whether a police officer, acting reasonably, would have made the stop for the reason given.

A

Petitioners contend that the standard they propose is consistent with our past cases' disapproval of police attempts to use valid bases of action against citizens as pretexts for pursuing other investigatory agendas. We are reminded that in *Florida v. Wells*, 495 U.S. 1, 4, 110 S.Ct. 1632, 1635, 109 L.Ed.2d 1 (1990), we stated that "an inventory search[1] must not be used as a ruse for a general rummaging in order to discover incriminating evidence"; that in *Colorado v. Bertine*, 479 U.S. 367, 372, 107 S.Ct. 738, 741, 93 L.Ed.2d 739 (1987), in approving an inventory search, we apparently thought it significant that there had been "no showing that the police, who were following standard procedures, acted in bad faith or for the sole purpose of investigation"; and that in *New York v. Burger*, 482 U.S. 691, 716–717, n. 27, 107 S Ct. 2636, 2651, n. 27, 96 L.Ed. 2d 601 (1987), we observed, in upholding the constitutionality of a warrantless administrative inspection,[2] that the search did not appear to be "a 'pretext' for obtaining evidence of * * * violation of * * * penal laws." But only an undiscerning reader would regard these cases as endorsing the principle that ulterior motives can invalidate police conduct that is justifiable on the basis of probable cause to believe that a violation of law has occurred. In each case we were addressing the validity of a search conducted in the *absence* of probable cause. Our quoted statements simply explain that the exemption from the need for probable cause (and warrant), which is accorded to searches made for the purpose of inventory or administrative regulation, is not accorded to searches that are *not* made for those purposes.

Petitioners also rely upon *Colorado v. Bannister*, 449 U.S. 1, 101 S.Ct. 42, 66 L Ed.2d 1 (1980) (*per curiam*), a case which, like this one, involved a traffic stop as the prelude to a plain-view sighting and arrest on charges wholly unrelated to the basis for the stop. Petitioners point to our statement that "there was no evidence whatsoever that the officer's

---

1. An inventory search is the search of property lawfully seized and detained, in order to ensure that it is harmless, to secure valuable items (such as might be kept in a towed car), and to protect against false claims of loss or damage.

2. An administrative inspection is the inspection of business premises conducted by authorities responsible for enforcing a pervasive regulatory scheme—for example, unannounced inspection of a mine for compliance with health and safety standards.

presence to issue a traffic citation was a pretext to confirm any other previous suspicion about the occupants" of the car. That dictum *at most* demonstrates that the Court in *Bannister* found no need to inquire into the question now under discussion; not that it was certain of the answer. And it may demonstrate even less than that: if by "pretext" the Court meant that the officer really had not seen the car speeding, the statement would mean only that there was no reason to doubt probable cause for the traffic stop.

It would, moreover, be anomalous, to say the least, to treat a statement in a footnote in the *per curiam Bannister* opinion as indicating a reversal of our prior law. Petitioners' difficulty is not simply a lack of affirmative support for their position. Not only have we never held, outside the context of inventory search or administrative inspection (discussed above), that an officer's motive invalidates objectively justifiable behavior under the Fourth Amendment; but we have repeatedly held and asserted the contrary. In *United States v. Villamonte–Marquez*, 462 U.S. 579, 584, n. 3, 103 S.Ct. 2573, 2577, n. 3, 77 L.Ed.2d 22 (1983), we held that an otherwise valid warrantless boarding of a vessel by customs officials was not rendered invalid "because the customs officers were accompanied by a Louisiana state policeman, and were following an informant's tip that a vessel in the ship channel was thought to be carrying marihuana." We flatly dismissed the idea that an ulterior motive might serve to strip the agents of their legal justification. In *United States v. Robinson* [p. 226] we held that a traffic-violation arrest (of the sort here) would not be rendered invalid by the fact that it was "a mere pretext for a narcotics search"; and that a lawful postarrest search of the person would not be rendered invalid by the fact that it was not motivated by the officer-safety concern that justifies such searches. And in *Scott v. United States*, 436 U.S. 128, 138, 98 S.Ct. 1717, 1723, 56 L.Ed. 2d 168 (1978), in rejecting the contention that wiretap evidence was subject to exclusion because the agents conducting the tap had failed to make any effort to comply with the statutory requirement that unauthorized acquisitions be minimized, we said that "[s]ubjective intent alone * * * does not make otherwise lawful conduct illegal or unconstitutional." We described *Robinson* as having established that "the fact that the officer does not have the state of mind which is hypothecated by the reasons which provide the legal justification for the officer's action does not invalidate the action taken as long as the circumstances, viewed objectively, justify that action."

We think these cases foreclose any argument that the constitutional reasonableness of traffic stops depends on the actual motivations of the individual officers involved. We of course agree with petitioners that the Constitution prohibits selective enforcement of the law based on considerations such as race. But the constitutional basis for objecting to intentionally discriminatory application of laws is the Equal Protection Clause, not the Fourth Amendment.[d] Subjective intentions play no role in ordinary, probable-cause Fourth Amendment analysis.

B

Recognizing that we have been unwilling to entertain Fourth Amendment challenges based on the actual motivations of individual officers, petitioners disavow any intention to make the individual officer's subjective good faith the touchstone of "reasonableness." They insist that the standard they have put forward—whether the officer's conduct deviated materially from usual police practices, so that a reasonable officer in the same circumstances would not have made the stop for the reasons given—is an "objective" one.

But although framed in empirical terms, this approach is plainly and indisputably driven by subjective considerations. Its whole purpose is to prevent the police from doing under the guise of enforcing the traffic code what they would like to do for different reasons. Petitioners' proposed standard may not use the word "pretext," but it is designed to combat nothing other than the perceived "danger" of the pretextual stop, albeit only indirectly and over the run of cases. Instead of asking whether the individual officer had the proper state of mind, the petitioners would have us ask, in effect, whether (based on general police practices) it is plausible to believe that the officer had the proper state of mind.

Why one would frame a test designed to combat pretext in such fashion that the court cannot take into account *actual and admitted pretext* is a curiosity that can only be explained by the fact that our cases have foreclosed the more sensible option. If those cases were based only upon the evidentiary difficulty of establishing subjective intent, petitioners' attempt to root out subjective vices through objective means might make sense. But they were not based only upon that, or indeed even principally upon that. Their principal basis—which applies equally to attempts to reach subjective intent through ostensibly objective means—is simply that the Fourth Amendment's concern with "reasonableness" allows certain actions to be taken in certain circumstances, *whatever* the subjective intent. But even if our concern had been only an evidentiary one, petitioners' proposal would by no means assuage it. Indeed, it seems to us somewhat easier to figure out the intent of an individual officer than to plumb the collective consciousness of law enforcement in order to

---

d. "The equal protection clause of the Fourteenth Amendment provides citizens a degree of protection independent of the Fourth Amendment * * *." United States v. Avery, 128 F.3d 974 (6th Cir.1997). Among other things, it protects:

from police action * * * based solely on impermissible racial considerations. * * * A person cannot become the target of a police investigation solely on the basis of skin color [or ethnic origin]. * * * If law enforcement adopts a policy, employs a practice, or in a given situation takes steps to initiate an investigation of a citizen based solely upon that citizens's race, without more, then a violation of the Equal Protection Clause has occurred. *Id.*

A violation of equal protection "can be proved through direct evidence, which seldom exists, or inferences that can be drawn from valid relevant statistical evidence of disparate impact or other circumstantial evidence." However, such statistical evidence "is limited to creation of a rebuttable, prima facie case that race is a motivating factor in the challenged action." *Id.*

determine whether a "reasonable officer" would have been moved to act upon the traffic violation. While police manuals and standard procedures may sometimes provide objective assistance, ordinarily one would be reduced to speculating about the hypothetical reaction of a hypothetical constable—an exercise that might be called virtual subjectivity.

Moreover, police enforcement practices, even if they could be practicably assessed by a judge, vary from place to place and from time to time. We cannot accept that the search and seizure protections of the Fourth Amendment are so variable, and can be made to turn upon such trivialities. The difficulty is illustrated by petitioners' arguments in this case. Their claim that a reasonable officer would not have made this stop is based largely on District of Columbia police regulations which permit plainclothes officers in unmarked vehicles to enforce traffic laws "only in the case of a violation that is so grave as to pose an *immediate threat* to the safety of others." Metropolitan Police Department—Washington, D. C., General Order 303.1, pt. 1, Objectives and Policies (A)(2)(4) (Apr. 30, 1992). This basis of invalidation would not apply in jurisdictions that had a different practice. And it would not have applied even in the District of Columbia, if Officer Soto had been wearing a uniform or patrolling in a marked police cruiser. * * *

III

In what would appear to be an elaboration on the "reasonable officer" test, petitioners argue that the balancing inherent in any Fourth Amendment inquiry requires us to weigh the governmental and individual interests implicated in a traffic stop such as we have here. That balancing, petitioners claim, does not support investigation of minor traffic infractions by plainclothes police in unmarked vehicles; such investigation only minimally advances the government's interest in traffic safety, and may indeed retard it by producing motorist confusion and alarm—a view said to be supported by the Metropolitan Police Department's own regulations generally prohibiting this practice. And as for the Fourth Amendment interests of the individuals concerned, petitioners point out that our cases acknowledge that even ordinary traffic stops entail "a possibly unsettling show of authority"; that they at best "interfere with freedom of movement, are inconvenient, and consume time" and at worst "may create substantial anxiety." That anxiety is likely to be even more pronounced when the stop is conducted by plainclothes officers in unmarked cars.

It is of course true that in principle every Fourth Amendment case, since it turns upon a "reasonableness" determination, involves a balancing of all relevant factors. With rare exceptions not applicable here, however, the result of that balancing is not in doubt where the search or seizure is based upon probable cause. * * *

Where probable cause has existed, the only cases in which we have found it necessary actually to perform the "balancing" analysis involved searches or seizures conducted in an extraordinary manner, unusually harmful to an individual's privacy or even physical interests—such as, for example, seizure by means of deadly force, see *Tennessee v. Garner*, 471 U.S. 1, 105 S.Ct. 1694, 85 L.Ed.2d 1 (1985), unannounced entry into a home, see *Wilson v. Arkansas*, 514 U.S. 927, 115 S.Ct. 1914, 131 L.Ed.2d 976 (1995), * * * or physical penetration of the body, see *Winston v. Lee*, 470 U.S. 753, 105 S.Ct. 1611, 84 L.Ed. 2d 662 (1985). The making of a traffic stop out-of-uniform does not remotely qualify as such an extreme practice, and so is governed by the usual rule that probable cause to believe the law has been broken "outbalances" private interest in avoiding police contact. * * *

For the run-of-the-mine case, which this surely is, we think there is no realistic alternative to the traditional common-law rule that probable cause justifies a search and seizure. * * *

Here the District Court found that the officers had probable cause to believe that petitioners had violated the traffic code. That rendered the stop reasonable under the Fourth Amendment, the evidence thereby discovered admissible, and the upholding of the convictions by the Court of Appeals for the District of Columbia Circuit correct.

Notes and Questions

1. Professor Wayne LaFave has characterized the Court's analysis in *Whren* as, "to put it mildly, quite disappointing. * * * Certainly one would have expected more from an opinion which drew neither a dissent nor a cautionary concurrence from any member of the Court." 1 Wayne R. LaFave, Search and Seizure 149 (4th ed. 2004). According to one court, "[b]y all indications, pretextual traffic stops have increased markedly all over the country since the *Whren* decision." Whitehead v. State, 116 Md.App. 497, 698 A.2d 1115 (Md.App.1997).

2. *The "pervasive police practice" of pretextual stops and arrests (with race added in).* A police officer explains why he will pull over a car on the road: "I have what you might call a profile. I pull up alongside a car with black males in it. Something don't match—maybe the style of the car with the guys in it. * * * We go from there." Jeffrey Goldberg, *What Cops Talk About When They Talk About Race*, New York Times Magazine, June 20, 1999, at 51.

Race may explain why Peter Lawson Jones, an African–American lawyer was pulled over in his new Mercury Sable in a white neighborhood by a police officer for allegedly running a stop sign. When the officer learned that Jones was not only an attorney but a state legislator, no ticket was issued. Hope Viner Samborn, *Profiled and Pulled Over*, American Bar Association Journal, October, 1999, at 18.

Or consider Robert Wilkins, an African–American Harvard Law School graduate who was pulled over for speeding as he was returning home from a family funeral. Instead of issuing a speeding citation at that time, the officer sought consent to search the car. When Wilkins refused, he was held for thirty minutes until a drug-sniffing dog could be brought to the scene. Only when nothing was discovered did the officer get around to issuing a speeding citation. David Cole, No Equal Justice 34–35 (1999).

Statistical evidence seemingly reenforces these anecdotes. A Department of Justice report during the Bush Administration stated that, in the year 2005, "white, black, and Hispanic drivers were stopped by police at similar rates," but that "blacks and Hispanics were more likely than whites to be searched by police." Bureau of Justice Statistics, Special Report: Contacts Between Police and the Public, 2005 (April 2007, NCJ 215243). This report does not seem to explain the reason—racial or otherwise—for this discrepancy. Can you suggest a justifiable basis for the results? For more specific data demonstrating racial and ethnic disparities, see p. 402, Note 5.

3.   The Supreme Court rarely rules unanimously on any controversial legal issue. Why do you think the justices were united on this subject?

4.   *Subjective versus objective standards.* If you dislike the outcome in *Whren*, can you suggest a workable standard for adjudicating allegations of pretextual searches and seizures? The petitioners in *Whren* suggested an objective standard, *i.e.*, would a reasonable police officer have stopped and issued a ticket for the traffic violation in question. Why did the Court reject this standard? Is this a suitable standard?

Some critics eschew an exclusively objective standard. They favor a test that permits courts to consider whether the particular officer subjectively acted as the result of illegitimate motives. According to Professor Morgan Cloud, a "test that denies [judges] the power to examine important elements of the encounter—like the subjective motives of the actors—is misguided." Morgan Cloud, *Judges, "Testilying," and the Constitution*, 69 S. Cal. L. Rev. 1341, 1386 (1996). Do you see anything wrong with such a subjective standard?

Would it be appropriate for a court to hold that an officer's deviation from usual police practices in the jurisdiction constitutes prima facie evidence of an improper motive which, in the absence of a proven justification, renders a traffic stop constitutionally unreasonable?

3.   CARS AND CONTAINERS

CHAMBERS v. MARONEY

Supreme Court of the United States, 1970.
399 U.S. 42, 90 S.Ct. 1975, 26 L.Ed.2d 419.

MR. JUSTICE WHITE delivered the opinion of the Court. * * *

I

During the night of May 20, 1963, a Gulf service station in North Braddock, Pennsylvania, was robbed by two men, each of whom carried and displayed a gun. The robbers took the currency from the cash register; the service station attendant, one Stephen Kovacich, was directed to place the coins in his right-hand glove, which was then taken by the robbers. Two teenagers, who had earlier noticed a blue compact station wagon circling the block in the vicinity of the Gulf station, then saw the station wagon speed away from a parking lot close to the Gulf station. About the same time, they learned that the Gulf station had been robbed. They reported to police, who arrived immediately, that four men were in the station wagon and one was wearing a green sweater. Kovacich told the police that one of the men who robbed him was wearing a green sweater and the other was wearing a trench coat. A description of the car and the two robbers was broadcast over the police radio. Within an hour, a light blue compact station wagon answering the description and carrying four men was stopped by the police about two miles from the Gulf station. Petitioner was one of the men in the station wagon. He was wearing a green sweater and there was a trench coat in the car. The occupants were arrested and the car was driven to the police station. In the course of a thorough search of the car at the station, the police found concealed in a compartment under the dashboard two .38–caliber revolvers * * *, a right-hand glove containing small change, and certain cards bearing the name of Raymond Havicon, the attendant at a Boron service station in McKeesport, Pennsylvania, who had been robbed at gunpoint on May 13, 1963. * * *

Petitioner was indicted for both robberies. * * * The materials taken from the station wagon were introduced into evidence * * *. [Petitioner was convicted of both offenses.] * * *

II * * *

* * * [T]he search that produced the incriminating evidence was made at the police station some time after the arrest and cannot be justified as a search incident to an arrest: "Once an accused is under arrest and in custody, then a search made at another place, without a warrant, is simply not incident to the arrest." *Preston v. United States*, 376 U.S. 364, 367, 84 S.Ct. 881, 883, 11 L.Ed.2d 777 (1964). * * *

There are, however, alternative grounds arguably justifying the search of the car in this case. * * * Here * * * the police had probable cause to believe that the robbers, carrying guns and the fruits of the crime, had fled the scene in a light blue compact station wagon which would be carrying four men, one wearing a green sweater and another wearing a trench coat. As the state courts correctly held, there was probable cause to arrest the occupants of the station wagon that the officers stopped; just as obviously was there probable cause to search the car for guns and stolen money.

In terms of the circumstances justifying a warrantless search, the Court has long distinguished between an automobile and a home or office. In *Carroll v. United States*, 267 U.S. 132, 45 S.Ct. 280, 69 L.Ed. 543 (1925), the issue was the admissibility in evidence of contraband liquor seized in a warrantless search of a car on the highway. After surveying the law from the time of the adoption of the Fourth Amendment onward, the Court held that automobiles and other conveyances may be searched without a warrant in circumstances that would not justify the search without a warrant of a house or an office, provided that there is probable cause to believe that the car contains articles that the officers are entitled to seize. The Court expressed its holding as follows:

"* * * [T]he guaranty of freedom from unreasonable searches and seizures by the Fourth Amendment has been construed, practically since the beginning of the Government, as recognizing a necessary difference between a search of a store, dwelling house or other structure in respect of which a proper official warrant readily may be obtained, and a search of a ship, motor boat, wagon or automobile, for contraband goods, where it is not practicable to secure a warrant because the vehicle can be quickly moved out of the locality or jurisdiction in which the warrant must be sought.

"Having thus established that contraband goods concealed and illegally transported in an automobile or other vehicle may be searched for without a warrant, we come now to consider under what circumstances such search may be made. * * * [T]hose lawfully within the country, entitled to use the public highways, have a right to free passage without interruption or search unless there is known to a competent official authorized to search, probable cause for believing that their vehicles are carrying contraband or illegal merchandise. * * *

"* * * The right to search and the validity of the seizure are not dependent on the right to arrest. They are dependent on the reasonable cause the seizing officer has for belief that the contents of the automobile offend against the law." * * *

Neither *Carroll* nor other cases in this Court require or suggest that in every conceivable circumstance the search of an auto even with probable cause may be made without the extra protection for privacy that a warrant affords. But the circumstances that furnish probable cause to search a particular auto for particular articles are most often unforeseeable; moreover, the opportunity to search is fleeting since a car is readily movable. Where this is true, as in *Carroll* and the case before us now, if an effective search is to be made at any time, either the search must be made immediately without a warrant or the car itself must be seized and held without a warrant for whatever period is necessary to obtain a warrant for the search.[9]

* * * Only in exigent circumstances will the judgment of the police as to probable cause serve as a sufficient authorization for a search. *Carroll* holds a search warrant unnecessary where there is probable cause to search an automobile stopped on the highway; the car is movable, the occupants are alerted, and the car's contents may never be found again if a warrant must be obtained. Hence an immediate search is constitutionally permissible.

---

9. Following the car until a warrant can be obtained seems an impractical alternative since, among other things, the car may be taken out of the jurisdiction. Tracing the car and searching it hours or days later would of course permit instruments or fruits of crime to be removed from the car before the search.

Arguably, because of the preference for a magistrate's judgment, only the immobilization of the car should be permitted until a search warrant is obtained; arguably, only the "lesser" intrusion is permissible until the magistrate authorizes the "greater." But which is the "greater" and which the "lesser" intrusion is itself a debatable question and the answer may depend on a variety of circumstances. For constitutional purposes, we see no difference between on the one hand seizing and holding a car before presenting the probable cause issue to a magistrate and on the other hand carrying out an immediate search without a warrant. Given probable cause to search, either course is reasonable under the Fourth Amendment.

On the facts before us, the blue station wagon could have been searched on the spot when it was stopped since there was probable cause to search and it was a fleeting target for a search. The probable-cause factor still obtained at the station house and so did the mobility of the car unless the Fourth Amendment permits a warrantless seizure of the car and the denial of its use to anyone until a warrant is secured. In that event there is little to choose in terms of practical consequences between an immediate search without a warrant and the car's immobilization until a warrant is obtained. The same consequences may not follow where there is unforeseeable cause to search a house. But as *Carroll* held, for the purposes of the Fourth Amendment there is a constitutional difference between houses and cars. * * *

Mr. Justice BLACKMUN took no part in the consideration or decision of this case.

[Justice Stewart's concurring opinion is omitted.]

Mr. Justice HARLAN, concurring in part and dissenting in part. * * *

II

In sustaining the search of the automobile I believe the Court ignores the framework of our past decisions circumscribing the scope of permissible search without a warrant. * * *

Where officers have probable cause to search a vehicle on a public way, a * * * limited exception to the warrant requirement is reasonable because "the vehicle can be quickly moved out of the locality or jurisdiction in which the warrant must be sought." *Carroll v. United States.* Because the officers might be deprived of valuable evidence if required to obtain a warrant before effecting any search or seizure, I agree with the Court that they should be permitted to take the steps necessary to preserve evidence and to make a search possible. The Court holds that those steps include making a warrantless search of the entire vehicle on the highway * * * and indeed appears to go further and to condone the removal of the car to the police station for a warrantless search there at the convenience of the police. I cannot agree that this result is consistent with our insistence in other areas that departures from the warrant requirement strictly conform to the exigency presented.

The Court concedes that the police could prevent removal of the evidence by temporarily seizing the car for the time necessary to obtain a warrant. It does not dispute that such a course would fully protect the interests of effective law enforcement; rather it states that whether temporary seizure is a "lesser" intrusion than warrantless search "is itself a debatable question and the answer may depend on a variety of circumstances."[8] I believe it clear that a warrantless search involves the greater sacrifice of Fourth Amendment values.

The Fourth Amendment proscribes, to be sure, unreasonable "seizures" as well as "searches." However, in the circumstances in which this problem is likely to occur, the lesser intrusion will almost always be the simple seizure of the car for the period—perhaps a day—necessary to enable the officers to obtain a search warrant. In the first place, as this case shows, the very facts establishing probable cause to search will often also justify arrest of the occupants of the vehicle. Since the occupants themselves are to be taken into custody, they will suffer minimal further inconvenience from the temporary immobilization of their vehicle. Even where no arrests are made, persons who wish to avoid a search—either to protect their privacy or to conceal incriminating evidence—will almost certainly prefer a brief loss of the use of the vehicle in exchange for the opportunity to have a magistrate pass upon the justification for the search. To be sure, one can conceive of instances in which the occupant, having nothing to hide and lacking concern for the privacy of the automobile, would be more deeply offended by a temporary immobilization of his vehicle than by a prompt search of it. However, such a person always remains free to consent to an immediate search, thus avoiding any delay. Where consent is not forthcoming, the occupants of the car have an interest in privacy that is protected by the Fourth Amendment even where the circumstances justify a temporary seizure. The Court's endorsement of a warrantless invasion of that privacy where another course would suffice is simply inconsistent with our repeated stress on the Fourth Amendment's mandate of " 'adherence to judicial processes.' " * * *

NOTES AND QUESTIONS

1. *Carroll v. United States*, discussed in *Chambers*, involved a prosecution under the National Prohibition Act. The occupants of the car in question were not arrested (and could not lawfully have been arrested) until federal agents searched the car and discovered illegal liquor concealed inside the car. In contrast, the car occupants in *Chambers* were arrested *before* the search. If one considers the practicability of seeking a warrant, is this factual distinction relevant?

What if a court seeks to weigh the interests of a car driver against the interests of law enforcement, in order to determine whether a particular

---

8. The Court, unable to decide whether search or temporary seizure is the "lesser" intrusion, in this case authorizes both. * * * [T]he Court approves the searches without even an inquiry into the officers' ability promptly to take their case before a magistrate.

warrantless car search is reasonable. In this regard, the driver has three interests at stake: an interest in locomotion (continuing to travel); an interest in control over his property; and an interest in the secrecy of the car's contents. Note, *Warrantless Searches and Seizures of Automobiles*, 87 Harv. L. Rev. 835, 841 (1974). What are the competing legitimate interests of the police? Balancing these interests, do you think the police acted reasonably in *Carroll* in conducting the warrantless search on the highway (assuming, as the Court held, that the police had probable cause to believe the car was transporting contraband)? Do you think the police acted reasonably in *Chambers* in conducting the warrantless search at the police station?

Why does Justice White believe that the *Carroll* principle applies in the *Chambers* circumstances? Are you persuaded by his explanation, or does Justice Harlan have the better side of the argument?

2. *From Carroll to Chambers to another "C" car case.* Just a year after *Chambers*, the Supreme Court considered another case involving a warrantless automobile search. In Coolidge v. New Hampshire, 403 U.S. 443, 91 S.Ct. 2022, 29 L.Ed.2d 564 (1971), a police investigation of the murder of a fourteen-year-old girl focused on Edward Coolidge. Initially, the police questioned him and asked him to take a lie detector test, which he did. At all times, Coolidge was cooperative. Subsequently, the police determined that they had sufficient evidence to arrest Coolidge, which they did in his home.

At the time of the arrest, two Coolidge cars were parked in the driveway. More than two hours after Coolidge was taken into custody, the cars were seized without a warrant. One of the cars was searched and vacuumed for microscopic evidence two days later, again a year later, and a third time five months after the latter search. You may assume that the police had probable cause for these searches. Given that assumption, if you represented Coolidge, what would be the basis of your objection? If you were the prosecutor, how would you justify the warrantless searches of the car?

In a four-justice plurality opinion, Justice Stewart ruled that the warrantless car searches were unconstitutional, notwithstanding probable cause:

[T]he most basic constitutional rule in this area is that "searches conducted outside the judicial process, without prior approval by judge or magistrate, are *per se* unreasonable under the Fourth Amendment— subject only to a few specifically established and well-delineated exceptions." * * * "[T]he burden is on those seeking the exemption to show the need for it." * * *

* * * [E]ven granting that the police had probable cause to search the car, the application of the *Carroll* case to these facts would extend it far beyond its original rationale. * * *

* * * As we said in *Chambers*, "exigent circumstances" justify the warrantless search of "an automobile *stopped on the highway*," where there is probable cause, because the car is "movable, the occupants are alerted, and the car's contents may never be found again if a warrant must be obtained." "[T]he opportunity to search is fleeting * * *."

In this case, the police had known for some time of the probable role of the Pontiac car in the crime. Coolidge was aware that he was a suspect in the * * * murder, but he had been extremely cooperative throughout the investigation, and there was no indication that he meant to flee. He had already had ample opportunity to destroy any evidence he thought incriminating. There is no suggestion that, on the night in question, the car was being used for any illegal purpose, and it was regularly parked in the driveway of his house. The opportunity for search was thus hardly "fleeting." The objects that the police are assumed to have had probable cause to search for in the car were neither stolen nor contraband nor dangerous. * * *18

The word "automobile" is not a talisman in whose presence the Fourth Amendment fades away and disappears. And surely there is nothing in this case to invoke the meaning and purpose of the rule of *Carroll v. United States*—no alerted criminal bent on flight, no fleeting opportunity on an open highway after a hazardous chase, no contraband or stolen goods or weapons, no confederates waiting to move the evidence, not even the inconvenience of a special police detail to guard the immobilized automobile. In short, by no possible stretch of the legal imagination can this be made into a case where "it is not practicable to secure a warrant," and the "automobile exception," despite its label, is simply irrelevant.

Since *Carroll* would not have justified a warrantless search of the Pontiac at the time Coolidge was arrested, the later search at the station house was plainly illegal, at least so far as the automobile exception is concerned. *Chambers* is of no help to the State, since that case held only that, where the police may stop and search an automobile under *Carroll*, they may also seize it and search it later at the police station.

Justice White and Chief Justice Burger concurred with the plurality that two of the three searches of the Coolidge car were improper:

Chambers upheld the seizure and subsequent search of automobiles at the station house rather than requiring the police to search cars immediately at the places where they are found. But *Chambers* did not authorize indefinite detention of automobiles so seized; it contemplated some expedition in completing the searches so that automobiles could be released and returned to their owners. In the present case, however, Coolidge's Pontiac was not released quickly but was retained in police

---

18. It is frequently said that occupied automobiles stopped on the open highway may be searched without a warrant because they are "mobile," or "movable." * * * In this case it is, of course, true that even though Coolidge was in jail, his wife was miles away in the company of two plainclothesmen, and the Coolidge property was under the guard of two other officers, the automobile was in a literal sense "mobile." A person who had the keys and could slip by the guard could drive it away. We attach no constitutional significance to this sort of mobility.

First, a good number of the containers that the police might discover on a person's property and want to search are equally movable, *e.g.*, trunks, suitcases, boxes, briefcases, and bags. How are such objects to be distinguished from an unoccupied automobile * * * sitting on the owner's property? It is true that the automobile has wheels and its own locomotive power. But given the virtually universal availability of automobiles in our society there is little difference between driving the container itself away and driving it away in a vehicle brought to the scene for that purpose. * * * [I]f *Carroll v. United States* permits a warrantless search of an unoccupied vehicle, on private property and beyond the scope of a valid search incident to an arrest, then it would permit as well a warrantless search of a suitcase or a box. We have found no case that suggests such an extension of *Carroll*.

custody for more than a year and was searched not only immediately after seizure but also on two other occasions: one of them 11 months and the other 14 months after seizure. Since fruits of the later searches as well as the earlier one were apparently introduced in evidence, I cannot look to *Chambers* and would invalidate the later searches * * *. It is only because of the long detention of the car that I find *Chambers* inapplicable, however, and I disagree strongly with the majority's reasoning for refusing to apply it. * * *

For Fourth Amendment purposes, the difference between a moving and movable vehicle is tenuous at best. It is a metaphysical distinction without roots in the commonsense standard of reasonableness governing search and seizure cases. Distinguishing the case before us from the *Carroll-Chambers* line of cases further enmeshes Fourth Amendment law in litigation breeding refinements having little relation to reality. I suggest that in the interest of coherence and credibility we either overrule our prior cases and treat automobiles precisely as we do houses or apply those cases to readily movable as well as moving vehicles and thus treat searches of automobiles as we do the arrest of a person.

Is *Coolidge* consistent with *Chambers*? Whose reasoning—Stewart's or White's—do you find more persuasive?

3. *In search of a new rationale. Carroll, Chambers,* and *Coolidge* all focused on the mobility of motor vehicles (although notice in *Coolidge* how differently Justices White and Stewart viewed the concept of mobility) as the basis for warrantless searches. After *Coolidge*, the Supreme Court developed an additional, non-mobility-based rationale for warrantless car searches, as the next case demonstrates.

CALIFORNIA v. CARNEY

Supreme Court of the United States, 1985.
471 U.S. 386, 105 S.Ct. 2066, 85 L.Ed.2d 406.

CHIEF JUSTICE BURGER delivered the opinion of the Court.

We granted certiorari to decide whether law enforcement agents violated the Fourth Amendment when they conducted a warrantless search, based on probable cause, of a fully mobile "motor home" located in a public place.

I

On May 31, 1979, Drug Enforcement Agency Agent Robert Williams watched respondent, Charles Carney, approach a youth in downtown San Diego. The youth accompanied Carney to a Dodge Mini Motor Home parked in a nearby lot. Carney and the youth closed the window shades in the motor home, including one across the front window. Agent Williams had previously received uncorroborated information that the same motor home was used by another person who was exchanging marihuana for sex. Williams, with assistance from other agents, kept the motor home under surveillance for the entire one and one-quarter hours that Carney and the youth remained inside. When the youth left the motor home, the agents followed and stopped him. The youth told the agents that he had received marihuana in return for allowing Carney sexual contacts.

At the agents' request, the youth returned to the motor home and knocked on its door; Carney stepped out. The agents identified themselves as law enforcement officers. Without a warrant or consent, one agent entered the motor home and observed marihuana, plastic bags, and a scale of the kind used in weighing drugs on a table. Agent Williams took Carney into custody and took possession of the motor home. A subsequent search of the motor home at the police station revealed additional marihuana in the cupboards and refrigerator.

Respondent was charged with possession of marihuana for sale. At a preliminary hearing, he moved to suppress the evidence discovered in the motor home. The Magistrate denied the motion * * *.

Respondent renewed his suppression motion in the Superior Court. The Superior Court also rejected the claim * * *. Respondent then pleaded *nolo contendere* to the charges against him, and was placed on probation for three years. * * *

II

* * * There are, of course, exceptions to the general rule that a warrant must be secured before a search is undertaken; one is the so-called "automobile exception" at issue in this case. This exception to the warrant requirement was first set forth by the Court 60 years ago in *Carroll v. United States*, 267 U.S. 132, 45 S.Ct. 280, 69 L.Ed. 543 (1925). There, the Court recognized that the privacy interests in an automobile are constitutionally protected; however, it held that the ready mobility of the automobile justifies a lesser degree of protection of those interests. The Court rested this exception on a long-recognized distinction between stationary structures and vehicles * * *.

The capacity to be "quickly moved" was clearly the basis of the holding in *Carroll*, and our cases have consistently recognized ready mobility as one of the principal bases of the automobile exception. * * *

However, although ready mobility alone was perhaps the original justification for the vehicle exception, our later cases have made clear that ready mobility is not the only basis for the exception. The reasons for the vehicle exception, we have said, are twofold. "Besides the element of mobility, less rigorous warrant requirements govern because the expectation of privacy with respect to one's automobile is significantly less than that relating to one's home or office." [*South Dakota v. Opperman*, 428 U.S. 364, 96 S.Ct. 3092, 49 L.Ed.2d 1000 (1976).] * * *

These reduced expectations of privacy derive not from the fact that the area to be searched is in plain view, but from the pervasive regulation of vehicles capable of traveling on the public highways. As we explained in *South Dakota v. Opperman*, an inventory search case:

"Automobiles, unlike homes, are subjected to pervasive and continuing governmental regulation and controls, including periodic inspection and licensing requirements. As an everyday occurrence, police stop and examine vehicles when license plates or inspection stickers have expired, or if other violations, such as exhaust fumes or excessive noise, are noted, or if headlights or other safety equipment are not in proper working order."

The public is fully aware that it is accorded less privacy in its automobiles because of this compelling governmental need for regulation. * * * In short, the pervasive schemes of regulation, which necessarily lead to reduced expectations of privacy, and the exigencies attendant to ready mobility justify searches without prior recourse to the authority of a magistrate so long as the overriding standard of probable cause is met.

When a vehicle is being used on the highways, or if it is readily capable of such use and is found stationary in a place not regularly used for residential purposes—temporary or otherwise—the two justifications for the vehicle exception come into play. First, the vehicle is obviously readily mobile by the turn of an ignition key, if not actually moving. Second, there is a reduced expectation of privacy stemming from its use as a licensed motor vehicle subject to a range of police regulation inapplicable to a fixed dwelling. At least in these circumstances, the overriding societal interests in effective law enforcement justify an immediate search before the vehicle and its occupants become unavailable.

While it is true that respondent's vehicle possessed some, if not many of the attributes of a home, it is equally clear that the vehicle falls clearly within the scope of the exception laid down in *Carroll* and applied in succeeding cases. Like the automobile in *Carroll*, respondent's motor home was readily mobile. Absent the prompt search and seizure, it could readily have been moved beyond the reach of the police. Furthermore, the vehicle was licensed to "operate on public streets; [was] serviced in public places; * * * and [was] subject to extensive regulation and inspection." And the vehicle was so situated that an objective observer would conclude that it was being used not as a residence, but as a vehicle.

Respondent urges us to distinguish his vehicle from other vehicles within the exception because it was *capable of functioning as a home*. In our increasingly mobile society, many vehicles used for transportation can be and are being used not only for transportation but for shelter, *i.e.,* as a "home" or "residence." To distinguish between respondent's motor home and an ordinary sedan for purposes of the vehicle exception would require that we apply the exception depending upon the size of the vehicle and the quality of its appointments. Moreover, to fail to apply the exception to vehicles such as a motor home ignores the fact that a motor home lends itself easily to use as an instrument of illicit drug traffic and other illegal activity. * * * We decline today to distinguish between "worthy" and "unworthy" vehicles which are either on the public roads and highways, or situated such that it is reasonable to conclude that the vehicle is not being used as a residence.

Our application of the vehicle exception has never turned on the other uses to which a vehicle might be put. The exception has historically turned on the ready mobility of the vehicle, and on the presence of the vehicle in a setting that objectively indicates that the vehicle is being used for transportation.[3] * * *

The judgment of the California Supreme Court is reversed * * *.

Justice STEVENS, with whom Justice BRENNAN and Justice MARSHALL join, dissenting.

The character of "the place to be searched" plays an important role in Fourth Amendment analysis. In this case, police officers searched a Dodge/Midas Mini Motor Home. The California Supreme Court correctly characterized this vehicle as a "hybrid" which combines "the mobility attribute of an automobile * * * with most of the privacy characteristics of a house."

The hybrid character of the motor home places it at the crossroads between the privacy interests that generally forbid warrantless invasions of the home, *Payton v. New York* [p. 171], and the law enforcement interests that support the exception for warrantless searches of automobiles based on probable cause. By choosing to follow the latter route, the Court * * * has accorded priority to an exception rather than to the general rule, and * * * has abandoned the limits on the exception imposed by prior cases. * * *

II * * *

In *United States v. Ross*, [456 U.S. 798, 102 S.Ct. 2157, 72 L.Ed.2d 572 (1982),] the Court reaffirmed the primary importance of the general rule condemning warrantless searches, and emphasized that the exception permitting the search of automobiles without a warrant is a narrow one. * * * Given this warning and the presumption of regularity that attaches to a warrant, it is hardly unrealistic to expect experienced law enforcement officers to obtain a search warrant when one can easily be secured.

* * * If the motor home were parked in the exact middle of the intersection between the general rule and the exception for automobiles, priority should be given to the rule rather than the exception.

III

The motor home, however, was not parked in the middle of that intersection. Our prior cases teach us that inherent mobility is not a

---

3. We need not pass on the application of the vehicle exception to a motor home that is situated in a way or place that objectively indicates that it is being used as a residence. Among the factors that might be relevant in determining whether a warrant would be required in such a circumstance is its location, whether the vehicle is readily mobile or instead, for instance, elevated on blocks, whether the vehicle is licensed, whether it is connected to utilities, and whether it has convenient access to a public road.

sufficient justification for the fashioning of an exception to the warrant requirement, especially in the face of heightened expectations of privacy in the location searched. Motor homes, by their common use and construction, afford their owners a substantial and legitimate expectation of privacy when they dwell within. When a motor home is parked in a location that is removed from the public highway, I believe that society is prepared to recognize that the expectations of privacy within it are not unlike the expectations one has in a fixed dwelling. As a general rule, such places may only be searched with a warrant based upon probable cause. Warrantless searches of motor homes are only reasonable when the motor home is traveling on the public streets or highways, or when exigent circumstances otherwise require an immediate search without the expenditure of time necessary to obtain a warrant. * * *

In this case, the motor home was parked in an off-the-street lot only a few blocks from the courthouse in downtown San Diego where dozens of magistrates were available to entertain a warrant application. The officers clearly had the element of surprise with them, and with curtains covering the windshield, the motor home offered no indication of any imminent departure. The officers plainly had probable cause to arrest the respondent and search the motor home, and on this record, it is inexplicable why they eschewed the safe harbor of a warrant.[17] * * *

Unlike a brick bungalow or a frame Victorian, a motor home seldom serves as a permanent lifetime abode. The motor home in this case, however, was designed to accommodate a breadth of ordinary everyday living. Photographs in the record indicate that its height, length, and beam provided substantial living space inside: stuffed chairs surround a table; cupboards provide room for storage of personal effects; bunk beds provide sleeping space; and a refrigerator provides ample space for food and beverages. Moreover, curtains and large opaque walls inhibit viewing the activities inside from the exterior of the vehicle. The interior configuration of the motor home establishes that the vehicle's size, shape, and mode of construction should have indicated to the officers that it was a vehicle containing mobile living quarters. * * *

In my opinion, searches of places that regularly accommodate a wide range of private human activity are fundamentally different from searches of automobiles which primarily serve a public transportation function. Although it may not be a castle, a motor home is usually the functional equivalent of a hotel room, a vacation and retirement home, or a hunting and fishing cabin. These places may be as spartan as a humble cottage when compared to the most majestic mansion, but the highest and most legitimate expectations of privacy associated with these temporary abodes should command the respect of this Court. In my opinion, a warrantless search of living quarters in a motor home is "presumptively unreasonable absent exigent circumstances."

---

17. This willingness to search first and later seek justification has properly been characterized as "a decision roughly comparable in prudence to determining whether an electrical wire is charged by grasping it." *United States v. Mitchell*, 538 F.2d 1230, 1233 (C.A.5 1976) (en banc).

NOTES AND QUESTIONS

1. What, if anything, is left of *Coolidge* (p. 271, Note 2) after *Carney*?

2. *The reduced-expectation-of-privacy rationale.* Is the Court correct that we have a reduced expectation of privacy in our automobiles because of pervasive governmental regulation of them? If so, does this mean that a municipality could conduct random inspections of homes for building, health, and safety code violations, and then claim that we have a reduced expectation of privacy in our "castles" because *they* are pervasively regulated?

Are there other grounds for claiming that we have a lesser expectation of privacy in our cars than we do in our homes? Yes, according to Cardwell v. Lewis, 417 U.S. 583, 94 S.Ct. 2464, 41 L.Ed.2d 325 (1974):

> One has a lesser expectation of privacy in a motor vehicle because its function is transportation and it seldom serves as one's residence or as the repository of personal effects. A car has little capacity for escaping public scrutiny. It travels public thoroughfares where both its occupants and its contents are in plain view.

Do these arguments withstand scrutiny? Why, or why not?

3. *Automobile inventories: another warrant "exception."* A warrantless search of a car may be permissible on various grounds. First, if the police have probable cause to search a car, the *Carroll-Chambers-Carney* "automobile exception" comes into play. Second, if an occupant (or recent occupant) of an automobile is arrested, the police may sometimes conduct, as an incident of the arrest, a contemporaneous search of the passenger compartment of the vehicle, even without probable cause to search. (pp. 235–258).

Still another basis for a car search is the "automobile inventory" warrant exception. In South Dakota v. Opperman, 428 U.S. 364, 96 S.Ct. 3092, 49 L.Ed.2d 1000 (1976), *O*'s automobile was towed to a city impound lot, as permitted by local ordinance, after it was ticketed twice for being parked in a restricted zone. Pursuant to standard operating procedures, officers unlocked the vehicle and, using a standard inventory form, inventoried the contents of the car. In the glove compartment, the police discovered marijuana. *O* was prosecuted for possession of the marijuana discovered during the warrantless, suspicionless search.

The Court determined that the probable cause and warrant requirements of the Fourth Amendment do not apply to routine inventory searches:

> The standard of probable cause is peculiarly related to criminal investigations, not routine, non-criminal procedures. The probable-cause approach is unhelpful when analysis centers upon the reasonableness of routine administrative caretaking functions, particularly when no claim is made that the protective procedures are a subterfuge for criminal investigations.
>
> In view of the noncriminal context of inventory searches, and the inapplicability in such a setting of the requirement of probable cause, courts have held—and quite correctly—that search warrants are not required, linked as the warrant requirement textually is to the probable-

cause concept. We have frequently observed that the warrant requirement assures that legal inferences and conclusions as to probable cause will be drawn by a neutral magistrate unrelated to the criminal investigative-enforcement process. With respect to noninvestigative police inventories of automobiles lawfully within governmental custody, however, the policies underlying the warrant requirement * * * are inapplicable.

With the warrant clause eliminated from analysis, the Court focused exclusively on the reasonableness requirement of the Fourth Amendment. In this regard, the Court balanced the competing interests. From the car owner's perspective there is his lesser expectation of privacy in the contents of the automobile. The Court then considered the government's side of the equation:

> When vehicles are impounded, local police departments generally follow a routine practice of securing and inventorying the automobiles' contents. These procedures developed in response to three distinct needs: the protection of the owner's property while it remains in police custody; the protection of the police against claims or disputes over lost or stolen property; and the protection of the police from potential danger. The practice has been viewed as essential to respond to incidents of theft or vandalism. In addition, police frequently attempt to determine whether a vehicle has been stolen and thereafter abandoned.

Balancing the competing interests, the Court unsurprisingly concluded that routine inventory searches are reasonable. Essential to this reasoning, however, is the requirement that the police follow standard procedures, *i.e.*, that they do not exceed the scope of their own rules. The police should not have unfettered discretion in conducting an inventory, in part to ensure that the inventory is "routine," rather than "a pretext concealing an investigatory police motive." *Id.*

For example, in Florida v. Wells, 495 U.S. 1, 110 S.Ct. 1632, 109 L.Ed.2d 1 (1990), the Court unanimously held that highway patrol officers were not permitted to open a locked suitcase they discovered during an inventory search because "the Florida Highway Patrol had no policy whatever with respect to the opening of closed containers encountered during an inventory search." A five-justice majority stated in dictum, however, that

> in forbidding uncanalized discretion to police officers conducting inventory searches, there is no reason to insist that they be conducted in a totally mechanical "all or nothing" fashion. * * * A police officer may be allowed sufficient latitude to determine whether a particular container should or should not be opened in light of the nature of the search and characteristics of the container itself. Thus, while policies of opening all containers or of opening no containers are unquestionably permissible, it would be equally permissible, for example, to allow the opening of closed containers whose contents officers determine they are unable to ascertain from examining the containers' exteriors. The allowance of the exercise of judgment based on concerns related to the purposes of an inventory search does not violate the Fourth Amendment.

4. *Containers in cars.* In *Chambers*, the police discovered criminal evidence concealed in a compartment of the vehicle they searched. In *Coolidge*, the police found particles of gun powder, apparently on the car upholstery or

floor. In *Carney*, drugs and related paraphernalia were in plain view on a table inside the motor home. That is, in each of these cases, the criminal evidence inside the car was in the open.

Suppose in an otherwise valid car search the police discover a closed container, such as a briefcase, an envelope, or paper bag. May the police open the container as part of the car search, or must they seize it, take it to the police station, and there hold it while they apply for a search warrant? We turn now to the container-in-car cases, which begin appropriately enough, with another "C" case.

UNITED STATES v. CHADWICK

Supreme Court of the United States, 1977.
433 U.S. 1, 97 S.Ct. 2476, 53 L.Ed.2d 538.

MR. CHIEF JUSTICE BURGER delivered the opinion of the Court. * * *

(1)

On May 8, 1973, Amtrak railroad officials in San Diego observed respondents Gregory Machado and Bridget Leary load a brown footlocker onto a train bound for Boston. Their suspicions were aroused when they noticed that the trunk was unusually heavy for its size, and that it was leaking talcum powder, a substance often used to mask the odor of marihuana or hashish. Because Machado matched a profile used to spot drug traffickers, the railroad officials reported these circumstances to federal agents in San Diego, who in turn relayed the information, together with detailed descriptions of Machado and the footlocker, to their counter-parts in Boston.

When the train arrived in Boston two days later, federal narcotics agents were on hand. Though the officers had not obtained an arrest or search warrant, they had with them a police dog trained to detect marihuana. The agents identified Machado and Leary and kept them under surveillance as they claimed their suitcases and the footlocker, which had been transported by baggage cart from the train to the departure area. Machado and Leary lifted the footlocker from the baggage cart, placed it on the floor and sat down on it.

The agents then released the dog near the footlocker. Without alert-ing respondents, the dog signaled the presence of a controlled substance inside. Respondent Chadwick then joined Machado and Leary, and they engaged an attendant to move the footlocker outside to Chadwick's waiting automobile. Machado, Chadwick, and the attendant together lifted the 200–pound footlocker into the trunk of the car, while Leary waited in the front seat. At that point, while the trunk of the car was still open and before the car engine had been started, the officers arrested all three. A search disclosed no weapons, but the keys to the footlocker were apparent-ly taken from Machado.

Respondents were taken to the Federal Building in Boston; the agents followed with Chadwick's car and the footlocker. As the Government concedes, from the moment of respondents' arrests at about 9 p.m., the footlocker remained under the exclusive control of law enforcement officers at all times. The footlocker and luggage were placed in the Federal Building, where, as one of the agents later testified, "there was no risk that whatever was contained in the footlocker trunk would be removed by the defendants or their associates." The agents had no reason to believe that the footlocker contained explosives or other inherently dangerous items, or that it contained evidence which would lose its value unless the footlocker were opened at once. Facilities were readily available in which the footlocker could have been stored securely; it is not contended that there was any exigency calling for an immediate search.

At the Federal Building an hour and a half after the arrests, the agents opened the footlocker and luggage. They did not obtain respondents' consent; they did not secure a search warrant. The footlocker was locked with a padlock and a regular trunk lock. * * * Large amounts of marihuana were found in the footlocker.

Respondents were indicted for possession of marihuana with intent to distribute it * * *, and for conspiracy * * *. Before trial, they moved to suppress the marihuana obtained from the footlocker. In the District Court, the Government sought to justify its failure to secure a search warrant under the "automobile exception" of *Chambers v. Maroney*, [p. 266], and as a search incident to the arrests. * * * [T]he District Court rejected both justifications. The court saw the relationship between the footlocker and Chadwick's automobile as merely coincidental, and held that the double-locked, 200–pound footlocker was not part of "the area from within which [respondents] might gain possession of a weapon or destructible evidence." * * *

(2)

In this Court the Government * * * contends that the Fourth Amendment Warrant Clause protects only interests traditionally identified with the home. Recalling the colonial writs of assistance, which were often executed in searches of private dwellings, the Government claims that the Warrant Clause was adopted primarily, if not exclusively, in response to unjustified intrusions into private homes on the authority of general warrants. The Government argues there is no evidence that the Framers of the Fourth Amendment intended to disturb the established practice of permitting warrantless searches outside the home, or to modify the initial clause of the Fourth Amendment by making warrantless searches supported by probable cause *per se* unreasonable.

Drawing on its reading of history, the Government argues that only homes, offices, and private communications implicate interests which lie at the core of the Fourth Amendment. Accordingly, it is only in these contexts that the determination whether a search or seizure is reasonable should turn on whether a warrant has been obtained. In all other situations, the Government contends, less significant privacy values are at stake, and the reasonableness of a government intrusion should depend solely on whether there is probable cause to believe evidence of criminal conduct is present. Where personal effects are lawfully seized outside the home on probable cause, the Government would thus regard searches without a warrant as not "unreasonable."

We do not agree that the Warrant Clause protects only dwellings and other specifically designated locales. As we have noted before, the Fourth Amendment "protects people, not places," *Katz v. United States* [p. 84]; more particularly, it protects people from unreasonable government intrusions into their legitimate expectations of privacy. In this case, the Warrant Clause makes a significant contribution to that protection. The question, then, is whether a warrantless search in these circumstances was unreasonable.

(3) * * *

Although the searches and seizures which deeply concerned the colonists, and which were foremost in the minds of the Framers, were those involving invasions of the home, it would be a mistake to conclude, as the Government contends, that the Warrant Clause was therefore intended to guard only against intrusions into the home. First, the Warrant Clause does not in terms distinguish between searches conducted in private homes and other searches. There is also a strong historical connection between the Warrant Clause and the initial clause of the Fourth Amendment, which draws no distinctions among "persons, houses, papers, and effects" in safeguarding against unreasonable searches and seizures.

Moreover, if there is little evidence that the Framers intended the Warrant Clause to operate outside the home, there is no evidence at all that they intended to exclude from protection of the Clause all searches occurring outside the home. The absence of a contemporary outcry against warrantless searches in public places was because, aside from searches incident to arrest, such warrantless searches were not a large issue in colonial America. Thus, silence in the historical record tells us little about the Framers' attitude toward application of the Warrant Clause to the search of respondents' footlocker. What we do know is that the Framers were men who focused on the wrongs of that day but who intended the Fourth Amendment to safeguard fundamental values which would far outlast the specific abuses which gave it birth.

Moreover, in this area we do not write on a clean slate. * * *

* * * [Our] cases illustrate the applicability of the Warrant Clause beyond the narrow limits suggested by the Government. They also reflect the settled constitutional principle, discussed earlier, that a fundamental purpose of the Fourth Amendment is to safeguard individuals from unreasonable government invasions of legitimate privacy interests, and not simply those interests found inside the four walls of the home.

In this case, important Fourth Amendment privacy interests were at stake. By placing personal effects inside a double-locked footlocker, respondents manifested an expectation that the contents would remain free from public examination. No less than one who locks the doors of his home against intruders, one who safeguards his personal possessions in this manner is due the protection of the Fourth Amendment Warrant Clause. There being no exigency, it was unreasonable for the Government to conduct this search without the safe-guards a judicial warrant provides.

(4)

The Government does not contend that the footlocker's brief contact with Chadwick's car makes this an automobile search, but it is argued that the rationale of our automobile search cases demonstrates the reasonableness of permitting warrantless searches of luggage; the Government views such luggage as analogous to motor vehicles for Fourth Amendment purposes. * * * But this Court has recognized significant differences between motor vehicles and other property which permit warrantless searches of automobiles in circumstances in which warrantless searches would not be reasonable in other contexts.

Our treatment of automobiles has been based in part on their inherent mobility, which often makes obtaining a judicial warrant impracticable. Nevertheless, we have also sustained "warrantless searches of vehicles * * * in cases in which the possibilities of the vehicle's being removed or evidence in it destroyed were remote, if not nonexistent."

The answer lies in the diminished expectation of privacy which surrounds the automobile * * *.

The factors which diminish the privacy aspects of an automobile do not apply to respondents' footlocker. Luggage contents are not open to public view, except as a condition to a border entry or common carrier travel; nor is luggage subject to regular inspections and official scrutiny on a continuing basis. Unlike an automobile, whose primary function is transportation, luggage is intended as a repository of personal effects. In sum, a person's expectations of privacy in personal luggage are substantially greater than in an automobile.

Nor does the footlocker's mobility justify dispensing with the added protections of the Warrant Clause. Once the federal agents had seized it at the railroad station and had safely transferred it to the Boston Federal Building under their exclusive control, there was not the slightest danger that the footlocker or its contents could have been removed before a valid search warrant could be obtained.[7] The initial seizure and detention of the footlocker, the validity of which respondents do not contest, were sufficient to guard against any risk that evidence might be lost. With the footlocker safely immobilized, it was unreasonable to undertake the additional and greater intrusion of a search without a warrant.[8]

---

7. This may often not be the case when automobiles are seized. Absolutely secure storage facilities may not be available, and the size and inherent mobility of a vehicle make it susceptible to theft or intrusion by vandals.

8. Respondents' principal privacy interest in the footlocker was, of course, not in the container itself, which was exposed to public view, but in its contents. A search of the interior was therefore

Finally, the Government urges that the Constitution permits the warrantless search of any property in the possession of a person arrested in public, so long as there is probable cause to believe that the property contains contraband or evidence of crime. Although recognizing that the footlocker was not within respondents' immediate control, the Government insists that the search was reasonable because the footlocker was seized contemporaneously with respondents' arrests and was searched as soon thereafter as was practicable. The reasons justifying search in a custodial arrest are quite different. * * *

Such searches may be conducted without a warrant, and they may also be made whether or not there is probable cause to believe that the person arrested may have a weapon or is about to destroy evidence. The potential dangers lurking in all custodial arrests make warrantless searches of items within the "immediate control" area reasonable without requiring the arresting officer to calculate the probability that weapons or destructible evidence may be involved. However, warrantless searches of luggage or other property seized at the time of an arrest cannot be justified as incident to that arrest either if the "search is remote in time or place from the arrest," or no exigency exists. Once law enforcement officers have reduced luggage or other personal property not immediately associated with the person of the arrestee to their exclusive control, and there is no longer any danger that the arrestee might gain access to the property to seize a weapon or destroy evidence, a search of that property is no longer an incident of the arrest.

Here the search was conducted more than an hour after federal agents had gained exclusive control of the footlocker and long after respondents were securely in custody; the search therefore cannot be viewed as incidental to the arrest or as justified by any other exigency. Even though on this record the issuance of a warrant by a judicial officer was reasonably predictable, a line must be drawn. In our view, when no exigency is shown to support the need for an immediate search, the Warrant Clause places the line at the point where the property to be searched comes under the exclusive dominion of police authority. Respondents were therefore entitled to the protection of the Warrant Clause with the evaluation of a neutral magistrate, before their privacy interests in the contents of the footlocker were invaded. * * *

Mr. Justice BRENNAN, concurring.

I fully join the Chief Justice's thorough opinion for the Court. I write only to comment upon two points made by my Brother Blackmun's dissent.

---

a far greater intrusion into Fourth Amendment values than the impoundment of the footlocker. Though surely a substantial infringement of respondents' use and possession, the seizure did not diminish respondents' legitimate expectation that the footlocker's contents would remain private.

It was the greatly reduced expectation of privacy in the automobile, coupled with the transportation function of the vehicle, which made the Court in *Chambers* unwilling to decide whether an immediate search of an automobile, or its seizure and indefinite immobilization, constituted a greater interference with the rights of the owner. This is clearly not the case with locked luggage.

First, I agree wholeheartedly with my Brother Blackmun that it is "unfortunate" that the Government in this case "sought * * * to vindicate an extreme view of the Fourth Amendment." It is unfortunate, in my view, * * * because it is deeply distressing that the Department of Justice, whose mission is to protect the constitutional liberties of the people of the United States, should even appear to be seeking to subvert them by extreme and dubious legal arguments. It is gratifying that the Court today unanimously rejects the Government's position.

Second, it should be noted that while Part II of the dissent suggests a number of possible alternative courses of action that the agents could have followed without violating the Constitution, no decision of this Court is cited to support the constitutionality of these courses * * *. In my view, it is not at all obvious that the agents could legally have searched the footlocker had they seized it after Machado and Leary had driven away with it in their car[1] or "at the time and place of the arrests."[2]

Mr. Justice BLACKMUN, with whom Mr. Justice REHNQUIST joins, dissenting.

I think it somewhat unfortunate that the Government sought a reversal in this case primarily to vindicate an extreme view of the Fourth Amendment that would restrict the protection of the Warrant Clause to private dwellings and a few other "high privacy" areas. I reject this argument for the reasons stated in Parts (2) and (3) of the Court's opinion, with which I am in general agreement. * * *

I

One line of recent decisions establishes that no warrant is required for the arresting officer to search the clothing and effects of one placed in custodial arrest. The rationale for this was explained in *United States v. Robinson*, [p. 226] * * *.

A second series of decisions concerns the consequences of custodial arrest of a person driving an automobile. The car may be impounded and, with probable cause, its contents (including locked compartments) subsequently examined without a warrant. *Chambers v. Maroney*, [p. 266]. * * *

I would apply the rationale of these two lines of authority and hold generally that a warrant is not required to seize and search any movable property in the possession of a person properly arrested in a public place.

---

1. While the contents of the car could have been searched pursuant to the automobile exception, it is by no means clear that the contents of locked containers found inside a car are subject to search under this exception, any more than they would be if the police found them in any other place.

2. When Machado and Leary were "standing next to [the] open automobile trunk containing the footlocker," and even when they "were seated on it," it is not obvious to me that the contents of the heavy, securely locked footlocker were within the area of their "immediate control" for purposes of the search-incident-to-arrest doctrine, the justification for which is the possibility that the arrested person might have immediate access to weapons that might endanger the officer's safety or assist in his escape, or to items of evidence that he might conceal or destroy. I would think that the footlocker in this case hardly was " 'within [respondents'] immediate control'— construing that phrase to mean the area from within which [they] might gain possession of a weapon or destructible evidence."

A person arrested in a public place is likely to have various kinds of property with him: items inside his clothing, a briefcase or suitcase, packages, or a vehicle. In such instances the police cannot very well leave the property on the sidewalk or street while they go to get a warrant. The items may be stolen by a passer-by or removed by the suspect's confederates. Rather than requiring the police to "post a guard" over such property, I think it is surely reasonable for the police to take the items along to the station with the arrested person. * * *

As the Court in *Robinson* recognized, custodial arrest is such a serious deprivation that various lesser invasions of privacy may be fairly regarded as incidental. An arrested person, of course, has an additional privacy interest in the objects in his possession at the time of arrest. To be sure, allowing impoundment of those objects pursuant to arrest, but requiring a warrant for examination of their contents, would protect that incremental privacy interest in cases where the police assessment of probable cause is subsequently rejected by a magistrate. But a countervailing consideration is that a warrant would be routinely forthcoming in the vast majority of situations where the property has been seized in conjunction with the valid arrest of a person in a public place. I therefore doubt that requiring the authorities to go through the formality of obtaining a warrant in this situation would have much practical effect in protecting Fourth Amendment values.

I believe this sort of practical evaluation underlies the Court's decisions permitting clothing, personal effects, and automobiles to be searched without a warrant as an incident of arrest, even though it would be possible simply to impound these items until a warrant could be obtained. The Court's opinion does not explain why a wallet carried in the arrested person's clothing, but not the footlocker in the present case, is subject to "reduced expectations of privacy caused by the arrest." Nor does the Court explain how such items as purses or briefcases fit into the dichotomy. Perhaps the holding in the present case will be limited in the future to objects that are relatively immobile by virtue of their size or absence of a means of propulsion. * * *

II

The approach taken by the Court has the perverse result of allowing fortuitous circumstances to control the outcome of the present case. The agents probably could have avoided having the footlocker search held unconstitutional either by delaying the arrest for a few minutes or by conducting the search on the spot rather than back at their office. Probable cause for the arrest was present from the time respondents Machado and Leary were seated on the footlocker inside Boston's South Station and the agents' dog signaled the presence of marihuana. Rather than make an arrest at this moment, the agents commendably sought to determine the possible involvement of others in the illegal scheme. They waited a short time until respondent Chadwick arrived and the footlocker had been loaded into the trunk of his car, and then made the arrest. But if the agents had postponed the arrest just a few minutes longer until the respondents started to drive away, then the car could have been seized, taken to the agents' office, and all its contents—including the footlocker—searched without a warrant.

Alternatively, the agents could have made a search of the footlocker at the time and place of the arrests. Machado and Leary were standing next to an open automobile trunk containing the footlocker, and thus it was within the area of their "immediate control." And certainly the footlocker would have been properly subject to search at the time if the arrest had occurred a few minutes earlier while Machado and Leary were seated on it.

In many cases, of course, small variations in the facts are determinative of the legal outcome. Criminal law necessarily involves some line drawing. But I see no way that these alternative courses of conduct, which likely would have been held constitutional under the Fourth Amendment, would have been any more solicitous of the privacy or well-being of the respondents. * * * It is decisions of the kind made by the Court today that make criminal law a trap for the unwary policeman and detract from the important activities of detecting criminal activity and protecting the public safety.

NOTES AND QUESTIONS

1. What do you think of the Justice Department's interpretation of the Fourth Amendment? Is it "extreme," as Justice Blackmun asserted?

2. Why did the district court describe the relationship between the footlocker and Chadwick's car as "coincidental"?

3. *Cars versus containers.* At the time of the respective searches, was the Chambers car more mobile than the Chadwick footlocker? How does *Chadwick* distinguish *Chambers*? Are you persuaded?

4. *Searches incident to lawful arrests.* According to Chief Justice Burger, exigencies aside, a warrant is required "at the point where the property to be searched comes under the exclusive dominion of police authority." If so, why didn't Officer Jenks have to obtain a warrant in *United States v. Robinson* (p. 226), in order to open up the cigarette package he found on Robinson's person, once the container was in Jenks's possession?

5. *Fortuities (part 1).* Justice Blackmun criticized the majority for devising a rule that permits fortuitous circumstances to control outcomes. He reasoned that if the police had searched the footlocker at the scene, a warrant would not have been required. Why does he say that? Is he right?

6. *Fortuities (part 2).* Justice Blackmun also suggested that if the agents had delayed their arrests for a few moments until the car was on the road, they could then have seized the footlocker and searched it at headquarters without a warrant. Why does he say that? Is he right?

7. *Containers "coincidentally" in cars.* In Arkansas v. Sanders, 442 U.S. 753, 99 S.Ct. 2586, 61 L.Ed.2d 235 (1979), the Supreme Court considered the

Blackmun scenario mentioned in Note 6. In *Sanders*, the police had probable cause to believe that Sanders would arrive at the airport with a green suitcase filled with marijuana. The officers put the airport under surveillance. They observed Sanders, and later a second man, place a closed but unlocked green suitcase into a taxicab trunk and, shortly thereafter, drive away. The officers stopped the taxi within a few blocks, opened the trunk, took out the suitcase, and opened it, all without a search warrant. At a subsequent trial, Sanders and his partner sought to exclude the marijuana found inside.

Notice that *Sanders* involves a container coincidentally in a car when it was seized. That is, as in *Chadwick*, the police in *Sanders* had probable cause to search a particular container before it was placed in an automobile. But here, unlike in *Chadwick*, the police did not confront the suspects until the vehicle was on the highway. As a consequence, unlike in *Chadwick*, the prosecutor in *Sanders* argued to the Supreme Court that the search was justifiable under the "automobile search" exception to the warrant require-ment. As Justice Powell put it for the Court, "we thus are presented with the task of determining whether the warrantless search of respondent's suitcase falls on the *Chadwick* or the *Chambers/Carroll* side of the Fourth Amendment line." The majority concluded that it fell on the *Chadwick* side:

> [A] suitcase taken from an automobile stopped on the highway is not necessarily attended by any lesser expectation of privacy than is associat-ed with luggage taken from other locations. One is not less inclined to place private, personal possessions in a suitcase merely because the suitcase is to be carried in an automobile rather than transported by other means or temporarily checked or stored. Indeed, the very purpose of a suitcase is to serve as a repository for personal items when one wishes to transport them. Accordingly, the reasons for not requiring a warrant for the search of an automobile do not apply to searches of personal luggage taken by police from automobiles. We therefore find no justifica-tion for the extension of *Carroll* and its progeny to the warrantless search of one's personal luggage merely because it was located in an automobile lawfully stopped by the police.

Do you agree? Why should the police be permitted to search a glove compartment or car trunk without a warrant on the highway or at the police station, but not be able to search a suitcase found in the same vehicle, assuming probable cause exists for either search?

8. *The relative Fourth Amendment worthiness of different containers.* *Chadwick* involved a double-locked footlocker. In *Sanders* (Note 7), the container was an unlocked suitcase. In both cases, the Court held that the police needed a warrant to search the container. However, are there contain-ers that by their nature may be opened without a warrant? Yes, according to *Sanders*:

> Not all containers and packages found by police during the course of a search will deserve the full protection of the Fourth Amendment. Thus, some containers (for example a kit of burglar tools or a gun case) by their very nature cannot support any reasonable expectation of privacy because their contents can be inferred from their outward appearance. Similarly,

in some cases the contents of a package will be open to "plain view," thereby obviating the need for a warrant.

These exceptions aside, however, all containers are treated alike. The Court has refused to draw a distinction between "worthy" and "unworthy" containers. The Court stated in United States v. Ross, 456 U.S. 798, 102 S.Ct. 2157, 72 L.Ed.2d 572 (1982):

> Even though * * * a distinction perhaps could evolve in a series of cases in which paper bags, locked trunks, lunch buckets, and orange crates were placed on one side of the line or the other, the central purpose of the Fourth Amendment forecloses such a distinction. For just as the most frail cottage in the kingdom is absolutely entitled to the same guarantees of privacy as the most majestic mansion, so also may a traveler who carries a toothbrush and a few articles of clothing in a paper bag or knotted scarf claim an equal right to conceal his possessions from official inspection as the sophisticated executive with the locked attaché case.

9. *Cars with "coincidental" containers.* In *Chadwick* and *Sanders* (Note 7) the police had prior probable cause to search a container that was placed in a car. Suppose, however, the police have probable case to search a car, during which search they inadvertently come across a container. We might call this a car-with-a-coincidental-container case, to distinguish it from *Chadwick* and *Sanders*, which were containers-coincidentally-in-car cases.

In Robbins v. California, 453 U.S. 420, 101 S.Ct. 2841, 69 L.Ed.2d 744 (1981), police officers stopped a car being driven erratically. When they approached the vehicle, they smelled marijuana smoke, which gave them probable cause to search the car. During the ensuing search the police found containers, which they opened. Writing for a four-justice plurality, Justice Stewart concluded that the warrantless search was impermissible under *Chadwick* and *Sanders*.

The Court quickly reversed directions, however, in United States v. Ross, 456 U.S. 798, 102 S.Ct. 2157, 72 L.Ed.2d 572 (1982). In *Ross*, the police had probable case to believe that a particular individual was selling drugs from the trunk of his car at a specified location. When the police discovered the car and suspect, now on the road, they stopped the automobile and searched the car trunk. Inside, they found a closed brown paper bag, which they opened and in which they discovered heroin.

Justice Stevens, writing for a seven-justice majority, overruled *Robbins* and "rejected some of the reasoning in *Sanders*." Stevens pointed out that a warrant to search a home provides the police with implicit authority to open any container—for example, a dresser drawer, a jewelry box, a briefcase—that might contain the criminal evidence for which they are searching. Likewise, "[a] warrant to search a vehicle would support a search of every part of the vehicle"—including containers therein—"that might contain the object of the search." Therefore, the Court reasoned, the same rule should apply to *warrantless* car searches: When the police have probable cause to search a car without a warrant under the *Carroll-Chambers-Carney* line of cases, they may also search any container found during the car search that is large enough to hold the evidence for which they are looking.

Thus, immediately after *Ross*, an uneasy—and complicated—car/container distinction existed. If the police had probable cause to search a car, they could search fixed parts thereof (*e.g.*, glove compartments, trunks) as well as movable containers carried within it (assuming they could conceal the object of the search). But, if the police had probable cause to search a specific container, which coincidentally was found in a car, they could search the car on the highway (or tow it to the police station, per *Chambers v. Maroney*), without a warrant in order to find and seize the container, but they needed a warrant to open the container (per *Chadwick* and whatever remained of *Arkansas v. Sanders* after *Ross*).

Then, along came the next case.

CALIFORNIA v. ACEVEDO

Supreme Court of the United States, 1991.
500 U.S. 565, 111 S.Ct. 1982, 114 L.Ed.2d 619.

JUSTICE BLACKMUN delivered the opinion of the Court. * * *

I

[Jamie Daza picked up a package from a Federal Express office, sent from Hawaii, that the police knew from prior inspection contained marijuana. Officers observed Daza take the package to his home. They kept the Daza residence under surveillance, while another officer left to obtain a warrant to search the Daza residence. Before a warrant could be obtained, the following events ensued.]

* * * [R]espondent Charles Steven Acevedo arrived. He entered Daza's apartment, stayed for about 10 minutes, and reappeared carrying a brown paper bag that looked full. The officers noticed that the bag was the size of one of the wrapped marijuana packages sent from Hawaii. Acevedo walked to a silver Honda in the parking lot. He placed the bag in the trunk of the car and started to drive away. Fearing the loss of evidence, officers in a marked police car stopped him. They opened the trunk and the bag, and found marijuana. * * *

The California Court of Appeal * * * concluded that the marijuana found in the paper bag in the car's trunk should have been suppressed. The court concluded that the officers had probable cause to believe that the paper bag contained drugs but lacked probable cause to suspect that Acevedo's car, itself, otherwise contained contraband. Because the officers' probable cause was directed specifically at the bag, the court held that the case was controlled by *United States v. Chadwick*, [p. 280] rather than by *United States v. Ross* [p. 289, Note 9]. Although the court agreed that the officers could seize the paper bag, it held that, under *Chadwick*, they could not open the bag without first obtaining a warrant for that purpose. * * *

We granted certiorari to reexamine the law applicable to a closed container in an automobile, a subject that has troubled courts and law enforcement officers since it was first considered in *Chadwick*. * * *

III * * *

This Court in *Ross* rejected *Chadwick*'s distinction between containers and cars. It concluded that the expectation of privacy in one's vehicle is equal to one's expectation of privacy in the container, and noted that "the privacy interests in a car's trunk or glove compartment may be no less than those in a movable container." It also recognized that it was arguable that the same exigent circumstances that permit a warrantless search of an automobile would justify the warrantless search of a movable container. In deference to the rule of *Chadwick* and [*Arkansas v.*] *Sanders* [p. 287, Note 7], however, the Court put that question to one side. It concluded that the time and expense of the warrant process would be misdirected if the police could search every cubic inch of an automobile until they [inadvertently] discovered a paper sack, at which point the Fourth Amendment required them to take the sack to a magistrate for permission to look inside. We now must decide the question deferred in *Ross*: whether the Fourth Amendment requires the police to obtain a warrant to open the sack in a movable vehicle simply because they lack probable cause to search the entire car. We conclude that it does not.

IV

Dissenters in *Ross* asked why the suitcase in *Sanders* was "more private, less difficult for police to seize and store, or in any other relevant respect more properly subject to the warrant requirement, than a container that police discover in a probable-cause search of an entire automobile?" We now agree that a container found after a general search of the automobile and a container found in a car after a limited search for the container are equally easy for the police to store and for the suspect to hide or destroy. In fact, we see no principled distinction in terms of either the privacy expectation or the exigent circumstances between the paper bag found by the police in *Ross* and the paper bag found by the police here. Furthermore, by attempting to distinguish between a container for which the police are specifically searching and a container which they come across in a car, we have provided only minimal protection for privacy and have impeded effective law enforcement.

The line between probable cause to search a vehicle and probable cause to search a package in that vehicle is not always clear, and separate rules that govern the two objects to be searched may enable the police to broaden their power to make warrantless searches and disserve privacy interests. * * * At the moment when officers stop an automobile, it may be less than clear whether they suspect with a high degree of certainty that the vehicle contains drugs in a bag or simply contains drugs. If the police know that they may open a bag only if they are actually searching the entire car, they may search more extensively than they otherwise would in order to establish the general probable cause required by *Ross*. * * *

To the extent that the *Chadwick-Sanders* rule protects privacy, its protection is minimal. Law enforcement officers may seize a container and hold it until they obtain a search warrant. *Chadwick*. "Since the police, by hypothesis, have probable cause to seize the property, we can assume that a warrant will be routinely forthcoming in the overwhelming majority of cases." *Sanders* (dissenting opinion). And the police often will be able to search containers without a warrant, despite the *Chadwick-Sanders* rule, as a search incident to a lawful arrest. * * *

Finally, the search of a paper bag intrudes far less on individual privacy than does the incursion sanctioned long ago in *Carroll*. In that case, prohibition agents slashed the upholstery of the automobile. This Court nonetheless found their search to be reasonable under the Fourth Amendment. If destroying the interior of an automobile is not unreasonable, we cannot conclude that looking inside a closed container is. In light of the minimal protection to privacy afforded by the *Chadwick-Sanders* rule, and our serious doubt whether that rule substantially serves privacy interests, we now hold that the Fourth Amendment does not compel separate treatment for an automobile search that extends only to a container within the vehicle.

V

The *Chadwick-Sanders* rule not only has failed to protect privacy but also has confused courts and police officers and impeded effective law enforcement. * * *

The discrepancy between the two rules has led to confusion for law enforcement officers. For example, when an officer, who has developed probable cause to believe that a vehicle contains drugs, begins to search the vehicle and immediately discovers a closed container, which rule applies? The defendant will argue that the fact that the officer first chose to search the container indicates that his probable cause extended only to the container and that *Chadwick* and *Sanders* therefore require a warrant. On the other hand, the fact that the officer first chose to search in the most obvious location should not restrict the propriety of the search. The *Chadwick* rule, as applied in *Sanders*, has devolved into an anomaly such that the more likely the police are to discover drugs in a container, the less authority they have to search it. We have noted the virtue of providing " ' "clear and unequivocal" guidelines to the law enforcement profession.' " The *Chadwick-Sanders* rule is the antithesis of a " ' 'clear and unequivocal' guideline." * * *

* * * We conclude that it is better to adopt one clear-cut rule to govern automobile searches and eliminate the warrant requirement for closed containers set forth in *Sanders*.

VI

The interpretation of the *Carroll* doctrine set forth in *Ross* now applies to all searches of containers found in an automobile. In other words, the police may search without a warrant if their search is supported by probable cause. The Court in *Ross* * * * went on to note:

"Probable cause to believe that a container placed in the trunk of a taxi contains contraband or evidence does not justify a search of the entire cab." We reaffirm that principle. In the case before us, the police had probable cause to believe that the paper bag in the automobile's trunk contained marijuana. That probable cause now allows a warrantless search of the paper bag. The facts in the record reveal that the police did not have probable cause to believe that contraband was hidden in any other part of the automobile and a search of the entire vehicle would have been without probable cause and unreasonable under the Fourth Amendment.

Our holding today neither extends the *Carroll* doctrine nor broadens the scope of the permissible automobile search delineated in *Carroll*, *Chambers*, and *Ross*. It remains a "cardinal principle that 'searches conducted outside the judicial process, without prior approval by judge or magistrate, are *per se* unreasonable under the Fourth Amendment— subject only to a few specifically established and well-delineated exceptions.' " * * *

Until today, this Court has drawn a curious line between the search of an automobile that coincidentally turns up a container and the search of a container that coincidentally turns up in an automobile. The protections of the Fourth Amendment must not turn on such coincidences. We therefore interpret *Carroll* as providing one rule to govern all automobile searches. The police may search an automobile and the containers within it where they have probable cause to believe contraband or evidence is contained.

Justice SCALIA, concurring in the judgment.

I agree with the dissent that it is anomalous for a briefcase to be protected by the "general requirement" of a prior warrant when it is being carried along the street, but for that same briefcase to become unprotected as soon as it is carried into an automobile. On the other hand, I agree with the Court that it would be anomalous for a locked compartment in an automobile to be unprotected by the "general requirement" of a prior warrant, but for an unlocked briefcase within the automobile to be protected. I join in the judgment of the Court because I think its holding is more faithful to the text and tradition of the Fourth Amendment, and if these anomalies in our jurisprudence are ever to be eliminated that is the direction in which we should travel.* * *

[Scalia described the Court's inconsistent approach to the "warrant requirement." See p. 185. He then proceeded:] Unlike the dissent, therefore, I do not regard today's holding as some momentous departure, but rather as merely the continuation of an inconsistent jurisprudence that has been with us for years. Cases like *United States v. Chadwick* and *Arkansas v. Sanders* have taken the "preference for a warrant" seriously, while cases like *United States v. Ross* and *Carroll v. United States* have not. There can be no clarity in this area unless we make up our minds, and unless the principles we express comport with the actions we take.

In my view, the path out of this confusion should be sought by returning to the first principle that the "reasonableness" requirement of the Fourth Amendment affords the protection that the common law afforded. I have no difficulty with the proposition that that includes the requirement of a warrant, where the common law required a warrant; and it may even be that changes in the surrounding legal rules * * * may make a warrant indispensable to reasonableness where it once was not. But the supposed "general rule" that a warrant is always required does not appear to have any basis in the common law, and confuses rather than facilitates any attempt to develop rules of reasonableness in light of changed legal circumstances, as the anomaly eliminated and the anomaly created by today's holding both demonstrate.

And there are more anomalies still. Under our precedents (as at common law), a person may be arrested outside the home on the basis of probable cause, without an arrest warrant. Upon arrest, the person, as well as the area within his grasp, may be searched for evidence related to the crime. Under these principles, if a known drug dealer is carrying a briefcase reasonably believed to contain marijuana (the unauthorized possession of which is a crime), the police may arrest him and search his person on the basis of probable cause alone. And, under our precedents, upon arrival at the station house, the police may inventory his possessions, including the briefcase, even if there is no reason to suspect that they contain contraband. *Illinois v. Lafayette*, [p. 234, Note 3]. According to our current law, however, the police may not, on the basis of the same probable cause, take the less intrusive step of stopping the individual on the street and demanding to see the contents of his briefcase. That makes no sense *a priori*, and in the absence of any common-law tradition supporting such a distinction, I see no reason to continue it.

* * *

I would reverse the judgment in the present case, not because a closed container carried inside a car becomes subject to the "automobile" exception to the general warrant requirement, but because the search of a closed container, outside a privately owned building, with probable cause to believe that the container contains contraband, and when it in fact does contain contraband, is not one of those searches whose Fourth Amendment reasonableness depends upon a warrant. For that reason I concur in the judgment of the Court.

Justice WHITE, dissenting.

Agreeing as I do with most of Justice Stevens' opinion and with the result he reaches, I dissent and would affirm the judgment below.

Justice STEVENS, with whom Justice MARSHAL joins, dissenting.

At the end of its opinion, the Court pays lipservice to the proposition that should provide the basis for a correct analysis of the legal question presented by this case: It is " 'a cardinal principle that "searches conducted outside the judicial process, without prior approval by judge or magistrate, are *per se* unreasonable under the Fourth Amendment—subject only to a few specifically established and well-delineated exceptions." ' "

Relying on arguments that conservative judges have repeatedly rejected in past cases, the Court today—despite its disclaimer to the contrary—enlarges the scope of the automobile exception to this "cardinal principle," which undergirded our Fourth Amendment jurisprudence * * * .
* * *

II

In its opinion today, the Court recognizes that the police did not have probable cause to search respondent's vehicle and that a search of anything but the paper bag that respondent had carried from Daza's apartment and placed in the trunk of his car would have been unconstitutional. Moreover, as I read the opinion, the Court assumes that the police could not have made a warrantless inspection of the bag before it was placed in the car. Finally, the Court also does not question the fact that, under our prior cases, it would have been lawful for the police to seize the container and detain it (and respondent) until they obtained a search warrant. Thus, all of the relevant facts that governed our decisions in *Chadwick* and *Sanders* are present here whereas the relevant fact that justified the vehicle search in *Ross* is not present.

The Court does not attempt to identify any exigent circumstances that would justify its refusal to apply the general rule against warrantless searches. Instead, it advances these three arguments: First, the rules identified in the foregoing cases are confusing and anomalous. Second, the rules do not protect any significant interest in privacy. And, third, the rules impede effective law enforcement. None of these arguments withstands scrutiny.

The "Confusion" * * *

The decided cases * * * provide no support for the Court's concern about "confusion." The Court * * * cites no evidence * * * that anyone * * * has been unable to understand the " 'inherent opaqueness' " of this uncomplicated issue. * * *

The Court summarizes the alleged "anomaly" created by the coexistence of *Ross*, *Chadwick*, and *Sanders* with the statement that "the more likely the police are to discover drugs in a container, the less authority they have to search it." This juxtaposition is only anomalous, however, if one accepts the flawed premise that the degree to which the police are likely to discover contraband is correlated with their authority to search *without a warrant*. Yet, even proof beyond a reasonable doubt will not justify a warrantless search that is not supported by one of the exceptions to the warrant requirement. And, even when the police have a warrant or an exception applies, once the police possess probable cause, the extent to which they are more or less certain of the contents of a container has no bearing on their authority to search it.

To the extent there was any "anomaly" in our prior jurisprudence, the Court has "cured" it at the expense of creating a more serious paradox. For surely it is anomalous to prohibit a search of a briefcase while the owner is carrying it exposed on a public street yet to permit a search once the owner has placed the briefcase in the locked trunk of his car. One's privacy interest in one's luggage can certainly not be diminished by one's removing it from a public thoroughfare and placing it—out of sight—in a privately owned vehicle. Nor is the danger that evidence will escape increased if the luggage is in a car rather than on the street. In either location, if the police have probable cause, they are authorized to seize the luggage and to detain it until they obtain judicial approval for a search. Any line demarking an exception to the warrant requirement will appear blurred at the edges, but the Court has certainly erred if it believes that, by erasing one line and drawing another, it has drawn a clearer boundary.

The Privacy Argument

The Court's statement that *Chadwick* and *Sanders* provide only "minimal protection to privacy" is also unpersuasive. Every citizen clearly has an interest in the privacy of the contents of his or her luggage, briefcase, handbag or any other container that conceals private papers and effects from public scrutiny. That privacy interest has been recognized repeatedly in cases spanning more than a century.

Under the Court's holding today, the privacy interest that protects the contents of a suitcase or a briefcase from a warrantless search when it is in public view simply vanishes when its owner climbs into a taxicab. Unquestionably the rejection of the *Sanders* line of cases by today's decision will result in a significant loss of individual privacy.

To support its argument that today's holding works only a minimal intrusion on privacy, the Court suggests that "[i]f the police know that they may open a bag only if they are actually searching the entire car, they may search more extensively than they otherwise would in order to establish the general probable cause required by *Ross*." * * * [T]his fear is unexplained and inexplicable. Neither evidence uncovered in the course of a search nor the scope of the search conducted can be used to provide *post hoc* justification for a search unsupported by probable cause at its inception. * * *

The Burden on Law Enforcement

The Court's suggestion that *Chadwick* and *Sanders* have created a significant burden on effective law enforcement is unsupported, inaccurate, and, in any event, an insufficient reason for creating a new exception to the warrant requirement. * * *

Even if the warrant requirement does inconvenience the police to some extent, that fact does not distinguish this constitutional requirement from any other procedural protection secured by the Bill of Rights. It is merely a part of the price that our society must pay in order to preserve its freedom. * * *

NOTES AND QUESTIONS

1. Who has the best side of the argument, Justice Blackmun, Justice Scalia, or Justice Stevens? Does Justice Scalia's position remind you of any Fourth Amendment argument that the Court previously repudiated?

2. Shortly after *Acevedo* was decided, Professor James Tomkovicz wrote:

A case that ostensibly focused on a relatively narrow issue yielded the unmistakable seeds of yet another quantum change in the Court's attitude toward the warrant requirement. While the holding of *Acevedo* was technically confined to the "automobile doctrine" issue upon which the Court granted review, the opinion's reasoning suggested that the Court is on the brink of "clarifying" Fourth Amendment law at the expense of the warrant requirement.

James J. Tomkovicz, California v. Acevedo: *The Walls Close In On the Warrant Requirement*, 29 Am. Crim. L. Rev. 1103, 1105–06 (1992).

Can you point to language or reasoning in the Blackmun opinion supporting this observation?

3. *Acevedo* overruled *Sanders*. Did it overrule *Chadwick*? If not, why not? If not, what is left of the *Chadwick* doctrine?

4. *Problem.* Would the following warrantless search variations on *Acevedo* be permissible?

A. The police in *Acevedo* open the trunk, immediately spot the paper bag, open it, and find marijuana. The police proceed to search the remainder of the trunk. They find and seize transparent bags of cocaine hidden under a blanket. They search the passenger compartment. Under the front seat, they find a small quantity of marijuana.

B. The same as A., except that when the police open the paper bag in the trunk they discover that it contains non-contraband lawful items. They proceed to search the remainder of the trunk, as in A.

C. The police open the trunk, and do not immediately see the paper bag. They hunt through the trunk. They do not find the paper bag, but they do discover a briefcase. They open it, find the brown paper bag inside, and open it.

D. The police stop Acevedo, but do not arrest him, before he enters the car. They seize and open the paper bag.

E. The police stop Acevedo before he enters the car. They arrest him for possession of marijuana, seize the paper bag, and open it.

5. *Containers belonging to passengers.* Does probable cause to search a car entitle the police to open containers they have reason to know belong to an occupant whom they lack probable cause to arrest? In Wyoming v. Houghton, 526 U.S. 295, 119 S.Ct. 1297, 143 L.Ed.2d 408 (1999), the police lawfully stopped a vehicle containing a male driver and two female front seat

passengers. The police uncontestedly obtained probable cause to search the car for drugs after they lawfully seized an illegal syringe from the driver, who admitted that he used it to take drugs. During the car search, the police discovered a purse in the back seat that one of the passengers, Houghton, claimed belonged to her. At the time, the officers did *not* have probable cause to suspect her of drug use, nor was the driver under arrest.

The Supreme Court, 6–3, per Justice Scalia, announced that "police officers with probable cause to search a car may inspect [any] passengers' belongings found in the car that are capable of concealing the object of the search." According to Scalia, "[p]assengers, no less than drivers, possess a reduced expectation of privacy with regard to the property that they transport in cars * * *." Moreover, "the degree of intrusiveness upon personal privacy and indeed even personal dignity" of a property search is less than the intrusiveness of a search of one's person. The Court concluded that the Government's legitimate interest in effective law enforcement justified a search of all car containers that might hold drugs, and not simply those containers apparently belonging to the driver.

What is the broader significance of *Houghton*? If the driver had been under arrest, but police lacked probable cause to search the car, would the search of the purse have been permissible? What if the police want to search Houghton's person, on the ground that *she* is a container that may possess contraband or a weapon?

4. PLAIN VIEW (AND TOUCH) DOCTRINES

HORTON v. CALIFORNIA

Supreme Court of the United States, 1990.
496 U.S. 128, 110 S.Ct. 2301, 110 L.Ed.2d 112.

Jᴜsᴛɪᴄᴇ Sᴛᴇᴠᴇɴs delivered the opinion of the Court.

In this case we revisit an issue that was considered, but not conclusively resolved, in *Coolidge v. New Hampshire*, 403 U.S. 443, 91 S.Ct. 2022, 29 L.Ed.2d 564 (1971): Whether the warrantless seizure of evidence of crime in plain view is prohibited by the Fourth Amendment if the discovery of the evidence was not inadvertent. We conclude that even though inadvertence is a characteristic of most legitimate "plain view" seizures, it is not a necessary condition.

I

Petitioner was convicted of the armed robbery of Erwin Wallaker, the treasurer of the San Jose Coin Club. When Wallaker returned to his home after the Club's annual show, he entered his garage and was accosted by two masked men, one armed with a machine gun and the other with an electrical shocking device, sometimes referred to as a "stun gun." The two men shocked Wallaker, bound and handcuffed him, and robbed him of jewelry and cash. * * *

Sergeant LaRault, an experienced police officer, investigated the crime and determined that there was probable cause to search petitioner's home for the proceeds of the robbery and for the weapons used by the robbers. His affidavit for a search warrant referred to police reports that described the weapons as well as the proceeds, but the warrant issued by the Magistrate only authorized a search for the proceeds, including three specifically described rings.

Pursuant to the warrant, LaRault searched petitioner's residence, but he did not find the stolen properly. During the course of the search, however, he discovered the weapons in plain view and seized them. Specifically, he seized an Uzi machine gun, a .38–caliber revolver, two stun guns, a handcuff key, a San Jose Coin Club advertising brochure, and a few items of clothing identified by the victim. LaRault testified that while he was searching for the rings, he also was interested in finding other evidence connecting petitioner to the robbery. Thus, the seized evidence was not discovered "inadvertently."

The trial court refused to suppress the evidence found in petitioner's home and, after a jury trial, petitioner was found guilty and sentenced to prison. * * *

II * * *

The right to security in person and property protected by the Fourth Amendment may be invaded in quite different ways by searches and seizures. A search compromises the individual interest in privacy; a seizure deprives the individual of dominion over his or her person or property. The "plain view" doctrine is often considered an exception to the general rule that warrantless searches are presumptively unreasonable, but this characterization overlooks the important difference between searches and seizures. If an article is already in plain view, neither its observation nor its seizure would involve any invasion of privacy. A seizure of the article, however, would obviously invade the owner's possessory interest. If "plain view" justifies an exception from an otherwise applicable warrant requirement, therefore, it must be an exception that is addressed to the concerns that are implicated by seizures rather than by searches.

The criteria that generally guide "plain view" seizures were set forth in *Coolidge v. New Hampshire*. The Court held that the police, in seizing two automobiles parked in plain view on the defendant's driveway in the course of arresting the defendant, violated the Fourth Amendment. Accordingly, particles of gun powder that had been subsequently found in vacuum sweepings from one of the cars could not be introduced in evidence against the defendant. The State endeavored to justify the seizure of the automobiles, and their subsequent search at the police station, on four different grounds, including the "plain view" doctrine. The scope of that doctrine as it had developed in earlier cases was fairly summarized in these three paragraphs from Justice Stewart's [plurality] opinion:

"It is well established that under certain circumstances the police may seize evidence in plain view without a warrant. But it is important to keep in mind that, in the vast majority of cases, *any* evidence seized by the police will be in plain view, at least at the moment of seizure. The problem with the 'plain view' doctrine has been to identify the circumstances in which plain view has legal significance rather than being simply the normal concomitant of any search, legal or illegal.

"An example of the applicability of the 'plain view' doctrine is the situation in which the police have a warrant to search a given area for specified objects, and in the course of the search come across some other article of incriminating character. Where the initial intrusion that brings the police within plain view of such an article is supported, not by a warrant, but by one of the recognized exceptions to the warrant requirement, the seizure is also legitimate. Thus the police may inadvertently come across evidence while in 'hot pursuit' of a fleeing suspect. *Warden v. Hayden* [p. 211]. And an object that comes into view during a search incident to arrest that is appropriately limited in scope under existing law may be seized without a warrant. *Chimel v. California* [p. 218]. Finally, the 'plain view' doctrine has been applied where a police officer is not searching for evidence against the accused, but nonetheless inadvertently comes across an incriminating object.

"What the 'plain view' cases have in common is that the police officer in each of them had a prior justification for an intrusion in the course of which he came inadvertently across a piece of evidence incriminating the accused. The doctrine serves to supplement the prior justification—whether it be a warrant for another object, hot pursuit, search incident to lawful arrest, or some other legitimate reason for being present unconnected with a search directed against the accused—and permits the warrantless seizure. Of course, the extension of the original justification is legitimate only where it is immediately apparent to the police that they have evidence before them; the 'plain view' doctrine may not be used to extend a general exploratory search from one object to another until something incriminating at last emerges."

Justice Stewart then described the two limitations on the doctrine that he found implicit in its rationale: First, that "plain view *alone* is never enough to justify the warrantless seizure of evidence"; and second, that "the discovery of evidence in plain view must be inadvertent."

* * * Before discussing the second limitation, which is implicated in this case, it is therefore necessary to explain why the first adequately supports the Court's judgment.

It is, of course, an essential predicate to any valid warrantless seizure of incriminating evidence that the officer did not violate the Fourth Amendment in arriving at the place from which the evidence could be plainly viewed. There are, moreover, two additional conditions that must be satisfied to justify the warrantless seizure. First, not only must the item be in plain view; its incriminating character must also be "immediately apparent." Thus, in *Coolidge*, the cars were obviously in plain view, but their probative value remained uncertain until after the interiors were swept and examined microscopically. Second, not only must the officer be lawfully located in a place from which the object can be plainly seen, but he or she must also have a lawful right of access to the object itself.[7] * * * [W]e are satisfied that the absence of inadvertence was not essential to the court's rejection of the State's "plain-view" argument in *Coolidge*.

III

Justice Stewart concluded that the inadvertence requirement was necessary to avoid a violation of the express constitutional requirement that a valid warrant must particularly describe the things to be seized. He explained:

> "The rationale of the exception to the warrant requirement, as just stated, is that a plain-view seizure will not turn an initially valid (and therefore limited) search into a 'general' one, while the inconvenience of procuring a warrant to cover an inadvertent discovery is great. But where the discovery is anticipated, where the police know in advance the location of the evidence and intend to seize it, the situation is altogether different. The requirement of a warrant to seize imposes no inconvenience whatever, or at least none which is constitutionally cognizable in a legal system that regards warrantless searches as '*per se* unreasonable' in the absence of 'exigent circumstances.'
>
> "If the initial intrusion is bottomed upon a warrant that fails to mention a particular object, though the police know its location and intend to seize it, then there is a violation of the express constitutional requirement of 'Warrants * * * particularly describing * * * [the] things to be seized.' "

We find two flaws in this reasoning. First, evenhanded law enforcement is best achieved by the application of objective standards of conduct, rather than standards that depend upon the subjective state of mind of the officer. The fact that an officer is interested in an item of evidence and fully expects to find it in the course of a search should not invalidate its seizure if the search is confined in area and duration by the terms of a warrant or a valid exception to the warrant requirement. If the officer has knowledge approaching certainty that the item will be found, we see no reason why he or she would deliberately omit a particular description of the item to be seized from the application for a search warrant. Specifica-

---

7. "This is simply a corollary of the familiar principle discussed above, that no amount of probable cause can justify a warrantless search or seizure absent 'exigent circumstances.' Incontrovertible testimony of the senses that an incriminating object is on premises belonging to a criminal suspect may establish the fullest possible measure of probable cause. But even where the object is contraband, this Court has repeatedly stated and enforced the basic rule that the police may not enter and make a warrantless seizure." *Coolidge*.

tion of the additional item could only permit the officer to expand the scope of the search. On the other hand, if he or she has a valid warrant to search for one item and merely a suspicion concerning the second, whether or not it amounts to probable cause, we fail to see why that suspicion should immunize the second item from seizure if it is found during a lawful search for the first. The hypothetical case put by Justice White in his dissenting opinion in *Coolidge* is instructive:

> "Let us suppose officers secure a warrant to search a house for a rifle. While staying well within the range of a rifle search, they discover two photographs of the murder victim, both in plain sight in the bedroom. Assume also that the discovery of the one photograph was inadvertent but finding the other was anticipated. The Court would permit the seizure of only one of the photographs. But in terms of the 'minor' peril to Fourth Amendment values there is surely no difference between these two photographs: the interference with possession is the same in each case and the officers' appraisal of the photograph they expected to see is no less reliable than their judgment about the other. And in both situations the actual inconvenience and danger to evidence remain identical if the officers must depart and secure a warrant."

Second, the suggestion that the inadvertence requirement is necessary to prevent the police from conducting general searches, or from converting specific warrants into general warrants, is not persuasive because that interest is already served by the requirements that no warrant issue unless it "particularly describ[es] the place to be searched and the persons or things to be seized," and that a warrantless search be circumscribed by the exigencies which justify its initiation. Scrupulous adherence to these requirements serves the interests in limiting the area and duration of the search that the inadvertence requirement inadequately protects. Once those commands have been satisfied and the officer has a lawful right of access, however, no additional Fourth Amendment interest is furthered by requiring that the discovery of evidence be inadvertent. If the scope of the search exceeds that permitted by the terms of a validly issued warrant or the character of the relevant exception from the warrant requirement, the subsequent seizure is unconstitutional without more. * * *

In this case, the scope of the search was not enlarged in the slightest by the omission of any reference to the weapons in the warrant. Indeed, if the three rings and other items named in the warrant had been found at the outset—or petitioner had them in his possession and had responded to the warrant by producing them immediately—no search for weapons could have taken place. * * *

As we have already suggested, by hypothesis the seizure of an object in plain view does not involve an intrusion on privacy. If the interest in privacy has been invaded, the violation must have occurred before the object came into plain view and there is no need for an inadvertence limitation on seizures to condemn it. The prohibition against general searches and general warrants serves primarily as a protection against unjustified intrusions on privacy. But reliance on privacy concerns that support that prohibition is misplaced when the inquiry concerns the scope of an exception that merely authorizes an officer with a lawful right of access to an item to seize it without a warrant.

In this case the items seized from petitioner's home were discovered during a lawful search authorized by a valid warrant. When they were discovered, it was immediately apparent to the officer that they constituted incriminating evidence. He had probable cause, not only to obtain a warrant to search for the stolen property, but also to believe that the weapons and handguns had been used in the crime he was investigating. The search was authorized by the warrant; the seizure was authorized by the "plain-view" doctrine. The judgment is affirmed. * * *

Justice BRENNAN, with whom Justice MARSHALL joins, dissenting. * * *

I

* * * The Amendment protects two distinct interests. The prohibition against unreasonable searches and the requirement that a warrant "particularly describ[e] the place to be searched" protect an interest in privacy. The prohibition against unreasonable seizures and the requirement that a warrant "particularly describ[e] * * * the * * * things to be seized" protect a possessory interest in property. The Fourth Amendment, by its terms, declares the privacy and possessory interests to be equally important. As this Court recently stated: "Although the interest protected by the Fourth Amendment injunction against unreasonable searches is quite different from that protected by its injunction against unreasonable seizures, neither the one nor the other is of inferior worth or necessarily requires only lesser protection." *Arizona v. Hicks*, [p. 304].

The Amendment protects these equally important interests in precisely the same manner: by requiring a neutral and detached magistrate to evaluate, before the search or seizure, the government's showing of probable cause and its particular description of the place to be searched and the items to be seized. Accordingly, just as a warrantless search is *per se* unreasonable absent exigent circumstances, so too a seizure of personal property is *"per se* unreasonable within the meaning of the Fourth Amendment unless it is accomplished pursuant to a judicial warrant issued upon probable cause and particularly describing the items to be seized." * * * A decision to invade a possessory interest in property is too important to be left to the discretion of zealous officers "engaged in the often competitive enterprise of ferreting out crime." * * *

The plain-view doctrine is an exception to the general rule that a seizure of personal property must be authorized by a warrant. As Justice Stewart explained in *Coolidge*, we accept a warrantless seizure when an officer is lawfully in a location and inadvertently sees evidence of a crime because of "the inconvenience of procuring a warrant" to seize this newly discovered piece of evidence. But "where the discovery is anticipated, where the police know in advance the location of the evidence and intend to seize it," the argument that procuring a warrant would be "inconvenient" loses much, if not all, of its force. Barring an exigency, there is no reason why the police officers could not have obtained a warrant to seize this evidence before entering the premises. The rationale behind the inadvertent discovery requirement is simply that we will not excuse officers from the general requirement of a warrant to seize if the officers know the location of evidence, have probable cause to seize it, intend to seize it, and yet do not bother to obtain a warrant particularly describing that evidence. * * *

* * * The inadvertent discovery requirement is essential if we are to take seriously the Fourth Amendment's protection of possessory interests as well as privacy interests. The Court today eliminates a rule designed to further possessory interests on the ground that it fails to further privacy interests. I cannot countenance such constitutional legerdemain. * * *

NOTES AND QUESTIONS

1. The dissent stated that, under the Fourth Amendment, "privacy and possessory interests [are] equally important"? Textual and historical issues aside, do *you* consider your personal possessory and privacy interests of equal magnitude? Why, or why not?

ARIZONA v. HICKS

Supreme Court of the United States, 1987.
480 U.S. 321, 107 S.Ct. 1149, 94 L.Ed.2d 347.

JUSTICE SCALIA delivered the opinion of the Court. * * *

I

On April 18, 1984, a bullet was fired through the floor of respondent's apartment, striking and injuring a man in the apartment below. Police officers arrived and entered respondent's apartment to search for the shooter, for other victims, and for weapons. They found and seized three weapons, including a sawed-off rifle, and in the course of their search also discovered a stocking-cap mask.

One of the policemen, Officer Nelson, noticed two sets of expensive stereo components, which seemed out of place in the squalid and otherwise ill-appointed four-room apartment. Suspecting that they were stolen, he read and recorded their serial numbers—moving some of the components, including a Bang and Olufsen turntable, in order to do so—which he then reported by phone to his headquarters. On being advised that the turntable had been taken in an armed robbery, he seized it immediately. It was later determined that some of the other serial numbers matched those on other stereo equipment taken in the same armed robbery, and a warrant was obtained and executed to seize that equipment as well. Respondent was subsequently indicted for the robbery. * * *

II

As an initial matter, the State argues that Officer Nelson's actions constituted neither a "search" nor a "seizure" within the meaning of the Fourth Amendment. We agree that the mere recording of the serial numbers did not constitute a seizure. To be sure, that was the first step in a process by which respondent was eventually deprived of the stereo equipment. In and of itself, however, it did not "meaningfully interfere" with respondent's possessory interest in either the serial numbers or the equipment, and therefore did not amount to a seizure.

Officer Nelson's moving of the equipment, however, did constitute a "search" separate and apart from the search for the shooter, victims, and weapons that was the lawful objective of his entry into the apartment. Merely inspecting those parts of the turntable that came into view during the latter search would not have constituted an independent search, because it would have produced no additional invasion of respondent's privacy interest. But taking action, unrelated to the objectives of the authorized intrusion, which exposed to view concealed portions of the apartment or its contents, did produce a new invasion of respondent's privacy unjustified by the exigent circumstance that validated the entry. This is why, contrary to Justice Powell's suggestion [in dissent], the "distinction between 'looking' at a suspicious object in plain view and 'moving' it even a few inches" is much more than trivial for purposes of the Fourth Amendment. It matters not that the search uncovered nothing of any great personal value to respondent—serial numbers rather than (what might conceivably have been hidden behind or under the equipment) letters or photographs. A search is a search, even if it happens to disclose nothing but the bottom of a turntable.

III

The remaining question is whether the search was "reasonable" under the Fourth Amendment. * * *

* * * "It is well established that under certain circumstances the police may *seize* evidence in plain view without a warrant," *Coolidge v. New Hampshire* (emphasis added). * * * It would be absurd to say that an object could lawfully be seized and taken from the premises, but could not be moved for closer examination. It is clear, therefore, that the search here was valid if the "plain view" doctrine would have sustained a seizure of the equipment.

There is no doubt it would have done so if Officer Nelson had probable cause to believe that the equipment was stolen. The State has conceded, however, that he had only a "reasonable suspicion," by which it means something less than probable cause. We have not ruled on the question whether probable cause is required in order to invoke the "plain view" doctrine. * * *

We now hold that probable cause is required. To say otherwise would be to cut the "plain view" doctrine loose from its theoretical and practical moorings. The theory of that doctrine consists of extending to nonpublic places such as the home, where searches and seizures without a warrant are presumptively unreasonable, the police's longstanding authority to make warrantless seizures in public places of such objects as weapons and contraband. And the practical justification for that extension is the desirability of sparing police, whose viewing of the object in the course of a lawful search is as legitimate as it would have been in a public place, the inconvenience and the risk—to themselves or to preservation of the evidence—of going to obtain a warrant. Dispensing with the need for a warrant is worlds apart from permitting a lesser standard of *cause* for the seizure than a warrant would require, *i.e.*, the standard of probable cause. No reason is apparent why an object should routinely be seizable on lesser grounds, during an unrelated search and seizure, than would have been needed to obtain a warrant for that same object if it had been known to be on the premises.

We do not say, of course, that a seizure can never be justified on less than probable cause. We have held that it can—where, for example, the seizure is minimally intrusive and operational necessities render it the only practicable means of detecting certain types of crime. No special operational necessities are relied on here, however—but rather the mere fact that the items in question came lawfully within the officer's plain view. That alone cannot supplant the requirement of probable cause.

The same considerations preclude us from holding that, even though probable cause would have been necessary for a *seizure*, the *search* of objects in plain view that occurred here could be sustained on lesser grounds. A dwelling-place search, no less than a dwelling-place seizure, requires probable cause, and there is no reason in theory or practicality why application of the "plain view" doctrine would supplant that requirement. Although the interest protected by the Fourth Amendment injunction against unreasonable searches is quite different from that protected by its injunction against unreasonable seizures, neither the one nor the other is of inferior worth or necessarily requires only lesser protection. We have not elsewhere drawn a categorical distinction between the two insofar as concerns the degree of justification needed to establish the reasonableness of police action, and we see no reason for a distinction in the particular circumstances before us here. Indeed, to treat searches more liberally would especially erode the plurality's warning in *Coolidge* that "the 'plain view' doctrine may not be used to extend a general exploratory search from one object to another until something incriminating at last emerges." In short, whether legal authority to move the equipment could be found only as an inevitable concomitant of the authority to seize it, or also as a consequence of some independent power to search certain objects in plain view, probable cause to believe the equipment was stolen was required.

Justice O'Connor's dissent suggests that we uphold the action here on the ground that it was a "cursory inspection" rather than a "full-blown search," and could therefore be justified by reasonable suspicion instead of probable cause. As already noted, a truly cursory inspection—one that involves merely looking at what is already exposed to view, without disturbing it—is not a "search" for Fourth Amendment purposes, and therefore does not even require reasonable suspicion. We are unwilling to send police and judges into a new thicket of Fourth Amendment law, to seek a creature of uncertain description that is neither a "plain view" inspection nor yet a "full-blown search." Nothing in the prior opinions of this Court supports such a distinction * * *.

Justice Powell's dissent reasonably asks what it is we would have had Officer Nelson do in these circumstances. The answer depends, of course, upon whether he had probable cause to conduct a search * * *. If he had, then he should have done precisely what he did. If not, then he should have followed up his suspicions, if possible, by means other than a search—just as he would have had to do if, while walking along the street, he had noticed the same suspicious stereo equipment sitting inside a house a few feet away from him, beneath an open window. It may well be that, in such circumstances, no effective means short of a search exist. But there is nothing new in the realization that the Constitution sometimes insulates the criminality of a few in order to protect the privacy of us all. Our disagreement with the dissenters pertains to where the proper balance should be struck; we choose to adhere to the textual and traditional standard of probable cause. * * *

[Justice White's concurring opinion is omitted.]

Justice POWELL, with whom THE CHIEF JUSTICE and Justice O'CONNOR join, dissenting. * * *

It is fair to ask what Officer Nelson should have done in these circumstances. Accepting the State's concession that he lacked probable cause, he could not have obtained a warrant to seize the stereo components. Neither could he have remained on the premises and forcibly prevented their removal. * * *

The Court holds that there was an unlawful search of the turntable. It agrees that the "mere recording of the serial numbers did not constitute a seizure." Thus, if the computer had identified as stolen property a component with a visible serial number, the evidence would have been admissible. But the Court further holds that "Officer Nelson's moving of the equipment * * * did constitute a 'search' * * *." It perceives a constitutional distinction between reading a serial number on an object and moving or picking up an identical object to see its serial number. * * * With all respect, this distinction between "looking" at a suspicious object in plain view and "moving" it even a few inches trivializes the

Fourth Amendment.[4] The Court's new rule will cause uncertainty, and could deter conscientious police officers from lawfully obtaining evidence necessary to convict guilty persons. * * * Accordingly, I dissent.

Justice O'CONNOR, with whom THE CHIEF JUSTICE and Justice POWELL join, dissenting.

The Court today gives the right answer to the wrong question. The Court asks whether the police must have probable cause before either seizing an object in plain view or conducting a full-blown search of that object, and concludes that they must. I agree. In my view, however, this case presents a different question: whether police must have probable cause before conducting a cursory inspection of an item in plain view. Because I conclude that such an inspection is reasonable if the police are aware of facts or circumstances that justify a reasonable suspicion that the item is evidence of a crime, I would reverse the judgment of the Arizona Court of Appeals, and therefore dissent.

* * * [T]he dispute in this case focuses on the application of the "immediately apparent" requirement; at issue is whether a police officer's reasonable suspicion is adequate to justify a cursory examination of an item in plain view.

The purpose of the "immediately apparent" requirement is to prevent "general, exploratory rummaging in a person's belongings." If an officer could indiscriminately search every item in plain view, a search justified by a limited purpose—such as exigent circumstances—could be used to eviscerate the protections of the Fourth Amendment. In order to prevent such a general search, therefore, we require that the relevance of the item be "immediately apparent." * * *

Thus, I agree with the Court that even under the plain-view doctrine, probable cause is required before the police seize an item, or conduct a full-blown search of evidence in plain view. Such a requirement of probable cause will prevent the plain-view doctrine from authorizing general searches. This is not to say, however, that even a mere inspection of a suspicious item must be supported by probable cause. When a police officer makes a cursory inspection of a suspicious item in plain view in order to determine whether it is indeed evidence of a crime, there is no "exploratory rummaging." Only those items that the police officer "reasonably suspects" as evidence of a crime may be inspected, and perhaps more importantly, the scope of such an inspection is quite limited. In short, if police officers have a reasonable, articulable suspicion that an

---

4. Numerous articles that frequently are stolen have identifying numbers, including expensive watches and cameras, and also credit cards. Assume for example that an officer reasonably suspects that two identical watches, both in plain view, have been stolen. Under the Court's decision, if one watch is lying face up and the other lying face down, reading the serial number on one of the watches would not be a search. But turning over the other watch to read its serial number would be a search. Moreover, the officer's ability to read a serial number may depend on its location in a room and light conditions at a particular time. Would there be a constitutional difference if an officer, on the basis of a reasonable suspicion, used a pocket flashlight or turned on a light to read a number rather than moving the object to a point where a serial number was clearly visible?

object they come across during the course of a lawful search is evidence of crime, in my view they may make a cursory examination of the object to verify their suspicion. If the officers wish to go beyond such a cursory examination of the object, however, they must have probable cause. * * *

This distinction between searches based on their relative intrusiveness * * * is entirely consistent with our Fourth Amendment jurisprudence. We have long recognized that searches can vary in intrusiveness, and that some brief searches "may be so minimally intrusive of Fourth Amendment interests that strong countervailing governmental interests will justify a [search] based only on specific articulable facts" that the item in question is contraband or evidence of a crime. * * *

In my view, the balance of the governmental and privacy interests strongly supports a reasonable-suspicion standard for the cursory examination of items in plain view. * * *

Unfortunately, in its desire to establish a "bright-line" test, the Court has taken a step that ignores a substantial body of precedent and that places serious roadblocks to reasonable law enforcement practices. * * *

NOTES AND QUESTIONS

1. *Making sense of Hicks.* According to Justice Scalia, what element of "plain view" was not proven by the Government? Suppose that Officer Nelson had feared that a gun was hidden behind a closed curtain in the Hicks residence. Could he lawfully have opened the curtain, without a warrant, in the absence of probable cause?

In dictum, Justice Scalia stated that if Officer Nelson had had probable cause to believe that the stereo equipment was stolen, "he should have done precisely what he did." Does that seem correct? Why or why not?

2. *Plain touch.* The Supreme Court announced for the first time in Minnesota v. Dickerson, 508 U.S. 366, 113 S.Ct. 2130, 124 L.Ed.2d 334 (1993), that there is a comparable plain-*touch* doctrine:

> We think that [the plain-view] doctrine has an obvious application by analogy to cases in which an officer discovers contraband through the sense of touch during an otherwise lawful search. * * * If a police officer lawfully pats down a suspect's outer clothing [for weapons] and feels an object whose contour or mass makes its identity immediately apparent, there has been no invasion of the suspect's privacy beyond that already authorized by the officer's search for weapons; if the object is contraband, its warrantless seizure would be justified by the same practical considerations that inhere in the plain view context. * * *

Application of the plain-touch doctrine is considered in greater detail at p. 364, Note 7.

3. *Problem.* A police officer obtained a warrant to search *F*'s home and computer for marijuana and documents and computer files pertaining to marijuana sales. When the officer found the computer, he turned it on, went to the "Documents" sub-menu of the "Start" menu, and there discovered a

list of recently opened files. He opened the first file and, to his surprise, it was a child pornography image. He then opened two or three more documents on the list, and they also contained child pornography. Does the plain-view doctrine justify the warrantless seizure of these photographs? Frasier v. State, 794 N.E.2d 449 (Ind. App. 2003).

4. *Problem*. A police officer, with consent, entered *H*'s residence to investigate an allegation of an abandoned minor at the residence. Inside, the officer observed a pipe sitting on a table that, based on his experience and training was "predominantly used to smoke marijuana." The officer picked it up and smelled the odor of marijuana. The officer seized the pipe and arrested *H* for possession of drug paraphernalia. Did the officer's actions violate *Hicks*? Commonwealth v. Hatcher, 199 S.W.3d 124 (Ky. 2006).

5.   CONSENT

SCHNECKLOTH v. BUSTAMONTE

Supreme Court of the United States, 1973.
412 U.S. 218, 93 S.Ct. 2041, 36 L.Ed.2d 854.

MR. JUSTICE STEWART delivered the opinion of the Court.

It is well settled under the Fourth and Fourteenth Amendments that a search conducted without a warrant issued upon probable cause is "*per se* unreasonable * * * subject only to a few specifically established and well-delineated exceptions." It is equally well settled that one of the specifically established exceptions to the requirements of both a warrant and probable cause is a search that is conducted pursuant to consent. The constitutional question in the present case concerns the definition of "consent" in this Fourth and Fourteenth Amendment context.

I

[While on routine patrol at 2:40 a.m., a police officer stopped a car containing six persons because he observed that one headlight and the car's license plate light were burned out. The driver could not produce a license. The officer requested the occupants to get out of the car, and the officer requested permission from Joe Alcala, who claimed to be the brother of the car owner, to search the vehicle. Alcala purportedly replied, "Sure, go ahead." Two reinforcement officers arrived at the scene. According to the officer's uncontradicted testimony, nobody was threatened with arrest prior to this time; it "was all very congenial." Alcala actually helped in the search of the car by opening the trunk and glove compartment. Wadded up under the left rear seat, the police discovered three stolen checks, later linked to one of the passengers, Bustamonte, who was prosecuted for theft. The trial court denied the defendant's pretrial motion to suppress the evidence, after which he was convicted at trial.]

II

It is important to make it clear at the outset what is not involved in this case. The respondent concedes that a search conducted pursuant to a valid consent is constitutionally permissible. * * * And similarly the State concedes that "[w]hen a prosecutor seeks to rely upon consent to justify the lawfulness of a search, he has the burden of proving that the consent was, in fact, freely and voluntarily given."

The precise question in this case, then, is what must the prosecution prove to demonstrate that a consent was "voluntarily" given. * * * The Court of Appeals for the Ninth Circuit concluded that it is an essential part of the State's initial burden to prove that a person knows he has a right to refuse consent. The California courts have followed the rule that voluntariness is a question of fact to be determined from the totality of all the circumstances, and that the state of a defendant's knowledge is only one factor to be taken into account in assessing the voluntariness of a consent.

A

The most extensive judicial exposition of the meaning of "voluntariness" has been developed in those cases in which the Court has had to determine the "voluntariness" of a defendant's confession for purposes of the Fourteenth Amendment. * * * It is to that body of case law to which we turn for initial guidance on the meaning of "voluntariness" in the present context. * * *

In determining whether a defendant's will was overborne in a particular case, the Court has assessed the totality of all the surrounding circumstances—both the characteristics of the accused and the details of the interrogation. * * *

The significant fact about all of these decisions is that none of them turned on the presence or absence of a single controlling criterion; each reflected a careful scrutiny of all the surrounding circumstances. * * *

B

Similar considerations lead us to agree with the courts of California that the question whether a consent to a search was in fact "voluntary" or was the product of duress or coercion, express or implied, is a question of fact to be determined from the totality of all the circumstances. While knowledge of the right to refuse consent is one factor to be taken into account, the government need not establish such knowledge as the *sine qua non* of an effective consent. As with police questioning, two competing concerns must be accommodated in determining the meaning of a "voluntary" consent—the legitimate need for such searches and the equally important requirement of assuring the absence of coercion.

In situations where the police have some evidence of illicit activity, but lack probable cause to arrest or search, a search authorized by a valid consent may be the only means of obtaining important and reliable evidence. In the present case for example, while the police had reason to stop the car for traffic violations, the State does not contend that there was probable cause to search the vehicle or that the search was incident to a valid arrest of any of the occupants. Yet, the search yielded tangible evidence that served as a basis for a prosecution, and provided some assurance that others, wholly innocent of the crime, were not mistakenly brought to trial. And in those cases where there is probable cause to arrest or search, but where the police lack a warrant, a consent search may still be valuable. If the search is conducted and proves fruitless, that in itself may convince the police that an arrest with its possible stigma and embarrassment is unnecessary, or that a far more extensive search pursuant to a warrant is not justified. In short, a search pursuant to consent may result in considerably less inconvenience for the subject of the search, and, properly conducted, is a constitutionally permissible and wholly legitimate aspect of effective police activity.

But the Fourth and Fourteenth Amendments require that a consent not be coerced, by explicit or implicit means, by implied threat or covert force. For, no matter how subtly the coercion was applied, the resulting "consent" would be no more than a pretext for the unjustified police intrusion against which the Fourth Amendment is directed. * * *

The problem of reconciling the recognized legitimacy of consent searches with the requirement that they be free from any aspect of official coercion cannot be resolved by any infallible touchstone. * * * Just as was true with confessions, the requirement of a "voluntary" consent reflects a fair accommodation of the constitutional requirements involved. In examining all the surrounding circumstances to determine if in fact the consent to search was coerced, account must be taken of subtly coercive police questions, as well as the possibly vulnerable subjective state of the person who consents. Those searches that are the product of police coercion can thus be filtered out without undermining the continuing validity of consent searches. In sum, there is no reason for us to depart in the area of consent searches, from the traditional definition of "voluntariness."

The approach of the Court of Appeals for the Ninth Circuit finds no support in any of our decisions that have attempted to define the meaning of "voluntariness." Its ruling, that the State must affirmatively prove that the subject of the search knew that he had a right to refuse consent, would, in practice, create serious doubt whether consent searches could continue to be conducted. There might be rare cases where it could be proved from the record that a person in fact affirmatively knew of his right to refuse—such as a case where he announced to the police that if he didn't sign the consent form, "you [police] are going to get a search warrant"; or a case where by prior experience and training a person had clearly and convincingly demonstrated such knowledge. But more commonly where there was no evidence of any coercion, explicit or implicit, the prosecution would nevertheless be unable to demonstrate that the subject of the search in fact had known of his right to refuse consent. * * *

One alternative that would go far toward proving that the subject of a search did know he had a right to refuse consent would be to advise him of that right before eliciting his consent. That, however, is a suggestion that has been almost universally repudiated by both federal and state courts, and, we think, rightly so. For it would be thoroughly impractical to impose on the normal consent search the detailed requirements of an effective warning. Consent searches are part of the standard investigatory techniques of law enforcement agencies. They normally occur on the highway, or in a person's home or office, and under informal and unstructured conditions. The circumstances that prompt the initial request to search may develop quickly or be a logical extension of investigative police questioning. The police may seek to investigate further suspicious circumstances or to follow up leads developed in questioning persons at the scene of a crime. These situations are a far cry from the structured atmosphere of a trial where, assisted by counsel if he chooses, a defendant is informed of his trial rights. And, while surely a closer question, these situations are still immeasurably far removed from "custodial interrogation" where, in *Miranda v. Arizona*, [p. 581], we found that the Constitution required certain now familiar warnings as a prerequisite to police interrogation. * * *

In short, neither this Court's prior cases, nor the traditional definition of "voluntariness" requires proof of knowledge of a right to refuse as the *sine qua non* of an effective consent to a search.

C

It is said, however, that a "consent" is a "waiver" of a person's rights under the Fourth and Fourteenth Amendments. The argument is that by allowing the police to conduct a search, a person "waives" whatever right he had to prevent the police from searching. It is argued that under the doctrine of *Johnson v. Zerbst*, 304 U.S. 458, 464, 58 S.Ct. 1019, 1023, 82 L.Ed. 1461 [1938], to establish such a "waiver" the State must demonstrate "an intentional relinquishment or abandonment of a known right or privilege."

But these standards were enunciated in *Johnson* in the context of the safeguards of a fair criminal trial. Our cases do not reflect an uncritical demand for a knowing and intelligent waiver in every situation where a person has failed to invoke a constitutional protection. * * *

The requirement of a "knowing" and "intelligent" waiver was articulated in a case involving the validity of a defendant's decision to forgo a right constitutionally guaranteed to protect a fair trial and the reliability of the truth-determining process. *Johnson v. Zerbst*, *supra*, dealt with the denial of counsel in a federal criminal trial. * * *

There is a vast difference between those rights that protect a fair criminal trial and the rights guaranteed under the Fourth Amendment. Nothing, either in the purposes behind requiring a "knowing" and "intelligent" waiver of trial rights, or in the practical application of such a requirement suggests that it ought to be extended to the constitutional guarantee against unreasonable searches and seizures.

A strict standard of waiver has been applied to those rights guaranteed to a criminal defendant to insure that he will be accorded the greatest possible opportunity to utilize every facet of the constitutional model of a fair criminal trial. Any trial conducted in derogation of that model leaves open the possibility that the trial reached an unfair result precisely because all the protections specified in the Constitution were not provided. A prime example is the right to counsel. For without that right, a wholly innocent accused faces the real and substantial danger that simply because of his lack of legal expertise, he may be convicted. * * *

The protections of the Fourth Amendment are of a wholly different order, and have nothing whatever to do with promoting the fair ascertainment of truth at a criminal trial. * * *

Nor can it even be said that a search, as opposed to an eventual trial, is somehow "unfair" if a person consents to a search. While the Fourth and Fourteenth Amendments limit the circumstances under which the police can conduct a search, there is nothing constitutionally suspect in a person's voluntarily allowing a search. The actual conduct of the search may be precisely the same as if the police had obtained a warrant. And, unlike those constitutional guarantees that protect a defendant at trial, it cannot be said every reasonable presumption ought to be indulged against voluntary relinquishment. * * * Rather, the community has a real interest in encouraging consent, for the resulting search may yield necessary evidence for the solution and prosecution of crime, evidence that may insure that a wholly innocent person is not wrongly charged with a criminal offense.

* * * To be true to *Johnson* and its progeny, there must be examination into the knowing and understanding nature of the waiver, an examination that was designed for a trial judge in the structured atmosphere of a courtroom. * * * It would be unrealistic to expect that in the informal, unstructured context of a consent search, a policeman, upon pain of tainting the evidence obtained, could make the detailed type of examination demanded by *Johnson*. And, if for this reason a diluted form of "waiver" were found acceptable, that would itself be ample recognition of the fact that there is no universal standard that must be applied in every situation where a person forgoes a constitutional right.

Similarly, a "waiver" approach to consent searches would be thoroughly inconsistent with our decisions that have approved "third party consents." In *Coolidge v. New Hampshire*[, 403 U.S. 443, 91 S.Ct. 2022, 29 L.Ed.2d 564 (1971)], where a wife surrendered to the police guns and clothing belonging to her husband, we found nothing constitutionally impermissible in the admission of that evidence at trial since the wife had not been coerced. * * * Yet it is inconceivable that the Constitution could countenance the waiver of a defendant's right to counsel by a third party, or that a waiver could be found because a trial judge reasonably, though mistakenly, believed a defendant had waived his right to plead not guilty.

In short, there is nothing in the purposes or application of the waiver requirements of *Johnson v. Zerbst* that justifies, much less compels, the easy equation of a knowing waiver with a consent search. * * *

D

Much of what has already been said disposes of the argument that the Court's decision in the *Miranda* case requires the conclusion that knowledge of a right to refuse is an indispensable element of a valid consent. The considerations that informed the Court's holding in *Miranda* are simply inapplicable in the present case. * * *

In this case, there is no evidence of any inherently coercive tactics—either from the nature of the police questioning or the environment in which it took place. Indeed, since consent searches will normally occur on a person's own familiar territory, the specter of incommunicado police interrogation in some remote station house is simply inapposite. There is no reason to believe, under circumstances such as are present here, that the response to a policeman's question is presumptively coerced; and there is, therefore, no reason to reject the traditional test for determining the voluntariness of a person's response. * * *

It is also argued that the failure to require the Government to establish knowledge as a prerequisite to a valid consent, will relegate the Fourth Amendment to the special province of "the sophisticated, the knowledgeable and the privileged." We cannot agree. The traditional definition of voluntariness we accept today has always taken into account evidence of minimal schooling, low intelligence, and the lack of any effective warnings to a person of his rights; and the voluntariness of any statement taken under those conditions has been carefully scrutinized to determine whether it was in fact voluntarily given.

E

Our decision today is a narrow one. We hold only that when the subject of a search is not in custody and the State attempts to justify a search on the basis of his consent, the Fourth and Fourteenth Amendments require that it demonstrate that the consent was in fact voluntarily given, and not the result of duress or coercion, express or implied. Voluntariness is a question of fact to be determined from all the circumstances, and while the subject's knowledge of a right to refuse is a factor to be taken into account, the prosecution is not required to demonstrate such knowledge as a prerequisite to establishing a voluntary consent. * * *

[The concurring opinions of Justices Blackmun and Powell, and the dissenting opinions of Justices Douglas and Brennan, are omitted.]

Mr. Justice MARSHALL, dissenting. * * *

I * * *

A

The Court assumes that the issue in this case is: what are the standards by which courts are to determine that consent is voluntarily given? It then imports into the law of search and seizure standards developed to decide entirely different questions about coerced confessions.

The Fifth Amendment, in terms, provides that no person "shall be compelled in any criminal case to be a witness against himself." * * * The inquiry in a case where a confession is challenged as having been elicited in an unconstitutional manner is, therefore, whether the behavior of the police amounted to compulsion of the defendant. Because of the nature of the right to be free of compulsion, it would be pointless to ask whether a defendant knew of it before he made a statement; no sane person would knowingly relinquish a right to be free of compulsion. Thus, the questions of compulsion and of violation of the right itself are inextricably intertwined. The cases involving coerced confessions, therefore, pass over the question of knowledge of that right as irrelevant, and turn directly to the question of compulsion. * * *

B

In contrast, this case deals not with "coercion," but with "consent," a subtly different concept to which different standards have been applied in the past. Freedom from coercion is a substantive right, guaranteed by the Fifth and Fourteenth Amendments. Consent, however, is a mechanism by which substantive requirements, otherwise applicable, are avoided. * * * Thus, consent searches are permitted, not because * * * an exception to the requirements of probable cause and warrant is essential to proper law enforcement, but because we permit our citizens to choose whether or not they wish to exercise their constitutional rights. Our prior decisions simply do not support the view that a meaningful choice has been made solely because no coercion was brought to bear on the subject. * * *

II * * *

If consent to search means that a person has chosen to forgo his right to exclude the police from the place they seek to search, it follows that his consent cannot be considered a meaningful choice unless he knew that he could in fact exclude the police. * * * I would therefore hold, at a minimum, that the prosecution may not rely on a purported consent to search if the subject of the search did not know that he could refuse to give consent. * * *

If one accepts this view, the question then is a simple one: must the Government show that the subject knew of his rights, or must the subject show that he lacked such knowledge?

I think that any fair allocation of the burden would require that it be placed on the prosecution. * * *

If the burden is placed on the defendant, all the subject can do is to testify that he did not know of his rights. And I doubt that many trial judges will find for the defendant simply on the basis of that testimony. Precisely because the evidence is very hard to come by, courts have traditionally been reluctant to require a party to prove negatives such as the lack of knowledge.

In contrast, there are several ways by which the subject's knowledge of his rights may be shown. The subject may affirmatively demonstrate such knowledge by his responses at the time the search took place * * *. Where, as in this case, the person giving consent is someone other than the defendant, the prosecution may require him to testify under oath. Denials of knowledge may be disproved by establishing that the subject had, in the recent past, demonstrated his knowledge of his rights, for example, by refusing entry when it was requested by the police. The prior experience or training of the subject might in some cases support an inference that he knew of his right to exclude the police.

The burden on the prosecutor would disappear, of course, if the police, at the time they requested consent to search, also told the subject that he had a right to refuse consent and that his decision to refuse would be respected. The Court's assertions to the contrary notwithstanding, there is nothing impractical about this method of satisfying the prosecution's burden of proof. * * *

The Court contends that if an officer paused to inform the subject of his rights, the informality of the exchange would be destroyed. I doubt that a simple statement by an officer of an individual's right to refuse consent would do much to alter the informality of the exchange, except to alert the subject to a fact that he surely is entitled to know. It is not without significance that for many years the agents of the Federal Bureau of Investigation have routinely informed subjects of their right to refuse consent, when they request consent to search. * * *

I must conclude, with some reluctance, that when the Court speaks of practicality, what it really is talking of is the continued ability of the police to capitalize on the ignorance of citizens so as to accomplish by subterfuge what they could not achieve by relying only on the knowing relinquishment of constitutional rights. Of course it would be "practical" for the police to ignore the commands of the Fourth Amendment, if by practicality we mean that more criminals will be apprehended, even though the constitutional rights of innocent people also go by the board. But such a practical advantage is achieved only at the cost of permitting the police to disregard the limitations that the Constitution places on their behavior, a cost that a constitutional democracy cannot long absorb. * * *

NOTES AND QUESTIONS

1. *A view from the trenches.* There are no precise data on how often searches are conducted on the basis of consent, but one study reported that the two most common warrant "exceptions" are consent and search incident to a lawful arrest, with one detective suggesting that as many as 98 percent of warrantless searches fall under the "consent" umbrella. Richard Van Duizend et al., The Search Warrant Process: Preconceptions, Perceptions, and Prac-

tices 21 (1984). Even if this figure is inflated, it suggests that consent issues are of profound importance in the "real world" of searches and seizures.

2.   Warrant exceptions require a rationale. As we have seen, warrantless car searches are justified on the grounds of mobility and the lesser expectation of privacy we possess in vehicles. Warrantless searches incident to arrest are justified on the ground that the police must protect themselves from possible attack and prevent destruction of evidence. Why is a warrantless search based on consent allowed? What does *Schneckloth* suggest?

3.   Arnold H. Loewy, *Cops, Cars, and Citizens: Fixing the Broken Balance*, 76 St. John's L. Rev. 535, 554 (2002):

> From the detainees' perspective [in *Schneckloth*], there was little that appeared voluntary. They were stopped at 2:40 in the morning, asked (ordered?) to exit the car, and witnessed the arrival of two reinforcement police officers. They were then asked to search the car without being told that "no" was an option. Can anyone not thoroughly steeped in legal fiction really believe that they thought "no" was one of their options?

Do you agree with Loewy? If so, why did the Supreme Court rule as it did?

4.   *Why do guilty people consent?* "Every year I witness the same mass incredulity. Why, one hundred criminal procedure students jointly wonder, would someone 'voluntarily' consent to allow a police officer to search the trunk of his car, knowing that massive amounts of cocaine are easily visible there?" Marcy Strauss, *Reconstructing Consent*, 92 J. Crim. L. & Criminology 211, 211 (2001). Have you thought the same thing?

One court has gone so far as to observe that "no sane man who denies his guilt would actually be willing that policemen search his room for contraband which is certain to be discovered." Higgins v. United States, 209 F.2d 819 (D.C. Cir. 1954). Do you agree? If so, why *do* courts so often find that voluntary consent has been granted? Is it that "observers outside the situation"—including judges—"systematically overestimate the extent to which citizens in police encounters feel free to refuse [consent]"? Janice Nadler, *No Need to Shout: Bus Sweeps and the Psychology of Coercion*, 2002 Sup. Ct. Rev. 153, 156. Or, is there another explanation?

5.   *More of the same.* In Ohio v. Robinette, 519 U.S. 33, 117 S.Ct. 417, 136 L.Ed.2d 347 (1996), *O*, an officer, lawfully detained *R* for speeding. After checking *R*'s license and finding no outstanding violations, *O* asked *R* to get out of the car, after which he issued *R* a verbal warning for speeding and returned the license. *O* then said, "[o]ne question before you get gone. Are you carrying any illegal contraband in your car? Any weapons of any kind, drugs, anything like that?" After *R* said that he was not in possession of contraband, *O* sought and obtained consent to search the car. The search turned up a small amount of marijuana and, in a film cannister, a pill later determined to be a controlled substance.

R argued that his consent was involuntary because he was not informed by *O* that he was free to go after return of his driver's license. As in *Schneckloth*, the Court here ruled that, although knowledge is a factor to be taken into account in voluntariness analysis, there is no categorical requirement that police officers inform "detainees that they are free to go before a consent to search may be deemed voluntary."

6. *Another view from the trenches.* The facts in *Robinette* (Note 5) repeat themselves often, with slight variations. Consider: A deputy sheriff pulled over three young men he saw drinking beer while driving in a rural area. Having open beer in the car was not a violation of state law, but the deputy surely had probable cause to think the driver might be intoxicated. The deputy ordered the driver to undergo a field sobriety test. Luckily for the driver, he had had only one beer and thus passed the test. Disgruntled, the deputy said (possibly a general question always to ask): "You boys mind if I take a look in your trunk." After a brief pause, the driver said, "No, sir." In the trunk, in plain view, was a modest amount of cocaine and some drug paraphernalia. The deputy seized these items and arrested all three men, who turned out to be college students.

Defendants retained one of the authors of this book to represent them. In the preliminary interview, their lawyer asked the obvious question: "You knew that stuff was in the trunk?" "Yes." "You're college students. College students are usually at least as smart as average people, so here it comes: why in the world did you consent?"

The sheepish response, which may explain a lot about this kind of consent case, was: "I thought if I didn't consent, the deputy would hold us and get a warrant; also, I thought if we were cooperative, he might overlook the small amount."

"You thought a deputy sheriff was going to overlook Schedule 2 drugs?"

Shrug: "I thought it was our only chance. If he got a warrant, I knew we were finished."

Is this valid consent under the majority opinion in *Schneckloth*? If so, does this case persuade you that Justice Marshall got the better of the argument in the case?

7. In *Bumper v. North Carolina*, 391 U.S. 543, 88 S.Ct. 1788, 20 L.Ed.2d 797 (1968), four white law enforcement officers went to the house of Hattie Leath, a 66-year-old African-American widow. According to the Court, the house was "located in a rural area at the end of an isolated mile-long dirt road." Ms. Leath met the officers at the front door. One of the officers told her, "I have a search warrant to search your house." She replied, "go ahead," and opened the door. At trial, the Government did not rely on a warrant to justify the search, but instead claimed that Ms. Leath voluntarily consented. The Supreme Court disagreed:

> When a prosecutor seeks to rely upon consent to justify the lawful-ness of a search, he has the burden of proving that the consent was, in fact, freely and voluntarily given. This burden cannot be discharged by showing no more than acquiescence to a claim of lawful authority. * * *

> When a law enforcement officer claims authority to search a home under a warrant, he announces in effect that the occupant has no right to resist the search. The situation is instinct with coercion—albeit colorably lawful coercion. Where there is coercion there cannot be consent.

Is *Bumper* consistent with the totality-of-circumstances test of voluntariness announced years later in *Schneckloth*?

Suppose Ms. Leath had told the officers, "I don't care about the warrant, feel free to search my house." Valid consent?

8. *Consent, race, and class.* Apparently most or all of the occupants of the Schneckloth vehicle were Hispanic. Should the Court have considered the possible disparate effect of the rule it was announcing in *Schneckloth* on persons of different races, cultures, and economic classes? Consider:

> Such reliance on ignorance and thinly veiled coercion is deeply troubling. As a very different Supreme Court said in 1964, "no system of criminal justice can, or should survive if it comes to depend for its continued effectiveness on the citizens' abdication through unawareness of their constitutional rights." [Escobedo v. Illinois, 378 U.S. 478, 490, 84 S.Ct. 1758, 12 L.Ed.2d 977 (1964).] The current system created two Fourth Amendments—one for people who are aware of their right to say no and confident enough to assert the right against a police officer, and another for those who do not know their rights or are afraid to assert them.

> This doubtful standard would be problematic even if it did not closely parallel race and class lines. * * * [T]he consent doctrine in application is likely to reflect race and class divisions. Because a consent search requires no objective individualized suspicion, it is more likely to be directed at poor young black men than wealthy white elderly women. In addition, those who are white and wealthy are more likely to know their rights and to feel secure in asserting them.

David Cole, No Equal Justice 31 (1999). Is Professor Cole correct? If so, in light of *Schneckloth*'s announcement of a totality-of-circumstances test, should a court take into consideration the race and class of the suspect in determining the voluntariness of consent?

In this regard, Professor Cole, *id.* at 33–34, reports:

> [O]ne of my students reports that when she attempted to teach the consent doctrine to prisoners at a federal prison in Virginia, her predominantly black and Hispanic students ridiculed the notion. They maintained that although it might be true that she, a white woman, had the right to consent, if they declined consent, the police would either beat them or go ahead and search anyway, and then testify that they had consented. It is of course difficult to verify such statements, but that perception itself will factor into a citizen's decision to assert her rights.

9. Even if a person voluntarily consents to a search, she can set limits of a temporal nature ("You may search my house for exactly two minutes and no more.") or limit the scope of the search ("You may search my kitchen and living room, but not the bedroom."). The latter issue is considered more fully at p. 343, Note 4.

A person may also withdraw consent after it is granted. The police must honor the citizen's wishes, unless their pre-withdrawal search gives them independent grounds to proceed. But, the issue of whether a defendant has truly withdrawn consent, like voluntariness, can be a difficult one to resolve.

For example, in Carter v. State, 762 So.2d 1024 (Fla.App.2000), *C* consented in writing to a search of his bedroom in a robbery investigation. He asked if he could be present during the search, and the police agreed. Thereafter, *C* became angry and unruly when a third party arrived at the scene and identified him as the robber. Because *C* did not settle down, the police moved him to the police car, where *C* said, "That's not fair. You promised that I would be able to be there when you searched." Has *C* withdrawn his consent?

10. *Problem.* Assume that the police believe that there is evidence of *D*'s involvement in a crime on her computer, but they lack probable cause to seek a warrant to search it. Therefore, they seek and obtain valid consent to search the computer for the evidence. Two days later, however, *D*'s lawyer advises her to withdraw her consent, which she does. But, now consider this twist: Apparently what the police typically do in such cases is get a computer forensic expert to create an image of the suspect's hard drive, so that there are two copies of the data—the original and the "image copy." This is done because ordinary searching of a hard drive can alter the data it contains. Typically, the image copy is made quickly after the police take possession of the computer, but well before they actually search the image. (This is because the image copy is a so-called "bitstream copy," which looks like a lot of "1"s" and "0's," and actual translation takes considerable time.)

Assume that *D*'s withdrawal of consent occurs *after* the image copy is made but *before* it is searched. The police return the computer but later search the image copy. Is this permissible?

GEORGIA v. RANDOLPH

Supreme Court of the United States, 2006.
547 U.S. 103, 126 S.Ct. 1515, 164 L.Ed.2d 208.

JUSTICE SOUTER delivered the opinion of the Court [in which Stevens, Kennedy, Ginsburg, and Breyer, JJ., joined].

The Fourth Amendment recognizes a valid warrantless entry and search of premises when police obtain the voluntary consent of an occupant who shares * * * authority over the area in common with a co-occupant who later objects to the use of evidence so obtained. *United States v. Matlock,* 415 U.S. 164, 94 S.Ct. 988, 39 L.Ed.2d 242 (1974). The question here is whether such an evidentiary seizure is likewise lawful with the permission of one occupant when the other, who later seeks to suppress the evidence, is present at the scene and expressly refuses to consent. We hold that, in the circumstances here at issue, a physically present co-occupant's stated refusal to permit entry prevails, rendering the warrantless search unreasonable and invalid as to him.

I

Respondent Scott Randolph and his wife, Janet, separated in late May 2001, when she left the marital residence in Americus, Georgia, and went to stay with her parents in Canada, taking their son and some belongings. In July, she returned to the Americus house with the child, though the record does not reveal whether her object was reconciliation or retrieval of remaining possessions.

On the morning of July 6, she complained to the police that after a domestic dispute her husband took their son away, and when officers reached the house she told them that her husband was a cocaine user whose habit had caused financial troubles. * * * Shortly after the police arrived, Scott Randolph returned and explained that he had removed the child to a neighbor's house out of concern that his wife might take the boy out of the country again; he denied cocaine use, and countered that it was in fact his wife who abused drugs and alcohol.

* * * Sergeant Murray asked Scott Randolph for permission to search the house, which he unequivocally refused.

The sergeant turned to Janet Randolph for consent to search, which she readily gave. She led the officer upstairs to a bedroom that she identified as Scott's, where the sergeant noticed a section of a drinking straw with a powdery residue he suspected was cocaine. * * * The police took the straw to the police station * * *. * * * Scott Randolph was indicted for possession of cocaine.

He moved to suppress the evidence, as products of a warrantless search of his house unauthorized by his wife's consent over his express refusal. The trial court denied the motion, ruling that Janet Randolph had common authority to consent to the search.

The Court of Appeals of Georgia reversed, and was itself sustained by the State Supreme Court * * *. * * *

We granted certiorari to resolve a split of authority on whether one occupant may give law enforcement effective consent to search shared premises, as against a co-tenant who is present and states a refusal to permit the search.[5] We now affirm.

II

To the Fourth Amendment rule ordinarily prohibiting the warrantless entry of a person's house as unreasonable *per se,* one "jealously and carefully drawn" exception recognizes the validity of searches with the voluntary consent of an individual possessing authority. That person might be the householder against whom evidence is sought, or a fellow occupant who shares common authority over property, when the suspect is absent, *Matlock, supra.* * * * None of our co-occupant consent-to-search cases, however, has presented the further fact of a second occupant physically present and refusing permission to search, and later moving to suppress evidence so obtained. The significance of such a refusal turns on the underpinnings of the co-occupant consent rule, as recognized since *Matlock*.

---

5. All four Courts of Appeals to have considered this question have concluded that consent remains effective in the face of an express objection. Of the state courts that have addressed the question, the majority have reached that conclusion as well.

A

The defendant in that case was arrested in the yard of a house where he lived with a Mrs. Graff and several of her relatives, and was detained in a squad car parked nearby. When the police went to the door, Mrs. Graff admitted them and consented to a search of the house. In resolving the defendant's objection to use of the evidence taken in the warrantless search, we said that "the consent of one who possesses common authority over premises or effects is valid as against the absent, nonconsenting person with whom that authority is shared." Consistent with our prior understanding that Fourth Amendment rights are not limited by the law of property, we explained that the third party's "common authority" is not synonymous with a technical property interest:

"The authority which justified the third-party consent does not rest upon the law of property, with its attendant historical and legal refinement, but rests rather on mutual use of the property by persons generally having joint access or control for most purposes, so that it is reasonable to recognize that any of the co-inhabitants has the right to permit the inspection in his own right and that the others have assumed the risk that one of their number might permit the common area to be searched."

* * *

The constant element in assessing Fourth Amendment reasonableness in the consent cases, then, is the great significance given to widely shared social expectations, which are naturally enough influenced by the law of property, but not controlled by its rules. *Matlock* accordingly not only holds that a solitary co-inhabitant may sometimes consent to a search of shared premises, but stands for the proposition that the reasonableness of such a search is in significant part a function of commonly held under-standing about the authority that co-inhabitants may exercise in ways that affect each other's interests.

B

Matlock's example of common understanding is readily apparent. When someone comes to the door of a domestic dwelling with a baby at her hip, as Mrs. Graff did, she shows that she belongs there, and that fact standing alone is enough to tell a law enforcement officer or any other visitor that if she occupies the place along with others, she probably lives there subject to the assumption tenants usually make about their common authority when they share quarters. They understand that any one of them may admit visitors, with the consequence that a guest obnoxious to one may nevertheless be admitted in his absence by another. As *Matlock* put it, shared tenancy is understood to include an "assumption of risk," on which police officers are entitled to rely, and although some group living together might make an exceptional arrangement that no one could admit a guest without the agreement of all, the chance of such an eccentric scheme is too remote to expect visitors to investigate a particular household's rules before accepting an invitation to come in. So, *Matlock* relied on what was usual and placed no burden on the police to eliminate the possibility of atypical arrangements, in the absence of reason to doubt that the regular scheme was in place.

It is also easy to imagine different facts on which, if known, no common authority could sensibly be suspected. A person on the scene who identifies himself, say, as a landlord or a hotel manager calls up no customary understanding of authority to admit guests without the consent of the current occupant. A tenant in the ordinary course does not take rented premises subject to any formal or informal agreement that the landlord may let visitors into the dwelling, and a hotel guest customarily has no reason to expect the manager to allow anyone but his own employees into his room. In these circumstances, neither state-law property rights, nor common contractual arrangements, nor any other source points to a common understanding of authority to admit third parties generally without the consent of a person occupying the premises. And when it comes to searching through bureau drawers, there will be instances in which even a person clearly belonging on premises as an occupant may lack any perceived authority to consent; "a child of eight might well be considered to have the power to consent to the police crossing the threshold into that part of the house where any caller, such as a pollster or salesman, might well be admitted," but no one would reasonably expect such a child to be in a position to authorize anyone to rummage through his parents' bedroom.

C

Although we have not dealt directly with the reasonableness of police entry in reliance on consent by one occupant subject to immediate challenge by another, we took a step toward the issue in an earlier case dealing with the Fourth Amendment rights of a social guest arrested at premises the police entered without a warrant or the benefit of any exception to the warrant requirement. *Minnesota v. Olson,* [p. 458, Note 6, infra], held that overnight houseguests have a legitimate expectation of privacy in their temporary quarters because "it is unlikely that [the host] will admit someone who wants to see or meet with the guest over the objection of the guest." If that customary expectation of courtesy or deference is a foundation of Fourth Amendment rights of a houseguest, it presumably should follow that an inhabitant of shared premises may claim at least as much, and it turns out that the co-inhabitant naturally has an even stronger claim.

To begin with, it is fair to say that a caller standing at the door of shared premises would have no confidence that one occupant's invitation was a sufficiently good reason to enter when a fellow tenant stood there saying, "stay out." Without some very good reason, no sensible person would go inside under those conditions. Fear for the safety of the occupant issuing the invitation, or of someone else inside, would be thought to justify entry, but the justification then would be the personal risk, the threats to life or limb, not the disputed invitation.

The visitor's reticence without some such good reason would show not timidity but a realization that when people living together disagree over the use of their common quarters, a resolution must come through voluntary accommodation, not by appeals to authority. Unless the people living together fall within some recognized hierarchy, like a household of parent and child or barracks housing military personnel of different grades, there is no societal understanding of superior and inferior, a fact reflected in a standard formulation of domestic property law * * *. * * * In sum, there is no common understanding that one co-tenant generally has a right or authority to prevail over the express wishes of another, whether the issue is the color of the curtains or invitations to outsiders.

D

Since the co-tenant wishing to open the door to a third party has no recognized authority in law or social practice to prevail over a present and objecting co-tenant, his disputed invitation, without more, gives a police officer no better claim to reasonableness in entering than the officer would have in the absence of any consent at all. Accordingly, in the balancing of competing individual and governmental interests entailed by the bar to unreasonable searches, the cooperative occupant's invitation adds nothing to the government's side to counter the force of an objecting individual's claim to security against the government's intrusion into his dwelling place. Since we hold to the "centuries-old principle of respect for the privacy of the home," "it is beyond dispute that the home is entitled to special protection as the center of the private lives of our people." We have, after all, lived our whole national history with an understanding of "the ancient adage that a man's home is his castle [to the point that t]he poorest man may in his cottage bid defiance to all the forces of the Crown."[4]

Disputed permission is thus no match for this central value of the Fourth Amendment, and the State's other countervailing claims do not add up to outweigh it.[5] Yes, we recognize the consenting tenant's interest as a citizen in bringing criminal activity to light. And we understand a co-tenant's legitimate self-interest in siding with the police to deflect suspicion raised by sharing quarters with a criminal.

---

4. In the dissent's view, the centuries of special protection for the privacy of the home are over. The principal dissent equates inviting the police into a co-tenant's home over his contemporaneous objection with reporting a secret, and the emphasis it places on the false equation suggests a deliberate intent to devalue the importance of the privacy of a dwelling place. The same attitude that privacy of a dwelling is not special underlies the dissent's easy assumption that privacy shared with another individual is privacy waived for all purposes including warrantless searches by the police.

5. A generalized interest in expedient law enforcement cannot, without more, justify a warrantless search. *Coolidge* v. *New Hampshire,* 403 U.S. 443, 481, 91 S.Ct. 2022, 29 L.Ed.2d 564 (1971) ("The warrant requirement * * * is not an inconvenience to be somehow 'weighed' against the claims of police efficiency").

But society can often have the benefit of these interests without relying on a theory of consent that ignores an inhabitant's refusal to allow a warrantless search. The co-tenant acting on his own initiative may be able to deliver evidence to the police, and can tell the police what he knows, for use before a magistrate in getting a warrant.[6] The reliance on a co-tenant's information instead of disputed consent accords with the law's general partiality toward "police action taken under a warrant [as against] searches and seizures without one" * * *.

Nor should this established policy of Fourth Amendment law be undermined by the principal dissent's claim that it shields spousal abusers and other violent co-tenants who will refuse to allow the police to enter a dwelling when their victims ask the police for help. It is not that the dissent exaggerates violence in the home; we recognize that domestic abuse is a serious problem in the United States.

But this case has no bearing on the capacity of the police to protect domestic victims. * * * No question has been raised, or reasonably could be, about the authority of the police to enter a dwelling to protect a resident from domestic violence; so long as they have good reason to believe such a threat exists, it would be silly to suggest that the police would commit a tort by entering, say, to give a complaining tenant the opportunity to collect belongings and get out safely, or to determine whether violence (or threat of violence) has just occurred or is about to (or soon will) occur, however much a spouse or other co-tenant objected. (And since the police would then be lawfully in the premises, there is no question that they could seize any evidence in plain view or take further action supported by any consequent probable cause.) Thus, the question whether the police might lawfully enter over objection in order to provide any protection that might be reasonable is easily answered yes. The undoubted right of the police to enter in order to protect a victim, however, has nothing to do with the question in this case, whether a search with the consent of one co-tenant is good against another, standing at the door and expressly refusing consent. * * *

The dissent's red herring aside, we know, of course, that alternatives to disputed consent will not always open the door to search for evidence that the police suspect is inside. The consenting tenant may simply not disclose enough information, or information factual enough, to add up to a showing of probable cause, and there may be no exigency to justify fast action. But nothing in social custom or its reflection in private law argues

---

6. Sometimes, of course, the very exchange of information like this in front of the objecting inhabitant may render consent irrelevant by creating an exigency that justifies immediate action on the police's part; if the objecting tenant cannot be incapacitated from destroying easily disposable evidence during the time required to get a warrant, see *Illinois v. McArthur,* [p. 207, Note 6, *supra*] (denying suspect access to his trailer home while police applied for a search warrant), a fairly perceived need to act on the spot to preserve evidence may justify entry and search under the exigent circumstances exception to the warrant requirement.

Additional exigent circumstances might justify warrantless searches. See, *e.g., Warden, Md. Penitentiary v. Hayden,* [p. 211, *supra*] (hot pursuit); *Chimel v. California,* [p. 218, *supra*] (protecting the safety of the police officers) * * *.

for placing a higher value on delving into private premises to search for evidence in the face of disputed consent, than on requiring clear justification before the government searches private living quarters over a resident's objection. We therefore hold that a warrantless search of a shared dwelling for evidence over the express refusal of consent by a physically present resident cannot be justified as reasonable as to him on the basis of consent given to the police by another resident.[8]

E

There are two loose ends, the first being the explanation given in *Matlock* for the constitutional sufficiency of a co-tenant's consent to enter and search: it "rests * * * on mutual use of the property by persons generally having joint access or control for most purposes, so that it is reasonable to recognize that any of the co-inhabitants has the right to permit the inspection in his own right * * *." If *Matlock's* co-tenant is giving permission "in his own right," how can his "own right" be eliminated by another tenant's objection? The answer appears in the very footnote from which the quoted statement is taken: the "right" to admit the police to which *Matlock* refers is not an enduring and enforceable ownership right as understood by the private law of property, but is instead the authority recognized by customary social usage as having a substantial bearing on Fourth Amendment reasonableness in specific circumstances. Thus, to ask whether the consenting tenant has the right to admit the police when a physically present fellow tenant objects is not to question whether some property right may be divested by the mere objection of another. It is, rather, the question whether customary social understanding accords the consenting tenant authority powerful enough to prevail over the co-tenant's objection. The *Matlock* Court did not purport to answer this question, a point made clear by another statement (which the dissent does not quote): the Court described the co-tenant's consent as good against "the absent, nonconsenting resident."

The second loose end is the significance of *Matlock* * * * and [*Illinois v.*] *Rodriguez* [p. 336, infra] after today's decision. Although the *Matlock* defendant was not present with the opportunity to object, he was in a squad car not far away; the *Rodriguez* defendant was actually asleep in the apartment, and the police might have roused him with a knock on the door before they entered with only the consent of an apparent co-tenant. If those cases are not to be undercut by today's holding, we have to admit that we are drawing a fine line; if a potential defendant with self-interest in objecting is in fact at the door and objects, the co-tenant's permission does not suffice for a reasonable search, whereas the potential objector, nearby but not invited to take part in the threshold colloquy, loses out.

---

8. The dissent is critical that our holding does not pass upon the constitutionality of such a search as to a third tenant against whom the government wishes to use evidence seized after a search with consent of one co-tenant subject to the contemporaneous objection of another. We decide the case before us, not a different one.

This is the line we draw, and we think the formalism is justified. So long as there is no evidence that the police have removed the potentially objecting tenant from the entrance for the sake of avoiding a possible objection, there is practical value in the simple clarity of complementary rules, one recognizing the co-tenant's permission when there is no fellow occupant on hand, the other according dispositive weight to the fellow occupant's contrary indication when he expresses it. * * * Better to accept the formalism of distinguishing *Matlock* from this case than to impose a requirement [of seeking out any co-tenant to determine his wishes], time-consuming in the field and in the courtroom, with no apparent systemic justification. * * *

III

This case invites a straightforward application of the rule that a physically present inhabitant's express refusal of consent to a police search is dispositive as to him, regardless of the consent of a fellow occupant. * * * The State does not argue that she gave any indication to the police of a need for protection inside the house that might have justified entry into the portion of the premises where the police found the powdery straw * * *. Nor does the State claim that the entry and search should be upheld under the rubric of exigent circumstances, owing to some apprehension by the police officers that Scott Randolph would destroy evidence of drug use before any warrant could be obtained.

The judgment of the Supreme Court of Georgia is therefore affirmed.

Justice ALITO took no part in the consideration or decision of this case.

Justice STEVENS, concurring.

The study of history for the purpose of ascertaining the original understanding of constitutional provisions is much like the study of legislative history for the purpose of ascertaining the intent of the law-makers who enact statutes. In both situations the facts uncovered by the study are usually relevant but not necessarily dispositive. This case illustrates why even the most dedicated adherent to an approach to constitutional interpretation that places primary reliance on the search for original understanding would recognize the relevance of changes in our society.

At least since 1604 it has been settled that in the absence of exigent circumstances, a government agent has no right to enter a "house" or "castle" unless authorized to do so by a valid warrant. Every occupant of the home has a right-protected by the common law for centuries and by the Fourth Amendment since 1791—to refuse entry. When an occupant gives his or her consent to enter, he or she is waiving a valuable constitutional right. * * * The issue in this case relates to the content of the advice that the officer should provide when met at the door by a man and a woman who are apparently joint tenants or joint owners of the property.

In the 18th century, when the Fourth Amendment was adopted, the advice would have been quite different from what is appropriate today. Given the then-prevailing dramatic differences between the property rights of the husband and the far lesser rights of the wife, only the consent of the husband would matter. Whether "the master of the house" consented or objected, his decision would control. Thus if "original under-standing" were to govern the outcome of this case, the search was clearly invalid because the husband did not consent. History, however, is not dispositive because it is now clear, as a matter of constitutional law, that the male and the female are equal partners.

In today's world the only advice that an officer could properly give should make it clear that each of the partners has a constitutional right that he or she may independently assert or waive. Assuming that both spouses are competent, neither one is a master possessing the power to override the other's constitutional right to deny entry to their castle.

With these observations, I join the Court's opinion.

Justice BREYER, concurring.

If Fourth Amendment law forced us to choose between two bright-line rules, (1) a rule that always found one tenant's consent sufficient to justify a search without a warrant and (2) a rule that never did, I believe we should choose the first. That is because, as the Chief Justice's dissent points out, a rule permitting such searches can serve important law enforcement needs (for example, in domestic abuse cases) and the consent-ing party's joint tenancy diminishes the objecting party's reasonable expectation of privacy.

But the Fourth Amendment does not insist upon bright-line rules. Rather, it recognizes that no single set of legal rules can capture the ever changing complexity of human life. It consequently uses the general terms "unreasonable searches and seizures." And this Court has continuously emphasized that "[r]easonableness * * * is measured * * * by examining the totality of the circumstances."

The circumstances here include the following: The search at issue was a search solely for evidence. The objecting party was present and made his objection known clearly and directly to the officers seeking to enter the house. The officers did not justify their search on grounds of possible evidence destruction. And, as far as the record reveals, the officers might easily have secured the premises and sought a warrant permitting them to enter. Thus, the "totality of the circumstances" present here do not suffice to justify abandoning the Fourth Amendment's traditional hostility to police entry into a home without a warrant.

I stress the totality of the circumstances, however, because, were the circumstances to change significantly, so should the result. The Court's opinion does not apply where the objector is not present "and object[ing]."

Moreover, the risk of an ongoing crime or other exigent circumstance can make a critical difference. Consider, for example, instances of domestic abuse. * * * [L]aw enforcement officers must be able to respond effectively when confronted with the possibility of abuse.

If a possible abuse victim invites a responding officer to enter a home or consents to the officer's entry request, that invitation (or consent) itself could reflect the victim's fear about being left alone with an abuser. It could also indicate the availability of evidence, in the form of an immediate willingness to speak, that might not otherwise exist. In that context, an invitation (or consent) would provide a special reason for immediate, rather than later, police entry. And, entry following invitation or consent by one party ordinarily would be reasonable even in the face of direct objection by the other. That being so, contrary to the Chief Justice's suggestion, today's decision will not adversely affect ordinary law enforcement practices.

Given the case-specific nature of the Court's holding, and with these understandings, I join the Court's holding and its opinion.

Chief Justice ROBERTS, with whom Justice SCALIA joins, dissenting.

* * * The rule the majority fashions does not implement the high office of the Fourth Amendment to protect privacy, but instead provides protection on a random and happenstance basis, protecting, for example, a co-occupant who happens to be at the front door when the other occupant consents to a search, but not one napping or watching television in the next room. And the cost of affording such random protection is great, as demonstrated by the recurring cases in which abused spouses seek to authorize police entry into a home they share with a nonconsenting abuser.

The correct approach to the question presented is clearly mapped out in our precedents: The Fourth Amendment protects privacy. If an individual shares information, papers, *or places* with another, he assumes the risk that the other person will in turn share access to that information or those papers *or places* with the government. And just as an individual who has shared illegal plans or incriminating documents with another cannot interpose an objection when that other person turns the information over to the government, just because the individual happens to be present at the time, so too someone who shares a place with another cannot interpose an objection when that person decides to grant access to the police, simply because the objecting individual happens to be present.

A warrantless search is reasonable if police obtain the voluntary consent of a person authorized to give it. Co-occupants have "assumed the risk that one of their number might permit [a] common area to be searched." *United States v. Matlock.* Just as Mrs. Randolph could walk upstairs, come down, and turn her husband's cocaine straw over to the police, she can consent to police entry and search of what is, after all, her home, too.

I

* * * One element that can make a warrantless government search of a home " 'reasonable' " is voluntary consent. * * * Today's opinion creates an exception to this otherwise clear rule: A third-party consent search is unreasonable, and therefore constitutionally impermissible, if the co-occupant against whom evidence is obtained was present and objected to the entry and search.

This exception is based on what the majority describes as "widely shared social expectations" that "when people living together disagree over the use of their common quarters, a resolution must come through voluntary accommodation." But this fundamental predicate to the majority's analysis gets us nowhere: Does the objecting cotenant accede to the consenting cotenant's wishes, or the other way around? The majority's assumption about voluntary accommodation simply leads to the common stalemate of two gentlemen insisting that the other enter a room first.

Nevertheless, the majority is confident in assuming—confident enough to incorporate its assumption into the Constitution—that an invited social guest who arrives at the door of a shared residence, and is greeted by a disagreeable co-occupant shouting " 'stay out,' " would simply go away. * * * But it seems equally accurate to say—based on the majority's conclusion that one does not have a right to prevail over the express wishes of his co-occupant—that the objector has no "authority" to insist on getting *his* way over his co-occupant's wish that her guest be admitted.

The fact is that a wide variety of differing social situations can readily be imagined, giving rise to quite different social expectations. A relative or good friend of one of two feuding roommates might well enter the apartment over the objection of the other roommate. The reason the invitee appeared at the door also affects expectations: A guest who came to celebrate an occupant's birthday, or one who had traveled some distance for a particular reason, might not readily turn away simply because of a roommate's objection. The nature of the place itself is also pertinent: Invitees may react one way if the feuding roommates share one room, differently if there are common areas from which the objecting roommate could readily be expected to absent himself. Altering the numbers might well change the social expectations: Invitees might enter if two of three co-occupants encourage them to do so, over one dissenter.

The possible scenarios are limitless, and slight variations in the fact pattern yield vastly different expectations about whether the invitee might be expected to enter or to go away. Such shifting expectations are not a promising foundation on which to ground a constitutional rule, particularly because the majority has no support for its basic assumption * * * beyond a hunch about how people would typically act in an atypical situation. * * *

* * * [T]he Fourth Amendment precedents the majority cites refer * * * to a "legitimate expectation of *privacy*." Whatever social expectation

the majority seeks to protect, it is not one of privacy. The very predicate giving rise to the question in cases of shared information, papers, containers, or places is that privacy has been shared with another. Our common social expectations may well be that the other person will not, in turn, share what we have shared with them with another—including the police—but that is the risk we take in sharing. * * *

A wide variety of often subtle social conventions may shape expectations about how we act when another shares with us what is otherwise private, and those conventions go by a variety of labels—courtesy, good manners, custom, protocol, even honor among thieves. The Constitution, however, protects not these but privacy, and once privacy has been shared, the shared information, documents, or places remain private only at the discretion of the confidant.

II * * *

The common thread in our decisions upholding searches conducted pursuant to third-party consent is an understanding that a person "assume[s] the risk" that those who have access to and control over his shared property might consent to a search. In *Matlock,* we explained that this assumption of risk is derived from a third party's "joint access or control for most purposes" of shared property. And we concluded that shared use of property makes it "reasonable to recognize that any of the co-inhabitants has the right to permit the inspection in his own right."

In this sense, the risk assumed by a joint occupant is comparable to the risk assumed by one who reveals private information to another. If a person has incriminating information, he can keep it private in the face of a request from police to share it, because he has that right under the Fifth Amendment. If a person occupies a house with incriminating information in it, he can keep that information private in the face of a request from police to search the house, because he has that right under the Fourth Amendment. But if he shares the information—or the house—with another, that other can grant access to the police in each instance.[1]

To the extent a person wants to ensure that his possessions will be subject to a consent search only due to his *own* consent, he is free to place

---

1. The majority considers this comparison to be a "false equation," and even discerns "a deliberate intent to devalue the importance of the privacy of a dwelling place." But the differences between the majority and this dissent reduce to this: Under the majority's view, police may not enter and search when an objecting co-occupant is *present at the door,* but they *may* do so when he is asleep in the next room; under our view, the co-occupant's consent is effective in both cases. It seems a bit overwrought to characterize the former approach as affording great protection to a man in his castle, the latter as signaling that "the centuries of special protection for the privacy of the home are over." * * *

The majority also mischaracterizes this dissent as assuming that "privacy shared with another individual is privacy waived for all purposes including warrantless searches by the police." The point, of course, is not that a person waives his privacy by sharing space with others such that police may enter at will, but that sharing space necessarily entails a limited yielding of privacy *to the person with whom the space is shared,* such that the other person shares authority to consent to a search of the shared space.

these items in an area over which others do *not* share access and control, be it a private room or a locked suitcase under a bed. * * *

III * * *

Just as the source of the majority's rule is not privacy, so too the interest it protects cannot reasonably be described as such. That interest is not protected if a co-owner happens to be absent when the police arrive, in the backyard gardening, asleep in the next room, or listening to music through earphones so that only his co-occupant hears the knock on the door. That the rule is so random in its application confirms that it bears no real relation to the privacy protected by the Fourth Amendment. What the majority's rule protects is not so much privacy as the good luck of a co-owner who just happens to be present at the door when the police arrive. Usually when the development of Fourth Amendment jurisprudence leads to such arbitrary lines, we take it as a signal that the rules need to be rethought. We should not embrace a rule at the outset that its *sponsors* appreciate will result in drawing fine, formalistic lines. * * *

The scope of the majority's rule is not only arbitrary but obscure as well. The majority repeats several times that a present co-occupant's refusal to permit entry renders the search unreasonable and invalid "as to him." This implies entry and search would be reasonable "as to" someone else, presumably the consenting co-occupant and any other absent co-occupants. The normal Fourth Amendment rule is that items discovered in plain view are admissible if the officers were legitimately on the premises; if the entry and search were reasonable "as to" Mrs. Randolph, based on her consent, it is not clear why the cocaine straw should not be admissible "as to" Mr. Randolph, as discovered in plain view during a legitimate search "as to" Mrs. Randolph. * * *

While the majority's rule protects something random, its consequences are particularly severe. * * * Under the majority's rule, there will be many cases in which a consenting co-occupant's wish to have the police enter is overridden by an objection from another present co-occupant. What does the majority imagine will happen, in a case in which the consenting co-occupant is concerned about the other's criminal activity, once the door clicks shut? The objecting co-occupant may pause briefly to decide whether to destroy any evidence of wrongdoing or to inflict retribution on the consenting co-occupant first, but there can be little doubt that he will attend to both in short order. It is no answer to say that the consenting co-occupant can depart with the police; remember that it is her home, too, and the other co-occupant's very presence, which allowed him to object, may also prevent the consenting co-occupant from doing more than urging the police to enter.

Perhaps the most serious consequence of the majority's rule is its operation in domestic abuse situations, a context in which the present question often arises. * * * The Court concludes that because "no sensible person would go inside" in the face of disputed consent, and the consenting cotenant thus has "no recognized authority" to insist on the guest's admission, a "police officer [has] no better claim to reasonableness in entering than the officer would have in the absence of any consent at all." But the police officer's superior claim to enter is obvious: Mrs. Randolph did not invite the police to join her for dessert and coffee; the officer's precise purpose in knocking on the door was to assist with a dispute between the Randolphs—one in which Mrs. Randolph felt the need for the protective presence of the police. The majority's rule apparently forbids police from entering to assist with a domestic dispute if the abuser whose behavior prompted the request for police assistance objects.

The majority acknowledges these concerns, but dismisses them on the ground that its rule can be expected to give rise to exigent situations, and police can then rely on an exigent circumstances exception to justify entry. This is a strange way to justify a rule, and the fact that alternative justifications for entry might arise does not show that entry pursuant to consent is unreasonable. * * *

Considering the majority's rule is solely concerned with protecting a person who happens to be present at the door when a police officer asks his co-occupant for consent to search, but not one who is asleep in the next room or in the backyard gardening, the majority has taken a great deal of pain in altering Fourth Amendment doctrine, for precious little (if any) gain in privacy. Perhaps one day, as the consequences of the majority's analytic approach become clearer, today's opinion will be treated the same way the majority treats our opinion[] in *Matlock*—as a "loose end" to be tied up.

One of the concurring opinions states that if it had to choose between a rule that a cotenant's consent was valid or a rule that it was not, it would choose the former. The concurrence advises, however, that "no single set of legal rules can capture the ever changing complexity of human life," and joins what becomes the majority opinion, "[g]iven the case-specific nature of the Court's holding." * * * The end result is a complete lack of practical guidance for the police in the field, let alone for the lower courts. * * *

Justice SCALIA, dissenting.

I join the dissent of The Chief Justice, but add these few words in response to Justice Stevens' concurrence.

It is not as clear to me as it is to Justice Stevens that, at the time the Fourth Amendment was adopted, a police officer could enter a married woman's home over her objection, and could not enter with only her consent. * * * It is entirely clear, however, that *if* the matter *did* depend solely on property rights, a latter-day alteration of property rights would also produce a latter-day alteration of the Fourth Amendment outcome—without altering the Fourth Amendment itself.

Justice Stevens' attempted critique of originalism confuses the original import of the Fourth Amendment with the background sources of law to which the Amendment, on its original meaning, referred. From the date of its ratification until well into the 20th century, violation of the Amendment was tied to common-law trespass. On the basis of that connection, someone who had power to license the search of a house by a private party could authorize a police search. As property law developed, individuals who previously could not authorize a search might become able to do so, and those who once could grant such consent might no longer have that power. But changes in the law of property to which the Fourth Amendment referred would not alter the Amendment's meaning: that anyone capable of authorizing a search by a private party could consent to a warrantless search by the police.

There is nothing new or surprising in the proposition that our unchanging Constitution refers to other bodies of law that might themselves change. * * * This reference to changeable law presents no problem for the originalist. * * *

In any event, Justice Stevens' panegyric to the *equal* rights of women under modern property law does not support his conclusion that "[a]ssuming * * * both spouses are competent, neither one is a master possessing the power to override the other's constitutional right to deny entry to their castle." The issue at hand is what to do when there is a *conflict* between two equals. Now that women have authority to consent, as Justice Stevens claims men alone once did, it does not follow that the spouse who *refuses* consent should be the winner of the contest. Justice Stevens could just as well have followed the same historical developments to the opposite conclusion * * *

Finally, I must express grave doubt that today's decision deserves Justice Stevens' celebration as part of the forward march of women's equality. Given the usual patterns of domestic violence, how often can police be expected to encounter the situation in which a man urges them to enter the home while a woman simultaneously demands that they stay out? The most common practical effect of today's decision, insofar as the contest between the sexes is concerned, is to give men the power to stop women from allowing police into their homes—which is, curiously enough, *precisely* the power that Justice Stevens disapprovingly presumes men had in 1791.

[The dissenting opinion of Justice Thomas is omitted.]

NOTES AND QUESTIONS

1.   As a matter of policy (especially in light of the problem of domestic violence), whose opinion—Justice Souter's or Chief Justice Roberts'—do you find more persuasive? Which opinion seems more correct in terms of the Fourth Amendment case law you have studied to date?

2.   In his dissent, the Chief Justice wrote:

What does the majority imagine will happen, in a case in which the consenting co-occupant is concerned about the other's criminal activity, once the door clicks shut? The objecting co-occupant may pause briefly to decide whether to destroy any evidence of wrongdoing or to inflict retribution on the consenting co-occupant first, but there can be little doubt that he will attend to both in short order.

Do you agree with the Chief Justice's observations? If so, does this help or hurt the dissent's Fourth Amendment argument?

3.   Justice Breyer states that if he were forced to choose one of the two bright-line rules he sets out in his concurrence, he would choose the first one he set out. If *you* had to choose one of the two bright-line rules, which one would *you* choose, and why?

4.   Justices Stevens' and Scalia's opinions are interesting reading, although they offer little to the "consent" debate. What you see here is an ongoing debate between those justices, most notably Justices Scalia and Thomas, who characterize themselves as "originalists"—persons who believe that the text of the Constitution means whatever the Framers of the text had in mind and does not change over time—and those justices, such as Justice Stevens, who reject originalism.

5.   Notice certain language in the last paragraph of the Chief Justice's dissent. He stated that Justice Breyer "joins *what becomes the majority opinion* * * *." What might this italicized language suggest about how the justices initially voted in this case?

6.   Assume in each of the following cases, *W* (Wife) and *H* (Husband) have joint authority over their home. In view of *Randolph*, is a search of their home valid on consent grounds (ignore any other possible justifications for entry) if: (a) *W*, outside the residence, consents to the search; *H*, inside the house and approached by the police who intend to execute a warrant to arrest him, barricades himself inside, United States v. McKerrell, 491 F.3d 1221 (10th Cir. 2007); (b) *H*, at work, refuses consent to search their home; *W*, at home, thereafter consents, United States v. Hudspeth, 518 F.3d 954 (8th Cir. 2008) (en banc); and (c) police arrive on a "domestic abuse" call, *W* reports the abuse and states that there are illegal items inside belonging to *H*, *W* consents to the search, *H* objects, police (validly) arrest *H* for domestic battery, remove *H* from the premises, and then enter based on *W*'s consent, United States v. Henderson, 536 F.3d 776 (7th Cir. 2008).

ILLINOIS v. RODRIGUEZ

Supreme Court of the United States, 1990.
497 U.S. 177, 110 S.Ct. 2793, 111 L.Ed.2d 148.

JUSTICE SCALIA delivered the opinion of the Court. * * *

I * * *

On July 26, 1985, police were summoned to the residence of Dorothy Jackson on South Wolcott in Chicago. They were met by Ms. Jackson's daughter, Gail Fischer, who showed signs of a severe beating. She told the officers that she had been assaulted by respondent Edward Rodriguez earlier that day in an apartment on South California Avenue. Fischer stated that Rodriguez was then asleep in the apartment, and she consented to travel there with the police in order to unlock the door with her key so that the officers could enter and arrest him. During this conversation, Fischer several times referred to the apartment on South California as "our" apartment, and said that she had clothes and furniture there. It is unclear whether she indicated that she currently lived at the apartment, or only that she used to live there.

The police officers drove to the apartment on South California, accompanied by Fischer. They did not obtain an arrest warrant for Rodriguez, nor did they seek a search warrant for the apartment. At the apartment, Fischer unlocked the door with her key and gave the officers permission to enter. They moved through the door into the living room, where they observed in plain view drug paraphernalia and containers filled with white powder that they believed (correctly, as later analysis showed) to be cocaine. * * * The officers arrested Rodriguez and seized the drugs and related paraphernalia.

Rodriguez was charged with possession of a controlled substance with intent to deliver. He moved to suppress all evidence seized at the time of his arrest, claiming that Fischer had vacated the apartment several weeks earlier and had no authority to consent to the entry. The Cook County Circuit Court granted the motion, holding that at the time she consented to the entry Fischer did not have common authority over the apartment. The Court concluded that Fischer was not a "usual resident" but rather an "infrequent visitor" at the apartment on South California, based upon its findings that Fischer's name was not on the lease, that she did not contribute to the rent, that she was not allowed to invite others to the apartment on her own, that she did not have access to the apartment when respondent was away, and that she had moved some of her possessions from the apartment. The Circuit Court also rejected the State's contention that, even if Fischer did not possess common authority over the premises, there was no Fourth Amendment violation if the police *reasonably believed* at the time of their entry that Fischer possessed the authority to consent. * * *

II * * *

As we stated in [*United States v.*] *Matlock*, [415 U.S. 164, 94 S.Ct. 988, 39 L.Ed.2d 242 (1974)], "[c]ommon authority" rests "on mutual use of the property by persons generally having joint access or control for most purposes * * *." The burden of establishing that common authority rests upon the State. On the basis of this record, it is clear that burden was not sustained. The evidence showed that although Fischer, with her two small children, had lived with Rodriguez beginning in December 1984, she had moved out on July 1, 1985, almost a month before the search at issue here, and had gone to live with her mother. * * * She had a key to the apartment, which she said at trial she had taken without Rodriguez's knowledge * * *. On these facts the State has not established that, with respect to the South California apartment, Fischer had "joint access or control for most purposes." * * *

III

A

The State contends that, even if Fischer did not in fact have authority to give consent, it suffices to validate the entry that the law enforcement officers reasonably believed she did. * * *

B

On the merits of the issue, respondent asserts that permitting a reasonable belief of common authority to validate an entry would cause a defendant's Fourth Amendment rights to be "vicariously waived." We disagree.

We have been unyielding in our insistence that a defendant's waiver of his trial rights cannot be given effect unless it is "knowing" and "intelligent." *Johnson v. Zerbst*, 304 U.S. 458, 58 S.Ct. 1019, 82 L.Ed. 1461 (1938). We would assuredly not permit, therefore, evidence seized in violation of the Fourth Amendment to be introduced on the basis of a trial court's mere "reasonable belief"—derived from statements by unauthorized persons—that the defendant has waived his objection. But one must make a distinction between, on the one hand, trial rights that *derive* from the violation of constitutional guarantees and, on the other hand, the nature of those constitutional guarantees themselves.* * *

What Rodriguez is assured by the trial right of the exclusionary rule, where it applies, is that no evidence seized in violation of the Fourth Amendment will be introduced at his trial unless he consents. What he is assured by the Fourth Amendment itself, however, is not that no government search of his house will occur unless he consents; but that no such search will occur that is "unreasonable." There are various elements, of course, that can make a search of a person's house "reasonable"—one of which is the consent of the person or his cotenant. The essence of respondent's argument is that we should impose upon this element a requirement that we have not imposed upon other elements that regularly compel government officers to exercise judgment regarding the facts: namely, the requirement that their judgment be not only responsible but correct.

The fundamental objective that alone validates all unconsented government searches is, of course, the seizure of persons who have committed or are about to commit crimes, or of evidence related to crimes. But "reasonableness," with respect to this necessary element, does not demand that the government be factually correct in its assessment that that is what a search will produce. Warrants need only be supported by "probable cause," which demands no more than a proper "assessment of probabilities in particular factual contexts * * *." If a magistrate, based upon seemingly reliable but factually inaccurate information, issues a warrant for the search of a house in which the sought-after felon is not present, has never been present, and was never likely to have been present, the owner of that house suffers one of the inconveniences we all expose ourselves to as the cost of living in a safe society; he does not suffer a violation of the Fourth Amendment.

Another element often, though not invariably, required in order to render an unconsented search "reasonable" is, of course, that the officer be authorized by a valid warrant. Here also we have not held that "reasonableness" precludes error with respect to those factual judgments that law enforcement officials are expected to make. [Justice Scalia then recounted the facts in *Maryland v. Garrison*, p. 208, Note 7, in which the Court upheld a search in which the police mistakenly searched the wrong residence.] * * *

It would be superfluous to multiply these examples. It is apparent that in order to satisfy the "reasonableness" requirement of the Fourth Amendment, what is generally demanded of the many factual determinations that must regularly be made by agents of the government—whether the magistrate issuing a warrant, the police officer executing a warrant, or the police officer conducting a search or seizure under one of the exceptions to the warrant requirement—is not that they always be correct, but that they always be reasonable. As we put it in *Brinegar v. United States*, 338 U.S. 160, 176, 69 S.Ct. 1302, 1311, 93 L.Ed. 1879 (1949):

> "Because many situations which confront officers in the course of executing their duties are more or less ambiguous, room must be allowed for some mistakes on their part. But the mistakes must be those of reasonable men, acting on facts leading sensibly to their conclusions of probability."

We see no reason to depart from this general rule with respect to facts bearing upon the authority to consent to a search. Whether the basis for such authority exists is the sort of recurring factual question to which law enforcement officials must be expected to apply their judgment; and all the Fourth Amendment requires is that they answer it reasonably. The Constitution is no more violated when officers enter without a warrant because they reasonably (though erroneously) believe that the person who has consented to their entry is a resident of the premises, than it is violated when they enter without a warrant because they reasonably (though erroneously) believe they are in pursuit of a violent felon who is about to escape.* * * *

* * * [W]hat we hold today does not suggest that law enforcement officers may always accept a person's invitation to enter premises. Even when the invitation is accompanied by an explicit assertion that the person lives there, the surrounding circumstances could conceivably be

---

* Justice Marshall's dissent rests upon a rejection of the proposition that searches pursuant to valid third-party consent are "generally reasonable." Only a warrant or exigent circumstances, he contends, can produce "reasonableness"; consent validates the search only because the object of the search thereby "limit[s] his expectation of privacy," so that the search becomes not really a search at all. We see no basis for making such an artificial distinction. To describe a consented search as a noninvasion of privacy and thus a nonsearch is strange in the extreme. And while it must be admitted that this ingenious device can explain why consented searches are lawful, it cannot explain why seemingly consented searches are "unreasonable," which is all that the Constitution forbids. * * *

such that a reasonable person would doubt its truth and not act upon it without further inquiry. As with other factual determinations bearing upon search and seizure, determination of consent to enter must "be judged against an objective standard: would the facts available to the officer at the moment * * * 'warrant a man of reasonable caution in the belief' " that the consenting party had authority over the premises? If not, then warrantless entry without further inquiry is unlawful unless authority actually exists. But if so, the search is valid.

In the present case, the Appellate Court found it unnecessary to determine whether the officers reasonably believed that Fischer had the authority to consent, because it ruled as a matter of law that a reasonable belief could not validate the entry. Since we find that ruling to be in error, we remand for consideration of that question.* * *

Justice MARSHALL, with whom Justice BRENNAN and Justice STEVENS join, dissenting. * * *

* * * The Court holds that the warrantless entry into Rodriguez's home was nonetheless valid if the officers reasonably believed that Fischer had authority to consent. The majority's defense of this position rests on a misconception of the basis for third-party consent searches. That such searches do not give rise to claims of constitutional violations rests not on the premise that they are "reasonable" under the Fourth Amendment, but on the premise that a person may voluntarily limit his expectation of privacy by allowing others to exercise authority over his possessions. Thus, an individual's decision to permit another "joint access [to] or control [over the property] for most purposes," *United States v. Matlock*, limits that individual's reasonable expectation of privacy and to that extent limits his Fourth Amendment protections. If an individual has not so limited his expectation of privacy, the police may not dispense with the safeguards established by the Fourth Amendment. * * *

I * * *

Unlike searches conducted pursuant to the recognized exceptions to the warrant requirement, third-party consent searches are not based on an exigency and therefore serve no compelling social goal. Police officers, when faced with the choice of relying on consent by a third party or securing a warrant, should secure a warrant and must therefore accept the risk of error should they instead choose to rely on consent.

II

Our prior cases discussing searches based on third-party consent have never suggested that such searches are "reasonable." In *United States v. Matlock*, this Court upheld a warrantless search conducted pursuant to the consent of a third party who was living with the defendant. The Court rejected the defendant's challenge to the search, stating that a person who permits others to have "joint access or control for most purposes * * * assume[s] the risk that [such persons] might permit the common area to be searched." As the Court's assumption-of-risk analysis makes clear, third-party consent limits a person's ability to challenge the reasonableness of the search only because that person voluntarily has relinquished some of his expectation of privacy by sharing access or control over his property with another person.

A search conducted pursuant to an officer's reasonable but mistaken belief that a third party had authority to consent is thus on an entirely different constitutional footing from one based on the consent of a third party who in fact has such authority. Even if the officers reasonably believed that Fischer had authority to consent, she did not, and Rodriguez's expectation of privacy was therefore undiminished. Rodriguez accordingly can challenge the warrantless intrusion into his home as a violation of the Fourth Amendment. * * *

III

* * * [T]he majority seeks to rely on cases suggesting that reasonable but mistaken factual judgments by police will not invalidate otherwise reasonable searches. * * *

* * * The cases the majority cites * * * provide no support for its holding. In *Brinegar v. United States*, for example, the Court confirmed the unremarkable proposition that police need only probable cause, not absolute certainty, to justify the arrest of a suspect on a highway. As *Brinegar* makes clear, the possibility of factual error is built into the probable cause standard, and such a standard, by its very definition, will in some cases result in the arrest of a suspect who has not actually committed a crime. Because probable cause defines the reasonableness of searches and seizures outside of the home, a search is reasonable under the Fourth Amendment whenever that standard is met, notwithstanding the possibility of "mistakes" on the part of police. * * *

The majority's reliance on *Maryland v. Garrison* is also misplaced. * * * As in *Brinegar*, the Court's decision was premised on the general reasonableness of the type of police action involved. Because searches based on warrants are generally reasonable, the officers' reasonable mistake of fact did not render their search "unreasonable." * * *

IV

* * * That a person who allows another joint access to his property thereby limits his expectation of privacy does not justify trampling the rights of a person who has not similarly relinquished any of his privacy expectation.

* * * [B]y allowing a person to be subjected to a warrantless search in his home without his consent and without exigency, the majority has taken away some of the liberty that the Fourth Amendment was designed to protect.

NOTES AND QUESTIONS

1. According to Justice Scalia, what is the justification for warrantless consent searches? Do you find the rationale in accord with *Schneckloth* and *Randolph*? Does Justice Marshall provide a plausible explanation of consent searches? For a rigorous analysis (and criticism) of *Rodriguez*, see Thomas Y. Davies, *Denying a Right by Disregarding Doctrine: How Illinois v. Rodriguez Demeans Consent, Trivializes Fourth Amendment Reasonableness, and Exaggerates the Excusability of Police Error*, 59 Tenn L. Rev. 1 (1991).

2. As developed at the trial court level and as is set out in the first paragraph of the Court's opinion, Gail Fischer told the police that she had clothing and some of her furniture at the apartment in question. Why would she have said this if it were her apartment? Don't these remarks put a reasonable officer on notice that this may not have been her apartment? In this regard, consider the following conversation between Michael R. Dreeben, who argued on behalf of the United States as *amicus curiae* in support of the State of Illinois, and Justices Stevens and O'Connor, during oral arguments in the *Rodriguez* case:

QUESTION: * * * [D]o you think the police officer had any duty to ask the young lady if she lived there? * * *

MR. DREEBEN: No. I don't think they did, Justice Stevens. And the reason that they didn't have a specific duty to ask that particular question is that they were summoned to the scene of what they understood was a battery victim. * * * They learned that she had been beaten by her boyfriend at an apartment that they—she described as "our apartment." There's testimony that she said that many of her things were there. * * *

QUESTION: Well, it would have been pretty simple for them to ask a few more questions, wouldn't it?

MR. DREEBEN: Yes, Justice O'Connor.

QUESTION: And, you're asking for an exception to the warrant requirement which is something paramount in the Fourth Amendment requirements. It seems to me you're suggesting that we just open the door wide without any corresponding obligation on the part of the police to make reasonable inquiry.

MR. DREEBEN: Justice O'Connor, I think it would be fully appropriate for this Court to hold that appropriate inquiry is necessary when the facts are ambiguous and clarification is what a reasonable police officer would do.

In your view, is this a case in which "the facts are ambiguous and clarification is what a reasonable police officer would do"?

3. Does this case have Fourth Amendment implications that extend beyond consent searches? For example, suppose that when Rodriguez was arrested, the police conducted a search incident to the arrest and discovered additional contraband in a dresser drawer thirty feet away from the handcuffed arrestee. If you represented Rodriguez and sought to have that evi-

dence suppressed, what would you argue? If you were the prosecutor, how would you respond based on *Rodriguez*?

4. *Scope of consent.* A consent search is invalid, even if the consent was voluntary, if the police exceed the scope of the consent granted. In Florida v. Jimeno, 500 U.S. 248, 111 S.Ct. 1801, 114 L.Ed.2d 297 (1991), Officer Trujillo, who had stopped Jimeno's car for a traffic violation, told Jimeno (based on earlier information) that he had reason to believe that Jimeno was carrying narcotics in the car. Trujillo asked permission to search the vehicle and reportedly received consent. In the search, the officer found a folded paper bag on the car's floorboard, which he opened. It contained cocaine. Jimeno moved to suppress the cocaine on the ground that his consent to search the car, even if voluntary, did not extend to the closed paper bag inside the car. The Court, per Chief Justice Rehnquist, rejected the argument:

> The touchstone of the Fourth Amendment is reasonableness. The Fourth Amendment does not proscribe all state-initiated searches and seizures; it merely proscribes those which are unreasonable. *Illinois v. Rodriguez.* * * * The standard for measuring the scope of a suspect's consent under the Fourth Amendment is that of "objective" reasonableness—what would the typical reasonable person have understood by the exchange between the officer and the suspect? The question before us, then, is whether it is reasonable for an officer to consider a suspect's general consent to a search of his car to include consent to examine a paper bag lying on the floor of the car. We think that it is.

> The scope of a search is generally defined by its expressed object. In this case, the terms of the search's authorization were simple. Respondent granted Officer Trujillo permission to search his car, and did not place any explicit limitation on the scope of the search. Trujillo had informed Jimeno that he believed Jimeno was carrying narcotics, and that he would be looking for narcotics in the car. We think that it was objectively reasonable for the police to conclude that the general consent to search respondents' car included consent to search containers within that car which might bear drugs. A reasonable person may be expected to know that narcotics are generally carried in some form of a container. * * * The authorization to search in this case, therefore, extended beyond the surfaces of the car's interior to the paper bag lying on the car's floor.

> The facts of this case are therefore different from those in *State v. Wells*, [539 So.2d 464 (1989)], on which the Supreme Court of Florida relied in affirming the suppression order in this case. There the Supreme Court of Florida held that consent to search the trunk of a car did not include authorization to pry open a locked briefcase found inside the trunk. It is very likely unreasonable to think that a suspect, by consenting to the search of his trunk, has agreed to the breaking open of a locked briefcase within the trunk, but it is otherwise with respect to a closed paper bag.

Did the Court adequately distinguish the facts in *Wells*? Would the consent here have been valid if Officer Trujillo had not told Jimeno that he was looking for drugs? What if Trujillo had told Jimeno that he wanted to search the car for a stolen large-screen television set?

5. *Problems.* In light of everything you have learned, what result in the following "consent" cases?

A. *O* obtained consent to search *D*'s luggage at a train station. Inside the luggage, he found a can labeled "tamales in gravy." *O* shook the can and it seemed to contain a dry substance, like salt. *O* proceeded to open the can and found a bag of methamphetamine. United States v. Osage, 235 F.3d 518 (10th Cir.2000).

B. *M* gave a border patrol agent consent to "take in the look in the back" of a commercial truck. The trailer contained a load of white cardboard boxes wrapped in plastic. The officer used a pocket knife to slice a piece of tape and open a box, in which the agent discovered marijuana. United States v. Mendoza–Gonzalez, 318 F.3d 663 (5th Cir. 2003).

C. At 3:30 a.m., *S*, a passenger in a vehicle stopped in a public parking lot, voluntarily consented to a search of his person for drugs. As part of that search, one of the police officers pulled open the waistbands of *S*'s sweat pants and underwear and peered inside with a flashlight. *S* objected, but by the time he did, the officer has already observed the white cap of what appeared to be a pill bottle tucked in between *S*'s inner thigh and testicles. Should the pill bottle, which was seized, be suppressed? State v. Stone, 362 N.C. 50, 653 S.E.2d 414 (2007).

D. The police lawfully stopped a vehicle driven by X, in which *D* was a passenger, for having only one working headlight. Outside *D*'s hearing, the officer received consent from *X* to search the car for "multiple things, bodies, weapons, guns, drugs." The search turned up two suitcases in the trunk. Without inquiring about the ownership of the suitcases, the officer opened one of the unlocked suitcases and found illegal drugs. The suitcase belonged to *D*, not *X*. State v. Frank, 650 N.W.2d 213 (Minn. App. 2002).

E. REASONABLENESS CLAUSE: THE DIMINISHING ROLES OF WARRANTS AND PROBABLE CAUSE

1. THE *TERRY* DOCTRINE

a. Terry v. Ohio: The Opinion

SCOTT E. SUNDBY—A RETURN TO FOURTH AMENDMENT BASICS: UNDOING THE MISCHIEF OF *CAMARA* AND *TERRY*

72 Minnesota Law Review 383 (1988), 383–95.

In its fourth amendment jurisprudence, the United States Supreme Court has struggled continually, and unsuccessfully, to develop a coherent analytical framework.* * *

* * * Many of the Court's present fourth amendment ills are symptoms of its failure to meet two basic challenges presented by the fourth

amendment's text. First, the reasonableness clause's general proscription against "unreasonable searches and seizures" must be reconciled with the warrant clause's mandate that "no Warrants shall issue, but upon probable cause." Second, the concept of reasonableness must be defined to reflect the amendment's underlying values and purposes. * * *

The two challenges of fourth amendment interpretation are formidable standing alone, and the Court's decisions in *Camara v. Municipal Court*[7] and *Terry v. Ohio*[8] have compounded the difficulty. Faced with novel fourth amendment questions, the Court in *Camara* and *Terry* turned to a broad reasonableness standard and an ill-defined balancing test for the immediate solutions. The combined effect of the *Camara* and *Terry* holdings, however, has proven to be something of a Faustian pact. The decisions allowed the fourth amendment's scope to extend to government activities like housing inspections, but in the process they significantly undermined the role of probable cause and set the stage for the long-term expansion of the reasonableness balancing test without proper justification or limits. * * *

I.   THE RISE OF REASONABLENESS IN FOURTH AMENDMENT ANALYSIS

A.   *When the Warrant Clause was King*

Prior to *Camara*, fourth amendment analysis had a relatively high amount of predictability: the Court presumed that a warrant based on probable cause was required before the police could perform a search or arrest. The Court's strong preference for the warrant requirement relegated the amendment's reasonableness clause, which bans "unreasonable searches and seizures," to a secondary role. The Court used the concept of reasonableness primarily to justify making an exception to the warrant requirement when exigent circumstances dictated excusing the police from procuring a warrant. Although reasonableness sometimes necessitated making an exception for obtaining a warrant, probable cause remained sacrosanct, immune from modification even in the name of reasonableness. * * *

The Court's almost exclusive focus on the warrant clause yielded predictability and strong protections, but it was not without costs. Because requiring a warrant based on probable cause would have precluded suspicionless government inspections, the Court did not extend the amendment's coverage very far beyond the context of criminal arrests and searches. When the fourth amendment governed, therefore, it provided the full protections of the warrant clause—but the protections generally did not apply to government intrusions other than criminal investigations.

The Court's warrant clause emphasis and corresponding reluctance to expand fourth amendment protections beyond criminal investigations largely explain its holding in *Frank v. Maryland*.[16] In *Frank* the Court

---

7.   387 U.S. 523 (1967).

8.   392 U.S. 1 (1968).

16.   359 U.S. 360 (1959). In *Frank* a city health inspector looking for a source of rats in the neighborhood found the defendant's house in an "extreme state of decay" and asked the

addressed the issue whether the defendant's conviction for resisting a warrantless inspection of his house violated the fourth amendment. Upholding the conviction and fine, the *Frank* majority espoused the traditional view that if inspections like those at issue were subject to full fourth amendment protections, the search would have to satisfy the warrant requirement. Yet requiring a warrant based on probable cause for housing inspections would defeat the inspections' objective of maintaining community health. Resisting efforts to modify the warrant and probable cause requirements, the majority adopted an all-or-nothing view that if the Constitution required a search warrant, "the requirement [could not] be flexibly interpreted to dispense with the rigorous constitutional restrictions for its issue."

Consistent with the Court's warrant clause orientation, the *Frank* majority also argued that because Frank's asserted privacy interest did not concern a criminal investigation, his claim, at most, touched "upon the periphery" of the important fourth amendment interests protected against invasion by government officials. Stressing that the housing inspection was not a search for criminal evidence, Justice Frankfurter argued that the Constitution's prohibition against official invasion arose almost entirely from the individual's fundamental right to be secure from evidentiary searches made in connection with criminal prosecutions. The majority pointed to the historical acceptance of warrantless inspections, not as an enforcement mechanism of the criminal law, but "as an adjunct to a regulatory scheme for the general welfare." Consequently, the majority concluded that any legitimate liberty interest Frank had was overwhelmed by the government's need for inspection and the desirability of not tampering with the fourth amendment's rigorous protections.

B. *Camara: Reasonableness Gets a Foot in the Door*

In *Camara v. Municipal Court*, the Court overruled its holding in *Frank* that the fourth amendment's full protections did not extend to housing inspections. Writing for the majority, Justice White rejected the "rather remarkable premise" in *Frank* that because housing inspections were not criminal investigations, they were merely on the periphery of the fourth amendment. He argued that inspection programs in fact went to the fourth amendment's central purpose of "safeguard[ing] the privacy and security of individuals against arbitrary invasions by government officials." Given that purpose, the majority concluded that it would be anomalous to suggest that an individual enjoys full fourth amendment protection only when suspected of criminal conduct.

---

defendant's permission to inspect the basement. The defendant refused permission, and after a subsequent attempt to gain entry, the inspector swore out a complaint for the defendant's arrest based on a city code section providing:

> "Whenever the Commissioner of Health shall have cause to suspect that a nuisance exists in any house, cellar or enclosure, he may demand entry therein in the day time, and if the owner or occupier shall refuse or delay to open the same and admit a free examination, he shall forfeit and pay for every such refusal the sum of Twenty Dollars."

Unshackling the fourth amendment from *Frank*'s restrictive reading of the amendment's purpose, however, was only the first step. The majority still had to address *Frank*'s perceived dilemma that application of the fourth amendment to administrative inspections would either dilute the amendment's protections or preclude blanket inspections altogether. In deciding how to apply the amendment, the Court did not adopt a new mode of fourth amendment analysis. Rather, it chose to assess the government inspection program within the traditional warrant and probable cause framework. Justifying its choice, the Court explained that it had adhered consistently to the governing principle that "[e]xcept in certain carefully defined classes of cases, a search of private property without proper consent is 'unreasonable' unless it has been authorized by a valid search warrant."

Having elected to continue its historical warrant clause emphasis, the necessity of modifying the clause's requirements to permit the housing inspections was evident. Traditional probable cause required facts sufficient to justify a reasonably cautious person in believing that another had committed or was committing a crime. Whether a search or arrest was reasonable depended at a minimum upon a showing of individualized suspicion amounting to probable cause. The fourth amendment would have precluded the government's power to conduct area housing inspections, a power all agreed was necessary, if probable cause required a showing of specific violations for each inspection. Consequently, the *Camara* majority redefined probable cause: rather than requiring individualized suspicion, probable cause was recast as standing for a broader concept of reasonableness based on a weighing of the governmental and individual interests. Under the new definition, probable cause existed and the warrant clause was satisfied once the Court concluded that the area housing inspections, although lacking individualized suspicion, were "reasonable." Probable cause, therefore, still served the formal function of a prerequisite for the issuance of a warrant, but its traditional requirement of particularized suspicion became merely one example of probable cause's meaning in a particular setting.

Ironically, in redefining probable cause as a flexible concept, the Court's effort to satisfy the warrant clause gave reasonableness a foot in the door as an independent factor in fourth amendment analysis. Prior to *Camara* the warrant clause had dictated the meaning of the reasonableness clause. A search or arrest was reasonable only when a warrant based on probable cause issued. *Camara*, in contrast, reversed the roles of probable cause and reasonableness. Instead of probable cause defining a reasonable search, after *Camara*, reasonableness, in the form of a balancing test, defined probable cause. Allowing reasonableness to define probable cause expanded the range of acceptable government behavior beyond intrusions based on individualized suspicion to include activities in which the government interest outweighed the individual's privacy interests. Reasonableness, in the form of a balancing test, had finally gained entrance into fourth amendment analysis, albeit through the back door of the warrant clause. * * *

Building upon *Camara*, the Court's decision in *Terry v. Ohio* provided reasonableness an even greater role as an independent factor in fourth amendment analysis.

JOSHUA DRESSLER & ALAN C. MICHAELS— UNDERSTANDING CRIMINAL PROCEDURE

(Volume 1) (Fourth edition 2006), 277–279.

The Fourth Amendment was once considered a monolith. "Probable cause" had a single meaning, and "searches" and "seizures" were all-or-nothing concepts. The monolith was cracked by the Supreme Court in *Camara v. Municipal Court*. In *Camara*, the justices recognized a different form of "probable cause," applicable to administrative-search cases, that does not require individualized suspicion and which is based on the general Fourth Amendment standard of "reasonableness." To determine "reasonableness," the *Camara* Court invoked a balancing test, in which the individual's and society's interests in a given type of administrative search were weighed against each other.

If *Camara* cracked the Fourth Amendment monolith, *Terry v. Ohio* broke it entirely. Although the issue in *Terry* was described by the Court as "quite narrow"—"whether it is always unreasonable for a policeman to seize a person and subject him to a limited search for weapons unless there is probable cause to arrest"—the significance of the case to Fourth Amendment jurisprudence is, quite simply, monumental. In terms of the daily activities of the police, as well as the experiences of persons "on the street," there is no Supreme Court Fourth Amendment case—not even *Katz v. United States*—of greater practical impact.

The significance of *Terry* will be seen in [the materials that follow], but a brief overview is appropriate. First, *Terry* transported *Camara*'s "reasonableness" balancing test from the realm of administrative searches to traditional criminal investigations, and used it to determine the reasonableness of certain warrantless searches and seizures, rather than merely to define "probable cause." The result has been a significant diminution in the role of the Warrant Clause in Fourth Amendment jurisprudence. That is, *Terry* provided the impetus, as well as the framework, for a move by the Supreme Court away from the proposition that warrantless searches are *per se* unreasonable, to the competing view that the appropriate test of police conduct "is not whether it is reasonable to procure a search warrant, but whether the search was reasonable." Warrantless police conduct became much easier to justify after *Terry*.

Second, *Terry* recognized that searches and seizures can vary in their intrusiveness. The Court no longer treats all searches and all seizures alike.* * *

Third, as a corollary of the last point, because of *Terry* the police may now conduct a wide array of searches and seizures that are considered less-than-ordinarily intrusive, on the basis of a lesser standard of cause than "probable cause" * * *. * * *

At least one other aspect of *Terry* deserves note here. Professor Akhil Amar suggests that this case may provide "one of the most open Fourth Amendment discussions of race to date."[10] Whether or not this assertion is accurate,[11] there is no gainsaying that when the police forcibly stop (seize) persons on the street to question them or to conduct full or cursory searches, highly sensitive issues of racial profiling (and to a lesser extent, issues of ethnicity, class, and gender) come to the fore.

Some scholars believe that the *Terry* opinion (or, at least, the *Terry* doctrine as it has come to be interpreted over the years), and its move away from the warrant requirement, has done much to exacerbate racial tensions between the police and members of minority communities. Others believe that the Court's movement in this case to a reasonableness standard is good, in part because it will force courts to confront issues, such as race and class, "honestly and openly." Whoever is right in this regard, Chief Justice Earl Warren was surely correct when he observed in *Terry* that "[w]e would be less than candid if we did not acknowledge that this [case] thrusts to the fore, difficult and troublesome issues regarding a sensitive area of police activity."

TERRY v. OHIO

Supreme Court of the United States, 1968.
392 U.S. 1, 88 S.Ct. 1868, 20 L.Ed.2d 889.

MR. CHIEF JUSTICE WARREN delivered the opinion of the Court. * * *

Petitioner Terry was convicted of carrying a concealed weapon and sentenced to the statutorily prescribed term of one to three years in the penitentiary. * * * Officer McFadden testified that while he was patrolling in plain clothes in downtown Cleveland at approximately 2:30 in the afternoon of October 31, 1963, his attention was attracted by two men, Chilton and Terry, standing on the corner of Huron Road and Euclid Avenue. He had never seen the two men before, and he was unable to say precisely what first drew his eye to them. However, he testified that he had been a policeman for 39 years and a detective for 35 and that he had been assigned to patrol this vicinity of downtown Cleveland for shoplifters and pickpockets for 30 years. He explained that he had developed routine habits of observation over the years and that he would "stand and watch people or walk and watch people at many intervals of the day." He added:

---

10. Akhil Reed Amar, *Fourth Amendment First Principles*, 107 Harv. L. Rev. 757, 808 (1994).

11. It is not a universally held view. *E.g.*, Anthony C. Thompson, *Stopping the Usual Suspects: Race and the Fourth Amendment*, 74 N.Y.U. L. Rev. 956 (1999) (contending that the Supreme Court intentionally disguised the race-based aspects of the search and seizure in *Terry*).

"Now, in this case when I looked over they didn't look right to me at the time."[e]

His interest aroused, Officer McFadden took up a post of observation in the entrance to a store 300 to 400 feet away from the two men. [He observed one of the men walk up the street, stop, peer into a store window, walk on, turn around, look in again, and then rejoin the second man and confer. The second man then repeated the process. This was done five or six times by each man] At one point, while the two were standing together on the corner, a third man approached them and engaged them briefly in conversation. This man then left the two others and walked west on Euclid Avenue. Chilton and Terry resumed their measured pacing, peering, and conferring. After this had gone on for 10 to 12 minutes, the two men walked off together, heading west on Euclid Avenue, following the path taken earlier by the third man.

By this time Officer McFadden had become thoroughly suspicious. He testified that after observing their elaborately casual and oft-repeated reconnaissance of the store window on Huron Road, he suspected the two men of "casing a job, a stick-up," and that he considered it his duty as a police officer to investigate further. He added that he feared "they may have a gun." * * * Deciding that the situation was ripe for direct action, Officer McFadden approached the three men, identified himself as a police officer and asked for their names. At this point his knowledge was confined to what he had observed. * * * When the men "mumbled something" in response to his inquiries, Officer McFadden grabbed petitioner Terry, spun him around so that they were facing the other two, with Terry between McFadden and the others, and patted down the outside of his clothing. In the left breast pocket of Terry's overcoat Officer McFadden felt a pistol. He * * * removed a .38–caliber revolver from the pocket and ordered all three men to face the wall with their hands raised. Officer McFadden proceeded to pat down the outer clothing of Chilton and the third man, Katz.[f] He discovered another revolver in the outer pocket of Chilton's overcoat, but no weapons were found on Katz. The officer testified that he only patted the men down to see whether they had weapons, and that he did not put his hands beneath the outer garments of

---

e.   Thirty years after the case, Terry's defense counsel remembers Officer McFadden's testimony as follows:

He was asked specifically what attracted him to them. On one occasion he said, "Well, to tell the truth, I just didn't like 'em." He was asked how long he'd been a police officer. "39 years." How long had he been a detective? "35 years." What did he think they were doing? "Well," he said, "I suspected that they were casing a joint for the purpose of robbing it." "Well," he was asked, "have you ever in your 39 years as a police officer, 35 as a detective, had the opportunity to observe anybody casing a place for a stickup?" He said, "No, I haven't." "Then what attracted you to them?" He indicated he just didn't like them.

Louis Stokes, *Representing John W. Terry*, 72 St. John's L. Rev. 727, 729–30 (1998).

As for McFadden himself, defense counsel Stokes respected him, *id.* at 729:

He was a real character—a tall, stately guy, and basically a good policeman. Mac, as we called him, was really a guy that we really liked. He was straight. One thing about him—as a police officer, he came straight down the line. You did not have to worry about him misrepresenting what the facts were.

f.   Although the *Terry* opinion was not explicit, Terry and Chilton were African–Americans; Katz was white. *Id.* at 729.

either Terry or Chilton until he felt their guns. * * * Officer McFadden seized Chilton's gun, asked the proprietor of the store to call a police wagon, and took all three men to the station, where Chilton and Terry were formally charged with carrying concealed weapons. * * *

I * * *

* * * Unquestionably petitioner was entitled to the protection of the Fourth Amendment as he walked down the street in Cleveland. The question is whether in all the circumstances of this on-the-street encounter, his right to personal security was violated by an unreasonable search and seizure.

We would be less than candid if we did not acknowledge that this question thrusts to the fore difficult and troublesome issues regarding a sensitive area of police activity—issues which have never before been squarely presented to this Court. * * *

On the one hand, it is frequently argued that in dealing with the rapidly unfolding and often dangerous situations on city streets the police are in need of an escalating set of flexible responses, graduated in relation to the amount of information they possess. For this purpose it is urged that distinctions should be made between a "stop" and an "arrest" (or a "seizure" of a person), and between a "frisk" and a "search." Thus, it is argued, the police should be allowed to "stop" a person and detain him briefly for questioning upon suspicion that he may be connected with criminal activity. Upon suspicion that the person may be armed, the police should have the power to "frisk" him for weapons. If the "stop" and the "frisk" give rise to probable cause to believe that the suspect has committed a crime, then the police should be empowered to make a formal "arrest," and a full incident "search" of the person. This scheme is justified in part upon the notion that a "stop" and a "frisk" amount to a mere "minor inconvenience and petty indignity," which can properly be imposed upon the citizen in the interest of effective law enforcement on the basis of a police officer's suspicion.

On the other side the argument is made that the authority of the police must be strictly circumscribed by the law of arrest and search as it has developed to date in the traditional jurisprudence of the Fourth Amendment. It is contended with some force that there is not—and cannot be—a variety of police activity which does not depend solely upon the voluntary cooperation of the citizen and yet which stops short of an arrest based upon probable cause to make such an arrest. The heart of the Fourth Amendment, the argument runs, is a severe requirement of specific justification for any intrusion upon protected personal security, coupled with a highly developed system of judicial controls to enforce upon the agents of the State the commands of the Constitution. Acquiescence by the courts in the compulsion inherent in the field interrogation practices at issue here, it is urged, would constitute an abdication of judicial control over, and indeed an encouragement of, substantial interference with liberty and personal security by police officers whose judgment is necessarily colored by their primary involvement in "the often competitive enterprise of ferreting out crime." This, it is argued, can only serve to exacerbate police-community tensions in the crowded centers of our Nation's cities.

In this context we approach the issues in this case mindful of the limitations of the judicial function in controlling the myriad daily situations in which policemen and citizens confront each other on the street. * * * Ever since its inception, the rule excluding evidence seized in violation of the Fourth Amendment has been recognized as a principal mode of discouraging lawless police conduct. * * *

The exclusionary rule has its limitations, however, as a tool of judicial control. It cannot properly be invoked to exclude the products of legitimate police investigative techniques on the ground that much conduct which is closely similar involves unwarranted intrusions upon constitutional protections. Moreover, in some contexts the rule is ineffective as a deterrent. Street encounters between citizens and police officers are incredibly rich in diversity. They range from wholly friendly exchanges of pleasantries or mutually useful information to hostile confrontations of armed men involving arrests, or injuries, or loss of life. Moreover, hostile confrontations are not all of a piece. Some of them begin in a friendly enough manner, only to take a different turn upon the injection of some unexpected element into the conversation. Encounters are initiated by the police for a wide variety of purposes, some of which are wholly unrelated to a desire to prosecute for crime. Doubtless some police "field interrogation" conduct violates the Fourth Amendment. But a stern refusal by this Court to condone such activity does not necessarily render it responsive to the exclusionary rule. Regardless of how effective the rule may be where obtaining convictions is an important objective of the police, it is powerless to deter invasions of constitutionally guaranteed rights where the police either have no interest in prosecuting or are willing to forgo successful prosecution in the interest of serving some other goal.

Proper adjudication of cases in which the exclusionary rule is invoked demands a constant awareness of these limitations. The wholesale harassment by certain elements of the police community, of which minority groups, particularly Negroes, frequently complain, will not be stopped by the exclusion of any evidence from any criminal trial. Yet a rigid and unthinking application of the exclusionary rule, in futile protest against practices which it can never be used effectively to control, may exact a high toll in human injury and frustration of efforts to prevent crime. No judicial opinion can comprehend the protean variety of the street encounter, and we can only judge the facts of the case before us. Nothing we say today is to be taken as indicating approval of police conduct outside the legitimate investigative sphere. Under our decision, courts still retain their traditional responsibility to guard against police conduct which is overbearing or harassing, or which trenches upon personal security without the objective evidentiary justification which the Constitution requires. When such conduct is identified, it must be condemned by the judiciary and its fruits must be excluded from evidence in criminal trials. And, of course, our approval of legitimate and restrained investigative conduct undertaken on the basis of ample factual justification should in no way discourage the employment of other remedies than the exclusionary rule to curtail abuses for which that sanction may prove inappropriate.

Having thus roughly sketched the perimeters of the constitutional debate over the limits on police investigative conduct in general and the background against which this case presents itself, we turn our attention to the quite narrow question posed by the facts before us: whether it is always unreasonable for a policeman to seize a person and subject him to a limited search for weapons unless there is probable cause for an arrest.
* * *

II

Our first task is to establish at what point in this encounter the Fourth Amendment becomes relevant. That is, we must decide whether and when Officer McFadden "seized" Terry and whether and when he conducted a "search." There is some suggestion in the use of such terms as "stop" and "frisk" that such police conduct is outside the purview of the Fourth Amendment because neither action rises to the level of a "search" or "seizure" within the meaning of the Constitution. We emphatically reject this notion. It is quite plain that the Fourth Amendment governs "seizures" of the person which do not eventuate in a trip to the station house and prosecution for crime—"arrests" in traditional terminology. It must be recognized that whenever a police officer accosts an individual and restrains his freedom to walk away, he has "seized" that person. And it is nothing less than sheer torture of the English language to suggest that a careful exploration of the outer surfaces of a person's clothing all over his or her body in an attempt to find weapons is not a "search." Moreover, it is simply fantastic to urge that such a procedure performed in public by a policeman while the citizen stands helpless, perhaps facing a wall with his hands raised, is a "petty indignity."[13] It is a serious intrusion upon the sanctity of the person, which may inflict great indignity and arouse strong resentment, and it is not to be undertaken lightly.

The danger in the logic which proceeds upon distinctions between a "stop" and an "arrest," or "seizure" of the person, and between a "frisk" and a "search" is twofold. It seeks to isolate from constitutional scrutiny the initial stages of the contact between the policeman and the citizen. And by suggesting a rigid all-or-nothing model of justification and regulation under the Amendment, it obscures the utility of limitations upon the scope, as well as the initiation, of police action as a means of constitutional

---

13. Consider the following apt description:

"[T]he officer must feel with sensitive fingers every portion of the prisoner's body. A thorough search must be made of the prisoner's arms and armpits, waistline and back, the groin and area about the testicles, and entire surface of the legs down to the feet." Priar & Martin, Searching and Disarming Criminals, 45 J. Crim. L. C. & P. S. 481 (1954).

regulation. This Court has held in the past that a search which is reasonable at its inception may violate the Fourth Amendment by virtue of its intolerable intensity and scope. The scope of the search must be "strictly tied to and justified by" the circumstances which rendered its initiation permissible.

The distinctions of classical "stop-and-frisk" theory thus serve to divert attention from the central inquiry under the Fourth Amendment— the reasonableness in all the circumstances of the particular governmental invasion of a citizen's personal security. "Search" and "seizure" are not talismans. We therefore reject the notions that the Fourth Amendment does not come into play at all as a limitation upon police conduct if the officers stop short of something called a "technical arrest" or a "full-blown search."

In this case there can be no question, then, that Officer McFadden "seized" petitioner and subjected him to a "search" when he took hold of him and patted down the outer surfaces of his clothing. We must decide whether at that point it was reasonable for Officer McFadden to have interfered with petitioner's personal security as he did.[16] And in determining whether the seizure and search were "unreasonable" our inquiry is a dual one—whether the officer's action was justified at its inception, and whether it was reasonably related in scope to the circumstances which justified the interference in the first place.

III

If this case involved police conduct subject to the Warrant Clause of the Fourth Amendment, we would have to ascertain whether "probable cause" existed to justify the search and seizure which took place. However, that is not the case. We do not retreat from our holdings that the police must, whenever practicable, obtain advance judicial approval of searches and seizures through the warrant procedure, or that in most instances failure to comply with the warrant requirement can only be excused by exigent circumstances. But we deal here with an entire rubric of police conduct—necessarily swift action predicated upon the on-the-spot observations of the officer on the beat—which historically has not been, and as a practical matter could not be, subjected to the warrant procedure. Instead, the conduct involved in this case must be tested by the Fourth Amendment's general proscription against unreasonable searches and seizures.

Nonetheless, the notions which underlie both the warrant procedure and the requirement of probable cause remain fully relevant in this

---

16. We thus decide nothing today concerning the constitutional propriety of an investigative "seizure" upon less than probable cause for purposes of "detention" and/or interrogation. Obviously, not all personal intercourse between policemen and citizens involves "seizures" of persons. Only when the officer, by means of physical force or show of authority, has in some way restrained the liberty of a citizen may we conclude that a "seizure" has occurred. We cannot tell with any certainty upon this record whether any such "seizure" took place here prior to Officer McFadden's initiation of physical contact for purposes of searching Terry for weapons, and we thus may assume that up to that point no intrusion upon constitutionally protected rights had occurred.

context. In order to assess the reasonableness of Officer McFadden's conduct as a general proposition, it is necessary "first to focus upon the governmental interest which allegedly justifies official intrusion upon the constitutionally protected interests of the private citizen," for there is "no ready test for determining reasonableness other than by balancing the need to search [or seize] against the invasion which the search [or seizure] entails." *Camara v. Municipal Court*, 387 U.S. 523, 534–535, 536–537, 87 S.Ct. 1727, 1735, 18 L.Ed.2d 930 (1967). And in justifying the particular intrusion the police officer must be able to point to specific and articulable facts which, taken together with rational inferences from those facts, reasonably warrant that intrusion. The scheme of the Fourth Amendment becomes meaningful only when it is assured that at some point the conduct of those charged with enforcing the laws can be subjected to the more detached, neutral scrutiny of a judge who must evaluate the reasonableness of a particular search or seizure in light of the particular circumstances. And in making that assessment it is imperative that the facts be judged against an objective standard: would the facts available to the officer at the moment of the seizure or the search "warrant a man of reasonable caution in the belief" that the action taken was appropriate? * * * Anything less would invite intrusions upon constitutionally guaranteed rights based on nothing more substantial than inarticulate hunches, a result this Court has consistently refused to sanction. * * *

Applying these principles to this case, we consider first the nature and extent of the governmental interests involved. One general interest is of course that of effective crime prevention and detection; it is this interest which underlies the recognition that a police officer may in appropriate circumstances and in an appropriate manner approach a person for purposes of investigating possibly criminal behavior even though there is no probable cause to make an arrest. It was this legitimate investigative function Officer McFadden was discharging when he decided to approach petitioner and his companions. He had observed Terry, Chilton, and Katz go through a series of acts, each of them perhaps innocent in itself, but which taken together warranted further investigation. There is nothing unusual in two men standing together on a street corner, perhaps waiting for someone. Nor is there anything suspicious about people in such circumstances strolling up and down the street, singly or in pairs. Store windows, moreover, are made to be looked in. But the story is quite different where, as here, two men hover about a street corner for an extended period of time, at the end of which it becomes apparent that they are not waiting for anyone or anything; where these men pace alternately along an identical route, pausing to stare in the same store window roughly 24 times; where each completion of this route is followed immediately by a conference between the two men on the corner; where they are joined in one of these conferences by a third man who leaves swiftly; and where the two men finally follow the third and rejoin him a couple of blocks away. It would have been poor police work indeed for an officer of

30 years' experience in the detection of thievery from stores in this same neighborhood to have failed to investigate this behavior further.

The crux of this case, however, is not the propriety of Officer McFadden's taking steps to investigate petitioner's suspicious behavior, but rather, whether there was justification for McFadden's invasion of Terry's personal security by searching him for weapons in the course of that investigation. We are now concerned with more than the governmental interest in investigating crime; in addition, there is the more immediate interest of the police officer in taking steps to assure himself that the person with whom he is dealing is not armed with a weapon that could unexpectedly and fatally be used against him. Certainly it would be unreasonable to require that police officers take unnecessary risks in the performance of their duties. American criminals have a long tradition of armed violence, and every year in this country many law enforcement officers are killed in the line of duty, and thousands more are wounded. Virtually all of these deaths and a substantial portion of the injuries are inflicted with guns and knives.

In view of these facts, we cannot blind ourselves to the need for law enforcement officers to protect themselves and other prospective victims of violence in situations where they may lack probable cause for an arrest. When an officer is justified in believing that the individual whose suspicious behavior he is investigating at close range is armed and presently dangerous to the officer or to others, it would appear to be clearly unreasonable to deny the officer the power to take necessary measures to determine whether the person is in fact carrying a weapon and to neutralize the threat of physical harm.

We must still consider, however, the nature and quality of the intrusion on individual rights which must be accepted if police officers are to be conceded the right to search for weapons in situations where probable cause to arrest for crime is lacking. Even a limited search of the outer clothing for weapons constitutes a severe, though brief, intrusion upon cherished personal security, and it must surely be an annoying, frightening, and perhaps humiliating experience. * * *

Petitioner * * * says it is unreasonable for the policeman to [frisk a suspect] * * * until such time as the situation evolves to a point where there is probable cause to make an arrest. * * *

There are two weaknesses in this line of reasoning, however. First, it fails to take account of traditional limitations upon the scope of searches, and thus recognizes no distinction in purpose, character, and extent between a search incident to an arrest and a limited search for weapons. The former, although justified in part by the acknowledged necessity to protect the arresting officer from assault with a concealed weapon, is also justified on other grounds, and can therefore involve a relatively extensive exploration of the person. A search for weapons in the absence of probable cause to arrest, however, must, like any other search, be strictly circumscribed by the exigencies which justify its initiation. Thus it must be limited to that which is necessary for the discovery of weapons which might be used to harm the officer or others nearby, and may realistically be characterized as something less than a "full" search, even though it remains a serious intrusion.

A second, and related, objection to petitioner's argument is that it assumes that the law of arrest has already worked out the balance between the particular interests involved here—the neutralization of danger to the policeman in the investigative circumstance and the sanctity of the individual. But this is not so. An arrest is a wholly different kind of intrusion upon individual freedom from a limited search for weapons, and the interests each is designed to serve are likewise quite different. An arrest is the initial stage of a criminal prosecution. It is intended to vindicate society's interest in having its laws obeyed, and it is inevitably accompanied by future interference with the individual's freedom of movement, whether or not trial or conviction ultimately follows. The protective search for weapons, on the other hand, constitutes a brief, though far from inconsiderable, intrusion upon the sanctity of the person.
* * *

Our evaluation of the proper balance that has to be struck in this type of case leads us to conclude that there must be a narrowly drawn authority to permit a reasonable search for weapons for the protection of the police officer, where he has reason to believe that he is dealing with an armed and dangerous individual, regardless of whether he has probable cause to arrest the individual for a crime. The officer need not be absolutely certain that the individual is armed; the issue is whether a reasonably prudent man in the circumstances would be warranted in the belief that his safety or that of others was in danger. And in determining whether the officer acted reasonably in such circumstances, due weight must be given, not to his inchoate and unparticularized suspicion or "hunch," but to the specific reasonable inferences which he is entitled to draw from the facts in light of his experience.

IV

* * * We think on the facts and circumstances Officer McFadden detailed before the trial judge a reasonably prudent man would have been warranted in believing petitioner was armed and thus presented a threat to the officer's safety while he was investigating his suspicious behavior. The actions of Terry and Chilton were consistent with McFadden's hypothesis that these men were contemplating a daylight robbery—which, it is reasonable to assume, would be likely to involve the use of weapons—and nothing in their conduct from the time he first noticed them until the time he confronted them and identified himself as a police officer gave him sufficient reason to negate that hypothesis. Although the trio had departed the original scene, there was nothing to indicate abandonment of an intent to commit a robbery at some point. Thus, when Officer McFadden approached the three men gathered before the display window at Zucker's store he had observed enough to make it quite reasonable to fear that they

were armed; and nothing in their response to his hailing them, identifying himself as a police officer, and asking their names served to dispel that reasonable belief. * * *

The manner in which the seizure and search were conducted is, of course, as vital a part of the inquiry as whether they were warranted at all. The Fourth Amendment proceeds as much by limitations upon the scope of governmental action as by imposing preconditions upon its initiation. * * *

We need not develop at length in this case, however, the limitations which the Fourth Amendment places upon a protective seizure and search for weapons. These limitations will have to be developed in the concrete factual circumstances of individual cases. See *Sibron v. New York*, [392 U.S. 40, 88 S.Ct. 1889, 20 L.Ed.2d 917], decided today. Suffice it to note that such a search, unlike a search without a warrant incident to a lawful arrest, is not justified by any need to prevent the disappearance or destruction of evidence of crime. The sole justification of the search in the present situation is the protection of the police officer and others nearby, and it must therefore be confined in scope to an intrusion reasonably designed to discover guns, knives, clubs, or other hidden instruments for the assault of the police officer.

The scope of the search in this case presents no serious problem in light of these standards. Officer McFadden patted down the outer clothing of petitioner and his two companions. He did not place his hands in their pockets or under the outer surface of their garments until he had felt weapons, and then he merely reached for and removed the guns. * * * Officer McFadden confined his search strictly to what was minimally necessary to learn whether the men were armed and to disarm them once he discovered the weapons. He did not conduct a general exploratory search for whatever evidence of criminal activity he might find.

V

We conclude that the revolver seized from Terry was properly admitted in evidence against him. At the time he seized petitioner and searched him for weapons, Officer McFadden had reasonable grounds to believe that petitioner was armed and dangerous, and it was necessary for the protection of himself and others to take swift measures to discover the true facts and neutralize the threat of harm if it materialized. The policeman carefully restricted his search to what was appropriate to the discovery of the particular items which he sought. Each case of this sort will, of course, have to be decided on its own facts. We merely hold today that where a police officer observes unusual conduct which leads him reasonably to conclude in light of his experience that criminal activity may be afoot and that the persons with whom he is dealing may be armed and presently dangerous, where in the course of investigating this behavior he identifies himself as a policeman and makes reasonable inquiries, and where nothing in the initial stages of the encounter serves to dispel his reasonable fear for his own or others' safety, he is entitled for the protection of himself and others in the area to conduct a carefully limited search of the outer clothing of such persons in an attempt to discover weapons which might be used to assault him. Such a search is a reasonable search under the Fourth Amendment, and any weapons seized may properly be introduced in evidence against the person from whom they were taken.

Affirmed.

[Justice BLACK concurred in the judgment and Chief Justice Warren's opinion except as to matters omitted from the excerpt above.]

Mr. Justice HARLAN, concurring.

While I unreservedly agree with the Court's ultimate holding in this case, I am constrained to fill in a few gaps, as I see them, in its opinion.* * *

In the first place, if the frisk is justified in order to protect the officer during an encounter with a citizen, the officer must first have constitutional grounds to insist on an encounter, to make a *forcible* stop. Any person, including a policeman, is at liberty to avoid a person he considers dangerous. If and when a policeman has a right instead to disarm such a person for his own protection, he must first have a right not to avoid him but to be in his presence. That right must be more than the liberty (again, possessed by every citizen) to address questions to other persons, for ordinarily the person addressed has an equal right to ignore his interrogator and walk away; he certainly need not submit to a frisk for the questioner's protection. I would make it perfectly clear that the right to frisk in this case depends upon the reasonableness of a forcible stop to investigate a suspected crime.

Where such a stop is reasonable, however, the right to frisk must be immediate and automatic if the reason for the stop is, as here, an articulable suspicion of a crime of violence. Just as a full search incident to a lawful arrest requires no additional justification, a limited frisk incident to a lawful stop must often be rapid and routine. There is no reason why an officer, rightfully but forcibly confronting a person suspected of a serious crime, should have to ask one question and take the risk that the answer might be a bullet. * * *

Mr. Justice WHITE, concurring.

* * * I think an additional word is in order concerning the matter of interrogation during an investigative stop. There is nothing in the Constitution which prevents a policeman from addressing questions to anyone on the street. * * * Of course, the person stopped is not obliged to answer, and answers may not be compelled, and refusal to answer furnishes no basis for an arrest, although it may alert the officer to the need for continued observation. * * *

Mr. Justice DOUGLAS, dissenting. * * *

The opinion of the Court disclaims the existence of "probable cause." * * * Had a warrant been sought, a magistrate would * * * have been unauthorized to issue one, for he can act only if there is a showing of "probable cause." We hold today that the police have greater authority to make a "seizure" and conduct a "search" than a judge has to authorize such action. We have said precisely the opposite over and over again.

* * * [P]olice officers up to today have been permitted to effect arrests or searches without warrants only when the facts within their personal knowledge would satisfy the constitutional standard of *probable cause.* * * * The term "probable cause" rings a bell of certainty that is not sounded by phrases such as "reasonable suspicion." Moreover, the meaning of "probable cause" is deeply imbedded in our constitutional history. * * *

To give the police greater power than a magistrate is to take a long step down the totalitarian path. Perhaps such a step is desirable to cope with modern forms of lawlessness. But if it is taken, it should be the deliberate choice of the people through a constitutional amendment. * * *

NOTES AND QUESTIONS

1. *What happened to probable cause?* Officer McFadden clearly did not have time to obtain a warrant to search Terry, Chilton, and Katz. The Supreme Court, therefore, could uncontroversially have justified the lack of a warrant on the basis of exigency, but how does the Chief Justice explain away the probable cause requirement?

2. *Thinking about the implications of Terry.* Professor Akhil Amar, no fan of the "warrant requirement" view of the Fourth Amendment (see p. 186), has written that there are "in effect two inconsistent *Terry* opinions," a "good *Terry*" and "bad *Terry*." Akhil Reed Amar, *Terry and Fourth Amendment First Principles*, 72 St. John's L. Rev. 1097, 1097 (1998). He has described the "good *Terry*" opinion this way:

> First, it embraced a broad definition of "searches" and "seizures," enabling the Fourth Amendment to apply to myriad ways in which government might intrude upon citizens' persons, houses, papers, and effects. Second, the good *Terry* did not insist that all such broadly defined searches and seizures be preceded by warrants. Third, and more dramatic still, the good *Terry* did not insist that all warrantless intrusions be justified by probable cause. The stunning logical lesson of the good *Terry* is thus that a warrantless search or seizure may sometimes lawfully occur in a situation where a warrant could not issue (because probable cause is lacking). Fourth, in place of the misguided notions that every search or seizure always requires a warrant, and always requires probable cause, the good *Terry* insisted that the Fourth Amendment means what it says and says what it means: All searches and seizures must be reasonable. Reasonableness—not the warrant, not probable cause—thus emerged as the central Fourth Amendment mandate and touchstone. Fifth, the good *Terry* identified some of the basic components of Fourth Amendment reasonableness so that the concept would make common sense and

constitutional sense. Reasonable intrusions must be *proportionate* to legitimate governmental purposes—more intrusive government action requires more justification. Reasonableness must focus not only on privacy and secrecy but also on *bodily integrity* and *personal dignity*: Cops act unreasonably not just when they paw through my pockets without good reason, but also when they beat me up for fun or toy with me for sport. Reasonableness also implicates *race*—a complete Fourth Amendment analysis, the good *Terry* insisted, must be sensitive to the possibility of racial oppression and harassment. If we wrongly think that the basic Fourth Amendment mandates are warrants and probable cause, we will have difficulty explicitly factoring race into the equation, but the spacious concept of reasonableness allows us to look race square in the eye, constitutionally.

Id. at 1098–1099.

Do you applaud some or all of these features of *Terry?*

Professor Scott Sundby is less enamored with *Terry,* particularly with its departure from the probable cause requirement:

It is mighty hard to argue with reasonableness. * * * After all, a flexible "reasonableness" based Fourth Amendment standard holds forth the promise of both accommodating a wide variety of governmental interests * * * while still being able to address a myriad of concerns about government overstepping * * *. A "one-size-fits-all" Fourth Amendment reasonableness standard seems to offer the best of all worlds: An ability to have an expansive Fourth Amendment that can be finely calibrated to meet the particularities of any situation.

Let me suggest, however, that when it comes to the Fourth Amendment there can be an unreasonable side to reasonableness, that "more can be less." * * *

My limited goal * * * is to suggest that if one looks at the Fourth Amendment's underlying values, in particular the value of mutual "government-citizen trust," probable cause should be viewed as a norm for a "reasonable" search or seizure. Consequently, any departures from probable cause should be deemed "reasonable" only as limited exceptions allowed under narrow circumstances. * * *

Viewing the Fourth Amendment as founded only upon privacy as a bedrock value * * * is to ignore that the Amendment is part of a larger constitutional setting. Once placed within a broader context of our whole constitutional system, the Amendment becomes much more than merely a constitutional outpost for individual privacy. Instead, the Amendment also becomes part of the mutually reinforcing consent that flows between the citizenry and the government, a form of reciprocal trust: The citizenry gives its consent and trust to the government to be governed and the government, in turn, trusts the citizenry to exercise its liberties responsibly. * * *

This idea of trust is why probable cause must be the center of the Fourth Amendment universe rather than * * * merely one satellite in orbit around a general reasonableness balancing test.

Scott E. Sundby, *An Ode to Probable Cause: A Brief Response to Professors Amar and Slobogin*, 72 St. John's L. Rev. 1133, 1133–1135, 1137–1138 (1998).

3. *Terry and race.* Professor Amar applauded *Terry* for bringing race into the Fourth Amendment picture (Note 2). Not everyone, however, believes that *Terry* handled the race issue adequately:

> When one examines the history and modern exercise of police "stop and frisk" practices, the old adage "the more things change, the more they stay the same," aptly describes the experience of many black men when confronted by police officers. Before the "due process revolution" of the 1960s, a retired, white Detroit police officer told the United States Civil Rights Commission the following:
>
>> I would estimate—and this I have heard in the station also—that if you stop and search 50 Negroes and you get one good arrest out of it that's a good percentage; it's a good day's work. So, in my opinion, there are 49 Negroes whose rights have been misused, and that goes on every day.
>
> * * * [T]hings have not changed much; black men continue to be subjected to arbitrary searches and "frisks" by police. * * *

> The irony, of course, is that the police power to "frisk" suspicious persons is the product of a Supreme Court that did more to promote the legal rights of black Americans than any other court. The Warren Court, led by Chief Justice Earl Warren, played an instrumental role in ending racial * * * discrimination in the United States. * * *

> Thus, it seems paradoxical to criticize the Warren Court as insensitive to the experience of blacks, particularly blacks targeted by police officials. Yet, the Court's ruling in *Terry v. Ohio*, which upheld the power of police to "frisk" persons they suspect are dangerous, merits criticism.* * *

> The *Terry* Court was correct to recognize that the degree of resentment in the black community provoked by stop and frisk policies was a pertinent element in deciding the reasonableness of this practice under the Fourth Amendment. * * * The Court does not promote Fourth Amendment values by ignoring evidence of racial impact. * * *

> My view that *Terry* was wrongly decided emanates from three propositions which bear emphasis. First, long before *Terry* came to the Court, the law was settled on the amount of evidence needed for a warrantless search. In a string of cases involving car searches, the Court left no doubt that the Fourth Amendment required probable cause of criminal conduct before officers could search the inside of a car. * * * If probable cause was the constitutional minimum to justify a car search, then surely an equivalent degree of evidence is required before that officer can undertake "a careful exploration of the outer surfaces of a person's clothing all over his or her body in an attempt to find weapons." * * *

> Second, presenting the issue in *Terry* as a conflict between "police safety" and individual freedom, misunderstands the reality of street encounters. No matter how the Court ruled in *Terry*, police officers would continue frisking people they viewed as a threat to their safety. Once this

pragmatic fact was conceded, the crucial question in *Terry* was who would bear the burden when officers searched without probable cause: The government, which would suffer the suppression of evidence, or the individual, who was the target of a search forbidden by the Constitution?

Finally, the *Terry* Court succumbed to pressure to weaken constitutional principle when it was clear that many politicians, and a large segment of the public, had signaled their disapproval of the Court's effort to extend meaningful constitutional protection to those who needed it the most: Poor and minority persons suspected of criminal behavior. A more confident Court would have surveyed the legal landscape, recognized that stop and frisk practices could not be reconciled with a robust Fourth Amendment, and begun the fight to ensure that blacks, the poor, and other "undesirables," would enjoy the same constitutional privileges possessed by the elite of American society.

Tracey Maclin, *Terry v. Ohio's Fourth Amendment Legacy: Black Men and Police Discretion*, 72 St. John's L. Rev. 1271, 1275–1276, 1285–1287 (1998).

Do you agree with Professor Maclin's concerns? If so, how should the Supreme Court have handled the stop-and-frisk issues raised in the case? Would your solution resolve Maclin's concern about racial harassment? This subject is considered in detail in David A. Harris, *Factors for Reasonable Suspicion: When Black and Poor Means Stopped and Frisked*, 69 Ind. L.J. 659 (1994), and Sheri Lynn Johnson, *Race and the Decision To Detain a Suspect*, 93 Yale L.J. 214 (1983).

4. *Some legal history: the Terry conference.* Professor John Q. Barrett has researched notes kept by Justices Brennan, Douglas and Fortas relating to the justices' conference in the *Terry* case. See John Q. Barrett, *Deciding the Stop and Frisk Cases: A Look Inside the Supreme Court's Conference*, 72 St. John's L. Rev. 749 (1998). Among the notable matters revealed from the notes are:

A. In conference, the Court unanimously voted to affirm Terry's conviction. Justice Douglas, who later would dissent, said little at the conference but indicated his agreement with Chief Justice Warren's view of the case.

B. The justices fairly quickly accepted the defendant's proposition that frisks are Fourth Amendment "searches." There was less agreement on the "stop" issue. Justice Black expressed the view that stops were not Fourth Amendment seizures, because an officer's "right to stop [and] ask questions is part of [the] body of [common] law." He said that the Fourth Amendment "does not fit into it until there is an arrest."

C. There is no record of any member of the Court analyzing the facts of the case through the lens of the reasonableness clause.

D. Perhaps most stunningly in view of the Court's eventual analysis, Professor Barrett discovered that the justices were originally wedded to the probable cause requirement, *i.e.*, they believed that McFadden's activities needed to be justified on grounds of probable cause. The Chief Justice stated that his opinion would "rest solely on 'probable cause'—I would not disregard probable cause." Indeed, Black urged the Chief Justice "to stick by 'probable cause' " and not to require a lesser standard of suspicion. Justices Harlan and Brennan agreed.

E.   Justice Warren indicated that he wanted to "use the case to lay down hard rules for stop and frisk," and to make clear that a "statute can't enlarge a policeman's rights." Justice Fortas suggested that the Court move cautiously, on a case-by-case basis.

5.   Suppose that a police officer, based on her personal observations, reasonably suspects (but lacks probable cause to believe) that a customer in a store is about to shoplift some merchandise. Applying *Terry*, may the officer briefly detain the customer for questioning? May she pat down the suspected shoplifter?

6.   *The "Terry doctrine" after a crime has been committed.* *Terry* and most Supreme Court cases interpreting it have involved circumstances in which the police believed "crime was afoot." In United States v. Hensley, 469 U.S. 221, 105 S.Ct. 675, 83 L.Ed.2d 604 (1985), the Court unanimously ruled that the *Terry* doctrine also applies when an officer seeks to investigate a *completed* felony: Stops are allowed if the "police have a reasonable suspicion, grounded in specific and articulable facts, that a person they encounter was involved in or is wanted in connection with a completed felony."

7.   *Pat-downs (part 1).* When a frisk is permissible under *Terry*, what may the officer do when she feels some object during the pat-down? You will remember (p. 309, Note 2) that the Court recognized a "plain touch" doctrine in Minnesota v. Dickerson, 508 U.S. 366, 113 S.Ct. 2130, 124 L.Ed.2d 334 (1993). Consider how the officer in *Dickerson* conducted a frisk (you may assume the officer had a right to conduct the pat-down):

> The officers pulled their squad car into the alley and ordered respondent to stop and submit to a patdown search. The search revealed no weapons, but the officer conducting the search did take an interest in a small lump in respondent's nylon jacket. The officer later testified:
>
> > "[A]s I pat-searched the front of his body, I felt a lump, a small lump, in the front pocket. I examined it with my fingers and it slid and it felt to be a lump of crack cocaine in cellophane."

The officer then reached into respondent's pocket and retrieved a small plastic bag containing one fifth of one gram of crack cocaine.

Although the officer in *Dickerson* had grounds to pat-down the suspect, the Court held that the crack cocaine here was improperly seized:

> [T]he dispositive question before this Court is whether the officer who conducted the search was acting within the lawful bounds marked by *Terry* at the time he gained probable cause to believe that the lump in respondent's jacket was contraband. * * * The Minnesota Supreme Court, after "a close examination of the record," held that the officer's own testimony "belies any notion that he 'immediately' " recognized the lump as crack cocaine. Rather, the court concluded, the officer determined that the lump was contraband only after "squeezing, sliding and otherwise manipulating the contents of the defendant's pocket"—a pocket which the officer already knew contained no weapon.

Under the State Supreme Court's interpretation of the record before it, it is clear that the court was correct in holding that the police officer in this case overstepped the bounds of the "strictly circumscribed" search for weapons allowed under *Terry.* * * * Here, the officer's continued exploration of respondent's pocket after having concluded that it contained no weapon was unrelated to "[t]he sole justification of the search [under *Terry*:] * * * the protection of the police officer and others nearby." It therefore amounted to the sort of evidentiary search that *Terry* expressly refused to authorize * * *.

8. *Pat-downs (part 2).* Do you agree with the Court that a pat-down constitutes a less serious intrusion that a "full search" of, for example, a suspect's pockets or briefcase? *Should* a frisk be permissible on less than probable cause? In a concurring opinion in *Dickerson, id.,* Justice Scalia expressed misgivings with this aspect of *Terry*:

> I frankly doubt * * * whether the fiercely proud men who adopted our Fourth Amendment would have allowed themselves to be subjected, on mere *suspicion* of being armed and dangerous, to such indignity [as a frisk] * * *. * * * On the other hand, even if a "frisk" prior to arrest would have been considered impermissible in 1791, perhaps it was considered permissible by 1868, when the Fourteenth Amendment (the basis for applying the Fourth Amendment to the States) was adopted. Or perhaps it is only since that time that concealed weapons capable of harming the interrogator quickly and from beyond arm's reach have become common—which might alter the judgment of what is "reasonable" under the original standard. But technological changes were no more discussed in *Terry* than was the original state of the law.
>
> If I were of the view that *Terry* was (insofar as the power to "frisk" is concerned) incorrectly decided, I might—even if I felt bound to adhere to that case—vote to exclude the evidence incidentally discovered, on the theory that half a constitutional guarantee is better than none. * * * As a policy matter, it may be desirable to *permit* "frisks" for weapons, but not to *encourage* "frisks" for drugs by admitting evidence other than weapons.

What do you think of Scalia's half-a-constitutional-right suggestion?

9. *Pat-downs (part 3).* At 2:15 a.m., the police received a tip (not amounting to probable cause, but you may assume for current purposes constituting reasonable suspicion) that a man seated in a nearby vehicle was carrying narcotics and had a gun at his waist. The officer, *O,* approached the vehicle to investigate. He tapped on the car window and asked the occupant, *W,* to open the door. Instead, *W* rolled down the window. When he did, *O* reached inside the car and—without conducting a pat-down—removed a revolver from *W*'s waistband. *W,* charged with illegal possession of a handgun, moved to suppress the weapon.

The Supreme Court in Adams v. Williams, 407 U.S. 143, 92 S.Ct. 1921, 32 L.Ed.2d 612 (1972), upheld *O*'s actions. Why would the Court have authorized the non-pat-down search under the principles of *Terry*? Beyond the pat-down issue, if you had represented *W,* can you think of another argument you could make, based solely on language found in the majority opinion in *Terry*, to argue that *O* acted unlawfully?

10. *When the purpose of the seizure changes: traffic stops that become something more.* The Court stated in *Terry* (end of Part II) that "in determining whether the seizure and search were 'unreasonable' our inquiry in a dual one—whether the officer's action was justified at its inception, and whether it was reasonably related in scope to the circumstances which justified the interference in the first place." In *Terry*, Office McFadden seized Terry and the other suspects in order to investigate a possible imminent robbery; the subsequent pat-down weapons search was reasonably related in scope to the purpose of the initial seizure. In contrast, in *Minnesota v. Dickerson* (Note 7), a pat-down for weapons that turned into a pat-down for drugs fell outside the scope of the *Terry* doctrine and, therefore, was unreasonable.

What if the police temporarily detain a person lawfully on a traffic violation, and then use the opportunity to conduct an investigation unrelated to the reason for the original seizure? For example, in Illinois v. Caballes, 543 U.S. 405, 125 S.Ct. 834, 160 L.Ed.2d 842 (2005), the police lawfully stopped *C*, an automobile driver, to write a warning ticket for speeding. While the vehicle was by the roadside, another officer used a "well-trained narcotics-detection dog" to sniff the vehicle for drugs. The police lacked reasonable suspicion to believe that the vehicle contained drugs.

As we have learned (p. 113, Note 5), the dog-sniffing procedure does not constitute a Fourth Amendment search. However, notice that use of the dog was unrelated to the original justification for the vehicle stop. According to the defense, therefore, "the use of the dog converted the citizen-police encounter from a lawful traffic stop into a drug investigation, and because the shift in purpose was not supported by any reasonable suspicion that [*C*] possessed narcotics, it was unlawful."

The Court, 6–2, rejected this argument. Writing for the majority, Justice Stevens *did* state that "a seizure that is justified solely by the interest in issuing a warning ticket can become unlawful if it is prolonged beyond the time reasonably required to complete that mission." Here, however, the state courts determined that the dog-sniffing procedure did not extend the duration of *C*'s seizure. As for the shift in purpose, Stevens stated that using a dog to sniff for drugs does "not change the character of a traffic stop that is lawful at its inception and otherwise executed in a reasonable manner, unless the dog sniff itself infringed [*C*'s] constitutionally protected interest in privacy." Here, "any interest in possessing contraband cannot be deemed legitimate," and thus, governmental conduct that *only* reveals the possession of contraband "compromises no legitimate privacy interest."

Justice Ginsburg, joined by Justice Souter, disagreed:

A drug-detection dog is an intimidating animal. Injecting such an animal into a routine traffic stop changes the character of the encounter between the police and the motorist. The stop becomes broader, more adversarial, and (in at least some cases) longer. [*C*] * * * was exposed to the embarrassment and intimidation of being investigated, on a public thoroughfare, for drugs. Even if the drug sniff is not characterized as a Fourth Amendment "search," the sniff surely broadened the scope of the traffic-violation-related seizure. * * * Under today's decision, every traffic stop could become an occasion to call in the dogs, to the distress and embarrassment of the law-abiding population. * * * Nor would motorists have constitutional grounds for complaint should police with dogs stationed at long traffic lights, circle cars waiting for the red signal to turn green.

Dog-sniffing aside, the Court recently, and unanimously, stated the rule for traffic stops that become investigations of possible criminal activity:

> A lawful roadside stop begins when a vehicle is pulled over for investigation of a traffic violation. The temporary seizure * * * ordinarily continues, and remains reasonable, for the duration of the stop. Normally, the stop ends when the police have no further need to control the scene, and inform the driver and passengers they are free to leave. An officer's inquiries into matters unrelated to the justification for the traffic stop * * * do not convert the encounter into something other than a lawful seizure, so long as those inquiries do not measurably extend the duration of the stop.

Arizona v. Johnson, 555 U.S. ___, 129 S.Ct. 781, 172 L.Ed.2d 694 (2009).

11. *Problem.* Consider the facts in Sibron v. New York, 392 U.S. 40, 88 S.Ct. 1889, 20 L.Ed.2d 917 (1968), a companion case to *Terry*: O, a police officer, observed S talk with known drug addicts over the course of an eight-hour period. Suspecting that S was selling drugs, O confronted S inside a restaurant, and told him to come outside. Outside, O said, "You know what I am after." S mumbled something and reached into his pocket, at which point O thrust his hand into the pocket and pulled out packets of heroin.

Should the heroin be suppressed at S's trial? What if the officer had not thrust his hand in S's pocket, but instead had ordered him to empty his pockets. Would this be permissible under *Terry*? See United States v. Reyes, 349 F.3d 219 (5th Cir. 2003).

12. *Follow-up tid-bit.* At about the time the Court was hearing the *Terry* case, Terry was confined to an asylum for the criminally insane; prior to the Court hearing, Chilton was shot to death while perpetrating a robbery in Columbus, Ohio. Reuben M. Payne, *The Prosecutor's Perspective on Terry: Detective McFadden Had a Right to Protect Himself*, 72 St. John's L. Rev. 733, 733 (1998). McFadden did take the third individual, Katz, into custody, but no charges were ultimately brought against him.

b. Drawing Lines: "Terry Seizures" versus De Facto Arrests

DUNAWAY v. NEW YORK

Supreme Court of the United States, 1979.
442 U.S. 200, 99 S.Ct. 2248, 60 L.Ed.2d 824.

MR. JUSTICE BRENNAN delivered the opinion of the Court. * * *

I

On March 26, 1971, the proprietor of a pizza parlor in Rochester, N.Y., was killed during an attempted robbery. On August 10, 1971,

Detective Anthony Fantigrossi of the Rochester Police was told by another officer that an informant had supplied a possible lead implicating petitioner in the crime. Fantigrossi questioned the supposed source of the lead—a jail inmate awaiting trial for burglary—but learned nothing that supplied "enough information to get a warrant" for petitioner's arrest. Nevertheless, Fantigrossi ordered other detectives to "pick up" petitioner and "bring him in." Three detectives located petitioner at a neighbor's house on the morning of August 11. Petitioner was taken into custody; although he was not told he was under arrest, he would have been physically restrained if he had attempted to leave. He was driven to police headquarters in a police car and placed in an interrogation room, where he was questioned by officers after being given the warnings required by *Miranda v. Arizona* [p. 581]. Petitioner waived counsel and eventually made statements and drew sketches that incriminated him in the crime. * * *

II * * *

* * * There can be little doubt that petitioner was "seized" in the Fourth Amendment sense when he was taken involuntarily to the police station. And respondent State concedes that the police lacked probable cause to arrest petitioner before his incriminating statement during interrogation. Nevertheless respondent contends that the seizure of petitioner did not amount to an arrest and was therefore permissible under the Fourth Amendment because the police had a "reasonable suspicion" that petitioner possessed "intimate knowledge about a serious and unsolved crime." We disagree.

Before *Terry v. Ohio*, the Fourth Amendment's guarantee against unreasonable seizures of persons was analyzed in terms of arrest, probable cause for arrest, and warrants based on such probable cause. The basic principles were relatively simple and straightforward: The term "arrest" was synonymous with those seizures governed by the Fourth Amendment. While warrants were not required in all circumstances, the requirement of probable cause, as elaborated in numerous precedents, was treated as absolute. * * *

Terry for the first time recognized an exception to the requirement that Fourth Amendment seizures of persons must be based on probable cause. That case involved a brief, on-the-spot stop on the street and a frisk for weapons, a situation that did not fit comfortably within the traditional concept of an "arrest." Nevertheless, the Court held that even this type of "necessarily swift action predicated upon the on-the-spot observations of the officer on the beat" constituted a "serious intrusion upon the sanctity of the person, which may inflict great indignity and arouse strong resentment," and therefore "must be tested by the Fourth Amendment's general proscription against unreasonable searches and seizures." However, since the intrusion involved in a "stop and frisk" was so much less severe than that involved in traditional "arrests," the Court declined to stretch the concept of "arrest"—and the general rule requiring probable cause to make arrests "reasonable" under the Fourth Amendment—to cover such intrusions. Instead, the Court treated the stop-and-frisk intrusion as a *sui generis* "rubric of police conduct." * * * Thus, *Terry* departed from traditional Fourth Amendment analysis in two respects. First, it defined a special category of Fourth Amendment "seizures" so substantially less intrusive than arrests that the general rule requiring probable cause to make Fourth Amendment "seizures" reasonable could be replaced by a balancing test. Second, the application of this balancing test led the Court to approve this narrowly defined less intrusive seizure on grounds less rigorous than probable cause, but only for the purpose of a pat-down for weapons.

Because *Terry* involved an exception to the general rule requiring probable cause, this Court has been careful to maintain its narrow scope. * * *

Respondent State now urges the Court to apply a balancing test, rather than the general rule, to custodial interrogations, and to hold that "seizures" such as that in this case may be justified by mere "reasonable suspicion." *Terry* and its progeny clearly do not support such a result. * * *

In contrast to the brief and narrowly circumscribed intrusions involved in those cases, the detention of petitioner was in important respects indistinguishable from a traditional arrest. Petitioner was not questioned briefly where he was found. Instead, he was taken from a neighbor's home to a police car, transported to a police station, and placed in an interrogation room. He was never informed that he was "free to go"; indeed, he would have been physically restrained if he had refused to accompany the officers or had tried to escape their custody. The application of the Fourth Amendment's requirement of probable cause does not depend on whether an intrusion of this magnitude is termed an "arrest" under state law. The mere facts that petitioner was not told he was under arrest, was not "booked," and would not have had an arrest record if the interrogation had proved fruitless, while not insignificant for all purposes, obviously do not make petitioner's seizure even roughly analogous to the narrowly defined intrusions involved in *Terry* and its progeny. Indeed, any "exception" that could cover a seizure as intrusive as that in this case would threaten to swallow the general rule that Fourth Amendment seizures are "reasonable" only if based on probable cause.

The central importance of the probable-cause requirement to the protection of a citizen's privacy afforded by the Fourth Amendment's guarantees cannot be compromised in this fashion. * * *

In effect, respondent urges us to adopt a multifactor balancing test of "reasonable police conduct under the circumstances" to cover all seizures that do not amount to technical arrests. But the protections intended by the Framers could all too easily disappear in the consideration and balancing of the multifarious circumstances presented by different cases, especially when that balancing may be done in the first instance by police officers engaged in the "often competitive enterprise of ferreting out crime." A single, familiar standard is essential to guide police officers, who have only limited time and expertise to reflect on and balance the social and individual interests involved in the specific circumstances they confront. * * * For all but those narrowly defined intrusions, the requisite "balancing" has been performed in centuries of precedent and is embodied in the principle that seizures are "reasonable" only if supported by probable cause. * * *

* * * We accordingly hold that the Rochester police violated the Fourth and Fourteenth Amendments when, without probable cause, they seized petitioner and transported him to the police station for interrogation. * * *

Mr. Justice POWELL took no part in the consideration or decision of this case.

Mr. Justice WHITE, concurring.

The opinion of the Court might be read to indicate that *Terry v. Ohio* is an almost unique exception to a hard-and-fast standard of probable cause. As our prior cases hold, however, the key principle of the Fourth Amendment is reasonableness—the balancing of competing interests. But if courts and law enforcement officials are to have workable rules, this balancing must in large part be done on a categorical basis—not in an ad hoc, case-by-case fashion by individual police officers. On the other hand, the need for rules of general applicability precludes neither the recognition in particular cases of extraordinary private or public interests, nor the generic recognition of certain exceptions to the normal rule of probable cause where more flexibility is essential. *Cf., e.g., Terry v. Ohio.* It is enough, for me, that the police conduct here is similar enough to an arrest that the normal level of probable cause is necessary before the interests of privacy and personal security must give way.

[The concurring opinion of Justice Stevens is omitted.]

Mr. Justice REHNQUIST, with whom THE CHIEF JUSTICE joins, dissenting. * * *

I

* * * In my view, this is a case where the defendant voluntarily accompanied the police to the station to answer their questions.

* * * According to the testimony of the police officers, one officer approached a house where petitioner was thought to be located and knocked on the door. When a person answered the door, the officer identified himself and asked the individual his name. After learning that the person who answered the door was petitioner, the officer asked him if he would accompany the officers to police headquarters for questioning, and petitioner responded that he would. Petitioner was not told that he was under arrest or in custody and was not warned not to resist or flee. No weapons were displayed and petitioner was not handcuffed. Each officer testified that petitioner was not touched or held during the trip

downtown; his freedom of action was not in any way restrained by the police. In short, the police behavior in this case was entirely free of "physical force or show of authority." * * *

* * * I do not dispute the fact that a police request to come to the station may indeed be an "awesome experience." But I do not think that that fact alone means that in every instance where a person assents to a police request to come to headquarters, there has been a "seizure" within the meaning of the Fourth Amendment. The question turns on whether the officer's conduct is objectively coercive or physically threatening, not on the mere fact that a person might in some measure feel cowed by the fact that a request is made by a police officer.

Therefore, although I agree that the police officers in this case did not have that degree of suspicion or probable cause that would have justified them in physically compelling petitioner to accompany them to the police station for questioning, I do not believe that the record demonstrates as a fact that this is what happened. No involuntary detention for questioning was shown to have taken place. The Fourth Amendment, accordingly, does not require suppression of petitioner's statements. * * *

Notes and Questions

1. Does the dissent disagree with the majority's claim that the police may not compel a person to come to the police station for questioning on less than probable cause? What is the basis of the disagreement between the majority and the dissent?

2. Would the seizure have been permissible if the police had found Dunaway in his front yard and had taken him to their police vehicle and questioned him there about the crime? What if they had taken him against his will from his front yard into his home for questioning?

3. *Drawing lines: moving the suspect (part 1).* In Florida v. Royer, 460 U.S. 491, 103 S.Ct. 1319, 75 L.Ed.2d 229 (1983), two police detectives at Miami International Airport became suspicious of Royer, whose characteristics fit a drug-courier profile and who had paid cash for a one-way ticket to New York. Royer was about to embark on the flight when the detectives approached him. Upon request, he produced his airline ticket and driver's license. The ticket was under an assumed name. The detectives informed Royer that they were narcotics investigators and that they suspected him of transporting narcotics. Without returning the ticket or license, they asked him to accompany them to a small room, which was equipped with a desk and two chairs, adjacent to the airport concourse, where he was alone with the two officers. Meanwhile, one of the detectives retrieved Royer's luggage from the airline and brought it to the room. Royer consented to a search of his luggage that turned up marijuana. During the encounter, the police concededly lacked probable cause to arrest Royer.

Justice White, joined by Justices Marshall, Powell, and Stevens, concluded that the marijuana seized from the luggage had to be suppressed:

We have concluded * * * that at the time Royer produced the key to his suitcase, the detention to which he was then subjected was a more serious intrusion on his personal liberty than is allowable on mere suspicion of criminal activity.

* * * What had begun as a consensual inquiry in a public place had escalated into an investigatory procedure in a police interrogation room, where the police, unsatisfied with previous explanations, sought to confirm their suspicions. The officers had Royer's ticket, they had his identification, and they had seized his luggage. Royer was never informed that he was free to board his plane if he so chose, and he reasonably believed that he was being detained. At least as of that moment, any consensual aspects of the encounter had evaporated * * *. As a practical matter, Royer was under arrest. * * *

We also think that the officers' conduct was more intrusive than necessary to effectuate an investigative detention otherwise authorized by the *Terry* line of cases. First, by returning his ticket and driver's license, and informing him that he was free to go if he so desired, the officers might have obviated any claim that the encounter was anything but a consensual matter from start to finish. Second, there are undoubtedly reasons of safety and security that would justify moving a suspect from one location to another during an investigatory detention, such as from an airport concourse to a more private area. There is no indication in this case that such reasons prompted the officers to transfer the site of the encounter from the concourse to the interrogation room. * * * The record does not reflect any facts which would support a finding that the legitimate law enforcement purposes which justified the detention in the first instance were furthered by removing Royer to the police room prior to the officers' attempt to gain his consent to a search of his luggage. * * *

Third, the State has not touched on the question whether it would have been feasible to investigate the contents of Royer's bags in a more expeditious way. The courts are not strangers to the use of trained dogs to detect the presence of controlled substances in luggage. There is no indication here that this means was not feasible and available. If it had been used, Royer and his luggage could have been momentarily detained while this investigative procedure was carried out. Indeed, it may be that no detention at all would have been necessary. A negative result would have freed Royer in short order; a positive result would have resulted in his justifiable arrest on probable cause.

4. *Drawing lines: moving the suspect (part 2).* In Pennsylvania v. Mimms, 434 U.S. 106, 98 S.Ct. 330, 54 L.Ed.2d 331 (1977), *O* validly stopped *M* in his vehicle in order to issue him a traffic citation. *O* ordered *M* out of the car, as he routinely did with all traffic violators. When *M* complied, *O* observed a large bulge under *M*'s jacket. *O* frisked *M*, felt a gun, and seized it. The bulge would not have been observed had *O* not ordered *M* out of the car, so the issue in the case centered around that action.

The state court held that *O* did not have a right to order *M* out of the vehicle because he lacked a reasonable belief that the driver posed a threat to his safety. The Supreme Court disagreed. Balancing the competing interests, it ruled that when an officer legally stops a driver on the highway, he may order the driver out of the car without further justification. It described the interest in police safety as "legitimate and weighty." On the other side of the scale is the driver's interest, having been lawfully stopped, to be permitted to stay in his car:

> We think this additional intrusion [of getting out of the car] can only be described as *de minimis*. The driver is being asked to expose very little more of his person than is already exposed. The police have already lawfully decided that the driver shall be briefly detained: the only question is whether he shall spend that period sitting in the driver's seat of his car or standing alongside it.

What if a driver, stopped for a ticket, has a passenger in his car. Is the officer justified in ordering *her* out of the car, too? In Maryland v. Wilson, 519 U.S. 408, 117 S.Ct. 882, 137 L.Ed.2d 41 (1997), the Court, 7–2, said yes. "On the public interest side of the balance, the same weighty interest in officer safety is present regardless of whether the occupant of the stopped car is a driver or passenger." In support, the Court cited FBI statistics that in one year alone, 5,762 officers were assaulted, and 11 killed, during traffic pursuits and stops.

"On the personal liberty side of the balance," the Court stated, "the case for the passengers is * * * stronger than that for the driver. There is probable cause to believe that the driver has committed a minor vehicular offense, but there is no reason to stop or detain the passengers." However, practically speaking, since innocent passengers are inevitably seized when the driver is stopped, the Court concluded that a change in circumstances—being ordered out of the car—was again too minor an additional intrusion to outweigh police safety.

Do you see the balance that way? What if an officer not only routinely orders drivers and passengers out of vehicles, but also requires them to keep their hands up while she issues driving citations?

What if the speeding vehicle is a taxicab, and the passenger wants to leave to find another cab. May an officer order her to *remain* until he completes ticketing the driver?

5. *Drawing lines: length of the detention.* In *Terry v. Ohio*, Officer McFadden only detained Terry and Chilton briefly before he determined that he had grounds to arrest them for possession of concealed weapons. In *Royer* (Note 3), the Court believed that the police did not act expeditiously in conducting their investigation. Does this mean, therefore, that a *Terry*-type seizure may not lawfully extend beyond a few minutes? Not necessarily.

In United States v. Sharpe, 470 U.S. 675, 105 S.Ct. 1568, 84 L.Ed.2d 605 (1985), federal drug agent Cooke patrolling a highway for drug trafficking observed a suspicious camper truck apparently traveling in tandem with a Pontiac. He radioed for assistance, and state highway patrolman Thrasher responded. They attempted to pull the cars over. The driver of the Pontiac pulled to the side, but the camper truck driver did not stop immediately. Thrasher successfully pursued the camper, which eventually pulled over.

Agent Cooke obtained identification from the Pontiac driver and then unsuccessfully attempted to reach Thrasher by radio. Cooke radioed for more assistance. When it arrived, he left the officers with the Pontiac and drove to the spot where Thrasher had pulled over the camper. When he smelled marijuana coming from the truck, he opened it, found bales of marijuana, and arrested the driver. The Court of Appeals held that the 20–minute detention of Savage, the driver of the camper, "failed to meet * * * [*Terry*'s] requirement of brevity." The Supreme Court, per Chief Justice Burger, saw it differently:

> [T]he court [below] concluded that the length of the detention alone transformed it from a *Terry* stop into a *de facto* arrest. Counsel for respondents * * * assert that conclusion as their principal argument before this Court, relying particularly upon our decisions in *Dunaway v. New York*; *Florida v. Royer*; and *United States v. Place* [p. 417, Note 4]. That reliance is misplaced.

> * * * *Dunaway* is simply inapposite here: the Court was not concerned with the length of the defendant's detention, but with events occurring during the detention.[4]

> In *Royer*, * * * [a]s in *Dunaway*, * * * the focus was primarily on facts other than the duration of the defendant's detention—particularly the fact that the police confined the defendant in a small airport room for questioning.

> The plurality in *Royer* did note that "an investigative detention must be temporary and last no longer than is necessary to effectuate the purpose of the stop." The Court followed a similar approach in *Place*. * * * "[I]n assessing the effect of the length of the detention, we take into account whether the police diligently pursue their investigation."

> Here, the Court of Appeals did not conclude that the police acted less than diligently, or that they *unnecessarily* prolonged Savage's detention. *Place* and *Royer* thus provide no support for the Court of Appeals' analysis.

> Admittedly, *Terry*, *Dunaway*, *Royer*, and *Place*, considered together, may in some instances create difficult line-drawing problems in distinguishing an investigative stop from a *de facto* arrest. Obviously, if an investigative stop continues indefinitely, at some point it can no longer be justified as an investigative stop. But our cases impose no rigid time limitation on *Terry* stops. While it is clear that "the brevity of the invasion of the individual's Fourth Amendment interests is an important factor in determining whether the seizure is so minimally intrusive as to be justifiable on reasonable suspicion," *United States v. Place*, we have emphasized the need to consider the law enforcement purposes to be served by the stop as well as the time reasonably needed to effectuate those purposes. Much as a "bright line" rule would be desirable, in evaluating whether an investigative detention is unreasonable, common

---

4. The pertinent facts relied on by the Court in *Dunaway* were that (1) the defendant was taken from a private dwelling; (2) he was transported unwillingly to the police station; and (3) he there was subjected to custodial interrogation resulting in a confession.

sense and ordinary human experience must govern over rigid criteria. * * *

In assessing whether a detention is too long in duration to be justified as an investigative stop, we consider it appropriate to examine whether the police diligently pursued a means of investigation that was likely to confirm or dispel their suspicions quickly, during which time it was necessary to detain the defendant. A court making this assessment should take care to consider whether the police are acting in a swiftly developing situation, and in such cases the court should not indulge in unrealistic second-guessing. A creative judge engaged in *post hoc* evaluation of police conduct can almost always imagine some alternative means by which the objectives of the police might have been accomplished. But "[t]he fact that the protection of the public might, in the abstract, have been accomplished by 'less intrusive' means does not, by itself, render the search unreasonable." The question is not simply whether some other alternative was available, but whether the police acted unreasonably in failing to recognize or to pursue it.

We readily conclude that, given the circumstances facing him, Agent Cooke pursued his investigation in a diligent and reasonable manner. During most of Savage's 20–minute detention, Cooke was attempting to contact Thrasher and enlisting the help of the local police who remained with Sharpe while Cooke left to pursue Officer Thrasher and the pickup. Once Cooke reached Officer Thrasher and Savage, he proceeded expeditiously * * *.

Clearly this case does not involve any delay unnecessary to the legitimate investigation of the law enforcement officers. Respondents presented no evidence that the officers were dilatory in their investigation. The delay in this case was attributable almost entirely to the evasive actions of Savage, who sought to elude the police as Sharpe moved his Pontiac to the side of the road. Except for Savage's maneuvers, only a short and certainly permissible pre-arrest detention would likely have taken place.

Is *Sharpe* consistent with *Terry*? With *Royer*?

6. *Problem*. Customs officials at L.A. International Airport had reason to suspect Rosa Montoya De Hernandez, who was a Columbia citizen, of being a "balloon swallower," *i.e.*, one who smuggles narcotics into the country hidden in balloons in her alimentary canal. The officials gave the suspect the option of undergoing an x-ray (she refused because she claimed that she was pregnant) or of being returned to her home country. She chose the latter option, but officials could not get her on a flight home due to visa problems. Therefore, "the officers decided on an alternative course: they would simply lock De Hernandez away in an adjacent manifest room 'until her peristaltic functions produced a monitored bowel movement.' The officers explained to De Hernandez that she could not leave until she had excreted by squatting over a wastebasket pursuant to the watchful eyes of two attending matrons."

The suspect was put incommunicado in a small room that contained only hard chairs and a table, where she remained for more than 16 hours during which she did not defecate. At that point, customs officials sought and received a court order authorizing a pregnancy test, which turned out negative, and a rectal examination that confirmed the existence of a balloon containing a foreign substance. Overall, the detention lasted nearly 24 hours. Is this a *Terry* seizure or *de facto* arrest? See United States v. Montoya de Hernandez, 473 U.S. 531, 105 S.Ct. 3304, 87 L.Ed.2d 381 (1985).

c. Drawing Lines: Seizure versus Non–Seizure Encounters

UNITED STATES v. MENDENHALL

Supreme Court of the United States, 1980.
446 U.S. 544, 100 S.Ct. 1870, 64 L.Ed.2d 497.

MR. JUSTICE STEWART announced the judgment of the Court and delivered an opinion, in which MR. JUSTICE REHNQUIST joined.**

* * *

I

* * * The respondent arrived at the Detroit Metropolitan Airport on a commercial airline flight from Los Angeles early in the morning on February 10, 1976. As she disembarked from the airplane, she was observed by two agents of the DEA [Drug Enforcement Administration], who were present at the airport for the purpose of detecting unlawful traffic in narcotics. After observing the respondent's conduct, which appeared to the agents to be characteristic of persons unlawfully carrying narcotics,[1] the agents approached her as she was walking through the concourse, identified themselves as federal agents, and asked to see her identification and airline ticket. The respondent produced her driver's license, which was in the name of Sylvia Mendenhall, and, in answer to a question of one of the agents, stated that she resided at the address appearing on the license. The airline ticket was issued in the name of "Annette Ford." When asked why the ticket bore a name different from her own, the respondent stated that she "just felt like using that name." In response to a further question, the respondent indicated that she had been in California only two days. Agent Anderson then specifically identified himself as a federal narcotics agent and, according to his testimony, the respondent "became quite shaken, extremely nervous. She had a hard time speaking."

After returning the airline ticket and driver's license to her, Agent Anderson asked the respondent if she would accompany him to the airport

---

** THE CHIEF JUSTICE, Mr. Justice BLACKMUN, and Mr. Justice POWELL also join all but Part II-a of this opinion.

1. The agent testified that the respondent's behavior fit the so-called "drug courier profile"—an informally compiled abstract of characteristics thought typical of persons carrying illicit drugs. In this case the agents thought it relevant that (1) the respondent was arriving on a flight from Los Angeles, a city believed by the agents to be the place of origin for much of the heroin brought to Detroit; (2) the respondent was the last person to leave the plane, "appeared to be very nervous," and "completely scanned the whole area where [the agents] were standing"; (3) after leaving the plane the respondent proceeded past the baggage area without claiming any luggage; and (4) the respondent changed airlines for her flight out of Detroit.

DEA office for further questions. She did so, although the record does not indicate a verbal response to the request. The office, which was located up one flight of stairs about 50 feet from where the respondent had first been approached, consisted of a reception area adjoined by three other rooms. At the office the agent asked the respondent if she would allow a search of her person and handbag and told her that she had the right to decline the search if she desired. She responded: "Go ahead." She then handed Agent Anderson her purse, which contained a receipt for an airline ticket that had been issued to "F. Bush" three days earlier for a flight from Pittsburgh through Chicago to Los Angeles. The agent asked whether this was the ticket that she had used for her flight to California, and the respondent stated that it was.

A female police officer then arrived to conduct the search of the respondent's person. She asked the agents if the respondent had consented to be searched. The agents said that she had, and the respondent followed the policewoman into a private room. There the policewoman again asked the respondent if she consented to the search, and the respondent replied that she did. The policewoman explained that the search would require that the respondent remove her clothing. The respondent stated that she had a plane to catch and was assured by the policewoman that if she were carrying no narcotics, there would be no problem. The respondent then began to disrobe without further comment. As the respondent removed her clothing, she took from her undergarments two small packages, one of which appeared to contain heroin, and handed both to the policewoman. The agents then arrested the respondent for possessing heroin. * * *

II

* * * Here the Government concedes that its agents had neither a warrant nor probable cause to believe that the respondent was carrying narcotics when the agents conducted a search of the respondent's person. It is the Government's position, however, that the search was conducted pursuant to the respondent's consent, and thus was excepted from the requirements of both a warrant and probable cause. Evidently, the Court of Appeals concluded that the respondent's apparent consent to the search was in fact not voluntarily given and was in any event the product of earlier official conduct violative of the Fourth Amendment. We must first consider, therefore, whether such conduct occurred, either on the concourse or in the DEA office at the airport.

A * * *

We adhere to the view that a person is "seized" only when, by means of physical force or a show of authority, his freedom of movement is restrained. Only when such restraint is imposed is there any foundation whatever for invoking constitutional safeguards. * * *

Moreover, characterizing every street encounter between a citizen and the police as a "seizure," while not enhancing any interest secured by the

Fourth Amendment, would impose wholly unrealistic restrictions upon a wide variety of legitimate law enforcement practices. The Court has on other occasions referred to the acknowledged need for police questioning as a tool in the effective enforcement of the criminal laws. * * *

We conclude that a person has been "seized" within the meaning of the Fourth Amendment only if, in view of all of the circumstances surrounding the incident, a reasonable person would have believed that he was not free to leave.[6] Examples of circumstances that might indicate a seizure, even where the person did not attempt to leave, would be the threatening presence of several officers, the display of a weapon by an officer, some physical touching of the person of the citizen, or the use of language or tone of voice indicating that compliance with the officer's request might be compelled. In the absence of some such evidence, otherwise inoffensive contact between a member of the public and the police cannot, as a matter of law, amount to a seizure of that person.

On the facts of this case, no "seizure" of the respondent occurred. The events took place in the public concourse. The agents wore no uniforms and displayed no weapons. They did not summon the respondent to their presence, but instead approached her and identified themselves as federal agents. They requested, but did not demand to see the respondent's identification and ticket. Such conduct, without more, did not amount to an intrusion upon any constitutionally protected interest. The respondent was not seized simply by reason of the fact that the agents approached her, asked her if she would show them her ticket and identification, and posed to her a few questions. Nor was it enough to establish a seizure that the person asking the questions was a law enforcement official. In short, nothing in the record suggests that the respondent had any objective reason to believe that she was not free to end the conversation in the concourse and proceed on her way, and for that reason we conclude that the agents' initial approach to her was not a seizure.

Our conclusion that no seizure occurred is not affected by the fact that the respondent was not expressly told by the agents that she was free to decline to cooperate with their inquiry, for the voluntariness of her responses does not depend upon her having been so informed. We also reject the argument that the only inference to be drawn from the fact that the respondent acted in a manner so contrary to her self-interest is that she was compelled to answer the agents' questions. It may happen that a person makes statements to law enforcement officials that he later regrets, but the issue in such cases is not whether the statement was self-protective, but rather whether it was made voluntarily. * * *

B

Although we have concluded that the initial encounter between the DEA agents and the respondent on the concourse at the Detroit Airport

---

6. We agree with the District Court that the subjective intention of the DEA agent in this case to detain the respondent, had she attempted to leave, is irrelevant except insofar as that may have been conveyed to the respondent.

did not constitute an unlawful seizure, it is still arguable that the respondent's Fourth Amendment protections were violated when she went from the concourse to the DEA office. Such a violation might in turn infect the subsequent search of the respondent's person. * * *

The question whether the respondent's consent to accompany the agents was in fact voluntary or was the product of duress or coercion, express or implied, is to be determined by the totality of all the circumstances, and is a matter which the Government has the burden of proving. The respondent herself did not testify at the hearing. The Government's evidence showed that the respondent was not told that she had to go to the office, but was simply asked if she would accompany the officers. There were neither threats nor any show of force. The respondent had been questioned only briefly, and her ticket and identification were returned to her before she was asked to accompany the officers.

On the other hand, it is argued that the incident would reasonably have appeared coercive to the respondent, who was 22 years old and had not been graduated from high school. It is additionally suggested that the respondent, a female and a Negro, may have felt unusually threatened by the officers, who were white males. While these factors were not irrelevant, neither were they decisive, and the totality of the evidence in this case was plainly adequate to support the District Court's finding that the respondent voluntarily consented to accompany the officers to the DEA office.

C

Because the search of the respondent's person was not preceded by an impermissible seizure of her person, it cannot be contended that her apparent consent to the subsequent search was infected by an unlawful detention. There remains to be considered whether the respondent's consent to the search was for any other reason invalid. * * *

III

We conclude that the District Court's determination that the respondent consented to the search of her person "freely and voluntarily" was sustained by the evidence and that the Court of Appeals was, therefore, in error in setting it aside. Accordingly, the judgment of the Court of Appeals is reversed, and the case is remanded to that court for further proceedings. * * *

Mr. Justice POWELL, with whom THE CHIEF JUSTICE and Mr. Justice BLACKMUN join, concurring in part and concurring in the judgment.

I join Parts I, II–B, II–C, and III of the Court's opinion. Because neither of the courts below considered the question, I do not reach the Government's contention that the agents did not "seize" the respondent within the meaning of the Fourth Amendment. In my view, we may assume for present purposes that the stop did constitute a seizure.[1] I would hold—as did the District Court—that the federal agents had reasonable suspicion that the respondent was engaging in criminal activity, and, therefore, that they did not violate the Fourth Amendment by stopping the respondent for routine questioning. * * *

II

[Justice Powell set out the reasons why, in the opinion of the concurring justices, the DEA agents possessed reasonable suspicion that Mendenhall was involved in illegal drug activities.]

III

* * * The public interest in preventing drug traffic is great, and the intrusion upon the respondent's privacy was minimal. The specially trained agents acted pursuant to a well-planned, and effective, federal law enforcement program. They observed respondent engaging in conduct that they reasonably associated with criminal activity. Furthermore, the events occurred in an airport known to be frequented by drug couriers.[6] In light of all of the circumstances, I would hold that the agents possessed reasonable and articulable suspicion of criminal activity when they stopped the respondent in a public place and asked her for identification. * * *

Mr. Justice WHITE, with whom Mr. Justice BRENNAN, Mr. Justice MARSHALL, and Mr. Justice STEVENS join, dissenting.

The Court today concludes that agents of the Drug Enforcement Administration (DEA) acted lawfully in stopping a traveler changing planes in an airport terminal and escorting her to a DEA office for a strip-search of her person. This result is particularly curious because a majority of the Members of the Court refuse to reject the conclusion that Ms. Mendenhall was "seized," while a separate majority decline to hold that there were reasonable grounds to justify a seizure. * * *

I * * *

Throughout the lower court proceedings in this case, the Government never questioned that the initial stop of Ms. Mendenhall was a "seizure" that required reasonable suspicion. Rather, the Government sought to justify the stop by arguing that Ms. Mendenhall's behavior had given rise to reasonable suspicion because it was consistent with portions of the so-

---

1. Mr. Justice Stewart concludes in Part II–A that there was no "seizure" within the meaning of the Fourth Amendment. * * * I do not necessarily disagree with the views expressed in Part II–A. For me, the question whether the respondent in this case reasonably could have thought she was free to "walk away" when asked by two Government agents for her driver's license and ticket is extremely close.

6. The results of the Drug Enforcement Agency's efforts at the Detroit Airport support the conclusion that considerable drug traffic flows through the Detroit Airport. Contrary to Mr. Justice White's apparent impression, I do not believe that these statistics establish by themselves the reasonableness of this search. Nor would reliance upon the "drug courier profile" necessarily demonstrate reasonable suspicion. Each case raising a Fourth Amendment issue must be judged on its own facts.

called "drug courier profile," an informal amalgam of characteristics thought to be associated with persons carrying illegal drugs. Having failed to convince the Court of Appeals that the DEA agents had reasonable suspicion for the stop, the Government seeks reversal here by arguing for the first time that no "seizure" occurred, an argument that Mr. Justice Stewart now accepts, thereby pretermitting the question whether there was reasonable suspicion to stop Ms. Mendenhall. Mr. Justice Stewart's opinion * * * addresses a fact-bound question with a totality-of-circumstances assessment that is best left in the first instance to the trial court, particularly since the question was not litigated below and hence we cannot be sure is adequately addressed by the record before us.

Mr. Justice Stewart believes that a "seizure" within the meaning of the Fourth Amendment occurs when an individual's freedom of movement is restrained by means of physical force or a show of authority. Although it is undisputed that Ms. Mendenhall was not free to leave after the DEA agents stopped her and inspected her identification, Mr. Justice Stewart concludes that she was not "seized" because he finds that, under the totality of the circumstances, a reasonable person would have believed that she was free to leave. While basing this finding on an alleged absence from the record of objective evidence indicating that Ms. Mendenhall was not free to ignore the officer's inquiries and continue on her way, Mr. Justice Stewart's opinion brushes off the fact that this asserted evidentiary deficiency may be largely attributable to the fact that the "seizure" question was never raised below. In assessing what the record does reveal, the opinion discounts certain objective factors that would tend to support a "seizure" finding,[3] while relying on contrary factors inconclusive even under its own illustrations of how a "seizure" may be established.[4] * * * Even if one believes the Government should be permitted to raise the "seizure" question in this Court, the proper course would be to direct a remand to the District Court for an evidentiary hearing on the question, rather than to decide it in the first instance in this Court.

II

Assuming, as we should, that Ms. Mendenhall was "seized" within the meaning of the Fourth Amendment when she was stopped by the DEA agents, the legality of that stop turns on whether there were reasonable grounds for suspecting her of criminal activity at the time of the stop. * * *

None of the aspects of Ms. Mendenhall's conduct, either alone or in combination, were sufficient to provide reasonable suspicion that she was engaged in criminal activity. * * *

---

3. Not the least of these factors is the fact that the DEA agents for a time took Ms. Mendenhall's plane ticket and driver's license from her. It is doubtful that any reasonable person about to board a plane would feel free to leave when law enforcement officers have her plane ticket.

4. Mr. Justice Stewart notes, for example, that a "seizure" might be established even if the suspect did not attempt to leave, by the nature of the language or tone of voice used by the officers, factors that were never addressed at the suppression hearing, very likely because the "seizure" question was not raised.

III

Whatever doubt there may be concerning whether Ms. Mendenhall's Fourth Amendment interests were implicated during the initial stages of her confrontation with the DEA agents, she undoubtedly was "seized" within the meaning of the Fourth Amendment when the agents escorted her from the public area of the terminal to the DEA office for questioning and a strip-search of her person. * * * Like the "seizure" in *Dunaway*, the nature of the intrusion to which Ms. Mendenhall was subjected when she was escorted by DEA agents to their office and detained there for questioning and a strip-search was so great that it "was in important respects indistinguishable from a traditional arrest." Although Ms. Mendenhall was not told that she was under arrest, she in fact was not free to refuse to go to the DEA office and was not told that she was. Furthermore, once inside the office, Ms. Mendenhall would not have been permitted to leave without submitting to a strip-search. * * *

* * * There was no evidence in the record to support the District Court's speculation, made before *Dunaway* was decided, that Ms. Mendenhall accompanied "Agent Anderson to the airport DEA Office 'voluntarily in a spirit of apparent cooperation with the [agent's] investigation.' " Ms. Mendenhall did not testify at the suppression hearing and the officers presented no testimony concerning what she said, if anything, when informed that the officers wanted her to come with them to the DEA office. Indeed, the only testimony concerning what occurred between Agent Anderson's "request" and Ms. Mendenhall's arrival at the DEA office is the agent's testimony that if Ms. Mendenhall had wanted to leave at that point she would have been forcibly restrained. * * *

* * * While the Government need not prove that Ms. Mendenhall knew that she had a right to refuse to accompany the officers, it cannot rely solely on acquiescence to the officers' wishes to establish the requisite consent. The Court of Appeals properly understood this in rejecting the District Court's "findings" of consent.

* * * [I]t is unbelievable[15] that this sequence of events involved no invasion of a citizen's constitutionally protected interest in privacy. The rule of law requires a different conclusion. * * *

NOTES AND QUESTIONS

1. How many (and which) justices believe that Mendenhall was seized? How many (and which) justices believe that the police had sufficient justification to seize Mendenhall?

Do *you* believe that Mendenhall was seized? If so, at what point did the seizure occur? Did it occur when the DEA agents first came up to Mendenhall and identified themselves? Would *you* have felt free to ignore the agents at this point and move on? If she was not seized then, was she seized when they

---

15. "Will you walk into my parlour?" said the spider to a fly.

(You may find you have consented, without ever knowing why.)

asked for her ticket and license? Or, when they took her to the DEA office in the airport? If she was seized in your opinion, what level of seizure occurred— a *Terry*-level seizure or a *Dunaway*-type seizure (that is, a seizure tantamount to an arrest)?

2. *Variation on the facts.* Suppose that when the officers obtained Mendenhall's license and ticket, they had used her license to check her identity on a computer to see if she had any outstanding arrest warrants, a process taking five minutes. Would *that* have converted the encounter into a seizure? See Reynolds v. State, 130 Md.App. 304, 746 A.2d 422 (1999).

3. Reconsider the facts in *Florida v. Royer* (p. 371, Note 3) in light of *Mendenhall*. Since we know that the Court ruled that Royer was seized (indeed, virtually arrested) when he was taken to the small room, how do we distinguish that outcome from *Mendenhall*?

4. *The potential role of race and other characteristics in "seizure" analysis.* To what extent is it relevant to the analysis that Mendenhall was an African–American woman, and that the police were white males? Consider the following:

> Two years ago, a provocative assertion appeared in the editorial pages of the New York Times. It read: "The black American finds that the most prominent reminder of his second-class citizenship are the police." The author of this sentence, Don Jackson, knew what he was talking about because he is a former police officer, who also happened to be a black man. Part of the foundation for Mr. Jackson's charge is a deep-seated distrust between police officers and black citizens. * * *
>
> * * * [M]y thesis is that police encounters involving black men contain a combination of fear, distrust, anger and coercion that make these encounters unique and always potentially explosive. * * *
>
> To be sure, when whites are stopped by the police, they too feel uneasy and often experience fear. Inherent in any police encounter, even for whites, is the fear that the officer will abuse his authority by being arrogant, or act in a manner that causes the individual to feel more nervous than necessary. * * *
>
> But I wonder whether the average white person worries that an otherwise routine police encounter may lead to a violent confrontation. When they are stopped by the police, do whites contemplate the possibility that they will be physically abused for questioning why an officer has stopped them? White teenagers who walk the streets or hang-out in the local mall, do they worry about being strip-searched by the police? Does the average white person ever see himself experiencing what Rodney King * * * went through during [his] encounter[] with the police?

Tracey Maclin, *"Black and Blue Encounters"—Some Preliminary Thoughts About Fourth Amendment Seizures: Should Race Matter?*, 26 Val. U. L. Rev. 243, 243, 254–56 (1991).

If this mutual distrust exists, and if African–Americans, especially black males, fear the police in a way that white males do not, should the law take this difference into account in measuring police conduct? Specifically, if the question is whether a "reasonable person" in the suspect's situation would believe that he is not free to leave, should we incorporate the suspect's race in that analysis (as Professor Maclin ultimately recommends), or should the law apply a race-blind approach? If the race of the suspect *should* be considered, are there other characteristics that should be included?

5. *Problem.* Officer, in police uniform, comes to *S*'s home at midnight and knocks at the door. *S*'s roommate opens the door. Officer asks if *S* is at home. Told that "he is, but is asleep," Officer insists that the roommate awaken *S*. When *S* arrives at the door, Officer tells him he is investigating a traffic violation and asks him to step outside the house. Seizure? State v. Scott, 138 N.M. 751, 126 P.3d 567 (2005).

UNITED STATES v. DRAYTON

Supreme Court of the United States, 2002.
536 U.S. 194, 122 S.Ct. 2105, 153 L.Ed.2d 242.

JUSTICE KENNEDY delivered the opinion of the Court. * * *

I

On February 4, 1999, respondents Christopher Drayton and Clifton Brown, Jr., were traveling on a Greyhound bus en route from Ft. Lauderdale, Florida, to Detroit, Michigan. The bus made a scheduled stop in Tallahassee, Florida. The passengers were required to disembark so the bus could be refueled and cleaned. As the passengers reboarded, the driver checked their tickets and then left to complete paperwork inside the terminal. As he left, the driver allowed three members of the Tallahassee Police Department to board the bus as part of a routine drug and weapons interdiction effort. The officers were dressed in plain clothes and carried concealed weapons and visible badges.

Once onboard Officer Hoover knelt on the driver's seat and faced the rear of the bus. He could observe the passengers * * * without blocking the aisle or otherwise obstructing the bus exit. Officers Lang and Blackburn went to the rear of the bus. Blackburn remained stationed there, facing forward. Lang worked his way toward the front of the bus, speaking with individual passengers as he went. He asked the passengers about their travel plans and sought to match passengers with luggage in the overhead racks. To avoid blocking the aisle, Lang stood next to or just behind each passenger with whom he spoke.

According to Lang's testimony, passengers who declined to cooperate with him or who chose to exit the bus at any time would have been allowed to do so without argument. In Lang's experience, however, most people are willing to cooperate. Some passengers go so far as to commend the police for their efforts to ensure the safety of their travel. Lang could recall five to six instances in the previous year in which passengers had declined to have their luggage searched. It also was common for passengers to leave the bus for a cigarette or a snack while the officers were on board. Lang sometimes informed passengers of their right to refuse to cooperate. On the day in question, however, he did not.

Respondents were seated next to each other on the bus. Drayton was in the aisle seat, Brown in the seat next to the window. Lang approached respondents from the rear and leaned over Drayton's shoulder. He held up his badge long enough for respondents to identify him as a police officer. With his face 12–to–18 inches away from Drayton's, Lang spoke in a voice just loud enough for respondents to hear:

"I'm Investigator Lang with the Tallahassee Police Department. We're conducting bus interdiction *[sic]*, attempting to deter drugs and illegal weapons being transported on the bus. Do you have any bags on the bus?"

Both respondents pointed to a single green bag in the overhead luggage rack. Lang asked, "Do you mind if I check it?," and Brown responded, "Go ahead." Lang handed the bag to Officer Blackburn to check. The bag contained no contraband.

Officer Lang noticed that both respondents were wearing heavy jackets and baggy pants despite the warm weather. In Lang's experience drug traffickers often use baggy clothing to conceal weapons or narcotics. The officer thus asked Brown if he had any weapons or drugs in his possession. And he asked Brown: "Do you mind if I check your person?" Brown answered, "Sure," and cooperated by leaning up in his seat, pulling a cell phone out of his pocket, and opening up his jacket. Lang reached across Drayton and patted down Brown's jacket and pockets, including his waist area, sides, and upper thighs. In both thigh areas, Lang detected hard objects similar to drug packages detected on other occasions. Lang arrested and handcuffed Brown. Officer Hoover escorted Brown from the bus.

Lang then asked Drayton, "Mind if I check you?" Drayton responded by lifting his hands about eight inches from his legs. Lang conducted a patdown of Drayton's thighs and detected hard objects similar to those found on Brown. He arrested Drayton and escorted him from the bus. A further search revealed that respondents had duct-taped plastic bundles of powder cocaine between several pairs of their boxer shorts. Brown possessed three bundles containing 483 grams of cocaine. Drayton possessed two bundles containing 295 grams of cocaine.

Respondents * * * moved to suppress the cocaine, arguing that the consent to the patdown search was invalid. * * * The District Court determined that the police conduct was not coercive and respondents' consent to the search was voluntary. The District Court pointed to the fact that the officers were dressed in plain clothes, did not brandish their badges in an authoritative manner, did not make a general announcement to the entire bus, and did not address anyone in a menacing tone of voice. It noted that the officers did not block the aisle or the exit, and stated that it was "obvious that [respondents] can get up and leave, as can the people ahead of them." The District Court concluded: "[E]verything that took place between Officer Lang and Mr. Drayton and Mr. Brown suggests that it was cooperative. There was nothing coercive, there was nothing confrontational about it."

The Court of Appeals for the Eleventh Circuit reversed and remanded with instructions to grant respondents' motions to suppress. The court held that * * * bus passengers do not feel free to disregard police officers' requests to search absent "some positive indication that consent could have been refused."

We granted certiorari. The respondents, we conclude, were not seized and their consent to the search was voluntary; and we reverse.

II

Law enforcement officers do not violate the Fourth Amendment's prohibition of unreasonable seizures merely by approaching individuals on the street or in other public places and putting questions to them if they are willing to listen. Even when law enforcement officers have no basis for suspecting a particular individual, they may pose questions, ask for identification, and request consent to search luggage—provided they do not induce cooperation by coercive means. See *Florida v. Bostick,* 501 U.S. 429, 111 S.Ct. 2382, 115 L.Ed.2d 389 (1991). If a reasonable person would feel free to terminate the encounter, then he or she has not been seized.

The Court has addressed on a previous occasion the specific question of drug interdiction efforts on buses. In *Bostick,* two police officers requested a bus passenger's consent to a search of his luggage. The passenger agreed, and the resulting search revealed cocaine in his suitcase. The Florida Supreme Court suppressed the cocaine. In doing so it adopted a *per se* rule that due to the cramped confines onboard a bus the act of questioning would deprive a person of his or her freedom of movement and so constitute a seizure under the Fourth Amendment.

This Court reversed. *Bostick* first made it clear that for the most part *per se* rules are inappropriate in the Fourth Amendment context. The proper inquiry necessitates a consideration of "all the circumstances surrounding the encounter." The Court noted next that the traditional rule, which states that a seizure does not occur so long as a reasonable person would feel free "to disregard the police and go about his business," is not an accurate measure of the coercive effect of a bus encounter. A passenger may not want to get off a bus if there is a risk it will depart before the opportunity to reboard. A bus rider's movements are confined in this sense, but this is the natural result of choosing to take the bus; it says nothing about whether the police conduct is coercive. The proper inquiry "is whether a reasonable person would feel free to decline the officers' requests or otherwise terminate the encounter." Finally, the Court rejected Bostick's argument that he must have been seized because no reasonable person would consent to a search of luggage containing drugs. The reasonable person test, the Court explained, is objective and "presupposes an *innocent* person."

In light of the limited record, *Bostick* refrained from deciding whether a seizure occurred. The Court, however, identified two factors "particularly worth noting" on remand. First, although it was obvious that an officer was armed, he did not remove the gun from its pouch or use it in a threatening way. Second, the officer advised the passenger that he could refuse consent to the search. * * *

Applying the *Bostick* framework to the facts of this particular case, we conclude that the police did not seize respondents when they boarded the bus and began questioning passengers. The officers gave the passengers no reason to believe that they were required to answer the officers' questions. When Officer Lang approached respondents, he did not brandish a weapon or make any intimidating movements. He left the aisle free so that respondents could exit. He spoke to passengers one by one and in a polite, quiet voice. Nothing he said would suggest to a reasonable person that he or she was barred from leaving the bus or otherwise terminating the encounter.

There were ample grounds for the District Court to conclude that "everything that took place between Officer Lang and [respondents] suggests that it was cooperative" and that there "was nothing coercive [or] confrontational" about the encounter. There was no application of force, no intimidating movement, no overwhelming show of force, no brandishing of weapons, no blocking of exits, no threat, no command, not even an authoritative tone of voice. It is beyond question that had this encounter occurred on the street, it would be constitutional. The fact that an encounter takes place on a bus does not on its own transform standard police questioning of citizens into an illegal seizure. Indeed, because many fellow passengers are present to witness officers' conduct, a reasonable person may feel even more secure in his or her decision not to cooperate with police on a bus than in other circumstances.

Respondents make much of the fact that Officer Lang displayed his badge. In * * * *INS v. Delgado,* 466 U.S. 210, 212–213, 104 S.Ct. 1758, 80 L.Ed.2d 247 (1984), the Court held that Immigration and Naturalization Service (INS) agents' wearing badges and questioning workers in a factory did not constitute a seizure. And while neither Lang nor his colleagues were in uniform or visibly armed, those factors should have little weight in the analysis. Officers are often required to wear uniforms and in many circumstances this is cause for assurance, not discomfort. Much the same can be said for wearing sidearms. That most law enforcement officers are armed is a fact well known to the public. The presence of a holstered firearm thus is unlikely to contribute to the coerciveness of the encounter absent active brandishing of the weapon.

Officer Hoover's position at the front of the bus also does not tip the scale in respondents' favor. Hoover did nothing to intimidate passengers, and he said nothing to suggest that people could not exit and indeed he left the aisle clear. In *Delgado,* the Court determined there was no seizure even though several uniformed INS officers were stationed near the exits of the factory. The Court noted: "The presence of agents by the exits posed no reasonable threat of detention to these workers, * * * the mere possibility that they would be questioned if they sought to leave the buildings should not have resulted in any reasonable apprehension by any of them that they would be seized or detained in any meaningful way."

Finally, the fact that in Officer Lang's experience only a few passengers have refused to cooperate does not suggest that a reasonable person would not feel free to terminate the bus encounter. In Lang's experience it was common for passengers to leave the bus for a cigarette or a snack while the officers were questioning passengers. And of more importance, bus passengers answer officers' questions and otherwise cooperate not because of coercion but because the passengers know that their participation enhances their own safety and the safety of those around them. * * *

Drayton contends that even if Brown's cooperation with the officers was consensual, Drayton was seized because no reasonable person would feel free to terminate the encounter with the officers after Brown had been arrested. The Court of Appeals did not address this claim; and in any event the argument fails. The arrest of one person does not mean that everyone around him has been seized by police. If anything, Brown's arrest should have put Drayton on notice of the consequences of continuing the encounter by answering the officers' questions. Even after arresting Brown, Lang addressed Drayton in a polite manner and provided him with no indication that he was required to answer Lang's questions.

We turn now from the question whether respondents were seized to whether they were subjected to an unreasonable search, *i.e.,* whether their consent to the suspicionless search was involuntary. * * * Nothing Officer Lang said indicated a command to consent to the search. Rather, when respondents informed Lang that they had a bag on the bus, he asked for their permission to check it. And when Lang requested to search Brown and Drayton's persons, he asked first if they objected, thus indicating to a reasonable person that he or she was free to refuse. Even after arresting Brown, Lang provided Drayton with no indication that he was required to consent to a search. To the contrary, Lang asked for Drayton's permission to search him ("Mind if I check you?"), and Drayton agreed.

The Court has rejected in specific terms the suggestion that police officers must always inform citizens of their right to refuse when seeking permission to conduct a warrantless consent search. *Schneckloth v. Bustamonte,* [p. 310, supra]. "While knowledge of the right to refuse consent is one factor to be taken into account, the government need not establish such knowledge as the *sine qua non* of an effective consent." *Ibid.* Nor do this Court's decisions suggest that even though there are no *per se* rules, a presumption of invalidity attaches if a citizen consented without explicit notification that he or she was free to refuse to cooperate. Instead, the Court has repeated that the totality of the circumstances must control, without giving extra weight to the absence of this type of warning.

Although Officer Lang did not inform respondents of their right to refuse the search, he did request permission to search, and the totality of the circumstances indicates that their consent was voluntary, so the searches were reasonable.

In a society based on law, the concept of agreement and consent should be given a weight and dignity of its own. Police officers act in full accord with the law when they ask citizens for consent. It reinforces the rule of law for the citizen to advise the police of his or her wishes and for the police to act in reliance on that understanding. When this exchange takes place, it dispels inferences of coercion. * * *

The judgment of the Court of Appeals is reversed, and the case is remanded for further proceedings consistent with this opinion. * * *

Justice SOUTER, with whom Justice STEVENS and Justice GINSBURG join, dissenting.

Anyone who travels by air today submits to searches of the person and luggage as a condition of boarding the aircraft. It is universally accepted that such intrusions are necessary to hedge against risks that, nowadays, even small children understand. The commonplace precautions of air travel have not, thus far, been justified for ground transportation, however, and no such conditions have been placed on passengers getting on trains or buses. There is therefore an air of unreality about the Court's explanation that bus passengers consent to searches of their luggage to "enhanc[e] their own safety and the safety of those around them." Nor are the other factual assessments underlying the Court's conclusion in favor of the Government more convincing. * * *

Florida v. Bostick established the framework for determining whether the bus passengers were seized in the constitutional sense. * * *

Before applying the standard in this case, it may be worth getting some perspective from different sets of facts. A perfect example of police conduct that supports no colorable claim of seizure is the act of an officer who simply goes up to a pedestrian on the street and asks him a question. A pair of officers questioning a pedestrian, without more, would presumably support the same conclusion. Now consider three officers, one of whom stands behind the pedestrian, another at his side toward the open sidewalk, with the third addressing questions to the pedestrian a foot or two from his face. Finally, consider the same scene in a narrow alley. On such barebones facts, one may not be able to say a seizure occurred, even in the last case, but one can say without qualification that the atmosphere of the encounters differed significantly from the first to the last examples. In the final instance there is every reason to believe that the pedestrian would have understood, to his considerable discomfort, what Justice Stewart described as the "threatening presence of several officers," *United States v. Mendenhall,* [p. 376, supra]. The police not only carry legitimate authority but also exercise power free from immediate check, and when the attention of several officers is brought to bear on one civilian the imbalance of immediate power is unmistakable. We all understand this, as well as we understand that a display of power rising to Justice Stewart's "threatening" level may overbear a normal person's ability to act freely, even in the absence of explicit commands or the formalities of detention. As common as this understanding is, however, there is little sign of it in the Court's opinion. My own understanding of the relevant facts and their significance follows. * * *

* * * [F]or reasons unexplained, the [bus] driver with the tickets entitling the passengers to travel * * * yielded his custody of the bus and its seated travelers to three police officers, whose authority apparently superseded the driver's own. The officers took control of the entire passenger compartment, one stationed at the door keeping surveillance of all the occupants, the others working forward from the back. With one officer right behind him and the other one forward, a third officer accosted each passenger at quarters extremely close and so cramped that as many as half the passengers could not even have stood to face the speaker. None was asked whether he was willing to converse with the police or to take part in the enquiry. Instead the officer said the police were "conducting bus interdiction," in the course of which they "would like * * * cooperation." The reasonable inference was that the "interdiction" was not a consensual exercise, but one the police would carry out whatever the circumstances; that they would prefer "cooperation" but would not let the lack of it stand in their way. There was no contrary indication that day, since no passenger had refused the cooperation requested, and there was no reason for any passenger to believe that the driver would return and the trip resume until the police were satisfied. The scene was set and an atmosphere of obligatory participation was established by this introduction. Later requests to search prefaced with "Do you mind * * * '" would naturally have been understood in the terms with which the encounter began.

It is very hard to imagine that either Brown or Drayton would have believed that he stood to lose nothing if he refused to cooperate with the police, or that he had any free choice to ignore the police altogether. No reasonable passenger could have believed that, only an uncomprehending one. It is neither here nor there that the interdiction was conducted by three officers, not one, as a safety precaution. The fact was that there were three, and when Brown and Drayton were called upon to respond, each one was presumably conscious of an officer in front watching, one at his side questioning him, and one behind for cover, in case he became unruly, perhaps, or "cooperation" was not forthcoming. The situation is much like the one in the alley, with civilians in close quarters, unable to move effectively, being told their cooperation is expected. While I am not prepared to say that no bus interrogation and search can pass the *Bostick* test without a warning that passengers are free to say no, the facts here surely required more from the officers than a quiet tone of voice. A police officer who is certain to get his way has no need to shout. * * *

* * * I respectfully dissent.

Notes and Questions

1. *Bus sweeps*. The Supreme Court first considered the Fourth Amendment validity of so-called "bus sweeps" in *Florida v. Bostick*, discussed in detail in *Drayton*. Consider what Justice Thurgood Marshall said in his dissent in *Bostick*:

> At issue in this case is a "new and increasingly common tactic in the war on drugs": the suspicionless police sweep of buses in interstate or intrastate travel. Typically under this technique, a group of state or federal officers will board a bus while it is stopped at an intermediate point on its route. Often displaying badges, weapons or other indicia of authority, the officers identify themselves and announce their purpose to intercept drug traffickers. They proceed to approach individual passengers, requesting them to show identification, produce their tickets, and explain the purpose of their travels. Never do the officers advise the passengers that they are free not to speak with the officers. An "interview" of this type ordinarily culminates in a request for consent to search the passenger's luggage.

> These sweeps are conducted in "dragnet" style. The police admittedly act without an "articulable suspicion" in deciding which buses to board and which passengers to approach for interviewing.[1] By proceeding systematically in this fashion, the police are able to engage in a tremendously high volume of searches.

What do you think Justice Marshall had in mind when he added footnote 1 to his dissent?

2. Look at the first paragraph of the dissenting opinion in *Drayton*. What do you think Justice Souter may have in mind, but which remains unstated, when he contrasts air travel to ground transportation, and accuses the majority of "an air of unreality" because it fails to draw such a distinction? Do you think Justice Souter is correct in his criticism?

3. Look at the last main paragraph of the majority opinion ("In a society based on law * * * "). In what way does Justice Kennedy's statement here arguably state new law?

CALIFORNIA v. HODARI D.

Supreme Court of the United States, 1991.
499 U.S. 621, 111 S.Ct. 1547, 113 L.Ed.2d 690.

JUSTICE SCALIA delivered the opinion of the Court.

Late one evening in April 1988, Officers Brian McColgin and Jerry Pertoso were on patrol in a high-crime area of Oakland, California. They were dressed in street clothes but wearing jackets with "Police" embossed on both front and back. Their unmarked car * * * rounded the corner,

---

1. That is to say, the police who conduct these sweeps decline to offer a reasonable, articulable suspicion of criminal wrongdoing sufficient to justify a warrantless "stop" or "seizure" of the confronted passenger. It does not follow, however, that the approach of passengers during a sweep is completely random. * * * [T]he basis of the decision to single out particular passengers during a suspicionless sweep is less likely to be *inarticulable* than *unspeakable*.

[and] they saw four or five youths huddled around a small red car parked at the curb. When the youths saw the officers' car approaching they apparently panicked, and took flight. The respondent here, Hodari D., and one companion ran west through an alley; the others fled south. The red car also headed south, at a high rate of speed.

The officers were suspicious and gave chase. [Officer Pertoso gave chase by foot. Just before he reached Hodari, the youth tossed away what appeared to be a small rock.] * * * A moment later, Pertoso tackled Hodari, handcuffed him, and radioed for assistance. Hodari was found to be carrying $130 in cash and a pager; and the rock he had discarded was found to be crack cocaine. * * *

As this case comes to us, the only issue presented is whether, at the time he dropped the drugs, Hodari had been "seized" within the meaning of the Fourth Amendment.[1] If so, respondent argues, the drugs were the fruit of that seizure and the evidence concerning them was properly excluded. If not, the drugs were abandoned by Hodari and lawfully recovered by the police, and the evidence should have been admitted. * * *

* * * From the time of the founding to the present, the word "seizure" has meant a "taking possession." For most purposes at common law, the word connoted not merely grasping, or applying physical force to, the animate or inanimate object in question, but actually bringing it within physical control. * * * To constitute an arrest, however—the quintessential "seizure of the person" under our Fourth Amendment jurisprudence—the mere grasping or application of physical force with lawful authority, whether or not it succeeded in subduing the arrestee, was sufficient. * * *

To say that an arrest is effected by the slightest application of physical force, despite the arrestee's escape, is not to say that for Fourth Amendment purposes there is a *continuing* arrest during the period of fugitivity. If, for example, Pertoso had laid his hands upon Hodari to arrest him, but Hodari had broken away and had *then* cast away the cocaine, it would hardly be realistic to say that that disclosure had been made during the course of an arrest. The present case, however, is even one step further removed. It does not involve the application of any physical force; Hodari was untouched by Officer Pertoso at the time he discarded the cocaine. His defense relies instead upon the proposition that a seizure occurs "when the officer, by means of physical force *or show of authority*, has in some way restrained the liberty of a citizen." *Terry v. Ohio* (emphasis added). Hodari contends (and we accept as true for purposes of this decision) that Pertoso's pursuit qualified as a "show of authority" calling upon Hodari to halt. The narrow question before us is

---

1. California conceded below that Officer Pertoso did not have the "reasonable suspicion" required to justify stopping Hodari. That it would be unreasonable to stop, for brief inquiry, young men who scatter in panic upon the mere sighting of the police is not self-evident, and arguably contradicts proverbial common sense. See Proverbs 28:1 ("The wicked flee when no man pursueth"). We do not decide that point here, but rely entirely upon the State's concession.

whether, with respect to a show of authority as with respect to application of physical force, a seizure occurs even though the subject does not yield. We hold that it does not.

The language of the Fourth Amendment, of course, cannot sustain respondent's contention. The word "seizure" readily bears the meaning of a laying on of hands or application of physical force to restrain movement, even when it is ultimately unsuccessful. ("She seized the purse-snatcher, but he broke out of her grasp.") It does not remotely apply, however, to the prospect of a policeman yelling "Stop, in the name of the law!" at a fleeing form that continues to flee. That is no seizure. Nor can the result respondent wishes to achieve be produced—indirectly, as it were—by suggesting that Pertoso's uncomplied-with show of authority was a common-law arrest, and then appealing to the principle that all common-law arrests are seizures. An arrest requires *either* physical force (as described above) *or*, where that is absent, *submission* to the assertion of authority. * * *

We do not think it desirable, even as a policy matter, to stretch the Fourth Amendment beyond its words and beyond the meaning of arrest, as respondent urges. Street pursuits always place the public at some risk, and compliance with police orders to stop should therefore be encouraged. Only a few of those orders, we must presume, will be without adequate basis, and since the addressee has no ready means of identifying the deficient ones it almost invariably is the responsible course to comply. * * *

Respondent contends that his position is sustained by the so-called *Mendenhall* test, formulated by Justice Stewart's opinion in *United States v. Mendenhall*, [p. 376], and adopted by the Court in later cases: "[a] person has been 'seized' within the meaning of the Fourth Amendment only if, in view of all the circumstances surrounding the incident, a reasonable person would have believed that he was not free to leave." In seeking to rely upon that test here, respondent fails to read it carefully. It says that a person has been seized "only if," not that he has been seized "whenever"; it states a *necessary*, but not a *sufficient*, condition for seizure—or, more precisely, for seizure effected through a "show of authority." * * *

In sum, assuming that Pertoso's pursuit in the present case constituted a "show of authority" enjoining Hodari to halt, since Hodari did not comply with that injunction he was not seized until he was tackled. The cocaine abandoned while he was running was in this case not the fruit of a seizure, and his motion to exclude evidence of it was properly denied. * * *

Justice STEVENS, with whom Justice MARSHALL joins, dissenting. * * *

II * * *

Whatever else one may think of today's decision, it unquestionably represents a departure from earlier Fourth Amendment case law. The notion that our prior cases contemplated a distinction between seizures effected by a touching on the one hand, and those effected by a show of force on the other hand, and that all of our repeated descriptions of the *Mendenhall* test stated only a necessary, but not a sufficient, condition for finding seizures in the latter category, is nothing if not creative lawmaking. Moreover, by narrowing the definition of the term seizure, instead of enlarging the scope of reasonable justifications for seizures, the Court has significantly limited the protection provided to the ordinary citizen by the Fourth Amendment. * * *

III

In this case the officer's show of force—taking the form of a head-on chase—adequately conveyed the message that respondent was not free to leave. * * * There was an interval of time between the moment that respondent saw the officer fast approaching and the moment when he was tackled, and thus brought under the control of the officer. The question is whether the Fourth Amendment was implicated at the earlier or the later moment.

Because the facts of this case are somewhat unusual, it is appropriate to note that the same issue would arise if the show of force took the form of a command to "freeze," a warning shot, or the sound of sirens accompanied by a patrol car's flashing lights. In any of these situations, there may be a significant time interval between the initiation of the officer's show of force and the complete submission by the citizen. At least on the facts of this case, the Court concludes that the timing of the seizure is governed by the citizen's reaction, rather than by the officer's conduct. One consequence of this conclusion is that the point at which the interaction between citizen and police officer becomes a seizure occurs, not when a reasonable citizen believes he or she is no longer free to go, but, rather, only after the officer exercises control over the citizen.

In my view, our interests in effective law enforcement and in personal liberty would be better served by adhering to a standard that "allows the police to determine in advance whether the conduct contemplated will implicate the Fourth Amendment." * * *

If an officer effects an arrest by touching a citizen, apparently the Court would accept the fact that a seizure occurred, even if the arrestee should thereafter break loose and flee. In such a case, the constitutionality of the seizure would be evaluated as of the time the officer acted. * * * It is anomalous, at best, to fashion a different rule for the subcategory of "show of force" arrests.

In cases within this new subcategory, there will be a period of time during which the citizen's liberty has been restrained, but he or she has not yet completely submitted to the show of force. A motorist pulled over by a highway patrol car cannot come to an immediate stop, even if the motorist intends to obey the patrol car's signal. If an officer decides to make [a random stop or one based solely on a hunch] * * *, and, after flashing his lights, but before the vehicle comes to a complete stop, sees that the license plate has expired, can he justify his action on the ground that the seizure became lawful after it was initiated but before it was completed? In an airport setting, may a drug enforcement agent now approach a group of passengers with his gun drawn, announce a "baggage search," and rely on the passengers' reactions to justify his investigative stops? The holding of today's majority fails to recognize the coercive and intimidating nature of such behavior and creates a rule that may allow such behavior to go unchecked. * * *

Some sacrifice of freedom always accompanies an expansion in the Executive's unreviewable law enforcement powers. A court more sensitive to the purposes of the Fourth Amendment would insist on greater rewards to society before decreeing the sacrifice it makes today. * * *

NOTES AND QUESTIONS

1.   In *Hodari D.*, the defendant tossed away rock cocaine during his flight from the officer. What is the lesson of the Court's ruling to officers who, as here, pursue individuals whom they lack reasonable suspicion to detain?

2.   Justice Souter, writing for a unanimous Supreme Court in Brendlin v. California, 551 U.S. 249, 127 S.Ct. 2400, 168 L.Ed.2d 132 (2007), recently summarized the "seizure of person" line of cases this way:

> A person is seized by the police and thus entitled to challenge the government's action under the Fourth Amendment when the officer, " 'by means of physical force or show of authority,' " terminates or restrains his freedom of movement, *"through means intentionally applied,"* Brower v. *County of Inyo*, 489 U.S. 593, 597, 109 S.Ct. 1378, 103 L.Ed.2d 628 (1989) (emphasis in original). Thus, an "unintended person * * * [may be] the object of the detention," so long as the detention is "willful" and not merely the consequence of "an unknowing act." [C]f. *County of Sacramento* v. *Lewis*, 523 U.S. 833, 844, 118 S.Ct. 1708, 140 L.Ed.2d 1043 (1998) (no seizure where a police officer accidentally struck and killed a motorcycle passenger during a high-speed pursuit). A police officer may make a seizure by a show of authority and without the use of physical force, but there is no seizure without actual submission * * *.

> When the actions of the police do not show an unambiguous intent to restrain or when an individual's submission to a show of governmental authority takes the form of passive acquiescence, there needs to be some test for telling when a seizure occurs in response to authority, and when it does not. The test was devised by Justice Stewart in *United States* v. *Mendenhall*, [p. 376], who wrote that a seizure occurs if "in view of all of the circumstances surrounding the incident, a reasonable person would have believed that he was not free to leave." Later on, the Court adopted Justice Stewart's touchstone, but added that when a person "has no desire to leave" for reasons unrelated to the police presence, the "coercive effect of the encounter" can be measured better by asking whether "a reasonable person would feel free to decline the officers' requests or

otherwise terminate the encounter"; see * * * *United States* v. *Drayton*, [p. 384].

Based on this summary of the law, the Court held that a car passenger, and not only the driver, is seized as the result of a police-ordered traffic stop:

> The law is settled that in Fourth Amendment terms a traffic stop entails a seizure of the driver "even though the purpose of the stop is limited and the resulting detention quite brief." And although we have not, until today, squarely answered the question whether a passenger is also seized, we have said over and over in dicta that during a traffic stop an officer seizes everyone in the vehicle, not just the driver. * * *

> A traffic stop necessarily curtails the travel a passenger has chosen just as much as it halts the driver, diverting both from the stream of traffic to the side of the road, and the police activity that normally amounts to intrusion on "privacy and personal security" does not normally (and did not here) distinguish between passenger and driver. An officer who orders one particular car to pull over acts with an implicit claim of right based on fault of some sort, and a sensible person would not expect a police officer to allow people to come and go freely from the physical focal point of an investigation into faulty behavior or wrongdoing. If the likely wrongdoing is not the driving, the passenger will reasonably feel subject to suspicion owing to close association; but even when the wrongdoing is only bad driving, the passenger will expect to be subject to some scrutiny, and his attempt to leave the scene would be so obviously likely to prompt an objection from the officer that no passenger would feel free to leave in the first place. * * *

> [T]he * * * Supreme Court [of California] shied away from the rule we apply today for fear that it "would encompass even those motorists following the vehicle subject to the traffic stop who, by virtue of the original detention, are forced to slow down and perhaps even come to a halt in order to accommodate that vehicle's submission to police authority." But an occupant of a car who knows that he is stuck in traffic because another car has been pulled over (like the motorist who can't even make out why the road is suddenly clogged) would not perceive a show of authority as directed at him or his car. Such incidental restrictions on freedom of movement would not tend to affect an individual's "sense of security and privacy in traveling in an automobile." * * *[6]

> * * * Holding that the passenger in a private car is not (without more) seized in a traffic stop would invite police officers to stop cars with passengers regardless of probable cause or reasonable suspicion of anything illegal. The fact that evidence uncovered as a result of an arbitrary traffic stop would still be admissible against any passengers would be a powerful incentive to run the kind of "roving patrols" that would still violate the driver's Fourth Amendment right.

---

6. California claims that, under today's rule, "all taxi cab and bus passengers would be 'seized' under the Fourth Amendment when the cab or bus driver is pulled over by the police for running a red light." But the relationship between driver and passenger is not the same in a common carrier as it is in a private vehicle, and the expectations of police officers and passengers differ accordingly. In those cases, as here, the crucial question would be whether a reasonable person in the passenger's position would feel free to take steps to terminate the encounter.

3. *Problem.* Officers, in their police vehicle, flashed their red lights to stop a car. After two blocks, the driver pulled into the driveway of his home. Passenger *M* got out of the car. One officer called out, "Hold up." *M* replied, "What do you want?," began to back away slowly, and then fled. During pursuit, *M* threw down an object later determined to be contraband. Was *M* seized? If so, at what moment? See United States v. Morgan, 936 F.2d 1561 (10th Cir.1991).

Suppose, instead, the following facts: *M* and his companion are walking along a downtown street; an officer pulls out his badge and says, "Police officers, we need to talk to you"; *M* says, "What do you want?," backs away, and then flees. Does this change the seizure analysis? Do you need more facts to answer the question? See State v. Rogers, 186 Ariz. 508, 924 P.2d 1027 (1996).

4. *Problem.* In a Detroit area "infamous for racial tension," a police officer observed three African–American youths riding their bicycle one block north of Eight Mile Road, the dividing point between largely-black Detroit and a white suburb. "After a quick interrogation and a racist joke, the officer allegedly ordered the youths to take their bicycles 'back across Eight Mile,' and watched while they did so." Stephen E. Henderson, *"Move On" Orders as Fourth Amendment Seizures*, 2008 B.Y.U. L. Rev. 1, 23. Did the officer's "move on" order constitute a seizure?

d. "Reasonable Suspicion"

ALABAMA v. WHITE

Supreme Court of the United States, 1990.
496 U.S. 325, 110 S.Ct. 2412, 110 L.Ed.2d 301.

JUSTICE WHITE delivered the opinion of the Court. * * *

On April 22, 1987, at approximately 3 p.m., Corporal B. H. Davis of the Montgomery Police Department received a telephone call from an anonymous person, stating that Vanessa White would be leaving 235–C Lynwood Terrace Apartments at a particular time in a brown Plymouth station wagon with the right taillight lens broken, that she would be going to Dobey's Motel, and that she would be in possession of about an ounce of cocaine inside a brown attaché case. Corporal Davis and his partner, Corporal P. A. Reynolds, proceeded to the Lynwood Terrace Apartments. The officers saw a brown Plymouth station wagon with a broken right taillight in the parking lot in front of the 235 building. The officers observed respondent leave the 235 building, carrying nothing in her hands, and enter the station wagon. They followed the vehicle as it drove the most direct route to Dobey's Motel. When the vehicle reached the Mobile Highway, on which Dobey's Motel is located, Corporal Reynolds requested a patrol unit to stop the vehicle. The vehicle was stopped at approximately 4:18 p.m., just short of Dobey's Motel. Corporal Davis asked respondent to step to the rear of her car, where he informed her that she had been stopped because she was suspected of carrying cocaine in the vehicle. He asked if they could look for cocaine, and respondent said they could look. The officers found a locked brown attaché case in the car, and, upon request, respondent provided the combination to the lock. The officers found marijuana in the attaché case and placed respondent under arrest. During processing at the station, the officers found three milligrams of cocaine in respondent's purse.

* * * The Court of Criminal Appeals of Alabama held that the officers did not have the reasonable suspicion necessary under *Terry v. Ohio* to justify the investigatory stop of respondent's car, and that the marijuana and cocaine were fruits of respondent's unconstitutional detention. * * * We now reverse. * * *

Illinois v. Gates, [p. 150], dealt with an anonymous tip in the probable-cause context. The Court there abandoned the "two-pronged test" of *Aguilar v. Texas*, 378 U.S. 108, 84 S.Ct. 1509, 12 L.Ed.2d 723 (1964), and *Spinelli v. United States*, [p. 142], in favor of a "totality of the circumstances" approach to determining whether an informant's tip establishes probable cause. *Gates* made clear, however, that those factors that had been considered critical under *Aguilar* and *Spinelli*—an informant's "veracity," "reliability," and "basis of knowledge"—remain "highly relevant in determining the value of his report." These factors are also relevant in the reasonable suspicion context, although allowance must be made in applying them for the lesser showing required to meet that standard.

The opinion in *Gates* recognized that an anonymous tip alone seldom demonstrates the informant's basis of knowledge or veracity inasmuch as ordinary citizens generally do not provide extensive recitations of the basis of their everyday observations and given that the veracity of persons supplying anonymous tips is "by hypothesis largely unknown, and unknowable." This is not to say that an anonymous caller could never provide the reasonable suspicion necessary for a *Terry* stop. But the tip in *Gates* was not an exception to the general rule, and the anonymous tip in this case is like the one in *Gates*: "[It] provides virtually nothing from which one might conclude that [the caller] is either honest or his information reliable; likewise, the [tip] gives absolutely no indication of the basis for the [caller's] predictions regarding [Vanessa White's] criminal activities." By requiring "[s]omething more," as *Gates* did, we merely apply what we said in *Adams* [*v. Williams*, 407 U.S. 143, 92 S.Ct. 1921, 32 L.Ed.2d 612 (1972)]: "Some tips, completely lacking in indicia of reliability, would either warrant no police response or require further investigation before a forcible stop of a suspect would be authorized." Simply put, a tip such as this one, standing alone, would not " 'warrant a man of reasonable caution in the belief' that [a stop] was appropriate."

As there was in *Gates*, however, in this case there is more than the tip itself. The tip was not as detailed, and the corroboration was not as complete, as in *Gates*, but the required degree of suspicion was likewise not as high. We discussed the difference in the two standards last Term in *United States v. Sokolow*, 490 U.S. 1, 109 S.Ct. 1581, 104 L.Ed.2d 1 (1989):

"The officer [making a *Terry* stop] * * * must be able to articulate something more than an 'inchoate and unparticularized suspicion or "hunch." ' The Fourth Amendment requires 'some minimal level of objective justification' for making the stop. That level of suspicion is considerably less than proof of wrongdoing by a preponderance of the evidence. We have held that probable cause means 'a fair probability that contraband or evidence of a crime will be found,' and the level of suspicion required for a *Terry* stop is obviously less demanding than for probable cause."

Reasonable suspicion is a less demanding standard than probable cause not only in the sense that reasonable suspicion can be established with information that is different in quantity or content than that required to establish probable cause, but also in the sense that reasonable suspicion can arise from information that is less reliable than that required to show probable cause. * * * Both factors—quantity and quality—are considered in the "totality of the circumstances—the whole picture," that must be taken into account when evaluating whether there is reasonable suspicion. Thus, if a tip has a relatively low degree of reliability, more information will be required to establish the requisite quantum of suspicion than would be required if the tip were more reliable. * * * Contrary to the court below, we conclude that when the officers stopped respondent, the anonymous tip had been sufficiently corroborated to furnish reasonable suspicion that respondent was engaged in criminal activity and that the investigative stop therefore did not violate the Fourth Amendment.

It is true that not every detail mentioned by the tipster was verified, such as the name of the woman leaving the building or the precise apartment from which she left; but the officers did corroborate that a woman left the 235 building and got into the particular vehicle that was described by the caller. With respect to the time of departure predicted by the informant, Corporal Davis testified that the caller gave a particular time when the woman would be leaving, but he did not state what that time was. He did testify that, after the call, he and his partner proceeded to the Lynwood Terrace Apartments to put the 235 building under surveillance. Given the fact that the officers proceeded to the indicated address immediately after the call and that respondent emerged not too long thereafter, it appears from the record before us that respondent's departure from the building was within the time frame predicted by the caller. As for the caller's prediction of respondent's destination, it is true that the officers stopped her just short of Dobey's Motel and did not know whether she would have pulled in or continued on past it. But given that the 4–mile route driven by respondent was the most direct route possible to Dobey's Motel, but nevertheless involved several turns, we think respondent's destination was significantly corroborated.

The Court's opinion in *Gates* gave credit to the proposition that because an informant is shown to be right about some things, he is probably right about other facts that he has alleged, including the claim that the object of the tip is engaged in criminal activity. Thus, it is not unreasonable to conclude in this case that the independent corroboration by the police of significant aspects of the informer's predictions imparted some degree of reliability to the other allegations made by the caller.

We think it also important that, as in *Gates*, "the anonymous [tip] contained a range of details relating not just to easily obtained facts and conditions existing at the time of the tip, but to future actions of third parties ordinarily not easily predicted." The fact that the officers found a car precisely matching the caller's description in front of the 235 building is an example of the former. Anyone could have "predicted" that fact because it was a condition presumably existing at the time of the call. What was important was the caller's ability to predict respondent's *future behavior*, because it demonstrated inside information—a special familiarity with respondent's affairs. The general public would have had no way of knowing that respondent would shortly leave the building, get in the described car, and drive the most direct route to Dobey's Motel. Because only a small number of people are generally privy to an individual's itinerary, it is reasonable for police to believe that a person with access to such information is likely to also have access to reliable information about that individual's illegal activities. When significant aspects of the caller's predictions were verified, there was reason to believe not only that the caller was honest but also that he was well informed, at least well enough to justify the stop.

Although it is a close case, we conclude that under the totality of the circumstances the anonymous tip, as corroborated, exhibited sufficient indicia of reliability to justify the investigatory stop of respondent's car. * * *

Justice STEVENS, with whom Justice BRENNAN and Justice MARSHALL join, dissenting.

Millions of people leave their apartments at about the same time every day carrying an attaché case and heading for a destination known to their neighbors. Usually, however, the neighbors do not know what the briefcase contains. An anonymous neighbor's prediction about somebody's time of departure and probable destination is anything but a reliable basis for assuming that the commuter is in possession of an illegal substance—particularly when the person is not even carrying the attaché case described by the tipster.

The record in this case does not tell us how often respondent drove from the Lynwood Terrace Apartments to Dobey's Motel; for all we know, she may have been a room clerk or telephone operator working the evening shift. It does not tell us whether Office Davis made any effort to ascertain the informer's identity, his reason for calling, or the basis of his prediction about respondent's destination. Indeed, for all that this record tells us, the tipster may well have been another police officer who had a "hunch" that respondent might have cocaine in her attaché case.

Anybody with enough knowledge about a given person to make her the target of a prank, or to harbor a grudge against her, will certainly be able to formulate a tip about her like the one predicting Vanessa White's excursion. In addition, under the Court's holding, every citizen is subject to being seized and questioned by any officer who is prepared to testify that the warrantless stop was based on an anonymous tip predicting whatever conduct the officer just observed. Fortunately, the vast majority of those in our law enforcement community would not adopt such a practice. But the Fourth Amendment was intended to protect the citizen from the overzealous and unscrupulous officer as well as from those who are conscientious and truthful. This decision makes a mockery of that protection. * * *

NOTES AND QUESTIONS

1. Do you believe that the police had sufficient grounds to stop White?

2. The *White* Court unsurprisingly stated that reasonable suspicion "can be established with information that is different in quantity * * * than that required to establish probable cause." But, it also stated that "reasonable suspicion" is a less demanding standard "in the sense that reasonable suspicion can arise from information that is less reliable than that required to show probable cause." *Should* this be the rule?

3. The *White* Court quoted *Adams v. Williams*, the pertinent facts of which are summarized on p. 365, Note 9. Take another look at that Note. Now, here are some additional facts: The officer approached the Williams vehicle after "a person known to [the officer] * * * informed him that an individual seated in a nearby vehicle was carrying narcotics and had a gun at his waist." The officer knew the tipster because he had provided information once before, regarding homosexual activity. That information did *not* result in an arrest because the officer could not substantiate the claim. The *Williams* majority concluded, nonetheless, that reasonable suspicion in *this* case existed:

> [W]e believe that [the officer] acted justifiably in responding to his informant's tip. The informant was known to him personally and had provided him with information in the past. This is a stronger case than obtains in the case of an anonymous telephone tip. The informant here came forward personally to give information that was immediately verifiable at the scene. Indeed, under Connecticut law, the informant might have been subject to immediate arrest for making a false complaint had [the officer]'s investigation proved the tip incorrect. Thus, while the Court's decisions indicate that this informant's unverified tip may have been insufficient for a narcotics arrest or search warrant, the information carried enough indicia of reliability to justify the officer's forcible stop of Williams.

Are you persuaded that the officer had reasonable suspicion, justifying a seizure or search of Williams? If so, what type of tip would *not* justify a similar police response? If you disagree with the Court, what would you have wanted the officer to do with the tipster's information?

4. An important factor in *Alabama v. White*, one that put the police conduct on the proper side of the "reasonable suspicion" line, was that the anonymous informant accurately predicted future behavior of the suspect. Even with that, you will notice that the Court characterized the facts as presenting "a close case" on the issue of reasonable suspicion. In this regard, consider Florida v. J.L., 529 U.S. 266, 120 S.Ct. 1375, 146 L.Ed.2d 254 (2000).

In *J.L.*, an anonymous caller told police that "a young black male standing at a particular bus stop and wearing a plaid shirt was carrying a gun." Two officers went to the location and observed three black males, one wearing a plaid shirt, "just hanging out [there]." Nothing about their behavior apart from the tip aroused suspicion, and no gun was visible. Nonetheless, the officers seized J.L., a minor, and frisked him. The Court *unanimously* held that the anonymous tip exhibited insufficient indicia of reliability to provide reasonable suspicion for the police action. Speaking for the Court, Justice Ginsburg wrote:

> The tip in the instant case lacked the moderate indicia of reliability present in *White* and essential to the Court's decision in that case. The anonymous call concerning J.L. provided no predictive information and therefore left the police without means to test the informant's knowledge or credibility. * * * All the police had to go on in this case was the bare report of an unknown, unaccountable informant who neither explained how he knew about the gun nor supplied any basis for believing he had inside information about J.L. If *White* was a close case on the reliability of anonymous tips, this one surely falls on the other side of the line.

> Florida contends that the tip was reliable because its description of the suspect's visible attributes proved accurate: There really was a young black male wearing a plaid shirt at the bus stop. * * *

> An accurate description of a subject's readily observable location and appearance is of course reliable in this limited sense: It will help the police correctly identify the person whom the tipster means to accuse. Such a tip, however, does not show that the tipster has knowledge of concealed criminal activity. The reasonable suspicion here at issue requires that a tip be reliable in its assertion of illegality, not just in its tendency to identify a determinate person.

Reconsider *Adams v. Williams* (Note 3). Is *J.L.* distinguishable?

5. *Racial profiling and reasonable suspicion.* Racial profiling (that is, the use of race or ethnicity as a criterion in conducting stops, searches, and other law enforcement investigative procedures) is a serious issue in light of the Supreme Court's ruling in *Whren v. United States*, p. 259, but it is magnified by *Terry v. Ohio* and the lower standard of cause that an officer may use to temporarily detain a person on the street or in a car.

For example, an officer might use something as minor as an apparent crack in a vehicle windshield as justification to stop a driver on the ground that it constitutes reasonable suspicion that the driver is violating a statute that prohibits driving "in such unsafe condition as to endanger any person." Muse v. State, 146 Md.App. 395, 807 A.2d 113 (2002). The officer might then use this stop in order to seek consent to conduct a drug or weapons search of the car—a search that she might not have sought to conduct if the driver had been white. Indeed, the officer might not have stopped the car with the cracked windshield in the first place but for the fact the driver was black or Hispanic.

That such racial profiling happens is not speculative. In Maryland, from 1995 through 1997, a survey indicated that 70% of drivers stopped on Interstate 95 were African–American, although 17.5% of the traffic and speeders on the road were black. David Cole, No Equal Justice 36 (1999). Videotapes in one Florida county demonstrated that 5% of the drivers appeared to be dark-skinned, but 70% of the drivers stopped were African–American or Hispanic, and more than 80% of cars searched on the highway were persons of color. Traffic tickets, however, were given in less than 1% of the stops. *Id.* at 37, 807 A.2d 113. A study of more than one million police traffic stops in Texas in 2002 and 2003 found that African–American and Hispanic drivers were far more likely to undergo searches than whites, although not in fact more likely to be carrying contraband or drugs. Ralph Blumenthal, *Study in Texas Sees Race Bias in Searches*, N.Y. Times, Feb. 25, 2005., at A14. A study of the Miami–Dade, Florida police department found that, although there was no demonstrated pattern of discriminatory action by police officers toward minority citizens when making traffic stops, African–Americans and Hispanics *were* the subject of disparate treatment after the lawful stops. Geoffrey P. Albert et al., *Investigating Racial Profiling by the Miami–Dade Police Department: A Multimethod Approach*, 6 Criminology & Pub. Pol'y 25 (2007).

All of this having been said, *are* there times when the fact that a person is of a particular race or ethnic group *is* relevant in evaluating reasonable suspicion? Consider this remark:

> [M]ost criminologists who have studied the matter have concluded that blacks (and men and young people) do in fact commit crime in a higher per capita rate than whites (and women and older people). Thus, all other things being equal, it is rational to be more suspicious of a young black man than an elderly white woman. But that it may be rational does not make it right.

Cole, supra, at 42. If it *is rational* to be more suspicious of young black men than elderly white women, why *isn't* it *right* to be more suspicious? Or, *is* it? If so, when should it be permissible?

In this regard, consider: A woman reported to the police that a young, black male broke into her home, attacked her, and then fled with a small wound on his hand. The police used a canine unit to track the attacker to a nearby university campus, at which point the dog lost the trail. The police then obtained a list of all black male students from the university and attempted to locate and, where necessary, seize them in order to examine them for the tell-tale wound. Brown v. City of Oneonta, 221 F.3d 329 (2d Cir. 2000). Were these seizures justifiable? *Should* they be?

Or, consider this: Shortly after the 9/11 terrorist attack the Justice Department began interviewing more than 5000 people nationwide, almost all of whom were Middle Eastern men between the ages of eighteen and twenty-three whose non-immigrant visas were near expiration. The purpose of the interviews was to determine whether the men had information relating to terrorist activities. Samuel R. Gross & Debra Livingston, *Racial Profiling Under Attack*, 102 Colum. L. Rev. 1413, 1417 (2002). Is *this* racial profiling? To the extent that some of the interviews turned into Fourth Amendment seizures (the men did not come voluntarily for questioning), are they constitutional? *Should* they be?

Finally, consider this thought experiment: Assume that a town near the Mexican border experiences a huge influx of Hispanics into their community in a short period of time. Therefore, federal agents begin stopping all persons of apparent Hispanic-origin to check their citizenship. Is this rational? Is it right? Is this situation different in some meaningful way than the previous examples?

For more on the subject of racial profiling, see Albert W. Alschuler, *Racial Profiling and the Constitution*, 2002 U. Chi. L. Forum 163; Sherry F. Colb, *Profiling With Apologies*, 1 Ohio St. J. Crim. L. 611 (2004); Sharon L. Davies, *Profiling Terror*, 1 Ohio St. J. Crim. L. 45 (2003); and David A. Harris, Profiles in Injustice: Why Racial Profiling Cannot Work (2002).

6. *Converting reasonable suspicion into an arrest?* May the police leap-frog from a *Terry* seizure based on reasonable suspicion into an arrest by simply asking the seized individual for her name and, if she refuses to answer, arresting her for that failure? Perhaps so, if a state enacts a law requiring a properly detained individual to identify herself to the police.

In Hiibel v. Sixth Judicial District Court of Nevada, Humboldt County, 542 U.S. 177, 124 S.Ct. 2451, 159 L.Ed.2d 292 (2004), a deputy sheriff was dispatched to investigate a report of a man assaulting a woman. When the officer arrived at the scene, he found a man standing outside a truck, with a young woman sitting inside it. The man appeared intoxicated. The deputy asked the man, later identified to be Larry Hiibel, for identification. At least eleven times Hiibel refused to provide identification. Consequently, the deputy arrested him for "willfully resist[ing], delay[ing], or obstruct[ing] a public officer in discharging or attempting to discharge any legal duty of his office." The government reasoned that Hiibel had violated this statute because another statute, a so-called "stop and identify" statute, authorized police officers to "detain any person whom the officer encounters under circumstances which reasonably indicate that the person has committed, is committing or is about to commit a crime," and to "ascertain [the individual's] identity." The latter statute provided that "[a]ny person so detained shall identify himself."

Stop-and-identify statutes violate the Constitution if they are written so broadly or vaguely as to give the police undue discretion in the enforcement of the law. And such laws cannot be enforced if the stop—the initial seizure that presages the request for identification—is unlawful for want of reasonable suspicion. But, what about here, where Hiibel conceded that the deputy had grounds to conduct a *Terry*-level seizure?

Justice Kennedy, writing for the majority, explained that properly crafted and enforced stop-and-identify laws are constitutional:

Our decisions make clear that questions concerning a suspect's identity are a routine and accepted part of many *Terry* stops.

Obtaining a suspect's name in the course of a *Terry* stop serves important government interests. Knowledge of identity may inform an officer that a suspect is wanted for another offense, or has a record of violence or mental disorder. On the other hand, knowing identity may help clear a suspect and allow the police to concentrate their efforts elsewhere. Identity may prove particularly important in cases such as this, where the police are investigating what appears to be a domestic assault. Officers called to investigate domestic disputes need to know whom they are dealing with in order to assess the situation, the threat to their own safety, and possible danger to the potential victim. * * *

The principles of *Terry* permit a State to require a suspect to disclose his name in the course of a *Terry* stop. The reasonableness of a seizure under the Fourth Amendment is determined "by balancing its intrusion on the individual's Fourth Amendment interests against its promotion of legitimate government interests." The Nevada statute [in this case] satisfies that standard. The request for identity has an immediate relation to the purpose, rationale, and practical demands of a *Terry* stop. The threat of criminal sanction helps ensure that the request for identity does not become a legal nullity. On the other hand, the Nevada statute does not alter the nature of the stop itself: it does not change its duration, or its location. A state law requiring a suspect to disclose his name in the course of a valid *Terry* stop is consistent with Fourth Amendment prohibitions against unreasonable searches and seizures.

Petitioner argues that the Nevada statute circumvents the probable cause requirement, in effect allowing an officer to arrest a person for being suspicious. According to petitioner, this creates a risk of arbitrary police conduct that the Fourth Amendment does not permit. * * * Petitioner's concerns are met by the requirement that a *Terry* stop must be justified at its inception and "reasonably related in scope to the circumstances which justified" the initial stop. Under these principles, an officer may not arrest a suspect for failure to identify himself if the request for identification is not reasonably related to the circumstances justifying the stop. * * * It is clear in this case that the request for identification was "reasonably related in scope to the circumstances which justified" the stop.

7. *Problems.* Is there reasonable suspicion of unlawful activity in the following cases:

A. State police received an anonymous tip that on a specified date, at a particular time, a drug sale would take place in a particular restaurant by a person who would drive to the restaurant in a specifically described car, wearing specified clothing. The officer went to the restaurant and observed S, who fit the description given, drive up to the restaurant in a car meeting the description provided, get out, enter the restaurant, and order food. The officer detained S on these facts. State v. Stickle, 792 N.E.2d 51 (Ind. App. 2003).

B. An anonymous caller told police that an African–American male was sitting on a porch "doing drugs" and had previously been driving a blue car.

Officers went to the address. They observed two black males on the porch, and a blue car out front. One of the men, *J*, hollered something to the other man. The other man fled. The officers seized *J*, who did not flee. State v. Jordan, 817 N.E.2d 864 (Ohio 2004).

C. An off-duty police officer observed a robbery in progress in a bank. He called the police dispatcher on his cell phone. He then pulled his car around to the front of the bank where he observed the person drive away on a white motorcycle. He followed the motorcycle to an enclosed parking lot where he lost sight of it. Fifteen seconds later, the officer saw a white van pull out of the area where he had last seen the motorcycle and head towards the only exit in the lot. The officer advised dispatch that he believed the suspect was now driving a white van. Based on this information, two on-duty police officers pulled the van over and ordered the driver out of the van by gunpoint. Is this a valid *Terry* stop? United States v. Thomas, 249 F.3d 725 (8th Cir. 2001).

ILLINOIS v. WARDLOW

Supreme Court of the United States, 2000.
528 U.S. 119, 120 S.Ct. 673, 145 L.Ed.2d 570.

CHIEF JUSTICE REHNQUIST delivered the opinion of the Court. * * *

On September 9, 1995, Officers Nolan and Harvey were working as uniformed officers in the special operations section of the Chicago Police Department. The officers were driving the last car of a four car caravan converging on an area known for heavy narcotics trafficking in order to investigate drug transactions. The officers were traveling together because they expected to find a crowd of people in the area, including lookouts and customers.

As the caravan passed 4035 West Van Buren, Officer Nolan observed respondent Wardlow standing next to the building holding an opaque bag. Respondent looked in the direction of the officers and fled. Nolan and Harvey turned their car southbound, watched him as he ran through * * * an alley, and eventually cornered him on the street. Nolan then exited his car and stopped respondent. He immediately conducted a protective pat-down search for weapons because in his experience it was common for there to be weapons in the near vicinity of narcotics transactions. During the frisk, Officer Nolan * * * felt a heavy, hard object similar to the shape of a gun. The officer then opened the bag and discovered a .38–caliber handgun with five live rounds of ammunition. The officers arrested Wardlow.

The Illinois trial court denied respondent's motion to suppress, finding the gun was recovered during a lawful stop and frisk. * * * Wardlow was convicted of unlawful use of a weapon by a felon. The Illinois Appellate Court reversed Wardlow's conviction, concluding that the gun should have been suppressed because Officer Nolan did not have reasonable suspicion sufficient to justify an investigative stop pursuant to *Terry v. Ohio.*

The Illinois Supreme Court agreed. While rejecting the Appellate Court's conclusion that Wardlow was not in a high crime area, the Illinois Supreme Court determined that sudden flight in such an area does not create a reasonable suspicion justifying a *Terry* stop. * * * [T]he court explained that although police have the right to approach individuals and ask questions, the individual has no obligation to respond. The person may decline to answer and simply go on his or her way, and the refusal to respond, alone, does not provide a legitimate basis for an investigative stop. The court then determined that flight may simply be an exercise of this right to "go on one's way," and, thus, could not constitute reasonable suspicion justifying a *Terry* stop.

The Illinois Supreme Court also rejected the argument that flight combined with the fact that it occurred in a high crime area supported a finding of reasonable suspicion * * *.

This case, involving a brief encounter between a citizen and a police officer on a public street, is governed by the analysis we first applied in *Terry*. * * *[1]

* * * An individual's presence in an area of expected criminal activity, standing alone, is not enough to support a reasonable, particularized suspicion that the person is committing a crime. But officers are not required to ignore the relevant characteristics of a location in determining whether the circumstances are sufficiently suspicious to warrant further investigation. Accordingly, we have previously noted the fact that the stop occurred in a "high crime area" among the relevant contextual considerations in a *Terry* analysis.

In this case, moreover, it was not merely respondent's presence in an area of heavy narcotics trafficking that aroused the officers' suspicion but his unprovoked flight upon noticing the police. Our cases have also recognized that nervous, evasive behavior is a pertinent factor in determining reasonable suspicion. Headlong flight—wherever it occurs—is the consummate act of evasion: it is not necessarily indicative of wrongdoing, but it is certainly suggestive of such. In reviewing the propriety of an officer's conduct, courts do not have available empirical studies dealing with inferences drawn from suspicious behavior, and we cannot reasonably demand scientific certainty from judges or law enforcement officers where none exists. Thus, the determination of reasonable suspicion must be based on commonsense judgments and inferences about human behavior. We conclude Officer Nolan was justified in suspecting that Wardlow was involved in criminal activity, and, therefore, in investigating further.

Such a holding is entirely consistent with our decision in *Florida v. Royer* [p. 371, Note 3], where we held that when an officer, without reasonable suspicion or probable cause, approaches an individual, the individual has a right to ignore the police and go about his business. * * *

---

1. We granted certiorari solely on the question of whether the initial stop was supported by reasonable suspicion. Therefore, we express no opinion as to the lawfulness of the frisk independently of the stop.

But unprovoked flight is simply not a mere refusal to cooperate. Flight, by its very nature, is not "going about one's business"; in fact, it is just the opposite. Allowing officers confronted with such flight to stop the fugitive and investigate further is quite consistent with the individual's right to go about his business or to stay put and remain silent in the face of police questioning.

Respondent and *amici* also argue that there are innocent reasons for flight from police and that, therefore, flight is not necessarily indicative of ongoing criminal activity. This fact is undoubtedly true, but does not establish a violation of the Fourth Amendment. Even in *Terry*, the conduct justifying the stop was ambiguous and susceptible of an innocent explanation. * * * *Terry* recognized that the officers could detain the individuals to resolve the ambiguity.

In allowing such detentions, *Terry* accepts the risk that officers may stop innocent people. Indeed, the Fourth Amendment accepts that risk in connection with more drastic police action; persons arrested and detained on probable cause to believe they have committed a crime may turn out to be innocent. The *Terry* stop is a far more minimal intrusion, simply allowing the officer to briefly investigate further. * * *

The judgment of the Supreme Court of Illinois is reversed * * *. * * *

Justice STEVENS, with whom Justice SOUTER, Justice GINSBURG, and Justice BREYER join, concurring in part and dissenting in part.

The State of Illinois asks this Court to announce a "bright-line rule" authorizing the temporary detention of anyone who flees at the mere sight of a police officer. Respondent counters by asking us to adopt the opposite *per se* rule—that the fact that a person flees upon seeing the police can never, by itself, be sufficient to justify a temporary investigative stop of the kind authorized by *Terry v. Ohio*. * * *

Although I agree with the Court's rejection of the *per se* rules proffered by the parties, unlike the Court, I am persuaded that in this case the brief testimony of the officer who seized respondent does not justify the conclusion that he had reasonable suspicion to make the stop. Before discussing the specific facts of this case, I shall comment on the parties' requests for a *per se* rule.

I * * *

* * * A pedestrian may break into a run for a variety of reasons—to catch up with a friend a block or two away, to seek shelter from an impending storm, to arrive at a bus stop before the bus leaves, to get home in time for dinner, to resume jogging after a pause for rest, to avoid contact with a bore or a bully, or simply to answer the call of nature—any of which might coincide with the arrival of an officer in the vicinity. A pedestrian might also run because he or she has just sighted one or more police officers. In the latter instance, the State properly points out "that the fleeing person may be, *inter alia*, (1) an escapee from jail; (2) wanted

on a warrant, (3) in possession of contraband, (*i.e.*, drugs, weapons, stolen goods, etc.); or (4) someone who has just committed another type of crime." In short, there are unquestionably circumstances in which a person's flight is suspicious, and undeniably instances in which a person runs for entirely innocent reasons.

Given the diversity and frequency of possible motivations for flight, it would be profoundly unwise to endorse either *per se* rule. The inference we can reasonably draw about the motivation for a person's flight, rather, will depend on a number of different circumstances. Factors such as the time of day, the number of people in the area, the character of the neighborhood, whether the officer was in uniform, the way the runner was dressed, the direction and speed of the flight, and whether the person's behavior was otherwise unusual might be relevant in specific cases. This number of variables is surely sufficient to preclude either a bright-line rule that always justifies, or that never justifies, an investigative stop based on the sole fact that flight began after a police officer appeared nearby. * * *

Even assuming we know that a person runs because he sees the police, the inference to be drawn may still vary from case to case. Flight to escape police detection, we have said, may have an entirely innocent motivation * * *. [Innocent people flee, *inter alia*, out of fear of being wrongfully arrested or forced to appear as a witness to a crime.]

In addition to these concerns, a reasonable person may conclude that an officer's sudden appearance indicates nearby criminal activity. And where there is criminal activity there is also a substantial element of danger—either from the criminal or from a confrontation between the criminal and the police. These considerations can lead to an innocent and understandable desire to quit the vicinity with all speed.

Among some citizens, particularly minorities and those residing in high crime areas, there is also the possibility that the fleeing person is entirely innocent, but, with or without justification, believes that contact with the police can itself be dangerous, apart from any criminal activity associated with the officer's sudden presence. For such a person, unprovoked flight is neither "aberrant" nor "abnormal." Moreover, these concerns and fears are known to the police officers themselves, and are validated by law enforcement investigations into their own practices. Accordingly, the evidence supporting the reasonableness of these beliefs is too pervasive to be dismissed as random or rare, and too persuasive to be disparaged as inconclusive or insufficient. In any event, just as we do not require "scientific certainty" for our commonsense conclusion that unprovoked flight can sometimes indicate suspicious motives, neither do we require scientific certainty to conclude that unprovoked flight can occur for other, innocent reasons.[12] * * *

---

12. As a general matter, local courts often have a keener and more informed sense of local police practices and events that may heighten these concerns at particular times or locations.

II

Guided by that totality-of-the-circumstances test, the Court concludes that Officer Nolan had reasonable suspicion to stop respondent. In this respect, my view differs from the Court's. * * *

Officer Nolan and his partner were in the last of the four patrol cars that "were all caravaning eastbound down Van Buren." Nolan first observed respondent "in front of 4035 West Van Buren." Wardlow "looked in our direction and began fleeing." Nolan then "began driving southbound down the street observing [respondent] running through the gangway and the alley southbound," and observed that Wardlow was carrying a white, opaque bag under his arm. * * *

This terse testimony is most noticeable for what it fails to reveal. Though asked whether he was in a marked or unmarked car, Officer Nolan could not recall the answer. He was not asked whether any of the other three cars in the caravan were marked, or whether any of the other seven officers were in uniform. Though he explained that the size of the caravan was because "[n]ormally in these different areas there's an enormous amount of people, sometimes lookouts, customers," Officer Nolan did not testify as to whether *anyone* besides Wardlow was nearby 4035 West Van Buren. Nor is it clear that that address was the intended destination of the caravan. * * * Officer Nolan's testimony also does not reveal how fast the officers were driving. It does not indicate whether he saw respondent notice the other patrol cars. And it does not say whether the caravan, or any part of it, had already passed Wardlow by before he began to run.

Indeed, the Appellate Court thought the record was even "too vague to support the inference that * * * defendant's flight was related to his expectation of police focus on him." Presumably, respondent did not react to the first three cars, and we cannot even be sure that he recognized the occupants of the fourth as police officers. The adverse inference is based entirely on the officer's statement: "He looked in our direction and began fleeing."

No other factors sufficiently support a finding of reasonable suspicion. * * *

The State, along with the majority of the Court, relies as well on the assumption that this flight occurred in a high crime area. Even if that assumption is accurate, it is insufficient because even in a high crime neighborhood unprovoked flight does not invariably lead to reasonable suspicion. On the contrary, because many factors providing innocent motivations for unprovoked flight are concentrated in high crime areas, the character of the neighborhood arguably makes an inference of guilt less appropriate, rather than more so. Like unprovoked flight itself, presence in a high crime neighborhood is a fact too generic and susceptible to innocent explanation to satisfy the reasonable suspicion inquiry. * * *

Thus, a reviewing court may accord substantial deference to a local court's determination that fear of the police is especially acute in a specific location or at a particular time.

NOTES AND QUESTIONS

1. Does "unprovoked flight" + "high-crime area" = "reasonable suspicion"? Can you posit a set of facts in which this is *not* an accurate formula?

2. Lenese C. Herbert, *Can't You See What I'm Saying? Making Expressive Conduct a Crime in High–Crimes Areas*, 9 Geo. J. Pov. L. & Pol'y 135, 135–36, 165 (2002):

> As an eager young Assistant United States Attorney who "papered" countless complaints, conducted numerous hearings, and tried a substantial number of cases, I learned how to decode police officer jargon and law enforcement terminology. One of the most commonly used—yet seldom defined—phrases was "high-crime area." * * * Before court appearance, I would often question police officers about this characterization. In court, however, judges * * * never asked officers for data to support assertions that an area was high-crime. Even defense counsel seldom explored what this classification meant, the bases for it, or its relevance. * * *

> I suspected that the police were using a code language to suggest that their actions were justified because they were directed at "high-crime people": poor, undereducated, black and brown males who live in or frequent depressed * * * inner-city neighborhoods, or who look as if they do. In practice, police have the implicit authorization to create and apply an inferior set of rights to individuals in high-crime areas, presumably because those individuals are regarded as being less worthy than other citizens. * * *

> * * * The *Wardlow* Court * * * has virtually relinquished the protection and safeguarding of the rights of the policed to the police themselves.

Are these criticisms fair?

3. *Problem.* Officers on patrol observed a car leaving the area with one headlight out and an expired inspection sticker. The officers signaled for the car to stop. The driver complied. As the officers approached the driver's side, *B*, a passenger in the front seat, jumped out and ran away. One officer gave chase and tackled him. Reasonable suspicion for *this* seizure? United States v. Bonner, 363 F.3d 213 (3d Cir. 2004). Does your answer depend on whether this occurred: (a) near a housing project in a poor part of town; or (b) in the Beverly Hills, California business district?

e. Extending the Terry Doctrine

MARYLAND v. BUIE

Supreme Court of the United States, 1990.
494 U.S. 325, 110 S.Ct. 1093, 108 L.Ed.2d 276.

JUSTICE WHITE delivered the opinion of the Court.

A "protective sweep" is a quick and limited search of premises, incident to an arrest and conducted to protect the safety of police officers or others. It is narrowly confined to a cursory visual inspection of those places in which a person might be hiding. In this case we must decide what level of justification is required by the Fourth and Fourteenth Amendments before police officers, while effecting the arrest of a suspect in his home pursuant to an arrest warrant, may conduct a warrantless protective sweep of all or part of the premises. * * *

I

On February 3, 1986, two men committed an armed robbery of a Godfather's Pizza restaurant in Prince George's County, Maryland. One of the robbers was wearing a red running suit. That same day, Prince George's County police obtained arrest warrants for respondent Jerome Edward Buie and his suspected accomplice in the robbery, Lloyd Allen. Buie's house was placed under police surveillance.

On February 5, the police executed the arrest warrant for Buie. They first had a police department secretary telephone Buie's house to verify that he was home. The secretary spoke to a female first, then to Buie himself. Six or seven officers proceeded to Buie's house. Once inside, the officers fanned out through the first and second floors. Corporal James Rozar announced that he would "freeze" the basement so that no one could come up and surprise the officers. With his service revolver drawn, Rozar twice shouted into the basement, ordering anyone down there to come out. When a voice asked who was calling, Rozar announced three times: "this is the police, show me your hands." Eventually, a pair of hands appeared around the bottom of the stairwell and Buie emerged from the basement. He was arrested, searched, and handcuffed by Rozar. Thereafter, Detective Joseph Frolich entered the basement "in case there was someone else" down there. He noticed a red running suit lying in plain view on a stack of clothing and seized it.

The trial court denied Buie's motion to suppress the running suit * * * . * * *

II

It is not disputed that until the point of Buie's arrest the police had the right, based on the authority of the arrest warrant, to search anywhere in the house that Buie might have been found, including the basement. * * * There is also no dispute that if Detective Frolich's entry into the basement was lawful, the seizure of the red running suit, which was in plain view and which the officer had probable cause to believe was evidence of a crime, was also lawful under the Fourth Amendment. The issue in this case is what level of justification the Fourth Amendment required before Detective Frolich could legally enter the basement to see if someone else was there.

Petitioner, the State of Maryland, argues that, under a general reasonableness balancing test, police should be permitted to conduct a protective sweep whenever they make an in-home arrest for a violent crime. * * *

III

It goes without saying that the Fourth Amendment bars only unreasonable searches and seizures. Our cases show that in determining reasonableness, we have balanced the intrusion on the individual's Fourth Amendment interests against its promotion of legitimate governmental interests. Under this test, a search of the house or office is generally not reasonable without a warrant issued on probable cause. There are other contexts, however, where the public interest is such that neither a warrant nor probable cause is required.

The *Terry* [*v. Ohio*] case is most instructive for present purposes. There we held that an on-the-street "frisk" for weapons must be tested by the Fourth Amendment's general proscription against unreasonable searches because such a frisk involves "an entire rubric of police conduct—necessarily swift action predicated upon the on-the-spot observations of the officer on the beat—which historically has not been, and as a practical matter could not be, subjected to the warrant procedure." We stated that there is " 'no ready test for determining reasonableness other than by balancing the need to search * * * against the invasion which the search * * * entails.' " Applying that balancing test, it was held that although a frisk for weapons "constitutes a severe, though brief, intrusion upon cherished personal security," such a frisk is reasonable when weighed against the "need for law enforcement officers to protect themselves and other prospective victims of violence in situations where they may lack probable cause for an arrest." We therefore authorized a limited patdown for weapons where a reasonably prudent officer would be warranted in the belief, based on "specific and articulable facts," and not on a mere "inchoate and unparticularized suspicion or 'hunch,' " "that he is dealing with an armed and dangerous individual." * * *

The ingredients to apply the balance struck in *Terry* * * * are present in this case. Possessing an arrest warrant and probable cause to believe Buie was in his home, the officers were entitled to enter and to search anywhere in the house in which Buie might be found. Once he was found, however, the search for him was over, and there was no longer that particular justification for entering any rooms that had not yet been searched.

That Buie had an expectation of privacy in those remaining areas of his house, however, does not mean such rooms were immune from entry. In *Terry* * * * we were concerned with the immediate interest of the police officer[] in taking steps to assure [himself] that the persons with whom [he was] dealing were not armed with, or able to gain immediate control of, a weapon that could unexpectedly and fatally be used against [him]. In the instant case, there is an analogous interest of the officers in taking steps to assure themselves that the house in which a suspect is being, or has just been, arrested is not harboring other persons who are dangerous and who could unexpectedly launch an attack. The risk of danger in the context of an arrest in the home is as great as, if not greater than, it is in an on-the-street or roadside investigatory encounter. A *Terry* * * * frisk occurs before a police-citizen confrontation has escalated to the point of arrest. A protective sweep, in contrast, occurs as an adjunct to the serious step of taking a person into custody for the purpose of prosecuting him for a crime. Moreover, unlike an encounter on the street or along a highway, an in-home arrest puts the officer at the disadvantage of being on his adversary's "turf." An ambush in a confined setting of unknown configuration is more to be feared than it is in open, more familiar surroundings.

We recognized in *Terry* that "[e]ven a limited search of the outer clothing for weapons constitutes a severe, though brief, intrusion upon cherished personal security, and it must surely be an annoying, frightening, and perhaps humiliating experience." But we permitted the intrusion, which was no more than necessary to protect the officer from harm. Nor do we here suggest, as the State does, that entering rooms not examined prior to the arrest is a *de minimis* intrusion that may be disregarded. We are quite sure, however, that the arresting officers are permitted in such circumstances to take reasonable steps to ensure their safety after, and while making, the arrest. That interest is sufficient to outweigh the intrusion such procedures may entail.

We agree with the State * * * that a warrant was not required. We also hold that as an incident to the arrest the officers could, as a precautionary matter and without probable cause or reasonable suspicion, look in closets and other spaces immediately adjoining the place of arrest from which an attack could be immediately launched. Beyond that, however, we hold that there must be articulable facts which, taken together with the rational inferences from those facts, would warrant a reasonably prudent officer in believing that the area to be swept harbors an individual posing a danger to those on the arrest scene. * * *

We should emphasize that such a protective sweep, aimed at protecting the arresting officers, if justified by the circumstances, is nevertheless not a full search of the premises, but may extend only to a cursory inspection of those spaces where a person may be found.[3] The sweep lasts no longer than is necessary to dispel the reasonable suspicion of danger and in any event no longer than it takes to complete the arrest and depart the premises.

---

3. Our reliance on the cursory nature of the search is not inconsistent with our statement in *Arizona v. Hicks*, [p. 304], that "[a] search is a search," or with our refusal in *Hicks* to sanction a standard less than probable cause on the ground that the search of a stereo was a "cursory inspection," rather than a "full-blown search." When the officer in *Hicks* moved the turntable to look at its serial number, he was searching for evidence plain and simple. There was no interest in officer safety or other exigency at work in that search. A protective sweep is without question a "search," as was the patdown in *Terry*; they are permissible on less than probable cause only because they are limited to that which is necessary to protect the safety of officers and others.

IV

* * * To reach our conclusion today * * *, we need not disagree with the Court's statement in *Chimel*, that "the invasion of privacy that results from a top-to-bottom search of a man's house [cannot be characterized] as 'minor,'" nor hold that "simply because some interference with an individual's privacy and freedom of movement has lawfully taken place, further intrusions should automatically be allowed despite the absence of a warrant that the Fourth Amendment would otherwise require." The type of search we authorize today is far removed from the "top-to-bottom" search involved in *Chimel*; moreover, it is decidedly not "automati[c]," but may be conducted only when justified by a reasonable, articulable suspicion that the house is harboring a person posing a danger to those on the arrest scene. * * *

We * * * remand this case to the Court of Appeals of Maryland for further proceedings not inconsistent with this opinion. * * *

Justice STEVENS, concurring.

Today the Court holds that reasonable suspicion, rather than probable cause, is necessary to support a protective sweep while an arrest is in progress. I agree with that holding and with the Court's opinion, but I believe it is important to emphasize that the standard applies only to *protective* sweeps. Officers conducting such a sweep must have a reasonable basis for believing that their search will reduce the danger of harm to themselves or of violent interference with their mission; in short, the search must be protective.

In this case, to justify Officer Frolich's entry into the basement, it is the State's burden to demonstrate that the officers had a reasonable basis for believing not only that someone in the basement might attack them or otherwise try to interfere with the arrest, but also that it would be safer to go down the stairs instead of simply guarding them from above until respondent had been removed from the house. The fact that respondent offered no resistance when he emerged from the basement is somewhat inconsistent with the hypothesis that the danger of an attack by a hidden confederate persisted after the arrest. * * *

Indeed, were the officers concerned about safety, one would expect them to do what Officer Rozar did before the arrest: guard the basement door to prevent surprise attacks. As the Court indicates, Officer Frolich might, at the time of the arrest, reasonably have "look[ed] in" the already open basement door to ensure that no accomplice had followed Buie to the stairwell. But Officer Frolich did not merely "look in" the basement; he entered it. That strategy is sensible if one wishes to search the basement. It is a surprising choice for an officer, worried about safety, who need not risk entering the stairwell at all.

The State may thus face a formidable task on remand. However, the Maryland courts are better equipped than are we to review the record. * * * I therefore agree that a remand is appropriate.

[The concurring opinion of Justice Kennedy is omitted.]

Justice BRENNAN, with whom Justice MARSHALL joins, dissenting.
* * *

* * * [T]he Court's implicit judgment that a protective sweep constitutes a "minimally intrusive" search akin to that involved in *Terry* markedly undervalues the nature and scope of the privacy interests involved.

While the Fourth Amendment protects a person's privacy interests in a variety of settings, "physical entry of the home is the chief evil against which the wording of the Fourth Amendment is directed." The Court discounts the nature of the intrusion because it believes that the scope of the intrusion is limited. The Court explains that a protective sweep's scope is "narrowly confined to a cursory visual inspection of those places in which a person might be hiding," and confined in duration to a period "no longer than is necessary to dispel the reasonable suspicion of danger and in any event no longer than it takes to complete the arrest and depart the premises." But these spatial and temporal restrictions are not particularly limiting. A protective sweep would bring within police purview virtually all personal possessions within the house not hidden from view in a small enclosed space. Police officers searching for potential ambushers might enter every room including basements and attics; open up closets, lockers, chests, wardrobes, and cars; and peer under beds and behind furniture. The officers will view letters, documents, and personal effects that are on tables or desks or are visible inside open drawers; books, records, tapes, and pictures on shelves; and clothing, medicines, toiletries and other paraphernalia not carefully stored in dresser drawers or bathroom cupboards. While perhaps not a "full-blown" or "top-to-bottom" search, a protective sweep is much closer to it than to a "limited patdown for weapons" * * *. * * * The "ingredient" of a minimally intrusive search is absent, and the Court's holding today therefore unpalatably deviates from *Terry* and its progeny.[6]

In light of the special sanctity of a private residence and the highly intrusive nature of a protective sweep, I firmly believe that police officers must have probable cause to fear that their personal safety is threatened by a hidden confederate of an arrestee before they may sweep through the entire home. * * * I respectfully dissent.

---

6. The Court's decision also to expand the "search incident to arrest" exception previously recognized in *Chimel v. California*, allowing police officers without *any* requisite level of suspicion to look into "closets and other spaces immediately adjoining the place of arrest from which an attack could be immediately launched," is equally disquieting. *Chimel* established that police officers may presume as a matter of law, without need for factual support in a particular case, that arrestees might take advantage of weapons or destroy evidence in the area "within [their] immediate control"; therefore, a protective search of that area is *per se* reasonable under the Fourth Amendment. I find much less plausible the Court's implicit assumption today that arrestees are likely to sprinkle hidden allies throughout the rooms in which they might be arrested. Hence there is no comparable justification for permitting arresting officers to presume as a matter of law that they are threatened by ambush from "immediately adjoining" spaces.

NOTES AND QUESTIONS

1.   On remand, the Court of Appeals of Maryland, 4–3, upheld the sweep. Buie v. State, 320 Md. 696, 580 A.2d 167 (1990).

2.   During a protective sweep, what may a police officer do if she finds a person hidden in a closet? Watching television in a family room? May she fully search the person? Automatically conduct a pat-down? May she conduct a search of the *grabbing area of that* person, even if this includes searching small areas, such as drawers, where a gun (but not another person) might be discovered?

3.   Is the *Buie* "protective sweep" rule limited to cases in which the police are in a home to make an arrest? What if the police are lawfully in a house to investigate a crime but are not yet prepared to make an arrest? And, does the protective sweep doctrine apply to an automobile? For example, what if the police stop a van driven by a person whom they reasonably suspect just committed an armed robbery nearby. If the officers cannot see inside the tinted windows of the van to see if others are inside, may they conduct a protective sweep pursuant to *Buie*? See United States v. Thomas, 249 F.3d 725 (8th Cir. 2001).

4.   *Brief seizure of property?* In United States v. Place, 462 U.S. 696, 103 S.Ct. 2637, 77 L.Ed.2d 110 (1983), the Supreme Court extended the *Terry* analysis of temporary seizures of persons to personalty. In *Place*, law enforcement officers at Miami International Airport grew suspicious of Raymond Place's behavior and, after an initial investigation, alerted Drug Enforcement Administration (DEA) authorities in New York, where Place was traveling. When Place arrived at New York's LaGuardia airport, two DEA agents were waiting for him. Place's behavior there reasonably aroused the agents' suspicion. Therefore, they approached Place, identified themselves as federal narcotics agents, requested and received his identification, and then sought consent to search Place's two pieces of luggage. When Place refused, the agents informed him that would take the bags to seek a search warrant. Instead, they took the luggage to Kennedy Airport where they subjected the two bags to a "sniff test" by a trained canine, which reacted positively to one bag. This occurred about ninety minutes after the initial seizure of the luggage. Because it was late in the afternoon on Friday, the agents held both bags until Monday morning, at which time a magistrate issued a warrant to search one bag. Upon opening it, the agents discovered a large quantity of cocaine.

Justice O'Connor, writing for six members of the Court held that the principles of *Terry v. Ohio*—namely, that the reasonableness of a seizure is determined by balancing the competing interests—applied to Place's luggage:

> We examine first the governmental interest offered as a justification for a brief seizure of luggage from the suspect's custody for the purpose of pursuing a limited course of investigation. The Government contends that, where the authorities possess specific and articulable facts warranting a reasonable belief that a traveler's luggage contains narcotics, the

governmental interest in seizing the luggage briefly to pursue further investigation is substantial. We agree. * * *

Against this strong governmental interest, we must weigh the nature and extent of the intrusion upon the individual's Fourth Amendment rights when the police briefly detain luggage for limited investigative purposes. On this point, respondent Place urges that the rationale for a *Terry* stop of the person is wholly inapplicable to investigative detentions of personalty. Specifically, the *Terry* exception to the probable-cause requirement is premised on the notion that a *Terry*-type stop of the person is substantially less intrusive of a person's liberty interests than a formal arrest. In the property context, however, Place urges, there are no degrees of intrusion. Once the owner's property is seized, the dispossession is absolute.

We disagree. The intrusion on possessory interests occasioned by a seizure of one's personal effects can vary both in its nature and extent. The seizure may be made after the owner has relinquished control of the property to a third party or, as here, from the immediate custody and control of the owner. Moreover, the police may confine their investigation to an on-the-spot inquiry—for example, immediate exposure of the luggage to a trained narcotics detection dog—or transport the property to another location. Given the fact that seizures of property can vary in intrusiveness, some brief detentions of personal effects may be so minimally intrusive of Fourth Amendment interests that strong countervailing governmental interests will justify a seizure based only on specific articulable facts that the property contains contraband or evidence of a crime.

In sum, we conclude that when an officer's observations lead him reasonably to believe that a traveler is carrying luggage that contains narcotics, the principles of *Terry* and its progeny would permit the officer to detain the luggage briefly to investigate the circumstances that aroused his suspicion, provided that the investigative detention is properly limited in scope.

Although the Government won *that* legal argument, it ultimately lost the Fourth Amendment claim in *this* case:

The premise of the Government's argument is that seizures of property are generally less intrusive than seizures of the person. While true in some circumstances, that premise is faulty on the facts we address in this case. The precise type of detention we confront here is seizure of personal luggage from the immediate possession of the suspect for the purpose of arranging exposure to a narcotics detection dog. Particularly in the case of detention of luggage within the traveler's immediate possession, the police conduct intrudes on both the suspect's possessory interest in his luggage as well as his liberty interest in proceeding with his itinerary. The person whose luggage is detained is technically still free to continue his travels or carry out other personal activities pending release of the luggage. * * * Nevertheless, such a seizure can effectively restrain the person since he is subjected to the possible disruption of his travel plans in order to remain with his luggage or to arrange for its return. Therefore, when the police seize luggage from the suspect's custody, we think the limitations applicable to investigative detentions of the person should define the permissible scope of an investigative detention of the person's luggage on less than probable cause. Under this standard, it is clear that the police conduct here exceeded the permissible limits of a *Terry*-type investigative stop.

The length of the detention of respondent's luggage alone precludes the conclusion that the seizure was reasonable in the absence of probable cause. Although we have recognized the reasonableness of seizures longer than the momentary ones involved in *Terry*, * * * the brevity of the invasion of the individual's Fourth Amendment interests is an important factor in determining whether the seizure is so minimally intrusive as to be justifiable on reasonable suspicion. Moreover, in assessing the effect of the length of the detention, we take into account whether the police diligently pursue their investigation. We note that here the New York agents knew the time of Place's scheduled arrival at LaGuardia, had ample time to arrange for their additional investigation at that location, and thereby could have minimized the intrusion on respondent's Fourth Amendment interests. Thus, although we decline to adopt any outside time limitation for a permissible *Terry* stop, we have never approved a seizure of the person for the prolonged 90–minute period involved here and cannot do so on the facts presented by this case.

Although the 90–minute detention of respondent's luggage is sufficient to render the seizure unreasonable, the violation was exacerbated by the failure of the agents to accurately inform respondent of the place to which they were transporting his luggage, of the length of time he might be dispossessed, and of what arrangements would be made for return of the luggage if the investigation dispelled the suspicion. In short, we hold that the detention of respondent's luggage in this case went beyond the narrow authority possessed by police to detain briefly luggage reasonably suspected to contain narcotics.

Does any of the Court's analysis here seem to conflict with anything else you have read in the *Terry* materials?

5. *"Car frisks."* We have seen that the police may ordinarily search a car without a warrant to the extent they have probable cause. They may also search portions of it as an incident to a lawful arrest of a car occupant (or a recent one), even without probable cause, if the interior of the car is in the arrestee's grabbing area. But, now suppose the police conduct a lawful *Terry*-level stop of a driver. May the police, short of probable cause, search the car to protect themselves from possible weapons that might be hidden inside?

In Michigan v. Long, 463 U.S. 1032, 103 S.Ct. 3469, 77 L.Ed.2d 1201 (1983), two officers on patrol in a rural area of Michigan, shortly after midnight, observed a car driving erratically and swerve off into a shallow ditch. The officer stopped to investigate. Long, the only occupant of the car, exited his vehicle and, leaving the car door open, met the officers at the rear of his car. One officer asked Long for his driver's license, but Long—who now appeared to the officers to be "under the influence of something"—did not respond, but turned away and began walking to the open door of his car. The officers followed him, at which point they observed a large hunting knife on the floorboard of the driver's side of the car. At that point, the officers stopped Long from moving closer to the car. They subjected him to a *Terry* frisk, which revealed no weapons.

One officer then shone his flashlights into the car, "to search for other weapons." As the Court described it, "[t]he officer noticed that something was protruding from under the armrest on the front seat. He knelt in the vehicle and lifted the armrest. He saw an open pouch on the front seat, and upon flashing his light on the pouch, determined that it contained what appeared to be marihuana." A further search of the passenger compartment of the vehicle did not turn up other contraband. Long was arrested for possession of marijuana.

The Supreme Court granted certiorari in the case "to consider the important question of the authority of a police officer to protect himself by conducting a *Terry*-type search of the passenger compartment of a motor vehicle during the lawful investigatory stop of the occupant of the vehicle." The Court, per Justice O'Connor, upheld what has since been characterized as a *Terry* "frisk" of the passenger compartment of an automobile:

> Although *Terry* itself involved the stop and subsequent patdown search of a person, we were careful to note that "[w]e need not develop at length in this case, however, the limitations which the Fourth Amendment places upon a protective search and seizure for weapons. These limitations will have to be developed in the concrete factual circumstances of individual cases." Contrary to Long's view, *Terry* need not be read as restricting the preventative search to the person of the detained suspect.
>
> In two cases in which we applied *Terry* to specific factual situations, we recognized that investigative detentions involving suspects in vehicles are especially fraught with danger to police officers. In *Pennsylvania v. Mimms*, [p. 372, Note 4], we held that police may order persons out of an automobile during a stop for a traffic violation, and may frisk those persons for weapons if there is a reasonable belief that they are armed and dangerous. Our decision rested in part on the "inordinate risk confronting an officer as he approaches a person seated in an automobile." In *Adams v. Williams*, [p. 365, Note 9], we held that the police, acting on an informant's tip, may reach into the passenger compartment of an automobile to remove a gun from a driver's waistband even where the gun was not apparent to police from outside the car and the police knew of its existence only because of the tip. Again, our decision rested in part on our view of the danger presented to police officers in "traffic stop" and automobile situations.
>
> Finally, we have also expressly recognized that suspects may injure police officers and others by virtue of their access to weapons, even though they may not themselves be armed. * * *
>
> Our past cases indicate then that protection of police and others can justify protective searches when police have a reasonable belief that the suspect poses a danger, that roadside encounters between police and suspects are especially hazardous, and that danger may arise from the

possible presence of weapons in the area surrounding a suspect. These principles compel our conclusion that the search of the passenger compartment of an automobile, limited to those areas in which a weapon may be placed or hidden, is permissible if the police officer possesses a reasonable belief based on "specific and articulable facts which, taken together with the rational inferences from those facts, reasonably warrant" the officer in believing that the suspect is dangerous and the suspect may gain immediate control of weapons. "[T]he issue is whether a reasonably prudent man in the circumstances would be warranted in the belief that his safety or that of others was in danger." If a suspect is "dangerous," he is no less dangerous simply because he is not arrested. If, while conducting a legitimate *Terry* search of the interior of the automobile, the officer should, as here, discover contraband other than weapons, he clearly cannot be required to ignore the contraband, and the Fourth Amendment does not require its suppression in such circumstances.

Having announced the new rule, the Court turned to the question of whether the officers here had the requisite grounds to conduct the weapons search of the passenger compartment of the car:

> The circumstances of this case clearly justified Deputies Howell and Lewis in their reasonable belief that Long posed a danger if he were permitted to reenter his vehicle. The hour was late and the area rural. Long was driving his automobile at excessive speed, and his car swerved into a ditch. The officers had to repeat their questions to Long, who appeared to be "under the influence" of some intoxicant. Long was not frisked until the officers observed that there was a large knife in the interior of the car into which Long was about to reenter. The subsequent search of the car was restricted to those areas to which Long would generally have immediate control, and that could contain a weapon. The trial court determined that the leather pouch containing marihuana could have contained a weapon. It is clear that the intrusion was "strictly circumscribed by the exigencies which justifi[ed] its initiation."

Do you agree with the Court's new rule? Even if you do, do you think the police needed to search the vehicle in *this* case? Justice Brennan, writing also for Justice Marshall, dissented:

> [T]he scope of a search is determined not only by reference to its purpose, but also by reference to its intrusiveness. Yet the Court today holds that a search of a car (and the containers within it) that is not even occupied by the suspect is only as intrusive as, or perhaps less intrusive than, thrusting a hand into a pocket after an initial patdown has suggested the presence of concealed objects that might be used as weapons.

> The Court suggests no limit on the "area search" it now authorizes. * * * Presumably a weapon "may be placed or hidden" anywhere in a car. A weapon also might be hidden in a container in the car. In this case, the Court upholds the officer's search of a leather pouch because it "could have contained a weapon." In addition, the Court's requirement that an officer have a reasonable suspicion that a suspect is armed and dangerous does little to check the initiation of an area search. In this case, the

officers saw a hunting knife in the car, but the Court does not base its holding that the subsequent search was permissible on the ground that possession of the knife may have been illegal under state law. An individual can lawfully possess many things that can be used as weapons. A hammer, or a baseball bat, can be used as a very effective weapon. * * * Based on these facts, one might reasonably conclude that respondent was drunk. A drunken driver is indeed dangerous while driving, but not while stopped on the roadside by the police. Even when an intoxicated person lawfully has in his car an object that could be used as a weapon, it requires imagination to conclude that he is presently dangerous. Even assuming that the facts in this case justified the officers' initial "frisk" of respondent, they hardly provide adequate justification for a search of a suspect's car and the containers within it. This represents an intrusion not just different in degree, but in kind, from the intrusion sanctioned by *Terry.* In short, the implications of the Court's decision are frightening.

6. *Problem.* R's live-in girlfriend called 911 to report that R was drunk and talking about committing suicide. While she was on the telephone, two gunshots were fired. The 911 dispatcher directed her to leave the house and wait for the police. A SWAT team arrived shortly thereafter and surrounded the house. The girlfriend informed them that R was the only person inside. After a lengthy standoff, an officer used a stun gun on R, who was sitting on a windowsill with his legs hanging out an open window as he drunkenly cursed at the officers. R was formally arrested outside the house for possession of a firearm. He told the officers that nobody else was inside the house. Nonetheless, the SWAT team secured the house and then broke through a barricaded door and entered the premises. Inside they seized a shotgun and made photographs of spent shells and the holes R had shot into the ceiling. The police justified the entry as a protective sweep. Was the entry valid on that or any other ground? Commonwealth v. Robertson, 275 Va. 559, 659 S.E.2d 321 (2008).

2. REASONABLENESS IN A "SPECIAL NEEDS" (AND NON–CRIMINAL?) CONTEXT

INTRODUCTION

It is necessary to draw a distinction between searches and seizures conducted by police in furtherance of their criminal law enforcement responsibilities and searches and seizures conducted by police, and by other public officials, in furtherance of "community caretaking functions" or, more generally, non-law enforcement purposes. It is necessary to draw this line because the Supreme Court sometimes does. Unfortunately, the line-drawing is exceptionally difficult, because the distinction, if it even exists, is not easy to draw.

If you think back over this chapter, nearly every case we have considered involved a search or seizure in a criminal investigation. But, there have been some exceptions. For example, we had a Note (p. 278,

Note 3) relating to automobile inventories: When an automobile must be towed as the result of illegal parking, for example, the police may routinely inspect the contents of the car, not as part of a criminal investigation, but simply to make sure that belongings are properly inventoried for safekeeping and other purposes. South Dakota v. Opperman, 428 U.S. 364, 96 S.Ct. 3092, 49 L.Ed.2d 1000 (1976), held that because such inventories are not criminal investigations, the warrant clause including the probable cause requirement do not apply. The reasonableness clause, alone, must be considered, and the Court held that the police may inventory automobiles under specified circumstances in the absence of probable cause *or even reasonable suspicion.*

Opperman has come to be seen as stating a special inventory "exception" to the warrant "requirement." But that may primarily be a function of history. Over time, the Supreme Court has come to recognize another general warrant "exception," sometimes described as the "special needs" exception, which could easily encompass inventories. A search or seizure comes within the "special needs" category when a perceived need, beyond the normal need for criminal law enforcement, makes the warrant and/or probable-cause requirements of the Fourth Amendment impracticable or, simply, irrelevant. In "special needs" circumstances, the Court evaluates the governmental activity by applying the reasonableness balancing standard.

One scholar has observed that "little or no effort has been made to explain what these 'special needs' are; the term turns out to be no more than a label that indicates when a lax standard will apply." William J. Stuntz, *Implicit Bargains, Government Power, and the Fourth Amendment*, 44 Stan. L. Rev. 553, 554 (1992). An interesting feature of the doctrine is that, in this area, often "the Court [has] one of its rare opportunities to hear face-to-face, as Fourth Amendment claimants, those law-abiding citizens for whose ultimate benefits the constitutional restraints on public power were primarily intended." Stephen J. Schulhofer, *On the Fourth Amendment Rights of the Law–Abiding Public*, 1989 Sup. Ct. Rev. 87, 88. Yet, as we will see, in these cases not only are traditional warrants inapplicable, but the Supreme Court sometimes dispenses with the requirement of suspicion of wrongdoing on the part of the "victim" of the search or seizure.

A final point, as we start looking at this field: This "exception" to the warrant "requirement" is part of a still-developing understanding by the high court that the warrant clause has no meaningful role to play in the non-criminal law enforcement context. Therefore, we should not look at the cases in this area as primarily stating a "special needs" exception to the warrant "requirement," but rather as cases that have forced the Court to navigate the shadowy area between criminal investigations and other public functions that invade the privacy and/or possessory interests of citizens.

NOTES AND QUESTIONS

1. *Administrative searches.* In 1967 (long before recognition of a "special needs" doctrine), the Supreme Court considered the applicability of the Fourth Amendment in the enforcement of housing code regulations, Camara v. Municipal Court, 387 U.S. 523, 87 S.Ct. 1727, 18 L.Ed.2d 930 (1967), and safety code provisions affecting commercial buildings, See v. City of Seattle, 387 U.S. 541, 87 S.Ct. 1737, 18 L.Ed.2d 943 (1967). *Camara* and *See* were decided during the peak of the dominance of the warrant clause. In general, the cases provide that, except in the event of emergency or consent, residences and commercial buildings may not be entered to inspect for administrative code violations without an administrative search warrant. The "probable cause" for these administrative warrants can be supplied by a showing of non-arbitrary justification to inspect the particular premises, *e.g.*, that all the buildings in the area are due to being inspected. This kind of "probable cause" obviously does not require particularized suspicion of criminal wrong-doing or even of administrative code violations in a specific building.

Since the *Camara-See* doctrine was laid down, and as the Supreme Court's devotion to warrants has receded, the Court has approved *warrantless* administrative searches of "closely [governmentally] regulated industries," even in the absence of emergency or consent. As the Court explained in New York v. Burger, 482 U.S. 691, 107 S.Ct. 2636, 96 L.Ed.2d 601 (1987),

> [b]ecause the owner or operator of commercial premises in a "closely regulated" industry has a reduced expectation of privacy, the warrant and probable-cause requirements, which fulfill the traditional Fourth Amendment standard of reasonableness for a government search, have lessened application in this context. Rather, we conclude that, as in other situations of "special need," where the privacy interests of the owner are weakened and the government interests in regulating particular businesses are concomitantly heightened, a warrantless inspection of commercial premises may well be reasonable within the meaning of the Fourth Amendment.

Burger is an especially interesting case because, unlike most administrative searches that are conducted by employees of administrative agencies, the searches here were performed by police officers, who entered the defendant's automobile junkyard without a warrant or probable cause of criminal wrong-doing. Pursuant to statute, they asked to see Burger's business license and record of automobiles and parts on the premises. He admitted he had neither and thus was in plain violation of the administrative regulations for junk-yards. The officers then searched the junkyard, where they discovered stolen vehicle parts that led to Burger's arrest for possession of stolen property.

The Court upheld the search. It did so despite the fact that the searches were conducted by police officers, and that the officers, serving as agents of an administrative agency, could have cited Burger for violation of administrative regulations once he admitted the lack of records to them, without ever conducting the search that turned up criminal wrongdoing. As the case was recently explained, "the Court relied on the 'plain administrative purposes' of the scheme to reject the contention that the statute was in fact 'designed to gather evidence to enable convictions under the penal laws'." Ferguson v. City of Charleston, 532 U.S. 67, 121 S.Ct. 1281, 149 L.Ed.2d 205 (2001) (quoting from *Burger*). The Court did not focus on the motives of the officers in this case. All that mattered was that the administrative regulations had a non-penal purpose.

2. *Birth of the "special needs" doctrine.* The Court gave birth to the "special needs" doctrine, although its express mention arose only in a concurring opinion, in New Jersey v. T.L.O, 469 U.S. 325, 105 S.Ct. 733, 83 L.Ed.2d 720 (1985). In *T.L.O.*, two public school students were caught smoking on school grounds, in violation of school rules. When one of them denied she smoked, the vice-principal demanded her purse, opened it, and observed a package of cigarettes. As he pulled them out, he discovered cigarette paper, which is often used to make marijuana cigarettes. This led to a full search of T.L.O.'s purse, which turned up evidence implicating her in marijuana sales. The criminal evidence was handed over to the police and used in a juvenile court proceeding against her.

The Supreme Court held that neither the warrant requirement nor probable cause applies to searches by public school officials. It quickly disposed of the warrant requirement, stating that it is "unsuited to the school environment," because it would "unduly interfere with the maintenance of the swift and informal disciplinary proceedings needed in the schools." As for probable cause, the majority observed that "[w]here a careful balancing of governmental and public interests suggests that the public interest is best served by a Fourth Amendment standard of reasonableness that stops short of probable cause, we have not hesitated to adopt such a standard." Here, the Court ruled, public school teachers and administrators may search students without a warrant if two conditions are met: (1) "there are reasonable grounds"—not necessarily "probable cause" in the criminal law context—"for suspecting that the search will turn up evidence that the student has violated or is violating either the law or the rules of the school"; and (2) once initiated, the search is "not excessively intrusive in light of the age and sex of the student and the nature of the infraction." The Supreme Court concluded that the initial search for cigarettes in this case, based on the report of her smoking, "was in no sense unreasonable for Fourth Amendment purposes."

3. *A "special needs" school search that went too far.* In Safford Unified School District #1 v. Redding, 557 U.S. ___, 129 S.Ct. 2633, 174, L.Ed.2d 354 (2009), the Court confronted the issue of "whether a 13-year-old student's Fourth Amendment right was violated when she was subjected to a search of her bra and underpants by school officials acting on reasonable suspicion that she had brought forbidden prescription and over-the-counter drugs to school." The Court stated that characterizing the search—requiring the student "to remove her clothes down to her underwear, and then 'pull out' her bra and the elastic band on her underpants"—as a "strip search is a fair way to speak of it." (The search failed to turn up any pills.)

Every member of the Court except Justice Thomas concluded that the strip search violated the Fourth Amendment. The Court, per Justice Souter, stated that it violated the "rule of reasonableness as stated in *T.L.O.*":

Here, the content of the suspicion failed to match the degree of intrusion. [The principal who ordered the search] knew beforehand that the pills were prescription-strength ibuprofen and over-the-counter nax-proxen, common pain relievers equivalent to two Advil, or one Aleve. He must have been aware of the nature and limited threat of the specific drugs he was searching for * * *. [The principal] had no reason to suspect that large quantities of the drugs were being passed around, or that individual students were receiving great numbers of pills. * * *

In sum, what was missing from the suspected facts that pointed to [the student] was any indication of danger to the students from the power of the drugs or their quantity, and any reason [specific to this student] to suppose that [she] was carrying pills in her underwear. * * *

We * * * mean * * * to make it clear that the *T.L.O.* concern to limit a school search to reasonable scope requires the support of reasonable suspicion of danger or of resort to underwear for hiding evidence of wrongdoing before a search can reasonably make the quantum leap from outer clothes and backpacks to exposure of intimate parts. The meaning of such a search, and the degradation its subject may reasonably feel, place a search that intrusive in a category of its own demanding its own specific suspicions.

4. *Border searches.* Special rules also apply in the international border context. At the border and its functional equivalent (*e.g.*, at an airport where an international flight arrives), a person may be stopped (seized) and her belongings searched without a warrant and in the absence of individualized suspicion of wrongdoing, "pursuant to the long-standing right of the sovereign to protect itself" from the entry of persons and things dangerous to the nation. United States v. Ramsey, 431 U.S. 606, 97 S.Ct. 1972, 52 L.Ed.2d 617 (1977). In dictum the *Ramsey* Court did state, however, that "[w]e * * * leave open the question 'whether, and under what circumstances, a border search might be deemed "unreasonable" because of the particularly offensive manner it is carried out.' "[g]

The law of border searches is somewhat more complicated away from the border. Particularly on highways in the vicinity of the Mexican border, federal agents often stop vehicles to question occupants regarding their citizenship. The Court has distinguished here between seizures conducted by "roving border patrols" (where agents stop a car without notice on a little-traveled road) and those that occur at a fixed interior checkpoint (a permanent stop along a well-traveled highway). With *roving* border patrols, the Supreme Court has determined that the agents need reasonable suspicion of criminal activity to detain the car occupants briefly. United States v. Brignoni–Ponce,

---

g. In United States v. Flores–Montano, 541 U.S. 149, 124 S.Ct. 1582, 158 L.Ed.2d 311 (2004), the Supreme Court unanimously held that a suspicionless international border search is constitutionally reasonable even when border agents, without reasonable suspicion, seize a person's car at the international border, remove the gas task (a process that took almost an hour), and search it. In language not at all surprising in the aftermath of the September 11 attacks on the United States, Chief Justice Rehnquist observed that "[t]he Government's interest in preventing the entry of unwanted persons and effects is at its zenith at the international border." He stated that "[i]t is difficult to imagine how the search of a gas tank, which should be solely a repository for fuel, could be more of an invasion of privacy than the search of the automobile's passenger compartment."

422 U.S. 873, 95 S.Ct. 2574, 45 L.Ed.2d 607 (1975). However, in United States v. Martinez–Fuerte, 428 U.S. 543, 96 S.Ct. 3074, 49 L.Ed.2d 1116 (1976), the Court ruled that vehicle occupants may be stopped for questioning at *fixed* interior checkpoints without individualized suspicion of wrongdoing.

The Court distinguished fixed checkpoints from roving patrols on two grounds. First, the subjective intrusion on the security of lawful travelers— their fear and surprise level—"is appreciably less in the case of a [fixed] checkpoint stop." Second, agents at fixed checkpoints have less discretionary enforcement authority than roving agents: the location of the checkpoint is fixed, and they may only stop those that pass through it.

MICHIGAN DEPARTMENT OF STATE POLICE v. SITZ
Supreme Court of the United States, 1990.
496 U.S. 444, 110 S.Ct. 2481, 110 L.Ed.2d 412.

CHIEF JUSTICE REHNQUIST delivered the opinion of the Court.

This case poses the question whether a State's use of highway sobriety checkpoints violates the Fourth and Fourteenth Amendments to the United States Constitution. We hold that it does not and therefore reverse the contrary holding of the Court of Appeals of Michigan.

Petitioners, the Michigan Department of State Police and its director, established a sobriety checkpoint pilot program in early 1986. The director appointed a Sobriety Checkpoint Advisory Committee comprising representatives of the State Police force, local police forces, state prosecutors, and the University of Michigan Transportation Research Institute. Pursuant to its charge, the advisory committee created guidelines setting forth procedures governing checkpoint operations, site selection, and publicity.

Under the guidelines, checkpoints would be set up at selected sites along state roads. All vehicles passing through a checkpoint would be stopped and their drivers briefly examined for signs of intoxication. In cases where a checkpoint officer detected signs of intoxication, the motorist would be directed to a location out of the traffic flow where an officer would check the motorist's driver's license and car registration and, if warranted, conduct further sobriety tests. Should the field tests and the officer's observations suggest that the driver was intoxicated, an arrest would be made. All other drivers would be permitted to resume their journey immediately.

The first—and to date the only—sobriety checkpoint operated under the program was conducted in Saginaw County with the assistance of the Saginaw County Sheriff's Department. During the 75–minute duration of the checkpoint's operation, 126 vehicles passed through the checkpoint. The average delay for each vehicle was approximately 25 seconds. Two drivers were detained for field sobriety testing, and one of the two was arrested for driving under the influence of alcohol. A third driver who drove through without stopping was pulled over by an officer in an observation vehicle and arrested for driving under the influence.

On the day before the operation of the Saginaw County checkpoint, respondents filed a complaint in the Circuit Court of Wayne County seeking declaratory and injunctive relief from potential subjection to the checkpoints. * * *

After the trial, at which the court heard extensive testimony concerning, *inter alia*, the "effectiveness" of highway sobriety checkpoint programs, the court ruled that the Michigan program violated the Fourth Amendment * * *. On appeal, the Michigan Court of Appeals affirmed the holding * * *. * * *

To decide this case the trial court performed a balancing test derived from our opinion in *Brown v. Texas*, 443 U.S. 47, 99 S.Ct. 2637, 61 L.Ed.2d 357 (1979). As described by the Court of Appeals, the test involved "balancing the state's interest in preventing accidents caused by drunk drivers, the effectiveness of sobriety checkpoints in achieving that goal, and the level of intrusion on an individual's privacy caused by the checkpoints." The Court of Appeals agreed that "the *Brown* three-prong balancing test was the correct test to be used to determine the constitutionality of the sobriety checkpoint plan." * * *

Petitioners concede, correctly in our view, that a Fourth Amendment "seizure" occurs when a vehicle is stopped at a checkpoint. The question thus becomes whether such seizures are "reasonable" under the Fourth Amendment.

* * * We address only the initial stop of each motorist passing through a checkpoint and the associated preliminary questioning and observation by checkpoint officers. Detention of particular motorists for more extensive field sobriety testing may require satisfaction of an individualized suspicion standard.

No one can seriously dispute the magnitude of the drunken driving problem or the States' interest in eradicating it. Media reports of alcohol-related death and mutilation on the Nation's roads are legion. The anecdotal is confirmed by the statistical. "Drunk drivers cause an annual death toll of over 25,000 and in the same time span cause nearly one million personal injuries and more than five billion dollars in property damage." For decades, this Court has "repeatedly lamented the tragedy."

Conversely, the weight bearing on the other scale—the measure of the intrusion on motorists stopped briefly at sobriety checkpoints—is slight. We reached a similar conclusion as to the intrusion on motorists subjected to a brief stop at a highway checkpoint for detecting illegal aliens. See [*United States v.*] *Martinez-Fuerte*, [p. 426, Note 4.] We see virtually no difference between the levels of intrusion on law-abiding motorists from the brief stops necessary to the effectuation of these two types of checkpoints, which to the average motorist would seem identical save for the nature of the questions the checkpoint officers might ask. The trial court and the Court of Appeals, thus, accurately gauged the "objective" intrusion, measured by the duration of the seizure and the intensity of the investigation, as minimal.

With respect to what it perceived to be the "subjective" intrusion on motorists, however, the Court of Appeals found such intrusion substantial. * * *

We believe the Michigan courts misread our cases concerning the degree of "subjective intrusion" and the potential for generating fear and surprise. The "fear and surprise" to be considered are not the natural fear of one who has been drinking over the prospect of being stopped at a sobriety checkpoint but, rather, the fear and surprise engendered in law-abiding motorists by the nature of the stop. * * * The intrusion resulting from the brief stop at the sobriety checkpoint is for constitutional purposes indistinguishable from the checkpoint stops we upheld in *Martinez-Fuerte*.

The Court of Appeals went on to consider as part of the balancing analysis the "effectiveness" of the proposed checkpoint program. Based on extensive testimony in the trial record, the court concluded that the checkpoint program failed the "effectiveness" part of the test, and that this failure materially discounted petitioners' strong interest in implementing the program. We think the Court of Appeals was wrong on this point as well.

The actual language from *Brown v. Texas*, upon which the Michigan courts based their evaluation of "effectiveness," describes the balancing factor as "the degree to which the seizure advances the public interest." This passage from *Brown* was not meant to transfer from politically accountable officials to the courts the decision as to which among reasonable alternative law enforcement techniques should be employed to deal with a serious public danger. Experts in police science might disagree over which of several methods of apprehending drunken drivers is preferable as an ideal. But for purposes of Fourth Amendment analysis, the choice among such reasonable alternatives remains with the governmental officials who have a unique understanding of, and a responsibility for, limited public resources, including a finite number of police officers. * * *

In *Delaware v. Prouse*, [440 U.S. 648, 99 S.Ct. 1391, 59 L.Ed.2d 660 (1979),] we disapproved random stops made by Delaware Highway Patrol officers in an effort to apprehend unlicensed drivers and unsafe vehicles. We observed that *no* empirical evidence indicated that such stops would be an effective means of promoting roadway safety * * *. * * *

Unlike *Prouse*, this case involves neither a complete absence of empirical data nor a challenge to random highway stops. During the operation of the Saginaw County checkpoint, the detention of the 126 vehicles that entered the checkpoint resulted in the arrest of two drunken drivers. Stated as a percentage, approximately 1.6 percent of the drivers passing through the checkpoint were arrested for alcohol impairment. In addition, an expert witness testified at the trial that experience in other States demonstrated that, on the whole, sobriety checkpoints resulted in drunken driving arrests of around 1 percent of all motorists stopped. By way of comparison, the record from one of the consolidated cases in

Martinez-Fuerte showed that in the associated checkpoint, illegal aliens were found in only 0.12 percent of the vehicles passing through the checkpoint. The ratio of illegal aliens detected to vehicles stopped (considering that on occasion two or more illegal aliens were found in a single vehicle) was approximately 0.5 percent. We concluded that this "record * * * provides a rather complete picture of the effectiveness of the San Clemente checkpoint," and we sustained its constitutionality. We see no justification for a different conclusion here.

In sum, the balance of the State's interest in preventing drunken driving, the extent to which this system can reasonably be said to advance that interest, and the degree of intrusion upon individual motorists who are briefly stopped, weighs in favor of the state program. We therefore hold that it is consistent with the Fourth Amendment. * * *

[Justice Blackmun's concurrence in the judgment is omitted.]

Justice BRENNAN, with whom Justice MARSHALL joins, dissenting. * * *

* * * Some level of individualized suspicion is a core component of the protection the Fourth Amendment provides against arbitrary government action. By holding that no level of suspicion is necessary before the police may stop a car for the purpose of preventing drunken driving, the Court potentially subjects the general public to arbitrary or harassing conduct by the police. * * *

* * * That stopping every car *might* make it easier to prevent drunken driving is an insufficient justification for abandoning the requirement of individualized suspicion. * * * Without proof that the police cannot develop individualized suspicion that a person is driving while impaired by alcohol, I believe the constitutional balance must be struck in favor of protecting the public against even the "minimally intrusive" seizures involved in this case. * * *

Justice STEVENS, with whom Justice BRENNAN and Justice MARSHALL join as to Parts I and II, dissenting. * * *

I

There is a critical difference between a seizure that is preceded by fair notice and one that is effected by surprise. That is one reason why a border search, or indeed any search at a permanent and fixed checkpoint, is much less intrusive than a random stop. A motorist with advance notice of the location of a permanent checkpoint has an opportunity to avoid the search entirely, or at least to prepare for, and limit, the intrusion on her privacy.

No such opportunity is available in the case of a random stop or a temporary checkpoint, which both depend for their effectiveness on the element of surprise. A driver who discovers an unexpected checkpoint on a familiar local road will be startled and distressed. She may infer, correctly, that the checkpoint is not simply "business as usual," and may likewise infer, again correctly, that the police have made a discretionary decision to focus their law enforcement efforts upon her and others who pass the chosen point.* * *

* * * [I]t is significant that many of the stops at permanent checkpoints occur during daylight hours, whereas the sobriety checkpoints are almost invariably operated at night. A seizure followed by interrogation and even a cursory search at night is surely more offensive than a daytime stop that is almost as routine as going through a toll gate. * * *

These fears are not, as the Court would have it, solely the lot of the guilty. * * * Unwanted attention from the local police need not be less discomforting simply because one's secrets are not the stuff of criminal prosecutions. Moreover, those who have found—by reason of prejudice or misfortune—that encounters with the police may become adversarial or unpleasant without good cause will have grounds for worrying at any stop designed to elicit signs of suspicious behavior. * * *

II

The Court, unable to draw any persuasive analogy to *Martinez-Fuerte*, rests its decision today on application of a more general balancing test taken from *Brown v. Texas*. In that case the appellant, a pedestrian, had been stopped for questioning in an area of El Paso, Texas, that had "a high incidence of drug traffic" because he "looked suspicious." He was then arrested and convicted for refusing to identify himself to police officers. We set aside his conviction because the officers stopped him when they lacked any reasonable suspicion that he was engaged in criminal activity. In our opinion, we stated:

> "Consideration of the constitutionality of such seizures involves a weighing of the gravity of the public concerns served by the seizure, the degree to which the seizure advances the public interest, and the severity of the interference with individual liberty."

The gravity of the public concern with highway safety that is implicated by this case is, of course, undisputed. Yet, that same grave concern was implicated in *Delaware v. Prouse*. Moreover, I do not understand the Court to have placed any lesser value on the importance of the drug problem implicated in *Brown v. Texas* * * *. A different result in this case must be justified by the other two factors in the *Brown* formulation.

As I have already explained, I believe the Court is quite wrong in blithely asserting that a sobriety checkpoint is no more intrusive than a permanent checkpoint. * * * [T]he surprise intrusion upon individual liberty is not minimal. On that issue, my difference with the Court may amount to nothing less than a difference in our respective evaluations of the importance of individual liberty, a serious, albeit inevitable, source of constitutional disagreement. On the degree to which the sobriety checkpoint seizures advance the public interest, however, the Court's position is wholly indefensible.

The Court's analysis of this issue resembles a business decision that measures profits by counting gross receipts and ignoring expenses. The evidence in this case indicates that sobriety checkpoints result in the arrest of a fraction of one percent of the drivers who are stopped, but there is absolutely no evidence that this figure represents an increase over the number of arrests that would have been made by using the same law enforcement resources in conventional patrols. Thus, although the *gross* number of arrests is more than zero, there is a complete failure of proof on the question whether the wholesale seizures have produced any *net* advance in the public interest in arresting intoxicated drivers. * * *

III

The most disturbing aspect of the Court's decision today is that it appears to give no weight to the citizen's interest in freedom from suspicionless unannounced investigatory seizures. * * * [T]he Court places a heavy thumb on the law enforcement interest by looking only at gross receipts instead of net benefits. Perhaps this tampering with the scales of justice can be explained by the Court's obvious concern about the slaughter on our highways and a resultant tolerance for policies designed to alleviate the problem by "setting an example" of a few motorists. This possibility prompts two observations.

First, my objections to random seizures or temporary checkpoints do not apply to a host of other investigatory procedures that do not depend upon surprise and are unquestionably permissible. * * * It is, for example, common practice to require every prospective airline passenger, or every visitor to a public building, to pass through a metal detector that will reveal the presence of a firearm or an explosive. Permanent, nondiscretionary checkpoints could be used to control serious dangers at other publicly operated facilities. Because concealed weapons obviously represent one such substantial threat to public safety, I would suppose that all subway passengers could be required to pass through metal detectors, so long as the detectors were permanent and every passenger was subjected to the same search. Likewise, I would suppose that a State could condition access to its toll roads upon not only paying the toll but also taking a uniformly administered breathalizer test. * * * This procedure would not be subject to the constitutional objections that control this case: The checkpoints would be permanently fixed, the stopping procedure would apply to all users of the toll road in precisely the same way, and police officers would not be free to make arbitrary choices about which neighborhoods should be targeted or about which individuals should be more thoroughly searched. * * *

Second, sobriety checkpoints are elaborate, and disquieting, publicity stunts. The possibility that anybody, no matter how innocent, may be stopped for police inspection is nothing if not attention getting. * * *

This is a case that is driven by nothing more than symbolic state action—an insufficient justification for an otherwise unreasonable program of random seizures. Unfortunately, the Court is transfixed by the wrong symbol—the illusory prospect of punishing countless intoxicated motorists—when it should keep its eyes on the road plainly marked by the Constitution. * * *

NOTES AND QUESTIONS

1. Is an otherwise permissible suspicionless checkpoint valid if there is no empirical data supporting its use? What if the data suggest that the checkpoints are useless or even counter-productive?

2. In *Delaware v. Prouse*, distinguished by the Chief Justice in *Sitz*, the Court held that

> except in those situations in which there is at least articulable and reasonable suspicion that a motorist is unlicensed or that an automobile is not registered * * *, stopping an automobile and detaining the driver in order to check his driver's license and the registration of the automobile are unreasonable under the Fourth Amendment. This holding does not preclude * * * States from developing methods for spot checks that involve less intrusion or that do not involve the unconstrained exercise of discretion. Questioning of all oncoming traffic at roadblock-type stops is one possible alternative.

Why would be it less objectionable to stop and question everyone? Does this "misery loves company" approach to the Fourth Amendment make sense?

CITY OF INDIANAPOLIS v. EDMOND

Supreme Court of the United States, 2000.
531 U.S. 32, 121 S.Ct. 447, 148 L.Ed.2d 333.

JUSTICE O'CONNOR delivered the opinion of the Court.

In *Michigan Dept. of State Police v. Sitz* [p. 427], and *United States v. Martinez–Fuerte* [p. 426 Note 4], we held that brief, suspicionless seizures at highway checkpoints for the purposes of combating drunk driving and intercepting illegal immigrants were constitutional. We now consider the constitutionality of a highway checkpoint program whose primary purpose is the discovery and interdiction of illegal narcotics.

I

In August 1998, the city of Indianapolis began to operate vehicle checkpoints on Indianapolis roads in an effort to interdict unlawful drugs. The city conducted six such roadblocks between August and November that year, stopping 1,161 vehicles and arresting 104 motorists. Fifty-five arrests were for drug-related crimes, while 49 were for offenses unrelated to drugs. The overall "hit rate" of the program was thus approximately nine percent.

* * * At each checkpoint location, the police stop a predetermined number of vehicles. Approximately 30 officers are stationed at the checkpoint. Pursuant to written directives issued by the chief of police, at least

one officer approaches the vehicle, advises the driver that he or she is being stopped briefly at a drug checkpoint, and asks the driver to produce a license and registration. The officer also looks for signs of impairment and conducts an open-view examination of the vehicle from the outside. A narcotics-detection dog walks around the outside of each stopped vehicle.

The directives instruct the officers that they may conduct a search only by consent or based on the appropriate quantum of particularized suspicion. The officers must conduct each stop in the same manner until particularized suspicion develops, and the officers have no discretion to stop any vehicle out of sequence. * * *

The affidavit of Indianapolis Police Sergeant Marshall DePew * * * provides further insight concerning the operation of the checkpoints. According to Sergeant DePew, checkpoint locations are selected * * * based on such considerations as area crime statistics and traffic flow. The checkpoints are generally operated during daylight hours and are identified with lighted signs reading, " 'NARCOTICS CHECKPOINT ___ MILE AHEAD, NARCOTICS K–9 IN USE, BE PREPARED TO STOP.' " * * * Sergeant DePew also stated that the average stop for a vehicle not subject to further processing lasts two to three minutes or less.

Respondents were each stopped at a narcotics checkpoint in late September 1998.* * * Respondents claimed that the roadblocks violated the Fourth Amendment of the United States Constitution * * *. Respondents requested declaratory and injunctive relief for the class, as well as damages and attorney's fees for themselves. * * *

II

The Fourth Amendment requires that searches and seizures be reasonable. A search or seizure is ordinarily unreasonable in the absence of individualized suspicion of wrongdoing. While such suspicion is not an "irreducible" component of reasonableness, we have recognized only limited circumstances in which the usual rule does not apply. For example, we have upheld certain regimes of suspicionless searches where the program was designed to serve "special needs, beyond the normal need for law enforcement." We have also allowed searches for certain administrative purposes without particularized suspicion of misconduct, provided that those searches are appropriately limited. See, *e.g., New York v. Burger,* [p. 424, Note 1].

We have also upheld brief, suspicionless seizures of motorists at a fixed Border Patrol checkpoint designed to intercept illegal aliens, *Martinez-Fuerte, supra,* and at a sobriety checkpoint aimed at removing drunk drivers from the road, *Michigan Dept. of State Police v. Sitz.* In addition, in *Delaware v. Prouse,* we suggested that a similar type of roadblock with the purpose of verifying drivers' licenses and vehicle registrations would be permissible. In none of these cases, however, did we indicate approval of a checkpoint program whose primary purpose was to detect evidence of ordinary criminal wrongdoing.

In *Martinez-Fuerte,* we entertained Fourth Amendment challenges to stops at two permanent immigration checkpoints located on major United States highways less than 100 miles from the Mexican border. We noted at the outset the particular context in which the constitutional question arose, describing in some detail the "formidable law enforcement problems" posed by the northbound tide of illegal entrants into the United States. * * * In *Martinez-Fuerte,* we found that the balance tipped in favor of the Government's interests in policing the Nation's borders. In so finding, we emphasized the difficulty of effectively containing illegal immigration at the border itself. We also stressed the impracticality of the particularized study of a given car to discern whether it was transporting illegal aliens, as well as the relatively modest degree of intrusion entailed by the stops.

Our subsequent cases have confirmed that considerations specifically related to the need to police the border were a significant factor in our *Martinez-Fuerte* decision. * * *

In *Sitz,* we evaluated the constitutionality of a Michigan highway sobriety checkpoint program. * * * The gravity of the drunk driving problem and the magnitude of the State's interest in getting drunk drivers off the road weighed heavily in our determination that the program was constitutional.

In *Prouse,* we invalidated a discretionary, suspicionless stop for a spot check of a motorist's driver's license and vehicle registration. * * * We nonetheless acknowledged the States' "vital interest in ensuring that only those qualified to do so are permitted to operate motor vehicles, that these vehicles are fit for safe operation, and hence that licensing, registration, and vehicle inspection requirements are being observed." Accordingly, we suggested that "[q]uestioning of all oncoming traffic at roadblock-type stops" would be a lawful means of serving this interest in highway safety.

We further indicated in *Prouse* that we considered the purposes of such a hypothetical roadblock to be distinct from a general purpose of investigating crime. The State proffered the additional interests of "the apprehension of stolen motor vehicles and of drivers under the influence of alcohol or narcotics" in its effort to justify the discretionary spot check. We attributed the entirety of the latter interest to the State's interest in roadway safety. We also noted that the interest in apprehending stolen vehicles may be partly subsumed by the interest in roadway safety. We observed, however, that "[t]he remaining governmental interest in controlling automobile thefts is not distinguishable from the general interest in crime control." Not only does the common thread of highway safety thus run through *Sitz* and *Prouse,* but *Prouse* itself reveals a difference in the Fourth Amendment significance of highway safety interests and the general interest in crime control.

III

* * * [W]hat principally distinguishes these checkpoints from those we have previously approved is their primary purpose.

As petitioners concede, the Indianapolis checkpoint program unquestionably has the primary purpose of interdicting illegal narcotics. In their stipulation of facts, the parties repeatedly refer to the checkpoints as "drug checkpoints" * * *. In addition, the first document attached to the parties' stipulation is entitled "DRUG CHECKPOINT CONTACT OFFICER DIRECTIVES BY ORDER OF THE CHIEF OF POLICE." These directives instruct officers to "[a]dvise the citizen that they are being stopped briefly at a drug checkpoint." * * * Further, according to Sergeant DePew, the checkpoints are identified with lighted signs [announcing a "NARCOTICS CHECKPOINT"]. * * *

We have never approved a checkpoint program whose primary purpose was to detect evidence of ordinary criminal wrongdoing. * * * [E]ach of the checkpoint programs that we have approved was designed primarily to serve purposes closely related to the problems of policing the border or the necessity of ensuring roadway safety. Because the primary purpose of the Indianapolis narcotics checkpoint program is to uncover evidence of ordinary criminal wrongdoing, the program contravenes the Fourth Amendment.

Petitioners propose several ways in which the narcotics-detection purpose of the instant checkpoint program may instead resemble the primary purposes of the checkpoints in *Sitz* and *Martinez-Fuerte*. Petitioners state that the checkpoints in those cases had the same ultimate purpose of arresting those suspected of committing crimes. Securing the border and apprehending drunk drivers are, of course, law enforcement activities, and law enforcement officers employ arrests and criminal prosecutions in pursuit of these goals. If we were to rest the case at this high level of generality, there would be little check on the ability of the authorities to construct roadblocks for almost any conceivable law enforcement purpose. Without drawing the line at roadblocks designed primarily to serve the general interest in crime control, the Fourth Amendment would do little to prevent such intrusions from becoming a routine part of American life.

Petitioners also emphasize the severe and intractable nature of the drug problem as justification for the checkpoint program. * * * But the gravity of the threat alone cannot be dispositive of questions concerning what means law enforcement officers may employ to pursue a given purpose. Rather, in determining whether individualized suspicion is required, we must consider the nature of the interests threatened and their connection to the particular law enforcement practices at issue. We are particularly reluctant to recognize exceptions to the general rule of individualized suspicion where governmental authorities primarily pursue their general crime control ends.

Nor can the narcotics-interdiction purpose of the checkpoints be rationalized in terms of a highway safety concern similar to that present in *Sitz*. The detection and punishment of almost any criminal offense serves broadly the safety of the community, and our streets would no doubt be safer but for the scourge of illegal drugs. Only with respect to a smaller class of offenses, however, is society confronted with the type of immediate, vehicle-bound threat to life and limb that the sobriety checkpoint in *Sitz* was designed to eliminate.

Petitioners also liken the anticontraband agenda of the Indianapolis checkpoints to the antismuggling purpose of the checkpoints in *Martinez-Fuerte.* Petitioners cite this Court's conclusion in *Martinez-Fuerte* that the flow of traffic was too heavy to permit "particularized study of a given car that would enable it to be identified as a possible carrier of illegal aliens," and claim that this logic has even more force here. The problem with this argument is that the same logic prevails any time a vehicle is employed to conceal contraband or other evidence of a crime. This type of connection to the roadway is very different from the close connection to roadway safety that was present in *Sitz* and *Prouse.* Further, the Indianapolis checkpoints are far removed from the border context that was crucial in *Martinez-Fuerte.* * * *

The primary purpose of the Indianapolis narcotics checkpoints is in the end to advance "the general interest in crime control." We decline to suspend the usual requirement of individualized suspicion where the police seek to employ a checkpoint primarily for the ordinary enterprise of investigating crimes. * * *

Of course, there are circumstances that may justify a law enforcement checkpoint where the primary purpose would otherwise, but for some emergency, relate to ordinary crime control. For example, * * * the Fourth Amendment would almost certainly permit an appropriately tailored roadblock set up to thwart an imminent terrorist attack or to catch a dangerous criminal who is likely to flee by way of a particular route. The exigencies created by these scenarios are far removed from the circumstances under which authorities might simply stop cars as a matter of course to see if there just happens to be a felon leaving the jurisdiction. While we do not limit the purposes that may justify a checkpoint program to any rigid set of categories, we decline to approve a program whose primary purpose is ultimately indistinguishable from the general interest in crime control.

Petitioners argue that our prior cases preclude an inquiry into the purposes of the checkpoint program. For example, they cite *Whren v. United States* [p. 259], * * * to support the proposition that "where the government articulates and pursues a legitimate interest for a suspicionless stop, courts should not look behind that interest to determine whether the government's 'primary purpose' is valid." * * *

In *Whren,* we held that an individual officer's subjective intentions are irrelevant to the Fourth Amendment validity of a traffic stop that is justified objectively by probable cause to believe that a traffic violation has occurred. * * * In so holding, we expressly distinguished cases where we had addressed the validity of searches conducted in the absence of probable cause.

Whren therefore reinforces the principle that, while "[s]ubjective intentions play no role in ordinary, probable-cause Fourth Amendment analysis," programmatic purposes may be relevant to the validity of Fourth Amendment intrusions undertaken pursuant to a general scheme without individualized suspicion. * * *

Petitioners argue that the Indianapolis checkpoint program is justified by its lawful secondary purposes of keeping impaired motorists off the road and verifying licenses and registrations. If this were the case, however, law enforcement authorities would be able to establish checkpoints for virtually any purpose so long as they also included a license or sobriety check. For this reason, we examine the available evidence to determine the primary purpose of the checkpoint program. * * * [A] program driven by an impermissible purpose may be proscribed while a program impelled by licit purposes is permitted, even though the challenged conduct may be outwardly similar. While reasonableness under the Fourth Amendment is predominantly an objective inquiry, our special needs and administrative search cases demonstrate that purpose is often relevant when suspicionless intrusions pursuant to a general scheme are at issue.[2]

It goes without saying that our holding today does nothing to alter the constitutional status of the sobriety and border checkpoints that we approved in *Sitz* and *Martinez-Fuerte,* or of the type of traffic checkpoint that we suggested would be lawful in *Prouse.* The constitutionality of such checkpoint programs still depends on a balancing of the competing interests at stake and the effectiveness of the program. * * *

Our holding also does not affect the validity of border searches or searches at places like airports and government buildings, where the need for such measures to ensure public safety can be particularly acute. * * * Finally, we caution that the purpose inquiry in this context is to be conducted only at the programmatic level and is not an invitation to probe the minds of individual officers acting at the scene.

Because the primary purpose of the Indianapolis checkpoint program is ultimately indistinguishable from the general interest in crime control, the checkpoints violate the Fourth Amendment. * * *

Chief Justice REHNQUIST, with whom Justice THOMAS joins, and with whom Justice SCALIA joins as to Part I, dissenting.

I

[The Chief Justice summarized what he characterized as "blackletter roadblock seizure law." He then proceeded:] This case follows naturally from *Martinez-Fuerte* and *Sitz.* Petitioners acknowledge that the "primary

---

2. Because petitioners concede that the primary purpose of the Indianapolis checkpoints is narcotics detection, we need not decide whether the State may establish a checkpoint program with the primary purpose of checking licenses or driver sobriety and a secondary purpose of interdicting narcotics. Specifically, we express no view on the question whether police may expand the scope of a license or sobriety checkpoint seizure in order to detect the presence of drugs in a stopped car.

purpose" of these roadblocks is to interdict illegal drugs, but this fact should not be controlling. Even accepting the Court's conclusion that the checkpoints at issue in *Martinez-Fuerte* and *Sitz* were not primarily related to criminal law enforcement,[2] the question whether a law enforcement purpose could support a roadblock seizure is not presented in this case. The District Court found that another "purpose of the checkpoints is to check driver's licenses and vehicle registrations," and the written directives state that the police officers are to "[l]ook for signs of impairment." The use of roadblocks to look for signs of impairment was validated by *Sitz,* and the use of roadblocks to check for driver's licenses and vehicle registrations was expressly recognized in *Delaware v. Prouse.* That the roadblocks serve these legitimate state interests cannot be seriously disputed * * *. And it would be speculative to conclude * * * that petitioners would not have operated these roadblocks but for the State's interest in interdicting drugs.

Because of the valid reasons for conducting these roadblock seizures, it is constitutionally irrelevant that petitioners also hoped to interdict drugs. * * *

With these checkpoints serving two important state interests, the remaining prongs of the *Brown v. Texas* balancing test are easily met. The seizure is objectively reasonable as it lasts, on average, two to three minutes and does not involve a search. The subjective intrusion is likewise limited as the checkpoints are clearly marked and operated by uniformed officers who are directed to stop every vehicle in the same manner. * * * Finally, the checkpoints' success rate—49 arrests for offenses unrelated to drugs—only confirms the State's legitimate interests in preventing drunken driving and ensuring the proper licensing of drivers and registration of their vehicles.

These stops effectively serve the State's legitimate interests; they are executed in a regularized and neutral manner; and they only minimally intrude upon the privacy of the motorists. They should therefore be constitutional.* * *

Justice THOMAS, dissenting.

Taken together, our decisions in *Michigan Dept. of State Police v. Sitz* and *United States v. Martinez–Fuerte* stand for the proposition that suspicionless roadblock seizures are constitutionally permissible if conducted according to a plan that limits the discretion of the officers conducting the stops. I am not convinced that *Sitz* and *Martinez-Fuerte* were correctly decided. Indeed, I rather doubt that the Framers of the Fourth Amendment would have considered "reasonable" a program of indiscriminate stops of individuals not suspected of wrongdoing.

Respondents did not, however, advocate the overruling of *Sitz* and *Martinez-Fuerte,* and I am reluctant to consider such a step without the benefit of briefing and argument. For the reasons given by The Chief

---

2. This gloss is not at all obvious. * * *

Justice, I believe that those cases compel upholding the program at issue here. I, therefore, join his opinion.

NOTES AND QUESTIONS

1. In your view, is *Edmond* distinguishable from *Sitz, Martinez-Fuerte*, and the dictum in *Prouse* (approving carefully drafted, suspicionless roadblocks used to verify drivers' licenses and vehicle registrations)?

2. Look again at footnote 2 of the majority opinion. The footnote resulted in the following tongue-in-cheek observation of Professor Wayne LaFave, posing as David Letterman:

> Now, I'm no Supreme Court justice, nor one of them there high-priced lawyers with the shiny suits and ring on the pinky finger, or even one of those legal pundits that jabber on TV all the time. I'm just a simple late-show host and TV celebrity, but I think I've got about an ounce of common sense, which is all it takes to see that if these drug checkpoints are bad, it shouldn't make any difference what purpose is listed first and what is listed second. And if the Court doesn't make that clear when the time comes, I guarantee that you'll hear about it on this show during our occasional "Stupid Supreme Court Tricks" segment.

Wayne R. LaFave, *The Fourth Amendment as a "Big Time" TV Fad*, 53 Hastings L.J.265, 274 (2001).

3. *How far does Edmond reach?* In Illinois v. Lidster, 540 U.S. 419, 124 S.Ct. 885, 157 L.Ed.2d 843 (2004), local police in Illinois set up a highway checkpoint designed to elicit information from motorists about a fatal hit-and-run accident that had occurred in roughly the same place a week earlier. The blockage resulted in a traffic slow-down, leading to lines of up to fifteen cars in each lane, a delay of a few minutes, and a brief ten-to-fifteen-second conversation with officers. Justice Breyer delivered the opinion of the Court:

> The checkpoint stop here differs significantly from that in *Edmond*. The stop's primary law enforcement purpose was *not* to determine whether a vehicle's occupants were committing a crime, but to ask vehicle occupants, as members of the public, for their help in providing information about a crime in all likelihood committed by others. The police expected the information elicited to help them apprehend, not the vehicle's occupants, but other individuals.
>
> *Edmond*'s language, as well as its context, makes clear that the constitutionality of this latter, information-seeking kind of stop was not then before the Court. * * * We concede that *Edmond* describes the law enforcement objective there in question as a "general interest in crime control," but it specifies that the phrase "general interest in crime control" does not refer to every "law enforcement" objective. We must read this and related general language in *Edmond* as we often read general language in judicial opinions—as referring in context to circumstances similar to the circumstances then before the Court and not referring to quite different circumstances that the Court was not then considering.

Neither do we believe, *Edmond* aside, that the Fourth Amendment would have us apply an *Edmond*-type rule of automatic unconstitutionality to brief, information-seeking highway stops of the kind now before us. * * * The Fourth Amendment does not treat a motorist's car as his castle. And special law enforcement concerns will sometimes justify highway stops without individualized suspicion. Moreover, unlike *Edmond*, the context here (seeking information from the public) is one in which, by definition, the concept of individualized suspicion has little role to play. Like certain other forms of police activity, say, crowd control or public safety, an information-seeking stop is not the kind of event that involves suspicion, or lack of suspicion, of the relevant individual.

For another thing, information-seeking highway stops are less likely to provoke anxiety or to prove intrusive. The stops are likely brief. The police are not likely to ask questions designed to elicit self-incriminating information. * * *

* * * Any accompanying traffic delay should prove no more onerous than many that typically accompany normal traffic congestion. And the resulting voluntary questioning of a motorist is as likely to prove important for police investigation as is the questioning of a pedestrian. * * *

Finally, we do not believe that an *Edmond*-type rule is needed to prevent an unreasonable proliferation of police checkpoints. Practical considerations—namely, limited police resources and community hostility to related traffic tie-ups—seem likely to inhibit any such proliferation. And, of course, the Fourth Amendment's normal insistence that the stop be reasonable in context will still provide an important legal limitation on police use of this kind of information-seeking checkpoint.

These considerations, taken together, convince us that an *Edmond*-type presumptive rule of unconstitutionality does not apply here. That does not mean the stop is automatically, or even presumptively, constitutional. It simply means that we must judge its reasonableness, hence, its constitutionality, on the basis of the individual circumstances. And as this Court said in *Brown v. Texas* [discussed in *Sitz, supra*], in judging reasonableness, we look to "the gravity of the public concerns served by the seizure, the degree to which the seizure advances the public interest, and the severity of the interference with individual liberty."

The Court proceeded to apply *Brown* and determined that the relevant public concern was grave; the checkpoint advanced the grave public concern to a significant degree; and "[m]ost importantly, the stops interfered only minimally with liberty of the sort the Fourth Amendment seeks to protect." Justice Breyer found that, objectively, the seizures were brief and minimal, and even viewed subjectively, "the contact provided little reason for anxiety or alarm," as the police stopped all vehicles systematically and "there is no allegation here that the police acted in a discriminatory or otherwise unlawful manner while questioning motorists during stops."

4. *Drug testing.* Suspicionless drug testing (by means of urinalysis, breathalyzer, or blood) has been upheld by the Supreme Court in various circumstances: drug testing of railroad personnel involved in train accidents, Skinner v. Railway Labor Executives' Association, 489 U.S. 602, 109 S.Ct.

1402, 103 L.Ed.2d 639 (1989); random drug testing of federal customs officers who carry weapons or are involved in drug interdiction, National Treasury Employees Union v. Von Raab, 489 U.S. 656, 109 S.Ct. 1384, 103 L.Ed.2d 685 (1989); and random urine testing of school students involved in athletics, Vernonia School District 47J v. Acton, 515 U.S. 646, 115 S.Ct. 2386, 132 L.Ed.2d 564 (1995), or other extracurricular activities, Board of Education of Independent School District No. 92 of Pottawatomie County v. Earls, 536 U.S. 822, 122 S.Ct. 2559, 153 L.Ed.2d 735 (2002) (policy required all middle and high school students participating in any extracurricular activity to consent to drug testing).

In drug testing cases, the Court considers the "nature and immediacy" of the government's concerns regarding drug use. In some cases, the Court has found a "compelling," "substantial," or "important" governmental or societal need for drug testing that could not be accommodated by application of ordinary probable cause or reasonable suspicion standards. In *Skinner*, evidence was introduced that there was a link between drug and alcohol use by railroad employees and train accidents. In *Von Raab*, there was a felt need to ensure that federal officers involved in handling weapons or investigating drug offenses were themselves free of drugs. In *Vernonia*, the School District had experienced serious academic disruption due to drug use by students, especially student-athletes. In *Pottawatomie County*, the student drug problem was not as severe as in *Vernonia*, but the school district "provided sufficient evidence" of drug use in its schools "to shore up the need for its drug testing program."

Weighed against the interest in random drug testing is the privacy interest of those subjected to the testing. The *Skinner* Court concluded that the bodily intrusion involved in blood testing is minimal; and breath testing is less intrusive still. As for urine testing, however, the justices agreed that the excretory function "traditionally [is] shielded by great privacy." But, in each of the cases, the testing regulations ensured that the individuals were not observed while they urinated. Also weighing against the privacy interests of the individuals was the fact that, with the employees, their expectation of privacy was "diminished by reason of their participation in an industry * * * regulated pervasively to ensure safety"; and in *Vernonia*, the Court stated that "[c]entral * * * to the present case is the fact that the subjects of the [drug] Policy are (1) children, who (2) have been committed to the temporary custody of the State as schoolmaster."

Not all suspicionless drug testing is allowed. The Fourth Amendment "shields society" from urinalysis drug testing that "diminishes personal privacy [solely] for a symbol's sake." In Chandler v. Miller, 520 U.S. 305, 117 S.Ct. 1295, 137 L.Ed.2d 513 (1997), the Supreme Court ruled, 8–1, that Georgia's requirement that candidates for state office pass a drug test did "not fit within the closely guarded category of constitutionally permissible suspicionless searches." The statute required candidates for state office to submit to urinalysis testing within thirty days prior to qualifying for nomination or election. A candidate who tested positive for illegal drugs could not be placed on the ballot.

The Court found no special need for the testing. First, the law was not passed in response to any suspicion of drug use by state officials. Second, because the test date was no secret, a drug-taking candidate could "abstain for a pretest period sufficient to avoid detection." Thus, the scheme was "not well designed to identify candidates who violate antidrug laws." And, finally, unlike *Skinner* and *Von Raab*, in which it was not feasible to subject employees to day-to-day scrutiny for drugs, "[c]andidates for public office * * * are subject to relentless scrutiny—by their peers, the public, and the press." Consequently, all that was left to the testing regime was "the image the State seeks to protect." "However well-meant," the Court said, "the Fourth Amendment shields society against that state action."

What if the reason for the testing is, quite simply, to promote enforcement of criminal laws? And, is it relevant to the legitimacy of drug testing that law enforcement officials are involved in the testing process? In Ferguson v. City of Charleston, 532 U.S. 67, 121 S.Ct. 1281, 149 L.Ed.2d 205 (2001), the Supreme Court invalidated a program (Policy M–7) to identify and test pregnant mothers suspected of drug use, which program was formulated by a task force composed of representatives of the Charleston public hospital operated by the Medical University of South Carolina (MUSC), police, and local officials. The Court described the procedure as follows:

> The first three pages of Policy M–7 set forth the procedure to be followed by the hospital staff to "identify/assist pregnant patients suspected of drug abuse." The first section, entitled the "Identification of Drug Abusers," provided that a patient should be tested for cocaine through a urine drug screen if she met one or more of nine criteria. It also stated that a chain of custody should be followed when obtaining and testing urine samples, presumably to make sure that the results could be used in subsequent criminal proceedings. The policy also provided for education and referral to a substance abuse clinic for patients who tested positive. Most important, it added the threat of law enforcement intervention that "provided the necessary 'leverage' to make the [p]olicy effective." That threat was, as respondents candidly acknowledge, essential to the program's success in getting women into treatment and keeping them there.
>
> The threat of law enforcement involvement was set forth in two protocols, the first dealing with the identification of drug use during pregnancy, and the second with identification of drug use after labor. Under the latter protocol, the police were to be notified without delay and the patient promptly arrested. Under the former, after the initial positive drug test, the police were to be notified (and the patient arrested) only if the patient tested positive for cocaine a second time or if she missed an appointment with a substance abuse counselor. [Subsequently], however, the policy was modified at the behest of the solicitor's office to give the patient who tested positive during labor, like the patient who tested positive during a prenatal care visit, an opportunity to avoid arrest by consenting to substance abuse treatment.

Justice Stevens, writing for five members of the Court (including now-retired Justices O'Connor and Souter), ruled that Policy M–7 did not fall within the "special needs" exception to the warrant requirement:

Because the hospital seeks to justify its authority to conduct drug tests and to turn the results over to law enforcement agents without the knowledge or consent of the patients, this case differs from * * * previous cases in which we have considered whether comparable drug tests "fit within the closely guarded category of constitutionally permissible suspicionless searches." In three of those cases, we sustained drug tests for railway employees involved in train accidents, for United States Customs Service employees seeking promotion to certain sensitive positions, and for high school students participating in interscholastic sports. In the fourth case, we struck down such testing for candidates for designated state offices as unreasonable. * * *

The critical difference between those four drug-testing cases and this one * * * lies in the nature of the "special need" asserted as justification for the warrantless searches. In each of those earlier cases, the "special need" that was advanced as a justification for the absence of a warrant or individualized suspicion was one divorced from the State's general interest in law enforcement. * * * In this case, however, the central and indispensable feature of the policy from its inception was the use of law enforcement to coerce the patients into substance abuse treatment. * * *

Respondents argue in essence that their ultimate purpose—namely, protecting the health of both mother and child—is a beneficent one. * * * In this case, a review of the M–7 policy plainly reveals that the purpose actually served by the MUSC searches "is ultimately indistinguishable from the general interest in crime control." *Indianapolis v. Edmond.*

In looking to the programmatic purpose, we consider all the available evidence in order to determine the relevant primary purpose. * * * "[I]t * * * is clear from the record that an initial and continuing focus of the policy was on the arrest and prosecution of drug-abusing mothers * * * ." Tellingly, the document codifying the policy incorporates the police's operational guidelines. It devotes its attention to the chain of custody, the range of possible criminal charges, and the logistics of police notification and arrests. Nowhere, however, does the document discuss different courses of medical treatment for either mother or infant, aside from treatment for the mother's addiction.

Moreover, throughout the development and application of the policy, the Charleston prosecutors and police were extensively involved in the day-to-day administration of the policy. * * *

While the ultimate goal of the program may well have been to get the women in question into substance abuse treatment and off of drugs, the immediate objective of the searches was to generate evidence *for law enforcement purposes* in order to reach that goal. The threat of law enforcement may ultimately have been intended as a means to an end, but the direct and primary purpose of MUSC's policy was to ensure the use of those means. In our opinion, this distinction is critical. Because law enforcement involvement always serves some broader social purpose or objective, under respondents' view, virtually any nonconsensual suspicionless search could be immunized under the special needs doctrine by defining the search solely in terms of its ultimate, rather than immediate, purpose. Such an approach is inconsistent with the Fourth Amendment. Given the primary purpose of the Charleston program, which was to use the threat of arrest and prosecution in order to force women into treatment, and given the extensive involvement of law enforcement officials at every stage of the policy, this case simply does not fit within the closely guarded category of "special needs."

The majority held that absent consent or an exigency, the urine testing here required a search warrant.

5. *Problem.* A Missouri police department set up a narcotics roadblock, but with a twist. One evening, they put warnings on a highway: "DRUG ENFORCEMENT CHECKPOINT ONE MILE AHEAD" and "POLICE DRUG DOGS WORKING." In fact, however, the checkpoint was set up immediately following the signs, at an exit selected because it did not provide gas or food services. The only lawful purpose for getting off at that exit was to go to a local high school (where no events were occurring that evening), a local church, or one of several residences.

In this case, the defendant "suddenly veered off onto the off ramp." The police at the checkpoint stopped him (as they did all others who exited at that point). The defendant appeared nervous, had glazed and bloodshot eyes, and smelled of alcohol. The defendant consented to a vehicle search, which turned up large quantities of drugs. Are the drugs admissible in a criminal prosecution? State v. Mack, 66 S.W.3d 706 (Mo.2002).

6. *Problem.* Consider the following New York City anti-terrorist checkpoint program for its subways: Officers are assigned to random-and-changing checkpoints. They are required to select every fifth or tenth person (based on passenger volume) and search the subway rider's belongings. Only belongings large enough to carry an explosive device may be opened, and the inspection is limited to "what is minimally necessary to ensure that [it] * * * does not contain an explosive device." The preferred inspection method involves physical manipulation of the contents by the subway rider or, if necessary, by the officer. The officer is not permitted to request or record a passenger's personal information (e.g., name, address, demographic data). In general, the typical inspection lasts a matter of seconds. This program is conducted in the absence of any specific terrorist threat, and the City cannot provide studies demonstrating that such a program deters terrorists. Constitutional? MacWade v. Kelly, 460 F.3d 260 (2nd Cir. 2006).

CHAPTER 5

REMEDIES FOR FOURTH AMENDMENT VIOLATIONS

■ ■ ■

A. STANDING

THE STARTING POINT

There are two important Fourth Amendment rules considered in this chapter: the "exclusionary rule" and a doctrine that the Supreme Court used to call (and many lawyers still call) "standing."

As discussed more fully later in this chapter, the exclusionary rule—the rule that evidence obtained in violation of the Fourth Amendment is suppressed at trial—is typically justified on deterrence grounds: The police will be less likely to violate the Fourth Amendment if they know that the fruits of their unconstitutional conduct will be excluded from a criminal trial. Before evidence can be excluded, however, a court must determine whether the person seeking exclusion has the right to bring the Fourth Amendment claim. This is the "standing" requirement.

In this regard consider Alderman v. United States, 394 U.S. 165, 89 S.Ct. 961, 22 L.Ed.2d 176 (1969): Alderman and Aderisio were charged with conspiracy to transmit murderous threats in interstate commerce. They sought, as co-defendants and accused co-conspirators, to have incriminating statements they made excluded because one or both of them were the subject of unlawful governmental electronic surveillance. Justice White, writing for the Court, explained that the issue of exclusion had to be determined on an individual basis—*each* defendant would have to prove that he, *personally*, had "standing" to raise the Fourth Amendment claim. *Alderman* explained the law of standing this way:

> The established principle is that suppression of the product of a Fourth Amendment violation can be successfully urged only by those whose rights were violated by the search itself, not by those who are aggrieved solely by the introduction of damaging evidence. Coconspirators and codefendants have been accorded no special standing. * * *

The rule is stated in Jones v. United States, 362 U.S. 257, 261, 80 S.Ct. 725, 731, 4 L.Ed.2d 697 (1960):

446

"In order to qualify as a 'person aggrieved by an unlawful search and seizure' one must have been a victim of a search or seizure, one against whom the search was directed, as distinguished from one who claims prejudice only through the use of evidence gathered as a consequence of a search or seizure directed at someone else. * * *

"Ordinarily, then, it is entirely proper to require of one who seeks to challenge the legality of a search as the basis for suppressing relevant evidence that he allege, and if the allegation be disputed that he establish, that he himself was the victim of an invasion of privacy." * * *

We adhere to * * * the general rule that Fourth Amendment rights are personal rights which, like some other constitutional rights, may not be vicariously asserted. * * *

The necessity for [proving standing is] * * * not eliminated by recognizing and acknowledging the deterrent aim of the [exclusionary] rule. * * * The deterrent values of preventing the incrimination of those whose rights the police have violated have been considered sufficient to justify the suppression of probative evidence even though the case against the defendant is weakened or destroyed. We adhere to that judgment. But we are not convinced that the additional benefits of extending the exclusionary rule to other defendants would justify further encroachment upon the public interest in prosecuting those accused of crime and having them acquitted or convicted on the basis of all the evidence which exposes the truth.

NOTES AND QUESTIONS

1. The Court ruled in *Alderman* that a person has standing to contest electronic surveillance, and thus is entitled to suppression of unlawfully heard conversations, if: (a) government agents unlawfully overheard that person's conversations, regardless of where they occurred; or (b) if the conversations occurred on that person's premises, whether or not she was present or participated in the conversations. In what way is a person a "victim" in each of these circumstances?

2. Consider the facts in United States v. Payner, 447 U.S. 727, 100 S.Ct. 2439, 65 L.Ed.2d 468 (1980):

In 1965, the Internal Revenue Service launched an investigation into the financial activities of American citizens in the Bahamas. The project, known as "Operation Trade Winds," was headquartered in Jacksonville, Fla. Suspicion focused on the Castle Bank in 1972 * * *. Special Agent Richard Jaffe of the Jacksonville office asked Norman Casper, a private investigator and occasional informant, to learn what he could about the Castle Bank and its depositors. To that end, Casper cultivated his friendship with Castle Bank vice president Michael Wolstencroft. Casper introduced Wolstencroft to Sybol Kennedy, a private investigator and former employee. When Casper discovered that the banker intended to spend a few days in Miami in January 1973, he devised a scheme to gain access to the bank records he knew Wolstencroft would be carrying in his briefcase. Agent Jaffe approved the basic outline of the plan.

Wolstencroft arrived in Miami on January 15 and went directly to Kennedy's apartment. At about 7:30 p. m., the two left for dinner at a Key Biscayne restaurant. Shortly thereafter, Casper entered the apartment using a key supplied by Kennedy. He removed the briefcase and delivered it to Jaffe. While the agent supervised the copying of approximately 400 documents taken from the briefcase, a "lookout" observed Kennedy and Wolstencroft at dinner. The observer notified Casper when the pair left the restaurant, and the briefcase was replaced. The documents photographed that evening included papers evidencing a close working relationship between the Castle Bank and the Bank of Perrine, Fla. Subpoenas issued to the Bank of Perrine ultimately uncovered [evidence that defendant Payner had falsified his tax records by denying that he maintained a foreign bank account at the Castle Bank, in the Bahama Islands].

The District Court found that the United States, acting through Jaffe, "knowingly and willfully participated in the unlawful seizure of Michael Wolstencroft's briefcase. * * * "

Based on *Alderman*, would you say Payner has standing to contest the Government's activities? Why or why not?

3. *"Atomistic" versus "regulatory" perspectives of the Fourth Amendment.* Can you see how the "standing" requirement can undercut the deterrence goal of the exclusionary rule? In this regard, consider Richard B. Kuhns, *The Concept of Personal Aggrievement in Fourth Amendment Standing Cases,* 65 Iowa L. Rev. 493, 495–96, 499, 501 (1980):

> Supreme Court decisions interpreting and applying the fourth amendment reflect what Professor Anthony Amsterdam has characterized as two distinct perspectives of the prohibition against unreasonable searches and seizures.[20] The Court has often viewed the fourth amendment as a protection of certain individual rights. From this perspective the fourth amendment, in the words of Professor Amsterdam, is "a collection of protections of atomistic spheres of interest of individual citizens." In contrast to this "atomistic" perspective, the Court has sometimes discussed the fourth amendment from what Professor Amsterdam has characterized as a "regulatory" perspective—one that views the amendment as "a regulatory canon requiring government to order its law enforcement procedures in a fashion that keeps us collectively secure * * * against unreasonable searches and seizures." The most important question from the atomistic perspective is whether an individual's rights have been violated, whereas from the regulatory perspective, the critical question is whether the government has engaged in an activity that, if left unregulated, would pose a threat to the security of people generally.
>
> The answers to these two questions will often be the same. For example, when the police make an arrest without probable cause to

---

20.   Amsterdam, *Perspectives on the Fourth Amendment*, 58 Minn. L. Rev. 349, 362–72 (1974).

believe that the arrestee has committed a crime, the arrestee's rights have been violated, and the police have engaged in a type of conduct that the fourth amendment was designed to regulate. * * *

Nonetheless, * * * there are cases in which the result is likely to depend on which perspective of the fourth amendment is dominant in a court's thinking. * * *

Perhaps the clearest manifestation of the Supreme Court's adherence to the regulatory perspective of the fourth amendment appears in the Court's discussions of the exclusionary rule. In recent years, for example, the Court has urged that the rule's primary [regulatory] purpose "is to deter future unlawful police conduct and thereby effectuate the guarantee of the Fourth Amendment * * *." * * *

In contrast to the regulatory objectives of the exclusionary rule, the concept of personal aggrievement, which is the core of the standing requirement, is essentially atomistic * * *.

In *Payner*, Note 2, *supra*, how would a court applying the atomistic perspective deal with the unlawful conduct proved in that case? What would a court following the regulatory approach do about the evidence?

4. If *Alderman* teaches us that a person may not successfully assert a Fourth Amendment claim unless she has standing to contest the search, *i.e.*, that she was the victim of the Fourth Amendment violation, the question to which we must now turn is, precisely, when *is* an individual a "victim" of an unlawful search. The materials that follow focus on this issue.

RAKAS v. ILLINOIS

Supreme Court of the United States, 1978.
439 U.S. 128, 99 S.Ct. 421, 58 L.Ed.2d 387.

MR. JUSTICE REHNQUIST delivered the opinion of the Court. * * *

I

Because we are not here concerned with the issue of probable cause, a brief description of the events leading to the search of the automobile will suffice. A police officer on a routine patrol received a radio call notifying him of a robbery of a clothing store in Bourbonnais, Ill., and describing the getaway car. Shortly thereafter, the officer spotted an automobile which he thought might be the getaway car. After following the car for some time and after the arrival of assistance, he and several other officers stopped the vehicle. The occupants of the automobile, petitioners and two female companions, were ordered out of the car and, after the occupants had left the car, two officers searched the interior of the vehicle. They discovered a box of rifle shells in the glove compartment, which had been locked, and a sawed-off rifle under the front passenger seat. After discovering the rifle and the shells, the officers took petitioners to the station and placed them under arrest.

Before trial petitioners moved to suppress the rifle and shells seized from the car on the ground that the search violated the Fourth and

Fourteenth Amendments. They conceded that they did not own the automobile and were simply passengers; the owner of the car had been the driver of the vehicle at the time of the search. Nor did they assert that they owned the rifle or the shells seized.[1] The prosecutor challenged petitioners' standing to object to the lawfulness of the search of the car because neither the car, the shells nor the rifle belonged to them. The trial court agreed that petitioners lacked standing and denied the motion to suppress the evidence. * * *

II * * *

A

[The Court rejected the petitioners' initial argument that, because they were targets of the search, *i.e.*, that the search was directed at obtaining incriminating evidence against them, they should have standing on that basis alone—even if they were not "victims" of the search—to contest the legality of the police action. The Court explained its reasoning:]

Conferring standing to raise vicarious Fourth Amendment claims would necessarily mean a more widespread invocation of the exclusionary rule during criminal trials. The Court's opinion in *Alderman* [p. 446] counseled against such an extension of the exclusionary rule * * *. Each time the exclusionary rule is applied it exacts a substantial social cost for the vindication of Fourth Amendment rights. Relevant and reliable evidence is kept from the trier of fact and the search for truth at trial is deflected. Since our cases generally have held that one whose Fourth Amendment rights are violated may successfully suppress evidence obtained in the course of an illegal search and seizure, misgivings as to the benefit of enlarging the class of persons who may invoke that rule are properly considered when deciding whether to expand standing to assert Fourth Amendment violations.

B

* * * [H]aving rejected petitioners' target theory and reaffirmed the principle that the "rights assured by the Fourth Amendment are personal rights, [which] * * * may be enforced by exclusion of evidence only at the instance of one whose own protection was infringed by the search and seizure," the question necessarily arises whether it serves any useful analytical purpose to consider this principle a matter of standing, distinct from the merits of a defendant's Fourth Amendment claim. We can think of no decided cases of this Court that would have come out differently had we concluded, as we do now, that the type of standing requirement * * * reaffirmed today is more properly subsumed under substantive Fourth

---

1. * * * The proponent of a motion to suppress has the burden of establishing that his own Fourth Amendment rights were violated by the challenged search or seizure. The prosecutor argued that petitioners lacked standing to challenge the search because they did not own the rifle, the shells or the automobile. Petitioners did not contest the factual predicates of the prosecutor's argument * * *. * * *

Amendment doctrine. Rigorous application of the principle that the rights secured by this Amendment are personal, in place of a notion of "standing," will produce no additional situations in which evidence must be excluded. The inquiry under either approach is the same. But we think the better analysis forthrightly focuses on the extent of a particular defendant's rights under the Fourth Amendment, rather than on any theoretically separate, but invariably intertwined concept of standing. * * *

Analyzed in these terms, the question is whether the challenged search and seizure violated the Fourth Amendment rights of a criminal defendant who seeks to exclude the evidence obtained during it. That inquiry in turn requires a determination of whether the disputed search and seizure has infringed an interest of the defendant which the Fourth Amendment was designed to protect. We are under no illusion that by dispensing with the rubric of standing * * * we have rendered any simpler the determination of whether the proponent of a motion to suppress is entitled to contest the legality of a search and seizure. But by frankly recognizing that this aspect of the analysis belongs more properly under the heading of substantive Fourth Amendment doctrine than under the heading of standing, we think the decision of this issue will rest on sounder logical footing.

C

Here petitioners, who were passengers occupying a car which they neither owned nor leased, seek to analogize their position to that of the defendant in *Jones v. United States*[, 362 U.S. 257, 80 S.Ct. 725, 4 L.Ed.2d 697 (1960)]. In *Jones*, petitioner was present at the time of the search of an apartment which was owned by a friend. The friend had given Jones permission to use the apartment and a key to it, with which Jones had admitted himself on the day of the search. He had a suit and shirt at the apartment and had slept there "maybe a night," but his home was elsewhere. At the time of the search, Jones was the only occupant of the apartment because the lessee was away for a period of several days. Under these circumstances, this Court stated that while one wrongfully on the premises could not move to suppress evidence obtained as a result of searching them, "anyone legitimately on premises where a search occurs may challenge its legality." Petitioners argue that their occupancy of the automobile in question was comparable to that of *Jones* in the apartment and that they therefore have standing to contest the legality of the search—or as we have rephrased the inquiry, that they, like Jones, had their Fourth Amendment rights violated by the search.

We do not question the conclusion in *Jones* that the defendant in that case suffered a violation of his personal Fourth Amendment rights if the search in question was unlawful. Nonetheless, we believe that the phrase "legitimately on premises" coined in *Jones* creates too broad a gauge for measurement of Fourth Amendment rights. For example, applied literally, this statement would permit a casual visitor who has never seen, or been permitted to visit, the basement of another's house to object to a search of the basement if the visitor happened to be in the kitchen of the house at the time of the search. Likewise, a casual visitor who walks into a house one minute before a search of the house commences and leaves one minute after the search ends would be able to contest the legality of the search. The first visitor would have absolutely no interest or legitimate expectation of privacy in the basement, the second would have none in the house, and it advances no purpose served by the Fourth Amendment to permit either of them to object to the lawfulness of the search.[11]

We think that *Jones* on its facts merely stands for the unremarkable proposition that a person can have a legally sufficient interest in a place other than his own home so that the Fourth Amendment protects him from unreasonable governmental intrusion into that place. In defining the scope of that interest, we adhere to the view expressed in *Jones* and echoed in later cases that arcane distinctions developed in property and tort law between guests, licensees, invitees, and the like, ought not to control. But the *Jones* statement that a person need only be "legitimately on premises" in order to challenge the validity of the search of a dwelling place cannot be taken in its full sweep beyond the facts of that case.

* * * [T]he holding in *Jones* can best be explained by the fact that Jones had a legitimate expectation of privacy in the premises he was using and therefore could claim the protection of the Fourth Amendment with respect to a governmental invasion of those premises, even though his "interest" in those premises might not have been a recognized property interest at common law.[12] * * *

D

Judged by the foregoing analysis, petitioners' claims must fail. They asserted neither a property nor a possessory interest in the automobile, nor an interest in the property seized. And as we have previously indicated, the fact that they were "legitimately on [the] premises" in the sense that they were in the car with the permission of its owner is not determinative of whether they had a legitimate expectation of privacy in the particular areas of the automobile searched. It is unnecessary for us to decide here whether the same expectations of privacy are warranted in a car as would be justified in a dwelling place in analogous circumstances. We have on numerous occasions pointed out that cars are not to be

---

11. This is not to say that such visitors could not contest the lawfulness of the seizure of evidence or the search if their own property were seized during the search.

12. Obviously, however, a "legitimate" expectation of privacy by definition means more than a subjective expectation of not being discovered. A burglar plying his trade in a summer cabin during the off season may have a thoroughly justified subjective expectation of privacy, but it is not one which the law recognizes as "legitimate." His presence, in the words of *Jones*, is "wrongful"; his expectation is not "one that society is prepared to recognize as 'reasonable.'" And it would, of course, be merely tautological to fall back on the notion that those expectations of privacy which are legitimate depend primarily on cases deciding exclusionary-rule issues in criminal cases. Legitimation of expectations of privacy by law must have a source outside of the Fourth Amendment, either by reference to concepts of real or personal property law or to understandings that are recognized and permitted by society. * * *

treated identically with houses or apartments for Fourth Amendment purposes. But here petitioners' claim is one which would fail even in an analogous situation in a dwelling place, since they made no showing that they had any legitimate expectation of privacy in the glove compartment or area under the seat of the car in which they were merely passengers. Like the trunk of an automobile, these are areas in which a passenger *qua* passenger simply would not normally have a legitimate expectation of privacy.

Jones v. United States * * * involved significantly different factual circumstances. Jones not only had permission to use the apartment of his friend, but had a key to the apartment with which he admitted himself on the day of the search and kept possessions in the apartment. Except with respect to his friend, Jones had complete dominion and control over the apartment and could exclude others from it. Likewise in *Katz* [p. 84], the defendant occupied the telephone booth, shut the door behind him to exclude all others and paid the toll, which "entitled [him] to assume that the words he utter[ed] into the mouthpiece [would] not be broadcast to the world." Katz and Jones could legitimately expect privacy in the areas which were the subject of the search and seizure each sought to contest. No such showing was made by these petitioners with respect to those portions of the automobile which were searched and from which incriminating evidence was seized.[17] * * *

Mr. Justice POWELL, with whom THE CHIEF JUSTICE joins, concurring.

I concur in the opinion of the Court, and add these thoughts. * * *

We are concerned here with an automobile search. Nothing is better established in Fourth Amendment jurisprudence than the distinction between one's expectation of privacy in an automobile and one's expectation when in other locations. We have repeatedly recognized that this expectation in "an automobile * * * [is] significantly different from the traditional expectation of privacy and freedom in one's residence." * * *

A distinction also properly may be made in some circumstances between the Fourth Amendment rights of passengers and the rights of an individual who has exclusive control of an automobile or of its locked compartments. * * * Here there were three passengers and a driver in the automobile searched. None of the passengers is said to have had control of the vehicle or the keys. It is unrealistic—as the shared experience of us all bears witness—to suggest that these passengers had any reasonable

---

17. * * * [T]he dissenters repeatedly state or imply that we now "hold" that a passenger lawfully in an automobile "may not invoke the exclusionary rule and challenge a search of that vehicle unless he happens to own or have a possessory interest in it." It is not without significance that these statements of today's "holding" come from the dissenting opinion, and not from the Court's opinion. The case before us involves the search of and seizure of property from the glove compartment and area under the seat of a car in which petitioners were riding as passengers. Petitioners claimed only that they were "legitimately on [the] premises" and did not claim that they had any legitimate expectation of privacy in the areas of the car which were searched. We cannot, therefore, agree with the dissenters' insistence that our decision will encourage the police to violate the Fourth Amendment.

expectation that the car in which they had been riding would not be searched after they were lawfully stopped and made to get out. The minimal privacy that existed simply is not comparable to that, for example, of an individual in his place of abode; of one who secludes himself in a telephone booth; or of the traveler who secures his belongings in a locked suitcase or footlocker.[4] * * *

Mr. Justice WHITE, with whom Mr. Justice BRENNAN, Mr. Justice MARSHALL, and Mr. Justice STEVENS join, dissenting.

The Court today holds that the Fourth Amendment protects property, not people, and specifically that a legitimate occupant of an automobile may not invoke the exclusionary rule and challenge a search of that vehicle unless he happens to own or have a possessory interest in it. Though professing to acknowledge that the primary purpose of the Fourth Amendment's prohibition of unreasonable searches is the protection of privacy—not property—the Court nonetheless effectively ties the application of the Fourth Amendment and the exclusionary rule in this situation to property law concepts. Insofar as passengers are concerned, the Court's opinion today declares an "open season" on automobiles. However unlawful stopping and searching a car may be, absent a possessory or ownership interest, no "mere" passenger may object, regardless of his relationship to the owner. * * *

III

* * * Our starting point is "[t]he established principle * * * that suppression of the product of a Fourth Amendment violation can be successfully urged only by those whose rights were violated by the search itself * * *." Though the Amendment protects one's liberty and property interests against unreasonable seizures of self[5] and effects,[6] "the primary object of the Fourth Amendment [is] * * * the protection of privacy." And privacy is the interest asserted here, so the first step is to ascertain whether the premises searched "fall within a protected zone of privacy." * * *

It is true that the Court asserts that it is not limiting the Fourth Amendment bar against unreasonable searches to the protection of property rights, but in reality it is doing exactly that.[14] Petitioners were in a

---

4. The sawed-off rifle in this case was merely pushed beneath the front seat, presumably by one of the petitioners. In that position, it could have slipped into full or partial view in the event of an accident, or indeed upon any sudden stop. As the rifle shells were in the locked glove compartment, this might have presented a closer case if it had been shown that one of the petitioners possessed the keys or if a rifle had not been found in the automobile. * * *

5. * * * [P]etitioners of course have standing to challenge the legality of the stop, and the evidence found may be a fruit of that stop. Petitioners have not argued that theory here * * *. * * *

6. * * * Petitioners never asserted a property interest in the items seized from the automobile. * * *

14. The Court's reliance on property law concepts is additionally shown by its suggestion that visitors could "contest the lawfulness of the seizure of evidence or the search if their own property were seized during the search." What difference should that property interest make to constitutional protection against unreasonable searches, which is concerned with privacy? * * *

private place with the permission of the owner, but the Court states that that is not sufficient to establish entitlement to a legitimate expectation of privacy. But if that is not sufficient, what would be? We are not told, and it is hard to imagine anything short of a property interest that would satisfy the majority. * * * The Court approves the result in *Jones*, but it fails to give any explanation why the facts in *Jones* differ, in a fashion material to the Fourth Amendment, from the facts here.[15] More importantly, how is the Court able to avoid answering the question why presence in a private place with the owner's permission is insufficient? * * *

IV

The Court's holding is contrary not only to our past decisions and the logic of the Fourth Amendment but also to the everyday expectations of privacy that we all share. Because of that, it is unworkable in all the various situations that arise in real life. If the owner of the car had not only invited petitioners to join her but had said to them, "I give you a temporary possessory interest in my vehicle so that you will share the right to privacy that the Supreme Court says that I own," then apparently the majority would reverse. But people seldom say such things, though they may mean their invitation to encompass them if only they had thought of the problem. If the nonowner were the spouse or child of the owner, would the Court recognize a sufficient interest? If so, would distant relatives somehow have more of an expectation of privacy than close friends? What if the nonowner were driving with the owner's permission? Would nonowning drivers have more of an expectation of privacy than mere passengers? What about a passenger in a taxicab? * * * Why should Fourth Amendment rights be present when one pays a cabdriver for a ride but be absent when one is given a ride by a friend?

The distinctions the Court would draw are based on relationships between private parties, but the Fourth Amendment is concerned with the relationship of one of those parties to the government. Divorced as it is from the purpose of the Fourth Amendment, the Court's essentially property-based rationale can satisfactorily answer none of the questions posed above. That is reason enough to reject it. The *Jones* rule is relatively easily applied by police and courts; the rule announced today will not provide law enforcement officials with a bright line between the protected and the unprotected. Only rarely will police know whether one private party has or has not been granted a sufficient possessory or other interest by another private party. Surely in this case the officers had no such knowledge. The Court's rule will ensnare defendants and police in need-

---

15. Jones had permission to use the apartment, had slept in it one night, had a key, had left a suit and a shirt there, and was the only occupant at the time of the search. Petitioners here had permission to be in the car and were occupying it at the time of the search. Thus the only distinguishing fact is that Jones could exclude others from the apartment by using his friend's key. But petitioners and their friend the owner had excluded others by entering the automobile and shutting the doors. Petitioners did not need a key because the owner was present. * * *

less litigation over factors that should not be determinative of Fourth Amendment rights.

More importantly, the ruling today undercuts the force of the exclusionary rule in the one area in which its use is most certainly justified— the deterrence of bad-faith violations of the Fourth Amendment. This decision invites police to engage in patently unreasonable searches every time an automobile contains more than one occupant. Should something be found, only the owner of the vehicle, or of the item, will have standing to seek suppression, and the evidence will presumably be usable against the other occupants. The danger of such bad faith is especially high in cases such as this one where the officers are only after the passengers and can usually infer accurately that the driver is the owner. * * *

NOTES AND QUESTIONS

1. *A procedural matter.* Judges hear Fourth Amendment suppression motions prior to trial. Notice the problem potentially confronting a defendant who seeks to have evidence seized by the police excluded from the trial: In order to raise the Fourth Amendment claim, she must first prove standing (or, after *Rakas*, must prove that it was *her* Fourth Amendment rights that were violated). To do this, the defendant may need to testify at the suppression hearing and, for example, assert ownership of a briefcase that was searched (and in which contraband was discovered), allegedly without probable cause.

The defendant's testimony that she owned the briefcase may benefit the defendant in the suppression hearing by giving her a right to challenge the police action, but what if she loses on her Fourth Amendment claim? May the prosecutor now use at trial the defendant's inculpatory pretrial admission that it was her briefcase in which contraband was discovered? If so, defendants who need to testify to prove standing may be deterred from raising legitimate Fourth Amendment claims for fear that their testimony will be used against them at trial. To mitigate this problem, the Supreme Court held in Simmons v. United States, 390 U.S. 377, 88 S.Ct. 967, 19 L.Ed.2d 1247 (1968), that "when a defendant testifies in support of a motion to suppress evidence on Fourth Amendment grounds, his testimony may not thereafter be admitted against him at trial on the issue of guilt unless he makes no objection."

Does *Simmons* relieve a defendant of *all* risks from testifying at the suppression hearing?

2. *Is "standing" a relevant concept after Rakas?* Justice Rehnquist in *Rakas* dispenses with the concept of "standing," as such, in the Fourth Amendment context. Previously, a defense lawyer would seek to prove that her client had standing to challenge the police action; if that obstacle was overcome, she would raise the merits of the Fourth Amendment claim. Now, *Rakas* teaches, there is just one step: to answer the substantive question of whether *the defendant's* Fourth Amendment rights were violated. But, this approach of converting a two-step process into one can result in unintended confusion, as Justice Blackmun has observed:

In my view, *Rakas v. Illinois* recognized two analytically distinct but "invariably intertwined" issues of substantive Fourth Amendment jurisprudence. The first is "whether [a] disputed search or seizure has infringed an interest of the defendant which the Fourth Amendment was designed to protect"; the second is whether "the challenged search or seizure violated [that] Fourth Amendment righ[t]." The first of these questions is answered by determining whether the defendant has a "legitimate expectation of privacy" that has been invaded by a governmental search or seizure. The second is answered by determining whether applicable cause and warrant requirements have been properly observed.

I agree with the Court that these two inquiries "merge into one," in the sense that both are to be addressed under the principles of Fourth Amendment analysis developed in *Katz v. United States* and its progeny. But I do not read today's decision, or *Rakas*, as holding that it is improper for lower courts to treat these inquiries as distinct components of a Fourth Amendment claim. Indeed, I am convinced that it would invite confusion to hold otherwise. It remains possible for a defendant to prove that his legitimate interest of privacy was invaded, and yet fail to prove that the police acted illegally in doing so. And it is equally possible for a defendant to prove that the police acted illegally, and yet fail to prove that his own privacy interest was affected.

Rawlings v. Kentucky, 448 U.S. 98, 100 S.Ct. 2556, 65 L.Ed.2d 633 (1980).

Can you see why Justice Blackmun might be correct in this regard? If not, you will hopefully see why, after you read the next case.

3. Look carefully at the majority opinion. *Did* the Court state that the petitioners lacked a legitimate expectation of privacy in the areas of the car that were searched? Hint: Look at footnote 17 and the text linked to it. Why does one of the authors of this casebook describe footnote 17 as the "*chutzpah*" footnote. (Ask around if you need help on the meaning of *that* word.)

4. Do *you* believe that the front seat passenger had a reasonable expectation of privacy regarding the search under his seat, where the sawed-off rifle was discovered? Why or why not? What about the glove compartment search?

5. *Open season on automobiles*? The dissent in *Rakas* accused the majority of declaring "open season" on automobiles in regard to passengers therein. Is that so? Suppose the police stop a car on a public road and search the trunk without consent or probable cause. The police find a blood-stained jacket in the trunk, which they seize. Subsequently, the prosecutor seeks to introduce the jacket in a murder prosecution of Bob, who was in the car. After *Rakas*, may Bob successfully challenge the police action in the following circumstances? Why, or why not?

A. At the time of the search, Alice, the car owner, was driving the vehicle, and Bob, a friend, was her front seat passenger.

B. The same as A., but Bob was driving, while Alice sat in the front seat.

C. The same as A., but the two were driving across country. Alice and Bob alternated driving, and Alice furnished Bob with a spare car key for the trip.

D. The same as A., but Bob wants to contest the car stop, rather than the trunk search.

E. The same as A., but Bob claims ownership of the jacket.

6. *Are homes like cars when it comes to issues of standing?* In Minnesota v. Olson, 495 U.S. 91, 110 S.Ct. 1684, 109 L.Ed.2d 85 (1990), the police, without a warrant or consent, entered a residence in which they believed Olson, a robbery-murder suspect, was staying as an overnight guest. The officers searched the residence until they discovered him hiding in a closet. In an opinion written by Justice White, the Court held that Olson had standing to contest the warrantless search:

> To hold that an overnight guest has a legitimate expectation of privacy in his host's home merely recognizes the everyday expectations of privacy that we all share. Staying overnight in another's home is a longstanding social custom that serves functions recognized as valuable by society. We stay in others' homes when we travel to a strange city for business or pleasure, when we visit our parents, children, or more distant relatives out of town, when we are in between jobs or homes, or when we house-sit for a friend. We will all be hosts and we will all be guests many times in our lives. From either perspective, we think that society recognizes that a houseguest has a legitimate expectation of privacy in his host's home.

> From the overnight guest's perspective, he seeks shelter in another's home precisely because it provides him with privacy, a place where he and his possessions will not be disturbed by anyone but his host and those his host allows inside. We are at our most vulnerable when we are asleep because we cannot monitor our own safety or the security of our belongings. It is for this reason that, although we may spend all day in public places, when we cannot sleep in our own home we seek out another private place to sleep, whether it be a hotel room, or the home of a friend. Society expects at least as much privacy in these places as in a telephone booth * * *.

> That the guest has a host who has ultimate control of the house is not inconsistent with the guest having a legitimate expectation of privacy. The houseguest is there with the permission of his host, who is willing to share his house and his privacy with his guest. It is unlikely that the guest will be confined to a restricted area of the house; and when the host is away or asleep, the guest will have a measure of control over the premises. The host may admit or exclude from the house as he prefers, but it is unlikely that he will admit someone who wants to see or meet with the guest over the objection of the guest. On the other hand, few houseguests will invite others to visit them while they are guests without consulting their hosts; but the latter, who have the authority to exclude despite the wishes of the guest, will often be accommodating. The point is that hosts will more likely than not respect the privacy interests of their guests, who are entitled to a legitimate expectation of privacy despite the fact that they have no legal interest in the premises and do not have the legal authority to determine who may or may not enter the household. If the untrammeled power to admit and exclude were essential to Fourth

Amendment protection, an adult daughter temporarily living in the home of her parents would have no legitimate expectation of privacy because her right to admit or exclude would be subject to her parents' veto.

Chief Justice Rehnquist and Justice Blackmun dissented, but did not write an opinion.

Is *Olson* consistent with *Rakas*?

MINNESOTA v. CARTER

Supreme Court of the United States, 1998.
525 U.S. 83, 119 S.Ct. 469, 142 L.Ed.2d 373.

Chief Justice Rehnquist delivered the opinion of the Court.

Respondents and the lessee of an apartment were sitting in one of its rooms, bagging cocaine. While so engaged they were observed by a police officer, who looked through a drawn window blind. The Supreme Court of Minnesota held that the officer's viewing was a search which violated respondents' Fourth Amendment rights. We hold that no such violation occurred.

James Thielen, a police officer in the Twin Cities' suburb of Eagan, Minnesota, went to an apartment building to investigate a tip from a confidential informant. The informant said that he had walked by the window of a ground-floor apartment and had seen people putting a white powder into bags. The officer looked in the same window through a gap in the closed blind and observed the bagging operation for several minutes. He then notified headquarters, which began preparing affidavits for a search warrant while he returned to the apartment building. * * *

* * * A search of the apartment pursuant to a warrant revealed cocaine residue [and plastic baggies] on the kitchen table * * *. Thielen identified Carter, Johns, and Thompson as the three people he had observed placing the powder into baggies. The police later learned that while Thompson was the lessee of the apartment, Carter and Johns lived in Chicago and had come to the apartment for the sole purpose of packaging the cocaine. Carter and Johns had never been to the apartment before and were only in the apartment for approximately 2½ hours. In return for the use of the apartment, Carter and Johns had given Thompson one-eighth of an ounce of the cocaine.

Carter and Johns * * * moved to suppress all evidence obtained from the apartment * * *. * * * The Minnesota trial court held that since, unlike the defendant in *Minnesota v. Olson* [p. 458, Note 6], Carter and Johns were not overnight social guests but temporary out-of-state visitors, they were not entitled to claim the protection of the Fourth Amendment against the government intrusion into the apartment. The trial court also concluded that Thielen's observation was not a search within the meaning of the Fourth Amendment. After a trial, Carter and Johns were each convicted of both offenses. * * *

A divided Minnesota Supreme Court reversed, holding that respondents had "standing" to claim the protection of the Fourth Amendment because they had " 'a legitimate expectation of privacy in the invaded place.' " * * * Based upon its conclusion that the respondents had "standing" to raise their Fourth Amendment claims, the court went on to hold that Thielen's observation constituted a search of the apartment under the Fourth Amendment, and that the search was unreasonable. * * *

The Minnesota courts analyzed whether respondents had a legitimate expectation of privacy under the rubric of "standing" doctrine, an analysis which this Court expressly rejected 20 years ago in *Rakas*. * * * Central to our analysis [in *Rakas*] was the idea that in determining whether a defendant is able to show the violation of his (and not someone else's) Fourth Amendment rights, the "definition of those rights is more properly placed within the purview of substantive Fourth Amendment law than within that of standing." Thus, we held that in order to claim the protection of the Fourth Amendment, a defendant must demonstrate that he personally has an expectation of privacy in the place searched, and that his expectation is reasonable * * *. * * *

The text of the Amendment suggests that its protections extend only to people in "their" houses. But we have held that in some circumstances a person may have a legitimate expectation of privacy in the house of someone else. In *Minnesota v. Olson*, for example, we decided that an overnight guest in a house had the sort of expectation of privacy that the Fourth Amendment protects. * * *

Respondents here were obviously not overnight guests, but were essentially present for a business transaction and were only in the home a matter of hours. There is no suggestion that they had a previous relationship with Thompson, or that there was any other purpose to their visit. Nor was there anything similar to the overnight guest relationship in *Olson* to suggest a degree of acceptance into the household. While the apartment was a dwelling place for Thompson, it was for these respondents simply a place to do business.

Property used for commercial purposes is treated differently for Fourth Amendment purposes than residential property. "An expectation of privacy in commercial premises, however, is different from, and indeed less than, a similar expectation in an individual's home." And while it was a "home" in which respondents were present, it was not their home. Similarly, the Court has held that in some circumstances a worker can claim Fourth Amendment protection over his own workplace. See, *e.g.*, *O'Connor v. Ortega*, 480 U.S. 709, 107 S.Ct. 1492, 94 L.Ed.2d 714 (1987). But there is no indication that respondents in this case had nearly as significant a connection to Thompson's apartment as the worker in *O'Connor* had to his own private office.

If we regard the overnight guest in *Minnesota v. Olson* as typifying those who may claim the protection of the Fourth Amendment in the home of another, and one merely "legitimately on the premises" as typifying those who may not do so, the present case is obviously somewhere in between. But the purely commercial nature of the transaction engaged in here, the relatively short period of time on the premises, and the lack of any previous connection between respondents and the householder, all lead us to conclude that respondents' situation is closer to that of one simply permitted on the premises. We therefore hold that any search which may have occurred did not violate their Fourth Amendment rights.

Because we conclude that respondents had no legitimate expectation of privacy in the apartment, we need not decide whether the police officer's observation constituted a "search." The judgment of the Supreme Court of Minnesota is accordingly reversed * * *. * * *

Justice SCALIA, with whom Justice THOMAS joins, concurring.

I join the opinion of the Court because I believe it accurately applies our recent case law, including *Minnesota v. Olson*. I write separately to express my view that that case law * * * gives short shrift to the text of the Fourth Amendment, and to the well and long understood meaning of that text. Specifically, it leaps to apply the fuzzy standard of "legitimate expectation of privacy"—a consideration that is often relevant to whether a search or seizure covered by the Fourth Amendment is "unreasonable"—to the threshold question whether a search or seizure covered by the Fourth Amendment *has occurred*. If that latter question is addressed first and analyzed under the text of the Constitution as traditionally understood, the present case is not remotely difficult.

The Fourth Amendment protects "[t]he right of the people to be secure *in their* persons, houses, papers, and effects, against unreasonable searches and seizures * * *." It must be acknowledged that the phrase "their * * * houses" in this provision is, in isolation, ambiguous. It could mean "their respective houses," so that the protection extends to each person only in his *own* house. But it could also mean "their respective and each other's houses," so that each person would be protected even when visiting the house of someone else. As today's opinion for the Court suggests, however, it is not linguistically possible to give the provision the latter, expansive interpretation with respect to "houses" without giving it the same interpretation with respect to the nouns that are parallel to "houses"—"persons, * * * papers, and effects"—which would give me a constitutional right not to have your person unreasonably searched. This is so absurd that it has to my knowledge never been contemplated. The obvious meaning of the provision is that *each* person has the right to be secure against unreasonable searches and seizures in *his own* person, house, papers, and effects. * * *

That "their * * * houses" was understood to mean "their respective houses" would have been clear to anyone who knew the English and early American law of arrest and trespass that underlay the Fourth Amendment. The people's protection against unreasonable search and seizure in their "houses" was drawn from the English common-law maxim, "A man's home is *his* castle." As far back as *Semayne's Case* of 1604, the leading English case for that proposition * * *, the King's Bench proclaimed that "the house of any one is not a castle or privilege but for himself, and shall not extend to protect any person who flies to his house." * * *

Of course this is not to say that the Fourth Amendment protects only the Lord of the Manor who holds his estate in fee simple. People call a house "their" home when legal title is in the bank, when they rent it, and even when they merely occupy it rent-free—*so long as they actually live there.* * * *

Thus, in deciding the question presented today we write upon a slate that is far from clean. The text of the Fourth Amendment, the common-law background against which it was adopted, and the understandings consistently displayed after its adoption make the answer clear. * * * We went to the absolute limit of what text and tradition permit in *Minnesota v. Olson*, when we protected a mere overnight guest against an unreasonable search of his hosts' apartment. But whereas it is plausible to regard a person's overnight lodging as at least his "temporary" residence, it is entirely impossible to give that characterization to an apartment that he uses to package cocaine. Respondents here were not searched in "their * * * hous[e]" under any interpretation of the phrase that bears the remotest relationship to the well understood meaning of the Fourth Amendment.

The dissent believes that "[o]ur obligation to produce coherent results" requires that we ignore this clear text and four-century-old tradition, and apply instead the notoriously unhelpful test adopted in a "benchmar[k]" decision that is 31 years old[,] citing *Katz v. United States*. In my view, the only thing the past three decades have established about the *Katz* test (which has come to mean the test enunciated by Justice Harlan's separate concurrence in *Katz*) is that, unsurprisingly, those "actual (subjective) expectation[s] of privacy" "that society is prepared to recognize as 'reasonable,'" bear an uncanny resemblance to those expectations of privacy that this Court considers reasonable. When that self-indulgent test is employed (as the dissent would employ it here) to determine whether a "search or seizure" within the meaning of the Constitution has *occurred* (as opposed to whether that "search or seizure" is an "unreasonable" one), it has no plausible foundation in the text of the Fourth Amendment. That provision did not guarantee some generalized "right of privacy" and leave it to this Court to determine which particular manifestations of the value of privacy "society is prepared to recognize as 'reasonable.'" Rather, it enumerated ("persons, houses, papers, and effects") the objects of privacy protection to which the *Constitution* would extend, leaving further expansion to the good judgment, not of this Court, but of the people through their representatives in the legislature.[3]

---

3. The dissent asserts that I "undervalu[e]" the *Katz* Court's observation that "the Fourth Amendment protects people, not places." That catchy slogan would be a devastating response to

The dissent may be correct that a person invited into someone else's house to engage in a common business (even common monkey-business, so to speak) *ought* to be protected against government searches of the room in which that business is conducted; and that persons invited in to deliver milk or pizza (whom the dissent dismisses as "classroom hypotheticals," as opposed, presumably, to flesh-and-blood hypotheticals) ought *not* to be protected against government searches of the rooms that they occupy. I am not sure of the answer to those policy questions. But I am sure that the answer is not remotely contained in the Constitution, which means that it is left—as *many*, indeed *most*, important questions are left—to the judgment of state and federal legislators. We go beyond our proper role as judges in a democratic society when we restrict the people's power to govern themselves over the full range of policy choices that the Constitution has left available to them.

Justice KENNEDY, concurring.

I join the Court's opinion, for its reasoning is consistent with my view that almost all social guests have a legitimate expectation of privacy, and hence protection against unreasonable searches, in their host's home. * * *

The dissent, as I interpret it, does not question *Rakas* or the principle that not all persons in the company of the property owner have the owner's right to assert the spatial protection. *Rakas*, it is true, involved automobiles, where the necessities of law enforcement permit more latitude to the police than ought to be extended to houses. The analysis in *Rakas* was not conceived, however, as a utilitarian exception to accommodate the needs of law enforcement. The Court's premise was a more fundamental one. Fourth Amendment rights are personal, and when a person objects to the search of a place and invokes the exclusionary rule, he or she must have the requisite connection to that place. * * *

The settled rule is that the requisite connection is an expectation of privacy that society recognizes as reasonable. The application of that rule involves consideration of the kind of place in which the individual claims the privacy interest and what expectations of privacy are traditional and well recognized. I would expect that most, if not all, social guests legitimately expect that, in accordance with social custom, the homeowner will exercise her discretion to include or exclude others for the guests' benefit. As we recognized in *Minnesota v. Olson*, where these social expectations

___

someone who maintained that a *location* could claim protection of the Fourth Amendment— someone who asserted, perhaps, that "primeval forests have rights, too." The issue here, however, is the less druidical one of whether respondents (who are people) have suffered a violation of *their* right "to be secure in their persons, houses, papers, and effects, against unreasonable searches and seizures." That the Fourth Amendment does not protect places is simply unresponsive to the question of whether the Fourth Amendment protects people in other people's homes. In saying this, I do not, as the dissent claims, clash with "the *leitmotif* of Justice Harlan's concurring opinion" in *Katz*; *au contraire* (or, to be more Wagnerian, *im Gegenteil*), in this regard I am entirely in harmony with that opinion, and it is the dissent that sings from another opera. See [*Katz*] (Harlan, J., concurring): "As the Court's opinion states, 'the Fourth Amendment protects people, not places.' The question, however, is what protection it affords to those people. Generally, as here, the answer to that question requires reference to a 'place.'"

exist—as in the case of an overnight guest—they are sufficient to create a legitimate expectation of privacy, even in the absence of any property right to exclude others. In this respect, the dissent must be correct that reasonable expectations of the owner are shared, to some extent, by the guest. This analysis suggests that, as a general rule, social guests will have an expectation of privacy in their host's home. That is not the case before us, however.

In this case respondents have established nothing more than a fleeting and insubstantial connection with Thompson's home. For all that appears in the record, respondents used Thompson's house simply as a convenient processing station, their purpose involving nothing more than the mechanical act of chopping and packing a substance for distribution. There is no suggestion that respondents engaged in confidential communications with Thompson about their transaction. Respondents had not been to Thompson's apartment before, and they left it even before their arrest. The Minnesota Supreme Court, which overturned respondents' convictions, acknowledged that respondents could not be fairly characterized as Thompson's "guests."

If respondents here had been visiting twenty homes, each for a minute or two, to drop off a bag of cocaine and were apprehended by a policeman wrongfully present in the nineteenth home; or if they had left the goods at a home where they were not staying and the police had seized the goods in their absence, we would have said that *Rakas* compels rejection of any privacy interest respondents might assert. So it does here, given that respondents have established no meaningful tie or connection to the owner, the owner's home, or the owner's expectation of privacy.

We cannot remain faithful to the underlying principle in *Rakas* without reversing in this case, and I am not persuaded that we need depart from it to protect the homeowner's own privacy interests. Respondents have made no persuasive argument that we need to fashion a *per se* rule of home protection, with an automatic right for all in the home to invoke the exclusionary rule, in order to protect homeowners and their guests from unlawful police intrusion. With these observations, I join the Court's opinion.

Justice BREYER, concurring in the judgment.

I agree with Justice Ginsburg that respondents can claim the Fourth Amendment's protection. Petitioner, however, raises a second question, whether under the circumstances Officer Thielen's observation made "from a public area outside the curtilage of the residence" violated respondents' Fourth Amendment rights. In my view, it did not. * * *

[Justice Breyer summarized in greater detail the facts in the case, including that the apartment in question was partly below ground level, that families living in the building frequently used the grassy area just outside the apartment's window for walking and playing, and that the officer here stood for nearly fifteen minutes about a foot from the window looking through a closed set of Venetian blinds, observing the illegal activities.]

Officer Thielen, then, stood at a place used by the public and from which one could see through the window into the kitchen. The precautions that the apartment's dwellers took to maintain their privacy would have failed in respect to an ordinary passerby standing in that place. Given this Court's well-established case law, I cannot say that the officer engaged in what the Constitution forbids, namely, an "unreasonable search." * * *

For these reasons, while agreeing with Justice Ginsburg, I also concur in the Court's judgment reversing the Minnesota Supreme Court.

Justice GINSBURG, with whom Justice STEVENS and Justice SOUTER join, dissenting.

The Court's decision undermines not only the security of short-term guests, but also the security of the home resident herself. In my view, when a homeowner or lessor personally invites a guest into her home to share in a common endeavor, whether it be for conversation, to engage in leisure activities, or for business purposes licit or illicit, that guest should share his host's shelter against unreasonable searches and seizures.

* * * First, the disposition I would reach in this case responds to the unique importance of the home—the most essential bastion of privacy recognized by the law. Second, even within the home itself, the position to which I would adhere would not permit "a casual visitor who has never seen, or been permitted to visit, the basement of another's house to object to a search of the basement if the visitor happened to be in the kitchen of the house at the time of the search." *Rakas*. Further, I would here decide only the case of the homeowner who chooses to share the privacy of her home and her company with a guest, and would not reach classroom hypotheticals like the milkman or pizza deliverer.

My concern centers on an individual's choice to share her home and her associations there with persons she selects. Our decisions indicate that people have a reasonable expectation of privacy in their homes in part because they have the prerogative to exclude others. The power to exclude implies the power to include. Our Fourth Amendment decisions should reflect these complementary prerogatives. * * *

Through the host's invitation, the guest gains a reasonable expectation of privacy in the home. *Minnesota v. Olson* so held with respect to an overnight guest. The logic of that decision extends to shorter term guests as well. * * * One need not remain overnight to anticipate privacy in another's home * * *. In sum, when a homeowner chooses to share the privacy of her home and her company with a short-term guest, the twofold requirement "emerg[ing] from prior decisions" has been satisfied: Both host and guest "have exhibited an actual (subjective) expectation of privacy"; that "expectation [is] one [our] society is prepared to recognize as 'reasonable.'" *Katz v. United States*.[2]

---

2. In his concurring opinion, Justice Kennedy maintains that respondents here * * * "established nothing more than a fleeting and insubstantial connection" with the host's home. As the

As the Solicitor General acknowledged, the illegality of the host-guest conduct, the fact that they were partners in crime, would not alter the analysis. * * * Indeed, it must be this way. If the illegality of the activity made constitutional an otherwise unconstitutional search, such Fourth Amendment protection, reserved for the innocent only, would have little force in regulating police behavior toward either the innocent or the guilty.

Our leading decision in *Katz* is key to my view of this case. * * * We were mindful that "the Fourth Amendment protects people, not places," and held that this electronic monitoring of a business call "violated the privacy upon which [the caller] justifiably relied while using the telephone booth." Our obligation to produce coherent results in this often visited area of the law requires us to inform our current expositions by benchmarks already established. * * * The Court's decision in this case veers sharply from the path marked in *Katz*. I do not agree that we have a more reasonable expectation of privacy when we place a business call to a person's home from a public telephone booth on the side of the street, than when we actually enter that person's premises to engage in a common endeavor.[3] * * *

NOTES AND QUESTIONS

1. Count votes in this case. Although Carter and Johns, the respondents, lost on their appeal, did the Court narrow or expand on the protections provided to guests in residences, as originally announced in *Minnesota v. Olson*? After *Carter*, when does a guest in a home have standing to contest a police search of the residence?

2. What is Justice Scalia's point regarding *Katz*? Are Justices Scalia and Thomas suggesting they would like to overrule or narrow *Katz*?

3. Why did Justice Breyer concur in the judgment, although he agrees with the dissent's observations on the "standing" issue? How did the dissenters respond to Breyer's opinion? In what way do the Breyer and Ginsburg opinions reinforce Justice Blackmun's observations (p. 456, Note 2) about the confusion that can result from *not* analyzing cases under the rubric of "standing"?

4. *Problem.* S, who was wanted by federal authorities in connection with a drug conspiracy and murder, drove all night from Michigan to Georgia. He

---

Minnesota Supreme Court reported, however, the stipulated facts showed that respondents were inside the apartment with the host's permission, remained inside for at least 2½ hours, and, during that time, engaged in concert with the host in a collaborative venture. These stipulated facts—which scarcely resemble a stop of a minute or two at the 19th of 20 homes to drop off a packet—securely demonstrate that the host intended to share her privacy with respondents, and that respondents, therefore, had entered into the homeland of Fourth Amendment protection. * * *

3. Justice Scalia's lively concurring opinion deplores our adherence to *Katz*. * * * Justice Scalia undervalues the clear opinion of the Court that "the Fourth Amendment protects people, not places." That core understanding is the *leitmotif* of Justice Harlan's concurring opinion. One cannot avoid a strong sense of *déjà vu* on reading Justice Scalia's elaboration. It so vividly recalls the opinion of Justice Black *in dissent* in *Katz*. * * *

arrived in the morning and promptly entered an apartment he had sublet from *L*, the leaseholder, for $2000. He went to sleep. Six hours later, the police entered, arrested *S*, and searched the premises, resulting in the seizure of evidence. United States v. Stuckey, 325 F.Supp.2d 793 (E.D. Mich. 2004). Standing?

5. In *Rakas v. Illinois*, the Court repeatedly observed that the petitioners in that case had not claimed ownership of the property seized. The implication seemed to be that if a person owns seized property, she has standing to contest the search resulting in its seizure. That implication, however, has proved false. In Rawlings v. Kentucky, 448 U.S. 98, 100 S.Ct. 2556, 65 L.Ed.2d 633 (1980), the Court ruled that the test enunciated in *Rakas*—whether the petitioner had a reasonable expectation of privacy in the area searched—is the exclusive test for determining whether a defendant may successfully challenge a search.

In *Rawlings*, the police, armed with a warrant to arrest *X*, entered a residence occupied by five persons. While unsuccessfully searching for *X*, the police smelled burnt marijuana and observed some marijuana seeds on the mantel in one bedroom. While two officers left to obtain a search warrant, other officers detained the occupants of the house, allowing them to leave only if they consented to a body search. Two of the occupants consented to a search and left.

Less than an hour later, the two officers returned with a search warrant. One of them walked over to Cox, a female sitting on the couch, and ordered her to empty the contents of her purse, which she did. Among the contents was a jar containing 1,800 tablets of LSD. At that point, Cox turned to Rawlings, a male who had been sitting next to her, and told him "to take what was his." He claimed ownership of the controlled substances. The trial court determined that Rawlings had known Cox for a few days and had recently slept on her couch at least twice, and—although there was a factual dispute on the matter—Rawlings had dumped the drugs in Cox's purse, with her knowledge, on the afternoon of the search.

The Court agreed with the lower court that Rawlings had not made a sufficient showing that his legitimate expectation of privacy was violated by the search of Cox's purse:

> We believe that the record in this case supports that conclusion. Petitioner, of course, bears the burden of proving not only that the search of Cox's purse was illegal, but also that he had a legitimate expectation of privacy in that purse. At the time petitioner dumped thousands of dollars worth of illegal drugs into Cox's purse, he had known her for only a few days. According to Cox's uncontested testimony, petitioner had never sought or received access to her purse prior to that sudden bailment. Nor did petitioner have any right to exclude other persons from access to Cox's purse. In fact, Cox testified that Bob Stallons, a longtime acquaintance and frequent companion of Cox's, had free access to her purse and on the very morning of the arrest had rummaged through its contents in search of a hairbrush. Moreover, even assuming that petitioner's version of the bailment is correct and that Cox did consent to the transfer of possession, the precipitous nature of the transaction hardly supports a

reasonable inference that petitioner took normal precautions to maintain his privacy. * * *

Petitioner contends nevertheless that, because he claimed ownership of the drugs in Cox's purse, he should be entitled to challenge the search regardless of his expectation of privacy. We disagree. While petitioner's ownership of the drugs is undoubtedly one fact to be considered in this case, *Rakas* emphatically rejected the notion that "arcane" concepts of property law ought to control the ability to claim the protections of the Fourth Amendment.

Are you persuaded by the Court's reasoning?

6.   *Variations on Rawlings.* Assume the following variations on the facts in *Rawlings*. Would Rawlings have standing to challenge the police conduct in these circumstances?

A.   When Cox emptied her purse as ordered, a police officer observed the drug vial, picked it up, but was unable to determine what was in it. He removed the lid and inspected the contents. Based on his observations, he concluded that the vial contained controlled substances and, therefore, seized it.

B.   When Cox emptied her purse, the officer discovered a sealed envelope belonging to Rawlings. Based on a hunch that the envelope contained illegal drugs, the officer seized the envelope and, four days later, subjected it to a dog sniff, which confirmed his hunch. The officer then opened the envelope and seized the drugs inside.

B.   EXCLUSIONARY RULE

1.   THE NATURE OF THE RULE

MAPP v. OHIO

Supreme Court of the United States, 1961.
367 U.S. 643, 81 S.Ct. 1684, 6 L.Ed.2d 1081.

[See p. 73 for the text of the case.]

2.   SHOULD THE RULE BE ABOLISHED?

Justice William Douglas predicted that *Mapp v. Ohio* would end the "storm of constitutional controversy" evoked by *Wolf v. Colorado*, which *Mapp* overruled. He was wrong. Debate regarding the exclusionary rule commenced almost as soon as the decision was announced, and it has not ceased.

The rule is criticized on various grounds. One dispute relates to the question of whether there is an historical foundation for the exclusionary rule. Most debate, however, has focused on the deterrence rationale of the rule: Does exclusion of evidence deter governmental misconduct; and even if it does, do the costs of the rule outweigh its benefits? Some of the arguments against and for the suppression doctrine are set out in the excerpt below.

JOSHUA DRESSLER & ALAN C. MICHAELS— UNDERSTANDING CRIMINAL PROCEDURE

(Volume 1) (Fourth edition 2006), 375–383.

§ 20.04   Exclusionary Rule: Should It Be Abolished? * * *

[C]   Does the Exclusionary Rule Deter Constitutional Violations? * * *

What the critics say: Early empirical studies suggest, and common sense tells us, that the exclusionary rule does not and cannot function as a meaningful deterrent. Most violations of the Fourth Amendment occur at its edges: an officer in good faith misunderstands a complex Fourth Amendment rule or interprets the facts regarding a search or seizure differently than a court does. These errors cannot be prevented; by definition, they are inadvertent. In any case, we would not want to deter good-faith police activity: all we can ask of the police is that they make reasonable, good-faith efforts to obey the Constitution.

In contrast, those who knowingly violate the Fourth Amendment *can* theoretically be deterred, but the exclusionary rule is too indirect and attenuated a form of punishment to do the job adequately. For the exclusionary rule to be fully effective, the undesired conduct must always be detected, and the "punishing stimulus" of the exclusion of evidence must be given *immediately* after *every* incident of misconduct. But, experience teaches us that most constitutionally questionable searches and seizures on the street are not litigated because the police do not make an arrest * * * or, when they do arrest, many harried defense lawyers plea bargain rather than litigate. Furthermore, suppression motions are often unsuccessful even when litigated. Bad faith officers believe, perhaps with reason, that by committing perjury they can avoid suppression of evidence. Finally, suppression of evidence, if it occurs at all, happens long after the wrongful conduct has occurred and may not even be communicated to the offending officer.

Beyond these deterrence problems, bad-faith officers may find the suppression of evidence, even if communicated to them, of marginal concern. * * * [T]he possibility that evidence may be excluded at trial does not diminish other powerful motivations to act unlawfully: malicious officers obtain considerable satisfaction from the knowledge that they have imposed other hardships on a suspect, such as invasion of privacy, the expense and ordeal of a criminal prosecution, family disruption, and loss of employment. * * *

What defenders of the rule say: As with all arguments regarding deterrence, it is easier to prove that a penalty has *not* had a deterrent effect than that it is to show that it has succeeded. * * *

Fair-minded critics of the exclusionary rule admit that "[n]o one actually knows how effective the exclusionary rule is as a deterrent."

Indeed, Professor Dallin Oaks, the author of the classic study most commonly cited by the rule's critics, candidly warned that his study "obviously fall[s] short of an empirical substantiation or refutation of the deterrent effect of the exclusionary rule." * * *

To a considerable extent, criticisms based on deterrence are misdirected. They seek to show that the exclusionary rule does not directly deter specific police officers. But, systemic (or general) deterrence, not specific deterrence, is the primary goal of the exclusionary rule. According to Justice Brennan, "the chief deterrent function of the rule is its tendency to promote institutional compliance with Fourth Amendment requirements on the part of law enforcement agencies generally." The exclusionary rule is meant to deter unconstitutional police conduct by promoting professionalism within the ranks, specifically by creating an incentive for police departments to hire individuals sensitive to civil liberties, to better train officers in the proper use of force, to keep officers updated on constitutional law, and to develop internal guidelines that reduce the likelihood of unreasonable arrests and searches.

There is anecdotal evidence that *Mapp* has had these effects in many police departments. * * * Various observers of police practices have reported that *Mapp* promoted professionalism. For example, [exclusionary rule critic] Oaks found that police adherence to constitutional doctrine increased after *Mapp* was decided, and that the rule "contributed to an increased awareness of constitutional requirements by the police," and more recent studies support this conclusion.

Furthermore, search warrants were sought more often after *Mapp* than before. Police departments and prosecutors that once paid no attention to the Fourth Amendment now "at least * * * consider the parameters of an unconstitutional search and seizure." And, flagrant cases of police misconduct—such as occurred in *Mapp*—appear to have diminished.

Some defenders of the exclusionary rule attack the issue differently. They reason that deterrence criticisms of the sort summarized earlier are disingenuous. According to Professors Wasserstrom and Seidman, "it is difficult to believe that the exclusionary rule debate would have the same intensity if the rule's opponents believed that it should be replaced by a more effective deterrent."[75] They point out that most critics of the rule, besides arguing that the rule does not deter, also claim that the rule results in too many criminals being set free. Yet, "[t]his state of affairs would be made worse, not better, if fourth amendment violations were more effectively deterred." * * * Thus, these scholars reason, "[i]t seems likely * * * that the real source of the opponents' discontent is not with the rule's *ineffectiveness* but with its *effectiveness*."

[D]   Is the Rule (Even If It Deters) Worth Its Cost?

[1]   Should This Question Even Be Asked? * * *

---

75. Silas J. Wasserstrom & Louis Michael Seidman, *The Fourth Amendment as Constitutional Theory*, 77 Geo. L.J. 19, 36–37 (1988).

* * * [C]ost-benefit calculations of the sort described here are not without critics. According to Justice Brennan, "the language of deterrence and of cost/benefit analysis ... can have a narcotic effect. It creates an illusion of technical precision and ineluctability." These critics maintain that it is nearly impossible to analyze objectively the costs and benefits of the rule, because the process involves "measuring imponderables and comparing incommensurables." For example, how much does privacy weigh in the balance? Is one unreasonable search that is deterred equal to one guilty person going free?

Some defenders of the exclusionary rule believe that courts ought to focus more on the principled, rather than pragmatic, grounds for the exclusionary rule. Courts ought to focus on the need to preserve judicial integrity—to "avoid the taint of partnership in official lawlessness"—by barring unconstitutionally seized evidence. The exclusionary rule, they argue, is defensible not because it deters the police (which it may or may not do) but because it is fair: it puts the citizen and the government back in the procedural position they would have found themselves if the Constitution had not been violated. * * *

[2] The "Costs"

[a] The Rule Protects the Wrong People

What the critics say: The purpose of a criminal trial is to learn the truth regarding a defendant's innocence or guilt, to "sort[] the innocent from the guilty." * * * The Fourth Amendment exclusionary rule, however, "deflects the truthfinding process" by excluding reliable evidence * * *.

As a result of the suppression of the truth, the exclusionary rule "often frees the guilty." * * * And, while the guilty go free, innocent people receive no benefit from the rule, because an innocent person has nothing to be seized. The innocent person must turn instead to a civil remedy to obtain redress if her privacy is unconstitutionally invaded.

What defenders of the rule say: First, the preceding argument is misdirected. If the criminal justice system is an obstacle course, it is the Fourth Amendment itself and not the exclusionary rule that constructs the barriers that make it harder to convict the guilty.

Second, the cost of guilty people going free is vastly overstated by the critics. A study by Professor Thomas Davies[88]—described by Professor Wayne LaFave as "the most careful and balanced assessment of all available empirical data"—suggests that the "most striking feature of the data is the concentration of illegal searches in drug arrests * * * and the extremely small effects in arrests for other offenses, including violent crimes." * * * Davies concluded that "available empirical evidence casts considerable doubt on both the alleged 'high costs' of the exclusionary rule

---

88. Thomas Y. Davies, *A Hard Look at What We Know (and Still Need to Learn) About the "Costs" of the Exclusionary Rule: The NIJ Study and Other Studies of "Lost" Arrests*, 1983 Am. B. Found. Res. J. 611.

and the purported prevalence of 'legal technicalities' as the cause of illegal searches."

Other studies support Davies' conclusions. A 1979 survey by the General Accounting Office—a study of a period when the Fourth Amendment was more vigorously enforced than today—showed that Fourth Amendment problems explained only 0.4 percent of the total number of cases declined for federal prosecution. * * *

Third, it is inaccurate to say that innocent people do not benefit from an exclusionary rule. If the rule serves its deterrent purpose, the police will not enter homes, search cars, or otherwise intrude upon the privacy of those about whom there is little objective evidence of guilt. * * * In any case, even if it were true that only the guilty derive benefit from the rule, this "does not suggest that the rule is not a necessary remedy, only that it is not a sufficient one."

[b]   The Rule Promotes Cynicism

What the critics say: The exclusionary rule promotes cynicism among members of the public and parties in the criminal justice system, including trial judges and even criminal defendants.

The exclusionary rule treats a criminal defendant as a "surrogate for the larger public interest in restraining the government. The criminal defendant is a kind of private attorney general." But, the defendant is "the worst kind" of surrogate, because he is "self-serving." As a person in possession of criminal evidence, he is "often unrepresentative of the larger class of law-abiding citizens, and his interests regularly conflict with theirs." No wonder, then, that a "solid majority of Americans rejects the idea that '[t]he criminal is to go free because the constable has blundered.' " * * *

This cynicism runs even deeper. Police officers lie in order to avoid suppression of evidence, and some trial judges wink at the dishonesty in order to avoid allowing guilty defendants to go free. * * *

The dishonesty inspired by the exclusionary rule even affects guilty defendants who are likely to think to themselves, "if the police are allowed to lie, and the judges permit it, why am I expected to act honestly?" The legal system, in short, pays a high cost in lost respect when it violates natural feelings of justice.

What defenders of the rule say: If the public is outraged by the exclusionary rule, it should not be. First, as noted above, fewer guilty people go free than is believed. Second, although the rule obstructs the truth by suppressing reliable evidence, responsibility for this should be placed at the door of the government, whose officers violated the Fourth Amendment. As Justice Harlan has explained, judges "do not release a criminal from jail because we like to do so, or because we think it is wise to do so, but only because the government has offended constitutional principles in the conduct of [the defendant's] case." * * *

[c] The Rule Results in Disproportionate Punishment

What the critics say: Even if the exclusionary rule should not be abandoned, the *Mapp* version of the doctrine goes too far because the "penalty" for violation of the Fourth Amendment is often disproportionate to the "crime" committed by the police.

First, *Mapp* applies as much to the inadvertent mistake of a good-faith police officer as it does to the malicious conduct of a bad-faith actor. Although "[f]reeing either a tiger or a mouse in a schoolroom is an illegal act, * * * no rational person would suggest that these two acts should be punished in the same way." Second, the rule does not distinguish between a trial for a serious crime and one for a minor offense. Therefore, a potentially dangerous offender may escape incarceration, even if the wrong committed by the officer was trivial in nature. Evidence of a crime should be excluded, if at all, when "the reprehensibility of the officer's illegality is greater than the defendant's."

What defenders of the rule say: The proportionality argument wrongly assumes that the exclusionary rule is intended as compensation of the victim for a Fourth Amendment violation. In fact, its purpose is to instill professionalism in police ranks, in order to prevent *future* violations. Just as punishment of a criminal is not calibrated to the facts of a particular case if we seek general deterrence, it is wrong to measure the effect of the exclusionary rule in an individual case.

NOTES AND QUESTIONS

1. *Alternative remedies.* One other point in the debate should be considered. Uncontroversially, there must be *some* remedy for Fourth Amendment violations. If not the exclusionary rule, what then?

Critics of the rule suggest a variety of potential remedies that singly or in combination might replace the exclusionary rule: common law or a newly created tort action; federal civil rights suits; criminal prosecutions of officers who maliciously violate the Fourth Amendment; injunctive relief; and/or police review boards with authority to suspend or fire officers for constitutional wrongdoing.

Defenders of the exclusionary rule agree that in a perfect world, a complete spectrum of civil and criminal remedies might work better than the exclusionary rule. They argue, however, that whatever its flaws, the exclusionary rule is the best *realistic* remedy. We cannot expect prosecutors to prosecute their normal allies, the police, for Fourth Amendment violations; civil actions, too, are hampered by government immunity doctrines and the fact that juries typically favor the police in civil actions except in the most egregious cases. Consequently, proponents of the exclusionary rule suggest, it is difficult to find lawyers willing to represent aggrieved citizens.

As you will see, the Supreme Court recently got into the "are there better remedies?" debate. See *Hudson v. Michigan*, p. 509.

2. Based on what you have learned so far this semester regarding the Fourth Amendment, do *you* believe that the exclusionary rule should be abolished?

3. *Mapp v. Ohio and the constitutionality of the exclusionary rule.* Look again at *Mapp v. Ohio.* Is the exclusionary rule constitutionally required, according to *Mapp?*

4. *United States v. Calandra and the constitutionality of the exclusionary rule.* The Supreme Court held in United States v. Calandra, 414 U.S. 338, 94 S.Ct. 613, 38 L.Ed.2d 561 (1974), that the Fourth Amendment exclusionary rule does not apply in grand jury proceedings. The Court's reasoning is significant:

> [T]he [exclusionary] rule is a judicially created remedy designed to safeguard Fourth Amendment rights generally through its deterrent effect, rather than a personal constitutional right of the party aggrieved.
>
> Despite its broad deterrent purpose, the exclusionary rule has never been interpreted to proscribe the use of illegally seized evidence in all proceedings or against all persons. As with any remedial device, the application of the rule has been restricted to those areas where its remedial objectives are thought most efficaciously served. * * *
>
> In deciding whether to extend the exclusionary rule to grand jury proceedings, we must weigh the potential injury to the historic role and functions of the grand jury against the potential benefits of the rule as applied in this context. It is evident that this extension of the exclusionary rule would seriously impede the grand jury. Because the grand jury does not finally adjudicate guilt or innocence, it has traditionally been allowed to pursue its investigative and accusatorial functions unimpeded by the evidentiary and procedural restrictions applicable to a criminal trial. Permitting witnesses to invoke the exclusionary rule before a grand jury would precipitate adjudication of issues hitherto reserved for the trial on the merits and would delay and disrupt grand jury proceedings. * * * In sum, we believe that allowing a grand jury witness to invoke the exclusionary rule would unduly interfere with the effective and expeditious discharge of the grand jury's duties.
>
> Against this potential damage to the role and functions of the grand jury, we must weigh the benefits to be derived from this proposed extension of the exclusionary rule. * * *
>
> Any incremental deterrent effect which might be achieved by extending the rule to grand jury proceedings is uncertain at best. Whatever deterrence of police misconduct may result from the exclusion of illegally seized evidence from criminal trials, it is unrealistic to assume that application of the rule to grand jury proceedings would significantly further that goal. Such an extension would deter only police investigation consciously directed toward the discovery of evidence solely for use in a grand jury investigation. The incentive to disregard the requirement of the Fourth Amendment solely to obtain an indictment from a grand jury is substantially negated by the inadmissibility of the illegally seized evidence in a subsequent criminal prosecution of the search victim. * * *

We therefore decline to embrace a view that would achieve a speculative and undoubtedly minimal advance in the deterrence of police misconduct at the expense of substantially impeding the role of the grand jury.

What is the significance of the Court's statement that "the rule is a judicially created remedy * * *, rather than a personal constitutional right of the party aggrieved"? Is that remark consistent with *Mapp*? Is the implication of *Calandra* that the exclusionary rule is *not* a component of the Fourth Amendment? If so, what are the implications?

5. *The "judicial integrity" rationale of the exclusionary rule.* As seen in Note 4, the Court in *United States v. Calandra* weighed the purported costs of the exclusionary rule against the incremental deterrent benefits of invoking the rule in grand jury proceedings. As the dissenters pointed out there, the majority did *not* consider a second rationale for the exclusionary doctrine:

> For the first time, the Court today discounts to the point of extinction the vital function of the rule to insure that the judiciary avoid even the slightest appearance of sanctioning illegal government conduct. This rejection of "the imperative of judicial integrity," openly invites "[t]he conviction that all government is staffed by * * * hypocrites[, a conviction] easy to instill and difficult to erase." When judges appear to become "accomplices in the willful disobedience of a Constitution they are sworn to uphold," we imperil the very foundation of our people's trust in their Government on which our democracy rests.

Why do you think the Court no longer recognizes the judicial integrity rationale of the exclusionary rule? In what way might its "extinction" undermine the position of advocates of the exclusionary rule?

6. *Comparative law.* Section 8 of the Canadian Charter of Rights and Freedoms provides, simply, that "[e]veryone has a right to be secure against unreasonable search or seizure." Unlike our Constitution, however, the Canadian charter expressly recognizes a general exclusionary rule. Section 24 of the Charter provides that

> [w]here * * * a court concludes that evidence was obtained in a manner that infringed or denied any rights or freedoms guaranteed by this Charter, the evidence shall be excluded if it is established that, having regard to all of the circumstances, the admission of it in the proceedings would bring the administration of justice into disrepute.

In New Zealand, as a result of a 2002 court decision, "[e]vidence is now excluded * * * only if the exclusion is held to be a proportional remedial response to the breach of the Bill of Rights at issue in the case. In order to make that determination, judges have to settle on what best serves the due administration of justice." Scott Optican, *Lessons From Down Under: A Dialogue on Police Search and Seizure in New Zealand and the United States*, 3 Ohio St. J. Crim. L. 257, 269 (2005). New Zealand courts balance various factors, including the nature of the violation, the seriousness of the crime allegedly committed by the defendant, and the importance of the evidence to the prosecutor's case. *Id.* at 269–70.

Do you prefer either of these approaches to the United States system?

3. WHEN THE EXCLUSIONARY RULE DOES NOT APPLY

a. In General

The exclusionary does not apply in various categories of circumstances. For example, "[i]n the complex and turbulent history of the [exclusionary] rule, the Court never has applied it to exclude evidence from a civil proceeding, federal or state." United States v. Janis, 428 U.S. 433, 96 S.Ct. 3021, 49 L.Ed.2d 1046 (1976). According to the Court, the deterrence benefit of extending the exclusionary rule to non-criminal proceedings (e.g., civil suits, deportation or disbarment proceedings, etc.) would be comparatively slight, whereas the social costs of exclusion would be great.

The exclusionary rule does not even apply in all criminal proceedings. Prosecutors may use evidence obtained in violation of the Fourth Amendment at grand jury proceedings. United States v. Calandra, 414 U.S. 338, 94 S.Ct. 613, 38 L.Ed.2d 561 (1974) (see p. 474, Note 4). Furthermore, courts have allowed use of unconstitutionally seized evidence in other criminal procedure settings, including at pre-trial preliminary hearings, in sentencing, and at probation and parole revocation hearings.

But, there is more. There are circumstances in which the exclusionary rule does not apply at criminal trials. First, the prosecutor may impeach a defendant's testimony by introducing evidence previously excluded on Fourth Amendment grounds. In Walder v. United States, 347 U.S. 62, 74 S.Ct. 354, 98 L.Ed. 503 (1954), the Supreme Court held that a defendant may not take advantage of a court's exclusion of narcotics found in his possession by testifying in direct examination that he has never possessed narcotics. In such circumstances, as Justice Frankfurter wrote for the Court:

> It is one thing to say that the Government cannot make an affirmative use of evidence unlawfully obtained. It is quite another to say that the defendant can turn the illegal method by which evidence in the Government's possession was obtained to his own advantage, and provide himself with a shield against contradiction of his untruths. Such an extension of the [exclusionary] doctrine would be a perversion of the Fourth Amendment.

In *Walder*, the prosecutor sought to impeach the testimony of the defendant given during *direct* examination. The exclusionary rule exception similarly applies if a prosecutor wishes to introduce unconstitutionally obtained evidence to impeach a defendant's *cross-examination* testimony. United States v. Havens, 446 U.S. 620, 100 S.Ct. 1912, 64 L.Ed.2d 559 (1980).

On the other hand, the Court held, 5–4, in James v. Illinois, 493 U.S. ⁀7, 110 S.Ct. 648, 107 L.Ed.2d 676 (1990), that the impeachment excep-
⁁oes not apply to a defendant's witnesses. In *James*, the defendant

did not testify, but the prosecutor wanted to impeach the testimony of the defendant's sole witness by introducing unconstitutionally seized evidence. The majority reasoned that expansion of the impeachment exception to *all* witnesses in *all* criminal trials—and not simply to defendants (who often choose not to testify anyway)—would unduly undermine the deterrent goal of the exclusionary rule. Also, the Court said, the threat of impeachment might deter defendants from calling witnesses who have legitimate exculpatory evidence to present to the jury, thereby disserving the truthfinding process.

There are also times when evidence obtained as a result of a Fourth Amendment violation may be used against a defendant in a prosecutor's *case-in-chief*. We turn now to that topic.

b.   Faulty Search Warrants Obtained in "Good Faith"

UNITED STATES v. LEON

Supreme Court of the United States, 1984.
468 U.S. 897, 104 S.Ct. 3405, 82 L.Ed.2d 677.

JUSTICE WHITE delivered the opinion of the Court.

This case presents the question whether the Fourth Amendment exclusionary rule should be modified so as not to bar the use in the prosecution's case in chief of evidence obtained by officers acting in reasonable reliance on a search warrant issued by a detached and neutral magistrate but ultimately found to be unsupported by probable cause. * * *

I

In August 1981, a confidential informant of unproven reliability informed an officer of the Burbank Police Department that two persons known to him as "Armando" and "Patsy" were selling large quantities of cocaine and methaqualone from their residence at 620 Price Drive in Burbank, Cal. [Based on this and other claims of the informant, the Burbank police initiated an investigation that focused on the Price Drive residence and, later, on two other residences.]

* * * Based on * * * observations summarized in the affidavit, Officer Cyril Rombach of the Burbank Police Department, an experienced and well-trained narcotics investigator, prepared an application for a warrant to search [three residences] and automobiles registered to each of the respondents for an extensive list of items believed to be related to respondents' drug-trafficking activities. Officer Rombach's extensive application was reviewed by several Deputy District Attorneys.

A facially valid search warrant was issued in September 1981 by a State Superior Court Judge. * * *

The respondents * * * filed motions to suppress the evidence seized pursuant to the warrant. The District Court held an evidentiary hearing and, while recognizing that the case was a close one, granted the motions to suppress * * *. It concluded that the affidavit was insufficient to establish probable cause * * *. In response to a request from the Government, the court made clear that Officer Rombach had acted in good faith, but it rejected the Government's suggestion that the Fourth Amendment exclusionary rule should not apply where evidence is seized in reasonable, good-faith reliance on a search warrant. * * *

The Government's petition for certiorari expressly declined to seek review of the lower courts' determinations that the search warrant was unsupported by probable cause and presented only the question "[w]hether the Fourth Amendment exclusionary rule should be modified so as not to bar the admission of evidence seized in reasonable, good-faith reliance on a search warrant that is subsequently held to be defective." We granted certiorari to consider the propriety of such a modification. * * *

II * * *

A

The Fourth Amendment contains no provision expressly precluding the use of evidence obtained in violation of its commands, and an examination of its origin and purposes makes clear that the use of fruits of a past unlawful search or seizure "work[s] no new Fourth Amendment wrong." The wrong condemned by the Amendment is "fully accomplished" by the unlawful search or seizure itself, and the exclusionary rule is neither intended nor able to "cure the invasion of the defendant's rights which he has already suffered." The rule thus operates as "a judicially created remedy designed to safeguard Fourth Amendment rights generally through its deterrent effect, rather than a personal constitutional right of the party aggrieved."

Whether the exclusionary sanction is appropriately imposed in a particular case, our decisions make clear, is "an issue separate from the question whether the Fourth Amendment rights of the party seeking to invoke the rule were violated by police conduct." Only the former question is currently before us, and it must be resolved by weighing the costs and benefits of preventing the use in the prosecution's case in chief of inherently trustworthy tangible evidence obtained in reliance on a search warrant issued by a detached and neutral magistrate that ultimately is found to be defective.

The substantial social costs exacted by the exclusionary rule for the vindication of Fourth Amendment rights have long been a source of concern. "Our cases have consistently recognized that unbending application of the exclusionary sanction to enforce ideals of governmental rectitude would impede unacceptably the truth-finding functions of judge and jury." An objectionable collateral consequence of this interference with the criminal justice system's truth-finding function is that some guilty defendants may go free or receive reduced sentences as a result of favorable plea bargains.[6] Particularly when law enforcement officers have acted in objective good faith or their transgressions have been minor, the magnitude of the benefit conferred on such guilty defendants offends basic concepts of the criminal justice system. Indiscriminate application of the exclusionary rule, therefore, may well "generat[e] disrespect for the law and administration of justice." Accordingly, "[a]s with any remedial device, the application of the rule has been restricted to those areas where its remedial objectives are thought most efficaciously served."

B

Close attention to those remedial objectives has characterized our recent decisions concerning the scope of the Fourth Amendment exclusionary rule. The Court has, to be sure, not seriously questioned, "in the absence of a more efficacious sanction, the continued application of the rule to suppress evidence from the [prosecution's] case where a Fourth Amendment violation has been substantial and deliberate * * *." Nevertheless, the balancing approach that has evolved in various contexts— including criminal trials—"forcefully suggest[s] that the exclusionary rule be more generally modified to permit the introduction of evidence obtained in the reasonable good-faith belief that a search or seizure was in accord with the Fourth Amendment." * * *

As yet, we have not recognized any form of good-faith exception to the Fourth Amendment exclusionary rule. But the balancing approach that has evolved during the years of experience with the rule provides strong support for the modification currently urged upon us. As we discuss below, our evaluation of the costs and benefits of suppressing reliable physical evidence seized by officers reasonably relying on a warrant issued by a detached and neutral magistrate leads to the conclusion that such evidence should be admissible in the prosecution's case in chief.

III

A

Because a search warrant "provides the detached scrutiny of a neutral magistrate, which is a more reliable safeguard against improper searches than the hurried judgment of a law enforcement officer 'engaged in the

---

6. Researchers have only recently begun to study extensively the effects of the exclusionary rule on the disposition of felony arrests. One study suggests that the rule results in the nonprosecution or nonconviction of between 0.6% and 2.35% of individuals arrested for felonies. Davies, A Hard Look at What We Know (and Still Need to Learn) About the "Costs" of the Exclusionary Rule: The NIJ Study and Other Studies of "Lost" Arrests, 1983 A.B.F. Res. J. 611, 621. The estimates are higher for particular crimes the prosecution of which depends heavily on physical evidence. Thus, the cumulative loss due to nonprosecution or nonconviction of individuals arrested on felony drug charges is probably in the range of 2.8% to 7.1%. * * * The exclusionary rule also has been found to affect the plea-bargaining process.

Many of these researchers have concluded that the impact of the exclusionary rule is insubstantial, but the small percentages with which they deal mask a large absolute number of felons who are released because the cases against them were based in part on illegal searches or seizures.* * * Because we find that the rule can have no substantial deterrent effect in the sorts of situations under consideration in this case, we conclude that it cannot pay its way in those situations.

often competitive enterprise of ferreting out crime,' " we have expressed a strong preference for warrants and declared that "in a doubtful or marginal case a search under a warrant may be sustainable where without one it would fall." Reasonable minds frequently may differ on the question whether a particular affidavit establishes probable cause, and we have thus concluded that the preference for warrants is most appropriately effectuated by according "great deference" to a magistrate's determination.

Deference to the magistrate, however, is not boundless. It is clear, first, that the deference accorded to a magistrate's finding of probable cause does not preclude inquiry into the knowing or reckless falsity of the affidavit on which that determination was based. *Franks v. Delaware*, [p. 165, Note 6]. Second, the courts must also insist that the magistrate purport to "perform his 'neutral and detached' function and not serve merely as a rubber stamp for the police." A magistrate failing to "manifest that neutrality and detachment demanded of a judicial officer when presented with a warrant application" and who acts instead as "an adjunct law enforcement officer" cannot provide valid authorization for an otherwise unconstitutional search. *Lo-Ji Sales, Inc. v. New York*, [p. 195].

Third, reviewing courts will not defer to a warrant based on an affidavit that does not "provide the magistrate with a substantial basis for determining the existence of probable cause." "Sufficient information must be presented to the magistrate to allow that official to determine probable cause; his action cannot be a mere ratification of the bare conclusions of others." Even if the warrant application was supported by more than a "bare bones" affidavit, a reviewing court may properly conclude that, notwithstanding the deference that magistrates deserve, the warrant was invalid because the magistrate's probable-cause determination reflected an improper analysis of the totality of the circumstances, or because the form of the warrant was improper in some respect.

Only in the first of these three situations, however, has the Court set forth a rationale for suppressing evidence obtained pursuant to a search warrant; in the other areas, it has simply excluded such evidence without considering whether Fourth Amendment interests will be advanced. To the extent that proponents of exclusion rely on its behavioral effects on judges and magistrates in these areas, their reliance is misplaced. First, the exclusionary rule is designed to deter police misconduct rather than to punish the errors of judges and magistrates. Second, there exists no evidence suggesting that judges and magistrates are inclined to ignore or subvert the Fourth Amendment or that lawlessness among these actors requires application of the extreme sanction of exclusion.[14]

Third, and most important, we discern no basis, and are offered none, for believing that exclusion of evidence seized pursuant to a warrant will

---

14. Although there are assertions that some magistrates become rubber stamps for the police and others may be unable effectively to screen police conduct, we are not convinced that this is a problem of major proportions.

have a significant deterrent effect on the issuing judge or magistrate. Many of the factors that indicate that the exclusionary rule cannot provide an effective "special" or "general" deterrent for individual offending law enforcement officers apply as well to judges or magistrates. And, to the extent that the rule is thought to operate as a "systemic" deterrent on a wider audience, it clearly can have no such effect on individuals empowered to issue search warrants. Judges and magistrates are not adjuncts to the law enforcement team; as neutral judicial officers, they have no stake in the outcome of particular criminal prosecutions. The threat of exclusion thus cannot be expected significantly to deter them. Imposition of the exclusionary sanction is not necessary meaningfully to inform judicial officers of their errors, and we cannot conclude that admitting evidence obtained pursuant to a warrant while at the same time declaring that the warrant was somehow defective will in any way reduce judicial officers' professional incentives to comply with the Fourth Amendment, encourage them to repeat their mistakes, or lead to the granting of all colorable warrant requests.[18]

B

If exclusion of evidence obtained pursuant to a subsequently invalidated warrant is to have any deterrent effect, therefore, it must alter the behavior of individual law enforcement officers or the policies of their departments. One could argue that applying the exclusionary rule in cases where the police failed to demonstrate probable cause in the warrant application deters future inadequate presentations or "magistrate shopping" and thus promotes the ends of the Fourth Amendment. Suppressing evidence obtained pursuant to a technically defective warrant supported by probable cause also might encourage officers to scrutinize more closely the form of the warrant and to point out suspected judicial errors. We find such arguments speculative and conclude that suppression of evidence obtained pursuant to a warrant should be ordered only on a case-by-case basis and only in those unusual cases in which exclusion will further the purposes of the exclusionary rule.[19]

We have frequently questioned whether the exclusionary rule can have any deterrent effect when the offending officers acted in the objectively reasonable belief that their conduct did not violate the Fourth Amendment. "No empirical researcher, proponent or opponent of the rule, has yet been able to establish with any assurance whether the rule has a deterrent effect * * *." But even assuming that the rule effectively deters some police misconduct and provides incentives for the law enforcement

---

18. * * * Federal magistrates * * * moreover, are subject to the direct supervision of district courts. They may be removed for "incompetency, misconduct, neglect of duty, or physical or mental disability." 28 U. S. C. § 631(i). If a magistrate serves merely as a "rubber stamp" for the police or is unable to exercise mature judgment, closer supervision or removal provides a more effective remedy than the exclusionary rule.

19. Our discussion of the deterrent effect of excluding evidence obtained in reasonable reliance on a subsequently invalidated warrant assumes, of course, that the officers properly executed the warrant and searched only those places and for those objects that it was reasonable to believe were covered by the warrant.

profession as a whole to conduct itself in accord with the Fourth Amendment, it cannot be expected, and should not be applied, to deter objectively reasonable law enforcement activity. * * *[20]

This is particularly true, we believe, when an officer acting with objective good faith has obtained a search warrant from a judge or magistrate and acted within its scope. In most such cases, there is no police illegality and thus nothing to deter. It is the magistrate's responsibility to determine whether the officer's allegations establish probable cause and, if so, to issue a warrant comporting in form with the requirements of the Fourth Amendment. In the ordinary case, an officer cannot be expected to question the magistrate's probable-cause determination or his judgment that the form of the warrant is technically sufficient. "[O]nce the warrant issues, there is literally nothing more the policeman can do in seeking to comply with the law." Penalizing the officer for the magistrate's error, rather than his own, cannot logically contribute to the deterrence of Fourth Amendment violations.

C

We conclude that the marginal or nonexistent benefits produced by suppressing evidence obtained in objectively reasonable reliance on a subsequently invalidated search warrant cannot justify the substantial costs of exclusion. We do not suggest, however, that exclusion is always inappropriate in cases where an officer has obtained a warrant and abided by its terms. * * * [T]he officer's reliance on the magistrate's probable-cause determination and on the technical sufficiency of the warrant he issues must be objectively reasonable,[23] and it is clear that in some

---

20. We emphasize that the standard of reasonableness we adopt is an objective one. Many objections to a good-faith exception assume that the exception will turn on the subjective good faith of individual officers. "Grounding the modification in objective reasonableness, however, retains the value of the exclusionary rule as an incentive for the law enforcement profession as a whole to conduct themselves in accord with the Fourth Amendment." The objective standard we adopt, moreover, requires officers to have a reasonable knowledge of what the law prohibits. As Professor Jerold Israel has observed:

"The key to the [exclusionary] rule's effectiveness as a deterrent lies, I believe, in the impetus it has provided to police training programs that make officers aware of the limits imposed by the fourth amendment and emphasize the need to operate within those limits. [An objective good-faith exception] is not likely to result in the elimination of such programs, which are now viewed as an important aspect of police professionalism. Neither is it likely to alter the tenor of those programs; the possibility that illegally obtained evidence may be admitted in borderline cases is unlikely to encourage police instructors to pay less attention to fourth amendment limitations. Finally, [it] should not encourage officers to pay less attention to what they are taught, as the requirement that the officer act in 'good faith' is inconsistent with closing one's mind to the possibility of illegality."

23. * * * [W]e * * * eschew inquiries into the subjective beliefs of law enforcement officers who seize evidence pursuant to a subsequently invalidated warrant. Although we have suggested that, "[o]n occasion, the motive with which the officer conducts an illegal search may have some relevance in determining the propriety of applying the exclusionary rule," we believe that "sending state and federal courts on an expedition into the minds of police officers would produce a grave and fruitless misallocation of judicial resources." Accordingly, our good-faith inquiry is confined to the objectively ascertainable question whether a reasonably well trained officer would have known that the search was illegal despite the magistrate's authorization. In making this determination, all of the circumstances—including whether the warrant application had previously been rejected by a different magistrate—may be considered.

circumstances the officer[24] will have no reasonable grounds for believing that the warrant was properly issued.

Suppression therefore remains an appropriate remedy if the magistrate or judge in issuing a warrant was misled by information in an affidavit that the affiant knew was false or would have known was false except for his reckless disregard of the truth. *Franks v. Delaware.* The exception we recognize today will also not apply in cases where the issuing magistrate wholly abandoned his judicial role in the manner condemned in *Lo-Ji Sales, Inc. v. New York*; in such circumstances, no reasonably well trained officer should rely on the warrant. Nor would an officer manifest objective good faith in relying on a warrant based on an affidavit "so lacking in indicia of probable cause as to render official belief in its existence entirely unreasonable." Finally, depending on the circumstances of the particular case, a warrant may be so facially deficient—*i.e.*, in failing to particularize the place to be searched or the things to be seized— that the executing officers cannot reasonably presume it to be valid.

In so limiting the suppression remedy, we leave untouched the probable cause standard and the various requirements for a valid warrant. The good-faith exception for searches conducted pursuant to warrants is not intended to signal our unwillingness strictly to enforce the requirements of the Fourth Amendment, and we do not believe that it will have this effect.* * *

IV

When the principles we have enunciated today are applied to the facts of this case, it is apparent that the judgment of the Court of Appeals cannot stand. * * *

In the absence of an allegation that the magistrate abandoned his detached and neutral role, suppression is appropriate only if the officers were dishonest or reckless in preparing their affidavit or could not have harbored an objectively reasonable belief in the existence of probable cause. * * * Officer Rombach's application for a warrant clearly was supported by much more than a "bare bones" affidavit. The affidavit related the results of an extensive investigation and, as the opinions of the divided panel of the Court of Appeals make clear, provided evidence sufficient to create disagreement among thoughtful and competent judges as to the existence of probable cause. Under these circumstances, the officers' reliance on the magistrate's determination of probable cause was objectively reasonable, and application of the extreme sanction of exclusion is inappropriate.

---

24. References to "officer" throughout this opinion should not be read too narrowly. It is necessary to consider the objective reasonableness, not only of the officers who eventually executed a warrant, but also of the officers who originally obtained it or who provided information material to the probable-cause determination. Nothing in our opinion suggests, for example, that an officer could obtain a warrant on the basis of a "bare bones" affidavit and then rely on colleagues who are ignorant of the circumstances under which the warrant was obtained to conduct the search.

Justice BLACKMUN, concurring. * * *

As the Court's opinion in this case makes clear, the Court has narrowed the scope of the exclusionary rule because of an empirical judgment that the rule has little appreciable effect in cases where officers act in objectively reasonable reliance on search warrants. Because I share the view that the exclusionary rule is not a constitutionally compelled corollary of the Fourth Amendment itself, I see no way to avoid making an empirical judgment of this sort, and I am satisfied that the Court has made the correct one on the information before it. * * *

What must be stressed, however, is that any empirical judgment about the effect of the exclusionary rule in a particular class of cases necessarily is a provisional one. By their very nature, the assumptions on which we proceed today cannot be cast in stone. To the contrary, they now will be tested in the real world of state and federal law enforcement, and this Court will attend to the results. If it should emerge from experience that, contrary to our expectations, the good-faith exception to the exclusionary rule results in a material change in police compliance with the Fourth Amendment, we shall have to reconsider what we have undertaken here. The logic of a decision that rests on untested predictions about police conduct demands no less.* * *

Justice BRENNAN, with whom Justice MARSHALL joins, dissenting.

Ten years ago in *United States v. Calandra*, [p. 474, Note 4], I expressed the fear that the Court's decision "may signal that a majority of my colleagues have positioned themselves to reopen the door [to evidence secured by official lawlessness] still further and abandon altogether the exclusionary rule in search-and-seizure cases." Since then, in case after case, I have witnessed the Court's gradual but determined strangulation of the rule. It now appears that the Court's victory over the Fourth Amendment is complete. That today's decisions represent the *piece de resistance* of the Court's past efforts cannot be doubted, for today the Court sanctions the use in the prosecution's case in chief of illegally obtained evidence against the individual whose rights have been violated—a result that had previously been thought to be foreclosed. * * *

I * * *

A

At bottom, the Court's decision turns on the proposition that the exclusionary rule is merely a " 'judicially created remedy designed to safeguard Fourth Amendment rights generally through its deterrent effect, rather than a personal constitutional right.' " The germ of that idea is found in *Wolf v. Colorado*, [p. 70], and although I had thought that such a narrow conception of the rule had been forever put to rest by our decision in *Mapp v. Ohio*, it has been revived by the present Court and reaches full flower with today's decision. The essence of this view * * * is that the sole "purpose of the Fourth Amendment is to prevent unreasonable governmental intrusions into the privacy of one's person, house, papers, or effects. The wrong condemned is the unjustified governmental invasion of these areas of an individual's life. That wrong * * * is *fully accomplished* by the original search without probable cause." This reading of the Amendment implies that its proscriptions are directed solely at those government agents who may actually invade an individual's constitutionally protected privacy. The courts are not subject to any direct constitutional duty to exclude illegally obtained evidence, because the question of the admissibility of such evidence is not addressed by the Amendment. This view of the scope of the Amendment relegates the judiciary to the periphery. Because the only constitutionally cognizable injury has already been "fully accomplished" by the police by the time a case comes before the courts, the Constitution is not itself violated if the judge decides to admit the tainted evidence. Indeed, the most the judge *can* do is wring his hands and hope that perhaps by excluding such evidence he can deter future transgressions by the police.

Such a reading appears plausible, because, as critics of the exclusionary rule never tire of repeating, the Fourth Amendment makes no express provision for the exclusion of evidence secured in violation of its commands. A short answer to this claim, of course, is that many of the Constitution's most vital imperatives are stated in general terms and the task of giving meaning to these precepts is therefore left to subsequent judicial decisionmaking in the context of concrete cases. * * *

A more direct answer may be supplied by recognizing that the Amendment, like other provisions of the Bill of Rights, restrains the power of the government as a whole; it does not specify only a particular agency and exempt all others. The judiciary is responsible, no less than the executive, for ensuring that constitutional rights are respected.

When that fact is kept in mind, the role of the courts and their possible involvement in the concerns of the Fourth Amendment comes into sharper focus. Because seizures are executed principally to secure evidence, and because such evidence generally has utility in our legal system only in the context of a trial supervised by a judge, it is apparent that the admission of illegally obtained evidence implicates the same constitutional concerns as the initial seizure of that evidence. Indeed, by admitting unlawfully seized evidence, the judiciary becomes a part of what is in fact a single governmental action prohibited by the terms of the Amendment. Once that connection between the evidence-gathering role of the police and the evidence-admitting function of the courts is acknowledged, the plausibility of the Court's interpretation becomes more suspect. Certainly nothing in the language or history of the Fourth Amendment suggests that a recognition of this evidentiary link between the police and the courts was meant to be foreclosed. It is difficult to give any meaning at all to the limitations imposed by the Amendment if they are read to proscribe only certain conduct by the police but to allow other agents of the same government to take advantage of evidence secured by the police in violation of its requirements. The Amendment therefore must be read to condemn not only the initial unconstitutional invasion of privacy—

which is done, after all, for the purpose of securing evidence—but also the subsequent use of any evidence so obtained. * * *

B * * *

* * * [T]he Court * * * has gradually pressed the deterrence rationale for the rule back to center stage. The various arguments advanced by the Court in this campaign have only strengthened my conviction that the deterrence theory is both misguided and unworkable. First, the Court has frequently bewailed the "cost" of excluding reliable evidence. In large part, this criticism rests upon a refusal to acknowledge the function of the Fourth Amendment itself. If nothing else, the Amendment plainly operates to disable the government from gathering information and securing evidence in certain ways. In practical terms, of course, this restriction of official power means that some incriminating evidence inevitably will go undetected if the government obeys these constitutional restraints. It is the loss of that evidence that is the "price" our society pays for enjoying the freedom and privacy safeguarded by the Fourth Amendment. Thus, some criminals will go free *not*, in Justice (then Judge) Cardozo's misleading epigram, "because the constable has blundered," but rather because official compliance with Fourth Amendment requirements makes it more difficult to catch criminals. Understood in this way, the Amendment directly contemplates that some reliable and incriminating evidence will be lost to the government; therefore, it is not the exclusionary rule, but the Amendment itself that has imposed this cost.

In addition, the Court's decisions over the past decade have made plain that the entire enterprise of attempting to assess the benefits and costs of the exclusionary rule in various contexts is a virtually impossible task for the judiciary to perform honestly or accurately. Although the Court's language in those cases suggests that some specific empirical basis may support its analyses, the reality is that the Court's opinions represent inherently unstable compounds of intuition, hunches, and occasional pieces of partial and often inconclusive data. * * *

By remaining within its redoubt of empiricism and by basing the rule solely on the deterrence rationale, the Court has robbed the rule of legitimacy. A doctrine that is explained as if it were an empirical proposition but for which there is only limited empirical support is both inherently unstable and an easy mark for critics. The extent of this Court's fidelity to Fourth Amendment requirements, however, should not turn on such statistical uncertainties. * * *

III

Even if I were to accept the Court's general approach to the exclusionary rule, I could not agree with today's result. * * *

At the outset, the Court suggests that society has been asked to pay a high price—in terms either of setting guilty persons free or of impeding the proper functioning of trials—as a result of excluding relevant physical evidence in cases where the police, in conducting searches and seizing evidence, have made only an "objectively reasonable" mistake concerning the constitutionality of their actions. But what evidence is there to support such a claim?

Significantly, the Court points to none, and, indeed, as the Court acknowledges, recent studies have demonstrated that the "costs" of the exclusionary rule—calculated in terms of dropped prosecutions and lost convictions—are quite low. Contrary to the claims of the rule's critics that exclusion leads to "the release of countless guilty criminals," these studies have demonstrated that federal and state prosecutors very rarely drop cases because of potential search and seizure problems. For example, a 1979 study prepared at the request of Congress by the General Accounting Office reported that only 0.4% of all cases actually declined for prosecution by federal prosecutors were declined primarily because of illegal search problems. If the GAO data are restated as a percentage of *all* arrests, the study shows that only 0.2% of all felony arrests are declined for prosecution because of potential exclusionary rule problems. Of course, these data describe only the costs attributable to the exclusion of evidence in all cases; the costs due to the exclusion of evidence in the narrower category of cases where police have made objectively reasonable mistakes must necessarily be even smaller. The Court, however, ignores this distinction and mistakenly weighs the aggregated costs of exclusion in *all* cases, irrespective of the circumstances that led to exclusion, against the potential benefits associated with only those cases in which evidence is excluded because police reasonably but mistakenly believe that their conduct does not violate the Fourth Amendment. When such faulty scales are used, it is little wonder that the balance tips in favor of restricting the application of the rule.

What then supports the Court's insistence that this evidence be admitted? Apparently, the Court's only answer is that even though the costs of exclusion are not very substantial, the potential deterrent effect in these circumstances is so marginal that exclusion cannot be justified. The key to the Court's conclusion in this respect is its belief that the prospective deterrent effect of the exclusionary rule operates only in those situations in which police officers, when deciding whether to go forward with some particular search, have reason to know that their planned conduct will violate the requirements of the Fourth Amendment. * * *

The flaw in the Court's argument, however, is that its logic captures only one comparatively minor element of the generally acknowledged deterrent purposes of the exclusionary rule. To be sure, the rule operates to some extent to deter future misconduct by individual officers who have had evidence suppressed in their own cases. But what the Court overlooks is that the deterrence rationale for the rule is not designed to be, nor should it be thought of as, a form of "punishment" of individual police officers for their failures to obey the restraints imposed by the Fourth Amendment. Instead, the chief deterrent function of the rule is its tendency to promote institutional compliance with Fourth Amendment requirements on the part of law enforcement agencies generally. Thus, as the Court has previously recognized, "over the long term, [the] demonstration [provided by the exclusionary rule] that our society attaches serious consequences to violation of constitutional rights is thought to encourage those who formulate law enforcement policies, and the officers who implement them, to incorporate Fourth Amendment ideals into their value system." It is only through such an institutionwide mechanism that information concerning Fourth Amendment standards can be effectively communicated to rank-and-file officers.

If the overall educational effect of the exclusionary rule is considered, application of the rule to even those situations in which individual police officers have acted on the basis of a reasonable but mistaken belief that their conduct was authorized can still be expected to have a considerable long-term deterrent effect. If evidence is consistently excluded in these circumstances, police departments will surely be prompted to instruct their officers to devote greater care and attention to providing sufficient information to establish probable cause when applying for a warrant, and to review with some attention the form of the warrant that they have been issued, rather than automatically assuming that whatever document the magistrate has signed will necessarily comport with Fourth Amendment requirements.

After today's decisions, however, that institutional incentive will be lost. * * *

Finally, even if one were to believe, as the Court apparently does, that police are hobbled by inflexible and hypertechnical warrant procedures, today's decisions cannot be justified. This is because, given the relaxed standard for assessing probable cause established just last Term in *Illinois v. Gates*, [p. 150], the Court's newly fashioned good-faith exception, when applied in the warrant context, will rarely, if ever, offer any greater flexibility for police than the *Gates* standard already supplies. In *Gates*, the Court held that "[t]he task of the issuing magistrate is simply to make a practical, common-sense decision whether, given all the circumstances set forth in the affidavit before him, * * * there is a fair probability that contraband or evidence of a crime will be found in a particular place." The task of a reviewing court is confined to determining whether "the magistrate had a 'substantial basis for * * * conclud[ing]' that probable cause existed." Given such a relaxed standard, it is virtually inconceivable that a reviewing court, when faced with a defendant's motion to suppress, could first find that a warrant was invalid under the new *Gates* standard, but then, at the same time, find that a police officer's reliance on such an invalid warrant was nevertheless "objectively reasonable" under the test announced today. Because the two standards overlap so completely, it is unlikely that a warrant could be found invalid under *Gates* and yet the police reliance upon it could be seen as objectively reasonable; otherwise, we would have to entertain the mind-boggling concept of objectively reasonable reliance upon an objectively unreasonable warrant. * * *

Justice STEVENS, [dissenting]. * * *

III * * *

The notion that a police officer's reliance on a magistrate's warrant is automatically appropriate is one the Framers of the Fourth Amendment would have vehemently rejected. The precise problem that the Amendment was intended to address was *the unreasonable issuance of warrants*. As we have often observed, the Amendment was actually motivated by the practice of issuing general warrants—warrants which did not satisfy the particularity and probable-cause requirements. The resentments which led to the Amendment were directed at the issuance of *warrants* unjustified by particularized evidence of wrongdoing. Those who sought to amend the Constitution to include a Bill of Rights repeatedly voiced the view that the evil which had to be addressed was the issuance of warrants on insufficient evidence. * * *

In short, the Framers of the Fourth Amendment were deeply suspicious of warrants; in their minds the paradigm of an abusive search was the execution of a warrant not based on probable cause. The fact that colonial officers had magisterial authorization for their conduct when they engaged in general searches surely did not make their conduct "reasonable." The Court's view that it is consistent with our Constitution to adopt a rule that it is presumptively reasonable to rely on a defective warrant is the product of constitutional amnesia.

IV * * *

* * * [T]he Court's creation of a double standard of reasonableness inevitably must erode the deterrence rationale that still supports the exclusionary rule. But we should not ignore the way it tarnishes the role of the judiciary in enforcing the Constitution. * * * Today, for the first time, this Court holds that although the Constitution has been violated, no court should do anything about it at any time and in any proceeding. In my judgment, the Constitution requires more. * * *

We could, of course, facilitate the process of administering justice to those who violate the criminal laws by ignoring the commands of the Fourth Amendment—indeed, by ignoring the entire Bill of Rights—but it is the very purpose of a Bill of Rights to identify values that may not be sacrificed to expediency. In a just society those who govern, as well as those who are governed, must obey the law. * * *

NOTES AND QUESTIONS

1. In Herring v. United States, 555 U.S. ___, 129 S.Ct. 695, 172 L.Ed.2d 496 (2009), the Supreme Court, while summarizing the holding of *Leon*, provided a worthwhile warning about the "good faith" label typically attached to the case:

When police act under a warrant that is invalid for lack of probable cause, the exclusionary rule does not apply if the police acted "in objectively reasonable reliance" on the subsequently invalidated search warrant. We (perhaps confusingly) called this objectively reasonable reliance "good faith."

2.   Who has the better side of the "good-faith" exclusionary rule argument, the majority or the dissenters in *Leon*?

The *Leon* rule has been rejected by various state courts, applying their own constitutions or statutes. See 1 Joshua Dressler & Alan C. Michaels, Understanding Criminal Procedure 389 n.137 (4th ed. 2006) (citing cases from Connecticut, Delaware, Georgia, Idaho, Iowa, Montana, New Hampshire, New Jersey, New Mexico, New York, North Carolina, Pennsylvania, South Carolina, and Vermont).

3.   The Supreme Court applied the "good faith" exception in a second case decided along with *Leon*. In Massachusetts v. Sheppard, 468 U.S. 981, 104 S.Ct. 3424, 82 L.Ed.2d 737 (1984), the Court permitted introduction of evidence obtained from a search conducted pursuant to a warrant that violated the Fourth Amendment particularity requirement. The Court explained how the problem arose:

> Because it was Sunday, the local court was closed, and the police had a difficult time finding a warrant application form. Detective O'Malley finally found a warrant form previously in use in the Dorchester District. The form was entitled "Search Warrant—Controlled Substance G. L. c. 276 §§ 1 through 3A." Realizing that some changes had to be made before the form could be used to authorize the search requested in the affidavit, Detective O'Malley deleted the subtitle "controlled substance" with a typewriter. He also substituted "Roxbury" for the printed "Dorchester" and typed Sheppard's name and address into blank spaces provided for that information. However, the reference to "controlled substance" was not deleted in the portion of the form that constituted the warrant application and that, when signed, would constitute the warrant itself.

> Detective O'Malley then took the affidavit and the warrant form to the residence of a judge who had consented to consider the warrant application. The judge examined the affidavit and stated that he would authorize the search as requested. Detective O'Malley offered the warrant form and stated that he knew the form as presented dealt with controlled substances. He showed the judge where he had crossed out the subtitles. After unsuccessfully searching for a more suitable form, the judge informed O'Malley that he would make the necessary changes so as to provide a proper search warrant. The judge then took the form, made some changes on it, and dated and signed the warrant. However, he did not change the substantive portion of the warrant, which continued to authorize a search for controlled substances; nor did he alter the form so as to incorporate the affidavit. The judge returned the affidavit and the warrant to O'Malley, informing him that the warrant was sufficient authority in form and content to carry out the search as requested. O'Malley took the two documents and, accompanied by other officers, proceeded to Sheppard's residence.

Although the warrant that was executed violated the Fourth Amendment, the Supreme Court concluded that the officers executing the warrant, which included Detective O'Malley, acted in objective good-faith.

The officers in this case took every step that could reasonably be expected of them. Detective O'Malley prepared an affidavit which was reviewed and approved by the District Attorney. He presented that affidavit to a neutral judge. The judge concluded that the affidavit established probable cause * * *. He was told by the judge that the necessary changes would be made. He then observed the judge make some changes and received the warrant and the affidavit. At this point, a reasonable police officer would have concluded, as O'Malley did, that the warrant authorized a search for the materials outlined in the affidavit.

Sheppard contends that since O'Malley knew the warrant form was defective, he should have examined it to make sure that the necessary changes had been made. However, that argument is based on the premise that O'Malley had a duty to disregard the judge's assurances that the requested search would be authorized and the necessary changes would be made. Whatever an officer may be required to do when he executes a warrant without knowing beforehand what items are to be seized,[6] we refuse to rule that an officer is required to disbelieve a judge who has just advised him, by word and by action, that the warrant he possesses authorizes him to conduct the search he has requested.

4. In *Sheppard* (Note 3), the Court determined that evidence seized pursuant to a defective warrant—invalid due to violation of the particularity clause of the Fourth Amendment—was admissible because the police acted in reasonable, good-faith reliance on the warrant. In contrast, consider Groh v. Ramirez, 540 U.S. 551, 124 S.Ct. 1284, 157 L.Ed.2d 1068 (2004), in which a federal agent prepared and signed an application for a warrant to search Ramirez's Montana ranch for specified weapons, explosives, and records. The agent supported the application with a detailed affidavit setting forth the agent's belief that the specified items were on the ranch. In turn, the affidavit was accompanied by a warrant form that an agent completed for the magistrate. However, in the portion of the warrant calling for a description of the "person or property" to be seized, the agent wrote only: "[T]here is now concealed [on the specified premises] a certain person or property, namely [a] single dwelling residence two story in height which is blue in color and has two additions attached to the east. The front entrance to the residence faces a southerly direction." Thus, the warrant failed entirely to specify the items to be seized; nor did the warrant incorporate by reference the itemized list of seizable items contained in the warrant application. The magistrate signed the warrant, after which agents executed the search, but discovered none of

---

6. Normally, when an officer who has not been involved in the application stage receives a warrant, he will read it in order to determine the object of the search. In this case, Detective O'Malley, the officer who directed the search, knew what items were listed in the affidavit presented to the judge, and he had good reason to believe that the warrant authorized the seizure of those items. Whether an officer who is less familiar with the warrant application or who has unalleviated concerns about the proper scope of the search would be justified in failing to notice a defect like the one in the warrant in this case is an issue we need not decide. We hold only that it was not unreasonable for the police in this case to rely on the judge's assurances that the warrant authorized the search they had requested.

the items they intended to seize. Ramirez brought suit for violation of his Fourth Amendment rights.

Justice Stevens, writing for five justices (including the now retired Justice O'Connor), determined that the warrant was "plainly invalid" in that it "failed altogether" to comply with the particularity requirement of the Fourth Amendment. Indeed, the majority stated, the warrant here "was so obviously deficient that we must regard the search as 'warrantless' within the meaning of our case law." Although the ultimate issue in the case was whether, in light of the Fourth Amendment violation, the agents were entitled to qualified immunity in Ramirez's civil action, the answer to *that* question led the justices to discuss the *Leon-Sheppard* rule. The majority opinion essentially suggested that, unlike in *Sheppard*, had evidence been seized at the ranch, it would have been excluded in a criminal prosecution of Ramirez.

Why would the evidence have been excluded here when it was *not* suppressed in *Sheppard*? The Court explained:

> In [*Sheppard*] we suggested that "the judge, not the police officers," may have committed "[a]n error of constitutional dimension," because the judge had assured the officers requesting the warrant that he would take the steps necessary to conform the warrant to constitutional require- ments. Thus, "it was not unreasonable for the police in [that] case to rely on the judge's assurances * * *." In this case, by contrast, [the agent] did not alert the Magistrate to the defect in the warrant that [he] drafted, and we therefore cannot know whether the Magistrate was aware of the scope of the search he was authorizing. Nor would it have been reason- able for petitioner to rely on that warrant that was so patently defective, even if the Magistrate was aware of the deficiency. See *United States v. Leon*.

5. According to *Illinois v. Gates*, a "probable cause" determination is a matter of "practical, common-sense" decisionmaking. In view of this stan- dard, is Professor LaFave correct when he observes that "a probable cause determination which is erroneous and thus lacking this sagaciousness is undeserving of * * * the appellation 'good faith' * * * "? Wayne R. LaFave, *Fourth Amendment Vagaries (Of Improbable Cause, Imperceptible Plain View, Notorious Privacy, and Balancing Askew)*, 74 J. Crim. L. & Criminology 1171, 1199 (1983).

Notwithstanding LaFave's observation, the Court in *Leon* ruled that the officers' reliance on the magistrate's erroneous determination of probable cause was objectively reasonable. In view of the *Gates* standard, how can this be?

According to *Leon*, when may an officer *not* reasonably rely on a magis- trate's probable cause determination?

6. Is the *Leon* standard exclusively objective, or are there circumstances in which a court may inquire into the thought processes of the officers seeking or executing a warrant? For example, suppose that an officer takes her warrant affidavit to the prosecutor for a legal judgment of its sufficiency. The prosecutor unequivocally states that it fails to show probable cause. Although

the officer now believes that the affidavit is inadequate, she applies for a warrant anyway, "just in case" she finds a sympathetic magistrate. Based on the same affidavit, a magistrate improperly issues a warrant. In determining whether the *Leon* exception to the exclusionary rule applies, is the officer's visit to the prosecutor relevant? If so, may defense counsel inquire into the officer's reasons for seeking a warrant despite the advice? May the lawyer elicit testimony, for example, that the officer had doubted that she had probable cause, but went ahead because she believed that the magistrate was "police-friendly"? See 1 Wayne R. LaFave, Search and Seizure 71–73 (4th ed. 2004).

7. Does the *Leon* exception apply if a magistrate signs a warrant without looking at the supporting affidavit? What if she skims the affidavit and signs the warrant five seconds later?

8. *Problem.* Based on a solid tip from an experienced police informant, *O* drafted an affidavit and search warrant for signature, and contacted *J*, a Superior Court judge, by telephone. Based on *O*'s representations of what was in the affidavit, *J* promised to sign the warrant as soon as *O* came to his chambers. When *O* arrived, he could not find *J*. Therefore, *O* called *M*, a retired judge, but one who had served as an Acting Judge on occasion at the specific order of the Presiding Judge. *M* had previously signed warrants for *O* in this capacity. *M* signed the warrant, although he lacked authority from the Presiding Judge to do so. *O* executed the invalid warrant. Does the *Leon* exception apply? United States v. Scott, 260 F.3d 512 (6th Cir.2001).

9. *Problem.* At the behest of the police, *I*, a confidential and reliable informant, entered *D*'s home and purchased drugs from *D* while the police observed from outside the home and thereafter confirmed the sale. *I* also told the police after the sale that he observed firearms and a stash of drugs in *D*'s house. Based on this information, the police prepared an affidavit, to apply for a warrant to search *D*'s house. They showed the affidavit to a county prosecutor, who signed off on it. The affidavit supporting the warrant indicated that *I* had purchased drugs, but failed to name *D* as the seller, nor did it state that the purchase occurred in *D*'s home. As for the firearms and stash of drugs, the affidavit stated that *I* observed the items in *D*'s home, but the affidavit did not indicate how or when *I* made these observations. Based on this affidavit, a magistrate issued a warrant. The police executed the warrant, and seized drugs and firearms from *D*'s home. In your view, is the warrant valid? If not, why not? If it is not valid, should the evidence be excluded, or admitted under *Leon*? United States v. Laughton, 409 F.3d 744 (6th Cir. 2005).

10. *The "good-faith" exception in non-warrant cases.* The "good faith" exception announced in *Leon* only applies to searches conducted with a warrant. Do the arguments in support of an exception to the exclusionary rule apply, however, with equal vigor in *non*-warrant cases? What does the language and reasoning of Justice White's opinion suggest to you?

We will return to this issue shortly. (See p. 525.)

c. Knock-and-Announce Rule

HUDSON v. MICHIGAN

Supreme Court of the United States, 2006.
547 U.S. 586, 126 S.Ct. 2159, 165 L.Ed.2d 56.

[See p. 509 for the text of this case.]

4. SCOPE OF THE EXCLUSIONARY RULE

a. In General

SILVERTHORNE LUMBER COMPANY
v. UNITED STATES

Supreme Court of the United States, 1920.
251 U.S. 385, 40 S.Ct. 182, 64 L.Ed. 319.

MR. JUSTICE HOLMES delivered the opinion of the court. * * *

The facts are simple. An indictment upon a single specific charge having been brought against the two Silverthornes mentioned, they both were arrested at their homes early in the morning of February 25, 1919, and were detained in custody a number of hours. While they were thus detained representatives of the Department of Justice and the United States marshal without a shadow of authority went to the office of their company and made a clean sweep of all the books, papers and documents found there. * * * An application was made as soon as might be to the District Court for a return of what thus had been taken unlawfully. It was opposed by the District Attorney * * *. * * * The District Court * * * found that all the papers had been seized in violation of the parties' constitutional rights. * * * The Government now, while in form repudiating and condemning the illegal seizure, seeks to maintain its right to avail itself of the knowledge obtained by that means which otherwise it would not have had.

The proposition could not be presented more nakedly. It is that although of course its seizure was an outrage which the Government now regrets, it may study the papers before it returns them, copy them, and then may use the knowledge [against the Silverthornes] * * *; that the protection of the Constitution covers the physical possession but not any advantages that the Government can gain over the object of its pursuit by doing the forbidden act. * * * In our opinion such is not the law. It reduces the Fourth Amendment to a form of words. The essence of a provision forbidding the acquisition of evidence in a certain way is that not merely evidence so acquired shall not be used before the Court but that it shall not be used at all. Of course this does not mean that the facts thus obtained become sacred and inaccessible. If knowledge of them is gained from an independent source they may be proved like any others, but the knowledge gained by the Government's own wrong cannot be used by it in the way proposed. * * *

N OTES AND Q UESTIONS

1. The scope of the exclusionary rule was stated this way in Walder v. United States, 347 U.S. 62, 74 S.Ct. 354, 98 L.Ed. 503 (1954):

> The Government cannot violate the Fourth Amendment * * * and use the fruits of such unlawful conduct to secure a conviction. *Nor can the Government make indirect use of such evidence for its case, or support a conviction on evidence obtained through leads from the unlawfully obtained evidence.* All these methods are outlawed, and convictions obtained by means of them are invalidated, because they encourage the kind of society that is obnoxious to free men. (Emphasis added.)

Thus, the suggestion here is that if the police seize item A, in violation of the Fourth Amendment, they may also not use item B if it is a fruit of the initial violation (a fruit of a poisonous tree.) But, read on.

2. The fruit-of-the-poisonous-tree doctrine is not as simple and straightforward as Note 1 might suggest. First, as noted in dictum at the end of *Silverthorne*, there is the "independent source" doctrine. Even if the defendant *was* the victim of a Fourth Amendment violation, perhaps the particular piece of evidence that she seeks to suppress was obtained lawfully. In other words, perhaps there *is* a poisonous tree, but *this* fruit comes from a different, *un*poisoned tree. This doctrine and the related "inevitable discovery" (or "hypothetical independent source") rule, are considered in subsection b. below.

Second, even if a particular piece of evidence *is* a fruit of the poisonous tree, i.e., does not come from an independent source, it may still be admissible, notwithstanding the sweeping italicized language in the *Walder* excerpt in Note 1. As Justice Frankfurter explained in Nardone v. United States, 308 U.S. 338, 60 S.Ct. 266, 84 L.Ed. 307 (1939), "[s]ophisticated argument may prove a causal connection between information obtained through illicit [police conduct] and the Government's proof. As a matter of good sense, however, such connection may have become so attenuated as to dissipate the taint." At some point, in other words, the law stops looking backwards in time and essentially says, "enough is enough, we are prepared to eat this fruit," i.e., to allow use of the secondary evidence at trial. We consider this attenuation factor in subsection c. below.

3. *Some help.* In analyzing any fruit-of-the-poisonous-tree case, study the facts carefully to: (a) identify the "tree" (the constitutional violation); (b) the fruit (the evidence the government seeks to introduce); (c) determine whether (b) comes from (a) (is there a causal link?); and (d) if the fruit *did* come from a poisonous tree, identify any facts that may justify the conclusion that the poison from the fruit has dissipated (the "attenuation" doctrine).

b. "Independent Source" and "Inevitable Discovery" Doctrines

MURRAY v. UNITED STATES

Supreme Court of the United States, 1988.
487 U.S. 533, 108 S.Ct. 2529, 101 L.Ed.2d 472.

J<small>USTICE</small> S<small>CALIA</small> delivered the opinion of the Court.

I

* * * [T]he facts are as follows: Based on information received from informants, federal law enforcement agents had been surveilling petitioner Murray and several of his co-conspirators. At about 1:45 p.m. on April 6, 1983, they observed Murray drive a truck and Carter drive a green camper, into a warehouse in South Boston. When the petitioners drove the vehicles out about 20 minutes later, the surveilling agents saw within the warehouse two individuals and a tractor-trailer rig bearing a long, dark container. Murray and [petitioner] Carter later turned over the truck and camper to other drivers, who were in turn followed and ultimately arrested, and the vehicles lawfully seized. Both vehicles were found to contain marijuana.

After receiving this information, several of the agents converged on the South Boston warehouse and forced entry. They found the warehouse unoccupied, but observed in plain view numerous burlap-wrapped bales that were later found to contain marijuana. They left without disturbing the bales, kept the warehouse under surveillance, and did not reenter it until they had a search warrant. In applying for the warrant, the agents did not mention the prior entry, and did not rely on any observations made during that entry. When the warrant was issued—at 10:40 p.m., approximately eight hours after the initial entry—the agents immediately reentered the warehouse and seized 270 bales of marijuana and notebooks listing customers for whom the bales were destined.

Before trial, petitioners moved to suppress the evidence found in the warehouse. The District Court denied the motion, rejecting petitioners' arguments that the warrant was invalid because the agents did not inform the Magistrate about their prior warrantless entry, and that the warrant was tainted by that entry. The First Circuit affirmed, assuming for purposes of its decision that the first entry into the warehouse was unlawful. * * *

II * * *

Almost simultaneously with our development of the exclusionary rule, in the first quarter of this century, we also announced what has come to be known as the "independent source" doctrine. *See Silverthorne Lumber Co. v. United States* [p. 494]. * * * The dispute here is over the scope of this doctrine. Petitioners contend that it applies only to evidence obtained for the first time during an independent lawful search. The Government argues that it applies also to evidence initially discovered during, or as a consequence of, an unlawful search, but later obtained independently from activities untainted by the initial illegality. We think the Government's view has better support in both precedent and policy.

Our cases have used the concept of "independent source" in a more general and a more specific sense. The more general sense identifies *all* evidence acquired in a fashion untainted by the illegal evidence-gathering activity. Thus, where an unlawful entry has given investigators knowledge of facts x and y, but fact z has been learned by other means, fact z can be said to be admissible because derived from an "independent source." This is how we used the term in *Segura v. United States*[, 468 U.S. 796, 104 S.Ct. 3380, 82 L.Ed.2d 599 (1984)]. In that case, agents unlawfully entered the defendant's apartment and remained there until a search warrant was obtained. The admissibility of what they discovered while waiting in the apartment was not before us, but we held that the evidence found for the first time during the execution of the valid and untainted search warrant was admissible because it was discovered pursuant to an "independent source."

The original use of the term, however, and its more important use for purposes of these cases, was more specific. It was originally applied in the exclusionary rule context, [in *Silverthorne*,] with reference to that particular category of evidence acquired by an untainted search *which is identical to the evidence unlawfully acquired*—that is, in the example just given, to knowledge of facts x and y derived from an independent source * * *.
* * *

Petitioners' asserted policy basis for excluding evidence which is initially discovered during an illegal search, but is subsequently acquired through an independent and lawful source, is that a contrary rule will remove all deterrence to, and indeed positively encourage, unlawful police searches. As petitioners see the incentives, law enforcement officers will routinely enter without a warrant to make sure that what they expect to be on the premises is in fact there. If it is not, they will have spared themselves the time and trouble of getting a warrant; if it is, they can get the warrant and use the evidence despite the unlawful entry. We see the incentives differently. An officer with probable cause sufficient to obtain a search warrant would be foolish to enter the premises first in an unlawful manner. By doing so, he would risk suppression of all evidence on the premises, both seen and unseen, since his action would add to the normal burden of convincing a magistrate that there is probable cause the much more onerous burden of convincing a trial court that no information gained from the illegal entry affected either the law enforcement officers' decision to seek a warrant or the magistrate's decision to grant it. Nor would the officer *without* sufficient probable cause to obtain a search warrant have any added incentive to conduct an unlawful entry, since whatever he finds cannot be used to establish probable cause before a magistrate.[2] * * *

III

To apply what we have said to the present cases: Knowledge that the marijuana was in the warehouse was assuredly acquired at the time of the unlawful entry. But it was also acquired at the time of entry pursuant to the warrant, and if that later acquisition was not the result of the earlier entry there is no reason why the independent source doctrine should not apply. Invoking the exclusionary rule would put the police (and society) not in the *same* position they would have occupied if no violation occurred, but in a *worse* one.

We think this is also true with respect to the tangible evidence, the bales of marijuana. * * * So long as a later, lawful seizure is genuinely independent of an earlier, tainted one (which may well be difficult to establish where the seized goods are kept in the police's possession) there is no reason why the independent source doctrine should not apply.

The ultimate question, therefore, is whether the search pursuant to warrant was in fact a genuinely independent source of the information and tangible evidence at issue here. This would not have been the case if the agents' decision to seek the warrant was prompted by what they had seen during the initial entry,[3] or if information obtained during that entry was presented to the Magistrate and affected his decision to issue the warrant. * * *

Accordingly, we vacate the judgment and remand these cases to the Court of Appeals with instructions that it remand to the District Court for determination whether the warrant-authorized search of the warehouse was an independent source of the challenged evidence in the sense we have described. * * *

Justice BRENNAN and Justice KENNEDY took no part in the consideration or decision of these cases.

---

2. Justice Marshall argues, in effect, that where the police cannot point to some historically verifiable fact demonstrating that the subsequent search pursuant to a warrant was wholly unaffected by the prior illegal search—*e.g.*, that they had already sought the warrant before entering the premises—we should adopt a *per se* rule of inadmissibility. We do not believe that such a prophylactic exception to the independent source rule is necessary. To say that a district court must be satisfied that a warrant would have been sought without the illegal entry is not to give dispositive effect to police officers' assurances on the point. Where the facts render those assurances implausible, the independent source doctrine will not apply. * * *

3. Justice Marshall argues that "the relevant question [is] whether, even if the initial entry uncovered no evidence, the officers would return immediately with a warrant to conduct a second search." We do not see how this is "relevant" at all. To determine whether the warrant was independent of the illegal entry, one must ask whether it would have been sought even if what actually happened had not occurred—not whether it would have been sought if something else had happened. That is to say, what counts is whether the actual illegal search had any effect in producing the warrant, not whether some hypothetical illegal search would have aborted the warrant. * * *

Justice MARSHALL, with whom Justice STEVENS and Justice O'CONNOR join, dissenting. * * *

* * * In holding that the independent source exception may apply to the facts of these cases, I believe the Court loses sight of the practical moorings of the independent source exception and creates an affirmative incentive for unconstitutional searches. * * *

Under the circumstances of these cases, the admission of the evidence "reseized" during the second search severely undermines the deterrence function of the exclusionary rule. Indeed, admission in these cases affirmatively encourages illegal searches. The incentives for such illegal conduct are clear. Obtaining a warrant is inconvenient and time consuming. Even when officers have probable cause to support a warrant application, therefore, they have an incentive first to determine whether it is worthwhile to obtain a warrant. Probable cause is much less than certainty, and many "confirmatory" searches will result in the discovery that no evidence is present, thus saving the police the time and trouble of getting a warrant. If contraband is discovered, however, the officers may later seek a warrant to shield the evidence from the taint of the illegal search. The police thus know in advance that they have little to lose and much to gain by forgoing the bother of obtaining a warrant and undertaking an illegal search.

The Court, however, "see[s] the incentives differently." Under the Court's view, today's decision does not provide an incentive for unlawful searches, because the officer undertaking the search would know that "his action would add to the normal burden of convincing a magistrate that there is probable cause the much more onerous burden of convincing a trial court that no information gained from the illegal entry affected either the law enforcement officers' decision to seek a warrant or the magistrate's decision to grant it." The Court, however, provides no hint of why this risk would actually seem significant to the officers. Under the circumstances of these cases, the officers committing the illegal search have both knowledge and control of the factors central to the trial court's determination. First, it is a simple matter, as was done in these cases, to exclude from the warrant application any information gained from the initial entry so that the magistrate's determination of probable cause is not influenced by the prior illegal search. Second, today's decision makes the application of the independent source exception turn entirely on an evaluation of the officers' intent. It normally will be difficult for the trial court to verify, or the defendant to rebut, an assertion by officers that they always intended to obtain a warrant, regardless of the results of the illegal search.[2] The testimony of the officers conducting the illegal search

---

2. Such an intent-based rule is of dubious value for other reasons as well. First, the intent of the officers prior to the illegal entry often will be of little significance to the relevant question: whether, even if the initial entry uncovered no evidence, the officers would return immediately with a warrant to conduct a second search. Officers who have probable cause to believe contraband is present genuinely might intend later to obtain a warrant, but after the illegal search uncovers no such contraband, those same officers might decide their time is better spent than to return with a warrant. In addition, such an intent rule will be difficult to apply. The Court fails to describe how a trial court will properly evaluate whether the law enforcement officers fully intended to obtain a warrant regardless of what they discovered during the illegal

is the only direct evidence of intent, and the defendant will be relegated simply to arguing that the officers should not be believed. Under these circumstances, the litigation risk described by the Court seems hardly a risk at all; it does not significantly dampen the incentive to conduct the initial illegal search.* * *

* * * In the instant cases, there are no "demonstrated historical facts" capable of supporting a finding that the subsequent warrant search was wholly unaffected by the prior illegal search. The same team of investigators was involved in both searches. The warrant was obtained immediately after the illegal search, and no effort was made to obtain a warrant prior to the discovery of the marijuana during the illegal search. The only evidence available that the warrant search was wholly independent is the testimony of the agents who conducted the illegal search. Under these circumstances, the threat that the subsequent search was tainted by the illegal search is too great to allow for the application of the independent source exception.[4] The Court's contrary holding lends itself to easy abuse, and offers an incentive to bypass the constitutional requirement that probable cause be assessed by a neutral and detached magistrate before the police invade an individual's privacy. * * *

In sum, under circumstances as are presented in these cases, when the very law enforcement officers who participate in an illegal search immediately thereafter obtain a warrant to search the same premises, I believe the evidence discovered during the initial illegal entry must be suppressed. Any other result emasculates the Warrant Clause and provides an intolerable incentive for warrantless searches. * * *

[The dissenting opinion of Justice Stevens is omitted.]

Notes and Questions

1. In *Murray*, the failure of the police to inform the magistrate of their unlawful confirmatory search strengthened their Fourth Amendment claim by avoiding possible taint in the warrant process. But, should an officer have a duty of candor that is violated by such non-disclosure when he seeks a warrant?

2. In *Murray*, suppose that a police officer had testified at the suppression hearing, "We were sure we had probable cause, so we planned on getting a warrant, but we were kinda worried that the defendants were going to come back and destroy the evidence. So, we went in, just in case, and then, when we

---

search. The obvious question is whose intent is relevant? Intentions clearly may differ both among supervisory officers and among officers who initiate the illegal search.

4. To conclude that the initial search had no effect on the decision to obtain a warrant, and thus that the warrant search was an "independent source" of the challenged evidence, one would have to assume that even if the officers entered the premises and discovered no contraband, they nonetheless would have gone to the Magistrate, sworn that they had probable cause to believe that contraband was in the building, and then returned to conduct another search. Although such a scenario is possible, I believe it is more plausible to believe that the officers would not have chosen to return immediately to the premises with a warrant to search for evidence had they not discovered evidence during the initial search.

saw we were wrong about the emergency, we went for the warrant. But, sure, if we had found nothing in the warehouse, we would not have applied for a warrant. Why would we have?'' According to Justice Scalia, based on this testimony, would the independent source doctrine apply? Should it?

3. Consider Craig M. Bradley, *Murray v. United States: The Bell Tolls for the Search Warrant Requirement*, 64 Ind. L.J. 907, 915–18 (1989):

> The pertinent question to ask about whether the exclusionary rule should be applied in a questionable case is not whether its operation would put the police in a worse position or whether the evidence would have been found "but for" the violation, but whether the operation of the rule would serve to deter the infraction in question. * * *

> Absent a clear rule that "evidence found on violated premises *must always* be suppressed," trial courts will be loath to suppress bales of marijuana, kilos of cocaine, and murder weapons when police make a colorable showing of pre-existing probable cause. This is why the Court has always recognized the need for a clear search warrant requirement * * *.

> While *Murray* will encourage the police to find evidence without a warrant, the most serious problem caused by the decision affects the innocent rather than the guilty. The purpose of the warrant requirement is not to slow the police down in their pursuit of the guilty, but to require that the decision of a "neutral and detached magistrate" is interposed between the police's impulse to search and their action on that impulse.

> * * * When * * * [non-exigent] warrantless searches are allowed to occur without any exclusionary sanction attaching, as in *Murray*, it greatly increases the chance that the police will search the innocent.

> Consider the position of the rational police officer. Assume that it is true, as the Court avers, that if he has ample probable cause and ample time, he will go ahead and get a warrant in order to avoid the additional explanations that a warrantless search will entail. But suppose, as is frequently the case, that his probable cause is shaky or nonexistent. *Murray* positively encourages him to proceed with an illegal search. If he finds nothing, he simply shrugs his shoulders and walks away. If he finds evidence, he leaves his partner to watch over it, repairs to the magistrate, and reports that "an anonymous reliable informant who has given information on three occasions in the past that has led to convictions called to tell me that he had just seen bales of marijuana stored at a warehouse at 123 Elm Street." The warrant issues and the marijuana is seized. Before trial (assuming that the defense has found out about the illegal search), the officer admits it, chalks it up to a fear that the evidence would be lost if the warehouse were not immediately secured, apologizes for being wrong in this assessment, and introduces the warrant affidavit to demonstrate an independent source. The Court, in allowing such behavior, has missed the point of the warrant requirement and the exclusionary rule—that it "reduce[s] the Fourth Amendment to a nullity" to allow warrantless searches to go unpunished. * * *

Of course, it has always been the case that the police could make up the existence of "Old Reliable," the informant, and use his fictitious "tip" as the basis for a search warrant. The problem with this tactic is that, if the police are wrong and no evidence is found, they are forced to return to the magistrate empty-handed. This is embarrassing to the police department and would only have to happen a few times before the magistrates and defense attorneys would realize that the police were liars. After *Murray*, there is no such fear, because the fictitious "Old Reliable" will *always be right!* His "tip" will always lead to evidence because the police will have found it in advance.

4. *Inevitable discovery doctrine.* In Nix v. Williams, 467 U.S. 431, 104 S.Ct. 2501, 81 L.Ed.2d 377 (1984), Williams was arraigned for the abduction of Pamela Powers, a 10–year-old girl who disappeared from a YMCA building in Des Moines, Iowa, where she had accompanied her parents to observe a sporting event. While in custody, the police subjected Williams to a so-called "Christian Burial Speech" that motivated him to lead authorities to the victim's body, so that she could receive a "Christian burial." At the time, a search for her body was underway and one search team was within two-and-a-half miles of the victim, but the search effort was called off when Williams agreed to cooperate. Williams was convicted of first-degree murder, in part based on his incriminating statements to the police while leading them to the body.

Williams appealed his conviction. As examined in *Brewer v. Williams* [p. 703], the Supreme Court overturned the conviction because the police violated Williams's Sixth Amendment right to counsel when they conducted the Christian Burial Speech. Consequently, at Williams's second trial, the Government was not permitted to introduce the defendant's statements to the police, nor did they seek to show that Williams led the police to the body, but they presented evidence of the condition of the victim's body when it was found, as well as articles and photographs of her clothing, and the results of post mortem medical and chemical tests on the body, all of which were concededly a fruit of the poisonous Sixth Amendment tree.

Because the Government could not show that they found the body independently, the independent-source doctrine was unavailable. Instead, it reasoned that, if the search had *not* been suspended and Williams had *not* led the police to the victim, her body would inevitably have been discovered in essentially the same condition within a short time. Therefore, the Government argued, the contested evidence should be admissible.

The Supreme Court unanimously agreed that the fruit-of-the-poisonous-tree doctrine (here, the Sixth Amendment version, but similarly pursuant to the Fourth Amendment) is subject to an "inevitable discovery" rule. As the Court put the rule: "If the prosecution can establish * * * that the information ultimately or inevitably would have been discovered by lawful means— here the volunteers' search—then the deterrence rationale has so little basis that the evidence should be received." If it were otherwise, the Court concluded, the Government would be put in a worse position than if no illegality had transpired.

What divided the *Williams* Court is whether the Government should carry a heavier burden to prove inevitable discovery than when it claims an independent source. Seven justices ruled that the same burden of proof—preponderance of the evidence—applies in both circumstances. Justices Brennan and Marshall felt a higher burden should be placed on the Government when evidence, in fact, is a fruit of the poisonous tree:

> The inevitable discovery exception necessarily implicates a hypothetical finding that differs in kind from the factual finding that precedes application of the independent source rule. To ensure that this hypothetical finding is narrowly confined to circumstances that are functionally equivalent to an independent source, and to protect fully the fundamental rights served by the exclusionary rule, [we] would require clear and convincing evidence before concluding that the government had met its burden of proof on this issue.

5. *But, wait!* There is more to be said about the independent-source doctrine, thanks to *Hudson v. Michigan*, to which we will turn very shortly (p. 509). Before that, however, we need to consider the attenuation doctrine, to which we *now* turn.

c. "Attenuation" (or "Dissipation of Taint") Doctrine

WONG SUN v. UNITED STATES

Supreme Court of the United States, 1963.
371 U.S. 471, 83 S.Ct. 407, 9 L.Ed.2d 441.

MR. JUSTICE BRENNAN delivered the opinion of the Court. * * *

About 2 a.m. on the morning of June 4, 1959, federal narcotics agents in San Francisco, after having had one Hom Way under surveillance for six weeks, arrested him and found heroin in his possession. Hom Way, who had not before been an informant, stated after his arrest that he had bought an ounce of heroin the night before from one known to him only as "Blackie Toy," proprietor of a laundry on Leavenworth Street.

About 6 a.m. that morning six or seven federal agents went to a laundry at 1733 Leavenworth Street. The sign above the door of this establishment said "Oye's Laundry." It was operated by the petitioner James Wah Toy. There is, however, nothing in the record which identifies James Wah Toy and "Blackie Toy" as the same person. The other federal officers remained nearby out of sight while Agent Alton Wong, who was of Chinese ancestry, rang the bell. When petitioner Toy appeared and opened the door, Agent Wong told him that he was calling for laundry and dry cleaning. Toy replied that he didn't open until 8 o'clock and told the agent to come back at that time. Toy started to close the door. Agent Wong thereupon took his badge from his pocket and said, "I am a federal narcotics agent." Toy immediately "slammed the door and started running" down the hallway through the laundry to his living quarters at the back where his wife and child were sleeping in a bedroom. Agent Wong and the other federal officers broke open the door and followed Toy down the hallway to the living quarters and into the bedroom. Toy reached into a nightstand drawer. Agent Wong thereupon drew his pistol, pulled Toy's hand out of the drawer, placed him under arrest and handcuffed him. There was nothing in the drawer and a search of the premises uncovered no narcotics.

One of the agents said to Toy " * * * [Hom Way] says he got narcotics from you." Toy responded, "No, I haven't been selling any narcotics at all. However, I do know somebody who has." When asked who that was, Toy said, "I only know him as Johnny. I don't know his last name." However, Toy described a house on Eleventh Avenue where he said Johnny lived; he also described a bedroom in the house where he said "Johnny kept about a piece" [an ounce—Eds.] of heroin, and where he and Johnny had smoked some of the drug the night before. The agents left immediately for Eleventh Avenue and located the house. They entered and found one Johnny Yee in the bedroom. After a discussion with the agents, Yee took from a bureau drawer several tubes containing in all just less than one ounce of heroin, and surrendered them. Within the hour Yee and Toy were taken to the Office of the Bureau of Narcotics. Yee there stated that the heroin had been brought to him some four days earlier by petitioner Toy and another Chinese known to him only as "Sea Dog."

Toy was questioned as to the identity of "Sea Dog" and said that "Sea Dog" was Wong Sun. Some agents, including Agent Alton Wong, took Toy to Wong Sun's neighborhood where Toy pointed out a multifamily dwelling where he said Wong Sun lived. Agent Wong rang a downstairs door bell and a buzzer sounded, opening the door. The officer identified himself as a narcotics agent to a woman on the landing and asked "for Mr. Wong." The woman was the wife of petitioner Wong Sun. She said that Wong Sun was "in the back room sleeping." Alton Wong and some six other officers climbed the stairs and entered the apartment. One of the officers went into the back room and brought petitioner Wong Sun from the bedroom in handcuffs. A thorough search of the apartment followed, but no narcotics were discovered.

Petitioner Toy and Johnny Yee were arraigned before a United States Commissioner on June 4 on a complaint charging a violation of 21 U.S.C. § 174. Later that day, each was released on his own recognizance. Petitioner Wong Sun was arraigned on a similar complaint filed the next day and was also released on his own recognizance. Within a few days, both petitioners and Yee were interrogated at the office of the Narcotics Bureau by Agent William Wong, also of Chinese ancestry. The agent advised each of the three of his right to withhold information which might be used against him, and stated to each that he was entitled to the advice of counsel, though it does not appear that any attorney was present during the questioning of any of the three. The officer also explained to each that no promises or offers of immunity or leniency were being or could be made.

The agent interrogated each of the three separately. After each had been interrogated the agent prepared a statement in English from rough notes. The agent read petitioner Toy's statement to him in English and interpreted certain portions of it for him in Chinese. Toy also read the statement in English aloud to the agent, said there were corrections to be made, and made the corrections in his own hand. Toy would not sign the statement, however; in the agent's words "he wanted to know first if the other persons involved in the case had signed theirs." Wong Sun had considerable difficulty understanding the statement in English and the agent restated its substance in Chinese. Wong Sun refused to sign the statement although he admitted the accuracy of its contents.

Hom Way did not testify at petitioners' trial. The Government offered Johnny Yee as its principal witness but excused him after he invoked the privilege against self-incrimination and flatly repudiated the statement he had given to Agent William Wong. That statement was not offered in evidence nor was any testimony elicited from him identifying either petitioner as the source of the heroin in his possession, or otherwise tending to support the charges against the petitioners.

The statute expressly provides that proof of the accused's possession of the drug will support a conviction under the statute unless the accused satisfactorily explains the possession. The Government's evidence tending to prove the petitioners' possession (the petitioners offered no exculpatory testimony) consisted of four items which the trial court admitted over timely objections that they were inadmissible as "fruits" of unlawful arrests or of attendant searches: (1) the statements made orally by petitioner Toy in his bedroom at the time of his arrest; (2) the heroin surrendered to the agents by Johnny Yee; (3) petitioner Toy's pretrial unsigned statement; and (4) petitioner Wong Sun's similar statement. The dispute below and here has centered around the correctness of the rulings of the trial judge allowing these items in evidence. * * *

We believe that significant differences between the cases of the two petitioners require separate discussion of each. We shall first consider the case of petitioner Toy.

I.

The Court of Appeals found there was neither reasonable grounds nor probable cause for Toy's arrest. * * *

* * * It remains to be seen what consequences flow from this conclusion.

II.

It is conceded that Toy's declarations in his bedroom are to be excluded if they are held to be "fruits" of the agents' unlawful action. * * *

The exclusionary rule has traditionally barred from trial physical, tangible materials obtained either during or as a direct result of an unlawful invasion. It follows from our holding in *Silverman v. United States*, 365 U.S. 505, 81 S.Ct. 679, 5 L.Ed.2d 734, that the Fourth Amendment may protect against the overhearing of verbal statements as well as against the more traditional seizure of "papers and effects." Similarly, testimony as to matters observed during an unlawful invasion has been excluded in order to enforce the basic constitutional policies. Thus, verbal evidence which derives so immediately from an unlawful entry and an unauthorized arrest as the officers' action in the present case is no less the "fruit" of official illegality than the more common tangible fruits of the unwarranted intrusion. Nor do the policies underlying the exclusionary rule invite any logical distinction between physical and verbal evidence. Either in terms of deterring lawless conduct by federal officers, or of closing the doors of the federal courts to any use of evidence unconstitutionally obtained, the danger in relaxing the exclusionary rules in the case of verbal evidence would seem too great to warrant introducing such a distinction.

The Government argues that Toy's statements to the officers in his bedroom, although closely consequent upon the invasion which we hold unlawful, were nevertheless admissible because they resulted from "an intervening independent act of a free will." This contention, however, takes insufficient account of the circumstances. Six or seven officers had broken the door and followed on Toy's heels into the bedroom where his wife and child were sleeping. He had been almost immediately handcuffed and arrested. Under such circumstances it is unreasonable to infer that Toy's response was sufficiently an act of free will to purge the primary taint of the unlawful invasion. * * *

III.

We now consider whether the exclusion of Toy's declarations requires also the exclusion of the narcotics taken from Yee, to which those declarations led the police. The prosecutor candidly told the trial court that "we wouldn't have found those drugs except that Mr. Toy helped us to." Hence this is not the case envisioned by this Court where the exclusionary rule has no application because the Government learned of the evidence "from an independent source"; nor is this a case in which the connection between the lawless conduct of the police and the discovery of the challenged evidence has "become so attenuated as to dissipate the taint." We need not hold that all evidence is "fruit of the poisonous tree" simply because it would not have come to light but for the illegal actions of the police. Rather, the more apt question in such a case is "whether, granting establishment of the primary illegality, the evidence to which instant objection is made has been come at by exploitation of that illegality or instead by means sufficiently distinguishable to be purged of the primary taint." Maguire, Evidence of Guilt, 221 (1959). We think it clear that the narcotics were "come at by the exploitation of that illegality" and hence that they may not be used against Toy.

IV.

[The Court determined that Toy's unsigned statement was inadmissible on non-constitutional grounds. Therefore, it did not reach the issue of "whether, in light of the fact that Toy was free on his own recognizance when he made the statement, that statement was a fruit of the illegal arrest."]

V.

We turn now to the case of the other petitioner, Wong Sun. We have no occasion to disagree with the finding of the Court of Appeals that his arrest, also, was without probable cause or reasonable grounds. At all events no evidentiary consequences turn upon that question. For Wong Sun's unsigned confession was not the fruit of that arrest, and was therefore properly admitted at trial. On the evidence that Wong Sun had been released on his own recognizance after a lawful arraignment, and had returned voluntarily several days later to make the statement, we hold that the connection between the arrest and the statement had "become so attenuated as to dissipate the taint." The fact that the statement was unsigned, whatever bearing this may have upon its weight and credibility, does not render it inadmissible; Wong Sun understood and adopted its substance, though he could not comprehend the English words. The petitioner has never suggested any impropriety in the interrogation itself which would require the exclusion of this statement.

We must then consider the admissibility of the narcotics surrendered by Yee. Our holding, *supra*, that this ounce of heroin was inadmissible against Toy does not compel a like result with respect to Wong Sun. The exclusion of the narcotics as to Toy was required solely by their tainted relationship to information unlawfully obtained from Toy, and not by any official impropriety connected with their surrender by Yee. The seizure of this heroin invaded no right of privacy of person or premises which would entitle Wong Sun to object to its use at his trial. * * *

[The concurring opinion of Justice Douglas, and the dissenting opinion of Justice Clark, joined by Justices Harlan, Stewart, and White, are omitted.]

NOTES AND QUESTIONS

1. What was the poisonous tree, *i.e.*, the initial illegality, in *Wong Sun*? What were the alleged fruits? Why did the Supreme Court treat Wong Sun differently than Toy?

2. *Removing the taint: factors.* Typically, dissipation-of-taint claims have been decided on their own facts. The Supreme Court in Brown v. Illinois, 422 U.S. 590, 95 S.Ct. 2254, 45 L.Ed.2d 416 (1975), and lower courts have applied at least four factors in determining when the connection between a Fourth Amendment violation and a fruit has become so attenuated as to dissipate the taint: (1) the length of time that has elapsed between the initial illegality and

the seizure of the fruit in question; (2) the flagrancy of the initial misconduct (dissipation of bad-faith violations takes longer than with good-faith violations); (3) the existence or absence of intervening causes of the seizure of the fruit; and (4) the presence or absence of an act of free will by the defendant resulting in the seizure of the fruit.

3. In *Wong Sun*, the Government sought to introduce statements made by Toy and Wong Sun. The criminal investigation here occurred before the Supreme Court announced its decision in *Miranda v. Arizona* (p. 581), so it did not have the opportunity to determine whether the act of giving *Miranda* warnings—among other things, telling the arrestee of his constitutional right to remain silent and of his right to have counsel present during any interrogation—in and of itself dissipates the taint from an earlier Fourth Amendment violation.

That issue arose in *Brown v. Illinois*, Note 2, supra. Brown was arrested at his apartment without probable cause, in violation of the Fourth Amendment. While in custody, he made incriminating statements after being read the *Miranda* warnings and voluntarily waiving his constitutional rights pursuant to *Miranda*. The Court rejected a proposed bright-line rule that *Miranda* warnings automatically untaint subsequent confessions. Whether a post-*Miranda*-warning statement, which is a fruit of a Fourth Amendment violation, is untainted is resolved on a case-by-case basis, based on the totality of the circumstances.

In *Brown*, the Court held that the State of Illinois had failed to sustain its burden of showing the requisite dissipation of taint, notwithstanding the *Miranda* warnings. The statement (the fruit) came less than two hours after the illegal arrest, and "there was no intervening event of significance whatsoever." Also, the Court noted that the illegality here (the unlawful arrest) "had a quality of purposefulness," in that the officers knew they were acting in violation of the Fourth Amendment.

4. In *Wong Sun*, the Court considered the admissibility of both tangible evidence (heroin) and verbal statements. The Court stated that "the policies underlying the exclusionary rule [do not] invite any logical distinction between physical and verbal evidence" in regard to the dissipation of taint. Do you agree? Are there reasons why courts might conclude that taint to physical evidence is more quickly dissipated than is the case with verbal evidence, or vice-versa?

In United States v. Ceccolini, 435 U.S. 268, 98 S.Ct. 1054, 55 L.Ed.2d 268 (1978), the police unlawfully obtained information that led them to a witness to a crime perpetrated by Ceccolini. Some months later, the witness agreed to testify against Ceccolini. According to the Court of Appeals, the witness's testimony should not have been permitted because "the road to [the] testimony from the [officer's] concededly unconstitutional search [was] both straight and uninterrupted."

The Supreme Court reversed. According to *Ceccolini*, "the exclusionary rule should be invoked with much greater reluctance where the claim is based on a causal relationship between a constitutional violation and the discovery of a live witness than when a similar claim is advanced to support suppression of an inanimate object." The Court reasoned as follows:

The greater the willingness of the witness to freely testify, the greater the likelihood that he or she will be discovered by legal means and, concomitantly, the smaller the incentive to conduct an illegal search to discover the witness. Witnesses are not like guns or documents which remain hidden from view until one turns over a sofa or opens a filing cabinet. Witnesses can, and often do, come forward and offer evidence entirely of their own volition. And evaluated properly, the degree of free will necessary to dissipate the taint will very likely be found more often in the case of live-witness testimony than other kinds of evidence. * * *

Another factor which * * * seems to us to differentiate the testimony of all live witnesses—even putative defendants—from the exclusion of the typical documentary evidence, is that such exclusion would perpetually disable a witness from testifying about relevant and material facts, regardless of how unrelated such testimony might be to the purpose of the originally illegal search or the evidence discovered thereby. Rules which disqualify knowledgeable witnesses from testifying at trial are, in the words of Professor McCormick, "serious obstructions to the ascertainment of truth" * * *. * * * In short, since the cost of excluding live-witness testimony often will be greater, a closer, more direct link between the illegality and that kind of testimony is required.

Are you persuaded?

5. *Problem.* O unlawfully arrested S without probable cause. (The nature of the offense is unclear.) Because O was male and S was female, O did not conduct a full search of S. At the police station, however, female officer F searched S and discovered four small bags of suspected illegal drugs on S. F momentarily put the bags on a nearby counter top. When F became distracted, S grabbed the suspected contraband, ran to a bathroom, and flushed most of the evidence down the toilet. The police charged S with destruction of evidence. (They did not charge her with possession of a controlled substance.) The government sought to introduce: (1) the drugs that S did not successfully flush down the toilet; and (2) the observations by officers present at the scene describing S's efforts to destroy the evidence. Admissible? State v. Schrecengost, 134 Idaho 547, 6 P.3d 403 (App.2000).

6. *But, wait!* As explained in Note 2, dissipation-of-taint analysis is usually resolved on a case-by-case basis by applying the factors laid out in that Note. But, as we say, wait—the Supreme Court recently threw a curve ball called *Hudson v. Michigan* (p. 509). What you have learned so far remains relevant, but there is more. . . .

5. THE EXCLUSIONARY RULE: UNDERGOING CHANGE

HUDSON v. MICHIGAN

Supreme Court of the United States, 2006.
547 U.S. 586, 126 S.Ct. 2159, 165 L.Ed.2d 56.

JUSTICE SCALIA delivered the opinion of the Court, except as to Part IV.

We decide whether violation of the knock-and-announce rule requires the suppression of all evidence found in the search.

I

Police obtained a warrant authorizing a search for drugs and firearms at the home of petitioner Booker Hudson. They discovered both. Large quantities of drugs were found, including cocaine rocks in Hudson's pocket. A loaded gun was lodged between the cushion and armrest of the chair in which he was sitting. Hudson was charged under Michigan law with unlawful drug and firearm possession.

This case is before us only because of the method of entry into the house. When the police arrived to execute the warrant, they announced their presence, but waited only a short time—perhaps "three to five seconds"—before turning the knob of the unlocked front door and entering Hudson's home. Hudson moved to suppress all the inculpatory evidence, arguing that the premature entry violated his Fourth Amendment rights.

The Michigan trial court granted his motion. On interlocutory review, the Michigan Court of Appeals reversed * * *. * * * Hudson was convicted of drug possession. He renewed his Fourth Amendment claim on appeal * * *. * * * We granted certiorari.

II

The common-law principle that law enforcement officers must announce their presence and provide residents an opportunity to open the door is an ancient one. See *Wilson v. Arkansas,* 514 U.S. 927, 931–932, 115 S.Ct. 1914, 131 L.Ed.2d 976 (1995). Since 1917, when Congress passed the Espionage Act, this traditional protection has been part of federal statutory law * * *. * * * Finally, in *Wilson,* we were asked whether the rule was also a command of the Fourth Amendment. Tracing its origins in our English legal heritage, we concluded that it was.

We recognized that the new constitutional rule we had announced is not easily applied. *Wilson* and cases following it have noted the many situations in which it is not necessary to knock and announce. [See generally pp. 199–207] * * *

When the knock-and-announce rule does apply, it is not easy to determine precisely what officers must do. How many seconds' wait are too few? Our "reasonable wait time" standard, see *United States v. Banks,* [p. 206, Note 5], is necessarily vague. * * * [I]t is unsurprising that * * * police officers about to encounter someone who may try to harm them will be uncertain how long to wait.

Happily, these issues do not confront us here. From the trial level onward, Michigan has conceded that the entry was a knock-and-announce violation. The issue here is remedy. *Wilson* specifically declined to decide whether the exclusionary rule is appropriate for violation of the knock-and-announce requirement. That question is squarely before us now.

III

A

In *Weeks v. United States,* [p. 67], we adopted the federal exclusionary rule for evidence that was unlawfully seized from a home without a warrant in violation of the Fourth Amendment. We began applying the same rule to the States, through the Fourteenth Amendment, in *Mapp v. Ohio,* [p. 73].

Suppression of evidence, however, has always been our last resort, not our first impulse. The exclusionary rule generates "substantial social costs," which sometimes include setting the guilty free and the dangerous at large. We have therefore been "cautio[us] against expanding" it, and "have repeatedly emphasized that the rule's 'costly toll' upon truth-seeking and law enforcement objectives presents a high obstacle for those urging [its] application." We have rejected "[i]ndiscriminate application" of the rule, and have held it to be applicable only "where its remedial objectives are thought most efficaciously served"—that is, "where its deterrence benefits outweigh its 'substantial social costs.'"

We did not always speak so guardedly. Expansive dicta in *Mapp,* for example, suggested wide scope for the exclusionary rule. * * * But we have long since rejected that approach. * * *

* * * [E]xclusion may not be premised on the mere fact that a constitutional violation was a "but-for" cause of obtaining evidence. Our cases show that but-for causality is only a necessary, not a sufficient, condition for suppression. In this case, of course, the constitutional violation of an illegal *manner* of entry was *not* a but-for cause of obtaining the evidence. Whether that preliminary misstep had occurred *or not,* the police would have executed the warrant they had obtained, and would have discovered the gun and drugs inside the house. But even if the illegal entry here could be characterized as a but-for cause of discovering what was inside, we have "never held that evidence is 'fruit of the poisonous tree' simply because 'it would not have come to light but for the illegal actions of the police.'" Rather, but-for cause, or "causation in the logical sense alone," can be too attenuated to justify exclusion. * * *

Attenuation can occur, of course, when the causal connection is remote. Attenuation also occurs when, even given a direct causal connection, the interest protected by the constitutional guarantee that has been violated would not be served by suppression of the evidence obtained. "The penalties visited upon the Government, and in turn upon the public, because its officers have violated the law must bear some relation to the purposes which the law is to serve." Thus, in *New York v. Harris,* 495 U.S. 14, 110 S.Ct. 1640, 109 L.Ed.2d 13 (1990), where an illegal warrantless arrest was made in Harris' house,[a] we held that

---

a. In *Harris,* police officers had probable cause to arrest Harris, but entered without a required arrest warrant. Harris received *Miranda* warrnings, waived his rights, and made an incriminating statement in his home. Later, at the police station, Harris made a second inculpatory statement. The in-home statement was suppressed as tainted, pursuant to attenua-

suppressing [Harris'] statement taken outside the house would not serve the purpose of the rule that made Harris' in-house arrest illegal. The warrant requirement for an arrest in the home is imposed to protect the home, and anything incriminating the police gathered from arresting Harris in his home, rather than elsewhere, has been excluded, as it should have been; the purpose of the rule has thereby been vindicated.

For this reason, cases excluding the fruits of unlawful warrantless searches say nothing about the appropriateness of exclusion to vindicate the interests protected by the knock-and-announce requirement. Until a valid warrant has issued, citizens are entitled to shield "their persons, houses, papers, and effects" from the government's scrutiny. Exclusion of the evidence obtained by a warrantless search vindicates that entitlement. The interests protected by the knock-and-announce requirement are quite different—and do not include the shielding of potential evidence from the government's eyes.

One of those interests is the protection of human life and limb, because an unannounced entry may provoke violence in supposed self-defense by the surprised resident. Another interest is the protection of property. Breaking a house (as the old cases typically put it) absent an announcement would penalize someone who " 'did not know of the process, of which, if he had notice, it is to be presumed that he would obey it * * *.' " The knock-and-announce rule gives individuals "the opportunity to comply with the law and to avoid the destruction of property occasioned by a forcible entry." And thirdly, the knock-and-announce rule protects those elements of privacy and dignity that can be destroyed by a sudden entrance. It gives residents the "opportunity to prepare themselves for" the entry of the police. "The brief interlude between announcement and entry with a warrant may be the opportunity that an individual has to pull on clothes or get out of bed." In other words, it assures the opportunity to collect oneself before answering the door.

What the knock-and-announce rule has never protected, however, is one's interest in preventing the government from seeing or taking evidence described in a warrant. Since the interests that *were* violated in this case have nothing to do with the seizure of the evidence, the exclusionary rule is inapplicable.

B

Quite apart from the requirement of unattenuated causation, the exclusionary rule has never been applied except "where its deterrence benefits outweigh its 'substantial social costs.' " The costs here are considerable. In addition to the grave adverse consequence that exclusion of relevant incriminating evidence always entails (viz., the risk of releasing dangerous criminals into society), imposing that massive remedy for a

---

tion principles enunciated in *Brown v. Illinois* (p. 507, Note 2). The sole issue on appeal was the admissibility of Harris's statement at the station house.

knock-and-announce violation would generate a constant flood of alleged failures to observe the rule, and claims that any asserted * * * justification for a no-knock entry had inadequate support. The cost of entering this lottery would be small, but the jackpot enormous: suppression of all evidence, amounting in many cases to a get-out-of-jail-free card. Courts would experience as never before the reality that "[t]he exclusionary rule frequently requires extensive litigation to determine whether particular evidence must be excluded." Unlike the warrant or *Miranda* requirements, compliance with which is readily determined (either there was or was not a warrant; either the *Miranda* warning was given, or it was not), what constituted a "reasonable wait time" in a particular case (or, for that matter, how many seconds the police in fact waited), or whether there was "reasonable suspicion" of the sort that would invoke [one of] the [knock-and-announce] exceptions, is difficult for the trial court to determine and even more difficult for an appellate court to review.

Another consequence of the incongruent remedy Hudson proposes would be police officers' refraining from timely entry after knocking and announcing. As we have observed, the amount of time they must wait is necessarily uncertain. If the consequences of running afoul of the rule were so massive, officers would be inclined to wait longer than the law requires—producing preventable violence against officers in some cases, and the destruction of evidence in many others. We deemed these consequences severe enough to produce our unanimous agreement that a mere "reasonable suspicion" that knocking and announcing "under the particular circumstances, would be dangerous or futile, or that it would inhibit the effective investigation of the crime," will cause the requirement to yield.

Next to these "substantial social costs" we must consider the deterrence benefits, existence of which is a necessary condition for exclusion. (It is not, of course, a sufficient condition: "[I]t does not follow that the Fourth Amendment requires adoption of every proposal that might deter police misconduct.") To begin with, the value of deterrence depends upon the strength of the incentive to commit the forbidden act. Viewed from this perspective, deterrence of knock-and-announce violations is not worth a lot. Violation of the warrant requirement sometimes produces incriminating evidence that could not otherwise be obtained. But ignoring knock-and-announce can realistically be expected to achieve absolutely nothing except the prevention of destruction of evidence and the avoidance of life-threatening resistance by occupants of the premises—dangers which, if there is even "reasonable suspicion" of their existence, *suspend the knock-and-announce requirement anyway*. Massive deterrence is hardly required.

It seems to us not even true, as Hudson contends, that without suppression there will be no deterrence of knock-and-announce violations at all. Of course even if this assertion were accurate, it would not necessarily justify suppression. Assuming (as the assertion must) that civil suit is not an effective deterrent, one can think of many forms of police misconduct that are similarly "undeterred." When, for example, a confessed suspect in the killing of a police officer, arrested (along with incriminating evidence) in a lawful warranted search, is subjected to physical abuse at the station house, would it seriously be suggested that the evidence must be excluded, since that is the only "effective deterrent"? And what, other than civil suit, is the "effective deterrent" of police violation of an already-confessed suspect's Sixth Amendment rights by denying him prompt access to counsel? Many would regard these violated rights as more significant than the right not to be intruded upon in one's nightclothes—and yet nothing but "ineffective" civil suit is available as a deterrent. And the police incentive for those violations is arguably greater than the incentive for disregarding the knock-and-announce rule.

We cannot assume that exclusion in this context is necessary deterrence simply because we found that it was necessary deterrence in different contexts and long ago. That would be forcing the public today to pay for the sins and inadequacies of a legal regime that existed almost half a century ago. Dollree Mapp could not turn to 42 U.S.C. § 1983 for meaningful relief; *Monroe v. Pape,* 365 U.S. 167, 81 S.Ct. 473, 5 L.Ed.2d 492 (1961), which began the slow but steady expansion of that remedy, was decided the same Term as *Mapp.* It would be another 17 years before the § 1983 remedy was extended to reach the deep pocket of municipalities. Citizens whose Fourth Amendment rights were violated by federal officers could not bring suit until 10 years after *Mapp,* with this Court's decision in *Bivens v. Six Unknown Fed. Narcotics Agents,* 403 U.S. 388, 91 S.Ct. 1999, 29 L.Ed.2d 619 (1971).

Hudson complains that "it would be very hard to find a lawyer to take a case such as this," but 42 U.S.C. § 1988(b) answers this objection. Since some civil-rights violations would yield damages too small to justify the expense of litigation, Congress has authorized attorney's fees for civil-rights plaintiffs. This remedy was unavailable in the heydays of our exclusionary-rule jurisprudence, because it is tied to the availability of a cause of action. For years after *Mapp,* "very few lawyers would even consider representation of persons who had civil rights claims against the police," but now "much has changed. Citizens and lawyers are much more willing to seek relief in the courts for police misconduct." M. Avery, D. Rudovsky, & K. Blum, Police Misconduct: Law and Litigation, p. v. (3d ed. 2005).[b] The number of public-interest law firms and lawyers who specialize in civil-rights grievances has greatly expanded.

Hudson points out that few published decisions to date announce huge awards for knock-and-announce violations. But this is an unhelpful statistic. Even if we thought that only large damages would deter police misconduct * * *, we do not know how many claims have been settled, or indeed how many violations have occurred that produced anything more

---

b. Justice Scalia failed to quote language from this book that immediately followed his quote: "But the development of the law has not been linear. In certain respects it is easier to challenge police misconduct in court. * * * In other respects, it is far more difficult." And, after *Hudson* was decided, the authors added a new footnote to their 2007 edition, characterizing the Court's quotation as "highly misleading."

than nominal injury. It is clear, at least, that the lower courts are allowing colorable knock-and-announce suits to go forward, unimpeded by assertions of qualified immunity. As far as we know, civil liability is an effective deterrent here, as we have assumed it is in other contexts.

Another development over the past half-century that deters civil-rights violations is the increasing professionalism of police forces, including a new emphasis on internal police discipline. Even as long ago as 1980 we felt it proper to "assume" that unlawful police behavior would "be dealt with appropriately" by the authorities, but we now have increasing evidence that police forces across the United States take the constitutional rights of citizens seriously. There have been "wide-ranging reforms in the education, training, and supervision of police officers." Numerous sources are now available to teach officers and their supervisors what is required of them under this Court's cases, how to respect constitutional guarantees in various situations, and how to craft an effective regime for internal discipline. Failure to teach and enforce constitutional requirements exposes municipalities to financial liability. Moreover, modern police forces are staffed with professionals; it is not credible to assert that internal discipline, which can limit successful careers, will not have a deterrent effect. There is also evidence that the increasing use of various forms of citizen review can enhance police accountability.

In sum, the social costs of applying the exclusionary rule to knock-and-announce violations are considerable; the incentive to such violations is minimal to begin with, and the extant deterrences against them are substantial—incomparably greater than the factors deterring warrantless entries when *Mapp* was decided. Resort to the massive remedy of suppressing evidence of guilt is unjustified.

IV

[The Court proceeded to discuss three prior high court opinions it felt "confirms our conclusion that suppression is unwarranted in this case."]

* * *

For the foregoing reasons we affirm the judgment of the Michigan Court of Appeals.

Justice KENNEDY, concurring in part and concurring in the judgment.

Two points should be underscored with respect to today's decision. First, the knock-and-announce requirement protects rights and expectations linked to ancient principles in our constitutional order. The Court's decision should not be interpreted as suggesting that violations of the requirement are trivial or beyond the law's concern. Second, the continued operation of the exclusionary rule, as settled and defined by our precedents, is not in doubt. Today's decision determines only that in the specific context of the knock-and-announce requirement, a violation is not sufficiently related to the later discovery of evidence to justify suppression.

As to the basic right in question, privacy and security in the home are central to the Fourth Amendment's guarantees as explained in our decisions and as understood since the beginnings of the Republic. This common understanding ensures respect for the law and allegiance to our institutions, and it is an instrument for transmitting our Constitution to later generations undiminished in meaning and force. It bears repeating that it is a serious matter if law enforcement officers violate the sanctity of the home by ignoring the requisites of lawful entry. Security must not be subject to erosion by indifference or contempt. * * *

Suppression is another matter. Under our precedents the causal link between a violation of the knock-and-announce requirement and a later search is too attenuated to allow suppression. When, for example, a violation results from want of a 20–second pause but an ensuing, lawful search lasting five hours discloses evidence of criminality, the failure to wait at the door cannot properly be described as having caused the discovery of evidence.

Today's decision does not address any demonstrated pattern of knock-and-announce violations. If a widespread pattern of violations were shown, and particularly if those violations were committed against persons who lacked the means or voice to mount an effective protest, there would be reason for grave concern. Even then, however, the Court would have to acknowledge that extending the remedy of exclusion to all the evidence seized following a knock-and-announce violation would mean revising the requirement of causation that limits our discretion in applying the exclusionary rule. That type of extension also would have significant practical implications, adding to the list of issues requiring resolution at the criminal trial questions such as whether police officers entered a home after waiting 10 seconds or 20.

In this case the relevant evidence was discovered not because of a failure to knock-and-announce, but because of a subsequent search pursuant to a lawful warrant. The Court in my view is correct to hold that suppression was not required. While I am not convinced that [the cases discussed in Part IV] have as much relevance here as Justice SCALIA appears to conclude, the Court's holding is fully supported by Parts I through III of its opinion. I accordingly join those Parts and concur in the judgment.

Justice BREYER, with whom Justice STEVENS, Justice SOUTER, and Justice GINSBURG join, dissenting. * * *

Today's opinion is * * * doubly troubling. It represents a significant departure from the Court's precedents. And it weakens, perhaps destroys, much of the practical value of the Constitution's knock-and-announce protection.

I

[Justice Breyer summarized knock-and-announce law, beginning with *Wilson v. Arkansas, supra*, which held that the "common-law 'knock and announce' principle forms a part of the reasonableness inquiry under the Fourth Amendment." He then summarized and quoted from Supreme Court cases originating and explaining the contours of the exclusionary rule in Fourth and Fourteenth Amendment cases.]

II

Reading our knock-and-announce cases * * * in light of this foundational Fourth Amendment case law, it is clear that the exclusionary rule should apply. For one thing, elementary logic leads to that conclusion. We have held that a court must "conside[r]" whether officers complied with the knock-and-announce requirement "in assessing the reasonableness of a search or seizure." The Fourth Amendment insists that an unreasonable search or seizure is, constitutionally speaking, an illegal search or seizure. And ever since *Weeks* (in respect to federal prosecutions) and *Mapp* (in respect to state prosecutions), "the use of evidence secured through an illegal search and seizure" is "barred" in criminal trials.

For another thing, the driving legal purpose underlying the exclusionary rule, namely, the deterrence of unlawful government behavior, argues strongly for suppression. * * * [T]he Court [has] based its holdings requiring suppression of unlawfully obtained evidence upon the recognition that admission of that evidence would seriously undermine the Fourth Amendment's promise. [Prior] cases recognized that failure to apply the exclusionary rule would make that promise a hollow one, reducing it to "a form of words," "of no value" to those whom it seeks to protect. Indeed, this Court in *Mapp* held that the exclusionary rule applies to the States in large part due to its belief that alternative state mechanisms for enforcing the Fourth Amendment's guarantees had proved "worthless and futile."

Why is application of the exclusionary rule any the less necessary here? Without such a rule, as in *Mapp*, police know that they can ignore the Constitution's requirements without risking suppression of evidence discovered after an unreasonable entry. As in *Mapp,* some government officers will find it easier, or believe it less risky, to proceed with what they consider a necessary search immediately and without the requisite constitutional (say, warrant or knock-and-announce) compliance.

Of course, the State or the Federal Government may provide alternative remedies for knock-and-announce violations. But that circumstance was true of *Mapp* as well. What reason is there to believe that those remedies * * *, which the Court found inadequate in *Mapp,* can adequately deter unconstitutional police behavior here? See Kamisar, In Defense of the Search and Seizure Exclusionary Rule, 26 Harv. J.L. & Pub. Pol'y 119, 126–129 (2003) (arguing that "five decades of post-*Weeks* 'freedom' from the inhibiting effect of the federal exclusionary rule failed to produce any meaningful alternative to the exclusionary rule in any jurisdiction" and that there is no evidence that "times have changed" post-*Mapp*).

The cases reporting knock-and-announce violations are legion. Indeed, these cases of reported violations seem sufficiently frequent and serious as to indicate "a widespread pattern" (KENNEDY, J., concurring in part and concurring in judgment). Yet the majority * * * has failed to cite a single reported case in which a plaintiff has collected more than nominal damages solely as a result of a knock-and-announce violation. Even Michigan concedes that, "in cases like the present one * * *, damages may be virtually non-existent." And Michigan's *amici* further concede that civil immunities prevent tort law from being an effective substitute for the exclusionary rule at this time.

As Justice Stewart, the author of a number of significant Fourth Amendment opinions, explained, the deterrent effect of damage actions "can hardly be said to be great," as such actions are "expensive, time-consuming, not readily available, and rarely successful." The upshot is that the need for deterrence—the critical factor driving this Court's Fourth Amendment cases for close to a century—argues with at least comparable strength for evidentiary exclusion here.

To argue, as the majority does, that new remedies, such as 42 U.S.C. § 1983 actions or better trained police, make suppression unnecessary is to argue that *Wolf*, not *Mapp*, is now the law. * * * To argue that there may be few civil suits because violations may produce nothing "more than nominal injury" is to confirm, not to deny, the inability of civil suits to deter violations. And to argue without evidence * * * that civil suits may provide deterrence because claims *may* "have been settled" is, perhaps, to search in desperation for an argument. Rather, the majority, as it candidly admits, has simply "assumed" that, "[a]s far as [it] know[s], civil liability is an effective deterrent," a support-free assumption that *Mapp* and subsequent cases make clear does not embody the Court's normal approach to difficult questions of Fourth Amendment law.

It is not surprising, then, that after looking at virtually every pertinent Supreme Court case decided since *Weeks,* I can find no precedent that might offer the majority support for its contrary conclusion. * * *

* * * The Court has decided more than 300 Fourth Amendment cases since *Weeks.* The Court has found constitutional violations in nearly a third of them. The nature of the constitutional violation varies. * * * But in every case involving evidence seized during an illegal search of a home (federally since *Weeks,* nationally since *Mapp*), the Court, with the exceptions mentioned, has either explicitly or implicitly upheld (or required) the suppression of the evidence at trial. In not one of those cases did the Court "questio[n], in the absence of a more efficacious sanction, the continued application of the [exclusionary] rule to suppress evidence from the State's case" in a criminal trial.

I can find nothing persuasive in the majority's opinion that could justify its refusal to apply the rule. * * *

[The majority cannot] justify its failure to respect the need for deterrence, as set forth consistently in the Court's prior case law, through its claim of "substantial social costs"—at least if it means that those "social costs" are somehow special here. The only costs it mentions are those that typically accompany *any* use of the Fourth Amendment's exclusionary principle: (1) that where the constable blunders, a guilty defendant may be set free (consider *Mapp* itself); (2) that defendants may assert claims where Fourth Amendment rights are uncertain * * *, and (3) that sometimes it is difficult to decide the merits of those uncertain claims. * * * The majority's "substantial social costs" argument is an argument against the Fourth Amendment's exclusionary principle itself. And it is an argument that this Court, until now, has consistently rejected.

III

The majority * * * make[s] several additional arguments. In my view, those arguments rest upon misunderstandings of the principles underlying this Court's precedents.

A

The majority first argues that "the constitutional violation of an illegal *manner* of entry was *not* a but-for cause of obtaining the evidence." But taking causation as it is commonly understood in the law, I do not see how that can be so. Although the police might have entered Hudson's home lawfully, they did not in fact do so. Their unlawful behavior inseparably characterizes their actual entry; that entry was a necessary condition of their presence in Hudson's home; and their presence in Hudson's home was a necessary condition of their finding and seizing the evidence. At the same time, their discovery of evidence in Hudson's home was a readily foreseeable consequence of their entry and their unlawful presence within the home.

Moreover, separating the "manner of entry" from the related search slices the violation too finely. As noted [earlier], we have described a failure to comply with the knock-and-announce rule, not as an independently unlawful event, but as a factor that renders the *search* "constitutionally defective."

The Court nonetheless accepts Michigan's argument that the requisite but-for-causation is not satisfied in this case because, whether or not the constitutional violation occurred (what the Court refers to as a "preliminary misstep"), "the police would have executed the warrant they had obtained, and would have discovered the gun and drugs inside the house." As support for this proposition, Michigan rests on this Court's inevitable discovery cases.

This claim, however, misunderstands the inevitable discovery doctrine. * * * That rule does not refer to discovery that would have taken place if the police behavior in question had (contrary to fact) been lawful. The doctrine does not treat as critical what *hypothetically could* have happened had the police acted lawfully in the first place. Rather, "independent" or "inevitable" discovery refers to discovery that did occur or that would have occurred (1) *despite* (not simply *in the absence of*) the unlawful behavior and (2) *independently* of that unlawful behavior. The government cannot, for example, avoid suppression of evidence seized without a warrant (or pursuant to a defective warrant) simply by showing that it could have obtained a valid warrant had it sought one. Instead, it must show that the same evidence "inevitably *would* have been discovered *by lawful means.*" * * *

Case law well illustrates the meaning of this principle. In *Nix* [*v. Williams*, p. 502, Note 4], *supra*, police officers violated a defendant's Sixth Amendment right by eliciting incriminating statements from him after he invoked his right to counsel. Those statements led to the discovery of the victim's body. The Court concluded that evidence obtained from the victim's body was admissible because it would ultimately or inevitably have been discovered by a volunteer search party effort that was ongoing—whether or not the Sixth Amendment violation had taken place. In other words, the evidence would have been found *despite,* and *independent of,* the Sixth Amendment violation. * * *

Thus, the Court's opinion reflects a misunderstanding of what inevitable discovery means when it says, "[i]n this case, of course, the constitutional violation of an illegal *manner* of entry was *not* a but-for cause of obtaining the evidence." The majority rests this conclusion on its next statement: "Whether that preliminary misstep has occurred *or not,* the police * * * would have discovered the gun and the drugs inside the house." Despite the phrase "of course," neither of these statements is correct. It is not true that, had the illegal entry not occurred, "police would have discovered the guns and drugs inside the house." Without that unlawful entry they would not have been inside the house; so there would have been no discovery.

Of course, had the police entered the house lawfully, they would have found the gun and drugs. But that fact is beside the point. The question is not what police might have done had they not behaved unlawfully. The question is what they did do. Was there set in motion an independent chain of events that would have inevitably led to the discovery and seizure of the evidence despite, and independent of, that behavior? The answer here is "no."

B

The majority, Michigan, and the United States point out that the officers here possessed a warrant authorizing a search. That fact, they argue, means that the evidence would have been discovered independently or somehow diminishes the need to suppress the evidence. But I do not see why that is so. The warrant in question * * * was an ordinary search warrant. It authorized a search that *complied with,* not a search that *disregarded,* the Constitution's knock-and-announce rule.

Would a warrant that authorizes entry into a home on Tuesday permit the police to enter on Monday? * * * It is difficult for me to see how the presence of a warrant that does not authorize the entry in question has anything to do with the "inevitable discovery" exception or otherwise diminishes the need to enforce the knock-and-announce requirement through suppression.

C * * *

The majority * * * says that evidence should not be suppressed once the causal connection between unlawful behavior and discovery of the evidence becomes too "attenuated." But the majority then makes clear that it is not using the word "attenuated" to mean what this Court's precedents have typically used that word to mean, namely, that the discovery of the evidence has come about long after the unlawful behavior took place or in an independent way, *i.e.,* through " 'means sufficiently distinguishable to be purged of the primary taint.' " *Wong Sun v. United States*.

Rather, the majority gives the word "attenuation" a new meaning * * *. "Attenuation," it says, "also occurs when, even given a direct causal connection, the interest protected by the constitutional guarantee that has been violated would not be served by suppression of the evidence obtained." The interests the knock-and-announce rule seeks to protect, the Court adds, are "human life" (at stake when a householder is "surprised"), "property" (such as the front door), and "those elements of privacy and dignity that can be destroyed by a sudden entrance," namely, "the opportunity to collect oneself before answering the door." Since none of those interests led to the discovery of the evidence seized here, there is no reason to suppress it.

There are three serious problems with this argument. First, it does not fully describe the constitutional values, purposes, and objectives underlying the knock-and-announce requirement. That rule does help to protect homeowners from damaged doors; it does help to protect occupants from surprise. But it does more than that. It protects the occupants' privacy by assuring them that government agents will not enter their home without complying with those requirements (among others) that diminish the offensive nature of any such intrusion. Many years ago, Justice Frankfurter wrote for the Court that the "knock at the door, * * * as a prelude to a search, without authority of law * * * [is] inconsistent with the conception of human rights enshrined in [our] history" and Constitution. How much the more offensive when the search takes place without any knock at all.

* * * The Court is therefore wrong to reduce the essence of its protection to "the right not to be intruded upon in one's nightclothes."

Second, whether the interests underlying the knock-and-announce rule are implicated in any given case is, in a sense, beside the point. As we have explained, failure to comply with the knock-and-announce rule renders the related search unlawful. And where a search is unlawful, the law insists upon suppression of the evidence consequently discovered, even if that evidence or its possession has little or nothing to do with the reasons underlying the unconstitutionality of a search. The Fourth Amendment does not seek to protect contraband, yet we have required suppression of contraband seized in an unlawful search. That is because the exclusionary rule protects more general "privacy values through deterrence of future police misconduct." The same is true here.

Third, the majority's interest-based approach departs from prior law. * * *

D

The United States, in its brief and at oral argument, has argued that suppression is "an especially harsh remedy given the nature of the violation in this case." This argument focuses upon the fact that entering a house after knocking and announcing can, in some cases, prove dangerous to a police officer. Perhaps someone inside has a gun, as turned out to be the case here. The majority adds that police officers about to encounter someone who may try to harm them will be "uncertain" as to how long to wait. It says that, "[i]f the consequences of running afoul" of the knock-and-announce "rule were so massive," *i.e.*, would lead to the exclusion of evidence, then "officers would be inclined to wait longer than the law requires—producing preventable violence against officers in some cases."

To argue that police efforts to assure compliance with the rule may prove dangerous, however, is not to argue against evidence suppression. It is to argue against the validity of the rule itself. Similarly, to argue that enforcement means uncertainty, which in turn means the potential for dangerous and longer-than-necessary delay, is (if true) to argue against meaningful compliance with the rule.

The answer to the first argument is that the rule itself does not require police to knock or to announce their presence where police have a "reasonable suspicion" that doing so "would be dangerous or futile" or "would inhibit the effective investigation of the crime by, for example, allowing the destruction of evidence."

The answer to the second argument is that States can, and many do, reduce police uncertainty while assuring a neutral evaluation of concerns about risks to officers or the destruction of evidence by permitting police to obtain a "no-knock" search warrant from a magistrate judge, thereby assuring police that a prior announcement is not necessary. While such a procedure cannot remove all uncertainty, it does provide an easy way for officers to comply with the knock-and-announce rule. * * *

Consider this very case. The police obtained a search warrant that authorized a search, not only for drugs, but also for *guns*. If probable cause justified a search for guns, why would it not also have justified a no-knock warrant, thereby diminishing any danger to the officers? Why (in a State such as Michigan that lacks no-knock warrants) would it not have justified the very no-knock entry at issue here? Indeed, why did the prosecutor not argue in this very case that, given the likelihood of guns, the no-knock entry was lawful? From what I have seen in the record, he would have won. And had he won, there would have been no suppression here.

That is the right way to win. * * *

IV * * *

There may be instances in the law where text or history or tradition leaves room for a judicial decision that rests upon little more than an unvarnished judicial instinct. But this is not one of them. Rather, our Fourth Amendment traditions place high value upon protecting privacy in the home. They emphasize the need to assure that its constitutional protections are effective, lest the Amendment "sound the word of promise to the ear but break it to the hope." They include an exclusionary principle, which since *Weeks* has formed the centerpiece of the criminal law's effort to ensure the practical reality of those promises. That is why the Court should assure itself that any departure from that principle is firmly grounded in logic, in history, in precedent, and in empirical fact. It has not done so. That is why, with respect, I dissent.

NOTES AND QUESTIONS

1. Professor Wayne LaFave, author of the leading treatise on the Fourth Amendment is no fan of *Hudson*, which he says "deserves a special niche in the Supreme Court's pantheon of Fourth Amendment jurisprudence, as one would be hard-pressed to find another case with so many bogus arguments piled atop one another." 6 Wayne R. LaFave, Search and Seizure § 11.4, at 34 (4th ed. Supp. 2008–2009). Putting aside your feelings for or against the exclusionary rule, do you believe the majority or the dissent is more consistent with exclusionary rule jurisprudence (specifically, independent-source, inevitable-discovery, and attenuation doctrines), as you just learned it in this chapter?

2. Is *Hudson* evidence of the beginning of the end of the Fourth Amendment exclusionary rule? David Moran, who represented Hudson in the United States Supreme Court, has written: "I have no idea whether my death will be noted in the *New York Times*. But if it is, I fear the headline of my obituary will look something like: 'Professor Dies; Lost *Hudson v. Michigan* in Supreme Court, Leading to Abolition of Exclusionary Rule.'" David A. Moran, *Waiting for the Other Shoe: Hudson and the Precarious State of Mapp*, 93 Iowa L. Rev. 1725, 1726 (2008). Another scholar has observed:

> [L]ike the bowls of porridge [in the story of Goldilocks] that were too hot, too cold, and just right, the chairs that were too large (or hard), too small (or soft), and just right, and the beds that were too hard, too soft, and, once again, just right—the future of the exclusionary rule foreshadowed in *Hudson* might lie at one extreme, at the other, or somewhere in between.

James J. Tomkovicz, *Hudson v. Michigan and the Future of Fourth Amendment Exclusion*, 93 Iowa L. Rev. 1819, 1820 (2008).

Writing in Spring 2008, both Moran and Tomkovicz believed that *Hudson* planted seeds that, at a minimum, could result in further narrowing of the exclusionary rule and, with changes in Supreme Court personnel, might result in its demise. As Professor Tomkovicz put it, "[f]or those inclined to discard a doctrine that has withstood a firestorm of criticism for nearly half a century, *Hudson* has stocked the shelves with arms and ammunition. The target awaits. Whether the Court will load and fire remains to be seen." *Id.* at 1887. Professor Moran predicted that the future of *Mapp v. Ohio* and the exclusionary rule depended on the Presidential election of 2008. If a "civil-libertarian Democratic President" were elected, he wrote, "it seems likely that a strong reaffirmation of *Mapp* would follow." Moran, *supra*, at 1740.

Time will tell. And, as you will see below, post-*Hudson*, the Supreme Court has spoken again regarding the exclusionary rule. But, let's stay with *Hudson* for awhile.

3. *Are the alternative remedies really good enough?* Justice Scalia wrote for the Court that "[w]e cannot assume that exclusion in this context is necessary * * * simply because we found that it was necessary * * * in different contexts and long ago. That would be forcing the public today to pay for the sins and inadequacies of a legal regime that existed almost half a century ago." Are things as rosy as he claims? According to Professor David Sklansky,

> systems of accountability for police misconduct have improved since the 1960s. But the particular system Justice Scalia talked about most in *Hudson*—civil damages action—is the one for which there is least evidence of significant improvement. * * * Chief among the new barriers to suing the police, of course, are the expanding doctrines of official immunity, which alone take [Avery, Rudovsky and Blum, the authors of the police misconduct book cited by Scalia] more than 120 pages to describe. More and more, these doctrines look like the Blob That Ate [Civil Rights] Section 1983.

David Alan Sklansky, *Is the Exclusionary Rule Obsolete?*, 5 Ohio St. J. Crim. L. 567, 571, 572 (2008).

Sklansky also is skeptical that civilian police review boards can satisfactorily replace the exclusionary rule. He writes that "[i]ronically, * * * one of the reasons citizens review panels have spread so broadly is that they have almost always proven much more sympathetic to rank-and-file officers than the [police] unions feared and than most of the original backers of the idea expected." *Id.* at 572.

4. Assuming that *Mapp v. Ohio* is not overruled (or until it is), does the Court's approach in *Hudson* suggest that, beyond knock-and-announce, there are other areas in which the exclusionary rule will no longer apply?

Is Professor Eric Johnson correct when he observes that application of *Hudson,* in particular its determination that the causal connection between the illegality (not waiting long enough before entering) and the evidence seized was not of the right kind (i.e., that exclusion of the evidence would not protect the interests that the knock-and-announce rule was intended to protect) "would, at the very least, make the exclusionary rule inapplicable to cases that have long been thought to fall at its core'"? Eric A. Johnson, *Causal Relevance in the Law of Search and Seizure*, 88 B.U. L. Rev. 113, 116 (2008). Johnson suggests that the logic of *Hudson* would mean that "the fruits of a warrantless residential search would not be subject to suppression if the police had probable cause to search the residence; what makes warrantless searches wrongful, after all, is the risk that the searches will be conducted on something less than probable cause." *Id*.

In turn, Professor Albert Alschuler suggests that:

> *Hudson*'s ruling on but-for causation would require a different result in all of the cases in which the police searched without a warrant they could have obtained. If the police had complied with the Constitution by securing this warrant, they would have discovered the challenged evidence, and if blocked from searching without a warrant, they probably would have taken the low-cost step of obtaining one. To echo the words of Judge Sam Ervin III, if they hadn't done it wrong, they would have done it right.

Albert W. Alschuler, *The Exclusionary Rule and Causation: Hudson v. Michigan and Its Ancestors*, 93 Iowa L. Rev. 1741, 1779 (2008). Alschuler writes that "[o]n the issue of but-for causation, the no-knock and no-warrant cases are indistinguishable."

5. And then there came ...

HERRING v. UNITED STATES

Supreme Court of the United States, 2009.
555 U.S. ___, 129 S.Ct. 695, 172 L.Ed.2d 496.

CHIEF JUSTICE ROBERTS delivered the opinion of the Court.

* * * What if an officer reasonably believes there is an outstanding arrest warrant, but that belief turns out to be wrong because of a negligent bookkeeping error by another police employee? The parties here agree that the ensuing arrest is still a violation of the Fourth Amendment, but dispute whether contraband found during a search incident to that arrest must be excluded in a later prosecution.

Our cases establish that such suppression is not an automatic consequence of a Fourth Amendment violation. Instead, the question turns on the culpability of the police and the potential of exclusion to deter wrongful police conduct. Here the error was the result of isolated negligence attenuated from the arrest. We hold that in these circumstances the jury should not be barred from considering all the evidence.

I

On July 7, 2004, Investigator Mark Anderson learned that Bennie Dean Herring had driven to the Coffee County Sheriff's Department to retrieve something from his impounded truck. Herring was no stranger to law enforcement, and Anderson asked the county's warrant clerk, Sandy Pope, to check for any outstanding warrants for Herring's arrest. When she found none, Anderson asked Pope to check with Sharon Morgan, her counterpart in neighboring Dale County. After checking Dale County's computer database, Morgan replied that there was an active arrest warrant for Herring's failure to appear on a felony charge. Pope relayed the information to Anderson and asked Morgan to fax over a copy of the warrant as confirmation. Anderson and a deputy followed Herring as he left the impound lot, pulled him over, and arrested him. A search incident to the arrest revealed methamphetamine in Herring's pocket, and a pistol (which as a felon he could not possess) in his vehicle.

There had, however, been a mistake about the warrant. The Dale County sheriff's computer records are supposed to correspond to actual arrest warrants, which the office also maintains. But when Morgan went to the files to retrieve the actual warrant to fax to Pope, Morgan was unable to find it. She called a court clerk and learned that the warrant had been recalled five months earlier. Normally when a warrant is recalled the court clerk's office or a judge's chambers calls Morgan, who enters the information in the sheriff's computer database and disposes of the physical copy. For whatever reason, the information about the recall of the warrant for Herring did not appear in the database. Morgan immediately called Pope to alert her to the mixup, and Pope contacted Anderson over a secure radio. This all unfolded in 10 to 15 minutes, but Herring had already been arrested and found with the gun and drugs, just a few hundred yards from the sheriff's office.

Herring was indicted in the District Court for the Middle District of Alabama for illegally possessing the gun and drugs * * *. He moved to suppress the evidence on the ground that his initial arrest had been illegal because the warrant had been rescinded. The Magistrate Judge recommended denying the motion because the arresting officers had acted in a good-faith belief that the warrant was still outstanding. Thus, * * * there was "no reason to believe that application of the exclusionary rule here would deter the occurrence of any future mistakes." The District Court adopted the Magistrate Judge's recommendation, and the Court of Appeals for the Eleventh Circuit affirmed.

The Eleventh Circuit found that the arresting officers in Coffee County "were entirely innocent of any wrongdoing or carelessness." The court assumed that whoever failed to update the Dale County sheriff's records was also a law enforcement official, but noted that "the conduct in question [wa]s a negligent failure to act, not a deliberate or tactical choice to act." Because the error was merely negligent and attenuated from the arrest, the Eleventh Circuit concluded that the benefit of suppressing the evidence "would be marginal or nonexistent," and the evidence was therefore admissible under the good-faith rule of *United States v. Leon,* [p. 477].

Other courts have required exclusion of evidence obtained through similar police errors, so we granted Herring's petition for certiorari to resolve the conflict. We now affirm the Eleventh Circuit's judgment.

II * * *

A

* * * [O]ur decisions establish an exclusionary rule that, when applicable, forbids the use of improperly obtained evidence at trial. We have stated that this judicially created rule is "designed to safeguard Fourth Amendment rights generally through its deterrent effect."

In analyzing the applicability of the rule, *Leon* admonished that we must consider the actions of all the police officers involved. The Coffee County officers did nothing improper. Indeed, the error was noticed so quickly because Coffee County requested a faxed confirmation of the warrant.

The Eleventh Circuit concluded, however, that somebody in Dale County should have updated the computer database to reflect the recall of the arrest warrant. The court also concluded that this error was negligent, but did not find it to be reckless or deliberate. That fact is crucial to our holding that this error is not enough by itself to require "the extreme sanction of exclusion."

B

1. The fact that a Fourth Amendment violation occurred * * * does not necessarily mean that the exclusionary rule applies. Indeed, exclusion "has always been our last resort, not our first impulse," *Hudson v. Michigan,* [p. 509], and our precedents establish important principles that constrain application of the exclusionary rule.

First, the exclusionary rule is not an individual right and applies only where it " 'result[s] in appreciable deterrence.' " * * * [2]

In addition, the benefits of deterrence must outweigh the costs. "We have never suggested that the exclusionary rule must apply in every circumstance in which it might provide marginal deterrence." * * * The principal cost of applying the rule is, of course, letting guilty and possibly dangerous defendants go free—something that "offends basic concepts of the criminal justice system." "[T]he rule's costly toll upon truth-seeking and law enforcement objectives presents a high obstacle for those urging [its] application."

These principles are reflected in the holding of *Leon*: When police act under a warrant that is invalid for lack of probable cause, the exclusionary rule does not apply if the police acted "in objectively reasonable reliance" on the subsequently invalidated search warrant. 468 U.S., at 922. We (perhaps confusingly) called this objectively reasonable reliance "good faith." In a companion case, *Massachusetts v. Sheppard,* [p. 490, Note 3], we held that the exclusionary rule did not apply when a warrant was invalid because a judge forgot to make "clerical corrections" to it.

---

2. Justice GINSBURG's dissent champions what she describes as " 'a more majestic conception' of * * * the exclusionary rule," which would exclude evidence even where deterrence does not justify doing so. Majestic or not, our cases reject this conception, and perhaps for this reason, her dissent relies almost exclusively on previous dissents to support its analysis.

Shortly thereafter we extended these holdings to warrantless administrative searches performed in good-faith reliance on a statute later declared unconstitutional. [Illinois v. Krull, 480 U.S. 340 (1987).] Finally, in [*Arizona v.*] *Evans,* 514 U.S. 1, 115 S.Ct. 1185, 131 L.Ed.2d 34, we applied this good-faith rule to police who reasonably relied on mistaken information in a court's database that an arrest warrant was outstanding. We held that a mistake made by a judicial employee could not give rise to exclusion for three reasons: The exclusionary rule was crafted to curb police rather than judicial misconduct; court employees were unlikely to try to subvert the Fourth Amendment; and "most important, there [was] no basis for believing that application of the exclusionary rule in [those] circumstances" would have any significant effect in deterring the errors. *Evans* left unresolved "whether the evidence should be suppressed if police personnel were responsible for the error," an issue not argued by the State in that case, but one that we now confront.

2.   The extent to which the exclusionary rule is justified by these deterrence principles varies with the culpability of the law enforcement conduct. As we said in *Leon,* "an assessment of the flagrancy of the police misconduct constitutes an important step in the calculus" of applying the exclusionary rule. Similarly, in *Krull* we elaborated that "evidence should be suppressed 'only if it can be said that the law enforcement officer had knowledge, or may properly be charged with knowledge, that the search was unconstitutional under the Fourth Amendment.'"

Anticipating the good-faith exception to the exclusionary rule, Judge Friendly wrote that "[t]he beneficent aim of the exclusionary rule to deter police misconduct can be sufficiently accomplished by a practice * * * outlawing evidence obtained by flagrant or deliberate violation of rights." The Bill of Rights as a Code of Criminal Procedure, 53 Calif. L.Rev. 929, 953 (1965) (footnotes omitted).

Indeed, the abuses that gave rise to the exclusionary rule featured intentional conduct that was patently unconstitutional. In *Weeks* [*v. United States*], [p. 67], * * * the officers had broken into the defendant's home (using a key shown to them by a neighbor), confiscated incriminating papers, then returned again with a U.S. Marshal to confiscate even more. Not only did they have no search warrant, * * * but they could not have gotten one had they tried. They were so lacking in sworn and particularized information that "not even an order of court would have justified such procedure." *Silverthorne Lumber Co. v. United States,* [p. 494], * * * was similar; federal officials "without a shadow of authority" went to the defendants' office and "made a clean sweep" of every paper they could find. Even the Government seemed to acknowledge that the "seizure was an outrage."

Equally flagrant conduct was at issue in *Mapp v. Ohio,* [p. 73], which * * * extended the exclusionary rule to the States. Officers forced open a door to Ms. Mapp's house, kept her lawyer from entering, brandished what the court concluded was a false warrant, then forced her into handcuffs and canvassed the house for obscenity. An error that arises from nonrecurring and attenuated negligence is thus far removed from the core concerns that led us to adopt the rule in the first place. And in fact since *Leon*, we have never applied the rule to exclude evidence obtained in violation of the Fourth Amendment, where the police conduct was no more intentional or culpable than this.

3. To trigger the exclusionary rule, police conduct must be sufficiently deliberate that exclusion can meaningfully deter it, and sufficiently culpable that such deterrence is worth the price paid by the justice system. As laid out in our cases, the exclusionary rule serves to deter deliberate, reckless, or grossly negligent conduct, or in some circumstances recurring or systemic negligence. The error in this case does not rise to that level.[4]
* * *

The pertinent analysis of deterrence and culpability is objective, not an "inquiry into the subjective awareness of arresting officers." We have already held that "our good-faith inquiry is confined to the objectively ascertainable question whether a reasonably well trained officer would have known that the search was illegal" in light of "all of the circumstances." These circumstances frequently include a particular officer's knowledge and experience, but that does not make the test any more subjective than the one for probable cause, which looks to an officer's knowledge and experience, but not his subjective intent.

We do not suggest that all recordkeeping errors by the police are immune from the exclusionary rule. In this case, however, the conduct at issue was not so objectively culpable as to require exclusion. * * *

If the police have been shown to be reckless in maintaining a warrant system, or to have knowingly made false entries to lay the groundwork for future false arrests, exclusion would certainly be justified under our cases should such misconduct cause a Fourth Amendment violation. * * * Petitioner's fears that our decision will cause police departments to deliberately keep their officers ignorant are thus unfounded.

The dissent also adverts to the possible unreliability of a number of databases not relevant to this case. In a case where systemic errors were demonstrated, it might be reckless for officers to rely on an unreliable warrant system. But there is no evidence that errors in Dale County's system are routine or widespread. * * * Because no such showings were made here, the Eleventh Circuit was correct to affirm the denial of the motion to suppress.

* * *

Petitioner's claim that police negligence automatically triggers suppression cannot be squared with the principles underlying the exclusion-

---

4. We do not quarrel with Justice GINSBURG's claim that "liability for negligence * * * creates an incentive to act with greater care," and we do not suggest that the exclusion of this evidence could have *no* deterrent effect. But our cases require any deterrence to "be weighed against the 'substantial social costs exacted by the exclusionary rule,'" and here exclusion is not worth the cost.

ary rule, as they have been explained in our cases. In light of our repeated holdings that the deterrent effect of suppression must be substantial and outweigh any harm to the justice system, we conclude that when police mistakes are the result of negligence such as that described here, rather than systemic error or reckless disregard of constitutional requirements, any marginal deterrence does not "pay its way." In such a case, the criminal should not "go free because the constable has blundered." *People v. Defore,* 242 N.Y. 13, 21, 150 N.E. 585, 587 (1926) (opinion of the Court by Cardozo, J.).

Justice GINSBURG, with whom Justice STEVENS, Justice SOUTER, and Justice BREYER join, dissenting. * * *

II

A

The Court states that the exclusionary rule is not a defendant's right; rather, it is simply a remedy applicable only when suppression would result in appreciable deterrence that outweighs the cost to the justice system.

The Court's discussion invokes a view of the exclusionary rule famously held by renowned jurists Henry J. Friendly and Benjamin Nathan Cardozo. Over 80 years ago, Cardozo, then seated on the New York Court of Appeals, commented critically on the federal exclusionary rule, which had not yet been applied to the States. He suggested that in at least some cases the rule exacted too high a price from the criminal justice system. In words often quoted, Cardozo questioned whether the criminal should "go free because the constable has blundered."

Judge Friendly later elaborated on Cardozo's query. "The sole reason for exclusion," Friendly wrote, "is that experience has demonstrated this to be the only effective method for deterring the police from violating the Constitution." He thought it excessive, in light of the rule's aim to deter police conduct, to require exclusion when the constable had merely "blundered"—when a police officer committed a technical error in an on-the-spot judgment, or made a "slight and unintentional miscalculation." * * *

B

Others have described "a more majestic conception" of the Fourth Amendment and its adjunct, the exclusionary rule. Protective of the fundamental "right of the people to be secure in their persons, houses, papers, and effects," the Amendment "is a constraint on the power of the sovereign, not merely on some of its agents." I share that vision of the Amendment.

The exclusionary rule is "a remedy necessary to ensure that" the Fourth Amendment's prohibitions "are observed in fact." The rule's service as an essential auxiliary to the Amendment earlier inclined the Court to hold the two inseparable.

Beyond doubt, a main objective of the rule "is to deter—to compel respect for the constitutional guaranty in the only effectively available way—by removing the incentive to disregard it." But the rule also serves other important purposes: It "enabl[es] the judiciary to avoid the taint of partnership in official lawlessness," and it "assur[es] the people—all potential victims of unlawful government conduct—that the government would not profit from its lawless behavior, thus minimizing the risk of seriously undermining popular trust in government."

The exclusionary rule, it bears emphasis, is often the only remedy effective to redress a Fourth Amendment violation. Civil liability will not lie for "the vast majority of [F]ourth [A]mendment violations—the frequent infringements motivated by commendable zeal, not condemnable malice." Criminal prosecutions or administrative sanctions against the offending officers and injunctive relief against widespread violations are an even farther cry.

III

The Court maintains that Herring's case is one in which the exclusionary rule could have scant deterrent effect and therefore would not "pay its way." I disagree.

A

The exclusionary rule, the Court suggests, is capable of only marginal deterrence when the misconduct at issue is merely careless, not intentional or reckless. The suggestion runs counter to a foundational premise of tort law—that liability for negligence, *i.e.,* lack of due care, creates an incentive to act with greater care. * * *

That the mistake here involved the failure to make a computer entry hardly means that application of the exclusionary rule would have minimal value. "Just as the risk of *respondeat superior* liability encourages employers to supervise * * * their employees' conduct [more carefully], so the risk of exclusion of evidence encourages policymakers and systems managers to monitor the performance of the systems they install and the personnel employed to operate those systems." * * *

B

Is the potential deterrence here worth the costs it imposes? In light of the paramount importance of accurate recordkeeping in law enforcement, I would answer yes * * *.

Electronic databases form the nervous system of contemporary criminal justice operations. In recent years, their breadth and influence have dramatically expanded. Police today can access databases that include not only the updated National Crime Information Center (NCIC), but also terrorist watchlists, the Federal Government's employee eligibility system, and various commercial databases. Moreover, States are actively expanding information sharing between jurisdictions. As a result, law enforcement has an increasing supply of information within its easy electronic reach.

The risk of error stemming from these databases is not slim. Herring's *amici* warn that law enforcement databases are insufficiently monitored and often out of date. Government reports describe, for example, flaws in NCIC databases, terrorist watchlist databases, and databases associated with the Federal Government's employment eligibility verification system

Inaccuracies in expansive, interconnected collections of electronic information raise grave concerns for individual liberty. * * *

C

The Court assures that "exclusion would certainly be justified" if "the police have been shown to be reckless in maintaining a warrant system, or to have knowingly made false entries to lay the groundwork for future false arrests." This concession provides little comfort.

First, by restricting suppression to bookkeeping errors that are deliberate or reckless, the majority leaves Herring, and others like him, with no remedy for violations of their constitutional rights. There can be no serious assertion that relief is available under 42 U.S.C. § 1983. The arresting officer would be sheltered by qualified immunity, and the police department itself is not liable for the negligent acts of its employees. Moreover, identifying the department employee who committed the error may be impossible.

Second, I doubt that police forces already possess sufficient incentives to maintain up-to-date records. * * *

Third, even when deliberate or reckless conduct is afoot, the Court's assurance will often be an empty promise: How is an impecunious defendant to make the required showing? If the answer is that a defendant is entitled to discovery (and if necessary, an audit of police databases), then the Court has imposed a considerable administrative burden on courts and law enforcement.

IV

Negligent recordkeeping errors by law enforcement threaten individual liberty, are susceptible to deterrence by the exclusionary rule, and cannot be remedied effectively through other means. Such errors present no occasion to further erode the exclusionary rule. The rule "is needed to make the Fourth Amendment something real; a guarantee that does not carry with it the exclusion of evidence obtained by its violation is a chimera." In keeping with the rule's "core concerns," suppression should have attended the unconstitutional search in this case. * * *

NOTES AND QUESTIONS

1. Shortly after *Herring* was decided, Kent Scheidegger, general counsel for the Criminal Justice Legal Foundation, a victims' rights group, told the New York Times that this case "jumped a firewall. I think *Herring* may be setting stage for the Holy Grail," by which he meant the overruling of *Mapp v. Ohio*. Adam Liptak, *Supreme Court Steps Closer to Repeal of Evidence Ruling*, New York Times, Jan. 31. 2009, at A1. Do you agree?

2. How should *Herring* be interpreted: Is the Court saying that, hereafter, the exclusionary rule *never* applies in the absence of proof of "deliberate, reckless, or grossly negligent conduct, or in some circumstances recurring or systemic negligence"? Or, is *Herring* limited to "clerical"-type errors in police computer databases? If it is the former, has the exclusionary rule already been overruled as a practical matter? How do you envision suppression hearing being held in the future?

Chapter 6

Confessions: The Voluntariness Requirement

■ ■ ■

A. TORTURE AND CONFESSIONS

HECTOR (A SLAVE) v. STATE

Supreme Court of Missouri, 1829.
2 Mo. 166.

M'GIRK, C.J. * * *

* * * A part of the testimony was, that about half past ten o'clock at night, when the burglary was discovered, certain persons caught Hector and began to flog him to make him confess what he knew concerning the burglary and stealing of the money * * *. That they continued flogging all night, that he screamed under the lash, and said if they would release him he would find the money. The State then examined one McKinney, who said, that about day break he was awakened by a loud hollowing or screaming in the rear of his house; that he arose, and on inquiry was informed by some persons there, near his house, that certain persons were flogging the slave Hector, to compel him to discover [to reveal his crime; eds.]. That when Hector heard the witness' voice he called on him to come to his assistance; that then the witness went to Hector, and told him if he took the money he ought to confess, and then asked Hector if he took the money. That Hector replied that he took the money, and that he would show the witness where it was, but that he did not wish the persons who had been flogging him to accompany him. * * * [T]hen Hector, the witness, and the other persons, went to the house of Mr. Menard [Hector's master] and did not find any money. That witness conceiving that Hector had deceived him, gave him several lashes with a cowskin, and then left him.

The prisoner's counsel then moved the court to exclude McKinney's testimony from the jury, on the ground that the confession of Hector was not freely and voluntarily made, but extorted by pain, & c., which motion the court overruled; and the prisoner's counsel also prayed the court to exclude from the consideration of the jury, all the confessions which were extorted from him, which the court refused.

But instructed the jury that they should exclude from their consideration any confession made by Hector under the influence of torture or pain, or hope or fear, but that the confessions of the defendant, which, in their opinion, was given freely and voluntarily, should be taken as good evidence against the prisoner, which instruction was objected to, & c.

The first question to be considered is, did the court err in refusing to exclude the testimony of McKinney from the jury? I think in this the court did err. Hector had been under the lash the greatest part of the night. This circumstance might of itself be sufficient to subdue him into any confession required. No doubt when he saw McKinney he hoped for some relief, and asked him for it, but he was told that if he was guilty he should confess, and then was asked if he took the money, to which he replied he had taken it and offered to show where it was. This all might have been done, and most probably was, to gain a respite from pain; which view of the subject is strengthened by the fact that no money was found where the party and prisoner went to look for it.

The court erred in instructing the jury that all the confessions, freely and voluntarily made, were evidence. And those not of this character not evidence. Whether a confession is sufficiently free and voluntary to be competent testimony, is a matter of law to be decided by the court and not by the jury. In this case there was another confession other than that made to McKinney that he took the money, which I consider made under the influence of pain, which should by the court have been excluded from the consideration of the jury.

BROWN v. MISSISSIPPI

Supreme Court of the United States, 1936.
297 U.S. 278, 56 S.Ct. 461, 80 L.Ed. 682.

Brown begins on p. 25.

NOTES & QUESTIONS

1. Is the misconduct more heinous in *Brown* than in *Hector* because the torture in *Brown* was at least in part authorized and conducted by law enforcement officers sworn to keep the peace? Leaving aside the source of the misconduct, is the coercion more severe in *Brown* than in *Hector*? If your answer is that the coercion is either more severe or the same in *Brown*, notice a curious, and very sad, fact.

Hector and *Brown* were separated by a century and the Civil War, the bloodiest war in our history. Hector won his case in the courts of a slave state. Brown lost his case in state court seventy years after slavery was abolished. It seems that things had not changed all that much in Mississippi. What had changed, of course, was that the Thirteenth, Fourteenth, and Fifteenth Amendments created legal tools to fight deep-seated racism. The Supreme Court in *Brown* relied on the due process clause of the Fourteenth Amendment to reverse the convictions and prevent the hanging of three probably innocent black defendants.

2. Would you be even a bit more inclined to admit Hector's confession if the money had been found where Hector said it was?

If the reliability of Hector's confession does not matter in finding the confession inadmissible, then what is the rationale behind suppression? Is it the likelihood that some people might confess falsely even if a particular suspect did not? Or is the problem with the confession purely the means used to obtain it, without regard to whether a person in Hector's situation might confess falsely?

3. Canvassing the authorities generally, John Henry Wigmore had no doubt that this kind of confession was inadmissible. 2 John Henry Wigmore, A Treatise on Evidence 159, § 833 (2d ed. 1923) (citing eight cases from 1829–1863). For more detail on how the law in slave cases generally tracked that of the law in cases involving whites, see Mark V. Tushnet, The American Law of Slavery: 1810–1860 (1981). At one point, Professor Tushnet concludes that Southern courts "may have wished to relax various technicalities in slave cases, but they ran the risk that elimination of concern for technicality in slave cases would reflect back onto cases involving whites, which formed part of the permissible range of analogy." *Id.* at 122.

TORTURE TO GET INFORMATION FROM SUSPECTED TERRORISTS: A NASTY BUSINESS

If one uses a purely utilitarian calculus, perhaps there are no limits on what can be done to obtain information if it would save more lives than it costs. Syndicated columnist Charles Krauthammer believes one should start with the most extreme case and reason from there. Suppose a nuclear bomb capable of killing a million people is set to go off in New York City and the authorities have captured one of the persons suspected of planting the bomb. If you were in charge of the interrogation, and believed that torture would force the suspect to reveal the location of the bomb, would you authorize torture?

CHARLES KRAUTHAMMER—THE TRUTH ABOUT TORTURE: IT'S TIME TO BE HONEST ABOUT DOING TERRIBLE THINGS

The Weekly Standard, 12/05/2005, Volume 011, Issue 12.

Now, on most issues regarding torture, I confess tentativeness and uncertainty. But on this issue, there can be no uncertainty: Not only is it permissible to hang this miscreant [who might know the location of the nuclear bomb] by his thumbs. It is a moral duty.

Yes, you say, but that's an extreme and very hypothetical case. Well, not as hypothetical as you think. Sure, the (nuclear) scale is hypothetical, but in the age of the car-and suicide-bomber, terrorists are often captured who have just set a car bomb to go off or sent a suicide bomber out to a coffee shop, and you only have minutes to find out where the attack is to take place. This "hypothetical" is common enough that the Israelis have a term for precisely that situation: the ticking time bomb problem.

And even if the example I gave were entirely hypothetical, the conclusion—yes, in this case even torture is permissible—is telling because it establishes the principle: Torture is not always impermissible. However rare the cases, there are circumstances in which, by any rational moral calculus, torture not only would be permissible but would be required (to acquire life-saving information). And once you've established the principle, to paraphrase George Bernard Shaw, all that's left to haggle about is the price. In the case of torture, that means that the argument is not *whether* torture is ever permissible, but *when*—i.e., under what obviously stringent circumstances: how big, how imminent, how preventable the ticking time bomb. * * *

Let's Take An Example that is far from hypothetical. You capture Khalid Sheikh Mohammed in Pakistan. He not only has already killed innocents, he is deeply involved in the planning for the present and future killing of innocents. He not only was the architect of the 9/11 attack that killed nearly three thousand people in one day, most of them dying a terrible, agonizing, indeed tortured death. But as the top al Qaeda planner and logistical expert he also knows a lot about terror attacks to come. He knows plans, identities, contacts, materials, cell locations, safe houses, cased targets, etc. What do you do with him?

We have recently learned that since 9/11 the United States has maintained a series of "black sites" around the world, secret detention centers where presumably high-level terrorists like Khalid Sheikh Mohammed have been imprisoned. The world is scandalized. Black sites? Secret detention? Jimmy Carter calls this "a profound and radical change in the * * * moral values of our country." The Council of Europe demands an investigation, calling the claims "extremely worrying." Its human rights commissioner declares "such practices" to constitute "a serious human rights violation, and further proof of the crisis of values" that has engulfed the war on terror. The gnashing of teeth and rending of garments has been considerable.

I myself have not gnashed a single tooth. My garments remain entirely unrent. Indeed, I feel reassured. It would be a gross dereliction of duty for any government *not* to keep Khalid Sheikh Mohammed isolated, disoriented, alone, despairing, cold and sleepless, in some godforsaken hidden location in order to find out what he knew about plans for future mass murder. What are we supposed to do? Give him a nice cell in a warm Manhattan prison, complete with Miranda rights, a mellifluent lawyer, and his own website? Are not those the kinds of courtesies we extended to the 1993 World Trade Center bombers, then congratulated ourselves on how we "brought to justice" those responsible for an attack that barely failed to kill tens of thousands of Americans, only to discover a decade later that we had accomplished nothing—indeed, that some of the disclosures at the trial had helped Osama bin Laden avoid U.S. surveillance?

Have we learned nothing from 9/11? Are we prepared to go back with complete amnesia to the domestic-crime model of dealing with terrorists, which allowed us to sleepwalk through the nineties while al Qaeda incubated and grew and metastasized unmolested until on 9/11 it finished what the first World Trade Center bombers had begun? * * *

Let's assume (and hope) that Khalid Sheikh Mohammed has been kept in one of these black sites, say, a cell somewhere in Romania, held entirely incommunicado and subjected to the kind of "coercive interrogation" that I described above. [Senator John] McCain has been going around praising the Israelis as the model of how to deal with terrorism and prevent terrorist attacks. He does so because in 1999 the Israeli Supreme Court outlawed all torture in the course of interrogation. But in reality, the Israeli case is far more complicated. And the complications reflect precisely the dilemmas regarding all coercive interrogation, the weighing of the lesser of two evils: the undeniable inhumanity of torture versus the abdication of the duty to protect the victims of a potentially preventable mass murder.

In a summary of Israel's policies, Glenn Frankel of the *Washington Post* noted that the 1999 Supreme Court ruling struck down secret guidelines established 12 years earlier that allowed interrogators to use the kind of physical and psychological pressure I described in imagining how KSM might be treated in America's "black sites."

"But after the second Palestinian uprising broke out a year later, and especially after a devastating series of suicide bombings of passenger buses, cafes and other civilian targets," writes Frankel, citing human rights lawyers and detainees, "Israel's internal security service, known as the Shin Bet or the Shabak, returned to physical coercion as a standard practice." Not only do the techniques used "command widespread support from the Israeli public," but "Israeli prime ministers and justice ministers with a variety of political views," including the most conciliatory and liberal, have defended these techniques "as a last resort in preventing terrorist attacks."

But let us push further into even more unpleasant territory, the territory that lies beyond mere coercive interrogation * * *.

This "going beyond" need not be cinematic and ghoulish * * * Consider, for example, injection with sodium pentathol. (Colloquially known as "truth serum," it is nothing of the sort. It is a barbiturate whose purpose is to sedate. Its effects are much like that of alcohol: disinhibiting the higher brain centers to make someone more likely to disclose information or thoughts that might otherwise be guarded.) Forcible sedation is a clear violation of bodily integrity. In a civilian context it would be considered assault. It is certainly impermissible under any prohibition of cruel, inhuman, or degrading treatment.

Let's posit that during the interrogation of Khalid Sheikh Mohammed, perhaps early on, we got intelligence about an imminent al Qaeda attack. And we had a very good reason to believe he knew about it.

And if we knew what he knew, we could stop it. If we thought we could glean a critical piece of information by use of sodium pentathol, would we be permitted to do so?

Less hypothetically, there is waterboarding, a terrifying and deeply shocking torture technique in which the prisoner has his face exposed to water in a way that gives the feeling of drowning. According to CIA sources cited by ABC News, Khalid Sheikh Mohammed "was able to last between two and 2 1/2 minutes before begging to confess." Should we regret having done that? Should we abolish by law that practice, so that it could never be used on the next Khalid Sheikh Mohammed having thus gotten his confession?

And what if he possessed information with less imminent implications? Say we had information about a cell that he had helped found or direct, and that cell was planning some major attack and we needed information about the identity and location of its members. A rational moral calculus might not permit measures as extreme as the nuke-in-Manhattan scenario, but would surely permit measures beyond mere psychological pressure.

Such a determination would not be made with an untroubled conscience. It would be troubled because there is no denying the monstrous evil that is any form of torture. And there is no denying how corrupting it can be to the individuals and society that practice it. But elected leaders, responsible above all for the protection of their citizens, have the obligation to tolerate their own sleepless nights by doing what is necessary—and only what is necessary, nothing more—to get information that could prevent mass murder.

Given the gravity of the decision, if we indeed cross the Rubicon—as we must—we need rules. * * *

* * * I would propose * * * a ban against all forms of torture, coercive interrogation, and inhuman treatment, except in two contingencies: (1) the ticking time bomb and (2) the slower-fuse high-level terrorist (such as KSM). Each contingency would have its own set of rules. In the case of the ticking time bomb, the rules would be relatively simple: Nothing rationally related to getting accurate information would be ruled out. The case of the high-value suspect with slow-fuse information is more complicated. The principle would be that the level of inhumanity of the measures used (moral honesty is essential here—we would be using measures that are by definition inhumane) would be proportional to the need and value of the information. Interrogators would be constrained to use the least inhumane treatment necessary relative to the magnitude and imminence of the evil being prevented and the importance of the knowledge being obtained.

NOTES & QUESTIONS

1. Krauthammer briefly described waterboarding. One of the CIA memos released by President Obama in 2009 contained a more detailed description, written in 2002 by an assistant attorney general to the general counsel of the CIA:

> [T]he individual is bound securely to an inclined bench * * *. The individual's feet are generally elevated. A cloth is placed over the forehead and eyes. Water is then applied to the cloth in a controlled manner. As this is done, the cloth is lowered until it covers both the nose and mouth. Once the cloth is saturated and completely covers the mouth and nose, air flow is slightly restricted for 20 to 40 seconds due to the presence of the cloth. This causes an increase in carbon dioxide level in the individual's blood [that] stimulates increased efforts to breathe. This effort plus the cloth produces the perception of "suffocation and incipient panic," i.e., the perception of drowning. The individual does not breathe any water into his lungs. During those 20 to 40 seconds, water is continuously applied from a height of twelve to twenty-four inches. After this period, the cloth is lifted, and the individual is allowed to breathe unimpeded for three or four full breaths. The sensation of drowning is immediately relieved by the removal of the cloth. The procedure may then be repeated. The water is usually applied from a canteen cup or small watering can with a spout. You have orally informed us that this procedure triggers an automatic physiological sensation of drowning that the individual cannot control even though he may be aware that he is in fact not drowning. You have also informed us that it is likely that this procedure would not last more than 20 minutes in any one application.

Jay S. Bybee, Assistant Attorney General, U.S. Department of Justice, Office of Legal Counsel, *Memorandum for Alberto R. Gonzales, Counsel for the President, Re: Standards of Conduct for Interrogation under 18 U.S.C. §§ 2340–2340A*, August 1, 2002 at 2, available at http://www.washingtonpost.com/wp-srv/politics/documents/cheney/torture_memo_aug2002.pdf.

Is this torture?

Do you agree with Krauthammer that even torture should be used in the ticking time bomb cases? If not, what do you think should be done in the nuclear bomb situation? If you are willing to use highly coercive techniques, but do not think the fruits of that coercion should be admitted into evidence, can you articulate why the statement, if accurate, should be excluded?

In 2003, President George W. Bush appointed Jay Bybee, the author of the 2002 memorandum quoted above, to the Ninth Circuit Court of Appeals. In April, 2009, *The New York Times* called on Congress to impeach Judge Bybee. Editorial, *Torturers' Manifesto*, The New York Times, April 19, 2009. Look at Article III. Do you see any problem with impeaching Bybee for the memo he wrote in 2002?

2. *Ticking time bombs: how realistic?* Two writers have cautioned that the "ticking time bomb" may be, in practice, quite unrealistic. Several

conditions, they argue, must be met for the utilitarian balance to favor torture:

> it must be certain that a bomb has been planted; that it is about to explode; that the interrogee has information essential for its disarmament; that this information can be extracted from him by torture, and only by torture, in time; that only the necessary amount of force will be used by the interrogators; that the information would prevent the explosion of the bomb; and so on.

Ra'em Segev & Mordechai Kremnitzer, *The Legality of Interrogation Torture: A Question of Formal Authorization or a Substantial Moral Problem* 35 (manuscript).

Do you agree with these writers about all the conditions that must exist before a utilitarian case can be made for torture or can some of the conditions be stated in a way that makes them easier to satisfy?

Sherry Colb has argued that the use of torture in the ticking time bomb situation presents a question of moral uniqueness that can be distinguished from the use of force in self defense. She identifies three conditions that must exist to justify the use of violence in either situation. The one that is always met in cases of self-defense but may, or may not, be met in the time bomb case is that there be a close link between the status of the target as a wrongdoer and the efficacy of the violence against him in saving life or limb. In some cases, the target of the torture may be innocent but nonetheless possesses information that could be used to save lives. See Sherry F. Colb, *Why Is Torture "Different" and How "Different" Is It?*, 30 Cardozo L. Rev. 1411 (2009).

3. *Moving away from hypothetical ticking bombs.* Suppose you were the leader of the Mumbai, India Intelligence Service and your top agents had arrested three of the terrorists who were going to kill innocent civilians on November 26, 2008. You have very good reason to believe that the plan will result in hundreds dead and wounded. Would you authorize coercion to learn what you could about the plot so that you might be able to stop it? How much coercion would you authorize? Suppose milder forms failed to persuade. Would you authorize as much as necessary to get answers? How could you be sure that those answers were the truth? Would you do, or authorize, what the Sri Lankan counter-terrorist officer did in the real life case that follows?

Before insurgents in Sri Lanka were apparently defeated in 2009, they had waged a terror war on the country's democratically-elected government for twenty-five years. The United Nations estimated that between 80,000 and 100,000 were killed during the terror war. C. Bryson Hull and Ranga Sirilal, "Last phase of Sri Lanka war killed 6,200 troops—govt, Thompson Reuters, May 22, 2009, available at http://www.reuters.com/article/latestCrisis/idUSSP 463682. In 2002, *Atlantic Monthly* writer Bruce Hoffman interviewed a "battle hardened Sri Lankan army officer charged with fighting the [terrorists] and protecting the lives" of innocent Sri Lankans. The officer described a "code red" when intelligence indicated a pending terrorist attack against public places. Three terrorist suspects were in custody, suspected of having planted a bomb in the city. The officer asked the location of the bomb, but the terrorists remained silent. The officer said he would kill them if they did not tell the location of the bomb. When they remained silent, he

> took his pistol from his gun belt, pointed it at the forehead of one of them, and shot him dead. The other two, he said, talked immediately; the bomb, which had been placed in a crowded railway station and set to explode during the evening rush hour, was found and defused, and countless lives were saved.

Bruce Hoffman, *A Nasty Business*, The Atlantic Monthly, January 2002, at 52. The officer who gave this information "hadn't exulted in his explanation or revealed any joy or even a hint of pleasure in what he had to do."

What is your view of this interrogation "technique"?

4. *Torture warrants.* Noted civil libertarian and Harvard law professor Alan Dershowitz appeared on *60 Minutes* on January 20, 2002, to make a startling recommendation: The law should authorize torture warrants for the ticking bomb cases. Mike Wallace looked stunned and said that "sounds medieval." Dershowitz responded that torture should be brought "into the legal system so that we can control it" rather than pretending it is not happening and winking our approval when it does. For Dershowitz, the issue is not torture or no torture. "If you've got the ticking time bomb case, the case of the terrorist who knew precisely where and when the bomb would go off, and it was the only way of saving 500 or 1,000 lives, every democratic society would, has, and will use torture."

And what of the constitutional issues? "It's not against the Fifth Amendment if it's not admitted in a criminal case against the defendant," Dershowitz said. [Dershowitz was quite the prophet. A year later, in a splintered opinion, five justices said almost what Dershowitz said. See *Chavez v. Martinez*, Note 8, p. 564. Eds.] As for due process, "The process that an alleged terrorist who was planning to kill thousands of people may be due is very different from the process that an ordinary criminal may be due."

Do you agree with Dershowitz's proposal? Why or why not?

5. *Torture nation?* Perhaps Americans are too sanguine about our legal system. John Parry has examined the history of how our police, our military, and our prison officials have used violence as a means to an end. It seems that while we mouth platitudes about abhorring torture, we tolerate a lot of it. Parry argues that "torture may be compatible with American values in practice and with the legal system we have constructed to serve those values," and he concludes that "being a torture nation could be as important a part of the U.S. legal and political system as the ban on torture." John T. Parry, *Torture Nation, Torture Law*, 97 Geo. L. J. 1001, 1003 (2009).

6. *Interrogation post–9/11.* Would your answers to the questions asked in the above Notes change if you had been an FBI or CIA agent with reliable information on September 10, 2001 that a suspect in your custody had information regarding a planned terrorist attack on the United States scheduled to occur within the next twenty-four to forty-eight hours? Though it is difficult to know exactly how a single event changes our attitudes, do you

think your answers to these questions are the same ones you would have provided prior to September 11?

If your mind has changed, does this suggest that you now believe your pre-September 11 ideas were wrong (naive?) or is it possible that your post-September 11 views are wrong (felt out of fear or anger)? Or, is there another way to characterize your pre- and post–11th attitudes?

7.   Much of the discussion in this section is utilitarian in cast. But there is another, perhaps more fundamental, rationale for suppressing the confessions in *Brown* and *Hector*—it is wrong, as a matter of morality or Kantian principles, to force someone to condemn himself. This rationale informs President Obama's position against torture. "I was clear throughout this campaign and was clear throughout this transition that under my administration the United States does not torture," Obama said, when asked at the news conference whether he would continue the Bush administration's policy of harsh interrogation. "We will abide by the Geneva Conventions. We will uphold our highest ideals." Associated Press, January 9, 2009, *Obama names intel picks, vows no torture*, available at http://www.msnbc.msn.com/id/28574408/.

The morality rationale also informs the so-called "privilege against compelled self-incrimination" that is contained in the Fifth Amendment: "Nor shall any person * * * be compelled in any criminal case to be a witness against himself." This part of the Constitution did not apply to the states until Malloy v. Hogan, 378 U.S. 1, 84 S.Ct. 1489, 12 L.Ed.2d 653 (1964), and much of the development of the privilege thus comes from federal cases. The Fifth Amendment privilege against compelled self-incrimination is the subject of Chapter 7.

B.   POLICE INTERROGATION WITHOUT TORTURE

LISENBA v. CALIFORNIA

Supreme Court of the United States, 1941.
314 U.S. 219, 62 S.Ct. 280, 86 L.Ed. 166.

Mr. Justice Roberts delivered the opinion of the Court. * * *

The petitioner, who used, and was commonly known by, the name of Robert S. James (and will be so called), and one Hope were indicted May 6, 1936, for the murder of James' wife on August 5, 1935. Hope pleaded guilty and was sentenced to life imprisonment. James pleaded not guilty, was tried, convicted, and sentenced to death. * * *

The State's theory is that the petitioner conceived the plan of marrying, insuring his wife's life by policies providing double indemnity for accidental death, killing her in a manner to give the appearance of accident, and collecting double indemnity.

James employed Mary E. Busch as a manicurist in his barber shop in March, 1935, and, about a month later, went through a marriage ceremony with her, which was not legal, as he then had a living wife. While they were affianced, insurance was negotiated on her life, with James as beneficiary. Upon the annulment of the earlier marriage, a lawful ceremony was performed. The petitioner made sure that the policies were not annulled by the fact that, when they were issued, Mary had not been his lawful wife.

The allegation is that James enlisted one Hope in a conspiracy to do away with Mary and collect and divide the insurance on her life. Hope testified that, at James' instigation, he procured rattlesnakes which were to bite and kill Mary; that they appeared not to be sufficiently venomous for the purpose, but he ultimately purchased others and delivered them to James; that James, on August 4, 1935, blindfolded his wife's eyes, tied her to a table, had Hope bring one of the snakes into the room, and caused the reptile to bite her foot; that, during the night, James told Hope the bite did not have the desired effect, and, in the early morning of August 5, he told Hope that he was going to drown his wife; that later he said to Hope, "That is that"; and still later, at his request, Hope aided him in carrying the body to the yard, and James placed the body face down at the edge of a fish pond with the head and shoulders in the water.

James was at his barber shop on August 5. On that evening he took two friends home for dinner. When they arrived the house was dark and empty, and, upon a search of the grounds, his wife's body was found in the position indicated. An autopsy showed the lungs were almost filled with water. The left great toe showed a puncture and the left leg was greatly swollen and almost black. Nothing came of the investigation of the death.

James attempted to collect double indemnity; the insurers refused to pay; suits were instituted and one of them settled. As a result of this activity, a fresh investigation of Mary James' death was instituted. On April 19, 1936, officers arrested James for the crime of incest.[a] He was booked on this charge on the morning of April 21, was given a hearing and remanded to jail. On May 2 and 3 he made statements respecting his wife's death to the prosecuting officials.

At the trial, in addition to that of Hope, testimony was adduced as to the finding and condition of the body, other evidence to connect James with the death, and expert testimony that the condition of the left leg could be attributed to rattlesnake bites. The purchase of snakes by Hope was proved by him and several other witnesses, one of whom said he sold the two snakes to Hope, one of which, Hope claimed, had bitten Mary James. Two snakes were brought into court, which the witness identified as those sold to Hope and by Hope resold to the witness.

James' statements were offered in evidence. Objection was made that they were not voluntary. Before they were admitted the trial judge heard testimony offered by the State and the defendant on that issue. He ruled that the confessions were admissible, and they were received in evidence.

---

a. No evidence appears in the opinion as to the basis for the charge of incest. Eds.

The State offered evidence with respect to the death of a former wife of James, in 1932. This tended to prove that, while driving down Pike's Peak, their automobile went off the road. James went for aid. When the persons called upon reached the automobile they found James' wife lying partly outside the car with her head badly crushed and a bloody hammer in the back of the car. James appeared unhurt. The woman recovered from her injuries, but, shortly afterwards, was discovered by James and another man, drowned in the bathtub in a house James had temporarily leased at Colorado Springs. James collected double indemnity from insurance companies for her death, the insurance having been placed at about the time he married her and her death having occurred within a few months thereafter. * * *

* * * The important question is whether the use of the confessions rendered petitioner's conviction a deprivation of his life without due process of law. Recital of the relevant facts is essential to a decision.

The petitioner, while having almost no formal education, is a man of intelligence and business experience. After his arrest, on the charge of incest, on the morning of Sunday, April 19, 1936, he was taken for a short time to the adjoining house and shown a dictaphone there installed. He was brought to the District Attorney's offices, where he was lodged in the Bureau of Investigation. He says that during the two or three hours he stayed there he was not questioned. He was taken into an office where the District Attorney showed him a statement made by a Miss Wright respecting the incest charge and asked him what he cared to say about it. He replied that he would not talk about it. He was questioned for about an hour. He says he was asked about his wife's death; others who were present deny this.

He was held in the District Attorney's suite until 5 or 6 o'clock, was given supper at a café, and then conducted to the house next door to his home, where he arrived about 7 or 7:30. Various officers questioned him there, in relays throughout the night, concerning his wife's death. He sat in a chair fully dressed and had no sleep. Monday morning he was taken out for breakfast and went with the officers to point out to them a house at 9th and Alvarado Streets, after which he was taken to the District Attorney's offices. He was brought back to the house next door to his home, and the questioning was resumed, and continued until about 3 o'clock Tuesday morning when, he says, he fainted; and others present say he fell asleep and slept until 7 or 8 o'clock. After he had breakfasted he was booked at the jail, arraigned before a magistrate, and committed on the incest charge.

James testified that about 10 P.M. Monday, April 20, the officers began to beat him; that his body was made black and blue; that the beating impaired his hearing, and caused a hernia; that later that night an Assistant District Attorney questioned him and that, after this ordeal, he collapsed. It is admitted that an officer slapped his face that night. This is said to have occurred as the result of an offensive remark James made concerning his wife; he denies having made the remark. In corroboration of James' testimony two witnesses said they noticed that one or both of his ears were bruised and swollen when he was lodged in the jail. All of this testimony is contradicted by numerous witnesses for the State, save only that it is admitted James was repeatedly and persistently questioned at intervals during the period from Sunday night until Tuesday morning. It is testified that, except for the one slap, no one laid a hand on James; that no inducement was held out to him; that no threats were made; that he answered questions freely and intelligently; and that he was at ease, cool, and collected. He admits that no promises or threats were made or maltreatment administered on the occasions when he was in the District Attorney's office. It is significant that James stated to one of the other officers that Officer Southard had slapped him and that when, May 2, the District Attorney asked how he had been treated he again referred to the slap. In neither case did he say anything of any other mistreatment. During the period April 19–21 James made no incriminating admission or confession.

* * * It is not suggested that James was not allowed to see his attorney as often as he desired or that any obstacle was interposed to the attorney's interviewing him between April 21 and May 2.

There is no claim that from April 21, when he was lodged in the jail, until May 2, he was interviewed, questioned, threatened, or mistreated by anyone. During this period his attorney told him that he would be indicted for his wife's murder and should not answer any questions unless his attorney was present.

May 1, Hope was arrested and made a statement. On the morning of May 2, James was brought from his cell to the chaplain's room in the prison and confronted with Hope. An Assistant District Attorney outlined Hope's story and asked James whether he had anything to say, to which he replied: "Nothing."

He went back to his cell and, about noon, an order of court was obtained to remove him from the prison. He was taken to his former home by two deputy sheriffs. The evidence does not disclose clearly either the purpose or the incidents of this trip. He was then brought to the District Attorney's office and that official began to question him. He requested that his attorney be sent for. In his presence a telephone call was made which disclosed that Mr. Silverman was not in Los Angeles. He asked that another attorney be summoned. He states that the District Attorney said it would take too long to acquaint any other attorney with the facts; others say that James did not give the name of the other attorney he wanted and it took some time to discover whom he had in mind. The attorney was not summoned.

The District Attorney and, at times, others questioned James until supper time. Sandwiches and coffee were procured. James says he had coffee but someone took his sandwiches. There is testimony that he had them. The questioning, based on Hope's confession, was continued into the night without James having refused to answer questions or having made any incriminating answers.

There is a sharp conflict as to how the session terminated. James says that Officer Southard, who had struck him on April 20, occupied the room alone with him, all others having left; that the officer told him he had been lying all evening and that if he did not tell the truth the officer would take him back to the house and beat him; that this so frightened him that he agreed to do his best to recite to the District Attorney the same story Hope had told. There is much evidence that no such incident occurred. Deputy Sheriff Killion says that sometime before midnight the others had left petitioner alone with him and that petitioner turned to him and said something to the effect: "Why can't we go out and get something to eat; if we do I'll tell you the story." To this Killion replied that they could go out. Killion and another Deputy Sheriff, Gray, a lady friend, and another person accompanied petitioner to a public café, where they had a supper and afterwards had cigars. James testified that neither Killion nor Gray nor the District Attorney ever laid hand on him, threatened him or offered him any inducement to confess.

The State's evidence is that after they started to smoke, James told a story, of which Killion took notes. Killion narrated at the trial what James had told him. * * *

Hope's statement laid on James the initiation of the murder plot, the attempt to consummate it with snake poison, the drowning and the disposition of her body. The account James gave Killion and the District Attorney, which he now says was an attempt to retell the tale Hope had told, which had been constantly dinned into his ears, is by no means a reiteration of Hope's story. On the contrary, James insisted that Hope suggested the destruction of Mary James, and the rattlesnake expedient, which Hope carried out; that when this failed Hope suggested that he, Hope, burn down the house to make it appear that Mrs. James died by accident; and that Hope also volunteered to commit an abortion on Mrs. James and also to do away with her. James asserted that, while he was absent from his home on the morning of August 5, 1935, Hope drowned his wife in the bathtub and told James that he had done so.

It is also to be noted that James' statement presents a lurid picture of the heavy drinking and intoxication of Hope, James, and Mary James during the three days anterior to the death of the latter. The effort evidently was to suggest that all were more or less irresponsible for their actions.

If Hope's story is true, James planned and accomplished the murder of his wife to obtain the insurance on her life. If James' statement is true, Hope planned the murder, James desired to abandon the scheme and thought that all Hope ultimately intended to do was to commit an abortion on James' wife and was shocked and surprised to learn that Hope had murdered her.

James said during supper at the café, and stated on another occasion, that there were not enough men in the District Attorney's office to make him talk, and if Hope had not talked he would never have told the story.

Scrutiny of the two statements indicates that James carefully considered what Hope had said and made up his mind to tell a story consistent with his intimacy with Hope, and with various incidents James could not deny, and then depict a drunken orgy as a result of which his will power was so enfeebled that he could not resist Hope's determination to make away with Mrs. James.

At the trial James contradicted the essential particulars of Hope's testimony and most of his own confession, including the evidence respecting the snakes. He swore all Hope was to do was to attempt an abortion; he believed Hope did not accomplish this, and that his wife died as a result of falling into the pond in a fainting fit due to her pregnancy.

The evidence as to the treatment of James and the conduct of officials and officers, from the moment of his arrest until the close of his statement to the District Attorney, was heard preliminarily by the trial judge in order to determine whether the State had, as required by California law, carried its burden of proving the confessions voluntary. The ruling was that it had; and the confessions were admitted. The trial judge, at defendant's request, charged the jury, in accordance with the State law, that the confessions must be utterly disregarded unless they were voluntary, that is, not the result of inducements, promises, threats, violence, or any form of coercion.

The failure of the arresting officers promptly to produce the petitioner before an examining magistrate, their detention of him in their custody from Sunday morning to Tuesday morning, and any assault committed upon him, were violations of state statutes and criminal offenses.

We find no authority for the issue of the court order under which the sheriff's deputies took the accused from jail to his former home, and to the District Attorney's office for questioning. The denial of opportunity to consult counsel, requested on May 2nd, was a misdemeanor. It may be assumed this treatment of the petitioner also deprived him of his liberty without due process and that the petitioner would have been afforded preventive relief if he could have gained access to a court to seek it.

But illegal acts, as such, committed in the course of obtaining a confession, whatever their effect on its admissibility under local law, do not furnish an answer to the constitutional question we must decide. The effect of the officers' conduct must be appraised by other considerations in determining whether the use of the confessions was a denial of due process. Moreover, petitioner does not, and cannot, ask redress in this proceeding for any disregard of due process prior to his trial. The gravamen of his complaint is the unfairness of the use of his confessions, and what occurred in their procurement is relevant only as it bears on that issue.

On the other hand, the fact that the confessions have been conclusively adjudged by the decision below to be admissible under State law, notwithstanding the circumstances under which they were made, does not answer the question whether due process was lacking. The aim of the rule that a confession is inadmissible unless it was voluntarily made is to exclude false evidence. Tests are invoked to determine whether the inducement to speak was such that there is a fair risk the confession is false.[14] These vary in the several States. This Court has formulated those which are to govern in trials in the federal courts. The Fourteenth Amendment leaves California free to adopt, by statute or decision, and to enforce, such rule as she elects, whether it conform to that applied in the federal or in other state courts. But the adoption of the rule of her choice cannot foreclose inquiry as to whether, in a given case, the application of that rule works a deprivation of the prisoner's life or liberty without due process of law. The aim of the requirement of due process is not to exclude presumptively false evidence, but to prevent fundamental unfairness in the use of evidence whether true or false. The criteria for decision of that question may differ from those appertaining to the State's rule as to the admissibility of a confession.

As applied to a criminal trial, denial of due process is the failure to observe that fundamental fairness essential to the very concept of justice. In order to declare a denial of it we must find that the absence of that fairness fatally infected the trial; the acts complained of must be of such quality as necessarily prevents a fair trial. Such unfairness exists when a coerced confession is used as a means of obtaining a verdict of guilt. We have so held in every instance in which we have set aside for want of due process a conviction based on a confession.

To extort testimony from a defendant by physical torture in the very presence of the trial tribunal is not due process. The case stands no better if torture induces an extrajudicial confession which is used as evidence in the courtroom. * * *

The concept of due process would void a trial in which, by threats or promises in the presence of court and jury, a defendant was induced to testify against himself. The case can stand no better if, by resort to the same means, the defendant is induced to confess and his confession is given in evidence. As we have said, "due process of law * * * commands that no such practice * * * shall send any accused to his death."

Where the claim is that the prisoner's statement has been procured by such means, we are bound to make an independent examination of the record to determine the validity of the claim. The performance of this duty cannot be foreclosed by the finding of a court, or the verdict of a jury, or both. * * *

There are cases, such as this one, where the evidence as to the methods employed to obtain a confession is conflicting, and in which, although denial of due process was not an issue in the trial, an issue has

---

14. Wigmore, Evidence, 3rd Ed., §§ 823, 824.

been resolved by court and jury, which involves an answer to the due process question. In such a case, we accept the determination of the triers of fact, unless it is so lacking in support in the evidence that to give it effect would work that fundamental unfairness which is at war with due process. * * *

In view of the conflicting testimony, we are unable to say that the finding below was erroneous so far as concerns the petitioner's claims of physical violence, threats, or implied promises of leniency. There remains the uncontradicted fact that on two occasions, separated by an interval of eleven days, the petitioner was questioned for protracted periods. He made no admission implicating him in his wife's death during, or soon after, the interrogations of April 19, 20, and 21. If, without more, eleven days later, confessions had been forthcoming we should have no hesitation in overruling his contention respecting the admission of his confessions.

Does the questioning on May 2nd, in and of itself, or in the light of his earlier experience, render the use of the confessions a violation of due process? If we are so to hold it must be upon the ground that such a practice, irrespective of the result upon the petitioner, so tainted his statements that, without considering other facts disclosed by the evidence, and without giving weight to accredited findings below that his statements were free and voluntary, as a matter of law, they were inadmissible in his trial. This would be to impose upon the state courts a stricter rule than we have enforced in federal trials. There is less reason for such a holding when we reflect that we are dealing with the system of criminal administration of California, a quasi-sovereign; that if federal power is invoked to set aside what California regards as a fair trial, it must be plain that a federal right has been invaded.

We have not hesitated to set aside convictions based in whole, or in substantial part, upon confessions extorted in graver circumstances. These were secured by protracted and repeated questioning of ignorant and untutored persons, in whose minds the power of officers was greatly magnified; who sensed the adverse sentiment of the community and the danger of mob violence; who had been held incommunicado, without the advice of friends or of counsel; some of whom had been taken by officers at night from the prison into dark and lonely places for questioning. This case is outside the scope of those decisions.

Like the Supreme Court of California, we disapprove the violations of law involved in the treatment of the petitioner, and we think it right to add that where a prisoner, held incommunicado, is subjected to questioning by officers for long periods, and deprived of the advice of counsel, we shall scrutinize the record with care to determine whether, by the use of his confession, he is deprived of liberty or life through tyrannical or oppressive means. Officers of the law must realize that if they indulge in such practices they may, in the end, defeat rather than further the ends of justice. Their lawless practices here took them close to the line. But on the facts as we have endeavored fairly to set them forth, and in the light of the findings in the state courts, we cannot hold that the illegal conduct in which the law enforcement officers of California indulged, by the prolonged questioning of the prisoner before arraignment, and in the absence of counsel, or their questioning on May 2, coerced the confessions, the introduction of which is the infringement of due process of which the petitioner complains. The petitioner has said that the interrogation would never have drawn an admission from him had his confederate not made a statement; he admits that no threats, promises, or acts of physical violence were offered him during this questioning or for eleven days preceding it. Counsel had been afforded full opportunity to see him and had advised him. He exhibited a self-possession, a coolness, and an acumen throughout his questioning, and at his trial, which negatives the view that he had so lost his freedom of action that the statements made were not his but were the result of the deprivation of his free choice to admit, to deny, or to refuse to answer. * * *

Mr. Justice BLACK, dissenting, with whom Mr. Justice DOUGLAS concurs.

I believe the confession used to convict James was the result of coercion and compulsion, and that the judgment should be reversed for that reason. The testimony of the officers to whom the confession was given is enough, standing alone, to convince me that it could not have been free and voluntary. * * *

NOTES AND QUESTIONS

1. What violations of law did the state authorities commit in their treatment of the defendant? The Court concedes that these violations deprived James of due process of law and yet still affirmed his convictions. What role does the Court's concern with federalism play in its reasoning process?

2. John Henry Wigmore, perhaps America's greatest evidence scholar, identified three possible tests for deciding when to suppress confessions.

(1) The first is, Was the inducement of a nature calculated under the circumstances to induce a confession irrespective of its truth or falsity? (2) Another is, Was there a threat or a promise, a fear or a hope? (3) The third test, Was the confession voluntary? is practically colorless and unserviceable when the nature of the inducement is in the question, and is almost always translated secondarily, before application, into terms of one of the other two tests.

2 John Henry Wigmore, A Treatise on Evidence, § 831, pp. 154–55 (2d ed. 1923).

Wigmore gave as an example of the "unserviceable" nature of the voluntariness test: "As between the rack and a false confession, the latter would usually be considered the less disagreeable; but it is nonetheless voluntarily chosen." *Id.* at § 824, p. 145. The point is that all conscious choices are, in some sense, voluntary.

Aristotle saw the same problem over two thousand years earlier:

> Some acts are performed out of fear of greater evils or for some good thing. * * * This is the case with throwing cargo overboard in storms. In general, no one willingly throws things overboard; but all people of sense do so to save their own lives and those of other people. These actions are mixed, but they are more like voluntary acts. We choose or decide to do them at the time they are carried out, and the end or goal of the act is fitted to the occasion. * * * Such acts, then, are voluntary; but perhaps in a general way they are involuntary, since no one would choose any such act of itself.

Aristotle, *Ethics*, Book III § 1 (A. E. Wardman & J. L. Creed, trans. 1963).

Here is Professor Albert Alschuler's response to Aristotle's anguish over determining which acts are voluntary:

> Country lawyers are often better philosophers than philosophers are. Most lawyers have known for a long time that the term coercion cannot be defined, that judges place this label on results for many diverse reasons, and that the word coercion metamorphoses remarkably with the factual circumstances in which legal actors press it into service.

Albert W. Alschuler, *Constraint and Confession*, 74 Den. U. L. Rev. 957 (1997).

Accepting the Wigmore–Aristotle–Alschuler skepticism about the definition of voluntariness, one is left with the question of whether courts should admit the confession.

Wigmore thought the only legitimate inquiry was:

> Human nature being what it is, *were the prospects attending confession* (involving the equalization or averaging of the benefit of realizing the promise or the benefit of escaping from the threat, against the drawbacks moral and legal of furnishing damaging evidence), *as weighed at the time against the prospects attending non-confession* (involving a similar averaging), *such as to have created, in any considerable degree, a risk that a false confession would be made?* Putting it more briefly and roughly, Was the inducement such that there was any fair risk of a false confession?

Id. at § 824, pp. 145–46 (emphasis in original).

3. Using Wigmore's test, do you have reservations about the outcome of *Lisenba*—that is, did the police interrogation create a "fair risk" that the confession was false?

Using whatever due process test you think appropriate, do you agree with the *Lisenba* Court that James's confession is admissible? If not, how would you articulate the due process interest of the suspect that was violated? Is it relevant that James did not confess until confronted with Hope's statement that James had "planned and accomplished the murder of his wife to obtain the insurance"? Is it relevant that James did not "confess" in the full sense of taking all responsibility but sought, instead, to shift a large measure of the blame to Hope? Why might these facts be relevant to voluntariness?

4. The English common law of evidence waxed and waned on the issue of admissibility of out-of-court statements. In 1736, an English treatise for the first time expressed concern about coerced confessions. Parliament in 1554

and 1555 required that justices of the peace examine those accused of a crime and then make any statements available to the prosecutor for use at trial. Hale's *Pleas of the Crown* cautions the justices to testify at trial that the prisoner confessed to them "freely and without any menace, or undue terror imposed upon him." 2 Matthew Hale, The History of the Pleas of the Crown 284 (1736).

Sir William Blackstone prepared eight editions of his *Commentaries on the Law of England*, probably the most influential treatise on the law of England. The first was published in 1765, two decades after Hale's treatise appeared, yet the initial edition contains no concern about confessions. Indeed, no concern appears until the eighth edition, published in 1778. A new insertion into the section about treason suddenly expresses profound skepticism, noting that out-of-court statements "are the weakest and most suspicious of all testimony; ever liable to be obtained by artifice, false hopes, promises of favour, or menaces; seldom remembered accurately, or reported with due precision; and incapable in their nature of being disproved by other negative evidence." 4 W. Blackstone, Commentaries 357 (8th ed. 1778).

Blackstone's skepticism about confessions manifests more than one rationale. Part of the concern is with reliability of the evidence ("seldom remembered accurately, or reported with due precision"). Concern about "menaces," and "false hopes [and] promises of favor," also suggests a reliability rationale. But it is not clear how a confession taken by "artifice" is unreliable. If police falsely tell a suspect that his fingerprints were found at the scene of the crime, this artifice would likely work only on suspects who are guilty. Indeed, police themselves acknowledge that lying about the evidence is a high-risk game; if the suspect knows he wasn't there (but his confederate was) or was there but wore gloves, he will see the falsehood and realize that the police need a confession. This awareness should stiffen his resolve not to confess.

Another rationale is needed to explain the common law concern with "artifice." One rationale might be called "mental freedom"—recognizing that even guilty suspects still retain their dignity and status as human beings, the State should not deprive them of the "mental freedom" to decide whether to confess. *Lisenba* seems to recognize this component of due process at the end of the opinion when it considered whether James had so lost "his freedom of action that the statements made were not his but were the result of the deprivation of his free choice to admit, to deny, or to refuse to answer." Some pressure to confess might fall short of coercion and still deny sufficient "mental freedom."

At least some trickery is also inconsistent with mental freedom. Consider the highly religious suspect who confesses to a "priest" who is a police detective. The confession is non-coerced and reliable (what highly religious person would falsely tell a priest that he had committed a crime?). Yet it was not made with the mental freedom to decide to confess to the police. You will see the mental freedom rationale in a highly-developed state in *Miranda*, p. 581.

Three rationales for suppressing confessions thus overlap and intertwine into an analytical stew: (1) to prevent unreliable evidence from reaching the jury; (2) to use only statements taken without coercion; (3) to prove guilt only with statements that manifest a minimal level of mental freedom, whether or not the statements were coerced. The Court has a more respectful term for its voluntariness inquiry than "analytical stew," noting that "a complex of values underlies the stricture against use by the state of confessions which, by way of convenient shorthand, this Court terms involuntary." Blackburn v. Alabama, 361 U.S. 199, 80 S.Ct. 274, 4 L.Ed.2d 242 (1960). "Complex" is a good word for the Court's involuntariness doctrine. Perhaps the best attempt to explain the complexity is Joseph D. Grano, Confessions, Truth and the Law (1993).

5. *And what of God's coercion?* In Colorado v. Connelly, 479 U.S. 157, 107 S.Ct. 515, 93 L.Ed.2d 473 (1986), Connelly approached a Denver police officer on the street and confessed to an unsolved murder. Connelly was suffering from chronic schizophrenia, including command hallucinations. One of his hallucinations involved the "voice of God" that "instructed [him] to withdraw money from the bank, to buy an airplane ticket, and to fly from Boston to Denver." When Connelly "arrived from Boston, God's voice became stronger and told [him] either to confess to the killing or to commit suicide. Reluctantly following the command of the voices," Connelly approached a police officer and confessed.

There was no dispute that Connelly confessed to the crime because he thought he had the grisly choice of confessing to murder or committing suicide. Did that make the confession involuntary? Focusing on the lack of state action, the Court held that the confession was, for purposes of the due process clause, voluntary.

Our "involuntary confession" jurisprudence is entirely consistent with the settled law requiring some sort of "state action" to support a claim of violation of the Due Process Clause of the Fourteenth Amendment. The Colorado trial court, of course, found that the police committed no wrongful acts, and that finding has been neither challenged by respondent nor disturbed by the Supreme Court of Colorado. The latter court, however, concluded that sufficient state action was present by virtue of the admission of the confession into evidence in a court of the State.

The difficulty with the approach of the Supreme Court of Colorado is that it fails to recognize the essential link between coercive activity of the State, on the one hand, and a resulting confession by a defendant, on the other. The flaw in respondent's constitutional argument is that it would expand our previous line of "voluntariness" cases into a far-ranging requirement that courts must divine a defendant's motivation for speaking or acting as he did even though there be no claim that governmental conduct coerced his decision.

The most outrageous behavior by a private party seeking to secure evidence against a defendant does not make that evidence inadmissible under the Due Process Clause. We have also observed that "[j]urists and scholars uniformly have recognized that the exclusionary rule imposes a substantial cost on the societal interest in law enforcement by its proscription of what concededly is relevant evidence." Moreover, suppressing respondent's statements would serve absolutely no purpose in enforcing constitutional guarantees. The purpose of excluding evidence seized in violation of the Constitution is to substantially deter future violations of the Constitution. Only if we were to establish a brand new constitutional right—the right of a criminal defendant to confess to his crime only when totally rational and properly motivated—could respondent's present claim be sustained.

6. Justice Brennan in his dissent in *Connelly* contended that, state action or not, Connelly's confession was unreliable and his conviction, therefore, a violation of due process on that ground alone. The *Connelly* majority conceded that a "statement rendered by one in the condition of respondent might be proved to be quite unreliable, but this is a matter to be governed by the evidentiary laws of the forum." Justice Brennan in dissent found the record "barren of any corroboration of the mentally ill defendant's confession." In Brennan's view, "There is not a shred of competent evidence in this record linking the defendant to the charged homicide. There is only Mr. Connelly's confession."

But in 2009, Professor William Pizzi pointed out that Brennan's assertion is, on its face, an overstatement. After all, Connelly led the police to the victim's body. More fundamentally, Pizzi explains why the record was otherwise barren of evidence connecting Connelly. When the trial judge suppressed all of Connelly's statements as involuntary, the state filed an interlocutory appeal to the state supreme court. That court's ruling affirming the trial court was then appealed to the United States Supreme Court. There was little evidence connecting Connelly to the murder *because the case had never been tried.* To put it mildly, this renders seriously misleading the claim that the record was "barren" of evidence corroborating the confession.

Pizzi also discloses what happened to Connelly on remand: the prosecutor offered, and the defense accepted, a plea bargain to second degree murder that required Connelly to serve a total of a little under six years. He left the state of Colorado in the spring of 1990 and Pizzi could locate no information about what happened to Francis Barry Connelly since then. William T. Pizzi, *Colorado v. Connelly: What Really Happened,* 7 Ohio St. J. Crm. L. 377 (2009).

7. *The implications of Connelly.* A neighborhood watch, with no connections to the local police or prosecutors, apprehended a man believed to be fleeing from an attempted rape. When he refused to answer their questions, the watch members threatened him with violence. He confessed to trying to force the victim to have sex with him. Will any right in the Bill of Rights lead to exclusion of the confession?

SPANO v. NEW YORK

Supreme Court of the United States, 1959.
360 U.S. 315, 79 S.Ct. 1202, 3 L.Ed.2d 1265.

MR. CHIEF JUSTICE WARREN delivered the opinion of the Court.

This is another in the long line of cases presenting the question whether a confession was properly admitted into evidence under the

Fourteenth Amendment. As in all such cases, we are forced to resolve a conflict between two fundamental interests of society; its interest in prompt and efficient law enforcement, and its interest in preventing the rights of its individual members from being abridged by unconstitutional methods of law enforcement. Because of the delicate nature of the constitutional determination which we must make, we cannot escape the responsibility of making our own examination of the record.

The State's evidence reveals the following: Petitioner Vincent Joseph Spano is a derivative citizen of this country, having been born in Messina, Italy. He was 25 years old at the time of the shooting in question and had graduated from junior high school. He had a record of regular employment. The shooting took place on January 22, 1957.

On that day, petitioner was drinking in a bar. The decedent, a former professional boxer weighing almost 200 pounds who had fought in Madison Square Garden, took some of petitioner's money from the bar. Petitioner followed him out of the bar to recover it. A fight ensued, with the decedent knocking petitioner down and then kicking him in the head three or four times. Shock from the force of these blows caused petitioner to vomit. After the bartender applied some ice to his head, petitioner left the bar, walked to his apartment, secured a gun, and walked eight or nine blocks to a candy store where the decedent was frequently to be found. He entered the store in which decedent, three friends of decedent, at least two of whom were ex-convicts, and a boy who was supervising the store were present. He fired five shots, two of which entered the decedent's body, causing his death. The boy was the only eyewitness; the three friends of decedent did not see the person who fired the shot. Petitioner then disappeared for the next week or so.

On February 1, 1957, the Bronx County Grand Jury returned an indictment for first-degree murder against petitioner.[b] * * *

On February 3, 1957, petitioner called one Gaspar Bruno, a close friend of 8 or 10 years' standing who had attended school with him. Bruno was a fledgling police officer, having at that time not yet finished attending police academy. According to Bruno's testimony, petitioner told him "that he took a terrific beating, that the deceased hurt him real bad and he dropped him a couple of times and he was dazed; he didn't know what he was doing and that he went and shot at him." Petitioner told Bruno that he intended to get a lawyer and give himself up. Bruno relayed this information to his superiors.

The following day, February 4, at 7:10 p.m., petitioner, accompanied by counsel, surrendered himself to the authorities * * *. His attorney had cautioned him to answer no questions, and left him in the custody of the officers. He was promptly taken to the office of the Assistant District Attorney and at 7:15 p.m. the questioning began * * *. The record reveals

---

   b. *Spano* was decided before *Massiah v. United States*, p. 696. Today, as the concurring opinions in *Spano* anticipate, this case would be decided as a Sixth Amendment case and Spano would win easily. Eds.

that the questioning was both persistent and continuous. Petitioner, in accordance with his attorney's instructions, steadfastly refused to answer. * * * Detective Farrell testified [about Spano]:

> "Q. What did he say?
>
> "A. He said 'you would have to see my attorney. I tell you nothing but my name.' * * *
>
> "Q. Did you continue to examine him?
>
> "A. Verbally, yes, sir."

He asked one officer, Detective Ciccone, if he could speak to his attorney, but that request was denied. Detective Ciccone testified that he could not find the attorney's name in the telephone book.[1] He was given two sandwiches, coffee and cake at 11 p.m.

At 12:15 a.m. on the morning of February 5, after five hours of questioning in which it became evident that petitioner was following his attorney's instructions, on the Assistant District Attorney's orders petitioner was transferred to the 46th Squad, Ryer Avenue Police Station. The Assistant District Attorney also went to the police station and to some extent continued to participate in the interrogation. Petitioner arrived at 12:30 and questioning was resumed at 12:40. * * * But petitioner persisted in his refusal to answer, and again requested permission to see his attorney, this time from Detective Lehrer. His request was again denied.

It was then that those in charge of the investigation decided that petitioner's close friend, Bruno, could be of use. He had been called out on the case around 10 or 11 p.m., although he was not connected with the 46th Squad or Precinct in any way. Although, in fact, his job was in no way threatened, Bruno was told to tell petitioner that petitioner's telephone call had gotten him "in a lot of trouble," and that he should seek to extract sympathy from petitioner for Bruno's pregnant wife and three children. Bruno developed this theme with petitioner without success, and petitioner, also without success, again sought to see his attorney, a request which Bruno relayed unavailingly to his superiors. After this first session with petitioner, Bruno was again directed by Lt. Gannon to play on petitioner's sympathies, but again no confession was forthcoming. But the Lieutenant a third time ordered Bruno falsely to importune his friend to confess, but again petitioner clung to his attorney's advice. Inevitably, in the fourth such session directed by the Lieutenant, lasting a full hour, petitioner succumbed to his friend's prevarications and agreed to make a statement. * * *

* * * [T]he officers also elicited a statement from petitioner that the deceased was always "on [his] back," "always pushing" him and that he was "not sorry" he had shot the deceased. All three detectives testified to that statement at the trial. * * *

---

1. How this could be so when the attorney's name, Tobias Russo, was concededly in the telephone book does not appear. The trial judge sustained objections by the Assistant District Attorney to questions designed to delve into this mystery.

At the trial, the confession was introduced in evidence over appropriate objections. The jury was instructed that it could rely on it only if it was found to be voluntary. The jury returned a guilty verdict and petitioner was sentenced to death. * * *

The abhorrence of society to the use of involuntary confessions does not turn alone on their inherent untrustworthiness. It also turns on the deep-rooted feeling that the police must obey the law while enforcing the law; that in the end life and liberty can be as much endangered from illegal methods used to convict those thought to be criminals as from the actual criminals themselves. Accordingly, the actions of police in obtaining confessions have come under scrutiny in a long series of cases. Those cases suggest that in recent years law enforcement officials have become increasingly aware of the burden which they share, along with our courts, in protecting fundamental rights of our citizenry, including that portion of our citizenry suspected of crime. The facts of no case recently in this Court have quite approached the brutal beatings in *Brown v. Mississippi*, [p. 25], or the 36 consecutive hours of questioning present in *Ashcraft v. State of Tennessee*, 322 U.S. 143, 64 S.Ct. 921, 88 L.Ed. 1192 (1944). But as law enforcement officers become more responsible, and the methods used to extract confessions more sophisticated, our duty to enforce federal constitutional protections does not cease. It only becomes more difficult because of the more delicate judgments to be made. Our judgment here is that, on all the facts, this conviction cannot stand.

Petitioner was a foreign-born young man of 25 with no past history of law violation or of subjection to official interrogation, at least insofar as the record shows. He had progressed only one-half year into high school and the record indicates that he had a history of emotional instability.[3] He did not make a narrative statement, but was subject to the leading questions of a skillful prosecutor in a question and answer confession. He was subjected to questioning not by a few men, but by many. * * * All played some part, and the effect of such massive official interrogation must have been felt. Petitioner was questioned for virtually eight straight hours before he confessed, with his only respite being a transfer to an arena presumably considered more appropriate by the police for the task at hand. Nor was the questioning conducted during normal business hours, but began in early evening, continued into the night, and did not bear fruition until the not-too-early morning. The drama was not played out, with the final admissions obtained, until almost sunrise. In such circumstances slowly mounting fatigue does, and is calculated to, play its part. The questioners persisted in the face of his repeated refusals to answer on the advice of his attorney, and they ignored his reasonable requests to contact the local attorney whom he had already retained and

---

3. Medical reports from New York City's Fordham Hospital introduced by defendant showed that he had suffered a cerebral concussion in 1955. He was described by a private physician in 1951 as "an extremely nervous tense individual who is emotionally unstable and maladjusted," and was found unacceptable for military service in 1951, primarily because of "Psychiatric disorder." He failed the Army's FAQT–1 intelligence test. His mother had been in mental hospitals on three separate occasions.

who had personally delivered him into the custody of these officers in obedience to the bench warrant.

The use of Bruno, characterized in this Court by counsel for the State as a "childhood friend" of petitioner's, is another factor which deserves mention in the totality of the situation. Bruno's was the one face visible to petitioner in which he could put some trust. There was a bond of friendship between them going back a decade into adolescence. It was with this material that the officers felt that they could overcome petitioner's will. They instructed Bruno falsely to state that petitioner's telephone call had gotten him into trouble, that his job was in jeopardy, and that loss of his job would be disastrous to his three children, his wife and his unborn child. And Bruno played this part of a worried father, harried by his superiors, in not one, but four different acts, the final one lasting an hour. Petitioner was apparently unaware of John Gay's famous couplet:

> "An open foe may prove a curse,
>
> But a pretended friend is worse,"

and he yielded to his false friend's entreaties.

We conclude that petitioner's will was overborne by official pressure, fatigue and sympathy falsely aroused, after considering all the facts in their post-indictment setting. Here a grand jury had already found sufficient cause to require petitioner to face trial on a charge of first-degree murder, and the police had an eyewitness to the shooting. The police were not therefore merely trying to solve a crime, or even to absolve a suspect. They were rather concerned primarily with securing a statement from defendant on which they could convict him. The undeviating intent of the officers to extract a confession from petitioner is therefore patent. When such an intent is shown, this Court has held that the confession obtained must be examined with the most careful scrutiny, and has reversed a conviction on facts less compelling than these. Accordingly, we hold that petitioner's conviction cannot stand under the Fourteenth Amendment. * * *

Mr. Justice DOUGLAS, with whom Mr. Justice BLACK and Mr. Justice BRENNAN join, concurring. [omitted]

Mr. Justice STEWART, whom Mr. Justice DOUGLAS and Mr. Justice BRENNAN join, concurring.

While I concur in the opinion of the Court, it is my view that the absence of counsel when this confession was elicited was alone enough to render it inadmissible under the Fourteenth Amendment.

Let it be emphasized at the outset that this is not a case where the police were questioning a suspect in the course of investigating an unsolved crime. When the petitioner surrendered to the New York authorities he was under indictment for first degree murder.

Under our system of justice an indictment is supposed to be followed by an arraignment and a trial. At every stage in those proceedings the accused has an absolute right to a lawyer's help if the case is one in which a death sentence may be imposed. *Powell v. Alabama*, [p. 13]. Indeed the right to the assistance of counsel whom the accused has himself retained is absolute, whatever the offense for which he is on trial.

What followed the petitioner's surrender in this case was not arraignment in a court of law, but an all-night inquisition in a prosecutor's office, a police station, and an automobile. Throughout the night the petitioner repeatedly asked to be allowed to send for his lawyer, and his requests were repeatedly denied. He finally was induced to make a confession. That confession was used to secure a verdict sending him to the electric chair.

Our Constitution guarantees the assistance of counsel to a man on trial for his life in an orderly courtroom, presided over by a judge, open to the public, and protected by all the procedural safeguards of the law. Surely a Constitution which promises that much can vouchsafe no less to the same man under midnight inquisition in the squad room of a police station.

NOTES AND QUESTIONS

1. It will likely come as no surprise to you that judges, being former advocates, tend to state the facts in a way that supports the holding. In *Spano*, for example, Chief Justice Warren wrote, "Inevitably, in the fourth such [interrogation] session * * *, lasting a full hour, petitioner succumbed * * *." There was no dissent in *Spano*, but if you were writing a dissent, how would you describe these same facts?

2. As Spano shot the victim in the presence of witnesses, why did the police or the prosecution even need Spano's confession?

3. What is the most important reason the Court ruled in Spano's favor? Is it the denial of counsel? Lack of sufficient mental freedom? Spano's "overborne will"? Doubts about the reliability of the confession (and thus the accuracy of the conviction)? Were you surprised that no one dissented?

4. *When values and attitudes change over time, law changes.* Compare the Court's approach to state interrogation in *Spano* (1959) with that in *Lisenba* (1941). They are very different, almost diametrically opposed. Why would the Court so change its basic approach? It is easy to forget that judges are part of the culture, and change as the culture changes. One fundamental change in the world between *Lisenba* and *Spano* was the end of World War II, with the public revelation of Nazi atrocities. There is little doubt that these developments influenced the Supreme Court. Professor Carol Steiker provides an account of Justice Jackson's service as head of the American prosecution team at the Nazi war crimes trial in Nuremberg, which according to Steiker made him a "fervent believer" that searches should be authorized by warrants in most cases. Carol S. Steiker, *Second Thoughts About First Principles*, 107 Harv. L. Rev. 820, 842 (1994). The same concern about totalitarian government probably moved the Court toward a voluntariness test that more easily condemned police interrogation.

Consider, in that regard, Justice Black's opinion for the Court in Ashcraft v. Tennessee, 322 U.S. 143, 64 S.Ct. 921, 88 L.Ed. 1192 (1944) (note the date):

> The Constitution of the United States stands as a bar against the conviction of any individual in an American court by means of a coerced confession. There have been, and are now, certain foreign nations with governments dedicated to an opposite policy: governments which convict individuals with testimony obtained by police organizations possessed of unrestrained power to seize persons suspected of crimes against the state, hold them in secret custody, and wring from them confessions by physical or mental torture. So long as the Constitution remains the basic law of this Republic, America will not have that kind of government.

5. Police suspected Oreste Fulminante of the brutal murder of his eleven-year-old stepdaughter, Jeneane Hunt. She "had been shot twice in the head at close range with a large caliber weapon, and a ligature was around her neck." No charges were filed initially, and Fulminante left the state. He was later convicted of federal charges of possession of a firearm by a felon. While in a federal correctional facility, Fulminante

> became friends with another inmate, Anthony Sarivola, then serving a 60–day sentence for extortion. The two men came to spend several hours a day together. Sarivola, a former police officer, had been involved in loansharking for organized crime but then became a paid informant for the Federal Bureau of Investigation. While [in prison], he masqueraded as an organized crime figure. After becoming friends with Fulminante, Sarivola heard a rumor that Fulminante was suspected of killing a child in Arizona. Sarivola then raised the subject with Fulminante in several conversations, but Fulminante repeatedly denied any involvement in Jeneane's death. During one conversation, he told Sarivola that Jeneane had been killed by bikers looking for drugs; on another occasion, he said he did not know what had happened. Sarivola passed this information on to an agent of the Federal Bureau of Investigation, who instructed Sarivola to find out more.

> Sarivola learned more one evening in October 1983, as he and Fulminante walked together around the prison track. Sarivola said that he knew Fulminante was "starting to get some tough treatment and whatnot" from other inmates because of the rumor. Sarivola offered to protect Fulminante from his fellow inmates, but told him, " 'You have to tell me about it,' you know. I mean, in other words, 'For me to give you any help.' " Fulminante then admitted to Sarivola that he had driven Jeneane to the desert on his motorcycle, where he choked her, sexually assaulted her, and made her beg for her life, before shooting her twice in the head.

Fulminate was convicted of first-degree murder and sentenced to death based, in part, on the confession he gave Sarivola. "Fulminante appealed, arguing, among other things, that his confession to Sarivola was the product of coercion and that its admission at trial violated his rights to due process under the Fifth and Fourteenth Amendments to the United States Constitution." In Arizona v. Fulminante, 499 U.S. 279, 111 S.Ct. 1246, 113 L.Ed.2d 302 (1991), the Supreme Court agreed.

In applying the totality of the circumstances test to determine that the confession to Sarivola was coerced, the Arizona Supreme Court focused on a number of relevant facts. First, the court noted that "because [Fulminante] was an alleged child murderer, he was in danger of physical harm at the hands of other inmates." In addition, Sarivola was aware that Fulminante had been receiving " 'rough treatment from the guys.' " Using his knowledge of these threats, Sarivola offered to protect Fulminante in exchange for a confession to Jeneane's murder, and "in response to Sarivola's offer of protection, [Fulminante] confessed." Agreeing with Fulminante that "Sarivola's promise was 'extremely coercive,' " the Arizona Court declared: "The confession was obtained as a direct result of extreme coercion and was tendered in the belief that the defendant's life was in jeopardy if he did not confess. This is a true coerced confession in every sense of the word."[2] * * *

Although the question is a close one, we agree with the Arizona Supreme Court's conclusion that Fulminante's confession was coerced. The Arizona Supreme Court found a credible threat of physical violence unless Fulminante confessed. Our cases have made clear that a finding of coercion need not depend upon actual violence by a government agent; a credible threat is sufficient. As we have said, "coercion can be mental as well as physical, and * * * the blood of the accused is not the only hallmark of an unconstitutional inquisition." As in *Payne* [*v. Arkansas*, 356 U.S. 560, 78 S.Ct. 844, 2 L.Ed.2d 975 (1958)], where the Court found that a confession was coerced because the interrogating police officer had promised that if the accused confessed, the officer would protect the accused from an angry mob outside the jailhouse door, so too here, the Arizona Supreme Court found that it was fear of physical violence, absent protection from his friend (and Government agent) Sarivola, which motivated Fulminante to confess. Accepting the Arizona court's finding, permissible on this record, that there was a credible threat of physical violence, we agree with its conclusion that Fulminante's will was overborne in such a way as to render his confession the product of coercion.

Do you agree that Sarivola coerced Fulminante to confess? The majority conceded that the question was close, and four members of the Court dissented on the coercion point.

The admissibility of a confession such as that made by respondent Fulminante depends upon whether it was voluntarily made. "The ultimate test remains that which has been the only clearly established test in Anglo–American courts for two hundred years: the test of voluntariness. Is the confession the product of an essentially free and unconstrained

---

2. There are additional facts in the record, not relied upon by the Arizona Supreme Court, which also support a finding of coercion. Fulminante possesses low average to average intelligence; he dropped out of school in the fourth grade. He is short in stature and slight in build. Although he had been in prison before, he had not always adapted well to the stress of prison life. While incarcerated at the age of 26, he had "felt threatened by the [prison] population," and he therefore requested that he be placed in protective custody. Once there, however, he was unable to cope with the isolation and was admitted to a psychiatric hospital. The Court has previously recognized that factors such as these are relevant in determining whether a defendant's will has been overborne. In addition, we note that Sarivola's position as Fulminante's friend might well have made the latter particularly susceptible to the former's entreaties. See *Spano v. New York*, p. 555.

choice by its maker? If it is, if he has willed to confess, it may be used against him. If it is not, if his will has been overborne and his capacity for self-determination critically impaired, the use of his confession offends due process." * * *

Exercising our responsibility to make the independent examination of the record necessary to decide this federal question, I am at a loss to see how the Supreme Court of Arizona reached the conclusion that it did. Fulminante offered no evidence that he believed that his life was in danger or that he in fact confessed to Sarivola in order to obtain the proffered protection. Indeed, he had stipulated that "at no time did the defendant indicate he was in fear of other inmates nor did he ever seek Mr. Sarivola's 'protection.'" Sarivola's testimony that he told Fulminante that "if [he] would tell the truth, he could be protected," adds little if anything to the substance of the parties' stipulation. The decision of the Supreme Court of Arizona rests on an assumption that is squarely contrary to this stipulation, and one that is not supported by any testimony of Fulminante.

The facts of record in the present case are quite different from those present in cases where we have found confessions to be coerced and involuntary. Since Fulminante was unaware that Sarivola was an FBI informant, there existed none of "the danger of coercion resulting from the interaction of custody and official interrogation." The fact that Sarivola was a government informant does not by itself render Fulminante's confession involuntary, since we have consistently accepted the use of informants in the discovery of evidence of a crime as a legitimate investigatory procedure consistent with the Constitution. The conversations between Sarivola and Fulminante were not lengthy, and the defendant was free at all times to leave Sarivola's company. Sarivola at no time threatened him or demanded that he confess; he simply requested that he speak the truth about the matter. Fulminante was an experienced habitue of prisons and presumably able to fend for himself. In concluding on these facts that Fulminante's confession was involuntary, the Court today embraces a more expansive definition of that term than is warranted by any of our decided cases.

It might surprise you to learn that the five-justice majority finding in Fulminante's favor included Justice Scalia and that Justice Souter joined Chief Justice Rehnquist's dissent. Which opinion would you have joined? Can *Spano* be distinguished?

6. *Involuntariness factors.*

A. *Characteristics of the suspect.* What is the relevance of the facts about Spano (background, age, etc.)? Assume that Spano had been a contract killer for the mob. Would that change your notion of the mental freedom issue? Of the "overborne will" issue? You saw in *Fulminante*, Note 4, that the Court took into account the characteristics of Fulminante that suggested that he might need protection inside prison. Should that matter?

B. *Morality of police conduct.* A perplexing question in the law of voluntariness is to what extent is voluntariness an empirical "fact in the universe," as opposed to a normative inquiry based on a court's judgment about the morality of the police conduct? For example, if the police intentionally exploit a suspect's highly religious nature, should courts be more likely to find the pressure overbearing than if the police were unaware of the suspect's religious nature but asked precisely the same questions in the same way? If you say "yes," you favor a normative view of voluntariness that turns, at least in part, on a moral judgment about what the police did. If you say "no, pressure is pressure regardless of police motives," you tend toward an empirical, Aristotelian view of voluntariness.

7. *Problems of due process voluntariness.*

A. *Physician 1.* Police call a physician to treat suspect *L*'s painful sinus condition. The physician, a psychiatrist who works for the police, tells *L* how much better he would feel if he unburdened himself about the crime of murdering his elderly parents with a hammer. *L* does not know that the physician is a psychiatrist. *L* confesses to the police shortly after the physician leaves. Is there any reason to think the confession is unreliable? *Cf.* Leyra v. Denno, 347 U.S. 556, 74 S.Ct. 716, 98 L.Ed. 948 (1954). Would it matter to due process voluntariness if the psychiatrist did *not* work for the police? Does the case come out the same way if the police provide a police officer who pretends to be a physician? An officer who pretends to be a priest?

B. *Physician 2.* Same as prior Problem, but this time, the physician engages in a lengthy interrogation (over an hour) during which he keeps suggesting details about how *L* killed his parents: his mother first, slipping up behind her, because *L* was going to kill his father when he came home, and he didn't want his mother to interfere. *L* responds over and over that he simply does not remember. As the interrogation becomes more intense, *L* responds to suggestions about how he killed his parents by saying, "That must have been the way I did it," or "It must have been me; no one else was in the house." After an hour, *L* says he is ready to talk to the police captain, and he gives a confession that contains the details suggested by the psychiatrist. Voluntary? What if, after confessing to the captain, *L* confesses within three hours to state prosecutors? Are these confessions consistent with due process?

C. *Physician 3.* After three hours of questioning, *S* requests drugs to ameliorate the pain of narcotics withdrawal. According to later expert testimony, the drugs supplied by the police physician included a drug that functioned as a "truth serum." Neither the police interrogators nor the physician intended that effect; no one even had a reason to know that the drug would have this effect on *S*. Moreover, the police were unaware of the effect as they continued to question *S* and to take his confession. Does lack of bad faith have anything to do with the voluntariness inquiry? See Townsend v. Sain, 372 U.S. 293, 83 S.Ct. 745, 9 L.Ed.2d 770 (1963).

8. Federal law, 42 U.S.C. § 1983, authorizes a civil lawsuit for damages if a state actor violates rights under the federal Constitution or federal law. In Chavez v. Martinez, 538 U.S. 760, 123 S.Ct. 1994, 155 L.Ed.2d 984 (2003), Oliverio Martinez brought suit under § 1983 against the police officer who caused him to confess. The issue was not whether the confession was admissible, as in *Brown v. Mississippi*, p. 25, but whether the interrogation violated his due process rights at the moment that the questioning took place. The facts revealed a persistent interrogation of a suspect who had been shot

and thought he was dying. Here is a portion of Justice Kennedy's opinion, concurring in part and dissenting in part:

> The District Court found that Martinez "had been shot in the face, both eyes were injured; he was screaming in pain, and coming in and out of consciousness while being repeatedly questioned about details of the encounter with the police." His blinding facial wounds made it impossible for him visually to distinguish the interrogating officer from the attending medical personnel. The officer made no effort to dispel the perception that medical treatment was being withheld until Martinez answered the questions put to him. There was no attempt through *Miranda* warnings or other assurances to advise the suspect that his cooperation should be voluntary. Martinez begged the officer to desist and provide treatment for his wounds, but the questioning persisted despite these pleas and despite Martinez's unequivocal refusal to answer questions.

In a badly-splintered opinion, the Court held that the due process inquiry in civil cases was the "shock the conscience" test of Rochin v. California, p. 72, Note 2. It appears, therefore, that suspects have a due process right not to have involuntary confessions admitted in a criminal case against them but no right to sue for a due process violation unless the police conduct "shocks the conscience."

Five justices voted to remand *Martinez* to allow the lower courts to determine whether the *Rochin* standard was met. Is your conscience shocked? The Ninth Circuit remanded to the district court for "the resolution of contested facts." In 2007, a federal jury could not reach a verdict and the judge declared a mistrial. A newspaper article said a new trial would be held but we found no evidence of a second trial. See Stephanie Hoops, *Mistrial in civil rights suit*, Ventura County Star, April 27, 2007. Evidence at the trial revealed that Martinez lost his eyesight and was partially paralyzed as a result of the police shooting.

CHAPTER 7

POLICE INTERROGATION: THE SELF-INCRIMINATION CLAUSE

■ ■ ■

"No person * * * shall be compelled in any criminal case to be a witness against himself * * *." U.S. Const. amend. V.

"The self-incrimination clause of the Fifth Amendment is an unsolved riddle of vast proportions, a Gordian knot in the middle of our Bill of Rights." Akhil Reed Amar, The Constitution and Criminal Procedure 46 (1997).

A. THE TEXT AND THE ROAD TO *MIRANDA*

We begin with a foundational textual question: At what point is a person being compelled to be a witness against himself? Is it when the government actor compels a statement or only when the statement is introduced at trial? You might think that an unimportant distinction, and it is for routine criminal cases. That explains why the Court did not settle the question until 2003 and why the question arose in a *civil* suit. Oliverio Martinez brought suit under 42 U.S.C. § 1983 against the police officer who coerced him to confess, claiming that the officer violated his constitutional right not to be compelled to be a witness against himself.

To unravel that question requires understanding the doctrine of immunity. The Court held in Kastigar v. United States, p. 864, that witnesses called to testify before grand juries can be compelled to testify if they are given what is known as "use-and-derivative-use immunity." This doctrine forbids use of the compelled testimony, and everything derived from it, in a criminal case against the person providing the testimony. It applies to state and federal courts, regardless of which sovereign obtains the testimony by granting immunity. The underlying theory of *Kastigar* is that the witness is not being compelled to be a witness against himself if the compelled testimony is never used in a criminal case against him. Implicit in *Kastigar* is the premise that a violation of the Fifth Amendment occurs only when the compelled testimony is used in a criminal case. That premise proves crucial in the next case.

CHAVEZ v. MARTINEZ

Supreme Court of the United States, 2003.
538 U.S. 760, 123 S.Ct. 1994, 155 L.Ed.2d 984.

Justice Thomas announced the judgment of the Court and delivered an opinion [in which The Chief Justice joins in its entirety, and in which Justice O'Connor and Justice Scalia join as to the portions excerpted here Eds.].

This case involves a § 1983 suit arising out of petitioner Ben Chavez's allegedly coercive interrogation of respondent Oliverio Martinez. The United States Court of Appeals for the Ninth Circuit held that Chavez was not entitled to a defense of qualified immunity because he violated Martinez's clearly established constitutional rights. We conclude that Chavez did not deprive Martinez of a constitutional right.

I

[A brief summary of the facts can be found at Chapter 6, p. 564, Note 8. Eds.].

Martinez was never charged with a crime, and his answers were never used against him in any criminal prosecution. Nevertheless, Martinez filed suit under 42 U.S.C. § 1983, maintaining that Chavez's actions violated his Fifth Amendment right not to be "compelled in any criminal case to be a witness against himself," as well as his Fourteenth Amendment substantive due process right to be free from coercive questioning. * * *

The Ninth Circuit [ultimately] concluded that the Fifth and Fourteenth Amendment rights asserted by Martinez were clearly established by federal law, explaining that a reasonable officer "would have known that persistent interrogation of the suspect despite repeated requests to stop violated the suspect's Fifth and Fourteenth Amendment right to be free from coercive interrogation." * * *

II * * *

A.

1

The Fifth Amendment, made applicable to the States by the Fourteenth Amendment requires that "no person * * * shall be compelled *in any criminal case* to be a *witness* against himself." (emphases added). We fail to see how, based on the text of the Fifth Amendment, Martinez can allege a violation of this right, since Martinez was never prosecuted for a crime, let alone compelled to be a witness against himself in a criminal case.

Although Martinez contends that the meaning of "criminal case" should encompass the entire criminal investigatory process, including police interrogations, we disagree. In our view, a "criminal case" at the very least requires the initiation of legal proceedings. We need not decide today the precise moment when a "criminal case" commences; it is enough to say that police questioning does not constitute a "case" any more than a private investigator's precomplaint activities constitute a "civil case." Statements compelled by police interrogations of course may not be used against a defendant at trial, see *Brown v. Mississippi* [p. 25, Note 4], but it is not until their use in a criminal case that a violation of the Self–Incrimination Clause occurs.

Here, Martinez was never made to be a "witness" against himself in violation of the Fifth Amendment's Self–Incrimination Clause because his statements were never admitted as testimony against him in a criminal case. Nor was he ever placed under oath and exposed to " 'the cruel trilemma of self-accusation, perjury or contempt.' " The text of the Self–Incrimination Clause simply cannot support the Ninth Circuit's view that the mere use of compulsive questioning, without more, violates the Constitution.

2

Nor can the Ninth Circuit's approach be reconciled with our case law. It is well established that the government may compel witnesses to testify at trial or before a grand jury, on pain of contempt, so long as the witness is not the target of the criminal case in which he testifies. Even for persons who have a legitimate fear that their statements may subject them to criminal prosecution, we have long permitted the compulsion of incriminating testimony so long as those statements (or evidence derived from those statements) cannot be used against the speaker in any criminal case. We have also recognized that governments may penalize public employees and government contractors (with the loss of their jobs or government contracts) to induce them to respond to inquiries, so long as the answers elicited (and their fruits) are immunized from use in any criminal case against the speaker. By contrast, no "penalty" may ever be imposed on someone who exercises his core Fifth Amendment right not to be a "witness" against himself in a "criminal case." Our holdings in these cases demonstrate that, contrary to the Ninth Circuit's view, mere coercion does not violate the text of the Self–Incrimination Clause absent use of the compelled statements in a criminal case against the witness.

We fail to see how Martinez was any more "compelled in any criminal case to be a witness against himself" than an immunized witness forced to testify on pain of contempt. One difference, perhaps, is that the immunized witness *knows* that his statements will not, and may not, be used against him, whereas Martinez likely did not. But this does not make the statements of the immunized witness any less "compelled" and lends no support to the Ninth Circuit's conclusion that coercive police interrogations, absent the use of the involuntary statements in a criminal case, violate the Fifth Amendment's Self–Incrimination Clause. * * *

3

Although our cases have permitted the Fifth Amendment's self-incrimination privilege to be asserted in noncriminal cases [such as grand jury hearings, administrative hearings, and civil trials; Eds.], that does not alter our conclusion that a violation of the constitutional *right* against self-incrimination occurs only if one has been compelled to be a witness against himself in a criminal case.

In the Fifth Amendment context, we have created prophylactic rules designed to safeguard the core constitutional right protected by the Self–Incrimination Clause. Among these rules is an evidentiary privilege that protects witnesses from being forced to give incriminating testimony, even in noncriminal cases, unless that testimony has been immunized from use and derivative use in a future criminal proceeding before it is compelled.

By allowing a witness to insist on an immunity agreement *before* being compelled to give incriminating testimony in a noncriminal case, the privilege preserves the core Fifth Amendment right from invasion by the use of that compelled testimony in a subsequent criminal case. Because the failure to assert the privilege will often forfeit the right to exclude the evidence in a subsequent "criminal case," it is necessary to allow assertion of the privilege prior to the commencement of a "criminal case" to safeguard the core Fifth Amendment trial right. If the privilege could not be asserted in such situations, testimony given in those judicial proceedings would be deemed "voluntary"; hence, insistence on a prior grant of immunity is essential to memorialize the fact that the testimony had indeed been compelled and therefore protected from use against the speaker in any "criminal case."

Rules designed to safeguard a constitutional right, however, do not extend the scope of the constitutional right itself, just as violations of judicially crafted prophylactic rules do not violate the constitutional rights of any person. As we explained, we have allowed the Fifth Amendment privilege to be asserted by witnesses in noncriminal cases in order to safeguard the core constitutional right defined by the Self–Incrimination Clause—the right not to be compelled in any criminal case to be a witness against oneself. * * *

Our views on the proper scope of the Fifth Amendment's Self–Incrimination Clause do not mean that police torture or other abuse that results in a confession is constitutionally permissible so long as the statements are not used at trial; it simply means that the Fourteenth Amendment's Due Process Clause, rather than the Fifth Amendment's Self–Incrimination Clause, would govern the inquiry in those cases and provide relief in appropriate circumstances. [See p. 564, Note 8. Eds.]

Justice SOUTER delivered an opinion, * * * Part I of which is an opinion concurring in the judgment. [Only Justice Breyer joined Part I. Eds.].

I

Respondent Martinez's claim under 42 U.S.C. § 1983 for violation of his privilege against compelled self-incrimination should be rejected and his case remanded for further proceedings. I write separately because I believe that our decision requires a degree of discretionary judgment greater than Justice Thomas acknowledges. As he points out, the text of the Fifth Amendment (applied here under the doctrine of Fourteenth Amendment incorporation) focuses on courtroom use of a criminal defendant's compelled, self-incriminating testimony, and the core of the guarantee against compelled self-incrimination is the exclusion of any such evidence. * * *

[Justice Souter discusses cases—for example, *Miranda v. Arizona*, p. 581, suggesting to him that extensions of the core constitutional protection are justified "if clearly shown to be desirable means to protect the basic right against the invasive pressures of contemporary society." Eds.] All of this law is outside the Fifth Amendment's core, with each case expressing a judgment that the core guarantee, or the judicial capacity to protect it, would be placed at some risk in the absence of such complementary protection.

I do not, however, believe that Martinez can make the "powerful showing," subject to a realistic assessment of costs and risks, necessary to expand protection of the privilege against compelled self-incrimination to the point of the civil liability he asks us to recognize here. The most obvious drawback inherent in Martinez's purely Fifth Amendment claim to damages is its risk of global application in every instance of interrogation producing a statement inadmissible under Fifth and Fourteenth Amendment principles, or violating one of the complementary rules we have accepted in aid of the privilege against evidentiary use. If obtaining Martinez's statement is to be treated as a stand-alone violation of the privilege subject to compensation, why should the same not be true whenever the police obtain any involuntary self-incriminating statement, or whenever the government so much as threatens a penalty in derogation of the right to immunity * * *? Martinez offers no limiting principle or reason to foresee a stopping place short of liability in all such cases.

Recognizing an action for damages in every such instance not only would revolutionize Fifth and Fourteenth Amendment law, but would beg the question that must inform every extension or recognition of a complementary rule in service of the core privilege: why is this new rule necessary in aid of the basic guarantee? Martinez has offered no reason to believe that the guarantee has been ineffective in all or many of those circumstances in which its vindication has depended on excluding testimonial admissions or barring penalties. And I have no reason to believe the law has been systemically defective in this respect.

Justice SCALIA, concurring in part in the judgment [omitted].

Justice STEVENS, concurring in part and dissenting in part [omitted].

Justice KENNEDY, with whom Justice STEVENS joins, and with whom Justice GINSBURG joins as to Parts II and III, concurring in part and dissenting in part. * * *

II

Justice Souter and Justice Thomas are wrong, in my view, to maintain that in all instances a violation of the Self–Incrimination Clause simply does not occur unless and until a statement is introduced at trial, no matter how severe the pain or how direct and commanding the official compulsion used to extract it.* * *

Our cases and our legal tradition establish that the Self–Incrimination Clause is a substantive constraint on the conduct of the government, not merely an evidentiary rule governing the work of the courts. The Clause must provide more than mere assurance that a compelled statement will not be introduced against its declarant in a criminal trial. Otherwise there will be too little protection against the compulsion the Clause prohibits. * * *

The conclusion that the Self–Incrimination Clause is not violated until the government seeks to use a statement in some later criminal proceeding strips the Clause of an essential part of its force and meaning. This is no small matter. It should come as an unwelcome surprise to judges, attorneys, and the citizenry as a whole that if a legislative committee or a judge in a civil case demands incriminating testimony without offering immunity, and even imposes sanctions for failure to comply, that the witness and counsel cannot insist the right against compelled self-incrimination is applicable then and there. Justice Souter and Justice Thomas, I submit, should be more respectful of the understanding that has prevailed for generations now. To tell our whole legal system that when conducting a criminal investigation police officials can use severe compulsion or even torture with no present violation of the right against compelled self-incrimination can only diminish a celebrated provision in the Bill of Rights. A Constitution survives over time because the people share a common, historic commitment to certain simple but fundamental principles which preserve their freedom. Today's decision undermines one of those respected precepts. * * *

Justice GINSBURG, concurring in part and dissenting in part.

* * * I would hold that the Self–Incrimination Clause applies at the time and place police use severe compulsion to extract a statement from a suspect. The evidence in this case * * * supports the conclusion "that the suspect thought his treatment would be delayed, and thus his pain and condition worsened, by refusal to answer questions." I write separately to state my view that, even if no finding were made concerning Martinez's belief that refusal to answer would delay his treatment, or Chavez's intent to create such an impression, the interrogation in this case would remain a clear instance of the kind of compulsion no reasonable officer would have thought constitutionally permissible.* * *

In common with the Due Process Clause, the privilege against self-incrimination safeguards "the freedom of the individual from the arbitrary power of governmental authorities." Closely connected "with the struggle to eliminate torture as a governmental practice," the privilege is rightly regarded as "one of the great landmarks in man's struggle to make himself civilized." Its core idea is captured in the Latin maxim, *"Nemo tenetur prodere se ipsum,"* in English, "No one should be required to accuse himself." As an "expression of our view of civilized governmental conduct," the privilege should instruct and control all of officialdom, the police no less than the prosecutor. * * *

NOTES AND QUESTIONS

1. Do not forget that the Court remanded the case for the lower courts to determine whether Chavez violated Martinez's due process rights, an action that culminated in a civil trial on the merits. See p. 564, Note 8.

2. *You really need to count votes in this case!* How many justices believe that Martinez showed no violation of his Fifth Amendment privilege? How many justices believe that no person can ever show a violation of the Fifth Amendment privilege from police interrogation as long as the statement is not offered against the speaker? How does Justice Souter's approach differ from the plurality's? What principle underlies Justice Kennedy's dissent?

Is Justice Thomas's view of the Fifth Amendment privilege built primarily on text, cases, or policy? Which opinion in *Chavez* do you prefer?

3. Justice Thomas, for the plurality, discusses prophylactic rules designed to protect the privilege, such as the right not to answer questions before a grand jury or a congressional committee. How does Thomas square this right with the facts in *Chavez*? Suppose Martinez had been called before a grand jury and compelled to answer questions. What would be his only remedy, in the plurality's view?

4. Oddly, the Court's "plain meaning" reading of the text is contrary to the history of the self-incrimination clause. Tom Davies argues that the thrust of the privilege was to ensure that no one would have to respond to an accusation, and thus potentially incriminate himself, unless evidence was produced from sources other than the accused. It thus gave the accused a weapon he could use to avoid government questioning until a *prima facie* case was made to a justice of the peace and then a grand jury. See Thomas Y. Davies, *Farther and Farther from the Original Fifth Amendment: The Recharacterization of the Right Against Self–Incrimination as a "Trial Right" in Chavez v. Martinez*, 70 Tenn. L. Rev. 987 (2003).

For an argument that *Martinez* potentially undermines the Court's doctrine in other civil contexts, such as administrative and congressional hearings, see Michael J. Zydney Mannheimer, *Ripeness of Self–Incrimination Clause Disputes*, 95 J. Crim. L. & Criminology 1261 (2005).

5. *Exclusionary rules.* You will recall from your study of the Fourth Amendment that the text is all rights and no remedy. Notice that the text of the Fifth Amendment privilege is all remedy and no rights! In the view of the *Chavez* plurality, the police can torture someone without violating the Fifth Amendment privilege. But if a statement is compelled, the text of the Fifth Amendment itself requires exclusion.

6. Can you think of an example of a police interrogation that might produce the "powerful showing" necessary for Justices Souter and Breyer to find a violation of the Fifth Amendment privilege absent introduction of the statement? If, as seems likely, it will be the rare police interrogation that permits a defendant to make that "powerful showing," *Chavez* will have no effect on prosecution of routine criminal cases. Statements taken in violation of the self-incrimination clause will continue to be suppressed at trial. *Chavez* has, however, changed the way police interrogation is understood as a constitutional matter, as we will seek to demonstrate throughout the chapter.

7. *Another foundational principle: What constitutes "being a witness"?* In Schmerber v. California, 384 U.S. 757, 86 S.Ct. 1826, 16 L.Ed.2d 908 (1966), the police ordered a hospital to withdraw blood over Schmerber's objection. There is no doubt that Schmerber was compelled to give up his blood. The issue was whether this compulsion is protected by the Fifth Amendment prohibition of compelling a person "to be a witness against himself." Was Schmerber being a "witness against himself" when he gave up his blood?

The Court by a 5–4 margin rejected Schmerber's claim. Citing little authority, the Court held "that the privilege protects an accused only from being compelled to testify against himself, or otherwise provide the State with evidence of a testimonial or communicative nature." The Court noted that the

> distinction which has emerged [from the cases], often expressed in different ways, is that the privilege is a bar against compelling "communications" or "testimony," but that compulsion which makes a suspect or accused the source of "real or physical evidence" does not violate it.
>
> Although we agree that this distinction is a helpful framework for analysis, * * * [t]here will be many cases in which such a distinction is not readily drawn. Some tests seemingly directed to obtain "physical evidence," for example, lie detector tests measuring changes in body function during interrogation, may actually be directed to eliciting responses which are essentially testimonial. To compel a person to submit to testing in which an effort will be made to determine his guilt or innocence on the basis of physiological responses, whether willed or not, is to evoke the spirit and history of the Fifth Amendment. * * *
>
> In the present case, however, no such problem of application is presented. Not even a shadow of testimonial compulsion upon or enforced communication by the accused was involved either in the extraction or in the chemical analysis. Petitioner's testimonial capacities were in no way implicated; indeed, his participation, except as a donor, was irrelevant to the results of the test, which depend on chemical analysis and on that alone. Since the blood test evidence, although an incriminating product of compulsion, was neither petitioner's testimony nor evidence relating to some communicative act or writing by the petitioner, it was not inadmissible on privilege grounds.

Thus, requiring a suspect to stand in a line-up, provide a writing sample, or speak certain words does not implicate the suspect's right not to be compelled to be a witness against himself.

8. Justice Ginsburg reminds us in *Chavez* that the "core idea" of "the Fifth Amendment privilege is captured in the Latin maxim, '*Nemo tenetur prodere se ipsum*,' in English, 'No one should be required to accuse himself.' " In 1964, Justice Goldberg wrote for the Court in Murphy v. Waterfront Commission, 378 U.S. 52, 84 S.Ct. 1594, 12 L.Ed.2d 678 (1964), that the "privilege against self-incrimination registers an important advance in the development of our liberty—one of the great landmarks in man's struggle to make himself civilized." It manifested "our respect for the inviolability of the human personality and of the right of each individual to a private enclave where he may lead a private life." (Internal quotation marks omitted. Eds.) Yet if we put *Chavez* and *Schmerber* together, we discover that the police may coerce us to give blood, a DNA sample, or a confession, and the Fifth Amendment is not violated unless the State seeks to offer the confession in court. Goldberg's vision of the Fifth Amendment has not flourished.

COMMENT ON THE ROAD TO *MIRANDA*

The history of the Fifth Amendment right against compelled self-incrimination—often called the privilege against self-incrimination—is far from clear, though some parts are reasonably well understood. Here is how Chief Justice Earl Warren, in *Miranda*, p. 581, explained the critical period in the development of this right in England:

> We sometimes forget how long it has taken to establish the privilege against self-incrimination, the sources from which it came and the fervor with which it was defended. Its roots go back into ancient times. Perhaps the critical historical event shedding light on its origins and evolution was the trial of one John Lilburn, a vocal anti-Stuart Leveller,[a] who was made to take the Star Chamber Oath in 1637. The oath would have bound him to answer to all questions posed to him on any subject. The Trial of John Lilburn and John Wharton, 3 How. St. Tr. 1315 (1637). He resisted the oath and declaimed the proceedings, stating:
>
> > 'Another fundamental right I then contended for, was, that no man's conscience ought to be racked by oaths imposed, to answer to questions concerning himself in matters criminal, or pretended to be so.'
>
> On account of the Lilburn Trial, Parliament abolished the inquisitorial Court of Star Chamber and went further in giving him generous reparation. The lofty principles to which Lilburn had appealed during his trial gained popular acceptance in England. These sentiments worked their way over to the Colonies and were implanted after great struggle into the Bill of Rights. Those who framed our Constitution and the Bill of Rights were ever aware of subtle encroachments on individual liberty. They knew that 'illegitimate and

---

a. The Stuart monarch in 1637 was Charles I, who, twelve years later, would be executed on orders from Parliament. England was declared a republic, an experiment that would die shortly after Oliver Cromwell, the Lord Protector of England, died in 1658. The Levellers were a political movement that espoused popular sovereignty and thus were antithetical to the monarchy. Eds.

unconstitutional practices get their first footing * * * by silent approaches and slight deviations from legal modes of procedure.' The privilege was elevated to constitutional status and has always been 'as broad as the mischief against which it seeks to guard.' *Counselman v. Hitchcock*, 142 U.S. 547, 562, 12 S.Ct. 195, 198, 35 L.Ed. 1110 (1892). We cannot depart from this noble heritage.

Once we leave Lilburn, and the right not to be forced to take an oath, the historical path to the modern role of the privilege is surprisingly opaque. Begin with the notion that the Star Chamber was not a common law court but a supervisory body that drew its authority from the king and thus from its beginning had greater powers and more flexibility than the English common law courts. The English monarchs in the sixteenth and seventeenth centuries expanded the power of the Star Chamber beyond its original role of seeking to ensure the fair enforcement of the laws. It became a tool in the seemingly endless conflict between English Protestants and Catholics, a tool used ruthlessly by the Stuart monarchs to pursue and destroy their enemies.

Thus, the test of wills between the religious dissenters and the Star Chamber in the seventeenth century was *not* about being compelled to confess to crimes. Rather, the objection was to the Star Chamber itself and its power to compel those called before it to obey an institution that, to many English subjects, lacked legitimacy. So, in that way, the Star Chamber was sui generis. The common law courts, on the other hand, had been around since the twelfth century, were not under the direct control of the monarch, and had the moral authority necessary to enforce their judgments. Moreover, the common law courts lacked the powers of the Star Chamber. Indeed, the criminal courts of the period lacked the authority to require a criminal defendant to take an oath, and defendants were not even permitted to testify under oath. The common law disability of defendants to testify was a rule of evidence based on the presumed bias of the defendant; it also applied to the victim of the crime.

That defendants could not testify under oath in the eighteenth century undermines what appears to be the "plain meaning" of the text—a ban on compelling defendants to testify in their criminal cases. Why would the Framers bother to prohibit that which could not have occurred?

It thus seems likely that the Framers intended the privilege to protect only against American versions of the Star Chamber, quasi-criminal tribunals that used the oath and contempt power to seek to expose and punish enemies of the State. The Framers would have understood the distinction between compelling a witness to take an oath before the Star Chamber and compelling a confession from a suspect. By 1783, the English courts were dealing with compelled confessions by refusing to allow them into evidence. That common law rule was probably part of the English "law of the land" and likely included as part of the protection offered Americans by the due process clause in the Fifth Amendment. The best reading of history, then, is that the Fifth Amendment took care of two problems of compulsion. The privilege forbids compelling individuals to take an oath; they can refuse by claiming their Fifth Amendment privilege. The due process clause forbids compelling confessions from those suspected of crime.

While we cannot be certain about the Framers' intent, we can begin the modern story in 1892. By then, the federal government and almost all states had, by statute, removed the common-law disability of criminal defendants to testify. The government argued in Counselman v. Hitchcock, 142 U.S. 547, 12 S.Ct. 195, 35 L.Ed. 1110 (1892), that the role of the privilege was *only* to prevent compelling testimony from defendants at their criminal trials. The Court rejected that narrow focus and found a pre-trial role for the privilege in protecting those who are called before grand juries:

> It is impossible that the meaning of the constitutional provision can only be that a person shall not be compelled to be a witness against himself in a criminal prosecution against himself. It would doubtless cover such cases; but it is not limited to them. The object was to insure that a person should not be compelled, when acting as a witness in any investigation, to give testimony which might tend to show that he himself had committed a crime. The privilege is limited to criminal matters, but it is as broad as the mischief against which it seeks to guard.

After *Counselman*, the privilege protects defendants from being subpoenaed to testify at their criminal trial and also protects witnesses in any type of formal hearing, such as congressional hearings or commission hearings, from being forced to take an oath and testify. See, e.g., Murphy v. Waterfront Commission, 378 U.S. 52, 84 S.Ct. 1594, 12 L.Ed.2d 678 (1964). This aspect of the privilege is considered in more detail in Chapter 13.

What *Counselman* did not contemplate was that the privilege might protect suspects who were being questioned by police. Compelled confessions were inadmissible, as we saw in Chapter 6, but that doctrine was based on the common law of confessions and not on the privilege. All of that would change, however, when the Supreme Court decided the next case, five years after *Counselman*.

BRAM v. UNITED STATES
Supreme Court of the United States, 1897.
168 U.S. 532, 18 S.Ct. 183, 42 L.Ed. 568.

MR. JUSTICE WHITE delivered the opinion of the Court.

[A murder occurred on a ship in the North Atlantic. Crewman Brown was the initial suspect. When the ship made port, a Canadian customs official had a second suspect, Bram, stripped to search his clothes for evidence of the murder. The official, Power, questioned Bram either while his clothes were being removed or after he was "denuded." Power testified as follows. Eds.]

"I said to him: 'Bram, we are trying to unravel this horrible mystery.'
I said: 'Your position is rather an awkward one. I have had Brown in
this office, and he made a statement that he saw you do the murder.'
He said: 'He could not have seen me. Where was he?' I said: 'He
states he was at the wheel.' 'Well,' he said, 'he could not see me from
there.'"

The contention is that the foregoing conversation, between the detective and the accused, was competent only as a confession by him made;
that it was offered as such; and that it was erroneously admitted, as it was
not shown to have been voluntary. * * * In criminal trials, in the courts
of the United States, wherever a question arises whether a confession is
incompetent because not voluntary, the issue is controlled by that portion
of the fifth amendment to the constitution of the United States commanding that no person "shall be compelled in any criminal case to be a witness
against himself." The legal principle by which the admissibility of the
confession of an accused person is to be determined is expressed in the
text-books.

In 3 Russ. Crimes (6th Ed.) 478, it is stated as follows:

"But a confession, in order to be admissible, must be free and
voluntary; that is, must not be extracted by any sort of threats or
violence, nor obtained by any direct or implied promises, however
slight, nor by the exertion of any improper influence. * * * A confession can never be received in evidence where the prisoner has been
influenced by any threat or promise; for the law cannot measure the
force of the influence used, or decide upon its effect upon the mind of
the prisoner, and therefore excludes the declaration if any degree of
influence has been exerted." * * *

[The Court also quoted from Hawkins' Pleas of the Crown (6th Ed.,
by Leach, published in 1787). Eds.] In section 3, c. 46, it is stated that
examinations by the common law before a secretary of state or other
magistrate for treason or other crimes not within the statutes of Philip
and Mary, and also the confession of the defendant himself in discourse
with private persons, might be given in evidence against the party confessing. A note (2) to this section, presumably inserted by the editor (see note
to Gilham's Case, 1 Moody, 194, 195), reads as follows:

The human mind, under the pressure of calamity, is easily
seduced, and is liable, in the alarm of danger, to acknowledge indiscriminately a falsehood or a truth, as different agitations may prevail.
A confession, therefore, whether made upon an official examination or
in discourse with private persons, which is obtained from a defendant,
either by the flattery of hope, or by the impressions of fear, however
slightly the emotions may be implanted, is not admissible evidence;
for the law will not suffer a prisoner to be made the deluded
instrument of his own conviction. * * *

* * * As said in the passage from Russell on Crimes already quoted:
"The law cannot measure the force of the influence used, or decide upon

its effect upon the mind of the prisoner, and therefore excludes the declaration if any degree of influence has been exerted." In the case before us we find that an influence was exerted, and, as any doubt as to whether the confession was voluntary must be determined in favor of the accused, we cannot escape the conclusion that error was committed by the trial court in admitting the confession under the circumstances disclosed by the record. * * *

Mr. Justice BREWER, dissenting. * * *

The witness Power, when called, testified positively that no threats were made nor any inducements held out to Bram; and this general declaration he affirmed and reaffirmed in response to inquiries made by the court and the defendant's counsel. The court therefore properly overruled the objection at that time made to his testifying to the statements of defendant. It is not suggested that there was error in this ruling, and the fact that inducements were held out is deduced only from the testimony subsequently given by Power of the conversation between him and Bram. The first part of that conversation is as follows: "When Mr. Bram came into my office, I said to him: 'Bram, we are trying to unravel this horrible mystery.' I said: 'Your position is rather an awkward one. I have had Brown in this office, and he made a statement that he saw you do the murder.' He said: 'He could not have seen me. Where was he?' I said: 'He states he was at the wheel.' 'Well,' he said, 'he could not see me from there." In this there is nothing which by any possibility can be tortured into a suggestion of threat or a temptation of hope. Power simply stated the obvious fact that they were trying to unravel a horrible mystery, and the further fact that Brown had charged the defendant with the crime, and the replies of Bram were given as freely and voluntarily as it is possible to conceive.

NOTES AND QUESTIONS

1. Do you agree that Bram's statements were compelled or is Justice Brewer right that his statements were given freely and voluntarily? How should a court weigh the fact that Bram was questioned while being "denuded"?

2. *The "free agent" concept.* One way to understand *Bram* is to consider it the lineal heir of *Rex v. Thompson*, 168 Eng. Rep. 248 (Cent.Crim.Ct. 1783), in which the English trial judge suppressed a confession obtained by the "threat" to take the suspect before a magistrate if he did not provide "a more satisfactory account" of the events. The court wrote, "Too great a chastity cannot be preserved on this point. * * * It is almost impossible to be too careful upon this subject." The confession must be suppressed, the court held, because "[t]he prisoner was hardly a free agent at the time" he responded to the statement indicating that he might be taken before a magistrate.

Bram cited and quoted many English cases applying the "free agent" concept. For example, the Court described *Thompson* as a case in which there was

> a declaration to a suspected person that, unless he gave a more satisfactory account of his connection with a stolen bank note, his interrogator would take him before a magistrate, was held equivalent to stating that it would be better to confess, and to have operated to lead the prisoner to believe that he would not be taken before a magistrate if he confessed. Baron Hotham, after commenting upon the evidence, in substance said that the prisoner was hardly a free agent at the time, as, though the language addressed to him scarcely amounted to a threat, it was certainly a strong invitation to the prisoner to confess, the manner in which it had been expressed rendering it more efficacious.

The Court here implies that a confession can be involuntary even if the authorities have not threatened the suspect. Involuntariness can be found in the "strong invitation" to confess.

Wigmore was harshly critical of cases like *Thompson* and *Bram*, concluding that it "cannot be denied" that "absurdities have disfigured the law of the admissibility of confessions," giving it a "sentimental irrationality" that had "obstructed the administration of justice." 2 John Henry Wigmore, A Treatise on Evidence 159, § 865 (2d ed. 1923). For a thoughtful explanation of how English law came to develop the "free agent" concept in the law of confessions, see John H. Langbein, The Origins of Adversary Criminal Trial 229–233 (2003).

3. *Why not a federal rule of evidence?* None of the cases that *Bram* cited, including *Thompson*, were based on the privilege not to testify as a witness. Instead, they were based on a common-law rule of evidence that barred the use of involuntary confessions. The *Bram* Court could have reached the same result by reading the common law rule of evidence into the Fifth Amendment due process clause. Indeed, when the Court later began reviewing state court convictions based on confessions, as we saw in Chapter 6, it read the Fourteenth Amendment due process clause to forbid convictions based on compelled confessions. Why *Bram* chose the Fifth Amendment privilege to create a federal law of confessions is a mystery, one that has far-reaching consequences in the vast *Miranda v. Arizona* doctrine.

4. *The collapse of the voluntariness test*. We saw in Chapter 6 that voluntariness is not an easy empirical or philosophical "fact" to determine. As Lawrence Herman has cogently put the problems with voluntariness:

> A careful reading of the Court's more than forty involuntary confession cases discloses not one but five different objectives. * * * (1) to deter the police from engaging in conduct that may produce an unreliable confession; (2) to deter the police from engaging in conduct so offensive to the minimum standards of a civilized society that it shocks the conscience of the Court; (3) to deter the police from engaging in less-than-shocking misconduct; (4) to deter the police from using the techniques of an inquisitorial system and to encourage them to use the techniques of an accusatorial system; and (5) to deter the police from overbearing the suspect's will.

> Your initial reaction may be that these objectives at last give us the definitional tool we need. Precisely the opposite is true, however. Each of

the objectives is problematic in one or more ways, and the very number of them obfuscates rather than clarifies. * * *

* * * Small wonder, then, that in a period of thirty years or so, the Supreme Court granted review in over thirty-five cases in which confessions had been held voluntary. Small wonder, too, that the Court reversed the conviction in most of these cases. And small wonder that the Court became disaffected from its own work product. All students of the Court recognize that it cannot police the application of doctrine by lower courts. All it can hope to do is make doctrine intelligible and give illustrative examples. The Court tried to do that in the confession cases, and it failed. Given the inherent vagueness of the crucial concepts and the many rationales underlying the rule, failure was foreordained. So also was the search for an alternative.

Lawrence Herman, *The Supreme Court, the Attorney General, and the Good Old Days of Police Interrogation*, 48 Ohio St. L.J. 733, 749–50, 754–55 (1987).

5. *Right to counsel as a limit on interrogation.* One attempt to provide limits on interrogation more precise than the voluntariness test was Escobedo v. Illinois, 378 U.S. 478, 84 S.Ct. 1758, 12 L.Ed.2d 977 (1964). Two years before *Miranda*, the Court held that the *Sixth Amendment* was violated when the police denied Escobedo's request to speak to his lawyer during an interrogation that took place before charges were filed. The Sixth Amendment provides: "In all criminal prosecutions, the accused shall enjoy the right * * * to have the Assistance of Counsel for his defence." The dissents soundly criticized the majority for applying the Sixth Amendment right to counsel in a pre-indictment case. Do you see the interpretive difficulty?

Justice White's dissent in *Escobedo* presaged what the Court would do in *Miranda*:

> The Court may be concerned with a narrower matter: the unknowing defendant who responds to police questioning because he mistakenly believes that he must and that his admissions will not be used against him. But this worry hardly calls for the broadside the Court has now fired. The failure to inform an accused that he need not answer and that his answers may be used against him is very relevant indeed to whether the disclosures are compelled. Cases in this Court, to say the least, have never placed a premium on ignorance of constitutional rights. If an accused is told he must answer and does not know better, it would be very doubtful that the resulting admissions could be used against him.

Justice White lost the *Escobedo* battle but won the war. The Court would, in *Miranda*, change course from the Sixth Amendment to the Fifth Amendment.

6. *Enter the Fifth Amendment privilege, or Kamisar leads and the Court follows.* In 1965, a year after *Escobedo* attempted to ground interrogation limits in the Sixth Amendment, and a year before *Miranda*, Professor Yale Kamisar argued that the Fifth Amendment privilege should be extended to the interrogation room. A privilege limited to the courtroom was not particularly valuable, Kamisar argued:

The courtroom is a splendid place where defense attorneys bellow and strut and prosecuting attorneys are hemmed in at many turns. But what happens before an accused reaches the safety and enjoys the comfort of this veritable mansion? Ah, there's the rub. Typically he must first pass through a much less pretentious edifice, a police station with bare back rooms and locked doors.

Yale Kamisar, *Equal Justice in the Gatehouses and Mansions of American Criminal Procedure: From Powell to Gideon, from Escobedo to * * * *, in Criminal Justice in Our Time, 19 (A.E. Dick Howard, ed. 1965).

Noting that wealthy privileged suspects routinely faced police interrogators with counsel at their side, Kamisar argued that "respect for the individual and securing equal treatment in law enforcement" require the State to make counsel available to suspects who face police interrogation and to warn them that they need not answer. He concluded: "To the extent the Constitution permits the wealthy and educated to 'defeat justice,' if you will, *why shouldn't* all defendants be given a like opportunity?" *Id*. at 79–80.

7.   By 1966 it was clear to the Court that a more precise rule was needed to govern police interrogation. It was also clear that *Escobedo* was not a very good rule. Leaving aside the interpretive difficulty in grounding the rule in the Sixth Amendment, there was the problem that few suspects had counsel or would know to ask to speak to their lawyer as required before the *Escobedo* rule provided help. No, what the Court needed was an all-encompassing rule. Enter *Miranda*.

B. *MIRANDA* SPAWNS A NEW LAW OF CONFESSIONS

MIRANDA v. ARIZONA

Supreme Court of the United States, 1966.
384 U.S. 436, 86 S.Ct. 1602, 16 L.Ed.2d 694.

MR. CHIEF JUSTICE WARREN delivered the opinion of the Court.

The cases before us raise questions which go to the roots of our concepts of American criminal jurisprudence: the restraints society must observe consistent with the Federal Constitution in prosecuting individuals for crime. More specifically, we deal with the admissibility of statements obtained from an individual who is subjected to custodial police interrogation and the necessity for procedures which assure that the individual is accorded his privilege under the Fifth Amendment to the Constitution not to be compelled to incriminate himself. * * *

We start here, as we did in *Escobedo* [p. 580, Note 5], with the premise that our holding is not an innovation in our jurisprudence, but is an application of principles long recognized and applied in other settings. We have undertaken a thorough re-examination of the *Escobedo* decision and the principles it announced, and we reaffirm it. That case was but an explication of basic rights that are enshrined in our Constitution—that "No person * * * shall be compelled in any criminal case to be a witness against himself," and that "the accused shall * * * have the Assistance of Counsel"—rights which were put in jeopardy in that case through official overbearing. These precious rights were fixed in our Constitution only after centuries of persecution and struggle. And in the words of Chief Justice Marshall, they were secured "for ages to come, and * * * designed to approach immortality as nearly as human institutions can approach it." * * *

Our holding will be spelled out with some specificity in the pages which follow but briefly stated it is this: the prosecution may not use statements, whether exculpatory or inculpatory, stemming from custodial interrogation of the defendant unless it demonstrates the use of procedural safeguards effective to secure the privilege against self-incrimination. By custodial interrogation, we mean questioning initiated by law enforcement officers after a person has been taken into custody or otherwise deprived of his freedom of action in any significant way.[4] * * *

I

The constitutional issue we decide in each of these cases is the admissibility of statements obtained from a defendant questioned while in custody or otherwise deprived of his freedom of action in any significant way. In each, the defendant was questioned by police officers, detectives, or a prosecuting attorney in a room in which he was cut off from the outside world. In none of these cases was the defendant given a full and effective warning of his rights at the outset of the interrogation process. In all the cases, the questioning elicited oral admissions, and in three of them, signed statements as well which were admitted at their trials. They all thus share salient features—incommunicado interrogation of individuals in a police-dominated atmosphere, resulting in self-incriminating statements without full warnings of constitutional rights.

An understanding of the nature and setting of this in-custody interrogation is essential to our decisions today. The difficulty in depicting what transpires at such interrogations stems from the fact that in this country they have largely taken place incommunicado. * * *

Again we stress that the modern practice of in-custody interrogation is psychologically rather than physically oriented. As we have stated before, " * * * [T]his Court has recognized that coercion can be mental as well as physical, and that the blood of the accused is not the only hallmark of an unconstitutional inquisition." Interrogation still takes place in privacy. Privacy results in secrecy and this in turn results in a gap in our knowledge as to what in fact goes on in the interrogation rooms. A valuable source of information about present police practices, however, may be found in various police manuals and texts which document procedures employed with success in the past, and which recommend various other effective tactics. These texts are used by law enforcement

---

4. This is what we meant in *Escobedo* when we spoke of an investigation which had focused on an accused.

agencies themselves as guides.[9] It should be noted that these texts professedly present the most enlightened and effective means presently used to obtain statements through custodial interrogation. By considering these texts and other data, it is possible to describe procedures observed and noted around the country.

The officers are told by the manuals that the "principal psychological factor contributing to a successful interrogation is *privacy*—being alone with the person under interrogation." The efficacy of this tactic has been explained as follows:

> "If at all practicable, the interrogation should take place in the investigator's office or at least in a room of his own choice. The subject should be deprived of every psychological advantage. In his own home he may be confident, indignant, or recalcitrant. He is more keenly aware of his rights and more reluctant to tell of his indiscretions or criminal behavior within the walls of his home. Moreover his family and other friends are nearby, their presence lending moral support. In his own office, the investigator possesses all the advantages. The atmosphere suggests the invincibility of the forces of the law."

To highlight the isolation and unfamiliar surroundings, the manuals instruct the police to display an air of confidence in the suspect's guilt and from outward appearance to maintain only an interest in confirming certain details. The guilt of the subject is to be posited as a fact. The interrogator should direct his comments toward the reasons why the subject committed the act, rather than court failure by asking the subject whether he did it. Like other men, perhaps the subject has had a bad family life, had an unhappy childhood, had too much to drink, had an unrequited desire for women. The officers are instructed to minimize the moral seriousness of the offense, to cast blame on the victim or on society. These tactics are designed to put the subject in a psychological state where his story is but an elaboration of what the police purport to know already—that he is guilty. Explanations to the contrary are dismissed and discouraged.

The texts thus stress that the major qualities an interrogator should possess are patience and perseverance. One writer describes the efficacy of these characteristics in this manner:

> "In the preceding paragraphs emphasis has been placed on kindness and stratagems. The investigator will, however, encounter many situations where the sheer weight of his personality will be the deciding factor. Where emotional appeals and tricks are employed to

---

9. The methods described in Inbau & Reid, Criminal Interrogation and Confessions (1962), are a revision and enlargement of material presented in three prior editions of a predecessor text, Lie Detection and Criminal Interrogation (3d ed. 1953). * * * Similarly, the techniques described in O'Hara, Fundamentals of Criminal Investigation (1956), were gleaned from long service as observer, lecturer in police science, and work as a federal criminal investigator. All these texts have had rather extensive use among law enforcement agencies and among students of police science, with total sales and circulation of over 44,000.

no avail, he must rely on an oppressive atmosphere of dogged persistence. He must interrogate steadily and without relent, leaving the subject no prospect of surcease. He must dominate his subject and overwhelm him with his inexorable will to obtain the truth. He should interrogate for a spell of several hours pausing only for the subject's necessities in acknowledgment of the need to avoid a charge of duress that can be technically substantiated. In a serious case, the interrogation may continue for days, with the required intervals for food and sleep, but with no respite from the atmosphere of domination. It is possible in this way to induce the suspect to talk without resorting to duress or coercion. The method should be used only when the guilt of the suspect appears highly probable."

The manuals suggest that the suspect be offered legal excuses for his actions in order to obtain an initial admission of guilt. Where there is a suspected revenge-killing, for example, the interrogator may say:

"Joe, you probably didn't go out looking for this fellow with the purpose of shooting him. My guess is, however, that you expected something from him and that's why you carried a gun—for your own protection. You knew him for what he was, no good. Then when you met him he probably started using foul, abusive language and he gave some indication that he was about to pull a gun on you, and that's when you had to act to save your own life. That's about it, isn't it, Joe?"

Having then obtained the admission of shooting, the interrogator is advised to refer to circumstantial evidence which negates the self-defense explanation. This should enable him to secure the entire story. One text notes that "Even if he fails to do so, the inconsistency between the subject's original denial of the shooting and his present admission of at least doing the shooting will serve to deprive him of a self-defense 'out' at the time of trial." * * *

The interrogators sometimes are instructed to induce a confession out of trickery. The technique here is quite effective in crimes which require identification or which run in series. In the identification situation, the interrogator may take a break in his questioning to place the subject among a group of men in a line-up. "The witness or complainant (previously coached, if necessary) studies the line-up and confidently points out the subject as the guilty party." Then the questioning resumes "as though there were now no doubt about the guilt of the subject." A variation on this technique is called the "reverse line-up":

"The accused is placed in a line-up, but this time he is identified by several fictitious witnesses or victims who associated him with different offenses. It is expected that the subject will become desperate and confess to the offense under investigation in order to escape from the false accusations." * * *

[The Court described other strategies, including the "Mutt and Jeff" act in which one officer plays the good cop and one the brutal bad cop who can be kept under control only if the suspect cooperates with the good cop. Another strategy discourages silence: "Suppose you were in my shoes and I were in yours and you called me in to ask me about this and I told you 'I don't want to answer any of your questions.' You'd think I had something to hide, and you'd probably be right in thinking that." Finally, one strategy discourages requests to talk to a lawyer or to a relative: "Joe I'm only looking for the truth, and if you're telling the truth, that's it. You can handle this by yourself." The Court noted, "Few will persist in their initial refusal to talk, it is said, if this monologue is employed correctly."]

From these representative samples of interrogation techniques, the setting prescribed by the manuals and observed in practice becomes clear. In essence, it is this: To be alone with the subject is essential to prevent distraction and to deprive him of any outside support. The aura of confidence in his guilt undermines his will to resist. He merely confirms the preconceived story the police seek to have him describe. Patience and persistence, at times relentless questioning, are employed. To obtain a confession, the interrogator must "patiently maneuver himself or his quarry into a position from which the desired objective may be attained." When normal procedures fail to produce the needed result, the police may resort to deceptive stratagems such as giving false legal advice. It is important to keep the subject off balance, for example, by trading on his insecurity about himself or his surroundings. The police then persuade, trick, or cajole him out of exercising his constitutional rights. * * *

In the cases before us today, given this background, we concern ourselves primarily with this interrogation atmosphere and the evils it can bring. In No. 759, *Miranda v. Arizona*, the police arrested the defendant and took him to a special interrogation room where they secured a confession. In No. 760, *Vignera v. New York*, the defendant made oral admissions to the police after interrogation in the afternoon, and then signed an inculpatory statement upon being questioned by an assistant district attorney later the same evening. In No. 761, *Westover v. United States*, the defendant was handed over to the Federal Bureau of Investigation by local authorities after they had detained and interrogated him for a lengthy period, both at night and the following morning. After some two hours of questioning, the federal officers had obtained signed statements from the defendant. Lastly, in No. 584, *California v. Stewart*, the local police held the defendant five days in the station and interrogated him on nine separate occasions before they secured his inculpatory statement.

In these cases, we might not find the defendants' statements to have been involuntary in traditional terms. Our concern for adequate safeguards to protect precious Fifth Amendment rights is, of course, not lessened in the slightest. In each of the cases, the defendant was thrust into an unfamiliar atmosphere and run through menacing police interrogation procedures. The potentiality for compulsion is forcefully apparent, for example, in *Miranda*, where the indigent Mexican defendant was a seriously disturbed individual with pronounced sexual fantasies, and in *Stewart*, in which the defendant was an indigent Los Angeles Negro who had dropped out of school in the sixth grade. To be sure, the records do not evince overt physical coercion or patent psychological ploys. The fact remains that in none of these cases did the officers undertake to afford appropriate safeguards at the outset of the interrogation to insure that the statements were truly the product of free choice.

It is obvious that such an interrogation environment is created for no purpose other than to subjugate the individual to the will of his examiner. This atmosphere carries its own badge of intimidation. To be sure, this is not physical intimidation, but it is equally destructive of human dignity. The current practice of incommunicado interrogation is at odds with one of our Nation's most cherished principles—that the individual may not be compelled to incriminate himself. Unless adequate protective devices are employed to dispel the compulsion inherent in custodial surroundings, no statement obtained from the defendant can truly be the product of his free choice.

From the foregoing, we can readily perceive an intimate connection between the privilege against self-incrimination and police custodial questioning. It is fitting to turn to history and precedent underlying the Self–Incrimination Clause to determine its applicability in this situation.

II.

We sometimes forget how long it has taken to establish the privilege against self-incrimination, the sources from which it came and the fervor with which it was defended. Its roots go back into ancient times. * * *

Thus we may view the historical development of the privilege as one which groped for the proper scope of governmental power over the citizen. As a "noble principle often transcends its origins," the privilege has come rightfully to be recognized in part as an individual's substantive right, a "right to a private enclave where he may lead a private life. That right is the hallmark of our democracy." We have recently noted that the privilege against self-incrimination—the essential mainstay of our adversary system—is founded on a complex of values. All these policies point to one overriding thought: the constitutional foundation underlying the privilege is the respect a government—state or federal—must accord to the dignity and integrity of its citizens. To maintain a "fair state-individual balance," to require the government "to shoulder the entire load," to respect the inviolability of the human personality, our accusatory system of criminal justice demands that the government seeking to punish an individual produce the evidence against him by its own independent labors, rather than by the cruel, simple expedient of compelling it from his own mouth. In sum, the privilege is fulfilled only when the person is guaranteed the right "to remain silent unless he chooses to speak in the unfettered exercise of his own will."

The question in these cases is whether the privilege is fully applicable during a period of custodial interrogation. In this Court, the privilege has consistently been accorded a liberal construction. We are satisfied that all the principles embodied in the privilege apply to informal compulsion exerted by law-enforcement officers during in-custody questioning. An individual swept from familiar surroundings into police custody, surrounded by antagonistic forces, and subjected to the techniques of persuasion described above cannot be otherwise than under compulsion to speak. As a practical matter, the compulsion to speak in the isolated setting of the police station may well be greater than in courts or other official investigations, where there are often impartial observers to guard against intimidation or trickery.

This question, in fact, could have been taken as settled in federal courts almost 70 years ago, when, in *Bram v. United States*, p. 576, this Court held:

> "In criminal trials, in the courts of the United States, wherever a question arises whether a confession is incompetent because not voluntary, the issue is controlled by that portion of the Fifth Amendment * * * commanding that no person 'shall be compelled in any criminal case to be a witness against himself.' " * * *

Because of the adoption by Congress of Rule 5(a) of the Federal Rules of Criminal Procedure, and the Court's effectuation of that Rule in *McNabb* [*v. United States*, 318 U.S. 332, 63 S.Ct. 608, 87 L.Ed. 819 (1943)] and *Mallory v. United States*, 354 U.S. 449, 77 S.Ct. 1356, 1 L.Ed.2d 1479 (1957)], we have had little occasion in the past quarter century to reach the constitutional issues in dealing with federal interrogations. These supervisory rules, requiring production of an arrested person before a commissioner "without unnecessary delay" and excluding evidence obtained in default of that statutory obligation, were nonetheless responsive to the same considerations of Fifth Amendment policy that unavoidably face us now as to the States. In *McNabb* and in *Mallory*, we recognized both the dangers of interrogation and the appropriateness of prophylaxis stemming from the very fact of interrogation itself.

Our decision in *Malloy v. Hogan*, 378 U.S. 1, 84 S.Ct. 1489, 12 L.Ed.2d 653 (1964), necessitates an examination of the scope of the privilege in state cases as well. In *Malloy*, we squarely held the privilege applicable to the States, and held that the substantive standards underlying the privilege applied with full force to state court proceedings. * * * Aside from the holding itself, the reasoning in *Malloy* made clear what had already become apparent—that the substantive and procedural safeguards surrounding admissibility of confessions in state cases had become exceedingly exacting, reflecting all the policies embedded in the privilege. The voluntariness doctrine in the state cases, as *Malloy* indicates, encompasses all interrogation practices which are likely to exert such pressure upon an individual as to disable him from making a free and rational choice. The implications of this proposition were elaborated in our decision in *Escobedo*, decided one week after *Malloy* applied the privilege to the States.

Our holding there stressed the fact that the police had not advised the defendant of his constitutional privilege to remain silent at the outset of the interrogation, and we drew attention to that fact at several points in the decision. This was no isolated factor, but an essential ingredient in our decision. The entire thrust of police interrogation there, as in all the cases today, was to put the defendant in such an emotional state as to impair his capacity for rational judgment. The abdication of the constitutional privilege—the choice on his part to speak to the police—was not made knowingly or competently because of the failure to apprise him of his rights; the compelling atmosphere of the in-custody interrogation, and not an independent decision on his part, caused the defendant to speak.

A different phase of the *Escobedo* decision was significant in its attention to the absence of counsel during the questioning. There, as in the cases today, we sought a protective device to dispel the compelling atmosphere of the interrogation. In *Escobedo*, however, the police did not relieve the defendant of the anxieties which they had created in the interrogation rooms. Rather, they denied his request for the assistance of counsel. This heightened his dilemma, and made his later statements the product of this compulsion. The denial of the defendant's request for his attorney thus undermined his ability to exercise the privilege—to remain silent if he chose or to speak without any intimidation, blatant or subtle. The presence of counsel, in all the cases before us today, would be the adequate protective device necessary to make the process of police interrogation conform to the dictates of the privilege. His presence would insure that statements made in the government-established atmosphere are not the product of compulsion.

It was in this manner that *Escobedo* explicated another facet of the pre-trial privilege, noted in many of the Court's prior decisions: the protection of rights at trial. That counsel is present when statements are taken from an individual during interrogation obviously enhances the integrity of the fact-finding processes in court. The presence of an attorney, and the warnings delivered to the individual, enable the defendant under otherwise compelling circumstances to tell his story without fear, effectively, and in a way that eliminates the evils in the interrogation process. Without the protections flowing from adequate warning and the rights of counsel, "all the careful safeguards erected around the giving of testimony, whether by an accused or any other witness, would become empty formalities in a procedure where the most compelling possible evidence of guilt, a confession, would have already been obtained at the unsupervised pleasure of the police."

III

Today, then, there can be no doubt that the Fifth Amendment privilege is available outside of criminal court proceedings and serves to protect persons in all settings in which their freedom of action is curtailed in any significant way from being compelled to incriminate themselves. We have concluded that without proper safeguards the process of in-custody interrogation of persons suspected or accused of crime contains inherently compelling pressures which work to undermine the individual's will to resist and to compel him to speak where he would not otherwise do so freely. In order to combat these pressures and to permit a full opportunity to exercise the privilege against self-incrimination, the accused must be adequately and effectively apprised of his rights and the exercise of those rights must be fully honored.

It is impossible for us to foresee the potential alternatives for protecting the privilege which might be devised by Congress or the States in the exercise of their creative rule-making capacities. Therefore we cannot say that the Constitution necessarily requires adherence to any particular solution for the inherent compulsions of the interrogation process as it is presently conducted. Our decision in no way creates a constitutional straitjacket which will handicap sound efforts at reform, nor is it intended to have this effect. We encourage Congress and the States to continue their laudable search for increasingly effective ways of protecting the rights of the individual while promoting efficient enforcement of our criminal laws. However, unless we are shown other procedures which are at least as effective in apprising accused persons of their right of silence and in assuring a continuous opportunity to exercise it, the following safeguards must be observed.

At the outset, if a person in custody is to be subjected to interrogation, he must first be informed in clear and unequivocal terms that he has the right to remain silent. For those unaware of the privilege, the warning is needed simply to make them aware of it—the threshold requirement for an intelligent decision as to its exercise. More important, such a warning is an absolute prerequisite in overcoming the inherent pressures of the interrogation atmosphere. It is not just the subnormal or woefully ignorant who succumb to an interrogator's imprecations, whether implied or expressly stated, that the interrogation will continue until a confession is obtained or that silence in the face of accusation is itself damning and will bode ill when presented to a jury. Further, the warning will show the individual that his interrogators are prepared to recognize his privilege should he choose to exercise it.

The Fifth Amendment privilege is so fundamental to our system of constitutional rule and the expedient of giving an adequate warning as to the availability of the privilege so simple, we will not pause to inquire in individual cases whether the defendant was aware of his rights without a warning being given. Assessments of the knowledge the defendant possessed, based on information as to his age, education, intelligence, or prior contact with authorities, can never be more than a speculation. More important, whatever the background of the person interrogated, a warning at the time of the interrogation is indispensable to overcome its pressures and to insure that the individual knows he is free to exercise the privilege at that point in time.

The warning of the right to remain silent must be accompanied by the explanation that anything said can and will be used against the individual in court. This warning is needed in order to make him aware not only of the privilege, but also of the consequences of forgoing it. It is only through an awareness of these consequences that there can be any assurance of real understanding and intelligent exercise of the privilege. Moreover, this warning may serve to make the individual more acutely aware that he is faced with a phase of the adversary system—that he is not in the presence of persons acting solely in his interest.

The circumstances surrounding in-custody interrogation can operate very quickly to overbear the will of one merely made aware of his privilege by his interrogators. Therefore, the right to have counsel present at the interrogation is indispensable to the protection of the Fifth Amendment privilege under the system we delineate today. Our aim is to assure that the individual's right to choose between silence and speech remains unfettered throughout the interrogation process. A once-stated warning, delivered by those who will conduct the interrogation, cannot itself suffice to that end among those who most require knowledge of their rights. A mere warning given by the interrogators is not alone sufficient to accomplish that end. Prosecutors themselves claim that the admonishment of the right to remain silent without more "will benefit only the recidivist and the professional." Even preliminary advice given to the accused by his own attorney can be swiftly overcome by the secret interrogation process. Thus, the need for counsel to protect the Fifth Amendment privilege comprehends not merely a right to consult with counsel prior to questioning, but also to have counsel present during any questioning if the defendant so desires.

The presence of counsel at the interrogation may serve several significant subsidiary functions as well. If the accused decides to talk to his interrogators, the assistance of counsel can mitigate the dangers of untrustworthiness. With a lawyer present the likelihood that the police will practice coercion is reduced, and if coercion is nevertheless exercised the lawyer can testify to it in court. The presence of a lawyer can also help to guarantee that the accused gives a fully accurate statement to the police and that the statement is rightly reported by the prosecution at trial.

An individual need not make a pre-interrogation request for a lawyer. While such request affirmatively secures his right to have one, his failure to ask for a lawyer does not constitute a waiver. No effective waiver of the right to counsel during interrogation can be recognized unless specifically made after the warnings we here delineate have been given. The accused who does not know his rights and therefore does not make a request may be the person who most needs counsel. * * *

Accordingly we hold that an individual held for interrogation must be clearly informed that he has the right to consult with a lawyer and to have the lawyer with him during interrogation under the system for protecting the privilege we delineate today. As with the warnings of the right to remain silent and that anything stated can be used in evidence against him, this warning is an absolute prerequisite to interrogation. No amount of circumstantial evidence that the person may have been aware of this right will suffice to stand in its stead. Only through such a warning is there ascertainable assurance that the accused was aware of this right.

If an individual indicates that he wishes the assistance of counsel before any interrogation occurs, the authorities cannot rationally ignore or deny his request on the basis that the individual does not have or cannot afford a retained attorney. The financial ability of the individual has no relationship to the scope of the rights involved here. The privilege against self-incrimination secured by the Constitution applies to all individuals. The need for counsel in order to protect the privilege exists for the indigent as well as the affluent. In fact, were we to limit these constitutional rights to those who can retain an attorney, our decisions today would be of little significance. The cases before us as well as the vast majority of confession cases with which we have dealt in the past involve those unable to retain counsel. While authorities are not required to relieve the accused of his poverty, they have the obligation not to take advantage of indigence in the administration of justice. * * *

In order fully to apprise a person interrogated of the extent of his rights under this system then, it is necessary to warn him not only that he has the right to consult with an attorney, but also that if he is indigent a lawyer will be appointed to represent him. Without this additional warning, the admonition of the right to consult with counsel would often be understood as meaning only that he can consult with a lawyer if he has one or has funds to obtain one. The warning of a right to counsel would be hollow if not couched in terms that would convey to the indigent—the person most often subjected to interrogation—the knowledge that he too has a right to have counsel present. As with the warnings of the right to remain silent and of the general right to counsel, only by effective and express explanation to the indigent of this right can there be assurance that he was truly in a position to exercise it.

Once warnings have been given, the subsequent procedure is clear. If the individual indicates in any manner, at any time prior to or during questioning, that he wishes to remain silent, the interrogation must cease. At this point he has shown that he intends to exercise his Fifth Amendment privilege; any statement taken after the person invokes his privilege cannot be other than the product of compulsion, subtle or otherwise. Without the right to cut off questioning, the setting of in-custody interrogation operates on the individual to overcome free choice in producing a statement after the privilege has been once invoked. If the individual states that he wants an attorney, the interrogation must cease until an attorney is present. At that time, the individual must have an opportunity to confer with the attorney and to have him present during any subsequent questioning. If the individual cannot obtain an attorney and he indicates that he wants one before speaking to police, they must respect his decision to remain silent. * * *

If the interrogation continues without the presence of an attorney and a statement is taken, a heavy burden rests on the government to demonstrate that the defendant knowingly and intelligently waived his privilege against self-incrimination and his right to retained or appointed counsel. This Court has always set high standards of proof for the waiver of constitutional rights, and we re-assert these standards as applied to in-custody interrogation. Since the State is responsible for establishing the isolated circumstances under which the interrogation takes place and has the only means of making available corroborated evidence of warnings given during incommunicado interrogation, the burden is rightly on its shoulders.

An express statement that the individual is willing to make a statement and does not want an attorney followed closely by a statement could constitute a waiver. But a valid waiver will not be presumed simply from the silence of the accused after warnings are given or simply from the fact that a confession was in fact eventually obtained. A statement we made in *Carnley v. Cochran*, 369 U.S. 506, 516, 82 S.Ct. 884, 8 L.Ed.2d 70 (1962), is applicable here:

> "Presuming waiver from a silent record is impermissible. The record must show, or there must be an allegation and evidence which show, that an accused was offered counsel but intelligently and understandingly rejected the offer. Anything less is not waiver."

Moreover, where in-custody interrogation is involved, there is no room for the contention that the privilege is waived if the individual answers some questions or gives some information on his own prior to invoking his right to remain silent when interrogated.

Whatever the testimony of the authorities as to waiver of rights by an accused, the fact of lengthy interrogation or incommunicado incarceration before a statement is made is strong evidence that the accused did not validly waive his rights. In these circumstances the fact that the individual eventually made a statement is consistent with the conclusion that the compelling influence of the interrogation finally forced him to do so. It is inconsistent with any notion of a voluntary relinquishment of the privilege. Moreover, any evidence that the accused was threatened, tricked, or cajoled into a waiver will, of course, show that the defendant did not voluntarily waive his privilege. The requirement of warnings and waiver of rights is a fundamental with respect to the Fifth Amendment privilege and not simply a preliminary ritual to existing methods of interrogation.

The warnings required and the waiver necessary in accordance with our opinion today are, in the absence of a fully effective equivalent, prerequisites to the admissibility of any statement made by a defendant. No distinction can be drawn between statements which are direct confessions and statements which amount to "admissions" of part or all of an offense. The privilege against self-incrimination protects the individual from being compelled to incriminate himself in any manner; it does not distinguish degrees of incrimination. Similarly, for precisely the same reason, no distinction may be drawn between inculpatory statements and statements alleged to be merely "exculpatory." If a statement made were in fact truly exculpatory it would, of course, never be used by the prosecution. In fact, statements merely intended to be exculpatory by the defendant are often used to impeach his testimony at trial or to demonstrate untruths in the statement given under interrogation and thus to prove guilt by implication. These statements are incriminating in any meaningful sense of the word and may not be used without the full warnings and effective waiver required for any other statement. In *Escobedo* itself, the defendant fully intended his accusation of another as the slayer to be exculpatory as to himself.

The principles announced today deal with the protection which must be given to the privilege against self-incrimination when the individual is first subjected to police interrogation while in custody at the station or otherwise deprived of his freedom of action in any significant way. It is at this point that our adversary system of criminal proceedings commences, distinguishing itself at the outset from the inquisitorial system recognized in some countries. Under the system of warnings we delineate today or under any other system which may be devised and found effective, the safeguards to be erected about the privilege must come into play at this point.

Our decision is not intended to hamper the traditional function of police officers in investigating crime. When an individual is in custody on probable cause, the police may, of course, seek out evidence in the field to be used at trial against him. Such investigation may include inquiry of persons not under restraint. General on-the-scene questioning as to facts surrounding a crime or other general questioning of citizens in the fact-finding process is not affected by our holding. It is an act of responsible citizenship for individuals to give whatever information they may have to aid in law enforcement. In such situations the compelling atmosphere inherent in the process of in-custody interrogation is not necessarily present. * * *

To summarize, we hold that when an individual is taken into custody or otherwise deprived of his freedom by the authorities in any significant way and is subjected to questioning, the privilege against self-incrimination is jeopardized. Procedural safeguards must be employed to protect the privilege, and unless other fully effective means are adopted to notify the person of his right to silence and to assure that the exercise of the right will be scrupulously honored, the following measures are required. He must be warned prior to any questioning that he has the right to remain silent, that anything he says can be used against him in a court of law, that he has the right to the presence of an attorney, and that if he cannot afford an attorney one will be appointed for him prior to any questioning if he so desires. Opportunity to exercise these rights must be afforded to him throughout the interrogation. After such warnings have been given, and such opportunity afforded him, the individual may knowingly and intelligently waive these rights and agree to answer questions or make a statement. But unless and until such warnings and waiver are demonstrated by the prosecution at trial, no evidence obtained as a result of interrogation can be used against him. * * *

V

Because of the nature of the problem and because of its recurrent significance in numerous cases, we have to this point discussed the relationship of the Fifth Amendment privilege to police interrogation without specific concentration on the facts of the cases before us. We turn now to these facts to consider the application to these cases of the constitutional principles discussed above. In each instance, we have concluded that statements were obtained from the defendant under circumstances that did not meet constitutional standards for protection of the privilege.

No. 759. *Miranda v. Arizona.*

On March 13, 1963, petitioner, Ernesto Miranda, was arrested at his home and taken in custody to a Phoenix police station. He was there identified by the complaining witness. The police then took him to "Interrogation Room No. 2" of the detective bureau. There he was questioned by two police officers. The officers admitted at trial that Miranda was not advised that he had a right to have an attorney present. Two hours later, the officers emerged from the interrogation room with a written confession signed by Miranda. At the top of the statement was a typed paragraph stating that the confession was made voluntarily, without threats or promises of immunity and "with full knowledge of my legal rights, understanding any statement I make may be used against me."

At his trial before a jury, the written confession was admitted into evidence over the objection of defense counsel, and the officers testified to the prior oral confession made by Miranda during the interrogation. Miranda was found guilty of kidnapping and rape. He was sentenced to 20 to 30 years' imprisonment on each count, the sentences to run concurrently. On appeal, the Supreme Court of Arizona held that Miranda's constitutional rights were not violated in obtaining the confession and affirmed the conviction. In reaching its decision, the court emphasized heavily the fact that Miranda did not specifically request counsel.

We reverse. From the testimony of the officers and by the admission of respondent, it is clear that Miranda was not in any way apprised of his right to consult with an attorney and to have one present during the interrogation, nor was his right not to be compelled to incriminate himself effectively protected in any other manner. Without these warnings the statements were inadmissible. The mere fact that he signed a statement which contained a typed-in clause stating that he had "full knowledge" of his "legal rights" does not approach the knowing and intelligent waiver required to relinquish constitutional rights. * * *

[The Court reversed the other three convictions as well. The opinion of Justice Clark, dissenting in three of the cases, including *Miranda*, and concurring in the result in one of the cases, is omitted.]

Mr. Justice HARLAN, with whom Mr. Justice STEWART and Mr. Justice WHITE join, dissenting. * * *

I * * *

While the fine points of [the majority's] scheme are far less clear than the Court admits, the tenor is quite apparent. The new rules are not designed to guard against police brutality or other unmistakably banned forms of coercion. Those who use third-degree tactics and deny them in court are equally able and destined to lie as skillfully about warnings and waivers. Rather, the thrust of the new rules is to negate all pressures, to reinforce the nervous or ignorant suspect, and ultimately to discourage any confession at all. The aim in short is toward "voluntariness" in a utopian sense, or to view it from a difference angle, voluntariness with a vengeance.

To incorporate this notion into the Constitution requires a strained reading of history and precedent and a disregard of the very pragmatic concerns that alone may on occasion justify such strains. * * *

III * * *

What the Court largely ignores is that its rules impair, if they will not eventually serve wholly to frustrate, an instrument of law enforcement that has long and quite reasonably been thought worth the price paid for it. There can be little doubt that the Court's new code would markedly decrease the number of confessions. * * *

While passing over the costs and risks of its experiment, the Court portrays the evils of normal police questioning in terms which I think are exaggerated. Albeit stringently confined by the due process standards interrogation is no doubt often inconvenient and unpleasant for the suspect. However, it is no less so for a man to be arrested and jailed, to have his house searched, or to stand trial in court, yet all this may properly happen to the most innocent given probable cause, a warrant, or an indictment. Society has always paid a stiff price for law and order, and peaceful interrogation is not one of the dark moments of the law. * * *

Mr. Justice WHITE, with whom Mr. Justice HARLAN and Mr. Justice STEWART join, dissenting. * * *

III * * *

Although in the Court's view in-custody interrogation is inherently coercive, the Court says that the spontaneous product of the coercion of arrest and detention is still to be deemed voluntary. An accused, arrested on probable cause, may blurt out a confession which will be admissible despite the fact that he is alone and in custody, without any showing that he had any notion of his right to remain silent or of the consequences of his admission. Yet, under the Court's rule, if the police ask him a single question such as "Do you have anything to say?" or "Did you kill your wife?" his response, if there is one, has somehow been compelled, even if the accused has been clearly warned of his right to remain silent. Common sense informs us to the contrary. While one may say that the response was "involuntary" in the sense the question provoked or was the occasion for the response and thus the defendant was induced to speak out when he might have remained silent if not arrested and not questioned, it is patently unsound to say the response is compelled. * * *

On the other hand, even if one assumed that there was an adequate factual basis for the conclusion that all confessions obtained during in-custody interrogation are the product of compulsion, the rule propounded by the Court would still be irrational, for, apparently, it is only if the accused is also warned of his right to counsel and waives both that right and the right against self-incrimination that the inherent compulsiveness of interrogation disappears. But if the defendant may not answer without a warning a question such as "Where were you last night?" without having his answer be a compelled one, how can the Court ever accept his negative answer to the question of whether he wants to consult his retained counsel or counsel whom the court will appoint? And why if counsel is present and the accused nevertheless confesses, or counsel tells the accused to tell the truth, and that is what the accused does, is the situation any less coercive insofar as the accused is concerned? The Court apparently realizes its dilemma of foreclosing questioning without the necessary warnings but at the same time permitting the accused, sitting in the same chair in front of the same policemen, to waive his right to consult an attorney. It expects, however, that the accused will not often waive that right; and if it is claimed that he has, the State faces a severe, if not impossible, burden of proof. * * *

In sum, for all the Court's expounding on the menacing atmosphere of police interrogation procedures, it has failed to supply any foundation for the conclusions it draws or the measures it adopts.

IV   * * *

The most basic function of any government is to provide for the security of the individual and of his property. These ends of society are served by the criminal laws which for the most part are aimed at the prevention of crime. Without the reasonably effective performance of the task of preventing private violence and retaliation, it is idle to talk about human dignity and civilized values. * * *

In some unknown number of cases the Court's rule will return a killer, a rapist or other criminal to the streets and to the environment which produced him, to repeat his crime whenever it pleases him. As a consequence, there will not be a gain, but a loss, in human dignity. The real concern is not the unfortunate consequences of this new decision on the criminal law as an abstract, disembodied series of authoritative proscriptions, but the impact on those who rely on the public authority for protection and who without it can only engage in violent self-help with guns, knives and the help of their neighbors similarly inclined. There is, of course, a saving factor: the next victims are uncertain, unnamed and unrepresented in this case. * * *

Notes and Questions

1. *Is Miranda legitimate?* The point to a Constitution, of course, is to enshrine certain principles so fundamental that they should stand even when a majority of the country thinks otherwise. This role is often called "counter-majoritarian" because it stands in the way of the ordinary democratic process. But when the Court seems to depart from the text or the meaning of the Constitution in implementing its view of fairness or justice, its counter-majoritarian function is potentially more controversial, and its legitimacy potentially weakened. We will shortly see, in Part C., both of those effects from *Miranda.*

When the Court is tempted to find new rights in old language, perhaps it should pause to consider how our society has become more partisan, the tenor of our discussions more shrill, the debates over Supreme Court nominees more contentious, and the decisions of the Court more indecipherable to the majority of our citizenry. Judging from the large percentage of our society that chooses not to take advantage of its right to vote, it appears that we have become increasingly disengaged from and cynical towards the democratic process as a means of effective societal change. Application of the Constitution's counter-majoritarian purposes has not come without a price.

Assume, for the moment, that the Framers did not intend the privilege to apply to voluntary, pre-trial confessions, given in ignorance of a "right" to remain silent and in the absence of an attorney. Does that historical understanding make *Miranda* an illegitimate usurpation of the democratic process? Putting history to one side, do you think the text of the Fifth Amendment can be stretched to fit *Miranda* and thus give it legitimacy?

2. Does the *Miranda* Court see the interrogation problem as police compulsion or, rather, as the police cajoling suspects in a way that creates or exploits the natural tendency to appear co-operative? That tendency would naturally lead suspects to talk even when it is not in their best interests. Perhaps the *Miranda* warnings were intended to create a set of preferences that exist in opposition to the preferences that police wish suspects to have. See Louis Michael Seidman, *Rubashov's Question: Self–Incrimination and the Problem of Coerced Preferences*, 2 Yale J. L. & Human. 149 (1990).

Police are, of course, quintessential authority figures. Moreover, as Professor Kent Greenawalt provocatively argued in *Silence as a Moral and Constitutional Right*, 23 Wm. & Mary L. Rev. 15 (1981), the ordinary morality we apply in our day-to-day lives usually requires a response when someone accuses us of malfeasance or misfeasance. If your co-worker, for instance, asks why you failed to cover for her as you promised, the future working relationship will be strained if you respond, "I don't have to answer that question." If you do answer, moreover, it is odd to think of that answer as compelled by the questioner. It seems more likely that you evaluated the consequences of answering and not answering, and chose by an exercise of your will to answer.

Why consider this choice to be "compulsion"? Examine the text of the Fifth Amendment. What is the textual basis for a "right to remain silent"?

3. *The fox-hunt analogy.* The *Miranda* dissents raise, in one form or another, the normative question: What is wrong with taking advantage of the weakness of guilty suspects to obtain a confession? One answer is Professor William Stuntz's. He argued that the *Miranda* Court misread the self-incrimination clause as protecting privacy rather than freedom from coercion. *Miranda*'s limits on police questioning, on this view, began with the premise that "the information belonged to the defendant, it was private, and the government had no right to get it unless the defendant chose—*really* chose—to give it up." William J. Stuntz, *The Substantive Origins of Criminal Procedure,* 105 Yale L.J. 393, 441 (1995).

Professor Gerald Caplan put it as follows:

> Perhaps the impulse to allow even the unquestionably guilty some prospect of escaping detection or conviction is universal. Wigmore referred to this impulse as the "instinct of giving the game fair play." Pound characterized it as "the sporting theory" of justice, and Bentham derisively labeled it "the fox hunter's reason." Under this view, fairness is given that special definition that sportsmen reserve for their games. Bentham elaborated on his analogy to the fox hunt: "The fox is to have a fair chance for his life: he must have * * * leave to run a certain length of way, for the express purpose of giving him a chance for escape." Fairness, so defined, dictates that neither side should have an undue advantage; the police and the criminal should be on roughly equal footing and the rules of the game should be drawn to avoid favoring one side or the other. As Justice Fortas put it in a well-known article (written before he joined the Court), the accused and the accuser are "equals, meeting in battle." The state was sovereign, but so was the individual. The individual possessed the "sovereign right * * * to meet the state on terms as equal as their respective strength would permit * * * strength against strength, resource against resource, argument against argument." * * *

> [T]he *Miranda* approach reflects a bias against self-accusation on principle. This bias has roots in the desire to treat suspects equally. Suspects who do not know their rights, or do not assert them, as a consequence of some handicap—poverty, lack of education, emotional instability—should not, it is felt, fare worse than more accomplished suspects who know and have the capacity to assert their rights. This "equal protection" appeal finds its way repeatedly into judicial opinions and legal commentary. In *Miranda* itself, Chief Justice Warren referred approvingly to [a] California Supreme Court's decision * * * , which stressed that "the defendant who does not realize his rights under the law and who therefore does not request counsel is the very defendant who most needs counsel." A few years earlier, Professor Beisel similarly argued that only the "frightened, the insecure, the weak, and untrained, the bewildered, the stupid, the naive, the credulous" confess. More recently, Professor Kamisar asserted that the pre-*Miranda* voluntariness test favored the more sophisticated suspects because it probably did not

permit greater-than-average pressures to be applied against stronger-than-average suspects.

To the extent that these observations are true—and they seem true enough—they suggest two distinct remedies. One would be to make it more difficult to convict those who are most vulnerable; the other would be to develop ways to bring those hardier, more knowledgeable persons—the hired killer, the calculating embezzler, the experienced burglar—to justice. The critics * * * have preferred the former. They do not see the lack of stamina and professionalism of the suspect as conferring a benefit on society by facilitating the identification of wrongdoers.

But guilt is personal. That another, equally guilty, person got away with murder because of some fortuitous factor—he was more experienced in dealing with the police, he had a poorly developed sense of guilt, he had a smart lawyer, he knew his rights—or even because of discrimination, does not make the more vulnerable murderer less guilty. To hold otherwise is to confuse justice with equality. "Both are desirable. However, neither can replace the other." Since sophisticated suspects ordinarily will choose not to confess (with or without knowledge of their rights), "[t]o strive for equality * * * is to strive to eliminate confessions." Thus, the *Miranda* Court elected to let one person get away with murder because of the advantage possessed by another.

Gerald M. Caplan, *Questioning Miranda*, 38 Vand. L. Rev. 1417, 1441–42, 1456–58 (1985).

4. *Miranda: more pros and cons.* Professor Caplan characterizes part of *Miranda*'s rationale, also present in Professor Kamisar's 1965 essay (p. 580, Note 6), as an appeal to "equal protection" principles—*i.e,* suspects should be treated equally during police interrogation without regard to whether they are rich or poor, knowledgeable or ignorant, frightened or confident. What is Caplan's response to this argument? Are you persuaded? Professor Joseph Grano argued for equality based on permitting police to refuse to allow any suspect to have a lawyer (this of course would require overruling *Miranda*). Joseph D. Grano, Confessions, Truth, and the Law 37 (1993). Isn't Grano right that there is no Sixth Amendment right to counsel in the interrogation room? The contrary argument is textually difficult because the Amendment applies only to "criminal prosecutions," and almost all police interrogation takes place before formal charges are filed. For a response to *Miranda*'s critics, see Stephen J. Schulhofer, *Reconsidering Miranda*, 54 U. Chi. L. Rev. 435 (1987).

The Supreme Court has spoken of the privilege in stirring language. For example, "the roots of the privilege * * * tap the basic stream of religious and political principle because the privilege reflects the limits of the individual's attornment to the state and—in a philosophical sense—insists upon the equality of the individual and the state." In re Gault, 387 U.S. 1, 87 S.Ct. 1428, 18 L.Ed.2d 527 (1967). Before he joined the Court, Abe Fortas wrote: "A man may be punished, even put to death by the state, but * * * he should not be made to prostrate himself before its majesty. Mea culpa belongs to a man and his God. It is a plea that cannot be exacted from free men by human authority." Abe Fortas, *The Fifth Amendment: Nemo Tenetur Prodere Seipsum*, 25 Clev. B. Ass'n J. 91, 100 (1954).

The Court noted in 1964 that "the privilege, while sometimes 'a shelter to the guilty,' is often 'a protection to the innocent.' " Does the privilege only "sometimes" shelter the guilty but "often" protect the innocent? It does not seem likely. To be sure, an innocent defendant might make a poor witness or have a felony record that can be introduced to impeach his credibility if he testifies. Professor Stephen Schulhofer notes that the defendant "may look sleazy. He may be inarticulate, nervous, or easily intimidated. His vague memory on some of the details may leave him vulnerable to a clever cross-examination." Stephen J. Schulhofer, *Some Kind Words for the Privilege Against Self–Incrimination*, 26 Val. U. L. Rev. 311, 330 (1991). But Judge Henry Friendly concluded that the privilege "so much more often shelters the guilty" that its "occasional effect in protecting the innocent would be an altogether insufficient reason" to find the privilege beneficial. Henry J. Friendly, *The Fifth Amendment Tomorrow: The Case for Constitutional Change*, 37 U. Cin. L. Rev. 671, 687 (1968).

Professor Donald Dripps has remarked, with characteristic economy that "[t]he privilege is at best an anachronism and at worst a constitutional blunder." Donald Dripps, *Akhil Amar On Criminal Procedure and Constitutional Law: "Here I Go Down That Wrong Road Again,"* 74 N. C. L. Rev. 1559, 1635 (1996). As you proceed through this chapter, you should consider whether you agree more with Professor Dripps's characterization of the Fifth Amendment privilege or, instead, Justice Goldberg's observations in *Murphy*, quoted at p. 574, Note 8.

5. Would *Miranda* apply to suspects who do not know that they are being questioned by police? Do you see the argument that it would not apply? With only Justice Marshall dissenting, the Court held in Illinois v. Perkins, 496 U.S. 292, 110 S.Ct. 2394, 110 L.Ed.2d 243 (1990), that encounters between suspects and undercover officers are not subject to *Miranda*, noting that "warnings are not required when the suspect is unaware that he is speaking to a law enforcement officer and gives a voluntary statement." The Court stated the rationale this way:

> Conversations between suspects and undercover agents do not implicate the concerns underlying *Miranda*. The essential ingredients of a "police-dominated atmosphere" and compulsion are not present when an incarcerated person speaks freely to someone that he believes to be a fellow inmate. Coercion is determined from the perspective of the suspect. When a suspect considers himself in the company of cellmates and not officers, the coercive atmosphere is lacking.

In his dissent, Justice Marshall raised the specter of the police posing as a priest or as the suspect's lawyer. Are those distinguishable from what happened in *Perkins*? What arguments would you make on behalf of those suspects?

6. *Where are they now?* The Court's sweeping judgment in *Miranda* was hardly the end of Ernest Miranda's contact with the criminal justice system. The state re-prosecuted—without the confession given to the police, of course—and the second trial ended again in a conviction. The principal

evidence was a confession Miranda made to his girl friend when she visited him in jail a few days after he had confessed to the police. Liva Baker, Miranda: Crime, Law and Politics 291 (1983). Miranda's second conviction was affirmed on appeal, and the United States Supreme Court denied certiorari. Thus, Ernest Miranda served a prison term for the very rape that led to the most controversial criminal procedure ruling in the history of the Supreme Court.

But that is not the end of the story. After Miranda was paroled, he returned to Phoenix, and worked for a time as an appliance store deliveryman. On January 31, 1976, he played poker with two Mexican immigrants in La Ampola, a "dusty bar in the Deuce section of Phoenix." A fistfight escalated into a knife attack on Miranda. He was stabbed twice and was dead on arrival at Good Samaritan Hospital. Miranda was 34 years old. The police apprehended one of the immigrants, later charged as an accomplice in the killing of Miranda. The officers read the suspect his *Miranda* rights. Baker, at 408.

THINKING ABOUT *MIRANDA:* A LAWYER'S (AND LAW STUDENT'S) CHECKLIST

You have read *Miranda*, seen the *Perkins* clarification, p. 600, Note 5, and learned what happened to Miranda the man. Now we begin the road of learning what happened to *Miranda*—the doctrine—after the case was decided. Before we begin the story, it is worth setting out the basic issues that a lawyer or law student needs to consider when a *Miranda* issue potentially arises in a specific case.

First, there is the triggering mechanism for *Miranda* warnings— custodial interrogation. We will see later that the Supreme Court treats this concept as if it were two independent elements, "custody" and "interrogation." And, both elements can be difficult to discern in specific cases.

Second, assuming a finding of "custodial interrogation," *Miranda* warnings are ordinarily required. But, as *Miranda* teaches, a suspect may waive her "*Miranda* rights." What constitutes a valid waiver can also be a complicated matter. By far, waiver is the most litigated *Miranda* issue in criminal proceedings.

Third, if *Miranda* warnings are not given when they should be, or if they are given but a valid waiver is not secured, the suspect's statements received by the police are generally inadmissible. But, there is another question that may come to your mind: What about any "fruits" of the *Miranda* violation? Are *they* subject to exclusion as well, in the same way as "fruits of the poisonous tree" are handled in the Fourth Amendment? Wait until you see what the Supreme Court has said about that!

Fourth, are there exceptions to the *Miranda* rule? That is, are there circumstances in which the police do *not* have to give *Miranda* warnings in advance of custodial interrogation, or are there circumstances in which the remedy for violation of the *Miranda* rule does *not* include total exclusion of the original *Miranda*-less statement?

It would be nice if we could look at *Miranda* law in the organized manner set out above, but the Supreme Court's torturous path through the *Miranda* thicket hinders such a straight-forward approach. As it turns out, the Supreme Court, almost from the start of the post-*Miranda* era, began to back away from the case's implications, but did so in a somewhat odd way: It began to re-characterize *Miranda*'s relationship to the Fifth Amendment. As you will see, that re-characterization has an impact on how the *Miranda* doctrine is applied. Re-characterization led to reshaping. So, rather than turn to the *Miranda* issues in the order we set them out above—the way a lawyer might analyze a *Miranda* problem today—we will start with a description of the stormy seas in which the decision found itself, and see how those seas re-shaped the case. Warning: Even in the "stormy seas" there is law to learn. In particular, be on the lookout for the Court's approach to the "fruits" issue, and to the "exceptions to *Miranda*" question.

C. STORMY SEAS FOR *MIRANDA*

1. THE POLITICAL REACTION TO *MIRANDA*: NIXON, GEORGE WALLACE, AND THE OMNIBUS CRIME CONTROL ACT

The reaction to *Miranda* was intense. Police and district attorneys railed against what they saw as a major blow to their ability to solve crimes. Newspaper editorials were generally opposed. By the summer of 1968, both Richard Nixon and George Wallace sought to use the Warren Court as a campaign issue against Democrat Hubert Humphrey. George Wallace, running for president on the American Independent Party ticket, made the following remarks during a rally in Cicero, Illinois, remarks that were a standard part of his campaign speech. The Supreme Court, Wallace said, was a "sorry, lousy, no-account outfit." Murderers and rapists are "just laughing while the police are crying for help." If a criminal "knocks you over the head," he will be "out of jail before you're out of the hospital and the policeman who arrested him will be on trial. But some psychologist says, 'well he's not to blame, society's to blame. His father didn't take him to see the Pittsburgh Pirates when he was a little boy.'" Then, a promise from Wallace: "If we were President now, you wouldn't get stabbed or raped in the shadow of the White House, even if we had to call out 30,000 troops and equip them with two-foot-long bayonets and station them every few feet apart." Liva Baker, Miranda: Crime, Law and Politics 243–44 (1983).

According to Baker, Richard Nixon's strategy was to appear as a "more respectable alternative" to Wallace, "countering his rhetoric 'with a velvet-glove version of the mailed fist.'" Again according to Baker, although there were many contentious issues in the 1968 campaign

(Vietnam, welfare, inflation, taxes, President Johnson's War on Poverty, Social Security), "the issue that stood out, its theme in every speech at every airport and on every makeshift stage, the one that was remembered most vividly years later, was [Nixon's] appeal for 'law and order.'" *Id.* at 244.

Focusing specifically on *Miranda*, Nixon said in Ohio two weeks before the election:

> I was in Philadelphia the other day. I found that a cab driver who had been cruelly murdered and robbed, and the man who murdered and robbed him had confessed the crime, was set free because of a Supreme Court decision. An old woman, who had been brutally robbed and then murdered—the man who confessed the crime was set free because of a Supreme Court decision. * * * And an old man who had been robbed and clubbed to death—and the man who confessed the crime was set free in Las Vegas. My friends, when that's happening in thousands of cases all over America, I say this. Some of our courts have gone too far in their decisions weakening the peace forces as against the criminal forces in the United States of America. And we're going to change that.

Id. at 248.

Just as telling as the attacks on the Court and on *Miranda* by Wallace and Nixon was Hubert Humphrey's failure to defend the Court. Only one position was presented to the American voter in 1968: The Court had gone too far in the direction of protecting criminals; the criminal forces were gaining an upper hand over the peace forces; something had to be done to right the ship. The voters spoke, giving 57% to Nixon and Wallace, and only 43% to Humphrey. In four years, Democratic votes for president declined from Lyndon Johnson's 61% to Humphrey's 43%. Many issues drove voters into the arms of Richard Nixon, including the hugely unpopular Vietnam War, the protests and counter-protests about the war, the race riots that erupted in over one hundred American cities in the summer of 1968, and the rioting at the Democratic convention that was put down by the heavy hand of Mayor Daley's police in riot gear. By the election in November, 1968, almost thirty thousand Americans had been killed in Vietnam and thousands more had been killed or injured in rioting throughout the country. Still, the unpopularity of the Warren Court played a part in the decline of Democratic fortunes. As Fred Graham put it:

> Where its predecessors had been bold, *Miranda* was to be brazen—*Gideon v. Wainwright* [p. 950] had created a constitutional right to counsel in felony cases at a time when all but five states already provided it; *Mapp v. Ohio* [p. 73] had extended the exclusionary rule to illegal searches after roughly one-half of the states had adopted the same rule; *Miranda* was to impose limits on police interrogation that no state had even approached * * *.

Fred P. Graham, The Self–Inflicted Wound 158 (1970). Ultimately, the question was not so much whether "suspects should be warned of their rights, but whether *Miranda* was worth the price." *Id.* at 192.

In a 1968 campaign speech, Nixon promised "legislation to restore the balance" between the "peace forces" and "criminal forces." Baker, *supra*, at 245–46. Congress beat him to the punch, passing in the summer the Omnibus Crime Control and Safe Streets Act of 1968. What follows gives some sense of the rhetoric on the floor of the Congress.

[Senator McClellan:] [C]rime and the threat of crime, rioting, and violence, stalk America. Our streets are unsafe. Our Citizens are fearful, terrorized, and outraged. * * *

The war on crime must be fought on many fronts. * * * Court decisions that dispense "unequal" justice to society and which protect and liberate guilty and confirmed criminals to pursue and repeat their nefarious crimes should be reversed and overruled. * * * The confusion and disarray injected into law enforcement by [*Miranda* and other cases] are deplorable and demoralizing. * * *

* * * Look at that chart [of the crime rate]. Look at it and weep for your country. * * *

* * * [I]f this effort to deal with these erroneous Court decisions is defeated, every gangster and overlord of the underworld; every syndicate chief, racketeer, captain, lieutenant, sergeant, private, punk, and hoodlum in organized crime; every murderer, rapist, robber, burglar, arsonist, thief, and conman will have cause to rejoice and celebrate.

* * * [A]nd every innocent, law-abiding, and God-fearing citizen in this land will have cause to weep and despair.

114 Cong. Rec. 11,200–01, 14,146, 14,155.

Part of the resulting bill was 18 U.S.C. § 3501, a statute intended to "overrule" *Miranda*. We will return to § 3501 later in the chapter.

And Nixon was doing his part. His first appointment to the Court was conservative jurist Warren E. Burger to replace Chief Justice Earl Warren in 1969. Within the next three years, Nixon would replace Abe Fortas and Hugo Black with Harry Blackmun and Lewis Powell. Three-fifths of the *Miranda* majority would be gone by 1972. Nixon also replaced Justice Harlan with Justice William Rehnquist. Although Justice Harlan dissented in *Miranda*, he believed in an old-fashioned form of stare decisis in which he would follow a decision with which he disagreed unless he could persuade a majority to overrule the disfavored decision. Thus, he could be counted on to follow *Miranda*. Justice Rehnquist did not share Harlan's view of stare decisis. Many Court watchers and scholars thought it was just a matter of finding the right case, and *Miranda* would be overruled. Like many predictions of the future, this one was spectacularly wrong. Instead of being overruled, *Miranda* was limited by later Courts stressing that it was not required by the Fifth Amendment.

NOTES AND QUESTIONS

1.　For an account of the politics and debate surrounding § 3501, see Yale Kamisar, *Can (Did) Congress "Overrule" Miranda?*, 85 Cornell L. Rev. 883 (2000).

2.　As the Court made plain near the end of Part II of its *Miranda* opinion, one of the pre-*Miranda* efforts to regulate police interrogation was based on Federal Rule of Criminal Procedure 5(a), which requires officers to bring arrestees before a federal magistrate "without unnecessary delay." In 1943, the Court created a remedy of exclusion for violations of this rule. Statements taken after the permissible time period had passed had to be suppressed. See McNabb v. United States, 318 U.S. 332, 63 S.Ct. 608, 87 L.Ed. 819 (1943); see also Mallory v. United States, 354 U.S. 449, 77 S.Ct. 1356, 1 L.Ed.2d 1479 (1957).

Part of 18 U.S.C. § 3501 was a limitation on the *McNabb-Mallory* rule that, the Court held in 2009, makes the rule inapplicable when the statements are made in the first six hours after arrest. See Corley v. United States, 556 U.S. ___, 129 S.Ct. 1558, 173 L.Ed.2d 443 (2009). Notice the significance of this ruling: A statement obtained from an arrestee who has been held by federal agents longer than six hours before being brought before a federal magistrate is potentially inadmissible in a federal trial *even if Miranda warnings were given and properly waived, and even if the statement was not coerced under traditional due process or self-incrimination grounds!* To be sure, if the delay is longer than six hours, the majority made plain that the government can argue that the delay was reasonable or necessary and thus avoid suppression.

2.　THE DOCTRINAL REACTION TO *MIRANDA*: CLARIFYING *MIRANDA*'S STATUS

INTRODUCTORY COMMENT

As the 1960s turned into the 1970s, the Supreme Court began to draw a distinction between the Fifth Amendment privilege and *Miranda*'s role as a procedural protection of that privilege. In Harris v. New York, 401 U.S. 222, 91 S.Ct. 643, 28 L.Ed.2d 1 (1971), the Court held that a confession taken in violation of *Miranda* could be used to impeach the defendant's testimony if he testified in his defense at trial. On the surface, *Harris* is not surprising. After all, evidence taken in violation of the Fourth Amendment can be used to impeach a defendant's testimony. See pp. 476–477. But New Jersey v. Portash, 440 U.S. 450, 99 S.Ct. 1292, 59 L.Ed.2d 501 (1979), made clear that *Miranda* was not coextensive with the Fifth Amendment privilege. *Portash* held that "a defendant's compelled statements, as opposed to statements taken in violation of *Miranda*, may not be put to any testimonial use against him in a criminal trial." Thus, unlike evidence seized in violation of the Fourth Amendment, or evidence seized in violation of *Miranda*, compelled confessions cannot be used for *any* purpose. To arrive at this doctrinal position, *Portash* drew an explicit distinction between a *Miranda* violation and a violation of "the constitutional privilege against compulsory self-incrimination in its most pristine form." Whatever *Miranda*'s status, it clearly was not a "pristine form" of the privilege.

Chronologically between *Harris* and *Portash* falls Michigan v. Tucker, 417 U.S. 433, 94 S.Ct. 2357, 41 L.Ed.2d 182 (1974). *Tucker* involved unusual facts. Police interrogated Tucker before *Miranda* was decided and thus the failure to provide warnings was truly a good-faith failure. Second, the evidence offered at a trial that took place after *Miranda* was not Tucker's statements but, rather, the statements of a witness whose name Tucker provided the police to substantiate his alibi. Clearly, the equities were in favor of permitting the witness to testify. Indeed, four years later, the Court ruled based on the attenuation-of-taint principle, that witnesses discovered through a constitutional violation can, in most cases, testify in the trial of the person whose rights were violated. Cf. United States v. Ceccolini, p. 508, Note 4 (Fourth Amendment violation).

But the Court, instead, chose to deny that Tucker's constitutional rights had been violated, holding that a violation of *Miranda* did not constitute a violation of the underlying Fifth Amendment right itself. The Court noted that *Miranda* warnings are "not themselves rights protected by the Constitution but [are] instead measures to insure that the right against compulsory self-incrimination [is] protected." The only harm in *Tucker* was that the police conduct departed "from the prophylactic standards later laid down by this Court in *Miranda* to safeguard" the Fifth Amendment privilege.

Because the violation in *Tucker* was of a prophylactic rule, the Court balanced the additional deterrence that would result from not allowing the witness to testify—Tucker's statements to the police had been suppressed—against the value of having all relevant and trustworthy evidence presented to the fact-finder. That balance tilted in favor of having the witness testify.

By the end of the 1970s, *Miranda* was understood to be a "prophylactic" standard designed to safeguard the Fifth Amendment privilege.

NOTES AND QUESTIONS

1. If the *Miranda* rights are not themselves "rights protected by the Constitution," might there be times when the warnings need not be given? Return to p. 56, Note 1.B. (the shallow grave case). If police did not give warnings and the suspect told the location of the grave, could that (should that) be admissible?

2. Michael Mannheimer has developed an account of "testimonial evidence" that brings together the confrontation clause and the self-incrimination clause. Part of his unifying theory is that both clauses are implicated only when the statement is offered as evidence, as opposed to being offered simply to show that it was made. Using that theory, *Harris* correctly decided that statements taken in violation of *Miranda* were admissible to impeach because

they were not being offered as evidence and thus did not implicate the self-incrimination clause. On the other hand, Mannheimer argues, *Portash* was incorrectly decided. It does not matter under Mannheimer's theory whether the violation was of the "pristine" constitutional provision or the *Miranda* prophylaxis. What is key is that the self-incrimination clause does not forbid the use of statements simply to show that they were made. See Michael J. Zydney Mannheimer, *Toward a Unified Theory of Testimonial Evidence under the Fifth and Sixth Amendments*, 80 Temple L. Rev. 1135 (2007).

3. After the *Harris-Tucker-Portash* start, the Court continued down the prophylaxis path. And what was the ultimate outcome? Read on and you will see.

NEW YORK v. QUARLES

Supreme Court of the United States, 1984.
467 U.S. 649, 104 S.Ct. 2626, 81 L.Ed.2d 550.

JUSTICE REHNQUIST delivered the opinion of the Court. * * *

On September 11, 1980, at approximately 12:30 a.m., Officer Frank Kraft and Officer Sal Scarring were on road patrol in Queens, N.Y., when a young woman approached their car. She told them that she had just been raped by a black male, approximately six feet tall, who was wearing a black jacket with the name "Big Ben" printed in yellow letters on the back. She told the officers that the man had just entered an A & P supermarket located nearby and that the man was carrying a gun.

The officers drove the woman to the supermarket, and Officer Kraft entered the store while Officer Scarring radioed for assistance. Officer Kraft quickly spotted respondent, who matched the description given by the woman, approaching a checkout counter. Apparently upon seeing the officer, respondent turned and ran toward the rear of the store, and Officer Kraft pursued him with a drawn gun. When respondent turned the corner at the end of an aisle, Officer Kraft lost sight of him for several seconds, and upon regaining sight of respondent, ordered him to stop and put his hands over his head.

Although more than three other officers had arrived on the scene by that time, Officer Kraft was the first to reach respondent. He frisked him and discovered that he was wearing a shoulder holster which was then empty. After handcuffing him, Officer Kraft asked him where the gun was. Respondent nodded in the direction of some empty cartons and responded, "the gun is over there." Officer Kraft thereafter retrieved a loaded .38–caliber revolver from one of the cartons, formally placed respondent under arrest, and read him his *Miranda* rights from a printed card. Respondent indicated that he would be willing to answer questions without an attorney present. Officer Kraft then asked respondent if he owned the gun and where he had purchased it. Respondent answered that he did own it and that he had purchased it in Miami, Fla.

In the subsequent prosecution of respondent for criminal possession of a weapon,[2] the judge excluded the statement, "the gun is over there," and the gun because the officer had not given respondent the warnings required by our decision in *Miranda v. Arizona* before asking him where the gun was located. The judge excluded the other statements about respondent's ownership of the gun and the place of purchase, as evidence tainted by the prior *Miranda* violation. * * *

[The New York Court of Appeals] * * * rejected the State's argument that the exigencies of the situation justified Officer Kraft's failure to read respondent his *Miranda* rights until after he had located the gun. * * * For the reasons which follow, we believe that this case presents a situation where concern for public safety must be paramount to adherence to the literal language of the prophylactic rules enunciated in *Miranda*.

The Fifth Amendment guarantees that "[n]o person * * * shall be compelled in any criminal case to be a witness against himself." In *Miranda* this Court for the first time extended the Fifth Amendment privilege against compulsory self-incrimination to individuals subjected to custodial interrogation by the police. The Fifth Amendment itself does not prohibit all incriminating admissions; "[a]bsent some officially coerced self-accusation, the Fifth Amendment privilege is not violated by even the most damning admissions." The *Miranda* Court, however, presumed that interrogation in certain custodial circumstances is inherently coercive and held that statements made under those circumstances are inadmissible unless the suspect is specifically informed of his *Miranda* rights and freely decides to forgo those rights. [As we said in *Michigan v. Tucker*, p. 606, the] prophylactic *Miranda* warnings therefore are "not themselves rights protected by the Constitution but [are] instead measures to insure that the right against compulsory self-incrimination [is] protected." Requiring *Miranda* warnings before custodial interrogation provides "practical reinforcement" for the Fifth Amendment right.

In this case we have before us no claim that respondent's statements were actually compelled by police conduct which overcame his will to resist. Thus the only issue before us is whether Officer Kraft was justified in failing to make available to respondent the procedural safeguards associated with the privilege against compulsory self-incrimination since *Miranda*.[5]

The New York Court of Appeals was undoubtedly correct in deciding that the facts of this case come within the ambit of the *Miranda* decision

---

2. The State originally charged respondent with rape, but the record provides no information as to why the State failed to pursue that charge.

5. The dissent curiously takes us to task for "endors[ing] the introduction of coerced self-incriminating statements in criminal prosecutions," and for "sanction[ing] *sub silentio* criminal prosecutions based on compelled self-incriminating statements." Of course our decision today does nothing of the kind. As the *Miranda* Court itself recognized, the failure to provide *Miranda* warnings in and of itself does not render a confession involuntary, and respondent is certainly free on remand to argue that his statement was coerced under traditional due process standards. Today we merely reject the only argument that respondent has raised to support the exclusion of his statement, that the statement must be *presumed* compelled because of Officer Kraft's failure to read him his *Miranda* warnings.

as we have subsequently interpreted it. We agree that respondent was in police custody * * *. Here Quarles was surrounded by at least four police officers and was handcuffed when the questioning at issue took place. As the New York Court of Appeals observed, there was nothing to suggest that any of the officers were any longer concerned for their own physical safety. The New York Court of Appeals' majority declined to express an opinion as to whether there might be an exception to the *Miranda* rule if the police had been acting to protect the public, because the lower courts in New York had made no factual determination that the police had acted with that motive.

We hold that on these facts there is a "public safety" exception to the requirement that *Miranda* warnings be given before a suspect's answers may be admitted into evidence, and that the availability of that exception does not depend upon the motivation of the individual officers involved. In a kaleidoscopic situation such as the one confronting these officers, where spontaneity rather than adherence to a police manual is necessarily the order of the day, the application of the exception which we recognize today should not be made to depend on *post hoc* findings at a suppression hearing concerning the subjective motivation of the arresting officer. Undoubtedly most police officers, if placed in Officer Kraft's position, would act out of a host of different, instinctive, and largely unverifiable motives—their own safety, the safety of others, and perhaps as well the desire to obtain incriminating evidence from the suspect.

Whatever the motivation of individual officers in such a situation, we do not believe that the doctrinal underpinnings of *Miranda* require that it be applied in all its rigor to a situation in which police officers ask questions reasonably prompted by a concern for the public safety. The *Miranda* decision was based in large part on this Court's view that the warnings which it required police to give to suspects in custody would reduce the likelihood that the suspects would fall victim to constitutionally impermissible practices of police interrogation in the presumptively coercive environment of the station house. The dissenters warned that the requirement of *Miranda* warnings would have the effect of decreasing the number of suspects who respond to police questioning. The *Miranda* majority, however, apparently felt that whatever the cost to society in terms of fewer convictions of guilty suspects, that cost would simply have to be borne in the interest of enlarged protection for the Fifth Amendment privilege.

The police in this case, in the very act of apprehending a suspect, were confronted with the immediate necessity of ascertaining the whereabouts of a gun which they had every reason to believe the suspect had just removed from his empty holster and discarded in the supermarket. So long as the gun was concealed somewhere in the supermarket, with its actual whereabouts unknown, it obviously posed more than one danger to the public safety: an accomplice might make use of it, a customer or employee might later come upon it.

In such a situation, if the police are required to recite the familiar *Miranda* warnings before asking the whereabouts of the gun, suspects in Quarles' position might well be deterred from responding. Procedural safeguards which deter a suspect from responding were deemed acceptable in *Miranda* in order to protect the Fifth Amendment privilege; when the primary social cost of those added protections is the possibility of fewer convictions, the *Miranda* majority was willing to bear that cost. Here, had *Miranda* warnings deterred Quarles from responding to Officer Kraft's question about the whereabouts of the gun, the cost would have been something more than merely the failure to obtain evidence useful in convicting Quarles. Officer Kraft needed an answer to his question not simply to make his case against Quarles but to insure that further danger to the public did not result from the concealment of the gun in a public area.

We conclude that the need for answers to questions in a situation posing a threat to the public safety outweighs the need for the prophylactic rule protecting the Fifth Amendment's privilege against self-incrimination. We decline to place officers such as Officer Kraft in the untenable position of having to consider, often in a matter of seconds, whether it best serves society for them to ask the necessary questions without the *Miranda* warnings and render whatever probative evidence they uncover inadmissible, or for them to give the warnings in order to preserve the admissibility of evidence they might uncover but possibly damage or destroy their ability to obtain that evidence and neutralize the volatile situation confronting them.[7]

In recognizing a narrow exception to the *Miranda* rule in this case, we acknowledge that to some degree we lessen the desirable clarity of that rule. * * * But as we have pointed out, we believe that the exception which we recognize today lessens the necessity of that on-the-scene balancing process. The exception will not be difficult for police officers to apply because in each case it will be circumscribed by the exigency which justifies it. We think police officers can and will distinguish almost instinctively between questions necessary to secure their own safety or the safety of the public and questions designed solely to elicit testimonial evidence from a suspect.

The facts of this case clearly demonstrate that distinction and an officer's ability to recognize it. Officer Kraft asked only the question necessary to locate the missing gun before advising respondent of his rights. It was only after securing the loaded revolver and giving the warnings that he continued with investigatory questions about the owner-

---

7. The dissent argues that a public safety exception to *Miranda* is unnecessary because in every case an officer can simply ask the necessary questions to protect himself or the public, and then the prosecution can decline to introduce any incriminating responses at a subsequent trial. But absent actual coercion by the officer, there is no constitutional imperative requiring the exclusion of the evidence that results from police inquiry of this kind; and we do not believe that the doctrinal underpinnings of *Miranda* require us to exclude the evidence, thus penalizing officers for asking the very questions which are the most crucial to their efforts to protect themselves and the public.

ship and place of purchase of the gun. The exception which we recognize today, far from complicating the thought processes and the on-the-scene judgments of police officers, will simply free them to follow their legitimate instincts when confronting situations presenting a danger to the public safety.[8]

We hold that the Court of Appeals in this case erred in excluding the statement, "the gun is over there," and the gun because of the officer's failure to read respondent his *Miranda* rights before attempting to locate the weapon. Accordingly we hold that it also erred in excluding the subsequent statements as illegal fruits of a *Miranda* violation. We therefore reverse and remand for further proceedings not inconsistent with this opinion. * * *

Justice O'CONNOR, concurring in the judgment in part and dissenting in part.

* * * Were the Court writing from a clean slate, I could agree with its holding. But *Miranda* is now the law and, in my view, the Court has not provided sufficient justification for departing from it or for blurring its now clear strictures. Accordingly, I would require suppression of the initial statement taken from respondent in this case. [In an omitted part of her opinion, Justice O'Connor agreed that the gun was admissible and thus concurred in that part of the Court's judgment. Her view, which later formed the holding in *Oregon v. Elstad*, p. 616, was that a Miranda violation has no "fruit" beyond the statement itself.] * * *

I * * *

In my view, a "public safety" exception unnecessarily blurs the edges of the clear line heretofore established and makes *Miranda*'s requirements more difficult to understand. In some cases, police will benefit because a reviewing court will find that an exigency excused their failure to administer the required warnings. But in other cases, police will suffer because, though they thought an exigency excused their noncompliance, a reviewing court will view the "objective" circumstances differently and require exclusion of admissions thereby obtained. The end result will be a fine-spun new doctrine on public safety exigencies incident to custodial interrogation, complete with the hair-splitting distinctions that currently plague our Fourth Amendment jurisprudence. * * *

---

8. Although it involves police questions in part relating to the whereabouts of a gun, *Orozco v. Texas*, 394 U.S. 324, 89 S.Ct. 1095, 22 L.Ed.2d 311 (1969), is in no sense inconsistent with our disposition of this case. In *Orozco* four hours after a murder had been committed at a restaurant, four police officers entered the defendant's boardinghouse and awakened the defendant, who was sleeping in his bedroom. Without giving him *Miranda* warnings, they began vigorously to interrogate him about whether he had been present at the scene of the shooting and whether he owned a gun. The defendant eventually admitted that he had been present at the scene and directed the officers to a washing machine in the backroom of the boardinghouse where he had hidden the gun. We held that all the statements should have been suppressed. In *Orozco*, however, the questions about the gun were clearly investigatory; they did not in any way relate to an objectively reasonable need to protect the police or the public from any immediate danger associated with the weapon. In short there was no exigency requiring immediate action by the officers beyond the normal need expeditiously to solve a serious crime. * * *

* * * In my view, since there is nothing about an exigency that makes custodial interrogation any less compelling, a principled application of *Miranda* requires that respondent's statement be suppressed. * * *

Justice MARSHALL, with whom Justice BRENNAN and Justice STEVENS join, dissenting. * * *

I * * *

The majority's entire analysis rests on the factual assumption that the public was at risk during Quarles' interrogation. This assumption is completely in conflict with the facts as found by New York's highest court. * * *

The New York court's conclusion that neither Quarles nor his missing gun posed a threat to the public's safety is amply supported by the evidence presented at the suppression hearing. Again contrary to the majority's intimations, no customers or employees were wandering about the store in danger of coming across Quarles' discarded weapon. Although the supermarket was open to the public, Quarles' arrest took place during the middle of the night when the store was apparently deserted except for the clerks at the checkout counter. The police could easily have cordoned off the store and searched for the missing gun. Had they done so, they would have found the gun forthwith. The police were well aware that Quarles had discarded his weapon somewhere near the scene of the arrest. * * *

III

* * * The majority has lost sight of the fact that *Miranda v. Arizona* and our earlier custodial-interrogation cases all implemented a constitutional privilege against self-incrimination. The rules established in these cases were designed to protect criminal defendants against prosecutions based on coerced self-incriminating statements. The majority today turns its back on these constitutional considerations, and invites the government to prosecute through the use of what necessarily are coerced statements.

A

The majority's error stems from a serious misunderstanding of *Miranda v. Arizona* and of the Fifth Amendment upon which that decision was based. The majority implies that *Miranda* consisted of no more than a judicial balancing act in which the benefits of "enlarged protection for the Fifth Amendment privilege" were weighed against "the cost to society in terms of fewer convictions of guilty suspects." Supposedly because the scales tipped in favor of the privilege against self-incrimination, the *Miranda* Court erected a prophylactic barrier around statements made during custodial interrogations. The majority now proposes to return to the scales of social utility to calculate whether *Miranda*'s prophylactic rule remains cost-effective when threats to the public's safety are added to the balance. * * *

Whether society would be better off if the police warned suspects of their rights before beginning an interrogation or whether the advantages of giving such warnings would outweigh their costs did not inform the *Miranda* decision. On the contrary, the *Miranda* Court was concerned with the proscriptions of the Fifth Amendment, and, in particular, whether the Self–Incrimination Clause permits the government to prosecute individuals based on statements made in the course of custodial interrogations. * * *

In fashioning its "public-safety" exception to *Miranda*, the majority makes no attempt to deal with the constitutional presumption established by that case. The majority does not argue that police questioning about issues of public safety is any less coercive than custodial interrogations into other matters. The majority's only contention is that police officers could more easily protect the public if *Miranda* did not apply to custodial interrogations concerning the public's safety. But *Miranda* was not a decision about public safety; it was a decision about coerced confessions. Without establishing that interrogations concerning the public's safety are less likely to be coercive than other interrogations, the majority cannot endorse the "public-safety" exception and remain faithful to the logic of *Miranda v. Arizona*.

<h2 style="text-align:center">B</h2>

The majority's avoidance of the issue of coercion may not have been inadvertent. It would strain credulity to contend that Officer Kraft's questioning of respondent Quarles was not coercive. In the middle of the night and in the back of an empty supermarket, Quarles was surrounded by four armed police officers. His hands were handcuffed behind his back. The first words out of the mouth of the arresting officer were: "Where is the gun?" In the majority's phrase, the situation was "kaleidoscopic." Police and suspect were acting on instinct. Officer Kraft's abrupt and pointed question pressured Quarles in precisely the way that the *Miranda* Court feared the custodial interrogations would coerce self-incriminating testimony.

That the application of the "public-safety" exception in this case entailed coercion is no happenstance. The majority's *ratio decidendi* is that interrogating suspects about matters of public safety *will* be coercive. In its cost-benefit analysis, the Court's strongest argument in favor of a "public-safety" exception to *Miranda* is that the police would be better able to protect the public's safety if they were not always required to give suspects their *Miranda* warnings. The crux of this argument is that, by deliberately withholding *Miranda* warnings, the police can get information out of suspects who would refuse to respond to police questioning were they advised of their constitutional rights. The "public-safety" exception is efficacious precisely because it permits police officers to coerce criminal defendants into making involuntary statements.

* * * Though the majority's opinion is cloaked in the beguiling language of utilitarianism, the Court has sanctioned *sub silentio* criminal

prosecutions based on compelled self-incriminating statements. I find this result in direct conflict with the Fifth Amendment's dictate that "[n]o person * * * shall be compelled in any criminal case to be a witness against himself."

The irony of the majority's decision is that the public's safety can be perfectly well protected without abridging the Fifth Amendment. If a bomb is about to explode or the public is otherwise imminently imperiled, the police are free to interrogate suspects without advising them of their constitutional rights. Such unconsented questioning may take place not only when police officers act on instinct but also when higher faculties lead them to believe that advising a suspect of his constitutional rights might decrease the likelihood that the suspect would reveal life-saving information. If trickery is necessary to protect the public, then the police may trick a suspect into confessing. While the Fourteenth Amendment sets limits on such behavior, nothing in the Fifth Amendment or our decision in *Miranda v. Arizona* proscribes this sort of emergency questioning. All the Fifth Amendment forbids is the introduction of coerced statements at trial. * * *

NOTES AND QUESTIONS

1.   On the facts as given by the majority and dissent, who gets the better of the argument that there was a legitimate threat to public safety? Is the majority or Justice Marshall right about whether *Quarles* can be decided within the conceptual framework of the *Miranda* opinion?

2.   Broadly construed, a "public safety" exception might swallow up much of the *Miranda* rule. One might think that in every arrest for a drug or violent crime, the police officer would ask whether the suspect was armed and lots of suspects would say something against their interest. But when author Thomas in 2002 drew a sample of 216 state and federal cases that discuss *Miranda*, he found that only four cases presented the public safety opinion. See George C. Thomas III, *Stories About* Miranda, 102 Mich. L. Rev. 1959 (2004). Three courts applied to it admit the statements and one found that the case did not fit *Quarles*.

3.   *911 calls and Quarles.* Police responded to a 911 call reporting that Ms. B had attempted suicide. The officers who answered the call were aware that Ms. B had obtained a restraining order against her estranged husband, who opened the door and admitted the police. He attempted to hand his cell phone to the officer, stating, "Can you speak to my attorney?" The officer ignored the phone and tried to assist Ms. B who was bleeding and motionless on the couch. After calling for assistance, the officer asked Mr. B when he had last heard from his wife. He said he had seen or talked to her around four o'clock. He then asked again "can you please talk to my attorney?" Two other officers arrived and Mr. B asked them to please talk to his attorney. Police ignored the request because they were attending to Ms. B. At one point, an officer took the phone and threw it across the room.

Does *Miranda* bar admission of Mr. B's answer to the question of when had he last heard from his wife? See State v. Boretsky, 186 N.J. 271, 894 A.2d 659 (2006).

4. *Miranda as due process?* It is odd to think that *Miranda* sometimes offers less protection from police-coerced statements than the due process clause, but that is the necessary implication of footnote 5 in the *Quarles* majority opinion. Can you offer a theory that would explain this?

5. *Problems.* Assume that no *Miranda* warnings were given in the following Problems, and concern yourself only with whether the case is a proper one for the "public safety" exception.

A. *L* walks into the police station and cries out, "I killed her, I killed her, I killed her." The police officer knew that *L*'s wife was missing. "Are you *L*?" "Yes." "Where is Mrs. *L*?" "At the boathouse." "Where exactly at the boathouse?" "In the last bay, in the van." Police take *L* to the boathouse. They inspect the van and find a large fiberglass box but no other sign of the victim. Police ask *L*, "Is she in the box?" "Yes." See State v. Lockhart, 830 A.2d 433 (Me. 2003).

B. A suspected purse snatcher bites the officer who catches and subdues him. The two are taken to the same hospital, where the detective asks the suspect whether he has any diseases. The suspect apologizes for biting the detective and offers to take a blood test. Is this statement admissible? See Thomas v. State, 128 Md.App. 274, 737 A.2d 622 (1999).

C. A bank robber, *F*, is shot by the bank security guard but manages to flee a Dallas bank. As he runs from the bank, a salesman from a nearby car dealership chases him. When *F* collapses in a field near the bank, the car salesman draws his gun and covers the wounded *F*. Two police officers arrive and draw their guns on the car salesman until they are persuaded that *F* is the suspect. The officers then aim their guns at *F* and tell him to put his hands over his head. He responds that he is wounded and cannot raise his arms. After frisking *F*, the police officers ascertain that he is wounded, yet keep their guns pointed at him. The officers ask the following questions: "Who shot you?", "Who was with you?", and "Where is the gun?" Are the answers admissible? See Fleming v. Collins, 954 F.2d 1109 (5th Cir.1992) (*en banc*).

D. After police arrest *L* on outstanding warrants, the officer notices that he is chewing and swallowing plastic bags. When she asks what is in the bags, the "savvy" suspect replies, "Methamphetamine." The State seeks to introduce the statement on the ground that the officer was concerned about the suspect's health and needed to know what he was ingesting. Which way do you rule as judge? See United States v. Lutz, 207 F.Supp.2d 1247 (D. Kan.2002).

E. *C* was arrested for conspiracy to distribute a large quantity of cocaine. Before searching *C* prior to placing him in detention at the station, the officer asked whether he had any drugs or needles on his person. He responded, "I don't use drugs. I sell them." Admissible? Would it matter if the officer testified that he asked the same question of every person arrested for a drug offense? See United States v. Carrillo, 16 F.3d 1046 (9th Cir.1994).

6. *Quarles* recognized a "public safety" exception to *Miranda*. It did so by distinguishing between compulsion—a pure violation of the Fifth Amendment—and a violation of the mere "prophylactic *Miranda* warn-

ings." In the next case, we see this distinction made more explicit, and the Supreme Court again finds that the implications of a *Miranda* violation are not the same as a violation of the Fifth Amendment in its pristine form.

OREGON v. ELSTAD

Supreme Court of the United States, 1985.
470 U.S. 298, 105 S.Ct. 1285, 84 L.Ed.2d 222.

JUSTICE O'CONNOR delivered the opinion of the Court.

This case requires us to decide whether an initial failure of law enforcement officers to administer the warnings required by *Miranda v. Arizona*, without more, "taints" subsequent admissions made after a suspect has been fully advised of and has waived his *Miranda* rights. Respondent, Michael James Elstad, was convicted of burglary by an Oregon trial court. The Oregon Court of Appeals reversed, holding that respondent's signed confession, although voluntary, was rendered inadmissible by a prior remark made in response to questioning without benefit of *Miranda* warnings. * * *

I

In December 1981, the home of Mr. and Mrs. Gilbert Gross, in the town of Salem, Polk County, Ore., was burglarized. Missing were art objects and furnishings valued at $150,000. A witness to the burglary contacted the Polk County Sheriff's office, implicating respondent Michael Elstad, an 18-year-old neighbor and friend of the Grosses' teenage son. Thereupon, Officers Burke and McAllister went to the home of respondent Elstad, with a warrant for his arrest. Elstad's mother answered the door. She led the officers to her son's room where he lay on his bed, clad in shorts and listening to his stereo. The officers asked him to get dressed and to accompany them into the living room. Officer McAllister asked respondent's mother to step into the kitchen, where he explained that they had a warrant for her son's arrest for the burglary of a neighbor's residence. Officer Burke remained with Elstad in the living room. He later testified:

> "I sat down with Mr. Elstad and I asked him if he was aware of why Detective McAllister and myself were there to talk with him. He stated no, he had no idea why we were there. I then asked him if he knew a person by the name of Gross, and he said yes, he did, and also added that he heard that there was a robbery at the Gross house. And at that point I told Mr. Elstad that I felt he was involved in that, and he looked at me and stated, 'Yes, I was there.' "

The officers then escorted Elstad to the back of the patrol car. As they were about to leave for the Polk County Sheriff's office, Elstad's father arrived home and came to the rear of the patrol car. The officers advised him that his son was a suspect in the burglary. Officer Burke testified that Mr. Elstad became quite agitated, opened the rear door of the car and admonished his son: "I told you that you were going to get into trouble. You wouldn't listen to me. You never learn."

Elstad was transported to the Sheriff's headquarters and approximately one hour later, Officers Burke and McAllister joined him in McAllister's office. McAllister then advised respondent for the first time of his *Miranda* rights, reading from a standard card. Respondent indicated he understood his rights, and, having these rights in mind, wished to speak with the officers. Elstad gave a full statement, explaining that he had known that the Gross family was out of town and had been paid to lead several acquaintances to the Gross residence and show them how to gain entry through a defective sliding glass door. The statement was typed, reviewed by respondent, read back to him for correction, initialed and signed by Elstad and both officers. As an afterthought, Elstad added and initialed the sentence, "After leaving the house Robby & I went back to [the] van & Robby handed me a small bag of grass." Respondent concedes that the officers made no threats or promises either at his residence or at the Sheriff's office. * * *

Following his conviction [of burglary], respondent appealed to the Oregon Court of Appeals * * *. The State conceded that Elstad had been in custody when he made his statement, "I was there," and accordingly agreed that this statement was inadmissible as having been given without the prescribed *Miranda* warnings. But the State maintained that any conceivable "taint" had been dissipated prior to the respondent's written confession by McAllister's careful administration of the requisite warnings. * * *

II

The arguments advanced in favor of suppression of respondent's written confession rely heavily on metaphor. One metaphor, familiar from the Fourth Amendment context, would require that respondent's confession, regardless of its integrity, voluntariness, and probative value, be suppressed as the "tainted fruit of the poisonous tree" of the *Miranda* violation. A second metaphor questions whether a confession can be truly voluntary once the "cat is out of the bag." Taken out of context, each of these metaphors can be misleading. They should not be used to obscure fundamental differences between the role of the Fourth Amendment exclusionary rule and the function of *Miranda* in guarding against the prosecutorial use of compelled statements as prohibited by the Fifth Amendment. The Oregon court assumed and respondent here contends that a failure to administer *Miranda* warnings necessarily breeds the same consequences as police infringement of a constitutional right, so that evidence uncovered following an unwarned statement must be suppressed as "fruit of the poisonous tree." We believe this view misconstrues the nature of the protections afforded by *Miranda* warnings and therefore misreads the consequences of police failure to supply them.

A * * *

Respondent's contention that his confession was tainted by the earlier failure of the police to provide *Miranda* warnings and must be excluded as "fruit of the poisonous tree" assumes the existence of a constitutional violation. This figure of speech is drawn from *Wong Sun v. United States*, [p. 503], in which the Court held that evidence and witnesses discovered as a result of a search in violation of the Fourth Amendment must be excluded from evidence. The *Wong Sun* doctrine applies as well when the fruit of the Fourth Amendment violation is a confession. It is settled law that "a confession obtained through custodial interrogation after an illegal arrest should be excluded unless intervening events break the causal connection between the illegal arrest and the confession so that the confession is 'sufficiently an act of free will to purge the primary taint.'"

But as we explained in *Quarles* [p. 607] and *Tucker* [p. 606], a procedural *Miranda* violation differs in significant respects from violations of the Fourth Amendment, which have traditionally mandated a broad application of the "fruits" doctrine. The purpose of the Fourth Amendment exclusionary rule is to deter unreasonable searches, no matter how probative their fruits. * * * Where a Fourth Amendment violation "taints" the confession, a finding of voluntariness for the purposes of the Fifth Amendment is merely a threshold requirement in determining whether the confession may be admitted in evidence. Beyond this, the prosecution must show a sufficient break in events to undermine the inference that the confession was caused by the Fourth Amendment violation.

The *Miranda* exclusionary rule, however, serves the Fifth Amendment and sweeps more broadly than the Fifth Amendment itself. It may be triggered even in the absence of a Fifth Amendment violation. The Fifth Amendment prohibits use by the prosecution in its case in chief only of *compelled* testimony. Failure to administer *Miranda* warnings creates a presumption of compulsion. Consequently, unwarned statements that are otherwise voluntary within the meaning of the Fifth Amendment must nevertheless be excluded from evidence under *Miranda*. Thus, in the individual case, *Miranda*'s preventive medicine provides a remedy even to the defendant who has suffered no identifiable constitutional harm.

But the *Miranda* presumption, though irrebuttable for purposes of the prosecution's case in chief, does not require that the statements and their fruits be discarded as inherently tainted. Despite the fact that patently *voluntary* statements taken in violation of *Miranda* must be excluded from the prosecution's case, the presumption of coercion does not bar their use for impeachment purposes on cross-examination. * * * Where an unwarned statement is preserved for use in situations that fall outside the sweep of the *Miranda* presumption, "the primary criterion of admissibility [remains] the 'old' due process voluntariness test."

* * * In deciding "how sweeping the judicially imposed consequences" of a failure to administer *Miranda* warnings should be, the

Tucker Court noted that neither the general goal of deterring improper police conduct nor the Fifth Amendment goal of assuring trustworthy evidence would be served by suppression of the witness' testimony. [As noted on p. 606, the police learned the name of a witness from Tucker without giving him *Miranda* warnings. Eds.] The unwarned confession must, of course, be suppressed, but the Court ruled that introduction of the third-party witness' testimony did not violate Tucker's Fifth Amendment rights.

We believe that this reasoning applies with equal force when the alleged "fruit" of a noncoercive *Miranda* violation is neither a witness nor an article of evidence but the accused's own voluntary testimony. As in *Tucker*, the absence of any coercion or improper tactics undercuts the twin rationales—trustworthiness and deterrence—for a broader rule. Once warned, the suspect is free to exercise his own volition in deciding whether or not to make a statement to the authorities. The Court has often noted: " '[A] living witness is not to be mechanically equated with the proffer of inanimate evidentiary objects illegally seized. * * * [T]he living witness is an individual human personality whose attributes of will, perception, memory and *volition* interact to determine what testimony he will give.' " * * *

* * * If errors are made by law enforcement officers in administering the prophylactic *Miranda* procedures, they should not breed the same irremediable consequences as police infringement of the Fifth Amendment itself. It is an unwarranted extension of *Miranda* to hold that a simple failure to administer the warnings, unaccompanied by any actual coercion or other circumstances calculated to undermine the suspect's ability to exercise his free will, so taints the investigatory process that a subsequent voluntary and informed waiver is ineffective for some indeterminate period. Though *Miranda* requires that the unwarned admission must be suppressed, the admissibility of any subsequent statement should turn in these circumstances solely on whether it is knowingly and voluntarily made.

B

The Oregon court, however, believed that the unwarned remark compromised the voluntariness of respondent's later confession. It was the court's view that the prior *answer* and not the unwarned questioning impaired respondent's ability to give a valid waiver and that only lapse of time and change of place could dissipate what it termed the "coercive impact" of the inadmissible statement. When a prior statement is actually coerced, the time that passes between confessions, the change in place of interrogations, and the change in identity of the interrogators all bear on whether that coercion has carried over into the second confession. The failure of police to administer *Miranda* warnings does not mean that the statements received have actually been coerced, but only that courts will presume the privilege against compulsory self-incrimination has not been intelligently exercised. * * * In these circumstances, a careful and thorough administration of *Miranda* warnings serves to cure the condition that rendered the unwarned statement inadmissible. The warning conveys the relevant information and thereafter the suspect's choice whether to exercise his privilege to remain silent should ordinarily be viewed as an "act of free will." * * *

* * * We must conclude that, absent deliberately coercive or improper tactics in obtaining the initial statement, the mere fact that a suspect has made an unwarned admission does not warrant a presumption of compulsion. A subsequent administration of *Miranda* warnings to a suspect who has given a voluntary but unwarned statement ordinarily should suffice to remove the conditions that precluded admission of the earlier statement. In such circumstances, the finder of fact may reasonably conclude that the suspect made a rational and intelligent choice whether to waive or invoke his rights.

III

Though belated, the reading of respondent's rights was undeniably complete. McAllister testified that he read the *Miranda* warnings aloud from a printed card and recorded Elstad's responses. There is no question that respondent knowingly and voluntarily waived his right to remain silent before he described his participation in the burglary. It is also beyond dispute that respondent's earlier remark was voluntary, within the meaning of the Fifth Amendment. Neither the environment nor the manner of either "interrogation" was coercive. The initial conversation took place at midday, in the living room area of respondent's own home, with his mother in the kitchen area, a few steps away. Although in retrospect the officers testified that respondent was then in custody [and thus warnings were required, eds.], at the time he made his statement he had not been informed that he was under arrest. The arresting officers' testimony indicates that the brief stop in the living room before proceeding to the station house was not to interrogate the suspect but to notify his mother of the reason for his arrest.

The State has conceded the issue of custody and thus we must assume that Burke breached *Miranda* procedures in failing to administer *Miranda* warnings before initiating the discussion in the living room. This breach may have been the result of confusion as to whether the brief exchange qualified as "custodial interrogation" or it may simply have reflected Burke's reluctance to initiate an alarming police procedure before McAllister had spoken with respondent's mother. Whatever the reason for Burke's oversight, the incident had none of the earmarks of coercion. Nor did the officers exploit the unwarned admission to pressure respondent into waiving his right to remain silent.

Respondent, however, has argued that he was unable to give a fully *informed* waiver of his rights because he was unaware that his prior statement could not be used against him. Respondent suggests that Officer McAllister, to cure this deficiency, should have added an additional warning to those given him at the Sheriff's office. Such a requirement is neither practicable nor constitutionally necessary. In many cases, a breach of *Miranda* procedures may not be identified as such until long after full *Miranda* warnings are administered and a valid confession obtained. The standard *Miranda* warnings explicitly inform the suspect of his right to consult a lawyer before speaking. Police officers are ill-equipped to pinch-hit for counsel, construing the murky and difficult questions of when "custody" begins or whether a given unwarned statement will ultimately be held admissible.

This Court has never embraced the theory that a defendant's ignorance of the full consequences of his decisions vitiates their voluntariness. If the prosecution has actually violated the defendant's Fifth Amendment rights by introducing an inadmissible confession at trial, compelling the defendant to testify in rebuttal, the rule announced in *Harrison v. United States* 392 U.S. 219, 88 S.Ct. 2008, 20 L.Ed.2d 1047 (1968), precludes use of that testimony on retrial. "Having 'released the spring' by using the petitioner's unlawfully obtained confessions against him, the Government must show that its illegal action did not induce his testimony." But the Court has refused to find that a defendant who confesses, after being falsely told that his codefendant has turned State's evidence, does so involuntarily. The Court has also rejected the argument that a defendant's ignorance that a prior coerced confession could not be admitted in evidence compromised the voluntariness of his guilty plea. Likewise, in *California v. Beheler*, [463 U.S. 1121, 103 S.Ct. 3517, 77 L.Ed.2d 1275 (1983)], the Court declined to accept defendant's contention that, because he was unaware of the potential adverse consequences of statements he made to the police, his participation in the interview was involuntary. Thus we have not held that the *sine qua non* for a knowing and voluntary waiver of the right to remain silent is a full and complete appreciation of all of the consequences flowing from the nature and the quality of the evidence in the case. * * *

Justice BRENNAN, with whom Justice MARSHALL joins, dissenting. * * *

Even while purporting to reaffirm [*Miranda*'s] constitutional guarantees, the Court has engaged of late in a studied campaign to strip the *Miranda* decision piecemeal and to undermine the rights *Miranda* sought to secure. Today's decision not only extends this effort a further step, but delivers a potentially crippling blow to *Miranda* and the ability of courts to safeguard the rights of persons accused of crime. For at least with respect to successive confessions, the Court today appears to strip remedies for *Miranda* violations of the "fruit of the poisonous tree" doctrine prohibiting the use of evidence presumptively derived from official illegality.[2] * * *

---

2. The Court repeatedly casts its analysis in terms of the "fruits" of a *Miranda* violation, but its dicta nevertheless surely should not be read as necessarily foreclosing application of derivative-evidence rules where the *Miranda* violation produces evidence other than a subsequent confession by the accused.

Today's decision, in short, threatens disastrous consequences far beyond the outcome in this case. * * *

I * * *

The Court today * * * [adopts] a rule that "the psychological impact of *voluntary* disclosure of a guilty secret" neither "qualifies as state compulsion" nor "compromises the voluntariness" of subsequent confessions. So long as a suspect receives the usual *Miranda* warnings before further interrogation, the Court reasons, the fact that he "is free to exercise his own volition in deciding whether or not to make" further confessions "ordinarily" is a sufficient "cure" and serves to break any causal connection between the illegal confession and subsequent statements.

The Court's marble-palace psychoanalysis is tidy, but it flies in the face of our own precedents, demonstrates a startling unawareness of the realities of police interrogation, and is completely out of tune with the experience of state and federal courts over the last 20 years. Perhaps the Court has grasped some psychological truth that has eluded persons far more experienced in these matters; if so, the Court owes an explanation of how so many could have been so wrong for so many years. * * *

[The opinion of Justice STEVENS, dissenting, is omitted.]

NOTES AND QUESTIONS

1. *Custody.* When you get to the custody materials, beginning on p. 645, you should reconsider whether the State should have conceded the custody issue.

2. Do you think the Court is saying that *Miranda* is not required by the Constitution?

3. Does the Court hold that no second statement would ever be suppressed if it followed an un-warned incriminating statement or only that *in this case* the statement was admissible? Or is there a third way to read *Elstad*?

4. *Problem.* Police question a 17–year-old suspect held in custody without providing *Miranda* warnings. He admits his involvement in a burglary. One officer turns to the other and, in ear-shot of the suspect, asks him to let the suspect "know about his rights" because he has "already told us about going into the house [and] I don't think that's going to change [his] desire to cooperate with us." Police give *Miranda* warnings. He asks whether he is under arrest and the police tell him he is not. He later confesses to a murder as well as the burglary. Argue for suppression of this confession. Ramirez v. State, 739 So.2d 568 (Fla. 1999).

5. Justice Brennan believed that the *Elstad* Court was engaging in a "fruits" analysis—see footnote 2 in his opinion. The Oregon Court of Appeals had used a fruits analysis. Look carefully at the majority opinion. Is the Court talking about fruit of the poisoned tree, and finding no poisoned tree, or is it plausible to argue that *Elstad* is really holding something else?

After a brief detour to (finally?) settle *Miranda*'s constitutional status, we will return to the "fruits" issue.

6. We saw earlier that Congress in 1968 railed against *Miranda* and enacted the 1968 Omnibus Crime Control and Safe Streets Act. Two of its provisions follow.

§ 3501. Admissibility of confessions

(a) In any criminal prosecution brought by the United States or by the District of Columbia, a confession, as defined in subsection (e) hereof, shall be admissible in evidence if it is voluntarily given. Before such confession is received in evidence, the trial judge shall, out of the presence of the jury, determine any issue as to voluntariness. If the trial judge determines that the confession was voluntarily made it shall be admitted in evidence and the trial judge shall permit the jury to hear relevant evidence on the issue of voluntariness and shall instruct the jury to give such weight to the confession as the jury feels it deserves under all the circumstances.

(b) The trial judge in determining the issue of voluntariness shall take into consideration all the circumstances surrounding the giving of the confession, including (1) the time elapsing between arrest and arraignment of the defendant making the confession, if it was made after arrest and before arraignment, (2) whether such defendant knew the nature of the offense with which he was charged or of which he was suspected at the time of making the confession, (3) whether or not such defendant was advised or knew that he was not required to make any statement and that any such statement could be used against him, (4) whether or not such defendant had been advised prior to questioning of his right to the assistance of counsel; and (5) whether or not such defendant was without the assistance of counsel when questioned and when giving such confession.

Do you thinking, in light of the cases you have read so far, that this part of the statute is constitutional?

7. *Quarles* held that *Miranda* warnings are not always required. *Elstad* pointedly said that the *Miranda* exclusionary rule "serves the Fifth Amendment and sweeps more broadly than the Fifth Amendment itself." So in 2000, the Court found itself at a cross-roads: Was *Miranda* "fully" constitutional, "partly" constitutional, or not constitutional at all? Notice what the answer to this question could mean. If *Miranda* really isn't a constitutional rule, why couldn't Congress legislate a different solution to the interrogation problem, as it attempted in § 3501, above? And, for that matter, why couldn't the states ignore *Miranda* if it is not a constitutional rule? In the next case, the Supreme Court answered these questions. Or, did it?

DICKERSON v. UNITED STATES

Supreme Court of the United States, 2000.
530 U.S. 428, 120 S.Ct. 2326, 147 L.Ed.2d 405.

CHIEF JUSTICE REHNQUIST delivered the opinion of the Court.

In *Miranda v. Arizona*, we held that certain warnings must be given before a suspect's statement made during custodial interrogation could be admitted in evidence. In the wake of that decision, Congress enacted 18 U.S.C. § 3501, which in essence laid down a rule that the admissibility of such statements should turn only on whether or not they were voluntarily made. We hold that *Miranda*, being a constitutional decision of this Court, may not be in effect overruled by an Act of Congress, and we decline to overrule *Miranda* ourselves. We therefore hold that *Miranda* and its progeny in this Court govern the admissibility of statements made during custodial interrogation in both state and federal courts.

Petitioner Dickerson was indicted for bank robbery, conspiracy to commit bank robbery, and using a firearm in the course of committing a crime of violence * * *. Before trial, Dickerson moved to suppress a statement he had made at a Federal Bureau of Investigation field office, on the grounds that he had not received "*Miranda* warnings" before being interrogated. [The Fourth Circuit held] that petitioner had not received *Miranda* warnings before making his statement. But it went on to hold that § 3501, which in effect makes the admissibility of statements such as Dickerson's turn solely on whether they were made voluntarily, was satisfied in this case. It then concluded that our decision in *Miranda* was not a constitutional holding, and that therefore Congress could by statute have the final say on the question of admissibility. * * *

We begin with a brief historical account of the law governing the admission of confessions. Prior to *Miranda*, we evaluated the admissibility of a suspect's confession under a voluntariness test. The roots of this test developed in the common law, as the courts of England and then the United States recognized that coerced confessions are inherently untrustworthy. Over time, our cases recognized two constitutional bases for the requirement that a confession be voluntary to be admitted into evidence: the Fifth Amendment right against self-incrimination and the Due Process Clause of the Fourteenth Amendment.* * *

We have never abandoned this due process jurisprudence, and thus continue to exclude confessions that were obtained involuntarily.* * *

In *Miranda*, we noted that the advent of modern custodial police interrogation brought with it an increased concern about confessions obtained by coercion. Because custodial police interrogation, by its very nature, isolates and pressures the individual, we stated that "even without employing brutality, the 'third degree' or [other] specific stratagems, * * * custodial interrogation exacts a heavy toll on individual liberty and trades on the weakness of individuals." We concluded that the coercion inherent in custodial interrogation blurs the line between voluntary and involuntary statements, and thus heightens the risk that an individual will not be "accorded his privilege under the Fifth Amendment * * * not to be compelled to incriminate himself." Accordingly, we laid down "concrete constitutional guidelines for law enforcement agencies and courts to follow." Those guidelines established that the admissibility in evidence of any statement given during custodial interrogation of a suspect would

depend on whether the police provided the suspect with four warnings.
* * *

Given § 3501's express designation of voluntariness as the touchstone of admissibility, its omission of any warning requirement, and the instruction for trial courts to consider a nonexclusive list of factors relevant to the circumstances of a confession, we agree with the Court of Appeals that Congress intended by its enactment to overrule *Miranda*. Because of the obvious conflict between our decision in *Miranda* and § 3501, we must address whether Congress has constitutional authority to thus supersede *Miranda*. If Congress has such authority, § 3501's totality-of-the-circumstances approach must prevail over *Miranda*'s requirement of warnings; if not, that section must yield to *Miranda*'s more specific requirements.

The law in this area is clear. This Court has supervisory authority over the federal courts, and we may use that authority to prescribe rules of evidence and procedure that are binding in those tribunals. However, the power to judicially create and enforce nonconstitutional "rules of procedure and evidence for the federal courts exists only in the absence of a relevant Act of Congress." Congress retains the ultimate authority to modify or set aside any judicially created rules of evidence and procedure that are not required by the Constitution.

But Congress may not legislatively supersede our decisions interpreting and applying the Constitution. This case therefore turns on whether the *Miranda* Court announced a constitutional rule or merely exercised its supervisory authority to regulate evidence in the absence of congressional direction. * * * Relying on the fact that we have created several exceptions to *Miranda*'s warnings requirement and that we have repeatedly referred to the *Miranda* warnings as "prophylactic," the Court of Appeals concluded that the protections announced in *Miranda* are not constitutionally required.

We disagree with the Court of Appeals' conclusion, although we concede that there is language in some of our opinions that supports the view taken by that court. But first and foremost of the factors on the other side—that *Miranda* is a constitutional decision—is that both *Miranda* and two of its companion cases applied the rule to proceedings in state courts—to wit, Arizona, California, and New York. Since that time, we have consistently applied Miranda's rule to prosecutions arising in state courts. It is beyond dispute that we do not hold a supervisory power over the courts of the several States. * * *

The *Miranda* opinion itself begins by stating that the Court granted certiorari "to explore some facets of the problems * * * of applying the privilege against self-incrimination to in-custody interrogation, *and to give concrete constitutional guidelines for law enforcement agencies and courts to follow*." (emphasis added). * * *

Additional support for our conclusion that *Miranda* is constitutionally based is found in the *Miranda* Court's invitation for legislative action to protect the constitutional right against coerced self-incrimination. After discussing the "compelling pressures" inherent in custodial police interrogation, the *Miranda* Court concluded that, "in order to combat these pressures and to permit a full opportunity to exercise the privilege against self-incrimination, the accused must be adequately and effectively appraised of his rights and the exercise of those rights must be fully honored." However, the Court emphasized that it could not foresee "the potential alternatives for protecting the privilege which might be devised by Congress or the States," and it accordingly opined that the Constitution would not preclude legislative solutions that differed from the prescribed *Miranda* warnings but which were "at least as effective in apprising accused persons of their right of silence and in assuring a continuous opportunity to exercise it."

The Court of Appeals also relied on the fact that we have, after our *Miranda* decision, made exceptions from its rule in cases such as *New York v. Quarles* [p. 607], and *Harris v. New York* [p. 616]. But we have also broadened the application of the *Miranda* doctrine * * *. These decisions illustrate the principle—not that *Miranda* is not a constitutional rule—but that no constitutional rule is immutable. No court laying down a general rule can possibly foresee the various circumstances in which counsel will seek to apply it, and the sort of modifications represented by these cases are as much a normal part of constitutional law as the original decision.

The Court of Appeals also noted that in *Oregon v. Elstad,* [p. 616], we stated that " 'the *Miranda* exclusionary rule * * * serves the Fifth Amendment and sweeps more broadly than the Fifth Amendment itself.' " Our decision in that case—refusing to apply the traditional "fruits" doctrine developed in Fourth Amendment cases—does not prove that *Miranda* is a nonconstitutional decision, but simply recognizes the fact that unreasonable searches under the Fourth Amendment are different from unwarned interrogation under the Fifth Amendment. * * *

The dissent argues that it is judicial overreaching for this Court to hold § 3501 unconstitutional unless we hold that the *Miranda* warnings are required by the Constitution, in the sense that nothing else will suffice to satisfy constitutional requirements. But we need not go farther than *Miranda* to decide this case. In *Miranda*, the Court noted that reliance on the traditional totality-of-the-circumstances test raised a risk of overlooking an involuntary custodial confession, a risk that the Court found unacceptably great when the confession is offered in the case in chief to prove guilt. The Court therefore concluded that something more than the totality test was necessary. As discussed above, § 3501 reinstates the totality test as sufficient. Section 3501 therefore cannot be sustained if *Miranda* is to remain the law.

Whether or not we would agree with *Miranda*'s reasoning and its resulting rule, were we addressing the issue in the first instance, the principles of *stare decisis* weigh heavily against overruling it now. While " '*stare decisis* is not an inexorable command,' " particularly when we are interpreting the Constitution, "even in constitutional cases, the doctrine carries such persuasive force that we have always required a departure from precedent to be supported by some 'special justification.' "

We do not think there is such justification for overruling *Miranda*. *Miranda* has become embedded in routine police practice to the point where the warnings have become part of our national culture. While we have overruled our precedents when subsequent cases have undermined their doctrinal underpinnings, we do not believe that this has happened to the *Miranda* decision. If anything, our subsequent cases have reduced the impact of the *Miranda* rule on legitimate law enforcement while reaffirming the decision's core ruling that unwarned statements may not be used as evidence in the prosecution's case in chief.

The disadvantage of the *Miranda* rule is that statements which may be by no means involuntary, made by a defendant who is aware of his "rights," may nonetheless be excluded and a guilty defendant go free as a result. But experience suggests that the totality-of-the-circumstances test which § 3501 seeks to revive is more difficult than *Miranda* for law enforcement officers to conform to, and for courts to apply in a consistent manner. The requirement that *Miranda* warnings be given does not, of course, dispense with the voluntariness inquiry. But as we said in *Berkemer v. McCarty* [p. 648], "cases in which a defendant can make a colorable argument that a self-incriminating statement was 'compelled' despite the fact that the law enforcement authorities adhered to the dictates of *Miranda* are rare."

In sum, we conclude that *Miranda* announced a constitutional rule that Congress may not supersede legislatively. Following the rule of *stare decisis*, we decline to overrule *Miranda* ourselves. * * *

Justice SCALIA, with whom Justice THOMAS joins, dissenting.

Those to whom judicial decisions are an unconnected series of judgments that produce either favored or disfavored results will doubtless greet today's decision as a paragon of moderation, since it declines to overrule *Miranda*. Those who understand the judicial process will appreciate that today's decision is not a reaffirmation of *Miranda*, but a radical revision of the most significant element of *Miranda* (as of all cases): the rationale that gives it a permanent place in our jurisprudence.

Marbury v. Madison, 1 Cranch 137 (1803), held that an Act of Congress will not be enforced by the courts if what it prescribes violates the Constitution of the United States. That was the basis on which *Miranda* was decided. One will search today's opinion in vain, however, for a statement (surely simple enough to make) that what 18 U.S.C. § 3501 prescribes—the use at trial of a voluntary confession, even when a *Miranda* warning or its equivalent has failed to be given—violates the Constitution. The reason the statement does not appear is not only (and perhaps not so much) that it would be absurd, inasmuch as § 3501 excludes from trial precisely what the Constitution excludes from trial, viz., compelled confessions; but also that Justices whose votes are needed to compose today's majority are on record as believing that a violation of *Miranda* is *not* a violation of the Constitution. And so, to justify today's agreed-upon result, the Court must adopt a significant *new*, if not entirely comprehensible, principle of constitutional law. As the Court chooses to describe that principle, statutes of Congress can be disregarded, not only when what they prescribe violates the Constitution, but when what they prescribe contradicts a decision of this Court that "announced a constitutional rule." As I shall discuss in some detail, the only thing that can possibly mean in the context of this case is that this Court has the power, not merely to apply the Constitution but to expand it, imposing what it regards as useful "prophylactic" restrictions upon Congress and the States. That is an immense and frightening antidemocratic power, and it does not exist.

It takes only a small step to bring today's opinion out of the realm of power-judging and into the mainstream of legal reasoning: The Court need only go beyond its carefully couched iterations that "*Miranda* is a constitutional decision," that "*Miranda* is constitutionally based," that *Miranda* has "constitutional underpinnings," and come out and say quite clearly: "We reaffirm today that custodial interrogation that is not preceded by *Miranda* warnings or their equivalent violates the Constitution of the United States." It cannot say that, because a majority of the Court does not believe it. The Court therefore acts in plain violation of the Constitution when it denies effect to this Act of Congress.

I * * *

It was once possible to characterize the so-called *Miranda* rule as resting (however implausibly) upon the proposition that what the statute here before us permits—the admission at trial of un-*Mirandized* confessions—violates the Constitution. That is the fairest reading of the *Miranda* case itself. * * *

So understood, *Miranda* was objectionable for innumerable reasons, not least the fact that cases spanning more than 70 years had rejected its core premise that, absent the warnings and an effective waiver of the right to remain silent and of the (thitherto unknown) right to have an attorney present, a statement obtained pursuant to custodial interrogation was necessarily the product of compulsion. Moreover, history and precedent aside, the decision in *Miranda*, if read as an explication of what the Constitution *requires*, is preposterous. There is, for example, simply no basis in reason for concluding that a response to the very first question asked, by a suspect who already *knows* all of the rights described in the *Miranda* warning, is anything other than a volitional act. And even if one assumes that the elimination of compulsion absolutely requires informing even the most knowledgeable suspect of his right to remain silent, it cannot conceivably require the right to have *counsel* present. There is a world of difference, which the Court recognized under the traditional voluntariness test but ignored in *Miranda*, between compelling a suspect to incriminate himself and preventing him from foolishly doing so of his own accord. Only the latter (which is *not* required by the Constitution) could explain the Court's inclusion of a right to counsel and the requirement that it, too, be knowingly and intelligently waived. Counsel's presence is not required to tell the suspect that he *need* not speak; the interrogators can do that. The only good reason for having counsel there is that he can be counted on to advise the suspect that he *should* not speak. * * *

For these reasons, and others more than adequately developed in the *Miranda* dissents and in the subsequent works of the decision's many critics, any conclusion that a violation of the *Miranda* rules *necessarily* amounts to a violation of the privilege against compelled self-incrimination can claim no support in history, precedent, or common sense, and as a result would at least presumptively be worth reconsidering even at this late date. But that is unnecessary, since the Court has (thankfully) long since abandoned the notion that failure to comply with *Miranda*'s rules is itself a violation of the Constitution.

II

As the Court today acknowledges, since *Miranda* we have explicitly, and repeatedly, interpreted that decision as having announced, not the circumstances in which custodial interrogation runs afoul of the Fifth or Fourteenth Amendment, but rather only "prophylactic" rules that go beyond the right against compelled self-incrimination. * * *

In light of these cases, and our statements to the same effect in others, it is simply no longer possible for the Court to conclude, even if it wanted to, that a violation of *Miranda*'s rules is a violation of the Constitution. But as I explained at the outset, that is what is required before the Court may disregard a law of Congress governing the admissibility of evidence in federal court. The Court today insists that the *decision* in *Miranda* is a "constitutional" one; that it has "constitutional underpinnings"; a "constitutional basis" and a "constitutional origin"; that it was "constitutionally based"; and that it announced a "constitutional rule." It is fine to play these word games; but what makes a decision "constitutional" in the only sense relevant here—in the sense that renders it impervious to supersession by congressional legislation such as § 3501—is the determination that the Constitution *requires* the result that the decision announces and the statute ignores. By disregarding congressional action that concededly does not violate the Constitution, the Court flagrantly offends fundamental principles of separation of powers, and arrogates to itself prerogatives reserved to the representatives of the people. * * *

III

There was available to the Court a means of reconciling the established proposition that a violation of *Miranda* does not itself offend the Fifth Amendment with the Court's assertion of a right to ignore the present statute. That means of reconciliation was argued strenuously by both petitioner and the United States, who were evidently more concerned than the Court is with maintaining the coherence of our jurisprudence. It is not mentioned in the Court's opinion because, I assume, a majority of the Justices intent on reversing believes that incoherence is the lesser evil. They may be right.

Petitioner and the United States contend that there is nothing at all exceptional, much less unconstitutional, about the Court's adopting prophylactic rules to buttress constitutional rights, and enforcing them against Congress and the States. * * *

I applaud * * * the refusal of the Justices in the majority to enunciate this boundless doctrine of judicial empowerment as a means of rendering today's decision rational. In nonetheless joining the Court's judgment, however, they overlook two truisms: that actions speak louder than silence, and that (in judge-made law at least) logic will out. Since there is in fact no other principle that can reconcile today's judgment with the post-*Miranda* cases that the Court refuses to abandon, what today's decision will stand for, whether the Justices can bring themselves to say it or not, is the power of the Supreme Court to write a prophylactic, extraconstitutional Constitution, binding on Congress and the States.

IV * * *

Today's judgment converts *Miranda* from a milestone of judicial overreaching into the very Cheops' Pyramid (or perhaps the Sphinx would be a better analogue) of judicial arrogance. In imposing its Court-made code upon the States, the original opinion at least *asserted* that it was demanded by the Constitution. Today's decision does not pretend that it is—and yet *still* asserts the right to impose it against the will of the people's representatives in Congress. * * * This is not the system that was established by the Framers, or that would be established by any sane supporter of government by the people.

I dissent from today's decision, and, until § 3501 is repealed, will continue to apply it in all cases where there has been a sustainable finding that the defendant's confession was voluntary.

NOTES AND QUESTIONS

1. The Court claims that *Miranda* is "a constitutional decision of this Court" that "may not be in effect overruled by an Act of Congress." Justice Scalia in dissent claims that *Miranda* is not constitutional in the relevant sense. Can you articulate the difference in the way the majority and the dissent are using the characterization "constitutional"?

2. Do you think it is appropriate for a justice to promise (threaten) to apply a statute that the Court has held is unconstitutional?

3. Which of the cases stressing Miranda's prophlyactic status seems most at risk now that we know that *Miranda* is based on the Constitution?

4. *Miranda death grip.* William Pizzi and Morris Hoffman argue that the members of the Court "remain locked in an increasingly bizarre kind of

Miranda death grip"—unwilling to treat a violation of *Miranda* as a violation of the "pristine" self-incrimination clause and yet unwilling to live without *Miranda*. In their view, the Court should either overrule most of the exceptions that resulted from *Miranda*'s prophylactic status or overrule *Miranda* itself. See William T. Pizzi & Morris B. Hoffman, Taking *Miranda*'s Pulse, 58 Vand. L. Rev. 813, 848–49 (2005).

5. Is Justice Scalia right that "logic will out," that the only way to reconcile *Dickerson* "with the post-*Miranda* cases that the Court refuses to abandon" is "the power of the Supreme Court to write a prophylactic, extra-constitutional Constitution, binding on Congress and the States?"

6. *What a web Miranda weaves. Dickerson* said that *Miranda* "has become embedded in routine police practice to the point where the warnings have become part of our national culture." Indeed, the warnings may be "embedded" beyond our national culture even if the underlying right is not. One of the casebook authors saw a detective comedy/drama show on a Canadian TV station. A Canadian officer arrests a suspect, who says, "Aren't you going to read me my *Miranda* rights?" Cop: "This is Canada, not the U.S. You don't have any rights here."

7. Now that we have, ahem, settled the question of *Miranda*'s constitutionality, we return to the fruits issue.

MISSOURI v. SEIBERT

Supreme Court of the United States, 2004.
542 U.S. 600, 124 S.Ct. 2601, 159 L.Ed.2d 643.

JUSTICE SOUTER announced the judgment of the Court and delivered an opinion, in which JUSTICE STEVENS, JUSTICE GINSBURG, and JUSTICE BREYER join.

This case tests a police protocol for custodial interrogation that calls for giving no warnings of the rights to silence and counsel until interrogation has produced a confession. Although such a statement is generally inadmissible, since taken in violation of *Miranda v. Arizona*, the interrogating officer follows it with *Miranda* warnings and then leads the suspect to cover the same ground a second time. The question here is the admissibility of the repeated statement. Because this midstream recitation of warnings after interrogation and unwarned confession could not effectively comply with *Miranda*'s constitutional requirement, we hold that a statement repeated after a warning in such circumstances is inadmissible.

I

Respondent Patrice Seibert's 12–year-old son Jonathan had cerebral palsy, and when he died in his sleep she feared charges of neglect because of bedsores on his body. In her presence, two of her teenage sons and two of their friends devised a plan to conceal the facts surrounding Jonathan's death by incinerating his body in the course of burning the family's mobile home, in which they planned to leave Donald Rector, a mentally ill teenager living with the family, to avoid any appearance that Jonathan had been unattended. Seibert's son Darian and a friend set the fire, and Donald died.

Five days later, the police awakened Seibert at 3 a.m. at a hospital where Darian was being treated for burns. In arresting her, Officer Kevin Clinton followed instructions from Rolla, Missouri, officer Richard Hanrahan that he refrain from giving *Miranda* warnings. After Seibert had been taken to the police station and left alone in an interview room for 15 to 20 minutes, Hanrahan questioned her without *Miranda* warnings for 30 to 40 minutes, squeezing her arm and repeating "Donald was also to die in his sleep." After Seibert finally admitted she knew Donald was meant to die in the fire, she was given a 20–minute coffee and cigarette break. Officer Hanrahan then turned on a tape recorder, gave Seibert the *Miranda* warnings, and obtained a signed waiver of rights from her. He resumed the questioning with "Ok, 'trice, we've been talking for a little while about what happened on Wednesday the twelfth, haven't we?," and confronted her with her prewarning statements:

> Hanrahan: "Now, in discussion you told us, you told us that there was an understanding about Donald."
>
> Seibert: "Yes."
>
> Hanrahan: "Did that take place earlier that morning?"
>
> Seibert: "Yes."
>
> Hanrahan: "And what was the understanding about Donald?"
>
> Seibert: "If they could get him out of the trailer, to take him out of the trailer."
>
> Hanrahan: "And if they couldn't?"
>
> Seibert: "I, I never even thought about it. I just figured they would."
>
> Hanrahan: " 'Trice, didn't you tell me that he was supposed to die in his sleep?"
>
> Seibert: "If that would happen, 'cause he was on that new medicine, you know * * * ' "
>
> Hanrahan: "The Prozac? And it makes him sleepy. So he was supposed to die in his sleep?"
>
> Seibert: "Yes."

* * * At the suppression hearing, Officer Hanrahan testified that he made a "conscious decision" to withhold *Miranda* warnings, thus resorting to an interrogation technique he had been taught: question first, then give the warnings, and then repeat the question "until I get the answer that she's already provided once." He acknowledged that Seibert's ultimate statement was "largely a repeat of information * * * obtained" prior to the warning.

* * * On appeal, the Missouri Court of Appeals affirmed, treating this case as indistinguishable from *Oregon v. Elstad* [p. 616]. The Supreme Court of Missouri reversed, holding that "in the circumstances here,

where the interrogation was nearly continuous, * * * the second statement, clearly the product of the invalid first statement, should have been suppressed." The court distinguished *Elstad* on the ground that warnings had not intentionally been withheld there, and reasoned that "Officer Hanrahan's intentional omission of a *Miranda* warning was intended to deprive Seibert of the opportunity knowingly and intelligently to waive her *Miranda* rights." Since there were "no circumstances that would seem to dispel the effect of the *Miranda* violation," the court held that the postwarning confession was involuntary and therefore inadmissible. To allow the police to achieve an "end run" around *Miranda*, the court explained, would encourage *Miranda* violations and diminish *Miranda*'s role in protecting the privilege against self-incrimination. * * *

We granted certiorari to resolve a split in the Courts of Appeals. We now affirm.

II * * *

In *Miranda*, we explained that the "voluntariness doctrine in the state cases * * * encompasses all interrogation practices which are likely to exert such pressure upon an individual as to disable him from making a free and rational choice." We appreciated the difficulty of judicial enquiry *post hoc* into the circumstances of a police interrogation and recognized that "the coercion inherent in custodial interrogation blurs the line between voluntary and involuntary statements, and thus heightens the risk" that the privilege against self-incrimination will not be observed. Hence our concern that the "traditional totality-of-the-circumstances" test posed an "unacceptably great" risk that involuntary custodial confessions would escape detection.

Accordingly, "to reduce the risk of a coerced confession and to implement the Self–Incrimination Clause," this Court in *Miranda* concluded that "the accused must be adequately and effectively apprised of his rights and the exercise of those rights must be fully honored." *Miranda* conditioned the admissibility at trial of any custodial confession on warning a suspect of his rights: failure to give the prescribed warnings and obtain a waiver of rights before custodial questioning generally requires exclusion of any statements obtained. Conversely, giving the warnings and getting a waiver has generally produced a virtual ticket of admissibility; maintaining that a statement is involuntary even though given after warnings and voluntary waiver of rights requires unusual stamina, and litigation over voluntariness tends to end with the finding of a valid waiver. To point out the obvious, this common consequence would not be common at all were it not that *Miranda* warnings are customarily given under circumstances allowing for a real choice between talking and remaining silent.

III * * *

The technique of interrogating in successive, unwarned and warned phases raises a new challenge to *Miranda*. Although we have no statistics on the frequency of this practice, it is not confined to Rolla, Missouri. An officer of that police department testified that the strategy of withholding *Miranda* warnings until after interrogating and drawing out a confession was promoted not only by his own department, but by a national police training organization and other departments in which he had worked. Consistently with the officer's testimony, the Police Law Institute, for example, instructs that "officers may conduct a two-stage interrogation * * *. At any point during the pre-*Miranda* interrogation, usually after arrestees have confessed, officers may then read the *Miranda* warnings and ask for a waiver. If the arrestees waive their *Miranda* rights, officers will be able to repeat any *subsequent* incriminating statements later in court" (emphasis in original).[2] The upshot of all this advice is a question-first practice of some popularity, as one can see from the reported cases describing its use, sometimes in obedience to departmental policy.

IV

* * * The object of [the] question-first [interrogation method] is to render *Miranda* warnings ineffective by waiting for a particularly opportune time to give them, after the suspect has already confessed.

Just as "no talismanic incantation [is] required to satisfy [*Miranda*'s] strictures," it would be absurd to think that mere recitation of the litany suffices to satisfy *Miranda* in every conceivable circumstance. "The inquiry is simply whether the warnings reasonably 'convey to [a suspect] his rights as required by *Miranda*.' " The threshold issue when interrogators question first and warn later is thus whether it would be reasonable to find that in these circumstances the warnings could function "effectively" as *Miranda* requires. Could the warnings effectively advise the suspect that he had a real choice about giving an admissible statement at that juncture? Could they reasonably convey that he could choose to stop talking even if he had talked earlier? For unless the warnings could place a suspect who has just been interrogated in a position to make such an informed choice, there is no practical justification for accepting the formal warnings as compliance with *Miranda*, or for treating the second stage of interrogation as distinct from the first, unwarned and inadmissible segment.[4]

---

2. Emphasizing the impeachment exception to the *Miranda* rule approved by this Court, some training programs advise officers to omit *Miranda* warnings altogether or to continue questioning after the suspect invokes his rights. [See] Weisselberg, Saving *Miranda*, 84 Cornell L. Rev. 109, 110, 132–139 (1998) (collecting California training materials encouraging questioning "outside *Miranda*"). This training is reflected in the reported cases involving deliberate questioning after invocation of *Miranda* rights. Scholars have noted the growing trend of such practices. See, *e.g.*, Leo, Questioning the Relevance of *Miranda* in the Twenty–First Century, 99 Mich. L. Rev. 1000, 1010 (2001); Weisselberg, In the Stationhouse After *Dickerson*, 99 Mich. L. Rev. 1121, 1123–1154 (2001). * * *

4. Respondent Seibert argues that her second confession should be excluded from evidence under the doctrine known by the metaphor of the "fruit of the poisonous tree," developed in the Fourth Amendment context in *Wong Sun v. United States* [p. 503]: evidence otherwise admissible but discovered as a result of an earlier violation is excluded as tainted, lest the law encourage future violations. But the Court in *Elstad* rejected the *Wong Sun* fruits doctrine for analyzing the admissibility of a subsequent warned confession following "an initial failure * * * to administer

There is no doubt about the answer that proponents of question-first give to this question about the effectiveness of warnings given only after successful interrogation, and we think their answer is correct. By any objective measure, applied to circumstances exemplified here, it is likely that if the interrogators employ the technique of withholding warnings until after interrogation succeeds in eliciting a confession, the warnings will be ineffective in preparing the suspect for successive interrogation, close in time and similar in content. After all, the reason that question-first is catching on is as obvious as its manifest purpose, which is to get a confession the suspect would not make if he understood his rights at the outset; the sensible underlying assumption is that with one confession in hand before the warnings, the interrogator can count on getting its duplicate, with trifling additional trouble. Upon hearing warnings only in the aftermath of interrogation and just after making a confession, a suspect would hardly think he had a genuine right to remain silent, let alone persist in so believing once the police began to lead him over the same ground again. A more likely reaction on a suspect's part would be perplexity about the reason for discussing rights at that point, bewilderment being an unpromising frame of mind for knowledgeable decision. What is worse, telling a suspect that "anything you say can and will be used against you," without expressly excepting the statement just given, could lead to an entirely reasonable inference that what he has just said will be used, with subsequent silence being of no avail. Thus, when *Miranda* warnings are inserted in the midst of coordinated and continuing interrogation, they are likely to mislead and "deprive a defendant of knowledge essential to his ability to understand the nature of his rights and the consequences of abandoning them." * * *

V

Missouri argues that a confession repeated at the end of an interrogation sequence envisioned in a question-first strategy is admissible on the authority of *Oregon v. Elstad*, but the argument disfigures that case. In *Elstad*, the police went to the young suspect's house to take him into custody on a charge of burglary. Before the arrest, one officer spoke with the suspect's mother, while the other one joined the suspect in a "brief stop in the living room" where the officer said he "felt" the young man was involved in a burglary. The suspect acknowledged he had been at the scene. This Court noted that the pause in the living room "was not to interrogate the suspect but to notify his mother of the reason for his arrest" and described the incident as having "none of the earmarks of coercion." The Court, indeed, took care to mention that the officer's initial

the warnings required by *Miranda*." * * * *Elstad* held that "a suspect who has once responded to unwarned yet uncoercive questioning is not thereby disabled from waiving his rights and confessing after he has been given the requisite *Miranda* warnings." In a sequential confession case, clarity is served if the later confession is approached by asking whether in the circumstances the *Miranda* warnings given could reasonably be found effective. If yes, a court can take up the standard issues of voluntary waiver and voluntary statement; if no, the subsequent statement is inadmissible for want of adequate *Miranda* warnings, because the earlier and later statements are realistically seen as parts of a single, unwarned sequence of questioning.

failure to warn was an "oversight" that "may have been the result of confusion as to whether the brief exchange qualified as 'custodial interrogation' or * * * may simply have reflected * * * reluctance to initiate an alarming police procedure before [an officer] had spoken with respondent's mother." At the outset of a later and systematic station house interrogation going well beyond the scope of the laconic prior admission, the suspect was given *Miranda* warnings and made a full confession. In holding the second statement admissible and voluntary, *Elstad* rejected the "cat out of the bag" theory that any short, earlier admission, obtained in arguably innocent neglect of *Miranda*, determined the character of the later, warned confession; on the facts of that case, the Court thought any causal connection between the first and second responses to the police was "speculative and attenuated." Although the *Elstad* Court expressed no explicit conclusion about either officer's state of mind, it is fair to read *Elstad* as treating the living room conversation as a good-faith *Miranda* mistake, not only open to correction by careful warnings before systematic questioning in that particular case, but posing no threat to warn-first practice generally.

The contrast between *Elstad* and this case reveals a series of relevant facts that bear on whether *Miranda* warnings delivered midstream could be effective enough to accomplish their object: the completeness and detail of the questions and answers in the first round of interrogation, the overlapping content of the two statements, the timing and setting of the first and the second, the continuity of police personnel, and the degree to which the interrogator's questions treated the second round as continuous with the first. In *Elstad*, it was not unreasonable to see the occasion for questioning at the station house as presenting a markedly different experience from the short conversation at home; since a reasonable person in the suspect's shoes could have seen the station house questioning as a new and distinct experience, the *Miranda* warnings could have made sense as presenting a genuine choice whether to follow up on the earlier admission.

At the opposite extreme are the facts here, which by any objective measure reveal a police strategy adapted to undermine the *Miranda* warnings.[6] The unwarned interrogation was conducted in the station house, and the questioning was systematic, exhaustive, and managed with psychological skill. When the police were finished there was little, if anything, of incriminating potential left unsaid. The warned phase of questioning proceeded after a pause of only 15 to 20 minutes, in the same place as the unwarned segment. When the same officer who had conducted the first phase recited the *Miranda* warnings, he said nothing to counter the probable misimpression that the advice that anything Seibert said could be used against her also applied to the details of the inculpatory statement previously elicited. In particular, the police did not advise that

---

6. Because the intent of the officer will rarely be as candidly admitted as it was here (even as it is likely to determine the conduct of the interrogation), the focus is on facts apart from intent that show the question-first tactic at work.

her prior statement could not be used.[7] Nothing was said or done to dispel the oddity of warning about legal rights to silence and counsel right after the police had led her through a systematic interrogation, and any uncertainty on her part about a right to stop talking about matters previously discussed would only have been aggravated by the way Officer Hanrahan set the scene by saying "we've been talking for a little while about what happened on Wednesday the twelfth, haven't we?" The impression that the further questioning was a mere continuation of the earlier questions and responses was fostered by references back to the confession already given. It would have been reasonable to regard the two sessions as parts of a continuum, in which it would have been unnatural to refuse to repeat at the second stage what had been said before. These circumstances must be seen as challenging the comprehensibility and efficacy of the *Miranda* warnings to the point that a reasonable person in the suspect's shoes would not have understood them to convey a message that she retained a choice about continuing to talk.[8]

VI

* * * Because the question-first tactic effectively threatens to thwart *Miranda*'s purpose of reducing the risk that a coerced confession would be admitted, and because the facts here do not reasonably support a conclusion that the warnings given could have served their purpose, Seibert's postwarning statements are inadmissible. * * *

Justice BREYER, concurring.

In my view, the following simple rule should apply to the two-stage interrogation technique: Courts should exclude the "fruits" of the initial unwarned questioning unless the failure to warn was in good faith. I believe this is a sound and workable approach to the problem this case presents. Prosecutors and judges have long understood how to apply the "fruits" approach, which they use in other areas of law. And in the workaday world of criminal law enforcement the administrative simplicity of the familiar has significant advantages over a more complex exclusionary rule.

I believe the plurality's approach in practice will function as a "fruits" test. The truly "effective" *Miranda* warnings on which the plurality insists will occur only when certain circumstances—a lapse in time, a change in location or interrogating officer, or a shift in the focus of the questioning—intervene between the unwarned questioning and any postwarning statement.

---

7. We do not hold that a formal addendum warning that a previous statement could not be used would be sufficient to change the character of the question-first procedure to the point of rendering an ensuing statement admissible, but its absence is clearly a factor that blunts the efficacy of the warnings and points to a continuing, not a new, interrogation.

8. Because we find that the warnings were inadequate, there is no need to assess the actual voluntariness of the statement.

I consequently join the plurality's opinion in full. I also agree with Justice Kennedy's opinion insofar as it is consistent with this approach and makes clear that a good-faith exception applies.

Justice KENNEDY, concurring in the judgment.

The interrogation technique used in this case is designed to circumvent *Miranda*. It undermines the *Miranda* warning and obscures its meaning. The plurality opinion is correct to conclude that statements obtained through the use of this technique are inadmissible. Although I agree with much in the careful and convincing opinion for the plurality, my approach does differ in some respects, requiring this separate statement. * * *

In my view, *Elstad* was correct in its reasoning and its result. *Elstad* reflects a balanced and pragmatic approach to enforcement of the *Miranda* warning. An officer may not realize that a suspect is in custody and warnings are required. The officer may not plan to question the suspect or may be waiting for a more appropriate time. Skilled investigators often interview suspects multiple times, and good police work may involve referring to prior statements to test their veracity or to refresh recollection. In light of these realities it would be extravagant to treat the presence of one statement that cannot be admitted under *Miranda* as sufficient reason to prohibit subsequent statements preceded by a proper warning. That approach would serve "neither the general goal of deterring improper police conduct nor the Fifth Amendment goal of assuring trustworthy evidence would be served by suppression of the * * * testimony."

This case presents different considerations. The police used a two-step questioning technique based on a deliberate violation of *Miranda*. The *Miranda* warning was withheld to obscure both the practical and legal significance of the admonition when finally given. * * *

* * * When an interrogator uses this deliberate, two-step strategy, predicated upon violating *Miranda* during an extended interview, postwarning statements that are related to the substance of prewarning statements must be excluded absent specific, curative steps.

The plurality concludes that whenever a two-stage interview occurs, admissibility of the postwarning statement should depend on "whether the *Miranda* warnings delivered midstream could have been effective enough to accomplish their object" given the specific facts of the case. This test envisions an objective inquiry from the perspective of the suspect, and applies in the case of both intentional and unintentional two-stage interrogations. In my view, this test cuts too broadly. *Miranda*'s clarity is one of its strengths, and a multifactor test that applies to every two-stage interrogation may serve to undermine that clarity. I would apply a narrower test applicable only in the infrequent case, such as we have here, in which the two-step interrogation technique was used in a calculated way to undermine the *Miranda* warning.

The admissibility of postwarning statements should continue to be governed by the principles of *Elstad* unless the deliberate two-step strategy was employed. If the deliberate two-step strategy has been used, postwarning statements that are related to the substance of prewarning statements must be excluded unless curative measures are taken before the postwarning statement is made. Curative measures should be designed to ensure that a reasonable person in the suspect's situation would understand the import and effect of the *Miranda* warning and of the *Miranda* waiver. For example, a substantial break in time and circumstances between the prewarning statement and the *Miranda* warning may suffice in most circumstances, as it allows the accused to distinguish the two contexts and appreciate that the interrogation has taken a new turn. Alternatively, an additional warning that explains the likely inadmissibility of the prewarning custodial statement may be sufficient. No curative steps were taken in this case, however, so the postwarning statements are inadmissible and the conviction cannot stand.

For these reasons, I concur in the judgment of the Court.

Justice O'CONNOR, with whom THE CHIEF JUSTICE, Justice SCALIA, and Justice THOMAS join, dissenting.

The plurality devours *Oregon v. Elstad* even as it accuses petitioner's argument of "disfiguring" that decision. I believe that we are bound by *Elstad* to reach a different result, and I would vacate the judgment of the Supreme Court of Missouri.

I

On two preliminary questions I am in full agreement with the plurality. First, the plurality appropriately follows *Elstad* in concluding that Seibert's statement cannot be held inadmissible under a "fruit of the poisonous tree" theory. Second, the plurality correctly declines to focus its analysis on the subjective intent of the interrogating officer.

A

This Court has made clear that there simply is no place for a robust deterrence doctrine with regard to violations of *Miranda*. * * *

Although the analysis the plurality ultimately espouses examines the same facts and circumstances that a "fruits" analysis would consider (such as the lapse of time between the two interrogations and change of questioner or location), it does so for entirely different reasons. The fruits analysis would examine those factors because they are relevant to the balance of deterrence value versus the "drastic and socially costly course" of excluding reliable evidence. The plurality, by contrast, looks to those factors to inform the *psychological* judgment regarding whether the suspect has been informed effectively of her right to remain silent. The analytical underpinnings of the two approaches are thus entirely distinct, and they should not be conflated just because they function similarly in practice.

B

The plurality's rejection of an intent-based test is also, in my view, correct. Freedom from compulsion lies at the heart of the Fifth Amendment, and requires us to assess whether a suspect's decision to speak truly was voluntary. Because voluntariness is a matter of the suspect's state of mind, we focus our analysis on the way in which suspects experience interrogation.

Thoughts kept inside a police officer's head cannot affect that experience. * * * A suspect who experienced the exact same interrogation as Seibert, save for a difference in the undivulged, subjective intent of the interrogating officer when he failed to give *Miranda* warnings, would not experience the interrogation any differently. * * * "Although highly inappropriate, even deliberate deception of an attorney could not possibly affect a suspect's decision to waive his *Miranda* rights unless he were at least aware of the incident."

* * * Moreover, recognizing an exception to *Elstad* for intentional violations would require focusing constitutional analysis on a police officer's subjective intent, an unattractive proposition that we all but uniformly avoid. In general, "we believe that 'sending state and federal courts on an expedition into the minds of police officers would produce a grave and fruitless misallocation of judicial resources.' " * * *

These evidentiary difficulties have led us to reject an intent-based test in several criminal procedure contexts. For example, in *New York v. Quarles*, one of the factors that led us to reject an inquiry into the subjective intent of the police officer in crafting a test for the "public safety" exception to *Miranda* was that officers' motives will be "largely unverifiable." Similarly, our opinion in *Whren v. United States* [p. 259] made clear that "the evidentiary difficulty of establishing subjective intent" was one of the reasons (albeit not the principal one) for refusing to consider intent in Fourth Amendment challenges generally.

For these reasons, I believe that the approach espoused by Justice Kennedy is ill advised. Justice Kennedy would extend *Miranda*'s exclusionary rule to any case in which the use of the "two-step interrogation technique" was "deliberate" or "calculated." This approach untethers the analysis from facts knowable to, and therefore having any potential directly to affect, the suspect. * * *

II

The plurality's adherence to *Elstad*, and mine to the plurality, end there. * * *

* * * The plurality might very well think that we struck the balance between Fifth Amendment rights and law enforcement interests incorrectly in *Elstad*; but that is not normally a sufficient reason for ignoring the dictates of *stare decisis*.

I would analyze the two-step interrogation procedure under the voluntariness standards central to the Fifth Amendment and reiterated in *Elstad*. *Elstad* commands that if Seibert's first statement is shown to have been involuntary, the court must examine whether the taint dissipated through the passing of time or a change in circumstances: "When a prior statement is actually coerced, the time that passes between confessions, the change in place of interrogations, and the change in identity of the interrogators all bear on whether that coercion has carried over into the second confession." In addition, Seibert's second statement should be suppressed if she showed that it was involuntary despite the *Miranda* warnings. Although I would leave this analysis for the Missouri courts to conduct on remand, I note that, unlike the officers in *Elstad*, Officer Hanrahan referred to Seibert's unwarned statement during the second part of the interrogation when she made a statement at odds with her unwarned confession. Such a tactic may bear on the voluntariness inquiry.

* * *

Because I believe that the plurality gives insufficient deference to *Elstad* and that Justice Kennedy places improper weight on subjective intent, I respectfully dissent.

NOTES AND QUESTIONS

1. *Counting votes.* It is time to count votes in *Seibert* to determine where *Elstad-Seibert* puts us now. Justice O'Connor, who wrote *Elstad*, sharply disputes the plurality's interpretation of what the Court did in *Elstad*. Who gets the better of that argument? What do you think of Justice Kennedy's opinion?

2. Given that no opinion attracted five votes in *Seibert*, what is the narrow holding in *Seibert*? See Marks v. United States, 430 U.S. 188, 97 S.Ct. 990, 51 L.Ed.2d 260 (1977).

3. The Court cites three articles that discuss what it calls a "growing trend" toward not giving *Miranda* warnings as part of a plan to use incriminating statements to impeach. See Richard A. Leo, *Questioning the Relevance of Miranda in the Twenty–First Century*, 99 Mich. L. Rev. 1000, 1010 (2001); Charles D. Weisselberg, *In the Stationhouse After Dickerson*, 99 Mich. L. Rev. 1121, 1123–1154 (2001); Charles D. Weisselberg, *Saving Miranda*, 84 Cornell L. Rev. 109, 110, 132–139 (1998). In light of *Seibert*, what do you think about the constitutionality of this practice?

Charles Weisselberg researched police training methods in California in the wake of *Seibert* and found that the training generally emphasized "the deliberate conduct of the officers in *Seibert*, distinguishing *Elstad* as a good-faith mistake." Charles D. Weisselberg, *Mourning Miranda*, 96 Cal. L. Rev. 1519, 1553 (2008). For example, the California Peace Officers Legal Sourcebook "says unequivocally that [o]fficers should not attempt to exploit the *Elstad* rule."

4. *The three step, five factor Seibert shuffle. Seibert* is an attempt to limit calculated police avoidance of *Miranda*, but it is far from easy to apply either

the plurality's test or that of Justice Kennedy. A Westlaw search of all state and federal cases for "Missouri v. Seibert" on January 4, 2009 produced a universe of 528 cases. A random sample of twenty state cases showed six that found a *Seibert* violation, usually on facts not as extreme as *Seibert*, and fourteen that found no violation. One court has identified five factors critical to the plurality in *Seibert* and then synthesized Souter's and Kennedy's opinions. According to this district judge, a court should consider

(1) the completeness and detail of the questions and answers in the first round of interrogation, (2) the overlapping content of the two statements, (3) the timing and setting of the first and second, (4) the continuity of police personnel, and (5) the degree to which the interrogator's questions treated the second round as continuous with the first. * * *

[A] court applying *Seibert* should follow three steps. First, the court should determine whether law enforcement personnel deliberately employed the two-round interrogation strategy for the purpose of sidestepping *Miranda*. Justice Kennedy's concurrence requires this. [If not, then the inquiry is at an end and no *Miranda* violation occurs. If the procedure was deliberately employed to sidestep *Miranda*, then] to determine whether a given situation is more like that in *Elstad* or *Seibert*, the court should apply the five factors the *Seibert* plurality enunciated. Finally, if after applying these factors, the court concludes that the facts are more like those in *Seibert* than *Elstad*, it should follow a third, final step: determining whether the interrogator took any curative measures. Assuming that he or she did not, the confession is inadmissible.

United States v. Long Tong Kiam, 343 F. Supp. 2d. 398, 407, 409 (E.D. Pa. 2004).

Question: Does law *have* to be this hard?

5. *Problems.*

A.   Police arrived at *A*'s place of work and asked him "if he would come to the sheriff's office for a videotaped informational interview. They represented that, after the interview, they would provide [him] with a ride to wherever [he] wished to be taken. Defendant agreed." No *Miranda* warnings were given. Police asked *A* to describe his activities on the day of a murder, and did not interrupt or contradict him as he answered questions for an hour. After a brief break, police resumed questioning, now in a more confrontational style, challenging *A*'s statements and warning him that "it will [all] come down on" him if he did not agree to cooperate with the police and that he was "accountable for what has taken place." The officer showed *A* "a picture of the electric chair and told [him] that he was facing it if some prosecutor wanted to make headlines."

At 2 hours and 17 minutes into the interview, the police detective said, "I don't think you thought Jorge was going to die. You just thought Jorge would get a beating?" *A* agreed and asked the detective, "If I tell you who pulled the trigger, will you let me leave?" He also asked, "My name never comes up?" The detective replied, "If you are 100% truthful, I will be on the phone. You don't have to leave. I'll be on the phone with * * * the State's Attorney's Office and [will] protect you."

With this assurance, *A* confessed participation in the events leading to the murder. The police still did not give *Miranda* warnings but asked *A* to go over the story again, starting at the beginning, which he did. Three hours into the interview, police gave *Miranda* warnings to *A*, saying that it was "just for formality." *A* then gave a third statement that was substantially similar to the previous two unwarned statements. He was then handcuffed and led out of the interview room (so much for the implied promise to let him go!). Is the third statement admissible? See People v. Alfaro, 386 Ill.App.3d 271, 324 Ill.Dec. 858, 896 N.E.2d 1077 (2008).

B.   *L* was arrested for the abduction of two victims. At the police station, one agent sat with the suspect while other agents looked for a tape recorder so that the defendant's interview could be recorded if the defendant agreed to speak with them. The agent sitting with *L* knew that no *Miranda* warnings had been given to him. The agent said nothing to *L*. After several minutes sitting in silence, *L*'s demeanor changed and he began to cry. The agent said, "I hope you know what kind of trouble you are in." *L* replied, "Yes, I know. I killed her." He said that he told her to get down on her knees and that the gun did not go off until the third time he pulled the trigger. After *L* said this, the agent left the room to report this information to other agents because, up until that moment, the law enforcement agencies had hoped that the victim was still alive. The defendant said nothing further at that time and was not asked any additional questions. When the officers located a tape recorder, they administered *Miranda* warnings. *L* signed the waiver form and gave a detailed confession that included the abduction of both victims, the theft of the victims' jewelry, credit cards, bank cards, and property, the sexual assault and murder of one victim, and the attempted murder of a second victim. Is the post-warnings confession admissible? See State v. Lebron, 979 So.2d 1093 (Fla. App. 2008).

6.   *Physical fruits: What Elstad did not decide. Elstad* left one fruits issue undecided. Can physical evidence, as distinguished from a statement made by a third party (as in *Tucker*, p. 606) or another confession of the defendant (as in *Elstad*), be used in evidence if discovered because of a violation of *Miranda*? We know from Chapter 5 that the Fourth Amendment rule, though subject to exceptions, is that physical evidence found by means of the violation is inadmissible.

The Court decided the *Miranda* physical fruits issue the same day it decided *Seibert*. In United States v. Patane, 542 U.S. 630, 124 S.Ct. 2620, 159 L.Ed.2d 667 (2004), officers arrested Patane for violating a restraining order and one officer began to recite the *Miranda* warnings. Patane stopped him after the "right to remain silent" and said that he knew his rights. The officers did not attempt to finish the warnings. The government conceded in the Supreme Court that Patane's responses to later questions were inadmissible at trial under *Miranda*, "despite the partial warning and respondent's assertions that he knew his rights."

A detective then asked about a .40 Glock pistol that he believed Patane possessed. Though initially "reluctant to discuss the matter," Patane finally told the detective "that the pistol was in his bedroom. [Patane] then gave

Detective Benner permission to retrieve the pistol. Detective Benner found the pistol and seized it.''

As the government conceded a failure to comply with *Miranda*, the issue was whether the *Miranda* violation made the gun inadmissible at Patane's trial for unlawful possession of the firearm. Five members of the Court agreed it was admissible, but it took two theories to produce a judgment affirming Patane's conviction.

Justice Thomas, joined by Chief Justice Rehnquist and Justice Scalia, delivered the Court's judgment in an opinion that re-iterated *Miranda*'s prophylactic status. As *Miranda* exists to protect against violations of the self-incrimination clause, it is ''not implicated by the admission into evidence of the physical fruit of a voluntary statement.'' In Thomas's words: ''Potential violations occur, if at all, only upon the admission of unwarned statements into evidence at trial. And, at that point, 'the exclusion of unwarned state-ments * * * is a complete and sufficient remedy' for any perceived *Miranda* violation.''

Justice Kennedy, joined by Justice O'Connor, concurred in the judgment. To their way of thinking, a simple cost-benefit balance produced a decision to admit physical evidence discovered through unwarned statements. ''In light of the important probative value of reliable physical evidence, it is doubtful that exclusion can be justified by a deterrence rationale sensitive to both law enforcement interests and a suspect's rights during an in-custody interroga-tion.''

Justice Souter, joined by Justices Stevens and Ginsburg, dissented, pre-dicting a loss of deterrence: ''There is no way to read this case except as an unjustifiable invitation to law enforcement officers to flout *Miranda* when there may be physical evidence to be gained.'' Justice Breyer also dissented.

7.   Despite the lack of a majority opinion, does *Patane* settle the physical fruits issue?

8.   *Dickerson fall-out.* The debate about the constitutional nature of *Miranda* continues in a post-*Dickerson* world. The key to Souter's dissent in *Patane* was the Court's failure to credit *Miranda*'s presumption of coercion. No one doubts that ''the Fifth Amendment privilege against compelled self-incrimination extends to the exclusion of derivative evidence.'' In Souter's view, it was only by denying *Miranda* ''full constitutional stature'' that the Court could find five votes to admit the pistol.

But not a single justice in *Seibert* suggested that *Dickerson* somehow undermined *Elstad*. *Seibert* is thus good evidence that the Court ''can have its cake and eat it, too''—that it can have a constitutional *Miranda* that has numerous exceptions and special rules. It appears that *Miranda* will co-exist indefinitely with police interrogation—the spider and its prey.

We turn now to the doctrinal web that the spider has spun. One reason to adopt rules to govern police interrogation, rather than relying on the norm of suppressing involuntary confessions, was to achieve greater clarity in the doctrine. Ask yourself, as you reflect on the chapter, whether that goal has been achieved.

D. *MIRANDA* CUSTODY

OREGON v. MATHIASON

Supreme Court of the United States, 1977.
429 U.S. 492, 97 S.Ct. 711, 50 L.Ed.2d 714.

PER CURIAM.

Respondent Carl Mathiason was convicted of first-degree burglary after a bench trial in which his confession was critical to the State's case. At trial he moved to suppress the confession as the fruit of questioning by the police not preceded by the warnings required in *Miranda v. Arizona*. * * *

The Supreme Court of Oregon described the factual situation surrounding the confession as follows:

"An officer of the State Police investigated a theft at a residence near Pendleton. He asked the lady of the house which had been burglarized if she suspected anyone. She replied that the defendant was the only one she could think of. The defendant was a parolee and a 'close associate' of her son. The officer tried to contact defendant on three or four occasions with no success. Finally, about 25 days after the burglary, the officer left his card at defendant's apartment with a note asking him to call because 'I'd like to discuss something with you.' The next afternoon the defendant did call. The officer asked where it would be convenient to meet. The defendant had no preference; so the officer asked if the defendant could meet him at the state patrol office in about an hour and a half, about 5:00 p.m. The patrol office was about two blocks from defendant's apartment. The building housed several state agencies.

"The officer met defendant in the hallway, shook hands and took him into an office. The defendant was told he was not under arrest. The door was closed. The two sat across a desk. The police radio in another room could be heard. The officer told defendant he wanted to talk to him about a burglary and that his truthfulness would possibly be considered by the district attorney or judge. The officer further advised that the police believed defendant was involved in the burglary and [falsely stated that] defendant's fingerprints were found at the scene. The defendant sat for a few minutes and then said he had taken the property. This occurred within five minutes after defendant had come to the office. The officer then advised defendant of his *Miranda* rights and took a taped confession.

"At the end of the taped conversation the officer told defendant he was not arresting him at this time; he was released to go about his job and return to his family. The officer said he was referring the case to the district attorney for him to determine whether criminal charges would be brought. It was 5:30 p.m. when the defendant left the office.

"The officer gave all the testimony relevant to this issue. The defendant did not take the stand either at the hearing on the motion to suppress or at the trial."

The Supreme Court of Oregon reasoned from these facts that:

"We hold the interrogation took place in a 'coercive environment.' The parties were in the offices of the State Police; they were alone behind closed doors; the officer informed the defendant he was a suspect in a theft and the authorities had evidence incriminating him in the crime; and the defendant was a parolee under supervision. We are of the opinion that this evidence is not overcome by the evidence that the defendant came to the office in response to a request and was told he was not under arrest."

Our decision in *Miranda* set forth rules of police procedure applicable to "custodial interrogation." "By custodial interrogation, we mean questioning initiated by law enforcement officers after a person has been taken into custody or otherwise deprived of his freedom of action in any significant way." Subsequently we have found the *Miranda* principle applicable to questioning which takes place in a prison setting during a suspect's term of imprisonment on a separate offense, and to questioning taking place in a suspect's home, after he has been arrested and is no longer free to go where he pleases.

In the present case, however, there is no indication that the questioning took place in a context where respondent's freedom to depart was restricted in any way. He came voluntarily to the police station, where he was immediately informed that he was not under arrest. At the close of a 1/2–hour interview respondent did in fact leave the police station without hindrance. It is clear from these facts that Mathiason was not in custody "or otherwise deprived of his freedom of action in any significant way."

Such a noncustodial situation is not converted to one in which *Miranda* applies simply because a reviewing court concludes that, even in the absence of any formal arrest or restraint on freedom of movement, the questioning took place in a "coercive environment." Any interview of one suspected of a crime by a police officer will have coercive aspects to it, simply by virtue of the fact that the police officer is part of a law enforcement system which may ultimately cause the suspect to be charged with a crime. But police officers are not required to administer *Miranda* warnings to everyone whom they question. Nor is the requirement of warnings to be imposed simply because the questioning takes place in the station house, or because the questioned person is one whom the police suspect. *Miranda* warnings are required only where there has been such a restriction on a person's freedom as to render him "in custody." It was *that* sort of coercive environment to which *Miranda* by its terms was made applicable, and to which it is limited.

The officer's false statement about having discovered Mathiason's fingerprints at the scene was found by the Supreme Court of Oregon to be another circumstance contributing to the coercive environment which makes the *Miranda* rationale applicable. Whatever relevance this fact may have to other issues in the case, it has nothing to do with whether respondent was in custody for purposes of the *Miranda* rule.

The petition for certiorari is granted, the judgment of the Oregon Supreme Court is reversed, and the case is remanded for proceedings not inconsistent with this opinion. * * *

Mr. Justice BRENNAN would grant the writ but dissents from the summary disposition and would set the case for oral argument.

Mr. Justice MARSHALL, dissenting. * * *

The Court today holds that for constitutional purposes [the pressures on respondent are] irrelevant because respondent had not " 'been taken into custody or otherwise deprived of his freedom of action in any significant way.' " I do not believe that such a determination is possible on the record before us. It is true that respondent was not formally placed under arrest, but surely formalities alone cannot control. At the very least, if respondent entertained an objectively reasonable belief that he was not free to leave during the questioning, then he was "deprived of his freedom of action in a significant way." Plainly the respondent could have so believed, after being told by the police that they thought he was involved in a burglary and that his fingerprints had been found at the scene. Yet the majority is content to note that "there is no indication that * * * respondent's freedom to depart was restricted in any way," as if a silent record (and no state-court findings) means that the State has sustained its burden of demonstrating that respondent received his constitutional due.

More fundamentally, however, I cannot agree with the Court's conclusion that if respondent were not in custody no warnings were required. I recognize that *Miranda* is limited to custodial interrogations, but that is because, as we noted last Term, the facts in the *Miranda* cases raised only this "narrow issue." The rationale of *Miranda*, however, is not so easily cabined. * * *

In my view, even if respondent were not in custody, the coercive elements in the instant case were so pervasive as to require *Miranda*-type warnings. Respondent was interrogated in "privacy" and in "unfamiliar surroundings," factors on which *Miranda* places great stress. The investigation had focused on respondent. And respondent was subjected to some of the "deceptive stratagems" which called forth the *Miranda* decision. I therefore agree with the Oregon Supreme Court that to excuse the absence of warnings given these facts is "contrary to the rationale expressed in *Miranda*." * * *

[The opinion of Justice Stevens, dissenting, is omitted.]

NOTES AND QUESTIONS

1. Suppose you had to choose between one of the following descriptions of *Mathiason*: (a) it applied a "bright-line" rule about custody; (b) it drew on *Miranda*'s rationale to understand custody. (This returns us to the rule versus norm question. See p. 34, Note 2.) Defend your choice.

2. With respect to the police lying to Mathiason about his fingerprints being found at the scene of the crime, the Court remarked: "Whatever relevance this fact may have to other issues in the case, it has nothing to do with whether respondent was in custody for purposes of the *Miranda* rule." Why not? Would it matter, on the custody issue, whether the fingerprint statement was true or false?

3. Police have probable cause to arrest *D* and intend to arrest him. They tell him he is not under arrest and question him without giving *Miranda* warnings. At the end of the questioning, police permit *D* to leave but arrest him in the parking lot. Custody? Does it matter if the police arrest him in the interrogation room?

4. *The ordeal.* A prostitute is found murdered and police interview her former high-school boyfriend, *D*, on three separate occasions. He was told each time that he was not under arrest; each time he voluntarily appeared at the police station. The third interview lasted eleven hours, with bathroom breaks and three other brief breaks where *D* was left alone. His car keys were taken from him to perform a consensual search of his car and never returned. Roughly ten hours into the interview, *D* asked if he could leave and return the next day to continue and the police said, "No, you're here now. Why don't we go ahead and get this all wrapped up." An hour later, he confessed. Only after the confession was reduced to writing did the police give him *Miranda* warnings. The trial court held the confession admissible because, like Mathiason, *D* was told he was not under arrest and showed up voluntarily for the interview. Do you agree? Do you believe this outcome is consistent with the rationale of *Miranda*? See Commonwealth v. DiStefano, 782 A.2d 574 (Pa.Super.2001).

BERKEMER v. McCARTY

Supreme Court of the United States, 1984.
468 U.S. 420, 104 S.Ct. 3138, 82 L.Ed.2d 317.

JUSTICE MARSHALL delivered the opinion of the Court.

This case presents two related questions: First, does our decision in *Miranda v. Arizona* govern the admissibility of statements made during custodial interrogation by a suspect accused of a misdemeanor traffic offense? Second, does the roadside questioning of a motorist detained pursuant to a traffic stop constitute custodial interrogation for the purposes of the doctrine enunciated in *Miranda*?

I

A

The parties have stipulated to the essential facts. On the evening of March 31, 1980, Trooper Williams of the Ohio State Highway Patrol observed respondent's car weaving in and out of a lane on Interstate Highway 270. After following the car for two miles, Williams forced respondent to stop and asked him to get out of the vehicle. When respondent complied, Williams noticed that he was having difficulty standing. At that point, "Williams concluded that [respondent] would be charged with a traffic offense and, therefore, his freedom to leave the scene was terminated." However, respondent was not told that he would be taken into custody. Williams then asked respondent to perform a field sobriety test, commonly known as a "balancing test." Respondent could not do so without falling.

While still at the scene of the traffic stop, Williams asked respondent whether he had been using intoxicants. Respondent replied that "he had consumed two beers and had smoked several joints of marijuana a short time before." Respondent's speech was slurred, and Williams had difficulty understanding him. Williams thereupon formally placed respondent under arrest and transported him in the patrol car to the Franklin County Jail.

At the jail, respondent was given an intoxilyzer test to determine the concentration of alcohol in his blood. The test did not detect any alcohol whatsoever in respondent's system. Williams then resumed questioning respondent in order to obtain information for inclusion in the State Highway Patrol Alcohol Influence Report. Respondent answered affirmatively a question whether he had been drinking. When then asked if he was under the influence of alcohol, he said, "I guess, barely." Williams next asked respondent to indicate on the form whether the marihuana he had smoked had been treated with any chemicals. In the section of the report headed "Remarks," respondent wrote, "No ang[el] dust or PCP in the pot. Rick McCarty."

At no point in this sequence of events did Williams or anyone else tell respondent that he had a right to remain silent, to consult with an attorney, and to have an attorney appointed for him if he could not afford one.

B

Respondent was charged with operating a motor vehicle while under the influence of alcohol and/or drugs * * *.

Respondent moved to exclude the various incriminating statements he had made to Trooper Williams on the ground that introduction into evidence of those statements would violate the Fifth Amendment insofar as he had not been informed of his constitutional rights prior to his interrogation. * * *

II * * *

In the years since the decision in *Miranda*, we have frequently reaffirmed the central principle established by that case: if the police take a suspect into custody and then ask him questions without informing him of the rights enumerated [in *Miranda*], his responses cannot be introduced into evidence to establish his guilt.

Petitioner asks us to carve an exception out of the foregoing principle. When the police arrest a person for allegedly committing a misdemeanor traffic offense and then ask him questions without telling him his consti-tutional rights, petitioner argues, his responses should be admissible against him. We cannot agree.

One of the principal advantages of the doctrine that suspects must be given warnings before being interrogated while in custody is the clarity of that rule. * * *

The exception to *Miranda* proposed by petitioner would substantially undermine this crucial advantage of the doctrine. The police often are unaware when they arrest a person whether he may have committed a misdemeanor or a felony. Consider, for example, the reasonably common situation in which the driver of a car involved in an accident is taken into custody. Under Ohio law, both driving while under the influence of intoxicants and negligent vehicular homicide are misdemeanors, while reckless vehicular homicide is a felony. When arresting a person for causing a collision, the police may not know which of these offenses he may have committed. Indeed, the nature of his offense may depend upon circumstances unknowable to the police, such as whether the suspect has previously committed a similar offense or has a criminal record of some other kind. It may even turn upon events yet to happen, such as whether a victim of the accident dies. It would be unreasonable to expect the police to make guesses as to the nature of the criminal conduct at issue before deciding how they may interrogate the suspect.

Equally importantly, the doctrinal complexities that would confront the courts if we accepted petitioner's proposal would be Byzantine. Diffi-cult questions quickly spring to mind: For instance, investigations into seemingly minor offenses sometimes escalate gradually into investigations into more serious matters; at what point in the evolution of an affair of this sort would the police be obliged to give *Miranda* warnings to a suspect in custody? What evidence would be necessary to establish that an arrest for a misdemeanor offense was merely a pretext to enable the police to interrogate the suspect (in hopes of obtaining information about a felony) without providing him the safeguards prescribed by *Miranda*? The litigation necessary to resolve such matters would be time-consuming and disruptive of law enforcement. And the end result would be an elaborate set of rules, interlaced with exceptions and subtle distinctions, discrimi-nating between different kinds of custodial interrogations. Neither the police nor criminal defendants would benefit from such a development.

Absent a compelling justification we surely would be unwilling so seriously to impair the simplicity and clarity of the holding of *Miranda*. Neither of the two arguments proffered by petitioner constitutes such a justification. Petitioner first contends that *Miranda* warnings are unnec-essary when a suspect is questioned about a misdemeanor traffic offense, because the police have no reason to subject such a suspect to the sort of interrogation that most troubled the Court in *Miranda*. We cannot agree that the dangers of police abuse are so slight in this context. For example, the offense of driving while intoxicated is increasingly regarded in many jurisdictions as a very serious matter. Especially when the intoxicant at issue is a narcotic drug rather than alcohol, the police sometimes have difficulty obtaining evidence of this crime. Under such circumstances, the incentive for the police to try to induce the defendant to incriminate himself may well be substantial. Similar incentives are likely to be present when a person is arrested for a minor offense but the police suspect that a more serious crime may have been committed. * * *

Petitioner's second argument is that law enforcement would be more expeditious and effective in the absence of a requirement that persons arrested for traffic offenses be informed of their rights. Again, we are unpersuaded. The occasions on which the police arrest and then interrogate someone suspected only of a misdemeanor traffic offense are rare. The police are already well accustomed to giving *Miranda* warnings to persons taken into custody. Adherence to the principle that *all* suspects must be given such warnings will not significantly hamper the efforts of the police to investigate crimes.

We hold therefore that a person subjected to custodial interrogation is entitled to the benefit of the procedural safeguards enunciated in *Miranda*, regardless of the nature or severity of the offense of which he is suspected or for which he was arrested.

The implication of this holding is that * * * the statements made by respondent at the County Jail were inadmissible. There can be no question that respondent was "in custody" at least as of the moment he was formally placed under arrest and instructed to get into the police car. Because he was not informed of his constitutional rights at that juncture, respondent's subsequent admissions should not have been used against him.

III

To assess the admissibility of the self-incriminating statements made by respondent prior to his formal arrest, we are obliged to address a second issue concerning the scope of our decision in *Miranda*: whether the roadside questioning of a motorist detained pursuant to a routine traffic stop should be considered "custodial interrogation." Respondent urges that it should, on the ground that *Miranda* by its terms applies whenever "a person has been taken into custody *or otherwise deprived of his freedom of action in any significant way.*" Petitioner contends that a holding that every detained motorist must be advised of his rights before being questioned would constitute an unwarranted extension of the *Miranda* doctrine.

It must be acknowledged at the outset that a traffic stop significantly curtails the "freedom of action" of the driver and the passengers, if any, of the detained vehicle. Under the law of most States, it is a crime either to ignore a policeman's signal to stop one's car or, once having stopped, to drive away without permission. Certainly few motorists would feel free either to disobey a directive to pull over or to leave the scene of a traffic stop without being told they might do so. Partly for these reasons, we have long acknowledged that "stopping an automobile and detaining its occupants constitute a 'seizure' within the meaning of [the Fourth] Amendmen[t], even though the purpose of the stop is limited and the resulting detention quite brief."

However, we decline to accord talismanic power to the phrase in the *Miranda* opinion emphasized by respondent. Fidelity to the doctrine announced in *Miranda* requires that it be enforced strictly, but only in those types of situations in which the concerns that powered the decision are implicated. Thus, we must decide whether a traffic stop exerts upon a detained person pressures that sufficiently impair his free exercise of his privilege against self-incrimination to require that he be warned of his constitutional rights.

Two features of an ordinary traffic stop mitigate the danger that a person questioned will be induced "to speak where he would not otherwise do so freely." First, detention of a motorist pursuant to a traffic stop is presumptively temporary and brief. The vast majority of roadside detentions last only a few minutes. A motorist's expectations, when he sees a policeman's light flashing behind him, are that he will be obliged to spend a short period of time answering questions and waiting while the officer checks his license and registration, that he may then be given a citation, but that in the end he most likely will be allowed to continue on his way. In this respect, questioning incident to an ordinary traffic stop is quite different from stationhouse interrogation, which frequently is prolonged, and in which the detainee often is aware that questioning will continue until he provides his interrogators the answers they seek.

Second, circumstances associated with the typical traffic stop are not such that the motorist feels completely at the mercy of the police. To be sure, the aura of authority surrounding an armed, uniformed officer and the knowledge that the officer has some discretion in deciding whether to issue a citation, in combination, exert some pressure on the detainee to respond to questions. But other aspects of the situation substantially offset these forces. Perhaps most importantly, the typical traffic stop is public, at least to some degree. Passersby, on foot or in other cars, witness the interaction of officer and motorist. This exposure to public view both reduces the ability of an unscrupulous policeman to use illegitimate means to elicit self-incriminating statements and diminishes the motorist's fear that, if he does not cooperate, he will be subjected to abuse. The fact that the detained motorist typically is confronted by only one or at most two policemen further mutes his sense of vulnerability. In short, the atmosphere surrounding an ordinary traffic stop is substantially less "police dominated" than that surrounding the kinds of interrogation at issue in *Miranda* itself, and in the subsequent cases in which we have applied *Miranda*.

In both of these respects, the usual traffic stop is more analogous to a so-called "*Terry* stop," than to a formal arrest. Under the Fourth Amendment, we have held, a policeman who lacks probable cause but whose "observations lead him reasonably to suspect" that a particular person has committed, is committing, or is about to commit a crime, may detain that person briefly in order to "investigate the circumstances that provoke suspicion." "[T]he stop and inquiry must be 'reasonably related in scope to the justification for their initiation.' " Typically, this means that the officer may ask the detainee a moderate number of questions to determine his identity and to try to obtain information confirming or dispelling the officer's suspicions. But the detainee is not obliged to respond. And, unless the detainee's answers provide the officer with probable cause to arrest him, he must then be released. The comparatively nonthreatening character of detentions of this sort explains the absence of any suggestion in our opinions that *Terry* stops are subject to the dictates of *Miranda*. The similarly noncoercive aspect of ordinary traffic stops prompts us to hold that persons temporarily detained pursuant to such stops are not "in custody" for the purposes of *Miranda*.

Respondent contends that to "exempt" traffic stops from the coverage of *Miranda* will open the way to widespread abuse. Policemen will simply delay formally arresting detained motorists, and will subject them to sustained and intimidating interrogation at the scene of their initial detention. The net result, respondent contends, will be a serious threat to the rights that the *Miranda* doctrine is designed to protect.

We are confident that the state of affairs projected by respondent will not come to pass. It is settled that the safeguards prescribed by *Miranda* become applicable as soon as a suspect's freedom of action is curtailed to a "degree associated with formal arrest." If a motorist who has been detained pursuant to a traffic stop thereafter is subjected to treatment that renders him "in custody" for practical purposes, he will be entitled to the full panoply of protections prescribed by *Miranda*.

Admittedly, our adherence to the doctrine just recounted will mean that the police and lower courts will continue occasionally to have difficulty deciding exactly when a suspect has been taken into custody. Either a rule that *Miranda* applies to all traffic stops or a rule that a suspect need not be advised of his rights until he is formally placed under arrest would provide a clearer, more easily administered line. However, each of these two alternatives has drawbacks that make it unacceptable. The first would substantially impede the enforcement of the Nation's traffic laws—by compelling the police either to take the time to warn all detained motorists of their constitutional rights or to forgo use of self-incriminating statements made by those motorists—while doing little to protect citizens' Fifth Amendment rights. The second would enable the police to circumvent the constraints on custodial interrogations established by *Miranda*.

Turning to the case before us, we find nothing in the record that indicates that respondent should have been given *Miranda* warnings at any point prior to the time Trooper Williams placed him under arrest. For the reasons indicated above, we reject the contention that the initial stop of respondent's car, by itself, rendered him "in custody." And respondent has failed to demonstrate that, at any time between the initial stop and the arrest, he was subjected to restraints comparable to those associated with a formal arrest. Only a short period of time elapsed between the stop and the arrest. At no point during that interval was respondent informed that his detention would not be temporary. Although Trooper Williams apparently decided as soon as respondent stepped out of his car that respondent would be taken into custody and charged with a traffic offense, Williams never communicated his intention to respondent. A policeman's unarticulated plan has no bearing on the question whether a suspect was "in custody" at a particular time; the only relevant inquiry is how a reasonable man in the suspect's position would have understood his situation. Nor do other aspects of the interaction of Williams and respondent support the contention that respondent was exposed to "custodial interrogation" at the scene of the stop. From aught that appears in the stipulation of facts, a single police officer asked respondent a modest number of questions and requested him to perform a simple balancing test at a location visible to passing motorists. Treatment of this sort cannot fairly be characterized as the functional equivalent of formal arrest.

We conclude, in short, that respondent was not taken into custody for the purposes of *Miranda* until Williams arrested him. Consequently, the statements respondent made prior to that point were admissible against him. * * *

[The opinion of Justice Stevens, concurring in part and concurring in the judgment is omitted].

NOTES AND QUESTIONS

1. The State argued for a blanket *Miranda* exception for traffic stops on the ground that they are generically different from other kinds of police interference with freedom to depart, and that *Miranda* would interfere with the efficient prosecution of traffic offenders. The Court rather casually rejected that argument. Yet in the part of the opinion holding that traffic stops do not *always* constitute custody, the Court embraced the argument that traffic stops are different from the custody that *Miranda* had in mind. How can the Court have it both ways?

2. Consider the *Berkemer* fact pattern with the following change: Before the officer administers the sobriety test, Rick says, "My house is right over there. My mother is expecting me home. Can I go tell her what's happening?" The officer says, "No." Custody? What if Rick tries to leave and the officer physically stops him? Would it matter if Rick were sixteen and driving on a learner's permit? What if the officer handcuffs him? See Stone v. City of Huntsville, 656 So.2d 404 (Ala.Crim.App.1994).

3. Put yourself in Rick McCarty's place after the officer orders him to perform a "simple balancing test," and he falls down. Would you expect the officer to let you climb to your feet, get into your car, and drive away? Suppose that, while prone on the ground, Rick McCarty had said, "I guess I'm

in a whole lot of trouble," and the officer did not respond. Custody? What if the officer had answered, "Yes"?

4. *Trying to clarify Berkemer*. In 1995, the Court attempted, in dicta, to clarify the *Miranda* custody issue:

> Two discrete inquiries are essential to the determination: first, what were the circumstances surrounding the interrogation; and second, given those circumstances, would a reasonable person have felt he or she was not at liberty to terminate the interrogation and leave. Once the scene is set and the players' lines and actions are reconstructed, the court must apply an objective test to resolve the ultimate inquiry: was there a formal arrest or restraint on freedom of movement of the degree associated with a formal arrest.

Thompson v. Keohane, 516 U.S. 99, 116 S.Ct. 457, 133 L.Ed.2d 383 (1995). If you were a trial judge deciding a *Miranda* custody issue, would you find the new version helpful? How does it guide your thinking?

5. *Revisiting Mathiason*. Does the *Berkemer* approach give the same result on the *Mathiason* facts? Consider this variation on *Mathiason*: *D* threatens his wife when she moves out, and a week later her daughter and grandchildren are murdered in her new apartment. The police approach *D* at work and tell him that he is not a suspect but they need to ask him some questions in light of his prior threats. He agrees to accompany them to the police station. They inform him that department policy requires them to handcuff him and put him in the back of the car for the ride to the station. Police remove the handcuffs as soon as they reach the station and take him to an interview room. There he is interrogated, makes incriminating statements, and is released, just as Mathiason was. Custody? Dye v. State, 717 N.E.2d 5 (Ind.1999).

6. *Problems*.

A. A police officer observes two groups of young men eyeing each other. Three of the men have their hands in their pockets, which the officer took as a "gang sign." He lawfully frisks one of these three, feels a bulge in his waistband, and pulls out a fourteen–inch hunting knife. He asks, "What are you doing with this?" The suspect responds that he was going to scare the other gang members with it. Is the response admissible? See Argueta v. State, 136 Md.App. 273, 764 A.2d 863 (2001).

B. *D* solicits *X*, an undercover officer, to kill *D*'s wife. *D*'s plan was to be at home, having a pool party, at the time his wife is killed at another location. Six police cars arrive during the pool party to arrest *D*, but because of the trees surrounding his house, none of the cars are visible to anyone at the party. A single officer (with arrest warrant in back pocket) goes to the pool area and asks to speak to *D* (other officers are hiding all over *D*'s property). Officer tells *D* that someone just shot his wife. Feigning shock and dismay, *D* answers questions the officer asks (without giving *Miranda* warnings). This exchange takes place in front of fourteen of *D*'s closest friends. After the questioning, officer pulls out an arrest warrant and arrests *D*. Are the answers to the questions admissible under *Berkemer*?

C. Return to p. 642, Problem 5. A. Is this custody?

D.   Police suspected *B* of possessing child pornography on his computer. Detectives in plain clothes went to *B*'s work station where an officer asked *B* "to remove himself from the computer." When he "was hesitant," the officer "reiterated the request a few times more." *B* complied and was "instructed" to go to a company conference room. Before the interview began, a detective told *B* that he was "not under arrest. You're not being arrested. You'll walk out of here when we're done." The detective did not, however, ever tell *B* explicitly that he was free to leave. He asked *B* for his car keys to allow the officers to execute a search warrant without having to break into the vehicle. *B* "resisted for a few minutes," but then told the detective where to find his car keys.

The detective then questioned *B* about his involvement in possessing and uploading images of child pornography. His "tone was calm and measured throughout." *B* "participated actively, saying that 'I understand what you're doing. I understand what you're saying. I'm more than happy to go with you through the process." He admitted to possessing and uploading child pornography.

Not all of the interrogation, however, was calm. *B* said to the detective at one point: "I don't want you to get mad again, because you make that face * * * I don't want you to get mad, to start threatening and this and that, I want to steer clear of that." Near the end of the interview, the detective told *B* that "the big thing is, it's your laptop * * * I'm not going to lie to you * * * we've got your email connected to the images, it's a done thing."

Also near the end of the interrogation, *B* asked: "[A]t what point in this game do I need to get a lawyer?" The detective replied: "Me? I'd wait until you get arrested, but that's me. Like I said at the beginning, you're not under arrest, you're going to walk out of here." The detective also told *B* that he was "more than welcome to walk right out and call [a lawyer]," But he never called a lawyer. After the detective announced that the interview was finished, *B* prolonged it by asking questions for about ten minutes. After about two and a half hours, *B* walked out of the conference room without being arrested. The government concedes that Bassignani was not given *Miranda* warnings.

Custody? See United States v. Bassignani, 560 F.3d 989, 09 Cal. Daily. Op. Serv. 3766 (9th Cir. 2009).

E. *MIRANDA* INTERROGATION

RHODE ISLAND v. INNIS

Supreme Court of the United States, 1980.
446 U.S. 291, 100 S.Ct. 1682, 64 L.Ed.2d 297.

MR. JUSTICE STEWART delivered the opinion of the Court. * * *

I

On the night of January 12, 1975, John Mulvaney, a Providence, R.I., taxicab driver, disappeared after being dispatched to pick up a customer. His body was discovered four days later buried in a shallow grave in Coventry, R.I. He had died from a shotgun blast aimed at the back of his head.

On January 17, 1975, shortly after midnight, the Providence police received a telephone call from Gerald Aubin, also a taxicab driver, who reported that he had just been robbed by a man wielding a sawed-off shotgun. Aubin further reported that he had dropped off his assailant near Rhode Island College in a section of Providence known as Mount Pleasant. [Aubin later identified a photo of respondent. Eds.] * * *

At approximately 4:30 a. m. on the same date, Patrolman Lovell, while cruising the streets of Mount Pleasant in a patrol car, spotted the respondent standing in the street facing him. When Patrolman Lovell stopped his car, the respondent walked towards it. Patrolman Lovell then arrested the respondent, who was unarmed, and advised him of his so-called *Miranda* rights. While the two men waited in the patrol car for other police officers to arrive, Patrolman Lovell did not converse with the respondent other than to respond to the latter's request for a cigarette.

Within minutes, Sergeant Sears arrived at the scene of the arrest, and he also gave the respondent the *Miranda* warnings. Immediately thereafter, Captain Leyden and other police officers arrived. Captain Leyden advised the respondent of his *Miranda* rights. The respondent stated that he understood those rights and wanted to speak with a lawyer. Captain Leyden then directed that the respondent be placed in a "caged wagon," a four-door police car with a wire screen mesh between the front and rear seats, and be driven to the central police station. Three officers, Patrolmen Gleckman, Williams, and McKenna, were assigned to accompany the respondent to the central station. They placed the respondent in the vehicle and shut the doors. Captain Leyden then instructed the officers not to question the respondent or intimidate or coerce him in any way. The three officers then entered the vehicle, and it departed.

While en route to the central station, Patrolman Gleckman initiated a conversation with Patrolman McKenna concerning the missing shotgun. As Patrolman Gleckman later testified:

> "A.   At this point, I was talking back and forth with Patrolman McKenna stating that I frequent this area while on patrol and [that because a school for handicapped children is located nearby,] there's a lot of handicapped children running around in this area, and God forbid one of them might find a weapon with shells and they might hurt themselves."

Patrolman McKenna apparently shared his fellow officer's concern:

> "A.   I more or less concurred with him [Gleckman] that it was a safety factor and that we should, you know, continue to search for the weapon and try to find it."

While Patrolman Williams said nothing, he overheard the conversation between the two officers:

> "A.   He [Gleckman] said it would be too bad if the little—I believe he said a girl—would pick up the gun, maybe kill herself."

The respondent then interrupted the conversation, stating that the officers should turn the car around so he could show them where the gun was located. At this point, Patrolman McKenna radioed back to Captain Leyden that they were returning to the scene of the arrest and that the respondent would inform them of the location of the gun. At the time the respondent indicated that the officers should turn back, they had traveled no more than a mile, a trip encompassing only a few minutes.

The police vehicle then returned to the scene of the arrest where a search for the shotgun was in progress. There, Captain Leyden again advised the respondent of his *Miranda* rights. The respondent replied that he understood those rights but that he "wanted to get the gun out of the way because of the kids in the area in the school." The respondent then led the police to a nearby field, where he pointed out the shotgun under some rocks by the side of the road.

On March 20, 1975, a grand jury returned an indictment charging the respondent with the kidnaping, robbery, and murder of John Mulvaney. Before trial, the respondent moved to suppress the shotgun and the statements he had made to the police regarding it. After an evidentiary hearing at which the respondent elected not to testify, the trial judge found that the respondent had been "repeatedly and completely advised of his *Miranda* rights." He further found that it was "entirely understandable that [the officers in the police vehicle] would voice their concern [for the safety of the handicapped children] to each other." The judge then concluded that the respondent's decision to inform the police of the location of the shotgun was "a waiver, clearly, and on the basis of the evidence that I have heard, and [*sic*] intelligent waiver, of his [*Miranda*] right to remain silent." Thus, without passing on whether the police officers had in fact "interrogated" the respondent, the trial court sustained the admissibility of the shotgun and testimony related to its discovery. That evidence was later introduced at the respondent's trial, and the jury returned a verdict of guilty on all counts. * * *

II * * *

In the present case, the parties are in agreement that the respondent was fully informed of his *Miranda* rights and that he invoked his *Miranda* right to counsel when he told Captain Leyden that he wished to consult with a lawyer. It is also uncontested that the respondent was "in custody" while being transported to the police station.

The issue, therefore, is whether the respondent was "interrogated" by the police officers in violation of the respondent's undisputed right under *Miranda* to remain silent until he had consulted with a lawyer.[2] In resolving this issue, we first define the term "interrogation" under *Miranda* before turning to a consideration of the facts of this case.

---

    2. Since we conclude that the respondent was not "interrogated" for *Miranda* purposes, we do not reach the question whether the respondent waived his right under *Miranda* to be free from interrogation until counsel was present.

A

The starting point for defining "interrogation" in this context is, of course, the Court's *Miranda* opinion. There the Court observed that "[b]y custodial interrogation, we mean *questioning* initiated by law enforcement officers after a person has been taken into custody or otherwise deprived of his freedom of action in any significant way." This passage and other references throughout the opinion to "questioning" might suggest that the *Miranda* rules were to apply only to those police interrogation practices that involve express questioning of a defendant while in custody.

We do not, however, construe the *Miranda* opinion so narrowly. The concern of the Court in *Miranda* was that the "interrogation environment" created by the interplay of interrogation and custody would "subjugate the individual to the will of his examiner" and thereby undermine the privilege against compulsory self-incrimination. The police practices that evoked this concern included several that did not involve express questioning. For example, one of the practices discussed in *Miranda* was the use of line-ups in which a coached witness would pick the defendant as the perpetrator. This was designed to establish that the defendant was in fact guilty as a predicate for further interrogation. A variation on this theme discussed in *Miranda* was the so-called "reverse line-up" in which a defendant would be identified by coached witnesses as the perpetrator of a fictitious crime, with the object of inducing him to confess to the actual crime of which he was suspected in order to escape the false prosecution. The Court in *Miranda* also included in its survey of interrogation practices the use of psychological ploys, such as to "posi[t]" "the guilt of the subject," to "minimize the moral seriousness of the offense," and "to cast blame on the victim or on society." It is clear that these techniques of persuasion, no less than express questioning, were thought, in a custodial setting, to amount to interrogation.[3]

This is not to say, however, that all statements obtained by the police after a person has been taken into custody are to be considered the product of interrogation. * * * [T]he special procedural safeguards outlined in *Miranda* are required not where a suspect is simply taken into custody, but rather where a suspect in custody is subjected to interrogation. "Interrogation," as conceptualized in the *Miranda* opinion, must reflect a measure of compulsion above and beyond that inherent in custody itself.

We conclude that the *Miranda* safeguards come into play whenever a person in custody is subjected to either express questioning or its functional equivalent. That is to say, the term "interrogation" under *Miranda* refers not only to express questioning, but also to any words or actions on the part of the police (other than those normally attendant to arrest and custody) that the police should know are reasonably likely to elicit an

---

3. To limit the ambit of *Miranda* to express questioning would "place a premium on the ingenuity of police to devise methods of indirect interrogation, rather than to implement the plain mandate of *Miranda*."

incriminating response from the suspect. The latter portion of this definition focuses primarily upon the perceptions of the suspect, rather than the
intent of the police. This focus reflects the fact that the *Miranda* safeguards were designed to vest a suspect in custody with an added measure
of protection against coercive police practices, without regard to objective
proof of the underlying intent of the police. A practice that the police
should know is reasonably likely to evoke an incriminating response from
a suspect thus amounts to interrogation.[7] But, since the police surely
cannot be held accountable for the unforeseeable results of their words or
actions, the definition of interrogation can extend only to words or actions
on the part of police officers that they *should have known* were reasonably
likely to elicit an incriminating response.[8]

B

Turning to the facts of the present case, we conclude that the
respondent was not "interrogated" within the meaning of *Miranda*. It is
undisputed that the first prong of the definition of "interrogation" was
not satisfied, for the conversation between Patrolmen Gleckman and
McKenna included no express questioning of the respondent. Rather, that
conversation was, at least in form, nothing more than a dialogue between
the two officers to which no response from the respondent was invited.

Moreover, it cannot be fairly concluded that the respondent was
subjected to the "functional equivalent" of questioning. It cannot be said,
in short, that Patrolmen Gleckman and McKenna should have known that
their conversation was reasonably likely to elicit an incriminating response from the respondent. There is nothing in the record to suggest that
the officers were aware that the respondent was peculiarly susceptible to
an appeal to his conscience concerning the safety of handicapped children.
Nor is there anything in the record to suggest that the police knew that
the respondent was unusually disoriented or upset at the time of his
arrest.[9]

The case thus boils down to whether, in the context of a brief
conversation, the officers should have known that the respondent would
suddenly be moved to make a self-incriminating response. Given the fact
that the entire conversation appears to have consisted of no more than a
few off hand remarks, we cannot say that the officers should have known

---

7. This is not to say that the intent of the police is irrelevant, for it may well have a bearing
on whether the police should have known that their words or actions were reasonably likely to
evoke an incriminating response. In particular, where a police practice is designed to elicit an
incriminating response from the accused, it is unlikely that the practice will not also be one which
the police should have known was reasonably likely to have that effect.

8. Any knowledge the police may have had concerning the unusual susceptibility of a
defendant to a particular form of persuasion might be an important factor in determining
whether the police should have known that their words or actions were reasonably likely to elicit
an incriminating response from the suspect.

9. The record in no way suggests that the officers' remarks were designed to elicit a response.
It is significant that the trial judge, after hearing the officers' testimony, concluded that it was
"entirely understandable that [the officers] would voice their concern [for the safety of the
handicapped children] to each other."

that it was reasonably likely that Innis would so respond. This is not a case where the police carried on a lengthy harangue in the presence of the suspect. Nor does the record support the respondent's contention that, under the circumstances, the officers' comments were particularly "evocative." It is our view, therefore, that the respondent was not subjected by the police to words or actions that the police should have known were reasonably likely to elicit an incriminating response from him.

The Rhode Island Supreme Court erred, in short, in equating "subtle compulsion" with interrogation. That the officers' comments struck a responsive chord is readily apparent. Thus, it may be said, as the Rhode Island Supreme Court did say, that the respondent was subjected to "subtle compulsion." But that is not the end of the inquiry. It must also be established that a suspect's incriminating response was the product of words or actions on the part of the police that they should have known were reasonably likely to elicit an incriminating response.[10] This was not established in the present case. * * *

[The opinion of Justice White, concurring, is omitted.]

Mr. Chief Justice BURGER, concurring in the judgment. * * *

The meaning of *Miranda* has become reasonably clear and law enforcement practices have adjusted to its strictures; I would neither overrule *Miranda*, disparage it, nor extend it at this late date. * * *

Mr. Justice MARSHALL, with whom Mr. Justice BRENNAN joins, dissenting.

I am substantially in agreement with the Court's definition of "interrogation" within the meaning of *Miranda*. In my view, the *Miranda* safeguards apply whenever police conduct is intended or likely to produce a response from a suspect in custody. As I read the Court's opinion, its definition of "interrogation" for *Miranda* purposes is equivalent, for practical purposes, to my formulation, since it contemplates that "where a police practice is designed to elicit an incriminating response from the accused, it is unlikely that the practice will not also be one which the police should have known was reasonably likely to have that effect." Thus, the Court requires an objective inquiry into the likely effect of police conduct on a typical individual, taking into account any special susceptibility of the suspect to certain kinds of pressure of which the police know or have reason to know.

I am utterly at a loss, however, to understand how this objective standard as applied to the facts before us can rationally lead to the conclusion that there was no interrogation. * * *

---

10. By way of example, if the police had done no more than to drive past the site of the concealed weapon while taking the most direct route to the police station, and if the respondent, upon noticing for the first time the proximity of the school for handicapped children, had blurted out that he would show the officers where the gun was located, it could not seriously be argued that this "subtle compulsion" would have constituted "interrogation" within the meaning of the *Miranda* opinion.

One can scarcely imagine a stronger appeal to the conscience of a suspect—*any* suspect—than the assertion that if the weapon is not found an innocent person will be hurt or killed. And not just any innocent person, but an innocent child—a little girl—a helpless, handicapped little girl on her way to school. The notion that such an appeal could not be expected to have any effect unless the suspect were known to have some special interest in handicapped children verges on the ludicrous. As a matter of fact, the appeal to a suspect to confess for the sake of others, to "display some evidence of decency and honor," is a classic interrogation technique. * * *

I firmly believe that this case is simply an aberration, and that in future cases the Court will apply the standard adopted today in accordance with its plain meaning.

Mr. Justice STEVENS, dissenting. * * *

I * * *

The difference between the approach required by a faithful adherence to *Miranda* and the stinted test applied by the Court today can be illustrated by comparing three different ways in which Officer Gleckman could have communicated his fears about the possible dangers posed by the shotgun to handicapped children. He could have:

(1) directly asked Innis:

Will you please tell me where the shotgun is so we can protect handicapped school children from danger?

(2) announced to the other officers in the wagon:

If the man sitting in the back seat with me should decide to tell us where the gun is, we can protect handicapped children from danger.

or (3) stated to the other officers:

It would be too bad if a little handicapped girl would pick up the gun that this man left in the area and maybe kill herself.

In my opinion, all three of these statements should be considered interrogation because all three appear to be designed to elicit a response from anyone who in fact knew where the gun was located.[12] Under the Court's test, on the other hand, the form of the statements would be critical. The third statement would not be interrogation because in the Court's view there was no reason for Officer Gleckman to believe that Innis was susceptible to this type of an implied appeal; therefore, the

---

12. See White, *Rhode Island v. Innis*: The Significance of a Suspect's Assertion of His Right to Counsel, 17 Am.Crim.L.Rev. 53, 68 (1979), where the author proposes the same test and applies it to the facts of this case, stating:

"Under the proposed objective standard, the result is obvious. Since the conversation indicates a strong desire to know the location of the shotgun, any person with knowledge of the weapon's location would be likely to believe that the officers wanted him to disclose its location. Thus, a reasonable person in Innis's position would believe that the officers were seeking to solicit precisely the type of response that was given."

statement would not be reasonably likely to elicit an incriminating response. Assuming that this is true, then it seems to me that the first two statements, which would be just as unlikely to elicit such a response, should also not be considered interrogation. But, because the first statement is clearly an express question, it *would* be considered interrogation under the Court's test. The second statement, although just as clearly a deliberate appeal to Innis to reveal the location of the gun, would presumably not be interrogation because (a) it was not in form a direct question and (b) it does not fit within the "reasonably likely to elicit an incriminating response" category that applies to indirect interrogation.

As this example illustrates, the Court's test creates an incentive for police to ignore a suspect's invocation of his rights in order to make continued attempts to extract information from him. If a suspect does not appear to be susceptible to a particular type of psychological pressure, the police are apparently free to exert that pressure on him despite his request for counsel, so long as they are careful not to punctuate their statements with question marks. And if, contrary to all reasonable expectations, the suspect makes an incriminating statement, that statement can be used against him at trial. The Court thus turns *Miranda*'s unequivocal rule against any interrogation at all into a trap in which unwary suspects may be caught by police deception. * * *

NOTES AND QUESTIONS

1. Do you think Chief Justice Burger concurs in the judgment out of respect for *stare decisis* or for some other reason?

2. Is the test for interrogation objective or subjective? Some of both? Why should the officer's intent make any difference? Indeed, why should the test focus on the *officer* at all?

3. *The question-mark rule.* J found one of two men in the drunk tank lying in a pool of blood. The other inmate was asleep on his bunk. As J was unlocking the door, she yelled to the sleeping inmate: "What happened?" The inmate awoke and said, "I killed the son of a bitch last night; he would not shut up." This case implies a rule that one should not irritate cellmates, but does it fit the *Innis* rule about express questioning? State v. Bennett, 30 Utah 2d 343, 517 P.2d 1029 (1973). Is there custody?

4. *The functional equivalent of questioning.* The second half of the *Innis* test is designed to cover situations in which the police create a situation that produces the same kind of pressure on the suspect that a direct question would. Given that the pressure in *Innis* itself was held insufficient to constitute the functional equivalent of questioning, consider the following cases:

A. *F* was arrested for murdering a woman during a robbery in which furs were stolen. Later, *F* asked a detective if he could speak with a district attorney. The detective responded: "You have to tell me what you want to talk to him about so I can relate that to him. Otherwise, he won't come." *F* said nothing further, and the detective left only to return with some of the stolen furs (recovered from the apartment of a co-defendant). The detective placed the furs right in front of the cell, about a foot away from *F*. *F* immediately grabbed the wire mesh and asked to speak to the district attorney. Told that the D.A. could not do anything for him, he said, "I can't afford to do a lot of time. What can I tell you?" Was this statement obtained through interrogation? See People v. Ferro, 63 N.Y.2d 316, 472 N.E.2d 13, 482 N.Y.S.2d 237 (1984).

B. Police took *J* into custody for the murder of his baby. They gave him *Miranda* warnings, and he said he understood his rights and would talk to them "but I want my lawyer present when I talk." The police said no lawyer was then available, but one would be appointed for him when he was transferred to the jail. *J* said, "Well, I want to tell you about it." One detective then said to *J*, "God takes care of little babies. The baby is already in heaven." *J* asked the detective: "Are you a religious man?" The detective responded, "Not as religious as I should be." *J* then began telling police how he had hit the baby and thrown it into the back yard. Interrogation? See State v. Jones, 386 So.2d 1363 (La.1980).

C. *H* was a suspect in the burglary and sexual assault of *V*. *H* permitted two police officers to take his picture and agreed to accompany them to *V*'s home. En route, *H* told the officers that he knew nothing about the crime. Upon arrival, one officer remained with *H* in the squad car and the other officer entered *V*'s home, where *V* identified *H* from a photograph array. The officer returned to the squad car and said to *H*, "You're a liar." *H* responded, "You're right. I did it." Was *H* subject to interrogation? Was he in custody? See People v. Huffman, 61 N.Y.2d 795, 473 N.Y.S.2d 945, 462 N.E.2d 122 (1984).

D. Police arrested *Y* for robbery and took him to the station, where he waived his *Miranda* rights. Agent *S* interrogated *Y*, who continually denied his involvement. When *Y*'s accomplice confessed in another room, *S* told *Y*, who then invoked his right to counsel. *S* terminated the interview and got up to leave the room. As he reached the door, however, he turned around and said, "I want you to remember me, and I want you to remember my face, and I want you to remember that I gave you a chance." Did this constitute interrogation? See United States v. Young, 46 M.J. 768 (Army Crim.App. 1997).

5. *S* walks into the sheriff's office and states, "I done it; I done it; arrest me; arrest me." A deputy asks, "What did you do?" He replies, "I killed my wife." "What did you kill her with?" asks the deputy. "With an axe, that's all I had." Are any of these statements admissible under *Miranda*? People v. Savage, 102 Ill.App.2d 477, 242 N.E.2d 446 (1968). What if the deputy's second response is "calm down; you're no murderer"? Interrogation? Custody?

6. *A doctrinal exception to Miranda.* Police order *M*, suspected of drunk driving, to perform three field sobriety tests. He performs poorly because, he tells the officer, he had "been drinking." Police arrest *M* and take him to a booking center where it is routine procedure to videotape all conversations with arrestees. The officer asks *M* his name, address, height, weight, eye color, date of birth, and current age. He answers all questions but "stumbl[es]

over his address and age." He is then ordered to perform the three sobriety tests that he had performed earlier. No *Miranda* warnings are given. Can the videotape be introduced to show that he (a) slurred his words and (b) performed the sobriety tests badly?

One answer to that question is to announce a "routine booking question exception" to *Miranda*, and four members of the Court embraced that answer in Pennsylvania v. Muniz, 496 U.S. 582, 110 S.Ct. 2638, 110 L.Ed.2d 528 (1990). The theory here is that routine questions do not seek incriminating answers. A majority of the Court would later embrace this theory when the answer sought was a suspect's identity. In Hiibel v. Sixth Judicial District Court of Nevada, Humboldt County, 542 U.S. 177, 124 S.Ct. 2451, 159 L.Ed.2d 292 (2004), the Court held that providing one's name to the police is not incriminating.

> In this case petitioner's refusal to disclose his name was not based on any articulated real and appreciable fear that his name would be used to incriminate him, or that it 'would furnish a link in the chain of evidence needed to prosecute' him. As best we can tell, petitioner refused to identify himself only because he thought his name was none of the officer's business. Even today, petitioner does not explain how the disclosure of his name could have been used against him in a criminal case. While we recognize petitioner's strong belief that he should not have to disclose his identity, the Fifth Amendment does not override the Nevada Legislature's judgment to the contrary absent a reasonable belief that the disclosure would tend to incriminate him.

7. *A foundational exception to Miranda.* Four members of the *Muniz* Court embraced a very different theory that focused on the *answers* rather than the *questions*. In *Schmerber v. California*, p. 573, Note 7, the Court held that blood is not testimonial and thus compelling a suspect to provide blood is not making him be a witness against himself. Drawing on *Schmerber* four members of the *Muniz* Court would have held that the answers to booking questions are not testimonial. For another four justices, booking questions are a categorical exception to *Miranda*. Only Justice Marshall would have suppressed the answers to the booking questions.

8. *Synergy between custody and interrogation.* One goal of the *Miranda* Court was to cut through the formalistic doctrines that made the Fifth Amendment privilege beyond the reach of many suspects. But the Court's rather rigid application of the custody and interrogation requirements has led to a new type of formalism in the current *Miranda* doctrine. For example, the Court often seems to view "custody" and "interrogation" as separate requirements, deciding the "custody" issue first and then, only if the suspect was in custody, addressing the interrogation issue. For an argument that this *Miranda* formalism should be rejected in favor of a model that views custody and interrogation as "augmenting the other, rather than merely being added to the other," see Daniel Yeager, *Rethinking Custodial Interrogation*, 28 Am. Crim. L. Rev. 1, 50 (1990). In Yeager's model, high "levels" of either interrogation or custody have a synergistic multiplier effect on low "levels" of the other variable to create coercive interrogation sooner than it would under the Court's doctrine.

F. WAIVER AND INVOCATION OF THE *MIRANDA* RIGHTS

The *Miranda* Court was careful to emphasize that suspects could waive the rights that the Court found implicit in the privilege against self-incrimination. Once a court determines that the suspect was in custody, and was interrogated, the next step is waiver.

NORTH CAROLINA v. BUTLER

Supreme Court of the United States, 1979.
441 U.S. 369, 99 S.Ct. 1755, 60 L.Ed.2d 286.

MR. JUSTICE STEWART delivered the opinion of the Court. * * *

[Butler was arrested by an FBI agent and subsequently] convicted in a North Carolina trial court of kidnaping, armed robbery, and felonious assault. * * *

* * * FBI Agent Martinez testified that at the time of the arrest he fully advised the respondent of the rights delineated in the *Miranda* case. * * * [A]fter the agents determined that the respondent had an 11th grade education and was literate, he was given the Bureau's "Advice of Rights" form which he read. When asked if he understood his rights, he replied that he did. The respondent refused to sign the waiver at the bottom of the form. He was told that he need neither speak nor sign the form, but that the agents would like him to talk to them. The respondent replied: "I will talk to you but I am not signing any form." He then made inculpatory statements. Agent Martinez testified that the respondent said nothing when advised of his right to the assistance of a lawyer. At no time did the respondent request counsel or attempt to terminate the agents' questioning.

At the conclusion of this testimony the respondent moved to suppress the evidence of his incriminating statements on the ground that he had not waived his right to the assistance of counsel at the time the statements were made. The court denied the motion, finding that

> "the statement made by the defendant, William Thomas Butler, to Agent David C. Martinez, was made freely and voluntarily to said agent after having been advised of his rights as required by the *Miranda* ruling, including his right to an attorney being present at the time of the inquiry and that the defendant, Butler, understood his rights; [and] that he effectively waived his rights, including the right to have an attorney present during the questioning by his indication that he was willing to answer questions, having read the rights form together with the Waiver of Rights * * *."

The respondent's statements were then admitted into evidence, and the jury ultimately found the respondent guilty of each offense charged.

On appeal, the North Carolina Supreme Court reversed the convictions and ordered a new trial. It found that the statements had been admitted in violation of the requirements of the *Miranda* decision, noting that the respondent had refused to waive in writing his right to have counsel present and that there had not been a *specific* oral waiver. As it had in at least two earlier cases, the court read the *Miranda* opinion as

"provid[ing] in plain language that waiver of the right to counsel during interrogation will not be recognized unless such waiver is 'specifically made' after the *Miranda* warnings have been given."

We conclude that the North Carolina Supreme Court erred in its reading of the *Miranda* opinion. There, this Court said:

"If the interrogation continues without the presence of an attorney and a statement is taken, a heavy burden rests on the government to demonstrate that the defendant knowingly and intelligently waived his privilege against self-incrimination and his right to retained or appointed counsel."

The Court's opinion went on to say:

"An express statement that the individual is willing to make a statement and does not want an attorney followed closely by a statement could constitute a waiver. But a valid waiver will not be presumed simply from the silence of the accused after warnings are given or simply from the fact that a confession was in fact eventually obtained."

Thus, the Court held that an express statement can constitute a waiver, and that silence alone after such warnings cannot do so. But the Court did not hold that such an express statement is indispensable to a finding of waiver.

An express written or oral statement of waiver of the right to remain silent or of the right to counsel is usually strong proof of the validity of that waiver, but is not inevitably either necessary or sufficient to establish waiver. The question is not one of form, but rather whether the defendant in fact knowingly and voluntarily waived the rights delineated in the *Miranda* case. As was unequivocally said in *Miranda*, mere silence is not enough. That does not mean that the defendant's silence, coupled with an understanding of his rights and a course of conduct indicating waiver, may never support a conclusion that a defendant has waived his rights. The courts must presume that a defendant did not waive his rights; the prosecution's burden is great; but in at least some cases waiver can be clearly inferred from the actions and words of the person interrogated.

The Court's opinion in *Miranda* explained the reasons for the prophylactic rules it created:

"We have concluded that without proper safeguards the process of in-custody interrogation of persons suspected or accused of crime contains inherently compelling pressures which work to undermine the individual's will to resist and to compel him to speak where he would not otherwise do so freely. In order to combat these pressures and to permit a full opportunity to exercise the privilege against self-incrimination, the accused must be adequately and effectively apprised of his rights and the exercise of those rights must be fully honored.''

The *per se* rule that the North Carolina Supreme Court has found in *Miranda* does not speak to these concerns. There is no doubt that this respondent was adequately and effectively apprised of his rights. The only question is whether he waived the exercise of one of those rights, the right to the presence of a lawyer. Neither the state court nor the respondent has offered any reason why there must be a negative answer to that question in the absence of an *express* waiver. This is not the first criminal case to question whether a defendant waived his constitutional rights. It is an issue with which courts must repeatedly deal. Even when a right so fundamental as that to counsel at trial is involved, the question of waiver must be determined on ''the particular facts and circumstances surrounding that case, including the background, experience, and conduct of the accused.''

We see no reason to discard that standard and replace it with an inflexible *per se* rule in a case such as this. * * * By creating an inflexible rule that no implicit waiver can ever suffice, the North Carolina Supreme Court has gone beyond the requirements of federal organic law. It follows that its judgment cannot stand, since a state court can neither add to nor subtract from the mandates of the United States Constitution. * * *

Mr. Justice POWELL took no part in the consideration or decision of this case.

[The opinion of Justice Blackmun, concurring, is omitted.]

Mr. Justice BRENNAN, with whom Mr. Justice MARSHALL and Mr. Justice STEVENS joins, dissenting. * * *

The rule announced by the Court today allows a finding of waiver based upon ''infer[ence] from the actions and words of the person interrogated.'' The Court thus shrouds in half-light the question of waiver, allowing courts to construct inferences from ambiguous words and gestures. But the very premise of *Miranda* requires that ambiguity be interpreted against the interrogator. That premise is the recognition of the ''compulsion inherent in custodial'' interrogation, and of its purpose ''to subjugate the individual to the will of [his] examiner.'' Under such conditions, only the most explicit waivers of rights can be considered knowingly and freely given. * * *

Faced with ''actions and words'' of uncertain meaning, some judges may find waivers where none occurred. Others may fail to find them where they did. In the former case, the defendant's rights will have been violated; in the latter, society's interest in effective law enforcement will have been frustrated. A simple prophylactic rule requiring the police to obtain an express waiver of the right to counsel before proceeding with interrogation eliminates these difficulties. And since the Court agrees that *Miranda* requires the police to obtain some kind of waiver—whether express or implied—the requirement of an express waiver would impose no burden on the police not imposed by the Court's interpretation. It would merely make that burden explicit. Had Agent Martinez simply elicited a clear answer from Willie Butler to the question, "Do you waive your right to a lawyer?" this journey through three courts would not have been necessary.

NOTES AND QUESTIONS

1. *The eighty percent solution.* Studies show that roughly eighty percent of suspects waive their *Miranda* rights. See Paul G. Cassell & Bret S. Hayman, *Police Interrogation in the 1990s: An Empirical Study of the Effects of Miranda*, 43 UCLA L. Rev. 839 (1996); Richard A. Leo, *Inside the Interrogation Room*, 86 J. Crim. L. & Criminology 266, 282–83 (1996). George C. Thomas III, *Stories About Miranda*, 102 Mich. L. Rev. 1959 (2004).

Does this mean *Miranda* is ineffective or only that most suspects want to tell their side of the story? For an argument that the latter character trait explains more of the waiver rate than most scholars believe, see George C. Thomas III, *Miranda's Illusion: Telling Stories in the Police Interrogation Room*, 81 Texas L. Rev. 1091 (2003) (essay on Welsh S. White, *Miranda's Waning Protections* (2001)).

2. *Problems.*

A. Suppose Butler had said to the agent, "I will talk to you but I'm not giving up my rights." Would this be a valid waiver of *Miranda*?

B. Reading from a waiver card, an officer concludes by saying, "With these warnings in mind, do you waive your rights as I have described them to you and agree to talk to me?" The suspect said "No," at the same time smiling and nodding. With no further discussion of waiver, the officer proceeds with questioning, and the suspect makes incriminating responses. Is this a waiver under *Butler*?

3. *Elements of a valid waiver.* The *Miranda* Court drew the waiver requirements from the law of the waiver of the right to counsel. See Johnson v. Zerbst, 304 U.S. 458, 58 S.Ct. 1019, 82 L.Ed. 1461 (1938). Thus, the waiver must be a voluntary, knowing, and intelligent relinquishment of the *Miranda* rights.

A. *Voluntary.* We know from Chapter 6 that the Court uses "voluntary" to mean actions by a person whose will is not overborne by the State. (Applying the standard is not easy, but the standard is familiar.) The *Miranda* Court arguably sought to elevate the standard for finding voluntariness when it commented that "a heavy burden rests on the government to demonstrate that the defendant knowingly and intelligently waived" his *Miranda* rights. Justice White predicted that the Court would eventually return to plain old voluntariness as the proper waiver standard. *Butler* seems to support that view. What could it mean in the substantive law of waiver to say that the government has a "heavy burden" to show waiver? What might it mean procedurally?

Prior to *Butler*, the Court had held that the standard for *Miranda* waiver was preponderance of the evidence. Lego v. Twomey, 404 U.S. 477, 92 S.Ct.

619, 30 L.Ed.2d 618 (1972). Putting *Butler* and *Lego* together creates "an historical irony. *Miranda* was intended as a bright-line alternative to the much-criticized, totality-of-the-circumstances 'voluntariness' standard that preceded it. Yet, through the vehicle of *Miranda* waiver law, 'voluntariness' jurisprudence has returned." 1 Joshua Dressler & Alan C. Michaels, Understanding Criminal Procedure 502 (4th ed. 2006).

B. *Knowing/intelligent.* If a suspect hears the warnings, indicates that she understands them, then answers police questions in the absence of a lawyer, it would seem to imply that she did so knowingly and intelligently. But the requirement of knowing and intelligent raises the issue of how complete the knowledge must be. For example, though it might benefit suspects to know that parole requirements had just been tightened (or parole abolished) for the crime for which they were arrested, this knowledge seems too peripheral to be required. But other types of knowledge might be necessary. Consider the following test: A suspect "must have 'full awareness' of the consequences of abandoning the *Miranda* rights, but need not have awareness of the *full* consequences." *Id.*

4. *Must the suspect know the crime the police are seeking to ask him about?* The answer is no. In Colorado v. Spring, 479 U.S. 564, 107 S.Ct. 851, 93 L.Ed.2d 954 (1987), *S* was arrested for interstate possession of stolen firearms. He waived his *Miranda* rights, and the police questioned him not about the stolen firearms but about a murder with which *S* had not been charged. The Court held that a waiver of *Miranda* is to interrogation in general and not to interrogation about a particular crime. Thus—using language that will become important in the next chapter—*Miranda* is *not* "crime-specific."

5. *Waiver is personal.* *B* was arrested for murder. As a result of the efforts of *B*'s sister, a lawyer called the police station and informed a detective that she would act as *B*'s lawyer in the event police intended to question him. The detective told the lawyer that *B* would not be interrogated that night. Less than an hour later, however, police began a series of interrogations of *B*. Prior to each session, police informed *B* of his *Miranda* rights, and he signed written forms waiving the right to counsel. At no time did the police inform *B* that a lawyer had offered to represent him during interrogation. *B* ultimately signed three written statements fully admitting the murder. In Moran v. Burbine, 475 U.S. 412, 106 S.Ct. 1135, 89 L.Ed.2d 410 (1986), the Court held that these were valid *Miranda* waivers even though he did not know his lawyer was trying to reach him.

> Events occurring outside of the presence of the suspect and entirely unknown to him surely can have no bearing on the capacity to comprehend and knowingly relinquish a constitutional right. Under the analysis of the Court of Appeals, the same defendant, armed with the same information and confronted with precisely the same police conduct, would have knowingly waived his *Miranda* rights had a lawyer not telephoned the police station to inquire about his status. Nothing in any of our waiver decisions or in our understanding of the essential components of a valid waiver requires so incongruous a result. No doubt the additional information would have been useful to respondent; perhaps even it might

have affected his decision to confess. But we have never read the Constitution to require that the police supply a suspect with a flow of information to help him calibrate his self-interest in deciding whether to speak or stand by his rights. Once it is determined that a suspect's decision not to rely on his rights was uncoerced, that he at all times knew he could stand mute and request a lawyer, and that he was aware of the State's intention to use his statements to secure a conviction, the analysis is complete and the waiver is valid as a matter of law. * * *

Nor are we prepared to adopt a rule requiring that the police inform a suspect of an attorney's efforts to reach him. While such a rule might add marginally to *Miranda*'s goal of dispelling the compulsion inherent in custodial interrogation, overriding practical considerations counsel against its adoption. * * * We have little doubt that the approach urged by respondent and endorsed by the Court of Appeals would have the inevitable consequence of muddying *Miranda*'s otherwise relatively clear waters. The legal questions it would spawn are legion: To what extent should the police be held accountable for knowing that the accused has counsel? Is it enough that someone in the station house knows, or must the interrogating officer himself know of counsel's efforts to contact the suspect? Do counsel's efforts to talk to the suspect concerning one criminal investigation trigger the obligation to inform the defendant before interrogation may proceed on a wholly separate matter? * * *

The Court also rejected Burbine's due process claim, albeit expressing a "distaste for the deliberate misleading of an officer of the court." Justice Stevens sarcastically said in his dissent that the majority, "finding its conscience troubled but not shocked," rejected the due process challenge in "precisely five sentences." (We return to *Burbine* in a Note in Chapter 8, to show that it does not fit the Court's right-to-counsel doctrine either.)

For a rejection of *Moran v. Burbine* on state constitutional law grounds, see Commonwealth v. Mavredakis, 430 Mass. 848, 725 N.E.2d 169 (2000) (declaring that the Massachusetts Declaration of Rights required a "bright-line rule" that "police must stop questioning and inform a suspect immediately" of attempts by a lawyer to contact the suspect).

6. *J* is fifteen years old and a suspect in a murder. His mother is with him at the police station. When police give him warnings and ask whether he wishes to answer questions, *J* answers "no." His mother turns to him and says, "No, we need to get this straightened out. We'll talk with him anyway." *J* looks at his mother for a time and then nods his head. The detective asks if he wishes to answer without a lawyer being present and this time he answers "yes." Is this a valid waiver? See State v. Johnson, 136 N.C.App. 683, 525 S.E.2d 830 (2000).

7. *Voluntariness problems persist.* Voluntariness remains part of confession law not just in the guise of *Miranda* waiver, but also in measuring the effect of interrogation techniques that follow a valid waiver.

A. *Shackles?* Police arrested *H* for murder and provided *Miranda* warnings. He agreed to talk to the police and denied involvement. He was taken to the police station, "placed in a 10 foot by 10 foot interview room" where "the handcuffs were removed, and he was shackled to the floor." He was "allowed to take bathroom breaks as needed,'' but otherwise remained shackled to the floor for seven hours. Police interrogated him for about two and one-half hours while he was shackled. Police falsely implied that the victim's blood was on the suspect's coat, that several people saw him at the scene of the murder, and that people were picking his photo out of photo arrays. Indeed, four witnesses had in fact picked a different man's picture out of the photo array but the police did not disclose this fact. Are his statements admissible? See State v. Harris, 279 Kan. 163, 105 P.3d 1258 (2005).

B. *We are brothers.* Detective Boyce questioned suspect Miller about the murder of a seventeen-year-old girl after Miller waived his *Miranda* rights. Audio tapes of the interview showed that Detective Boyce made no threats while questioning Miller. Instead, Boyce assumed a friendly, understanding manner and spoke in a soft tone of voice. Boyce's major theme throughout the interrogation was that whoever had committed such a heinous crime had mental problems and was desperately in need of psychological treatment.

Boyce: You can see it, Frank, you can feel it, you can feel it but you are not responsible. This is what I'm trying to tell you, but you've got to come forward and tell me. Don't, don't, don't let it eat you up, don't, don't fight it. You've got to rectify it, Frank. We've got to get together on this thing, or I, I mean really, you need help, you need proper help, and you know it, my God, you know, in God's name, you, you, you know it. You are not a criminal, you are not a criminal. * * * Frank, listen to me, honest to God, I'm, I'm telling you, Frank (inaudible). I know, it's going to bother you, Frank, it's going to bother you. It's there, it's not going to go away, it's there. It's right in front of you, Frank. Am I right or wrong?

Miller: Yeah. * * *

Boyce: First thing we have to do is let it all come out. Don't fight it because it's worse, Frank, it's worse. It's hurting me because I feel it. I feel it wanting to come out, but it's hurting me, Frank. * * * Let it come out, Frank. I'm here, I'm here with you now. I'm on your side, I'm on your side, Frank. I'm your brother, you and I are brothers, Frank. We are brothers, and I want to help my brother. * * * We have, we have a relationship, don't we? Have I been sincere with you, Frank? * * * No, listen to me, Frank, please listen to me. The issue now is what happened. The issue now is truth. Truth is the issue now. You've got to believe this, and the truth prevails in the end, Frank. You have to believe that and I'm sincere when I'm saying it to you. You've got to be truthful with yourself. * * * That's the most important thing, not, not what has happened, Frank. The fact that you were truthful, you came forward and you said, look I have a problem. I didn't mean to do what I did. I have a problem, this is what's important, Frank. This is very important, I got, I, I got to get closer to you, Frank, I got to make you believe this and I'm, and I'm sincere when I tell you this. You got to tell me exactly what happened, Frank. That's very important. I know how you feel inside, Frank, it's eating you up, am I right? It's eating you up, Frank. You've got to come forward. You've got to do it for yourself, for your family, for your father, this is what's important, the truth, Frank.

The interview lasted less than an hour. After Miller confessed, he collapsed in a state of shock. He slid off his chair and onto the floor with a blank stare on his face. The police officers sent for a first-aid squad that took him to the hospital. Is the confession voluntary? Does *Miranda* help in any way with this kind of issue? See Miller v. Fenton, 796 F.2d 598 (3d Cir.1986).

8. *How often do police use coercion in post-waiver interrogations?* Professor Richard Leo's field work found very few examples of coercive police techniques following waiver. As he observed 182 interrogations, Leo looked for any coercive tactic from a list of ten tactics—a list comprehensive enough to "generally resolve any doubts in favor of the suspect, not the police." Despite his broad definition of coercion, Leo found evidence of coercive tactics in only four (or 2%) of the cases. Richard A. Leo, *Inside the Interrogation Room*, 86 J. Crim. L. & Criminology 266, 282–83 (1996).

9. *Why not videotape?* A slow but steady movement toward requiring police to videotape interrogations can be discerned in courts and legislatures. Unlike the *Miranda* revolution, which was imposed from the top by a bare majority of the Court, this revolution began at the level of individual police departments. William Geller estimated that in 1990 about one-third of all police and sheriffs' departments serving populations of 50,000 or more were videotaping at least some interrogations. William A. Geller, *Videotaping Interrogations and Confessions*," in Miranda: Law, Justice, and Policing (Richard A. Leo & George C. Thomas III eds., 1998).

According to Geller, the "vast majority" of agencies reported that "videotaping has led to improvements in police interrogation," including better preparation, lack of distractions formerly required to record written confessions, the monitoring of interrogations by supervisors to assess officer performance, the use of old tapes to train detectives (both beginners and veterans), and the use of tapes to show a recalcitrant suspect that his accomplice has implicated him. Geller, *supra*, at 307.

Prosecutors found the tapes useful in helping them "assess the state's case and prepare for trial," as well as in plea bargaining situations. *Id.* at 308. A tape of the defendant confessing in a sincere and contrite manner would indeed be a powerful incentive not to go to trial! For that reason, and others, defense lawyers' "opinions of videotapes were much more mixed * * *. Some were flatly opposed to videotaping, primarily because it generally gives the state a strategic edge." *Id.* at 309. But public defenders generally supported videotaping, both because of the "client-control benefits" of videotaping and because small details could be seen in the videotape that occasionally supported the client's version of the facts. One private lawyer gave the following assessment of videotaping confessions: "As a defense lawyer, I hate videotaping. As a citizen needing the protection of the police against criminals, I love it." *Id.*

Christopher Slobogin has recently outlined "why taping is needed despite the elaborate rules that now govern interrogation. Put simply, the reasoning is as follows: the *Miranda* regime has failed, voluntariness should once again be the focal point of interrogation regulation, and taping is necessary to push courts in that direction. Christopher Slobogin, *Toward Taping*, 1 Ohio St. J. Crim. L. 309, 309 (2003).

Do you think the Court should find a videotaping requirement in the Constitution? What rights might be read to require taping? See Christopher Slobogin, *id.* (identifying three constitutional "homes" for a taping requirement).

10. Complicating matters further is the issue of how to analyze invocations of the twin *Miranda* rights—the right to remain silent and the right to counsel. In a way, the invocation issue is the other side of the coin of the waiver issue. By definition, a suspect who is invoking her rights cannot be waiving her rights. But invocation means more than lack of waiver, of course. Invocation requires (or prevents) certain acts on the part of the interrogators, as the next case makes plain.

EDWARDS v. ARIZONA

Supreme Court of the United States, 1981.
451 U.S. 477, 101 S.Ct. 1880, 68 L.Ed.2d 378.

JUSTICE WHITE delivered the opinion of the Court. * * *

I

On January 19, 1976, a sworn complaint was filed against Edwards in Arizona state court charging him with robbery, burglary, and first-degree murder. An arrest warrant was issued pursuant to the complaint, and Edwards was arrested at his home later that same day. At the police station, he was informed of his rights as required by *Miranda v. Arizona*. Petitioner stated that he understood his rights, and was willing to submit to questioning. After being told that another suspect already in custody had implicated him in the crime, Edwards denied involvement and gave a taped statement presenting an alibi defense. He then sought to "make a deal." The interrogating officer told him that he wanted a statement, but that he did not have the authority to negotiate a deal. The officer provided Edwards with the telephone number of a county attorney. Petitioner made the call, but hung up after a few moments. Edwards then said: "I want an attorney before making a deal." At that point, questioning ceased and Edwards was taken to county jail.

At 9:15 the next morning, two detectives, colleagues of the officer who had interrogated Edwards the previous night, came to the jail and asked to see Edwards. When the detention officer informed Edwards that the detectives wished to speak with him, he replied that he did not want to talk to anyone. The guard told him that "he had" to talk and then took him to meet with the detectives. The officers identified themselves, stated they wanted to talk to him, and informed him of his *Miranda* rights. Edwards was willing to talk, but he first wanted to hear the taped statement of the alleged accomplice who had implicated him. After listening to the tape for several minutes, petitioner said that he would make a statement so long as it was not tape-recorded. The detectives informed him that the recording was irrelevant since they could testify in court concerning whatever he said. Edwards replied: "I'll tell you anything you want to know, but I don't want it on tape." He thereupon implicated himself in the crime.

Prior to trial, Edwards moved to suppress his confession on the ground that his *Miranda* rights had been violated when the officers returned to question him after he had invoked his right to counsel. * * * The [trial] court stated without explanation that it found Edwards' statement to be voluntary. Edwards was tried twice and convicted. Evidence concerning his confession was admitted at both trials.

On appeal, the Arizona Supreme Court held that Edwards had invoked both his right to remain silent and his right to counsel during the interrogation conducted on the night of January 19. The court then went on to determine, however, that Edwards had waived both rights during the January 20 meeting when he voluntarily gave his statement to the detectives after again being informed that he need not answer questions and that he need not answer without the advice of counsel. * * *

II

In *Miranda v. Arizona*, the Court determined that the Fifth and Fourteenth Amendments' prohibition against compelled self-incrimination required that custodial interrogation be preceded by advice to the putative defendant that he has the right to remain silent and also the right to the presence of an attorney. The Court also indicated the procedures to be followed subsequent to the warnings. If the accused indicates that he wishes to remain silent, "the interrogation must cease." If he requests counsel, "the interrogation must cease until an attorney is present."

Miranda thus declared that an accused has a Fifth and Fourteenth Amendment right to have counsel present during custodial interrogation. Here, the critical facts as found by the Arizona Supreme Court are that Edwards asserted his right to counsel and his right to remain silent on January 19, but that the police, without furnishing him counsel, returned the next morning to confront him and as a result of the meeting secured incriminating oral admissions. Contrary to the holdings of the state courts, Edwards insists that having exercised his right on the 19th to have counsel present during interrogation, he did not validly waive that right on the 20th. For the following reasons, we agree.

First, the Arizona Supreme Court applied an erroneous standard for determining waiver where the accused has specifically invoked his right to counsel. It is reasonably clear under our cases that waivers of counsel must not only be voluntary, but must also constitute a knowing and intelligent relinquishment or abandonment of a known right or privilege, a matter which depends in each case "upon the particular facts and circumstances surrounding that case, including the background, experience, and conduct of the accused." * * *

* * * Here, however sound the conclusion of the state courts as to the voluntariness of Edwards' admission may be, neither the trial court nor the Arizona Supreme Court undertook to focus on whether Edwards understood his right to counsel and intelligently and knowingly relinquished it. It is thus apparent that the decision below misunderstood the requirement for finding a valid waiver of the right to counsel, once invoked.

Second, although we have held that after initially being advised of his *Miranda* rights, the accused may himself validly waive his rights and respond to interrogation, the Court has strongly indicated that additional safeguards are necessary when the accused asks for counsel; and we now hold that when an accused has invoked his right to have counsel present during custodial interrogation, a valid waiver of that right cannot be established by showing only that he responded to further police-initiated custodial interrogation even if he has been advised of his rights. We further hold that an accused, such as Edwards, having expressed his desire to deal with the police only through counsel, is not subject to further interrogation by the authorities until counsel has been made available to him, unless the accused himself initiates further communication, exchanges, or conversations with the police.

Miranda itself indicated that the assertion of the right to counsel was a significant event and that once exercised by the accused, "the interrogation must cease until an attorney is present." Our later cases have not abandoned that view. * * * We reconfirm these [cases] and, to lend them substance, emphasize that it is inconsistent with *Miranda* and its progeny for the authorities, at their instance, to reinterrogate an accused in custody if he has clearly asserted his right to counsel.

In concluding that the fruits of the interrogation initiated by the police on January 20 could not be used against Edwards, we do not hold or imply that Edwards was powerless to countermand his election or that the authorities could in no event use any incriminating statements made by Edwards prior to his having access to counsel. Had Edwards initiated the meeting on January 20, nothing in the Fifth and Fourteenth Amendments would prohibit the police from merely listening to his voluntary, volunteered statements and using them against him at the trial. The Fifth Amendment right identified in *Miranda* is the right to have counsel present at any custodial interrogation. Absent such interrogation, there would have been no infringement of the right that Edwards invoked and there would be no occasion to determine whether there had been a valid waiver. *Rhode Island v. Innis* [p. 656] makes this sufficiently clear.[9]

---

9. If, as frequently would occur in the course of a meeting initiated by the accused, the conversation is not wholly one-sided, it is likely that the officers will say or do something that clearly would be "interrogation." In that event, the question would be whether a valid waiver of the right to counsel and the right to silence had occurred, that is, whether the purported waiver was knowing and intelligent and found to be so under the totality of the circumstances, including

But this is not what the facts of this case show. Here, the officers conducting the interrogation on the evening of January 19 ceased interrogation when Edwards requested counsel as he had been advised he had the right to do. The Arizona Supreme Court was of the opinion that this was a sufficient invocation of his *Miranda* rights, and we are in accord. It is also clear that without making counsel available to Edwards, the police returned to him the next day. This was not at his suggestion or request. Indeed, Edwards informed the detention officer that he did not want to talk to anyone. At the meeting, the detectives told Edwards that they wanted to talk to him and again advised him of his *Miranda* rights. Edwards stated that he would talk, but what prompted this action does not appear. He listened at his own request to part of the taped statement made by one of his alleged accomplices and then made an incriminating statement, which was used against him at his trial. We think it is clear that Edwards was subjected to custodial interrogation on January 20 within the meaning of *Rhode Island v. Innis*, and that this occurred at the instance of the authorities. His statement made without having had access to counsel, did not amount to a valid waiver and hence was inadmissible.

Accordingly, the holding of the Arizona Supreme Court that Edwards had waived his right to counsel was infirm, and the judgment of that court is reversed. * * *

[The opinion of Chief Justice Burger, concurring in the judgment, is omitted.]

Justice POWELL, with whom Justice REHNQUIST joins, concurring in the result.

Although I agree that the judgment of the Arizona Supreme Court must be reversed, I do not join the Court's opinion because I am not sure what it means. * * *

* * * [T]he Court—after reiterating the familiar principles of waiver—goes on to say:

"We further hold that an accused, such as Edwards, having expressed his desire to deal with the police only through counsel, is not subject to further interrogation by the authorities until counsel has been made available to him, *unless the accused [has] himself initiate[d] further communication, exchanges, or conversations with the police.*"

In view of the emphasis placed on "initiation," I find the Court's opinion unclear. If read to create a new *per se* rule, requiring a threshold inquiry as to precisely who opened any conversation between an accused and state officials, I cannot agree. I would not superimpose a new element of proof on the established doctrine of waiver of counsel. * * *

In sum, once warnings have been given and the right to counsel has been invoked, the relevant inquiry—whether the suspect now desires to talk to police without counsel—is a question of fact to be determined in

---

the necessary fact that the accused, not the police, reopened the dialogue with the authorities. * * *

light of all of the circumstances. Who "initiated" a conversation may be relevant to the question of waiver, but it is not the *sine qua non* to the inquiry. The ultimate question is whether there was a free and knowing waiver of counsel before interrogation commenced.

If the Court's opinion does nothing more than restate these principles, I am in agreement with it. I hesitate to join the opinion only because of what appears to be an undue and undefined, emphasis on a single element: "initiation." * * * My concern is that the Court's opinion today may be read as "constitutionalizing" not the generalized *Zerbst* [waiver] standard but a *single element of fact* among the various facts that may be relevant to determining whether there has been a valid waiver.

NOTES AND QUESTIONS

1. *How does an invocation of the right to remain silent compare to Edwards?* A single standard could measure the effect of all invocations of *Miranda*. The *Edwards* rule could apply to invocations of the right to remain silent as well as the right to counsel; the police would not then be permitted to attempt to question the suspect who invoked either right unless the suspect initiated the exchange. But the Court has not seen fit to apply the same broad rule to requests to remain silent.

In Michigan v. Mosley, 423 U.S. 96, 96 S.Ct. 321, 46 L.Ed.2d 313 (1975), decided five years before *Edwards*, Mosley was questioned by a detective of the armed robbery section of the detective bureau. The interrogation ended as soon as Mosley "said he did not want to answer any questions about the robberies." A few hours later, a detective from the homicide bureau questioned Mosley about a fatal shooting during a holdup attempt (not the same robbery that was the subject of the earlier interrogation).

> Before questioning Mosley about this homicide, Detective Hill carefully advised him of his "*Miranda* rights." Mosley read the notification form both silently and aloud, and Detective Hill then read and explained the warnings to him and had him sign the form. Mosley at first denied any involvement in the Williams murder, but after the officer told him that Anthony Smith had confessed to participating in the slaying and had named him as the "shooter," Mosley made a statement implicating himself in the homicide. The interrogation by Detective Hill lasted approximately 15 minutes, and at no time during its course did Mosley ask to consult with a lawyer or indicate that he did not want to discuss the homicide. In short, there is no claim that the procedures followed during Detective Hill's interrogation of Mosley, standing alone, did not fully comply with the strictures of the *Miranda* opinion.

The Court considered the various meanings that the *Miranda* Court could have intended when it stated that "interrogation must cease" when the person in custody indicates that "he wishes to remain silent."

> A reasonable and faithful interpretation of the *Miranda* opinion must rest on the intention of the Court in that case to adopt "fully effective means * * * to notify the person of his right of silence and to assure that

the exercise of the right will be scrupulously honored * * *." The critical safeguard identified in the passage at issue is a person's "right to cut off questioning." Through the exercise of his option to terminate questioning he can control the time at which questioning occurs, the subjects discussed, and the duration of the interrogation. The requirement that law enforcement authorities must respect a person's exercise of that option counteracts the coercive pressures of the custodial setting. We therefore conclude that the admissibility of statements obtained after the person in custody has decided to remain silent depends under *Miranda* on whether his "right to cut off questioning" was "scrupulously honored."

The Court held that, under the facts of the case, the previous request not to talk to a different detective, from a different police bureau, about a different crime, did not extend to a second interrogation that was also preceded by warnings. Thus, the suspect who requests her right to silence is protected differently from the one who demands her right to counsel.

Does *Mosley* make sense now that the Court has decided *Edwards*? Mosley invoked a right of silence that the *Miranda* Court created as a prophylactic rule to protect the Fifth Amendment privilege. Edwards, on the other hand, invoked the *Miranda* right to counsel designed to protect the right to silence designed to protect the privilege, in essence a prophylaxis to protect a prophylaxis. Why is the *Edwards* double prophylaxis entitled to greater protection than the prophylaxis it was designed to protect? Professor Yale Kamisar has concluded that "either *Mosley* was wrongly decided or *Edwards* was." Yale Kamisar, *The Edwards and Bradshaw Cases: The Court Giveth and the Court Taketh Away*, in 5 The Supreme Court: Trends and Developments 153, 157 (J. Choper, Y. Kamisar, & L. Tribe, eds. 1984). Is Professor Kamisar right?

2. *Problems of initiation/waiver.* A plurality of the Court sought to explain "initiation" two years after *Edwards* in Oregon v. Bradshaw, 462 U.S. 1039, 103 S.Ct. 2830, 77 L.Ed.2d 405 (1983). Initiation occurs only when an inquiry from the suspect can "be fairly said to represent a desire on the part of an accused to open up a more generalized discussion relating directly or indirectly to the investigation." Asking for a drink of water or to use a telephone would not constitute initiation because they are "routine incidents of the custodial relationship."

A.   Police arrested *B* for a misdemeanor after *B* admitted minor involvement in an offense. At that point, *B* requested counsel, and the police terminated the conversation. Later, when *B* was being transferred from the police station to the jail, *B* asked, "Well, what is going to happen to me now?" The officer responded, "You do not have to talk to me. You have requested an attorney, and I don't want you talking to me unless you so desire because anything you say—because—since you have requested an attorney, you know, it has to be at your own free will." *B* said he understood. During the following conversation, the officer suggested that *B* might "help himself" by taking a polygraph examination. *B* agreed, took the test, was told that the test revealed he was not telling the truth, and he then confessed. What are the issues under *Edwards*, and how would you resolve them?

B. What if the officer had replied to *B*'s initial question by saying, "That's up to you. If you pass a polygraph test, it'll help your case." Then *B* agrees to take the polygraph and everything happens as above. How is this case different?

C. A uniformed police officer arrested *C* and provided warnings, to which he responded by clearly requesting counsel. Later, at the station and after the complaining witness identified *C*, a detective said that he needed to ask *C* some questions for the booking process. The detective said that he was not going to ask *C* about the crime because he knew *C* had invoked his right to counsel. *C* became upset and said he wasn't about to talk to a patrol officer about the crime but that he wanted to talk to a detective. The detective read *C* his rights again, and *C* waived and made a statement. Admissible? See Cross v. State, 144 S.W.3d 521 (Tex. Crim. App. 2004).

3. *How broad is the Edwards rule?* In their separate *Edwards* opinions, Chief Justice Burger and Justice Powell expressed concern that the majority opinion could be read to require a rigid prophylactic rule as a way of protecting the prophylactic rule of *Miranda*. This is precisely the way *Edwards* is now understood.

In Minnick v. Mississippi, 498 U.S. 146, 111 S.Ct. 486, 112 L.Ed.2d 489 (1990), Minnick told FBI agents, "Come back Monday when I have a lawyer." In the interim, Minnick consulted with his lawyer on two or three occasions. Police from another jurisdiction appeared, and the jailers told Minnick that he had to talk to them. The police advised him of his *Miranda* rights, and he declined to sign a waiver form. During the interview that followed, Minnick answered the police questions. The Court held that Minnick's statements were inadmissible. Under *Edwards-Minnick*, once a suspect invokes his right to counsel, the police may not reinitiate interrogation *in the absence of counsel*. Or, as Justice Scalia put it, in dissent, the Court "establishe[d] an irrebuttable presumption that a criminal suspect, after invoking his *Miranda* right to counsel, can *never* validly waive that right during any police-initiated encounter, even after the suspect has been provided multiple *Miranda* warnings and has actually consulted his attorney." Criticizing the *Minnick* irrebuttable presumption, Scalia wrote:

> That Minnick's original request to see an attorney had been honored, that Minnick had consulted with his attorney on several occasions, and that the attorney had specifically warned Minnick not to speak to the authorities, are irrelevant. * * * The confession must be suppressed, not because it was "compelled," nor even because it was obtained from an individual who could realistically be assumed to be unaware of his rights, but simply because this Court sees fit to prescribe as a "systemic assuranc[e]," that a person in custody who has once asked for counsel cannot thereafter be approached by the police unless counsel is present. Of course the Constitution's proscription of compelled testimony does not remotely authorize this incursion upon state practices; and even our recent precedents are not a valid excuse. * * *

> Today's extension of the *Edwards* prohibition is the latest stage of prophylaxis built upon prophylaxis, producing a veritable fairyland castle of imagined constitutional restriction upon law enforcement. This newest

tower, according to the Court, is needed to avoid "inconsisten[cy] with [the] purpose" of *Edwards'* prophylactic rule, which was needed to protect *Miranda*'s prophylactic right to have counsel present, which was needed to protect the right against *compelled self-incrimination* found (at last!) in the Constitution.

It seems obvious to me that, even in *Edwards* itself but surely in today's decision, we have gone far beyond any genuine concern about suspects who do not *know* their right to remain silent, or who have been *coerced* to abandon it. Both holdings are explicable, in my view, only as an effort to protect suspects against what is regarded as their own folly. The sharp-witted criminal would know better than to confess; why should the dull-witted suffer for his lack of mental endowment? Providing him an attorney at every stage where he might be induced or persuaded (though not coerced) to incriminate himself will even the odds. Apart from the fact that this protective enterprise is beyond our authority under the Fifth Amendment or any other provision of the Constitution, it is unwise. The procedural protections of the Constitution protect the guilty as well as the innocent, but it is not their objective to set the guilty free. That some clever criminals may employ those protections to their advantage is poor reason to allow criminals who have not done so to escape justice.

Do you agree with Justice Scalia? What is the purpose of counsel in the *Miranda* context, as contrasted with the Sixth Amendment? That is, why do you think the Court requires that a suspect who requests counsel be furnished with a lawyer during police interrogation?

Is there *any* limit to the *Edwards-Minnick* rule? Is there *any* way for the police to cure an admitted violation of the *Edwards-Minnick* rule?

4. *What the Court giveth with one hand* * * *. As we saw in the last Note, *Minnick* expanded *Edwards* by making clear that suspects who invoke the *Miranda* right to counsel can never be reapproached in the absence of counsel, but the effect of *Edwards* has been tempered by the Court's view that the request for counsel has to be unambiguous before *Edwards* applies. In Davis v. United States, 512 U.S. 452, 114 S.Ct. 2350, 129 L.Ed.2d 362 (1994), the suspect initially waived his right to remain silent and to a lawyer both orally and in writing.

> About an hour and a half into the interview, petitioner said, "Maybe I should talk to a lawyer." According to the uncontradicted testimony of one of the interviewing agents, the interview then proceeded as follows:
>
>> "[We m]ade it very clear that we're not here to violate his rights, that if he wants a lawyer, then we will stop any kind of questioning with him, that we weren't going to pursue the matter unless we have it clarified is he asking for a lawyer or is he just making a comment about a lawyer, and he said, [']No, I'm not asking for a lawyer,' and then he continued on, and said, 'No, I don't want a lawyer.'"

After a short break, the agents reminded petitioner of his rights to remain silent and to counsel. The interview then continued for another hour, until petitioner said, "I think I want a lawyer before I say anything else." At that point, questioning ceased.

The Court characterized Davis's argument that his statements be suppressed as an "invitation to extend *Edwards* and require law enforcement officers to cease questioning immediately upon the making of an ambiguous or equivocal reference to an attorney." It declined to accept the argument, holding instead that

> the suspect must unambiguously request counsel. As we have observed, "a statement either is such an assertion of the right to counsel or it is not." Although a suspect need not "speak with the discrimination of an Oxford don," he must articulate his desire to have counsel present sufficiently clearly that a reasonable police officer in the circumstances would understand the statement to be a request for an attorney. If the statement fails to meet the requisite level of clarity, *Edwards* does not require that the officers stop questioning the suspect.

Four members of the *Davis* Court concurred in the judgment in an opinion by Justice Souter, agreeing that on the facts of the case no violation of *Edwards* occurred, but challenging the majority's assertion that *Edwards* did not require clarifying questions when officers are faced with an ambiguous request for counsel.

> Indeed, it is easy, amidst the discussion of layers of protection, to lose sight of a real risk in the majority's approach, going close to the core of what the Court has held that the Fifth Amendment requires. * * * When a suspect understands his (expressed) wishes to have been ignored (and by hypothesis, he has said something that an objective listener could "reasonably," although not necessarily, take to be a request), in contravention of the "rights" just read to him by his interrogator, he may well see further objection as futile and confession (true or not) as the only way to end his interrogation. * * *

> The other justifications offered for the "requisite level of clarity" rule, are that, whatever its costs, it will further society's strong interest in "effective law enforcement," and maintain the "ease of application" that has long been a concern of our *Miranda* jurisprudence. With respect to the first point, the margin of difference between the clarification approach advocated here and the one the Court adopts is defined by the class of cases in which a suspect, if asked, would make it plain that he meant to request counsel (at which point questioning would cease). While these lost confessions do exact a real price from society, it is one that *Miranda* itself determined should be borne.

5. *The "woman" question.* Professor Janet Ainsworth wrote on the *Davis* (Note 4) issue prior to the Court's opinion, based on what the lower courts had done. In developing her critique of the soon-to-be *Davis* approach, she first noted that "incorporation of unconscious androcentric assumptions into legal doctrine" is a "general phenomenon within the law."

> * * * [S]ociolinguistic research on typical male and female speech patterns indicates that men tend to use direct and assertive language, whereas women more often adopt indirect and deferential speech patterns. Because majority legal doctrine governing a person's rights during police interrogation favors linguistic behavior more typical of men than of

women, asking the "woman question" reveals a hidden bias in this ostensibly gender-neutral doctrine.

The sociolinguistic evidence that women disproportionately adopt indirect speech patterns predicts that legal rules requiring the use of direct and unqualified language will adversely affect female defendants more often than male defendants. * * *

The detrimental consequences of interrogation law, however, are not limited to female defendants. Asking the "woman question" provokes related inquiry into whether legal doctrine may similarly fail to incorporate the experiences and perspectives of other marginalized groups. * * * [T]he available evidence demonstrates that there are a number of ethnic speech communities whose members habitually adopt a speech register including indirect and qualified modes of expression very much like those observed in typical female language use.

Even within communities whose speech is not characterized by indirect modes of expression, individual speakers who are socially or situationally powerless frequently adopt an indirect speech register. In fact, several prominent researchers have concluded that the use of this characteristically "female" speech style correlates better with powerlessness than with gender. The psychosocial dynamics of the police interrogation setting inherently involve an imbalance of power between the suspect, who is situationally powerless, and the interrogator, whose role entails the exercise of power. Such asymmetries of power in the interrogation session increase the likelihood that a particular suspect will adopt an indirect, and thus seemingly equivocal, mode of expression. This study, which begins by focusing on the disadvantages to women defendants of current invocation doctrine, ultimately has far-reaching implications for various other classes of speakers that do not share the linguistic norm of assertive and direct expression.

Janet E. Ainsworth, *The Pragmatics of Powerlessness in Police Interrogation*, 103 Yale L.J. 259, 262–264 (1993).

Which position on the *Davis* issue do you find persuasive?

6.   *Problems of invocation and waiver of the right to counsel or silence.*

A.   Officers arrest a suspect and place him in a squad car. An officer reads him his *Miranda* rights and asks if he understands them. He says that he does. The officer then reads a waiver form and asks him if he is willing to waive his rights. He responds: "Get the f—out of my face. I don't have nothing to say. I refuse to sign [the waiver form]." Is this invocation? See United States v. Banks, 78 F.3d 1190, 1196–98 (7th Cir. 1996).

B.   Police ask *B* to come to the station to discuss a "police matter." When he arrives, police tell him he is not under arrest and is free to leave at any time. "Great," he says. "But I want a lawyer anyway, and I want a lawyer now." Police ignore the request and ask *B* questions. He quickly answers in an incriminating way. Police allow him to leave but, of course, arrest him later. Are his answers admissible? See Burket v. Angelone, 208 F.3d 172, 198 (4th Cir. 2000).

C. Police want to question H about a forgery charge. Police provide *Miranda* warnings, and H executes a standard waiver form. Over the course of approximately three hours, H freely answers questions about the forgeries. Sometime during the interrogation, the detectives begin questioning H about a murder that had not until then been mentioned. At this point, he says: "I think I need a lawyer because if I tell everything I know, how do I know I'm not going to wind up with a complicity charge?" Invocation? See State v. Henness, 79 Ohio St.3d 53, 679 N.E.2d 686 (1997).

D. A is in police custody. Before police ask any questions, or provide warnings, A says, "maybe I should talk to an attorney by the name of William Evans." He showed the police Evans's business card. The police officer left the room. When he returned, he made no mention of Evans but gave *Miranda* warnings to A, who signed a written waiver and gave a statement. Admissible? See Abela v. Martin, 380 F.3d 915 (6th Cir. 2004).

E. Federal agents give D his *Miranda* warnings and he first signs a waiver but then requests counsel. At this point, the agents ask booking questions—age, birth date and place, address, height, weight, Social Security number. They also request a hair sample, telling him that if he refuses, they will get a court order. He agrees to permit the agents to take a hair sample at the local hospital. He then begins to talk about the crime and signs a second waiver. He talks more after which he requests a lawyer and falls silent. The agents sit in silence for a time. D begins to talk again and then confesses. Is any of what D said admissible? See United States v. Dougall, 919 F.2d 932 (5th Cir.1990). Hint: Don't forget that some evidence is not testimonial.

F. Police arrest G for murder and, after he receives his *Miranda* warnings, he requests a lawyer. He makes no incriminating statements and, the next day, is released on bail only to be arrested twelve days later for a burglary that happened after his release. After receiving warnings this time, he waived his rights and confessed to the murder. Is this statement admissible under *Minnick*? See Commonwealth v. Gregory, 263 Va. 134, 557 S.E.2d 715 (2002).

7. *A final problem: pulling together Butler, Edwards, and Mosley.* Police arrest H for a fire in the apartment of his girlfriend, Deb. She is dead but police do not initially reveal this fact. They give him warnings and he signs a waiver form. He admits seeing her the evening of the fire. The officers tell him that others in the apartment complex heard H and Deb in a heated argument that afternoon. H repeatedly tells police he does not know what they are talking to him about. After the officers finally tell H that Deb is dead, the following exchange occurs:

H: What are you saying here?

Detective: What are we saying? We're saying that you took Deb's life.

H: You're saying I killed Deb?

Detective: Absolutely. There's no doubt about that. OK? We know that. * * * We just need to know why you did that, OK? We know you did that. That's not even a question here, Kevin. Understand that? We know that. We talked to a bunch of people here and—and we—we put the evidence together at the scene and it clearly points to you. OK? So, we need to know why. What was your—?

H: You think I killed her?

Detective: Did you—did you kill her because you were upset with her? Did you kill her because—

H: You think I killed—

Detective: Kevin, it's not that we think that, we know that. We need to know why you did that. That's all, OK? Tha—it's no question as to did you do that. That's not a question here, Kevin, OK? So—

H: Can I have a drink of water and then lock me up—I think we really should have an attorney.

Detective: We'll get you a drink of water.

H: I don't want to talk anymore please. (Pause). This is—this is really wrong. This woman has scars all over her from this [other man.] He's callin' her 50 times a week.

Detective: 'Kay. If you want to talk to an attorney, you understand that we have to stop talking to you. OK? And—and then your side of this story will never be known. That's your choice. That's a choice you're making.

H: So, that means what?

Detective: That means we're gonna put this thing together and we're gonna convict you of murder.

H: Of murder?

Detective: Absolutely. Yup.

H: Convict me of murdering her?

The interrogation continued and *H* made numerous statements regarding his involvement in Deb's death.

Did *H* invoke the right to counsel? To silence? Did the police violate any aspect of *Miranda* or did the original waiver solve any *Miranda* problems? See State v. Hannon, 636 N.W.2d 796 (Minn. 2001).

G. A YEAR ON THE KILLING STREETS: THE BITTER FRUIT OF WAIVER

Journalist David Simon observed the Baltimore Homicide Division for a year (1988). In the excerpt that follows, Simon describes the interrogation practices and strategies that he saw. Be warned: what follows is "street real," including vulgar and obscene language.

DAVID SIMON—HOMICIDE, A YEAR ON THE KILLING STREETS
(1991) 193–207.

You are a citizen of a free nation, having lived your adult life in a land of guaranteed civil liberties, and you commit a crime of violence, whereupon you are jacked up, hauled down to a police station and deposited in a claustrophobic anteroom with three chairs, a table and no windows. There you sit for a half hour or so until a police detective—a man you have never met before, a man who can in no way be mistaken for a friend—enters the room with a thin stack of lined notepaper and a ball-point pen.

The detective offers a cigarette, not your brand, and begins an uninterrupted monologue that wanders back and forth for a half hour more, eventually coming to rest in a familiar place: *"You have the absolute right to remain silent."*

Of course you do. You're a criminal. Criminals always have the right to remain silent. At least once in your miserable life, you spent an hour in front of a television set, listening to this book-'em-Danno routine. You think Joe Friday was lying to you? You think Kojak was making this horseshit up? No way, bunk, we're talking sacred freedoms here, notably your Fifth Fucking Amendment protection against self-incrimination, and hey, it was good enough for Ollie North, so who are you to go incriminating yourself at the first opportunity? Get it straight: A police detective, a man who gets paid government money to put you in prison, is explaining your absolute right to shut up before you say something stupid.

"Anything you say or write may be used against you in a court of law."

Yo, bunky, wake the fuck up. You're now being told that talking to a police detective in an interrogation room can only hurt you. If it could help you, they would probably be pretty quick to say that, wouldn't they? They'd stand up and say you have the right not to worry because what you say or write in this godforsaken cubicle is gonna be used to your benefit in a court of law. No, your best bet is to shut up. Shut up now.

"You have the right to talk with a lawyer at any time—before any questioning, before answering any questions, or during any questions."

Talk about helpful. Now the man who wants to arrest you for violating the peace and dignity of the state is saying you can talk to a trained professional, an attorney who has read the relevant portions of the Maryland Annotated Code or can at least get his hands on some Cliffs Notes. And let's face it, pal, you just carved up a drunk in a Dundalk Avenue bar, but that don't make you a neurosurgeon. Take whatever help you can get.

"If you want a lawyer and cannot afford to hire one, you will not be asked any questions, and the court will be requested to appoint a lawyer for you."

Translation: You're a derelict. No charge for derelicts.

At this point, if all lobes are working, you ought to have seen enough of this Double Jeopardy category to know that it ain't where you want to be. How about a little something from Criminal Lawyers and Their Clients for $50, Alex?

Whoa, bunk, not so fast.

"Before we get started, lemme just get through the paperwork," says the detective, who now produces an Explanation of Rights sheet, BPD Form 69, and passes it across the table.

"EXPLANATION OF RIGHTS," declares the top line in bold block letters. The detective asks you to fill in your name, address, age, and education, then the date and time. That much accomplished, he asks you to read the next section. It begins, "YOU ARE HEREBY ADVISED THAT:"

Read number one, the detective says. Do you understand number one?

"You have the absolute right to remain silent."

Yeah, you understand. We did this already.

"Then write your initials next to number one. Now read number two."

And so forth, until you have initialed each component of the Miranda warning. That done, the detective tells you to write your signature on the next line, the one just below the sentence that says, "I HAVE READ THE ABOVE EXPLANATION OF MY RIGHTS AND FULLY UNDERSTAND IT."

You sign your name and the monologue resumes. The detective assures you that he has informed you of these rights because he wants you to be protected, because there is nothing that concerns him more than giving you every possible assistance in this very confusing and stressful moment in your life. If you don't want to talk, he tells you, that's fine. And if you want a lawyer, that's fine, too, because first of all, he's no relation to the guy you cut up, and second, he's gonna get six hours overtime no matter what you do. But he wants you to know—and he's been doing this a lot longer than you, so take his word for it—that your rights to remain silent and obtain qualified counsel aren't all they're cracked up to be.

Look at it this way, he says, leaning back in his chair. Once you up and call for that lawyer, son, we can't do a damn thing for you. No sir, your friends in the city homicide unit are going to have to leave you locked in this room all alone and the next authority figure to scan your case will be a tie-wearing, three-piece bloodsucker—a no-nonsense prosecutor from the Violent Crimes Unit with the official title of assistant state's attorney for the city of Baltimore. And God help you then, son, because a ruthless fucker like that will have an O'Donnell Heights motorhead like yourself halfway to the gas chamber before you get three words out. Now's the time to speak up, right now when I got my pen and paper here on the table, because once I walk out of this room any chance you have of telling your side of the story is gone and I gotta write it up the way it looks. And the way it looks right now is first-fucking-degree murder. Felony murder, mister, which when shoved up a man's asshole is a helluva lot more painful than second-degree or maybe even manslaughter. What you say right here and now could make the difference, bunk. Did I mention that Maryland has a gas chamber? Big, ugly sumbitch at the penitentiary on Eager Street, not twenty blocks from here. You don't wanna get too close to that bad boy, lemme tell you.

A small, wavering sound of protest passes your lips and the detective leans back in his chair, shaking his head sadly.

What the hell is wrong with you, son? You think I'm fucking with you? Hey, I don't even need to bother with your weak shit. I got three witnesses in three other rooms who say you're my man. I got a knife from the scene that's going downstairs to the lab for latent prints. I got blood spatter on them Air Jordans we took off you ten minutes ago. Why the fuck do you think we took 'em? Do I look like I wear high-top tennis? Fuck no. You got spatter all over 'em, and I think we both know whose blood type it's gonna be. Hey, bunk, I'm only in here to make sure that there ain't nothing you can say for yourself before I write it all up.

You hesitate.

Oh, says the detective. You want to think about it. Hey, you think about it all you want, pal. My captain's right outside in the hallway, and he already told me to charge your ass in the first fuckin' degree. For once in your beshitted little life someone is giving you a chance and you're too fucking dumb to take it. What the fuck, you go ahead and think about it and I'll tell my captain to cool his heels for ten minutes. I can do that much for you. How 'bout some coffee? Another cigarette?

The detective leaves you alone in that cramped, windowless room. Just you and the blank notepaper and the Form 69 and * * * first-degree murder. First-degree murder with witnesses and fingerprints and blood on your Air Jordans. Christ, you didn't even notice the blood on your own fucking shoes. Felony murder, mister. First-fucking-degree. How many years, you begin to wonder, how many years do I get for involuntary manslaughter?

Whereupon the man who wants to put you in prison, the man who is not your friend, comes back in the room, asking if the coffee's okay.

Yeah, you say, the coffee's fine, but what happens if I want a lawyer?

The detective shrugs. Then we get you a lawyer, he says. And I walk out of the room and type up the charging documents for first-degree murder and you can't say a fucking thing about it. Look, bunk, I'm giving you a chance. He came at you, right? You were scared. It was self-defense.

Your mouth opens to speak.

He came at you, didn't he?

"Yeah," you venture cautiously, "he came at me."

Whoa, says the detective, holding up his hands. Wait a minute. If we're gonna do this, I gotta find your rights form. Where's the fucking form? Damn things are like cops, never around when you need 'em. Here it is, he says, pushing the explanation-of-rights sheet across the table and pointing to the bottom. Read that, he says.

"I am willing to answer questions and I do not want any attorney at this time. My decision to answer questions without having an attorney present is free and voluntary on my part."

As you read, he leaves the room and returns a moment later with a second detective as a witness. You sign the bottom of the form, as do both detectives.

The first detective looks up from the form, his eyes soaked with innocence. "He came at you, huh?"

"Yeah, he came at me."

Get used to small rooms, bunk, because you are about to be drop-kicked into the lost land of pretrial detention. Because it's one thing to be a murdering little asshole from Southeast Baltimore, and it's another to be stupid about it, and with five little words you have just elevated yourself to the ranks of the truly witless.

End of the road, pal. It's over. It's history. And if that police detective wasn't so busy committing your weak bullshit to paper, he'd probably look you in the eye and tell you so. He'd give you another cigarette and say, son, you are ignorance personified and you just put yourself in for the fatal stabbing of a human being. He might even tell you that the other witnesses in the other rooms are too drunk to identify their own reflections, much less the kid who had the knife, or that it's always a long shot for the lab to pull a latent off a knife hilt, or that your $95 sneakers are as clean as the day you bought them. If he was feeling particularly expansive, he might tell you that everyone who leaves the homicide unit in handcuffs does so charged with first-degree murder, that it's for the lawyers to decide what kind of deal will be cut. He might go on to say that even after all these years working homicides, there is still a small part of him that finds it completely mystifying that anyone ever utters a single word in a police interrogation. To illustrate the point, he could hold up your Form 69, on which you waived away every last one of your rights, and say, "Lookit here, pistonhead, I told you twice that you were deep in the shit and that whatever you said could put you in deeper." And if his message was still somehow beyond your understanding, he could drag your carcass back down the sixth-floor hallway, back toward the sign that says Homicide Unit in white block letters, the sign you saw when you walked off the elevator.

Now think hard: Who lives in a homicide unit? Yeah, right. And what do homicide detectives do for a living? Yeah, you got it, bunk. And what did you do tonight? You murdered someone.

So when you opened that mouth of yours, what the fuck were you thinking?

Homicide detectives in Baltimore like to imagine a small, open window at the top of the long wall in the large interrogation room. More to the point, they like to imagine their suspects imagining a small, open window at the top of the long wall. The open window is the escape hatch, the Out. It is the perfect representation of what every suspect believes when he opens his mouth during an interrogation. Every last one envisions himself parrying questions with the right combination of alibi and excuse; every last one sees himself coming up with the right words, then crawling out the window to go home and sleep in his own bed. More often than not, a guilty man is looking for the Out from his first moments in the interrogation room; in that sense, the window is as much the suspect's fantasy as the detective's mirage.

The effect of the illusion is profound, distorting as it does the natural hostility between hunter and hunted, transforming it until it resembles a relationship more symbiotic than adversarial. That is the lie, and when the roles are perfectly performed, deceit surpasses itself, becoming manipulation on a grand scale and ultimately an act of betrayal. Because what occurs in an interrogation room is indeed little more than a carefully staged drama, a choreographed performance that allows a detective and his suspect to find common ground where none exists. There, in a carefully controlled purgatory, the guilty proclaim their malefactions, though rarely in any form that allows for contrition or resembles an unequivocal admission. * * *

Once the minefield that is Miranda has been successfully negotiated, the detective must let the suspect know that his guilt is certain and easily established by the existing evidence. He must then offer the Out.

This, too, is role playing, and it requires a seasoned actor. If a witness or suspect is belligerent, you wear him down with greater belligerence. If the man shows fear, you offer calm and comfort. When he looks weak, you appear strong. When he wants a friend, you crack a joke and offer to buy him a soda. If he's confident, you are more so, assuring him that you are certain of his guilt and are curious only about a few select details of the crime. And if he's arrogant, if he wants nothing to do with the process, you intimidate him, threaten him, make him believe that making you happy may be the only thing between his ass and the Baltimore City Jail.

Kill your woman and a good detective will come to real tears as he touches your shoulder and tells you how he knows that you must have loved her, that it wouldn't be so hard for you to talk about if you didn't. Beat your child to death and a police detective will wrap his arm around you in the interrogation room, telling you about how he beats his own children all the time, how it wasn't your fault if the kid up and died on you. Shoot a friend over a poker hand and that same detective will lie about your dead buddy's condition, telling you that the victim is in stable condition at Hopkins and probably won't press charges, which wouldn't amount to more than assault with intent even if he does. Murder a man with an accomplice and the detective will walk your co-conspirator past the open door of your interrogation room, then say your bunky's going home tonight because he gave a statement making you the triggerman.

And if that same detective thinks you can be bluffed, he might tell you that they've got your prints on the weapon, or that there are two eyewitnesses who have picked your photo from an array, or that the victim made a dying declaration in which he named you as his assailant.

All of which is street legal. Reasonable deception, the courts call it. After all, what could be more reasonable than deceiving someone who has taken a human life and is now lying about it?

The deception sometimes goes too far, or at least it sometimes seems that way to those unfamiliar with the process. Not long ago, several veteran homicide detectives in Detroit were publicly upbraided and disciplined by their superiors for using the office Xerox machine as a polygraph device. It seems that the detectives, when confronted with a statement of dubious veracity, would sometimes adjourn to the Xerox room and load three sheets of paper into the feeder.

"Truth," said the first.

"Truth," said the second.

"Lie," said the third.

Then the suspect would be led into the room and told to put his hand against the side of the machine. The detectives would ask the man's name, listen to the answer, then hit the copy button.

Truth.

And where do you live?

Truth again.

And did you or did you not kill Tater, shooting him down like a dog in the 1200 block of North Durham Street?

Lie. Well, well: You lying motherfucker.

In Baltimore, the homicide detectives read newspaper accounts of the Detroit controversy and wondered why anyone had a problem. Polygraph by copier was an old trick; it had been attempted on more than one occasion in the sixth-floor Xerox room. * * *

Variations on the theme are limited only by a detective's imagination and his ability to sustain the fraud. But every bluff carries a corresponding risk, and a detective who tells a suspect his fingerprints are all over a crime scene loses all hope if the man knows he was wearing gloves. An interrogation room fraud is only as good as the material from which it was constructed—or, for that matter, as good as the suspect is witless—and a detective who underestimates his prey or overestimates his knowledge of the crime will lose precious credibility. Once a detective claims knowledge of a fact that the suspect knows to be untrue, the veil has been lifted, and the investigator is instead revealed as the liar. * * *

* * * [T]here can be no mistaking that critical moment, that light that shines from the other end of the tunnel when a guilty man is about to give it up. Later, after he's initialed each page and is alone again in the

cubicle, there will be only exhaustion and, in some cases, depression. If he gets to brooding, there might even be a suicide attempt.

But that is epilogue. The emotive crest of a guilty man's performance comes in those cold moments before he opens his mouth and reaches for the Out. Just before a man gives up life and liberty in an interrogation room, his body acknowledges the defeat: His eyes are glazed, his jaw is slack, his body lists against the nearest wall or table edge. Some put their heads against the tabletop to steady themselves. Some become physically sick, holding their stomachs as if the problem were digestive: a few actually vomit.

At that critical moment, the detectives tell their suspects that they really are sick—sick of lying, sick of hiding. They tell them it's time to turn over a new leaf, that they'll only begin to feel better when they start to tell the truth. Amazingly enough, many of them actually believe it. As they reach for the ledge of that high window, they believe every last word of it.

"He came at you, right?"

"Yeah, he came at me."

The Out leads in.

NOTES AND QUESTIONS

1. Was the suspect in the Simon excerpt treated fairly by the Baltimore detectives? Does it matter? Are you sympathetic to the suspect or did you find yourself hoping that the police would obtain a confession? Is the outcome just?

Simon's book gave rise to a television show named Homicide. For a riveting fictional account of a police interrogation, see the episode from the show's first season called "Three Men and Adena." Unlike the case in most TV police shows, the viewer *never knows* whether the suspect is guilty. Thus, the viewer is placed in the position of the interrogating officers, which makes the characters seem more real and less like actors.

2. Assuming the facts in the Simon excerpt can be proved, do you see a *Miranda* violation?

3. Even if the Simon excerpt shows a *Miranda* violation, it seems pretty clear that courts give police a substantial amount of room to trick suspects *after* they waive *Miranda*. Consider the following set of facts: J, a murder suspect, waived *Miranda* and was interviewed for three hours and released; the next day, again waiving *Miranda*, he was questioned and told that the clothes he wore the day of the murder were stained with blood, and that tracks made by his tennis shoes were found at the scene of the crime. Both statements were false. J did not confess. Ten days later, J voluntarily came to the police station and waived *Miranda*; he was shown a bloody fingerprint on a knife. The police said that the print on the knife was J's and that an eyewitness could identify J leaving the murdered woman's apartment carrying a knife. Both statements were false. In addition, the officers said that if J denied what he had done, they would "go into court and testify that he was a

black man out there viciously raping and killing white women." *J* confessed. Is it admissible under *Miranda*? Was it coerced under the due process clause? Should it matter that the case occurs in a Southern state? See State v. Jackson, 308 N.C. 549, 304 S.E.2d 134 (1983).

4. *Problems.* A. *P*, a murder suspect, was arrested and held for nineteen hours before police questioned him. During this period, police obtained information about the victim and the crime scene. Ten minutes into the interrogation, *P* waived his *Miranda* rights in writing. When told that he was suspected of the murder, he gave an alibi. Police then told him that they had spoken to an eyewitness. When *P* said nothing, police played an audiotape in which one police officer pretended to be an eyewitness being questioned by an officer. At one point the "eyewitness" identifies a picture of *P*. "Immediately after the investigators played the audiotape, defendant asked: 'Who was that motherfucker?' Defendant then confessed to murdering Hoke and agreed to give a taped statement." Admissible? See State v. Patton, 362 N.J.Super. 16, 826 A.2d 783 (2003). See also Commonwealth v. DiGiambattista, 442 Mass. 423, 813 N.E.2d 516 (Sup. Jud. Ct. 2004).

B. Police question *W* about her husband's murder. She waives her *Miranda* rights in writing, using a pen police provide. The pen has a powder on it that makes her hands glow under a certain light. They then tell her that the glow is gunpowder residue from killing her husband. After interviewing her off and on over the next eighteen hours, police secure two incriminating statements. Admissible? See Whittington v. State, 147 Md.App. 496, 809 A.2d 721 (2002). See also Sheriff v. Bessey, 112 Nev. 322, 914 P.2d 618 (1996); Arthur v. Commonwealth, 24 Va.App. 102, 480 S.E.2d 749 (1997).

C. The police suspect *C* of sexually assaulting and smothering his five-year-old niece. After an "extensive interview," police did not think that they had sufficient evidence with which to charge him. With the knowledge of the state attorney's office, the police fabricated two scientific reports that they used as ploys in interrogating the defendant. One false report was prepared on stationery of the Florida Department of Criminal Law Enforcement; another was prepared on stationery of Life Codes, Inc., a testing organization. These false reports indicated that a scientific test established that the semen stains on the victim's underwear came from the defendant. The police showed the reports to the defendant after he had formally waived his *Miranda* rights. He confessed. Admissible? See State v. Cayward, 552 So.2d 971 (Fla. App. 1989).

5. Professor Richard Leo's observational study of 182 police interrogations in 1992–93 is a gold mine of information. Richard A. Leo, *Inside the Interrogation Room*, 86 J. Crim. L. & Criminology 266 (1996). One conclusion was that 78% of suspects waived their *Miranda* rights. Perhaps this finding does not surprise you after reading Simon. We should be careful, however, about generalizing from the Simon excerpt. Some police probably view these techniques as objectionable. Even police who are willing to use the Simon techniques are probably not willing to spend the time to use them in very many cases. The crime under investigation in the excerpt, after all, was murder. Less serious cases, such as larceny and car theft, would not likely be seen as worth the time to engage in elaborate trickery and deception. FBI

data for the year 2000 show nationwide arrests for homicide totaled roughly 13,000 while arrests for burglary, larceny, and car theft totaled 1,500,000. 2000 FBI Uniform Crime Statistics, tbl. 29. If few interrogations in the latter category involve trickery and deception of the type Simon describes, and 78% of suspects still waive their *Miranda* rights, what might the reasons be?

6. *Suspects as thermometers?* Do you think the *Miranda* Court wanted to regulate police interrogation? The Court made a point to say that a suspect can invoke either the right to counsel or the right to remain silent at any time during interrogation. It seems likely that the Court thought a fair number of suspects would serve as "thermometers"—willing to talk until the discussion got too hot, at which point they would invoke and cause the interrogation to cease. A self-regulating procedure might have appealed to a Court that had struggled for decades trying to find a way to regulate police interrogation through judicial doctrine.

But as Professor William Stuntz has pointed out, if *Miranda* is to succeed as a self-regulating procedure, suspects must be generally willing to cut off questioning when it becomes too oppressive. William J. Stuntz, *Miranda's Mistake*, 99 Mich. L. Rev. 975 (2001). Two studies of police interrogation in the 1990s failed to find an appreciable number of that kind of suspect. A few suspects invoke their rights at the beginning, and many more waive their rights, but almost no one invokes in the midst of the interrogation. See Paul G. Cassell & Bret S. Hayman, *Police Interrogation in the 1990s: An Empirical Study of the Effects of Miranda*, 43 UCLA L. Rev. 839 (1996); Richard A. Leo, *Inside the Interrogation Room*, 86 J. Crim. L. & Criminology 266 (1996).

As Stuntz puts it:

> One of two things is true: Either there is a significant amount of abusive police questioning, or there isn't. If there is, *Miranda* is a failure; it does not protect the suspects who need protecting. If there isn't, *Miranda* is pointless—it gives a few Silent Types [those who invoke prior to interrogation] a very valuable entitlement, but to no good end. Either way, *Miranda* accomplishes nothing save distributive perversity. After thirty-five years, we can be reasonably confident of this much: Suspects cannot regulate police interrogation. The law of police interrogation is broken, and needs fixing.

Stuntz, *supra*, at 991–92.

But perhaps the Court did not care whether *Miranda* regulated interrogation. Perhaps, as Professor Lawrence Rosenthal provocatively argues, all "that *Miranda* expects of suspects is that they will knowingly and intelligently decide whether to waive their Fifth Amendment rights, and under settled waiver principles, suspects facing interrogation are perfectly competent to engage in such 'sorting.' " After all, the due process clause is still available to regulate abusive interrogation. See Lawrence Rosenthal, *Against Orthodoxy Miranda Is Not Prophylactic and the Constitution Is Not Perfect,* 10 Chapman L. Rev. 579, 604 (2007).

7. *Does Miranda help the police?* Is it possible that *Miranda* has helped police and prosecutors in obtaining statements? Empirical evidence indicates that the police almost always provide *Miranda* warnings. See the studies cited

in Note 6. This suggests that police do not view *Miranda* as a particularly difficult burden. Moreover, because the police almost always obtain waivers in cases where suspects incriminate themselves, the prosecutor comes to court with an oral or written waiver of the right not to be interrogated. This creates a pretty strong presumption that the suspect *wanted* to talk to the police. The waiver not only virtually guarantees that a court will find no *Miranda* violation, but also may reduce the willingness of courts to inquire into the coerciveness of the police interrogation that follows waiver. If *Miranda* has helped police and prosecutors more than defendants, it would be a remarkable irony.

> Charles Weisselberg presses deeper than irony, nothing that

> if *Miranda*'s system of warnings and waivers is not effective in protecting the Fifth Amendment privilege for many suspects, this wholesale displacement of the voluntariness doctrine is a sleight-of-hand; it is bottomed on a falsehood. I am not against warnings and waivers per se, just the assumed effect of them. For me, the main problem with *Miranda* is the judiciary's unjustified confidence in *Miranda*'s safeguards. There is an almost religious belief that the warnings and waivers actually work, and an apparent deafness to claims that they do not. I am not the first to observe that *Miranda* can be an obstacle to the more important assessment of voluntariness; Professor Alfredo Garcia has made the point with particular force. I once was a proponent of *Miranda*, but I now believe that its critics are right.

Charles D. Weisselberg, *Mourning Miranda*, 96 Cal. L. Rev. 1519, 1595–96 (2008). The provocative Garcia article to which Weisselberg refers is Alfredo Garcia, *Is Miranda Dead, Was It Overruled, or Is It Irrelevant?*, 10 St. Thomas L. Rev. 461 (1988).

8. *Hoax?* One scholar puts his criticism of *Miranda* more simply: "*Miranda v. Arizona* is a hoax." Christopher Slobogin, *Toward Taping*, 1 Ohio St. J. Crim. L. 309, 309 (2003).

9. *Mourning Miranda.* Charles Weisselberg offers the following sad farewell to *Miranda*:

> *Miranda* launched a forty-year experiment in reforming police practices. I think the Court was right to try; sometimes there can be no progress without experimentation. Now, four decades later, we know that a set of bright-line rules is not a panacea for the issues endemic in police interrogation. I mourn the passing of *Miranda*. I deeply regret that the justices' ambitions and expectations were not met. However, I think that the best way to mourn the loss is to learn from the experiment called *Miranda*, acknowledge its failures, and move forward.

Weisselberg, supra Note 7, at 1599–1600.

CHAPTER 8

POLICE INTERROGATION: THE SIXTH AMENDMENT RIGHT TO COUNSEL

■ ■ ■

A. ELICITING STATEMENTS IN THE ABSENCE OF COUNSEL

MASSIAH v. UNITED STATES

Supreme Court of the United States, 1964.
377 U.S. 201, 84 S.Ct. 1199, 12 L.Ed.2d 246.

MR. JUSTICE STEWART delivered the opinion of the Court.

The petitioner was indicted for violating the federal narcotics laws. He retained a lawyer, pleaded not guilty, and was released on bail. * * *

A few days later, and quite without the petitioner's knowledge, [co-defendant] Colson decided to cooperate with the government agents in their continuing investigation of the narcotics activities in which the petitioner, Colson, and others had allegedly been engaged. Colson permitted an agent named Murphy to install a Schmidt radio transmitter under the front seat of Colson's automobile, by means of which Murphy, equipped with an appropriate receiving device, could overhear from some distance away conversations carried on in Colson's car.

On the evening of November 19, 1959, Colson and the petitioner held a lengthy conversation while sitting in Colson's automobile, parked on a New York street. By prearrangement with Colson, and totally unbeknown to the petitioner, the agent Murphy sat in a car parked out of sight down the street and listened over the radio to the entire conversation. The petitioner made several incriminating statements during the course of this conversation. At the petitioner's trial these incriminating statements were brought before the jury through Murphy's testimony, despite the insistent objection of defense counsel. The jury convicted the petitioner of several related narcotics offenses, and the convictions were affirmed by the Court of Appeals.

The petitioner argues that it was an error of constitutional dimensions to permit the agent Murphy at the trial to testify to the petitioner's incriminating statements which Murphy had overheard under the circumstances disclosed by this record. This argument is based upon two distinct and independent grounds. [The Court did not reach the Fourth Amendment argument.] Secondly, it is said that the petitioner's Fifth and Sixth Amendment rights were violated by the use in evidence against him of incriminating statements which government agents had deliberately elicited from him after he had been indicted and in the absence of his retained counsel. * * *

In *Spano v. New York* [p. 555], this Court reversed a state criminal conviction because a confession had been wrongly admitted into evidence against the defendant at his trial. In that case the defendant had already been indicted for first-degree murder at the time he confessed. The Court held that the defendant's conviction could not stand under the Fourteenth Amendment. While the Court's opinion relied upon the totality of the circumstances under which the confession had been obtained, four concurring Justices pointed out that the Constitution required reversal of the conviction upon the sole and specific ground that the confession had been deliberately elicited by the police after the defendant had been indicted, and therefore at a time when he was clearly entitled to a lawyer's help. It was pointed out that under our system of justice the most elemental concepts of due process of law contemplate that an indictment be followed by a trial, "in an orderly courtroom, presided over by a judge, open to the public, and protected by all the procedural safeguards of the law." It was said that a Constitution which guarantees a defendant the aid of counsel at such a trial could surely vouchsafe no less to an indicted defendant under interrogation by the police in a completely extrajudicial proceeding. Anything less, it was said, might deny a defendant "effective representation by counsel at the only stage when legal aid and advice would help him." * * *

This view no more than reflects a constitutional principle established as long ago as *Powell v. Alabama* [p. 13] where the Court noted that " * * * during perhaps the most critical period of the proceedings * * * that is to say, from the time of their arraignment until the beginning of their trial, when consultation, thorough-going investigation and preparation [are] vitally important, the defendants * * * [are] as much entitled to such aid [of counsel] during that period as at the trial itself." * * *

Here we deal not with a state court conviction, but with a federal case, where the specific guarantee of the Sixth Amendment directly applies. We hold that the petitioner was denied the basic protections of that guarantee when there was used against him at his trial evidence of his own incriminating words, which federal agents had deliberately elicited from him after he had been indicted and in the absence of his counsel. It is true that in the *Spano* case the defendant was interrogated in a police station, while here the damaging testimony was elicited from the defendant without his knowledge while he was free on bail. But, as Judge Hays pointed out in his dissent in the Court of Appeals, "if such a rule is to have any efficacy it must apply to indirect and surreptitious interrogations as well as those conducted in the jailhouse. In this case, Massiah was more seriously imposed upon * * * because he did not even know that he was under interrogation by a government agent.''

* * * We do not question that in this case, as in many cases, it was entirely proper to continue an investigation of the suspected criminal activities of the defendant and his alleged confederates, even though the defendant had already been indicted. All that we hold is that the defendant's own incriminating statements, obtained by federal agents under the circumstances here disclosed, could not constitutionally be used by the prosecution as evidence against *him* at his trial. * * *

Mr. Justice WHITE, with whom Mr. Justice CLARK and Mr. Justice HARLAN join, dissenting. * * *

It is * * * a rather portentous occasion when a constitutional rule is established barring the use of evidence which is relevant, reliable and highly probative of the issue which the trial court has before it—whether the accused committed the act with which he is charged. Without the evidence, the quest for truth may be seriously impeded and in many cases the trial court, although aware of proof showing defendant's guilt, must nevertheless release him because the crucial evidence is deemed inadmissible. This result is entirely justified in some circumstances because exclusion serves other policies of overriding importance, as where evidence seized in an illegal search is excluded, not because of the quality of the proof, but to secure meaningful enforcement of the Fourth Amendment. But this only emphasizes that the soundest of reasons is necessary to warrant the exclusion of evidence otherwise admissible and the creation of another area of privileged testimony. With all due deference, I am not at all convinced that the additional barriers to the pursuit of truth which the Court today erects rest on anything like the solid foundations which decisions of this gravity should require. * * *

Whatever the content or scope of the rule may prove to be, I am unable to see how this case presents an unconstitutional interference with Massiah's right to counsel. Massiah was not prevented from consulting with counsel as often as he wished. No meetings with counsel were disturbed or spied upon. Preparation for trial was in no way obstructed. It is only a sterile syllogism—an unsound one, besides—to say that because Massiah had a right to counsel's aid before and during the trial, his out-of-court conversations and admissions must be excluded if obtained without counsel's consent or presence. The right to counsel has never meant as much before, and its extension in this case requires some further explanation, so far unarticulated by the Court. * * *

Applying the new exclusionary rule is peculiarly inappropriate in this case. At the time of the conversation in question, petitioner was not in custody but free on bail. He was not questioned in what anyone could call an atmosphere of official coercion. What he said was said to his partner in crime who had also been indicted. There was no suggestion or any possibility of coercion. What petitioner did not know was that Colson had decided to report the conversation to the police. Had there been no prior arrangements between Colson and the police, had Colson simply gone to the police after the conversation had occurred, his testimony relating Massiah's statements would be readily admissible at the trial, as would a recording which he might have made of the conversation. In such event, it would simply be said that Massiah risked talking to a friend who decided to disclose what he knew of Massiah's criminal activities. But if, as occurred here, Colson had been cooperating with the police prior to his meeting with Massiah, both his evidence and the recorded conversation are somehow transformed into inadmissible evidence despite the fact that the hazard to Massiah remains precisely the same—the defection of a confederate in crime. * * *

* * * It is one thing to establish safeguards against procedures fraught with the potentiality of coercion and to outlaw "easy but self-defeating ways in which brutality is substituted for brains as an instrument of crime detection." But here there was no substitution of brutality for brains, no inherent danger of police coercion justifying the prophylactic effect of another exclusionary rule. Massiah was not being interrogated in a police station, was not surrounded by numerous officers or questioned in relays, and was not forbidden access to others. Law enforcement may have the elements of a contest about it, but it is not a game. Massiah and those like him receive ample protection from the long line of precedents in this Court holding that confessions may not be introduced unless they are voluntary. In making these determinations the courts must consider the absence of counsel as one of several factors by which voluntariness is to be judged. This is a wiser rule than the automatic rule announced by the Court, which requires courts and juries to disregard voluntary admissions which they might well find to be the best possible evidence in discharging their responsibility for ascertaining truth.

NOTES AND QUESTIONS

1. Justice White's dissent characterized the *Massiah* rationale as a "thinly disguised constitutional policy of minimizing or entirely prohibiting the use in evidence of voluntary out-of-court admissions and confessions made by the accused." As we have seen, the Court would soon apply this policy with a vengeance in *Miranda* by giving all suspects the right to remain silent and the right to counsel. Predictably, Justice White dissented in *Miranda* as well.

2. In the mid-eighteenth century, the role of defense counsel was minimal. In one sample of New Jersey cases from 1749–57, roughly half of the defendants represented themselves, presenting evidence as best they could. But even when lawyers appeared for defendants, their role appeared to be summing up at the end of the trial by making any points of law that might be helpful. This is consistent with English law that prohibited lawyers in felony cases from presenting the defendant's case, though lawyers could debate "points of law." In one New Jersey case, the judge appointed counsel but apparently not until after the defendant had already presented her case; the

lawyer's job presumably was to sum up the case and argue points of law (she lost and was sentenced to hang). See George C. Thomas III, *Colonial Criminal Law and Procedure: The Royal Colony of New Jersey 1749–57*, 1 N.Y.U. J. L. & Liberty 671, 687–88 (2005).

Assuming that this was the model the Framers had in mind when they guaranteed the "assistance of counsel" for defendants, was it illegitimate for the *Massiah* Court to radically expand the meaning of assistance of counsel? Inappropriate? The wrong road taken?

3.   Think back to what constituted a valid waiver of *Miranda*. Using that test, do you think Massiah could have waived his right to counsel? Turning the question around, what purpose would Massiah's lawyer have served if he had been in the car with Massiah and Colson? If you don't like what the Government did in this case, what *precisely* is it that you think was improper?

Deliberate Elicitation: The Doctrine Evolves

In *Massiah*, the State was actively seeking to elicit statements from the accused in the absence of counsel. But the Court has decided two cases in which this was not so clear. In United States v. Henry, 447 U.S. 264, 100 S.Ct. 2183, 65 L.Ed.2d 115 (1980), Henry was indicted for bank robbery and held in jail. The government agents working on the robbery contacted Nichols, an inmate at the same jail as Henry, who "had been engaged to provide confidential information to the Federal Bureau of Investigation as a paid informant. * * * Nichols informed the agent that he was housed in the same cellblock with several federal prisoners awaiting trial, including Henry." Nichols testified at trial that Henry told him about the robbery.

As Henry had been indicted, he was in the same position as Massiah with regard to his right to counsel. But had Nichols deliberately elicited the admissions from Henry? Here is what the government agent said in his affidavit concerning the instructions given Nichols:

> "I recall telling Nichols at this time to be alert to any statements made by these individuals [the federal prisoners] regarding the charges against them. I specifically recall telling Nichols that he was not to question Henry or these individuals about the charges against them, however, if they engaged him in conversation or talked in front of him, he was requested to pay attention to their statements. I recall telling Nichols not to initiate any conversations with Henry regarding the bank robbery charges against Henry, but that if Henry initiated the conversations with Nichols, I requested Nichols to pay attention to the information furnished by Henry."

Was this "deliberate elicitation"? In an opinion by Chief Justice Burger, the Court held that it was. The Court reasoned that "[e]ven if the agent's statement that he did not intend that Nichols would take affirmative steps to secure incriminating information is accepted, he must have known that such propinquity likely would lead to that result." Moreover, the Court noted that "[i]n *Massiah*, no inquiry was made as to whether

Massiah or his codefendant first raised the subject of the crime under investigation."

True enough but the *Massiah* Court concluded that the agents had "deliberately elicited" statements from Massiah. Could the same be said in *Henry*? It seems that the Court in *Henry* was rejecting a narrow meaning of "deliberate elicitation." *Henry* seems to stand for the proposition that "deliberate elicitation" means "deliberately put an agent in a situation where it is likely that he will hear incriminating statements." Perhaps there is no Sixth Amendment distinction between intending to elicit statements and intending to put an agent in a position where he was likely to obtain statements.

The reason to treat those two situations alike, as *Massiah* noted, is that suspects like Henry and Massiah are "more seriously imposed upon because he did not know that his codefendant was a Government agent." This, of course, is because "[a]n accused speaking to a known Government agent is typically aware that his statements may be used against him," but not when "the accused is in the company of a fellow inmate who is acting by prearrangement as a Government agent."

But if *Henry* broadened the standard to include deliberately placing jail plants in the cell with the accused, its future is a bit uncertain after Kuhlmann v. Wilson, 477 U.S. 436, 106 S.Ct. 2616, 91 L.Ed.2d 364 (1986). In *Kuhlmann*, respondent was arraigned on charges arising from a robbery and murder.

> Before respondent arrived in the jail, [a prisoner named] Lee had entered into an arrangement with Detective Cullen, according to which Lee agreed to listen to respondent's conversations and report his remarks to Cullen. Since the police had positive evidence of respondent's participation, the purpose of placing Lee in the cell was to determine the identities of respondent's confederates. Cullen instructed Lee not to ask respondent any questions, but simply to "keep his ears open" for the names of the other perpetrators. Respondent first spoke to Lee about the crimes after he looked out the cellblock window at the Star Taxicab Garage, where the crimes had occurred. Respondent said, "someone's messing with me," and began talking to Lee about the robbery, narrating the same story that he had given the police at the time of his arrest. Lee advised respondent that this explanation "didn't sound too good," but respondent did not alter his story. Over the next few days, however, respondent changed details of his original account. Respondent then received a visit from his brother, who mentioned that members of his family were upset because they believed that respondent had murdered the dispatcher. After the visit, respondent again described the crimes to Lee. Respondent now admitted that he and two other men, whom he never identified, had planned and carried out the robbery, and had murdered the dispatcher. Lee informed Cullen of respondent's statements and furnished

Cullen with notes that he had written surreptitiously while sharing the cell with respondent.

The Court held that this situation was not covered by *Massiah*. Making almost no effort to distinguish *Henry*, the Court noted that

> the primary concern of the *Massiah* line of decisions is secret interrogation by investigatory techniques that are the equivalent of direct police interrogation. Since "the Sixth Amendment is not violated whenever—by luck or happenstance—the State obtains incriminating statements from the accused after the right to counsel has attached," a defendant does not make out a violation of that right simply by showing that an informant, either through prior arrangement or voluntarily, reported his incriminating statements to the police. Rather, the defendant must demonstrate that the police and their informant took some action, beyond merely listening, that was designed deliberately to elicit incriminating remarks.

NOTES AND QUESTIONS

1.   Can you distinguish the facts in *Kuhlmann* from those in *Henry*?

2.   *Trying to crack a meth ring.* Here are the facts in United States v. Johnson, 338 F.3d 918 (8th Cir. 2003):

> In 1993, a grand jury indicted Dustin Honken for conspiracy to distribute methamphetamine. A witness who was to testify against him disappeared, as did the witness's girlfriend and her two young daughters. Later, another witness in the case vanished. By March of 1995, the government was forced to abandon its case against Mr. Honken because of a dearth of witnesses to testify against him. However, the government continued its investigation. Angela Johnson, Mr. Honken's girlfriend at the time of the disappearances, was indicted in July of 2000 for aiding and abetting the murder of the five witnesses, aiding and abetting the solicitation of the murder of witnesses, and conspiring to interfere with witnesses. She was arrested on July 30, 2000. The government had Ms. Johnson sent to the Benton County Jail in Iowa.

> The government knew that Robert McNeese, an inmate with a history of trading information he gathered in prison for favorable treatment, was already housed at the Benton County Jail. By August 7, 2000, Mr. McNeese had established contact with Ms. Johnson. Thereafter, they communicated openly or surreptitiously as opportunities presented themselves. It is clear that some of the jailers knew that they were in contact and made only token efforts to sever the link between them. Detective Wright, who was in charge of investigating incidents at the jail, learned of these exchanges and ordered Mr. McNeese to stop communicating with Ms. Johnson. Detective Wright had Ms. Johnson moved to a new cell, but the move merely altered her channels of communication with Mr. McNeese, not the frequency of contacts.

> A month later, Mr. McNeese told a prison official that he had convinced Ms. Johnson that he could get a prisoner in another jail to

confess to the five murders she was charged with, so that Ms. Johnson could sue the government for false imprisonment and split the proceeds of such a suit with Mr. McNeese. Mr. McNeese had also obtained some incriminating admissions from Ms. Johnson. The official told Mr. McNeese not to deal with Ms. Johnson until the officer could get instructions on how the situation should be handled.

Five days later, on September 11, 2000, Mr. McNeese met with officials to receive "listening-post" instructions regarding Ms. Johnson. All parties agree that Mr. McNeese was acting as a government agent from this point forward. The next day he signed a plea agreement that had been drafted back on September 7, 2000, in another case. This agreement required that Mr. McNeese cooperate in cases that might arise in the Northern District of Iowa. Two weeks later, Mr. McNeese disclosed to the government the information that he had extracted from Ms. Johnson while they had been in jail together.

Are the admissions made to McNeese prior to September 11, 2000 admissible? If not, at what point did McNeese become part of a deliberate elicitation by the government?

3. *Miranda v. Massiah.* What result in the Note 2 case if *Miranda* were the only relevant protection?

4. The cases so far have involved police deception. *Massiah* was decided two years before *Miranda*. It might seem (it seemed to one of the authors of the casebook) that *Miranda* rendered *Massiah* superfluous in the context of overt police interrogation. *Miranda*, after all, created its own right to counsel that protected suspects from having to face police interrogation without the aid of counsel. Why wouldn't a violation of *Massiah* in the context of police interrogation always be a violation of *Miranda*? The next case raises, but does not dispose of, this question.

B. *MASSIAH* WAIVER

BREWER v. WILLIAMS

Supreme Court of the United States, 1977.
430 U.S. 387, 97 S.Ct. 1232, 51 L.Ed.2d 424.

MR. JUSTICE STEWART delivered the opinion of the Court. * * *

I

On the afternoon of December 24, 1968, a 10–year-old girl named Pamela Powers went with her family to the YMCA in Des Moines, Iowa, to watch a wrestling tournament in which her brother was participating. When she failed to return from a trip to the washroom, a search for her began. The search was unsuccessful.

Robert Williams, who had recently escaped from a mental hospital, was a resident of the YMCA. Soon after the girl's disappearance Williams was seen in the YMCA lobby carrying some clothing and a large bundle wrapped in a blanket. He obtained help from a 14–year-old boy in opening the street door of the YMCA and the door to his automobile parked outside. When Williams placed the bundle in the front seat of his car the boy "saw two legs in it and they were skinny and white." Before anyone could see what was in the bundle Williams drove away. His abandoned car was found the following day in Davenport, Iowa, roughly 160 miles east of Des Moines. A warrant was then issued in Des Moines for his arrest on a charge of abduction.

On the morning of December 26, a Des Moines lawyer named Henry McKnight went to the Des Moines police station and informed the officers present that he had just received a long-distance call from Williams, and that he had advised Williams to turn himself in to the Davenport police. Williams did surrender that morning to the police in Davenport, and they booked him on the charge specified in the arrest warrant and gave him the warnings required by *Miranda v. Arizona*. The Davenport police then telephoned their counterparts in Des Moines to inform them that Williams had surrendered. McKnight, the lawyer, was still at the Des Moines police headquarters, and Williams conversed with McKnight on the telephone. In the presence of the Des Moines chief of police and a police detective named Leaming, McKnight advised Williams that Des Moines police officers would be driving to Davenport to pick him up, that the officers would not interrogate him or mistreat him, and that Williams was not to talk to the officers about Pamela Powers until after consulting with McKnight upon his return to Des Moines. As a result of these conversations, it was agreed between McKnight and the Des Moines police officials that Detective Leaming and a fellow officer would drive to Davenport to pick up Williams, that they would bring him directly back to Des Moines, and that they would not question him during the trip.

In the meantime Williams was arraigned before a judge in Davenport on the outstanding arrest warrant. The judge advised him of his *Miranda* rights and committed him to jail. Before leaving the courtroom, Williams conferred with a lawyer named Kelly, who advised him not to make any statements until consulting with McKnight back in Des Moines.

Detective Leaming and his fellow officer arrived in Davenport about noon to pick up Williams and return him to Des Moines. Soon after their arrival they met with Williams and Kelly, who, they understood, was acting as Williams' lawyer. Detective Leaming repeated the *Miranda* warnings, and told Williams:

> "[W]e both know that you're being represented here by Mr. Kelly and you're being represented by Mr. McKnight in Des Moines, and * * * I want you to remember this because we'll be visiting between here and Des Moines."

Williams then conferred again with Kelly alone, and after this conference Kelly reiterated to Detective Leaming that Williams was not to be questioned about the disappearance of Pamela Powers until after he had consulted with McKnight back in Des Moines. When Leaming expressed some reservations, Kelly firmly stated that the agreement with McKnight was to be carried out—that there was to be no interrogation of Williams during the automobile journey to Des Moines. Kelly was denied permission to ride in the police car back to Des Moines with Williams and the two officers.

The two detectives, with Williams in their charge, then set out on the 160–mile drive. At no time during the trip did Williams express a willingness to be interrogated in the absence of an attorney. Instead, he stated several times that "[w]hen I get to Des Moines and see Mr. McKnight, I am going to tell you the whole story." Detective Leaming knew that Williams was a former mental patient, and knew also that he was deeply religious.

The detective and his prisoner soon embarked on a wide-ranging conversation covering a variety of topics, including the subject of religion. Then, not long after leaving Davenport and reaching the interstate highway, Detective Leaming delivered what has been referred to in the briefs and oral arguments as the "Christian burial speech." Addressing Williams as "Reverend," the detective said:

> "I want to give you something to think about while we're traveling down the road. * * * Number one, I want you to observe the weather conditions, it's raining, it's sleeting, it's freezing, driving is very treacherous, visibility is poor, it's going to be dark early this evening. They are predicting several inches of snow for tonight, and I feel that you yourself are the only person that knows where this little girl's body is, that you yourself have only been there once, and if you get a snow on top of it you yourself may be unable to find it. And, since we will be going right past the area on the way into Des Moines, I feel that we could stop and locate the body, that the parents of this little girl should be entitled to a Christian burial for the little girl who was snatched away from them on Christmas [E]ve and murdered. And I feel we should stop and locate it on the way in rather than waiting until morning and trying to come back out after a snow storm and possibly not being able to find it at all."

Williams asked Detective Leaming why he thought their route to Des Moines would be taking them past the girl's body, and Leaming responded that he knew the body was in the area of Mitchellville—a town they would be passing on the way to Des Moines.[1] Leaming then stated: "I do not want you to answer me. I don't want to discuss it any further. Just think about it as we're riding down the road."

As the car approached Grinnell, a town approximately 100 miles west of Davenport, Williams asked whether the police had found the victim's shoes. When Detective Leaming replied that he was unsure, Williams directed the officers to a service station where he said he had left the shoes; a search for them proved unsuccessful. As they continued towards Des Moines, Williams asked whether the police had found the blanket, and directed the officers to a rest area where he said he had disposed of the

---

1. The fact of the matter, of course, was that Detective Leaming possessed no such knowledge.

blanket. Nothing was found. The car continued towards Des Moines, and as it approached Mitchellville, Williams said that he would show the officers where the body was. He then directed the police to the body of Pamela Powers.

Williams was indicted for first-degree murder. Before trial, his counsel moved to suppress all evidence relating to or resulting from any statements Williams had made during the automobile ride from Davenport to Des Moines. After an evidentiary hearing the trial judge denied the motion. He found that "an agreement was made between defense counsel and the police officials to the effect that the Defendant was not to be questioned on the return trip to Des Moines," and that the evidence in question had been elicited from Williams during "a critical stage in the proceedings requiring the presence of counsel on his request." The judge ruled, however, that Williams had "waived his right to have an attorney present during the giving of such information."

The evidence in question was introduced over counsel's continuing objection at the subsequent trial. The jury found Williams guilty of murder [and the Iowa Supreme Court affirmed]. * * *

[The federal district court granted a petition for a writ of habeas corpus, concluding] as a matter of law that the evidence in question had been wrongly admitted at Williams' trial. This conclusion was based on three alternative and independent grounds: (1) that Williams had been denied his constitutional right to the assistance of counsel; (2) that he had been denied the constitutional protections defined by this Court's decisions in *Escobedo v. Illinois* [p. 580, Note 5] and *Miranda v. Arizona* [p. 581]; and (3) that in any event, his self-incriminatory statements on the automobile trip from Davenport to Des Moines had been involuntarily made. Further, the District Court ruled that there had been no waiver by Williams of the constitutional protections in question. * * *

II * * *

B

As stated above, the District Court based its judgment in this case on three independent grounds. The Court of Appeals appears to have affirmed the judgment on two of those grounds. We have concluded that only one of them need be considered here.

Specifically, there is no need to review in this case the doctrine of *Miranda v. Arizona*, a doctrine designed to secure the constitutional privilege against compulsory self-incrimination. It is equally unnecessary to evaluate the ruling of the District Court that Williams' self-incriminating statements were, indeed, involuntarily made. For it is clear that the judgment before us must in any event be affirmed upon the ground that Williams was deprived of a different constitutional right—the right to the assistance of counsel. * * *

There has occasionally been a difference of opinion within the Court as to the peripheral scope of this constitutional right. * * * Whatever else it may mean, the right to counsel granted by the Sixth and Fourteenth Amendments means at least that a person is entitled to the help of a lawyer at or after the time that judicial proceedings have been initiated against him "whether by way of formal charge, preliminary hearing, indictment, information, or arraignment."

There can be no doubt in the present case that judicial proceedings had been initiated against Williams before the start of the automobile ride from Davenport to Des Moines. A warrant had been issued for his arrest, he had been arraigned on that warrant before a judge in a Davenport courtroom, and he had been committed by the court to confinement in jail. The State does not contend otherwise.

There can be no serious doubt, either, that Detective Leaming deliberately and designedly set out to elicit information from Williams just as surely as—and perhaps more effectively than—if he had formally interrogated him. Detective Leaming was fully aware before departing for Des Moines that Williams was being represented in Davenport by Kelly and in Des Moines by McKnight. Yet he purposely sought during Williams' isolation from his lawyers to obtain as much incriminating information as possible. Indeed, Detective Leaming conceded as much when he testified at Williams' trial:

"Q. In fact, Captain, whether he was a mental patient or not, you were trying to get all the information you could before he got to his lawyer, weren't you?

"A. I was sure hoping to find out where that little girl was, yes, sir. * * *

"Q. Well, I'll put it this way: You was [sic] hoping to get all the information you could before Williams got back to McKnight, weren't you?

"A. Yes, sir."

The state courts clearly proceeded upon the hypothesis that Detective Leaming's "Christian burial speech" had been tantamount to interrogation. * * *

The circumstances of this case are thus constitutionally indistinguishable from those presented in *Massiah v. United States.* * * *

That the incriminating statements were elicited surreptitiously in the *Massiah* case, and otherwise here, is constitutionally irrelevant. Rather, the clear rule of *Massiah* is that once adversary proceedings have commenced against an individual, he has a right to legal representation when the government interrogates him.[8] It thus requires no wooden or technical application of the *Massiah* doctrine to conclude that Williams was entitled

---

8. The only other significant factual difference between the present case and *Massiah* is that here the police had agreed that they would not interrogate Williams in the absence of his counsel. This circumstance plainly provides petitioner with no argument for distinguishing away the protection afforded by *Massiah.* * * *

to the assistance of counsel guaranteed to him by the Sixth and Four-teenth Amendments.

III

The Iowa courts recognized that Williams had been denied the consti-tutional right to the assistance of counsel. They held, however, that he had waived that right during the course of the automobile trip from Davenport to Des Moines. * * *

In its lengthy opinion affirming this determination, the Iowa Supreme Court applied "the totality-of-circumstances test for a showing of waiver of constitutionally-protected rights in the absence of an express waiver," and concluded that "evidence of the time element involved on the trip, the general circumstances of it, and the absence of any request or expressed desire for the aid of counsel before or at the time of giving information, were sufficient to sustain a conclusion that defendant did waive his constitutional rights as alleged."

In the federal habeas corpus proceeding the District Court, believing that the issue of waiver was not one of fact but of federal law, held that the Iowa courts had "applied the wrong constitutional standards" in ruling that Williams had waived the protections that were his under the Constitution. * * *

The District Court and the Court of Appeals were * * * correct in their understanding of the proper standard to be applied in determining the question of waiver as a matter of federal constitutional law—that it was incumbent upon the State to prove "an intentional relinquishment or abandonment of a known right or privilege." *Johnson v. Zerbst*, [304 U.S. 458, 464, 58 S.Ct. 1019, 1023, 82 L.Ed. 1461 (1938)]. That standard has been reiterated in many cases. We have said that the right to counsel does not depend upon a request by the defendant, and that courts indulge in every reasonable presumption against waiver. This strict standard applies equally to an alleged waiver of the right to counsel whether at trial or at a critical stage of pretrial proceedings.

We conclude, finally, that the Court of Appeals was correct in holding that, judged by these standards, the record in this case falls far short of sustaining petitioner's burden. It is true that Williams had been informed of and appeared to understand his right to counsel. But waiver requires not merely comprehension but relinquishment, and Williams' consistent reliance upon the advice of counsel in dealing with the authorities refutes any suggestion that he waived that right. He consulted McKnight by long-distance telephone before turning himself in. He spoke with McKnight by telephone again shortly after being booked. After he was arraigned, Williams sought out and obtained legal advice from Kelly. Williams again consulted with Kelly after Detective Leaming and his fellow officer arrived in Davenport. Throughout, Williams was advised not to make any state-ments before seeing McKnight in Des Moines, and was assured that the police had agreed not to question him. His statements while in the car that he would tell the whole story *after* seeing McKnight in Des Moines were the clearest expressions by Williams himself that he desired the presence of an attorney before any interrogation took place. But even before making these statements, Williams had effectively asserted his right to counsel by having secured attorneys at both ends of the automobile trip, both of whom, acting as his agents, had made clear to the police that no interrogation was to occur during the journey. Williams knew of that agreement and, particularly in view of his consistent reliance on counsel, there is no basis for concluding that he disavowed it.

Despite Williams' express and implicit assertions of his right to counsel, Detective Leaming proceeded to elicit incriminating statements from Williams. Leaming did not preface this effort by telling Williams that he had a right to the presence of a lawyer, and made no effort at all to ascertain whether Williams wished to relinquish that right. The circumstances of record in this case thus provide no reasonable basis for finding that Williams waived his right to the assistance of counsel.

The Court of Appeals did not hold, nor do we, that under the circumstances of this case Williams *could not*, without notice to counsel, have waived his rights under the Sixth and Fourteenth Amendments. It only held, as do we, that he did not.

IV

The crime of which Williams was convicted was senseless and brutal, calling for swift and energetic action by the police to apprehend the perpetrator and gather evidence with which he could be convicted. No mission of law enforcement officials is more important. Yet "[d]isinterested zeal for the public good does not assure either wisdom or right in the methods it pursues." Although we do not lightly affirm the issuance of a writ of habeas corpus in this case, so clear a violation of the Sixth and Fourteenth Amendments as here occurred cannot be condoned. The pressures on state executive and judicial officers charged with the administration of the criminal law are great, especially when the crime is murder and the victim a small child. But it is precisely the predictability of those pressures that makes imperative a resolute loyalty to the guarantees that the Constitution extends to us all. * * *

Mr. Justice MARSHALL, concurring.

I concur wholeheartedly in my Brother Stewart's opinion for the Court, but add these words in light of the dissenting opinions filed today. The dissenters have, I believe, lost sight of the fundamental constitutional backbone of our criminal law. They seem to think that Detective Leaming's actions were perfectly proper, indeed laudable, examples of "good police work." In my view, good police work is something far different from catching the criminal at any price. It is equally important that the police, as guardians of the law, fulfill their responsibility to obey its commands scrupulously. For "in the end life and liberty can be as much endangered from illegal methods used to convict those thought to be criminals as from the actual criminals themselves."

In this case, there can be no doubt that Detective Leaming consciously and knowingly set out to violate Williams' Sixth Amendment right to counsel and his Fifth Amendment privilege against self-incrimination, as Leaming himself understood those rights. * * *

Leaming knowingly isolated Williams from the protection of his lawyers and during that period he intentionally "persuaded" him to give incriminating evidence. It is this intentional police misconduct—not good police practice—that the Court rightly condemns. The heinous nature of the crime is no excuse, as the dissenters would have it, for condoning knowing and intentional police transgression of the constitutional rights of a defendant. If Williams is to go free—and given the ingenuity of Iowa prosecutors on retrial or in a civil commitment proceeding, I doubt very much that there is any chance a dangerous criminal will be loosed on the streets, the bloodcurdling cries of the dissents notwithstanding—it will hardly be because he deserves it. It will be because Detective Leaming, knowing full well that he risked reversal of Williams' conviction, intentionally denied Williams the right of *every* American under the Sixth Amendment to have the protective shield of a lawyer between himself and the awesome power of the State. * * *

Mr. Justice POWELL, concurring. * * *

I * * *

* * * It is clear from the record, as both of the federal courts below found, that there was no evidence of a knowing and voluntary waiver of the right to have counsel present beyond the fact that Williams ultimately confessed. It is settled law that an inferred waiver of a constitutional right is disfavored. I find no basis in the record of this case—or in the dissenting opinions—for disagreeing with the conclusion of the District Court that "the State has produced no affirmative evidence whatsoever to support its claim of waiver."

The dissenting opinion of the Chief Justice states that the Court's holding today "conclusively presumes a suspect is legally incompetent to change his mind and tell the truth until an attorney is present." I find no justification for this view. On the contrary, the opinion of the Court is explicitly clear that the right to assistance of counsel may be waived, after it has attached, without notice to or consultation with counsel. We would have such a case here if petitioner had proved that the police refrained from coercion and interrogation, as they had agreed, and that Williams freely on his own initiative had confessed the crime. * * *

Mr. Justice STEVENS, concurring. * * *

Nothing that we write, no matter how well reasoned or forcefully expressed, can bring back the victim of this tragedy or undo the consequences of the official neglect which led to the respondent's escape from a state mental institution. The emotional aspects of the case make it difficult to decide dispassionately, but do not qualify our obligation to apply the law with an eye to the future as well as with concern for the result in the particular case before us.

Underlying the surface issues in this case is the question whether a fugitive from justice can rely on his lawyer's advice given in connection with a decision to surrender voluntarily. The defendant placed his trust in an experienced Iowa trial lawyer who in turn trusted the Iowa law enforcement authorities to honor a commitment made during negotiations which led to the apprehension of a potentially dangerous person. Under any analysis, this was a critical stage of the proceeding in which the participation of an independent professional was of vital importance to the accused and to society. At this stage—as in countless others in which the law profoundly affects the life of the individual—the lawyer is the essential medium through which the demands and commitments of the sovereign are communicated to the citizen. If, in the long run, we are seriously concerned about the individual's effective representation by counsel, the State cannot be permitted to dishonor its promise to this lawyer.

Mr. Chief Justice BURGER, dissenting.

The result in this case ought to be intolerable in any society which purports to call itself an organized society. It continues the Court—by the narrowest margin—on the much-criticized course of punishing the public for the mistakes and misdeeds of law enforcement officers, instead of punishing the officer directly, if in fact he is guilty of wrongdoing. It mechanically and blindly keeps reliable evidence from juries whether the claimed constitutional violation involves gross police misconduct or honest human error.

Williams is guilty of the savage murder of a small child; no member of the Court contends he is not. While in custody, and after no fewer than *five* warnings of his rights to silence and to counsel, he led police to the concealed body of his victim. The Court concedes Williams was not threatened or coerced and that he spoke and acted voluntarily and with full awareness of his constitutional rights. In the face of all this, the Court now holds that because Williams was prompted by the detective's statement—not interrogation but a statement—the jury must not be told how the police found the body.

Today's holding fulfills Judge (later Mr. Justice) Cardozo's grim prophecy that someday some court might carry the exclusionary rule to the absurd extent that its operative effect would exclude evidence relating to the body of a murder victim because of the means by which it was found. In so ruling the Court regresses to playing a grisly game of "hide and seek," once more exalting the sporting theory of criminal justice which has been experiencing a decline in our jurisprudence. With Justices White, Blackmun, and Rehnquist, I categorically reject the remarkable notion that the police in this case were guilty of unconstitutional misconduct, or any conduct justifying the bizarre result reached by the Court.
* * *

Under well-settled precedents which the Court freely acknowledges, it is very clear that Williams had made a valid waiver of his Fifth Amendment right to silence and his Sixth Amendment right to counsel when he led police to the child's body. Indeed, even under the Court's analysis I do not understand how a contrary conclusion is possible. * * *

The evidence is uncontradicted that Williams had abundant knowledge of his right to have counsel present and of his right to silence. Since the Court does not question his mental competence, it boggles the mind to suggest that Williams could not understand that leading police to the child's body would have other than the most serious consequences. All of the elements necessary to make out a valid waiver are shown by the record and acknowledged by the Court; we thus are left to guess how the Court reached its holding.

One plausible but unarticulated basis for the result reached is that once a suspect has asserted his right not to talk without the presence of an attorney, it becomes legally impossible for him to waive that right until he has seen an attorney. But constitutional rights are *personal*, and an otherwise valid waiver should not be brushed aside by judges simply because an attorney was not present. The Court's holding operates to "imprison a man in his privileges"; it conclusively presumes a suspect is legally incompetent to change his mind and tell the truth until an attorney is present. It denigrates an individual to a nonperson whose free will has become hostage to a lawyer so that until the lawyer consents, the suspect is deprived of any legal right or power to decide for himself that he wishes to make a disclosure. * * *

Mr. Justice WHITE, with whom Mr. Justice BLACKMUN and Mr. Justice REHNQUIST join, dissenting.

The respondent in this case killed a 10–year-old child. * * *

I

[During his recitation of the facts, Justice White noted that Williams began directing the police in search of incriminating evidence "[s]ome considerable time" after Leaming's "Christian burial speech." In footnote 3, White observed: "The trip was 160 miles long and was made in bad weather. Leaming's statement was made shortly after leaving Davenport. Respondent's statements about the victim's clothes were made shortly before arriving in Mitchellville, a near suburb of Des Moines." Eds.]

II

The strictest test of waiver which might be applied to this case is that set forth in *Johnson v. Zerbst*, and quoted by the majority. In order to show that a right has been waived under this test, the State must prove "an intentional relinquishment or abandonment of a known right or privilege." The majority creates no new rule preventing an accused who has retained a lawyer from waiving his right to the lawyer's presence during questioning. The majority simply finds that no waiver was *proved* in this case. I disagree. That respondent knew of his right not to say anything to the officers without advice and presence of counsel is established on this record to a moral certainty. He was advised of the right by three officials of the State—telling at least one that he understood the right—and by two lawyers. Finally, he further demonstrated his knowledge of the right by informing the police that he would tell them the story in the presence of McKnight when they arrived in Des Moines. The issue in this case, then, is whether respondent relinquished that right intentionally.

Respondent relinquished his right not to talk to the police about his crime when the car approached the place where he had hidden the victim's clothes. Men usually intend to do what they do, and there is nothing in the record to support the proposition that respondent's decision to talk was anything but an exercise of his own free will. Apparently, without any prodding from the officers, respondent—who had earlier said that he would tell the whole story when he arrived in Des Moines—spontaneously changed his mind about the timing of his disclosures when the car approached the places where he had hidden the evidence. However, even if his statements were influenced by Detective Leaming's above-quoted statement, respondent's decision to talk in the absence of counsel can hardly be viewed as the product of an overborne will. The statement by Leaming was not coercive; it was accompanied by a request that respondent not respond to it; and it was delivered hours before respondent decided to make any statement. Respondent's waiver was thus knowing and intentional.

The majority's contrary conclusion seems to rest on the fact that respondent "asserted" his right to counsel by retaining and consulting with one lawyer and by consulting with another. How this supports the conclusion that respondent's later relinquishment of his right not to talk in the absence of counsel was unintentional is a mystery. The fact that respondent consulted with counsel on the question whether he should talk to the police in counsel's absence makes his later decision to talk in counsel's absence *better* informed and, if anything, more intelligent.

The majority recognizes that even after this "assertion" of his right to counsel, it would have found that respondent waived his right not to talk in counsel's absence if his waiver had been express—*i.e.*, if the officers had asked him in the car whether he would be willing to answer questions in counsel's absence and if he had answered "yes." But waiver is not a formalistic concept. Waiver is shown whenever the facts establish that an accused knew of a right and intended to relinquish it. Such waiver, even if not express,[5] was plainly shown here. The only other conceivable basis for the majority's holding is the implicit suggestion that the right involved in

---

5. * * * [T]he issue is, as the majority recognizes, one of the proof necessary to establish waiver. If an intentional relinquishment of the right to counsel under *Miranda* is established by proof that the accused was informed of his right and then voluntarily answered questions in counsel's absence, then similar proof establishes an intentional relinquishment of the *Massiah* right to counsel.

Massiah v. United States, as distinguished from the right involved in *Miranda v. Arizona*, is a right not to be *asked* any questions in counsel's absence rather than a right not to *answer* any questions in counsel's absence, and that the right not to be *asked* questions must be waived *before* the questions are asked. Such wafer-thin distinctions cannot determine whether a guilty murderer should go free. The only conceivable purpose for the presence of counsel during questioning is to protect an accused from making incriminating *answers*. Questions, unanswered, have no significance at all. Absent coercion—no matter how the right involved is defined—an accused is amply protected by a rule requiring waiver before or simultaneously with the giving by him of an answer or the making by him of a statement.

III

The consequence of the majority's decision is, as the majority recognizes, extremely serious. A mentally disturbed killer whose guilt is not in question may be released. Why? Apparently the answer is that the majority believes that the law enforcement officers acted in a way which involves some risk of injury to society and that such conduct should be deterred. However, the officers' conduct did not, and was not likely to, jeopardize the fairness of respondent's trial or in any way risk the conviction of an innocent man—the risk against which the Sixth Amendment guarantee of assistance of counsel is designed to protect. The police did nothing "wrong," let alone anything "unconstitutional." To anyone not lost in the intricacies of the prophylactic rules of *Miranda v. Arizona*, the result in this case seems utterly senseless; and for the reasons stated in Part II, even applying those rules as well as the rule of *Massiah v. United States*, the statements made by respondent were properly admitted. In light of these considerations, the majority's protest that the result in this case is justified by a "clear violation" of the Sixth and Fourteenth Amendments has a distressing hollow ring. I respectfully dissent.

[The dissenting opinion of Justice Blackmun, joined by Justices White and Rehnquist, is omitted].

NOTES AND QUESTIONS

1. While a law student, one of the authors of the casebook worked on *Brewer* when it was on appeal to the Eighth Circuit; his view was that the issue was better analyzed under *Miranda*. Others thought so, too. *Brewer* was widely viewed as the case the Court would use to overrule *Miranda*. Justice Blackmun noted in his *Brewer* dissent that twenty-two states "and others, as *amicus curiae*, strongly urge that" *Miranda* "be re-examined and overruled." Perhaps sensing *Miranda*'s vulnerability, the University of Iowa law professor in charge of the case—Robert Bartels—insisted that the Sixth Amendment argument was the defendant's best hope. As usual, the teacher was wiser than the student. But the key question is *why* the Court was more comfortable deciding the case under *Massiah*. What do you think?

2. The *Brewer* Court said that judicial proceedings began, and the Sixth Amendment attached, when Williams was arraigned before a judge on an arrest warrant. The Court does not tell us whether the State was represented by a prosecutor at that hearing, but Rothgery v. Gillespie County, 554 U.S. ___, 128 S.Ct. 2578, 171 L.Ed.2d 366 (2008), made clear that the Sixth Amendment attaches whether or not a prosecutor is present at the hearing and even if no one in the prosecutor's office knows about the hearing. It is the hearing itself that triggers the Sixth Amendment.

3. The bitter dispute in *Brewer* is framed in terms of waiver, not whether Leaming deliberately elicited Williams's statements. Are these different inquiries or just two sides of the same coin?

4. What did Officer Leaming do wrong? Is the problem the "Christian burial speech" or the "waiver" after the speech? If you think it is the latter, did the Court conclude that this was an involuntary waiver? An unintelligent one? Or is there another basis? The classic treatment of this question is Yale Kamisar, *Brewer v. Williams, Massiah and Miranda: What is "Interrogation"? When Does It Matter?*, 67 Geo. L.J. 1 (1978).

Other valuable perspectives on the *Brewer* interrogation issue can be found in Joseph D. Grano, *Rhode Island v. Innis: A Need to Reconsider the Constitutional Premises Underlying the Law of Confessions*, 17 Am. Crim. L. Rev. 1 (1979); and Stephen J. Schulhofer, *Confessions and the Court*, 79 Mich. L. Rev. 865 (1980) (reviewing Yale Kamisar, *Police Interrogation and Confessions* (1980)).

5. Chief Justice Burger stated in his dissent that, following the majority's reasoning, "[I]t becomes legally impossible for [Williams] to waive that right until he has seen an attorney." Is this what the majority says? Would that be a sensible outcome? Could Officer Leaming have done something differently that would have permitted Williams to waive before seeing McKnight?

Assume Officer Leaming gave the Christian burial speech, three hours passed, and Williams asked to telephone his boyhood minister. After a lengthy telephone call, Williams told the police: "I am a religious man. Having thought of nothing these last three hours except the nature of sin and forgiveness, I decided to call my minister, who said that my religious duty is to direct you to where I hid the body." A violation of *Massiah*, as amplified by *Brewer*? What if, instead, Williams tells police he is going to call his lawyer and returns after the call to say he is ready to talk? Does it matter what the lawyer advised him?

Alternatively, assume the police persuade a local radio weatherman to give the speech and leave the radio on for Williams to hear. Does this change anything in the *Massiah* analysis? Does it change the *Miranda* analysis? (The hypothetical is Professor Kamisar's; see Kamisar, Note 4.)

6. *Massiah "fruit."* What evidence is rendered inadmissible by the Sixth Amendment violation in *Brewer*? The Court held that the statements Williams made leading the police to the body were inadmissible, of course, but what about the body itself? This is one way to ask whether a *Massiah* violation has poisoned fruit, as in the case of a Fourth Amendment violation. You will recall

that *Miranda* is "fruitless." Is a *Massiah* violation more like a Fourth Amendment violation or more like a *Miranda* violation?

The Court in *Brewer* suggested in a footnote that the body might be admissible if it would have been discovered in any event. As you saw in *Nix v. Williams*, p. 502, Note 4, the Court later made a holding of this dicta. Notice, however, that this "inevitable discovery" exception is precisely that—an exception to a general rule that the fruit of a violation of *Massiah* must be suppressed. Do you see why *Massiah*, but not *Miranda*, generally requires suppression of evidence found by means of the violation?

7. *Brewer v. Williams: the rest of the story.* The State of Iowa retried Williams. For details on the retrial, including the defense theory of how Williams was factually innocent, see Phillip E. Johnson, *The Return of the "Christian Burial Speech" Case*, 32 Emory L.J. 349 (1983). In brief, the theory was that the victim was killed by someone else, a janitor at the YMCA who then hid the body in Williams's room. Upon discovering the body, and fearing the inevitable inference, Williams panicked, fled, and hid the body where it was ultimately found. According to the Eighth Circuit, the defense theory of innocence "is not so far-fetched as it sounds." Williams v. Nix, 700 F.2d 1164, 1168 (8th Cir.1983). Some evidence in Williams's favor: A witness heard the sounds of a struggle coming from the janitor's room shortly after the victim's disappearance, and the janitor made what one witness called "furtive preparations to depart" shortly after the crime occurred. Moreover, according to defense lawyers, the janitor had a history of child molestation.

As you saw in Chapter 5, in the inevitable discovery materials, Williams was again convicted, mostly on the testimony of the person who saw skinny white legs sticking out of the bundle that Williams put in his car. Iowa does not have the death penalty. Williams is still serving a life sentence at the Fort Madison, Iowa prison.

8. To appreciate the significance of the next case, you should know a little about Michigan v. Jackson, 475 U.S. 625, 106 S.Ct. 1404, 89 L.Ed.2d 631 (1986). When Jackson (who was indigent) was arraigned, he requested that counsel be appointed. The Court in *Jackson* held that this request created a Sixth Amendment *Edwards v. Arizona* (p. 674) rule forbidding the initiation of further interrogation by the police. Thus, even though Jackson never invoked his *Miranda* right to counsel, and could not benefit from *Edwards*, *Jackson* held that the Sixth Amendment protected him from police attempts to get him to answer questions. Stated differently, when Jackon waived *Miranda,* he did not waive his Sixth Amendment right to counsel. But what if a defendant does *not* request counsel after indictment? Is that a distinction with constitutional significance?

PATTERSON v. ILLINOIS

Supreme Court of the United States, 1988.
487 U.S. 285, 108 S.Ct. 2389, 101 L.Ed.2d 261 (1988).

JUSTICE WHITE delivered the opinion of the Court.

In this case, we are called on to determine whether the interrogation of petitioner after his indictment violated his Sixth Amendment right to counsel.

I

Before dawn on August 21, 1983, petitioner and other members of the "Vice Lords" street gang became involved in a fight with members of a rival gang, the "Black Mobsters." Some time after the fight, a former member of the Black Mobsters, James Jackson, went to the home where the Vice Lords had fled. A second fight broke out there, with petitioner and three other Vice Lords beating Jackson severely. The Vice Lords then put Jackson into a car, drove to the end of a nearby street, and left him face down in a puddle of water. Later that morning, police discovered Jackson, dead, where he had been left. * * *

On August 23, a Cook County grand jury indicted petitioner and two other gang members for the murder of James Jackson. Police Officer Michael Gresham, who had questioned petitioner earlier, removed him from the lockup where he was being held, and told petitioner that because he had been indicted he was being transferred to the Cook County jail. Petitioner asked Gresham which of the gang members had been charged with Jackson's murder, and upon learning that one particular Vice Lord had been omitted from the indictments, asked: "[W]hy wasn't he indicted, he did everything." Petitioner also began to explain that there was a witness who would support his account of the crime.

At this point, Gresham interrupted petitioner, and handed him a *Miranda* waiver form. The form contained five specific warnings, as suggested by this Court's *Miranda* decision, to make petitioner aware of his right to counsel and of the consequences of any statement he might make to police. Gresham read the warnings aloud, as petitioner read along with him. Petitioner initialed each of the five warnings, and signed the waiver form. Petitioner then gave a lengthy statement to police officers concerning the Jackson murder; petitioner's statement described in detail the role of each of the Vice Lords—including himself—in the murder of James Jackson.

Later that day, petitioner confessed involvement in the murder for a second time. This confession came in an interview with Assistant State's Attorney (ASA) George Smith. At the outset of the interview, Smith reviewed with petitioner the *Miranda* waiver he had previously signed, and petitioner confirmed that he had signed the waiver and understood his rights. Smith went through the waiver procedure once again: reading petitioner his rights, having petitioner initial each one, and sign a waiver form. In addition, Smith informed petitioner that he was a lawyer working with the police investigating the Jackson case. Petitioner then gave another inculpatory statement concerning the crime.

Before trial, petitioner moved to suppress his statements, arguing that they were obtained in a manner at odds with various constitutional guarantees. The trial court denied these motions, and the statements were used against petitioner at his trial. The jury found petitioner guilty of murder, and petitioner was sentenced to a 24-year prison term.

On appeal, petitioner argued that he had not "knowingly and intelligently" waived his Sixth Amendment right to counsel before he gave his uncounseled postindictment confessions. Petitioner contended that the warnings he received, while adequate for the purposes of protecting his *Fifth* Amendment rights as guaranteed by *Miranda,* did not adequately inform him of his *Sixth* Amendment right to counsel. The Illinois Supreme Court, however, rejected this theory, applying its previous decision * * * which had held that *Miranda* warnings were sufficient to make a defendant aware of his Sixth Amendment right to counsel during postindictment questioning.

In reaching this conclusion, the Illinois Supreme Court noted that this Court had reserved decision on this question on several previous occasions and that the lower courts are divided on the issue. We granted this petition for certiorari to resolve this split of authority and to address the issues we had previously left open.

II

There can be no doubt that petitioner had the right to have the assistance of counsel at his postindictment interviews with law enforcement authorities. Our cases make it plain that the Sixth Amendment guarantees this right to criminal defendants. Michigan v. Jackson, 475 U.S. 625, 629–630, 106 S.Ct. 1404, 1407–1408, 89 L.Ed.2d 631 (1986); *Brewer v. Williams*; *Massiah v. United States*.[3] Petitioner asserts that the questioning that produced his incriminating statements violated his Sixth Amendment right to counsel in two ways.

A

Petitioner's first claim is that because his Sixth Amendment right to counsel arose with his indictment, the police were thereafter barred from initiating a meeting with him. He equates himself with a preindictment suspect who, while being interrogated, asserts his Fifth Amendment right to counsel; under *Edwards v. Arizona,* [p. 674], such a suspect may not be questioned again unless he initiates the meeting. * * *

At bottom, petitioner's theory cannot be squared with our rationale in *Edwards,* the case he relies on for support. *Edwards* rested on the view that once "an accused * * * ha[s] expressed his desire to deal with the police only through counsel" he should "not [be] subject to further interrogation by the authorities until counsel has been made available to him, unless the accused himself initiates further communication." Preserving the integrity of an accused's choice to communicate with police only through counsel is the essence of *Edwards* and its progeny—not

---

3. We note as a matter of some significance that petitioner had not retained, or accepted by appointment, a lawyer to represent him at the time he was questioned by authorities. Once an accused has a lawyer, a distinct set of constitutional safeguards aimed at preserving the sanctity of the attorney-client relationship takes effect. The State conceded as much at argument.

Indeed, the analysis changes markedly once an accused even *requests* the assistance of counsel. See *Michigan v. Jackson, supra.*

barring an accused from making an *initial* election as to whether he will face the State's officers during questioning with the aid of counsel, or go it alone. If an accused "knowingly and intelligently" pursues the latter course, we see no reason why the uncounseled statements he then makes must be excluded at his trial.

B

Petitioner's principal and more substantial claim is that questioning him without counsel present violated the Sixth Amendment because he did not validly waive his right to have counsel present during the interviews. Since it is clear that after the *Miranda* warnings were given to petitioner, he not only voluntarily answered questions without claiming his right to silence or his right to have a lawyer present to advise him but also executed a written waiver of his right to counsel during questioning, the specific issue posed here is whether this waiver was a "knowing and intelligent" waiver of his Sixth Amendment right. See *Brewer v. Williams.*

In the past, this Court has held that a waiver of the Sixth Amendment right to counsel is valid only when it reflects "an intentional relinquishment or abandonment of a known right or privilege." In other words, the accused must "kno[w] what he is doing" so that "his choice is made with eyes open." In a case arising under the Fifth Amendment, we described this requirement as "a full awareness of both the nature of the right being abandoned and the consequences of the decision to abandon it." Whichever of these formulations is used, the key inquiry in a case such as this one must be: Was the accused, who waived his Sixth Amendment rights during postindictment questioning, made sufficiently aware of his right to have counsel present during the questioning, and of the possible consequences of a decision to forgo the aid of counsel? In this case, we are convinced that by admonishing petitioner with the *Miranda* warnings, respondent has met this burden and that petitioner's waiver of his right to counsel at the questioning was valid.[4]

First, the *Miranda* warnings given petitioner made him aware of his right to have counsel present during the questioning. By telling petitioner that he had a right to consult with an attorney, to have a lawyer present while he was questioned, and even to have a lawyer appointed for him if he could not afford to retain one on his own, Officer Gresham and ASA Smith conveyed to petitioner the sum and substance of the rights that the Sixth Amendment provided him. "Indeed, it seems self-evident that one who is told he" has such rights to counsel "is in a curious posture to later complain" that his waiver of these rights was unknowing. There is little

---

4. We emphasize the significance of the fact that petitioner's waiver of counsel was only for this limited aspect of the criminal proceedings against him—only for postindictment questioning. Our decision on the validity of petitioner's waiver extends only so far.

Moreover, even within this limited context, we note that petitioner's waiver was binding on him *only* so long as he wished it to be. Under this Court's precedents, at any time during the questioning petitioner could have changed his mind, elected to have the assistance of counsel, and immediately dissolve the effectiveness of his waiver with respect to any subsequent statements. Our decision today does nothing to change this rule.

more petitioner could have possibly been told in an effort to satisfy this portion of the waiver inquiry.

Second, the *Miranda* warnings also served to make petitioner aware of the consequences of a decision by him to waive his Sixth Amendment rights during postindictment questioning. Petitioner knew that any statement that he made could be used against him in subsequent criminal proceedings. This is the ultimate adverse consequence petitioner could have suffered by virtue of his choice to make uncounseled admissions to the authorities. This warning also sufficed—contrary to petitioner's claim here—to let petitioner know what a lawyer could "do for him" during the postindictment questioning: namely, advise petitioner to refrain from making any such statements. By knowing what could be done with any statements he might make, and therefore, what benefit could be obtained by having the aid of counsel while making such statements, petitioner was essentially informed of the possible consequences of going without counsel during questioning. If petitioner nonetheless lacked "a full and complete appreciation of all of the consequences flowing" from his waiver, it does not defeat the State's showing that the information it provided to him satisfied the constitutional minimum.

Our conclusion is supported by petitioner's inability, in the proceedings before this Court, to articulate with precision what additional information should have been provided to him before he would have been competent to waive his right to counsel. All that petitioner's brief and reply brief suggest is petitioner should have been made aware of his "right under the Sixth Amendment to the broad protection of counsel"—a rather nebulous suggestion—and the "gravity of [his] situation." But surely this latter "requirement" (if it is one) was met when Officer Gresham informed petitioner that he had been formally charged with the murder of James Jackson. Under close questioning on this same point at argument, petitioner likewise failed to suggest any meaningful additional information that he should have been, but was not, provided in advance of his decision to waive his right to counsel.[7] The discussions found in favorable court

---

7. Representative excerpts from the relevant portions of argument include the following:

"QUESTION: [Petitioner] . . . * * * was told that he had a right to counsel.

"MR. HONCHELL [petitioner's counsel]: He was told-the word 'counsel' was used. He was told he had a right to counsel. But not through information by which it would become meaningful to him, because the method that was used was not designed to alert the accused to the Sixth Amendment rights to counsel * * *.

"QUESTION: * * * You mean they should have said you have a Sixth Amendment right to counsel instead of just, you have a right to counsel?

"He knew he had a right to have counsel present before [he] made the confession. Now, what in addition did he have to know to make the waiver an intelligent one?

"MR. HONCHELL: He had to meaningfully know he had a Sixth Amendment right to counsel present because—

"QUESTION: What is the difference between meaningfully knowing and knowing?

"MR. HONCHELL: Because the warning here used did not convey or express what counsel was intended to do for him after indictment. * * * That there is a right to counsel who would act on his behalf and represent him.

"QUESTION: Well, okay. So it should have said, in addition to saying counsel, counsel who would act on your behalf and represent you? That would have been the magic solution?

decisions, on which petitioner relies, are similarly lacking.[8]

As a general matter, then, an accused who is admonished with the warnings prescribed by this Court in *Miranda* has been sufficiently apprised of the nature of his Sixth Amendment rights, and of the consequences of abandoning those rights, so that his waiver on this basis will be considered a knowing and intelligent one. We feel that our conclusion in a recent Fifth Amendment case is equally apposite here: "Once it is determined that a suspect's decision not to rely on his rights was uncoerced, that he at all times knew he could stand mute and request a lawyer, and that he was aware of the State's intention to use his statements to secure a conviction, the analysis is complete and the waiver is valid as a matter of law."

C

We consequently reject petitioner's argument, which has some acceptance from courts and commentators, that since "the sixth amendment right [to counsel] is far superior to that of the fifth amendment right" and since "[t]he greater the right the greater the loss from a waiver of that right," waiver of an accused's Sixth Amendment right to counsel should be "more difficult" to effectuate than waiver of a suspect's Fifth Amendment rights. While our cases have recognized a "difference" between the Fifth Amendment and Sixth Amendment rights to counsel, and the "policies" behind these constitutional guarantees, we have never suggested that one right is "superior" or "greater" than the other, nor is there any support in our cases for the notion that because a Sixth Amendment right may be involved, it is more difficult to waive than the Fifth Amendment counterpart. Instead, we have taken a more pragmatic approach to the waiver question—asking what purposes a lawyer can serve at the particular stage of the proceedings in question, and what assistance he could provide to an accused at that stage—to determine the scope of the Sixth Amendment right to counsel, and the type of warnings and procedures that should be required before a waiver of that right will be recognized.

At one end of the spectrum, we have concluded there is no Sixth Amendment right to counsel whatsoever at a postindictment photographic display identification, because this procedure is not one at which the accused "require [s] aid in coping with legal problems or assistance in meeting his adversary." At the other extreme, recognizing the enormous importance and role that an attorney plays at a criminal trial, we have

---

"MR. HONCHELL: That is a possible method, yes."

We do not believe that adding the words "who would act on your behalf and represent you" in Sixth Amendment cases would provide any meaningful improvement in the *Miranda* warnings.

8. * * * An exception to this is the occasional suggestion that, in addition to the *Miranda* warnings, an accused should be informed that he has been indicted before a postindictment waiver is sought. Because, in this case, petitioner concedes that he was so informed, we do not address the question whether or not an accused must be told that he has been indicted before a postindictment Sixth Amendment waiver will be valid. Nor do we even pass on the desirability of so informing the accused—a matter that can be reasonably debated. * * *

imposed the most rigorous restrictions on the information that must be conveyed to a defendant, and the procedures that must be observed, before permitting him to waive his right to counsel at trial. In these extreme cases, and in others that fall between these two poles, we have defined the scope of the right to counsel by a pragmatic assessment of the usefulness of counsel to the accused at the particular proceeding, and the dangers to the accused of proceeding without counsel. An accused's waiver of his right to counsel is "knowing" when he is made aware of these basic facts.

Applying this approach, it is our view that whatever warnings suffice for *Miranda*'s purposes will also be sufficient in the context of postindictment questioning. The State's decision to take an additional step and commence formal adversarial proceedings against the accused does not substantially increase the value of counsel to the accused at questioning, or expand the limited purpose that an attorney serves when the accused is questioned by authorities. With respect to this inquiry, we do not discern a substantial difference between the usefulness of a lawyer to a suspect during custodial interrogation, and his value to an accused at postindictment questioning.

Thus, we require a more searching or formal inquiry before permitting an accused to waive his right to counsel at trial than we require for a Sixth Amendment waiver during postindictment questioning—*not* because postindictment questioning is less important than a trial (the analysis that petitioner's "hierarchical" approach would suggest)—but because the full "dangers and disadvantages of self-representation," during questioning are less substantial and more obvious to an accused than they are at trial.[13] Because the role of counsel at questioning is relatively simple and limited, we see no problem in having a waiver procedure at that stage which is likewise simple and limited. So long as the accused is made aware of the "dangers and disadvantages of self-representation" during postindictment questioning, by use of the *Miranda* warnings, his waiver of his Sixth Amendment right to counsel at such questioning is "knowing and intelligent."

III

Before confessing to the murder of James Jackson, petitioner was meticulously informed by authorities of his right to counsel, and of the consequences of any choice not to exercise that right. On two separate occasions, petitioner elected to forgo the assistance of counsel, and speak directly to officials concerning his role in the murder. Because we believe that petitioner's waiver of his Sixth Amendment rights was "knowing and intelligent," we find no error in the decision of the trial court to permit petitioner's confessions to be used against him. Consequently, the judgment of the Illinois Supreme Court is

---

13. [A]n attorney's role at questioning is relatively limited. But at trial, counsel is required to help even the most gifted layman adhere to the rules of procedure and evidence, comprehend the subtleties of *voir dire,* examine and cross-examine witnesses effectively (including the accused), object to improper prosecution questions, and much more.

Affirmed.

Justice BLACKMUN, dissenting.

I agree with most of what Justice STEVENS says in his dissenting opinion. I, however, merely would hold that after formal adversary proceedings against a defendant have been commenced, the Sixth Amendment mandates that the defendant not be "subject to further interrogation by the authorities until counsel has been made available to him, unless the accused himself initiates further communication, exchanges, or conversations with the police." Michigan v. Jackson. * * *

Justice STEVENS, with whom Justice BRENNAN and Justice MARSHALL join, dissenting.

The Court should not condone unethical forms of trial preparation by prosecutors or their investigators. In civil litigation it is improper for a lawyer to communicate with his or her adversary's client without either notice to opposing counsel or the permission of the court. An attempt to obtain evidence for use at trial by going behind the back of one's adversary would be not only a serious breach of professional ethics but also a manifestly unfair form of trial practice. In the criminal context, the same ethical rules apply and, in my opinion, notions of fairness that are at least as demanding should also be enforced.

After a jury has been empaneled and a criminal trial is in progress, it would obviously be improper for the prosecutor to conduct a private interview with the defendant for the purpose of obtaining evidence to be used against him at trial. By "private interview" I mean, of course, an interview initiated by the prosecutor, or his or her agents, without notice to the defendant's lawyer and without the permission of the court. Even if such an interview were to be commenced by giving the defendant the five items of legal advice that are mandated by *Miranda,* I have no doubt that this Court would promptly and unanimously condemn such a shabby practice. As our holding in *Michigan v. Jackson* suggests, such a practice would not simply constitute a serious ethical violation, but would rise to the level of an impairment of the Sixth Amendment right to counsel.

The question that this case raises, therefore, is at what point in the adversary process does it become impermissible for the prosecutor, or his or her agents, to conduct such private interviews with the opposing party? Several alternatives are conceivable: when the trial commences, when the defendant has actually met and accepted representation by his or her appointed counsel, when counsel is appointed, or when the adversary process commences. In my opinion, the Sixth Amendment right to counsel demands that a firm and unequivocal line be drawn at the point at which adversary proceedings commence.

In prior cases this Court has used strong language to emphasize the significance of the formal commencement of adversary proceedings. * * *

Today, however, * * * the Court backs away from the significance previously attributed to the initiation of formal proceedings. In the majority's view, the purported waiver of counsel in this case is properly equated with that of an unindicted suspect. Yet, as recognized in [earlier cases], important differences separate the two. The return of an indictment, or like instrument, substantially alters the relationship between the state and the accused. Only after a formal accusation has "the government * * * committed itself to prosecute, and only then [have] the adverse positions of government and defendant * * * solidified." Moreover, the return of an indictment also presumably signals the government's conclusion that it has sufficient evidence to establish a prima facie case. As a result, any further interrogation can only be designed to buttress the government's case; authorities are no longer simply attempting " 'to solve a crime.' " Given the significance of the initiation of formal proceedings and the concomitant shift in the relationship between the state and the accused, I think it quite wrong to suggest that *Miranda* warnings—or for that matter, any warnings offered by an adverse party—provide a sufficient basis for permitting the undoubtedly prejudicial—and, in my view, unfair—practice of permitting trained law enforcement personnel and prosecuting attorneys to communicate with as-of-yet unrepresented criminal defendants.

It is well settled that there is a strong presumption against waiver of Sixth Amendment protections, and that a waiver may only be accepted if made with full awareness of "the dangers and disadvantages of self-representation." Warnings offered by an opposing party, whether detailed or cursory, simply cannot satisfy this high standard.

The majority premises its conclusion that *Miranda* warnings lay a sufficient basis for accepting a waiver of the right to counsel on the assumption that those warnings make clear to an accused "what a lawyer could 'do for him' during the postindictment questioning: namely, advise [him] to refrain from making any [incriminating] statements." Yet, this is surely a gross understatement of the disadvantage of proceeding without a lawyer and an understatement of what a defendant must understand to make a knowing waiver. The *Miranda* warnings do not, for example, inform the accused that a lawyer might examine the indictment for legal sufficiency before submitting his or her client to interrogation or that a lawyer is likely to be considerably more skillful at negotiating a plea bargain and that such negotiations may be most fruitful if initiated prior to any interrogation. Rather, the warnings do not even go so far as to explain to the accused the nature of the charges pending against him— advice that a court would insist upon before allowing a defendant to enter a guilty plea with or without the presence of an attorney. Without defining precisely the nature of the inquiry required to establish a valid waiver of the Sixth Amendment right to counsel, it must be conceded that at least minimal advice is necessary—the accused must be told of the "dangers and disadvantages of self-representation."

Yet, once it is conceded that certain advice is required and that after indictment the adversary relationship between the state and the accused has solidified, it inescapably follows that a prosecutor may not conduct private interviews with a charged defendant. As at least one Court of Appeals has recognized, there are ethical constraints that prevent a prosecutor from giving legal advice to an uncounseled adversary. Thus, neither the prosecutor nor his or her agents can ethically provide the unrepresented defendant with the kind of advice that should precede an evidence-gathering interview after formal proceedings have been commenced. Indeed, in my opinion even the *Miranda* warnings themselves are a species of legal advice that is improper when given by the prosecutor after indictment.

Moreover, there are good reasons why such advice is deemed unethical, reasons that extend to the custodial, postindictment setting with unequaled strength. First, the offering of legal advice may lead an accused to underestimate the prosecuting authorities' true adversary posture. For an incarcerated defendant—in this case, a 17–year-old who had been in custody for 44 hours at the time he was told of the indictment—the assistance of someone to explain why he is being held, the nature of the charges against him, and the extent of his legal rights, may be of such importance as to overcome what is perhaps obvious to most, that the prosecutor is a foe and not a friend. Second, the adversary posture of the parties, which is not fully solidified until formal charges are brought, will inevitably tend to color the advice offered. As hard as a prosecutor might try, I doubt that it is possible for one to wear the hat of an effective adviser to a criminal defendant while at the same time wearing the hat of a law enforcement authority. Finally, regardless of whether or not the accused actually understands the legal and factual issues involved and the state's role as an adversary party, advice offered by a lawyer (or his or her agents) with such an evident conflict of interest cannot help but create a public perception of unfairness and unethical conduct. * * *

In sum, without a careful discussion of the pitfalls of proceeding without counsel, the Sixth Amendment right cannot properly be waived. An adversary party, moreover, cannot adequately provide such advice. As a result, once the right to counsel attaches and the adversary relationship between the state and the accused solidifies, a prosecutor cannot conduct a private interview with an accused party without "dilut[ing] the protection afforded by the right to counsel," Although this ground alone is reason enough to never permit such private interviews, the rule also presents the added virtue of drawing a clear and easily identifiable line at the point between the investigatory and adversary stages of a criminal proceeding. Such clarity in definition of constitutional rules that govern criminal proceedings is important to the law enforcement profession as well as to the private citizen. It is true, of course, that the interest in effective law enforcement would benefit from an opportunity to engage in incommunicado questioning of defendants who, for reasons beyond their control, have not been able to receive the legal advice from counsel to which they are constitutionally entitled. But the Court's singleminded concentration on that interest might also lead to the toleration of similar practices at any stage of the trial. I think it clear that such private communications are intolerable not simply during trial, but at any point after adversary proceedings have commenced.

I therefore respectfully dissent.

NOTES AND QUESTIONS

1. Can you articulate the theory of the right to counsel that underlies the majority and the two dissents? Which view of the right to counsel do you prefer?

2. Look again at footnote 8 in the majority opinion. Do you think the Court would find a valid waiver of a defendant's Sixth Amendment right to counsel if he waived *Miranda* without knowing that he was under indictment?

3. Justice White dissented in *Massiah* and *Brewer*, and wrote the majority opinion in *Patterson*. Can you articulate his theory of the Sixth Amendment right to counsel when police are deliberately eliciting statements from an accused?

4. *The Moulton "background principle."* In Maine v. Moulton, 474 U.S. 159, 106 S.Ct. 477, 88 L.Ed.2d 481 (1985), the Court stressed the "background principle" that once an accused is represented by counsel, the state may approach only through counsel. This was significant to the holding in *Moulton* because, unlike *Massiah*, the police were not seeking information about the crime for which the accused was under indictment. After Moulton and a co-defendant were indicted on four counts of theft, both retained counsel. Later, the co-defendant told police that Moulton had threatened to kill one of the state's witnesses on the theft charges. The police chief put a "wire" on the co-defendant to record any conversation about threats to witnesses and to allow police to intervene in case Moulton realized the co-defendant was cooperating with the police.

The *Moulton* dissent described the recording "as part of a good-faith investigation of entirely separate crimes." Indeed, the recordings led to burglary, arson, and three new theft charges against Moulton. Statements about these crimes were, of course, admissible because they were not subject to an indictment at that time.

Statements were also made about the crimes under indictment, but these statements might be viewed as an inadvertent discovery, a sort of good-faith exception to *Massiah*. To meet this argument, the Court asserted that the "Sixth Amendment guarantees the accused, at least after the initiation of formal charges, the right to rely on counsel as a 'medium' between him and the State." The Court thus held that the statements relating to the crimes for which Moulton was under indictment were inadmissible as a violation of the Sixth Amendment.

5. *Michigan v. Jackson.* Notice that, as part of the lawyer-as-medium understanding of *Massiah*, the *Patterson* Court and both dissents cite *Michigan v. Jackson*. The *Patterson* majority distinguished *Jackson* on the ground that Patterson, unlike Jackson, did not request counsel after adversary proceedings had begun. See, e.g., footnote 3 in the majority opinion. Thus, following *Patterson*, defendants were treated differently for purposes of waiver

of the Sixth Amendment right to counsel during interrogation depending on whether they had requested counsel at a judicial proceeding. The *Patterson* dissenters argued that a request for counsel is not necessary once adversary proceedings have begun and, therefore, that Jackson and Patterson should be treated the same way.

The logic of the *Patterson* dissenters won the day but not in a way that they would have liked. In Montejo v. Louisiana, 556 U.S. ___, 129 S.Ct. 2079, 173 L.Ed.2d 955 (2009), the Court overruled *Jackson* and held that the Sixth Amendment creates no broader right to counsel during interrogation than *Miranda* provides. Thus, defendants like Patterson and Jackson are treated the same. Defendants who request counsel following indictment will be in the same position when being questioned by police or prosecutors as indicted defendants who did not request counsel. Both groups must invoke the *Miranda* right to counsel before police are forbidden from seeking *Miranda* waivers. Even more dramatic, defendants who request counsel after being indicted but before being interrogated will be in the same constitutional posture as suspects who have not been indicted.

After *Montejo*, is there anything left of the *Moulton* "counsel-as-medium" theory of the Sixth Amendment?

6. *Miranda and Massiah: two peas in a pod?* Now that *Jackson* has been overruled, is *Massiah*'s protection different from *Miranda*'s when the defendant is being questioned by police or prosecutors? One way to read *Brewer* is that showing waiver by showing that the suspect cooperated with police might be more difficult for the State to show under *Massiah* than under *Miranda*. Compare *North Carolina v. Butler*, p. 666, with the facts of *Brewer*. However that issue comes out, we now know that formal waivers of *Miranda* suffice to waive *Massiah* whether or not the defendant has requested counsel (*Montejo* and *Patterson*).

So is *Massiah* different from *Miranda* in any interesting or important way? Should the Court overrule *Massiah* now that *Miranda* is the 800–pound gorilla?

It may turn out that *Massiah* offers greater protection than *Miranda* along only one dimension: the facts of *Massiah* itself. *Massiah*, but not *Miranda*, applies when the police are trying to obtain information and the suspect is unaware that he is talking to the police. This principle explains not only *Massiah* but also *Henry*, p. 700, and *Moulton*, Note 3 above.

And, as we will see in the next case, *Massiah* also provides *less* protection along one dimension.

C. *MASSIAH* AND *MIRANDA*: A DIVERGENCE

McNEIL v. WISCONSIN

Supreme Court of the United States, 1991.
501 U.S. 171, 111 S.Ct. 2204, 115 L.Ed.2d 158.

JUSTICE SCALIA delivered the opinion of the Court.

This case presents the question whether an accused's invocation of his Sixth Amendment right to counsel during a judicial proceeding constitutes an invocation of his *Miranda* right to counsel.

I

Petitioner Paul McNeil was arrested in Omaha, Nebraska, in May 1987, pursuant to a warrant charging him with an armed robbery in West Allis, Wisconsin, a suburb of Milwaukee. Shortly after his arrest, two Milwaukee County deputy sheriffs arrived in Omaha to retrieve him. After advising him of his *Miranda* rights, the deputies sought to question him. He refused to answer any questions, but did not request an attorney. The deputies promptly ended the interview.

Once back in Wisconsin, petitioner was brought before a Milwaukee County Court Commissioner on the armed robbery charge. The Commissioner set bail and scheduled a preliminary examination. An attorney from the Wisconsin Public Defender's Office represented petitioner at this initial appearance.

Later that evening, Detective Joseph Butts of the Milwaukee County Sheriff's Department visited petitioner in jail. Butts had been assisting the Racine County, Wisconsin, police in their investigation of a murder, attempted murder, and armed burglary in the town of Caledonia; petitioner was a suspect. Butts advised petitioner of his *Miranda* rights, and petitioner signed a form waiving them. In this first interview, petitioner did not deny knowledge of the Caledonia crimes, but said that he had not been involved.

Butts returned two days later with detectives from Caledonia. He again began the encounter by advising petitioner of his *Miranda* rights and providing a waiver form. Petitioner placed his initials next to each of the warnings and signed the form. This time, petitioner admitted that he had been involved in the Caledonia crimes, which he described in detail. He also implicated two other men, Willie Pope and Lloyd Crowley. The statement was typed up by a detective and given to petitioner to review. Petitioner placed his initials next to every reference to himself and signed every page.

Butts and the Caledonia Police returned two days later, having in the meantime found and questioned Pope, who convinced them that he had not been involved in the Caledonia crimes. They again began the interview by administering the *Miranda* warnings and obtaining petitioner's signature and initials on the waiver form. Petitioner acknowledged that he had lied about Pope's involvement to minimize his own role in the Caledonia crimes and provided another statement recounting the events, which was transcribed, signed, and initialed as before. * * *

II

The Sixth Amendment provides that "[i]n all criminal prosecutions, the accused shall enjoy the right * * * to have the Assistance of Counsel for his defence." In *Michigan v. Jackson*, 475 U.S. 625, 106 S.Ct. 1404, 89 L.Ed.2d 631 (1986), we held that once this right to counsel has attached and has been invoked, any subsequent waiver during a police-initiated custodial interview is ineffective. It is undisputed, and we accept for purposes of the present case, that at the time petitioner provided the incriminating statements at issue, his Sixth Amendment right had attached and had been invoked with respect to the *West Allis armed robbery*, for which he had been formally charged.

The Sixth Amendment right, however, is offense specific. It cannot be invoked once for all future prosecutions, for it does not attach until a prosecution is commenced, that is, " 'at or after the initiation of adversary judicial criminal proceedings—whether by way of formal charge, preliminary hearing, indictment, information, or arraignment.' " And just as the right is offense specific, so also its *Michigan v. Jackson* effect of invalidating subsequent waivers in police-initiated interviews is offense specific. * * * Because petitioner provided the statements at issue here before his Sixth Amendment right to counsel with respect to the *Caledonia offenses* had been (or even could have been) invoked, that right poses no bar to the admission of the statements in this case.

Petitioner relies, however, upon a different "right to counsel," found not in the text of the Sixth Amendment, but in this Court's jurisprudence relating to the Fifth Amendment [*Miranda* prophylactic rights]. * * *

In *Edwards v. Arizona* [p. 674], we established a second layer of prophylaxis for the *Miranda* right to counsel: Once a suspect asserts the right, not only must the current interrogation cease, but he may not be approached for further interrogation "until counsel has been made available to him,"—which means, we have most recently held, that counsel must be present, *Minnick v. Mississippi*, 498 U.S. 146, 111 S.Ct. 486, 112 L.Ed.2d 489 (1990). If the police do subsequently initiate an encounter in the absence of counsel (assuming there has been no break in custody), the suspect's statements are presumed involuntary and therefore inadmissible as substantive evidence at trial, even where the suspect executes a waiver and his statements would be considered voluntary under traditional standards. This is "designed to prevent police from badgering a defendant into waiving his previously asserted *Miranda* rights." The *Edwards* rule, moreover, is *not* offense specific: Once a suspect invokes the *Miranda* right to counsel for interrogation regarding one offense, he may not be reapproached regarding *any* offense unless counsel is present.

Having described the nature and effects of both the Sixth Amendment right to counsel and the *Miranda-Edwards* "Fifth Amendment" right to counsel, we come at last to the issue here: Petitioner seeks to prevail by combining the two of them. He contends that, although he expressly waived his *Miranda* right to counsel on every occasion he was interrogated, those waivers were the invalid product of impermissible approaches, because his prior invocation of the offense specific Sixth Amendment right with regard to the West Allis burglary was also an invocation of the nonoffense-specific *Miranda-Edwards* right. We think that is false as a matter of fact and inadvisable (if even permissible) as a contrary-to-fact presumption of policy.

As to the former: The purpose of the Sixth Amendment counsel guarantee—and hence the purpose of invoking it—is to "protec[t] the unaided layman at critical confrontations" with his "expert adversary," the government, *after* "the adverse positions of government and defendant have solidified" with respect to a particular alleged crime. The purpose of the *Miranda-Edwards* guarantee, on the other hand—and hence the purpose of invoking it—is to protect a quite different interest: the suspect's "desire to deal with the police only through counsel." This is in one respect narrower than the interest protected by the Sixth Amendment guarantee (because it relates only to custodial interrogation) and in another respect broader (because it relates to interrogation regarding *any* suspected crime and attaches whether or not the "adversarial relationship" produced by a pending prosecution has yet arisen). To invoke the Sixth Amendment interest is, as a matter of *fact, not* to invoke the *Miranda-Edwards* interest. One might be quite willing to speak to the police without counsel present concerning many matters, but not the matter under prosecution. It can be said, perhaps, that it is *likely* that one who has asked for counsel's assistance in defending against a prosecution would want counsel present for all custodial interrogation, even interrogation unrelated to the charge. That is not necessarily true, since suspects often believe that they can avoid the laying of charges by demonstrating an assurance of innocence through frank and unassisted answers to questions. But even if it were true, the *likelihood* that a suspect would wish counsel to be present is not the test for applicability of *Edwards*. The rule of that case applies only when the suspect "ha[s] *expressed*" his wish for the particular sort of lawyerly assistance that is the subject of *Miranda*. It requires, at a minimum, some statement that can reasonably be construed to be an expression of a desire for the assistance of an attorney *in dealing with custodial interrogation by the police*. Requesting the assistance of an attorney at a bail hearing does not bear that construction. * * *

There remains to be considered the possibility that, even though the assertion of the Sixth Amendment right to counsel does not *in fact* imply an assertion of the *Miranda* "Fifth Amendment" right, we should declare it to be such as a matter of sound policy. Assuming we have such an expansive power under the Constitution, it would not wisely be exercised. Petitioner's proposed rule has only insignificant advantages. If a suspect does not wish to communicate with the police except through an attorney, he can simply tell them that when they give him the *Miranda* warnings. There is not the remotest chance that he will feel "badgered" by their asking to talk to him without counsel present, since the subject will not be the charge on which he has already requested counsel's assistance (for in that event *Jackson* would preclude initiation of the interview) and he will not have rejected uncounseled interrogation on *any* subject before (for in that event *Edwards* would preclude initiation of the interview). The proposed rule would, however, seriously impede effective law enforcement. The Sixth Amendment right to counsel attaches at the first formal proceeding against an accused, and in most States, at least with respect to serious offenses, free counsel is made available at that time and ordinarily requested. Thus, if we were to adopt petitioner's rule, most persons in pretrial custody for serious offenses would be *unapproachable* by police officers suspecting them of involvement in other crimes, *even though they have never expressed any unwillingness to be questioned*. Since the ready ability to obtain uncoerced confessions is not an evil but an unmitigated good, society would be the loser. Admissions of guilt resulting from valid *Miranda* waivers "are more than merely 'desirable'; they are essential to society's compelling interest in finding, convicting, and punishing those who violate the law."[2]

Petitioner urges upon us the desirability of providing a "clear and unequivocal" guideline for the police: no police-initiated questioning of any person in custody who has requested counsel to assist him in defense or in interrogation. But the police do not need our assistance to establish such a guideline; they are free, if they wish, to adopt it on their own. Of course it is our task to establish guidelines for judicial review. We like *them* to be "clear and unequivocal," but only when they guide sensibly and in a direction we are authorized to go. Petitioner's proposal would in our view do much more harm than good, and is not contained within, or even in furtherance of, the Sixth Amendment's right to counsel or the Fifth Amendment's right against compelled self-incrimination.[3] * * *

"This Court is forever adding new stories to the temples of constitutional law, and the temples have a way of collapsing when one story too many is added." We decline to add yet another story to *Miranda*. * * *

---

2. The dissent condemns these sentiments as "revealing a preference for an inquisitorial system of justice." We cannot imagine what this means. What makes a system adversarial rather than inquisitorial is not the presence of counsel, much less the presence of counsel where the defendant has not requested it; but rather, the presence of a judge who does not (as an inquisitor does) conduct the factual and legal investigation himself, but instead decides on the basis of facts and arguments pro and con adduced by the parties. In the inquisitorial criminal process of the civil law, the defendant ordinarily has counsel; and in the adversarial criminal process of the common law, he sometimes does not. Our system of justice is, and has always been, an inquisitorial one at the investigatory stage (even the grand jury is an inquisitorial body), and no other disposition is conceivable. Even if detectives were to bring impartial magistrates around with them to all interrogations, there would be no decision for the impartial magistrate to umpire. If all the dissent means by a "preference for an inquisitorial system" is a preference not to require the presence of counsel during an investigatory interview where the interviewee has not requested it—that is a strange way to put it, but we are guilty.

3. The dissent predicts that the result in this case will routinely be circumvented when, "[i]n future preliminary hearings, competent counsel * * * make sure that they, or their clients, make a statement on the record" invoking the *Miranda* right to counsel. We have in fact never held that a person can invoke his *Miranda* rights anticipatorily, in a context other than "custodial interrogation"—which a preliminary hearing will not always, or even usually, involve. If the *Miranda* right to counsel can be invoked at a preliminary hearing, it could be argued, there is no logical reason why it could not be invoked by a letter prior to arrest, or indeed even prior to identification as a suspect. Most rights must be asserted when the government seeks to take the action they protect against. The fact that we have allowed the *Miranda* right to counsel, once asserted, to be effective with respect to future custodial interrogation does not necessarily mean that we will allow it to be asserted initially outside the context of custodial interrogation, with similar future effect. Assuming, however, that an assertion at arraignment would be effective, and would be routinely made, the mere fact that adherence to the principle of our decisions will not have substantial consequences is no reason to abandon that principle. It would remain intolerable that a person in custody who had expressed *no* objection to being questioned would be unapproachable.

[The opinion of Justice Kennedy, concurring, is omitted.]

Justice STEVENS, with whom Justice MARSHALL and Justice BLACKMUN join, dissenting.

The Court's opinion demeans the importance of the right to counsel. As a practical matter, the opinion probably will have only a slight impact on current custodial interrogation procedures. As a theoretical matter, the Court's innovative development of an "offense-specific" limitation on the scope of the attorney-client relationship can only generate confusion in the law and undermine the protections that undergird our adversarial system of justice. As a symbolic matter, today's decision is ominous because it reflects a preference for an inquisitorial system that regards the defense lawyer as an impediment rather than a servant to the cause of justice.
* * *

NOTES AND QUESTIONS

1. Is it fair to say that Justice Scalia's opinion is truer to the constitutional text, while McNeil's argument is more concerned with the pragmatic effect of not having a bright-line rule? Which position do you prefer?

2. In footnote 3, Justice Scalia is skeptical about the idea that the Fifth Amendment right to counsel can be invoked at the preliminary hearing or in a letter to the police. For cases holding that *Miranda* rights may not be invoked unless interrogation is imminent, see United States v. Muick, 167 F.3d 1162 (7th Cir. 1999); United States v. Grimes, 142 F.3d 1342 (11th Cir.1998); Holland v. State, 813 So.2d 1007 (Fla. App. 2002); People v. Villalobos, 193 Ill.2d 229, 250 Ill.Dec. 17, 737 N.E.2d 639 (2000); People v. Avila, 75 Cal.App.4th 416, 89 Cal.Rptr.2d 320 (1999).

3. In Texas v. Cobb, 532 U.S. 162, 121 S.Ct. 1335, 149 L.Ed.2d 321 (2001), the Court emphasized that *McNeil* had held the Sixth Amendment right to counsel to be "offense specific." But what does it mean to say that the right is *"offense* specific"? Blackstone told us that murder is the same offense as manslaughter, for purposes of the common law prohibition of double jeopardy, but is murder the same double jeopardy offense as a burglary that led to a murder? If not, are these different *Sixth Amendment* offenses? Is there any reason why "offense" should be defined the same way for these different constitutional protections?

The Court answered these questions, by a 5–4 margin, in *Cobb*. The initial report to the sheriff was of a burglary and the disappearance of a woman and her sixteen-month-old daughter from the home. Cobb later confessed to the burglary but denied involvement in the disappearances. The state indicted Cobb for burglary, and the judge appointed counsel to represent him. Later, free on bond, Cobb told his father that he had killed the woman when she confronted him during the burglary. The father reported this information to the authorities, who arrested Cobb. He waived his *Miranda* rights and confessed to killing and burying both the mother and her infant. The details of the death of the infant were particularly gruesome. The trial court permitted the state to introduce this confession in Cobb's murder trial.

The Texas Court of Criminal Appeals reversed Cobb's conviction on the ground that the confession was inadmissible. Cobb's Sixth Amendment right to counsel protected him from any questioning about the burglary, the state court held, and the murders were the same Sixth Amendment "offense" because they were "very closely related factually" to the burglary.

The Supreme Court rejected the state court's test of "factual relation" and held that the test for "same offense" in the Sixth Amendment context is the same as in the Fifth Amendment double jeopardy clause, namely the so-called "*Blockburger*" test from Blockburger v. United States, 284 U.S. 299, 304, 52 S.Ct. 180, 182, 76 L.Ed. 306 (1932). This test finds different statutory offenses to be the same *only* when the elements of one offense are *necessarily* included in the elements of the other offense. One way to express this principle is to say that offenses are the same only when proving the elements of the greater will *always* prove the elements of the lesser.

For example, offense *A* with elements 1, 2, and 3 is the same double jeopardy offense as offense *B* with elements 1 and 2, but *A* is *not* the same offense as offense *C* with elements 1, 2, and 4. To use real life examples, if proving auto theft always proves joyriding, they are the same offense. This, of course, explains why murder is typically the same offense as manslaughter. Robbery would typically be the same offense as larceny (because robbery requires proof of taking the property of another—larceny—by force) but not the same offense as burglary (because robbery requires proof of force while burglary requires proof of breaking and entering a structure).

In *Cobb*, the offenses lacked the necessary elemental relationship. Murder requires proof of a killing while burglary requires proof of breaking and entering. That the murders occurred during the course of the burglary is, according to the Court, insufficient to make the offenses the same for Sixth Amendment purposes. Thus, the Sixth Amendment did not prohibit questioning Cobb about the murders after he had been indicted for the burglary.

Cobb claimed that "the offense-specific rule will prove 'disastrous' to suspects' constitutional rights and will 'permit law enforcement officers almost complete and total license to conduct unwanted and uncounseled interrogations.'" The Court was not persuaded. "Besides offering no evidence that such a parade of horribles has occurred" in the jurisdictions that apply the offense-specific rule, Cobb's argument

> fails to appreciate the significance of two critical considerations. First, there can be no doubt that a suspect must be apprised of his rights against compulsory self-incrimination and to consult with an attorney before authorities may conduct custodial interrogation. See *Miranda v. Arizona*. In the present case, police scrupulously followed *Miranda*'s dictates when questioning respondent. Second, it is critical to recognize that the Constitution does not negate society's interest in the ability of police to talk to witnesses and suspects, even those who have been charged with other offenses.

Justice Breyer dissented, joined by Justices Stevens, Souter, and Ginsburg. The dissent characterized the majority's holding as permitting police to "force a suspect who has asked for legal counsel to make a critical legal choice without the legal assistance that he has requested and that the Constitution guarantees." Moreover, the dissent found the majority's test of "same offense" inadequate both on policy grounds and because it is inconsistent with prior Sixth Amendment case law. The majority's rule will "significantly diminish[] the Sixth Amendment protections" found in earlier cases

> because criminal codes are lengthy and highly detailed, often proliferating "overlapping and related statutory offenses" to the point where prosecutors can easily "spin out a startlingly numerous series of offenses from a single * * * criminal transaction." Thus, an armed robber who reaches across a store counter, grabs the cashier, and demands "your money or your life," may through that single instance of conduct have committed several "offenses," in the majority's sense of the term, including armed robbery, assault, battery, trespass, use of a firearm to commit a felony, and perhaps possession of a firearm by a felon, as well. * * *

> The majority's rule permits law enforcement officials to question those charged with a crime without first approaching counsel, through the simple device of asking questions about any other related crime not actually charged in the indictment. Thus, the police could ask the individual charged with robbery about, say, the assault of the cashier not yet charged, or about any other uncharged offense (unless under *Blockburger*'s definition it counts as the "same crime"), all *without notifying counsel.* * * * What Sixth Amendment sense—what common sense—does such a rule make? * * *

> In fact, under the rule today announced by the majority, two of the seminal cases in our Sixth Amendment jurisprudence would have come out differently. In *Maine v. Moulton,* which the majority points out "expressly referred to the offense-specific nature of the Sixth Amendment right to counsel," we treated burglary and theft as the same offense for Sixth Amendment purposes. * * *

> In *Brewer v. Williams,* [p. 703], the effect of the majority's rule would have been even more dramatic. Because first-degree murder and child abduction each required proof of a fact not required by the other, and because at the time of the impermissible interrogation Williams had been charged only with abduction of a child, Williams' murder conviction should have remained undisturbed. This is not to suggest that this Court has previously addressed and decided the question presented by this case. Rather, it is to point out that the Court's conception of the Sixth Amendment right at the time that *Moulton* and *Brewer* were decided naturally presumed that it extended to factually related but uncharged offenses.

Given the values that underlie the *Massiah* right to counsel, who gets the better of the argument here? Should "offense" be defined more broadly than for Fifth Amendment double jeopardy purposes? The Texas Court of Criminal Appeals used a test of "close factual relation." Is this a better test than *Blockburger*?

4. It is unclear how much of the double jeopardy principles will be read into *Massiah* doctrine. For example, as you will see in Chapter 18, the Court views the federal government as a different sovereign, for double jeopardy purposes, from each of the states and each of the states as separate from the

other forty-nine. Under this "dual sovereignty" principle, a defendant who is convicted, or acquitted, of bank robbery in federal court can be prosecuted *for the very same robbery* in state court, and vice-versa. Should that principle apply to limit the *Massiah* doctrine? Compare United States v. Mills, 412 F.3d 325 (2d Cir. 2005) with United States v. Coker, 433 F.3d 39 (1st Cir. 2005).

5. *Precedent.* As the *Cobb* dissent concluded, *Maine v. Moulton* (p. 726, Note 4), and *Brewer v. Williams* (p. 703) would have been decided differently if the Cobb definition of "offense" had been applied to them. (Can you see why?) The Court, however, did not discuss the definition of "offense" in either case. If the Court rules in favor of a defendant, without mentioning a particular issue but necessarily resolving that issue in the defendant's favor, is the question settled for purposes of *stare decisis*? Was *Cobb* wrong in treating the "offense" issue as "previously undecided?"

6. *And what about waiver?* The Court also granted certiorari in *Cobb* to decide whether Cobb waived his Sixth Amendment right to counsel when he waived *Miranda* but, given the holding against him on the "same offense" issue, the Court did not reach the waiver question. Cobb had consulted with his appointed lawyer, who twice gave permission for police to talk to him, but Cobb apparently did not request a lawyer at any point in the process. Is Cobb's case distinguishable from *Montejo*?

D. SHEDDING LIGHT ON *MASSIAH*'S ANALYTICAL CORE

KANSAS v. VENTRIS

Supreme Court of the United States, 2009.
556 U.S. ___, 129 S.Ct. 1841, 173 L.Ed.2d 801.

JUSTICE SCALIA delivered the opinion of the Court.

We address in this case the question whether a defendant's incriminating statement to a jailhouse informant, concededly elicited in violation of Sixth Amendment strictures, is admissible at trial to impeach the defendant's conflicting statement.

I

In the early hours of January 7, 2004, after two days of no sleep and some drug use, Rhonda Theel and respondent Donnie Ray Ventris reached an ill-conceived agreement to confront Ernest Hicks in his home. The couple testified that the aim of the visit was simply to investigate rumors that Hicks abused children, but the couple may have been inspired by the potential for financial gain: Theel had recently learned that Hicks carried large amounts of cash.

The encounter did not end well. One or both of the pair shot and killed Hicks with shots from a .38–caliber revolver, and the companions drove off in Hicks's truck with approximately $300 of his money and his cell phone. On receiving a tip from two friends of the couple who had helped transport them to Hicks's home, officers arrested Ventris and

Theel and charged them with various crimes, chief among them murder and aggravated robbery. The State dropped the murder charge against Theel in exchange for her guilty plea to the robbery charge and her testimony identifying Ventris as the shooter.

Prior to trial, officers planted an informant in Ventris's holding cell, instructing him to "keep [his] ear open and listen" for incriminating statements. According to the informant, in response to his statement that Ventris appeared to have "something more serious weighing in on his mind," Ventris divulged that "[h]e'd shot this man in his head and in his chest" and taken "his keys, his wallet, about $350.00, and * * * a vehicle."

At trial, Ventris took the stand and blamed the robbery and shooting entirely on Theel. The government sought to call the informant, to testify to Ventris's prior contradictory statement; Ventris objected. The State conceded that there was "probably a violation" of Ventris's Sixth Amendment right to counsel but nonetheless argued that the statement was admissible for impeachment purposes because the violation "doesn't give the Defendant * * * a license to just get on the stand and lie." The trial court agreed and allowed the informant's testimony, but instructed the jury to "consider with caution" all testimony given in exchange for benefits from the State. The jury ultimately acquitted Ventris of felony murder and misdemeanor theft but returned a guilty verdict on the aggravated burglary and aggravated robbery counts.

The Kansas Supreme Court reversed the conviction, holding that "[o]nce a criminal prosecution has commenced, the defendant's statements made to an undercover informant surreptitiously acting as an agent for the State are not admissible at trial for any reason, including the impeachment of the defendant's testimony." Chief Justice McFarland dissented. We granted the State's petition for certiorari.

II

The Sixth Amendment, applied to the States through the Fourteenth Amendment, guarantees that "[i]n all criminal prosecutions, the accused shall * * * have the Assistance of Counsel for his defence." The core of this right has historically been, and remains today, "the opportunity for a defendant to consult with an attorney and to have him investigate the case and prepare a defense for trial." We have held, however, that the right extends to having counsel present at various pretrial "critical" interactions between the defendant and the State, including the deliberate elicitation by law enforcement officers (and their agents) of statements pertaining to the charge, *Massiah v. United States*. The State has conceded throughout these proceedings that Ventris's confession was taken in violation of dictates and was therefore not admissible in the prosecution's case in chief. Without affirming that this concession was necessary, see *Kuhlmann v. Wilson*, [p. 701], we accept it as the law of the case. The only question we answer today is whether the State must bear the additional consequence of inability to counter Ventris's contradictory testimony by placing the informant on the stand.

A

Whether otherwise excluded evidence can be admitted for purposes of impeachment depends upon the nature of the constitutional guarantee that is violated. Sometimes that explicitly mandates exclusion from trial, and sometimes it does not. The Fifth Amendment guarantees that no person shall be compelled to give evidence against himself, and so is violated whenever a truly coerced confession is introduced at trial, whether by way of impeachment or otherwise. The Fourth Amendment, on the other hand, guarantees that no person shall be subjected to unreasonable searches or seizures, and says nothing about excluding their fruits from evidence; exclusion comes by way of deterrent sanction rather than to avoid violation of the substantive guarantee. Inadmissibility has not been automatic, therefore, but we have instead applied an exclusionary-rule balancing test. The same is true for violations of the Fifth and Sixth Amendment prophylactic rules forbidding certain pretrial police conduct.

Respondent argues that the Sixth Amendment's right to counsel is a "right an accused is to enjoy a[t] trial." The core of the right to counsel is indeed a trial right, ensuring that the prosecution's case is subjected to "the crucible of meaningful adversarial testing." But our opinions under the Sixth Amendment, as under the Fifth, have held that the right covers pretrial interrogations to ensure that police manipulation does not render counsel entirely impotent—depriving the defendant of " 'effective representation by counsel at the only stage when legal aid and advice would help him.' "

Our opinion in *Massiah,* to be sure, was equivocal on what precisely constituted the violation. It quoted various authorities indicating that the violation occurred at the moment of the postindictment interrogation because such questioning " 'contravenes the basic dictates of fairness in the conduct of criminal causes.' " But the opinion later suggested that the violation occurred only when the improperly obtained evidence was "used against [the defendant] at his trial." That question was irrelevant to the decision in *Massiah* in any event. Now that we are confronted with the question, we conclude that the *Massiah* right is a right to be free of uncounseled interrogation, and is infringed at the time of the interrogation. That, we think, is when the "Assistance of Counsel" is denied.

It is illogical to say that the right is not violated until trial counsel's task of opposing conviction has been undermined by the statement's admission into evidence. A defendant is not denied counsel merely because the prosecution has been permitted to introduce evidence of guilt—even evidence so overwhelming that the attorney's job of gaining an acquittal is rendered impossible. In such circumstances the accused continues to enjoy the assistance of counsel; the assistance is simply not worth much. The assistance of counsel has been denied, however, at the prior critical stage which produced the inculpatory evidence. Our cases acknowledge that reality in holding that the stringency of the warnings necessary for a waiver of the assistance of counsel varies according to the usefulness of counsel to the accused at the particular [pretrial] proceeding. *Patterson v. Illinois* [, p. 716]. It is *that* deprivation which demands a remedy.

The United States [as *amicus curiae*] insists that "post-charge deliberate elicitation of statements without the defendant's counsel or a valid waiver of counsel is not intrinsically unlawful." That is true when the questioning is unrelated to charged crimes—the Sixth Amendment right is "offense specific," *McNeil v. Wisconsin* [, p. 727]. We have never said, however, that officers may badger counseled defendants about charged crimes so long as they do not use information they gain. The constitutional violation occurs when the uncounseled interrogation is conducted.

B

This case does not involve, therefore, the prevention of a constitutional violation, but rather the scope of the remedy for a violation that has already occurred. Our precedents make clear that the game of excluding tainted evidence for impeachment purposes is not worth the candle. The interests safeguarded by such exclusion are "outweighed by the need to prevent perjury and to assure the integrity of the trial process." "It is one thing to say that the Government cannot make an affirmative use of evidence unlawfully obtained. It is quite another to say that the defendant can * * * provide himself with a shield against contradiction of his untruths." Once the defendant testifies in a way that contradicts prior statements, denying the prosecution use of "the traditional truth-testing devices of the adversary process," is a high price to pay for vindication of the right to counsel at the prior stage.

On the other side of the scale, preventing impeachment use of statements taken in violation of *Massiah* would add little appreciable deterrence. Officers have significant incentive to ensure that they and their informants comply with the Constitution's demands, since statements lawfully obtained can be used for all purposes rather than simply for impeachment. And the *ex ante* probability that evidence gained in violation of *Massiah* would be of use for impeachment is exceedingly small. An investigator would have to anticipate both that the defendant would choose to testify at trial (an unusual occurrence to begin with) *and* that he would testify inconsistently despite the admissibility of his prior statement for impeachment. Not likely to happen—or at least not likely enough to risk squandering the opportunity of using a properly obtained statement for the prosecution's case in chief.

In any event, even if "the officer may be said to have little to lose and perhaps something to gain by way of possibly uncovering impeachment material," we have multiple times rejected the argument that this "speculative possibility" can trump the costs of allowing perjurious statements to go unchallenged. We have held in every other context that tainted evidence—evidence whose very introduction does not constitute the constitutional violation, but whose obtaining was constitutionally invalid—is admissible for impeachment. We see no distinction that would alter the balance here.*

* * *

We hold that the informant's testimony, concededly elicited in violation of the Sixth Amendment, was admissible to challenge Ventris's inconsistent testimony at trial. The judgment of the Kansas Supreme Court is reversed, and the case is remanded for further proceedings not inconsistent with this opinion. * * *

Justice STEVENS, with whom Justice GINSBURG joins, dissenting.

In *Michigan v. Harvey,* 494 U.S. 344, 110 S.Ct. 1176, 108 L.Ed.2d 293 (1990), the Court held that a statement obtained from a defendant in violation of the Sixth Amendment could be used to impeach his testimony at trial. As I explained in a dissent joined by three other Members of the Court, that holding eroded the principle that "those who are entrusted with the power of government have the same duty to respect and obey the law as the ordinary citizen." It was my view then, as it is now, that "the Sixth Amendment is violated when the fruits of the State's impermissible encounter with the represented defendant are used for impeachment just as it is when the fruits are used in the prosecutor's case in chief."

In this case, the State has conceded that it violated the Sixth Amendment as interpreted in *Massiah v. United States* when it used a jailhouse informant to elicit a statement from the defendant. No *Miranda* warnings were given to the defendant, nor was he otherwise alerted to the fact that he was speaking to a state agent. Even though the jury apparently did not credit the informant's testimony, the Kansas Supreme Court correctly concluded that the prosecution should not be allowed to exploit its pretrial constitutional violation during the trial itself. The Kansas Court's judgment should be affirmed.

This Court's contrary holding relies on the view that a defendant's pretrial right to counsel is merely "prophylactic" in nature. The majority argues that any violation of this prophylactic right occurs solely at the time the State subjects a counseled defendant to an uncounseled interrogation, not when the fruits of the encounter are used against the defendant at trial. This reasoning is deeply flawed.

The pretrial right to counsel is not ancillary to, or of lesser importance than, the right to rely on counsel at trial. The Sixth Amendment grants the right to counsel "[i]n all criminal prosecutions," and we have long recognized that the right applies in periods before trial commences.

---

* Respondent's *amicus* insists that jailhouse snitches are so inherently unreliable that this Court should craft a broader exclusionary rule for uncorroborated statements obtained by that means. Brief for National Association of Criminal Defense Lawyers 25–26. Our legal system, however, is built on the premise that it is the province of the jury to weigh the credibility of competing witnesses, and we have long purported to avoid "establish[ing] this Court as a rule-making organ for the promulgation of state rules of criminal procedure." It would be especially inappropriate to fabricate such a rule in this case, where it appears the jury took to heart the trial judge's cautionary instruction on the unreliability of rewarded informant testimony by acquitting Ventris of felony murder.

We have never endorsed the notion that the pretrial right to counsel stands at the periphery of the Sixth Amendment. To the contrary, we have explained that the pretrial period is "perhaps the most critical period of the proceedings" during which a defendant "requires the guiding hand of counsel." *Powell v. Alabama*, p. 13; *Maine v. Moulton*, p. 726, Note 4 (recognizing the defendant's "right to rely on counsel as a 'medium' between him and the State" in all critical stages of prosecution). Placing the prophylactic label on a core Sixth Amendment right mischaracterizes the sweep of the constitutional guarantee.

Treating the State's actions in this case as a violation of a prophylactic right, the Court concludes that introducing the illegally obtained evidence at trial does not itself violate the Constitution. I strongly disagree. While the constitutional breach began at the time of interrogation, the State's use of that evidence at trial compounded the violation. The logic that compels the exclusion of the evidence during the State's case in chief extends to any attempt by the State to rely on the evidence, even for impeachment. The use of ill-gotten evidence during any phase of criminal prosecution does damage to the adversarial process—the fairness of which the Sixth Amendment was designed to protect.

When counsel is excluded from a critical pretrial interaction between the defendant and the State, she may be unable to effectively counter the potentially devastating, and potentially false, evidence subsequently introduced at trial. Inexplicably, today's Court refuses to recognize that this is a constitutional harm. Yet in *Massiah,* the Court forcefully explained that a defendant is "denied the basic protections of the [Sixth Amendment] guarantee when there [is] used against him at his trial evidence of his own incriminating words" that were "deliberately elicited from him after he had been indicted and in the absence of counsel." Sadly, the majority has retreated from this robust understanding of the right to counsel.

Today's decision is lamentable not only because of its flawed underpinnings, but also because it is another occasion in which the Court has privileged the prosecution at the expense of the Constitution. Permitting the State to cut corners in criminal proceedings taxes the legitimacy of the entire criminal process. "The State's interest in truthseeking is congruent with the defendant's interest in representation by counsel, for it is an elementary premise of our system of criminal justice 'that partisan advocacy on both sides of a case will best promote the ultimate objective that the guilty be convicted and the innocent go free.' " Although the Court may not be concerned with the use of ill-gotten evidence in derogation of the right to counsel, I remain convinced that such shabby tactics are intolerable in all cases. I respectfully dissent.

NOTES AND QUESTIONS

1. The majority insists that the apt analogy for *Massiah* violations is with Fourth Amendment and *Miranda* violations, which occur at the time of the police action. Then the Court balances the additional deterrence that

would result from excluding the statements when offered to impeach (not very much) against the need to prevent perjury (high). That balance favors the State, as it did in the Fourth Amendment and *Miranda* contexts. How does the dissent's view differ from the majority's? Which do you prefer?

2. As the right to counsel is at least in part a trial right, unlike the right to be free from coercive police interrogation, there is much to be said for the dissent's theory of when the counsel violation occurs. That this argument garnered only two votes suggests two propositions. First, the current Court finds exclusionary rules distasteful. Second, today's Court might have decided *Massiah* differently, along the lines of Justice White's dissent. A more forthright approach in *Ventris* would have been to overrule *Massiah*, as Sherry Colb recommended in 2001. *Massiah* treats similarly situated defendants differently depending on whether charges have been filed. But, Colb argues, indictment is a meaningless threshold when the issue is whether defendants need legal advice about how to respond to police who are seeking statements from them. Why doesn't a defendant need advice of counsel the day before indictment just as much as he needs advice the day after indictment? See Sherry F. Colb, *Why the Supreme Court Should Overrule the Massiah Doctrine and Permit Miranda Alone to Govern Interrogations*, at http://writ.news.findlaw.com/colb/20010509.html.

Colb is also highly critical of *Ventris*, concluding that there is "something deeply dishonest about the [majority] opinion." *Kansas v. Ventris: The Supreme Court Misconstrues the Right to Counsel*, at http://writ.news.findlaw.com/colb/20090610.html. To Colb, the real rationale of *Ventris* is that the Court views *Massiah* as a prophylactic, designed to protect the "real" right to counsel. But Justice Scalia cannot embrace that rationale because he ridiculed it in *Dickerson v. United States*, p. 623, the case that "clarified" the status of *Miranda*.

3. A different approach governs statements compelled by threat of contempt after a grant of immunity. See New Jersey v. Portash, 440 U.S. 450, 99 S.Ct. 1292, 59 L.Ed.2d 501 (1979), where the Court reasoned that a "pristine" violation of the Fifth Amendment precluded any use of the statements. The Court rejected resort to the balancing test it had used in deciding that statements taken in violation of *Miranda* could be used to impeach.

> Balancing of interests was thought to be necessary in *Harris* [*v. New York*] * * * when the attempt to deter unlawful police conduct collided with the need to prevent perjury. Here, by contrast, we deal with the constitutional privilege against compulsory self-incrimination in its most pristine form. Balancing, therefore, is not simply unnecessary. It is impermissible.

The Court gave no explanation for why balancing is impermissible when a "pristine" violation of the self-incrimination clause occurs. Is this formalistic distinction persuasive? After all, a violation of the Fourth Amendment is a "pristine" violation and yet that evidence can be used to impeach.

For an argument that the Court's emerging theory of what constitutes testimonial evidence has undermined *Portash*, which should now be overruled, see Michael J. Zydney Mannheimer, *Toward a Unified Theory of Testimonial*

Evidence under the Fifth and Sixth Amendments, 80 Temple L. Rev. 1135 (2007).

4.   Justice Stevens wrote the Court's opinion in *Maine v. Moulton* (p. 726, Note 4), and is clearly unwilling to give up the idea of counsel as medium between the client and the State. See the fourth paragraph from the end of his dissent. As we pointed out in Note 5 after *Patterson* (p. 716), however, the Court no longer seems to put much stock in that metaphor.

5.   After reading *Ventris*, can you articulate the underlying analytical structure of the *Massiah* doctrine? Can you summarize the differences between the Fifth Amendment right to counsel and the Sixth Amendment right to counsel during interrogation? For one effort to do so, see 1 Joshua Dressler & Alan C. Michaels, Understanding Criminal Procedure § 25.08 (5th ed. 2010).

CHAPTER 9

ENTRAPMENT

■ ■ ■

INTRODUCTORY COMMENT

Entrapment is a criminal law defense. As with other defenses, a defendant who proves "entrapment" is entitled to be acquitted of an offense or to have the charge against her dismissed. Put another way, a finding of entrapment does more than result in exclusion of evidence at trial: It bars the successful prosecution of the defendant.

Entrapment is not a constitutional doctrine. That is, when a police officer "entraps" a person, she does not, *by that fact alone*, violate any provision of the Constitution. Therefore, no jurisdiction is required to recognize the entrapment defense. Nonetheless, every state and the federal courts recognize the claim in some form. And, as you will see at the end of this chapter, there remains a lingering question of whether entrapment-like techniques can become so outrageous that, at some point, the Constitution *is* offended.

Generally speaking, there are two approaches to entrapment, termed the "subjective" and "objective" tests of entrapment. In *Sherman v. United States*, the first case in this chapter, the majority opinion adopts the subjective test; the concurring justices prefer the objective standard. The subjective standard is followed in the federal courts and some states; other states apply an objective test.

SHERMAN v. UNITED STATES

Supreme Court of the United States, 1958.
356 U.S. 369, 78 S.Ct. 819, 2 L.Ed.2d 848.

MR. CHIEF JUSTICE WARREN delivered the opinion of the Court.

The issue before us is whether petitioner's conviction should be set aside on the ground that as a matter of law the defense of entrapment was established. Petitioner was convicted under an indictment charging three sales of narcotics in violation of 21 U. S. C. § 174. * * *

In late August 1951, Kalchinian, a government informer, first met petitioner at a doctor's office where apparently both were being treated to be cured of narcotics addiction. Several accidental meetings followed, either at the doctor's office or at the pharmacy where both filled their prescriptions from the doctor. From mere greetings, conversation progressed to a discussion of mutual experiences and problems, including their attempts to overcome addiction to narcotics. Finally Kalchinian asked petitioner if he knew of a good source of narcotics. He asked petitioner to supply him with a source because he was not responding to treatment. From the first, petitioner tried to avoid the issue. Not until after a number of repetitions of the request, predicated on Kalchinian's presumed suffering, did petitioner finally acquiesce. Several times thereafter he obtained a quantity of narcotics which he shared with Kalchinian. Each time petitioner told Kalchinian that the total cost of narcotics he obtained was twenty-five dollars and that Kalchinian owed him fifteen dollars. The informer thus bore the cost of his share of the narcotics plus the taxi and other expenses necessary to obtain the drug. After several such sales Kalchinian informed agents of the Bureau of Narcotics that he had another seller for them. On three occasions during November 1951, government agents observed petitioner give narcotics to Kalchinian in return for money supplied by the Government.

At the trial the factual issue was whether the informer had convinced an otherwise unwilling person to commit a criminal act or whether petitioner was already predisposed to commit the act and exhibited only the natural hesitancy of one acquainted with the narcotics trade. The issue of entrapment went to the jury, and a conviction resulted. Petitioner was sentenced to imprisonment for ten years. * * *

In *Sorrells v. United States*, 287 U.S. 435, 53 S.Ct. 210, 77 L.Ed. 413 [(1932)], this Court firmly recognized the defense of entrapment in the federal courts. The intervening years have in no way detracted from the principles underlying that decision. The function of law enforcement is the prevention of crime and the apprehension of criminals. Manifestly, that function does not include the manufacturing of crime. Criminal activity is such that stealth and strategy are necessary weapons in the arsenal of the police officer. However, "[a] different question is presented when the criminal design originates with the officials of the Government, and they implant in the mind of an innocent person the disposition to commit the alleged offense and induce its commission in order that they may prosecute." Then stealth and strategy become as objectionable police methods as the coerced confession and the unlawful search. Congress could not have intended that its statutes were to be enforced by tempting innocent persons into violations.

However, the fact that government agents "merely afford opportunities or facilities for the commission of the offense does not" constitute entrapment. Entrapment occurs only when the criminal conduct was "the product of the *creative* activity" of law-enforcement officials. To determine whether entrapment has been established, a line must be drawn between the trap for the unwary innocent and the trap for the unwary criminal. The principles by which the courts are to make this determination were outlined in *Sorrells*. On the one hand, at trial the accused may examine the conduct of the government agent; and on the other hand, the accused will be subjected to an "appropriate and searching inquiry into his own conduct and predisposition" as bearing on his claim of innocence.

We conclude from the evidence that entrapment was established as a matter of law. * * * We reach our conclusion from the undisputed testimony of the prosecution's witnesses.

It is patently clear that petitioner was induced by Kalchinian. The informer himself testified that, believing petitioner to be undergoing a cure for narcotics addiction, he nonetheless sought to persuade petitioner to obtain for him a source of narcotics. In Kalchinian's own words we are told of the accidental, yet recurring, meetings, the ensuing conversations concerning mutual experiences in regard to narcotics addiction, and then of Kalchinian's resort to sympathy. One request was not enough, for Kalchinian tells us that additional ones were necessary to overcome, first, petitioner's refusal, then his evasiveness, and then his hesitancy in order to achieve capitulation. Kalchinian not only procured a source of narcotics but apparently also induced petitioner to return to the habit. Finally, assured of a catch, Kalchinian informed the authorities so that they could close the net. The Government cannot disown Kalchinian and insist it is not responsible for his actions. Although he was not being paid, Kalchinian was an active government informer who had but recently been the instigator of at least two other prosecutions. * * * It makes no difference that the sales for which petitioner was convicted occurred after a series of sales. They were not independent acts subsequent to the inducement but part of a course of conduct which was the product of the inducement. * * *

The Government sought to overcome the defense of entrapment by claiming that petitioner evinced a "ready complaisance" to accede to Kalchinian's request. Aside from a record of past convictions, which we discuss in the following paragraph, the Government's case is unsupported. There is no evidence that petitioner himself was in the trade. When his apartment was searched after arrest, no narcotics were found. There is no significant evidence that petitioner even made a profit on any sale to Kalchinian. The Government's characterization of petitioner's hesitancy to Kalchinian's request as the natural wariness of the criminal cannot fill the evidentiary void.

The Government's additional evidence * * * that petitioner was ready and willing to sell narcotics should the opportunity present itself was petitioner's record of two past narcotics convictions. In 1942 petitioner was convicted of illegally selling narcotics; in 1946 he was convicted of illegally possessing them. However, a nine-year-old sales conviction and a five-year-old possession conviction are insufficient to prove petitioner had a readiness to sell narcotics at the time Kalchinian approached him, particularly when we must assume from the record he was trying to overcome the narcotics habit at the time.

The case at bar illustrates an evil which the defense of entrapment is designed to overcome. The government informer entices someone attempting to avoid narcotics not only into carrying out an illegal sale but also into returning to the habit of use. Selecting the proper time, the informer then tells the government agent. The set-up is accepted by the agent without even a question as to the manner in which the informer encountered the seller. Thus the Government plays on the weaknesses of an innocent party and beguiles him into committing crimes which he otherwise would not have attempted. Law enforcement does not require methods such as this. * * *

Mr. Justice FRANKFURTER, whom Mr. Justice DOUGLAS, Mr. Justice HARLAN, and Mr. Justice BRENNAN join, concurring in the result.

Although agreeing with the Court that the undisputed facts show entrapment as a matter of law, I reach this result by a route different from the Court's. * * *

It is surely sheer fiction to suggest that a conviction cannot be had when a defendant has been entrapped by government officers or informers because "Congress could not have intended that its statutes were to be enforced by tempting innocent persons into violations." In these cases raising claims of entrapment, the only legislative intention that can with any show of reason be extracted from the statute is the intention to make criminal precisely the conduct in which the defendant has engaged. That conduct includes all the elements necessary to constitute criminality. * * * [T]he defendant has violated the statutory command. * * * In these circumstances, conduct is not less criminal because the result of temptation, whether the tempter is a private person or a government agent or informer.

The courts refuse to convict an entrapped defendant, not because his conduct falls outside the proscription of the statute, but because, even if his guilt be admitted, the methods employed on behalf of the Government to bring about conviction cannot be countenanced. As Mr. Justice Holmes said in *Olmstead v. United States*, 277 U.S. 438, 470, 48 S.Ct. 564, 575, 72 L.Ed. 944, (dissenting), in another connection, "[* * *] [F]or my part I think it a less evil that some criminals should escape than that the Government should play an ignoble part." Insofar as they are used as instrumentalities in the administration of criminal justice, the federal courts have an obligation to set their face against enforcement of the law by lawless means or means that violate rationally vindicated standards of justice, and to refuse to sustain such methods by effectuating them. * * * Public confidence in the fair and honorable administration of justice, upon which ultimately depends the rule of law, is the transcending value at stake. * * *

The crucial question, not easy of answer, to which the court must direct itself is whether the police conduct revealed in the particular case falls below standards, to which common feelings respond, for the proper use of governmental power. For answer it is wholly irrelevant to ask if the "intention" to commit the crime originated with the defendant or government officers, or if the criminal conduct was the product of "the creative activity" of law-enforcement officials. Yet in the present case the Court repeats and purports to apply these unrevealing tests. Of course in every case of this kind the intention that the particular crime be committed originates with the police, and without their inducement the crime would not have occurred. But it is perfectly clear [that] * * * where the police in effect simply furnished the opportunity for the commission of the crime, that this is not enough to enable the defendant to escape conviction.

The intention referred to, therefore, must be a general intention or predisposition to commit, whenever the opportunity should arise, crimes of the kind solicited, and in proof of such a predisposition evidence has often been admitted to show the defendant's reputation, criminal activities, and prior disposition. The danger of prejudice in such a situation, particularly if the issue of entrapment must be submitted to the jury and disposed of by a general verdict of guilty or innocent, is evident. The defendant must either forego the claim of entrapment or run the substantial risk that, in spite of instructions, the jury will allow a criminal record or bad reputation to weigh in its determination of guilt of the specific offense of which he stands charged. Furthermore, a test that looks to the character and predisposition of the defendant rather than the conduct of the police loses sight of the underlying reason for the defense of entrapment. No matter what the defendant's past record and present inclinations to criminality, or the depths to which he has sunk in the estimation of society, certain police conduct to ensnare him into further crime is not to be tolerated by an advanced society. * * * Permissible police activity does not vary according to the particular defendant concerned; surely if two suspects have been solicited at the same time in the same manner, one should not go to jail simply because he has been convicted before and is said to have a criminal disposition. * * * Appeals to sympathy, friendship, the possibility of exorbitant gain, and so forth, can no more be tolerated when directed against a past offender than against an ordinary law-abiding citizen. A contrary view runs afoul of fundamental principles of equality under law, and would espouse the notion that when dealing with the criminal classes anything goes. * * * Past crimes do not forever outlaw the criminal and open him to police practices, aimed at securing his repeated conviction, from which the ordinary citizen is protected. * * *

This does not mean that the police may not act so as to detect those engaged in criminal conduct and ready and willing to commit further crimes should the occasion arise. Such indeed is their obligation. It does mean that in holding out inducements they should act in such a manner as is likely to induce to the commission of crime only these persons and not others who would normally avoid crime and through self-struggle resist ordinary temptations. This test shifts attention from the record and predisposition of the particular defendant to the conduct of the police and the likelihood, objectively considered, that it would entrap only those ready and willing to commit crime. It is as objective a test as the subject matter permits, and will give guidance in regulating police conduct that is lacking when the reasonableness of police suspicions must be judged or the criminal disposition of the defendant retrospectively appraised. * * *

What police conduct is to be condemned, because likely to induce those not otherwise ready and willing to commit crime, must be picked out from case to case as new situations arise involving different crimes and new methods of detection. * * * Particularly reprehensible in the present case was the use of repeated requests to overcome petitioner's hesitancy, coupled with appeals to sympathy based on mutual experiences with narcotics addiction. Evidence of the setting in which the inducement took place is of course highly relevant in judging its likely effect, and the court should also consider the nature of the crime involved, its secrecy and difficulty of detection, and the manner in which the particular criminal business is usually carried out.

As Mr. Justice Roberts convincingly urged in the *Sorrells* case, * * * "[t]he protection of its own functions and the preservation of the purity of its own temple belongs only to the court. It is the province of the court and of the court alone to protect itself and the government from such prostitution of the criminal law. The violation of the principles of justice by the entrapment of the unwary into crime should be dealt with by the court no matter by whom or at what stage of the proceedings the facts are brought to its attention." Equally important is the consideration that a jury verdict, although it may settle the issue of entrapment in the particular case, cannot give significant guidance for official conduct for the future. Only the court, through the gradual evolution of explicit standards in accumulated precedents, can do this with the degree of certainty that the wise administration of criminal justice demands.

NOTES AND QUESTIONS

1. Chief Justice Warren observed that no narcotics were found in Sherman's residence during the post-arrest search. Why is this relevant to the entrapment defense?

2. The majority opinion espoused a "subjective" test of entrapment. Justice Frankfurter advocated an "objective" test. What are the elements of each test? What are the procedural differences between the two versions of entrapment? Which test do *you* prefer?

3. What is the underlying theory of the entrapment defense? Is it that no offense occurs when the police entrap an actor? Or, is it that an offense occurs, but we do not blame the actor for committing it because of police entrapment? Or, does an offense occur *and* the actor is culpable for committing it, but we still release him from liability because of the police conduct? Which of these explanations is the soundest basis of the defense? If you favor the second answer—the actor is not culpable—why is someone like Sherman

excused for his actions? Is there any traditional criminal law defense analogous to entrapment?

4. *Problem*. In order to apprehend women pickpockets who were posing as prostitutes, a Minneapolis police officer pinned two $20 bills inside the front pocket of his coat so as to make portions of the bills visible. He then went into an alley at midnight and removed his penis from his pants as if to urinate. A woman drove by in a car, stopped, stuck her head out of the vehicle window, and propositioned him for sex. The officer answered, "OK with me," after which the woman (now out of the car) grabbed his penis, asked him what he wanted and how much he wanted to spend. While negotiating, the woman grabbed the $20 bills and fled. She was arrested on charges relating to prostitution and theft. R.T. Nybak, *Officer Nabs Prostitute Suspect with "Unbecoming" Technique*, Minneapolis Tribune, August 30, 1980, at 3A. Does the woman have a valid entrapment defense under the subjective test? Objective test?

JACOBSON v. UNITED STATES

Supreme Court of the United States, 1992.
503 U.S. 540, 112 S.Ct. 1535, 118 L.Ed.2d 174.

Justice White delivered the opinion of the Court. * * *

I

In February 1984, petitioner, a 56–year-old veteran-turned-farmer who supported his elderly father in Nebraska, ordered two magazines and a brochure from a California adult bookstore. The magazines, entitled Bare Boys I and Bare Boys II, contained photographs of nude preteen and teenage boys. The contents of the magazines startled petitioner, who testified that he had expected to receive photographs of "young men 18 years or older." * * *

The young men depicted in the magazines were not engaged in sexual activity, and petitioner's receipt of the magazines was legal under both federal and Nebraska law. Within three months, the law with respect to child pornography changed; Congress passed the [Child Protection Act of 1984] illegalizing the receipt through the mails of sexually explicit depictions of children. In the very month that the new provision became law, postal inspectors found petitioner's name on the mailing list of the California bookstore that had mailed him Bare Boys I and II. There followed over the next 2½ years repeated efforts by two Government agencies, through five fictitious organizations and a bogus pen pal, to explore petitioner's willingness to break the new law by ordering sexually explicit photographs of children through the mail.

The Government began its efforts in January 1985 when a postal inspector sent petitioner a letter supposedly from the American Hedonist Society, which in fact was a fictitious organization. The letter included a membership application and stated the Society's doctrine: that members had the "right to read what we desire, the right to discuss similar interests with those who share our philosophy, and finally that we have the right to seek pleasure without restrictions being placed on us by outdated puritan morality." Petitioner enrolled in the organization and returned a sexual attitude questionnaire that asked him to rank on a scale of one to four his enjoyment of various sexual materials, with one being "really enjoy," two being "enjoy," three being "somewhat enjoy," and four being "do not enjoy." Petitioner ranked the entry "[p]re-teen sex" as a two, but indicated that he was opposed to pedophilia.

For a time, the Government left petitioner alone. But then a new "prohibited mailing specialist" in the Postal Service found petitioner's name in a file, and in May 1986, petitioner received a solicitation from a second fictitious consumer research company, "Midlands Data Research," seeking a response from those who "believe in the joys of sex and the complete awareness of those lusty and youthful lads and lasses of the neophite [sic] age." The letter never explained whether "neophite" referred to minors or young adults. Petitioner responded: "Please feel free to send me more information, I am interested in teenage sexuality. Please keep my name confidential."

Petitioner then heard from yet another Government creation, "Heartland Institute for a New Tomorrow" (HINT), which proclaimed that it was "an organization founded to protect and promote sexual freedom and freedom of choice. We believe that arbitrarily imposed legislative sanctions restricting *your* sexual freedom should be rescinded through the legislative process." The letter also enclosed a second survey. Petitioner indicated that his interest in "[p]reteen sex-homosexual" material was above average, but not high. In response to another question, petitioner wrote: "Not only sexual expression but freedom of the press is under attack. We must be ever vigilant to counter attack right wing fundamentalists who are determined to curtail our freedoms."

HINT replied, portraying itself as a lobbying organization seeking to repeal "all statutes which regulate sexual activities, except those laws which deal with violent behavior, such as rape. HINT is also lobbying to eliminate any legal definition of 'the age of consent'." These lobbying efforts were to be funded by sales from a catalog to be published in the future "offering the sale of various items which we believe you will find to be both interesting and stimulating." HINT also provided computer matching of group members with similar survey responses; and, although petitioner was supplied with a list of potential "pen pals," he did not initiate any correspondence.

Nevertheless, the Government's "prohibited mailing specialist" began writing to petitioner, using the pseudonym "Carl Long." The letters employed a tactic known as "mirroring," which the inspector described as "reflect[ing] whatever the interests are of the person we are writing to." Petitioner responded at first, indicating that his interest was primarily in "male-male items." Inspector "Long" wrote back:

> "My interests too are primarily male-male items. Are you satisfied with the type of VCR tapes available? Personally, I like the amateur stuff better if its [sic] well produced as it can get more kinky and also seems more real. I think the actors enjoy it more."

Petitioner responded:

> "As far as my likes are concerned, I like good looking young guys (in their late teens and early 20's) doing their thing together."

Petitioner's letters to "Long" made no reference to child pornography. After writing two letters, petitioner discontinued the correspondence.

By March 1987, 34 months had passed since the Government obtained petitioner's name from the mailing list of the California bookstore, and 26 months had passed since the Postal Service had commenced its mailings to petitioner. Although petitioner had responded to surveys and letters, the Government had no evidence that petitioner had ever intentionally possessed or been exposed to child pornography. The Postal Service had not checked petitioner's mail to determine whether he was receiving questionable mailings from persons—other than the Government—involved in the child pornography industry.

At this point, a second Government agency, the Customs Service, included petitioner in its own child pornography sting, "Operation Borderline," after receiving his name on lists submitted by the Postal Service. Using the name of a fictitious Canadian company called "Produit Outaouais," the Customs Service mailed petitioner a brochure advertising photographs of young boys engaging in sex. Petitioner placed an order that was never filled.

The Postal Service also continued its efforts in the Jacobson case, writing to petitioner as the "Far Eastern Trading Company Ltd." The letter began:

> "As many of you know, much hysterical nonsense has appeared in the American media concerning 'pornography' and what must be done to stop it from coming across your borders. This brief letter does not allow us to give much comments; however, why is your government spending millions of dollars to exercise international censorship while tons of drugs, which makes yours the world's most crime ridden country are passed through easily."

The letter went on to say:

> "[W]e have devised a method of getting these to you without prying eyes of U.S. Customs seizing your mail. * * * After consultations with American solicitors, we have been advised that once we have posted our material through your system, it cannot be opened for any inspection without authorization of a judge."

The letter invited petitioner to send for more information. It also asked petitioner to sign an affirmation that he was "not a law enforcement officer or agent of the U.S. Government acting in an undercover capacity for the purpose of entrapping Far Eastern Trading Company, its agents or customers." Petitioner responded. A catalog was sent, and petitioner ordered Boys Who Love Boys, a pornographic magazine depicting young boys engaged in various sexual activities. Petitioner was arrested after a controlled delivery of a photocopy of the magazine.

When petitioner was asked at trial why he placed such an order, he explained that the Government had succeeded in piquing his curiosity:

> "Well, the statement was made of all the trouble and the hysteria over pornography and I wanted to see what the material was. It didn't describe the—I didn't know for sure what kind of sexual action they were referring to in the Canadian letter."

In petitioner's home, the Government found the Bare Boys magazines and materials that the Government had sent to him in the course of its protracted investigation, but no other materials that would indicate that petitioner collected, or was actively interested in, child pornography.

Petitioner was indicted for violating [the federal child pornography statute]. The trial court instructed the jury on the petitioner's entrapment defense, petitioner was convicted * * *. * * *

II

There can be no dispute about the evils of child pornography or the difficulties that laws and law enforcement have encountered in eliminating it. Likewise, there can be no dispute that the Government may use undercover agents to enforce the law. * * *

In their zeal to enforce the law, however, Government agents may not originate a criminal design, implant in an innocent person's mind the disposition to commit a criminal act, and then induce commission of the crime so that the Government may prosecute. Where the Government has induced an individual to break the law and the defense of entrapment is at issue, as it was in this case, the prosecution must prove beyond reasonable doubt that the defendant was disposed to commit the criminal act prior to first being approached by Government agents.[2]

---

2. Inducement is not at issue in this case. The Government does not dispute that it induced petitioner to commit the crime. The sole issue is whether the Government carried its burden of proving that petitioner was predisposed to violate the law *before* the Government intervened. The dissent is mistaken in claiming that this is an innovation in entrapment law and in suggesting that the Government's conduct prior to the moment of solicitation is irrelevant. * * * Indeed, the proposition that the accused must be predisposed prior to contact with law enforcement officers is so firmly established that the Government conceded the point at oral argument, submitting that the evidence it developed during the course of its investigation was probative because it indicated petitioner's state of mind *prior* to the commencement of the Government's investigation.

This long-established standard in no way encroaches upon Government investigatory activities. Indeed, the Government's internal guidelines for undercover operations provide that an inducement to commit a crime should not be offered unless:

> "(a) [T]here is a reasonable indication, based on information developed through informants or other means, that the subject is engaging, has engaged, or is likely to engage in illegal activity of a similar type; *or*

> "(b) The opportunity for illegal activity has been structured so that there is reason for believing that persons drawn to the opportunity, or brought to it, are predisposed to engage in

Thus, an agent deployed to stop the traffic in illegal drugs may offer the opportunity to buy or sell drugs and, if the offer is accepted, make an arrest on the spot or later. In such a typical case, or in a more elaborate "sting" operation involving government-sponsored fencing where the defendant is simply provided with the opportunity to commit a crime, the entrapment defense is of little use because the ready commission of the criminal act amply demonstrates the defendant's predisposition. Had the agents in this case simply offered petitioner the opportunity to order child pornography through the mails, and petitioner—who must be presumed to know the law—had promptly availed himself of this criminal opportunity, it is unlikely that his entrapment defense would have warranted a jury instruction.

But that is not what happened here. By the time petitioner finally placed his order, he had already been the target of 26 months of repeated mailings and communications from Government agents and fictitious organizations. Therefore, although he had become predisposed to break the law by May 1987, it is our view that the Government did not prove that this predisposition was independent and not the product of the attention that the Government had directed at petitioner since January 1985.

The prosecution's evidence of predisposition falls into two categories: evidence developed prior to the Postal Service's mail campaign, and that developed during the course of the investigation. The sole piece of preinvestigation evidence is petitioner's 1984 order and receipt of the Bare Boys magazines. But this is scant if any proof of petitioner's predisposition to commit an illegal act, the criminal character of which a defendant is presumed to know. It may indicate a predisposition to view sexually-oriented photographs that are responsive to his sexual tastes; but evidence that merely indicates a generic inclination to act within a broad range, not all of which is criminal, is of little probative value in establishing predisposition.

Furthermore, petitioner was acting within the law at the time he received these magazines. Receipt through the mails of sexually explicit depictions of children for noncommercial use did not become illegal under federal law until May 1984, and Nebraska had no law that forbade petitioner's possession of such material until 1988. Evidence of predisposition to do what once was lawful is not, by itself, sufficient to show predisposition to do what is now illegal, for there is a common understanding that most people obey the law even when they disapprove of it. * * * Hence, the fact that petitioner legally ordered and received the Bare Boys magazines does little to further the Government's burden of proving that petitioner was predisposed to commit a criminal act. This is particularly true given petitioner's unchallenged testimony was that he did not know until they arrived that the magazines would depict minors.

---

the contemplated illegal activity." Attorney General's Guidelines on FBI Undercover Operations (Dec. 31, 1980), reprinted in S. Rep. No. 97–682, p. 551 (1982).

The prosecution's evidence gathered during the investigation also fails to carry the Government's burden. Petitioner's responses to the many communications prior to the ultimate criminal act were at most indicative of certain personal inclinations, including a predisposition to view photographs of preteen sex and a willingness to promote a given agenda by supporting lobbying organizations. Even so, petitioner's responses hardly support an inference that he would commit the crime of receiving child pornography through the mails.[3] Furthermore, a person's inclinations and "fantasies * * * are his own and beyond the reach of government * * *."

On the other hand, the strong arguable inference is that, by waving the banner of individual rights and disparaging the legitimacy and constitutionality of efforts to restrict the availability of sexually explicit materials, the Government not only excited petitioner's interest in sexually explicit materials banned by law but also exerted substantial pressure on petitioner to obtain and read such material as part of a fight against censorship and the infringement of individual rights. * * *

Petitioner's ready response to these [anti-censorship] solicitations cannot be enough to establish beyond reasonable doubt that he was predisposed, prior to the Government acts intended to create predisposition, to commit the crime of receiving child pornography through the mails. The evidence that petitioner was ready and willing to commit the offense came only after the Government had devoted 2½ years to convincing him that he had or should have the right to engage in the very behavior proscribed by law. Rational jurors could not say beyond a reasonable doubt that petitioner possessed the requisite predisposition prior to the Government's investigation and that it existed independent of the Government's many and varied approaches to petitioner. * * *

Justice O'CONNOR, with whom THE CHIEF JUSTICE and Justice KENNEDY join, and with whom Justice SCALIA joins except as to Part II, dissenting.

Keith Jacobson was offered only two opportunities to buy child pornography through the mail. Both times, he ordered. Both times, he asked for opportunities to buy more. He needed no Government agent to coax, threaten, or persuade him; no one played on his sympathies, friendship, or suggested that his committing the crime would further a greater good. In fact, no Government agent even contacted him face to face. The Government contends that from the enthusiasm with which Mr. Jacobson responded to the chance to commit a crime, a reasonable jury could permissibly infer beyond a reasonable doubt that he was predisposed to commit the crime. I agree.

The first time the Government sent Mr. Jacobson a catalog of illegal materials, he ordered a set of photographs advertised as picturing "young

---

3. We do not hold, as the dissent suggests, that the Government was required to prove that petitioner knowingly violated the law. We simply conclude that proof that petitioner engaged in legal conduct and possessed certain generalized personal inclinations is not sufficient evidence to prove beyond a reasonable doubt that he would have been predisposed to commit the crime charged independent of the Government's coaxing.

boys in sex action fun." He enclosed the following note with his order: "I received your brochure and decided to place an order. If I like your product, I will order more later." For reasons undisclosed in the record, Mr. Jacobson's order was never delivered.

The second time the Government sent a catalog of illegal materials, Mr. Jacobson ordered a magazine called "Boys Who Love Boys," described as: "11 year old and 14 year old boys get it on in every way possible. Oral, anal sex and heavy masturbation. If you love boys, you will be delighted with this." Along with his order, Mr. Jacobson sent the following note: "Will order other items later. I want to be discreet in order to protect you and me."

Government agents admittedly did not offer Mr. Jacobson the chance to buy child pornography right away. Instead, they first sent questionnaires in order to make sure that he was generally interested in the subject matter. Indeed, a "cold call" in such a business would not only risk rebuff and suspicion, but might also shock and offend the uninitiated, or expose minors to suggestive materials. Mr. Jacobson's responses to the questionnaires gave the investigators reason to think he would be interested in photographs depicting preteen sex.

The Court, however, concludes that a reasonable jury could not have found Mr. Jacobson to be predisposed beyond a reasonable doubt on the basis of his responses to the Government's catalogs, even though it admits that, by that time, he was predisposed to commit the crime. The Government, the Court holds, failed to provide evidence that Mr. Jacobson's obvious predisposition at the time of the crime "was independent and not the product of the attention that the Government had directed at petitioner." In so holding, I believe the Court fails to acknowledge the reasonableness of the jury's inference from the evidence, redefines "predisposition," and introduces a new requirement that Government sting operations have a reasonable suspicion of illegal activity before contacting a suspect.

I

* * * [A] defendant's predisposition is to be assessed as of the time the Government agent first suggested the crime, not when the Government agent first became involved. Until the Government actually makes a suggestion of criminal conduct, it could not be said to have "implant[ed] in the mind of an innocent person the disposition to commit the alleged offense and induce its commission * * *." Even in *Sherman v. United States*, [p. 743], in which the Court held that the defendant had been entrapped as a matter of law, the Government agent had repeatedly and unsuccessfully coaxed the defendant to buy drugs, ultimately succeeding only by playing on the defendant's sympathy. The Court found lack of predisposition based on the Government's numerous unsuccessful attempts to induce the crime, not on the basis of preliminary contacts with the defendant.

Today, the Court holds that Government conduct may be considered to create a predisposition to commit a crime, even before any Government action to induce the commission of the crime. In my view, this holding changes entrapment doctrine. Generally, the inquiry is whether a suspect is predisposed before the Government induces the commission of the crime, not before the Government makes initial contact with him. There is no dispute here that the Government's questionnaires and letters were not sufficient to establish inducement; they did not even suggest that Mr. Jacobson should engage in any illegal activity. If all the Government had done was to send these materials, Mr. Jacobson's entrapment defense would fail. Yet the Court holds that the Government must prove not only that a suspect was predisposed to commit the crime before the opportunity to commit it arose, but also before the Government came on the scene.

The rule that preliminary Government contact can create a predisposition has the potential to be misread by lower courts as well as criminal investigators as requiring that the Government must have sufficient evidence of a defendant's predisposition *before it ever seeks to contact him.* Surely the Court cannot intend to impose such a requirement, for it would mean that the Government must have a reasonable suspicion of criminal activity before it begins an investigation, a condition that we have never before imposed. The Court denies that its new rule will affect run-of-the-mill sting operations, and one hopes that it means what it says. Nonetheless, after this case, every defendant will claim that something the Government agent did before soliciting the crime "created" a predisposition that was not there before. For example, a bribetaker will claim that the description of the amount of money available was so enticing that it implanted a disposition to accept the bribe later offered. A drug buyer will claim that the description of the drug's purity and effects was so tempting that it created the urge to try it for the first time. In short, the Court's opinion could be read to prohibit the Government from advertising the seductions of criminal activity as part of its sting operation, for fear of creating a predisposition in its suspects. That limitation would be especially likely to hamper sting operations such as this one, which mimic the advertising done by genuine purveyors of pornography. No doubt the Court would protest that its opinion does not stand for so broad a proposition, but the apparent lack of a principled basis for distinguishing these scenarios exposes a flaw in the more limited rule the Court today adopts.

The Court's rule is all the more troubling because it does not distinguish between Government conduct that merely highlights the temptation of the crime itself, and Government conduct that threatens, coerces, or leads a suspect to commit a crime in order to fulfill some other obligation. * * *

* * * While the Court states that the Government "exerted substantial pressure on petitioner to obtain and read such material as part of a fight against censorship and the infringement of individual rights," one looks at the record in vain for evidence of such "substantial pressure."

The most one finds is letters advocating legislative action to liberalize obscenity laws, letters which could easily be ignored or thrown away. * * * Mr. Jacobson's curiosity to see what " 'all the trouble and the hysteria' " was about, is certainly susceptible of more than one interpretation. And it is the jury that is charged with the obligation of interpreting it. In sum, the Court fails to construe the evidence in the light most favorable to the Government, and fails to draw all reasonable inferences in the Government's favor. It was surely reasonable for the jury to infer that Mr. Jacobson was predisposed beyond a reasonable doubt, even if other inferences from the evidence were also possible.

II

The second puzzling thing about the Court's opinion is its redefinition of predisposition. The Court acknowledges that "[p]etitioner's responses to the many communications prior to the ultimate criminal act were * * * indicative of certain personal inclinations, including a predisposition to view photographs of preteen sex * * *." If true, this should have settled the matter; Mr. Jacobson was predisposed to engage in the illegal conduct. Yet, the Court concludes, "petitioner's responses hardly support an inference that he would commit the crime of receiving child pornography through the mails."

The Court seems to add something new to the burden of proving predisposition. Not only must the Government show that a defendant was predisposed to engage in the illegal conduct, here, receiving photographs of minors engaged in sex, but also that the defendant was predisposed to break the law knowingly in order to do so. The statute violated here, however, does not require proof of specific intent to break the law; it requires only knowing receipt of visual depictions produced by using minors engaged in sexually explicit conduct. * * *

The crux of the Court's concern in this case is that the Government went too far and "abused" the " 'processes of detection and enforcement' " by luring an innocent person to violate the law. * * * It was, however, the jury's task, as the conscience of the community, to decide whether or not Mr. Jacobson was a willing participant in the criminal activity here or an innocent dupe. * * * There is no dispute that the jury in this case was fully and accurately instructed on the law of entrapment, and nonetheless found Mr. Jacobson guilty. Because I believe there was sufficient evidence to uphold the jury's verdict, I respectfully dissent.

Notes and Questions

1. Is Justice White correct in concluding that *no* reasonable juror could say "beyond a reasonable doubt that petitioner possessed the requisite predisposition"?

2. According to Dru Stevenson, *Entrapment by Numbers*, 16 U. Fla. J. L. & Pub. Pol'y 1, 2–3 (2005), entrapment claims appear to be decreasing in almost every state and in the federal courts from the peak years in the 1980s

and early 1990s. Today, entrapment claims are disproportionately raised in California, Florida, Michigan, Ohio, Tennessee, Texas, Virginia, and Washington. *Id* at 16 n. 37. Do you have any thoughts as to why entrapment claims peaked in the 1980s and have fallen off since then?

3. *"Outrageous conduct" defense and due process.* Can entrapment-like conduct ever violate the Constitution? In United States v. Russell, 411 U.S. 423, 93 S.Ct. 1637, 36 L.Ed.2d 366 (1973), the defendant was convicted of multiple counts of unlawful manufacture of methamphetamine ("speed"). An undercover federal agent, claiming to represent an organization interested in controlling drug manufacturing in the Pacific Northwest, offered to supply the defendant with a lawful, but difficult-to-obtain, chemical necessary for the production of speed, in exchange for one-half of the drugs produced. The defendant agreed to the arrangement.

The defendant's predisposition to commit the offense undermined his entrapment claim. He argued, however, that "a defense to a criminal charge may be founded upon an intolerable degree of governmental participation in the criminal enterprise." However, Justice Rehnquist, for five members of the Court, stated: "While we may some day be presented with a situation in which the conduct of law enforcement agents is so outrageous that due process principles would absolutely bar the government from invoking judicial processes to obtain a conviction, the instant case is distinctly not of that breed."

In Hampton v. United States, 425 U.S. 484, 489, 96 S.Ct. 1646, 48 L.Ed.2d 113 (1976), Chief Justice Rehnquist, writing now only for himself and two others, recanted his "maybe someday" dicta. In *Hampton*, a federal informant supplied heroin to the defendant and then brought him to another agent to whom the defendant sold the drug. As dissenting Justice Brennan put it, "[t]he Government [was] doing nothing less than buying contraband from itself through an intermediary and jailing the intermediary." Nonetheless, the Chief Justice stated that "[t]he limitations of the Due Process Clause of the Fifth Amendment come into play only when the Government activity in question violates some protected right of the *defendant*."

Five justices, however—two in concurrence and three in dissent—rejected Rehnquist's categorical rejection of a due process defense. As a result, an "outrageous conduct" due process defense has developed in lower courts. Nearly ever federal circuit court and many state courts now recognize, at least in dictum, a constitutional defense. One court has explained the defense this way:

> In evaluating whether the State's conduct violated due process, we focus on the State's behavior and not the Defendant's predisposition. There are several factors which courts consider when determining whether police conduct offends due process: whether the police conduct instigated a crime or merely infiltrated ongoing criminal activity; whether the defendant's reluctance to commit a crime was overcome by pleas of sympathy, promises of excessive profits, or persistent solicitation; whether the government controls the criminal activity or simply allows for the

criminal activity to occur; whether the police motive was to prevent crime or protect the public; and whether the government conduct itself amounted to criminal activity or conduct "repugnant to a sense of justice."

State v. Lively, 130 Wash.2d 1, 921 P.2d 1035 (1996).

Is the due process defense simply the Supreme Court-rejected objective standard of entrapment in disguise?

CHAPTER 10

EYEWITNESS IDENTIFICATION PROCEDURES

■ ■ ■

INTRODUCTION: THE PROBLEM

On January 3, 2008, Charles Chatman walked out of a Texas prison a free man. By then he had served twenty-seven years of a ninety-nine year prison sentence for a rape someone else had committed. Eyewitness misidentification was a major factor in Chatman's wrongful conviction. He was exonerated thanks to DNA testing.

Chatman's experience is hardly unique. He was the fifteenth wrongfully convicted prisoner exonerated in Dallas County, Texas in the first seven years of DNA testing. Ralph Blumenthal, *15th Dallas County Inmate Since '01 Is Freed by DNA*, N.Y. Times, Jan. 4, 2008, at A11. And, what is more significant at this point in the casebook is that *eyewitness misidentification is the single most common factor in wrongful convictions throughout the United States*. In a study of 200 DNA exonerations, faulty eyewitness identifications contributed to nearly eighty percent of the improper convictions. Brandon L. Garrett, *Judging Innocence*, 108 Colum. L. Rev. 55, 60 (2008); see also Samuel R. Gross et al., *Exonerations in the United States 1989 Through 2003*, 95 J. Crim. L. & Criminology 523, 542 (2005) (of 340 exonerations between 1980 and 2003, at least one eyewitness misidentified the defendant in sixty-four percent of the trials overall, ninety percent of the wrongful rape convictions, and about half of the homicides).

Although the recent advent of DNA testing has demonstrated that wrongful convictions are more common than previously believed (and, at that, we cannot know how many innocent persons are being convicted because DNA evidence is not left at most crime scenes), social scientists and lawyers have known for a very long time that eyewitness identifications are unreliable.

Why *are* misidentifications such a problem in the criminal justice system? What has the Supreme Court done to reduce the risk of misidentifications? The materials that follow respond to these questions. As you will see, the Supreme Court has done relatively little in the "eyewitness identification" area; however, some state courts and officials—perhaps stung by the high number of DNA exonerations that have occurred—have recently begun to look for means to reform the identification process.

In reading the materials in this chapter, which primarily but not exclusively focus on United States constitutional law, you will find it helpful to ask yourself: (1) What constitutional right is implicated?; (2) Did the identification procedure at issue occur before or after formal adversary proceedings commenced?; (3) Was the identification procedure corporeal (*i.e.*, the suspect was personally displayed to the witness) or noncorporeal (*e.g.*, a photograph of the suspect was displayed)?; and (4) Is the prosecutor trying to introduce the witness's *pre*trial identification into evidence at trial, or does she want the witness to conduct an *in*-court identification of the defendant, or both?

A. RIGHT TO COUNSEL

UNITED STATES v. WADE

Supreme Court of the United States, 1967.
388 U.S. 218, 87 S.Ct. 1926, 18 L.Ed.2d 1149.

MR. JUSTICE BRENNAN delivered the opinion of the Court.

The question here is whether courtroom identifications of an accused at trial are to be excluded from evidence because the accused was exhibited to the witnesses before trial at a post-indictment lineup conducted for identification purposes without notice to and in the absence of the accused's appointed counsel.

The federally insured bank in Eustace, Texas, was robbed on September 21, 1964. A man with a small strip of tape on each side of his face entered the bank, pointed a pistol at the female cashier and the vice president, the only persons in the bank at the time, and forced them to fill a pillowcase with the bank's money. The man then drove away with an accomplice who had been waiting in a stolen car outside the bank. On March 23, 1965, an indictment was returned against respondent, Wade, and two others for conspiring to rob the bank, and against Wade and the accomplice for the robbery itself. Wade was arrested on April 2, and counsel was appointed to represent him on April 26. Fifteen days later an FBI agent, without notice to Wade's lawyer, arranged to have the two bank employees observe a lineup made up of Wade and five or six other prisoners and conducted in a courtroom of the local county courthouse. Each person in the line wore strips of tape such as allegedly worn by the robber and upon direction each said something like "put the money in the bag," the words allegedly uttered by the robber. Both bank employees identified Wade in the lineup as the bank robber.

At trial, the two employees, when asked on direct examination if the robber was in the courtroom, pointed to Wade. The prior lineup identification was then elicited from both employees on cross-examination. At the close of testimony, Wade's counsel moved * * * to strike the bank officials' courtroom identifications on the ground that conduct of the lineup, without notice to and in the absence of his appointed counsel, violated his Fifth Amendment privilege against self-incrimination and his Sixth Amendment right to the assistance of counsel. The motion was denied, and Wade was convicted. * * * We granted certiorari, and set the case for oral argument with No. 223, *Gilbert v. California, post,* and No. 254, *Stovall v. Denno,* [p. 775], which present similar questions. * * *

II.   * * *

* * * [I]n this case it is urged that the assistance of counsel at the lineup was indispensable to protect Wade's most basic right as a criminal defendant—his right to a fair trial at which the witnesses against him might be meaningfully cross-examined. * * *

As early as *Powell v. Alabama* [p. 13], we recognized that the period from arraignment to trial was "perhaps the most critical period of the proceedings * * *," during which the accused "requires the guiding hand of counsel * * *," if the guarantee is not to prove an empty right.* * *

* * * It is central to that principle that in addition to counsel's presence at trial, the accused is guaranteed that he need not stand alone against the State at any stage of the prosecution, formal or informal, in court or out, where counsel's absence might derogate from the accused's right to a fair trial. * * *

In sum, the principle of *Powell v. Alabama* and succeeding cases requires that we scrutinize *any* pretrial confrontation of the accused to determine whether the presence of his counsel is necessary to preserve the defendant's basic right to a fair trial as affected by his right meaningfully to cross-examine the witnesses against him and to have effective assistance of counsel at the trial itself. It calls upon us to analyze whether potential substantial prejudice to defendant's rights inheres in the particular confrontation and the ability of counsel to help avoid that prejudice.

III.

The Government characterizes the lineup as a mere preparatory step in the gathering of the prosecution's evidence, not different—for Sixth Amendment purposes—from various other preparatory steps, such as systematized or scientific analyzing of the accused's fingerprints, blood sample, clothing, hair, and the like. We think there are differences which preclude such stages being characterized as critical stages at which the accused has the right to the presence of his counsel. Knowledge of the techniques of science and technology is sufficiently available, and the variables in techniques few enough, that the accused has the opportunity for a meaningful confrontation of the Government's case at trial through the ordinary processes of cross-examination of the Government's expert witnesses and the presentation of the evidence of his own experts. The denial of a right to have his counsel present at such analyses does not therefore violate the Sixth Amendment; they are not critical stages since there is minimal risk that his counsel's absence at such stages might derogate from his right to a fair trial.

IV.

But the confrontation compelled by the State between the accused and the victim or witnesses to a crime to elicit identification evidence is peculiarly riddled with innumerable dangers and variable factors which might seriously, even crucially, derogate from a fair trial. The vagaries of eyewitness identification are well-known; the annals of criminal law are rife with instances of mistaken identification. Mr. Justice Frankfurter once said: "What is the worth of identification testimony even when uncontradicted? The identification of strangers is proverbially untrustworthy. The hazards of such testimony are established by a formidable number of instances in the records of English and American trials. These instances are recent—not due to the brutalities of ancient criminal procedure." A major factor contributing to the high incidence of miscarriage of justice from mistaken identification has been the degree of suggestion inherent in the manner in which the prosecution presents the suspect to witnesses for pretrial identification. A commentator has observed that "[t]he influence of improper suggestion upon identifying witnesses probably accounts for more miscarriages of justice than any other single factor—perhaps it is responsible for more such errors than all other factors combined." Wall, EYE-WITNESS IDENTIFICATION IN CRIMINAL CASES 26. Suggestion can be created intentionally or unintentionally in many subtle ways. And the dangers for the suspect are particularly grave when the witness' opportunity for observation was insubstantial, and thus his susceptibility to suggestion the greatest.

Moreover, "[i]t is a matter of common experience that, once a witness has picked out the accused at the line-up, he is not likely to go back on his word later on, so that in practice the issue of identity may (in the absence of other relevant evidence) for all practical purposes be determined there and then, before the trial."

The pretrial confrontation for purpose of identification may take the form of a lineup, also known as an "identification parade" or "showup," as in the present case, or presentation of the suspect alone to the witness, as in *Stovall v. Denno, supra*. It is obvious that risks of suggestion attend either form of confrontation and increase the dangers inhering in eyewitness identification. But as is the case with secret interrogations, there is serious difficulty in depicting what transpires at lineups and other forms of identification confrontations. "Privacy results in secrecy and this in turn results in a gap in our knowledge as to what in fact goes on * * *." For the same reasons, the defense can seldom reconstruct the manner and mode of lineup identification for judge or jury at trial. Those participating in a lineup with the accused may often be police officers; in any event, the participants' names are rarely recorded or divulged at trial. The impediments to an objective observation are increased when the victim is the witness. Lineups are prevalent in rape and robbery prosecutions and present a particular hazard that a victim's understandable outrage may excite vengeful or spiteful motives. In any event, neither witnesses nor lineup participants are apt to be alert for conditions prejudicial to the suspect. And if they were, it would likely be of scant benefit to the suspect since neither witnesses nor lineup participants are likely to be schooled in the detection of suggestive influences.[13] Improper influences may go undetected by a suspect, guilty or not, who experiences the emotional tension which we might expect in one being confronted with potential accusers. Even when he does observe abuse, if he has a criminal record he may be reluctant to take the stand and open up the admission of prior convictions. Moreover, any protestations by the suspect of the fairness of the lineup made at trial are likely to be in vain; the jury's choice is between the accused's unsupported version and that of the police officers present. In short, the accused's inability effectively to reconstruct at trial any unfairness that occurred at the lineup may deprive him of his only opportunity meaningfully to attack the credibility of the witness' court-room identification. * * *

The potential for improper influence is illustrated by the circum-stances, insofar as they appear, surrounding the prior identifications in the three cases we decide today. In the present case, the testimony of the identifying witnesses elicited on cross-examination revealed that those witnesses were taken to the courthouse and seated in the courtroom to await assembly of the lineup. The courtroom faced on a hallway observa-ble to the witnesses through an open door. The cashier testified that she saw Wade "standing in the hall" within sight of an FBI agent. Five or six other prisoners later appeared in the hall. The vice president testified that he saw a person in the hall in the custody of the agent who "resembled the person that we identified as the one that had entered the bank."

The lineup in *Gilbert*, [388 U.S. 263, 87 S.Ct. 1951, 18 L.Ed.2d 1178 (1967)], was conducted in an auditorium in which some 100 witnesses to several alleged state and federal robberies charged to Gilbert made whole-sale identifications of Gilbert as the robber in each other's presence, a procedure said to be fraught with dangers of suggestion. And the vice of suggestion created by the identification in *Stovall* was the presentation to the witness of the suspect alone handcuffed to police officers. It is hard to imagine a situation more clearly conveying the suggestion to the witness that the one presented is believed guilty by the police.

The few cases that have surfaced therefore reveal the existence of a process attended with hazards of serious unfairness to the criminal accused and strongly suggest the plight of the more numerous defendants who are unable to ferret out suggestive influences in the secrecy of the confrontation. We do not assume that these risks are the result of police procedures intentionally designed to prejudice an accused. Rather we

---

13. An additional impediment to the detection of such influences by participants, including the suspect, is the physical conditions often surrounding the conduct of the lineup. In many, lights shine on the stage in such a way that the suspect cannot see the witness. In some a one-way mirror is used and what is said on the witness' side cannot be heard.

assume they derive from the dangers inherent in eyewitness identification and the suggestibility inherent in the context of the pretrial identification. Williams & Hammelmann, in one of the most comprehensive studies of such forms of identification, said, "[T]he fact that the police themselves have, in a given case, little or no doubt that the man put up for identification has committed the offense, and that their chief pre-occupation is with the problem of getting sufficient proof, because he has not 'come clean,' involves a danger that this persuasion may communicate itself even in a doubtful case to the witness in some way * * *." Identification Parades, Part I, [1963] Crim. L. Rev. 479, 483.

Insofar as the accused's conviction may rest on a courtroom identification in fact the fruit of a suspect pretrial identification which the accused is helpless to subject to effective scrutiny at trial, the accused is deprived of that right of cross-examination which is an essential safeguard to his right to confront the witnesses against him. And even though cross-examination is a precious safeguard to a fair trial, it cannot be viewed as an absolute assurance of accuracy and reliability. Thus in the present context, where so many variables and pitfalls exist, the first line of defense must be the prevention of unfairness and the lessening of the hazards of eyewitness identification at the lineup itself. The trial which might determine the accused's fate may well not be that in the courtroom but that at the pretrial confrontation, with the State aligned against the accused, the witness the sole jury, and the accused unprotected against the over-reaching, intentional or unintentional, and with little or no effective appeal from the judgment there rendered by the witness—"that's the man."

Since it appears that there is grave potential for prejudice, intentional or not, in the pretrial lineup, which may not be capable of reconstruction at trial, and since presence of counsel itself can often avert prejudice and assure a meaningful confrontation at trial,[26] there can be little doubt that

---

26. One commentator proposes a model statute providing not only for counsel, but other safeguards as well:

"Most, if not all, of the attacks on the lineup process could be averted by a uniform statute modeled upon the best features of the civilian codes. Any proposed statute should provide for the right to counsel during any lineup or during any confrontation. Provision should be made that any person, whether a victim or a witness, must give a description of the suspect before he views any arrested person. A written record of this description should be required, and the witness should be made to sign it. This written record would be available for inspection by defense counsel for copying before the trial and for use at the trial in testing the accuracy of the identification made during the lineup and during the trial.

"This ideal statute would require at least six persons in addition to the accused in a lineup, and these persons would have to be of approximately the same height, weight, coloration of hair and skin, and bodily types as the suspect. In addition, all of these men should, as nearly as possible, be dressed alike. If distinctive garb was used during the crime, the suspect should not be forced to wear similar clothing in the lineup unless all of the other persons are similarly garbed. A complete written report of the names, addresses, descriptive details of the other persons in the lineup, and of everything which transpired during the identification would be mandatory. This report would include everything stated by the identifying witness during this step, including any reasons given by him as to what features, etc., have sparked his recognition.

for Wade the post-indictment lineup was a critical stage of the prosecution at which he was "as much entitled to such aid [of counsel] * * * as at the trial itself." Thus both Wade and his counsel should have been notified of the impending lineup, and counsel's presence should have been a requisite to conduct of the lineup, absent an "intelligent waiver." No substantial countervailing policy considerations have been advanced against the requirement of the presence of counsel. Concern is expressed that the requirement will forestall prompt identifications and result in obstruction of the confrontations. As for the first, we note that in the two cases in which the right to counsel is today held to apply, counsel had already been appointed and no argument is made in either case that notice to counsel would have prejudicially delayed the confrontations. Moreover, we leave open the question whether the presence of substitute counsel might not suffice where notification and presence of the suspect's own counsel would result in prejudicial delay. And to refuse to recognize the right to counsel for fear that counsel will obstruct the course of justice is contrary to the basic assumptions upon which this Court has operated in Sixth Amendment cases. We rejected similar logic in *Miranda v. Arizona* concerning presence of counsel during custodial interrogation * * *. In our view counsel can hardly impede legitimate law enforcement; on the contrary, for the reasons expressed, law enforcement may be assisted by preventing the infiltration of taint in the prosecution's identification evidence. That result cannot help the guilty avoid conviction but can only help assure that the right man has been brought to justice.[29]

Legislative or other regulations, such as those of local police departments, which eliminate the risks of abuse and unintentional suggestion at lineup proceedings and the impediments to meaningful confrontation at trial may also remove the basis for regarding the stage as "critical." But neither Congress nor the federal authorities have seen fit to provide a solution. What we hold today "in no way creates a constitutional straitjacket which will handicap sound efforts at reform, nor is it intended to have this effect."

"This statute should permit voice identification tests by having each person in the lineup repeat identical innocuous phrases, and it would be impermissible to force the use of words allegedly used during a criminal act.

"The statute would enjoin the police from suggesting to any viewer that one or more persons in the lineup had been arrested as a suspect. If more than one witness is to make an identification, each witness should be required to do so separately and should be forbidden to speak to another witness until all of them have completed the process.

"The statute could require the use of movie cameras and tape recorders to record the lineup process in those states which are financially able to afford these devices. Finally, the statute should provide that any evidence obtained as the result of a violation of this statute would be inadmissible." Murray, The Criminal Lineup at Home and Abroad, 1966 Utah L. Rev. 610, 627–628.

29. Many other nations surround the lineup with safeguards against prejudice to the suspect. In England the suspect must be allowed the presence of his solicitor or a friend; Germany requires the presence of retained counsel; France forbids the confrontation of the suspect in the absence of his counsel; Spain, Mexico, and Italy provide detailed procedures prescribing the conditions under which confrontation must occur under the supervision of a judicial officer who sees to it that the proceedings are officially recorded to assure adequate scrutiny at trial.

V.

We come now to the question whether the denial of Wade's motion to strike the courtroom identification by the bank witnesses at trial because of the absence of his counsel at the lineup required, as the Court of Appeals held, the grant of a new trial at which such evidence is to be excluded. We do not think this disposition can be justified without first giving the Government the opportunity to establish by clear and convincing evidence that the in-court identifications were based upon observations of the suspect other than the lineup identification. Where, as here, the admissibility of evidence of the lineup identification itself is not involved, a *per se* rule of exclusion of courtroom identification would be unjustified. A rule limited solely to the exclusion of testimony concerning identification at the lineup itself, without regard to admissibility of the courtroom identification, would render the right to counsel an empty one. The lineup is most often used, as in the present case, to crystallize the witnesses' identification of the defendant for future reference. We have already noted that the lineup identification will have that effect. The State may then rest upon the witnesses' unequivocal courtroom identification, and not mention the pretrial identification as part of the State's case at trial. Counsel is then in the predicament in which Wade's counsel found himself—realizing that possible unfairness at the lineup may be the sole means of attack upon the unequivocal courtroom identification, and having to probe in the dark in an attempt to discover and reveal unfairness, while bolstering the government witness' courtroom identification by bringing out and dwelling upon his prior identification. Since counsel's presence at the lineup would equip him to attack not only the lineup identification but the courtroom identification as well, limiting the impact of violation of the right to counsel to exclusion of evidence only of identification at the lineup itself disregards a critical element of that right.

We think it follows that the proper test to be applied in these situations is that quoted in *Wong Sun v. United States*, [p. 503], " '[W]hether, granting establishment of the primary illegality, the evidence to which instant objection is made has been come at by exploitation of that illegality or instead by means sufficiently distinguishable to be purged of the primary taint.' Maguire, Evidence of Guilt 221 (1959)." Application of this test in the present context requires consideration of various factors; for example, the prior opportunity to observe the alleged criminal act, the existence of any discrepancy between any pre-lineup description and the defendant's actual description, any identification prior to lineup of another person, the identification by picture of the defendant prior to the lineup, failure to identify the defendant on a prior occasion, and the lapse of time between the alleged act and the lineup identification. It is also relevant to consider those facts which, despite the absence of counsel, are disclosed concerning the conduct of the lineup.[33] * * *

---

33. Thus it is not the case that [as the dissent asserts] "[i]t matters not how well the witness knows the suspect, whether the witness is the suspect's mother, brother, or long-time associate, and no matter how long or well the witness observed the perpetrator at the scene of the crime."

On the record now before us we cannot make the determination whether the in-court identifications had an independent origin. * * * We * * * think the appropriate procedure to be followed is to vacate the conviction pending a hearing to determine whether the in-court identifications had an independent source, * * * and for the District Court to reinstate the conviction or order a new trial, as may be proper. * * *

Mr. Justice WHITE, whom Mr. Justice HARLAN and Mr. Justice STEWART join, dissenting [on the Sixth Amendment issue].

The Court has again propounded a broad constitutional rule barring use of a wide spectrum of relevant and probative evidence, solely because a step in its ascertainment or discovery occurs outside the presence of defense counsel. * * *

The Court's opinion is far-reaching. It proceeds first by creating a new *per se* rule of constitutional law: a criminal suspect cannot be subjected to a pretrial identification process in the absence of his counsel without violating the Sixth Amendment. If he is, the State may not buttress a later courtroom identification of the witness by any reference to the previous identification. Furthermore, the courtroom identification is not admissible at all unless the State can establish by clear and convincing proof that the testimony is not the fruit of the earlier identification made in the absence of defendant's counsel—admittedly a heavy burden for the State and probably an impossible one. To all intents and purposes, courtroom identifications are barred if pretrial identifications have occurred without counsel being present.

The rule applies to any lineup, to any other techniques employed to produce an identification and *a fortiori* to a face-to-face encounter between the witness and the suspect alone, regardless of when the identification occurs, in time or place, and whether before or after indictment or information. It matters not how well the witness knows the suspect, whether the witness is the suspect's mother, brother, or long-time associate, and no matter how long or well the witness observed the perpetrator at the scene of the crime. The kidnap victim who has lived for days with his abductor is in the same category as the witness who has had only a fleeting glimpse of the criminal. Neither may identify the suspect without defendant's counsel being present. The same strictures apply regardless of the number of other witnesses who positively identify the defendant and regardless of the corroborative evidence showing that it was the defendant who had committed the crime.

The premise for the Court's rule is not the general unreliability of eyewitness identifications nor the difficulties inherent in observation, recall, and recognition. The Court assumes a narrower evil as the basis for

---

Such factors will have an important bearing upon the true basis of the witness' in-court identification. Moreover, the State's inability to bolster the witness' courtroom identification by introduction of the lineup identification itself, will become less significant the more the evidence of other opportunities of the witness to observe the defendant. Thus where the witness is a "kidnap victim who has lived for days with his abductor" the value to the State of admission of the lineup identification is indeed marginal, and such identification would be a mere formality.

its rule—improper police suggestion which contributes to erroneous identifications. The Court apparently believes that improper police procedures are so widespread that a broad prophylactic rule must be laid down, requiring the presence of counsel at all pretrial identifications, in order to detect recurring instances of police misconduct. I do not share this pervasive distrust of all official investigations. None of the materials the Court relies upon supports it. Certainly, I would bow to solid fact, but the Court quite obviously does not have before it any reliable, comprehensive survey of current police practices on which to base its new rule. Until it does, the Court should avoid excluding relevant evidence from state criminal trials. * * *

I share the Court's view that the criminal trial, at the very least, should aim at truthful factfinding, including accurate eyewitness identifications. I doubt, however, on the basis of our present information, that the tragic mistakes which have occurred in criminal trials are as much the product of improper police conduct as they are the consequence of the difficulties inherent in eyewitness testimony and in resolving evidentiary conflicts by court or jury. I doubt that the Court's new rule will obviate these difficulties, or that the situation will be measurably improved by inserting defense counsel into the investigative processes of police departments everywhere.

But, it may be asked, what possible state interest militates against requiring the presence of defense counsel at lineups? After all, the argument goes, he *may* do some good, he *may* upgrade the quality of identification evidence in state courts and he can scarcely do any harm. Even if true, this is a feeble foundation for fastening an ironclad constitutional rule upon state criminal procedures. Absent some reliably established constitutional violation, the processes by which the States enforce their criminal laws are their own prerogative. * * *

Beyond this, however, requiring counsel at pretrial identifications as an invariable rule trenches on other valid state interests. One of them is its concern with the prompt and efficient enforcement of its criminal laws. Identifications frequently take place after arrest but before an indictment is returned or an information is filed. The police may have arrested a suspect on probable cause but may still have the wrong man. Both the suspect and the State have every interest in a prompt identification at that stage, the suspect in order to secure his immediate release and the State because prompt and early identification enhances *accurate* identification and because it must know whether it is on the right investigative track. Unavoidably, however, the absolute rule requiring the presence of counsel will cause significant delay and it may very well result in no pretrial identification at all. Counsel must be appointed and a time arranged convenient for him and the witnesses. Meanwhile, it may be necessary to file charges against the suspect who may then be released on bail, in the federal system very often on his own recognizance, with neither the State nor the defendant having the benefit of a properly conducted identification procedure.

Nor do I think the witnesses themselves can be ignored. They will now be required to be present at the convenience of counsel rather than their own. Many may be much less willing to participate if the identification stage is transformed into an adversary proceeding not under the control of a judge. Others may fear for their own safety if their identity is known at an early date, especially when there is no way of knowing until the lineup occurs whether or not the police really have the right man.

Finally, I think the Court's new rule is vulnerable in terms of its own unimpeachable purpose of increasing the reliability of identification testimony.

Law enforcement officers have the obligation to convict the guilty and to make sure they do not convict the innocent. They must be dedicated to making the criminal trial a procedure for the ascertainment of the true facts surrounding the commission of the crime.[5] To this extent, our so-called adversary system is not adversary at all; nor should it be. But defense counsel has no comparable obligation to ascertain or present the truth. Our system assigns him a different mission. He must be and is interested in preventing the conviction of the innocent, but, absent a voluntary plea of guilty, we also insist that he defend his client whether he is innocent or guilty. The State has the obligation to present the evidence. Defense counsel need present nothing, even if he knows what the truth is. He need not furnish any witnesses to the police, or reveal any confidences of his client, or furnish any other information to help the prosecution's case. If he can confuse a witness, even a truthful one, or make him appear at a disadvantage, unsure or indecisive, that will be his normal course. Our interest in not convicting the innocent permits counsel to put the State to its proof, to put the State's case in the worst possible light, regardless of what he thinks or knows to be the truth. Undoubtedly there are some limits which defense counsel must observe but more often than not, defense counsel will cross-examine a prosecution witness, and impeach him if he can, even if he thinks the witness is telling the truth, just as he will attempt to destroy a witness who he thinks is lying. In this respect, as part of our modified adversary system and as part of the duty imposed on the most honorable defense counsel, we countenance or require conduct which in many instances has little, if any, relation to the search for truth.

I would not extend this system, at least as it presently operates, to police investigations and would not require counsel's presence at pretrial identification procedures. Counsel's interest is in not having his client

---

5. "The United States Attorney is the representative not of an ordinary party to a controversy, but of a sovereignty whose obligation to govern impartially is as compelling as its obligation to govern at all; and whose interest, therefore, in a criminal prosecution is not that it shall win a case, but that justice shall be done. As such, he is in a peculiar and very definite sense the servant of the law, the twofold aim of which is that guilt shall not escape or innocence suffer. He may prosecute with earnestness and vigor—indeed, he should do so. But, while he may strike hard blows, he is not at liberty to strike foul ones. It is as much his duty to refrain from improper methods calculated to produce a wrongful conviction as it is to use every legitimate means to bring about a just one." *Berger v. United States*, 295 U.S. 78, 88, 55 S.Ct. 629, 633, 79 L.Ed. 1314.

placed at the scene of the crime, regardless of his whereabouts. Some counsel may advise their clients to refuse to make any movements or to speak any words in a lineup or even to appear in one. To that extent the impact on truthful factfinding is quite obvious. Others will not only observe what occurs and develop possibilities for later cross-examination but will hover over witnesses and begin their cross-examination then, menacing truthful factfinding as thoroughly as the Court fears the police now do. Certainly there is an implicit invitation to counsel to suggest rules for the lineup and to manage and produce it as best he can. I therefore doubt that the Court's new rule, at least absent some clearly defined limits on counsel's role, will measurably contribute to more reliable pretrial identifications. My fears are that it will have precisely the opposite result. * * *

NOTES AND QUESTIONS

1. *Introducing evidence of the pretrial identification procedure.* In *Wade*, the prosecution did not seek to introduce evidence relating to the lineup. The only issue was the admissibility of the witness's *in*-court identification of Wade. However, in companion case *Gilbert v. California, supra,* the prosecutor elicited testimony at trial of the fact that witnesses had identified the defendant at a post-indictment pretrial lineup at which Gilbert was not represented by counsel. The Court held that

> [t]he State is * * * not entitled to an opportunity to show that that testimony had an independent source. Only a *per se* exclusionary rule as to such testimony can be an effective sanction to assure that law enforcement authorities will respect the accused's constitutional right to the presence of his counsel at the critical lineup.

How would you summarize the "*Wade-Gilbert* rule"? Specifically, under what circumstances does a defendant have a right to counsel at a lineup or other corporeal identification procedure? Does the rule apply to an identification that occurs *before* indictment? Before arrest? And, what are the evidentiary implications if the defendant's counsel right is violated?

2. Reconsider the second and third paragraphs of Justice White's dissent. Has he correctly stated the *Wade* rule, as you understand it from Note 1? Reconsider the fourth paragraph of his dissent. Do you believe that he accurately states the "premise for the Court's rule"?

3. *The problems with eyewitness identifications.* The *Wade* Court noted that "identification evidence is peculiarly riddled with innumerable dangers * * * which might seriously, even crucially, derogate from a fair trial." We have already noted the story of one man misidentified and consequently convicted of rape, and we have cited studies reporting that the most common single reason for wrongful convictions is eyewitness misidentification (p. 760). As two social scientists long ago put it, "people quite often do not see or hear things which are presented clearly to their senses, see or hear things which are not there, do not remember things which have happened to them, and remember things which did not happen." Felice J. Levine & June Louin Tapp,

The Psychology of Criminal Identification: The Gap from Wade to Kirby, 121 U. Pa. L. Rev. 1079, 1087–88 (1973).

Why and under what circumstances is eyewitness testimony particularly unreliable? Social scientists who have studied the subject provide various answers. (For cites to relevant literature and greater detail on the subject, see 1 Joshua Dressler & Alan C. Michaels, Understanding Criminal Procedure § 26.01 (4th ed. 2006).) First, people tend to see what they expect to see. A hunter looking for a deer in the forest may "see" a deer in the brush that turns out to be a human being. If a witness to a crime has an expectation of what a criminal should look like—the person's age, race, size, gender—she may unconsciously "see" the offender in a way that fits her preconception. Second, there is substantial evidence of unreliability in cross-racial identification cases, *i.e.*, when a person of one racial group attempts to identify a crime perpetrator of a different racial category.

Third, memory decays over time. Worse, memory is an "active, constructive process." Frederic D. Woocher, Note, *Did Your Eyes Deceive You? Expert Psychological Testimony on the Unreliability of Eyewitness Identification*, 29 Stan. L. Rev. 969, 983 (1977). That is, people dislike uncertainty; therefore, when a person experiences a memory gap, the individual unconsciously tries to fill in the memory holes with details that often are inaccurate.

Fourth, post-crime identification police procedures can aggravate the situation. For example, a lineup typically functions as a multiple-choice test in which eyewitness-participants believe—or are led to believe by the police—that "none of the above" is an unacceptable answer. Therefore, witnesses often give the "most correct" answer (pick the person whom they believe most resembles the culprit), rather than indicate that they do not recognize anyone in the lineup. And, once a witness identifies—correctly or incorrectly—someone from a lineup, she becomes psychologically committed to her identification. Her mind may even play tricks on her: when she thinks back to the crime, her "mind's eye" may now "remember" the person she selected from the lineup. It substitutes for her initial memory of the culprit.

4. *Remedies*. Jurors tend to place a high value on eyewitness testimony. They do not distinguish between high-risk and low-risk identifications. They tend to overestimate the accuracy of eyewitness testimony. What can be done, therefore, to reduce the inherent risks in eyewitness identification procedures? The *Wade* Court invited legislatures and police departments to reform their procedures and even quoted (footnote 26) from a scholarly article recommending a model statute to deal with the problem.

For many years, social scientists have urged changes in police procedures in order to enhance the reliability of the identification process. Until recently, their recommendations were largely ignored. In 2001, however, New Jersey took a significant step by initiating new lineup procedures. New Jersey Attorney General Guidelines for Preparing and Conducting Photo and Live Lineup Identification Procedures (April 18, 2001). Among the implemented changes are so-called "double-blind sequential lineups." That is, a witness is shown possible suspects one at a time ("Is (s)he the person you saw?") rather than as a group; and, whenever possible, not only the witness but the person conducting the identification does not know whom the suspect is. This reduces the risk that a police officer may intentionally or unintentionally influence the witness by way of a nod, an approving "right," or by suggesting that the witness "take another look" if she chooses the "wrong" person. And, more recently, the New Jersey Supreme Court exercised its constitutional rule-making authority to require, as a condition of admissibility of any out-of-court identification of a defendant, the production "to the extent feasible" of a record of the dialogue between police officials and the eyewitness conducted during the identification process. State v. Delgado, 188 N.J. 48, 902 A.2d 888 (2006).

Can you suggest additional curatives? Should the police be required to tell eyewitnesses that the offender may not be in the lineup? Should a defendant be permitted to introduce social science testimony regarding the general unreliability of eyewitness testimony? In regard to these questions see State v. Ledbetter, 275 Conn. 534, 881 A.2d 290 (2005) (ruling that officers administering identification procedures should advise the witness that the perpetrator may or may not be present in the procedure, or else evidence at trial of the identification must be accompanied by a jury instruction stating that "psychological studies have shown" that failure to so admonish eyewitnesses "increases the likelihood that the witness will select one of the individuals in the procedure, even when the perpetrator is not present"); and Johnson v. State, 272 Ga. 254, 526 S.E.2d 549 (2000); People v. Lee, 96 N.Y.2d 157, 726 N.Y.S.2d 361, 750 N.E.2d 63 (2001); State v. Copeland, 226 S.W.3d 287 (Tenn. 2007) (all holding that expert testimony about the unreliability of eyewitness testimony is eligible for admission in criminal trials).

5. Suppose that a police department routinely videotapes its lineups and furnishes the defense with an unedited copy of the procedure. Should the accused still have a constitutional right to the presence of counsel?

6. *The role of counsel at the lineup.* Reconsider Justice Brennan's opinion in *Wade*. What does he envision a lawyer doing during the identification process? What is Justice White's understanding in this regard?

What *should* be the role of a lawyer at a lineup? Should she serve simply as a passive observer who can reconstruct the events of the lineup at trial, point to alleged abuses, and thereby minimize the incriminating force of the identification? Or should she be permitted to make objections at the time of the lineup and suggest ways to improve the process? If the lawyer's role is passive, is *Wade* an adequate solution to the unreliability problem? If the lawyer's role is active, is Justice White correct in fearing that defense lawyers may make the process less efficient and, ultimately, less accurate?

For a moment, imagine that you are a Public Defender and are called to the police station to represent a person in a lineup. You look at the lineup and you believe that it is unduly suggestive (perhaps the others in the confrontation do not look like your client). What would you do? Would you complain to the police and urge them to find persons who look more like your client? Would you say nothing? What are the risks of being vocal? Of being passive?

7. *When is the right to counsel triggered?: the Kirby "clarification."* Look again at your answers to the questions asked at the end of Note 1. (You did answer them, right?) Specifically, as you read the majority opinion in *Wade, when* is the right to counsel triggered? Does it apply to an identification

that occurs *before* indictment? Before arrest? What is dissenting Justice White's answer?

As it turns out, the answer to the timing question may not have been what some of the *Wade* justices hoped or feared. In Kirby v. Illinois, 406 U.S. 682, 92 S.Ct. 1877, 32 L.Ed.2d 411 (1972), a case involving a corporeal identification that occurred after arrest but before indictment or arraignment, a plurality of the Court announced:

> In a line of constitutional cases in this Court stemming back to the Court's landmark opinion in *Powell v. Alabama* [p. 13], it has been firmly established that a person's Sixth and Fourteenth Amendment right to counsel attaches only at or after the time that adversary judicial proceedings have been initiated against him.

> This is not to say that a defendant in a criminal case has a constitutional right to counsel only at the trial itself. The *Powell* case makes clear that the right attaches at the time of arraignment, and the Court has recently held that it exists also at the time of a preliminary hearing. But the point is that, while members of the Court have differed as to the existence of the right to counsel in the contexts of some of the above cases, *all* of those cases have involved points of time at or after the initiation of adversary judicial criminal proceedings—whether by way of formal charge, preliminary hearing, indictment, information, or arraignment.[a] * * *

> The initiation of judicial criminal proceedings is far from a mere formalism. It is the starting point of our whole system of adversary criminal justice. For it is only then that the government has committed itself to prosecute, and only then that the adverse positions of government and defendant have solidified. It is then that a defendant finds himself faced with the prosecutorial forces of organized society, and immersed in the intricacies of substantive and procedural criminal law. It is this point, therefore, that marks the commencement of the "criminal prosecutions" to which alone the explicit guarantees of the Sixth Amendment are applicable. * * *

> What has been said is not to suggest that there may not be occasions during the course of a criminal investigation when the police do abuse identification procedures. Such abuses are not beyond the reach of the Constitution. As the Court pointed out in *Wade* itself, it is always necessary to "scrutinize *any* pretrial confrontation * * *."[b] The Due Process Clause of the Fifth and Fourteenth Amendments forbids a lineup that is unnecessarily suggestive and conducive to irreparable mistaken identification. *Stovall v. Denno* [p. 775]. When a person has not been formally charged with a criminal offense, *Stovall* strikes the appropriate constitutional balance between the right of a suspect to be protected from prejudicial procedures and the interest of society in the prompt and purposeful investigation of an unsolved crime.

---

    a. Although *Kirby* was a plurality opinion, the majority opinion in Moore v. Illinois, 434 U.S. 220, 98 S.Ct. 458, 54 L.Ed.2d 424 (1977), confirmed the line drawn here—initiation of adversary judicial proceedings—as the critical one in corporal identification cases.

    b. Is *Kirby* properly using this quote from *Wade*? Look back at the full quote on p. 762.

Is *Kirby* consistent with the underlying rationale of *Wade*? Justice White did not think so. He dissented again, stating simply that *"United States v. Wade* and *Gilbert v. California* govern this case and compel reversal of the judgment below."

8. What is the practical effect of *Kirby* (Note 7)?

9. *Post-indictment noncorporeal identifications.* In United States v. Ash, 413 U.S. 300, 93 S.Ct. 2568, 37 L.Ed.2d 619 (1973), the Supreme Court held that the *Wade-Gilbert* rule does not apply to photographic displays, even if such a procedure occurs after formal criminal proceedings have commenced.

In *Ash*, four witnesses identified Ash from a single black-and-white photograph. Then they were shown five color photographs, one of which included Ash. Three of the witnesses selected Ash, but the other was unable to make any selection. This occurred after Ash had been indicted, and in the absence of defense counsel. In light of *Wade*, can you think of any good reason for the no-right-to-counsel holding in *Ash*?

B. DUE PROCESS OF LAW

STOVALL v. DENNO

Supreme Court of the United States, 1967.
388 U.S. 293, 87 S.Ct. 1967, 18 L.Ed.2d 1199.

MR. JUSTICE BRENNAN delivered the opinion of the Court. * * *

Dr. Paul Behrendt was stabbed to death in the kitchen of his home in Garden City, Long Island, about midnight August 23, 1961. Dr. Behrendt's wife, also a physician, had followed her husband to the kitchen and jumped at the assailant. He knocked her to the floor and stabbed her 11 times. The police found a shirt on the kitchen floor and keys in a pocket which they traced to petitioner. They arrested him on the afternoon of August 24. An arraignment was promptly held but was postponed until petitioner could retain counsel.

Mrs. Behrendt was hospitalized for major surgery to save her life. The police, without affording petitioner time to retain counsel, arranged with her surgeon to permit them to bring petitioner to her hospital room about noon of August 25, the day after the surgery. Petitioner was handcuffed to one of five police officers who, with two members of the staff of the District Attorney, brought him to the hospital room. Petitioner was the only Negro in the room. Mrs. Behrendt identified him from her hospital bed after being asked by an officer whether he "was the man" and after petitioner repeated at the direction of an officer a "few words for voice identification." None of the witnesses could recall the words that were used. Mrs. Behrendt and the officers testified at the trial to her identification of the petitioner in the hospital room, and she also made an in-court identification of petitioner in the courtroom.

Petitioner was convicted and sentenced to death. * * *

[The Court first held that the *Wade-Gilbert* rule (p. 771, Note 1), announced the same day as this opinion, only applied prospectively, *i.e.*, to identification procedures conducted after the date of those decisions. Therefore, the Court ruled against petitioner on Sixth Amendment grounds.]

We turn now to the question whether petitioner, although not entitled to the application of *Wade* and *Gilbert* to his case, is entitled to relief on his claim that in any event the confrontation conducted in this case was so unnecessarily suggestive and conducive to irreparable mistaken identification that he was denied due process of law. This is a recognized ground of attack upon a conviction independent of any right to counsel claim. The practice of showing suspects singly to persons for the purpose of identification, and not as part of a lineup, has been widely condemned. However, a claimed violation of due process of law in the conduct of a confrontation depends on the totality of the circumstances surrounding it, and the record in the present case reveals that the showing of Stovall to Mrs. Behrendt in an immediate hospital confrontation was imperative. The Court of Appeals, *en banc*, stated,

> "Here was the only person in the world who could possibly exonerate Stovall. Her words, and only her words, 'He is not the man' could have resulted in freedom for Stovall. The hospital was not far distant from the courthouse and jail. No one knew how long Mrs. Behrendt might live. Faced with the responsibility of identifying the attacker, with the need for immediate action and with the knowledge that Mrs. Behrendt could not visit the jail, the police followed the only feasible procedure and took Stovall to the hospital room. Under these circumstances, the usual police station line-up, which Stovall now argues he should have had, was out of the question."

The judgment of the Court of Appeals is affirmed. * * *

Mr. Justice Douglas is of the view that the deprivation of the right to counsel in the setting of this case should be given retroactive effect * * *.

Mr. Justice Fortas would reverse and remand for a new trial on the ground that the State's reference at trial to the improper hospital identification violated petitioner's Fourteenth Amendment rights and was prejudicial. He would not reach the question of retroactivity of *Wade* and *Gilbert*.

[The concurring opinion of Justice White, with whom Justices Harlan and Stewart joined, is omitted. The dissenting opinion of Justice Black is omitted.]

NOTES AND QUESTIONS

1.   Is the Court here saying that the procedure was *not* suggestive? (Can you imagine a more suggestive procedure, short of the police pointing their finger at the suspect?) Or, is it that, although the procedure was unduly suggestive, the emergency justified the procedure? If it is the latter, and even

granting *arguendo* the emergency circumstances, couldn't the suggestive nature of the identification procedure have been mitigated?

MANSON v. BRATHWAITE

Supreme Court of the United States, 1977.
432 U.S. 98, 97 S.Ct. 2243, 53 L.Ed.2d 140.

Mr. Justice Blackmun delivered the opinion of the Court. * * *

This case presents the issue as to whether the Due Process Clause of the Fourteenth Amendment compels the exclusion, in a state criminal trial, apart from any consideration of reliability, of pretrial identification evidence obtained by a police procedure that was both suggestive and unnecessary. This Court's decision in *Stovall v. Denno* [p. 775] and *Neil v. Biggers*, 409 U.S. 188, 93 S.Ct. 375, 34 L.Ed.2d 401 (1972), are particularly implicated.

I

Jimmy D. Glover, a full-time trooper of the Connecticut State Police, in 1970 was assigned to the Narcotics Division in an undercover capacity. On May 5 of that year, about 7:45 p.m., e.d.t., and while there was still daylight, Glover and Henry Alton Brown, an informant, went to an apartment building at 201 Westland, in Hartford, for the purpose of purchasing narcotics from "Dickie Boy" Cicero, a known narcotics dealer. Cicero, it was thought, lived on the third floor of that apartment building. Glover and Brown entered the building, observed by backup Officers D'Onofrio and Gaffey, and proceeded by stairs to the third floor. Glover knocked at the door of one of the two apartments served by the stairway. The area was illuminated by natural light from a window in the third floor hallway. The door was opened 12 to 18 inches in response to the knock. Glover observed a man standing at the door and, behind him, a woman. Brown identified himself. Glover then asked for "two things" of narcotics. The man at the door held out his hand, and Glover gave him two $10 bills. The door closed. Soon the man returned and handed Glover two glassine bags. While the door was open, Glover stood within two feet of the person from whom he made the purchase and observed his face. Five to seven minutes elapsed from the time the door first opened until it closed the second time.

Glover and Brown then left the building. This was about eight minutes after their arrival. Glover drove to headquarters where he described the seller to D'Onofrio and Gaffey. Glover at that time did not know the identity of the seller. He described him as being "a colored man, approximately five feet eleven inches tall, dark complexion, black hair, short Afro style, and having high cheekbones, and of heavy build. He was wearing at the time blue pants and a plaid shirt." D'Onofrio, suspecting from this description that respondent might be the seller, obtained a photograph of respondent from the Records Division of the Hartford Police Department. He left it at Glover's office. D'Onofrio was not acquainted with respondent personally, but did know him by sight and had seen him "[s]everal times" prior to May 5. Glover, when alone, viewed the photograph for the first time upon his return to headquarters on May 7; he identified the person shown as the one from whom he had purchased the narcotics. * * *

Respondent was charged, in a two-count information, with possession and sale of heroin * * *. At his trial in January 1971, the photograph from which Glover had identified respondent was received in evidence * * *. Glover also testified that, although he had not seen respondent in the eight months that had elapsed since the sale, "there [was] no doubt whatsoever" in his mind that the person shown on the photograph was respondent. Glover also made a positive in-court identification * * *.

No explanation was offered by the prosecution for the failure to utilize a photographic array or to conduct a lineup.

Respondent, who took the stand in his own defense, testified that on May 5, the day in question, he had been ill at his Albany Avenue apartment ("a lot of back pains, muscle spasms * * * a bad heart * * * high blood pressure * * * neuralgia in my face, and sinus"), and that at no time on that particular day had he been at 201 Westland. His wife testified that she recalled, after her husband had refreshed her memory, that he was home all day on May 5. Doctor Wesley M. Vietzke, an internist and assistant professor of medicine at the University of Connecticut, testified that respondent had consulted him on April 15, 1970 * * * and heard his complaint about his back and facial pain, and discovered that he had high blood pressure. The physician found respondent, subjectively, "in great discomfort." Respondent in fact underwent surgery for a herniated disc * * * on August 17.

The jury found respondent guilty on both counts of the information.* * *

II * * *

Neil v. Biggers[, supra] * * * concerned a respondent who had been convicted * * * on evidence consisting in part of the victim's visual and voice identification of Biggers at a station-house showup seven months after the crime. * * * The Court expressed concern about the lapse of seven months * * *. The "central question," however, was "whether under the 'totality of the circumstances' the identification was reliable even though the confrontation procedure was suggestive." Applying that test, the Court found "no substantial likelihood of misidentification. [* * *]."

Biggers well might be seen to provide an unambiguous answer to the question before us: The admission of testimony concerning a suggestive and unnecessary identification procedure does not violate due process so long as the identification possesses sufficient aspects of reliability. In one passage, however, the Court observed that the challenged procedure occurred pre-*Stovall* and that a strict rule would make little sense with regard to a confrontation that preceded the Court's first indication that a suggestive procedure might lead to the exclusion of evidence. One perhaps might argue that, by implication, * * * a different rule could apply post-*Stovall*. The question before us, then, is simply whether the *Biggers* analysis applies to post-*Stovall* confrontations as well as those pre-*Stovall*. * * *

IV

Petitioner at the outset acknowledges that "the procedure in the instant case was suggestive [because only one photograph was used] and unnecessary" [because there was no emergency or exigent circumstance]. * * *

Since the decision in *Biggers*, the Courts of Appeals appear to have developed at least two approaches to such evidence. The first, or *per se* approach, employed by the Second Circuit in the present case, focuses on the procedures employed and requires exclusion of the out-of-court identification evidence, without regard to reliability, whenever it has been obtained through unnecessarily suggested confrontation procedures. The justifications advanced are the elimination of evidence of uncertain reliability, deterrence of the police and prosecutors, and the stated "fair assurance against the awful risks of misidentification."

The second, or more lenient, approach is one that continues to rely on the totality of the circumstances. It permits the admission of the confrontation evidence if, despite the suggestive aspect, the out-of-court identification possesses certain features of reliability. * * *

There are, of course, several interests to be considered and taken into account. The driving force behind *United States v. Wade, Gilbert v. California*, 388 U.S. 263, 87 S.Ct. 1951, 18 L.Ed.2d 1178 (1967) (right to counsel at a post-indictment lineup), and *Stovall*, all decided on the same day, was the Court's concern with the problems of eyewitness identification. * * * It must be observed that both approaches before us are responsive to this concern. The *per se* rule, however, goes too far since its application automatically and peremptorily, and without consideration of alleviating factors, keeps evidence from the jury that is reliable and relevant.

The second factor is deterrence. Although the *per se* approach has the more significant deterrent effect, the totality approach also has an influence on police behavior. The police will guard against unnecessarily suggestive procedures under the totality rule, as well as the *per se* one, for fear that their actions will lead to the exclusion of identifications as unreliable.

The third factor is the effect on the administration of justice. Here the *per se* approach suffers serious drawbacks. Since it denies the trier reliable evidence, it may result, on occasion, in the guilty going free. * * * And in those cases in which the admission of identification evidence is error under the *per se* approach but not under the totality approach—cases in which the identification is reliable despite an unnecessarily suggestive identification procedure—reversal is a Draconian sanction. * * *

We therefore conclude that reliability is the linchpin in determining the admissibility of identification testimony for both pre-and post-*Stovall* confrontations. The factors to be considered are set out in *Biggers*. These include the opportunity of the witness to view the criminal at the time of the crime, the witness' degree of attention, the accuracy of his prior description of the criminal, the level of certainty demonstrated at the confrontation, and the time between the crime and the confrontation. Against these factors is to be weighed the corrupting effect of the suggestive identification itself.

V

We turn, then, to the facts of this case and apply the analysis:

1. The opportunity to view. Glover testified that for two to three minutes he stood at the apartment door, within two feet of the respondent. The door opened twice, and each time the man stood at the door. * * * It was near sunset, to be sure, but the sun had not yet set, so it was not dark or even dusk or twilight. Natural light from outside entered the hallway through a window. There was natural light, as well, from inside the apartment.

2. The degree of attention. Glover was not a casual or passing observer, as is so often the case with eyewitness identification. Trooper Glover was a trained police officer on duty * * *. Glover himself was a Negro and unlikely to perceive only general features of "hundreds of Hartford black males," as the Court of Appeals stated. * * * [A]s a specially trained, assigned, and experienced officer, he could be expected to pay scrupulous attention to detail, for he knew that subsequently he would have to find and arrest his vendor. In addition, he knew that his claimed observations would be subject later to close scrutiny and examination at any trial.

3. The accuracy of the description. Glover's description was given to D'Onofrio within minutes after the transaction. It included the vendor's race, his height, his build, the color and style of his hair, and the high cheekbone facial feature. It also included clothing the vendor wore. No claim has been made that respondent did not possess the physical characteristics so described. D'Onofrio reacted positively at once. Two days later, when Glover was alone, he viewed the photograph D'Onofrio produced and identified its subject as the narcotics seller.

4. The witness' level of certainty. There is no dispute that the photograph in question was that of respondent. Glover, in response to a question whether the photograph was that of the person from whom he made the purchase, testified: "There is no question whatsoever." This positive assurance was repeated.

5. The time between the crime and the confrontation. Glover's description of his vendor was given to D'Onofrio within minutes of the

crime. The photographic identification took place only two days later. We do not have here the passage of weeks or months between the crime and the viewing of the photograph.

These indicators of Glover's ability to make an accurate identification are hardly outweighed by the corrupting effect of the challenged identification itself. Although identifications arising from single-photograph displays may be viewed in general with suspicion, we find in the instant case little pressure on the witness to acquiesce in the suggestion that such a display entails. D'Onofrio had left the photograph at Glover's office and was not present when Glover first viewed it two days after the event. There thus was little urgency and Glover could view the photograph at his leisure. And since Glover examined the photograph alone, there was no coercive pressure to make an identification arising from the presence of another. The identification was made in circumstances allowing care and reflection. * * *

Surely, we cannot say that under all the circumstances of this case there is "a very substantial likelihood of irreparable misidentification." Short of that point, such evidence is for the jury to weigh. We are content to rely upon the good sense and judgment of American juries, for evidence with some element of untrustworthiness is customary grist for the jury mill. Juries are not so susceptible that they cannot measure intelligently the weight of identification testimony that has some questionable feature.

Of course, it would have been better had D'Onofrio presented Glover with a photographic array including "so far as practicable * * * a reasonable number of persons similar to any person then suspected whose likeness is included in the array." * * * But we are not disposed to view D'Onofrio's failure as one of constitutional dimension to be enforced by a rigorous and unbending exclusionary rule. The defect, if there be one, goes to weight and not to substance. * * *

Mr. Justice STEVENS, concurring. * * *

* * * [I]n evaluating the admissibility of particular identification testimony it is sometimes difficult to put other evidence of guilt entirely to one side. Mr. Justice Blackmun's opinion for the Court carefully avoids this pitfall and correctly relies only on appropriate indicia of the reliability of the identification itself. Although I consider the factual question in this case extremely close, I am persuaded that the Court has resolved it properly.

Mr. Justice MARSHALL, with whom Mr. Justice BRENNAN joins, dissenting.

Today's decision can come as no surprise to those who have been watching the Court dismantle the protections against mistaken eyewitness testimony erected a decade ago in *United States v. Wade*; *Gilbert v. California*; and *Stovall v. Denno*. But it is still distressing to see the Court virtually ignore the teaching of experience embodied in those decisions and blindly uphold the conviction of a defendant who may well be innocent. * * *

II

* * * [I]n determining the admissibility of the post-*Stovall* identification in this case, the Court considers two alternatives, a *per se* exclusionary rule and a totality-of-the-circumstances approach. The Court weighs three factors in deciding that the totality approach, which is essentially the test used in *Biggers*, should be applied. In my view, the Court wrongly evaluates the impact of these factors.

First, the Court acknowledges that one of the factors, deterrence of police use of unnecessarily suggestive identification procedures, favors the *per se* rule. Indeed, it does so heavily, for such a rule would make it unquestionably clear to the police they must never use a suggestive procedure when a fairer alternative is available. I have no doubt that conduct would quickly conform to the rule.

Second, the Court gives passing consideration to the dangers of eyewitness identification recognized in [prior cases]. It concludes, however, that the grave risk of error does not justify adoption of the *per se* approach because that would too often result in exclusion of relevant evidence. In my view, this conclusion totally ignores the lessons of *Wade*. The dangers of mistaken identification are, as *Stovall* held, simply too great to permit unnecessarily suggestive identifications. * * *

Finally, the Court errs in its assessment of the relative impact of the two approaches on the administration of justice. * * * Relying on little more than a strong distaste for "inflexible rules of exclusion," the Court rejects the *per se* test. In so doing, the Court disregards two significant distinctions between the *per se* rule advocated in this case and the exclusionary remedies for certain other constitutional violations.

First, the *per se* rule here is not "inflexible." Where evidence is suppressed, for example, as the fruit of an unlawful search, it may well be forever lost to the prosecution. Identification evidence, however, can by its very nature be readily and effectively reproduced. The in-court identification, permitted under *Wade* and *Simmons* if it has a source independent of an uncounseled or suggestive procedure, is one example. Similarly, when a prosecuting attorney learns that there has been a suggestive confrontation, he can easily arrange another lineup conducted under scrupulously fair conditions. * * *

Second, other exclusionary rules have been criticized for preventing jury consideration of relevant and usually reliable evidence in order to serve interests unrelated to guilt or innocence, such as discouraging illegal searches or denial of counsel. Suggestively obtained eyewitness testimony is excluded, in contrast, precisely because of its unreliability and concomitant irrelevance. Its exclusion both protects the integrity of the truth-seeking function of the trial and discourages police use of needlessly inaccurate and ineffective investigatory methods.

Indeed, impermissibly suggestive identifications are not merely worthless law enforcement tools. They pose a grave threat to society at large in a more direct way than most governmental disobedience of the law. For if the police and the public erroneously conclude, on the basis of an unnecessarily suggestive confrontation, that the right man has been caught and convicted, the real outlaw must still remain at large. Law enforcement has failed in its primary function and has left society unprotected from the depredations of an active criminal.

For these reasons, I conclude that adoption of the *per se* rule would enhance, rather than detract from, the effective administration of justice. * * *

Even more disturbing than the Court's reliance on the totality test, however, is the analysis it uses, which suggests a reinterpretation of the concept of due process of law in criminal cases. The decision suggests that due process violations in identification procedures may not be measured by whether the government employed procedures violating standards of fundamental fairness. By relying on the probable accuracy of a challenged identification, instead of the necessity for its use, the Court seems to be ascertaining whether the defendant was probably guilty.* * * The Due Process Clause requires adherence to the same high standard of fundamental fairness in dealing with every criminal defendant, whatever * * * the strength of the State's case against him. * * *

III

* * * [I]t is my view that, assuming applicability of the totality test enunciated by the Court, the facts of the present case require [exclusion of the identification testimony].

I consider first the opportunity that Officer Glover had to view the suspect. Careful review of the record shows that he could see the heroin seller only for the time it took to speak three sentences of four or five short words, to hand over some money, and later after the door reopened, to receive the drugs in return. The entire face-to-face transaction could have taken as little as 15 or 20 seconds. But during this time, Glover's attention was not focused exclusively on the seller's face. He observed that the door was opened 12 to 18 inches, that there was a window in the room behind the door, and, most importantly, that there was a woman standing behind the man. Glover was, of course, also concentrating on the details of the transaction—he must have looked away from the seller's face to hand him the money and receive the drugs. The observation during the conversation thus may have been as brief as 5 or 10 seconds.

As the Court notes, Glover was a police officer trained in and attentive to the need for making accurate identifications. Nevertheless, both common sense and scholarly study indicate that while a trained observer such as a police officer "is somewhat less likely to make an erroneous identification than the average untrained observer, the mere fact that he has been so trained is no guarantee that he is correct in a specific case. His identification testimony should be scrutinized just as carefully as that of the normal witness." * * *

Another factor on which the Court relies—the witness' degree of certainty in making the identification—is worthless as an indicator that he is correct. Even if Glover had been unsure initially about his identification of respondent's picture, by the time he was called at trial to present a key piece of evidence for the State that paid his salary, it is impossible to imagine his responding negatively to such questions as "is there any doubt in your mind whatsoever" that the identification was correct. * * *

Next, the Court finds that because the identification procedure took place two days after the crime, its reliability is enhanced. While such temporal proximity makes the identification more reliable than one occurring months later, the fact is that the greatest memory loss occurs within hours after an event. * * *

Finally, the Court makes much of the fact that Glover gave a description of the seller to D'Onofrio shortly after the incident. * * * [T]he description given by Glover was actually no more than a general summary of the seller's appearance. We may discount entirely the seller's clothing, for that was of no significance later in the proceeding. Indeed, to the extent that Glover noticed clothes, his attention was diverted from the seller's face. * * * Conspicuously absent is any indication that the seller was a native of the West Indies, certainly something which a member of the black community could immediately recognize from both appearance and accent.

From all of this, I must conclude that the evidence of Glover's ability to make an accurate identification is far weaker than the Court finds it. In contrast, the procedure used to identify respondent was both extraordinarily suggestive and strongly conducive to error. In dismissing "the corrupting effect of the suggestive identification" procedure here, the Court virtually grants the police license to convict the innocent. By displaying a single photograph of respondent to the witness Glover under the circumstances in this record almost everything that could have been done wrong was done wrong.

In the first place, there was no need to use a photograph at all. Because photos are static, two-dimensional, and often outdated, they are "clearly inferior in reliability" to corporeal procedures. * * * With little inconvenience, a corporeal lineup including Brathwaite might have been arranged. Properly conducted, such a procedure would have gone far to remove any doubt about the fairness and accuracy of the identification.

Worse still than the failure to use an easily available corporeal identification was the display to Glover of only a single picture, rather than a photo array. * * *

The use of a single picture (or the display of a single live suspect, for that matter) is a grave error, of course, because it dramatically suggests to the witness that the person shown must be the culprit. Why else would the police choose the person? And it is deeply ingrained in human nature to agree with the expressed opinions of others—particularly others who should be more knowledgeable—when making a difficult decision. * * *

I must conclude that this record presents compelling evidence that there was "a very substantial likelihood of misidentification" of respondent Brathwaite. * * *

NOTES AND QUESTIONS

1. Who has the better side of the argument—the majority or the dissent—regarding the due process standard that ought to be applied in identification cases? Who has the better side of the argument regarding whether the identification procedure here violated due process under the totality-of-circumstances test?

2. *Problem.* A Western Union office was robbed by two men. The sole witness was Joseph David, the late-night manager of the office. A day after the robbery, a suspect turned himself into the police for the robbery and implicated Foster. Foster was arrested and immediately placed in a lineup with three other men. Foster was six feet tall; the other men were approximately six inches shorter. Foster (and nobody else) wore a leather jacket similar to one manager David had seen underneath the coveralls worn by the robber. David told the police he "thought" Foster was the robber, but said he could not positively identify him. David asked to speak to Foster, so the arrestee was brought into an office and told to sit across from David. David again indicated that he was uncertain.

Ten days later the police arranged a second lineup. Five men were in the lineup, including Foster. This time, all of the men were of similar height. David reported that he was "convinced" that Foster was the robber. Later, charges were brought against Foster.

At trial, David testified to the identification of petitioner in the two lineups and identified him again in the courtroom.

Are both out-of-court identifications admissible under the Sixth Amendment? Due process? What about the in-court identification? See Foster v. California, 394 U.S. 440, 89 S.Ct. 1127, 22 L.Ed.2d 402 (1969).

3. For an argument that the Warren Court failed to come to grips with the problem of unreliable eyewitness identifications, in part because of the apparent ease of the right-to-counsel solution, see George C. Thomas III, *The Criminal Procedure Road Not Taken: Due Process and the Protection of Innocence*, 3 Ohio St. J. Crim. L. 169 (2005).

CHAPTER 14

THE ROLE OF DEFENSE COUNSEL

■ ■ ■

In all criminal prosecutions, the accused shall enjoy the right * * * to have the Assistance of Counsel for his defence. U.S. Const. amend. VI.

* * *

"How can you defend those people?" is a question frequently put to criminal defense attorneys, often in a tone suggesting that it is not so much a question as a demand for an apology, as though a defense attorney needs to justify his work, in a way that a prosecutor doesn't. Because the question presumes that "those people" accused of crime are guilty, and that people who are guilty of crimes ought not to be defended, it reflects a profound misunderstanding of our criminal justice system and the defense attorney's role in it. James S. Kunen, How Can You Defend Those People?: The Making of a Criminal Lawyer xi (1983).

* * *

The first mention of "counsel" in Anglo–American law appears in the Laws of Henry I, collected around 1115. Here, "counsel" was meant quite literally:

> In [most] cases an accused person may seek counsel and obtain it from his friends and relatives (no law should forbid this), in particular the advice of those whom he brings with him or invites to attend his [case]; and in taking counsel he shall faithfully state the truth of the matter so that circumstances may appear to the best advantage with respect to the [case] or its peaceful settlement. * * *

> For it is often the case that a person sees less in his own cause than in someone else's and it is generally possible to amend in another person's mouth what may not be amended in his own.

Leges Henrici Primi, laws 46.4 & 46.6

Notice that even in the twelfth century, scribes recognized that to take maximum advantage of counsel, the accused should "faithfully state the truth of the matter." Beyond that, it is clear that the principal role of counsel was to provide advice about how to proceed in a case. That is still true today.

It is difficult to exaggerate the importance of the lawyer to the criminal process. The norms that we identified in Chapter 1 as underlying the process—accuracy, efficiency, fairness, and limiting the power of government—simply cannot be achieved if the lawyer for the defense or the prosecution is inept, incompetent, indifferent, or corrupt. Consider a hypothetical based on a real case. *D* is charged with a rape-murder. He denies guilt, claiming he wasn't there that night. While preparing for trial, the lawyer learns that the rapist was sterile *but the lawyer never asks D whether he was sterile and does not even tell D this fact about the case.* Thus, the client never had a chance to offer his thoughts on whether he should take a sperm test. Without evidence that he was not sterile, *D* is convicted and given a long sentence. On appeal, a different lawyer discovered the sterility issue, has *D* tested, and (guess what?) *D* is not sterile. Whether the original lawyer was guilty of ineffective assistance of counsel is an issue for Part D. For present purposes, it is easy to see that had the lawyer performed at a higher level, *D* would have been acquitted in the first place, an outcome that serves the norms of accuracy, fairness, and efficiency.

The ethics of representing criminal defendants thus include zealous and competent representation. The ethics of lawyering also include duties owed to the court. Prosecutors, of course, also have ethical duties to provide competent representation and, above that, to seek justice rather than merely to be an advocate. The prosecutor's duties were explored in connection with prosecutorial discretion and pre-trial discovery in Chapters 12 and 13. In this chapter, we consider the role, duties, and ethics of defense counsel.

A. THE ETHICS OF DEFENDING "THOSE" PEOPLE

1. A CASE STUDY: DEFENDING THE DEFENSELESS CLIENT

What follows is based on the New York City police treatment of suspect named Abner Louima. The worst of the abuse, allegedly committed by Officer Justin Volpe, was shoving a broom handle into Louima's rectum so violently that it caused serious internal injuries. Volpe was charged, along with three other officers, with violating the civil rights of Louima. Volpe faced life in prison for his part in the brutal treatment. For the facts of the case, as well as the commentary on the duties of defense counsel representing Volpe, we draw heavily from Abbe Smith, *Defending Defending: The Case for Unmitigated Zeal on Behalf of People Who Do Terrible Things*, 28 Hofstra L. Rev. 925 (2000).

First, let us assume you are a lawyer specializing in criminal defense work and Officer Volpe asks you to represent him. Does it matter to you whether Volpe is guilty? Should it? If he admits that he is guilty, you might decide you do not want to represent him. If so, do you have any obligation to provide him a defense?

Suppose Volpe denies any role in the abuse, but you do not believe him. You think you have before you "a sadistic, racist cop who, in some sort of monstrous rage, had brutalized an innocent, hard-working immigrant who had the misfortune to cross Volpe's path." Smith, *supra*, at 927. Now assume that you decide to represent Volpe. You have a sign on your desk that says "Presumption of Innocence Commences With Payment of Retainer." *Id*. Volpe pays. You are his lawyer. You have suspended your judgment about Volpe's moral culpability and your job is to minimize the legal consequences of what he did. Now should your belief about his guilt or innocence make any difference in how you approach your job?

Do you think the prosecutor will offer a favorable plea bargain in Volpe's case? Suppose a hard but fair plea offer is made and you suspect, the well-known "blue wall of silence" notwithstanding, that some of the police officers involved in the incident will testify against Volpe. You decide that it is in the best interests of your client to plead guilty. Should you simply provide advice and leave it up to Volpe or should you advocate for a guilty plea? If the latter, how intensely should you advocate?

> Although much has been written about lawyer-client counseling and the proper allocation of power in decision-making, nothing can prepare a criminal lawyer for the intensity of counseling clients about the decision to plead guilty or go to trial, especially where the stakes are high. The timing of this conversation is crucial and can sorely test even a good lawyer-client relationship. Sometimes the moment of reckoning is early on, and sometimes not until the eve of trial.

> Most experienced criminal defense lawyers have had grueling sessions during which they urge recalcitrant clients to plead guilty. These intense and often unpleasant encounters can ultimately be enlightening and even redemptive for the client. Sometimes there is enormous relief in accepting the reality of a situation, putting an end to the uncertainty, and admitting guilt. Of course, sometimes the client simply sees the writing on the wall and wishes to cut his or her losses.

Smith, *supra*, at 946–47.

If no plausible plea bargain is forthcoming, or Volpe simply refuses to accept, you must prepare a defense. Whether other police officers will incriminate Volpe is not certain, but you have one very real problem. Mr. Louima suffered a torn colon, lacerated bladder, and ruptured intestine, all of which is documented in the medical evidence. How to explain these injuries without admitting that *someone* put a broom stick violently into his rectum? And if someone did that, and if the other officers point the finger at Volpe, his case is hopeless.

One way to explain the terrible injuries—the way Volpe's lawyer chose in real life—is to suggest that "Louima's injuries were not the result of police brutality, but of consensual anal sex with another man." Smith, *supra*, at 930. Would you choose this path? Is there any ethical reason not to? Turning the question around, if this is the *only* half-way plausible alternative explanation, are you ethically obligated to present the explanation?

Perhaps. Alan Dershowitz has argued, "What a defense attorney 'may' do, he must do, if it is necessary to defend his client. A zealous defense attorney has a professional obligation to take every legal and ethically permissible step that will serve the client's best interest—even if the attorney finds the step personally distasteful." Smith, *supra*, at 958, quoting Alan M. Dershowitz, Reasonable Doubts: The O.J. Simpson Case and the Criminal Justice System 145 (1996).

But we have yet to answer the question of *whether* this is permissible defense conduct. Many commentators were harshly condemning of the "rough sex" defense, denouncing it as a "vile insinuation," a "vile fantasy," and as "a second rape." Smith, *supra*, at 930–31. Does it matter if you believe that Volpe is guilty and thus that your story cannot be true? What if you are not certain of Volpe's guilt, but you have no evidence to support the allegation of homosexual conduct? Even if you believe Volpe is innocent, can you allege "rough sex" without *any* evidence? Does it matter that Abner Louima is married and has two children?

To Lord Brougham in the early nineteenth century, the answer was that you can present the explanation without regard to your belief in your client's innocence or the truth of the story. Here is how Brougham put it:

> [A]n advocate, in the discharge of his duty, knows but one person in all the world, and that person is his client. To save that client by all means and expedients, and at all hazards and costs to other persons, and, amongst them to himself, is his first and only duty; and in performing this duty he must not regard the alarm, the torments, the destruction which he may bring upon others. Separating the duty of a patriot from that of an advocate, he must go on reckless of consequences, though it should be his unhappy fate to involve his country in confusion.

Smith, *supra*, at 928 n.23, citing 2 Trial of Queen Caroline 8 (London, Shackell & Arrowsmith 1820–21).

Now let us assume that Lord Brougham is right. But what if part of your calculation is not just to create doubt among the jury by offering an alternative explanation of the facts in evidence but, rather, to invoke jury antipathy toward homosexuals, to invite homophobia to cloud the minds of the jurors? Does this take the case out of Lord Brougham's prescription for defending defenseless clients?

Some argue yes, that it crosses an ethical line when a criminal defense lawyer exploits racism, sexism, homophobia, or ethnic bias. But why would it be ethically improper to exploit homophobia if it is ethically desirable (or at least ethically neutral) for a defense lawyer to suggest through cross-examination that the eyewitness is lying when the lawyer knows she is telling the truth? To answer that challenge, some have argued that criminal defense lawyers sometimes have a duty to the community that is at least as important as the duty to the client. Exploiting various nefarious attitudes that exist in society would presumably be more injurious than suggesting that eyewitnesses are lying. But Professor Abbe Smith is unpersuaded by this "progressive" scholarship.

Anthony Alfieri, the most prominent progressive scholar on this subject, wants to have it both ways: He would like criminal defense lawyers to be more "community-centered," and to embrace a "color-conscious, pluralist approach to advocacy that honors the integrity of diverse individual and collective * * * identities *without sacrificing effective representation.*" This is both untenable and disingenuous. In truth, he wants to transform criminal defense lawyers from defenders of individuals accused of crime to defenders of the community and of certain values he holds dear.

It is difficult, if not impossible, to zealously represent the criminally accused and simultaneously tend to the feelings of others. This is so in any political climate, but even more so in a time when criminal punishment is regarded as the answer to almost all of our social problems. We cannot seem to build prisons fast enough, and we are on the road to the virtual banishment of young African American men from society. It is simply wrong to place an additional burden on criminal defense lawyers to make the world a better place as they labor to represent individuals facing loss of liberty or life. * * *

There is nothing unethical about using racial, gender, ethnic, or sexual stereotypes in criminal defense. It is simply an aspect of zealous advocacy. Prejudice exists in the community and in the courthouse, and criminal defense lawyers would be foolhardy not to recognize this as a fact of life. Of course, most bias and prejudice works against the accused, disproportionate numbers of whom are poor and nonwhite. Defense lawyers must incorporate this knowledge, as well as knowledge about the stereotypes that might apply, to the prosecution and defense witnesses in all their trial decisions.

A trial is theater. Defense lawyers cannot afford to be color-blind, gender-blind, or even slightly near-sighted when it comes to race, gender, sexual orientation, and ethnicity, because jurors will be paying close attention and they have come to the trial with their own feelings about these issues. Many stereotypes arise in a criminal trial, whether or not they are actively exploited by either party. Sometimes the exploitation of stereotypes is unavoidable.

Smith, *supra*, at 951–52, 954–55, citing Anthony V. Alfieri, Defending Racial Violence, 95 Colum. L. Rev. 1301, 1320–21 (1995); Anthony V. Alfieri, *Race Trials*, 76 Tex. L. Rev. 1293, 1305–23 (1998).

For Professor Smith, defending the defenseless with vigorous arguments, even those designed to appeal to prejudices, poses no ethical problems.

Justin Volpe did a terrible thing, and he will pay the price for his brutal crime for a long time. Given his client's insistence on going to trial, Volpe's lawyer had no choice but to try to mount a vigorous defense, however ill fated. This was the right thing for Volpe's lawyer to do—for his client and for the rest of us.

Smith, *supra*, at 961.

NOTES AND QUESTIONS

1.   Justice White compared the role of defense counsel to that of the prosecutor in *United States v. Wade*, 388 U.S. 218, 87 S.Ct. 1926, 18 L.Ed.2d 1149 (1967) (White, J., dissenting in part):

> [D]efense counsel has no comparable obligation to ascertain or present the truth. Our system assigns him a different mission. * * * Defense counsel need present nothing, even if he knows what the truth is. He need not furnish any witnesses to the police, or reveal any confidences of his client, or furnish any other information to help the prosecution's case. If he can confuse a witness, even a truthful one, or make him appear at a disadvantage, unsure or indecisive, that will be his normal course. Our interest in not convicting the innocent permits counsel to put the State to its proof, to put the State's case in the worst possible light, regardless of what he thinks or knows to be the truth. Undoubtedly there are some limits which defense counsel must observe but more often than not, defense counsel will cross-examine a prosecution witness, and impeach him if he can, even if he thinks the witness is telling the truth, just as he will attempt to destroy a witness who he thinks is lying. In this respect, as part of our modified adversary system and as part of the duty imposed on the most honorable defense counsel, we countenance or require conduct which in many instances has little, if any, relation to the search for truth.

2.   A.   Would you represent Volpe and, if so, under what conditions concerning your belief as to his guilt?

B.   If you say you would not represent Volpe under any circumstances as a retained lawyer, assume that you are a public defender, the case has been assigned to you, and all your efforts to get it assigned elsewhere have failed. Given the Sixth Amendment, Volpe has the right to have *somebody* represent him. Do you think you could provide zealous representation? For an example of an appointed lawyer who might have faced an even more hopeless case, see *Messer v. Kemp*, 760 F.2d 1080 (11th Cir.1985), where two appointed lawyers had asked to be "relieved," citing "community pressure," but the third lawyer had to try the death penalty case all the way to the gruesome end.

C.   If a hard, but fair, guilty plea were offered, how strongly would you urge Volpe to take it?

D.   If the case goes to trial, would you (should you) raise the "rough sex" defense if you have no evidence that it is true? Would your degree of certainty of Volpe's guilt or innocence make any difference to your thinking on this issue?

In this regard, consider ABA Standards for Criminal Justice: Prosecution Function and Defense Function, 3d, 1993, Standard 4–7.6 (d): "Defense counsel should not ask a question which implies the existence of a factual predicate for which a good faith belief is lacking." Does this mean that, in the absence of proof, you cannot ask Louima whether anal sex caused his injuries?

3.   Do you agree with Professor Alfieri (quoted in the Smith excerpt) that a criminal defense lawyer can adopt a "community-centered" approach and provide zealous defense at the same time?

2.   ETHICS AND DUTIES OF DEFENSE COUNSEL

GERALD B. LEFCOURT—RESPONSIBILITIES OF A CRIMINAL DEFENSE ATTORNEY

30 Loyola of Los Angeles Law Review 59 (1996), 59–63.

Re-read the part of the Lefcourt excerpt at p. 23. It continues:

In twenty-five years of practice, I have seen all sides of the criminal defense bar. I have represented indigent defendants accused of killing police officers, college protesters accused of violating student codes, politicians accused of corruption, and wealthy professionals accused of sophisticated financial crimes. The fact is, in some ways, it is always the same. I truly believe that my responsibility as a lawyer to a client is the same no matter who the defendant and no matter what the crime, and I endeavor to discharge that responsibility as zealously as possible for all.

Society expects a lot from us, all the while bashing us in every possible way. Under the Sixth Amendment we are expected to provide the criminal defendant with a rigorous defense undivided by conflicts. At the same time, in many cases we must fight with judges and prosecutors just to get paid out of frozen funds. We have to worry about whether we will be subpoenaed or have our law offices searched. We have to worry about whether the government is secretly courting our clients to turn against us. And we are told by our friends and by the media that we should not be representing guilty defendants.

These are all situations that drive wedges between our clients and our solemn responsibilities. How do we handle this? What are our fundamental obligations?

I.   RESPONSIBILITIES TO THE CLIENT

First and foremost, defense attorneys must zealously and uncompromisingly represent the client. They must do so with all their ability and creativity, within the bounds of law. Defense attorneys must accept this duty as sacrosanct and be prepared to do whatever it takes to improve the client's position. That means they may have to offend. They may have to do the uncomfortable thing. They may have to have prosecutors and judges think of them as "the other," not one of them.

Of course, paramount is making use of one's own good judgment. While defense attorneys must take into consideration what the client wants, it is the lawyer's judgment that is being offered to the client, and the lawyer must not be afraid to use it. Defense counsel must be both an advisor and an advocate with courage and devotion. Indeed, some have described the role as a "learned friend," often the only one to whom a criminal defendant may turn in total confidence. The defendant needs counsel to evaluate the risks and advantages of alternative courses of action. But the defendant also needs a broad and comprehensive approach to the predicament.

Devoted service to the client does raise the issue of whether the attorney must do whatever the client wants. I believe that we must allow the client to make informed decisions about all matters, including strategy. An informed and participating client is a critical component of discharging our responsibilities. That is not the same thing as doing something illegal, and a lawyer should leave a case if a serious conflict arises. If defense counsel is truly repulsed by the client, the lawyer should not represent the individual. Lawyers are not busses, and they are not obligated to stop at every stop. * * *

Representing an innocent client is an easy situation for the public to support. In practice it is the hardest because of the overwhelming fear of loss. A factually guilty client, where guilt is apparent, raises society's challenge to the defense attorney: "How can you go into court knowing your client is guilty and try to get him or her off?" If this is a problem for you, you should not be a defense attorney. The committed defense attorney must be prepared to ensure that before the government takes away the client's liberty, the process of doing so is fair and true. Defense attorneys are not advocates for crime. They are as interested as anyone in a safe environment in which to live and raise their families. But they are, or should be, overwhelmingly interested in making sure that the government deprives no one of liberty without doing so consistent with the law. Otherwise, the government is just another thug interfering with a citizen's freedom.

NOTES AND QUESTIONS

1.   In the Volpe case study, you considered how it might feel to represent someone who is guilty of a horrific crime. Yet, as Lefcourt suggests, it might be worse to represent an innocent defendant. How would you feel if your innocent client were sentenced to a long prison sentence? To die?

2.   Does the Lefcourt excerpt make you more or less likely to make criminal defense work part of your career? More or less likely to go to work for a public defender's office?

3.   For those who are thinking about becoming prosecutors, what is your reaction to the picture drawn by Lefcourt?

4. If you had to name one personality aspect that Lefcourt might say was crucial to providing consistent, competent representation of "those people," what would it be?

5. *American Bar Association standards.* The overarching function of defense counsel "is to serve as the accused's counselor and advocate with courage and devotion and to render effective, quality representation." Standard 4–1.2. Within that overarching goal, defense counsel has a duty to interview the client and "probe for all legally relevant information without seeking to influence the direction of the client's response." Standard 4–3.2. Beyond interviewing the client, there is of course a duty to investigate the case, put this way in Standard 4–4.1:

> Defense counsel should conduct a prompt investigation of the circumstances of the case and explore all avenues leading to facts relevant to the merits of the case and the penalty in the event of conviction. The investigation should include efforts to secure information in the possession of the prosecution and law enforcement authorities. The duty to investigate exists regardless of the accused's admissions or statements to defense counsel of facts constituting guilt or the accused's stated desire to plead guilty.

For over seven hundred years, counsel in England provided advice but the accused actually pled the case. Though lawyers today do much of the pleading of the case, in some ways the client is still the principal and the lawyer merely the agent or the specialized assistant. For example, five categories of decisions belong to the client: (i) what pleas to enter, including whether to plead not guilty by reason of insanity; (ii) whether to accept a plea agreement; (iii) whether to waive jury trial; (iv) whether to testify in his or her own behalf; and (v) whether to appeal. *Id.*, Standard 4–5.2.

Other decisions in trial strategy and tactics "should be made by defense counsel after consultation with the client where feasible and appropriate. Such decisions include what witnesses to call, whether and how to conduct cross-examination, what jurors to accept or strike, what trial motions should be made, and what evidence should be introduced." *Id*, Standard 4–5.2(b).

6. Suppose your client insists on calling his girlfriend as an alibi witness. Having interviewed her, you think the prosecutor will destroy her on cross examination because you believe she is lying about the alibi. Must you call her? Apply Note 5.

7. *The Unabomber client.* Suppose you were appointed to represent Ted Kaczynski, charged with several bombings and killings. The Government has asked for the death penalty, and the prosecutors have overwhelming evidence of guilt—*e.g.*, a fully-armed bomb found in his tiny cabin, bomb-making parts and chemicals, carbon copies of the Unabomber's manifesto and taunting letters to victims and the news media, thousands of pages of diaries and journals that Kaczynski kept over a twenty-year period. The journals are filled with observations of a man who wanted only to kill his enemies by building a perfect bomb. All of this evidence, and more, will almost certainly be presented to the jury.

You believe your client is mentally ill. If his mental illness is insufficient to qualify for an insanity defense, at the very least it will be his best argument to the jury to impose life without parole rather than the death penalty. You have repeatedly given your client the benefit of your advice on this point, but he refuses to cooperate in the mental illness defense, and orders you not to raise it at trial or at the penalty phase. He tells you that if you raise the issue in court, even indirectly, he will fire you on the spot and represent himself.

What do you do? Let us assume that you are convinced that, without a mental illness defense, your client will be given the death penalty. Can you ignore his orders? What if you also believe that his decision not to plead mental illness is itself caused by his mental illness? Can you proceed with the defense without his permission?

For an argument that "the criminal process failed Kaczynski, his counsel, and the public," see Martin Sabelli & Stacey Leyton, *Train Wrecks and Freeway Crashes: An Argument For Fairness and Against Self Representation in the Criminal Justice System*, 91 J. Crim. L. & Criminology 161, 164 (2000). The authors conclude that to help avoid this kind of failure in the future, "the ethical rules must be modified to clearly allocate the authority to present evidence of mental illness to defense counsel, regardless of the defendant's wishes." *Id.* at 217. What do you think of that solution?

8. *Dealing with pain.* Writing about defense counsel, Susan Bandes concludes that "[t]here may be no other profession whose practitioners are required to deal with so much pain with so little support and guidance." Susan Bandes, *Repression and Denial in Criminal Lawyering*, 9 Buffalo Crim. L. Rev. 339, 342 (2006). As a result, defense lawyers adopt mechanisms to minimize the pain, "including avoidance, denial, suppression, repression," and splitting one's personal and professional life. *Id.* at 366. While some of these mechanisms are healthy in moderation, "the danger is that they will be used to excess, leading to burnout and other forms of distress—both personal and professional." *Id.* at 380.

NIX v. WHITESIDE

Supreme Court of the United States, 1986.
475 U.S. 157, 106 S.Ct. 988, 89 L.Ed.2d 123.

CHIEF JUSTICE BURGER delivered the opinion of the Court. * * *

Whiteside was convicted of second-degree murder by a jury verdict which was affirmed by the Iowa courts. The killing took place on February 8, 1977, in Cedar Rapids, Iowa. Whiteside and two others went to one Calvin Love's apartment late that night, seeking marihuana. Love was in bed when Whiteside and his companions arrived; an argument between Whiteside and Love over the marihuana ensued. At one point, Love directed his girlfriend to get his "piece," and at another point got up, then returned to his bed. According to Whiteside's testimony, Love then started to reach under his pillow and moved toward Whiteside. Whiteside stabbed Love in the chest, inflicting a fatal wound.

Whiteside was charged with murder, and when counsel was appointed he objected to the lawyer initially appointed, claiming that he felt uncomfortable with a lawyer who had formerly been a prosecutor. Gary L. Robinson was then appointed and immediately began an investigation. Whiteside gave him a statement that he had stabbed Love as the latter "was pulling a pistol from underneath the pillow on the bed." Upon questioning by Robinson, however, Whiteside indicated that he had not actually seen a gun, but that he was convinced that Love had a gun. No pistol was found on the premises; shortly after the police search following the stabbing, which had revealed no weapon, the victim's family had removed all of the victim's possessions from the apartment. Robinson interviewed Whiteside's companions who were present during the stabbing, and none had seen a gun during the incident. Robinson advised Whiteside that the existence of a gun was not necessary to establish the claim of self-defense, and that only a reasonable belief that the victim had a gun nearby was necessary even though no gun was actually present.

Until shortly before trial, Whiteside consistently stated to Robinson that he had not actually seen a gun, but that he was convinced that Love had a gun in his hand. About a week before trial, during preparation for direct examination, Whiteside for the first time told Robinson and his associate Donna Paulsen that he had seen something "metallic" in Love's hand. When asked about this, Whiteside responded:

> "[I]n Howard Cook's case there was a gun. If I don't say I saw a gun, I'm dead."

Robinson told Whiteside that such testimony would be perjury and repeated that it was not necessary to prove that a gun was available but only that Whiteside reasonably believed that he was in danger. On Whiteside's insisting that he would testify that he saw "something metallic" Robinson told him, according to Robinson's testimony:

> "[W]e could not allow him to [testify falsely] because that would be perjury, and as officers of the court we would be suborning perjury if we allowed him to do it; * * * I advised him that if he did do that it would be my duty to advise the Court of what he was doing and that I felt he was committing perjury; also, that I probably would be allowed to attempt to impeach that particular testimony."

Robinson also indicated he would seek to withdraw from the representation if Whiteside insisted on committing perjury.[2]

Whiteside testified in his own defense at trial and stated that he "knew" that Love had a gun and that he believed Love was reaching for a gun and he had acted swiftly in self-defense. On cross-examination, he admitted that he had not actually seen a gun in Love's hand. Robinson presented evidence that Love had been seen with a sawed-off shotgun on

---

2. Whiteside's version of the events at this pretrial meeting is considerably more cryptic:

"Q. And as you went over the questions, did the two of you come into conflict with regard to whether or not there was a weapon?

"A. I couldn't—I couldn't say a conflict. But I got the impression at one time that maybe if I didn't go along with—with what was happening, that it was no gun being involved, maybe that he will pull out of my trial."

other occasions, that the police search of the apartment may have been careless, and that the victim's family had removed everything from the apartment shortly after the crime. Robinson presented this evidence to show a basis for Whiteside's asserted fear that Love had a gun.

The jury returned a verdict of second-degree murder, and Whiteside moved for a new trial, claiming that he had been deprived of a fair trial by Robinson's admonitions not to state that he saw a gun or "something metallic." The trial court held a hearing, heard testimony by Whiteside and Robinson, and denied the motion. The trial court made specific findings that the facts were as related by Robinson. * * *

B * * *

The [Eighth Circuit] Court of Appeals accepted the findings of the trial judge, affirmed by the Iowa Supreme Court, that trial counsel believed with good cause that Whiteside would testify falsely and acknowledged that under *Harris v. New York*, 401 U.S. 222, 91 S.Ct. 643, 28 L.Ed.2d 1 (1971), a criminal defendant's privilege to testify in his own behalf does not include a right to commit perjury. Nevertheless, the court reasoned that an intent to commit perjury, communicated to counsel, does not alter a defendant's right to effective assistance of counsel and that Robinson's admonition to Whiteside that he would inform the court of Whiteside's perjury constituted a threat to violate the attorney's duty to preserve client confidences. According to the Court of Appeals, this threatened violation of client confidences breached the standards of effective representation set down in *Strickland v. Washington* [holding, p. 989, that the Sixth Amendment requires "reasonably effective" representation.] * * *

II * * *

C

* * * We must determine whether, in this setting, Robinson's conduct fell within the wide range of professional responses to threatened client perjury acceptable under the Sixth Amendment.

In *Strickland*, we recognized counsel's duty of loyalty and his "overarching duty to advocate the defendant's cause." Plainly, that duty is limited to legitimate, lawful conduct compatible with the very nature of a trial as a search for truth. Although counsel must take all reasonable lawful means to attain the objectives of the client, counsel is precluded from taking steps or in any way assisting the client in presenting false evidence or otherwise violating the law. This principle has consistently been recognized in most unequivocal terms by expositors of the norms of professional conduct since the first Canons of Professional Ethics were adopted by the American Bar Association in 1908. * * *

These principles have been carried through to contemporary codifications of an attorney's professional responsibility. Disciplinary Rule 7–102 of the Model Code of Professional Responsibility (1980), entitled "Representing a Client Within the Bounds of the Law," provides:

> "(A) In his representation of a client, a lawyer shall not: * * * (4) Knowingly use perjured testimony or false evidence. * * * (7) Counsel or assist his client in conduct that the lawyer knows to be illegal or fraudulent."

This provision has been adopted by Iowa, and is binding on all lawyers who appear in its courts. The more recent Model Rules of Professional Conduct (1983) similarly admonish attorneys to obey all laws in the course of representing a client. * * *

Both the Model Code of Professional Responsibility and the Model Rules of Professional Conduct also adopt the specific exception from the attorney-client privilege for disclosure of perjury that his client intends to commit or has committed. DR 4–101(C)(3) (intention of client to commit a crime); Rule 3.3 (lawyer has duty to disclose falsity of evidence even if disclosure compromises client confidences). Indeed, both the Model Code and the Model Rules do not merely *authorize* disclosure by counsel of client perjury; they *require* such disclosure.

These standards confirm that the legal profession has accepted that an attorney's ethical duty to advance the interests of his client is limited by an equally solemn duty to comply with the law and standards of professional conduct; it specifically ensures that the client may not use false evidence. This special duty of an attorney to prevent and disclose frauds upon the court derives from the recognition that perjury is as much a crime as tampering with witnesses or jurors by way of promises and threats, and undermines the administration of justice. * * *

* * * [A]n attorney's revelation of his client's perjury to the court is a professionally responsible and acceptable response to the conduct of a client who has actually given perjured testimony. Similarly, the Model Rules and the commentary, as well as the Code of Professional Responsibility adopted in Iowa, expressly permit withdrawal from representation as an appropriate response of an attorney when the client threatens to commit perjury. Withdrawal of counsel when this situation arises at trial gives rise to many difficult questions including possible mistrial and claims of double jeopardy.[6]

---

6. In the evolution of the contemporary standards promulgated by the American Bar Association, an early draft reflects a compromise suggesting that when the disclosure of intended perjury is made during the course of trial, when withdrawal of counsel would raise difficult questions of a mistrial holding, counsel had the option to let the defendant take the stand but decline to affirmatively assist the presentation of perjury by traditional direct examination. Instead, counsel would stand mute while the defendant undertook to present the false version in narrative form in his own words unaided by any direct examination. This conduct was thought to be a signal at least to the presiding judge that the attorney considered the testimony to be false and was seeking to disassociate himself from that course. Additionally, counsel would not be permitted to discuss the known false testimony in closing arguments. Most courts treating the subject rejected this approach and insisted on a more rigorous standard. The Eighth Circuit in this case and the Ninth Circuit have expressed approval of the "free narrative" standards.

The essence of the brief *amicus* of the American Bar Association reviewing practices long accepted by ethical lawyers is that under no circumstance may a lawyer either advocate or passively tolerate a client's giving false testimony. This, of course, is consistent with the governance of trial conduct in what we have long called "a search for truth." The suggestion sometimes made that "a lawyer must believe his client, not judge him" in no sense means a lawyer can honorably be a party to or in any way give aid to presenting known perjury.

D

Considering Robinson's representation of respondent in light of these accepted norms of professional conduct, we discern no failure to adhere to reasonable professional standards that would in any sense make out a deprivation of the Sixth Amendment right to counsel. Whether Robinson's conduct is seen as a successful attempt to dissuade his client from committing the crime of perjury, or whether seen as a "threat" to withdraw from representation and disclose the illegal scheme, Robinson's representation of Whiteside falls well within accepted standards of professional conduct and the range of reasonable professional conduct acceptable under *Strickland*. * * *

The Court of Appeals' holding that Robinson's "action deprived [Whiteside] of due process and effective assistance of counsel" is not supported by the record since Robinson's action, at most, deprived Whiteside of his contemplated perjury. Nothing counsel did in any way undermined Whiteside's claim that he believed the victim was reaching for a gun. Similarly, the record gives no support for holding that Robinson's action "also impermissibly compromised [Whiteside's] right to testify in his own defense by conditioning continued representation * * * and confidentiality upon [Whiteside's] *restricted* testimony." The record in fact shows the contrary: (a) that Whiteside did testify, and (b) he was "restricted" or restrained only from testifying falsely and was aided by Robinson in developing the basis for the fear that Love was reaching for a gun. Robinson divulged no client communications until he was compelled to do so in response to Whiteside's post-trial challenge to the quality of his performance. We see this as a case in which the attorney successfully dissuaded the client from committing the crime of perjury. * * *

The rule adopted by the Court of Appeals, which seemingly would require an attorney to remain silent while his client committed perjury, is wholly incompatible with the established standards of ethical conduct and the laws of Iowa and contrary to professional standards promulgated by that State. The position advocated by petitioner, on the contrary, is wholly consistent with the Iowa standards of professional conduct and law, with the overwhelming majority of courts, and with codes of professional ethics. Since there has been no breach of any recognized professional duty, it

---

The Rule finally promulgated in the current Model Rules of Professional Conduct rejects any participation or passive role whatever by counsel in allowing perjury to be presented without challenge.

follows that there can be no deprivation of the right to assistance of counsel under the *Strickland* standard. * * *

Justice BRENNAN, concurring in the judgment.

This Court has no constitutional authority to establish rules of ethical conduct for lawyers practicing in the state courts. Nor does the Court enjoy any statutory grant of jurisdiction over legal ethics. * * *

Unfortunately, the Court seems unable to resist the temptation of sharing with the legal community its vision of ethical conduct. But let there be no mistake: the Court's essay regarding what constitutes the correct response to a criminal client's suggestion that he will perjure himself is pure discourse without force of law. * * * *[T]hat* issue is a thorny one, but it is not an issue presented by this case. Lawyers, judges, bar associations, students, and others should understand that the problem has not now been "decided." * * *

Justice BLACKMUN, with whom Justice BRENNAN, Justice MARSHALL, and Justice STEVENS join, concurring in the judgment [omitted].

Justice STEVENS, concurring in the judgment.

Justice Holmes taught us that a word is but the skin of a living thought. A "fact" may also have a life of its own. From the perspective of an appellate judge, after a case has been tried and the evidence has been sifted by another judge, a particular fact may be as clear and certain as a piece of crystal or a small diamond. A trial lawyer, however, must often deal with mixtures of sand and clay. Even a pebble that seems clear enough at first glance may take on a different hue in a handful of gravel.

As we view this case, it appears perfectly clear that respondent intended to commit perjury, that his lawyer knew it, and that the lawyer had a duty—both to the court and to his client, for perjured testimony can ruin an otherwise meritorious case—to take extreme measures to prevent the perjury from occurring. The lawyer was successful and, from our unanimous and remote perspective, it is now pellucidly clear that the client suffered no "legally cognizable prejudice."

Nevertheless, beneath the surface of this case there are areas of uncertainty that cannot be resolved today. A lawyer's certainty that a change in his client's recollection is a harbinger of intended perjury—as well as judicial review of such apparent certainty—should be tempered by the realization that, after reflection, the most honest witness may recall (or sincerely believe he recalls) details that he previously overlooked. Similarly, the post-trial review of a lawyer's pretrial threat to expose perjury that had not yet been committed—and, indeed, may have been prevented by the threat—is by no means the same as review of the way in which such a threat may actually have been carried out. Thus, one can be convinced—as I am—that this lawyer's actions were a proper way to provide his client with effective representation without confronting the much more difficult questions of what a lawyer must, should, or may do after his client has given testimony that the lawyer does not believe. The answer to such questions may well be colored by the particular circumstances attending the actual event and its aftermath. * * *

NOTES AND QUESTIONS

1.   If you had been Robinson, what would you have done?

2.   Suppose your client said, "I recently underwent hypnosis and it refreshed my recollection of what I saw that night." You call the hypnotist, and she confirms the client's story and is willing to testify to the general reliability of hypnotically refreshed recollection. What do you do in this case?

3.   Suppose your client said, "I saw something metallic in Love's hand that night, which is why I told you I thought he had a gun. I never told you I didn't see something metallic. I told you I wasn't sure what I saw was a gun. If you thought I said otherwise, you were mistaken." Does Justice Steven's concurring opinion help here?

4.   *Standard to apply*. How certain should a defense lawyer be before she takes some kind of action, such as having the client testify in a narrative fashion? The Wisconsin Supreme Court recently considered two standards that might govern here. The State argued that defense counsel should be permitted to assume the client is going to testify falsely if the lawyer has "a firm factual basis" for her belief. The defendant urged that the right standard was whether the defense lawyer *knew* the defendant was going to testify falsely. The state court adopted the latter standard, elaborating: "Absent the most extraordinary circumstances, such knowledge must be based on the client's expressed admission of intent to testify untruthfully. While we recognize that the defendant's admission need not be phrased in 'magic words,' it must be unambiguous and directly made to the attorney." State v. McDowell, 272 Wis.2d 488, 681 N.W.2d 500 (2004). See also People v. Johnson, 62 Cal.App.4th 608, 72 Cal.Rptr.2d 805 (1998). Do you agree? Did the lawyer in *Nix* have that level of certainty?

5.   *Conflicting duties*. The ethical dilemma in *Nix* arises from the easy assumption that the lawyer has co-equal duties to her client and to the court. One does not have to accept this premise. Professor Monroe Freedman argues forcefully that the lawyer's first duty is to the client, which requires the lawyer to facilitate and argue the client's perjured testimony if the client cannot be persuaded not to commit perjury. See Monroe Freedman, *Professional Responsibility of the Criminal Defense Lawyer: The Three Hardest Questions*, 64 Mich. L. Rev. 1469 (1966). Does this appeal to you as a solution to the perjury dilemma?

B.   THE RIGHT TO HAVE APPOINTED COUNSEL

The first case in which the Court required a state to provide counsel for indigent defendants was *Powell v. Alabama*, p. 13, holding that "in a capital case, where the defendant is unable to employ counsel, and is incapable adequately of making his own defense because of ignorance, feeble-mindedness, illiteracy, or the like, it is the duty of the court, whether requested or not, to assign counsel for him as a necessary requisite of due process of law * * *." The inevitable question after *Powell* was whether its counsel rule would be limited to the narrow set of circumstances set out in the holding or expanded to include most or all indigent defendants.

In Betts v. Brady, 316 U.S. 455, 62 S.Ct. 1252, 86 L.Ed. 1595 (1942), the Court held that there was a due process right to appointed counsel at state expense only when the failure to appoint counsel would be "offensive to the common and fundamental ideas of fairness." This required a case by case determination, with much discretion in trial judges. At least viewed in light of present-day attitudes about fairness, *Betts* was highly unstable. Could courts continue to say that it is fair to convict indigent defendants of felonies without providing counsel? If not, then why not have a rule requiring appointment? Enter Clarence Gideon, a drifter convicted of breaking and entering a poolroom in Florida. He would provide the Court with a vehicle to change the law.

GIDEON v. WAINWRIGHT

Supreme Court of the United States, 1963.
372 U.S. 335, 83 S.Ct. 792, 9 L.Ed.2d 799.

MR. JUSTICE BLACK delivered the opinion of the Court.

Petitioner was charged in a Florida state court with having broken and entered a poolroom with intent to commit a misdemeanor. This offense is a felony under Florida law. Appearing in court without funds and without a lawyer, petitioner asked the court to appoint counsel for him, whereupon the following colloquy took place:

> "The COURT: Mr. Gideon, I am sorry, but I cannot appoint Counsel to represent you in this case. Under the laws of the State of Florida, the only time the Court can appoint Counsel to represent a Defendant is when that person is charged with a capital offense. I am sorry, but I will have to deny your request to appoint Counsel to defend you in this case.

> "The DEFENDANT: The United States Supreme Court says I am entitled to be represented by Counsel."

Put to trial before a jury, Gideon conducted his defense about as well as could be expected from a layman. He made an opening statement to the jury, cross-examined the State's witnesses, presented witnesses in his own defense, declined to testify himself, and made a short argument "emphasizing his innocence to the charge contained in the Information filed in this case." The jury returned a verdict of guilty, and petitioner was sentenced to serve five years in the state prison. * * * Since 1942, when *Betts v. Brady* was decided by a divided Court, the problem of a defendant's federal constitutional right to counsel in a state court has been a continuing source of controversy and litigation in both state and federal courts. To give this problem another review here, we granted certiorari. Since Gideon was proceeding *in forma pauperis*, we appointed counsel to represent him and requested both sides to discuss in their briefs and oral arguments the following: "Should this Court's holding in *Betts v. Brady* be reconsidered?"

I

The facts upon which Betts claimed that he had been unconstitutionally denied the right to have counsel appointed to assist him are strikingly like the facts upon which Gideon here bases his federal constitutional claim. Betts was indicted for robbery in a Maryland state court. On arraignment, he told the trial judge of his lack of funds to hire a lawyer and asked the court to appoint one for him. Betts was advised that it was not the practice in that county to appoint counsel for indigent defendants except in murder and rape cases. He then pleaded not guilty, had witnesses summoned, cross-examined the State's witnesses, examined his own, and chose not to testify himself. He was found guilty by the judge, sitting without a jury, and sentenced to eight years in prison. Like Gideon, Betts sought release by habeas corpus, alleging that he had been denied the right to assistance of counsel in violation of the Fourteenth Amendment. Betts was denied any relief, and on review this Court affirmed. It was held that a refusal to appoint counsel for an indigent defendant charged with a felony did not necessarily violate the Due Process Clause of the Fourteenth Amendment, which for reasons given the Court deemed to be the only applicable federal constitutional provision. The Court said:

> "Asserted denial [of due process] is to be tested by an appraisal of the totality of facts in a given case. That which may, in one setting, constitute a denial of fundamental fairness, shocking to the universal sense of justice, may, in other circumstances, and in the light of other considerations, fall short of such denial."

Treating due process as "a concept less rigid and more fluid than those envisaged in other specific and particular provisions of the Bill of Rights," the Court held that refusal to appoint counsel under the particular facts and circumstances in the *Betts* case was not so "offensive to the common and fundamental ideas of fairness" as to amount to a denial of due process. Since the facts and circumstances of the two cases are so nearly indistinguishable, we think the *Betts v. Brady* holding if left standing would require us to reject Gideon's claim that the Constitution guarantees him the assistance of counsel. Upon full reconsideration we conclude that *Betts v. Brady* should be overruled.

II

The Sixth Amendment provides, "In all criminal prosecutions, the accused shall enjoy the right * * * to have the Assistance of Counsel for his defence." We have construed this to mean that in federal courts counsel must be provided for defendants unable to employ counsel unless the right is competently and intelligently waived. Betts argued that this right is extended to indigent defendants in state courts by the Fourteenth Amendment. * * * In order to decide whether the Sixth Amendment's guarantee of counsel is of this fundamental nature, the Court in *Betts* set out and considered "[r]elevant data on the subject * * * afforded by constitutional and statutory provisions subsisting in the colonies and the states prior to the inclusion of the Bill of Rights in the national Constitution, and in the constitutional, legislative, and judicial history of the states to the present date." On the basis of this historical data the Court concluded that "appointment of counsel is not a fundamental right, essential to a fair trial." It was for this reason the *Betts* Court refused to accept the contention that the Sixth Amendment's guarantee of counsel for indigent federal defendants was extended to or, in the words of that Court, "made obligatory upon the states by the Fourteenth Amendment." Plainly, had the Court concluded that appointment of counsel for an indigent criminal defendant was "a fundamental right, essential to a fair trial," it would have held that the Fourteenth Amendment requires appointment of counsel in a state court, just as the Sixth Amendment requires in a federal court. * * *

We accept *Betts v. Brady*'s assumption, based as it was on our prior cases, that a provision of the Bill of Rights which is "fundamental and essential to a fair trial" is made obligatory upon the States by the Fourteenth Amendment. We think the Court in *Betts* was wrong, however, in concluding that the Sixth Amendment's guarantee of counsel is not one of these fundamental rights. Ten years before *Betts v. Brady*, this Court, after full consideration of all the historical data examined in *Betts*, had unequivocally declared that "the right to the aid of counsel is of this fundamental character." *Powell v. Alabama*. While the Court at the close of its *Powell* opinion did by its language, as this Court frequently does, limit its holding to the particular facts and circumstances of that case, its conclusions about the fundamental nature of the right to counsel are unmistakable. * * *

* * * The fact is that in deciding as it did—that "appointment of counsel is not a fundamental right, essential to a fair trial"—the Court in *Betts v. Brady* made an abrupt break with its own well-considered precedents. In returning to these old precedents, sounder we believe than the new, we but restore constitutional principles established to achieve a fair system of justice. Not only these precedents but also reason and reflection require us to recognize that in our adversary system of criminal justice, any person haled into court, who is too poor to hire a lawyer, cannot be assured a fair trial unless counsel is provided for him. This seems to us to be an obvious truth. Governments, both state and federal, quite properly spend vast sums of money to establish machinery to try defendants accused of crime. Lawyers to prosecute are everywhere deemed essential to protect the public's interest in an orderly society. Similarly, there are few defendants charged with crime, few indeed, who fail to hire the best lawyers they can get to prepare and present their defenses. That govern-

ment hires lawyers to prosecute and defendants who have the money hire lawyers to defend are the strongest indications of the wide-spread belief that lawyers in criminal courts are necessities, not luxuries. The right of one charged with crime to counsel may not be deemed fundamental and essential to fair trials in some countries, but it is in ours. From the very beginning, our state and national constitutions and laws have laid great emphasis on procedural and substantive safeguards designed to assure fair trials before impartial tribunals in which every defendant stands equal before the law. This noble ideal cannot be realized if the poor man charged with crime has to face his accusers without a lawyer to assist him. * * *

The Court in *Betts v. Brady* departed from the sound wisdom upon which the Court's holding in *Powell v. Alabama* rested. Florida, supported by two other States, has asked that *Betts v. Brady* be left intact. Twenty-two States, as friends of the Court, argue that *Betts* was "an anachronism when handed down" and that it should now be overruled. We agree.

[The separate opinion of Justice Douglas, and the opinion of Justice Clark, concurring in the result, are omitted.]

Mr. Justice HARLAN, concurring.

I agree that *Betts v. Brady* should be overruled, but consider it entitled to a more respectful burial than has been accorded, at least on the part of those of us who were not on the Court when that case was decided.

I cannot subscribe to the view that *Betts v. Brady* represented "an abrupt break with its own well-considered precedents." In 1932, in *Powell v. Alabama*, a capital case, this Court declared that under the particular facts there presented—"the ignorance and illiteracy of the defendants, their youth, the circumstances of public hostility * * * and above all that they stood in deadly peril of their lives"—the state court had a duty to assign counsel for the trial as a necessary requisite of due process of law. It is evident that these limiting facts were not added to the opinion as an after-thought; they were repeatedly emphasized, and were clearly regarded as important to the result.

Thus when this Court, a decade later, decided *Betts v. Brady*, it did no more than to admit of the possible existence of special circumstances in noncapital as well as capital trials, while at the same time insisting that such circumstances be shown in order to establish a denial of due process. The right to appointed counsel had been recognized as being considerably broader in federal prosecutions, see *Johnson v. Zerbst*, 304 U.S. 458, 58 S.Ct. 1019, 82 L.Ed. 1461, but to have imposed these requirements on the States would indeed have been "an abrupt break" with the almost immediate past. The declaration that the right to appointed counsel in state prosecutions, as established in *Powell v. Alabama*, was not limited to capital cases was in truth not a departure from, but an extension of, existing precedent. * * *

The special circumstances rule has been formally abandoned in capital cases, and the time has now come when it should be similarly abandoned in noncapital cases, at least as to offenses which, as the one involved here, carry the possibility of a substantial prison sentence. (Whether the rule should extend to all criminal cases need not now be decided.) This indeed does no more than to make explicit something that has long since been foreshadowed in our decisions. * * *

NOTES AND QUESTIONS

1. In considering whether *Betts* was a "break" with precedent, Black reads *Powell* broadly while Harlan reads it narrowly. Just based on what these two opinions tell us about *Powell*, which do you think is the better reading of *Powell*?

2. Look again at the language of the Sixth Amendment. Does the "right to the Assistance of Counsel" carry with it the correlative duty on the part of state governments to appoint and compensate counsel for indigent defendants?

Not according to *Betts*, which noted the English rule that denied representation by counsel in felony cases (oddly enough, counsel could represent misdemeanor, but not felony, defendants in England at that time). *Betts* read the eighteenth century state constitutional provisions as abrogating the English rule and thus *permitting* the assistance of counsel but not *compelling* appointment of counsel at state expense. The two ideas are conceptually very different. To have the right to do something (own property, for example) is not always the same as having the means to that right guaranteed. But some rights create a correlative duty on the part of government. The right to vote, for example, creates a duty on government to make available the means to vote (voting booths, ballots, etc.), and a duty to ensure that every vote is weighted roughly the same.

Betts accepted that the Sixth Amendment right to counsel creates a correlative duty on the *federal* government to provide counsel to all indigent federal defendants. But it did not find that duty in the due process clause of the Fourteenth Amendment and thus did not find any similar duty on States. *Betts* can thus be explained by the historic importance of federalism in the United States, but it does seem anachronistic in light of the crucial role that lawyers play in trials.

3. *Gideon's Trumpet.* When Clarence Earl Gideon's case was called for trial, the judge asked if he was ready. He responded: "I am not ready, your Honor." After more questioning from the judge, Gideon asked for counsel and the colloquy followed that you saw in *Gideon*. Anthony Lewis, Gideon's Trumpet 9–10 (1964). From prison, he filed a handwritten habeas petition in the Florida Supreme Court and, when he lost there, a handwritten petition for certiorari in the United States Supreme Court. *Id*. at 34–35. Perhaps signaling that the Supreme Court was ready to change its mind about the rule of *Betts*, the Court appointed Abe Fortas to represent Gideon. Fortas, who, of course, went on to become a justice, was in 1962, "a high-powered example of that high-powered species, the Washington lawyer." *Id*. at 48.

After preparing a brief on Gideon's behalf, Fortas sent a copy to Gideon at the state prison. He responded by thanking Fortas for the copy and added:

"Everone [sic] and myself thinks it is a very wonderful and brilliant document. I do not know how you have enticed the general public to take such a [sic] interest in this cause. But I must say it makes me feel very good." *Id.* at 138.

During oral argument Fortas sought rather ingeniously to make the federalism argument work for, rather than against, Gideon. He responded to Justice Harlan's argumentative question about federalism by stating that it was "a fundamental principle for which I personally have the highest regard and concern." Then he added the *tour de force*: "Betts against Brady does not incorporate a proper regard for federalism. It requires a case-by-case supervision by this Court of state criminal proceedings, and that cannot be wholesome. * * * Intervention should be in the least abrasive, the least corrosive way possible." *Id.* at 171–72. For Fortas, the "least abrasive" intervention was a bright-line rule that state judges could apply without having federal judges looking over their shoulder.

Justice Black dissented in *Betts*. He said to a friend shortly after *Gideon* was announced, "When *Betts v. Brady* was decided, I never thought I'd live to see it overruled." Lewis, *supra* at 192.

And what of Clarence Earl Gideon? Facing a second prosecution after remand, he rejected the trial lawyer the ACLU provided; after interviewing Gideon, this lawyer characterized him as "an irascible but spunky" man. *Id.* at 224. The trial judge then appointed a lawyer whom Gideon grudgingly accepted, the case proceeded to trial, and the jury acquitted. "After nearly two years in the state penitentiary Gideon was a free man. There were tears in his eyes, and he trembled even more than usual * * *." A newspaper reporter asked, "Do you feel like you accomplished something?" Gideon replied: "Well I did." *Id.* at 238.

4.   The *Gideon* Court was unanimous that *Betts* should be overruled, and that the right to counsel should extend at least to indigent state defendants like Gideon, who face felony charges. Can you determine from Justice Black's opinion whether *Gideon* applies more broadly than to felonies?

5.   Suppose the judge told *Gideon* prior to trial, "If you are convicted, I won't send you to prison, so I'm not going to give you a lawyer." Would that violate the Constitution as interpreted by *Gideon*?

6.   *Gideon's legacy*. None of the Justices in *Gideon* mentioned the problem of funding the new right to counsel in state courts. In 1963, relatively few federal crimes existed. The problem of paying for lawyers to represent indigent federal defendants was minuscule by comparison to indigent criminal defendants in state court. Three basic forms of public financing have evolved: public-defender programs, contract-attorney representation; and assigned-lawyer programs.

> A public-defender system is an organization of lawyers designated by a jurisdiction to provide representation to indigents in criminal cases. The attorneys who work in a public defender office are full-time salaried government employees working together under a single head defender who has responsibility for indigent representation in a particular jurisdiction—just as prosecutors are typically salaried government employees

working under a single district attorney for a jurisdiction. Virtually all states have at least a minority of counties with such defender programs.

Many counties have an assigned-counsel program. Under this approach, often inexperienced or under-employed private practitioners are placed on a list to provide representation to poor defendants on a case-by-case basis. They are paid by the hour (usually well below ordinary rates for attorneys in the community) or receive a flat fee per case.

A contract-attorney program is one in which a jurisdiction enters into an agreement with private attorneys, law firms, or bar associations to represent indigents in the community. Attorneys in such a system often maintain a substantial private practice apart from their contract work. They are paid either on a fixed-price basis (they agree to accept an undetermined number of cases for a determined flat fee) or on a fixed-fee-per-case basis. Frequently, the fees are so low that quality representation, particularly in capital cases, is difficult to obtain.

Today, most large counties employ some combination of these programs.

1 Joshua Dressler & Alan C. Michaels, Understanding Criminal Procedure § 28.03 [B][5] (5th ed. 2010).

7. *Is the state prosecuting and defending?* No matter which form of public financing is used to implement *Gideon*, the net effect is that the State is paying the lawyers on both sides. While this fact could hardly be characterized as a formal conflict of interest, it might lead to a more subtle problem. As long as the only client is the State, doesn't this create an incentive for everyone involved to process the cases as smoothly as possible? To plea bargain rather than engage in pre-trial discovery, investigation, and motion practice?

What would you say, as public defender, if your client said to you, "Who's paying your salary, dude? The same dudes as for the [bleeping] DA, right?"

In this context, Justice Blackmun once observed:

> The right to privately chosen and compensated counsel * * * serves broader institutional interests. The "virtual socialization of criminal defense work in this country that would be the result of a widespread abandonment of the right to retain chosen counsel too readily would standardize the provision of criminal-defense services and diminish defense counsel's independence. There is a place in our system of criminal justice for the maverick and the risk taker and for approaches that might not fit into the structured environment of a public defender's office, or that might displease a judge whose preference for nonconfrontational styles of advocacy might influence the judge's appointment decisions.

Caplin & Drysdale, Chartered v. United States, 491 U.S. 617, 109 S.Ct. 2646, 105 L.Ed.2d 528 (1989) (Blackmun, J., dissenting).

Perhaps the public financed "system is designed to institutionalize cost-efficient lawyering arrangements that depend on routinized case processing and discourage individual lawyers assigned to the poor from providing them with adversarial advocacy." Perhaps the "principal effects" of public financed criminal defense "have been to strengthen the private bar's monopoly over fee-paying cases and to enable the state to discipline the poor through the implementation of the criminal sanction." Perhaps the system is "in reality a triumph of the alliance between the organized bar and the state." That, at least, is the view of two scholars. *See* Michael McConville & Chester L. Mirsky, *Understanding Defense of the Poor in State Courts*, 10 Studies in Law, Politics, and Society 217 (1990).

SCOTT v. ILLINOIS

Supreme Court of the United States, 1979.
440 U.S. 367, 99 S.Ct. 1158, 59 L.Ed.2d 383.

MR. JUSTICE REHNQUIST delivered the opinion of the Court.

We granted certiorari in this case to resolve a conflict among state and lower federal courts regarding the proper application of our decision in *Argersinger v. Hamlin*, 407 U.S. 25, 92 S.Ct. 2006, 32 L.Ed.2d 530 (1972). Petitioner Scott was convicted of theft and fined $50 after a bench trial in the Circuit Court of Cook County, Ill. His conviction was affirmed by the state intermediate appellate court and then by the Supreme Court of Illinois, over Scott's contention that the Sixth and Fourteenth Amendments to the United States Constitution required that Illinois provide trial counsel to him at its expense.

Petitioner Scott was convicted of shoplifting merchandise valued at less than $150. The applicable Illinois statute set the maximum penalty for such an offense at a $500 fine or one year in jail, or both. The petitioner argues that a line of this Court's cases culminating in *Argersinger v. Hamlin*, requires state provision of counsel whenever imprisonment is an authorized penalty.

The Supreme Court of Illinois rejected this contention, quoting the following language from *Argersinger*:

"We hold, therefore, that absent a knowing and intelligent waiver, no person may be imprisoned for any offense, whether classified as petty, misdemeanor, or felony, unless he was represented by counsel at his trial."

"Under the rule we announce today, every judge will know when the trial of a misdemeanor starts that no imprisonment may be imposed, even though local law permits it, unless the accused is represented by counsel. He will have a measure of the seriousness and gravity of the offense and therefore know when to name a lawyer to represent the accused before the trial starts."

The Supreme Court of Illinois went on to state that it was "not inclined to extend *Argersinger*" to the case where a defendant is charged with a statutory offense for which imprisonment upon conviction is authorized but not actually imposed upon the defendant. We agree with the Supreme Court of Illinois that the Federal Constitution does not require a state trial court to appoint counsel for a criminal defendant such as petitioner, and we therefore affirm its judgment. * * *

There is considerable doubt that the Sixth Amendment itself, as originally drafted by the Framers of the Bill of Rights, contemplated any guarantee other than the right of an accused in a criminal prosecution in a federal court to employ a lawyer to assist in his defense. * * *

[We] held in *Duncan v. Louisiana*, p. 39, that the right to jury trial in federal court guaranteed by the Sixth Amendment was applicable to the States by virtue of the Fourteenth Amendment. The Court held, however: "It is doubtless true that there is a category of petty crimes or offenses which is not subject to the Sixth Amendment jury trial provision and should not be subject to the Fourteenth Amendment jury trial requirement here applied to the States. Crimes carrying possible penalties up to six months do not require a jury trial if they otherwise qualify as petty offenses * * *." In *Baldwin v. New York*, 399 U.S. 66, 69, 90 S.Ct. 1886, 1888, 26 L.Ed.2d 437 (1970), the controlling opinion of Mr. Justice White concluded that "no offense can be deemed 'petty' for purposes of the right to trial by jury where imprisonment for more than six months is authorized."

In *Argersinger* the State of Florida urged that a similar dichotomy be employed in the right-to-counsel area: Any offense punishable by less than six months in jail should not require appointment of counsel for an indigent defendant. The *Argersinger* Court rejected this analogy, however, observing that "the right to trial by jury has a different genealogy and is brigaded with a system of trial to a judge alone."

The number of separate opinions in *Gideon, Duncan, Baldwin*, and *Argersinger*, suggests that constitutional line drawing becomes more difficult as the reach of the Constitution is extended further, and as efforts are made to transpose lines from one area of Sixth Amendment jurisprudence to another. The process of incorporation creates special difficulties, for the state and federal contexts are often different and application of the same principle may have ramifications distinct in degree and kind. The range of human conduct regulated by state criminal laws is much broader than that of the federal criminal laws, particularly on the "petty" offense part of the spectrum. As a matter of constitutional adjudication, we are, therefore, less willing to extrapolate an already extended line when, although the general nature of the principle sought to be applied is clear, its precise limits and their ramifications become less so. We have now in our decided cases departed from the literal meaning of the Sixth Amendment. And we cannot fall back on the common law as it existed prior to the enactment of that Amendment, since it perversely gave less in the way of right to counsel to accused felons than to those accused of misdemeanors. * * *

Although the intentions of the *Argersinger* Court are not unmistakably clear from its opinion, we conclude today that *Argersinger* did indeed delimit the constitutional right to appointed counsel in state criminal proceedings. Even were the matter *res nova*, we believe that the central premise of *Argersinger*—that actual imprisonment is a penalty different in kind from fines or the mere threat of imprisonment—is eminently sound and warrants adoption of actual imprisonment as the line defining the constitutional right to appointment of counsel. *Argersinger* has proved reasonably workable, whereas any extension would create confusion and impose unpredictable, but necessarily substantial, costs on 50 quite diverse States. We therefore hold that the Sixth and Fourteenth Amendments to the United States Constitution require only that no indigent criminal defendant be sentenced to a term of imprisonment unless the State has afforded him the right to assistance of appointed counsel in his defense. * * *

Mr. Justice POWELL, concurring.

For the reasons stated in my opinion in *Argersinger v. Hamlin*, I do not think the rule adopted by the Court in that case is required by the Constitution. Moreover, the drawing of a line based on whether there is imprisonment (even for overnight) can have the practical effect of precluding provision of counsel in other types of cases in which conviction can have more serious consequences. The *Argersinger* rule also tends to impair the proper functioning of the criminal justice system in that trial judges, in advance of hearing any evidence and before knowing anything about the case except the charge, all too often will be compelled to forgo the legislatively granted option to impose a sentence of imprisonment upon conviction. Preserving this option by providing counsel often will be impossible or impracticable—particularly in congested urban courts where scores of cases are heard in a single sitting, and in small and rural communities where lawyers may not be available.

Despite my continuing reservations about the *Argersinger* rule, it was approved by the Court in the 1972 opinion and four Justices have reaffirmed it today. It is important that this Court provide clear guidance to the hundreds of courts across the country that confront this problem daily. Accordingly, and mindful of *stare decisis*, I join the opinion of the Court. I do so, however, with the hope that in due time a majority will recognize that a more flexible rule is consistent with due process and will better serve the cause of justice.

Mr. Justice BRENNAN, with whom Mr. Justice MARSHALL and Mr. Justice STEVENS join, dissenting. * * *

II

In my view petitioner could prevail in this case without extending the right to counsel beyond what was assumed to exist in *Argersinger*. Neither party in that case questioned the existence of the right to counsel in trials involving "non-petty" offenses punishable by more than six months in jail. The question the Court addressed was whether the right applied to some "petty" offenses to which the right to jury trial did not extend. The Court's reasoning in applying the right to counsel in the case before it—

that the right to counsel is more fundamental to a fair proceeding than the right to jury trial and that the historical limitations on the jury trial right are irrelevant to the right to counsel—certainly cannot support a standard for the right to counsel that is more restrictive than the standard for granting a right to jury trial. * * * *Argersinger* thus established a "two dimensional" test for the right to counsel: the right attaches to any "nonpetty" offense punishable by more than six months in jail and in addition to any offense where actual incarceration is likely regardless of the maximum authorized penalty.

The offense of "theft" with which Scott was charged is certainly not a "petty" one. It is punishable by a sentence of up to one year in jail. Unlike many traffic or other "regulatory" offenses, it carries the moral stigma associated with common-law crimes traditionally recognized as indicative of moral depravity. The State indicated at oral argument that the services of a professional prosecutor were considered essential to the prosecution of this offense. Likewise, nonindigent defendants charged with this offense would be well advised to hire the "best lawyers they can get." Scott's right to the assistance of appointed counsel is thus plainly mandated by the logic of the Court's prior cases, including *Argersinger* itself.

III

But rather than decide consonant with the assumption in regard to nonpetty offenses that was both implicit and explicit in *Argersinger*, the Court today retreats to the indefensible position that the *Argersinger* "actual imprisonment" standard is the *only* test for determining the boundary of the Sixth Amendment right to appointed counsel in state misdemeanor cases, thus necessarily deciding that in many cases (such as this one) a defendant will have no right to appointed counsel even when he has a constitutional right to a jury trial. This is simply an intolerable result. Not only is the "actual imprisonment" standard unprecedented as the exclusive test, but also the problems inherent in its application demonstrate the superiority of an "authorized imprisonment" standard that would require the appointment of counsel for indigents accused of any offense for which imprisonment for any time is authorized.

First, the "authorized imprisonment" standard more faithfully implements the principles of the Sixth Amendment identified in *Gideon*. The procedural rules established by state statutes are geared to the nature of the potential penalty for an offense, not to the actual penalty imposed in particular cases. The authorized penalty is also a better predictor of the stigma and other collateral consequences that attach to conviction of an offense. * * *

Second, the "authorized imprisonment" test presents no problems of administration. It avoids the necessity for time-consuming consideration of the likely sentence in each individual case before trial and the attendant problems of inaccurate predictions, unequal treatment, and apparent and actual bias. These problems with the "actual imprisonment" standard were suggested in my Brother Powell's concurrence in *Argersinger*, which was echoed in scholarly criticism of that decision. * * *

Perhaps the strongest refutation of respondent's alarmist prophecies that an "authorized imprisonment" standard would wreak havoc on the States is that the standard has not produced that result in the substantial number of States that already provide counsel in all cases where imprisonment is authorized—States that include a large majority of the country's population and a great diversity of urban and rural environments. Moreover, of those States that do not yet provide counsel in all cases where *any* imprisonment is authorized, many provide counsel when periods of imprisonment longer than 30 days, 3 months, or 6 months are authorized. In fact, Scott would be entitled to appointed counsel under the current laws of at least 33 States. * * *

IV

The Court's opinion turns the reasoning of *Argersinger* on its head. It restricts the right to counsel, perhaps the most fundamental Sixth Amendment right, more narrowly than the admittedly less fundamental right to jury trial. The abstract pretext that "constitutional line drawing becomes more difficult as the reach of the Constitution is extended further, and as efforts are made to transpose lines from one area of Sixth Amendment jurisprudence to another," cannot camouflage the anomalous result the Court reaches. Today's decision reminds one of Mr. Justice Black's description of *Betts v. Brady*: "an anachronism when handed down" that "ma[kes] an abrupt break with its own well-considered precedents."

Mr. Justice BLACKMUN, dissenting.

For substantially the reasons stated by Mr. Justice BRENNAN in Parts I and II of his dissenting opinion, I would hold that the right to counsel secured by the Sixth and Fourteenth Amendments extends at least as far as the right to jury trial secured by those Amendments. * * *

This resolution, I feel, would provide the "bright line" that defendants, prosecutors, and trial and appellate courts all deserve and, at the same time, would reconcile on a principled basis the important considerations that led to the decisions in *Duncan*, *Baldwin*, and *Argersinger*. * * *

NOTES AND QUESTIONS

1. Does the *Scott* rule apply to felonies?

2. As you will see in Chapter 16, Scott had a constitutional right to a jury trial. Consider the spectacle of a *pro se* defendant selecting a jury through the *voir dire* process and trying his case before that jury.

3. The "backward-looking" nature of *Argersinger* is in stark contrast to most rules of constitutional criminal procedure. Absent *Argersinger*, a judge in a misdemeanor or traffic court would not be called upon to make a prediction about the sanction to be imposed if the defendant is found guilty.

Argersinger *requires precisely that prediction. Is this a reason to reject the imprisonment test? See Sherry F. Colb,* Freedom From Incarceration: Why Is This Right Different From All Other Rights?, *69 N.Y.U. L. Rev. 781 (1994) (arguing that freedom from incarceration is a separate due process right and using* Argersinger *to demonstrate the Court's commitment to that right).*

4. Justice Rehnquist seems to concede that *Argersinger* did not compel a rejection of Scott's claim. Thus, the Court had a chance to examine the issue left open by *Argersinger*. What seems to be the key factor in ruling against Scott?

5. Justice Brennan notes that Scott would have had a right to counsel under state law in thirty-three states (but not Illinois). To what extent should this be relevant in interpreting the due process clause?

6. What does Justice Rehnquist mean when he claims that the Court has now "departed from the literal meaning of the Sixth Amendment"? Do you agree?

7. *Another prophylactic rule?* Many states require restitution from those convicted of crimes. One way to create incentives for defendants to pay these sums is to impose a jail sentence and suspend it on the condition that the defendant pay restitution plus any fines and court costs that might also be imposed. If the defendant does not pay, within whatever time period the court sets, the jail sentence can be "activated" by a showing of non-payment. Do indigent defendants facing that sentencing structure have a right to counsel under *Argersinger?*

Yes, the Court held by a 5–4 margin in Alabama v. Shelton, 535 U.S. 654, 122 S.Ct. 1764, 152 L.Ed.2d 888 (2002). Focusing on the fact that the Alabama probation revocation hearing would not permit the defendant to inquire into the basis of his conviction, the Court adopted what amounts to a prophylactic rule. Because defendants might later face incarceration without having had counsel at the trial where guilt was determined, the Court held that courts cannot impose suspended sentences on indigent defendants without providing counsel at trial or finding waiver.

8. *Right to counsel in bail hearings.* Do indigent defendants have a right to counsel at bail hearings? The answer is "sort of." See p. 794, Note 7.

9. To what extent is the *Powell-Gideon-Scott* line of cases based on a concern about inaccurate outcomes if defendants do not have lawyers (innocent defendants being convicted) and to what extent is it based on fairness (even guilty defendants deserve a fair procedure to determine their guilt)? These norms are discussed in Chapter 1. Though these norms overlap substantially in the cases we have read so far, a tension between them appears when the issue is the right to appointed counsel on appeal, as the next two cases demonstrate.

DOUGLAS v. CALIFORNIA

Supreme Court of the United States, 1963.
372 U.S. 353, 83 S.Ct. 814, 9 L.Ed.2d 811.

MR. JUSTICE DOUGLAS delivered the opinion of the Court.

Petitioners, Bennie Will Meyes and William Douglas, were jointly tried and convicted in a California court on an information charging them with 13 felonies. A single public defender was appointed to represent them. At the commencement of the trial, the defender moved for a continuance, stating that the case was very complicated, that he was not as prepared as he felt he should be because he was handling a different defense every day, and that there was a conflict of interest between the petitioners requiring the appointment of separate counsel for each of them. This motion was denied. Thereafter, petitioners dismissed the defender, claiming he was unprepared, and again renewed motions for separate counsel and for a continuance. These motions also were denied, and petitioners were ultimately convicted by a jury of all 13 felonies, which included robbery, assault with a deadly weapon, and assault with intent to commit murder. Both were given prison terms. Both appealed as of right to the California District Court of Appeal. That court affirmed their convictions. Both Meyes and Douglas then petitioned for further discretionary review in the California Supreme Court, but their petitions were denied without a hearing.

Although several questions are presented in the petition for certiorari, we address ourselves to only one of them. The record shows that petitioners requested, and were denied, the assistance of counsel on appeal, even though it plainly appeared they were indigents. In denying petitioners' requests, the California District Court of Appeal stated that it had "gone through" the record and had come to the conclusion that "no good whatever could be served by appointment of counsel." The District Court of Appeal was acting in accordance with a California rule of criminal procedure which provides that state appellate courts, upon the request of an indigent for counsel, may make "an independent investigation of the record and determine whether it would be of advantage to the defendant or helpful to the appellate court to have counsel appointed. * * * After such investigation, appellate courts should appoint counsel if in their opinion it would be helpful to the defendant or the court, and should deny the appointment of counsel only if in their judgment such appointment would be of no value to either the defendant or the court."

We agree, however, with Justice Traynor of the California Supreme Court, who said that the "[d]enial of counsel on appeal [to an indigent] would seem to be a discrimination at least as invidious as that condemned in *Griffin v. Illinois* * * *." In *Griffin v. Illinois*, 351 U.S. 12, 76 S.Ct. 585, 100 L.Ed. 891, we held that a State may not grant appellate review in such a way as to discriminate against some convicted defendants on account of their poverty. There * * *, the right to a free transcript on appeal was in issue. Here the issue is whether or not an indigent shall be denied the assistance of counsel on appeal. In either case the evil is the same: discrimination against the indigent. For there can be no equal justice where the kind of an appeal a man enjoys "depends on the amount of money he has."

In spite of California's forward treatment of indigents, under its present practice the type of an appeal a person is afforded in the District Court of Appeal hinges upon whether or not he can pay for the assistance of counsel. If he can the appellate court passes on the merits of his case only after having the full benefit of written briefs and oral argument by counsel. If he cannot the appellate court is forced to prejudge the merits before it can even determine whether counsel should be provided. At this stage in the proceedings only the barren record speaks for the indigent, and, unless the printed pages show that an injustice has been committed, he is forced to go without a champion on appeal. Any real chance he may have had of showing that his appeal has hidden merit is deprived him when the court decides on an *ex parte* examination of the record that the assistance of counsel is not required.

We are not here concerned with problems that might arise from the denial of counsel for the preparation of a petition for discretionary or mandatory review beyond the stage in the appellate process at which the claims have once been presented by a lawyer and passed upon by an appellate court. We are dealing only with the *first appeal*, granted as a matter of right to rich and poor alike, from a criminal conviction. We need not now decide whether California would have to provide counsel for an indigent seeking a discretionary hearing from the California Supreme Court after the District Court of Appeal had sustained his conviction, or whether counsel must be appointed for an indigent seeking review of an appellate affirmance of his conviction in this Court by appeal as of right or by petition for a writ of certiorari which lies within the Court's discretion. But it is appropriate to observe that a State can, consistently with the Fourteenth Amendment, provide for differences so long as the result does not amount to a denial of due process or an "invidious discrimination." Absolute equality is not required; lines can be and are drawn and we often sustain them. But where the merits of the one and only appeal an indigent has as of right are decided without benefit of counsel, we think an unconstitutional line has been drawn between rich and poor.

When an indigent is forced to run this gantlet of a preliminary showing of merit, the right to appeal does not comport with fair procedure. * * * The present case, where counsel was denied petitioners on appeal, shows that the discrimination is not between "possibly good and obviously bad cases," but between cases where the rich man can require the court to listen to argument of counsel before deciding on the merits, but a poor man cannot. There is lacking that equality demanded by the Fourteenth Amendment where the rich man, who appeals as of right, enjoys the benefit of counsel's examination into the record, research of the law, and marshalling of arguments on his behalf, while the indigent, already burdened by a preliminary determination that his case is without merit, is forced to shift for himself. The indigent, where the record is unclear or the errors are hidden, has only the right to a meaningless ritual, while the rich man has a meaningful appeal. * * *

[The opinion of Justice CLARK, dissenting, is omitted.]

Mr. Justice HARLAN, whom Mr. Justice STEWART joins, dissenting.

In holding that an indigent has an absolute right to appointed counsel on appeal of a state criminal conviction, the Court appears to rely both on the Equal Protection Clause and on the guarantees of fair procedure inherent in the Due Process Clause of the Fourteenth Amendment, with obvious emphasis on "equal protection." In my view the Equal Protection Clause is not apposite, and its application to cases like the present one can lead only to mischievous results. This case should be judged solely under the Due Process Clause, and I do not believe that the California procedure violates that provision.

EQUAL PROTECTION

To approach the present problem in terms of the Equal Protection Clause is, I submit, but to substitute resounding phrases for analysis. I dissented from this approach in *Griffin v. Illinois*, and I am constrained to dissent from the implicit extension of the equal protection approach here—to a case in which the State denies no one an appeal, but seeks only to keep within reasonable bounds the instances in which appellate counsel will be assigned to indigents.

The States, of course, are prohibited by the Equal Protection Clause from discriminating between "rich" and "poor" *as such* in the formulation and application of their laws. But it is a far different thing to suggest that this provision prevents the State from adopting a law of general applicability that may affect the poor more harshly than it does the rich, or, on the other hand, from making some effort to redress economic imbalances while not eliminating them entirely.

Every financial exaction which the State imposes on a uniform basis is more easily satisfied by the well-to-do than by the indigent. Yet I take it that no one would dispute the constitutional power of the State to levy a uniform sales tax, to charge tuition at a state university, to fix rates for the purchase of water from a municipal corporation, to impose a standard fine for criminal violations, or to establish minimum bail for various categories of offenses. Nor could it be contended that the State may not classify as crimes acts which the poor are more likely to commit than are the rich. And surely, there would be no basis for attacking a state law which provided benefits for the needy simply because those benefits fell short of the goods or services that others could purchase for themselves.

Laws such as these do not deny equal protection to the less fortunate for one essential reason: the Equal Protection Clause does not impose on the States "an affirmative duty to lift the handicaps flowing from differences in economic circumstances." To so construe it would be to read into the Constitution a philosophy of leveling that would be foreign to many of our basic concepts of the proper relations between government and society. The State may have a moral obligation to eliminate the evils of poverty, but it is not required by the Equal Protection Clause to give to some whatever others can afford.

* * * California does not discriminate between rich and poor in having a uniform policy permitting everyone to appeal and to retain counsel, and in having a separate rule dealing *only* with the standards for the appointment of counsel for those unable to retain their own attorneys. The sole classification established by this rule is between those cases that are believed to have merit and those regarded as frivolous. And, of course, no matter how far the state rule might go in providing counsel for indigents, it could never be expected to satisfy an affirmative duty—if one existed—to place the poor on the same level as those who can afford the best legal talent available.

Parenthetically, it should be noted that if the present problem may be viewed as one of equal protection, so may the question of the right to appointed counsel at trial, and the Court's analysis of that right in *Gideon v. Wainwright* is wholly unnecessary. The short way to dispose of *Gideon v. Wainwright*, in other words, would be simply to say that the State deprives the indigent of equal protection whenever it fails to furnish him with legal services, and perhaps with other services as well, equivalent to those that the affluent defendant can obtain.

The real question in this case, I submit, and the only one that permits of satisfactory analysis, is whether or not the state rule, as applied in this case, is consistent with the requirements of fair procedure guaranteed by the Due Process Clause. Of course, in considering this question, it must not be lost sight of that the State's responsibility under the Due Process Clause is to provide justice for all. Refusal to furnish criminal indigents with some things that others can afford may fall short of constitutional standards of fairness. The problem before us is whether this is such a case.

DUE PROCESS * * *

It was precisely towards providing adequate appellate review—as part of what the Court concedes to be "California's forward treatment of indigents"—that the State formulated the system which the Court today strikes down. That system requires the state appellate courts to appoint counsel on appeal for any indigent defendant except "if in their judgment such appointment would be of no value to either the defendant or the court." This judgment can be reached only after an independent investigation of the trial record by the reviewing court. And even if counsel is denied, a full appeal on the merits is accorded to the indigent appellant, together with a statement of the reasons why counsel was not assigned. There is nothing in the present case, or in any other case that has been cited to us, to indicate that the system has resulted in injustice. Quite the contrary, there is every reason to believe that California appellate courts have made a painstaking effort to apply the rule fairly and to live up to the State Supreme Court's mandate.

We have today held that in a case such as the one before us, there is an absolute right to the services of counsel at trial. *Gideon v. Wainwright.* But the appellate procedures involved here stand on an entirely different constitutional footing. *First*, appellate review is in itself not required by the Fourteenth Amendment, and thus the question presented is the narrow one whether the State's rules with respect to the appointment of counsel are so arbitrary or unreasonable, *in the context of the particular appellate procedure that it has established*, as to require their invalidation. *Second*, the kinds of questions that may arise on appeal are circumscribed by the record of the proceedings that led to the conviction; they do not encompass the large variety of tactical and strategic problems that must be resolved at the trial. *Third*, as California applies its rule, the indigent appellant receives the benefit of expert and conscientious legal appraisal of the merits of his case on the basis of the trial record, and whether or not he is assigned counsel, is guaranteed full consideration of his appeal. It would be painting with too broad a brush to conclude that under these circumstances an appeal is just like a trial. * * *

I cannot agree that the Constitution prohibits a State in seeking to redress economic imbalances at its bar of justice and to provide indigents with full review, from taking reasonable steps to guard against needless expense. This is all that California has done. Accordingly, I would affirm the state judgment.

NOTES AND QUESTIONS

1. What is the constitutional basis for the majority opinion? Sixth Amendment? Due process? Equal protection?

2. *Free transcripts*. As the Court noted in *Douglas*, Griffin v. Illinois, 351 U.S. 12, 76 S.Ct. 585, 100 L.Ed. 891 (1956), held that a state must provide a transcript free of charge to indigent defendants when it is necessary for them to obtain "adequate appellate review of their alleged trial errors." Can you distinguish *Griffin* from *Douglas*? Justice Harlan dissented in both, but could you have joined the majority in *Griffin* and the dissent in *Douglas*?

3. *Justice for sale*. The plurality opinion in *Griffin*, authored by Justice Black, contained stirring words about equal justice.

> Providing equal justice for poor and rich, weak and powerful alike is an age-old problem. People have never ceased to hope and strive to move closer to that goal. This hope, at least in part, brought about in 1215 the royal concessions of Magna Charta: "To no one will we sell, to no one will we refuse, or delay, right or justice. * * * No free man shall be taken or imprisoned, or disseised, or outlawed, or exiled, or anywise destroyed; nor shall we go upon him nor send upon him, but by the lawful judgement of his peers or by the law of the land." These pledges were unquestionably steps toward a fairer and more nearly equal application of criminal justice. In this tradition, our own constitutional guaranties of due process

and equal protection both call for procedures in criminal trials which allow no invidious discriminations between persons and different groups of persons. Both equal protection and due process emphasize the central aim of our entire judicial system—all people charged with crime must, so far as the law is concerned, "stand on an equality before the bar of justice in every American court."

Black's rhetoric expresses noble goals. Does it tell us anything about how to apply the equality principle in a case like *Douglas*?

4. Chapter 1 noted that fairness sometimes requires at least rough equality of treatment. How does Justice Harlan, in his dissent, find California's procedure consistent with due process fairness?

5. Justice Harlan turned out to be quite a prophet. The equal protection clause could not bear the weight that Justice Douglas put on it in the majority opinion in *Douglas*.

ROSS v. MOFFITT

Supreme Court of the United States, 1974.
417 U.S. 600, 94 S.Ct. 2437, 41 L.Ed.2d 341.

MR. JUSTICE REHNQUIST delivered the opinion of the Court.

We are asked in this case to decide whether *Douglas v. California*, which requires appointment of counsel for indigent state defendants on their first appeal as of right, should be extended to require counsel for discretionary state appeals and for applications for review in this Court. * * *

II * * *

The precise rationale for the *Griffin* and *Douglas* lines of cases has never been explicitly stated, some support being derived from the Equal Protection Clause of the Fourteenth Amendment, and some from the Due Process Clause of that Amendment. Neither Clause by itself provides an entirely satisfactory basis for the result reached, each depending on a different inquiry which emphasizes different factors. "Due process" emphasizes fairness between the State and the individual dealing with the State, regardless of how other individuals in the same situation may be treated. "Equal protection," on the other hand, emphasizes disparity in treatment by a State between classes of individuals whose situations are arguably indistinguishable. * * *

III * * *

We do not believe that the Due Process Clause requires North Carolina to provide respondent with counsel on his discretionary appeal to the State Supreme Court. At the trial stage of a criminal proceeding, the right of an indigent defendant to counsel is fundamental and binding upon the States by virtue of the Sixth and Fourteenth Amendments. But there are significant differences between the trial and appellate stages of a criminal proceeding. The purpose of the trial stage from the State's point of view is to convert a criminal defendant from a person presumed innocent to one found guilty beyond a reasonable doubt. To accomplish this purpose, the State employs a prosecuting attorney who presents evidence to the court, challenges any witnesses offered by the defendant, argues rulings of the court, and makes direct arguments to the court and jury seeking to persuade them of the defendant's guilt. Under these circumstances "reason and reflection require us to recognize that in our adversary system of criminal justice, any person haled into court, who is too poor to hire a lawyer, cannot be assured a fair trial unless counsel is provided for him."

By contrast, it is ordinarily the defendant, rather than the State, who initiates the appellate process, seeking not to fend off the efforts of the State's prosecutor but rather to overturn a finding of guilt made by a judge or a jury below. The defendant needs an attorney on appeal not as a shield to protect him against being "haled into court" by the State and stripped of his presumption of innocence, but rather as a sword to upset the prior determination of guilt. This difference is significant for, while no one would agree that the State may simply dispense with the trial stage of proceedings without a criminal defendant's consent, it is clear that the State need not provide any appeal at all. The fact that an appeal *has* been provided does not automatically mean that a State then acts unfairly by refusing to provide counsel to indigent defendants at every stage of the way. Unfairness results only if indigents are singled out by the State and denied meaningful access to the appellate system because of their poverty. That question is more profitably considered under an equal protection analysis.

IV * * *

Despite the tendency of all rights "to declare themselves absolute to their logical extreme," there are obviously limits beyond which the equal protection analysis may not be pressed without doing violence to principles recognized in other decisions of this Court. * * * The question is not one of absolutes, but one of degrees. In this case we do not believe that the Equal Protection Clause, when interpreted in the context of these cases, requires North Carolina to provide free counsel for indigent defendants seeking to take discretionary appeals to the North Carolina Supreme Court, or to file petitions for certiorari in this Court. * * *

The facts show that respondent, in connection with his Mecklenburg County conviction, received the benefit of counsel in examining the record of his trial and in preparing an appellate brief on his behalf for the state Court of Appeals. Thus, prior to his seeking discretionary review in the State Supreme Court, his claims had "once been presented by a lawyer and passed upon by an appellate court." We do not believe that it can be said, therefore, that a defendant in respondent's circumstances is denied meaningful access to the North Carolina Supreme Court simply because the State does not appoint counsel to aid him in seeking review in that court. At that stage he will have, at the very least, a transcript or other record of trial proceedings, a brief on his behalf in the Court of Appeals setting forth his claims of error, and in many cases an opinion by the Court of Appeals disposing of his case. These materials, supplemented by whatever submission respondent may make *pro se*, would appear to provide the Supreme Court of North Carolina with an adequate basis for its decision to grant or deny review.

We are fortified in this conclusion by our understanding of the function served by discretionary review in the North Carolina Supreme Court. The critical issue in that court, as we perceive it, is not whether there has been "a correct adjudication of guilt" in every individual case, see *Griffin v. Illinois*, but rather whether "the subject matter of the appeal has significant public interest," whether "the cause involves legal principles of major significance to the jurisprudence of the State," or whether the decision below is in probable conflict with a decision of the Supreme Court. The Supreme Court may deny certiorari even though it believes that the decision of the Court of Appeals was incorrect, since a decision which appears incorrect may nevertheless fail to satisfy any of the criteria discussed above. Once a defendant's claims of error are organized and presented in a lawyerlike fashion to the Court of Appeals, the justices of the Supreme Court of North Carolina who make the decision to grant or deny discretionary review should be able to ascertain whether his case satisfies the standards established by the legislature for such review.

This is not to say, of course, that a skilled lawyer, particularly one trained in the somewhat arcane art of preparing petitions for discretionary review, would not prove helpful to any litigant able to employ him. An indigent defendant seeking review in the Supreme Court of North Carolina is therefore somewhat handicapped in comparison with a wealthy defendant who has counsel assisting him in every conceivable manner at every stage in the proceeding. But both the opportunity to have counsel prepare an initial brief in the Court of Appeals and the nature of discretionary review in the Supreme Court of North Carolina make this relative handicap far less than the handicap borne by the indigent defendant denied counsel on his initial appeal as of right in *Douglas*. And the fact that a particular service might be of benefit to an indigent defendant does not mean that the service is constitutionally required. The duty of the State under our cases is not to duplicate the legal arsenal that may be privately retained by a criminal defendant in a continuing effort to reverse his conviction, but only to assure the indigent defendant an adequate opportunity to present his claims fairly in the context of the State's appellate process. We think respondent was given that opportunity under the existing North Carolina system.

V

Much of the discussion in the preceding section is equally relevant to the question of whether a State must provide counsel for a defendant seeking review of his conviction in this Court. North Carolina will have provided counsel for a convicted defendant's only appeal as of right, and the brief prepared by that counsel together with one and perhaps two North Carolina appellate opinions will be available to this Court in order that it may decide whether or not to grant certiorari. This Court's review, much like that of the Supreme Court of North Carolina, is discretionary and depends on numerous factors other than the perceived correctness of the judgment we are asked to review. * * *

Mr. Justice DOUGLAS, with whom Mr. Justice BRENNAN and Mr. Justice MARSHALL concur, dissenting.

I would affirm the judgment below because I am in agreement with the opinion of Chief Judge Haynsworth for a unanimous panel in the Court of Appeals. * * *

Chief Judge Haynsworth could find "no logical basis for differentiation between appeals of right and permissive review procedures in the context of the Constitution and the right to counsel." * * *

Douglas v. California was grounded on concepts of fairness and equality. The right to seek discretionary review is a substantial one, and one where a lawyer can be of significant assistance to an indigent defendant. It was correctly perceived below that the "same concepts of fairness and equality, which require counsel in a first appeal of right, require counsel in other and subsequent discretionary appeals."

NOTES AND QUESTIONS

1. *And who is Judge Haynsworth?* Justice Douglas twice refers, with respect, to Chief Judge Haynsworth. A trivia prize to the students who know the role Judge Haynsworth played in the Supreme Court nomination process. No fair looking it up on the internet.

2. *Another (losing) war story.* You may be cynical about the value of having had a lawyer prepare the first appeal if the defendant has to face the second level of appeal without a lawyer. We invite the cynics to read Tansil v. Tansil, 673 S.W.2d 131 (Tenn.1984), a case in which a civil appellant discharged the lawyer who had represented him at trial and in the intermediate appellate court. The appellant represented himself for the rest of the process. He filed a handwritten petition for discretionary review in the state supreme court, which was granted, and then a badly-typed and poorly-organized brief roughly based on his lawyer's brief in the court of appeals. He also argued the case before the Tennessee Supreme Court, at one point rising from his seat among the spectators to yell that appellee's lawyer was a liar. The Chief Justice threatened appellant with expulsion, and no more outbursts occurred. The *pro se* appellant won 5–0. (One of the authors of the present casebook represented appellee; how do you explain to your client that you lost to a *pro se* appellant?).

3. One way to read *Ross* is that indigents have a right to counsel for appeals as of right but not for permissive appeals. The next case shows that this is not the best reading.

4. *The Court clarifies the Douglas–Ross rationale.* The state system in Halbert v. Michigan, 545 U.S. 605, 125 S.Ct. 2582, 162 L.Ed.2d 552 (2005), is

complex but, in essence, Michigan did not allow automatic appeal from a conviction resulting from a guilty plea or a plea of nolo contendere. Instead, the state court of appeals could *permit* an appeal in those cases, depending on the merits of the application. The state in *Halbert* argued that the discretionary nature of the appeal meant that the case was governed by *Ross*, while the defendant argued that the lack of a lawyer to brief and file the first appeal moved the case within the ambit of *Douglas*. The Court agreed with the defendant, noting the emphasis in *Ross* on the fact that, under the state system there, a lawyer had already prepared one appeal and thus

> will have reviewed the trial court record, researched the legal issues, and prepared a brief reflecting that review and research. The defendant seeking second-tier review may also be armed with an opinion of the intermediate appellate court addressing the issues counsel raised. A first-tier review applicant, forced to act *pro se*, will face a record unreviewed by appellate counsel, and will be equipped with no attorney's brief prepared for, or reasoned opinion by, a court of review.

In Michigan, the court of appeals ruling on the application from a plea-convicted defendant "provides the first, and likely the only, direct review the defendant's conviction and sentence will receive." The Court then noted: "Navigating the appellate process without a lawyer's assistance is a perilous endeavor for a layperson, and well beyond the competence of individuals, like Halbert, who have little education, learning disabilities, and mental impairments." Michigan's system was thus unconstitutional under the authority of *Douglas* because it did not require lawyers for all defendants who wish to appeal their convictions to the first appellate court.

Justice Thomas's dissent, joined by Justice Scalia and, in large part by Chief Justice Rehnquist, argued that the risk to the innocent is less significant in *Halbert* than in *Douglas* because defendants who accept a conviction are less likely to be innocent. Moreover, "When a defendant pleads in open court, there is less need for counsel to develop the record and refine claims to present to an appellate court." Thus, because lawyers are less necessary, and the risk to the innocent, lower, the dissent did not find a violation of due process.

Which view of the right to counsel in the Michigan appellate system do you prefer?

5. We saw in Chapter 12 that defendants have a constitutional right to counsel during preliminary hearings, p. 832, even though no judgment on the merits of the case can be entered. What theory requires counsel during a preliminary hearing, but not on appeal to the state supreme court?

C. THE RIGHT TO DECIDE WHETHER TO HAVE COUNSEL

Does the right "to have the Assistance of Counsel for his defence" imply the right *not* to have a lawyer—that is the right to represent oneself?

FARETTA v. CALIFORNIA

Supreme Court of the United States, 1975.
422 U.S. 806, 95 S.Ct. 2525, 45 L.Ed.2d 562.

Mr. Justice Stewart delivered the opinion of the Court.

The Sixth and Fourteenth Amendments of our Constitution guarantee that a person brought to trial in any state or federal court must be afforded the right to the assistance of counsel before he can be validly convicted and punished by imprisonment. This clear constitutional rule has emerged from a series of cases decided here over the last 50 years. The question before us now is whether a defendant in a state criminal trial has a constitutional right to proceed *without* counsel when he voluntarily and intelligently elects to do so. Stated another way, the question is whether a State may constitutionally hale a person into its criminal courts and there force a lawyer upon him, even when he insists that he wants to conduct his own defense. It is not an easy question, but we have concluded that a State may not constitutionally do so.

I

Anthony Faretta was charged with grand theft in an information filed in the Superior Court of Los Angeles County, Cal. At the arraignment, the Superior Court Judge assigned to preside at the trial appointed the public defender to represent Faretta. Well before the date of trial, however, Faretta requested that he be permitted to represent himself. Questioning by the judge revealed that Faretta had once represented himself in a criminal prosecution, that he had a high school education, and that he did not want to be represented by the public defender because he believed that that office was "very loaded down with * * * a heavy case load." The judge responded that he believed Faretta was "making a mistake" and emphasized that in further proceedings Faretta would receive no special favors. Nevertheless, after establishing that Faretta wanted to represent himself and did not want a lawyer, the judge, in a "preliminary ruling," accepted Faretta's waiver of the assistance of counsel. The judge indicated, however, that he might reverse this ruling if it later appeared that Faretta was unable adequately to represent himself.

Several weeks thereafter, but still prior to trial, the judge *sua sponte* held a hearing to inquire into Faretta's ability to conduct his own defense, and questioned him specifically about both the hearsay rule and the state law governing the challenge of potential jurors.[3] After consideration of

---

3. The colloquy was as follows:

"THE COURT: In the Faretta matter, I brought you back down here to do some reconsideration as to whether or not you should continue to represent yourself.

"How have you been getting along on your research?

"THE DEFENDANT: Not bad, your Honor.

"Last night I put in the mail a 995 motion and it should be with the Clerk within the next day or two.

consideration of Faretta's answers, and observation of his demeanor, the

"THE COURT: Have you been preparing yourself for the intricacies of the trial of the matter?

"THE DEFENDANT: Well, your Honor, I was hoping that the case could possibly be disposed of on the 995.

"Mrs. Ayers informed me yesterday that it was the Court's policy to hear the pretrial motions at the time of trial. If possible, your Honor, I would like a date set as soon as the Court deems adequate after they receive the motion, sometime before trial.

"THE COURT: Let's see how you have been doing on your research.

"How many exceptions are there to the hearsay rule?

"THE DEFENDANT: Well, the hearsay rule would, I guess, be called the best evidence rule, your Honor. And there are several exceptions in case law, but in actual statutory law, I don't feel there is none.

"THE COURT: What are the challenges to the jury for cause?

"THE DEFENDANT: Well, there is twelve peremptory challenges.

"THE COURT: And how many for cause?

"THE DEFENDANT: Well, as many as the Court deems valid.

"THE COURT: And what are they? What are the grounds for challenging a juror for cause?

"THE DEFENDANT: Well, numerous grounds to challenge a witness—I mean, a juror, your Honor, one being the juror is perhaps suffered, was a victim of the same type of offense, might be prejudiced toward the defendant. Any substantial ground that might make the juror prejudice[d] toward the defendant.

"THE COURT: Anything else?

"THE DEFENDANT: Well, a relative perhaps of the victim.

"THE COURT: Have you taken a look at that code section to see what it is?

"THE DEFENDANT: Challenge a juror?

"THE COURT: Yes.

"THE DEFENDANT: Yes, your Honor. I have done—

"THE COURT: What is the code section?

"THE DEFENDANT: On voir diring a jury, your Honor?

"THE COURT: Yes.

"THE DEFENDANT: I am not aware of the section right offhand.

"THE COURT: What code is it in?

"THE DEFENDANT: Well, the research I have done on challenging would be in Witkins Jurisprudence.

"THE COURT: Have you looked at any of the codes to see where these various things are taken up?

"THE DEFENDANT: No, your Honor, I haven't.

"THE COURT: Have you looked in any of the California Codes with reference to trial procedure?

"THE DEFENDANT: Yes, your Honor.

"THE COURT: What codes?

"THE DEFENDANT: I have done extensive research in the Penal Code, your Honor, and the Civil Code.

"THE COURT: If you have done extensive research into it, then tell me about it.

"THE DEFENDANT: On empaneling a jury, your Honor?

"THE COURT: Yes.

"THE DEFENDANT: Well, the District Attorney and the defendant, defense counsel, has both the right to 12 peremptory challenges of a jury. These 12 challenges are undisputable. Any reason that the defense or prosecution should feel that a juror would be inadequate to try the case or to rule on a case, they may then discharge that juror.

"But if there is a valid challenge due to grounds of prejudice or some other grounds, that these aren't considered in the 12 peremptory challenges. There are numerous and the defendant, the defense and the prosecution both have the right to make any inquiry to the jury as to their feelings toward the case."

judge ruled that Faretta had not made an intelligent and knowing waiver of his right to the assistance of counsel, and also ruled that Faretta had no constitutional right to conduct his own defense. The judge, accordingly, reversed his earlier ruling permitting self-representation and again appointed the public defender to represent Faretta. Faretta's subsequent request for leave to act as co-counsel was rejected, as were his efforts to make certain motions on his own behalf.[5] Throughout the subsequent trial, the judge required that Faretta's defense be conducted only through the appointed lawyer from the public defender's office. At the conclusion of the trial, the jury found Faretta guilty as charged, and the judge sentenced him to prison. * * *

II

In the federal courts, the right of self-representation has been protected by statute since the beginnings of our Nation. Section 35 of the Judiciary Act of 1789, 1 Stat. 73, 92, enacted by the First Congress and signed by President Washington one day before the Sixth Amendment was proposed, provided that "in all the courts of the United States, the parties may plead and manage their own causes personally or by the assistance of * * * counsel * * *." The right is currently codified in 28 U.S.C. § 1654.

With few exceptions, each of the several States also accords a defendant the right to represent himself in any criminal case. The constitutions of 36 States explicitly confer that right. Moreover, many state courts have expressed the view that the right is also supported by the Constitution of the United States. * * *

III

This consensus is soundly premised. The right of self-representation finds support in the structure of the Sixth Amendment, as well as in the English and colonial jurisprudence from which the Amendment emerged.

A

The Sixth Amendment includes a compact statement of the rights necessary to a full defense:

> "In all criminal prosecutions, the accused shall enjoy the right * * * to be informed of the nature and cause of the accusation; to be confronted with the witnesses against him; to have compulsory process for obtaining witnesses in his favor, and to have the Assistance of Counsel for his defence."

Because these rights are basic to our adversary system of criminal justice, they are part of the "due process of law" that is guaranteed by the Fourteenth Amendment to defendants in the criminal courts of the States. The rights to notice, confrontation, and compulsory process, when taken

---

5. Faretta also urged without success that he was entitled to counsel of his choice, and three times moved for the appointment of a lawyer other than the public defender. These motions, too, were denied.

together, guarantee that a criminal charge may be answered in a manner now considered fundamental to the fair administration of American justice—through the calling and interrogation of favorable witnesses, the cross-examination of adverse witnesses, and the orderly introduction of evidence. In short, the Amendment constitutionalizes the right in an adversary criminal trial to make a defense as we know it.

The Sixth Amendment does not provide merely that a defense shall be made for the accused; it grants to the accused personally the right to make his defense. It is the accused, not counsel, who must be "informed of the nature and cause of the accusation," who must be "confronted with the witnesses against him," and who must be accorded "compulsory process for obtaining witnesses in his favor." Although not stated in the Amendment in so many words, the right to self-representation—to make one's own defense personally—is thus necessarily implied by the structure of the Amendment. The right to defend is given directly to the accused; for it is he who suffers the consequences if the defense fails.

The counsel provision supplements this design. It speaks of the "assistance" of counsel, and an assistant, however expert, is still an assistant. The language and spirit of the Sixth Amendment contemplate that counsel, like the other defense tools guaranteed by the Amendment, shall be an aid to a willing defendant—not an organ of the State interposed between an unwilling defendant and his right to defend himself personally. To thrust counsel upon the accused, against his considered wish, thus violates the logic of the Amendment. In such a case, counsel is not an assistant, but a master;[16] and the right to make a defense is stripped of the personal character upon which the Amendment insists. It is true that when a defendant chooses to have a lawyer manage and present his case, law and tradition may allocate to the counsel the power to make binding decisions of trial strategy in many areas. This allocation can only be justified, however, by the defendant's consent, at the outset, to accept counsel as his representative. An unwanted counsel "represents" the defendant only through a tenuous and unacceptable legal fiction. Unless the accused has acquiesced in such representation, the defense presented is not the defense guaranteed him by the Constitution, for, in a very real sense, it is not *his* defense.

B

The Sixth Amendment, when naturally read, thus implies a right of self-representation. This reading is reinforced by the Amendment's roots in English legal history. * * *

---

16. Such a result would sever the concept of counsel from its historic roots. The first lawyers were personal friends of the litigant, brought into court by him so that he might "take 'counsel' with them" before pleading. 1 F. Pollock & F. Maitland, The History of English Law 211 (2d ed. 1909). Similarly, the first "attorneys" were personal agents, often lacking any professional training, who were appointed by those litigants who had secured royal permission to carry on their affairs through a representative, rather than personally. *Id.*, at 212–213.

By the common law of [the 17th century], it was not representation by counsel but self-representation that was the practice in prosecutions for serious crime. At one time, every litigant was required to "appear before the court in his own person and conduct his own cause in his own words." While a right to counsel developed early in civil cases and in cases of misdemeanor, a prohibition against the assistance of counsel continued for centuries in prosecutions for felony or treason. Thus, in the 16th and 17th centuries the accused felon or traitor stood alone, with neither counsel nor the benefit of other rights—to notice, confrontation, and compulsory process—that we now associate with a genuinely fair adversary proceeding. The trial was merely a "long argument between the prisoner and the counsel for the Crown." As harsh as this now seems, at least "the prisoner was allowed to make what statements he liked. * * * Obviously this public oral trial presented many more opportunities to a prisoner than the secret enquiry based on written depositions, which, on the continent, had taken the place of a trial * * *." * * *

C

In the American Colonies the insistence upon a right of self-representation was, if anything, more fervent than in England.

The colonists brought with them an appreciation of the virtues of self-reliance and a traditional distrust of lawyers. When the Colonies were first settled, "the lawyer was synonymous with the cringing Attorneys–General and Solicitors–General of the Crown and the arbitrary Justices of the King's Court, all bent on the conviction of those who opposed the King's prerogatives, and twisting the law to secure convictions." This prejudice gained strength in the Colonies where "distrust of lawyers became an institution." Several Colonies prohibited pleading for hire in the 17th century. The prejudice persisted into the 18th century as "the lower classes came to identify lawyers with the upper class." The years of Revolution and Confederation saw an upsurge of antilawyer sentiment, a "sudden revival, after the War of the Revolution, of the old dislike and distrust of lawyers as a class." In the heat of these sentiments the Constitution was forged.

This is not to say that the Colonies were slow to recognize the value of counsel in criminal cases. Colonial judges soon departed from ancient English practice and allowed accused felons the aid of counsel for their defense. At the same time, however, the basic right of self-representation was never questioned. We have found no instance where a colonial court required a defendant in a criminal case to accept as his representative an unwanted lawyer. Indeed, even where counsel was permitted, the general practice continued to be self-representation.

The right of self-representation was guaranteed in many colonial charters and declarations of rights. These early documents establish that the "right to counsel" meant to the colonists a right to choose between pleading through a lawyer and representing oneself. After the Declaration of Independence, the right of self-representation, along with other rights basic to the making of a defense, entered the new state constitutions in wholesale fashion. The right to counsel was clearly thought to supplement the primary right of the accused to defend himself, utilizing his personal rights to notice, confrontation, and compulsory process. And when the Colonies or newly independent States provided by statute rather than by constitution for court appointment of counsel in criminal cases, they also meticulously preserved the right of the accused to defend himself personally. * * *

In sum, there is no evidence that the colonists and the Framers ever doubted the right of self-representation, or imagined that this right might be considered inferior to the right of assistance of counsel. To the contrary, the colonists and the Framers, as well as their English ancestors, always conceived of the right to counsel as an "assistance" for the accused, to be used at his option, in defending himself. The Framers selected in the Sixth Amendment a form of words that necessarily implies the right of self-representation. That conclusion is supported by centuries of consistent history.

IV

There can be no blinking the fact that the right of an accused to conduct his own defense seems to cut against the grain of this Court's decisions holding that the Constitution requires that no accused can be convicted and imprisoned unless he has been accorded the right to the assistance of counsel. For it is surely true that the basic thesis of those decisions is that the help of a lawyer is essential to assure the defendant a fair trial. And a strong argument can surely be made that the whole thrust of those decisions most inevitably lead to the conclusion that a State may constitutionally impose a lawyer upon even an unwilling defendant.

But it is one thing to hold that every defendant, rich or poor, has the right to the assistance of counsel, and quite another to say that a State may compel a defendant to accept a lawyer he does not want. The value of state-appointed counsel was not unappreciated by the Founders, yet the notion of compulsory counsel was utterly foreign to them. And whatever else may be said of those who wrote the Bill of Rights, surely there can be no doubt that they understood the inestimable worth of free choice.

It is undeniable that in most criminal prosecutions defendants could better defend with counsel's guidance than by their own unskilled efforts. But where the defendant will not voluntarily accept representation by counsel, the potential advantage of a lawyer's training and experience can be realized, if at all, only imperfectly. To force a lawyer on a defendant can only lead him to believe that the law contrives against him. Moreover, it is not inconceivable that in some rare instances, the defendant might in fact present his case more effectively by conducting his own defense. Personal liberties are not rooted in the law of averages. The right to defend is personal. The defendant, and not his lawyer or the State, will bear the personal consequences of a conviction. It is the defendant, therefore, who must be free personally to decide whether in his particular case counsel is to his advantage. And although he may conduct his own defense ultimately to his own detriment, his choice must be honored out of "that respect for the individual which is the lifeblood of the law."[46]

V

When an accused manages his own defense, he relinquishes, as a purely factual matter, many of the traditional benefits associated with the right to counsel. For this reason, in order to represent himself, the accused must "knowingly and intelligently" forgo those relinquished benefits. Although a defendant need not himself have the skill and experience of a lawyer in order competently and intelligently to choose self-representation, he should be made aware of the dangers and disadvantages of self-representation, so that the record will establish that "he knows what he is doing and his choice is made with eyes open."

Here, weeks before trial, Faretta clearly and unequivocally declared to the trial judge that he wanted to represent himself and did not want counsel. The record affirmatively shows that Faretta was literate, competent, and understanding, and that he was voluntarily exercising his informed free will. The trial judge had warned Faretta that he thought it was a mistake not to accept the assistance of counsel, and that Faretta would be required to follow all the "ground rules" of trial procedure. We need make no assessment of how well or poorly Faretta had mastered the intricacies of the hearsay rule and the California code provisions that govern challenges of potential jurors on *voir dire*. For his technical legal knowledge, as such, was not relevant to an assessment of his knowing exercise of the right to defend himself.

In forcing Faretta, under these circumstances, to accept against his will a state-appointed public defender, the California courts deprived him of his constitutional right to conduct his own defense. * * *

Mr. Chief Justice BURGER, with whom Mr. Justice BLACKMUN and Mr. Justice REHNQUIST join, dissenting. * * *

I

The most striking feature of the Court's opinion is that it devotes so little discussion to the matter which it concedes is the core of the decision,

---

46. We are told that many criminal defendants representing themselves may use the courtroom for deliberate disruption of their trials. But the right of self-representation has been recognized from our beginnings by federal law and by most of the States, and no such result has thereby occurred. Moreover, the trial judge may terminate self-representation by a defendant who deliberately engages in serious and obstructionist misconduct. Of course, a State may—even over objection by the accused—appoint a "standby counsel" to aid the accused if and when the accused requests help, and to be available to represent the accused in the event that termination of the defendant's self-representation is necessary.

The right of self-representation is not a license to abuse the dignity of the courtroom. Neither is it a license not to comply with relevant rules of procedural and substantive law. Thus, whatever else may or may not be open to him on appeal, a defendant who elects to represent himself cannot thereafter complain that the quality of his own defense amounted to a denial of "effective assistance of counsel."

that is, discerning an independent basis in the Constitution for the supposed right to represent oneself in a criminal trial. Its ultimate assertion that such a right is tucked between the lines of the Sixth Amendment is contradicted by the Amendment's language and its consistent judicial interpretation.

As the Court seems to recognize, the conclusion that the rights guaranteed by the Sixth Amendment are "personal" to an accused reflects nothing more than the obvious fact that it is he who is on trial and therefore has need of a defense. But neither that nearly trivial proposition nor the language of the Amendment, which speaks in uniformly mandatory terms, leads to the further conclusion that the right to counsel is merely supplementary and may be dispensed with at the whim of the accused. Rather, this Court's decisions have consistently included the right to counsel as an integral part of the bundle making up the larger "right to a defense as we know it." * * *

In short, both the "spirit and the logic" of the Sixth Amendment are that every person accused of crime shall receive the fullest possible defense; in the vast majority of cases this command can be honored only by means of the expressly guaranteed right to counsel, and the trial judge is in the best position to determine whether the accused is capable of conducting his defense. True freedom of choice and society's interest in seeing that justice is achieved can be vindicated only if the trial court retains discretion to reject any attempted waiver of counsel and insist that the accused be tried according to the Constitution. This discretion is as critical an element of basic fairness as a trial judge's discretion to decline to accept a plea of guilty. * * *

III

* * * I hesitate to participate in the Court's attempt to use history to take it where legal analysis cannot. Piecing together shreds of English legal history and early state constitutional and statutory provisions, without a full elaboration of the context in which they occurred or any evidence that they were relied upon by the drafters of our Federal Constitution, creates more questions than it answers and hardly provides the firm foundation upon which the creation of new constitutional rights should rest. We are well reminded that this Court once employed an exhaustive analysis of English and colonial practices regarding the right to counsel to justify the conclusion that it was fundamental to a fair trial and, less than 10 years later, used essentially the same material to conclude that it was not.

As if to illustrate this point, the single historical fact cited by the Court which would appear truly relevant to ascertaining the meaning of the Sixth Amendment proves too much. As the Court points out, § 35 of the Judiciary Act of 1789 provided a statutory right to self-representation in federal criminal trials. The text of the Sixth Amendment, which expressly provides only for a right to counsel, was proposed the day after the Judiciary Act was signed. It can hardly be suggested that the Members of the Congress of 1789, then few in number, were unfamiliar with the Amendment's carefully structured language, which had been under discussion since the 1787 Constitutional Convention. And it would be most remarkable to suggest, had the right to conduct one's own defense been considered so critical as to require constitutional protection, that it would have been left to implication. Rather, under traditional canons of construction, *inclusion* of the right in the Judiciary Act and its *omission* from the constitutional amendment drafted at the same time by many of the same men, supports the conclusion that the omission was intentional.

There is no way to reconcile the idea that the Sixth Amendment impliedly guaranteed the right of an accused to conduct his own defense with the contemporaneous action of the Congress in passing a statute explicitly giving that right. If the Sixth Amendment created a right to self-representation it was unnecessary for Congress to enact any statute on the subject at all. In this case, therefore, history ought to lead judges to conclude that the Constitution leaves to the judgment of legislatures, and the flexible process of statutory amendment, the question whether criminal defendants should be permitted to conduct their trials *pro se*. And the fact that we have not hinted at a contrary view for 185 years is surely entitled to some weight in the scales. * * *

Mr. Justice BLACKMUN, with whom THE CHIEF JUSTICE and Mr. Justice REHNQUIST join, dissenting.

III

* * * I note briefly the procedural problems that, I suspect, today's decision will visit upon trial courts in the future. Although the Court indicates that a *pro se* defendant necessarily waives any claim he might otherwise make of ineffective assistance of counsel, the opinion leaves open a host of other procedural questions. Must every defendant be advised of his right to proceed *pro se*? If so, when must that notice be given? Since the right to assistance of counsel and the right to self-representation are mutually exclusive, how is the waiver of each right to be measured? If a defendant has elected to exercise his right to proceed *pro se*, does he still have a constitutional right to assistance of standby counsel? How soon in the criminal proceeding must a defendant decide between proceeding by counsel or *pro se*? Must he be allowed to switch in midtrial? May a violation of the right to self-representation ever be harmless error? Must the trial court treat the *pro se* defendant differently than it would professional counsel? I assume that many of these questions will be answered with finality in due course. Many of them, however, such as the standards of waiver and the treatment of the *pro se* defendant, will haunt the trial of every defendant who elects to exercise his right to self-representation. * * *

If there is any truth to the old proverb that "one who is his own lawyer has a fool for a client," the Court by its opinion today now bestows a *constitutional* right on one to make a fool of himself.

NOTES AND QUESTIONS

1. Recall from p. 942, Note 5, that a defense lawyer makes every decision except what plea to enter, whether to accept a plea agreement, whether to waive jury trial, whether to testify in his or her own behalf, and whether to appeal. All the countless decisions about how to present a defense, how to challenge the prosecution's case, and how best to argue to the judge and jury are made by the lawyer. When a criminal defendant exercises his *Faretta* right to represent himself, he must make all those decisions. Which *Faretta* position, majority or dissent, do you prefer as a matter of policy? Does it seem at all odd to you that the eloquent defenders of *Gideon* in this case are the "conservative" justices?

2. Who gets the better of the argument from history? Perhaps more importantly, *why* does history seem to count so much on this issue?

3. The Court says that "even where counsel was permitted, the general practice continued to be self-representation" during the colonial era. Author Thomas reviewed the records of forty-eight trials in the New Jersey criminal courts from 1749 to 1757. In those records, defendants were represented by counsel in twenty-six cases. See George C. Thomas III, *Colonial Criminal Law and Procedure: The Royal Colony of New Jersey, 1749–57*, 1 N.Y.U. J. L. & Liberty 671, 689 (2005). Based on these data, the colonial cases were roughly evenly split between counseled and un-counseled criminal defendants. The acquittal rate was much higher (77%) in cases where the defendant was represented by counsel than in *pro se* cases (18%). Id. at 691. Before we feel too smug about those data, it is possible that a good deal of the difference is explained by self-selection. Defendants whose guilt was obvious, or who had worked out some kind of sentence deal with the prosecutor, would be less likely to spend money or try to persuade a friend to represent them.

4. Should the *Faretta* arguments, sounding in autonomy, history, and the text of the Sixth Amendment, apply equally to defendants who want to represent themselves on appeal? In Martinez v. Court of Appeal of California, 528 U.S. 152, 120 S.Ct. 684, 145 L.Ed.2d 597 (2000), the Court concluded that these concerns were less weighty. There was no right to appeal at common law, and no statutory right to appeal in federal court or state court until, at the earliest, the late nineteenth century. As to the textual argument, the Court reiterated that the Sixth Amendment applies only to rights "that are available in preparation for trial and at the trial itself. The Sixth Amendment does not include any right to appeal."

There remain the *Faretta* autonomy interests but, given that there is no Sixth Amendment right at stake, the Court found that the autonomy question had to be analyzed under the due process clause. One autonomy interest is the value of not forcing a lawyer on an appellant, who might "be skeptical of whether a lawyer, who is employed by the same government that is prosecuting him, will serve his cause with undivided loyalty." The other autonomy interest is that it is the appellant, just like the defendant in *Faretta*, who personally will bear the consequences of the proceeding. But there are costs associated with the exercise of autonomy in this context. As the Court noted, no one argues that *pro se* representation "is wise, desirable or efficient." Rather, it is usually a "bad defense, particularly when compared to a defense provided by an experienced criminal defense attorney."

Martinez concluded that the autonomy interests weigh less in the appellate context. "The status of the accused defendant, who retains a presumption of innocence throughout the trial process, changes dramatically when a jury returns a guilty verdict." Any autonomy interests "that survive a felony conviction are less compelling than those motivating the decision in *Faretta*. Yet the overriding state interest in the fair and efficient administration of justice remains as strong as at the trial level. Thus, the States are clearly within their discretion to conclude that the government's interests outweigh an invasion of the appellant's interest in self-representation."

Do you agree that the existence of a conviction impairs the autonomy interest implicit in deciding whether to represent oneself in an appellate procedure?

5.   Does the *Faretta* Court find that the Sixth Amendment entails a right to waive counsel or that the Sixth Amendment contains a positive right of self-representation?

6.   How many peremptory challenges do criminal defendants get in non-capital cases under your state law? If you don't know, perhaps Faretta is in better shape to defend himself than it might first appear. Why do you think the Court included footnote 3?

7.   *Standby counsel.* In footnote 46 of *Faretta*, the Court anticipated the desire of trial courts to appoint standby counsel. In McKaskle v. Wiggins, 465 U.S. 168, 104 S.Ct. 944, 79 L.Ed.2d 122 (1984), the issue was whether unwanted intervention by standby counsel was an unconstitutional erosion of the *pro se* defendant's right of self-representation.

The Court approached this difficult inquiry by keeping its focus on the autonomy dimension of the *Faretta* doctrine:

> First, the *pro se* defendant is entitled to preserve actual control over the case he chooses to present to the jury. This is the core of the *Faretta* right. If standby counsel's participation over the defendant's objection effectively allows counsel to make or substantially interfere with any significant tactical decision, or to control the questioning of witnesses, or to speak instead of the defendant on any matter of importance, the *Faretta* right is eroded.

> Second, participation by standby counsel without the defendant's consent should not be allowed to destroy the jury's perception that the defendant is representing himself. The defendant's appearance in the status of one conducting his own defense is important in a criminal trial, since the right to appear *pro se* exists to affirm the accused's individual dignity and autonomy.

Is this statement inconsistent with at least the surface meaning of *Faretta* footnote 46? Can you reconcile the two?

Professor Anne Bowen Poulin offers insight into why the relationship between the *pro se* defendant and standby counsel might be fractious. Anne

Bowen Poulin, *The Role of Standby Counsel in Criminal Cases: In the Twilight Zone of the Criminal Justice System*, 75 N.Y.U. L. Rev. 676 (2000). Many requests to proceed *pro se* result from a trial judge's refusal to appoint substitute counsel when the defendant has concluded that a fair trial is not possible with current counsel. If the judge grants the *pro se* request somewhat late in the process, which is when the motion is usually made, efficiency suggests not appointing a different lawyer to act as standby counsel. But to appoint the lawyer that the defendant has already rejected is only asking for trouble.

    8. *Professor Poulin on the role of standby counsel.* Professor Poulin's comprehensive examination of the proper role for standby counsel, Note 7, concludes that the role varies substantially by the stage of the proceedings at issue. The threat to the jury's "perception that the defendant is representing himself" is a problem only at the trial stage. But even at trial, Professor Poulin argues that standby counsel should do more than merely sit passively and wait for a plea for help. Instead, standby counsel "should actively guide the defendant through the procedures of the trial" and should "identify hurdles, inform the defendant, and help the defendant surmount them." *Id.* at 718.

    Do you think this a sound idea? Is it consistent with *Faretta* and *McKaskle*, Note 7?

    According to Poulin, at the pre-trial, evidence-gathering stage, the standby lawyer should be as active as possible. "Only if the defendant rejects standby counsel's offer of assistance has the professional obligation of standby counsel been satisfied." *Id.* at 716. Under this conception of the role of standby counsel, the lawyer would be the client's specialized assistant, much as serjeants assisted clients in English courts in the sixteenth and seventeenth centuries.

    9. *Competency to waive counsel.* In Godinez v. Moran, 509 U.S. 389, 113 S.Ct. 2680, 125 L.Ed.2d 321 (1993), the defendant had committed three cold blooded murders, including that of his ex-wife. He was evaluated by two psychiatrists, "both of whom concluded that he was competent to stand trial." The doctors prescribed medications because he was depressed and suicidal. While being treated for his depression, he sought to discharge his public defender and represent himself, with the plan of pleading guilty and not resisting the State's attempt to impose the death penalty.

    The issue in *Godinez* was whether defendants who are competent to stand trial are also competent to waive counsel and plead guilty. The standard for competence to stand trial is whether the defendant has both a "sufficient present ability to consult with his lawyer with a reasonable degree of rational understanding" and "a rational as well as factual understanding of the proceedings against him." *Godinez* reasoned that while defendants who plead guilty have to make many decisions and waive several rights, the defendant who stands trial has additional decisions to make about how to present a defense. Thus, the Court held that if the competence standard "is adequate for defendants who plead not guilty, it is necessarily adequate for those who plead guilty." The Court also held that a defendant who is competent to stand trial is competent to waive counsel en route to a guilty plea.

The Court then explained why the waiver of right to counsel does not require a greater capacity:

> Nor do we think that a defendant who waives his right to the assistance of counsel must be more competent than a defendant who does not, since there is no reason to believe that the decision to waive counsel requires an appreciably higher level of mental functioning than the decision to waive other constitutional rights. [Moran] suggests that a higher competency standard is necessary because a defendant who represents himself " 'must have greater powers of comprehension, judgment, and reason than would be necessary to stand trial with the aid of an attorney.' " But this argument has a flawed premise; the competence that is required of a defendant seeking to waive his right to counsel is the competence to *waive the right*, not the competence to represent himself. In *Faretta v. California*, we held that a defendant choosing self-representation must do so "competently and intelligently," but we made it clear that the defendant's "technical legal knowledge" is "not relevant" to the determination whether he is competent to waive his right to counsel, and we emphasized that although the defendant "may conduct his own defense ultimately to his own detriment, his choice must be honored."

The Court stressed that the validity of the guilty plea or the waiver of the right to counsel requires more than competence or capacity. It requires a finding that the plea or the waiver "is knowing and voluntary. In this sense there is a 'heightened' standard for pleading guilty and for waiving the right to counsel, but it is not a heightened standard of *competence*."

Justice Blackmun, joined by Justice Stevens, dissented on the ground that the trial judge was on notice of Moran's "self-destructive behavior" and "his deep depression" and should therefore "have conducted another competency evaluation to determine Moran's capacity to waive the right to counsel and represent himself, instead of relying upon the psychiatrists' reports that he was able to stand trial with the assistance of counsel."

On March 30, 1996, Moran was executed. *Nevada Executes Man Who Killed 3 People*, New York Times, March 31, 1996, Sect. 1, at 27.

FARETTA HELL
GRAPEFRUITS AND JUDGES: IS THIS
WHAT THE *FARETTA* COURT HAD IN MIND?

Colin Ferguson was charged with killing six railroad commuters and wounding nineteen others in a 1993 shooting rampage on the Long Island Railroad. Ferguson chose this location, rather than the New York City subways, because he did not want to embarrass African–American Mayor David Dinkins. *Gunman's Shooting Spree on Commuter Train Racially Motivated: Police Say*, Agence France–Presse (France), December 8, 1993, at 1. He entered the train with more than 100 rounds of ammunition already loaded in magazine clips. James Barron, *Suspect's Notes Suggest Motive*, The Patriot Ledger (Quincy, Mass.), December 9, 1993, at 17. He fired thirty to fifty rounds in the train, hitting the twenty-five victims. Pat

Milton, *Race-Obsessed Loner Blamed in Train Tragedy*, Associated Press, December 8, 1993. All of his victims were either Caucasian or Asian, and these individuals were deliberately targeted as evidenced by four pages of handwritten notes. The notes listed racism by these groups as his primary motivation. Two examples: "That Chinese fascist will never put me to shame again without cause"; and "The sloppy running of the No. 2 train. It is racism by Caucasians and Uncle Tom Negroes." *Id.*

While in jail awaiting trial, Ferguson accused guards of throwing a fire extinguisher and a milk crate at him. *Train Suspect Claims Abuse From Jailers*, The New Orleans Times–Picayune, December 18, 1993, at A10. He also claimed that the light in his cell was kept on twenty-four hours a day to prevent him from sleeping, and that guards were plotting to poison his food. *Id.* Nassau County Sheriff officials investigated these allegations and found no evidence of mistreatment. *Id.* Despite Ferguson's mental state while in jail, two court-appointed experts found him to be competent to stand trial. *Court Psychiatrist Says Ferguson is Competent to Stand Trial*, Associated Press, January 4, 1994.

His lawyers claimed he was paranoid and delusional. He accused the lawyers of plotting against him, fired them, and requested his right to represent himself. The trial judge found him fit to stand trial and, therefore, under *Godinez*, capable of representing himself. John T. McQuiston, *Accused Killer Asks Search for "Real Killer,"* N.Y. Times, December 15, 1994, at 12. While representing himself, Ferguson asked the court to allow him to hire a private investigator so he could find the real killer. *Id.*

During the ten-day trial, he attempted to subpoena President Clinton and former New York Governor Mario Cuomo because they met with some of the survivors of the shooting. Pat Milton, *Man Convicted of Murdering Six in Train Massacre*, Associated Press, February 17, 1995. He claimed that the only reason the indictment against him had ninety-three counts was that the shootings occurred in 1993. He also claimed that he was a victim of a government conspiracy. *Id.*

His claim that he was not the killer prompted ridicule throughout the trial. On cross-examination of a detective, Ferguson asked if the suspect was ever searched. The detective replied, "Did I ever search you, no." *Id.* He cross-examined the victims he was accused of wounding. One victim, Maryanne Phillips, responded to his cross-examination by stating, "I saw you shoot me." *Id.* When he made a reference to "the gunman," the witnesses would correct him by responding with the pronoun "you." Janet Cawley, *In Bizarre Trial, Accused Gunman Defends Self; "You Shot Us,"* *Train Survivors Testify*, Chicago Tribune, February 16, 1995, at 4. Ferguson changed his mind at least once but finally decided not to testify. In a twenty-minute monologue to the judge, with the jury out of the room, Ferguson alleged that he was the victim of a conspiracy that was somehow connected to the slaying in prison of mass murderer Jeffrey Dahmer. Pat Milton, *Ferguson Decides Not to Testify in Train–Massacre Trial*, Associated Press, February 16, 1995. He claimed the Dahmer murder was "a prelude against me. There's a conspiracy to murder me if I'm convicted." *Id.*

After ten hours of deliberation, the jury found Ferguson guilty of six counts of murder, nineteen counts of attempted murder, and three other counts. The judge sentenced him to 200 years. On appeal, his lawyer, Richard Barbuto, asked the New York courts to require a higher standard of competency for self-representation than the federal standard in *Godinez*. The Ferguson case, argued Barbuto, "resulted in a perversion of the criminal justice system process." The standard for self-representation "has to be more than being able to tell the difference between a judge and a grapefruit." Robin Topping, *LIRR Gunman Didn't Have a Clue in Court*, Newsday, June 25, 1996, at A29.

These antics might appear a "perversion" of the process to Ferguson's appellate lawyer, or to you, or to the editors of this casebook. But the New York Appellate Division devoted exactly one sentence to the argument that Ferguson was not competent to represent himself: "The [trial] court properly permitted the defendant to appear *pro se,* since a defendant who is competent to stand trial is necessarily competent to waive his right to counsel and proceed *pro se.*" People v. Ferguson, 670 N.Y.S.2d 327, 248 A.D.2d 725 (1998). The highest New York court denied leave to appeal.

NOTES AND QUESTIONS

1. *A third way.* The Court in *Godinez*—Note 9, p. 984—held that a defendant who is competent to stand trial is competent to waive counsel and plead guilty. But as the Court realized in Indiana v. Edwards, 554 U.S. ___, 128 S.Ct. 2379, 171 L.Ed.2d 345 (2008), the competence to waive counsel and plead guilty is not necessarily the same as the competence to waive counsel and represent oneself at trial. Edwards had been found to be schizophrenic but, after a stay in the state mental hospital, competent to stand trial. The trial judge, however, drew a distinction between competence to stand trial and competence to be his own lawyer: "With these findings, he's competent to stand trial but I'm not going to find he's competent to defend himself."

Edwards proceeded to trial represented by appointed counsel, was convicted of attempted murder, and claimed on appeal that his Sixth Amendment self-representation rights were violated. The Indiana Supreme Court agreed, concluding that *Faretta* and *Godinez* stood for the proposition that a defendant has a right to represent himself at trial if he is competent to stand trial. The Court disagreed, 7–2, finding nothing in the Sixth Amendment or the Court's precedents that would deny the state the right to force counsel on a defendant who is not mentally competent to represent himself:

> [T]he Constitution permits judges to take realistic account of the particular defendant's mental capacities by asking whether a defendant who seeks to conduct his own defense at trial is mentally competent to do so. That is to say, the Constitution permits States to insist upon representation by counsel for those competent enough to stand trial * * * but who

still suffer from severe mental illness to the point where they are not competent to conduct trial proceedings by themselves.

Notably, the Court in *Edwards* did not elaborate on its standard of "not competent to conduct trial proceedings." Presumably, Colin Ferguson would not meet whatever standard is finally adopted.

After *Edwards*, three levels of defendant competence seem to exist. A defendant might be incompetent to stand trial and thus must be released or made the subject of civil commitment proceedings. If competent to stand trial, a defendant might be competent to waive counsel and plead guilty but not competent to represent himself at trial. Finally, a defendant might be competent to waive counsel and represent himself at trial, in which case *Faretta* gives him the absolute right to do so.

2. *What Edwards fails to answer. Edwards* held that a state is *permitted* to require counsel when defendants fall below the standard of "not competent to conduct trial proceedings." Is the converse of this holding also implied—is a state *required* to appoint counsel for all defendants who wish to represent themselves but are not mentally competent to do so?

Though *Edwards* does not decide this issue, the Court offered a comment on the perception of fairness, noting that "proceedings must not only be fair, they must 'appear fair to all who observe them.' The majority referred to an *amicus* brief in which a psychiatrist observed his patient represent himself at trial and asked "how in the world can our legal system allow an insane man to defend himself?" Taken to its logical conclusion, this comment suggests that there may be a constitutional requirement for counsel when defendants who are "not competent to conduct trial proceedings" seek to represent themselves at trial. The possibility that this issue might be raised on appeal will probably encourage trial judges to err on the side of appointing counsel in close cases.

D. THE RIGHT TO EFFECTIVE ASSISTANCE OF COUNSEL

The right to counsel cases considered so far, from *Powell* to *Faretta*, can be described as the "structural" right to counsel. The Court in these cases decided *when* defendants have a right to counsel at state expense (or the right to proceed without counsel), but not *what* constitutes the "Assistance of Counsel." But there must also be a substantive component to the right to counsel. If the defense lawyer were in a coma during the trial, it could not be said that the accused had received the "Assistance of Counsel." From there, it is merely a matter of degree to questions about lawyers who are drunk, incompetent, depressed, asleep part of the time, or representing a co-defendant with conflicting interests. These questions of substance are not easy, and many commentators think the Supreme Court has failed to grapple meaningfully with them.

STRICKLAND v. WASHINGTON

Supreme Court of the United States, 1984.
466 U.S. 668, 104 S.Ct. 2052, 80 L.Ed.2d 674.

JUSTICE O'CONNOR delivered the opinion of the Court.

This case requires us to consider the proper standards for judging a criminal defendant's contention that the Constitution requires a conviction or death sentence to be set aside because counsel's assistance at the trial or sentencing was ineffective.

I

A

During a 10–day period in September 1976, respondent planned and committed three groups of crimes, which included three brutal stabbing murders, torture, kidnaping, severe assaults, attempted murders, attempted extortion, and theft. After his two accomplices were arrested, respondent surrendered to police and voluntarily gave a lengthy statement confessing to the third of the criminal episodes. The State of Florida indicted respondent for kidnaping and murder and appointed an experienced criminal lawyer to represent him.

Counsel actively pursued pretrial motions and discovery. He cut his efforts short, however, and he experienced a sense of hopelessness about the case, when he learned that, against his specific advice, respondent had also confessed to the first two murders. By the date set for trial, respondent was subject to indictment for three counts of first-degree murder and multiple counts of robbery, kidnaping for ransom, breaking and entering and assault, attempted murder, and conspiracy to commit robbery. Respondent waived his right to a jury trial, again acting against counsel's advice, and pleaded guilty to all charges, including the three capital murder charges.

In the plea colloquy, respondent told the trial judge that, although he had committed a string of burglaries, he had no significant prior criminal record and that at the time of his criminal spree he was under extreme stress caused by his inability to support his family. He also stated, however, that he accepted responsibility for the crimes. The trial judge told respondent that he had "a great deal of respect for people who are willing to step forward and admit their responsibility" but that he was making no statement at all about his likely sentencing decision.

Counsel advised respondent to invoke his right under Florida law to an advisory jury at his capital sentencing hearing. Respondent rejected the advice and waived the right. He chose instead to be sentenced by the trial judge without a jury recommendation.

In preparing for the sentencing hearing, counsel spoke with respondent about his background. He also spoke on the telephone with respondent's wife and mother, though he did not follow up on the one unsuccessful effort to meet with them. He did not otherwise seek out character witnesses for respondent. Nor did he request a psychiatric examination, since his conversations with his client gave no indication that respondent had psychological problems.

Counsel decided not to present and hence not to look further for evidence concerning respondent's character and emotional state. That decision reflected trial counsel's sense of hopelessness about overcoming the evidentiary effect of respondent's confessions to the gruesome crimes. It also reflected the judgment that it was advisable to rely on the plea colloquy for evidence about respondent's background and about his claim of emotional stress: the plea colloquy communicated sufficient information about these subjects, and by forgoing the opportunity to present new evidence on these subjects, counsel prevented the State from cross-examining respondent on his claim and from putting on psychiatric evidence of its own.

Counsel also excluded from the sentencing hearing other evidence he thought was potentially damaging. He successfully moved to exclude respondent's "rap sheet." Because he judged that a presentence report might prove more detrimental than helpful, as it would have included respondent's criminal history and thereby would have undermined the claim of no significant history of criminal activity, he did not request that one be prepared.

At the sentencing hearing, counsel's strategy was based primarily on the trial judge's remarks at the plea colloquy as well as on his reputation as a sentencing judge who thought it important for a convicted defendant to own up to his crime. Counsel argued that respondent's remorse and acceptance of responsibility justified sparing him from the death penalty. Counsel also argued that respondent had no history of criminal activity and that respondent committed the crimes under extreme mental or emotional disturbance, thus coming within the statutory list of mitigating circumstances. He further argued that respondent should be spared death because he had surrendered, confessed, and offered to testify against a codefendant and because respondent was fundamentally a good person who had briefly gone badly wrong in extremely stressful circumstances. The State put on evidence and witnesses largely for the purpose of describing the details of the crimes. Counsel did not cross-examine the medical experts who testified about the manner of death of respondent's victims.

The trial judge found several aggravating circumstances with respect to each of the three murders. He found that all three murders were especially heinous, atrocious, and cruel, all involving repeated stabbings. All three murders were committed in the course of at least one other dangerous and violent felony, and since all involved robbery, the murders were for pecuniary gain. All three murders were committed to avoid arrest for the accompanying crimes and to hinder law enforcement. In the course of one of the murders, respondent knowingly subjected numerous persons to a grave risk of death by deliberately stabbing and shooting the murder victim's sisters-in-law, who sustained severe—in one case, ultimately fatal—injuries.

With respect to mitigating circumstances, the trial judge made the same findings for all three capital murders. First, although there was no admitted evidence of prior convictions, respondent had stated that he had engaged in a course of stealing. In any case, even if respondent had no significant history of criminal activity, the aggravating circumstances "would still clearly far outweigh" that mitigating factor. Second, the judge found that, during all three crimes, respondent was not suffering from extreme mental or emotional disturbance and could appreciate the criminality of his acts. Third, none of the victims was a participant in, or consented to, respondent's conduct. Fourth, respondent's participation in the crimes was neither minor nor the result of duress or domination by an accomplice. Finally, respondent's age (26) could not be considered a factor in mitigation, especially when viewed in light of respondent's planning of the crimes and disposition of the proceeds of the various accompanying thefts.

In short, the trial judge found numerous aggravating circumstances and no (or a single comparatively insignificant) mitigating circumstance. With respect to each of the three convictions for capital murder, the trial judge concluded: "A careful consideration of all matters presented to the court impels the conclusion that there are insufficient mitigating circumstances * * * to outweigh the aggravating circumstances." He therefore sentenced respondent to death on each of the three counts of murder and to prison terms for the other crimes. The Florida Supreme Court upheld the convictions and sentences on direct appeal.

B

Respondent subsequently sought collateral relief in state court on numerous grounds, among them that counsel had rendered ineffective assistance at the sentencing proceeding. Respondent challenged counsel's assistance in six respects. He asserted that counsel was ineffective because he failed to move for a continuance to prepare for sentencing, to request a psychiatric report, to investigate and present character witnesses, to seek a presentence investigation report, to present meaningful arguments to the sentencing judge, and to investigate the medical examiner's reports or cross-examine the medical experts. In support of the claim, respondent submitted 14 affidavits from friends, neighbors, and relatives stating that they would have testified if asked to do so. He also submitted one psychiatric report and one psychological report stating that respondent, though not under the influence of extreme mental or emotional disturbance, was "chronically frustrated and depressed because of his economic dilemma" at the time of his crimes.

The trial court denied relief without an evidentiary hearing, finding that the record evidence conclusively showed that the ineffectiveness claim was meritless. Four of the assertedly prejudicial errors required little discussion. First, there were no grounds to request a continuance, so there was no error in not requesting one when respondent pleaded guilty. Second, failure to request a presentence investigation was not a serious error because the trial judge had discretion not to grant such a request and because any presentence investigation would have resulted in admission of respondent's "rap sheet" and thus would have undermined his assertion of no significant history of criminal activity. Third, the argument and memorandum given to the sentencing judge were "admirable" in light of the overwhelming aggravating circumstances and absence of mitigating circumstances. Fourth, there was no error in failure to examine the medical examiner's reports or to cross-examine the medical witnesses testifying on the manner of death of respondent's victims, since respondent admitted that the victims died in the ways shown by the unchallenged medical evidence.

The trial court dealt at greater length with the two other bases for the ineffectiveness claim. The court pointed out that a psychiatric examination of respondent was conducted by state order soon after respondent's initial arraignment. That report states that there was no indication of major mental illness at the time of the crimes. Moreover, both the reports submitted in the collateral proceeding state that, although respondent was "chronically frustrated and depressed because of his economic dilemma," he was not under the influence of extreme mental or emotional disturbance. All three reports thus directly undermine the contention made at the sentencing hearing that respondent was suffering from extreme mental or emotional disturbance during his crime spree. Accordingly, counsel could reasonably decide not to seek psychiatric reports; indeed, by relying solely on the plea colloquy to support the emotional disturbance contention, counsel denied the State an opportunity to rebut his claim with psychiatric testimony. In any event, the aggravating circumstances were so overwhelming that no substantial prejudice resulted from the absence at sentencing of the psychiatric evidence offered in the collateral attack.

The court rejected the challenge to counsel's failure to develop and to present character evidence for much the same reasons. The affidavits submitted in the collateral proceeding showed nothing more than that certain persons would have testified that respondent was basically a good person who was worried about his family's financial problems. Respondent himself had already testified along those lines at the plea colloquy. Moreover, respondent's admission of a course of stealing rebutted many of the factual allegations in the affidavits. For those reasons, and because the sentencing judge had stated that the death sentence would be appropriate even if respondent had no significant prior criminal history, no substantial prejudice resulted from the absence at sentencing of the character evidence offered in the collateral attack. * * *

C

Respondent * * * filed a petition for a writ of habeas corpus in the United States District Court for the Southern District of Florida. He advanced numerous grounds for relief, among them ineffective assistance of counsel based on the same errors, except for the failure to move for a continuance, as those he had identified in state court. The District Court held an evidentiary hearing to inquire into trial counsel's efforts to investigate and to present mitigating circumstances. Respondent offered the affidavits and reports he had submitted in the state collateral proceedings; he also called his trial counsel to testify. The State of Florida, over respondent's objection, called the trial judge to testify.

* * * On the legal issue of ineffectiveness, the District Court concluded that, although trial counsel made errors in judgment in failing to investigate nonstatutory mitigating evidence further than he did, no prejudice to respondent's sentence resulted from any such error in judgment. Relying in part on the trial judge's testimony but also on the same factors that led the state courts to find no prejudice, the District Court concluded that "there does not appear to be a likelihood, or even a significant possibility," that any errors of trial counsel had affected the outcome of the sentencing proceeding. * * *

[The Court of Appeals reversed and remanded for a new factfinding hearing.]

D

* * * [This case] presents a type of Sixth Amendment claim that this Court has not previously considered in any generality. The Court has considered Sixth Amendment claims based on actual or constructive denial of the assistance of counsel altogether, as well as claims based on state interference with the ability of counsel to render effective assistance to the accused. With the exception of *Cuyler v. Sullivan*, 446 U.S. 335, 100 S.Ct. 1708, 64 L.Ed.2d 333 (1980), however, which involved a claim that counsel's assistance was rendered ineffective by a conflict of interest, the Court has never directly and fully addressed a claim of "actual ineffectiveness" of counsel's assistance in a case going to trial. * * *

II

In a long line of cases that includes *Powell v. Alabama* [p. 13], *Johnson v. Zerbst*, 304 U.S. 458, 58 S.Ct. 1019, 82 L.Ed. 1461 (1938), and *Gideon v. Wainwright*, [p. 950], this Court has recognized that the Sixth Amendment right to counsel exists, and is needed, in order to protect the fundamental right to a fair trial. The Constitution guarantees a fair trial through the Due Process Clauses, but it defines the basic elements of a fair trial largely through the several provisions of the Sixth Amendment, including the Counsel Clause * * *.

[Using the Sixth Amendment as a guide], a fair trial is one in which evidence subject to adversarial testing is presented to an impartial tribunal for resolution of issues defined in advance of the proceeding. The right to counsel plays a crucial role in the adversarial system embodied in the Sixth Amendment, since access to counsel's skill and knowledge is necessary to accord defendants the "ample opportunity to meet the case of the prosecution" to which they are entitled.

Because of the vital importance of counsel's assistance, this Court has held that, with certain exceptions, a person accused of a federal or state crime has the right to have counsel appointed if retained counsel cannot be obtained. That a person who happens to be a lawyer is present at trial alongside the accused, however, is not enough to satisfy the constitutional command. The Sixth Amendment recognizes the right to the assistance of counsel because it envisions counsel's playing a role that is critical to the ability of the adversarial system to produce just results. An accused is entitled to be assisted by an attorney, whether retained or appointed, who plays the role necessary to ensure that the trial is fair.

For that reason, the Court has recognized that "the right to counsel is the right to the effective assistance of counsel." * * *

The Court has not elaborated on the meaning of the constitutional requirement of effective assistance in the latter class of cases—that is, those presenting claims of "actual ineffectiveness." In giving meaning to the requirement, however, we must take its purpose—to ensure a fair trial—as the guide. The benchmark for judging any claim of ineffectiveness must be whether counsel's conduct so undermined the proper functioning of the adversarial process that the trial cannot be relied on as having produced a just result.

The same principle applies to a capital sentencing proceeding such as that provided by Florida law. * * *

III

A convicted defendant's claim that counsel's assistance was so defective as to require reversal of a conviction or death sentence has two components. First, the defendant must show that counsel's performance was deficient. This requires showing that counsel made errors so serious that counsel was not functioning as the "counsel" guaranteed the defendant by the Sixth Amendment. Second, the defendant must show that the deficient performance prejudiced the defense. This requires showing that counsel's errors were so serious as to deprive the defendant of a fair trial, a trial whose result is reliable. Unless a defendant makes both showings, it cannot be said that the conviction or death sentence resulted from a breakdown in the adversary process that renders the result unreliable.

A

As all the Federal Courts of Appeals have now held, the proper standard for attorney performance is that of reasonably effective assistance. * * * When a convicted defendant complains of the ineffectiveness of counsel's assistance, the defendant must show that counsel's representation fell below an objective standard of reasonableness.

More specific guidelines are not appropriate. The Sixth Amendment refers simply to "counsel," not specifying particular requirements of effective assistance. It relies instead on the legal profession's maintenance of standards sufficient to justify the law's presumption that counsel will fulfill the role in the adversary process that the Amendment envisions. The proper measure of attorney performance remains simply reasonableness under prevailing professional norms.

Representation of a criminal defendant entails certain basic duties. Counsel's function is to assist the defendant, and hence counsel owes the client a duty of loyalty, a duty to avoid conflicts of interest. From counsel's function as assistant to the defendant derive the overarching duty to advocate the defendant's cause and the more particular duties to consult with the defendant on important decisions and to keep the defendant informed of important developments in the course of the prosecution. Counsel also has a duty to bring to bear such skill and knowledge as will render the trial a reliable adversarial testing process.

These basic duties neither exhaustively define the obligations of counsel nor form a checklist for judicial evaluation of attorney performance. In any case presenting an ineffectiveness claim, the performance inquiry must be whether counsel's assistance was reasonable considering all the circumstances. Prevailing norms of practice as reflected in American Bar Association standards and the like are guides to determining what is reasonable, but they are only guides. No particular set of detailed rules for counsel's conduct can satisfactorily take account of the variety of circumstances faced by defense counsel or the range of legitimate decisions regarding how best to represent a criminal defendant. Any such set of rules would interfere with the constitutionally protected independence of counsel and restrict the wide latitude counsel must have in making tactical decisions. Indeed, the existence of detailed guidelines for representation could distract counsel from the overriding mission of vigorous advocacy of the defendant's cause. Moreover, the purpose of the effective assistance guarantee of the Sixth Amendment is not to improve the quality of legal representation, although that is a goal of considerable importance to the legal system. The purpose is simply to ensure that criminal defendants receive a fair trial.

Judicial scrutiny of counsel's performance must be highly deferential. It is all too tempting for a defendant to second-guess counsel's assistance after conviction or adverse sentence, and it is all too easy for a court, examining counsel's defense after it has proved unsuccessful, to conclude that a particular act or omission of counsel was unreasonable. A fair assessment of attorney performance requires that every effort be made to eliminate the distorting effects of hindsight, to reconstruct the circumstances of counsel's challenged conduct, and to evaluate the conduct from counsel's perspective at the time. Because of the difficulties inherent in making the evaluation, a court must indulge a strong presumption that counsel's conduct falls within the wide range of reasonable professional assistance; that is, the defendant must overcome the presumption that, under the circumstances, the challenged action "might be considered sound trial strategy." There are countless ways to provide effective assistance in any given case. Even the best criminal defense attorneys would not defend a particular client in the same way.

The availability of intrusive post-trial inquiry into attorney performance or of detailed guidelines for its evaluation would encourage the proliferation of ineffectiveness challenges. Criminal trials resolved unfavorably to the defendant would increasingly come to be followed by a second trial, this one of counsel's unsuccessful defense. Counsel's performance and even willingness to serve could be adversely affected. Intensive scrutiny of counsel and rigid requirements for acceptable assistance could dampen the ardor and impair the independence of defense counsel, discourage the acceptance of assigned cases, and undermine the trust between attorney and client.

Thus, a court deciding an actual ineffectiveness claim must judge the reasonableness of counsel's challenged conduct on the facts of the particular case, viewed as of the time of counsel's conduct. A convicted defendant making a claim of ineffective assistance must identify the acts or omissions of counsel that are alleged not to have been the result of reasonable professional judgment. The court must then determine whether, in light of all the circumstances, the identified acts or omissions were outside the wide range of professionally competent assistance. In making that determination, the court should keep in mind that counsel's function, as elaborated in prevailing professional norms, is to make the adversarial testing process work in the particular case. At the same time, the court should recognize that counsel is strongly presumed to have rendered adequate assistance and made all significant decisions in the exercise of reasonable professional judgment.

These standards require no special amplification in order to define counsel's duty to investigate, the duty at issue in this case. * * * [S]trategic choices made after thorough investigation of law and facts relevant to plausible options are virtually unchallengeable; and strategic choices made after less than complete investigation are reasonable precisely to the extent that reasonable professional judgments support the limitations on investigation. In other words, counsel has a duty to make reasonable investigations or to make a reasonable decision that makes particular investigations unnecessary. In any ineffectiveness case, a particular decision not to investigate must be directly assessed for reasonableness in all the circumstances, applying a heavy measure of deference to counsel's judgments.

The reasonableness of counsel's actions may be determined or substantially influenced by the defendant's own statements or actions. Counsel's actions are usually based, quite properly, on informed strategic choices made by the defendant and on information supplied by the defendant. In particular, what investigation decisions are reasonable depends critically on such information. For example, when the facts that support a certain potential line of defense are generally known to counsel because of what the defendant has said, the need for further investigation may be considerably diminished or eliminated altogether. And when a defendant has given counsel reason to believe that pursuing certain investigations would be fruitless or even harmful, counsel's failure to pursue those investigations may not later be challenged as unreasonable. In short, inquiry into counsel's conversations with the defendant may be critical to a proper assessment of counsel's investigation decisions, just as it may be critical to a proper assessment of counsel's other litigation decisions.

B

An error by counsel, even if professionally unreasonable, does not warrant setting aside the judgment of a criminal proceeding if the error had no effect on the judgment. The purpose of the Sixth Amendment guarantee of counsel is to ensure that a defendant has the assistance necessary to justify reliance on the outcome of the proceeding. Accordingly, any deficiencies in counsel's performance must be prejudicial to the defense in order to constitute ineffective assistance under the Constitution.

In certain Sixth Amendment contexts, prejudice is presumed. Actual or constructive denial of the assistance of counsel altogether is legally presumed to result in prejudice. So are various kinds of state interference with counsel's assistance. Prejudice in these circumstances is so likely that case-by-case inquiry into prejudice is not worth the cost. Moreover, such circumstances involve impairments of the Sixth Amendment right that are easy to identify and, for that reason and because the prosecution is directly responsible, easy for the government to prevent.

One type of actual ineffectiveness claim warrants a similar, though more limited, presumption of prejudice. In *Cuyler v. Sullivan*, the Court held that prejudice is presumed when counsel is burdened by an actual conflict of interest. In those circumstances, counsel breaches the duty of loyalty, perhaps the most basic of counsel's duties. Moreover, it is difficult to measure the precise effect on the defense of representation corrupted by conflicting interests. Given the obligation of counsel to avoid conflicts of interest and the ability of trial courts to make early inquiry in certain situations likely to give rise to conflicts, it is reasonable for the criminal justice system to maintain a fairly rigid rule of presumed prejudice for conflicts of interest. Even so, the rule is not quite the *per se* rule of prejudice that exists for the Sixth Amendment claims mentioned above. Prejudice is presumed only if the defendant demonstrates that counsel "actively represented conflicting interests" and that "an actual conflict of interest adversely affected his lawyer's performance."

Conflict of interest claims aside, actual ineffectiveness claims alleging a deficiency in attorney performance are subject to a general requirement that the defendant affirmatively prove prejudice. The government is not responsible for, and hence not able to prevent, attorney errors that will result in reversal of a conviction or sentence. Attorney errors come in an infinite variety and are as likely to be utterly harmless in a particular case as they are to be prejudicial. They cannot be classified according to likelihood of causing prejudice. Nor can they be defined with sufficient precision to inform defense attorneys correctly just what conduct to avoid. Representation is an art, and an act or omission that is unprofessional in one case may be sound or even brilliant in another. Even if a defendant shows that particular errors of counsel were unreasonable, therefore, the defendant must show that they actually had an adverse effect on the defense.

It is not enough for the defendant to show that the errors had some conceivable effect on the outcome of the proceeding. Virtually every act or omission of counsel would meet that test, and not every error that conceivably could have influenced the outcome undermines the reliability of the result of the proceeding. Respondent suggests requiring a showing that the errors "impaired the presentation of the defense." That standard, however, provides no workable principle. Since any error, if it is indeed an error, "impairs" the presentation of the defense, the proposed standard is inadequate because it provides no way of deciding what impairments are sufficiently serious to warrant setting aside the outcome of the proceeding.

On the other hand, we believe that a defendant need not show that counsel's deficient conduct more likely than not altered the outcome in the case. This outcome-determinative standard has several strengths. It defines the relevant inquiry in a way familiar to courts, though the inquiry, as is inevitable, is anything but precise. The standard also reflects the profound importance of finality in criminal proceedings. Moreover, it comports with the widely used standard for assessing motions for new trial based on newly discovered evidence. Nevertheless, the standard is not quite appropriate.

Even when the specified attorney error results in the omission of certain evidence, the newly discovered evidence standard is not an apt source from which to draw a prejudice standard for ineffectiveness claims. The high standard for newly discovered evidence claims presupposes that all the essential elements of a presumptively accurate and fair proceeding were present in the proceeding whose result is challenged. An ineffective assistance claim asserts the absence of one of the crucial assurances that the result of the proceeding is reliable, so finality concerns are somewhat weaker and the appropriate standard of prejudice should be somewhat lower. The result of a proceeding can be rendered unreliable, and hence the proceeding itself unfair, even if the errors of counsel cannot be shown by a preponderance of the evidence to have determined the outcome.

Accordingly, the appropriate test for prejudice finds its roots in the test for materiality of exculpatory information not disclosed to the defense by the prosecution, [Chapter 13, C. 2], and in the test for materiality of testimony made unavailable to the defense by Government deportation of a witness, *United States v. Valenzuela–Bernal*, [458 U.S. 858, 102 S.Ct. 3440, 73 L.Ed.2d 1193 (1982)]. The defendant must show that there is a reasonable probability that, but for counsel's unprofessional errors, the result of the proceeding would have been different. A reasonable probability is a probability sufficient to undermine confidence in the outcome.

In making the determination whether the specified errors resulted in the required prejudice, a court should presume, absent challenge to the judgment on grounds of evidentiary insufficiency, that the judge or jury acted according to law. An assessment of the likelihood of a result more favorable to the defendant must exclude the possibility of arbitrariness, whimsy, caprice, "nullification," and the like. A defendant has no entitlement to the luck of a lawless decisionmaker, even if a lawless decision cannot be reviewed. The assessment of prejudice should proceed on the assumption that the decisionmaker is reasonably, conscientiously, and impartially applying the standards that govern the decision. It should not depend on the idiosyncracies of the particular decisionmaker, such as unusual propensities toward harshness or leniency. Although these factors may actually have entered into counsel's selection of strategies and, to that limited extent, may thus affect the performance inquiry, they are irrelevant to the prejudice inquiry. Thus, evidence about the actual process of decision, if not part of the record of the proceeding under review, and evidence about, for example, a particular judge's sentencing practices, should not be considered in the prejudice determination.

The governing legal standard plays a critical role in defining the question to be asked in assessing the prejudice from counsel's errors. When a defendant challenges a conviction, the question is whether there is a reasonable probability that, absent the errors, the factfinder would have had a reasonable doubt respecting guilt. When a defendant challenges a death sentence such as the one at issue in this case, the question is whether there is a reasonable probability that, absent the errors, the sentencer—including an appellate court, to the extent it independently reweighs the evidence—would have concluded that the balance of aggravating and mitigating circumstances did not warrant death.

In making this determination, a court hearing an ineffectiveness claim must consider the totality of the evidence before the judge or jury. Some of the factual findings will have been unaffected by the errors, and factual findings that were affected will have been affected in different ways. Some errors will have had a pervasive effect on the inferences to be drawn from the evidence, altering the entire evidentiary picture, and some will have had an isolated, trivial effect. Moreover, a verdict or conclusion only weakly supported by the record is more likely to have been affected by errors than one with overwhelming record support. Taking the unaffected findings as a given, and taking due account of the effect of the errors on the remaining findings, a court making the prejudice inquiry must ask if the defendant has met the burden of showing that the decision reached would reasonably likely have been different absent the errors.

IV

A number of practical considerations are important for the application of the standards we have outlined. Most important, in adjudicating a claim of actual ineffectiveness of counsel, a court should keep in mind that the principles we have stated do not establish mechanical rules. Although those principles should guide the process of decision, the ultimate focus of inquiry must be on the fundamental fairness of the proceeding whose result is being challenged. In every case the court should be concerned with whether, despite the strong presumption of reliability, the result of the particular proceeding is unreliable because of a breakdown in the adversarial process that our system counts on to produce just results. * * *

Although we have discussed the performance component of an ineffectiveness claim prior to the prejudice component, there is no reason for a court deciding an ineffective assistance claim to approach the inquiry in the same order or even to address both components of the inquiry if the defendant makes an insufficient showing on one. In particular, a court need not determine whether counsel's performance was deficient before examining the prejudice suffered by the defendant as a result of the alleged deficiencies. The object of an ineffectiveness claim is not to grade counsel's performance. If it is easier to dispose of an ineffectiveness claim on the ground of lack of sufficient prejudice, which we expect will often be so, that course should be followed. Courts should strive to ensure that ineffectiveness claims not become so burdensome to defense counsel that the entire criminal justice system suffers as a result. * * *

V

Having articulated general standards for judging ineffectiveness claims, we think it useful to apply those standards to the facts of this case in order to illustrate the meaning of the general principles. The record makes it possible to do so. There are no conflicts between the state and federal courts over findings of fact, and the principles we have articulated are sufficiently close to the principles applied both in the Florida courts and in the District Court that it is clear that the factfinding was not affected by erroneous legal principles.

Application of the governing principles is not difficult in this case. The facts as described above make clear that the conduct of respondent's counsel at and before respondent's sentencing proceeding cannot be found unreasonable. They also make clear that, even assuming the challenged conduct of counsel was unreasonable, respondent suffered insufficient prejudice to warrant setting aside his death sentence.

With respect to the performance component, the record shows that respondent's counsel made a strategic choice to argue for the extreme emotional distress mitigating circumstance and to rely as fully as possible on respondent's acceptance of responsibility for his crimes. Although counsel understandably felt hopeless about respondent's prospects, nothing in the record indicates, as one possible reading of the District Court's opinion suggests, that counsel's sense of hopelessness distorted his professional judgment. Counsel's strategy choice was well within the range of professionally reasonable judgments, and the decision not to seek more character or psychological evidence than was already in hand was likewise reasonable.

The trial judge's views on the importance of owning up to one's crimes were well known to counsel. The aggravating circumstances were utterly overwhelming. Trial counsel could reasonably surmise from his conversations with respondent that character and psychological evidence would be of little help. Respondent had already been able to mention at the plea colloquy the substance of what there was to know about his financial and emotional troubles. Restricting testimony on respondent's character to what had come in at the plea colloquy ensured that contrary character and psychological evidence and respondent's criminal history, which counsel had successfully moved to exclude, would not come in. On these facts, there can be little question, even without application of the presumption of adequate performance, that trial counsel's defense, though unsuccessful, was the result of reasonable professional judgment.

With respect to the prejudice component, the lack of merit of respondent's claim is even more stark. The evidence that respondent says his trial counsel should have offered at the sentencing hearing would barely have altered the sentencing profile presented to the sentencing judge. As the state courts and District Court found, at most this evidence shows that numerous people who knew respondent thought he was generally a good person and that a psychiatrist and a psychologist believed he was under considerable emotional stress that did not rise to the level of extreme disturbance. Given the overwhelming aggravating factors, there is no reasonable probability that the omitted evidence would have changed the conclusion that the aggravating circumstances outweighed the mitigating circumstances and, hence, the sentence imposed. Indeed, admission of the evidence respondent now offers might even have been harmful to his case: his "rap sheet" would probably have been admitted into evidence, and the psychological reports would have directly contradicted respondent's claim that the mitigating circumstance of extreme emotional disturbance applied to his case. * * *

Failure to make the required showing of either deficient performance or sufficient prejudice defeats the ineffectiveness claim. Here there is a double failure. More generally, respondent has made no showing that the justice of his sentence was rendered unreliable by a breakdown in the adversary process caused by deficiencies in counsel's assistance. Respondent's sentencing proceeding was not fundamentally unfair. * * *

Justice BRENNAN, concurring in part and dissenting in part.

I join the Court's opinion but dissent from its judgment. Adhering to my view that the death penalty is in all circumstances cruel and unusual punishment forbidden by the Eighth and Fourteenth Amendments, I would vacate respondent's death sentence and remand the case for further proceedings. * * *

I join the Court's opinion because I believe that the standards it sets out today will both provide helpful guidance to courts considering claims of actual ineffectiveness of counsel and also permit those courts to continue their efforts to achieve progressive development of this area of the law. * * *

Justice MARSHALL, dissenting. * * *

I * * *

A

My objection to the performance standard adopted by the Court is that it is so malleable that, in practice, it will either have no grip at all or will yield excessive variation in the manner in which the Sixth Amendment is interpreted and applied by different courts. To tell lawyers and the lower courts that counsel for a criminal defendant must behave "reasonably" and must act like "a reasonably competent attorney," is to tell them almost nothing. In essence, the majority has instructed judges called upon to assess claims of ineffective assistance of counsel to advert to their own intuitions regarding what constitutes "professional" representation, and has discouraged them from trying to develop more detailed standards governing the performance of defense counsel. In my view, the Court has thereby not only abdicated its own responsibility to interpret the Constitution, but also impaired the ability of the lower courts to exercise theirs. * * *

The majority defends its refusal to adopt more specific standards primarily on the ground that "[n]o particular set of detailed rules for counsel's conduct can satisfactorily take account of the variety of circumstances faced by defense counsel or the range of legitimate decisions regarding how best to represent a criminal defendant." I agree that counsel must be afforded "wide latitude" when making "tactical decisions" regarding trial strategy, but many aspects of the job of a criminal defense attorney are more amenable to judicial oversight. For example, much of the work involved in preparing for a trial, applying for bail, conferring with one's client, making timely objections to significant, arguably erroneous rulings of the trial judge, and filing a notice of appeal if there are colorable grounds therefor could profitably be made the subject of uniform standards. * * *

B

I object to the prejudice standard adopted by the Court for two independent reasons. First, it is often very difficult to tell whether a defendant convicted after a trial in which he was ineffectively represented would have fared better if his lawyer had been competent. Seemingly impregnable cases can sometimes be dismantled by good defense counsel. On the basis of a cold record, it may be impossible for a reviewing court confidently to ascertain how the government's evidence and arguments would have stood up against rebuttal and cross-examination by a shrewd, well-prepared lawyer. The difficulties of estimating prejudice after the fact are exacerbated by the possibility that evidence of injury to the defendant may be missing from the record precisely because of the incompetence of defense counsel. In view of all these impediments to a fair evaluation of the probability that the outcome of a trial was affected by ineffectiveness of counsel, it seems to me senseless to impose on a defendant whose lawyer has been shown to have been incompetent the burden of demonstrating prejudice.

Second and more fundamentally, the assumption on which the Court's holding rests is that the only purpose of the constitutional guarantee of effective assistance of counsel is to reduce the chance that innocent persons will be convicted. In my view, the guarantee also functions to ensure that convictions are obtained only through fundamentally fair procedures. The majority contends that the Sixth Amendment is not violated when a manifestly guilty defendant is convicted after a trial in which he was represented by a manifestly ineffective attorney. I cannot agree. Every defendant is entitled to a trial in which his interests are vigorously and conscientiously advocated by an able lawyer. A proceeding in which the defendant does not receive meaningful assistance in meeting the forces of the State does not, in my opinion, constitute due process. * * *

II

Even if I were inclined to join the majority's two central holdings, I could not abide the manner in which the majority elaborates upon its rulings. * * *

A

In defining the standard of attorney performance required by the Constitution, the majority appropriately notes that many problems confronting criminal defense attorneys admit of "a range of legitimate" responses. And the majority properly cautions courts, when reviewing a lawyer's selection amongst a set of options, to avoid the hubris of hindsight. The majority goes on, however, to suggest that reviewing courts should "indulge a strong presumption that counsel's conduct" was constitutionally acceptable, and should "appl[y] a heavy measure of deference to counsel's judgments."

I am not sure what these phrases mean, and I doubt that they will be self-explanatory to lower courts. If they denote nothing more than that a defendant claiming he was denied effective assistance of counsel has the burden of proof, I would agree. But the adjectives "strong" and "heavy" might be read as imposing upon defendants an unusually weighty burden of persuasion. If that is the majority's intent, I must respectfully dissent. The range of acceptable behavior defined by "prevailing professional norms" seems to me sufficiently broad to allow defense counsel the flexibility they need in responding to novel problems of trial strategy. To afford attorneys more latitude, by "strongly presuming" that their behavior will fall within the zone of reasonableness, is covertly to legitimate convictions and sentences obtained on the basis of incompetent conduct by defense counsel. * * *

IV

The views expressed in the preceding section oblige me to dissent from the majority's disposition of the case before us. It is undisputed that respondent's trial counsel made virtually no investigation of the possibility of obtaining testimony from respondent's relatives, friends, or former employers pertaining to respondent's character or background. Had counsel done so, he would have found several persons willing and able to testify that, in their experience, respondent was a responsible, non-violent man, devoted to his family, and active in the affairs of his church. Respondent contends that his lawyer could have and should have used that testimony to "humanize" respondent, to counteract the impression conveyed by the trial that he was little more than a cold-blooded killer. Had this evidence been admitted, respondent argues, his chances of obtaining a life sentence would have been significantly better.

Measured against the standards outlined above, respondent's contentions are substantial. Experienced members of the death-penalty bar have long recognized the crucial importance of adducing evidence at a sentencing proceeding that establishes the defendant's social and familial connections. See Goodpaster, The Trial for Life: Effective Assistance of Counsel in Death Penalty Cases, 58 N.Y.U. L.Rev. 299, 300–303, 334–335 (1983). The State makes a colorable—though in my view not compelling—argument that defense counsel in this case might have made a reasonable "strategic" decision not to present such evidence at the sentencing hearing on the assumption that an unadorned acknowledgment of respondent's responsibility for his crimes would be more likely to appeal to the trial judge, who was reputed to respect persons who accepted responsibility for their actions. But however justifiable such a choice might have been after counsel had fairly assessed the potential strength of the mitigating evidence available to him, counsel's failure to make any significant effort to find out what evidence might be garnered from respondent's relatives and acquaintances surely cannot be described as "reasonable." Counsel's failure to investigate is particularly suspicious in light of his candid admission that respondent's confessions and conduct in the course of the trial gave him a feeling of "hopelessness" regarding the possibility of saving respondent's life.

That the aggravating circumstances implicated by respondent's criminal conduct were substantial does not vitiate respondent's constitutional claim; judges and juries in cases involving behavior at least as egregious have shown mercy, particularly when afforded an opportunity to see other facets of the defendant's personality and life. Nor is respondent's contention defeated by the possibility that the material his counsel turned up might not have been sufficient to establish a statutory mitigating circumstance under Florida law; Florida sentencing judges and the Florida Supreme Court sometimes refuse to impose death sentences in cases "in which, even though *statutory* mitigating circumstances do not outweigh statutory aggravating circumstances, the addition of nonstatutory mitigating circumstances tips the scales in favor of life imprisonment."

If counsel had investigated the availability of mitigating evidence, he might well have decided to present some such material at the hearing. If he had done so, there is a significant chance that respondent would have been given a life sentence. In my view, those possibilities, conjoined with the unreasonableness of counsel's failure to investigate, are more than sufficient to establish a violation of the Sixth Amendment and to entitle respondent to a new sentencing proceeding. * * *

NOTES AND QUESTIONS

1. It is important, when representing clients who committed gruesome crimes, to attempt to see the defendant as a person. There are few individuals who are truly evil, who commit crimes for no reason or for reasons that are unfathomable to those of us who do not commit crimes. According to David von Drehle, David Washington, the defendant in *Strickland v. Washington*, "could often be heard weeping in his cell" on death row. Most of the men on death row "have nothing but empty space where their conscience should be," but observers thought that Washington's "remorse was real and gut-wrenching." David von Drehle, Among the Lowest of the Dead 134 (1995).

And how did someone who felt real remorse do the awful deeds that he did? Out of work, depressed, and worried about supporting his family, he was in a laundromat when a man identified himself as a minister and made a proposition—if Washington came to the minister's home, there might be money in it for him. What he did not know until later was that the proposition was sexual in nature; it included "that Washington strip and straddle his face." Washington would later explain: "I stabbed him about five times. The only thing going through my mind, I said, 'Here I am out here trying to get some money to feed my family, and here go a minister supposed to be a minister in the church, running around doing stuff like this.' " *Id.*

2. With this knowledge of David Washington, and attempting to put out of your mind that the evidence against him was overwhelming, how would you grade counsel's performance in handling the case? Consider yourself a professor who teaches a course in representing criminal defendants, forget about the crime committed, focus on the details of what counsel did and did not do, and give the lawyer in this case a grade from the following list: C (competent); D (less than competent but within the range of reasonable); D-(barely above the line of incompetence); F (incompetent). (If you think a grade of A or B is justified, see us after class!)

Put another way, imagine you were the lawyer in *Strickland* and you are later describing your performance to your spouse, your parents, or your children. Would you be proud of your accomplishment? Satisfied? Embarrassed?

3. We do not minimize the harm that David Washington caused or his blameworthiness for that harm. According to von Drehle, one of Washington's

crimes was to kidnap a student from the University of Miami, rob him, and stab him to death "as the young man recited the Lord's prayer." *Id.* at 134.

4. *Categories of denial of counsel.* The Court in *Strickland* draws a distinction between "actual or constructive denial of the assistance of counsel altogether," and the denial through "actual ineffectiveness." The difference is between not having a lawyer at all (or having one that the State has disabled in some significant way), and having one that is free to provide assistance of counsel but fails to do so. The former category is exemplified by *Gideon v. Wainwright*, p. 950, where the State refused to provide a lawyer to an indigent defendant, and Geders v. United States, 425 U.S. 80, 96 S.Ct. 1330, 47 L.Ed.2d 592 (1976), where the trial judge prohibited the defendant from consulting with his lawyer during an overnight recess. These cases are relatively easy; one merely has to decide whether the defendant had a right to have a lawyer (*Gideon*) or whether the restraints on the lawyer were an unjustifiable interference with the lawyer-client relationship (*Geders*).

The second category—no state interference but ineffective representation—is *Strickland*. These cases are much more difficult than the structural denial.

Insight in how to approach *Strickland* cases can be gained from a hybrid doctrine that bridges the gap between the categories—the conflict-of-interest cases. In Holloway v. Arkansas, 435 U.S. 475, 98 S.Ct. 1173, 55 L.Ed.2d 426 (1978), the trial judge refused to appoint separate counsel for defendants being tried jointly even though the single public defender stated that he was operating with a conflict of interest. The trial judge refused even to have a hearing on the conflict question. Here, because the State (through the judge) was directly interfering with the ability of the lawyer to provide zealous and loyal representation, the Court reversed without regard to whether the defendant could show actual prejudice. The Court held that when the trial judge is apprised of a potential conflict from joint representation, he must hold a hearing; the failure to hold a hearing requires automatic reversal on Sixth Amendment grounds.

Cuyler v. Sullivan, 446 U.S. 335, 347, 100 S.Ct. 1708, 64 L.Ed.2d 333 (1980), on the other hand, involved a retained lawyer, who did nothing to put the judge on notice that he was laboring under a conflict of interest. The Court rejected the facile distinction between retained and appointed lawyers, finding that ineffective assistance by retained lawyers is just as much a violation of the Sixth Amendment as if the lawyer is appointed. But the Court did find a major difference between *Cuyler* and *Holloway*—the lack of actual notice to the judge in *Cuyler* that a conflict might exist. In *Cuyler* the State did not directly abridge the lawyer's ability to defend the client by failing to inquire into the potential conflict, and no rule of automatic reversal thus applies. *Cuyler* is more like *Strickland*, requiring proof that an actual conflict existed (a form of ineffective assistance) and that the conflict "adversely affected" the lawyer's performance (a form of prejudice). *Holloway*, on the other hand, is more like *Gideon*—if the trial judge fails to inquire when put on notice, both lack of assistance and prejudice will be presumed.

In Mickens v. Taylor, 535 U.S. 162, 122 S.Ct. 1237, 152 L.Ed.2d 291 (2002), the Court made clear that *Holloway* mandates a hearing only when trial counsel objects to the dual representation. Thus, even when the trial judge *in fact* knows of the conflict, only an objection from counsel triggers the right to a hearing and an automatic reversal if no hearing is held. *Mickens* stressed, however, that if there is no objection, and the defendant demonstrates a conflict that "adversely affected the lawyer's performance," the defendant need not show "prejudice" in the *Strickland* sense—that the result would have been different. Prejudice is, in effect, presumed when defendant shows a conflict that adversely affected counsel's performance.

5. *Counsel of choice.* We know from *Faretta v. California*, p. 989, that a defendant can proceed without counsel and represent herself. We know from *Godinez v. Moran*, p. 984, Note 9, that a competent defendant can waive counsel and plead guilty. We know from dicta in several cases that a defendant generally has the right to retain counsel of choice.

But what if the judge concludes that the lawyer has a conflict of interest and the defendant is willing to waive the right to a conflict-free lawyer? In Wheat v. United States, 486 U.S. 153, 108 S.Ct. 1692, 100 L.Ed.2d 140 (1988), the Court held that a judge can refuse a waiver of a conflict of interest and thus refuse to give the defendant his counsel of choice. The defendant is not the only party with an interest to protect, according to the Court. "Federal courts have an independent interest in ensuring that criminal trials are conducted within the ethical standards of the profession and that legal proceedings appear fair to all who observe them." Moreover, the Court noted that the legal profession itself has an interest in ensuring that verdicts appear to be just.

6. *Criticisms of lawyers.* An exhaustive study of New York County in the mid–1980s revealed that private lawyers appointed to represent indigent defendants *did not interview their clients* in 82% of the non-homicide cases. Even in homicide cases, the lawyer interviewed the client only 26% of the time. Michael McConville & Chester Mirsky, *Criminal Defense of the Poor in New York City*, 15 N.Y.U. L. & Social Change 581, 758–62 (1986–87). While the "going rate" for legal time in New York City is probably five to ten times what the state pays for indigent defense, it is clearly unethical to neglect an appointed client because the lawyer doesn't think she can afford to work for the state rate. How could it ever be effective assistance under *Strickland* if the lawyer did not interview her client or conduct any investigation?

7. *Criticisms of Strickland.* The Court's opinion in *Strickland* has not met with favor among the commentators. One problem, identified by Professor Donald Dripps, is that the appellate review is of a record made by the lawyer charged with incompetence: "It is all but ludicrous to ask a reviewing court to assess a record made by counsel to determine how counsel erred. As one might expect, this inquiry has done little to improve the quality of defense representation." Donald A. Dripps, *Ineffective Assistance of Counsel: The Case for an Ex Ante Parity Standard*, 88 J. Crim. L. & Criminology 242, 243 (1997). As the title of this article implies, Professor Dripps would replace the *Strickland* after-the-fact inquiry with an ex ante standard that requires the judge to determine, prior to the trial, "whether the defendant's lawyer can effectively represent him. Because the effectiveness of counsel is relative to the opposition, the test should be whether the defendant is represented by a

lawyer roughly as good and roughly as well-prepared as counsel for the prosecution." *Id.* at 244.

8. *Why did Justice Brennan concur in Strickland?* Professor Vivian Berger, in the excerpt that follows, calls Brennan's concurrence "puzzling." We agree.

VIVIAN O. BERGER—THE SUPREME COURT AND DEFENSE COUNSEL: OLD ROADS, NEW PATHS—A DEAD END?

86 Columbia Law Review 9 (1986), 112–116.

The "moral bases of attribution in the counsel/client relationship" * * * are most tenuous in criminal proceedings. The bulk of clients do not choose their own lawyers and the stakes are liberty and, at times, even life. Yet in our complex, adversarial system, practical responsibility for the accused's cause will inevitably fall upon his professional representative unless he forgoes a lawyer entirely. * * *

Given this fact, the Court's long-awaited treatment of the subject was disappointing. The *Strickland* majority's weighty presumption of lawyer competence (despite an otherwise acceptable test of "reasonable" performance) appeared to abolish the problem by fiat. If the language of presumption and deference can be relegated to some extent to the realm of rhetoric, the burden that the Court imposed on defendants to demonstrate actual prejudice cannot. Altogether, the justices signaled an intent to shield at least appellate courts from more than minimal involvement with claims of inadequate representation, leaving it to defendants themselves and conscientious trial court judges to deal with the problem as best they can.

But if the Court paid mere lip service to the importance of effective assistance by defense counsel while offering little by way of concrete vindication of the right, one must ask, nonetheless, how much difference it would have made had a better opinion been written in *Strickland*. Few people would disagree that upsetting convictions is an inefficient way to guarantee effective assistance—not to mention the systemic costs that vacating judgments invariably inflicts. One can only speculate whether reversals of judgments or grants of the writ [of habeas corpus] educate the target population of lawyers. Very likely, these decisions have greater impact on the judiciary, teaching courts what types of conduct by attorneys will not pass constitutional muster.

I believe that the justices might have at least increased the probability of such beneficial fallout by declining to make the element of prejudice the centerpiece of their analysis. However, reformers attempting to enhance the quality of counsel's representation have fielded much more ambitious programs than simply varying the legal standards used to evaluate lawyer performance after the fact. Suggestions range from exhortations to trial judges to monitor attorneys in pending cases—by inquiring into counsel preparation and client satisfaction—to calls for broad systemic improvements. The latter include continuing legal education, professional certification or specialization requirements for practice in certain courts or subjects, more clinically oriented law school training, higher pay and greater auxiliary resources for assigned counsel, and structural changes in the delivery of defense services.

* * * Not surprisingly, none [of these proposals] promises to yield a ready panacea for the problem of ineffective assistance, and a number pose difficulties of their own; yet some merit further exploration. For present purposes, I wish to make only one point concerning such ideas: individually and as a group, they largely resist constitutionalization. In *Strickland*—which involved a state conviction—the Court was, of course, necessarily expounding the Constitution.

* * * [I]t is hard to find power in the federal courts to order expansive structural remedies addressed to the qualifications of counsel or the organization or funding of defender associations. The most generous conception of the Court's authority to mold constitutional "common law" could hardly sustain many needed forms of systemic relief, although it might conceivably permit some form of mandated trial court procedures designed to smoke out lawyer incompetence before irremediable damage occurs. * * * I believe that there is little in a practical vein the Court could have done, or can do in the future, to promote competent performance by counsel. If I am correct, perhaps Justice Brennan's puzzling concurrence with the *Strickland* majority stems from understandable reluctance to face that extremely discomfiting fact.* * *

In short, the Court's visions of the right to counsel and the role of counsel are incoherent, or downright cynical. In this area, most of the justices have failed to speak thoughtfully and candidly about the issues, an obligation that the Court as teacher owes us always. With regard to inadequate representation, even an honest acknowledgment of the Court's limitations might have encouraged further thought about solutions transcending the factual and legal bounds of particular cases as well as the jurisdictional constraints of a Court construing the Constitution. Thus, the road mapped in *Powell*, *Gideon*, and *Douglas* has petered out in a dead end, at least for now. Signposts for new directions for counsel will have to come from a different source.

BRUCE A. GREEN—LETHAL FICTION: THE MEANING OF "COUNSEL" IN THE SIXTH AMENDMENT

78 Iowa Law Review 433, 433, 437 (1993).

Charles Bell, Donald Paradis, and Shirley Tyler were tried in different states for murder. Each was convicted and sentenced to death. Charles Bell was represented at trial by a recent law school graduate who had never before tried a criminal case to completion. Donald Paradis's lawyer had passed the bar exam six months earlier, had never previously represented a criminal accused, and had not elected courses in criminal law, criminal procedure, or trial advocacy while in law school. Shirley Tyler's trial lawyer was also a member of the bar for only a few months. He had defended one previous assault case and one previous robbery case, each lasting half a day. Each condemned prisoner later asserted that he or she had been denied the Sixth Amendment right of a criminal accused "to have the assistance of counsel for his defence" on the ground that the defense attorney had rendered ineffective legal assistance. In asserting this claim, each undertook the difficult burden of demonstrating the likelihood that he or she had received a sentence of death only because of the attorney's unreasonably poor performance.

Not surprisingly, none of the three death-row defendants claimed to have been deprived of "counsel" altogether, since courts unwaveringly adhere to the view that "counsel" under the Sixth Amendment includes any duly licensed attorney. This Article argues, however, that a narrower construction of the constitutional term is warranted: "counsel" should include only those attorneys who are qualified to render legal assistance to a person accused of a crime. By that standard, these three defendants, and many others who similarly have been tried, convicted, and sentenced to death with an unqualified attorney by their side, have been deprived of their right to "counsel." * * *

[This Article] describes what redefining "counsel" would mean for the criminal justice system. To be regarded as "counsel" for constitutional purposes, a member of the bar should possess the skill and knowledge understood within the profession as prerequisites to defending criminal cases adequately. The right to "counsel," meaning a qualified advocate, would not supplant the presently recognized right to effective assistance of counsel, but would supplement it. Criminal defendants would be entitled, at the threshold, to a qualified attorney. In individual cases in which a seemingly capable lawyer provided substandard representation, a convicted defendant could claim that he was denied the right to effective assistance of counsel.

Because most lawyers do not possess the requisite skill and knowledge to be qualified to defend a criminal case, some mechanism to train and certify those lawyers must be established. Courts are undoubtedly capable of establishing such a mechanism. The judiciary is, after all, responsible for the existing licensing process, and some courts already have established processes either for certifying criminal lawyers as specialists or for determining which lawyers are qualified to serve by assignment in criminal cases. Moreover, legislatures are equally capable of devising a process for upgrading the quality of criminal defense lawyers. Congress, for one, recently considered legislation designed in part to improve the quality of defense lawyers in death penalty cases.

NOTES AND QUESTIONS

1. Perhaps the pithiest criticism of the *Strickland* test is that some defense counsel call it the "foggy mirror" test. "If you place a mirror in front of defense counsel during trial and it fogs, counsel is in fact effective."

Randall Coyne, Capital Punishment and the Judicial Process, Teacher's Manual 148 (1995).

2. To what extent do Professors Berger and Green agree on the nature of the problem? On the solution? Which solution is more easily within the reach of, say, a state supreme court that wanted to "raise the bar" of the *Strickland* standard under its own constitution? If you were the Chief Justice of your state supreme court, would you "raise the bar" or would you be satisfied with the *Strickland* standard?

3. *The end of the David Washington story.*

> He was ashamed and remorseful to the very end; he had that small credit. As his twelve-year-old daughter sobbed through their final visit, he cupped her trembling chin in his hand and said: "I want you to look at me, and I want you to see where I am * * * and I want you to do better."

David von Drehle, Among the Lowest of the Dead 254 (1995).

4. *Sleeping beauties.* According to a court clerk assigned to the trial judge, Calvin Burdine's lawyer slept "a lot" and "for long periods of time" during the prosecution's questioning of witnesses in a death penalty trial. Yet a Fifth Circuit panel held that this fact, by itself, did not automatically require a finding that the counsel was ineffective. Burdine v. Johnson, 231 F.3d 950 (5th Cir.2000). To be sure, an en banc decision overturned the panel, by a vote of nine to five—see Burdine v. Johnson, 262 F.3d 336 (5th Cir.2001)—but it might give one pause that five members of the Fifth Circuit did not believe that a sleeping lawyer is necessarily an ineffective one.

5. *The simple closing argument.* Death penalty cases require a separate sentencing phase, as you saw in *Strickland*. What if the defense lawyer failed to present *any* mitigating evidence in the sentencing phase and a court later found "sufficient grounds" to argue several mitigating factors, including "youth, intoxication, and family background"? The only defense at sentencing consisted of the following closing argument:

> Defense Counsel: Ladies and Gentlemen, I appreciate the time you took deliberating and the thought you put into this. I'm going to be extremely brief. I have a reputation for not being brief.
>
> Jesse, stand up. Jesse?

The Defendant: Sir?

Defense Counsel: Stand up.

> You are an extremely intelligent jury. You've got that man's life in your hands. You can take it or not. That's all I have to say.

Is this effective assistance under *Strickland*? See Romero v. Lynaugh, 884 F.2d 871 (5th Cir.1989).

6. *Thank God it's over.* In another death case, the crime was a brutal rape and murder of an eight-year-old girl; she suffered six stab wounds to the body and five knife slashes traversing her abdomen, along with numerous lacerations and abrasions on her face, neck, and upper chest. At the close of the *guilt* phase, defense counsel argued as follows:

I would be [dishonest] with each and every one of you if I tried to tell you the evidence said something other than what [the prosecutor] indicates occurred on that day so I'm not going to. * * * I don't think in a situation like this there's anything that I can say except to say thank God this is over. * * * I pray to God that none of you or myself, or the other people in this court room, will ever see anything like this again. I'm not going to be dishonest to y'all and say something to change what is, the evidence is, what the evidence is, the law the judge gives you as to how to consider this evidence. That's all I have. Thank you.

Assuming the evidence of guilt was overwhelming, does this closing argument at the guilt phase meet the *Strickland* standard? See Messer v. Kemp, 760 F.2d 1080 (11th Cir.1985).

7. *Forgiveness from heaven.* Same case as Note 6. The jury convicts. At the sentencing phase, the lawyer presents a single witness, the defendant's mother, and elicits from her that she and the defendant both expected the death penalty. She also testified that the defendant "has got saved, he's confessed his sins to Christ, and he told me, he said 'mama, the Lord has forgiven me * * *.'"

In the closing argument in the sentencing phase, the lawyer said to the jury, "[Your decision] is an awesome responsibility and I dare say I would rather be over here than in y'all's seats, because as a parent under these circumstances"—here he paused before continuing—"but that's for y'all to decide." Is this effective representation under *Strickland?*

For a biting critique of the representation of counsel in death cases, see Vivian O. Berger, *The Chiropractor as Brain Surgeon: Defense Lawyering in Capital Cases,* 18 N.Y.U. Rev. L. & Social Change 245 (1990); Stephen B. Bright, *Death By Lottery—Procedural Bar of Constitutional Claims in Capital Cases Due to Inadequate Representation of Indigent Defendants,* 92 W. Va. L. Rev. 679 (1990).

8. *An easy case (and defendant wins).* The principal issue in Kimmelman v. Morrison, 477 U.S. 365, 106 S.Ct. 2574, 91 L.Ed.2d 305 (1986), had to do with the proper jurisdiction of federal courts to hear habeas claims. The underlying constitutional claim was ineffective assistance of counsel and the Court unanimously held that counsel's performance was constitutionally deficient. The charge was rape, the defense was that it never happened, and an important piece of evidence was a bedsheet taken without a warrant from defendant's apartment. Here is how Justice Powell, concurring in the judgment, characterized the performance issue:

[Defendant]'s ineffective-assistance claim is uncomplicated. [Defendant] argues that his trial counsel incompetently failed to conduct any pretrial discovery. Had counsel conducted discovery, he would have known that the police had seized a bedsheet from [defendant]'s apartment without a warrant. The bedsheet contained hair samples matching hair of both [defendant] and the rape victim. The sheet also contained semen stains matching those found in the victim's underpants. The State introduced the bedsheet and accompanying expert analysis at trial, and the trial judge denied [defendant]'s belated motion to suppress on the ground that it was untimely. [Defendant] contends that the sheet would have been excluded on Fourth Amendment grounds had the suppression motion been timely filed. Thus, [defendant] argues, counsel's failure to conduct discovery led to the admission of evidence that was both damning and excludible.

Counsel's "explanation" for his failure to conduct discovery was two-fold. First, he "asserted that it was the State's obligation to inform him of its case against his client, even though he made no request for discovery." Second, counsel said "he had not expected to go to trial because he had been told that the victim did not wish to proceed." The Supreme Court unanimously held that these explanations were not sufficient to bring the case under the *Strickland* rule that trial strategy is generally not to be second-guessed. As the Court put it: "The justifications [defendant]'s attorney offered for his omission betray a startling ignorance of the law—or a weak attempt to shift blame for inadequate preparation." The Court remanded for a hearing on prejudice.

9. *Is the Court quietly requiring more competent lawyering in death cases?* Two of the Court's recent death cases suggest that *Strickland*'s refusal to engage in "Monday-morning quarter-backing" seems to be receding a bit. To be sure, *Strickland* claims in death cases are even more fact-sensitive and complex than in ordinary run-of-the mill cases, and it is difficult to generalize.

The defendant in Wiggins v. Smith, 539 U.S. 510, 123 S.Ct. 2527, 156 L.Ed.2d 471 (2003), convinced the Court that his lawyer was ineffective because he did not investigate the severe physical and sexual abuse at the hands of his mother and under the care of a series of foster parents. Notably, the Court was willing to rely on the standards for capital defense work articulated by the American Bar Association, which require "efforts to discover *all reasonably available* mitigating evidence and evidence to rebut any aggravating evidence that may be introduced by the prosecutor." ABA Guidelines for the Appointment and Performance of Counsel in Death Penalty Cases 11.4.1(C), p. 93 (1989) (emphasis added). Might Washington have proven lack of competence of his counsel if the *Strickland* Court had applied that standard? To be sure, the ABA Guidelines appeared five years after *Strickland* was decided, but evolving guidelines can be viewed as part of a partial retreat from *Strickland*.

In Rompilla v. Beard, 545 U.S. 374, 125 S.Ct. 2456, 162 L.Ed.2d 360 (2005), the defendant's trial lawyers worked harder than did Wiggins's lawyers to find mitigating evidence. They interviewed five family members in a "detailed manner" and reviewed the reports of three mental health experts who examined Rompilla. But the lawyers did not review a court file, readily available in the courthouse, containing material about one of Rompilla's prior convictions. The prosecutor had told defense counsel that he was going to use the rape victim's testimony in the prior case to prove Rompilla's violent character, which was relevant to an aggravating circumstance under the state death penalty law. Defense lawyers read the victim's testimony in the court file but did not examine the rest of the file. If defense lawyers had examined the file completely, they would have found a range of mitigating evidence about Rompilla's childhood and mental health that no other source had revealed. The Court held that this constituted deficient defense. Is this really more deficient than the utter failure of the lawyer in *Strickland* to investigate his client's possible emotional disturbance? Perhaps. Justice O'Connor, the author of *Strickland*, joined the *Rompilla* majority.

The capital defendant lost by a 5–4 margin in Schriro v. Landrigan, 550 U.S. 465, 127 S.Ct. 1933, 167 L.Ed.2d 836 (2007), but the critical fact seemed to be that Landrigan had instructed his lawyer not to present any mitigating evidence. This is similar to the "hopeless" counsel in *Strickland*, though the defendant in *Strickland* apparently did not give instructions not to present mitigating evidence. Thus, *Strickland* would be a stronger case than *Landrigan* and Landrigan came within one vote of winning his case in the current Court. Why would the 2007 Court be friendlier to an ineffective assistance claim than the 1984 Court that included, other than Marshall who dissented, Brennan, Stevens, and Blackmun? Perhaps the experience with *Strickland* has made the Court aware that it is too deferential.

10. *Problems.*

A. *Failure to introduce exculpatory evidence.* Three men are charged with rape. The state tests the victim for DNA and finds DNA from the other co-defendants but not from *Y*. *Y*'s defense is that he attempted to keep the other two from raping the victim and when he failed in that attempt, he went to another part of the house. The victim testifies that *Y* penetrated her. Defense counsel seeks to introduce the DNA evidence by asking *Y* whether he had received a copy of the results. The judge sustains the prosecution's hearsay objection and defense counsel makes no further attempt to introduce the results. The prosecutor later stated that he would have stipulated to the DNA results if counsel had asked. The state's theory of the case was that *Y* was a principal in the rape, not that he aided and abetted. People v. York, 312 Ill.App.3d 434, 245 Ill.Dec. 227, 727 N.E.2d 674 (2000). Ineffective assistance?

B. *Failure to change clothes.* Defendant *M*, charged with robbing a store during business hours, is borderline mentally retarded. The store's video camera captured the robbery, including that the robber was wearing a blue T-shirt with the words "Cameron Elementary Scotties" and a picture of a Scottish terrier dog. *M* is arrested the next day wearing a shirt identical to the one worn by the robber. His picture, wearing that shirt, is used in a photo lineup; no one else in the photo array is wearing a similar shirt. The clerk picks out *M*'s picture. Prior to trial, defense counsel fails to object to the photo array.

During at least part of the *voir dire*, *M* is wearing the same shirt. The clerk identifies *M* in court as the robber (by now he is wearing a different shirt). At the close of the trial, *M*'s lawyer moves for a mistrial on the ground that he has just realized that the T-shirt *M* wore during the *voir dire* was the same one the robber wore. The judge denies the motion, stating that these are "his clothes" and that it would be improper for him to appear in jail clothes. The jury convicts and the judge sentences *M* to eighty years in prison. Ineffective assistance? Is there a problem with prejudice? Mitchell v. State, 23 S.W.3d 582 (Tex.App.2000).

C. *Failure to do **anything**.* Prior to jury selection in *H*'s capital murder trial, defense counsel files a motion for continuance, stating that he is "totally unprepared to begin with this case." The judge denied the motion. Defense counsel questions the jury but at the close of *voir dire* refuses to exercise any of his client's peremptory challenges (available to exclude potential jurors if a challenge for cause fails). He renews his motion for a continuance and when the judge again denies it, states: "[I]f we are going ahead with this trial, * * * I will be physically present because I am sure the Court would require that, but I do not in any way intend to participate in the trial of this matter." He again asserts that he is unprepared and physically exhausted. He attends the trial but does not participate in any way. The jury convicted and, after a sentencing hearing, the judge sentenced *H* to die. State v. Harvey, 692 S.W.2d 290 (Mo.1985).

This is either the most fundamental failure imaginable or a clever strategy. Do you see how it could be a strategy? Is there a way for the judge to defeat the strategy short of having to grant the continuance?

12. *Strickland "batting average."* The Center for Capital Litigators in Columbia, South Carolina has collected citations and summaries of all published successful ineffective assistance of counsel claims since *Strickland*. As of December, 2001, the list contained roughly 1,200 state and federal cases. Running *Strickland* in Westlaw for the same time period produced about 37,000 entries. Thus, as the lower courts have understood and applied *Strickland*, lawyers provided constitutionally competent assistance in roughly 97% of the cases where their performance was challenged. Perhaps Justice O'Connor would say that this demonstrates the basic soundness of lawyering in criminal cases. Perhaps it does.

INDEX

References are to Pages

Page numbers 786–933, and 1016–1416, set out below, are found in Dressler and Thomas, CRIMINAL PROCEDURE: PROSECUTING CRIME and Dressler and Thomas, CRIMINAL PROCEDURE: PRINCIPLES, POLICIES AND PERSPECTIVES